The original decisions in this volume were prepared for translation by Vice-President Hassemer, Justices Bryde, Di Fabio, Eichberger, Gaier, Gerhardt, Hoffmann-Riem, Hohmann-Dennhardt, Landau, Lübbe-Wolff, Mellinghoff, Osterloh, Steiner and their research assistants. The translations were carried out by P. Aliferis (Hamburg), D. Elliott (Bonn), M. Hepner (London), M. Marks (Fürth), N. Mussett (Alfter), U. Reusch (Berlin), C. Thomas (Karlsruhe) and H. Weiland/R. A. Miller.
Coordination of the translation project: H. Weiland
Editorial supervision: M. Böckel

Decisions of the Bundesverfassungsgericht
– Federal Constitutional Court –
Federal Republic of Germany

Volume 5:

Family-Related Decisions

1957-2010

Edited by the
Federal Constitutional Court

Karlsruhe 2013

Nomos Verlagsgesellschaft
Baden-Baden

Die Deutsche Nationalbibliothek verzeichnet diese Publikation in der Deutschen Nationalbibliografie; detaillierte bibliografische Daten sind im Internet über http://dnb.d-nb.de abrufbar.

Die Deutsche Nationalbibliothek lists this publication in the Deutsche Nationalbibliografie; detailed bibliographic data is available in the Internet at http://dnb.d-nb.de.

ISBN 978-3-8329-6851-9

1. Auflage 2013

Contents

Preface by Prof. Dr. Andreas Voßkuhle		XVII
Explanations of Abbreviations in the Court's Case Numbers		XX
Justices of the Federal Constitutional Court, 1951-2013		XXIII
1. BVerfGE 6, 55	Order of the First Senate of 17 January 1957 – 1 BvL 4/54 **"Taxation of households case"** Article 6.1 of the Basic Law is a fundamental provision (binding value decision) and currently binding constitutional law	1
2. BVerfGE 10, 59	Judgment of the First Senate of 29 July 1959 – 1 BvR 205, 332, 333, 367/58, 1 BvL 27, 100/58 **"Case concerning parental power"** Decision regarding the equality of the mother and the father (father's final decision)	20
3. BVerfGE 22, 93	Order of the First Senate of 7 June 1967 – 1 BvR 76/62 **"Maintenance I case"** Taking Article 6.1 of the Basic Law into account in determining the maintenance of spouses living apart	40
4. BVerfGE 23, 258	Order of the First Senate of 7 May 1968 – 1 BvR 133/67 **"Duty to promote families case"** Decision on the duty of the state to promote families	45

5. BVerfGE 24, 119 | Order of the First Senate of 29 July 1968 – 1 BvL 20/63, 31/66, 5/67
"Adoption I case"
Substitution of parental consent to adoption 51

6. BVerfGE 28, 324 | Order of the First Senate of 27 May 1970 – 1 BvL 22/63, 27/64
"Marriage clause case"
Incompatibility of the marriage clauses in the orphans' pension in social pensions insurance with Article 6.1 of the Basic Law 75

7. BVerfGE 31, 58 | Order of the First Senate of 4 May 1971 – 1 BvR 636/68
"Spaniard case"
Validity of fundamental rights (here: Article 6.1 of the Basic Law) for German international private law; freedom of marriage (act of marriage between a Spanish man and a German woman divorced by a German court) 100

8. BVerfGE 42, 95 | Order of the Second Senate of 6 April 1976 – 2 BvR 61/76
"Pre-trial detention I case (visiting permission)"
Permission for spouses and children of pre-trial detainees to visit outside general visiting days 122

9. BVerfGE 51, 386 | Order of the First Senate of 18 July 1979 – 1 BvR 650/77
"Expulsion case"
Expulsion of a foreign national convicted of a criminal offence who is married to a German woman and has a legitimate child with her 127

10. BVerfGE 53, 224	Judgment of the First Senate of 28 February 1980 – 1 BvL 136/78, 1 BvR 890/77, 1300, 1440/78, 32/79 **"Divorce law case"** Dissolution of marriage according to the new law because of breakdown of marriage – also irrefutably presumed after three-year separation –; application to "prior marriages"; hardship clause	138
11. BVerfGE 55, 171	Order of the First Senate of 5 November 1980 – 1 BvR 349/80 **"Custody case"** Accommodation of the will of a child in a ruling on custody after divorce of the parents and ruling of the judge with jurisdiction on the question of the personal hearing of children under the age of 14	156
12. BVerfGE 57, 170	Order of the Second Senate of 5 February 1981 – 2 BvR 646/80 **"Pre-trial detention II case (correspondence by letter)"** Decision regarding the monitoring of letters during pre-trial detention; written correspondence between adult children and their parents	166
13. BVerfGE 60, 79	Order of the First Senate of 17 February 1982 – 1 BvR 188/80 **"Case concerning the separation of a child from its family"** Separation of a child from its family even where the parents fail without being at fault as the strongest encroachment on parental rights, only if principle of proportionality is strictly observed	191

14. BVerfGE 61, 358 | Judgment of the First Senate of 3 November 1982 – 1 BvL 25, 38, 40/80, 12/81
“Joint custody case”
Decision regarding the exclusion of the joint custody of divorced parents 203

15. BVerfGE 66, 84 | Order of the First Senate of 10 January 1984 – 1 BvL 5/83
“Maintenance priority case”
Priority under the law of maintenance for the divorced spouse with care of children 220

16. BVerfGE 72, 122 | Order of the First Senate of 18 June 1986 – 1 BvR 857/85
“Withdrawal of custody rights case”
Safeguarding the status of children as holders of fundamental rights in the proceedings (supplementary curator) 231

17. BVerfGE 76, 1 | Order of the Second Senate of 12 May 1987 – 2 BvR 1226/83, 101, 313/84
“Entry of aliens to join family members living in the Federal Republic”
Waiting periods for the entry of aliens (Turkish and Yugoslavian nationals) to join family members living in the Federal Republic of Germany 245

18. BVerfGE 79, 51 | Order of the First Senate of 12 October 1988 – 1 BvR 818/88
“Foster parents case”
Removal of a child from its foster family 287

19. BVerfGE 80, 81	Order of the Second Senate of 18 April 1989 – 2 BvR 1169/84 **“Case concerning the adoption of an adult foreigner”** Right of residence of an adult foreigner adopted by a German	301
20. BVerfGE 82, 6	Order of the First Senate of 3 April 1990 – 1 BvR 1186/89 **“Unmarried civil partner as tenant case”** Unmarried civil partner of a deceased tenant as “another family member” within the meaning of § 569a.2 sentence 1 of the Civil Code	311
21. BVerfGE 84, 168	Order of the First Senate of 7 May 1991 – 1 BvL 32/88 **“Case regarding custody rights for children born out of wedlock”** Joint parental custody for children born out of wedlock	320
22. BVerfGE 87, 1	Judgment of the First Senate of 7 July 1992 – 1 BvL 51/86, 50/87, 1 BvR 873/90, 761/91 **“Rubble women case”** Allowance of child-raising periods in the statutory pensions insurance of wage-earners and salaried employees (“rubble women”)	336
23. BVerfGE 93, 373	Order of the Second Senate of 16 January 1996 – 2 BvL 4/95 **“Case involving a divorced couple’s simultaneous membership of a municipal council”** Simultaneous membership of former spouses of the municipal council of a municipality with not more than 20,000 inhabitants	355

24. BVerfGE 96, 56 — Order of the First Senate of 6 May 1997 – 1 BvR 409/90
"Case concerning information about father's identity"
Decision regarding the obligation of a mother to provide information to her adult illegitimate child about the identity of the biological father 364

25. BVerfGE 97, 332 — Order of the First Senate of 10 March 1998 – 1 BvR 178/97
"Graduated kindergarten contributions case"
Kindergarten contributions graduated by family income 372

26. BVerfGE 99, 145 — Order of the Second Senate of 29 October 1998 – 2 BvR 1206/98
"Hague Child Abduction Convention case"
Hague Child Abduction Convention; accommodation of the best interests of the child in the special case of converse child return applications 386

27. BVerfGE 99, 216 — Order of the Second Senate of 10 November 1998 – 2 BvR 1057, 1226, 980/91
"Equalisation of family burdens case"
Exclusion of parents living in marital community from tax deduction of childcare costs as an extraordinary expense resulting from gainful employment and from granting of the household allowance 402

28. BVerfGE 99, 246 — Order of the Second Senate of 10 November 1998 – 2 BvL 42/93
"Minimum child income case"
Minimum child income for the 1987 assessment period to be allowed for in income tax 420

29. BVerfGE 99, 300 Order of the Second Senate of 24 November 1998 – 2 BvL 26/91, 5, 6, 7, 8, 9, 10/96, 3, 4, 5, 6/97
"Civil servants' children case" (state's obligation to take care of civil servants' welfare and family)
Remuneration of civil servants and judges with more than two children in the period from 1988 to 1996 432

30. BVerfGE 101, 361 Judgment of the First Senate of 15 December 1999 – 1 BvR 653/96
"Caroline of Monaco II case"
Publication of photographs from the daily and private life of prominent persons – Caroline of Monaco 450

31. BVerfGE 103, 89 Judgment of the First Senate of 6 February 2001 – 1 BvR 12/92
"Marriage covenant case"
Judicial review of agreements in a covenant of marriage concluded with a pregnant woman prior to the conclusion of marriage 475

32. BVerfGE 103, 242 Judgment of the First Senate of 3 April 2001 – 1 BvR 1629/94
"Long-term care insurance case"
Long-term care insurance contributions for child-caring and child-raising members of social long-term care insurance 491

33. BVerfGE 104, 373 Judgment of the First Senate of 30 January 2002 – 1 BvL 23/96
"Double family names case"
Exclusion of double family names 515

34. BVerfGE 105, 1 | Order of the First Senate of 5 February 2002 – 1 BvR 105, 559/95, 457/96
"Post-marital maintenance case"
Equivalence of family work and gainful employment in the assessment of post-marital maintenance 530

35. BVerfGE 105, 313 | Judgment of the First Senate of 17 July 2002 – 1 BvF 1, 2/01
"Civil Partnerships Act case"
Correction of an adopted bill; right of approval of the *Bundesrat*; compatibility with Articles 6.1, 3.1, 3.3 sentence 1 and 14.1 of the Basic Law 541

36. BVerfGE 106, 166 | Order of the First Senate of 29 October 2002 – 1 BvL 16, 17/95, 16/97
"Case involving the advantage acquired through additional counted children"
Decision regarding the equal treatment of different forms of family under the law on child benefit 577

37. BVerfGE 107, 104 | Judgment of the Second Senate of 16 January 2003 – 2 BvR 716/01
"Parental involvement in proceedings under the Juvenile Court Act case"
Exclusion of a father with parental rights from proceedings before a juvenile court which involve his son (§ 51.2 of the Juvenile Court Act) 591

38. BVerfGE 107, 150 Judgment of the First Senate of 29 January 2003 – 1 BvL 20/99, 1 BvR 933/01
"Case regarding parental custody for children born out of wedlock"
§ 1626a of the Civil Code is currently compatible with Article 6.2 and 6.5 of the Basic Law, lack of a transitional arrangement for old cases is unconstitutional 611

39. BVerfGE 107, 205 Judgment of the First Senate of 12 February 2003 – 1 BvR 624/01
"Family insurance case"
The constitutionality of family insurance (§ 10 of the Fifth Book of the Code of Social Law) 633

40. BVerfGE 108, 82 Order of the First Senate of 9 April 2003 – 1 BvR 1493/96, 1724/01
"Biological father case"
Decision regarding the legal position of the (putative) natural, but not legal, father and the constitutionality of §§ 1600 and 1685 of the Civil Code and § 1711 of the Civil Code old 642

41. BVerfGE 108, 351 Order of the First Senate of 7 October 2003 – 1 BvR 246/93, 2298/94
"Case relating to the splitting advantage in case of spousal maintenance"
Unconstitutionality of the consideration of fiscal advantages from a new marriage of a person obliged to provide maintenance in the assessment of the maintenance payable to the former spouse 669

42. BVerfGE 109, 256 | Judgment of the First Senate of 18 February 2004 – 1 BvR 193/97
“Joint family name case”
Unconstitutionality of § 1355.2 of the Civil Code, which prohibits spouses who wish to have a joint family name as their married name the selection of a married name acquired through previous conclusion of marriage | 681

43. BVerfGE 111, 307 | Order of the Second Senate of 14 October 2004 – 2 BvR 1481/04
“Görgülü I case”
Obligation to take into account the European Convention on Human Rights and the decisions of the European Court of Human Rights, and the limits of such obligation, in the context of the principle that the judge is bound by statute and law (Article 20.3 of the Basic Law) | 694

44. BVerfGK 4, 339 | Order of the Third Chamber of the First Senate of 28 December 2004 – 1 BvR 2790/04
“Görgülü II case”
Arbitrary review of an unappealable arrangement for access – binding effect of a decision of the European Court of Human Rights – weighing of consequences with regard to contact in the form of access | 714

45. BVerfGK 5, 161 | Order of the First Chamber of the First Senate of 5 April 2005 – 1 BvR 1664/04
“Görgülü III case”
Binding effect of a decision of the European Court of Human Rights – constitutional requirements placed on the removal of a child from its foster family | 724

46. BVerfGE 113, 88 | Judgment of the First Senate of 7 June 2005 – 1 BvR 1508/96
“Parental support case”
Constitutional limits where children are required by the social assistance funding agency to pay support for their parents as the result of an assigned right 732

47. BVerfGE 115, 259 | Order of the First Senate of 28 March 2006 – 1 BvL 10/01
“Maternity protection period case”
Incompatibility with Article 6.4 of the Basic Law of the employment promotion law in force between 1998 and 2002, according to which periods in which mothers interrupted employment requiring the payment of social security contributions because of the prohibitions under maternity protection law were not taken into account in the calculation of the qualifying period for receiving unemployment benefit 747

48. BVerfGE 117, 202 | Judgment of the First Senate of 13 February 2007 – 1 BvR 421/05
“Secret paternity test case”
Decision regarding the right of the legal father to know that his child is biologically his and the obligation of the legislature to make available a suitable procedure 759

49. BVerfGE 118, 45	Order of the First Senate of 28 February 2007 – 1 BvL 9/04 **"Childcare maintenance case"** Incompatibility of the different assessment of childcare maintenance because of the care or bringing up of children born in and out of wedlock (§§ 1570 and 1615 l.2 sentence 3 of the Civil Code) with Article 6.5 of the Basic Law	779
50. BVerfGE 121, 69	Judgment of the First Senate of 1 April 2008 – 1 BvR 1620/04 **"Parental duty of contact case"** Decision regarding the compulsory enforcement of an adjudged duty of contact pursuant to § 1684.1 of the Civil Code	804
51. BVerfGE 127, 132	Order of the First Senate of 21 July 2010 – 1 BvR 420/09 **"Case regarding custody rights of fathers of children born out of wedlock"** Decision regarding the parental right of the father of a child born out of wedlock; incompatibility of § 1626a.1 no. 1 and § 1672.1 of the Civil Code with Article 6.2 of the Basic Law	826
Appendix	The Basic Law for the Federal Republic of Germany	852
Index		937
Index of Statutes		957

Preface

by Prof. Dr. Andreas Voßkuhle
President of the German Federal Constitutional Court

The book which you are holding continues the Federal Constitutional Court's topical collection series of English translations of rulings. The first four volumes already dealt with a broad spectrum of the Court's case-law, covering the topics international law/law of the European Communities, freedom of speech, questions of law arising from German unification and the law of freedom of faith and the law of the churches. The present volume now adds important rulings on family-related issues, and hence introduces a further major field of German constitutional case-law.
According to Article 6.1 of the Basic Law for the Federal Republic of Germany, marriage and the family enjoy the special protection of the state. According to the case-law of the Federal Constitutional Court, this protection guaranteed by the Basic Law covers three levels. It contains first and foremost a fundamental defensive right which shields the individual against state interference in the protected area of marriage and the family and makes him or her free to conclude marriage and establish a family. Additionally, Article 6.1 of the Basic Law however also encompasses an institutional guarantee for marriage and the family. This guarantee obliges the legislature to uphold the core of the family law provisions, in particular of civil law, and prohibits the complete abolition or the undermining of the institution of marriage and the family. Finally, as a fundamental provision that determines values, Article 6 also has an extended application with regard to the entire legal system, and hence exerts an influence on the interpretation and application of non-constitutional law. At the same time, this provision gives rise to an obligation incumbent on the state to promote marriage and the family, to protect them against harm caused by other powers, as well as prohibiting the state to cause detriment to or discriminate against marriage and the family.
The case-law of the Federal Constitutional Court contains major rulings on all three of these dimensions of the fundamental right to protection of marriage and the family, a selection of which can be read in the present collection. The same applies to the individual fundamental rights that are safeguarded in Article 6.2 to Article 6.5, relating to more specific aspects of marriage and the family such as parental rights, mothers' right to protection and welfare, and the equal treatment of children born in and out of wedlock.
The breadth of the spectrum of legal areas and the considerable diversity of circumstances which have been dealt with by the Court in connection with marriage and

the family in its case-law is already shown if one takes a look at the table of contents of this volume with the brief titles of the rulings. The field encompasses many aspects of the (legal) relationships within marriage and the family, and ranges from questions on the conclusion of marriage, the law on maintenance, rights of custody, adoption and divorce, through to the right to know one's parentage. At the same time, however, the diverse influence of the protection of marriage and the family under the Basic Law on interpretation in such varied fields of the law as for instance social law, fiscal law, prison law, press or local authority law becomes clear. The interplay of marriage and the family with the principle of equal treatment contained in Article 3.2 of the Basic Law also deserves particular attention.

Using the rulings collected here, it is easy to see how constantly high the practical significance of the fundamental right under Article 6 of the Basic Law has been and continues to be in the more than 60-year history of the Federal Constitutional Court. It can however also be recognised that marriage and the family, which have a stabilising impact as institutions in society, are themselves subject to social change in a special way. Constitutional case-law is called upon in this respect to do justice to a changing environment in granting the protection of marriage and the family required by the Basic Law and to always answer new questions in a convincing manner. The Court benefits here to a considerable degree from the adjustable nature of the Basic Law, which is lean and open to developments within society. In the process of adjusting to the prerequisites of the Basic Law, the family law of the Federal Republic of Germany has been shaped and refined by the Federal Constitutional Court as hardly any other area of the law.

The English-speaking reader is now also to be able to gain an impression of this process using the present volume and to form his or her own picture. The rulings which have been included were translated into English in a form that is only slightly shortened after being selected by the members of both Senates of the Federal Constitutional Court. All the original German texts of the rulings are printed in the official collection of rulings of the Federal Constitutional Court and in the collection of chamber rulings published by the Association of the Justices of the Federal Constitutional Court. In order to make the rulings more accessible, the Basic Law is provided in English in the Annex. Finally, a new feature in comparison to the previous volumes should be pointed to: In those cases, not small in number in family law, in which legal amendments had to be carried out because of a ruling of the Court, information is provided at the end of each ruling regarding the corresponding reaction on the part of the legislature.

It is a great pleasure for me to add this volume to the series commenced by my predecessors as President of the Federal Constitutional Court Roman Herzog, Jutta Limbach and Hans-Jürgen Papier. I join with all the members of the Federal Constitutional Court in hoping that the family law rulings which have been collected will be useful to practitioners in constitutional courts and in the legal sciences in other countries, and that they will make a contribution towards establishing a dialogue between constitutional courts and academics all over the world.

Professor Dr. Andreas Voßkuhle
President of the Federal Constitutional Court

Karlsruhe, June 2013

Explanation of Abbreviations in the Court's Case Numbers

1.	BvA	=	Cases pursuant to Article 18 of the Basic Law (§ 13 no. 1 of the Federal Constitutional Court Act) Forfeiture of fundamental rights
2.	BvB	=	Cases pursuant to Article 21.2 of the Basic Law (§ 13 no. 2 of the Federal Constitutional Court Act) Unconstitutionality of political parties
3.	BvC	=	Cases pursuant to Article 41.2 of the Basic Law (§ 13 no. 3 of the Federal Constitutional Court Act) Scrutiny of elections and of the status as a member of the *Bundestag*
4.	BvD	=	Impeachment of the Federal President (Article 61 of the Basic Law) (§ 13 no. 4 of the Federal Constitutional Court Act)
5.	BvE	=	Cases pursuant to Article 93.1 no. 1 of the Basic Law (§ 13 no. 5 of the Federal Constitutional Court Act) *Organstreit* proceedings (Disputes between supreme federal bodies)
6.	BvF	=	Cases pursuant to Article 93.1 no. 2 of the Basic Law (§ 13 no. 6 of the Federal Constitutional Court Act) Abstract review of statutes (upon application by a constitutional body)
7.	BvG	=	Cases pursuant to Article 93.1 no. 3 and Article 84.4 sentence 2 of the Basic Law (§ 13 no. 7 of the Federal Constitutional Court Act) Disputes between the Federation and the *Länder* (states)
8.	BvH	=	Cases pursuant to Articles 93.1 no. 4 of the Basic Law (§ 13 no. 8 of the Federal Constitutional Court Act) Other disputes involving public law

9. BvJ = Impeachment of judges
(Article 98.2 and 98.5 of the Basic Law)
(§ 13 no. 9 of the Federal Constitutional Court Act)

10. BvK = Cases pursuant to Article 99 of the Basic Law
(§ 13 no. 10 of the Federal Constitutional Court Act)
Constitutional disputes within a *Land* (state)

11. BvL = Cases pursuant to Article100.1 of the Basic Law
(§ 13 no. 11 of the Federal Constitutional Court Act)
Concrete review of statutes (judicial referrals)

12. BvM = Cases pursuant to Article 100.2 of the Basic Law
(§ 13 no. 12 of the Federal Constitutional Court Act)
Review of public international law

13. BvN = Cases pursuant to Article 100.3 of the Basic Law
(§ 13 no. 13 of the Federal Constitutional Court Act)
Referrals from *Länder* constitutional courts

14. BvO = Cases pursuant to Article 126 of the Basic Law
(§ 13 no. 14 of the Federal Constitutional Court Act)
Continued applicability of law as federal law

15. BvP = Cases pursuant to Article 93.2 of the Basic Law
(§ 13 no. 15 of the Federal Constitutional Court Act)
Other referrals on account of federal laws

16. BvQ = Temporary injunction proceedings
(§ 32 of the Federal Constitutional Court Act)

17. BvR = Constitutional complaints
(Article 93.1 no. 4a and 4b of the Basic Law)
(§ 13 no. 8a of the Federal Constitutional Court Act)

18. BvT = Former types of proceedings conducted at the Federal
Constitutional Court until 1960

19.	BvW	=	Disagreements on whether a law complies with the requirements of Article 72.2 of the Basic Law (Article 93.1 no. 2a of the Basic Law) (§ 13 no. 6a of the Federal Constitutional Court Act)
20.	BvX	=	Submissions by the Federal Court of Justice (*Bundesgerichtshof*) pursuant to § 36.2 of the Law Governing the Legal Framework for Committees of Inquiry (*Untersuchungsausschussgesetz*)
21.	BvY		Submissions pursuant to Article 93.2 of the Basic Law
22.	PBvS	=	Retirement of a Federal Constitutional Court Justice due to disability for service or for other reasons (§ 105 of the Federal Constitutional Court Act)
23.	BvU/ PBvU	=	Plenum decisions (decisions of the two Senates sitting) (§ 16 of the Federal Constitutional Court Act)
24.	PBvV	=	Legal opinions issued by the Plenum (until 1952) (§ 97 of the Federal Constitutional Court Act)

JUSTICES OF THE FEDERAL CONSTITUTIONAL COURT, 1951–2013

	Justice		*Position*
	FIRST SENATE: BUNDESTAG ELECTED		
Seat 1	Höpker-Aschoff, Hermann† (1951–54)		President
	Wintrich, Josef† (1954–58)		President
	Müller, Gebhard† (1959–71)		President
	Benda, Ernst† (1971–83)		President
	Herzog, Roman (1983–87)		Vice-President
	by *Bundesrat* (1987–94)		President
	Haas, Evelyn (1994–2006)		Justice
	Schluckebier, Wilhelm (since 2006)		Justice
Seat 2	Zweigert, Kurt† (1951–52)		Justice
	Heck, Karl† (1954–65)		Justice
	Böhmer, Werner (1965–83)		Justice
	Niedermaier, Franz† (1983–86)		Justice
	Seidl, Otto	(1986–95)	Justice
		(1995–98)	Vice-President
	Papier, Hans-Jürgen	(1998–2002)	Vice-President
		(2002–10)	President
	Paulus, Andreas (since 2010)		Justice
Seat 3	Heiland, Gerhard† (1951–61)		Justice
	Haager, Karl† (1962–79)		Justice
	Heußner, Hermann† (1979–89)		Justice
	Kühling, Jürgen (1989–2001)		Justice
	Bryde, Brun-Otto (2001–11)		Justice
	Baer, Susanne (since 2011)		Justice

Seat 4	Scholtissek, Herbert† (1951–67)	Justice
	Brox, Hans† (1967–75)	Justice
	Katzenstein, Dietrich† (1975–87)	Justice
	Söllner, Alfred† (1987–95)	Justice
	Steiner, Udo (1995–2007)	Justice
	Kirchhof, Ferdinand (2007–10)	Justice
	(since 2010)	Vice-President
Seat 5	Zweigert, Konrad† (1951–56)	Justice
	Seat abolished in 1956	
Seat 6	Lehmann, Joachim† (1951–63)	Justice
	Seat abolished in 1963	

FIRST SENATE: BUNDESRAT ELECTED

Seat 1	Stein, Erwin† (1951–71)	Justice
	Faller, Hans† (1971–83)	Justice
	Henschel, Johann Friedrich† (1983–94)	Justice
	(1994–95)	Vice-President
	Hömig, Dieter (1995–2006)	Justice
	Eichberger, Michael (since 2006)	Justice
Seat 2	Wessel, Franz† (1951–58)	Justice
	Berger, Hugo† (1959–67)	Justice
	Zeidler, Wolfgang† (1967–70)	Justice
	Simon, Helmut (1970–87)	Justice
	Dieterich, Thomas (1987–94)	Justice
	Jaeger, Renate (1994–2004)	Justice
	Gaier, Reinhard (since 2004)	Justice
Seat 3	Scheffler, Erna† (1951–63)	Justice
	Rupp-von Brünneck, Wiltraut† (1963–77)	Justice
	Niemeyer, Gisela† (1977–89)	Justice
	Seibert, Helga† (1989–98)	Justice
	Hohmann-Dennhardt, Christine (1999–2011)	Justice
	Britz, Gabriele (since 2011)	Justice

Seat 4	Ritterspach, Theodor† (1951–75)	Justice
	Hesse, Konrad† (1975–87)	Justice
	Grimm, Dieter (1987–99)	Justice
	Hoffmann-Riem, Wolfgang (1999–2008)	Justice
	Masing, Johannes (since 2008)	Justice
Seat 5	Ellinghaus, Wilhelm† (1951–55)	Justice
	Kutscher, Hans† (1955–56)	Justice
	Seat abolished in 1956	
Seat 6	Drath, Martin† (1951–63)	Justice
	Seat abolished in 1963	

SECOND SENATE: BUNDESTAG ELECTED

Seat 1	Rupp, Hans† (1951–75)	Justice
	Zeidler, Wolfgang† (1975–83)	Vice-President
	(1983–87)	President
	Franßen, Everhardt (1987–91)	Justice
	Sommer, Bertold (1991–2003)	Justice
	Gerhardt, Michael (since 2003)	Justice
Seat 2	Henneka, Anton† (1951–68)	Justice
	Rinck, Hans-Justus† (1968–86)	Justice
	Graßhof, Karin (1986–98)	Justice
	Osterloh, Lerke (1998–2010)	Justice
	Hermanns, Monika (since 2010)	Justice
Seat 3	Federer, Julius† (1951–67)	Justice
	von Schlabrendorff, Fabian† (1967–75)	Justice
	Niebler, Engelbert† (1975–87)	Justice
	Kruis, Konrad (1987–98)	Justice
	Broß, Siegfried (1998–2010)	Justice
	Huber, Peter Michael (since 2010)	Justice

Seat 4	Leibholz, Gerhard† (1951–71)	Justice
	Hirsch, Martin† (1971–81)	Justice
	Mahrenholz, Ernst Gottfried (1981–87)	Justice
	(1987–94)	Vice-President
	Limbach, Jutta (1994)	Vice-President
	(1994–2002)	President
	Lübbe-Wolff, Gertrude (since 2002)	Justice
Seat 5	Roediger, Conrad Frederick† (1951–56)	Justice
	Seat abolished in 1956	
Seat 6	Klaas, Walter† (1951–63)	Justice
	Seat abolished in 1963	

SECOND SENATE: BUNDESRAT ELECTED

Seat 1	Katz, Rudolf† (1951–61)	Vice-President
	Wagner, Friedrich Wilhelm† (1961–67)	Vice-President
	Seuffert, Walter† (1967–75)	Vice-President
	Steinberger, Helmut (1975–87)	Justice
	Kirchhof, Paul (1987–99)	Justice
	Di Fabio, Udo (1999–2011)	Justice
	Müller, Peter (since 2011)	Justice
Seat 2	Geiger, Willi† (1951–77)	Justice
	Träger, Ernst (1977–89)	Justice
	Winter, Klaus† (1989–2000)	Justice
	Mellinghoff, Rudolf (2001–11)	Justice
	Kessal-Wulf, Sibylle (since 2011)	Justice
Seat 3	Fröhlich, Georg† (1951–56)	Justice
	Kutscher, Hans† (1956–70)	Justice
	Wand, Walter Rudi† (1970–83)	Justice
	Klein, Hans Hugo (1983–96)	Justice
	Jentsch, Hans-Joachim (1996–2005)	Justice
	Landau, Herbert (since 2005)	Justice

Seat 4	Leusser, Claus† (1951–52)		Justice
	Schunck, Egon† (1952–63)		Justice
	Geller, Gregor† (1963–71)		Justice
	Rottmann, Joachim (1971–83)		Justice
	Böckenförde, Ernst-Wolfgang (1983–96)		Justice
	Hassemer, Winfried	(1996–2002)	Justice
		(2002–08)	Vice-President
	Voßkuhle, Andreas	(2008–10)	Vice-President
		(since 2010)	President
Seat 5	Wolff, Bernhard† (1951–56)		Justice
	Seat abolished in 1956		
Seat 6	Friesenhahn, Ernst† (1951–63)		Justice
	Seat abolished in 1963		

† deceased

No. 1

BVerfGE 6, 55
of 17 January 1957 – 1 BvL 4/54 –
"Taxation of households case"

HEADNOTES:

1. **The provision under § 80.4 of the Federal Constitutional Court Act (*Bundesverfassungsgerichtsgesetz* – BVerfGG) is not applicable if the Federal Constitutional Court (*Bundesverfassungsgericht*) received a court's submission made pursuant to Article 100.1 of the Basic Law (*Grundgesetz* – GG) and § 80.1 of the Federal Constitutional Court Act prior to the entry into force of the Act Amending the Federal Constitutional Court Act (*Gesetz zur Änderung des Gesetzes über das Bundesverfassungsgericht*) of 21 July 1956 in such a manner that it fulfilled the then applicable rules of procedure.**
2. **The authorisation and obligation to make a submission to the Federal Constitutional Court pursuant to Article 100.1 of the Basic Law applies to all tribunals which are impartial, are entrusted with the tasks of a court on the basis of a formally applicable law, and are designated as a court.**
3. **Any unamended provision of a law which has otherwise been amended following the promulgation of the Basic Law cannot be regarded as pre-constitutional law within the meaning of the decision of 24 February 1953 (Decisions of the Federal Constitutional Court (*Entscheidungen des Bundesverfassungsgerichts* – BVerfGE) 2, 124 (128 et seq.)) if a legislature which is bound by the Basic Law has also incorporated that provision into its will.**
4. **The legislature's discretion is also restricted on account of fundamental provisions (*Grundsatznormen*) which express the constituent legislature's value determinations in regard to certain areas of the legal and social order. Where a statutory provision is found to be incompatible with such a special fundamental provision, a constitutional review of that same provision is no longer possible from the point of view of the general principle of equality (Article 3.1 of the Basic Law).**

5. **Article 6.1 of the Basic Law is not only a "classic fundamental right" guaranteeing the protection of the specific private sphere of marriage and the family and an institutional guarantee, but rather, over and above that, it is also a fundamental provision, i.e. a binding value determination pertaining to that entire realm of private and public law which concerns marriage and the family.**
   It is therefore at least constitutional law which is currently binding for the legislature insofar as it prohibits any encroachment on marriage and the family by means of interference on the part of the state. Placing spouses at a disadvantage on account of joint assessment for income tax purposes – § 26 of the Income Tax Act (*Einkommensteuergesetz* – EStG) as amended on 17 January 1952 – Income Tax Act 1951 – (Federal Law Gazette (*Bundesgesetzblatt* – BGBl.) I p. 33) constitutes such interference.
6. **Equal rights for women include women having the opportunity to earn an income on the free market under the same legal conditions as every male citizen.**

Order of the First Senate of 17 January 1957
– 1 BvL 4/54 –

in the proceedings on the constitutional review of § 26 of the Income Tax Act (*Einkommensteuergesetz* – EStG) as amended on 17 January 1952 – Income Tax Act 1951 – (Federal Law Gazette (*Bundesgesetzblatt* – BGBl.) I p. 33) on application by the Munich Finance Court (*Finanzgericht München*).

RULING:

§ 26 of the Income Tax Act as amended on 17 January 1952 – Income Tax Act 1951 – (Federal Law Gazette I p. 33) is void.

EXTRACT FROM GROUNDS:

A.

According to § I.1 of the Income Tax Act as amended on 17 January 1952 – Income Tax Act 1951 – (Federal Law Gazette I p. 33) "natural persons … are liable to pay income tax". The basis of assessment for income tax according to a progressive tariff is the taxable person's total income (§ 2.1).
Apart from joint assessment of the head of the household with those of his children for whom he is entitled to deduct an allowance (§ 27), only § 26, the provision under review in these proceedings, constitutes an exception to this principle of individual taxation:

"§ 26
Taxation of households: Spouses

> (1) Spouses shall be assessed jointly so long as both are subject to unlimited tax liability and are not permanently separated. These prerequisites must have existed for a minimum of four months during the tax assessment period.
> (2) The spouses' income shall be added together for the purposes of the joint assessment."

§ 43 of the Ordinance Implementing Income Tax Law (*Einkommensteuer-Durchführungsverordnung* – EStDV) as amended on 17 January 1952 – Income Tax Implementation Ordinance 1951 – (Federal Law Gazette I p. 54) stands in relation thereto:

"§ 43
Taxation of households with regard to spouses

> Income from the wife's dependent employment in a business which does not belong to her husband shall not be included in the joint assessment."

B.

I. Mr. and Mrs. S. from P. were assessed jointly for the year 1951 pursuant to § 26 of the Income Tax Act 1951 by the tax assessment notice issued by the Deggendorf Tax Office; Mr. S., a retired civil servant, had drawn a pension and Mrs. S. had earned an income from her retail business. Mr. and Mrs. S. raised an objection to the tax assessment notice; they above all complained about their joint assessment, since on account of the progressive nature of the tariff they thus had to pay more tax than if they had been assessed separately. The Tax Office rejected the objection to the joint assessment as unfounded. Mr. and Mrs. S. appealed that decision. By order of 21 December 1953 – FG II 293/53 – the presiding judge of the Second Chamber at the Munich Finance Court stayed the proceedings … until a decision had been passed by the Federal Constitutional Court (*Bundesverfassungsgericht*) on whether § 26 of the Income Tax Act 1951 was compatible with the Basic Law (*Grundgesetz* – GG). The Chamber confirmed this order by judgment of 25 February 1954 and submitted the files directly to the Federal Constitutional Court. The Finance Court is of the opinion that § 26 of the Income Tax Act 1951 is incompatible with Article 3.2 and Article 6.1 of the Basic Law – as well as with Article 3.1 of the Basic Law, as results from the reference to the Decisions of the Federal Court of Justice in Civil Matters (*Entscheidungen des Bundesgerichtshofes in Zivilsachen* – BGHZ) 11, Annex, p. 34 (78) – "on account of its interfering with equality in taxation for married citizens and unmarried citizens".

II. The Federal Constitutional Court first notified the Federal Finance Court (*Bundesfinanzhof*) of the submission by forwarding the files. Pursuant to § 82.1 and § 82.3 in conjunction with § 77 of the Federal Constitutional Court Act (*Bundesverfassungsgerichtsgesetz* – BVerfGG), the *Bundestag*, the *Bundesrat*, the Federal Government, the *Land* (state) governments and the parties to the original proceedings were given the opportunity to submit written observations. The Federal Minister of Finance availed himself of this opportunity to submit written observations on behalf of the Federal Government, without thereby becoming a party to the proceedings. Mr. and Mrs. S. and the Deggendorf Tax Office likewise submitted written observations.

…

C.

I. Sending the files directly to the Federal Constitutional Court contrary to § 80 of the Federal Constitutional Court Act as amended on 12 March 1951 constituted a procedural error, which was remedied by the Federal Constitutional Court forwarding the files to the Federal Finance Court (see Decisions of the Federal Constitutional Court (*Entscheidungen des Bundesverfassungsgerichts* – BVerfGE) 2, 124 (127)).

…

III. The application made by the Munich Finance Court is admissible.

1. The Munich Finance Court is a "court" within the meaning of Article 100.1 of the Basic Law.

The submission made within the meaning of Article 100.1 of the Basic Law is not the decision of the presiding judge of 21 December 1953, but rather the judgment of the Chamber of 25 February 1954; since only the court having to find in the matter of the appeal is authorised to make a submission (see BVerfGE 1, 80 (81)). …
On 25 February 1954 the Chamber sat with Dr. W., *Regierungsdirektor*, as its presiding judge, Mr. W., *Regierungsrat*, as the established associate judge, and three voluntary associate judges. This composition meets the requirements under § 2.3 of the Bavarian Act on the Restoration of Fiscal Court Jurisdiction (*Gesetz zur Wiederherstellung der Finanzgerichtsbarkeit*) of 19 May 1948 (Law and Ordinance Gazette (*Gesetz- und Verordnungsblatt* – GVBl.) p. 87). Concerns that Bavarian tax courts may not be "courts" within the meaning of the Basic Law might arise – despite their being designated "courts" – since the "established associate judges" could be recalled at any time (§ 2.4 sentence 4) and because the presiding judge and the established associate judge (permanent member) are described in the Act as "civil servants in the fiscal administration" (§ 2.3). In view of these provisions, it may be open to doubt whether the constitutional principles of the independence of the courts and the separation of powers are safeguarded and whether, therefore, taking recourse to the Bavarian tax courts provides the guarantee of recourse to the courts within the meaning of Article 19.4 of the Basic Law. However, no decision regarding this question need be taken in connection with the current review of the admissibility of the application for the judicial review of the constitutionality of a law.
It is true that pursuant to Article 100.1 of the Basic Law, only "courts" are authorised to make a submission to the Federal Constitutional Court. That should, however, not be interpreted such that it only refers to panels of judges which can be viewed in concrete terms as courts within the meaning of the Basic Law and whose activities as a panel of judges thus provide the guarantee of recourse to the courts under Article 19.4 of the Basic Law. The term "court", which is also used in this particular provision, has two different meanings here and in Article 100.1 of the Basic Law, since the two provisions serve different purposes. Article 19.4 of the Basic Law has the task in regard to constitutional law and constitutional policy of guaranteeing the legal protection of each citizen; for that reason the question of whether a panel of judges is a "court" within the meaning of this provision must be measured against a strict standard, i.e. the one established in the decision by the Federal Constitutional Court of 9 November 1955 (BVerfGE 4, 331 (344 et seq.)). By contrast, Article 100.1 of the Basic Law serves to safeguard the authority of the legislature in relation to the administration of justice and to safeguard a uniform administration of justice regarding constitutional issues (BVerfGE 1, 184 (197 et seq.); 2, 124 (128 et seq.)). This objective of constitutional law and constitutional

policy requires that the authorisation and obligation to make a submission to the Federal Constitutional Court pursuant to Article 100.1 of the Basic Law applies to all tribunals which are impartial, are entrusted with the tasks of a court on the basis of a formally applicable law, and are designated as a court. It is not open to any doubt that the Bavarian tax courts are "courts" at least in this sense. The Munich Finance Court is thus authorised to make a submission to the Federal Constitutional Court.

…

2. The provision under review here does not constitute pre-constitutional law within the meaning of the decision of 24 February 1953 (BVerfGE 2, 124 (128 et seq.)); it is thus subject to a review by the Federal Constitutional Court. Although the wording of § 26 of the Income Tax Act to be measured against the Basic Law in this instance has been applicable law since 1939, it does not constitute pre-constitutional law, since the federal legislature has repeatedly discussed and confirmed the need to retain the joint assessment of spouses in connection with consultations regarding amendments to income tax law.

Prior to the tax assessment period 1951, § 26 of the Income Tax Act has not been amended since the Income Tax Act of 16 October 1934 (Reich Law Gazette (*Reichsgesetzblatt* – RGBl.) I p. 1005) as far as content is concerned and not since 1939 as far as its wording is concerned (Promulgation of the Amendment to the Income Tax Act of 27 February 1939, Reich Law Gazette I p. 297); however, the remainder of the Income Tax Act has been amended on numerous occasions, for the tax assessment period 1951 by means of the Act Amending and Simplifying the Income Tax Act and the Corporation Tax Act (*Gesetz zur Änderung und Vereinfachung des Einkommensteuergesetzes und des Körperschaftsteuergesetzes – ESt- und KSt-Änderungsgesetz* 1951) of 21 June 1951 (Federal Law Gazette I p. 411).

The principles developed in the decision of 24 February 1953 cannot readily be applied to those provisions of such a law which has been amended following the promulgation of the Basic Law. The claim that the Federal Constitutional Court is not competent to review pre-constitutional provisions is based on its task of "preventing each individual court disregarding the will of the federal and *Land* legislature by not applying the laws enacted by them because in the opinion of the courts they violate the Basic Law or the federal hierarchy of federal and *Land* law" (BVerfGE 2, 124 (129)). This idea does not at any rate justify treating the unamended provisions of a law which has otherwise been amended following the promulgation of the Basic Law as pre-constitutional law if the legislature which is bound by the Basic Law, in this case the federal legislature, has also incorporated those provisions into its will. Whether that is the case must be determined on a case-by-case basis.

Here, the federal legislature's decision of will results from the fact that § 26 of the Income Tax Act had been thoroughly debated in the course of the legislative procedure and – at least in regard to consultations on the tax amendment law of 27 June 1951 – an amendment had explicitly been rejected [.] …
After that, the federal legislature explicitly confirmed that § 26 of the Income Tax Act was applicable, so that the Federal Constitutional Court has exclusive competency to reject it, as is the case with any newly enacted provision.

D.

The view held by the Munich Finance Court, namely that § 26 of the Income Tax Act 1951 is incompatible with the Basic Law, is well-founded.
I. The subject of the constitutional review is not the question of whether, abstractly, the joint assessment of several persons in general or of spouses in particular is compatible with the Basic Law; rather the issue here is whether the joint assessment of spouses within the framework of the Income Tax Act 1951, which is based on the *progressive* taxation of *individual* taxpayers, is unconstitutional. It may be constitutionally unobjectionable to base taxation not on the income of an individual person, but rather on the income of several persons living in one common household, either by choosing to apply the principle of taxation of households in the first place or by retaining the principle of taxation of individuals and introducing a proportional tariff. The decisive fact here is that spouses are placed at an overall economic disadvantage compared to other persons on account of joint assessment in view of the fact that the progressive tax tariff is geared to the performance of the individual – with joint and several liability associated with joint assessment also coming into play (§ 7.2 and 7.3 of the Tax Adjustment Act (*Steueranpassungsgesetz*) as amended on 1 December 1936 – Reich Law Gazette I p. 961 (977) –).
The two cases of joint assessment (§§ 26, 27 of the Income Tax Act) are extraneous to this modern system of income tax law, which is based on the principle of taxation of the individual. A historical review shows that this is a remnant of what was originally a general system of taxation of households.
The first law to introduce a tax in Germany which is to any significant degree comparable to the present-day income tax was the Prussian Act to Introduce a Class Tax (*Gesetz wegen Einführung einer Klassensteuer*) of 30 May 1820 (Law Collection for the Royal Prussian States (*Gesetz-Sammlung für die Königlichen Preußischen Staaten* – GS) p. 140). Here taxes were levied "on households as a rule" (§ 4(a)); "precise knowledge of financial circumstances" was to be avoided, and the person liable was to be taxed on the basis of a "grading based on a few and easily discernible features" (Instructions of 25 August 1820, printed in Schimmelfennig,

Die Preußischen direkten Steuern, Part 2, 1843, p. 10). The household comprised the "householder" or the "housewife" who was earning her own income plus those dependants they were providing with "accommodation and upkeep" (§ 4(b)). Those who were neither the head of their own household nor a member of a tax-paying household paid half of the tax rate applicable to their class (§ 3.1) as a tax on persons (§ 4(d)). This was, thus, real taxation of households, in which the whole family was treated as a single unit. Neither the Act of 1820 nor the Act on the Introduction of a Class and Classified Income Tax (*Gesetz, betr. die Einführung einer Klassen- und klassifizierten Einkommensteuer*) of 1 May 1851 (GS p. 193) included a duty of declaration. Households were classified according to tax classes based on estimates (§ 7.1 of the Act of 1851).
Subsequent legislation gradually took different groups of members of the household out of joint taxation. The Prussian Income Tax Act of 24 June 1891 (GS p. 175) already in actual fact only retained the taxation of spouses from the old system of taxation of households, although that was not explicitly expressed in the wording of the law (see Fuisting-Strutz, *Komm. z. (preuß.) EStG*, 8th ed., 1915, note 2 re § 10, p. 458); since from then on, in effect, only the spouses' income was added together (§ 11). The Income Tax Act in the version promulgated on 19 June 1906 (GS p. 259) unambiguously expressed that fact (§ 10); the word "household" was not even used, rather the text referred to the fact that the wife's income was added to the husband's income. However, as well as introducing the joint assessment of spouses (§ 16), the (Reich) Income Tax Act of 29 March 1920 (Reich Law Gazette I p. 359) reintroduced the limited inclusion of the income of underage children as well (§ 17); however, it was of little practical significance since the most frequent form of income generated by minors, namely income from dependent and non-dependent *employment*, was not included in the joint assessment and because, under civil law, the father had the right of direct use of the child's *property* anyway, i.e. it was his own income.
Finally, the Act Amending the Income Tax Act (*Änderungsgesetz zum Einkommensteuergesetz*) of 24 March 1921 (Reich Law Gazette p. 313) also introduced a limiting condition on the joint assessment of spouses: The wife's income from non-dependent employment and from dependent employment in a business not belonging to the husband was not included in the joint assessment, and the wife was assessed separately in this respect (§ 16.1 in conjunction with § 9). That regulation was retained in the Income Tax Act of 10 August 1925 – Reich Law Gazette I p. 189 – (§ 22.4 in conjunction with § 6.1; see Strutz, *Komm. z. EStG 1925*, vol. 2, 1929, notes 2 and 21 re § 22, pp. 136-137, 152-153).
However, tax legislation introduced by the National Socialists meant that these exceptions to the joint assessment of spouses were deleted in the Income Tax Act of

16 October 1934 (Reich Law Gazette I p. 1005) and all the wife's income was included in the joint assessment (§ 26). According to the then State Secretary in the Reich Ministry of Finance, the measure served labour market policy efforts to crowd women out of the labour market (Reinhardt, *Die neuen Steuergesetze*, 1934, p. 98). When, during the Second World War, women were needed as labour, the wife's income from dependent employment was excluded from joint taxation on the basis of § 19 of the Income Tax Implementation Ordinance 1941 of 7 December 1941 (Reich Law Gazette I p. 751), and the regulation included in the Income Tax Act of 1921 was thus partly reinstated. This legal situation regarding joint assessment of spouses remained until the fiscal year 1951 relevant here.

The joint assessment of spouses was thus originally part of a system of general taxation of households, and was also justified in that context. Since the legislature has abandoned the principle of taxation of households and adopted the principle of taxation of individuals, it constitutes an element that is, taken out of context, not compatible with today's income tax law.

Up until the end of the First World War, joint assessment was of little economic relevance either for the individual taxpayer or the state, since the progression of tariffs was very modest and the tax rates remained low. It was not until the idea had become established that, in the case of direct taxes, equality in taxation necessitated a steeper progressive gradation of the tax tariff, and since this gradation has led to considerable tension between the highest and lowest tax rate, joint assessment leads to substantial additional tax charges on spouses. This cannot even be balanced out by creating several tax classes, i.e. fixed – non-progressive – tax-free income parts for the wife (and for the children) which are incorporated into the tariff. These allowable deductions only take account of the increase in the subsistence minimum, which is linked to the individual taxpayer's obligation to pay his family members' upkeep, but do not change the principle of progressive taxation of individuals. At the same time, the additional tax charges associated with joint assessment have provided the state with an additional source of income, whilst in the past it merely served to simplify the administrative process (see Grounds for § 11 of the draft of a (Prussian) Income Tax Act: Annexes to the Stenographic Minutes on Negotiations in the House of Representatives during the 3rd Session of the 17th Electoral Term 1890/91, vol. 1, Doc. No. 5, p. 222).

II. Such additional tax charges on spouses which take marriage as their point of reference, as also result from § 26 of the Income Tax Act 1951, are incompatible with Article 6.1 of the Basic Law.

1. In contrast to Article 134 of the Weimar Constitution (*Weimarer Reichsverfassung*), the Basic Law does not contain an explicit provision regarding which principle is to be applied to how citizens contribute to public charges. However, there is

no doubt that the legislature is bound by the principle of equality in taxation which results from Article 3.1 of the Basic Law.
According to the case-law of the Federal Constitutional Court, the reasoning behind Article 3.1 of the Basic Law is “to a considerable degree that not all actual differences should lead to different treatment by the law, but rather only those actual dissimilarities which, out of consideration for justice and expediency, also differ in regard to their importance for the law. That decision is primarily left to the legislature to make” (BVerfGE 3, 225 (240)). However, the legislature’s discretion reaches its limits not only in the prohibition of arbitrariness and in how the general principle of equality (in particular Article 3.2 and 3.3 of the Basic Law) is given concrete form in various instances, but also in other fundamental provisions which express the constituent legislature’s value determinations in regard to certain areas of the legal and social order. Where such fundamental provisions are to be taken into consideration, a provision must first be reviewed to establish whether it is compatible with them; where the answer is negative, then it is no longer possible to carry out a review from the point of view of the general principle of equality (Article 3.1 of the Basic Law). Therefore, the Munich Finance Court correctly described Article 3.2 and Article 6.1 of the Basic Law as special review criteria. Since § 26 of the Income Tax Act 1951 takes the chargeable event of “marriage” as its point of reference, its constitutionality is primarily to be measured against Article 6.1 of the Basic Law.
2. Article 6.1 of the Basic Law is a fundamental provision that determines values. It places marriage and the family, as the nucleus of all human society whose significance cannot be compared to any other human relationship, under the special protection of the state.
First and foremost this is a determination in the sense of a classic fundamental right which, in view of experiences gained in the period under National Socialist rule, serves to protect the specific private sphere of marriage and the family from external coercion on the part of the state. By turning away from the all-powerful state which existed under National Socialist rule, the Basic Law pledged to safeguard a person’s autonomy and self-responsibility in regard to this area of life too.
Indisputably, the constitutional commitment to marriage and the family at the same time encompasses guaranteeing both lifestyles, i.e. it also comprises what is known as an institutional or agency guarantee. As such, it merely safeguards the fundamental structure of marriage and the family, so that in legal reality its legal effect only serves to constitutionally guarantee core provisions of marriage and family law.
However, the legal effect of Article 6.1 of the Basic Law goes beyond those functions. Like a whole series of constitutional provisions – especially those regulating

the citizen's relations with the state or the life of the community – Article 6.1 of the Basic Law fulfils several functions which are interconnected and overlap. It is the task of constitutional case-law to deduce the various functions of a constitutional provision, in particular those of a fundamental right. In doing so preference is to be given to that interpretation "which develops the legal effect of the provision in question to the greatest degree" (Thoma).

An interpretation of Article 6.1 of the Basic Law based on this principle shows that it not only contains a commitment and acts as an institutional guarantee, but rather that over and above that it also represents a fundamental provision, i.e. a binding value determination pertaining to that entire realm of private and public law which concerns marriage and the family.

According to its wording, Article 6.1 of the Basic Law per se demands that marriage and the family enjoy the special protection of the state. Even this broad wording clearly indicates its purpose – also – as a fundamental provision pertaining to all of that law which concerns marriage and the family. And this interpretation alone also does justice to the guiding principle of the social state under the rule of law and to the provision being included in that part of the constitution which contains fundamental rights.

That sense of Article 6.1 of the Basic Law which goes beyond the institutional guarantee is also confirmed by its genesis. It essentially retains the content of subsections 1 and 2 of Article 119 of the Weimar Constitution:

> "Marriage, as the foundation of the family and the preservation and expansion of the nation, enjoys the special protection of the Constitution. It is based on the equality of both sexes.
> The state and the local authorities are responsible for the preservation, recovery and social promotion of the family. Large families have the right to claim compensatory welfare support."

In this broader version, the safeguard provision also explicitly refers to the remainder of public and private law which concerns marriage and the family.

Despite the fact that Article 6.1 of the Basic Law is shorter than Article 119 of the Weimar Constitution, there is nothing which speaks in favour of the legislature of the Basic Law wanting to limit the scope of the safeguard provision compared to the Weimar Constitution to the institution-forming provisions of marriage and family law: The so-called "Herrenchiemsee Draft" contained no provision which corresponded to Article 119 of the Weimar Constitution. The first proposal, which was formulated by members of the CDU parliamentary group, summarised the safeguard provision for marriage and the family in one sentence:

"Marriage, as the legitimate form of the lasting relationship between man and woman and the family issuing from it, as well as the rights and duties resulting from marriage and membership of a family enjoy the special protection of the Constitution."
(24th Session of the Policy Committee, Stenographic Minutes (*StenProt.*), p. 34).

The proposal was initially justified by claiming that this version corresponded, as far as content was concerned, to the draft of the United Nations Universal Declaration of Human Rights, according to which the family is the natural and fundamental group unit of society and is entitled to protection (see *Jahrbuch des öffentlichen Rechts der Gegenwart. Neue Folge* – JöR NF, vol. 1, p. 93, note 2). In the course of the consultations, the CDU parliamentary group repeatedly pointed out that the Weimar Constitution had already ensured that marriage and the family enjoyed the protection of the state. The recurrent discussions never once touched on the fact that the constitutional guarantee only refers to the core area of marriage and family law, i.e. that it should mean less than the parallel provision in the Weimar Constitution.
The opinion expressed by the Federal Minister of Finance, namely that Article 6.1 of the Basic Law can therefore not be of any objective-legal significance for tax law because it essentially represents an institutional guarantee and, over and above that, is only programmatic in nature, finds no justification in a statement issued by the General Drafting Committee of the Parliamentary Council, to which the Federal Minister of Finance has made reference. It is a note referring to the then Article 7a (as amended in the first reading of the Main Committee), which read as follows:

"(1) Marriage, as the legitimate form of the lasting relationship between man and woman and the family it is endowed with, as well as the rights and duties resulting from marriage and membership of a family enjoy the special protection of the Constitution.
(2) Every mother shall be entitled to the same protection and support of the community.
(3) The legislature shall create the same conditions for the physical, mental and social development of children born out of wedlock as for children born in wedlock." (Parliamentary Council Printed Paper (*PR Drucks.*) No. 340).

The “note” added by the General Drafting Committee, as published in the Parliamentary Council Printed Paper No. 370 of 13 December 1948, reads as follows:

> “*Note regarding Article 7a:*
> If marriage and the family enjoy the protection of the state, then the resulting rights thus also enjoy that protection. For the rest, no reference to the legitimate form of the lasting relationship between man and woman is required if marriage per se enjoys the special protection of the state. *This Article is only of programmatic significance.** It in principle only establishes guidelines for the legislature and over and above that merely has the character of an interpretative provision for courts applying the law. The principle of only including directly applicable law in that section of the Constitution which contains fundamental rights has thus been broken.”

The note was, however, corrected (Parliamentary Council Printed Paper No. 394 of 18 December 1948, p. 3) and the amended wording was included in the printed version of the drafts of the Basic Law (phrases proposed by the technical committees, the General Drafting Committee, the Main Committee and the plenary: p. 87). The decisive sentence there reads as follows:

> “Article 7a *subsection* 3 is only of programmatic significance.”**

The concerns of the General Drafting Committee thus – contrary to the opinion of the Federal Minister of Finance – did not refer to subsection 1, the only one which is of interest here (the explanations in JöR NF vol. 1, p. 97-98, are incorrect).

…

The genesis of Article 6.1 of the Basic Law thus shows that the scope of the safeguard provision in regard to marriage and the family was, according to the will of the constituent legislature, not to be restricted more than the corresponding provision in the Weimar Constitution, and thus confirms the provision’s function as deduced from the interpretation of the text as a fundamental provision that determines values.

3. Article 6.1 of the Basic Law’s function as a fundamental provision that determines values provides the legal limits for the freedom of legislative discretion.

Like every constitutional provision, Article 6.1 of the Basic Law is only currently binding law for the legislature insofar as its wording is sufficiently clear to allow an

---

* Emphasis added by the Court.

** Emphasis added by the Court.

inferior provision to be measured against it. Here the degree of the precision results from the term "protection"; which means promoting the protected interest, protecting against interference or impairment and above all no interference on the part of the state. The special protection enjoyed by marriage and the family as laid down in Article 6.1 of the Basic Law thus comprises two aspects: in the *positive* sense, the state's task of not only protecting marriage and the family from encroachment by other authorities, but also of promoting it by suitable means; in the *negative* sense the prohibition of the state itself impairing or encroaching on marriage. It may remain open whether even when fulfilling the positive protective function under Article 6.1 of the Basic Law cases are imaginable in which its wording is sufficiently precise to allow an inferior provision to be measured against it. In any case, it clearly – in the negative sense – prohibits the state from encroaching on marriage and the family by interfering, and is thus current constitutional law.

Naturally, Article 6.1 of the Basic Law, even in its function as a fundamental provision, does not prohibit linking legal consequences with certain economic impacts to the chargeable event of "marriage", as the Federal Minister of Finance fears. For one thing, Article 6.1 of the Basic Law does not prohibit giving married couples preferential treatment, but rather only placing them at a disadvantage: The introduction of favourable tax law provisions (e.g. splitting) would thus be constitutionally unobjectionable in that respect. Furthermore, it is obvious that marriage can be the point of reference for economic legal consequences insofar as that corresponds to the nature of the sphere of life being regulated. That applies in particular to relations between family members and the benefit-providing administration, where the social state under the rule of law takes on the duties of care which used to be performed by the extended family or the maintenance obligations of a deceased person or a person who is unable to pay maintenance.

Further, the conclusion cannot be drawn from Article 6.1 of the Basic Law that such provisions are incompatible with the constitution which only in certain cases have the unintended incidental consequence of providing a gravamen for marriage.

4. As regards the constitutional review of § 26 of the Income Tax Act 1951, it is Article 6.1 of the Basic Law's effect as a current protective provision that is at any rate decisive; since the joint assessment of spouses in regard to income tax breaks through the principle of taxation of individuals, namely to the detriment of married couples, and thus constitutes interference with marriage. The objections raised against this conclusion lack justification.

Joint assessment cannot be justified by saying that it does not take marriage as its point of reference, but rather the (purported) savings made on account of running a common household and the resulting increase in "performance", so that the increased taxation of spouses merely constitutes an unintentional incidental consequence. But the remainder of income tax law does not take account, as a factor of performance, of the possibility of making savings in regard to the cost of living; this aspect is therefore extrinsic to the system. Above all, however, it is not correct to say that increased taxation of spouses is only an unintentional incidental consequence; since joint assessment is not only linked to marriage as a legal maxim, but the resulting effect of increased taxation is the actual, main purpose of this provision.

Were the increased performance on account of running a common household the actual point of reference, then taxes could not only be levied on the marital household, especially since it by no means constitutes the typical kind of household comprising several persons earning an income on the free market. Whilst, for example, in 1950, of a total of 12.6 million multi-person households there were 5.7 million households with more than one income earner (not including family members helping in a family business), there were only 0.74 million gainfully employed wives living in the same household as their husband that year, whereby wives helping out in their husband's business were not included (*Wirtschaft und Statistik*, 1954, pp. 214 and 326). Not even every seventh case in which several persons earning an independent income on the free market are living in one household is thus based on the wife earning an income. Abandoning the joint assessment of spouses would thus also not, as the Federal Minister of Finance believes, constitute injustice vis-à-vis the unmarried because they do not generally have the opportunity to keep house with other people.

The causality between marriage per se, not the running of a common household, and joint assessment is explicitly confirmed by the case-law of the Federal Finance Court. In a judgment of 2 July 1953 (Federal Tax Gazette (*Bundessteuerblatt* – BStBl.) 1953 III p. 256, no. 217) it dismissed the objections raised by two gainfully employed spouses (both managers of different businesses) against their joint assessment, although the spouses had both not changed and permanently maintained the households they had had prior to getting married, which were located around 10 km apart. In its decision the Federal Finance Court found that spouses can only be assessed separately "if the separation not only refers to the household and management of the household, but rather also to married life". According to the case-law of the Federal Finance Court, a couple are only permanently separated within the meaning of § 26.1 sentence 1 of the Income Tax Act if they are separated "from bed and board". It thus follows the casc-law of the Reich Finance Court (Reich Tax Gazette (*Reichssteuerblatt* – RStBl.) 1937 p. 435), which had for a long time already been included in the Income Tax Directives (*Einkommensteuer-Richtlinien* – EStR; e.g. Income Tax Directive 1951 of 31 May 1952 – Federal Tax Gazette 1952 I p. 289 (380) – section 190): "Spouses are permanently separated within the meaning of § 26 of the Income Tax Act if their separation covers married life, the household and management of the household, and one spouse intends to maintain this separation in the longer term."

Nor does the increased tax pressure associated with joint assessment have its roots, according to the essence of income tax law, in the very nature of marriage; since it is obvious that in the case of a mere tax provision, the point of reference of marriage is not in the nature of the matter, as is the case, for example, in family law or in certain areas of welfare law. If in income tax law the point of reference is to be the fact that marriage and the family are "not only" to be recognised as "the sum of two spouses and their children ..., but rather as a superior unit" (Memorandum of the Federal Minister of Finance regarding the question of taxation of spouses: Bundestag II/1953, Printed Paper 1866, Annex 1, p. 17), then that could at most justify placing spouses at an advantage when it comes to taxation. It is incomprehensible how placing spouses at a disadvantage when it comes to taxation could be justified by the higher moral value attached to that status on which their taxation is then based.

Furthermore, an attempt has been made to justify the discrimination of spouses associated with joint assessment by claiming that showing consideration for those married couples where only one spouse is earning an economic income, in particular those with large families, and that the supposed necessity of "getting wives back into the home" practically called for joint assessment in view of Article 6.1 of the Basic Law.

Rescinding joint assessment would – it has been said – mean unjust discrimination of families in which the wife and mother does not or cannot earn an economic income. It is not obvious to what extent a family with only *one* person earning an income should be placed at an unjust disadvantage compared to those married couples who both earn an income: since if one assumes that such "discrimination" exists, then it also exists vis-à-vis every other taxpayer who must bear the costs for a smaller number of people than a father who is the sole earner in the family, and this "discrimination" cannot be eliminated by subjecting, of the large number of those who are "positively discriminated", only those spouses with two independent incomes to higher rates of taxation. If one wants to do justice, from the point of view of the social welfare state and the protection of marriage and the family, to the special situation of the husband and father who must bear the costs for several persons, then there are various ways of doing so which have already been the subject of public debate (increasing allowable deductions, introducing so-called splitting). Joint assessment is unsuitable, since it only places a higher tax burden on some married couples without benefiting the others. If one interprets the objection that showing consideration for large families requires the joint assessment of spouses such that the additional income from joint assessment is to be used to benefit those families with many children, then that amounts to – apart from the fact that it would be impossible to monitor such use on the basis of applicable budgetary principles – the justification that the state's general financial requirements necessitate this income. However, the state's financial requirements are never suited to justifying an unconstitutional tax.

Joint assessment is to serve the purpose of "getting wives back into the home", the so-called educational effect, because the associated additional tax burden stops wives from entering gainful employment (see, e.g., Memorandum of the Federal Minister of Finance, p. 14). In principle no constitutional objections can be raised to a tax pursuing purposes other than merely generating income. However, that only applies with the caveat that these incidental purposes are themselves neutral as far as the constitution is concerned and are pursued by means of taxes that are constitutionally unobjectionable. In the case of joint assessment of spouses, however, the educational effect is firstly used to justify a provision that is already unconstitutional for other reasons. Secondly, the educational effect itself concerns an area which is already delimited by a decision under constitutional law on the basis of which the ordinary legislature is no longer entirely free to make determinations with regard to values: That results both from Article 6.1 of the Basic Law and from Article 3.2 and 3.3 of the Basic Law.

As already explained in the above, Article 6.1 of the Basic Law expresses, in the sense of a classic fundamental right, a commitment to the freedom of the specific private sphere of marriage and the family; it thus corresponds to a guiding principle of our constitution, namely the fundamental limitedness of all public authority in its means of having an influence on the free individual. The conclusion to be drawn from this idea is generally the recognition that there is a sphere of private life on which the state can have no influence (BVerfGE 5, 85 (200, 204); Judgment of 16 January 1957 – 1 BvR 253/56 –). The content of such private decision-making freedom on the part of married couples includes the decision regarding whether a wife will remain at home, whether she will help her husband in his business, or whether she will earn her own income on the free market. The goal of getting those wives who are earning an income "back into the home", which is used to justify joint assessment, corresponds to a specific idea of what constitutes the best type of marriage. The principle of protecting marriage and the family as set out in Article 6.1 of the Basic Law, however, applies to every marriage and family which corresponds to the legally standardised civil-law institutions of marriage and family in the Federal Republic of Germany today, that is, it leaves it up to the spouses to decide how to organise that private sphere. The legislature should therefore not directly force couples to organise the private sphere of marriage in a certain way. Where, however, such direct coercion is unconstitutional, then the same goal cannot also be suitable for legitimising a measure which, like joint assessment, indirectly serves that objective.

The fact that the so-called educational effect is unsuitable for justifying joint assessment also follows from the principle of equality of the sexes (Article 3.2 and 3.3 of the Basic Law). The Basic Law assumes that equality of the sexes is compatible with the protection of marriage and the family (see BVerfGE 3, 225 (241)), so that the legislation can also not assume that the two principles are contradictory. However, the principle of equal rights for women includes women having the opportunity to earn an income on the free market based on the same legal opportunities as every male citizen. Judging the gainful employment of women from the outset as being destructive to marriage contradicts not only the principle but also the wording of Article 3.2 of the Basic Law. The purpose of the law, namely to stop wives from engaging in gainful employment, is not suited to justifying joint assessment.

5. Based on all the above, the conclusion to be drawn is that § 26 of the Income Tax Act 1951 constitutes an exemption provision which places married couples at a disadvantage and thus violates the value determination under Article 6.1 of the Basic Law to the detriment of marriage.

It is thus not necessary to review whether § 26 of the Income Tax Act 1951 is also unconstitutional looked at from other aspects of constitutional law, in particular on account of a violation of Article 3 of the Basic Law. …

In view of this outcome, administrative considerations which have been drawn on in justification of joint assessment – for instance making it easier to record married couples compared to other common households and possibly preventing tax manipulation among spouses – cannot be the decisive issue. Compared to Article 6.1 of the Basic Law, they are by their very nature not suited to being used as legal arguments, since the precedence given to constitutional value judgments prohibits the legislature from giving scope to considerations of expediency which violate such value judgments. Nevertheless, that does not say that such administrative aspects should not be important if a tax law is only to be measured against the yardstick of Article 3.1 of the Basic Law, i.e. regarding its compatibility with the principle of general equality in taxation. For the rest, special statutory provisions which merely serve to prevent spouses circumventing the obligation to pay taxes by means of a pretext based on the civil-law distribution of incomes – especially from capital assets – would also never constitute discrimination against marriage and the family as prohibited under Article 6.1 of the Basic Law.

III. As a result, § 26 of the Income Tax Act 1951 is thus not compatible with Article 6.1 of the Basic Law and therefore void.

Although in individual cases – namely when the profits of one spouse are added to the losses of the other – joint assessment can also be advantageous for the taxpayers, the declaration of nullity as such must be made, since § 26 of the Income Tax Act 1951 – in contrast to, for instance, § 69.2 of the Emergency Aid Act (*Soforthilfegesetz*; BVerfGE 4, 331 (332)) – is a unitary provision which can only be valid or void in its entirety.

As a result of the Federal Constitutional Court's decision, the legislature replaced § 26 of the Income Tax Act 1951, the provision which had been declared void, with §§ 26 to 26e of the Income Tax Act as amended in 1957 on the basis of Article 1 no. 4 of the Act Amending Tax Law Provisions (Gesetz zur Änderung steuerrechtlicher Vorschriften) *of 26 July 1957 (Federal Law Gazette I p. 848). § 26 of the Income Tax Act subsequently read as follows:*

> *"Spouses who are both subject to unlimited tax liability and are not permanently separated and for whom these prerequisites have existed for at least four months during the tax assessment period shall be assessed separately pursuant to § 26a. They shall be assessed jointly pursuant to §§ 26b to 26e upon application."*

No. 2

BVerfGE 10, 59
of 29 July 1959 – 1 BvR 205, 332, 333, 367/58, 1 BvL 27, 100/58 –
"Case concerning parental power"

HEADNOTE:

The moral community between the parents and their joint, indivisible responsibility for the child in conjunction with the comprehensive requirement of equal rights under the constitution results in the absolute equality of the father and the mother in the area of parental power.

Judgment of the First Senate of 29 July 1959
– 1 BvR 205, 332, 333, 367/58, 1 BvL 27, 100/58 –
in the consolidated proceedings

I. regarding the constitutional complaints 1. of the lawyer Maria M., 2. of the wife Amalie T., 3. of the wife Gertrud G., 4. of the wife Ingeborg H. against § 1628 and § 1629.1 of the Civil Code (*Bürgerliches Gesetzbuch* – BGB) as amended by the Equal Rights Act (*Gleichberechtigungsgesetz*) of 18 June 1957 (Federal Law Gazette (*Bundesgesetzblatt* – BGBl.) I p. 609),
II. regarding the review under constitutional law of § 1629.1 of the Civil Code as amended by the Equal Rights Act of 18 June 1957 (Federal Law Gazette I p. 609) – referrals from the Local Court (*Amtsgericht*) of Cologne (referral decision of 24 July 1958 – 16 VII H 9642) and of the Local Court of Bensberg (referral decision of 13 November 1958 – 6 C 1098/58).

RULING:

§ 1628 and § 1629.1 of the Civil Code as amended by the Equal Rights Act of 18 June 1957 (Federal Law Gazette I p. 609) are void.

EXTRACT FROM GROUNDS:

A.

The provisions of the Civil Code on parental power were amended by the Equal Rights Act of 18 June 1957 (Federal Law Gazette I p. 609). According to § 1626.1 [of the Civil Code], a child who is not of age is subject to the parental power of its father and mother. According to subsection 2, unless otherwise stated in individual provisions, by virtue of their parental power the father and the mother are entitled and obliged to look after the child and its property; looking after the child and its property also includes representation of the child. According to § 1627, the parents shall exercise their parental power at their own responsibility and in mutual agreement for the benefit of the child, and they shall endeavour to reach agreement should differences of opinion arise.

§ 1628 and § 1629.1 of the Civil Code, the provisions under review in the present proceedings, read as follows:

§ 1628

If the parents are unable to agree, the father shall decide while taking into consideration the mother's opinion.

The guardianship court (*Vormundschaftsgericht*) may entrust the decision on an individual matter or on matters of a certain kind to the mother if the father's conduct in a matter of particular importance is not consistent with the child's best interests or if proper administration of the child's property requires such a transfer.

If the father persistently breaches his obligation to endeavour to reach agreement where differences of opinions arise and to take the mother's opinion into consideration when making his decisions, the guardianship court may entrust the mother with the decision in the personal and property matters of the child upon request, if this corresponds to the child's best interests.

§ 1629.1

The father is entitled to represent the child; the mother shall represent the child insofar as she exercises the parental power alone or insofar as she has been entrusted with the decision in accordance with § 1628.2 and 1628.3.

I.

The complainants are wives and the mothers of children who are minors. Their constitutional complaints directly challenge § 1628 and § 1629.1 of the Civil Code. The complainants argue that both provisions are contrary to Article 3.2 and Article 6.2 of the Basic Law (*Grundgesetz* – GG). They take the view that their status as mothers as guaranteed by the aforesaid provisions of the Basic Law is violated by the Civil Code.

II.

The applications submitted by the Local Courts of Cologne and Bensberg under Article 100.1 of the Basic Law are based on the following factual constellations:

Wilhelm Reinhard F., who is a minor, recognised his paternity of the child Heinz H. before the Local Court of Cologne and undertook to pay child maintenance in enforceable form. His father granted his consent in accordance with § 111 of the Civil Code. The judge of the guardianship court who was competent to decide on approval of the payment obligation considers such consent invalid, i.e. ineligible for approval, since the mother of the young father had not granted her consent in accordance with § 111 of the Civil Code. The judge takes the view that as a matter of principle the father is entitled to act as the legal representative of the minor solely together with the mother. The judge would therefore like to refuse to grant his approval.

T. company filed suit against Willi K., who is a minor, before the Local Court of Bensberg for payment of the price of a French correspondence course, arguing that the defendant had entered into the contract of sale with the approval of his father. The defendant is represented by his father during the proceedings. The court takes the view that representation by the father is not sufficient since the defendant can only be represented by both parents jointly. The court would therefore like to dismiss the suit by a judgment based on procedural aspects alone.

Both judges consider their intended judgments to be prevented by § 1629.1 of the Civil Code. They consider the provision incompatible with Article 3.2 of the Basic Law, the judge at the guardianship court in Cologne also with Article 6.2 of same Law. He therefore suspended the proceedings for approval, and the judge in Bensberg suspended the proceedings, and both requested a decision from the Federal Constitutional Court (*Bundesverfassungsgericht*) in accordance with Article 100.1 of the Basic Law as to whether § 1629.1 of the Civil Code is compatible with the Basic Law. It was argued that one could only speak of equality if the father and the mother have equal influence on measures concerning the child. However, the legitimate influence of the mother on the child's fate is diminished significantly by the authorisation to represent granted to the father alone. Practical reservations against joint representation of the child by both parents are irrelevant in the face of the unequivocal provisions of the Basic Law, it was argued, especially since joint representation was practised between 1 April 1953 and the entry into force of the Equal Rights Act (1 July 1958) without notable problems.

III.

The Federal Minister of Justice commented on the constitutional issues in the name of the Federal Government, without joining one of the proceedings for judicial review of legal provisions. In his view § 1628 and § 1629.1 of the Civil Code are compatible with the Basic Law.

…

IV.

…

V.

…

B.

All proceedings are admissible.

The constitutional complaints which directly challenge the provisions are admissible because the complainants as the mothers of children who are minors are affected themselves, presently and directly by the legislation (see Decisions of the Federal Constitutional Court (*Entscheidungen des Bundesverfassungsgerichts* – BVerfGE) 1, 97 (101)).

The legislation regulates the right of the father to make decisions where there are differences of opinion, and grants the authorisation to represent solely to the father as regards personal and property matters of the child. It thus determines the legal status of the mother within the family directly, without an act of execution by a public authority being required for enforcement of the legislation.

The decision referred by the Local Court of Cologne is admissible although it was rendered not within a lawsuit but, rather, in proceedings of voluntary jurisdiction (see BVerfGE 4, 45 (48)). The decision requests a comprehensive constitutional review of § 1629 of the Civil Code; it becomes clear from the context, however, that the provision in § 1629.1 alone is meant.

C.

§ 1628 and § 1629.1 of the Civil Code are not compatible with the Basic Law.

I.

According to Article 6.1 of the Basic Law, marriage and the family enjoy the special protection of the state. The structural principles determining these institutions arise initially from the regulation of life outside the confines of the law. Both institutions date from time immemorial and have essentially remained unchanged; to this extent the substance of the institutional guarantee under Article 6.1 of the Basic Law is compatible with conventional law. The Basic Law deems marriage to be an alliance between a man and a woman in conjugal community that in principle cannot be dissolved, and the family is the broad community of parents and children within which the parents have the primary right and obligation to look after and bring up the children. This systematic core of the institutions is inviolable with regard to the general sense of justice and the sense of right and wrong.

However, this does not exhaust the institutional substance of Article 6.1 of the Basic Law. Further crucial elements arise from the particular value determinations under the Basic Law. The comprehensive requirement of equal rights in Article 3.2 and 3.3 of the Basic Law especially comes into question in this respect. The makers of the Basic Law proceeded on the assumption that Article 6 is compatible with Article 3.2 of the Basic Law; the Federal Constitutional Court has confirmed this view as regards Article 6.1 of same Law, according to which men and women have equal rights within a marriage and within the family (BVerfGE 3, 225 (242)).

The requirement of equal rights for men and women within a marriage and within the family also applies unreservedly to the regulation of relations between parents and children. Article 6.2 of the Basic Law describes the care and upbringing of children as being "the natural right of parents and a duty primarily incumbent upon them". The close community between parents and their joint responsibility for the child results in the equality of the father and the mother in relations with the children. Since the responsibility is indivisible, it affects the parents equally. Their obligation to support and complement one another within that responsibility is reciprocal; there is equality between the father and the mother who are joined in moral community.

1. The history of the Basic Law confirms this interpretation. The provision in Article 6.1 and 6.2 in conjunction with Article 3.2 and 3.3 of the Basic Law goes back to Article 119.1 of the Weimar Constitution (*Weimarer Reichsverfassung*). It was argued expressly at the National Assembly during the consultations on the provision in opposition to the motion to include in the draft a sentence on the equality of men and women within marriage and the family, that the right of men to decide had to be upheld in case of disputes within the family. It was stated in response that "the provisions of the Civil Code presently in force result in injustice against women in many cases and hence against marriage" (constituent assembly of the German National Assembly, 70th session on 30 July 1919, Minutes p. 2087, (2126), and printed papers nos. 680 and 711). As a result of the consultations, a provision was included in Article 119.1 that marriage – as the basis of family life – is based on the equality of the two sexes.
The negotiations within the Parliamentary Council (*Parlamentarischer Rat*) leave no doubt that the makers of the constitution did not intend to fall short of the provisions of the Constitution of the Weimar Republic, but, rather, intended to realise the principle of equality comprehensively in all areas of the law and specifically within civil law. The Member of Parliament Dr. Strauss emphasised this through his reference to the burden placed on and shouldered by women in the wartime and the immediate post-war period. He stressed (Deliberations of the Main Committee, 42nd session on 18 January 1949, pp. 538-539) that:

> "… the principle of equality of men and women has become second nature to us to such an extent at least since 1918 that the debate is somewhat surprising to us … We agreed on the principle from the outset. It is also self-evident. Recent years especially have proven to all men including bachelors that the responsibilities of a woman are even more severe – also physically – than those of a man. Most German women have worked for years now, likewise the men, but in addition to the responsibilities of men they also have household responsibilities and the task of bringing up children. Many German men have only learned during these years what housework is, especially when they were compelled to participate in it. As a result there should be no doubt anywhere – apart from in a couple of country bumpkins – even among bachelors that we have to recognise and demand equal rights for women in all respects, not only as regards civil rights and duties, and that any legal contradictions have to be removed.
> We therefore have to find a wording which puts this aspect into full effect. This can be realised in accordance with our motion, by deleting the word 'civil' (*staatsbürgerlich*) and by setting a deadline in the transitional provisions, which to my knowledge has taken place, by which date the conflicting general law, es-

pecially the law on marital goods, has to be adjusted to this principle. I therefore believe, and the general public can now establish, that this matter has been clarified in a manner which no longer reveals any differences of opinion within the parliament."

There was general agreement on this point (see Members of Parliament Dr. v. Mangoldt, Dr. Weber and Dr. Dehler at the 26th session of the Policy Committee (*Grundsatzausschuß*) on 30 November 1948, Stenographic Minutes (*StenProt.*) p. 59/61; Mrs. Selbert at the 42nd session of the Main Committee on 18 January 1949, p. 540). Hence, the resolution of the Parliamentary Council seems to be a decision that was taken in full awareness of its implications, as the fulfilment of demands long raised which did not necessarily arise merely from the societal changes of the last century and the changed status of women in society and within the family; it was also and specifically justified by the actual living conditions prior to and during the coming into being of the Basic Law.

A glance at the efforts of women's associations aimed over decades at achieving equality suffices in order to remove any doubts that the Basic Law intended women as mothers to have equal rights. As early as 1895, a memorial by Sera Proelss and Marie Raschke, "*Die Frau im neuen bürgerlichen Gesetzbuch*" (p. 34), called for equal parental power for the father and the mother (see also, e.g., Marianne Weber, "*Ehefrau und Mutter in der Rechtsentwicklung*" (1907), pp. 457-458; memorial published by the German organisation of women's associations in 1923, pp. 37-38; expert opinions and papers for the 36th German Jurists Forum (*Deutscher Juristentag*) 1931 (vol. 1 pp. 584 et seq., 608 et seq.; vol. 2 pp. 92 et seq.)). It is not conceivable that the makers of a constitution wishing to achieve comprehensive equal rights for women also in civil law would have wanted to permit a limitation in this important area without saying so expressly.

2. In practice and academia, in the period between the entry into force of the principle of equal rights (1 April 1953) and the entry into force of the Equal Rights Act (1 July 1958), one proceeded predominantly on the assumption of absolute equality of parents within the family.

For safety's sake the administration at least assumed the necessity of joint representation of children by their parents. This is expressed for example in the decrees issued by the ministers of the interior in the *Länder* (states) in the area of the law on nationality, in which the subordinate authorities were instructed only to accept applications filed jointly by the father and the mother as of 1 April 1953. …

During those 5 years, under the leadership of the German Federal Court of Justice (*Bundesgerichtshof* – BGH), with only few exceptions the case-law advocated joint decisions and joint responsibility of parents, especially the Fourth Senate of the

Federal Court of Justice. In its decision of 2 May 1956 (Decisions of the Federal Court of Justice in Civil Matters (*Entscheidungen des Bundesgerichtshofes in Zivilsachen* – BGHZ 20, p. 313), the Federal Court of Justice issued the following headnotes on the right to make decisions:

> "In corresponding application of § 1797 and 1798 of the Civil Code, the guardianship court is competent to decide a dispute between the parents, who as a matter of principle share parental custody as of 31 March 1953, in a matter concerning custody, if the prerequisites of § 1666 are not met. The child's best interests alone are pivotal to the decision."

In its decision of 5 February 1958 (*Zeitschrift für das gesamte Familienrecht* – FamRZ 1958, p. 178), i.e. after publication of the Equal Rights Act, the Fourth Senate also held that a legitimate child who is a minor has to be represented by both parents jointly in the period between the entry into force of Article 3.2 of the Basic Law and the entry into force of the Equal Rights Act – i.e. during a period in which "the principle of equal rights has to be realised without express individual provisions that within a certain context are reserved to the legislative powers." …

The predominant opinion in academia was consistent with the prevailing practice within the administration and case-law. The issue already discussed in 1931 … was addressed again at the 38th German Jurists Forum in 1950. The civil law faction concurred with the view taken by the speaker Prof. Dr. Ulmer, that the Basic Law required a provision according to which the father and mother were to exercise parental power jointly; in case of significant disputes the guardianship court was to decide (38th German Jurists Forum (1950) B 53-54, 98-99, 102). …

Finally, the Equal Rights Act itself takes the constitutional requirement of equality into account as a structural element of the family, also in relations between parents and children: the provisions on parental power state firstly that the father and the mother are both entitled and under an obligation to care for the child and for its property and to represent the child; they have to exercise their parental power in mutual agreement in the best interest of the child (§ 1626 and § 1627 of the Civil Code). In line with this, the obligation to pay child maintenance which was previously imposed primarily on the father is now imposed equally on the mother as well (§ 1606 of the Civil Code).

II.

If the requirement of equal rights in Article 3.2 and 3.3 does affect the regulation of parental power via Article 6.1 and 6.2 of the Basic Law, it is first necessary to examine whether the principles on interpretation already developed in the case-law of the Federal Constitutional Court on Article 3.2 and 3.3 of the Basic Law permit a limitation of the mother's parental power. This is not the case.

1. The Federal Constitutional Court has held that the application of Article 3.1 of the Basic Law is always based on a comparison of living conditions, which are never the same in all aspects but only in some, and that in principle the legislature has to decide which aspects of the living conditions to be regulated determine equal or unequal treatment in the statutes (BVerfGE 6, 273 (280)). However, this does not permit the conclusion that where men and women are involved the legislature has the same freedom to use functional or biological differences rather than different aspects of living conditions as connecting factors and, therefore, to treat men and women differently.

Rather, according to the case-law of the Federal Constitutional Court, the freedom to regulate as regards the general principle of equality is limited specifically by "the specifications of the principle of equal rights within the constitution itself", i.e. especially in Article 3.2 and 3.3 of the Basic Law (BVerfGE 3, 225 (240)). The legislature's freedom to determine within the utmost bounds of justice the comparative couples to which it orients the solution of its respective legislative responsibility is not given in cases covered by Article 3.2 and 3.3 of the Basic Law. Here, the legislature is not permitted to take into account certain differences between people by way of differences in legal regulation since the makers of the constitution deemed such differences to be irrelevant to the future legal system they intended, in view of the equality of all people for the most part. If one wished to grant the legislature similar freedom within the area of application of Article 3.2 and 3.3 of the Basic Law as in the area of the general principle of equality, the unacceptable result would be that "a simple legislating majority and a seconding majority of members of the Federal Constitutional Court could after all introduce discrimination – e.g. against women, against Jews, against members of certain political parties or religious societies", provided the members of such constitutional organs were of the opinion that such discrimination was "reasonable" in the given circumstances (Thoma, *Deutsches Verwaltungsblatt* – DVBl. 1951, pp. 457, 459). The legislature's freedom to regulate is only upheld insofar as there are different viable ways to realise equality.

2. However, the Federal Constitutional Court held that the bans on differentiation in Article 3.2 and 3.3 of the Basic Law are limited to the limitations mentioned therein, whereas in the area of family law, for example, with regard to objective biological or functional differences (division of work), depending on the nature of the individual living conditions, a different legal regulation could be permissible or even necessary (BVerfGE 3, 225 (242)).

However, the demotion of women as mothers cannot be justified by reference to the above decision; the Federal Constitutional Court had in mind such differentiations on which the "demands made for realisation of equal rights are based as obvious prerequisites" (BVerfGE, loc. cit.), e.g. provisions on the protection of women as mothers and provisions on the particular nature of their work for the family community.

The Federal Constitutional Court also clarified that "objective" biological differences may only result in different treatment in law if they determine the living conditions to be regulated to such a degree that comparable elements are subordinated completely so that the unequal legal regulation does not fall within the terms "discrimination" or "favour" (BVerfGE 6, 389, (422)). This applies accordingly to differences made with regard to functional differences. Although the terms "favour" and "discriminate" were initially aimed at individual situations and hence cannot describe precisely the status of an individual within an institution that is a community, they do describe approximately a situation in which a member who in principle is equal is excluded from participating with equal responsibility in performance of the responsibilities of the community; such a demotion is covered by the ban on discrimination.

There is no discrimination against one or the other spouse in the above sense where the Civil Code (§ 1360 old) recognises that as a rule the wife fulfils her obligation to contribute to supporting the family by way of work by keeping house, whereas the husband fulfils his obligation through gainful employment (see BVerfGE 3, 225 (242)). This does not apply where fulfilment of the same responsibility incumbent on parents is indivisible, i.e. as regards their personal relations with the children. This situation in life has different aspects in the person of the father and the mother respectively – due to their sexes. However, Article 3.2 and 3.3 of the Basic Law excludes any connection with such differences of the male and female sexes in the social field, if the provision is to be meaningful at all; the reason is that every situation in life will involve such "different aspects". It is not necessary to discuss in further detail the argument that Article 3.2 and 3.3 of the Basic Law do not apply where "failure to take into account the particular nature of women or the other difference between the sexes would prevent women from realising their goals, i.e. from unfolding their personalities without changing their nature", the reason being that equality of the mother and the father as regards rights and obligations is not capable of impairing the realisation of the goals of women.

Crucial to the evaluation of the provisions on parental power under constitutional law is that the existing living conditions – may they be called biological or functional – do not characterise relations between the father and mother and the children so very differently that the comparable aspects are rendered subordinate.

Rather, these comparable aspects dominate to such an extent that the nature of relations between both parents and the children is identical.

III.

The legal treatment of the father and the mother in the provisions on parental power therefore has to be measured according to Article 3.2 and 3.3 of the Basic Law, without taking into account existing functional or biological differences. Hence the constitutional nature of a provision which affords unequal treatment to a father and a mother depends firstly on whether there is discrimination against the mother. If so, then in view of the requirement of equal rights the provision is only tenable under constitutional law if it is supported by overarching value determinations under constitutional law which prevail over the requirement of equal rights.

1. The provisions placed under scrutiny discriminate against women as mothers.

The right to decide (§ 1628 of the Civil Code) and its correspondence outside the home, the authority to represent (§ 1629.1 of the Civil Code) are statutory manifestations of parental power. Representation is entrusted to the father alone, and in case of dispute he alone is entitled to decide, the mother only accedes to his rights if the father is unable or not permitted to exercise them. It is obvious that the father and the mother are not being treated equally.

It is true that in modern law a father's authority is no longer, as in the past, a right of control, but rather a right entailing responsibility, a social right linked with the duty to act in the child's best interests. Yet this link to responsibility does mean that the father's more extensive competence stops being a privilege; the influence and authority are indivisibly linked with the responsibility and duty. The demand for equal rights for mothers under constitutional law is not met by the obligation imposed on the father to take the mother's opinion into consideration in case of disputes, or by the possibility for the mother to have recourse to a court in order to prevent a decision made by the father in matters of particular importance which is contrary to the child's best interests. As regards most issues, it is not clear how the father could take the mother's opinion into consideration after an attempt to reach agreement has failed; nor is the mother able to exercise her care and upbringing positively in line with her idea of the child's best interests to the same extent as the father; she can only attempt to prevent abuse of the right to decide by the father.

In case of differences of opinion, the decision made by the father is final in all matters that are not of particular significance for the child's best interests. The mother has no possibility to influence matters beyond an attempt to convince the father, either prior to or after his decision. This is clearly discriminatory against the mother; the discrimination is not counterbalanced by § 1628.3 of the Civil Code quite sim-

ply because it is difficult for the mother to prove the requirements of the provision, especially that of a "persistent" breach of duty by the father.
Yet the legislation makes it almost impossible for the mother to fulfil her duty of upbringing and care for the child in case of differences of opinion with the father, also in matters of particular importance. Even if a question of conscience for her is concerned, she is only able to challenge decisions and measures taken by the husband by having recourse to a court – here again, apart from the possibility of convincing the father.
Consequently, the legal influence of the mother on the fate of her children in case of disputes with the father is minor. The external constituents for an application under § 1628.2 of the Civil Code are for the most part consistent with the requirements for the involvement of the guardianship court under § 1666 of the Civil Code (see Bavarian Highest Regional Court (*Bayerisches Oberstes Landesgericht* – BayObLG), *Zeitschrift für das gesamte Familienrecht* 1959, p. 293 (294)). The main legal difference is that in the latter case there has to be fault. In practice, however, this is relatively unimportant because a violation of the child's best interests in a matter of particular importance will usually be due to fault. Moreover, the judge at the guardianship court may raise the accusation that the father is violating his children's best interests in abuse of his rights, without taking into account the father's reaction. The mother does have to pay consideration to his reaction, for it is difficult to believe that a marriage can be tolerably continued if the mother has applied for a transfer of the decision-making authority on the grounds that the decision made by the father in a matter of particular importance is contrary to the child's best interests.
The demotion of the mother presently at issue is not a borderline situation which has to be accepted due to its relative insignificance; rather, it concerns the nucleus of the equality between parents insofar as it has to be legally asserted. The mother is demoted in that her influence and authority diminish because the legislation entrusts the father with the right to decide in case of disputes; this discrimination is exacerbated by the fact that in connection with the right to decide, the authority to represent the child is assigned to the father alone so that decisions, also on vital issues, can be put into effect without the participation or even prior knowledge of the mother. This discrimination against the mother is particularly susceptible to examination under constitutional law, for several reasons: firstly, it strengthens legally the de facto stronger position of the husband and it weakens the position of the wife specifically in the area in which her nature is most profoundly rooted and unfolds – that of motherhood – whereas equal rights have been granted to women in almost all other areas in accordance with the Basic Law. Finally, the discrimination also affects women who continue their marriages, whereas in case of a divorce or sepa-

ration the legislation ensures absolute equality (§ 1671 and § 1672 of the Civil Code old).

The provision placed at the start of the new provision on parental power by the legislature does not counterbalance this discrimination, although the significance of its guiding principle should not be overlooked. Whereas under § 1627 of the Civil Code old, the father, by virtue of parental power, has the right and duty to care for the person and property of the child, the Equal Rights Act in the new version of § 1627 establishes the rule that the parents have to exercise their authority in mutual agreement in the interest of the child, and the legislation lends weight to this rule through the codicil that the parents must attempt to reach agreement in case of differences of opinion. This corresponds to the general belief that the child's best interests are best served by agreement between the father and the mother on the child's care and upbringing. The legislation also attempts to strengthen this belief through positive wording. However, the guiding principle established is marred, the requirement of equal responsibility for upbringing and care is invalidated by the provision in § 1628 that the father decides in case of dispute. Hence, the guiding principle merely reflects the basic situation in a family in which the parents agree or are willing to agree so that life regulates itself automatically irrespective of the legal system. However, the question of legal equality only becomes important if the parents are unable to agree, and for that case specifically the guiding principle has been abandoned by the law.

The effect of the provision is not limited to the referral of the mother to recourse to the guardianship court. In awareness of the fact that agreement between married couples would be more difficult if it was clear from the outset that the husband could decide in case of dispute, upon the request of its Committee on Legal Affairs (*Rechtsausschuss*) the *Bundestag* revoked the husband's right to decide in all matters concerning joint married life (§ 1354 of the Civil Code) (BT II/1935 on printed paper 3409, p. 35). Likewise, it is clear that the father's willingness to reach agreement is limited by the knowledge that in case of dispute he is entitled to make a decision on matters concerning the children. Hence, § 1628.1 indirectly and inevitably alters the status of the parents for the entire area of decision-making to the detriment of the inner cohesion of the family, and at the same time to the detriment of the mother and her influence on the children.

The view is expressed in the literature (Bosch, *Zeitschrift für das gesamte Familienrecht* 1959, p. 265 (266)) that there is no discrimination against the mother since § 1628.1 has to be "considered together" with § 1356.1 of the Civil Code. This allegedly confirms the natural division of parents' responsibilities: within the scope of her independent housekeeping, the wife is able to regulate independently and to decide the children's affairs within that context. As a result, the mother al-

legedly decides "almost all the time" and the father "very rarely and in exceptional cases".
There is no indication whatsoever of such an interpretation "in conformity with the constitution" in the legislative history; moreover, such an interpretation contradicts traditional principles of interpretation, namely that the specific and exhaustive provision in §§ 1626 et seq. for the special area of parental power supersede the general principle of independent housekeeping established in *one* sentence in the provision "general effects of marriage". It is also overlooked that crucial decisions on issues of care and upbringing cannot be subsumed under the term housekeeping.
2. The demotion of mothers in the regulation of parental power is not justified by overarching aspects of constitutional law, i.e. by value determinations to which the principle of the equality of women would be subordinated. The unity of the family and the child's best interests have been deemed such value determinations, in the absence however of convincing grounds.
a) The question of the interdependence of "equality" and "unity of the family" may not be asked focusing on whether the provision under scrutiny is still consistent with the unity of the family, which it doubtlessly is. Rather, the provisions of the Civil Code under scrutiny would be in line with the Basic Law only if equality of the parents within the family were impossible; for equality of parents is the principle of the Basic Law. Exceptions are only permitted where it can be proved that unreserved realisation of the principle would destroy or at least earnestly jeopardise the unity of the family.
b) The question whether the unity of the family necessarily requires the father's primary competence to decide in case of dispute has been discussed in many cases on the basis of concepts of natural law. However, the great variety of natural-law theories arising as soon as one leaves the area of fundamental legal principles, as demonstrated especially in the discussion of the relations between "natural law and historicity", "natural law and positive law", issues which are highly disputed among advocates of natural law, excludes an examination under constitutional law oriented towards such concepts. The Basic Law alone therefore comes into question as the standard for the examination to be conducted.
c) From the general system of values in the constitution, its commitment to human dignity, to personal freedom and equality, follows the rule as regards parental rights: "As much equal freedom as possible." The question remains however whether the father's right to decide is necessary because a majority decision is not possible within a community consisting of two persons and because a decision by a third-party instance is legally or factually impossible. The argument that in case of dispute one party within a community of two has to make a decision has become considerably less persuasive because it was submitted likewise in favour of the hus-

band's right to decide (§ 1354 of the Civil Code), yet did not prevent the legislature from deleting that provision completely and from relying on the ability of the married couple to see reason and the persuasive force of daily necessities. Apart from this, examples from different areas of the law refute the theory that one party within a community of two has to be entitled to decide. In the area of family law especially there have long since been cases of coordination, e.g. as regards the parents themselves (§ 1747 of the Civil Code, § 3.3 of the Marriage Act (*Ehegesetz*), § 2.2 of the Act on Religious Upbringing of Children (*Gesetz über die religiöse Kindererziehung* – RelKindErzG), with regard to several guardians (§ 1797 of the Civil Code), similarly with regard to adviser relationships (§ 1690 of the Civil Code old) and carer relationships (§ 1629 of the Civil Code old).

The formation of an intent within a community can be borne by a different principle than that of voting or a "tie-breaker", namely by the duty to reach agreement and loyalty to the community. This duty does not automatically work like a decision taken by voting or by one partner alone; however, it is strong enough to bring about necessary joint decisions (see BVerfGE 1, 299 (315)). In everyday life within a family such joint decisions arise automatically from the fact that parents let one another decide in those areas where one or the other is particularly involved. For the few fundamental decisions, the best interests of the child and of the family set the standard which as a rule will suffice to ensure that a specific decision is brought about by natural agreement or by compromises made by one side or both sides. During the five years of realisation of the equality of parents in practice, only in very few cases have the guardianship courts been called on by married couples who have not separated (see the figures provided by the Member of Parliament Dr. Dr. Marie-Elisabeth Lüders on the basis of official documents during consultation of the Equal Rights Act within the *Bundestag*: BT II/1953, Stenographic Minutes p. 11,778). This permits the assumption that one can trust this form of forming an intent, this congruence of views and willingness to compromise, so that the express installation of a decision-making instance is not necessary. If, in an exceptional case, it is not possible to reach agreement, then the absence of a decision would not necessarily be harmful at least if the guardianship court were able to address the matter under § 1666 of the Civil Code by virtue of legal provisions at the time the objective constituents arise, i.e. without fault on the part of one of the parents. This procedure has applied in Sweden in the area of personal care since 1920 (see Müller-Freienfels, *Juristenzeitung* – JZ 1957, p. 685 (695); Simson, *Zeitschrift für Ausländisches und Internationales Privatrecht* 1953, p. 141 (143)).

If, however, it is considered necessary to ensure the coming about of a decision by law, it would be in the tradition of German law to enable recourse to be had to the guardianship court in order to make a decision in the event that the parents' inability to reach agreement were to jeopardise the best interests of the children. The solution involving the guardianship court in one way or another has dominated the public discussion .... Contrary to the reservations expressed, the Federal Constitutional Court takes the view that with a restriction to the earnest case of a risk for the child's best interests, this solution would not be unconstitutional. The solution is not unconstitutional particularly if one recognises the principle of "subsidiarity" in the sense that the smaller community is to act primarily and that state measures are only to intervene if they are unavoidable, and if one also assumes that this principle is expressed in Article 6.2 of the Basic Law ("primarily"). However, the content of Article 6.1 and 6.2 of the Basic Law as a guarantee of freedom for marriage and the family also means that as a matter of principle, these institutions are permitted to take first place and that the state only interferes where they no longer suffice (see BVerfGE 7, 320 (323)). According to the above, the state has to exercise general restraint.

Consequently, according to the proposals discussed so far, the guardianship court would not be introduced as the primary decision-making entity of the family instead of the father.

Rather, within the space vacated by revocation of the husband's final right to decide, the married couple and the parents are to shape the fate of the family, especially the upbringing of the children, jointly in *equal* freedom and responsibility. As mentioned above, one may assume that the large majority of differences of opinion within this community will resolve themselves. According to the proposals discussed so far, the judge at the guardianship court will only be available as an "ultimate" decision-making instance if parents fail on a significant issue and if the child's best interests call for intervention. This would be consistent with the principle of subsidiarity of intervention by the state; the guardianship court would not play a role any different to the one it plays in numerous similar cases, where often no abuse of parental power or breach of duty by one of the parents has to exist (see – apart from § 1643 of the Civil Code – e.g. §§ 1630.2, 1666, 1671, 1672, 1727, 1750.1, 1751, 1797 of the Civil Code, § 3.3 of the Marriage Act, § 2.3 of the Act on Religious Upbringing of Children). In all these cases the guardianship court performs the "watchdog function" (Article 6.2 of the Basic Law) of the state community, the constitutional aim of which is to prevent objective harm to the child's best interests, irrespective of fault on the part of the parents.

Apart from this, from the viewpoint of the principle of subsidiarity, the general statutory attribution of the right to decide and authority to represent to the father meets with reservations because a general provision thus interferes with the unrestrained decision-making process in which both parents are constitutionally entitled to participate (see Elisabeth Schwarzhaupt, *Gesellschaft und bürgerliches Recht*, in:

Hessische Hochschulwochen, vol. 21 (1959), p. 38 (54)). Such a normative regulation of married life intervening in all marriages carries more weight than does the statutory making available of an instance of the judiciary in order to make decisions solely in case of severe conflicts. The principle of Article 6.1 and 6.2 of the Basic Law requires specifically that decision-making processes within the family remain open. This alone is consistent with the legislative obligation in a state such as Germany, that does not have an uniform world view, to standardise the law so that it leaves citizens with the freedom to realise their religious and ideological obligations with all consequences when living their married and family life (see v. Nell-Breuning, *Wirtschaft und Gesellschaft heute*, vol. II, p. 319). Hence the spouses have to be at liberty, also in the area of parental power, to conduct their marriage while upholding the equality of the sexes or to let the father decide in case of conflict. In fact, the process of forming an intent varies from family to family and from case to case. However, § 1628.1 of the Civil Code interferes with this natural process.

d) The practical considerations raised against the involvement of the guardianship court cannot carry any weight against the principle of equality, especially since it appears in the light of the experiences made between 1953 and 1958 that their significance is overestimated. A delay in making an important decision is possible where the father makes the decision alone ..., and likewise with the present regulation of parental power if the mother has recourse to the guardianship court.

The risk that the guardianship courts would be overtaxed quantitatively or as regards the substance of the decisions to be made by them has not been confirmed by experience, as shown by the above-mentioned communications of the Member of Parliament Dr. Dr. Lüders during consultations on the Equal Rights Act in the *Bundestag*. Nor have complaints been raised during those years that an issue submitted to a judge was not susceptible to being decided by a court of justice. The issues concern the child's best interests, as do those to be decided by a judge at the guardianship court in ordinary cases. Apart from this, if competence for a decision in the sense of one of the aforementioned legislative proposals is assigned to a judge at the guardianship court, as a rule the judge does not have to decide on the matter as such, but, rather, merely has to assign certain matters to one parent or, in an individual case, takes up the proposal made by one parent unless the proposals made by both parents jeopardise the child's best interests. The case-law from the relevant period shows that there were sufficient objective indications for the judge to form a judgment as to whether the father's or the mother's opinion is better for the child's best interests. This is proven particularly by the many years of case-law regarding the Act on Religious Upbringing of Children, which gave judges the task of clarifying the relationship with a certain religion within a specific marriage and family by way of an analysis of the actual situation, and of deciding about the stronger or weaker congruence of the one or other opinion with the situation in that family on the basis of the relevant facts thus established. The decisions to be made by judges at the guardianship courts in case of severe unsolvable conflicts would not be more complex in substance; appropriate objective criteria for the decision could be found.

e) Equality of the parents as regards the right to decide does not jeopardise the child's best interests.

The fundamental rule established in § 1627 of the Civil Code, according to which the father and the mother are entitled to the parental power which has to be exercised in mutual agreement in the best interest of the child, expresses in agreement with Article 6.2 of the Basic Law that a joint upbringing of the child in mutual agreement best serves the interests of the child. If the parents are unable to agree, in many cases the marriage will be troubled. Yet here especially the equal influence of the mother is more important in the child's interest, for experience has shown that in a fragile marriage there is often a risk that the father's interest in the child's well-being diminishes concurrently with his emotional removal from the mother. In such a situation the mother can only fulfil her obligation to the child if she is granted the same influence as the father by law. If the law makes this difficult by entrusting the father alone with decisions and by referring the mother to the courts, it induces the mother to accept decisions of the father for the sake of peace even if she should object to them for reasons of her conscience and the child's well-being.

This is not rebutted by the argument that even in case of equality of the parents, the mother can only enforce her views against the father with the aid of a judge. The reason is that the situation is psychologically different from the outset depending on whether both parents have the same influence and both have to reach agreement in principle, or whether one parent is aware that he has the right to decide. There is also a difference where the father or mother request a decision from the guardianship court either jointly or individually because they are unable to agree on what best serves the child's best interests, to where a request is made on the basis of § 1628.2 or even 1628.3 of the Civil Code.

The fact that equality of the parents is no less suitable to serve the child's best interests as is the father's right to decide is also indicated by the absolute equality in a number of particularly important cases under the law in force (in case of adoption – § 1747 of the Civil Code, in case of consent to marriage – § 3.3 of the Marriage Act, and in case of a change in the religious upbringing – § 2.2 of the Act on Religious Upbringing of Children –). It is not acceptable why securing the influence of the mother in other important decisions should be less important and contribute less to the child's best interests than it is in the above cases.

IV.

Since the father's right to decide constitutes discrimination against the mother which cannot be justified on the basis of overarching value determinations under constitutional law, § 1628.1 of the Civil Code is in violation of Article 6.1 and 6.2 in conjunction with Article 3.2 and 3.3 of the Basic Law; it is therefore void. The nullity of § 1628.1 of the Civil Code means that the two subsequent subsections become obsolete; they therefore also become void.

In its present form, § 1629.1 of the Civil Code cannot be upheld either. Apart from the fact that it refers expressly to § 1628.2 and 1628.3, it is closely connected with § 1628.1. The provision on the father's sole authority to represent is derived from his right to decide. § 1629.1 of the Civil Code "extends" this right to decide beyond the home: *since* the father alone decides in case of conflict, he is also to represent the child alone. This is shown clearly by the legislative history of the Equal Rights Act; it was not considered expedient to allow the mother to participate in representation with regard to decisions possibly made against her will (see government draft: BT II/1953, printed paper 224, p. 59). In the *Bundestag* the father's authority to represent was also treated as a consequence of his right to decide (BT III 1953 on printed paper 3409, p. 41). § 1629.1 of the Civil Code cannot be separated from this connection with the right to decide. If the provision could be understood independently of the provision in § 1628 of the Civil Code as an independent provision of the father's right to represent on his own, then a conflict with § 1626.2 final half-sentence would arise which would be difficult to explain. This clause states that the authority to represent is part of the right of parental custody, which on its part forms the nucleus of the parental power to which the father and the mother are jointly entitled. On that basis, without the connection with § 1628 of the Civil Code it would not be possible to understand why § 1629.1 should generally establish the father's sole authority to represent. If the provision can only be explained under the particular, close connection with § 1628.1, then it is unconstitutional for that reason alone and therefore void.

This does not mean that representation of the child by one parent alone always and as such amounts to discrimination against the other parent in violation of the Equal Rights Act. Representation by both parents jointly in all matters is feasible, as the experience over the five years of equality of parents has shown. However, there are cases where reasonable consideration of the requirements of legal relations renders representation by one parent alone necessary. In this respect the influence of the parent opposing the decision, who presumptively has the child's best interests in mind as well, may not remain without protection. Proposals in this vein have already been made in the discussion so far.

The gap in legislation that arose owing to the declaration of invalidity of § 1628 and § 1629.1 of the Civil Code by the Federal Constitutional Court was not closed by the legislature until the adoption of the Act Revising the Law on Parental Custody (Gesetz zur Neuregelung des Rechts der elterlichen Sorge) *of 18 July 1979 (Federal Law Gazette I, p. 1061). Article 1.3 and 1.4 of that Act rendered the wording of the provisions declared void as follows:*

§ 1628

> *(1) If the parents are unable to agree in a single matter or in a particular kind of matter of parental custody the arrangement of which is of substantial importance for the child, then the guardianship court may, on the application of a parent, assign the decision to one parent provided this corresponds to the child's best interests. The assignment may be subject to limitations or conditions.*
> *(2) Prior to the decision the guardianship court shall urge the parents to reach agreement on a solution that is consistent with the child's best interests.*

§ 1629.1

> *(1) Parental custody includes the representation of the child. The parents shall represent the child jointly; where a declaration of intent is to be made to the child, it is sufficient if it is made to one parent. One parent shall represent the child alone to the extent that he or she exercises parental custody alone or the decision has been assigned to him or her under § 1628.1.*

No. 3

BVerfGE 22, 93
of 7 June 1967 – 1 BvR 76/62 –
"Maintenance I case"

HEADNOTE:

–

Order of the First Senate of 7 June 1967
– 1 BvR 76/62 –

in the proceedings regarding the constitutional complaint of S., married woman – authorised representative: ..., lawyer – against the judgment of the Nuremberg-Fuerth Regional Court (*Landgericht*) of 15 December 1961 – 11 S 148/61.

RULING:

The constitutional complaint is rejected as unfounded.

EXTRACT FROM GROUNDS:

A.

The complainant, who was born in November 1928, has been married to a local government officer in the higher intermediate class since April 1948. Before the marriage, the complainant worked for about two-and-a-half years as the employee of a public authority. In August 1948 she gave up this occupation. In April 1960 the husband left the marital home. Since that date, the spouses have lived apart.
The complainant petitioned for maintenance, demanding a monthly payment of DM 300; the Nuremberg-Fuerth Regional Court, at second instance, ordered ... the husband to pay the following amounts to the complainant: DM 300 per month from

May 1960, DM 150 per month from April 1962, and DM 75 per month from October 1962. In other respects it found against the complainant. In the statement of reasons for its decision, the Regional Court stated in essence that although the husband had not been solely responsible for the separation, he was very predominantly responsible. The court left it undecided whether the complainant would also have been obliged to take up gainful employment if the parties had continued living together. It stated that it appeared grossly inequitable to allow the wife, who was thirty-two years old, in good health and childless, to live the life of a pensioner at the cost of her husband. The wife had been gainfully employed before the marriage and at the beginning of the marriage. She had later dedicated her working capacity to the marital household, and now, as a result of the separation, it was available again. Her occupational training made it possible for her, at least in the foreseeable future, to find a job approximately similar to her earlier occupation, a job which, moreover, would certainly be compatible with the financial and social status of her husband. However, the wife could not reasonably be expected to accept the first available vacancy on the job market. Until the end of March 1962, therefore, her husband would have to be fully responsible for his wife's maintenance. Even after taking up her own gainful employment, the wife, in view of her interruption of employment for more than twelve years, would need a certain initial period in which her income would still be substantially less than what she could eventually attain. It therefore appeared just, according to the court, for the husband to supplement her earnings by DM 150 per month for a transitional period of six months. As a result of this, the wife would maintain the financial and social situation that was appropriate for her, that she now held as the wife of a man with the civil-service grade of *Oberinspektor*. This aspect even compelled the court to grant her DM 75 per month for the following period, in which she would be earning a full income. For then too the wife had to be given the possibility of standing out from the ranks of her colleagues in the way she would be able to if her marriage had not broken down, and as was appropriate for her, even after the separation which was the fault of her spouse, as the wife of a municipal *Oberinspektor*.

As grounds for her constitutional complaint filed against the judgment of the Regional Court, the complainant submits that the interpretation of § 1361.2 of the Civil Code (*Bürgerliches Gesetzbuch* – BGB) in this decision is particularly likely to facilitate the dissolution of her marriage. If a husband who earns over DM 800 per month is obliged to pay only DM 75 maintenance per month to his wife after the separation for which he is at fault, this is a considerable financial relief for him, she states. However, she submits, this clearly conflicts with the goals of Article 6.1 of the Basic Law (*Grundgesetz* – GG), which is intended to preserve marriage. She states that the court also completely disregarded the fact that if it had not been for the marriage she could have undertaken further occupational training in that period and could have attained a considerably higher income than is possible for her now even if the monthly maintenance payment granted her by the Regional Court is taken into account.

...

B.

1. If spouses live apart, then under § 1361.1 of the Civil Code each spouse may only claim maintenance from the other if and to the extent that this is equitable. § 1361.2 of the Civil Code contains a special provision for the wife who is not gainfully employed for the situation where the husband is solely or very predominantly at fault for the separation.

In these circumstances, the wife may be ordered to earn her maintenance herself only if she would have been obliged to take up gainful employment even if the domestic community had continued or – and this may apply in the present situation – recourse to the husband, in the particular circumstances of the case, in particular with regard to the fact that the wife was gainfully employed at an earlier time or that the marriage was of short duration, would be *grossly inequitable*.

2. There are no reservations as to the constitutionality of § 1361.2 of the Civil Code ... either with regard to the protection of marriage and the family required by Article 6.1 of the Basic Law or with regard to equal rights for men and women under Article 3.2 of the Basic Law. This maintenance provision takes account of both constitutional precepts in providing for a particular protection of the wife who is not gainfully employed in the cases governed by it ... It proceeds on the assumption that the wife normally performs her duty of maintenance towards the family by running the household (§ 1360 sentence 2 of the Civil Code) and often, relying on the belief that the marriage will be a lasting one, does not engage in gainful employment outside the home, but devotes herself exclusively to the domestic sphere of the family. In the case where the conjugal community ends, this inevitably leads to substantial disadvantages for the earning situation of the wife, and this is even the case if she does not have children to take care of (see Decisions of the Federal Constitutional Court (*Entscheidungen des Bundesverfassungsgerichts* – BVerfGE) 17, 1 (21-22)). A housewife without any occupational training will in most cases be too old to make up for this, and is therefore dependent on taking an unskilled job, that is, a job with correspondingly low wages. A woman who has been trained for an occupation but has given it up because of her marriage will often have difficulty, even after a short interruption, but certainly after years outside employment, to return to this occupation, and she will normally not be able to attain the position that

she would probably have if her working life had not been interrupted. For this reason, § 1361.2 of the Civil Code requires that the division of labour in a marriage, which normally results from a unanimous decision of the spouses, should be taken into account in favour of the wife in the case of disturbances of the marriage that are not caused, solely or predominantly, by her. The partner who culpably prevents the continuation of conjugal community in the previous manner is not as a general rule to be able to require the wife to earn her maintenance by gainful employment outside the home from now on. The situation is to be different only if, in the circumstances of the individual case, the unchanged continuation of the husband's duty of full maintenance would be grossly inequitable. Seen in this light, the provision is an expression of the correctly understood principle of equal rights of women in marriage.
3. The way in which the Regional Court interpreted and applied this provision is also unobjectionable in constitutional law.
a) The Federal Constitutional Court (*Bundesverfassungsgericht*), in accordance with its established case-law, may review judicial decisions only to a limited extent (BVerfGE 18, 85 (92-93)). In the present case, review by the Federal Constitutional Court is also subject to strict limits because the decision as to whether an action is or is not grossly inequitable within the meaning of § 1361.2 of the Civil Code depends decisively on the assessment of the individual case, that is, on the ascertainment and evaluation of a large number of individual circumstances. …
In the present case, therefore, the Federal Constitutional Court can only review whether the decision challenged is based on a fundamentally erroneous view of the significance of the fundamental rights asserted (BVerfGE 18, 85 (92)). Article 6.1 and Article 3.2 of the Basic Law constitute binding value determinations for the whole area of private and public law relating to marriage and the family (see BVerfGE 6, 55 (72-73); 6, 386 (388)); they must therefore be complied with in the interpretation and application of non-constitutional law, in particular in the application of general clauses, such as the concept of gross inequity in the present case. In the interpretation of the law of maintenance too, the judge must take into consideration the constitutionally required protection of conjugal community, which is based on the equality of the sexes, and despite the judge's particularly broad competence to make a decision when applying an equity clause, he must not exercise this competence in a way that is likely to impair the existence of the marriage or, in the case of a marriage that is no longer intact, to accelcrate the process of breaking up. In interpreting § 1361.2 of the Civil Code, the judge must in particular comply with the basic principle of the provision, set out above, that is, the judge must take into consideration, for the benefit of the wife who is not gainfully employed, the long-term effect of the division of duties in marriage.

b) If one assesses the decision challenged in its full context without emphasising individual formulations, it cannot be found that the Regional Court disregarded these value standards. The decision does not reveal an incorrect understanding of the nature of conjugal community as protected by Article 6.1 in conjunction with Article 3.2 of the Basic Law, and is not based on a tendency that is inimical to marriage. The Regional Court also endeavoured to take into account the protective principle of § 1361.2 of the Civil Code. The court did not proceed on the assumption that in the case of a separation for which the husband is at fault, the wife is automatically obliged to take up gainful employment; it did not fail to recognise that such a duty can only be assumed to exist in exceptional cases, depending on the particular circumstances of the individual case. If the decision, despite this, confirmed the complainant's duty to engage in gainful employment, this was based on the judicial assessment of the special facts of the present case, such as the length of the marriage, the lack of children, the age and health of the complainant, her occupational training, the state of the labour market and the fact that the complainant lives with her parents. The court took into account the continuing effect of the division of labour in the marriage when, with consideration for the length of the marriage, it granted the complainant a transitional period until she finds appropriate and reasonable employment and, on the basis of the standard of living enjoyed in the marriage, held that the husband has a long-term obligation to make a maintenance payment supplementing her income from employment.
On this basis, the interpretation and application of § 1361.2 of the Civil Code on which the decision is based are constitutionally unobjectionable. …

Justices: Dr. Müller, Dr. Berger, Dr. Scholtissek, Dr. Stein, Ritterspach, Dr. Haager, Rupp-von Brünneck, Dr. Böhmer

No. 4

BVerfGE 23, 258
of 7 May 1968 – 1 BvR 133/67 –
"Duty to promote families case"

HEADNOTE:

A refusal to grant child benefit to children who do not have either their domicile or habitual residence within the territory of the German Reich in the borders of 31 December 1937 (§ 34.2 of the former Child Benefit Act (*Kindergeldgesetz*)) in the version of § 10 no. 10 of the Act to Supplement the Child Benefit Act (*Gesetz zur Ergänzung des Kindergeldgesetzes (Kindergeldergänzungsgesetz*)) of 23 December 1955 (Federal Law Gazette (*Bundesgesetzblatt* – BGBl.) I p. 841 –) did not violate the Basic Law (*Grundgesetz* – GG).

Order of the First Senate of 7 May 1968
pursuant to § 24 of the Federal Constitutional Court Act
– 1 BvR 133/67 –

in the proceedings regarding the constitutional complaint of the miner … – authorised representative: …, lawyer – against the judgment of the Federal Social Court (*Bundessozialgericht*) of 25 November 1966 – 7 RKg 12/65 – indirectly against § 34.2 of the Act on the Grant of Child Benefit and the Establishment of Family Equalisation Funds – Child Benefit Act (*Gesetz über die Gewährung von Kindergeld und die Errichtung von Familienausgleichskassen* (*Kindergeldgesetz* – KGG)) of 13 November 1954 – Federal Law Gazette I p. 333 – in the version of § 10 no. 10 of the Act to Supplement the Child Benefit Act (*Kindergeldergänzungsgesetz* – KGEG) of 23 December 1955 – Federal Law Gazette I p. 841 –.

RULING:

The constitutional complaint is rejected as unfounded.

EXTRACT FROM GROUNDS

A. – I.

Child benefit was originally only granted for the third and every child after that (§ 4.1 of the Act on the Grant of Child Benefit and the Establishment of Family Equalisation Funds – Child Benefit Act (KGG) of 13 November 1954 – Federal Law Gazette I p. 333 –). In this connection, it was originally irrelevant whether the child was living or residing inside or outside of the Federal Republic of Germany. Unless otherwise provided for in an international treaty, it was only foreign nationals whose children were not domiciled or habitually residing within the territorial area of the Act who did not receive any child benefit (§ 34.2 of the Child Benefit Act). This provision was amended with effect from 1 February 1956, and the version of it which is relevant in this case reads as follows:

> Children who do not have either their domicile or habitual residence in the territory of the German Reich in the borders of 31 December 1937 are not entitled to child benefit.

(§ 34.2 of the Child Benefit Act in the version of § 10 no. 10 of the Act to Supplement the Child Benefit Act (Child Benefit Supplementary Act – KGEG) of 23 December 1955 – Federal Law Gazette I p. 841 –).
The Federal Government was authorised to allow exceptions to this provision through the enactment of ordinances (§ 34.3 of the Child Benefit Act). It repeatedly exercised the authority given to it and allowed the grant of child benefit to workers employed in the Federal Republic of Germany whose children were living in the Netherlands, France, Italy, Spain, Greece and Turkey. In addition, workers from EEC countries were entitled to child benefit on the basis of international law (see Articles 39 et seq. of Council Regulation (EEC) No. 3 on the Social Security of Migrant Workers (*EWG-Verordnung Nr. 3 über die Soziale Sicherheit der Wanderarbeitnehmer*) of 25 September 1958 – Federal Law Gazette II 1959 p. 474 – and Article 67 of Regulation No. 4 on the Implementation and Supplementation of Regulation No. 3 on the Social Security of Migrant Workers (*Verordnung Nr. 4 zur Durchführung und Ergänzung der Verordnung Nr. 3 über die Soziale Sicherheit der Wanderarbeitnehmer*) of 3 December 1958 – Federal Law Gazette II 1959 p. 496 –).
Since 1 April 1961 child benefit has also been granted for the second child under certain circumstances (§ 1 of the Act on the Grant of Child Benefit Also to Second-Born Children and the Establishment of a Child Benefit Fund (Child Benefit Fund

Act) (*Gesetz über die Gewährung von Kindergeld für zweite Kinder und die Errichtung einer Kindergeldkasse* (*Kindergeldkassengesetz* – KGKG –)) of 18 July 1961 – Federal Law Gazette I p. 1001 –). To this extent too the provision in the Child Benefit Act applied so that child benefit was not granted to children living outside the territory of the German Reich in the borders of 31 December 1937; however, the Federal Government could make exceptions (§ 7 of the Child Benefit Fund Act in conjunction with § 34 of the Child Benefit Act). The Federal Government exercised this right in favour of the foreign and German workers employed in Germany whose children were domiciled or whose children habitually resided in EEC countries or in Spain, Greece or Turkey.

II.

The complainant was born in Poland and is a German national; he lives and works in the Federal Republic of Germany. He has two children from his first marriage who were born in 1944 and 1946; his first marriage has meanwhile been dissolved. The children live with their mother in Knurow, Poland. This town also belonged to Poland on 31 December 1937. The complainant was ordered to pay maintenance to both of his children, and he also fulfilled this obligation. In view of the fact that he had children living in Knurow, he applied in August 1961 for the grant of child benefit for the second child. The child benefit fund rejected his application by relying on § 34.2 of the Child Benefit Act in conjunction with § 7 of the Child Benefit Fund Act. The action brought by the complainant against the rejection was unsuccessful. In the end, the Federal Social Court rejected his appeal (judgment of 25 November 1966 (BSG 25, 295)).

The complainant had submitted predominantly constitutional doubts about § 34.2 of the Child Benefit Act in his appeal. The Federal Social Court rejected these submissions for the following reasons:

The provision is compatible with Article 3.1 of the Basic Law. According to the Federal Social Court, it is constitutionally legitimate to limit social support and care generally to the inhabitants of one's own territory. The Federal Social Court elaborated further that, also according to the purpose and content of the child benefit legislation, § 34.2 of the Child Benefit Act uses appropriate criteria for distinguishing between recipients. Child benefit is intended to compensate in part for the increased expenses incurred by a family as a result of having children. As a rule, the expenses only occur if the child is living in the family circle and receiving its support from it. The Federal Social Court was of the opinion that the complainant could not advance his own case by relying on the fact that the Federal Government had deviated in a few cases from the principle in § 34.2 of the Child Benefit Act by passing ordinances allowing child benefit to also be paid to children living abroad. The exceptions were based on reciprocal equal treatment principles and permitted exceptions to the territoriality principle where significant economic reasons and labour market policy were involved. The complainant's fundamental rights in Article 3.3 and Article 6.1 of the Basic Law were also not violated.

III.

The constitutional complaint is directed against § 34.2 of the Child Benefit Act and the judgment handed down by the Federal Social Court on 25 November 1966, which was based on this provision. The complainant is of the opinion that his fundamental rights in Article 3.1 and 3.3 and Article 6.1 of the Basic Law have been violated and submits the following reasons for this:
The incompatibility of § 34.2 of the Child Benefit Act with Article 3.1 of the Basic Law is self-evident. The entitlement of a German worker employed in the Federal Republic of Germany cannot be made dependent on whether the children he is obliged to support are living inside or outside the borders of the former German Reich. He would otherwise suffer unfair discrimination as compared with fellow citizens who were also working. In particular, the territorial principle advanced by the Federal Social Court must lead to his receiving child benefit; for he and not his children is entitled to same. If foreign guest workers receive child benefit – which is not objectionable – he as a German citizen working in Germany should not be in a worse position. The opinion of the Federal Social Court that a child that is not living within its family circle is not an additional burden is not correct; a child can more easily be fed within its family circle. He is being discriminated against by § 34.2 of the Child Benefit Act since he has had to leave his wife and children in his homeland, i.e. the discrimination is based on his homeland and origin; consequently, his fundamental right under Article 3.3 of the Basic Law is violated. Finally, the provision violates Article 6.1 of the Basic Law. The fact that he – in contrast to other citizens of the Federal Republic – does not receive any child benefit and nonetheless still has to make support payments is damaging to his current marriage and family.
The Federal Minister for Family and Youth (*Bundesminister für Familie und Jugend*) responded on behalf of the Federal Government. He considers § 34.2 of the Child Benefit Act compatible with the Basic Law.

B.

§ 34.2 of the Child Benefit Act in the version relevant for these proceedings was compatible with the Basic Law.

I.

Article 3.3 of the Basic Law is not violated. The refusal to grant child benefit does not constitute discrimination against him on account of his homeland and origin. Exclusion from benefits in § 34.2 of the Child Benefit Act does not depend on the social origin and roots of the entitled person or on his geographical homeland by birth or residence (see Decisions of the Federal Constitutional Court (*Entscheidungen des Bundesverfassungsgerichts* – BVerfGE 5, 17 (22)). Only the domicile or the habitual residence of the child for which the payment of child benefit is being considered is decisive. A person who has lived in the territory of the Federal Republic of Germany ever since his or her birth has just as little right to demand child benefit for a child living outside of the territory of the German Reich in the borders of 31 December 1937 as does a person living outside of the Federal Republic. The complainant would have had to have been refused child benefit on the basis of § 34.2 of the Child Benefit Act even if he did not originate from the territory of Poland today.

II.

§ 34.2 of the Child Benefit Act is also compatible with the general principle of equality.

Article 3.1 of the Basic Law prohibits the legislature from arbitrary unequal treatment of things whose essentials are identical. This fundamental right is violated unless there are circumstances or other obvious objective reason which allow for statutory distinctions (see BVerfGE 18, 121 (124)).

1. No violation of Article 3.1 of the Basic Law can be found in the fact that Germans with children who have their domicile or habitual residence outside of the territory of the German Reich in the borders of 31 December 1937 are in a less favourable position than Germans whose children live within the named territory. The reason for the different treatment is a result of thc goal of child benefit. Child benefit seeks to "equalise family burdens"; the aim is to equalise in part the higher expenses incurred by a family as a result of having children (see BVerfGE 11, 105 (115 et seq.); 22, 163 (168)). It is evident from the child benefit legislation and above all from the order of entitled persons set out therein (§ 3.1 of the Child Bene-

fit Act and § 7 of the Child Benefit Fund Act) that the relevant consideration for the regulation of child benefit is not the relief of the person who has to pay support but rather the assistance of the family in which the child permanently lives. Those persons who provide the child with a home and who look after its personal well-being and upbringing are to receive compensation from the community for the associated financial or at least personal sacrifice (see BVerfGE 22, 163 (169-170, 173)). This differentiation which results from the objectives of the child benefit rules cannot be described as inappropriate.
In this connection, one also has to consider that the child benefit legislation affects the state when it is in the role of the provider of benefits. The Federal Constitutional Court (*Bundesverfassungsgericht*) has already spoken out on many occasions in favour of the legislature being granted greater operating latitude in this area than in its dealings with encroachments on fundamental rights (BVerfGE 6, 55 (77); 11, 50 (60); 12, 151 (166); 17, 210 (216)).
2. No improper differentiation within the meaning of Article 3.1 of the Basic Law is made by the above-mentioned legislation granting child benefit to foreign and German workers for children living in certain countries. These exceptions are based on the one hand on domestic labour market policy and on the other hand on the obligations undertaken by the Federal Republic in international agreements, in particular within the EEC, which are based on reciprocity. These are objective reasons.

III.

Finally, Article 6.1 of the Basic Law is also not violated.
The duty which the state has in principle of promoting families does not extend so far as to oblige it to equalise every financial burden affecting them. The other submissions of this nature made by the complainant have already been dealt with in the comments on Article 3 of the Basic Law.

Justices: Dr. Müller, Dr. Stein, Ritterspach, Dr. Haager, Rupp-v. Brünneck, Dr. Böhmer, Dr. Brox, Dr. Zeidler

No. 5

BVerfGE 24, 119
of 29 July 1968 – 1 BvL 20/63, 31/66 and 5/67 –
"Adoption I case"

HEADNOTES:

1. **The principles developed in Decisions of the Federal Constitutional Court (*Entscheidungen des Bundesverfassungsgerichts* – BVerfGE) 11, 330 (334-335) on the admissibility of submissions according to Article 100.1 of the Basic Law (*Grundgesetz* – GG) do not apply if a court called to rule on an appeal on points of law or further complaint would remit the case to a prior instance for further clarification of the facts were the provision submitted for review to be valid.**
2. **"Separation from the family" within the meaning of Article 6.3 of the Basic Law means de facto separation whilst the parent-child relationship and the rights and obligations based thereon in principle continue.**
3. **Article 6.2 of the Basic Law guarantees to the parents, as educators, priority over the state. This parental right entails, as an essence-determining element, the duty to care for and bring up the children; parents who evade this obligation may not invoke the parental right towards state encroachments made in the child's best interests.**
4. **The state's watchdog function (Article 6.2 sentence 2 of the Basic Law) is based first and foremost on the need for protection of the child, who as a holder of fundamental rights has human dignity of its own and its own right to the development of its personality within the meaning of Article 1.1 and Article 2.1 of the Basic Law.**
5. **a) Substitution of parental consent to adoption in cases of the grievous and persistent failure of the parents (§ 1747.3 of the Civil Code (*Bürgerliches Gesetzbuch* – BGB)) does not breach Article 6.2 of the Basic Law and is also in accord with the value determination of Article 6.1 of the Basic Law.**
   b) The application of § 1747.3 of the Civil Code is also constitutionally permissible in the case of incognito adoptions.

Order of the First Senate of 29 July 1968
– 1 BvL 20/63, 31/66, 5/67 –

in the proceedings for a constitutional review of § 1747.3 of the Civil Code in the version of the Act Standardising and Amending Family Law Provisions – Family Law Amendment Act (*Gesetz zur Vereinheitlichung und Änderung familienrechtlicher Vorschriften – Familienrechtsänderungsgesetz*) of 11 August 1961 (Federal Law Gazette (*Bundesgesetzblatt* – BGBl.) I p. 1221) – suspension of proceedings and submission orders a) of the Stuttgart Higher Regional Court (*Oberlandesgericht*) of 8 November 1963 (8 W 160/63), b) of the Passau Regional Court (*Landgericht*) of 3 November 1966 (2 T 43/65) and c) of the Gronau/Westf. Local Court (*Amtsgericht*) of 31 March 1967 (VII – M – 366) –.

RULING:

§ 1747.3 of the Civil Code in the version of the Act Standardising and Amending Family Law Provisions (Family Law Amendment Act) of 11 August 1961 (Federal Law Gazette I p. 1221) is compatible with the Basic Law.

EXTRACT FROM GROUNDS:

A. – I.

Adoption requires a contract to be concluded between the adoptee and the adopter(s), and this contract to be confirmed by the Local Court which has jurisdiction (§§ 1741 and 1754 of the Civil Code). The contract is concluded for a child aged under 14 by its legal representative, and for a child aged over 14 by the child personally with the consent of his or her legal representative; the approval of the guardianship court (*Vormundschaftsgericht*) is required in both cases (§ 1751 of the Civil Code). According to § 1747.1 of the Civil Code, a child born in wedlock may only be adopted with the consent of his or her parents until reaching the age of 21, a child born out of wedlock until the same age only with the consent of his or her mother. The declaration of consent must be judicially or notarially recorded; it may not be issued by a representative and does not require the consent of the legal representative even in the case of those with limited capacity to contract; it is irrevocable (§ 1748 of the Civil Code). Consent is not required if the party entitled to give consent is permanently unable to submit a declaration or his or her whereabouts are

permanently unknown (§ 1747.1 sentence 2 in conjunction with § 1746.2 of the Civil Code).
The Family Law Amendment Act of 11 August 1961 (Federal Law Gazette I p. 1221) inserted subsection 3 below into § 1747:

§ 1747

(1) …
(2) …
(3) The guardianship court, on the application of the child, may substitute the consent of one parent where that parent has persistently and grossly violated his or her duties towards the child or has forfeited parental power (*elterliche Gewalt*), and if he or she maliciously refuses to give consent and it would be disproportionately disadvantageous to the child if the adoption did not take place.

II.

1. The insertion of this provision into the Civil Code is connected with general developments in adoption, the significance and function of which has undergone crucial changes in recent decades … The statistics record for instance a considerable increase in the number of adoptions since the nineteen twenties, which is partly a factor of the two Wars: 7,748 adoptions were concluded in Germany in 1965 with the cooperation of the youth welfare offices (see *Statistisches Jahrbuch für die Bundesrepublik Deutschland*, 1967, p. 413); the number of adoptions in the entire German Reich, by contrast, is estimated at only 4,000 per annum for the period from 1920-1933 … Whilst adoption previously focused on the interest of childless persons in passing on their family name and family inheritance, and adults were frequently adopted, today adoption principally serves the purpose of entrusting orphaned children and children whose parents are unable to bring them up to the permanent care of a family which is able to care for and bring them up, and at the same time of meeting the desire of men and women with no natural descendants to bring up a child as their own. Adoption hence fulfils a significant function for society: The adopted children as a rule live in much more favourable circumstances as a result of being taken into the new family, and are hence frequently safeguarded against dangers in their previous surroundings; as a side-effect, one must also point to the financial and other reductions in the burden on the public welfare funding organisations. Adoption particularly benefits children born out of wedlock. Apart from legitimation by subsequent marriage, it is for them a particularly suitable

means of obtaining integration into a complete family in compliance with the value determination contained in Article 6.5 of the Basic Law (see Decisions of the Federal Constitutional Court (*Entscheidungen des Bundesverfassungsgerichts* – BVerfGE) 22, 163 (173)).
The increasing understanding of adoption as a protective and welfare measure for children who cannot grow up with their natural parents has led to a great number of legal amendments in comparison with the original provision, which all in all are characterised by the emphasis placed on the child's best interests (see for instance the relaxations of the preconditions for adoption with regard to age and childlessness, protection against abuse and the restriction of adult adoption). This entails the lesser priority given to the private-law, legal-transaction element in favour of emphasising the public-law element, which finds its expression in the state provision of placement in adoption (see Act on Placement in Adoption (*Gesetz über die Vermittlung der Annahme an Kindes Statt*) of 29 March 1951 – Federal Law Gazette I p. 214), in the greater involvement of the youth welfare authorities and the courts, in the expansion of the power of the judge to rule on the establishment of adoption, and in the court revocation of adoption ex officio.
2. The provision submitted for review can be traced back to a proposal made by the Commission on the Reform of the Law on Adoption (*Kommission zur Reform des Adoptionsrechts*), established by the Working Group for Youth Support and Youth Welfare (*Arbeitsgemeinschaft für Jugendpflege und Jugendwohlfahrt* – AGJJ) (see reasoning on the Draft Family Law Amendment Act submitted by the Federal Government, *Bundestag* printed paper – BT-Drucks. III/530 p. 13). The Federal Government wished by including this proposal to facilitate the establishment of adoption in cases in which the refusal of parental consent constituted an abuse of rights because reservations had arisen in the majority of the case-law when it came to forgoing consent without a statutory empowerment in these cases (see *Bundestag* printed paper, loc. cit., p. 21). Whilst the *Bundesrat* approved the provision unamended in both passages (see Deliberations of the *Bundesrat* (*BR-Verhandlungen*), 195th session of 4 July 1958, p. 162 in conjunction with *Bundesrat* printed paper – *BR-Drucks.* 162/58, 236th session of 14 July 1961, pp. 181 et seq. in conjunction with *Bundesrat* printed paper 246/61), it encountered several Members' reservations in the *Bundestag* committees involved concerning partly constitutional, and partly legal-policy matters. The majority of the sub-committee established by the Committee on Legal Affairs wished to permit the substitution of parental consent only if the parents have forfeited parental power (§ 1676 of the Civil Code); when the representatives of the Federal Government declared the provision to be valueless with such a restriction, the sub-committee recommended deleting the provision altogether (see minutes of the 4th session of the sub-committee of 24 October 1960,

pp. 16 et seq.). The Committee on Legal Affairs did not comply with the recommendation of its sub-committee, but the majority voted for the provision in the version of the Government Draft, as did the *Bundestag* Committee on Family Affairs and Youth, which was consulted (see minutes of the 147th session of the Committee on Legal Affairs of 26 April 1961, pp. 19 et seq.; minutes of the 19th and 20th sessions of the Committee on Family Affairs and Youth of 5 and 19 March 1959). The provision was accepted in the second and third readings in the *Bundestag* on 28 June 1961, without a debate (Deliberations of the Bundestag (*BT-Verhandlungen*), third electoral term, 164th session, p. 9459 (9461)).

3. The tendency in legal development in Germany corresponds to developments in other European and non-European countries. Many foreign states have provisions in their law on adoption that are comparable with § 1747.3 of the Civil Code, according to which a waiver of parental consent or official substitution of consent is provided for under certain preconditions, e.g. Austria, Switzerland, France, Luxembourg, the Netherlands, Denmark, England and several states of the USA … The preconditions are much broader in some cases in these countries than in the German provision. For instance, according to French law, refusal of parental consent can be declared by the judge to be immaterial insofar as it constitutes an abuse of the discretion of the parent and the latter has not taken an interest in the well-being of the child, so that the child's best interests were placed at risk. In England, the court may permit adoption without parental consent if the parent in question has persistently and culpably failed to fulfil his or her obligations towards the child. According to the Austrian provision, the court may substitute consent on request by a partner to the contract if no justified grounds exist for refusal.

4. The application of § 1747.3 of the Civil Code is contentious in the legal literature. Several authors consider such a provision to be incompatible with Article 6.2 and 6.3 of the Basic Law … or have legal-policy reservations … They largely take as a basis the same reasons as the court submissions; in some cases, they fear a precedent for totalitarian encroachments on the family on the part of the state or consider a measure going so far to also not be necessary in the child's best interests. By contrast, other authors declare the impugned provision to be constitutional, factually justified and welcome. … Equally, the views in the courts are divergent. …

III.

Several courts have requested a ruling from the Federal Constitutional Court (*Bundesverfassungsgericht*) according to Article 100.1 of the Basic Law because they consider § 1747.3 of the Civil Code to be unconstitutional.

1. The proceedings on which the submission of the Stuttgart Higher Regional Court (*Zeitschrift für das gesamte Familienrecht* – FamRZ 1964, p. 51) is based relate to the adoption of a child born out of wedlock in 1953. The child grew up with its father's parents from the outset. The mother took the child back in 1960 after marrying another man. The child was however unable to become accustomed to its new surroundings, so that serious difficulties arose in bringing it up. The grandparents took the child back into their home at the insistence of the mother and step-father.
In 1962, custody was withdrawn from the mother at the request of the youth welfare office and transferred to the youth welfare office as curator. When the grandparents wished to adopt the child, the mother refused to consent, in contradistinction to her previous declarations.
The Local Court substituted consent according to § 1747.3 of the Civil Code; the mother's complaint to the Regional Court was unsuccessful. Both courts presumed that one of the rare cases applied here in which application of § 1747.3 of the Civil Code was absolutely necessary in the child's best interests. The child's mother was said to have persistently and grossly violated her parental duties; she was said to have no maternal feelings and to repeatedly take or demand measures which caused mental and emotional damage to the child. Also, the mother's husband was said to have no empathy with the child. It was said to be malicious for the mother to refuse to consent to adoption by the grandparents after she herself had very heartlessly abandoned the child to them. It was said that it would be disproportionately disadvantageous to the child, who regarded the foster parents as father and mother and was very fond of them, if the adoption did not take place. It was said that it had developed favourably with the grandparents, but was living in constant fear of being taken away again by the mother. Ongoing success in upbringing was said to require the child to finally find peace and for its development not to be continually disturbed by motions lodged by the mother.
The Higher Regional Court holds the view that the decision on the further complaint depends on the constitutionality of § 1747.3 of the Civil Code. If the provision is unconstitutional, there is said to be no legal basis for the substitution of the consent of the mother; the rulings of the Local Court and of the Regional Court would hence have to be rescinded and the child's motion rejected. If, by contrast, the provision was compatible with the constitution, the orders of the previous instances would have to be rescinded for a violation of § 12 of the Act on Matters of Non-Contentious Jurisdiction (*Gesetz über die Angelegenheiten der freiwilligen Gerichtsbarkeit* – FGG) and the case remitted to the Local Court for further clarification; in particular, detailed questioning of the child's mother, of her husband and of the foster parents would be indispensable.

The Higher Regional Court considers § 1747.3 of the Civil Code to be incompatible with Article 6.2 and 6.3 of the Basic Law and with the principle of the rule of law. Application of the provision was said to permanently deprive parents of parental power, and unmarried mothers of custody, in substantive terms; it was said that the child was forcibly "transferred" to another family. This measure was said to be irreparable since adoption could only be rescinded under special circumstances (§§ 1768, 1770a and 1770b of the Civil Code). At the same time, this was said to constitute deprivation of the parental right guaranteed in Article 6.2 sentence 1 of the Basic Law to which unmarried mothers were also entitled. As a real fundamental right, the parental right was said to grant a right to avert non-permissible encroachments on the part of the state; it was said to be identical for the field of care and upbringing to parental power in terms of its content.
Since according to Article 19.2 of the Basic Law a fundamental right may reportedly not be touched upon in any case in its essential content, it was said to not be possible to withdraw the parental right within the meaning of Article 6.2 of the Basic Law in terms of its substance, any more than parental power; it was said that encroachments by the guardianship court may only relate to the exercise of parental rights. This was also said to be favoured by the wording of Article 6.2 sentence 2 of the Basic Law, which was said not to contain any general proviso of legality; the "performance" (*Betätigung*) of parental rights and obligations could only mean the "exercise" (*Ausübung*) of parental power within the meaning of the Civil Code. Accordingly, deprivation of custody according to § 1666 of the Civil Code could be understood only as prohibition of exercise, as a special type of suspension of parental power. Equally, the "forfeiture" (*Verwirkung*) of parental power according to § 1676 of the Civil Code could only be interpreted in conformity with the constitution as a prohibition of the exercise of parental power since the final provision of Article 18 of the Basic Law on the forfeiture of fundamental rights did not mention the parental right. Article 6.3 of the Basic Law, which was said to be internally linked with subsection 2, was also said according to its wording and legislative history to lead to the conclusion that the legal removal of a child from its family by a state coercive measure was prohibited. The "separation" regulated on there was said to relate only to the de facto removal of the child from the parental home. Since the requirement of consent was said to be based on the natural parent-child relationship, i.e. the family tie, it was said that consent per se was not amenable to substitution.
Even if § 1747.3 of the Civil Code was intended to serve the child's best interests, it was said that this could not justify such a serious encroachment on the parental right, even if the parents had committed a serious crime towards the child. Deprivation of the entire parental status was said to encroach on the essence of the funda-

mental right because, unlike for instance the case of expropriation according to Article 14.3 of the Basic Law, no compensation was said to be conceivable here. There were also said to be other such rights that were not amenable to deprivation, such as German citizenship (Article 16.1 sentence 1 of the Basic Law).

§ 1747.3 of the Civil Code was furthermore said to be worded in too undetermined a manner. For reasons related to the rule of law, the preconditions for serious encroachments on rights of the individual had to be set in a clear, precise manner. These requirements were said to not be met by the terms "persistently and grossly violated", "malicious" and "disproportionate disadvantage". The lack of clarity inherent in the latter characteristic was said to be shown in the case-law regarding § 1727 of the Civil Code. § 1747.3 of the Civil Code was hence said to be suited to open the floodgates to the enforced removal of a child.

2. The proceedings on which the submission of the Passau Regional Court is based relate to the adoption of two siblings born in wedlock in 1962 and 1963, whose mother died at the birth of the younger child. The father has been punished eleven times for various crimes (including for theft, fraud, resistance to state authority and the rape of a 71-year-old woman). In view of the longer periods of incarceration, the guardianship court found that the parental power of the father had been suspended, and appointed the youth welfare office as guardian. The youth welfare office had initially placed the children in a home and later initiated adoption; both children have been in foster care with the envisioned adoptive parents since the beginning of 1966. Since the father refused to give his consent, the Local Court substituted the consent of the father to adoption "by the parents entered at No. 2/65 in the adoption list held by the district youth welfare office ..." (so-called incognito adoption); it presumed that the preconditions for the substitution of consent that were constitutionally admissible in narrowly restricted cases were met. The father submitted a complaint against this.

The Regional Court holds § 1747.3 of the Civil Code to be incompatible with Article 6.2 and 6.3 of the Basic Law since the latter are said to permit only a restriction in the exercise of parental power, but not a withdrawal in terms of its substance. However, adoption is said to be tantamount to this because the parental power of the biological parents is said to be substituted by that of the adoptive parents. Therefore, the essence of a fundamental right is said to be touched upon, contrary to the provision of Article 19.2 of the Basic Law.

In the case of incognito adoption, the substitution of consent is said, furthermore, to breach the fundamental right to a hearing in court according to Article 103.1 of the Basic Law. Since the name of the adoptive parents had to be kept confidential, it is said that the biological parents do not have an opportunity to form a picture of the personality of the adoptive parents on their own responsibility. Hence, it is said that they have no opportunity to influence the court's decision with regard to an aspect which is essential to the assessment of the facts. As long as the party entitled to give consent is not also able to make a statement on the personality of the adoptive parents, it is not possible to reliably assess whether he or she is maliciously refusing to give consent.

3. The proceedings on which the submission of the Gronau Local Court is based relate to substitution of consent to adoption of a boy born out of wedlock in 1952. The mother has three other children born out of wedlock, one of whom has the same father as the child intended to be put up for adoption. In 1954, this child was fostered by the mother, who at that time lived with two other children in one room, on its father and his wife, an agreement being reached that child maintenance was to be continued to be paid to the mother. When the payments ceased after several months, the mother demanded her child back without success. The mother had previously been a drinker and had at times looked after her three other children so badly that temporary withdrawal of custody had had to be ordered. The father of the child born out of wedlock now wishes to adopt the child together with his wife, but the mother, who is now also married, is refusing to give her consent.

The Local Court regards the fact of giving away the child and that the mother ceased to be concerned about her son after the unsuccessful attempt to retrieve the child as constituting a persistent gross violation of her obligations; refusal to consent to adoption is said to be malicious because this is said to be largely based on the mother already having previously refused to consent, upholding this position and not considering it necessary for one child to have a better life than his brother descending from the same progenitor. In the view of the court, the child is much better off in the household of his father than in that of his mother, with regard to whom a relapse into the previous conduct posing a danger to the children could not be ruled out. The Local Court would hence like to comply with the application to substitute consent according to § 1747.3 of the Civil Code, but considers itself prevented from doing so because it considers the provision to be incompatible with Article 6.2 and 6.3 of the Basic Law. In its reasoning, it concurs with the submission order of the Stuttgart Higher Regional Court of 8 November 1963 (see A III 1).

IV.

The Federal Minister of Justice, who made a statement for the Federal Government, considers the submission of the Stuttgart Higher Regional Court to be inadmissible because, given the current state of the proceedings, the ruling is said not to depend on the constitutionality of § 1747.3 of the Civil Code. … Moreover, he considers the provision submitted for review to be constitutional.

…

B.

The submissions are admissible.

I.

The Stuttgart Higher Regional Court intends to rule differently if the provision is invalid than if it is valid: In the first case, it intends to rescind the orders of the previous instances and at the same time itself to rule finally on the case, namely to reject the child's motion for substitution of the mother's consent to adoption. In the second case, it intends to also rescind the orders of the previous instances, but at the same time to remit the case to the Local Court for further investigations according to § 12 of the Act on Matters of Non-Contentious Jurisdiction. This further clarification of the facts could now admittedly lead to one or several of the preconditions provided in § 1747.3 of the Civil Code for the substitution of consent de facto not being met, so that the child's motion would already have to be rejected for this reason; in this respect, it has not yet been ascertained at present whether the ruling on the merits of the original proceedings is ultimately contingent on the constitutionality of the provision.

This however does not counter the admissibility of the submission because the submitting court is unable in this instance – unlike in the proceedings on which the ruling in BVerfGE 11, 330 (334-335) is based – to carry out the necessary investigations itself. The further complaint corresponds to an appeal on points of law in civil proceedings; the finding and evaluation of the facts is reserved for the trial court judge. A ruling concluding the appeal on points of law or further complaint stage, if it does not conclude the overall proceedings but remits the case, also differs in essential terms as against an interim ruling such as an order to take evidence within the same instance: In terms of its content, it contains a ruling regarding legal questions; it rescinds the factual ruling that had been valid until then and binds the lower court in the context of the reasoning which is material to the rescission. Above all, however, the question of procedural economy arises differently in case of remittal than it does with an interim ruling at the same instance. The point of view of preventing the Federal Constitutional Court from becoming overloaded with sets of proceedings on the constitutionality of a specific statute must take second place here behind the justified interest of those concerned by the proceedings and of the courts in avoiding, wherever possible, having to undergo the course of instances once more. Hence, the Federal Constitutional Court has already treated submissions from courts hearing appeals on points of law as admissible in similar cases (BVerfGE 16, 286 (293); see also 18, 257 (263)).

II.

The submission order of the Passau Regional Court permits one to recognise that, should § 1747.3 of the Civil Code be invalid, the court intends to allow the father's complaint and reject the child's motion for substitution of consent to adoption. By contrast, it does not become clear how the court would rule if the provision were to be constitutional, particularly whether it intends to adopt the factual finding and evaluation of the Local Court in this case. The submission can however be evaluated such that, in the view of the submitting court, the legislature intends § 1747.3 of the Civil Code to also embrace the case of incognito adoption and that this gives rise to an additional argument in favour of the unconstitutionality of the provision. The court also considers the provision to be contradictory because, on the one hand, it is also to apply to incognito adoptions, whilst on the other hand it is not possible to examine in this case whether the refusal to give consent is malicious. Given this interpretation, it is possible to regard the submission as admissible because one may not expect the court to predict the decision to be taken were the provision to be applied.

C.

§ 1747.3 of the Civil Code is compatible with the Basic Law.

I.

1. As a measure of the constitutional review, above all Article 6 of the Basic Law can be considered as the fundamental constitutional provision for the sphere of the family. Within this constitutional provision, as a community consisting of parents and children, the family is the subject of the provisions contained in subsections 1, 2 and 3, which are internally connected with one another, but each relate to specific aspects of the same subject. Parents within the meaning of Article 6.2 of the Basic Law are initially to be regarded as the parents of children born in wedlock; the protection of this provision however also benefits the mother of a child born out of wedlock.

The general provision is Article 6.1 of the Basic Law; it establishes a comprehensive protection principle addressing the state which is restricted neither by a proviso of legality nor by other means. The three-fold constitutional significance of this provision is already clarified by the case-law of the Federal Constitutional Court; it contains both an institutional guarantee, as well as a fundamental right to protection against disturbing encroachments on the part of the state, and over and above this a fundamental provision that determines values for the entire law relating to marriage and the family (BVerfGE 6, 55 (71-72)). In all these relationships, the family is to be regarded as a closed, independent sphere; the constitution obliges the state to respect and promote this unit and the self-responsibility of the family.

By contrast, Article 6.2 and 6.3 of the Basic Law, as more specific provisions, relate to the parent-child relationship, and at the same time determine the function of the state and its boundaries in this sphere. Subsection 2 sentence 1 emphasises the priority of parents in bringing up and caring for the children and guarantees it in constitutional terms; however, the word "primarily" (*zuvörderst*) already permits one to recognise that, in addition to the parents, the state also has a function as an educator, with corresponding obligations. Over and above this, subsection 2 sentence 2 imposes on the state the office of supervising the care and upbringing of the children by the parents. Subsection 3, finally, regulates a specific encroachment by the state on care and upbringing, and provides an explicit proviso of legality for this purpose.

2. The selection of one among the sub-regulations of Article 6 of the Basic Law which have been explained to be an anchor for the constitutional review of § 1747.3 of the Civil Code depends on the manner in which this provision affects the area protected by Article 6 of the Basic Law. It is to be presumed here that the substitution of parental consent to adoption which it permits does not yet amend the child's status under family law, since the impact of adoption under family law does not occur until the subsequent confirmation of the adoption contract (§§ 1741 sentence 2 and 1754.1 of the Civil Code). The court's substitution of consent however already entails an encroachment on the parent-child relationship; it takes from the parents the right, to which they are in principle entitled, to decide freely whether and how adoption is to occur. Admittedly, according to an almost universal view in the literature, this right is not an element of parental power or of the right to care for the person of the child, but is based in principle on the family relationship created by procreation and birth (see Engler in Staudinger, [*Kommentar zum BGB*, 10th/11th ed., 1966], *§ 1747*, marginal no. 1). Particularly parents who are not entitled to parental power or to care for the person of the child because for instance a case of forfeit applies or a measure according to § 1666.1 of the Civil Code has been carried out, retain the right to consent according to § 1747.1 of the Civil Code. On the

other hand, blood descent is not the decisive criterion; parental consent is only necessary with children under 21, and no consent by the child is required for the reverse case – the adoption by a parent; furthermore, an "ostensible father" is entitled to the right to consent on the one hand as long as he has not effectively challenged the child having been born in wedlock, whilst on the other hand it is prohibited to the father of a child born out of wedlock. The vital aspect for the requirement of parental consent is, accordingly, the entitlement and responsibility of the parents as recognised and guaranteed by the legal order for the care and upbringing of the child (see already *Motive zum BGB*, vol. IV, pp. 964-965).

This is confirmed if one includes the legal impact of adoption. A ruling according to § 1747.3 of the Civil Code as a rule creates the major precondition for the establishment of adoption since court confirmation of the adoption contract may only be refused if a statutory requirement of adoption is missing or if there are justified doubts as to adoption being used to bring about a family tie corresponding to a parent-child relationship. Legally valid adoption affects neither the general legal family tie, nor the blood tie to the child's previous family; the legal family relationship and the mutual maintenance rights and obligations based thereon, as well as the mutual inheritance rights, remain in place (§ 1764 of the Civil Code). A new family relationship is created only between the child and the adopter personally, whose family name the child receives in principle, but not between the child and the relatives of the adopter (§§ 1757.1, 1763, 1758 and 1758a of the Civil Code). Mutual maintenance obligations, accordingly, arise only between the adopter and the child, the maintenance obligation of the adoptive parent preceding the maintenance obligation of the previous family (§ 1766 of the Civil Code). The child only has an inheritance right towards the adopter, and not vice versa; this right may also be contracted out (§§ 1759 and 1767.1 of the Civil Code).

The impact of adoption on the parent-child relationship is very much more incisive. Since the child takes on the legal status of a child of the adopter born in wedlock, the latter has full parental power. The natural parents lose parental power, or the care for the person of the child if they only had the latter (§ 1765 of the Civil Code). Whether the same applies to the right of access has recently become contentious (see the overview in Schwoerer in Staudinger, loc. cit., *§ 1634*, marginal no. 34). The previously prevalent view, and the view which prevails today in practice at least, affirms this because the right of access is said to be a residual element of the right of care for the person of the child, not a consequence of the blood relationship, and because the child's best interests as a rule are said to be against the continuation of this right. If the parental power of the adopter ends or is suspended, the natural parents' care for the person of the child is only restored if they grant main-

tenance to the child; the right to represent the child continues to be excluded in any case (§ 1765.2 of the Civil Code).
Accordingly, the provision submitted for review does not, as held by the Federal Minister of Justice, primarily affect the legal affiliation of the child to a specific family and its general position in this family within the meaning of Article 6.1 of the Basic Law, but relates primarily to the parent-child relationship. § 1747.3 of the Civil Code is hence principally to be measured against Article 6.2 and 6.3 of the Basic Law.

II.

1. The area of freedom of parental activity is delimitated by subsections 2 and 3 of Article 6 of the Basic Law in relation to the state: These provisions guarantee the priority of the parents, their independence and their own responsibility in caring for and bringing up the children, but at the same time appoint the state community to watch over them. The parental right thus delimitated constitutes a fundamental right in the classic sense which grants to the parents a right to avert state encroachments insofar as these are not covered by the "state's watchdog function" (see BVerfGE 4, 52 (57); 7, 320 (323)).
Subsections 2 and 3 of Article 6 of the Basic Law are closely linked because subsection 3 regulates and at the same time restricts a specific encroachment on the parental right which can be considered because of the state's watchdog function: It grants a right to avert state measures which separate children from their families without a statutory basis and without meeting specific preconditions, and at the same time gives rise to a proviso for the legislature to permit separation under these conditions.
2. In the relationship between the two subsections, it might suggest itself to derive the review standard solely from subsection 3 because adoption facilitated by a measure according to § 1747.3 of the Civil Code dissolves the community of the child with its parents, and this could be regarded as a "separation" of the child from the family within the meaning of subsection 3. Accordingly, with regard to the constitutionality of the provision to be reviewed it would only be decisive whether the facts which it regulated corresponded to the preconditions contained in Article 6.3 of the Basic Law (failure of the parents and threat of neglect of the child), which would have to be affirmed in principle. Such subsumption of the legal transaction in question here under Article 6.3 of the Basic Law is however not tenable for the following reasons:
The wording of the constitutional provision, as the Stuttgart Higher Regional Court rightly emphasises, is already more in favour of understanding by "separation of

the family" only the actual separation, i.e. the "removal" of the child from its parents. This is however not actually the case with measures according to § 1747.3 of the Civil Code; in such cases, rather, the initiation of adoption has as a rule been preceded by the actual separation of the child from the parents because the parents, on the basis of § 1666.1 of the Civil Code, have been deprived of parental power, of the care for the person of the child or the right to determine the child's whereabouts or, once parental power has been forfeited, the youth welfare office and the guardianship court have arranged for alternative accommodation for the child or correctional education (*Fürsorgeerziehung*) has been ordered on the basis of §§ 64 et seq. of the Youth Welfare Act (*Jugendwohlfahrtsgesetz* – JWG). In this context, the practice of the youth welfare offices should also be referred to, which as a rule do not place a person in adoption until the child has been fostered on the adoptive parents for some time and the latter have proven themselves in this respect … Finally, with children born in wedlock, adoption against the will of the parents can only be considered if they no longer have parental power, including the right to legal representation, or no longer have this right without restriction because the cooperation of the legal representative that is necessary according to § 1751 of the Civil Code cannot be substituted by the guardianship court.

The interpretation gained from the wording and meaning of Article 6.3 of the Basic Law is supported by the legislative history …:

…

Accordingly, the legislature adopting the Basic Law did not consider the adoption of a child against the will of the parents in the context of Article 6.3 of the Basic Law. The provision is, rather, motivated in its fundamental tendency by the experience of the National Socialist period, and is intended to prevent the "removal" of children from their parents for the purpose of state coercive education, as is customary in totalitarian states (state youth, forced attendance at boarding schools, training camps) without affecting the known welfare measures. Accordingly, the provision has as its subject-matter partial encroachments on the part of the state on the parent-child relationship, and the rights and obligations based thereon continue in principle. Measures for the adoption of a child against the will of the natural parents do not differ from this as a result of the intensity of the encroachment, but as a result of the other purpose being pursued. They do not intend to suppress parental educational activity in favour of a the state exerting an influence on this process, but – because of the failure of the natural parents – to give rise to a new, functioning parent-child relationship the partners to which exercise the function of care and upbringing independently and autonomously, and in doing so are in turn protected against state encroachments through the guaranteed fundamental rights. Measures of this nature do not fall under Article 6.3 of the Basic Law, but are – as an aliud –

also not ruled out by this constitutional provision. Their permissibility is, rather, to be judged according to Article 6.2 of the Basic Law.

III.

1. The submission order of the Stuttgart Higher Regional Court and the proponents of the same view in the literature evidently presume that the object of protection of Article 6.2 of the Basic Law is a legal position which does not exhaust itself in exercising care and upbringing. It is to be awarded solely with biological parenthood and should also continue to exist if the parents have never concerned themselves with the care and upbringing of the child, or if they have grossly and culpably neglected this task. It is to continue as irremovable legal substance even if, to protect the child, the parents are excluded by a judicial pronouncement from exerting any influence on his or her care and upbringing, indeed even if they have lost parental power for ever as a result of a criminal offence against the child.

This view does not correspond to the wording and meaning of the constitutional provision. The fundamental right guaranteed therein refers to a specific task and to the activities to be carried out to this end, which is particularly stressed by the position of the words. The parents have the right to freely shape the care and upbringing of their children according to their own ideas and enjoy in this respect, on proviso of Article 7 of the Basic Law, priority as against other educators. This protection of fundamental rights may however only be claimed for an act which with the broadest recognition of the parents' personal responsibility can still be valued as care and upbringing, but not for the opposite: neglect of the child. The constitution makes this clear by linking the *right* to care and upbringing with the *obligation* to perform this activity. This obligation distinguishes the parental right from all other fundamental rights; it is also different in nature in comparison with the social duty constituted by property (see Article 14.2 of the Basic Law). Article 6.2 sentence 1 of the Basic Law indissolubly interlinks rights and obligations from the outset; an obligation is not a barrier limiting the right, but an essence-determining element of this "parental right", which in this respect can be more correctly designated as "parental responsibility" (see BVerfGE 10, 59 (67 and 76 et seq.); … Article 6.2 sentence 1 of the Basic Law hence protects the free decision of the parents as to how they wish to comply with this natural obligation; it does not protect those parents who evade this obligation.

2. The state's watchdog function according to Article 6.2 sentence 2 of the Basic Law applies if parents fail in this manner; the state is not merely entitled, but indeed obliged, to ensure the care and upbringing of the child. This obligation incumbent on the state follows not solely from the legitimate interest of the state commu-

nity in young people's upbringing (see § 1 of the Youth Welfare Act), for considerations ensuing from the social welfare state or for instance from general aspects of public order; it emerges primarily from the fact that, as a holder of fundamental rights, the child itself has a right to the protection of the state. The child is a being with personal human dignity and its own right to the development of its personality within the meaning of Article 1.1 and Article 2.1 of the Basic Law. A constitution which places human dignity at the centre of its value system cannot in the order of inter-personal relationships in principle grant to anyone rights to the person of another who is not at the same time bound by duties and respect for the human dignity of the other. The recognition of parental responsibility and of the concomitant rights is hence justified in the fact that the child requires protection and assistance in order to develop to become an autonomous personality within the social community, as corresponds to the perception of the Basic Law (see BVerfGE 7, 198 (205); see also the United Nations Declaration of the Rights of the Child of 20 November 1959 (Yearbook of the United Nations, 1959, p. 198)). The state must safeguard this, and where necessary protect the child, who is as yet unable to protect itself, against its development suffering as a result of the abuse of parental rights or of neglect.

In this sense, the child's best interests are the marker for the state's mandate according to Article 6.2 sentence 2 of the Basic Law (see BVerfGE 10, 59 (84)). This does not mean that any failure or any neglect entitles the state to remove the parents from care and upbringing, or indeed to take on this task itself; rather, it must always take account of the fundamental priority of the parents. What is more, however, the principle of proportionality applies here too. The nature and extent of the encroachment are determined according to the extent of the failure of the parents and according to what is necessary in the interest of the child. The state must therefore initially attempt wherever possible to achieve its goal by means of helping, supporting measures aiming to create or restore responsible conduct on the part of the natural parents. It is however not restricted to this, but can, if such measures are insufficient, withdraw either temporarily, or indeed permanently, from the parents their rights of upbringing and care; in these cases, it must at the same time positively create the circumstances for the child to grow up healthily.

3. According to these standards, § 1747.3 of the Civil Code does not overstep the boundaries drawn by the constitution for activity on the part of the state.

The provision does not contain an across-the-board, schematic restriction of parental rights in relation to adoption of the child, but only permits substitution of consent by a judicial ruling in individual cases after a review of the respective de facto circumstances. It hence corresponds to the principle that individual measures to avert a risk to the children take priority over across-the-board arrangements, and

the legislature must as a rule restrict itself to regulating the preconditions for an encroachment in individual cases (see BVerfGE 7, 320 (323-324)).
The application of the provision is, furthermore, tied to three narrowly limited preconditions, which additionally must apply cumulatively:
a) According to § 1676 of the Civil Code, the forfeit of parental power occurs automatically and irrevocably if a parent has committed a major crime or an intentional minor crime against the child, and hence has been sentenced with final effect to imprisonment or to a prison sentence of at least six months. This includes, primarily, cases of ill-treatment of children or of sexual offences. Persistent gross violation of the obligations towards the child is equivalent to the forfeit to be found by the guardianship court in individual cases. This precondition is likely to correspond in part to the elements of § 1666.1 of the Civil Code; what is more, the circumstances of the case must make the presumption appear to be justified that the conduct of the parents towards the child is unlikely to change in the period which is vital to the development of the child.
b) § 1747.3 of the Civil Code further requires that it would be disproportionately disadvantageous to the child if the adoption did not take place; this explicitly demands the weighing, which is in any case required by the constitutional principle of proportionality, between the interest of the child and the interest of the parent refusing to give consent. Adoption carried out against the will of the parents must be necessary in order to avert a danger to the healthy development of the child which has already occurred or which is threatening as a result of the parents' failure; it may not be applied until less drastic means are inadequate for this purpose, such as in particular temporary accommodation of the child in a home or in foster care. Which measure is necessary in each case can admittedly not be judged solely from the point of view of the parents. Because of the change of status particularly documented by the name change, adoption may appear to them as the most incisive on the scale of possible encroachments although in reality it does not differ markedly from forfeiting parental power or comprehensively withdrawing custody according to § 1666.1 of the Civil Code, since in such cases the parents are also completely excluded from caring for and bringing up the children. By contrast, however, according to the circumstances of the case the interests of the child may be particularly well promoted by adoption, as against permanent placement in a home (see on this also III 4 below).
c) Finally, refusal to give consent must be malicious. This characteristic will apply if the refusal stems from self-centred motives, for instance because the parent would like to have his or her consent "bought out" (see the case ruled on by the Hamburg Regional Court (FamRZ 1957, p. 328 et seq.)), or if it is based on an inimical stance towards the child, the adoptive parents or the competent authorities,

or otherwise takes place on the basis of an attitude which disregards the child's best interests.

If one takes all three preconditions together, the exceptional nature of the provision is clearly recognisable: It relates only to cases of particularly grievous, complete, persistent failure on the part of the parents in their responsibility towards their child. It is hence ultimately a manifestation of the general legal concept that the abusive exercise of a right is not protected by the legal order. What is more, the substitution of consent is handed down in court proceedings that are equipped with the corresponding guarantees, in which the facts must be comprehensively clarified ex officio. The decision of the guardianship court may be examined in two further instances. Protection against erroneous application of the provision is, furthermore, offered by the comprehensive consultation of official and judicial controls in the adoption procedure. The allegation that § 1747.3 of the Civil Code opens the floodgates to the forced removal of children appears to be vastly exaggerated under these circumstances. The provision, rather, provides the substantively and procedurally restricted empowerment in the above cases to largely dissolve the legal relationship between parents and children now only existing in formal terms; this satisfies the protection of the child required by the constitution, as well as the general value determination of Article 6 of the Basic Law favouring the family.

4. If the state community must intervene to compensate for the parents' failure in order to create the conditions for the healthy physical and emotional development of the child and for its sound integration into society, the state is faced here with the option to order correctional education, to otherwise accommodate the child in a home or to place it in foster care or, finally, to place it in adoption. From the point of view of the child, the latter two possibilities will as a rule be preferred in this situation. The traditional conviction that the experience of a harmonious, viable family community is simply irreplaceable for the normal development of the child is confirmed by the experience of the (youth) welfare authorities, as well as by the knowledge of modern psychology, psychiatry and paediatrics. The lack of such an order in childhood, i.e. in the first years of life, and above all the emotional neglect which this entails, frequently cause serious developmental disturbances and mental or moral defects which express themselves in criminal or antisocial conduct or in abnormal sexual leanings. Even in favourable circumstances, placement in a home cannot replace the security of the child in the family and the conditions prevailing there for the development of the child's personal skills and social contacts, especially as many homes lack adequate or sufficiently trained staff, suitable premises and particularly funding. Even with excellent external care, the lack of personal attention and of external development incentives, the frequent change in persons to closely relate to, and later uncertainty as to one's own origins and about the future,

may lead to development being held back, this phenomenon increasing with the duration of the stay in the home, and in serious cases leading to disease symptoms.
It already follows from this that, in the event of the persistent failure of the parents, the state must primarily endeavour to place the child in another family which voluntarily takes on the function of forming the natural tie, both in the interest of the child and of the public (see BVerfGE 22, 163 (173)). The two possibilities for this are accommodation in a foster family and adoption. According to practical experience, it is relatively not difficult to find suitable parents to foster a child in order to adopt it. By contrast, it is very difficult to find good foster parents if adoption is not being considered from the outset. Offers of foster places are not infrequently based primarily on the motive of earning money or the desire to acquire labour; damage caused to the children by selfish, uncaring or indeed criminal foster parents is frequently discovered too late because of a lack of supervisory staff. The development of harmonious relationships between the child and the foster parents may also be hindered by the conduct of parents who demand the child back for financial or other self-centred motives without themselves being able and willing to care for them and bring them up. By contrast, through adoption the child normally receives the preconditions for healthy physical and emotional development, above all the experience of being secure, which is vital to developing social relationships, and the permanent, uninterrupted affiliation to its family.
5. The limited permission of adoption against the will of the parents in the cases described is also in line with the general value determination expressed in Article 6.1 to 6.3 of the Basic Law in favour of the family. The Basic Law considers the family to constitute the core of any human community, the significance of which cannot be compared with any other human tie (BVerfGE 6, 55 (71)); it recognises its function for the care and upbringing of children and ensures its priority over collective forms of upbringing. However, better justice is done to this fundamental tendency if the state endeavours, in the situation depicted, to safeguard the family upbringing of the child which exceptionally cannot be provided in the natural family, by other means instead of selecting the administratively more convenient path of accommodation in state or other collective institutions.
6. If, therefore, measures according to § 1747.3 of the Civil Code are – under the described conditions – accordingly an admissible exercise of the state's watchdog function according to Article 6.2 sentence 2 of the Basic Law which is compatible with the general value determinations of Article 6 of the Basic Law, this at the same time unambiguously states that the provision submitted for review does not impinge on the parental right in its essence. The identification of the parental right as a "natural right" in Article 6.2 sentence 1 of the Basic Law does not contradict this (see also BVerfGE 10, 59 (81)). The parliament handing down the constitution

has presumed that those who give life to a child are by nature willing and called upon to shoulder the responsibility for its care and upbringing. If, by way of exception, this precondition is not met, substitution of consent to adoption replaces the parent-child relationship in a situation in which a constitutionally protectable right of the natural parents no longer exists. This is hence not a forced "parent *exchange*". The child only receives parents who deserve this name within the meaning of the Basic Law because they are willing to shoulder the obligations inseparably tied to the parental right (see also BVerfGE 10, 59 (67)) by virtue of adoption.

7. Further, the view that substitution of parental consent to adoption could at best be recognised if restricted to cases of forfeiture of parental power does not apply. It can in particular not be based on the prohibition of excessiveness. Since forfeiture links solely to the penalty, which depends not only on the degree of the concrete violation of the obligation towards the child, but is determined by many other elements (personality of the offender, significance and consequences of the offence, general prevention, etc.), it is not possible to say that in the case of a conviction meeting the elements of § 1676 of the Civil Code the violation of the obligation by the parent in question in each case is more serious than if no criminal proceedings have taken place. There are not infrequently cases of sadistic conduct on the part of parents or of gross physical or emotional neglect which are not covered by the Criminal Code (*Strafgesetzbuch* – StGB) or which cannot be prosecuted for other reasons. Hence, the forfeiture of parental power from the point of view of parental responsibility is not a criterion within the meaning of Article 6.2 of the Basic Law which is suitable in absolute terms for the permission of adoption against the will of the parents. Rather, reservations may exist, conversely, against taking the schematic regulation of § 1676 of the Civil Code as a starting point for the encroachment that is permitted in § 1747.3 of the Civil Code. Accordingly, for instance, a conviction for violation of the maintenance obligation or because of a crime against the child's property with a corresponding penalty satisfies the elements of § 1676 of the Civil Code without regard to the significance of the punishable act for the concrete parent-child relationship. This however does not give rise to a complaint about the provision which has been submitted for review because the margin of appreciation granted by the legislature to the guardianship judge certainly permits the latter to constitutionally apply it.

§ 1747.3 of the Civil Code is hence compatible with Article 6.2 of the Basic Law.

IV.

The provision also does not violate any other constitutional provisions.

1. There is no need for review against Article 2.1 of the Basic Law because its application to the parental right of upbringing is definitely ruled out by Article 6.2 of the Basic Law (BVerfGE 4, 52 (56)).
2. The reference to Article 18 of the Basic Law contained in the submission order of the Stuttgart Higher Regional Court disregards the definition of forfeit within the meaning of this constitutional provision and its constitutional function. § 1747.3 of the Civil Code merely lends concrete form to a restriction which from the outset is inherent in the fundamental right contained in Article 6.2 of the Basic Law. Its impact is limited to the individual act in question and to the relationship between the parents and a specific child.
3. A violation of the principle of the rule of law for a lack of definiteness of the provision submitted for review also does not apply (see BVerfGE 11, 234 (237); 17, 67 (82); 21, 245 (261)). The terms used therein are not less determined or less determinable than for instance the elements of § 1666.1 of the Civil Code, the application of which the Federal Constitutional Court has not found to be objectionable (see BVerfGE 4, 52 (57)).
The interpretation of the term "malicious" is not uniform in the case-law and literature to date. It is demanded in some cases that consent is refused on the basis of a reproachable, inimical stance; in some cases, it is considered to be adequate if alien motives apply which are by no means to be recognised, or if no objectively material reasons are submitted for refusal ... This difference in opinions is however not an indication of a lack of definiteness because the provision was not inserted until 1961 and, in consideration of the constitutional reservations, has so far been applied only hesitantly. Constitutionally, all the above interpretations are tenable; they show that it is certainly possible to derive criteria from the purpose of the provision and its wording for the interpretation of the content.

V.

The provision submitted for review also does not violate the constitution because it also applies to the case of incognito adoption.
1. The legal view applied to the review of admissibility regarding the applicability of § 1747.3 of the Civil Code to this special form of adoption also reveals itself as correct if one takes a closer view. The wording of the provision does not oppose such an approach; its meaning speaks in favour of it. The case-law and the prevailing view in the legal literature consider adoption in which the parents remain unaware of the name of the adoptive parents to be permissible if the consent of the parents nonetheless refers to an individually determined adoption relationship (see Decisions of the Federal Court of Justice in Civil Matters (*Entscheidungen des*

Bundesgerichtshofes in Zivilsachen – BGHZ 2, 287 (290 et seq.)). The procedure followed here is such that the youth welfare office or other state-recognised adoption agency selects the adoptive parents and enters them in a list; consent is declared to the adoption of the child by the adoptive parents listed under a certain number in this list. Material to permission for incognito adoption was above all the experience that even parents who initially consent to adoption later wish to re-establish contact with the child, and that this disturbs the process by which the child becomes familiar with the new surroundings and the development of a harmonious relationship with the adoptive parents. It suggests itself that the child's need for protection against such disturbances can arise particularly in cases which § 1747.3 of the Civil Code is intended to cover, namely with particularly irresponsible, unreasonable or unstable parents. According to the purpose of the provision, it can therefore be presumed that the possibility of substitution of parental consent is also to apply to incognito adoption; otherwise, the legislature, which was aware of the case-law on the permissibility of incognito adoption, would have restricted the provision correspondingly.

2. Constitutional permissibility is contingent solely on the priority of parents with regard to caring for and bringing up their children, which is protected by Article 6.2 of the Basic Law. In this respect, however, the legal and de facto impact of incognito adoption is the same as that of customary adoption. The difference merely lies in the fact that the legally continuing family relationships on the part of the parents can no longer be maintained in practice. This does not apply to the child since the names and addresses of all concerned are recorded in the files of the youth welfare office and the concerned courts, as well as – albeit with a note restricting access (see § 61 of the Civil Status Act (*Personenstandsgesetz* – PStG)) – in the civil status registries. The child or its legal representative may therefore take up contact with the parents or other relatives if this is in the interest of the child, for instance in order to assert a maintenance claim after the death of the adoptive parents. Furthermore, the child is already customarily informed of the fact of adoption while growing up or on reaching adulthood, so that he or she certainly has the opportunity to establish relationships with the natural parents on reaching majority.

Even if, however, one were to consider incognito adoption to constitute a more incisive encroachment on the area protected by Article 6.2 of the Basic Law, it would only constitute a difference of degree in the scale of the incursion which is to be evaluated according to the criteria developed above, and particularly according to consideration for the child's best interests and the principle of proportionality. If, accordingly, incognito adoption is necessary in order to ensure the healthy development of the child, the interest in maintaining family relationships must take a secondary position. Whether this precondition is met is to be ascertained in the framework of the weighing of interests which in any case is necessary under § 1747.3 of the Civil Code.

3. By contrast, the indication of the right of access of parents who do not have the care for the person of the child according to § 1634.1 of the Civil Code also cannot lead to another result. If one were to wish to recognise a right of access of the natural parents even after adoption has been finalised, should the designated requirements for substitution of consent to incognito adoption be met, at the same time in each case the preconditions would apply for exclusion of the right of access according to § 1634.2 of the Civil Code (see on this also BGHZ 2, 287 (292)).

4. In contradistinction to the view held by the Passau Regional Court, the individual elements of § 1747.3 of the Civil Code can also be evaluated with incognito adoption; in particular, the objection that the lack of awareness of the identity of the adoptive parents denies the parents a "responsible decision" concerning consent misses the mark. If the already stringent preconditions contained in § 1747.3 of the Civil Code for substitution of consent apply, and over and above this incognito adoption is necessary for the above reasons, these are not parents from whom one may anticipate a responsible decision at all, i.e. one which is orientated towards the child's best interests. Moreover, incognito adoption only means that the parents do not learn of the name and address of the adoptive parents; this does not rule out informing the parents of the general circumstances of the adoptive parents (nationality, denomination, economic and social circumstances), and this will as a rule be necessary.

5. Such an application of § 1747.3 of the Civil Code to incognito adoptions also does not violate Article 103.1 of the Basic Law. This constitutional provision guarantees to those concerned in court proceedings the right to make a statement on the facts on which the ruling is based prior to the ruling being handed down (BVerfGE 1, 418 (429); established case-law). In the proceedings according to § 1747.3 of the Civil Code, the parents may, as parties, fully assert their objections to adoption per se, as well as against any intended form of incognito adoption. This constitutes adequate protection of their procedural interests.

Justices: Dr. Müller, Dr. Stein, Ritterspach, Dr. Haager, Rupp-v. Brünneck, Dr. Brox, Dr. Zeidler

No. 6

BVerfGE 28, 324
of 27 May 1970 – 1 BvL 22/63, 27/64 –
"Marriage clause case"

HEADNOTE:

The marriage clauses in orphans' pensions in social pensions insurance (§ 44.1 sentence 2 of the Salaried Employees Insurance Act (*Angestelltenversicherungsgesetz* – AVG) and § 1267.1 sentence 2 of the Reich Insurance Code (*Reichsversicherungsordnung* – RVO) are incompatible with Article 6.1 of the Basic Law insofar as they exclude orphans undergoing training from drawing the pension on marriage even if their spouse is unable to provide maintenance.

Order of the First Senate of 27 May 1970
– 1 BvL 22/63, 27/64 –

in the proceedings for a constitutional review 1. of § 44.1 sentence 2 of the Salaried Employees Insurance Act (*Angestelltenversicherungsgesetz* – AVG) – suspension of proceedings and submission order of the Hamburg Social Court of 30 October 1963 (10 – AN 1510/60) – 1 BvL 22/63; 2. of § 1267.1 sentence 2 of the Reich Insurance Code (*Reichsversicherungsordnung* – RVO)) – suspension of proceedings and submission order of the Lüneburg Social Court of 26 October 1964 (S 1 J – 35/64) – 1 BvL 27/64 –.

RULING:

§ 44.1 sentence 2 of the Salaried Employees Insurance Act in the versions of Article 1 of the Act Reforming the Salaried Employees Insurance Act (*Angestelltenversicherungs-Neuregelungsgesetz*) of 23 February 1957 (Federal Law Gazette (*Bundesgesetzblatt* – BGBl.) I p. 88) and of § 7 no. 4 of the Act

Promoting a Voluntary Social Year (*Gesetz zur Förderung eines freiwilligen sozialen Jahres*) of 17 August 1964 (Federal Law Gazette I p. 640)

and

§ 1267.1 sentence 2 of the Reich Insurance Code in the versions of Article 1 no. 2 of the Act Reforming the Wage-Earners Pensions Insurance Act (*Arbeiterrentenversicherungs-Neuregelungsgesetz*) of 23 February 1957 (Federal Law Gazette I p. 45) and of § 6 no. 6 of the Act Promoting a Voluntary Social Year of 17 August 1964 (Federal Law Gazette I p. 640)

are incompatible with Article 6.1 of the Basic Law (*Grundgesetz* – GG) insofar as 18-year-old orphans who are in school or vocational training certainly are, if they are married, excluded from drawing the orphans' pension.

EXTRACT FROM GROUNDS:

A.

Both submissions relate to the constitutionality of so-called marriage clauses (also known as marriage discontinuation clauses or marriage exclusion clauses) for orphans' pensions in salaried employees' insurance and wage-earners' insurance. According to the provision contained in the Salaried Employees Insurance Act and in the Reich Insurance Code, the wording of which is identical, the children of a deceased insured party receive an orphans' pension if the general preconditions for drawing surviving dependants' pensions are met (§ 40 of the Salaried Employees Insurance Act and § 1263 of the Reich Insurance Code). The orphans' pension is granted to all children until they reach the age of 18, without regard for whether they are single or married (so-called general orphans' pension). By contrast, children aged over 18 only receive an orphans' pension if they meet particular preconditions, in particular if they are in school or vocational training; entitlement to this so-called extended orphans' pension is always conditional on the orphan being unmarried.

I.

… [The provisions in question read as follows] in the version applicable today:

§ 44.1 of the Salaried Employees Insurance Act = § 1267.1 of the Reich Insurance Code

(1) After the death of the insured party, his or her children shall receive an orphans' pension (...) until reaching the age of 18. The orphans' pension shall be paid at most until reaching the age of 25 for an unmarried child who is in school or vocational training, who is serving a voluntary social year within the meaning of the Act Promoting a Voluntary Social Year or who as a result of physical or mental afflictions is unable to maintain himself or herself. In the case of a interruption of or delay in school or vocational training caused by meeting the child's statutory military or alternative obligatory service, the orphans' pension shall also be granted for a period beyond the age of 25 corresponding to the time of such service.

II.

The submitting social courts consider it to be unconstitutional that the claim to an orphans' pension of an orphan who is over 18 and still in school or vocational training ceases to apply on the marriage of the orphan even if the spouse is unable to maintain the orphan, and especially to contribute towards the costs of vocational training. The submissions are based on the following sets of original proceedings:

1. Proceedings of the Hamburg Social Court – 1 BvL 22/63 –:
a) The plaintiff, who was born in 1936, received as a student an orphans' pension from the insured employees' insurance of his deceased father. At the end of November 1959, he married a girl who was expecting a child from him; the child was born in June 1960. The Federal Insurance Institute for Salaried Employees (*Bundesversicherungsanstalt für Angestellte*) discontinued payment of the orphans' pension from 1 December 1959. In 1960 the plaintiff took a job as a salaried employee and hence gave up his studies.
He lodged an action with the Social Court for continued payment of the pension until 31 May 1960 on grounds that discontinuation of the pension by virtue of marriage allegedly breached Article 6.1 of the Basic Law. His wife testified to the Social Court that she had not been admitted in the GDR to study medicine, and had therefore come to Hamburg. There she had commenced training as a welfare worker with the aid of support from public funds. This support had discontinued on her marriage; the plaintiff had met the costs of the last term of her training. She had taken her examination in March 1960, and had thereafter still worked for one year in order to receive state recognition. It emerges from the files from the Employment Office consulted by the Social Court that the support of DM 214 per month paid from there to the plaintiff's wife was indeed discontinued at the end of November 1959.

b) By its order of 30 October 1963 (*Die Sozialgerichtsbarkeit* 1964, p. 340), the Hamburg Social Court requested, according to Article 100.1 of the Basic Law, a ruling by the Federal Constitutional Court (*Bundesverfassungsgericht*) on

> "whether the characteristic 'unmarried' in § 44 of the Salaried Employees Insurance Act
> a) is in violation of Article 6.1 of the Basic Law if the spouse is economically unable to contribute towards the costs of vocational training,
> b) is in violation of Articles 6.1 and 6.5 of the Basic Law if this marriage is concluded because of pregnancy."

It reasoned the submission as follows:
If the provision submitted for review was unrestrictedly valid, the action would have to be rejected. The unambiguous wording of the provision was said not to permit any other interpretation that was in conformity with the constitution. If however the provision was invalid to the degree stated, the action would have to be allowed because the plaintiff's wife had not been obliged to maintain him. At that time, she had had neither assets nor an income. It had also not been reasonable to expect her to take up gainful employment in order to fund her husband's studies since she herself had still been in training. The provision was said to violate Article 6.1 of the Basic Law under conditions designated in the submission order because the discontinuation of the orphans' pension by virtue of marriage was said to act as an inhibition to the conclusion of marriage where fiancées were in an unfavourable economic situation. It was said that pension beneficiaries in poorer economic situations with spouses who had no assets were particularly affected in cases where the discontinuation of the pension influenced the decision on the continuation of training. In this respect, the provision presented for review was also said to touch upon the principle of the social welfare state.
Refusal of the pension solely because of marriage was said to signify placing married persons in a disadvantageous situation without justification in comparison with unmarried persons during vocational training. Since the intention of the statutory provision was to enable young people who had lost one or both parents to undergo thorough vocational training from their social insurance, it was said to run counter to the nature of the area of life regulated upon to take marriage as a reference point for such a disadvantage. Also persons who were in vocational training could be mature for marriage in terms of their character. Insofar as the foundation for earning a suitable living was still missing, it was said to be a task for the family of those en-

tering into marriage to help to provide them with this, and hence to facilitate the transition to an independent livelihood and full personal development.
The claim to the orphans' pension in social insurance was said to be maintenance-substituting in nature, and thus had to correspond to the regulation under civil law in accordance with which the relatives' maintenance obligation took priority if the spouse was unable to provide maintenance. During the lifetime of his father, the plaintiff would have retained the priority maintenance claim against the latter despite the marriage because his own income as a working student had been insufficient to cover the costs of studying, and because his wife had not been under an obligation to maintain him. It was said that there were no factually convincing reasons why the social pensions insurance violated the logic established by the law itself with the assumption of family maintenance obligations. The legislature's margin of appreciation consisting of the benefit-providing administration was said to be restricted by the prohibition contained in Article 6.1 of the Basic Law to damage or cause detriment to marriage. What is more, pensions insurance was said to have less of a welfare character than that of insurance; care for the surviving dependants was said to be among its main elements, and must hence be closely adapted to maintenance law under civil law. The connection with the ability to pay of the insured party during his or her lifetime was said to be maintained by virtue of the fact that the amount of the pension was orientated in line with the contribution, which in turn was said to correspond towards the income of the insured party. Whilst the orphans' pension did not depend on the need of the orphan in an individual case, the claim was said to be largely dependent on obligatory insurance which, in a generalising manner, assumed need. By contrast, the consideration, on which the discontinuation of the pension was based, that a person marrying no longer needed to invoke the insurance of the father or mother was said to be a generalisation which impermissibly led to a disadvantage. The disadvantageous consequences to which this led were said not to constitute unintentional side-effects in individual cases which had to be accepted: The marriage of a 24-year-old juvenile who was still undergoing training could not be regarded as an isolated case. The plaintiff may also not be expected to finance his studies by other means, for instance by the Honnef model, since these required additional preconditions to be met.
If a child was expected, the discontinuation of the claim to the orphans' pension by virtue of marriage was said to violate Article 6.5 of the Basic Law at the same time because it was said to inhibit parents' decision to marry and hence to make it difficult for them to comply with their moral duty towards the child. Also from this point of view, these were said not to be exceptional cases, given that a considerable number of all first-born children were procreated before marriage.

2. Proceedings of the Lüneburg Social Court – 1 BvL 27/64 –:

a) The plaintiff, who was born in 1939, as a student drew an orphans' pension from the wage-earners' insurance of his father, who had been killed in action. When he married in November 1963, the Hanover Land Insurance Facility (*Landesversicherungsanstalt*) discontinued payment of the pension. He filed an action against this with the Social Court and requested further payment of the pension on grounds that § 1267 of the Reich Insurance Code was allegedly unconstitutional. He claimed that his wife had no income or assets and that she could not provide him with any maintenance. It was said that she was also a student and had interrupted her studies because she was expecting a child from him. As a double orphan, she herself had drawn an orphans' pension, payment of which had however been discontinued on conclusion of marriage.

b) By its order of 26 October 1964 (*Zeitschrift für das gesamte Familienrecht* – FamRZ 1969, p. 34) the Social Court requested, according to Article 100.1 of the Basic Law, a ruling of the Federal Constitutional Court on the matter of

> "whether § 1267.1 of the Reich Insurance Code is compatible with the Basic Law for the Federal Republic of Germany insofar as it provides that only unmarried persons are entitled to an orphans' pension for children after reaching the age of 18".

It reasoned the submission as follows:

According to the wording of § 1267.1 of the Reich Insurance Code, which is not amenable to interpretation in this respect, if the provision was valid the action would have to be rejected. If however the provision was unconstitutional, the action would have to be allowed, with the consequence that the plaintiff would also receive an orphans' pension for the period from 1 November 1963 to 30 June 1964.

In the conviction of the court, the provision submitted for review violates Article 3.1 and Article 6.1 of the Basic Law. The general principle of equality was said to have been violated because the differentiation between married and unmarried orphans was not justified by a reason arising from the nature of the matter. The orphans' pension did have a maintenance-substituting function, and the maintenance claim against the parents to be substituted by the pension claim was said to discontinue in principle if the pension recipient acquired a maintenance claim against the spouse by virtue of conclusion of marriage. Since this consequence did not however occur in a not inconsiderable number of cases, it was said not to be expedient to link discontinuation of the pension solely to the conclusion of marriage. By contrast, without violating the principle of equality the legislature could make the pension claim dependent on whether the deceased parent – if he or she had remained

alive – would have been able to provide maintenance, and also on the spouse not being able to provide maintenance.
The consideration of the Federal Social Court (*Bundessozialgericht*) in the ruling of 24 February 1960 (Decisions of the Federal Social Court (*Entscheidungen des Bundessozialgerichts* – BSGE) 12, 27 (30)), namely that it was not a matter of actually granting maintenance since it also did not play any role with orphans under 18, was said not to be convincing. If with orphans under 18 the need was not examined in individual cases, this was said to be a regulation made for reasons of simplifying the administration as suggested by experience which made a permissible generalisation and did not place those concerned at a disadvantage.
Article 6.1 of the Basic Law was said to have been violated because the statutory provision could of necessity cause fiancées with a material orientation or with few funds to postpone their planned marriage until reaching the age of 25. They would indeed not be able to marry prior to that time in exceptional cases unless they wished to claim public welfare. The consideration of the Federal Social Court that it served the protection of marriage to keep the income of a spouse as low as possible so that the maintenance obligation of the other spouse remained unaffected was said to miss the mark. If the spouse did not have any income or assets, the previous recipient of the orphans' pension would, subsequent to marriage, not only have to ensure his or her own maintenance as previously, but also to pay for that of the spouse. Out of a sense of responsibility, he or she would therefore, under certain conditions, refrain from the conclusion of marriage despite urgent reasons such as pregnancy, in order not to endanger his or her maintenance and that of the spouse.

III.

1. The Federal Minister of Labour and Social Affairs, who made a statement in the name of the Federal Government, considers § 44.1 sentence 2 of the Salaried Employees Insurance Act and § 1267.1 sentence 2 of the Reich Insurance Code to be compatible with the Basic Law.
…
2. The Federation of German Pension Insurance Institutes (*Verband Deutscher Rentenversicherungsträger*) considers § 44.1 sentence 2 of the Salaried Employees Insurance Act to be compatible with the constitution for the same reasons as the Federal Minister of Labour.
3. The plaintiff of the original proceedings at the Hamburg Social Court mainly concurs with the statements of the submission order, with a detailed discussion of the ruling of the Federal Social Court of 24 February 1960 (BSGE 12, 27).

IV.

The constitutionality of the marriage clauses is contentious in the case-law and in legal literature. The discussion relates here not solely to the marriage clauses with the orphans' pensions in social insurance, but also to equivalent or similar provisions in other statutes.

1. In a wide variety of legal fields, the school or vocational training of a child or juvenile in conjunction with certain age limits is the linking point for a payment from public funds, whether the latter is granted to the child or juvenile himself or herself (e.g. orphans' pension, training allowance), or benefits the parents (e.g. child supplement, child benefit). The impact of marriage on the entitlement to draw a pension is not uniformly regulated; in the vast majority of cases, however, it leads to discontinuation of the payment. For instance, in all branches of social insurance the regulations of the orphans' pension and of the child supplement which an insured party receives who is entitled to a pension are identical to the provisions to be reviewed here in terms of their content, or indeed verbatim (see e.g. § 39.3 sentence 2 of the Salaried Employees Insurance Act); an exception applies only to the family allowance in unemployment insurance, which is to also be granted without restriction to married children of the unemployed person (see § 113.1 of the Employment Promotion Act (*Arbeitsförderungsgesetz*) of 25 June 1969 – Federal Law Gazette I p. 582 –). Equivalent marriage clauses can be found with child benefit (see § 2.2 of the Federal Child Benefit Act (*Bundeskindergeldgesetz* – BKGG) of 14 April 1964 – Federal Law Gazette I p. 265 –)[1], as well as with the orphans' pension and the child allowance according to the Federal War Victims' Pensions Act (*Bundesversorgungsgesetz* – BVG) (see § 45.3 and § 33b.4 of the Federal War Victims' Pensions Act in the version of 20 January 1967 – Federal Law Gazette I p. 141 –)[2], there, however, modified by the possibility of equalisation of hardships (see § 89 of the Federal War Victims' Pensions Act). By contrast, in the law on the equalisation of war burdens the maintenance assistance for double orphans and the child allowance for maintenance assistance are granted both for married and for unmarried children (see §§ 265.2 and 265.3, 269.2, 272.3, 273.2 and 275.2 of the Equalisation of War Burdens Act (*Lastenausgleichsgesetz* – LAG) in the version of 1 October 1969 – Federal Law Gazette I p. 1909 –).

Marriage clauses going even further than social insurance statutes are contained by the statutes of the Federation and of the *Länder* (states) on civil servants and remu-

---

1 see Decisions of the Federal Constitutional Court (*Entscheidungen des Bundesverfassungsgerichts* – BVerfGE) 29, no. 13, p. 71.

2 see BVerfGE 29, no. 12, p. 57.

neration: Not only the orphans' benefit for the children of civil servants aged over 18 who are at school or in vocational training, but even the orphans' benefit for children of civil servants under 18 discontinues on the marriage of the child (see 164.1 no. 1 of the Federal Civil Servants' Act (*Bundesbeamtengesetz*) in the version of 22 October 1965 – Federal Law Gazette I p. 1776 – and § 88.1 no. 1 of the Civil Service Law Framework Act (*Beamtenrechtsrahmengesetz*) in the version of 22 October 1965 – Federal Law Gazette I p. 1754 –). The same applies to the child allowance (see § 18.6 and § 57 of the Federal Civil Servants' Remuneration Act (*Bundesbesoldungsgesetz*) in the version of 18 December 1963 – Federal Law Gazette I p. 916 –)[3]. Only in the *Länder* Hamburg and Rhineland-Palatinate is a child allowance also granted for married civil servants' children if the spouse is unable to provide maintenance. The provision on the orphans' pension in federal compensation law is linked to the provision of the child allowance in federal remuneration law (see § 17.1 no. 3 of the Federal Compensation Act (*Bundesentschädigungsgesetz* – BEG) in the version of 14 September 1965 – Federal Law Gazette I p. 1315 –).

Married persons also have a right to training assistance according to the Training Assistance Act (*Ausbildungsförderungsgesetz*) of 19 September 1969 (Federal Law Gazette I p. 1719). Here, however, in contradistinction to the social benefits listed above, an individual needs assessment is carried out: The training allowance is conditional on the trainee not having the necessary means otherwise available; here, the income of the spouse is to be allowed for just as the individual's or that of the parents. The same regulation applies to other individual training allowances, particularly according to the so-called Honnef model (see *Deutscher Hochschulführer* 1969, 44th ed., p. 45).

2. Insofar as the supreme federal courts have been previously seized of marriage clauses, they have affirmed the constitutionality of the regulations in established case-law; see the rulings of the Federal Social Court on marriage clauses in the orphans' pension in the Federal War Victims' Pensions Act and re § 44.1 sentence 2 of the Salaried Employees Insurance Act (BSGE 12, 27; 25, 205), of the Federal Court of Justice (*Bundesgerichtshof*) on the marriage clause in orphans' pensions according to federal compensation law (FamRZ 1966, p. 448-449) and of the Federal Administrative Court (*Bundesverwaltungsgericht*) on the marriage clause with the child allowance in federal civil servants' remuneration law (Decisions of the Federal Administrative Court (*Entscheidungen des Bundesverwaltungsgerichts* – BVerwGE) 25, 123). Apart from the latter ruling, which is based on the special, traditional form taken by the child allowance in the law on civil servants' remunera-

3 see BVerfGE 29, no. 1, p. 1.

tion, this case-law is based on the same arguments as the Federal Government has presented to defend the provisions submitted for review ... In addition, the Federal Social Court stressed in the ruling on § 44.1 sentence 2 of the Salaried Employees Insurance Act that the disadvantage affecting the married orphan by the discontinuation of the pension had to be compared to the legal claims of married insured parties and their spouses arising according to social insurance law through the conclusion of marriage.

In contradistinction to this case-law, some lower courts consider the marriage clauses to be unconstitutional; see apart from the submissions on which this decision is based the submission order of the Lüneburg Social Court regarding § 2.2 of the Federal Child Benefit Act (FamRZ 1969, p. 158) and the submission orders of the Gelsenkirchen Administrative Court regarding the marriage clauses of the North Rhine-Westphalian remuneration and civil servants acts (FamRZ 1967, p. 45 (additionally p. 575) and 1968, p. 522).

3. The above supreme-court case-law has undergone increasing criticism in recent years. By far the greatest part of the legal literature considers the marriage clauses to be unconstitutional – in all fields of law ... The reasons brought forward for the unconstitutionality of the clauses are the same as were relevant to the submission orders (above II 1 b, 2 b); above all, the generalisation "married = looked after" on which the impugned provisions are based is regarded as not being constitutionally tenable. Over and above this, the clauses are also impugned for social, societal, economic and family policy reasons, and are no longer considered to constitute the state-of-the-art in view of the falling age at marriage and the extension of training time in many professions; the lack of standardisation of the various regulations is also criticised ...

V.

In the fifth electoral term of the German *Bundestag*, a number of Members of the CDU and the CSU introduced a draft Bill to relax the marriage clauses in all fields of law, which however was no longer deliberated on (*Bundestag* printed paper – BTDrucks. V/3111 of 27 June 1968; ...). This draft Bill was once more introduced, unchanged, in the present (sixth) electoral term by the CDU/CSU parliamentary group in the *Bundestag* and transferred to the competent *Bundestag* committees in the *Bundestag* session held on 10 December 1969 (see Stenographic Report (StenBer.) of the 19th session of the *Bundestag*, 6th electoral term, p. 693). According to the draft Bill, orphans' pensions or other benefits are to be continued to be granted to orphans or children in training after marriage if the spouse is unable to provide maintenance, and child allowances or other benefits to parents if the married child is still largely maintained by the beneficiary. It was stated as reasoning that the global concept pursued by the legislature that marriages were not concluded until there was an adequate financial foundation no longer corresponded to the de facto circumstances today. With the increased occurrence of early marriage and the extension of training, the conclusion of marriage between two young people who were still in training was said to be on the increase. In such cases, the loss of income caused by the discontinuation of payments on both sides was said to be considerable. The additional burden caused by the draft Bill was said to be estimated by the Federal Minister of Finance at DM 11 million for the Child Benefit Act and social insurance, DM 3.8 million for civil servants' remuneration law and DM 1 million for the Federal War Victims' Pensions Act.

The *Bundestag* Committee on Labour and Social Affairs, which was in charge, and the *Bundestag* Committee for Youth, Family Affairs and Health, which assisted in the deliberations, initially requested the Federal Government to provide a detailed portrayal of the problems of the marriage clauses, particularly of their financial impact, and for a progress report on the reform of the equalisation of family burdens (see minutes of the 7th session of the Committee which was in charge of 22 January 1970, pp. 8-9, and of the 7th session of the assisting Committee of 12 March 1970, p. 18). This statement is currently not yet available. In the response to a minor interpellation on the part of the *Bundestag* parliamentary groups of the SPD and FDP as to the possibilities to abolish the marriage clauses and the resulting financial consequences, the Federal Minister for Youth, Family and Health, after consultation with the federal ministers involved, affirmed the need for an amendment to the relevant provisions per se. The idea of the economic independence of married children which was material on creation of the marriage clauses hardly did justice to today's circumstances; what is more, there was said to be an unsuitable disharmony between the marriage clauses in public law, the regulation on the maintenance obligation in civil law, as well as the provisions on the allowance of the parents' income with individual training allowances for married persons. After carrying out a review of the cost question, the Federal Government would make a statement on whether it was able to favour a relaxation or deletion of the clauses, and submit a corresponding draft Bill after continuing the multi-annual financial planning (see *Bundestag* printed paper VI/197 of 17 December 1969).

B. – I.

Since the marriage clauses in § 44.1 sentence 2 of the Salaried Employees Insurance Act and § 1267.1 sentence 2 of the Reich Insurance Code are identical verbatim (apart from the quote of the respective statutory provision on the definition of a

child), the submissions of the two Social Courts have been consolidated for joint adjudication.
The submissions are correctly restricted to a partial regulation of both provisions, namely to the granting of the extended orphans' pension to unmarried orphans over 18 who are still in school and vocational training, since only this part of the provision is relevant to the decision on the original proceedings. By contrast, the further content of the provision – the granting of the extended orphans' pension to orphans over 18 during the serving of a voluntary social year or because the orphan is infirm – does not require consideration.

II.

The submitting courts are of the opinion that married orphans are placed at a disadvantage solely by the word "unmarried"; in their view, therefore, the term "orphan" in the social insurance statutes addresses both the unmarried and the married children of the deceased insured party, even though the latter form a family of their own on conclusion of marriage. This interpretation of the law corresponds to the general view in practice and in the legal literature (see Bogs, [*Verhandlungen des 43. Deutschen Juristentages*, vol. II] G 43; see also BVerwG of 2 December 1959 – V C 200.59 – partly reproduced in *Die Öffentliche Verwaltung* – DÖV 1960, p. 473-474 = *Deutsches Verwaltungsblatt* – DVBl.) 1960, p. 255); it is also confirmed by the legislative history. The unconstitutionality existing in the view of the courts is therefore not based on the use of this term, but solely on the word "unmarried" contained in that part of the provision.

III.

The Lüneburg Social Court simply submits this precondition for a claim for review, the Hamburg Social Court only insofar as by these means the continued payment of the extended orphans' pension is also ruled out if even if the spouse of the orphan is unable to pay. This difference in the wording of the two submission orders is however insignificant. The provision itself contains an absolute – not differentiating – marriage clause. The submitting courts consider it to be unconstitutional for precisely this reason, and further concur that the legislature could order the discontinuation of the orphans' pension without violating the constitution if and insofar as the spouse was able to pay the maintenance, including the costs of vocational training.

IV.

Both courts consider that the violation of the constitution underlying the provisions submitted for review must at least lead to the partial nullity of the provision. Whether this view is correct, or whether the alleged unconstitutionality can lead not to a declaration of nullity, but only to the ascertainment of the violation of the constitution by the Federal Constitutional Court, is void of significance for the admissibility of the submissions. The requested constitutional review is also material to the decision in the original proceedings in the latter case because the social courts would have to take a different decision than if the provision were valid: They would have to suspend the proceedings and await the decision of the legislature (see BVerfGE 22, 349 (360-361); 23, 74 (78)).

C.

The constitutional review hence encompasses both provisions of social insurance law insofar as, accordingly, in the group of children aged under 18 of a deceased insured party who are still in (school or vocational) training only the unmarried children receive the orphans' pension until reaching the age of 25, indeed under certain circumstances beyond this, whilst married children do not receive it under conditions which are otherwise identical. To this degree, the provisions are not compatible with Article 6.1 of the Basic Law insofar as, in each case, they exclude married children from drawing an orphans' pension.

I.

1. The provisions which are to be reviewed differentiate solely by civil status under otherwise identical circumstances: A comparison is carried out between unmarried orphans who on reaching the age of 18 are in school or vocational training on the one hand, and married orphans who on reaching the age of 18 are in school or vocational training on the other hand.

Such a differentiation is to be measured directly by the standard of Article 6.1 of the Basic Law. As a special review standard, this constitutional provision certainly precedes Article 3.1 of the Basic Law if the statutory provision is linked directly to the conclusion of marriage, that is as here the legal disadvantage (non-granting of the pension) affects only spouses, and not also third parties (see BVerfGE 9, 237 (242); 13, 290 (295 et seq.); 17, 210 (224)).

2. According to the established case-law of the Federal Constitutional Court (see BVerfGE 6, 55 (71, 76); 17, 210 (219-220); 24, 104 (109)), it emerges from Article

6.1 of the Basic Law, as a fundamental provision that determines values, for the state, positively, that there is an automatic responsibility to promote marriage and the family through suitable measures and to protect them against being placed at a disadvantage by other forces, and, negatively, a prohibition of damaging or otherwise causing detriment to marriage, regardless of whether this takes place through measures enacted against existing marriages or whether the willingness to conclude a marriage is placed at risk (see BVerfGE 12, 151 (167)). Accordingly, married persons may by no means be placed at a disadvantage *solely* because they are married, or in particular receive lower state benefits than single persons. The marital partnership and economic community may naturally be used as a link to economic legal consequences. Nonetheless, convincing factual reasons must emerge for a differentiation which imposes a burden on married persons from the nature of the circumstances which are regulated on: Allowance for the special situation of the spouses caused by the marital partnership and economic community may, particularly with the concrete measure, not contradict the ideas of justice of the community, and hence be regarded as constituting discrimination of marriage (see BVerfGE 6, 55 (77); 17, 210 (217, 220); 18, 97 (107); 22, 100 (105)).

II.

According to this standard, the provisions which are for review are not compatible with Article 6.1 of the Basic Law because an absolute exclusion of married orphans from the extended orphans' pension cannot be materially justified in view of the subject-matter and the purpose of the statutory regulation.

1. The surviving dependants' pension is a major element of social insurance. This serves the purpose of overall social security and social equalisation, that is protection of social existence against the vicissitudes of life (see BVerfGE 11, 105 (117)); in its present manifestation, which is by no means restricted any longer to averting extreme emergencies and caring for the socially weakest among the population, it is a particularly succinct expression of the principle of the social welfare state (Article 20.1 of the Basic Law). In the system of social insurance benefits, the orphans' pension is to grant to the child equalisation for the impairment of the family community, occurring as a result of the death of the father or mother, and of the natural economic structure of the family household. It hence has a maintenance-substituting character insofar as it is to replace the loss of family maintenance payments in full or at least in part (BVerfGE 17, 1 (8 et seq.)). The extended orphans' pension specifically corresponds to the needs of those who are still in training to cover their maintenance, including the costs of (preparatory) vocational training. If one looks at the situation solely from the point of view of the orphan with a pension entitle-

ment, it is evident that the marriage changes nothing as to this need for maintenance: Those who wish to continue the training that has been commenced are not yet able to maintain themselves, still less to fund their training; they continue to require the economic or financial assistance which, by its function, the orphans' pension is to grant. It can therefore only be asked whether the social benefit is dispensable because the married orphan is able to receive the assistance needed elsewhere or because other points of view relating to the purpose of the benefit justify refusal because of marriage.

2. This already makes it impossible to justify the marriage clauses merely by stating that the orphans' pension is a state benefit of the benefit-providing administration the granting or restriction of which is within the margin of appreciation of the legislature. These arguments disregard, first of all, the fact that social insurance, in particular pensions insurance, contains a major element of social welfare, but that its structure is characterised at least as strongly by the insurance-law component: Surviving dependants' pensions are based to a significant degree on the insured party's own payments (see BVerfGE 17, 1 (9 with further references)). Apart from this, and also in the framework of the benefit-providing administration, a margin of appreciation only exists for the question as to whether and to what degree a benefit is to be granted. The legislature may however not carry out an improper differentiation in defining the group of beneficiaries; it is bound not only by the general equality principle, but also by the specific value determinations of the constitution, as that of Article 6.1 of the Basic Law (see BVerfGE 12, 354 (367); 17, 1 (23); 17, 210 (217)).

3. For the same reasons, the marriage clauses cannot be based on the consideration of the extended orphans' pension constituting an "exception" in relation to the general orphans' pension, i.e. an additional financial benefit which is as such not necessary or required. Even if this were to be the case, the legislature, were it to grant such a benefit at all to orphans over 18 in training, could not differentiate at will within this group of individuals. By its structure and function, the extended orphans' pension is however not distinct from the general orphans' pension in any sense which is relevant here. If the statutory preconditions are met, a legal claim exists in the same way as a claim to the general orphans' pension does; the extended orphans' pension is also in fact not granted exceptionally. If in the course of legal developments the age limit for the duration of drawing the orphans' pension has been repeatedly increased and specifically expanded in line with the period of school or vocational training, this corresponds to the change in the general economic and social situation. The latter has led to a situation in which, on the one hand, an increasing demand for qualified labour exists, and the training times have been considerably extended in many occupations, and not only academic ones, whilst on

the other hand an ever increasing number of juveniles are aspiring to qualified vocational training. Finally, a major factor is that social insurance has covered an ever greater section of the population. For this reason, the extended orphans' pension may also not be qualified as an exception with regard to the "maintenance-substituting character" of the surviving dependants' pensions. As a result of the above developments, parents are having their children engage in school or vocational training beyond the age of 18 to a much greater degree than previously, and are hence complying with a family-law obligation, given that in accordance with § 1610.2 of the Civil Code (*Bürgerliches Gesetzbuch* – BGB) the maintenance of a person requiring education also includes the costs of education and preparatory training for a vocation. The extended orphans' pension hence merely signifies an adjustment of the social insurance benefit which would apply as an alternative if family maintenance were to fail, an adjustment with which the legislature has done justice to the changed situation.

4. Further, it is asserted in favour of the marriage clauses that, on marriage, the child leaves the closer family community with the parents and forms his or her own independent family which is no longer permitted to rely for its economic existence on the former family community and its continued effect in the shape of the orphans' pension ... This can be countered by stating that the relations under family law between parents and children are far less affected by the marriage of the child than by coming of age. Although the latter event removes the child from the power of the parents and makes him or her legally independent, and furthermore restricts the scope of the parents' maintenance obligation in all cases (see § 1603.1 and 1603.2 of the Civil Code), coming of age is devoid of significance for the granting of the extended orphans' pension. Nonetheless, the marriage of the child may in many cases constitute a major turning-point in his or her relationship with the parents; as a rule it is a major or indeed a decisive step towards the de facto, personal independence of the child, and leads in this respect to a relaxation or at least to a change in the link with the parents; above all, its effect is customarily that the child leaves the domestic community with the parents. If a child marries prior to concluding his or her vocational training, the economic circumstances of the young spouses however frequently force them to initially live with parents or parents-in-law; as students' marriages show, however, a separate household is frequently also formed in such circumstances.

Even if one considers these general consequences of the conclusion of marriage, they cannot justify refusing to grant the orphans' pension; the orphans' pension is not related to the domestic community and the inner bonds between parents and children. Its function can consist solely of equalising the economic need caused by the discontinuation of the maintenance payment of the deceased insured party (see

BVerfGE 17, 1 (11)). It is hence vital whether the marriage constitutes, in economic terms, a major change in the relationship between the parents and the children which could impact the granting of the pension right.
5. In concordance with the above supreme-court rulings, the Federal Government considers such an economic aspect which in its view is material to the marriage clauses (see A IV 2 above) to lie in the fact that marriage transfers the parents' maintenance obligation to the orphan's spouse. In fact, under civil law, the conclusion of marriage gives rise to a maintenance claim of each spouse towards the other, and this maintenance claim precedes the maintenance obligation of the parents, as well as of all other relatives (§§ 1360 sentence 1 and 1608 sentence 1 of the Civil Code). It may remain unconsidered here that by virtue of marriage the orphan also in turn takes on a maintenance obligation towards his or her spouse, so that the possible economic increment created by virtue of the acquisition of a new maintenance right can be compared to the possible strain entailed by one's own maintenance obligation. With regard to the maintenance-substituting character of the orphans' pension, it is a matter first and foremost of the removal of the burden on the parents provided for in civil law: The new "maintenance bond" is accordingly to take on in principle the economic function of the previous maintenance bond between parents and children.
There are admittedly doubts as to whether the spouse's maintenance obligation also covers the cost of the partner's school or vocational training, or whether it is a matter for the parents' family to continue to fund training already commenced at the time of marriage, in particular to what degree the wife is obliged, in view of § 1360 sentence 2 of the Civil Code, to enter into gainful employment outside the household in order to enable the husband to undergo vocational training ... These questions however do not require further discussion. Even if such a maintenance obligation of the spouse were to be unrestrictedly affirmed, the conclusion of marriage by the child, in contradistinction for instance to the re-marriage of a divorced spouse who is entitled to maintenance (see § 67 of the Marriage Act (*Ehegesetz*)), does not lead to the complete, final discontinuation of the previous relationship under the law on maintenance. Rather, the previous maintenance bond continues if the spouse is unable to provide maintenance. This is already the case according to the wording of § 1608 sentence 2 of the Civil Code and the prevailing opinion on this if and insofar as the spouse is unable to pay, when taking account of his or her other obligations and of his or her own suitable maintenance ... In individual cases, by contrast, the view is held that the limits of the spouse's ability to pay should be broader and determined according to § 1360 of the Civil Code ... It is however undisputed that in the case of the inability of the spouse to pay – however it is to be determined – his or her maintenance obligation does not arise from the outset since, in mainte-

nance law on the marital family, ability to pay is a precondition for the maintenance obligation … In this case, therefore, the parents must, as previously, pay for the maintenance of the married child, including the training costs, without regard for the marriage. Their payment may at best be reduced to the degree that the maintenance obligation towards married minor children is restricted to the maintenance amount owed to major children (see § 1603.1 and 1603.2 sentence 1 of the Civil Code); on the other hand, they may in principle no longer refer the married child to maintenance granted in kind (see § 1612.1 and 1612.2 sentence 1 of the Civil Code).

In consequence, it is therefore possible according to the structure under civil law that with the marriage of a child who is undergoing vocational training the maintenance obligation of the spouse substitutes that of the parents, but this consequence may indeed fail to take place for reasons provided for in the maintenance regulation itself. The latter will be the case if at the time of marriage the spouse himself or herself has commenced but not yet concluded vocational training, or if the marriage is concluded because of the immanent birth of a child and the wife is prevented from engaging in gainful employment by pregnancy or by later taking care of the child.

The proponents of the marriage clauses hold that these differing legal and factual effects of the regulation under maintenance law should remain unconsidered. They wrongly invoke here the independence of the surviving dependants' pensions under social insurance law as against private maintenance law. Namely, were there to be no link between the two regulations, there would be no reason why the – abstract or possible – coming into being of a maintenance claim under family law against the spouse should at all lead to discontinuation of the pension. Conversely, however, it also misses the mark if the obligation incumbent on the legislature to allow for § 1608 sentence 2 of the Civil Code in forming the pension in social insurance is already derived from the principle of the unity of the legal order … The regulation on the surviving dependants' pensions differs significantly in several points from the maintenance regulation according to the Civil Code, be it in the delimitation of the group of beneficiaries, in the determination of the period of payment or in the lack of consideration of ability to pay and need. This follows, partly, from the structural element which is derived from the law on insurance, partly from the economic and social purpose pursued, and partly from the need to generalise.

The differences which have been mentioned however change nothing as to the connection with family law emerging from the maintenance-substituting character of the surviving dependants' pensions. The regulation on the orphans' pension in terms of its content and purpose evidently presumes a maintenance obligation to exist on the part of the parents towards their children; this is also recognised in the case-law for equal and equivalent payments (see BSGE 12, 27 (29-30); 25, 205 (206-207, 209); Federal Court of Justice (BGH), FamRZ 1966, p. 448 (449)). As the Federal Constitutional Court stated in greater detail in the ruling of 24 July 1963 (BVerfGE 17, 1 (10-11, 23-24)), the substitute payments are to meet the need *typically* emerging here by virtue of the deceased's discontinuation of the maintenance payments. Such a generalising view already forms the basis for the distinction between the general and the extended orphans' pension. Both § 44 of the Salaried Employees Insurance Act and § 1267 of the Reich Insurance Code grant to each orphan, certainly until reaching the age of 18, a right to an orphans' pension because it can be presumed that orphans of this age are still at school or in vocational training with few exceptions, and are hence unable to make their own living. An orphans' pension is only granted over and above this age limit if it is demonstrated that the orphan is still in training, is serving a voluntary social year or is infirm, i.e. in turn in cases in which one may normally presume that the orphan will be unable to maintain himself or herself. The circumstance that the granting of the orphans' pension over and above this does not require a review of the de facto need of the orphan in the individual case is hence based on the generalisation required by the fact that social insurance is a mass administration. Insofar as, accordingly, the pension, in derogation from its purpose, is also granted to orphans who do not require maintenance because of other income or assets, this constitutes a benefit in exceptional cases which cannot call into question the constitutional permissibility of the generalisation (see BVerfGE 17, 1 (23-24)). The same considerations could also apply per se to a lack of consideration of the de facto or presumed ability to pay of the deceased insured party. However, it already emerges from the insurance concept that it may not be a matter of whether the insured party, were he or she to still be alive, would be able to pay maintenance. What is more, there is indeed a clear link between the orphans' pension and the actual income of the deceased insured party insofar as the amounts measured by the amount of the income in turn have a material impact on the amount of the pension.

6. The function of the orphans' pension as a substitute for parental maintenance may justify taking the fundamental transfer of the parents' maintenance obligation to the spouse as a reason to refuse to provide the pension right, but then also requires taking those cases into account in which the maintenance claim against the parents remains despite marriage. The proponents of the marriage clauses, by contrast, hold that the legislature should have neglected the cases of § 1608 sentence 2 of the Civil Code because it could have rightly presumed that a marrying child as a rule loses the maintenance claim against the parents, so that, typically, the need for a maintenance substitute also ceases to apply to the marrying orphan. Such a view however, in contradistinction to the favourable generalisations above, leads to a

generalisation which entails disadvantages, and which according to the case-law of the Federal Constitutional Court on Article 3 of the Basic Law is only to a limited degree permissible in social law (see BVerfGE 17, 1 (23-24); see also BVerfGE 17, 210 (221); 19, 101 (116)). Somewhat more stringent, or at least equal, requirements apply to the review by Article 6.1 of the Basic Law. The strict prohibition which can be derived from this constitutional provision of a differentiation of the benefits solely by civil status permits a restriction from the point of view of generalisation at best if these are clearly exceptional cases.

Accordingly, the regulations submitted for review do not stand up to the constitution. Solely the group which meets the preconditions for the extended orphans' pension in other respects is material here, i.e. orphans aged between 18 and 25 (in some cases 27) who study or are otherwise still in training. Related to this group of beneficiaries, orphans who marry without acquiring a maintenance claim against their spouse are by no means an exception which could be neglected according to the above information.

As long ago as 1960, the *Bundesrat* stated on the occasion of the deliberation on an amendment to § 27 of the Federal War Victims' Pensions Act that the general presumption that, on conclusion of marriage, the child or the orphan had sufficient funds from the household community was no longer justified under today's circumstances, as practical experience (students' marriages) had shown (*Bundesrat* printed paper – BRDrucks. 53/60 pp. 32-33, no. 61 re § 132 no. 6b of the government Draft to the Federal Social Assistance Act (*Bundessozialhilfegesetz*)). The Federal Social Court also allowed in the ruling on § 44.1 sentence 2 of the Salaried Employees Insurance Act that the lack of a maintenance claim against the spouse was not infrequent as a result of the not inconsiderable number of early marriages and the increasing demands as to qualified training and the concomitant longer duration of that training (see BSGE 25, 205 (209)). The reasoning of the above initiative draft Bill tends even more decidedly in this direction (A V above). Very recently, the 1970 Social Report, submitted to the legislative bodies by the Federal Government on 20 April 1970, stated in general terms on the marriage clauses that they no longer did justice to the current circumstances. It could not be presumed that married children over 18 – in contradistinction to unmarried ones – were typically able to fund training and maintenance themselves from their own funds or with the assistance of the spouse (see *Bundestag* printed paper VI/643 no. 69 p. 27, see also the response of the Federal Minister for Youth, Family and Health of 17 December 1969 to the minor interpellation of the SPD and FDP parliamentary groups of the *Bundestag* – *Bundestag* printed paper VI/197 –).

The above authors ... mostly consider it to be manifest according to general experience that the generalisations on which the marriage clauses are based no longer correspond to today's social circumstances and that thus, particularly if students' marriages are taken into account, not only individuals, but also a large share of the population would be affected … Partly, they take statistical information as a basis for this. The available statistical material is inadequate, however, since there is as yet no targeted statistical survey regarding the questions which are material here. The figures that are known are not based on a complete survey of the entire group of individuals still in vocational training in the corresponding age limits; furthermore, the cases in which withdrawal of the orphans' pension or of another social benefit caused training that had been commenced to be interrupted or the parents to discontinue their previous support, were not taken into account. Finally, there are no investigations to determine in how many cases an intended conclusion of marriage did not take place in order to avoid the discontinuation of a social benefit as a result of marriage. However, it can already be derived from the figures regarding students and students' marriages, that is marriages between students, that the marriage of a person still in training with a partner who is unable to provide maintenance because of not having completed vocational training or for other reasons, is at least no longer a rare exceptional case … The falling age at marriage acts together here with the extension of the duration of training and the increase in the number of those who opt for vocations with a longer period of training.

7. The marriage clauses can also not be supported with the consideration that their disadvantages had to be compared to the advantages accruing in social insurance law through a marriage in the shape of legal rights on the part of the orphan or of the spouse, such as the right of the orphan's spouse to family allowance in unemployment insurance, the right to family assistance according to § 205 of the Reich Insurance Code or the right of the orphan to surviving dependants' pension after the death of his or her spouse if the latter had social insurance (for instance BSGE 25, 205 (210)). Statutory provisions which by their structure and de facto impact place a certain group of marriages at a disadvantage may not be regarded as constitutionally unobjectionable because other provisions of the same Act or from the same legal area favour another group of marriages (BVerfGE 18, 97 (108)). These advantages link to completely different preconditions in the special situation of the individual family, and may only incidentally benefit the same individuals who are placed at a disadvantage by the marriage clauses (see BVerfGE 12, 151 (167-168)). It is certainly not relevant that a number of other social benefits are available for the promotion of training. Apart from the fact that these benefits differ from the orphans' pension according to their prerequisites, nature and scope– for instance assistance according to the Honnef model is in some cases only granted as a loan – these are not benefits specifically provided for married persons which in this sense

can compensate for the loss of the orphans' pension as a result of the marriage clauses.

8. It is also not the case that the marriage clauses are required in order to prevent the diversion of the orphans' pension because it would otherwise be used to substitute for the lack of payments provided by a spouse who is obliged to provide maintenance or to release the latter completely or partly from his or her obligation to provide maintenance (for instance BSGE 12, 27 (30)). If, according to § 1360 in conjunction with § 1608 sentence 1 of the Civil Code, the spouse is unable to provide maintenance, he or she is, as has been described, from the outset not subject to a maintenance obligation; the maintenance obligation is incumbent solely on the parents. The pension payment which is continued under such circumstances hence fully retains the maintenance-substituting character for which the deceased parent, were he or she to be still alive, would have to provide by virtue of his or her own obligation. It is also simply incomprehensible why the continued payment of the orphans' pension to an orphan who for lack of a maintenance claim against the needy spouse continues to require maintenance should not be compatible with the protection of marriage according to Article 6.1 of the Basic Law.

9. Finally, it is claimed in defence of the marriage clauses that according to the general moral and social value concepts the model of marriage that is material to the application of Article 6.1 of the Basic Law is contingent on the new family community being economically independent. Certainly, the orphan could not derive from Article 6.1 of the Basic Law a right to promotion of an early marriage without the spouses having a joint livelihood. It can be argued against this, initially, that the provisions to be reviewed are not about promoting marriages with no independent economic basis by additional state benefits or by other means, but about whether a social benefit provided generally as to vocational training may be withdrawn because of the beneficiary's marriage. Further, according to the statistical surveys, the average age on marriage has fallen continually since the Second World War. Among men, it was 28.4 years in 1947, 26.6 in 1957 and 26.0 in 1965, and 25.1, 24.1 and 23.7 years among women in the same years … The fall in the average age on marriage is also linked with a disproportionately large increase in the number of early marriages. Thus, the marriage frequency of minor-age men increased by 35 per cent between 1957 and 1965, and that of minor-age women by 80 per cent from 1954 to 1965 ….

It may certainly be desirable on principle for marriages not to be concluded until the foundation is ensured for an independent economic livelihood by means of completion of training for at least one of the spouses or by other means. The realisation of such an aspiration is however countered, on the one hand, by the extension of the training periods and on the other hand by the tendency emerging from the statistics that have been mentioned to conclude marriage at a younger age, in favour of which a number of family policy and other reasons may be invoked. It is however not necessary for the decision to be taken here to discuss which view deserves preference and whether and within what boundaries Article 6.1 of the Basic Law permits affecting the willingness to conclude marriage and to take as a basis here ideas of the nature mentioned at the outset. Such a model of marriage within society could not justify the differentiation made in granting the extended orphans' pension already because it is incompatible with Article 6.1 of the Basic Law if the general family-law regulation which is required by the constitution and necessary for the realisation of the value determination of Article 6.1 of the Basic Law permits the conclusion of marriage on reaching certain age limits without consideration of the spouses' economic circumstances, but social law disapproves of such conclusion of marriage and "punishes" it by withdrawing social benefits.

III.

1. The differentiation between married and unmarried orphans in the provisions submitted for review hence violates Article 6.1 of the Basic Law. Accordingly, it can be considered irrelevant whether a violation of the constitution might be considered from other points of view.

2. A full declaration of the nullity of the marriage clauses cannot be considered because it would lead to the orphans' pension having to be granted to all married orphans regardless. According to the above information, unconstitutionality is however based only on the absolute exclusion of married orphans from drawing the extended orphans' pension. By contrast, in accordance with the meaning and purpose of the pension provisions, it would not be constitutionally objectionable if the legislature did without a generalising provision and made refusal or continued payment of the orphans' pension after marriage dependent on whether or not a maintenance claim of the orphan against the spouse exists in the individual case.

Therefore, only a partial nullity declaration to the extent stipulated in the submission order at a) by the Hamburg Social Court could be considered. The Social Court holds that one could derive with certainty from the version of the provision submitted for review and its legislative history that the legislature, had it been aware of the unconstitutionality, would certainly have recognised a right to the extended orphans' pension for married orphans in the case of a lack of ability to pay on the part of the spouse. Even such a restricted nullity declaration would however be a too far-reaching incursion on the legislature's margin of appreciation because several possibilities exist to remedy the violation of the constitution (see BVerfGE 22, 349 (360-361); 23, 74 (78)).

The possibility of completely abolishing the extended orphans' pension cannot be considered; however, in view of the fluctuating legal development in this field and of the financial burden that is to be taken into account, it cannot be entirely ruled out that the legislature, in connection with the discontinuation of the absolute marriage clause, would delimitate the preconditions for the extended orphans' pension differently, with particular reference to the period of entitlement; equally, it could substitute the entire provision by a fundamental re-ordering of the financial assistance to vocational training. Further, a marriage clause that differentiated by the ability to pay of the spouse could also be differently regulated in terms of its form and content. Above all, however, attention should be paid to the indication of the Federal Government of the administrative difficulties resulting from a case-by-case review. Provisions have certainly existed for decades in other statutes with regard to comparable benefits which are determined for mass cases and nonetheless require an individual review of the income and assets of those concerned. However, it must be left to the legislature to decide whether it is possible and expedient to also introduce such a review with the extended orphans' pension, or whether instead it is justifiable and more expedient to eliminate the marriage clauses altogether and to grant the extended orphans' pension to all married orphans just as with the general orphans' pension. Therefore, the decision was to be restricted to ascertaining the breach of the constitution. The submitting courts must accordingly suspend the original proceedings until the legislature has replaced the unconstitutional provision with a provision that is compatible with the constitution.

3. The proceedings of the Lüneburg Social Court depend for the ruling on the validity of § 1267.1 sentence 2 of the Reich Insurance Code, both in the – earlier – version of the Act Reforming the Wage-Earners Pensions Insurance Act of 23 February 1957 (Federal Law Gazette I p. 45), and in the – applicable – version of § 6 no. 6 of the Act Promoting a Voluntary Social Year of 17 August 1964 (Federal Law Gazette I p. 640). Thus, the unconstitutionality of the provision was to be ascertained to the designated degree for both versions.

In the proceedings of the Hamburg Social Court, the ruling only depends on the validity of § 44.1 sentence 2 of the Salaried Employees Insurance Act in the – earlier – version of the Act Reforming the Salaried Employees Insurance Act of 23 February 1957 (Federal Law Gazette I p. 88). Since the provision in the – applicable – version of § 7 no. 4 of the Act Promoting a Voluntary Social Year of 17 August 1964 (Federal Law Gazette I p. 640) however contains the marriage clause unaltered, and in this respect is identical verbatim with § 1267.1 sentence 2 of the Reich Insurance Code in the applicable version, it appeared necessary in corresponding application of §§ 82.1 and 78 sentence 2 of the Federal Constitutional Court Act (*Bundesverfassungsgerichtsgesetz* – BVerfGG) to also have the finding of the unconstitutionality of § 44.1 sentence 2 of the Salaried Employees Insurance Act cover both versions of the provision to the extent that has been described.

Justices: Dr. Müller, Dr. Stein, Ritterspach, Dr. Haager, Rupp-v. Brünneck, Dr. Böhmer, Dr. Brox; Justice Dr. Zeidler retired from office after the order was drafted.

Following the Federal Constitutional Court's decision, the word "unmarried" was deleted from § 44.1 sentence 2 of the Salaried Employees Insurance Act with effect from 1 June 1970 by Article 3 of the Act Amending Social and Civil Law Provisions on Benefits for Married Children (Gesetz zur Änderung sozial- und beamtenrechtlicher Vorschriften über Leistungen für verheiratete Kinder) *of 25 January 1971 (Federal Law Gazette I p. 65).*

No. 7

BVerfGE 31, 58
of 4 May 1971 – 1 BvR 636/68 –
"Spaniard case"

HEADNOTES:

1. **The fundamental right enshrined in Article 6.1 of the Basic Law (*Grundgesetz* – GG) guarantees everyone – including a foreigner – the freedom to marry a partner of one's own choice (freedom of marriage).**
2. **The provisions of German international private law and the application of foreign law invoked thereby in individual cases must be measured against fundamental rights.**
3. **a) Article 13.1 of the Introductory Act to the Civil Code (*Einführungsgesetz zum Bürgerlichen Gesetzbuch* – EGBGB), according to which the capacity to marry of each person engaged to be married is assessed in the light of the law of his state of origin, does not violate Article 6.1 of the Basic Law.**
   b) Article 6.1 of the Basic Law is violated when a Spanish man who wishes to marry a German woman whose previous marriage with a German man has been divorced by a German court is denied exemption from furnishing a certificate of no impediment because Spanish law does not recognise the divorce.

Order of the First Senate of 4 May 1971
– 1 BvR 636/68 –

in the proceedings regarding the constitutional complaint filed by Mr. José Castello G., secondly by Ms. Hilde L. – authorised representative: ..., lawyer – against the order of the Hamm Higher Regional Court (*Oberlandesgericht*) of 3 September 1968 – 15 VA 4/67 –.

RULING:

1. The order of the Hamm Higher Regional Court of 3 September 1968 – 15 VA 4/67 – violates the complainants' fundamental right under Article 6.1 of the Basic Law. It is hereby reversed. The case is referred back to the Hamm Higher Regional Court.
2. The *Land* (state) North Rhine-Westphalia is ordered to reimburse the complainants their necessary expenses.

EXTRACT FROM GROUNDS:

The constitutional complaint concerns the question of whether it is compatible with Article 6.1 of the Basic Law for German authorities and courts to refuse to permit the act of marriage between a foreigner and a German national who has obtained a divorce from a German court because the home country of the foreign person engaged to be married does not recognise the divorce.

A. – I.

1. The complainants wish to marry one another. The male complainant, who has not previously been married, is a Spanish national; he has been living in the Federal Republic of Germany since 1962. He was a member of the Catholic Church, but declared his resignation of membership in 1967. The female complainant is a German national. She was previously married to a German national who, like her, is a member of the Protestant Church. This marriage – which was concluded only in a civil ceremony – was divorced by final judgment of the Bielefeld Regional Court of 20 January 1965.
2. As the Spanish authorities do not issue certificates of no impediment, the complainant applied to be exempted from furnishing a certificate of no impediment pursuant to § 10.2 of the Marriage Act (*Ehegesetz*) of 20 February 1946 (*Amtsblatt des Kontrollrates* – KRABl. p. 77) as amended by the Family Law Amendment Act (*Familienrechtsänderungsgesetz*) of 11 August 1961 (Federal Law Gazette (*Bundesgesetzblatt* – BGBl.) I p. 1221). The president of the Hamm Higher Regional Court rejected the application. The Hamm Higher Regional Court, to which the complainant resorted, declared the president of the Higher Regional Court's order of rejection lawful and provided the following grounds in essence:
According to Article 13.1 of the Introductory Act to the Civil Code, any impediments to marriage, especially the impediment of bigamous marriage, are to be as-

sessed for each person engaged to be married on the basis of the law of the country of which they are a national. That was why, in the male complainant's case, Spanish law was decisive. It recognised two forms of marriage (Article 42 of the Spanish Civil Code (*Código Civil*) of 24 July 1889 with numerous amendments): the canonical form of marriage, which is mandatory when at least one of those marrying is a member of the Catholic Church, and civil marriage. Regardless of which form of marriage was applicable in the present case, the German complainant's previous marriage was an impediment to the intended marriage (see Article 51 and Article 83 no. 5 of the Spanish Civil Code). A Spaniard could not even legally marry anyone abroad if one of the persons engaged to be married was legally married according to canon law. The female complainant's previous marriage had been legally concluded according to canon law, because, according to Canon 1099 § 2 of the Codex of the Canon Law (*Codex iuris canonici*), in the case of marriages concluded between non-Catholics the so-called tridentine form of marriage was not necessary, rather any other form of marriage also sufficed. Despite the legal force of the divorce obtained from a German court, this marriage still existed according to canon law; Spanish law, which also did not permit the divorce of civil marriages, refused to recognise each and every foreign divorce on account of its being contrary to the Spanish ordre public, or public policy. Accordingly, the female complainant's previous marriage provided the impediment of the bond of marriage, which was directed at both persons engaged to be married in equal measure in the form of a double prohibition in accordance with both canon and German civil law. Such application of Spanish law violated neither Article 30 of the Introductory Act to the Civil Code nor any of the legal provisions of the Basic Law.

3. In the further grounds for its decision the Higher Regional Court also made reference to its own previous case-law (see Hamm Higher Regional Court, *Zeitschrift für das gesamte Familienrecht* – FamRZ 1963, p. 566 and FamRZ 1968, p. 389) and to the Federal Court of Justice (*Bundesgerichtshof*), which, in view of the differences of opinion between several higher regional courts, had decided in two orders of 12 February 1964 (Decisions of the Federal Court of Justice in Civil Matters (*Entscheidungen des Bundesgerichtshofes in Zivilsachen* – BGHZ) 41, 136 and IV AR (VZ) 40/63 – unpublished –) in favour of the opinion of the Higher Regional Courts of Hamm, Celle (*Neue Juristische Wochenschrift* – NJW 1962, p. 20212 = FamRZ 1963, p. 91), Karlsruhe (*Die Justiz* 1962, p. 291) and Munich (NJW 1963, p. 2233)). The case adjudicated by the first-mentioned decision of the Federal Court of Justice corresponded to the facts underlying the present case – with the exception of the Spanish complainant's religious affiliation. The Federal Court of Justice found that although the previous marriage of the German person engaged to be married had been divorced by a German court, the desired exemption from furnish-

ing a certificate of no impediment could not be granted, and provided the following grounds, among others:
Article 13 of the Introductory Act to the Civil Code ensured that the planned marriage would be recognised as fully valid in regard to the future spouses' areas of life, especially in the foreign spouse's home country. That prevented marriages being concluded from which the foreign spouse could extricate himself at any time by returning to his home country and invoking the fact that the marriage was invalid according to the law of that country. The provision protected the German partner, who could be placed in a difficult legal position by entering into the marriage, particularly when moving with the foreign spouse to his home country. In particular, the German spouse's right to succeed to the foreign inheritance of his partner or the right to succeed and the rights to maintenance payments of any children born into the marriage could be jeopardised. In view of this concept of protection, German law referred to the foreign law and thus accepted conclusions which were in fact foreign to our legal order. It would, however, only be guaranteed that the marriage would be recognised in the home country of the foreign person engaged to be married, as was being sought, if the question of the validity of the previous marriage of one of the persons engaged to be married and its continued existence was assessed on the basis of foreign law.
Article 30 of the Introductory Act to the Civil Code proved no obstacle to the application of Spanish law. The applicability of foreign provisions, which was based on the idea of the indissolubility of the bond of marriage, was neither contra bonos mores not did it violate the purpose of a German law. Neither could the reference to the legal effect of a divorce decree issued to two German nationals provide the grounds for such a violation. As the German legislature declared foreign law binding on the German judge in the interest of the German spouse, German case-law did not suffer any loss of prestige if the authority of the divorce decree broke down on account of the boundaries drawn by substantive law.
The application of Spanish law which was necessary according to Article 13.1 of the Introductory Act to the Civil Code violated neither Article 12 and 14 of the European Convention on the Protection of Human Rights and Fundamental Freedoms, nor did it contradict the Basic Law. The connection to nationality under Article 13.1 of the Introductory Act to the Civil Code was compatible with Article 3.3 of the Basic Law; Article 2.1 and Article 6.1 of the Basic Law had not been violated either. The fundamental right to the freedom of marriage could only be exercised within the framework of the laws, including the foreign legal order described by our conflict of laws provisions. If these laws refused a bigamous marriage which existed according to their interpretation, this did not affect the essence of any fundamental right within the meaning of Article 19.2 of the Basic Law. The principles

of the Basic Law, to which German international private law was also subject, had not already been violated where the conflict rule referred to the foreign legal order in cases in which there was a link to another state and it contained different or even stricter provisions concerning the existence of impediments to marriage of whatever form. If the effects of a legal act, such as in this case the act of marriage, should go beyond the area of application of the Basic Law, its principles, such as for example the right to the freedom of marriage, even if it applies to everyone, cannot be applied contrary to the foreign law. In such cases the foreign legal provisions would not have to be measured against German constitutional law even if there was a strong domestic link.

4. As follows from the decision of the Federal Court of Justice itself, the legal issues dealt with there are controversial in the case-law and the literature … Whilst a number of legal authors and the majority of case-law in effect concur with the opinion expressed by the Federal Court of Justice and largely also with the grounds …, others have criticised it.

The majority of opponents are of the opinion that the continued existence of a divorced marriage follows German laws from the very outset. In part this is supported by arguing that the question of the legal effect of a German divorce decree is not to be answered according to German international private law, but according to German international procedural law, which for its part refers to German procedural law; accordingly, a divorce decree is said to dissolve the marriage with effect for and against everyone by virtue of its ability to shape a legal relationship …

The opponents' opinion is in part substantiated with the argument that the question raised when examining the impediment of bigamous marriage under Spanish (canon) law regarding whether the German person engaged to be married is still to be viewed as married cannot also be answered according to Spanish law (so-called dependent connection), but that it constitutes an independent preliminary question not covered by Article 13.1 of the Introductory Act to the Civil Code, which must be reviewed on the basis of that law which is decisive for the divorce, that is in the present case according to German law (so-called independent connection). It is argued that is the only way in which it can be guaranteed that domestic authorities and courts can uniformly review the question raised in various contexts concerning the continued existence of the previous marriage …

Some courts and authors hold the opinion that the application of Spanish law, which is shaped according to the principles of a specific denomination, violates the German ordre public (Article 30 of the Introductory Act to the Civil Code) or that it is not compatible with the Basic Law, in particular Article 6.1 of the Basic Law …

5. The case-law of the Federal Court of Justice (see also Decisions of the Federal Court of Justice in Civil Matters 46, 87) led the members of the Petitions Commit-

tee of the German Bundestag to introduce a draft law amending Article 13 of the Introductory Act to the Civil Code during the 4th and 5th electoral terms (see *Bundestag* printed papers (*Bundestagsdrucksachen* – BT-Drucks.) IV/3088 and V/359). According to a proposal put forward by the Commission on Matrimonial Law of the German Council for International Private Law (*Eherechtskommission des Deutschen Rates für Internationales Privatrecht*), a new requirement was to be introduced such that a marriage divorced with legal effect by a German court did not constitute an impediment to a new marriage even if the decree was not recognised by a foreign state. Consultations on the draft law were postponed in order not to pre-empt a new international regulation. Thus, both the Hague Conference on International Private Law and the International Commission of the Civil State (*Commission Internationale de l'État Civil* – CIEC), with the involvement of representatives of the Federal Republic of Germany, have over the past few years drafted conventions which obligate the contracting states to mutually recognise decisions in matrimonial issues and at the same time to prevent a new marriage following a divorce being refused because the law of a third-party state does not recognise the dissolution of the previous marriage …
6. Most Western European countries, just like the United States of America, permit an act of marriage in comparable cases regardless of whether the law of the home country of one of the persons engaged to be married is against divorce …; Denmark is one such example. That is the reason why foreigners resident in the Federal Republic of Germany have over the past few years often chosen to circumvent the German prohibition by getting married in Denmark, especially in the city of Tonder, which is close to the border. The legal effect of these so-called "Tonder marriages" is controversial. In German legal practice they are sometimes viewed as fully valid, although in the majority of cases they are seen as void, that is, valid until such time as they are declared void by court decision …

II.

1. The complainants jointly filed a constitutional complaint against the order issued by the Hamm Higher Regional Court on 3 September 1968 and submit the following observations:
The decision violates Article 6.1 of the Basic Law because it impairs their freedom to choose one's own spouse. Were Article 13 of the Introductory Act to the Civil Code applied in accordance with the Basic Law, the Higher Regional Court would have had to judge the question of whether the female complainant's previous marriage continued to exist according to German law alone and thus would have had to answer that question in the negative.

Article 3.3, Article 4.1, Article 33.3 and Article 140 of the Basic Law in conjunction with Article 136.2 of the Weimar Constitution (*Weimarer Reichsverfassung*) have been violated, they claim, because the decision imposes moral restrictions on the complainants for religious, legally irrelevant reasons and draws negative consequences from their religious affiliation. The violation against the state's duty to remain neutral as regards matters of religion also leads to the following absurd result: Had the female complainant been Catholic, her previous marriage would not be valid within the meaning of Catholic canon law, since it had only been concluded in a civil ceremony, and it would not pose any impediment to her marrying the male complainant.

Insofar as the Higher Regional Court refers to the protection of the German spouse in its application of the law, this constitutes interference with the future spouses' closest relationships, which is incompatible with Article 2.1 of the Basic Law. The court must allow the spouses themselves to decide whether they want to remain married; the complainants are consciously accepting the risk associated with getting married due to the Spanish law. Finally, the authority of the state is undermined if those wishing to get married are forced to circumvent the German prohibition by getting married abroad.

2. The Federal Minister of Justice, who submitted observations on behalf of the German Government, believes the constitutional complaint is well-founded …

B.

The constitutional complaint is admissible, also insofar as it is filed by the female complainant. The female complainant was not involved in the original proceedings before the Hamm Higher Regional Court; however, she is not only indirectly or factually, but also directly and legally affected by the decision issued against the male complainant (see Decisions of the Federal Constitutional Court (*Entscheidungen des Bundesverfassungsgerichts* – BVerfGE) 15, 256 (262-263); see also 21, 132 (136)). If one of the persons engaged to be married is prevented from marrying by an act of state, that interference affects both persons engaged to be married.

C.

The constitutional complaint is well-founded. The contested decision violates the complainants' fundamental rights under Article 6.1 of the Basic Law.

I.

1. According to the case-law of the Federal Constitutional Court, Article 6.1 of the Basic Law contains both a classic fundamental right to protection against state interference and an institutional guarantee, as well as a fundamental provision that determines values concerning the entire area of marriage and family law (BVerfGE 6, 55 (71 et seq.); 24, 119 (135)). As the decision of 7 October 1970 (BVerfGE 29, 166 (175 with further references)) explicitly states, a key component of the fundamental right is the right or the freedom to marry a partner of one's own choice (freedom of marriage).

2. The freedom of marriage and the ensuing right to avert any state-imposed obstructions apply to both German nationals within the meaning of Article 116 of the Basic Law and to foreign nationals and stateless persons. In contrast to some other provisions regarding fundamental rights, Article 6.1 of the Basic Law is not restricted to Germans, and in addition the fundamental right concerns an area of the most personal of lifestyle choices, which is of significance to all people (see BVerfGE 6, 55 (71 and 81)). According to Article 12 of the European Convention on the Protection of Human Rights and Fundamental Freedoms (the Convention) of 4 November 1950, which the Federal Republic of Germany has recognised as binding (see Federal Law Gazette 1952 II p. 685, 1954 II p. 14), "men and women have the right to marry and to found a family, according to the national laws governing the exercise of this right". Over and above the area of application of the Convention it also corresponds to international legal conviction that the freedom of marriage is a key human right. The Convention refers in its Preamble to the United Nations Universal Declaration of Human Rights of 10 December 1948, Article 16.1 sentence 1 of which reads as follows:

> Men and women of full age, without any limitation due to race, nationality or religion, have the right to marry and found a family.

The UN Convention on consent to marriage, minimum age for marriage and registration of marriages of 10 December 1962 (see Federal Law Gazette 1969 II p. 161, 1970 II p. 110), which entered into force for the Federal Republic of Germany on 7 October 1969, explicitly cites this provision in its Preamble and re-affirms the duty all states are under of "ensuring … complete freedom in the choice of a spouse".

II.

Since § 10 of the Marriage Act requires that when two foreign nationals marry a certificate of no impediment must be furnished or formal exemption from this obligation must be granted, the refusal to exempt the complainant interferes with his and the female complainant's fundamental right to the freedom of marriage. A review must therefore be carried out regarding whether this interference is covered by a legal regulation which is compatible with Article 6.1 of the Basic Law and its application pursuant to the constitution.

1. The general restrictions such as are laid down in Article 2.1 of the Basic Law in regard to the freedom of action do not apply to the freedom of marriage, which is based on Article 6.1 of the Basic Law. The opinion that the fundamental right to the freedom of marriage can only be exercised "within the framework of the laws" is at least unclear. The scope of Article 6.1 of the Basic Law is not exhausted in the legal provisions of marriage and family law which shape the institution of marriage (see BVerfGE 6, 55 (73)); the comprehensive requirement made of the state in the provision, namely to provide protection, is restricted neither by a proviso of legality nor in any other way (BVerfGE 24, 119 (135)). It is, therefore, also not correct when reviewing a legal provision of matrimonial law in non-constitutional law against Article 6.1 of the Basic Law to only take into account whether the essence of the fundamental right within the meaning of Article 19.2 of the Basic Law is being affected, since the ultimate boundary set by the guarantee of the essence under Article 19.2 of the Basic Law affects those cases in which the legislature is authorised to restrict a fundamental right.

2. Nevertheless, the freedom of marriage not only permits statutory regulations governing the forms of the act of marriage and its factual preconditions, but virtually makes them a prerequisite. This results from the inseparable link between the fundamental right and the institutional guarantee, which of necessity requires a legal order. In order to be realised, the value determination in Article 6.1 of the Basic Law requires a general regulation under family law which legally defines and delimits the long-term relationship between a man and a woman, which enjoys the protection of the constitution in the form of marriage (see BVerfGE 28, 324 (361)). However, this regulation must observe the key structural principles which determine the institution of marriage and which result from the connection between Article 6.1 of the Basic Law and existing, traditional ways of life in conjunction with the nature of the guaranteed fundamental right as a freedom right and other constitutional provisions – for instance the principle of monogamy – (see BVerfGE 10, 59 (66-67); 29, 166 (176)). Whereas traditional civil law also largely concurs with these structural principles, the content of the institutional guarantee cannot, vice

versa, be concluded from the non-constitutional law in the first place so that this could never contradict the constitution … Rather, the individual regulations of civil law must be measured against Article 6.1 of the Basic Law as a prior-ranking, leading provision which itself contains the fundamental principles (see BVerfGE 10, 59 (66); 24, 104 (109)). Certainly, the legislature here has quite considerable scope, for example when regulating the form of the act of marriage, marriageable age and the prerequisites for the dissolution of a marriage. Nevertheless, factual and formal prerequisites for marriage which are too strict or too lenient, for instance, could be incompatible with the freedom of marriage or other structural principles of marriage resulting from the constitution itself. Likewise, the application of a statutory provision can, in individual cases, violate that freedom or general constitutional principles, such as for example the principle of proportionality.

III.

The fact that the interference with the complainants' freedom of marriage is based on the application of foreign law invoked on account of a German conflict rule does not pose an obstacle to a constitutional review against this yardstick.

1. The contested decision derived the impediment of bigamous marriage from Spanish law, primarily from the reference made in the Spanish Civil Code to canon law. Whether the validity of the female complainant's previous marriage and the effectiveness of the dissolution of this marriage are to be evaluated according to canon law is not the matter under review here. As regards the second question, the Higher Regional Court after all makes reference to the Spanish ordre public regardless of the fact that canon law is invoked. Accordingly, every foreign divorce, regardless of whether the marriage was concluded as the canonical form of marriage or as a civil marriage, whether between domestic nationals or foreign nationals, Catholics or non-Catholics, is contrary to the Spanish ordre public insofar as there are any points of reference with the Spanish legal order whatsoever, such as the circumstance that one of the persons engaged to be married is a Spanish national … Correspondingly, the legal interpretation in the contested decision is not evidently incorrect in that regard and must, therefore, since it is a question of non-constitutional law, form the basis of a constitutional review.

2. According to one opinion prevalent in the case-law and the literature, in the field of international private law the influence of German constitutional law only comes into play with a large number of restrictions. The German conflict rules are themselves in fact still to be examined in regard to their compatibility with the Basic Law, especially with fundamental rights, even if this examination often, especially when reference is made to the technical, neutral nature of the legal provisions, re-

mains summary or is even restricted only to the prohibition of arbitrariness or the guarantee of the essence of a fundamental right under Article 19.2 of the Basic Law. By contrast, the application of foreign law invoked on account of the German conflict rule will in principle no longer be dependent on compliance with fundamental rights. The decision of the Federal Court of Justice, to which reference has variously been made, goes furthest in this direction, which itself aims to eliminate German constitutional law per se even if there is a strong domestic link in the matter to be adjudicated: Whenever effects of a legal act go beyond the area of application of the Basic Law, i.e. in the case of matters with any link to another state whatsoever, constitutional principles, including human rights, are not to be applied contrary to the foreign law (BGHZ 41, 136 (151)). A somewhat later decision of 29 April 1964 (BGHZ 42, 7 (12 et seq.)) modified this opinion to the extent that a certain examination of the foreign law to be applied according to international private law in regard to the value order established in the Basic Law is permitted, but *only* within the framework of Article 30 of the Introductory Act to the Civil Code. The Federal Court of Justice is of the opinion that constitutional provisions, being objective norms, insofar as they refer to private-law legal relations require that German private law be applied; consequently the personal and spatial scope of the constitutional law is delimited by the conflict rules. According to the Federal Court of Justice, it is also not appropriate and would contradict the principles of international law if the application of foreign legal rules were from the outset dependent on their compatibility with the Basic Law. The decision does not aim to permit such a far-reaching examination within the context of Article 30 of the Introductory Act to the Civil Code either; in accordance with the generally restrictive interpretation of the proviso clause, the German ordre public may only interfere where "key constitutional principles which form an absolute basis of German state or social life" or "indispensable requirements of German constitutional law" are violated. This prerequisite is only seen to have been fulfilled in the case of violations of fundamental rights where the essence of the fundamental right has been infringed.
Even when taking the aforementioned modification into account, the case-law of the highest court, which was decisive for the contested case, is therefore based on the fundamental opinion that fundamental rights in the field of international private law only develop their legal effect when and insofar as the German conflict rules, including Article 30 of the Introductory Act to the Civil Code, open up that possibility …
3. This opinion does not do justice to the precedence given to the constitution and the central importance of fundamental rights. Under international private law the guiding principle of Article 1.3 of the Basic Law is also assumed to apply, which directly binds all state power within the area of application of the Basic Law by the

fundamental rights. This firstly leads to the conclusion that in regard to the enactment of a conflict rule by the German legislature or its transference from pre-constitutional law the same applies as to other sub-constitutional laws. As national, domestic law …, the provisions of German international private law are to be measured entirely against the fundamental rights. Naturally, the examination may only go so far as to establish whether the general decision of the German legislature in favour of a specific principle of legislation, especially the choice of connections, is compatible with the fundamental rights. Insofar as foreign law is thereby invoked, it is hardly possible, given the differences and changeability of foreign regulations, for the legislature to assess what possible content an applicable foreign legal provision can have and what its effect will be under the conditions of each individual case.

It is thus even less permissible in this "leap into the dark" … not to undertake the constitutional review and to abandon the persons affected to the uncertain outcome of the respective application of the foreign law invoked on account of the conflict rule without the protection of fundamental rights. Fundamental rights form an inseparable part of the constitution; they are the actual core of the free democratic order of the life of the state in the Basic Law. Their scope can, therefore, not be dependent on the way in which a certain matter is regulated by non-constitutional law; it is, rather, directly to be concluded from the provisions of the constitution themselves … Nor would it be possible to justify any other opinion with the special nature of international private law. The applicable German conflict rules do not constitute the only conceivable way of regulating this area of the law. As a glance at foreign conflict rules and efforts to reform German international private law reveals, there are a number of possibilities here, each of which may have its advantages in one or other regard in respect of justice and expedience. If the aforementioned basic opinion were correct, then the legislature's decision to adopt one of the possible principles at the level of non-constitutional law, for example whether the connection in respect of an act of marriage is to be nationality, place of residence or place of marriage, would at the same time determine whether an area more or less "free of fundamental rights" was created for the matters for which the rules are to be introduced. Drawing on Article 30 of the Introductory Act to the Civil Code would also not change anything as long as this norm was not understood as providing a gateway for fundamental rights into international private law (see also VI 2 below), but, conversely, the narrowly interpreted features of the provision determine the – restricted – scope of application of fundamental rights. This would likewise lead to the result that a provision at the disposal of the non-constitutional legislature would have to determine the rank and scope of constitutional provisions.

Likewise, the prevailing opinion cannot be justified by the fact that the foreign legislature is only bound by the constitution of its own state and, in accordance with prevailing opinion, the foreign law to which reference is made by a German conflict rule does not stop being a foreign law on account of its application on domestic territory. Even if one proceeds on this assumption, when German authorities and courts apply it this constitutes exercise of German state power, which is bound by the requirements set out in Article 1.3 and Article 20.3 of the Basic Law.
This recognition that the fundamental rights' claim to validity also refers to the application of the foreign law invoked does not constitute an inadmissible extension of the area of application of the Basic Law vis-à-vis the foreign state or the forced imposition of German values on foreign states. The foreign law is not examined in general in regard to its correspondence with the Basic Law out of the context of its own constitution and its national area of application. Rather, it is only a matter of whether the domestic legal act by the German state power in respect of a concrete matter which has a more or less strong domestic link leads to a violation of a fundamental right. If it is shown that the application of the foreign law "breaks down" in the face of a fundamental right, this does not constitute general censorship of the foreign regulation, which was not created for application by German public authorities and may be justifiable or sensible in its own area, but only constitutes the conclusion that its concrete application is not compatible, in regard to one specific aspect, with our constitutional order. If such a procedure is from the outset burdened with the odium of discrimination against the foreign legislature, this can presumably be explained by its dependence on the categories of terms applied in Article 30 of the Introductory Act to the Civil Code, whose first alternative (contra bonos mores) at least according to the previous, narrow interpretation presupposes a condemnation of the foreign law or suggests this. However, only one reproach could – if at all – be made against the German legislature insofar as, for example when invoking foreign law, foreseeable conflicts with individual fundamental rights have not been taken into account by means of possible special regulations.
An application of fundamental rights under the aforementioned prerequisites also does not contradict general rules of international law, which must be observed as an element of federal law pursuant to Article 25 of the Basic Law. The Basic Law overall tends to be open towards international law. Both the Preamble and Article 1.2, Article 24 and Article 25 of the Basic Law, as well as the principles of pluralism and tolerance, which are characteristic of the constitutional system as a whole, indicate that the constitutions of other states are recognised as equal members of the international community and that their independent legal orders are respected (see BVerfGE 18, 112 (116 et seq.)). However, this fundamental philosophy does not yet lead to the conclusion that there exists an obligation in respect of

the unrestricted application of foreign law by domestic public authorities to matters with a link to another state; above all, the Basic Law nowhere contains a general proviso such that fundamental rights must therefore take second place. The declaration of belief in the inviolability and inalienability of human rights placed at the beginning of the text of the constitution as providing the basis of *every* human community, of peace and justice in the world (Article 1.2 of the Basic Law) is not compatible with the idea that the system of values established on the basis of the fundamental rights, particularly the safeguarding thereby of an area of freedom for each individual, could or must generally be put out of operation in order to give precedence to the legal order of another state.
The question of whether and what modifications could result from the explicitly permitted commitment of the Federal Republic of Germany to supranational communities on account of the Preamble to the Basic Law and Article 24.1 of the Basic Law (see BVerfGE 22, 293 (298-299)) can be ignored. The German legislature alone has laid down in international private law, without such binding effect, that the competent German public authorities apply foreign law. Where they take corresponding action, they can neither themselves disregard the protection of fundamental rights required by the constitution, nor can the German legislature release itself from the obligation to observe fundamental rights.
The objections discussed are in part based on the concern that a "normal" review of the application of foreign law against fundamental rights which is not only restricted to extreme cases would turn international private law upside down. Regardless of the fact that in large areas of this field of law conflicts with fundamental rights will probably hardly ever occur, such a concern would only be justified if one now wanted to treat the application of the foreign law at any rate in the same way as the application of standard German legal provisions to purely domestic matters. A proper interpretation of fundamental rights does in fact permit the special features of this case to be taken into account. Reference can already be made to the fact that even when formulating individual fundamental rights the constituent legislature drew a distinction between Germans and non-Germans. Regardless of that fact, a fundamental right can by its very nature require a certain relationship to the specific way of life in the area of application of the constitution, so that unrestricted assertion in entirely or mainly foreign matters would not do justice to the purpose of the protection of fundamental rights. The extent to which this is the case cannot be determined on a general basis. Rather, in each case the interpretation of the corresponding constitutional provision must decide whether it will, according to its wording, purpose and objective, apply to each conceivable application of public authority within the Federal Republic of Germany or whether it permits or requires a distinction to be drawn to cases with a more or less strong link to another state ...

Within the context of this determination of the scope of fundamental rights, which is to be developed from the constitution itself, the aforementioned basic position expressed in the constitution vis-à-vis other states and the international community may also have a role to play.
The fear that such an interpretation places too great a burden on judges and jeopardises legal certainty is unfounded. The task, by its very nature, is no different from the customary interpretation of the constitution in respect of domestic matters, especially in regard to the influence of fundamental rights on the interpretation of private law (see BVerfGE 7, 198 (205 et seq.); see also BVerfGE 25, 167 (181)). For the rest, the case-law and the literature have done a comparable, at least as difficult a job in developing international private law from a few incomplete legal provisions.

IV.

The conclusion to be drawn from the review of the decisive conflict rule in the present case against Article 6.1 of the Basic Law is that there has been no violation of the constitution:
1. The normal case for which Article 6.1 of the Basic Law was conceived concerns a marriage between two German nationals in Germany. The constitution grants these the fundamental right to marry a partner of their own choice if both fulfil the prerequisites of the "institutional rules" set by the German legislature, which must, for their part, correspond to the constitution (see C II above). German nationals who are engaged to be married correspondingly have an absolute right vis-à-vis the German authorities and courts that the marriage be permitted and no further obstacles be placed in the way of the marriage than those which are permissibly laid down by German laws.
2. In the special case of a marriage between two foreigners in the Federal Republic of Germany, the object of the human right to the freedom of marriage they are granted is that they must be permitted to marry in Germany and the German authorities are obligated to become involved to the required extent. However, that does not necessarily require that the foreigner who is engaged to be married must be subject to the same rules in respect of the prerequisites for the marriage as a German national who is engaged to be married in the normal case, i.e. that thus the law of the place of residence or of the place of marriage would have to apply. The German legislature's decision to apply the principle of nationality is based on the assumption that it is in the interest of those involved to be assessed, in personal matters, according to the law of their home country because, taking the more general view, nationality documents their continued personal affinity with that state and the law

directed at persons of their own nationality and created by the legislature of their own nationality is most familiar to them …

Reference should here also be made to efforts which are regularly in the well-understood interest of the foreign persons engaged to be married and rightly emphasised by the Federal Court of Justice to create, wherever possible, the prerequisites for the marriage to be recognised in the home countries the persons engaged to be married have possibly left only temporarily so as to ensure the marriage is guaranteed its continuance. These considerations, like the respect for the independence of other legal orders which underlies the constitution, can justify, in the aforementioned cases, in principle not deriving legal provisions in respect of the institution of marriage, as required under Article 6.1 of the Basic Law, from German but from the respective national rules.

3. For the same reasons no objections can be raised for constitutional-law reasons to the basic decision taken by the legislature of conflict rules in respect of marriages between Germans and foreigners, although from the point of view of the German partner not only German rules are applied but also foreign laws which have not originated according to the Basic Law's general constitutional principles and organisational provisions. If, according to Article 13.1 of the Introductory Act to the Civil Code, the act of marriage in such cases is not to be treated as a uniform procedure which was to be subjected as a whole either to the domestic or to the foreign legal order, but that the capacity to marry of each person engaged to be married is to be viewed separately and is to be assessed on the basis of each one's domestic law, this does not constitute an inappropriate solution to the conflict of interests which have been demonstrated.

Naturally, the application of both legal orders side by side can place greater restrictions on the German partner's freedom of marriage than would be the case if only German laws were applied. For example, the domestic law of the foreign national who is engaged to be married may prescribe a higher marriageable age or make stricter requirements in regard to the consent of third parties. In particular, however, when assessing the foreign partner's capacity to marry according to his own law, the German partner may also be involved by means of the legal concept of bilateral impediments to marriage and thereby personal reasons may lead to an impediment to marriage which would not apply if only German institutional regulations were applied. However, the possibilities vary so greatly in each individual case that the legislature's general decision to apply foreign law cannot bc called into question on that account.

Thus, the additional obstacle to the freedom of marriage resulting from the repercussions on the German national who is engaged to be married of personal impediments to marriage which are based on the personal situation of the foreign person

engaged to be married does not regularly constitute an excessive restriction on the freedom of marriage of the German holder of fundamental rights. It does not as a rule contradict the nature of marriage if the German person engaged to be married who would like to marry a foreign partner must accept special features in his personal status resulting from the legal order he has “brought with him”, especially since the national regulation in question may be closely related to the respective national character and national habits so that compliance with them can serve to ensure the marriage to be entered into continues to exist. As regards the possible cumulative effect of bilateral impediments to marriage, it is difficult to develop general regulations on account of the multifarious constellations. Rather, only the actual application of the law in individual cases will show whether the concerns raised against invoking foreign law in general can also support the concrete interference with the freedom of marriage and whether such interference is appropriate and reasonable in relation to the affected holder of fundamental rights.
Nor is any violation of Article 13.1 of the Introductory Act to the Civil Code against fundamental rights provisions other than Article 6.1 of the Basic Law discernible (see BGHZ 41, 136 (150)).

V.

1. On the other hand, the application of Spanish law, which according to Article 13 of the Introductory Act to the Civil Code is decisive, in the contested decision violates Article 6.1 of the Basic Law. It denies the female complainant the freedom to marry the male complainant, to which she would have a right were German law applied. The male complainant’s freedom of marriage is thereby also violated, since a uniform decision must of necessity be issued against both complainants regarding whether they can marry one another.
The interference with the female complainant’s freedom of marriage at issue here does not result from the aforementioned repercussions of a unilateral impediment to marriage resulting from the male complainant’s personal circumstances. Rather, the circumstances which pose an obstacle to the marriage derive from the female complainant’s personal situation, and the impediment of bigamous marriage resulting therefrom is in principle intrinsic to both legal orders in the same manner. When assessing the female complainant’s capacity to marry, according to Article 13.1 of the Introductory Act to the Civil Code following German law, the German authorities must also examine whether the female complainant is unmarried; they can only unequivocally answer this question in the affirmative because her previous marriage has been dissolved by a final court decision on account of the divorce. At the same time, however, the examination of the same factual and legal circumstances

within the framework of assessing the male complainant's capacity to marry results in the fact that the German authorities and courts answer the same question just as unequivocally in the negative because Spanish law does not recognise the divorce. This contradiction already speaks in favour of an inadmissible interference with the female complainant's freedom of marriage. It also seems hardly understandable why one's own state feigns the continuance of a marriage by applying Spanish law, a marriage which according to its own law it views as dissolved with final effect and with effect for and against everyone. This applies all the more since the previous marriage was dissolved by the German authorities and neither the marriage nor the divorce stands in any relationship whatsoever to any foreign legal order: A marriage between German nationals has been divorced according to German law by a German court.

It is, further, decisive that the different assessment of the female complainant's marital status is based on the Spanish ordre public, which combines the impediment of bigamous marriage with the idea of the indissolubility of marriage by secular act. Spanish law also in principle assumes that the capacity to marry of a German person who is engaged to be married is assessed based on German law; however, it recognises neither the German provisions regarding divorce nor the German divorce decrees on account of their contradicting its own basic values. If the German authorities and courts accept this rejection of German law, this constitutes inadmissible interference with the freedom of marriage. If a German who is engaged to be married is unmarried according to German law and thus unreservedly capable of marrying, his capacity to marry cannot be denied on the basis of foreign ideas regarding marriage in relation to the foreign person engaged to be married which are incompatible with Article 6.1 of the Basic Law and German regulations governing matrimonial law.

The contrary opinion in the contested decision and the case-law of the Federal Court of Justice ignores the fact that the matter in hand here is not that the foreign law is to be censured or that German values are to be forcibly imposed on foreign states, but rather that the Spanish forced imposition is to be rejected. The non-recognition of the German divorce decree on the grounds of the Spanish ordre public cannot be accepted from the point of view of the German legal order, since the matter to be assessed is a purely domestic one. Spanish law seeks to attribute to the female complainant's previous marriage the continued effect of a marriage which cannot be dissolved per se while the spouses are still alive, an effcct which the marriage concluded according to German law never had. Although even according to Article 6.1 of the Basic Law and German matrimonial law marriage is a community concluded for life, it is only "in principle", not absolutely, indissoluble (see BVerfGE 10, 59 (66)). The constitutional requirement that marriage be protected does not guarantee the institution of marriage abstractly, but only as regards the form that corresponds to the prevailing notions which are expressed in the statutory regulation and become decisive there (see BVerfGE 6, 55 (82); 9, 237 (242-243); 15, 328 (332)). Correspondingly, the constitution is founded upon the idea of a "secularised" civil-law marriage which also includes the possibility that spouses may be divorced under the prerequisites laid down in the law and thus to regain their freedom of marriage (see E. Scheffler [in: Bettermann-Nipperdey-Scheuner, *Die Grundrechte*, vol. IV/1, 1960], p. 283-284; see also *Motive zu dem Entwurfe eines Bürgerlichen Gesetzbuches*, vol. IV, pp. 562-563).

2. Nor can the interference with the female complainant's freedom of marriage be justified with efforts to ensure that a marriage is recognised by all and to avoid a "limping" marriage. The "principle of conformity of decisions in international jurisdiction" (*äußerer Entscheidungseinklang*) will continue to be an unfulfilled ideal in international private law until such time as all states at least apply the same regulations in their international private law or enter into corresponding obligations by treaties. "Limping" legal relations often arise in matters with a link to another state, especially when the application of the foreign law invoked on the basis of a conflict rule is excluded by the ordre public or a proviso clause. For example, the application of Article 13.3 and Article 17.3 of the Introductory Act to the Civil Code frequently leads to "limping" marriages or to "limping" divorces. Of course, recognition of the planned marriage in the home countries of both persons engaged to be married would better correspond to the constitutional requirement of protecting the continued existence of marriage; however, if this objective cannot be achieved on account of foreign values, then the complainants cannot be denied the right to marry in general on a matter of principle although such a marriage would be recognised as legally effective not only in the Federal Republic of Germany but also in practically all third countries.

The principle of conformity of decisions in international jurisdiction here also stands in insurmountable contrast to the principle of conformity of decisions in domestic jurisdiction (*innerer Entscheidungseinklang*), i.e. the uniform assessment of the female complainant's divorce and marital status by the domestic authorities and courts, in which both the involved citizens and the state order have a considerable interest. The president of the Higher Regional Court, the Higher Regional Court and the registrar who is bound by their decision regard the female complainant as still married in relationship to the male complainant, whilst in all other legal relations – marital status, maintenance and benefit claims, the law of inheritance etc. – she is treated as divorced with final effect in legal transactions and by every German public authority.

3. The contested decision can likewise not be supported by the consideration that the German woman engaged to be married and any children which may be born into the planned marriage would have to be protected against the disadvantages which could result from a conduct of the Spanish partner which was contrary to marriage because the marriage is not legally recognised in Spain. It cannot be derived from the case-law of the Federal Constitutional Court in respect of Article 6.1 of the Basic Law that the state of the person engaged to be married may impose such protection against her will; this is neither compatible with the fundamental right to the freedom of marriage nor with the spouses' self-responsibility, which is characteristic of the nature of marriage within the meaning of Article 6.1 of the Basic Law. The state is also neither authorised nor obligated to prevent marriage as a precaution in cases where its continued existence, for example on account of extreme age differences or weaknesses of character, appears questionable from the outset or when there are concerns that the woman will likely suffer severe disadvantages because, for instance, the husband has been divorced several times and is already culpably neglecting to make maintenance payments deriving from previous marriages. Correspondingly, it must in the present case also be left to the persons engaged to be married to take on the risk of a "limping" marriage after the competent authorities have pointed this out to them, as is their duty. For the rest, it has not yet been proven that such "limping" marriages are actually at considerably greater risk than other marriages between people of different nationalities …
From the point of view of protecting those involved one must also take account of the fact that human experience shows that persons engaged to be married who are denied the wedding they want to have do not usually separate but rather cohabit out of wedlock. By contrast, a "limping" marriage is at any rate the lesser of the two evils. It releases the wife and children from the blemish of illegality and grants them, at least in the Federal Republic of Germany and in all foreign states in which this marriage is recognised, the status relevant for maintenance claims and succession, as well as social benefits based on it.
4. Another result thereof is that the contested decision contains excessive and disproportionate interference with the female complainant's freedom of marriage. This fundamental right protects the innermost sphere of private life; the state cannot allow the realisation of the joint decision to finally fail without that being justified by a recognisable, higher interest. It is particularly in this area that the application of the law must not lose sight of the guiding principle in the Basic Law, namely that man is the focal point of the system of values set out in the constitution and that the statutory regulations are not a means in themselves. That is why the only possible way out of the legal dilemma cannot be seen as the nationalisation of the foreign person engaged to be married. Apart from the fact that the relatively strict legal pre-

requisites will often not be fulfilled, such a recommendation is tantamount to the capitulation of international private law, whose function is in fact to enable those concerned to make appropriate lifestyle choices without having to relinquish their affiliation to their home country.

VI.

1. As a result, therefore, the contested decision violates the complainants' fundamental right under Article 6.1 of the Basic Law, as in evaluating one of the domestic procedures relating to the female complainant's personal circumstances the court accepted the rejection of the German legal notions of marriage corresponding to Article 6.1 of the Basic Law on account of the Spanish ordre public and derived an impediment to marriage therefrom. Accordingly, no further review need be carried out regarding the question of whether there has been any other violation of fundamental rights in any other regard. The contested decision therefore had to be reversed and the case referred back to the Higher Regional Court.

2. As regards the new decision which must now be passed, there are various possibilities for applying the law in line with the constitution:

The unconstitutional outcome would, for example, be avoided if the court adopted one of the two opinions developed in international private law without reference to constitutional law, according to which the question of the continued existence of the divorced marriage is not to be answered according to the foreign law invoked on account of Article 13.1 of the Introductory Act to the Civil Code, but rather from the very outset according to German procedural or substantive law (see A I 4 above). Should this path not be deemed viable, then according to the principles developed above, the application of Spanish law would be precluded insofar as it leads to a violation of a fundamental right. This could either be achieved by viewing the fundamental rights as including an obstacle which directly limits the applicability of the law invoked on account of a conflict rule, or by drawing on Article 30 of the Introductory Act to the Civil Code. Were the second solution to be chosen, however, no distinction could be drawn between viable and non-viable violations of fundamental rights. Rather, the assertion of the fundamental right under Article 30 of the Introductory Act to the Civil Code would have to view the clause as a "gateway" for fundamental rights into international private law (see BVerfGE 7, 198 (206)), with the consequence that each violation of the fundamental right effected in each individual case by application of the foreign law would trigger interference by the German ordre public. The right measure would thereby result from an examination of whether and to what extent the specific fundamental right concerned would, according to its wording, content and function, taking account of the equal status of other states and the independence of their legal orders, necessitate its validity in matters with a link to another state.

Justices: Dr. Müller, Dr. Stein, Ritterspach, Dr. Haager, Rupp-v.Brünneck, Dr. Böhmer, Dr. Brox, Dr. Simon

No. 8

BVerfGE 42, 95
of 6 April 1976 – 2 BvR 61/76 –
"Pre-trial detention I case (visiting permission)"

HEADNOTE:

Protection of marriage and the family also takes on particular significance in detention as a fundamental provision that determines values. In exceptional situations demonstrating special circumstances, it may therefore be necessary to create visiting opportunities, in addition to the general visiting days, for visits by the spouses and children of pre-trial detainees.

Order of the Second Senate of 6 April 1976
– 2 BvR 61/76 –

in the proceedings regarding the constitutional complaint 1. of Mr. M., – authorised representative: ..., lawyer –, 2. of Mrs. M. against the order of the Essen Regional Court (*Landgericht*) of 3 December 1975 – 26 Qs 68/75 – *and* application for a temporary injunction.

RULING:

1. The order of the Essen Regional Court of 3 December 1975 – 32 Js 322/74 (26 Qs 68/75) – and the order of the Essen Local Court (*Amtsgericht*) of 29 September 1975 – 71 Gs 1352/75 (26 Qs 68/75) – violate the fundamental rights of the complainants under Article 6.1 of the Basic Law (*Grundgesetz* – GG). They are reversed. The case is referred back to the Essen Local Court.
The application for a temporary injunction is hereby disposed of.
2. The *Land* (state) North Rhine-Westphalia is ordered to refund the complainant's necessary expenses.

EXTRACT FROM GROUNDS:

A. – I.

The complainant has been in pre-trial detention since 13 November 1974 on suspicion of economic crimes. His spouse, the second complainant, continues to live with their two children in the shared home, which lies roughly 325 km from the prison.

On 24 August 1975 the second complainant asked to be granted in future visiting permission to visit the complainant on Saturdays, since she was in gainful employment and had a long distance to travel.

This request was rejected by the Local Court by its order of 29 September 1975. The Regional Court rejected as unfounded the complainant's complaint directed against this. In its order of 3 December 1975, the court stated that refusal to grant visiting permission on Saturdays did not violate the complainant's visiting rights. It was said to be certainly reasonable to expect his spouse to visit him during the week, using the leave to which she was entitled by law. It was said to be impossible to guarantee proper supervision of visits on Saturdays. Due to the special nature of the case, it was said to only be possible for this supervision to be carried out by an officer, either of the criminal police or of the public prosecution office where the investigations were being carried out, who was familiar with the subject-matter of the investigation because the complainant's spouse was accused of being an accessory to some of the offences of which the complainant was accused. If the visits were to be inadequately supervised, suspicion would arise of danger of collusion of facts, which moreover was also a reason for the complainant's detention. This suspicion was said to be strengthened in particular because the complainant was said to have attempted to send to his spouse several letters which had dealt with the subject-matter of the investigation proceedings in an impermissible manner. It was said to be an unreasonable burden on the small number of officers familiar with the case, as well as being impossible for organisational reasons, to supervise such visits on Saturdays, when they would be off-duty.

The complainant's constitutional complaint opposes this order. He complains of a violation of his fundamental rights under Articles 1.1, 2.2, 6.1, 6.2, 20 and 104.1 of the Basic Law. He claims that his spouse is unable to visit him on weekdays between Monday and Friday because she is forced to work to ensure her own livelihood and that of their two children. The impugned ruling is said to make visits by his spouse practically impossible, and to thereby violate his right to the protection of his marriage and family. Maintenance of the family ties is said to become all the more urgent the longer pre-trial detention lasts. … It must be possible to deploy suitable officers to supervise visits on Saturdays; there is said to be no apparent reason why supervision could only be carried out by the officers who are familiar with the investigation, either from the public prosecution office or from the criminal police.

At the same time, the complainant applied for a temporary injunction and requested for the impugned order of the Regional Court to be reversed and for the prison [authority] to be instructed to facilitate visits by his spouse on Saturdays.

The complainant's spouse joined the constitutional complaint. She claims that the impugned order also impairs in a most serious manner her right to the protection of her marriage and family. Because of the considerable distance between her home and the prison, and because her children have to go to school and she has to go to work, visits between Monday and Friday are alleged to entail significant sacrifices and difficulties. To date, she has been able to visit her husband occasionally by taking leave as specified in the collective agreement. She further alleges that she can prove that her employer has refused to continue to grant her leave for such visits in the future.

The second complainant visited the complainant once per month from August 1975 to February 1976 (with the exception of January 1976), in each instance on a Monday, Tuesday or Friday.

II.

…

B.

The constitutional complaint is admissible and well-founded.

I.

The impugned order violates the complainants' rights under Article 6.1 of the Basic Law.

1. According to § 119.3 of the Code of Criminal Procedure (*Strafprozeßordnung* – StPO), pre-trial detainees may only be subject to restrictions which are required by the purpose of pre-trial detention or to maintain order in the prison. As is the case with all provisions that restrict fundamental rights, this provision must also be measured against the standard of the fundamental rights which it restricts; its interpretation must take into account that a pre-trial detainee has not yet been convicted, and hence may only be subject to restrictions that are unavoidable (see Decisions of the

Federal Constitutional Court (*Entscheidungen des Bundesverfassungsgerichts* – BVerfGE) 15, 288 (295); 34, 384 (395-396); 35, 5 (9-10)) …

These unavoidable restrictions of necessity include all limitations that must be imposed on personal freedom by virtue of deprivation of liberty and placement in a prison, so to speak from the "nature of the matter". Therefore, only limited visits may be made to a pre-trial detainee by persons living outside the prison, and both pre-trial detainees and prospective visitors must accept such restrictions as a natural consequence of the deprivation of liberty. In addition, all individual restrictions and supervision measures are permissible that are necessary to prevent danger of escape or of collusion of facts. In the light of the above, it is necessary to consider the equipment of the prison in question in terms of the available premises and personnel, and any limitations on facilities used in managing visits resulting from these factors. The utmost limit of the permissibility of a restriction on visiting arrangements has not been exceeded, and hence constitutional law has not been violated, until refusal of visiting permission is necessary neither in order to ensure the purposes of detention, nor to ensure order in the prison, and the restriction imposes a burden on those concerned far in excess of what is typical of the situation. This applies above all when elements of the constitutionally established value order are affected as a result.

2. In the instant case, the Local Court and the Regional Court have not acted in compliance with Article 6.1 of the Basic Law insofar as it contains a fundamental provision that determines values.

a) Marriage and the family are particularly protected by the state (Article 6.1 of the Basic Law). The Federal Constitutional Court (*Bundesverfassungsgericht*) has drawn from this a series of legal consequences (BVerfGE 6, 55 (71 et seq.); 6, 386 (388); 24, 119 (135); 28, 104 (112); 31, 58 (67)). It is decisive here that the fundamental provision that determines values contained in Article 6.1 of the Basic Law also takes on particular significance in detention. Each instance of longer-term pre-trial detention, as a rule, places a considerable strain on the family relationships of the person concerned. Its execution impairs the necessary communication between the detainee and his or her family members who live in freedom, and can contribute towards their becoming fundamentally alienated from one another. The duty of the state, in fulfilment of its constitutional obligation to ensure the preservation of marriage and the family, is to limit such a detrimental impact of the deprivation of liberty as far as is possible and reasonable, whilst adequately satisfying the interests of the public.

It follows from this that the competent authorities must do what is necessary and reasonable to facilitate a suitable number of visits by the spouses and children of pre-trial detainees. In the interest of proper prison operation, in principle they too

may however only avail themselves of the general visiting days. Only in exceptional situations demonstrating special circumstances may it be necessary and indeed reasonable to expect the prison [authority] to create visiting opportunities, in addition to the general visiting days, for spouses and children of pre-trial detainees who are entitled to visit.
b) Such an exceptional case applies here. The complainant has been in pre-trial detention for roughly one-and-a-half years, so that the maintenance of his family ties appears to be particularly at risk. Complete rejection of Saturday visits has led in the past to the second complainant only being able to visit the complainant under disproportionate difficulties and sacrifices because of the considerable distance between the place of residence of the family and the prison, as well as because of her work.
The organisational and personnel difficulties sustained by the prison [authority] for weekend visits are unable to justify such a serious strain on the complainants' family ties. These difficulties are certainly not so insurmountable that the constitutional principle should take a back seat when effecting the necessary weighing of the fundamental provision that determines values contained in Article 6.1 of the Basic Law against the interests of the prison [authority].
In an exceptional case of this nature, visiting opportunities must therefore also be created at the weekend to a suitable and adequate degree (see BVerfGE 36, 264-265).
…
The impugned orders had to be reversed and the case had to be referred back to the Local Court (§ 95.2 of the Federal Constitutional Court Act (*Bundesverfassungsgerichtsgesetz* – BVerfGG)).

II.

With the ruling on the principal proceedings, the request for an injunction has been disposed of.

III.

…

Justices: Dr. Zeidler, Dr. Geiger, Wand, Hirsch, Dr. Rottmann, Dr. Steinberger

No. 9

BVerfGE 51, 386
of 18 July 1979 – 1 BvR 650/77 –
"Expulsion case"

HEADNOTES:

1. **The expulsion of a foreign national convicted of a criminal offence who is married to a German woman and has a legitimate child with her is permissible on the basis of discretionary considerations relating to crime prevention only if the criminal offence is particularly serious.**
2. **When a decision on the expulsion of such a foreign national is being made, particular importance must be attached to the possibility of limiting the effect in time of the expulsion.**

Order of the First Senate of 18 July 1979
– 1 BvR 650/77 –

in the proceedings regarding the constitutional complaint of Mrs. K. – authorised representative: …, lawyer – against (a) the order of the Federal Administrative Court (*Bundesverwaltungsgericht*) of 9 June 1977 – BVerwG I B 70.77 –, (b) the judgment of the Higher Administrative Court (*Oberverwaltungsgericht*) for the *Land* (state) North Rhine-Westphalia of 17 January 1977 – IV A 352/75 –, (c) the judgment of the Cologne Administrative Court (*Verwaltungsgericht*) of 30 October 1974 – 5 (4) K 2521/73 –, (d) the expulsion order of the City of Cologne (*Stadt Köln*) of 30 March 1972 as amended by the ruling of the Cologne District Chief Administrative Officer (*Regierungspräsident Köln*) of 11 October 1973 on the objection and the order of the City of Cologne of 4 January 1977.

RULING:

The constitutional complaint is rejected as unfounded.

EXTRACT FROM GROUNDS:

A.

The constitutional complaint concerns the question whether it is permissible for a foreign national who is married to a German woman and has a legitimate child with her to be expelled from the Federal Republic of Germany on the basis of discretionary considerations relating to crime prevention because he has been convicted of a drugs offence.

I.

The legal status of foreign nationals in the Federal Republic of Germany is regulated primarily by the Foreign Nationals Act (*Ausländergesetz* – AuslG) of 28 April 1965 (Federal Law Gazette (*Bundesgesetzblatt* – BGBl.) I p 353), most recently amended by Article 1 of the Act on Acceleration of the Asylum Procedure (*Gesetz zur Beschleunigung des Asylverfahrens*) of 25 July 1978 (Federal Law Gazette I p 1108), – hereinafter "the Foreign Nationals Act". Expulsion is permissible only for the reasons set out in detail in § 10.1 nos. 1 to 11 of the Foreign Nationals Act, in particular where the foreign national has been convicted of a criminal offence (§ 10.1 no. 2 of the Foreign Nationals Act). Expulsion causes the residence permit to expire (§ 9.1 sentence 1 no. 4 of the Foreign Nationals Act); an expelled foreign national is obliged to leave the country without delay (§ 12.1 sentence 2 of the Foreign Nationals Act) and may be deported (§ 13 of the Foreign Nationals Act). The effect of expulsion and deportation, regulated in § 15.1 sentence 1 of the Foreign Nationals Act, namely, that no residence permit can be granted, may be limited in time by the authority which expelled or deported the foreign national (§ 15.1 sentence 2 of the Foreign Nationals Act). § 15.1 sentence 3 of the Foreign Nationals Act provides for the possibility of a retrospective extension or shortening of the time limit.
The nationals of Member States of the European Communities occupy a privileged position among foreign nationals. They, together with the members of their families, enjoy a large degree of freedom of movement and enhanced protection against expulsion. In addition, the entry, residence and expulsion of foreign nationals are the subject-matter of numerous bilateral and multilateral agreements entered into by the Federal Republic, which take precedence over the provisions of the Foreign Nationals Act (§ 55.3 of the Foreign Nationals Act). Subject to the provisions on immigration, the Convention on Establishment between the German Reich and the Turkish Republic of 12 January 1927 (Reich Law Gazette (*Reichsgesetzblatt* – RG-

Bl.) II p. 76; Federal Law Gazette 1952 II p. 608) guarantees complete freedom of entry and establishment (Article 2), but at the same time reserves the right of the Contracting Parties to expel nationals of the other party by individual measures on the basis of a court judgment or pursuant to the statutes, ordinances concerning public morals, public health or the control of vagrancy or on grounds of the internal or external security of the state (Article 7). The European Agreement on Regulations governing the Movement of Persons between Member States of the Council of Europe (Federal Law Gazette 1959 II p. 389; Joint Ministerial Gazette (*Gemeinsames Ministerialblatt* – GMBl.) 1962 p. 102) leaves unaffected the right of each Contracting Party to forbid nationals of another Contracting Party whom it considers undesirable to stay in its territory (Article 6).
The General Administrative Regulations Relating to the Implementation of the Foreign Nationals Act (*Allgemeine Verwaltungsvorschrift zur Ausführung des Ausländergesetzes*) issued pursuant to § 51 of the Foreign Nationals Act, in the version promulgated on 10 May 1977 (Joint Ministerial Gazette p. 202), most recently amended by the General Administrative Regulations of 7 July 1978 (Joint Ministerial Gazette p. 368), direct that any expulsion of foreign nationals who are married to Germans or are responsible for the care for the person of a German child may be contemplated only where the reasons set out in the § 10.1 of the Foreign Nationals Act are serious in the particular case (no. 1a relating to § 10).

II.

1. The German complainant's Turkish husband, who was born in 1938, entered federal territory legally in October 1961 in order to take up employment and has since worked for various companies, generally as a locksmith. The residence permit first granted to him in December 1961 was regularly extended, most recently until 3 January 1973. The child of both spouses, born in June 1968, acquired German nationality in July 1975.
In December 1965, the complainant's husband was fined DM 120 for driving a vehicle on the public highway without a driving licence in June 1962. On 10 March 1972, he was finally convicted and sentenced to imprisonment for one year and three months and to a fine of DM 300 for handling tax-evaded goods and a related opium offence committed in September 1971. According to the findings of the criminal court, he, together with two compatriots, had handed over four kilograms of hashish to a police detective who had pretended to be a buyer of drugs. In October 1972 he was conditionally released from prison after the remainder of the sentence of approximately three months was suspended on probation for three years; the remainder of the sentence has since been remitted.

2. By order of 30 March 1972, the City of Cologne expelled the complainant's husband permanently from the Federal Republic of Germany, set him a period of one month after release from prison within which to leave the country and warned him that deportation could be imposed. The expulsion was based on § 10.1 no. 2 and no. 6 of the Foreign Nationals Act and essentially on the reasoning that illegal drug trafficking posed grave dangers to public security and public order in Germany. In addition, the complainant's husband had failed to disclose in an earlier declaration of residence the punishment imposed in 1965, had repeatedly infringed provisions of the law governing registration with the authorities and had thus clearly demonstrated that he was not willing to abide by the laws of Germany. The authority hearing the objection confirmed the order of the authority responsible for foreign nationals and held that the public interest in expulsion was justified on the basis of the concept of deterrence alone.

3. The complainant and her husband brought a legal action against the expulsion. After the complainant had withdrawn her action and been summoned as an interested party in the proceedings by the Administrative Court, she continued to argue that her husband should be allowed to remain in Germany, but made no separate application of her own.

The action was dismissed. In the grounds of the decision, however, the court pointed out that before the expulsion order, as a discretionary decision, is issued, the criminal records are, in principle, to be obtained. Only because it could be assumed that expulsion would have occurred in any event on account of the gravity of the offence, the failure to require the criminal records to be produced did not call into question the lawfulness of the expulsion order in this instance.

Both spouses appealed against the dismissal of the action. During the appeal proceedings, the authority responsible for foreign nationals limited the effect in time of the expulsion retrospectively to five years after the expulsion order ceased to be open to appeal.

The Higher Administrative Court dismissed the appeals of the complainant and her husband. In the grounds of the judgment it is again pointed out that the balance to be struck in accordance with objective principles between the circumstances for and against the expulsion of a foreign national for a conviction by a criminal court generally requires the authority responsible for foreign nationals to obtain the criminal records. That applies *a fortiori* where expulsion – as in this case – may be ordered only on account of particularly serious circumstances. Only because of the particular circumstances of the case was the exercise of discretion not defective.

According to the court, the expulsion, retrospectively limited in time and still based only on considerations relating to crime prevention, is justified under § 10.1 no. 2 of the Foreign Nationals Act on account of the drugs offence. The power of expul-

sion is not restricted either by Article 7.1 of the German-Turkish Convention on Establishment or by Article 6 of the European Agreement on Regulations governing the Movement of Persons between Member States of the Council of Europe.
It is appropriate, according to the court, to use expulsions to combat the selling of drugs involving foreign nationals. They are necessary in order to prevent other foreign nationals from committing identical or similar criminal offences. In relation to certain categories of cases, of which drug trafficking is one, the expectation that expulsions will have general preventive effects is in accordance with the law. The foreign national concerned is not being used as a mere means of deterring others. Since, by his criminal offence, he has given a possible incentive for disturbances affecting public security and public order, the potential risk which expulsion is intended to combat has at least been increased. Consequently, he is to be regarded as a "troublemaker" (*Störer*) within the meaning of police law and regulatory law.
Nor is expulsion precluded by protection of the marital community and the family unit. It is true, according to the court, that a separation of the spouses and the child born to them must be seriously contemplated, and that this may jeopardise the survival of the marriage and the family, even though it would only be for five years and short visits would be possible. However, Article 6.1 of the Basic Law (*Grundgesetz* – GG) does not grant absolute protection from expulsions; in cases of moderate and serious criminality it is reasonable that expulsion of the foreign national should have the consequence of a separation from his German wife and German child, because they could not be expected, nor would it be possible, for them to live abroad. The intensity and scale of the complainant's husband's involvement in drug trafficking activity and the considerable criminality which has come to light in that connection undermine the interests of the Federal Republic in a particularly serious manner and demonstrate that the consequences for his family of an expulsion for a limited time are not disproportionate.
The complaint against the denial of leave to appeal on points of law, which only the complainant's husband had lodged, was rejected by the Federal Administrative Court.
The complainant's husband continues to live in Germany; he is being allowed to stay pending the ruling on the constitutional complaint.

III.

By the constitutional complaint, the complainant alleges infringement of her fundamental rights under Article 6.1 and 6.2 and Article 11 of the Basic Law. She argues:

If she follows her husband to Turkey with their child, the family's means of livelihood will be destroyed and the education of the child, who is now over 10 years old, will be interrupted. If she remains in Germany, she will have to claim public assistance, because she cannot provide for her child on her own and cannot manage on her own salary. Although she is employed as a bookkeeper, she is reliant on her husband's maintenance payments. Even in the case of gross violations of the law, the state cannot accept the break-up of the family unit as a consequence of expulsion. Arguments relating to crime prevention must take second place to the state's duty to protect marriage and the family, particularly since the violations of the law took place a long time ago and her husband has had an unblemished criminal record since 1972.

IV.

1. The Federal Minister of the Interior has submitted observations on behalf of the Federal Government: He refers to his observations in the case 1 BvR 241/77 (see Decisions of the Federal Constitutional Court (*Entscheidungen des Bundesverfassungsgerichts* – BVerfGE) 50, 166 (171-172)) on the crime rate of foreign nationals and on the deterrent effect of expulsions of delinquent foreign nationals on grounds of crime prevention and makes the following supplementary observations on the drugs crime rate among foreign nationals:
... No ascertainable experience concerning the preventive effect of expulsions on the drugs crime rate is available. No statement can be made in that connection with regard to persons who are psychologically and physically drug-dependent. However, it is perfectly plausible that there may be a preventive effect on potential drug traffickers and drug smugglers who are not drug-dependent.
2. The Minister-President of the *Land* North Rhine-Westphalia refers to his observations in the case 1 BvR 241/77, in which he argued that police experience, which could not be proved by documents, tended to indicate that fear of possible expulsion prevented foreign nationals from committing criminal offences.
3. The Federal Administrative Court (*Bundesverwaltungsgericht*) stated as follows: Expulsion serves as a regulatory-law measure designed to prevent any future disturbance affecting the maintenance of public security and public order or any impairment of other important interests of the Federal Republic. The discretionary decision on expulsion following conviction of a criminal offence may, in certain categories of cases, having regard to the principle of proportionality, be based solely on considerations relating to crime prevention if experience shows that expulsion may have the effect of inducing other foreign nationals to conduct themselves in an orderly manner in Germany in view of the threat of expulsion which they too would

otherwise face. Before an expulsion is ordered, it must also be examined whether the protection of the foreign national's marriage and family takes priority over the public interest in his expulsion. The striking of a balance between the conflicting values and interests involved, which is necessary in that context, means that foreign nationals who are married to a German national ought to be expelled if the reasons for doing so are serious in an individual case and the presence of the foreign national cannot be tolerated further despite the marriage. This applies in cases of moderate and serious crime. If the marriage has resulted in children of German nationality, the family reasons pointing against expulsion could be strengthened even further.

...

B.

The constitutional complaint is admissible.

Admissibility is not precluded by the fact that the expulsion order is directed against the complainant's husband and she herself has not lodged a complaint against the denial of leave to appeal.

1. A constitutional complaint may be filed only by a person alleging that one of his fundamental rights or one of his rights equivalent to a fundamental right has been infringed by public authority (Article 93.1 no. 4a of the Basic Law, § 90.1 of the Federal Constitutional Court Act (*Bundesverfassungsgerichtsgesetz* – BVerfGG)). A constitutional complaint against a judicial decision further requires that the complainant is directly affected in law and not merely indirectly in fact by it and is thus aggrieved (BVerfGE 4, 96 (101); 28, 314 (320); 31, 58 (66-67); 34, 81 (97) with further references). This requirement may be satisfied even if the complainant was not himself a party to the original proceedings; the only decisive factor is whether the citizen is directly affected by the judicial sovereign act (BVerfGE 34, 81 (97)). That question must be answered in the affirmative in this case; this is because the complainant, as the wife of the expelled foreign national, has an interest meriting protection in his remaining in the country.

2. According to the principle of subsidiarity, which is enshrined in constitutional law (BVerfGE 42, 243 (249)), every complainant must, before filing a constitutional complaint, first try to eliminate the alleged infringement of fundamental rights by means of the other legal remedies available to him (BVerfGE 22, 287 (290); established case-law). In administrative proceedings, the complaint against denial of leave to appeal forms part of recourse to the courts within the meaning of § 90.2 BVerfGG if it is admissible and not manifestly lacking any prospect of success (BVerfGE 16, 1 (2-3). It is true that the complainant filed no such complaint. How-

ever, as the third party summoned in the proceedings on her husband's complaint against denial of leave to appeal, she was able to take procedural steps effectively herself within his claims (§ 66 of the Rules of Procedure of the Administrative Courts (*Verwaltungsgerichtsordnung* – VwGO)), and the decision of the Federal Administrative Court was also effective against her. Since the principle of subsidiarity of the constitutional complaint is intended to ensure that the complaint put forward undergoes proper preliminary examination at the appropriate levels of the courts (BVerfGE 4, 193 (198)) and is redressed as far as possible (BVerfGE 9, 3 (7)), that purpose is taken into account by the complainant's husband's complaint against the denial of leave to appeal. That exhaustion of the available remedies must also be attributed to the complainant.

C.

The constitutional complaint is unfounded.

I.

1. There are no constitutional objections to the provision of § 10.1 no. 2 of the Foreign Nationals Act, which allows expulsion of a foreign national convicted of a criminal offence. Since expulsion is at the discretion, to be exercised in accordance with objective principles, of the authority responsible for foreign nationals, sufficient scope remains in an individual case for account to be taken of higher-ranking constitutional law, in particular the principle of proportionality (BVerfGE 50, 166 (174) with further references). In the case of married foreign nationals, due regard must accordingly be had to the implications of Article 6.1 of the Basic Law.
2. Article 6.1 of the Basic Law contains both a classic fundamental right to protection from state intervention as an institutional guarantee and a fundamental provision that determines values for the whole sphere of private and public law concerning marriage and the family, and also applies to foreign nationals (BVerfGE 31, 58 (67)). It is true that Article 6.1 of the Basic Law does not absolutely protect the foreign spouse of a German national from deportation (BVerfGE 35, 382 (408)); however, the interest of the German spouse in continuing his marriage as a life-long relationship between partners having equal rights in Germany must be taken into account *proprio motu* in any discretionary decision on the expulsion of a foreign national (BVerfGE 19, 394 (397); 35, 382 (408)).
Since, in principle, it is for the spouses alone, autonomously and free from any exercise of influence by the state, to determine the territorial and social centre of their life together, the freedom of both spouses to decide to live together in Germany

merits special state protection if one of the spouses possesses German nationality. Convictions for criminal acts are not, in principle, sufficient to justify an expulsion which would jeopardise a marriage. However, where a danger of recidivism exists or where expulsion is intended to deter other foreign nationals, it must considered, on balance, whether the continued residence of the foreign national can nevertheless be tolerated or whether German spouses can be expected either to leave their spouses or to follow them and therefore abandon their homeland.

In the case of expulsions based on reasons relating to crime prevention, there must be a presumption, in the light of Article 6.1 of the Basic Law, that the constitutionally safeguarded interest in the maintenance of the marriage to a German citizen outweighs, in principle, the interest of deterrence. Only if the criminal offence is particularly serious and there is therefore an urgent need, over and above the sanction according to criminal law, to regard it as a ground for expulsion, in order to deter other foreign nationals from committing criminal offences of a similar nature and gravity, may the state's duty of protection in favour of the continued existence of the marriage of a German national be overridden. It must be assumed here that drugs offences are among those offences which are dangerous and difficult to combat.

Since Article 6.1 of the Basic Law covers not only marriage, but also the family with children, as a distinct personal sphere (BVerfGE 18, 97 (105-106), the state is obliged to respect and promote the unity and self-responsibility of the family (BVerfGE 10, 59 (83 et seq.); 17, 38 (50); 24, 119 (135)). Article 6.2 of the Basic Law guarantees the parental right in the interests of the child's best interests (BVerfGE 24, 119 (144); 37, 217 (252)) and protects the freedom of the parents to decide how they wish to fulfil their parental responsibility free from state interventions (BVerfGE 31, 194 (204 et seq.) with further references). The decision of a German national who is married to a foreign national and whose legitimate child possesses German nationality to live with his child in Germany is therefore covered by the guarantee in Article 6.1 and 6.2 of the Basic Law. The German parent's constitutionally protected interest in the family unit and in the joint upbringing of the child in Germany must therefore be taken into account when expulsion of the foreign parent is being decided upon. The existence of a legitimate child with German nationality cannot protect the foreign parent from expulsion in every case, but strengthens the protection against expulsion which, in view of the marriage to a German partner, exists anyway.

3. When a decision on the expulsion of a foreign national with a German spouse is being taken, particular importance must be attached to § 15.1 of the Foreign Nationals Act, since it enables the authority responsible for foreign nationals to set a time limit, at its discretion, to be exercised in accordance with objective principles, on

the effect of the expulsion and therefore on the prohibition of granting a new residence permit. By that provision, the legislature has created a suitable means under the rule of law of limiting the drastic consequences of an expulsion for the foreign national's personal lifestyle and, where considerations relating to crime prevention apply, of preventing the measure of expulsion under the law concerning foreign nationals from proving to be an inadequate intervention in relation to the intended purpose of deterring other foreign nationals. The social and economic disadvantages associated with leaving the Federal Republic only temporarily can still be considerable, but, in the light of the requirement of proportionality, are more bearable and reasonable than the consequences of an indefinite expulsion. The authority responsible for foreign nationals can accordingly do justice to the public interest in the expulsion of a foreign national who has committed criminal offences and been convicted with a response which is graduated in terms of time and at the same time takes sufficient account of his private interests.

4. A decision brought into conformity with the principle of proportionality on the validity of an expulsion ordered for reasons relating to crime prevention and on the limitation of its temporal effect further presupposes, as well as adherence to the scope of protection of Article 6.1 and 6.2 of the Basic Law in the case of a foreign national with a German spouse and a German child, that the authority responsible for foreign nationals carefully investigates and thoroughly assesses *proprio motu* the circumstances of the criminal offence and the personal circumstances of the person concerned. Without knowledge of the details of the commission of the offence and of the family and occupational situation, the implications of expulsion for the aforementioned constitutionally protected individual interests cannot, as a rule, be ascertained with sufficient certainty and weighed, in a case-based evaluation, against the interests of the general public which call for expulsion. Normally, therefore, before the decision on expulsion is taken, inspection of the criminal records is just as indispensable as ascertaining the family, employment and housing circumstances of the person concerned. If, in the light of the purpose of expulsion, it is not possible to assess immediately whether the setting of a time limit is appropriate, the authority responsible for foreign nationals must, if necessary, examine retrospectively the question of setting a time limit and shortening the time limit and, to that end, must monitor the development of the personal circumstances of the expellee and his family. A decision on a standard form concerning the expulsion of a foreign national, without an assessment of the specific facts and circumstances, could not stand up to constitutional scrutiny. This includes the obligation, to which attention is drawn by the Federal Administrative Court, of the authority responsible for foreign nationals to re-examine, if necessary, even after the expulsion order has become final and no longer open to appeal, whether, in the case of a change of rele-

vant circumstances, the maintenance of an expulsion order – even though subject to a time limit – violates Article 6.1 of the Basic Law.

II.

If the contested decisions are examined on the basis of those criteria, there is no indication that norms and criteria relating to fundamental rights were disregarded in the ascertainment and assessment of the facts and circumstances and in the interpretation and application of the provisions of § 10.1 no. 2 and § 15.1 sentence 2 of the Foreign Nationals Act, which form part of non-constitutional law (BVerfGE 42, 143 (148) with further references).

In view of the intensity and scale of the complainant's husband's involvement in drug trafficking, the administrative courts have presumed that the custodial sentence of one year and three months for that trafficking justifies his temporary expulsion. Because of the particular features of the present case, even the failure to obtain the records does not, according to the courts, call into question the lawfulness of the expulsion order. The power of expulsion is not limited under international agreements and expulsion is suitable and necessary in order to prevent other foreign nationals from committing identical or similar criminal offences. Having regard to the implications of Article 6.1 of the Basic Law, that finding is also constitutionally unobjectionable.

Since the date of delivery of the ruling on the objection (October 1973) is decisive for the expulsion order and for the factual circumstances on which it is based, it could not be relevant for the administrative court decisions that the criminal offence was committed as long ago as September 1971 and that the complainant's husband conducted himself in a manifestly unexceptionable manner in the intervening period. That development can be relevant only for subsequent decisions of the authority responsible for foreign nationals (see C I 4).

Justices: Dr. Benda, Dr. Simon, Dr. Faller, Dr. Katzenstein, Dr. Niemeyer, Dr. Heußner; Justices Dr. Böhmer and Dr. Hesse are unable to attend for signing.

No. 10

BVerfGE 53, 224
of 28 February 1980 – 1 BvL 136/78, 1 BvR 890/77, 1300, 1440/78, 32/79 –
"Divorce law case"

HEADNOTES:

1. **It does not violate Article 6.1 of the Basic Law (*Grundgesetz* – GG) that it has been possible since 1 July 1977 for marriages to be dissolved according to § 1565.1 of the Civil Code (*Bürgerliches Gesetzbuch* – BGB) if they have broken down (transition from the fault to the breakdown principle).**
2. **The irrefutable presumption of the breakdown of marriage after a three-year separation of the spouses (§ 1566.2 of the Civil Code) is compatible with Article 6.1 of the Basic Law.**
3. **Decision regarding the constitutional evaluation of the time limit on the non-economic hardship clause (§ 1568.2 of the Civil Code).**
4. **The legislature was constitutionally not prevented from introducing the new divorce law also for marriages which were concluded prior to 1 July 1977.**

Judgment of the First Senate of 28 February 1980
on the basis of the oral hearing of 27, 28 and 29 November 1979
– 1 BvL 136/78, 1 BvR 890/77, 1300, 1440/78, 32/79 –

in the proceedings I. for constitutional review of §§ 1565.1 sentence 1 and 1566 of the Civil Code – suspension of proceedings and submission order of the Aurich Local Court (*Amtsgericht*) of 1 December 1978 (11 F 19/77) – 1 BvL 136/78 –; II. concerning the constitutional complaints 1. of Ms. P. – authorised representative: ..., lawyer – a) directly against aa) the judgment of the Frankfurt am Main Higher Regional Court (*Oberlandesgericht*) of 24 April 1978 – 1 UF 509/77 –, bb) the partial judgment of the Wiesbaden Local Court of 7 September 1977 – 53 F 4/77 –, b) indirectly against §§ 1565.1 sentence 1 and 1566.2 and 1568.2 of the Civil Code and Article 12 no. 3.1 of the First Act Reforming the Law on Marriage and Family

– First Marriage Law Reform Act (*Erstes Gesetz zur Reform des Ehe- und Familienrechts* – 1. EheRG) of 14 June 1976 (Federal Law Gazette (*Bundesgesetzblatt* – BGBl.)) I p. 1421) – 1 BvR 890/77 –; 2. of Dr. H. – authorised representative: Dr. …, lawyer – a) directly against aa) the order of the Cologne Higher Regional Court of 20 October 1978 – 4 WF 206/78 –, bb) the order of the Bonn Local Court of 28 August 1978 – 24 a F 179/77 –, b) indirectly against §§ 1565.1, 1566.2 and 1568.2 of the Civil Code and Article 12 no. 3.1 of the First Marriage Law Reform Act – 1 BvR 1300/78 –; 3. of Ms. B. – authorised representatives: Dr. … and …, lawyers – a) directly against the judgment of the Stuttgart Higher Regional Court of 26 October 1978 – 16 UF 201/78 ES –, b) indirectly against §§ 1565.1, 1566.2 and 1568.2 of the Civil Code and Article 12 no. 3.1 of the First Marriage Law Reform Act – 1 BvR 1440/78 –; 4. of Ms. W. – authorised representatives: Dr. …, Dr. … and Dr. …, lawyers – a) directly against aa) the judgment of the Munich Higher Regional Court of 4 December 1978 – 2 UF 815/78 –, bb) the judgment of the Munich Local Court of 17 May 1978 – 86 F 1800/77 –, b) indirectly against §§ 1565.1, 1566.2 and 1568.2 of the Civil Code and Article 12 no. 3.1 of the First Marriage Law Reform Act – 1 BvR 32/79 –.

RULING:

I. § 1565.1 sentence 1 and § 1566.2 of the Civil Code in the version of Article 1 no. 20 of the First Act Reforming the Law on Marriage and Family (First Marriage Law Reform Act) of 14 June 1976 (Federal Law Gazette I p. 1421) are compatible with the Basic Law.
Article 12 no. 3.1 of the First Act Reforming the Law on Marriage and Family (First Marriage Law Reform Act) of 14 June 1976 (Federal Law Gazette I p. 1421) is compatible with the Basic Law insofar as it relates to these provisions.
II. The constitutional complaints are rejected as unfounded.

EXTRACT FROM GROUNDS:

A.

The subject-matter of the proceedings, which were combined for a joint hearing and ruling, is the question of whether material provisions of divorce law, which has been amended since 1 July 1977, and its application to marriages which were concluded prior to this time, are compatible with the Basic Law.

I.

1. The First Marriage Law Reform Act of 14 June 1976 (Federal Law Gazette I p. 1421) has newly defined the prerequisites under which marriages can be dissolved. The vital amendment as against the previous law lies in the transition from the fault principle to the breakdown principle. The fundamental provisions read as follows:

§ 1565

(1) A marriage may be dissolved by divorce if it has broken down. The marriage is deemed to have broken down if the conjugal community of the spouses no longer exists and it cannot be expected that the spouses restore it.
(2) Where the spouses have not yet lived apart for one year, the marriage may be dissolved by divorce only if the continuation of the marriage would constitute an unreasonable hardship for the petitioner for reasons that lie in the person of the other spouse.

§ 1566

(1) It is irrefutably presumed that the marriage has broken down if the spouses have lived apart for a year and both spouses petition for divorce or the respondent consents to divorce.
(2) It is irrefutably presumed that the marriage has broken down if the spouses have been living apart for three years.

§ 1567

(1) The spouses are deemed to be living apart if there is no domestic community between them and a spouse recognisably does not intend to create this because he or she rejects the conjugal community. The domestic community is also deemed to no longer exist if the spouses live apart in the matrimonial home.
(2) Living together for a short period which is intended to reconcile the spouses does not interrupt or suspend the periods laid down in section 1566.

§ 1568

(1) The marriage should not be dissolved by divorce, although it has broken down, if and for as long as the maintenance of the marriage, in the interest of minor children of the family, is, exceptionally, necessary for particular reasons or if and for as long as divorce, by reason of extraordinary circumstances, would constitute such a severe hardship for the respondent, who rejects it, that the

maintenance of the marriage, exceptionally, appears to be advisable, even taking into account the concerns of the petitioner.

(2) Subsection 1 shall not be applied if the spouses have been living apart for more than five years.

The amended divorce law came into force on 1 July 1977 (Article 12 no. 13 (a) of the First Marriage Law Reform Act). It also applies if the marriage was concluded prior to this time (Article 12 no. 3.1 of the First Marriage Law Reform Act).
The provision on the suspension of the divorce proceedings was reworded and expanded. It now reads as follows:

§ 614 of the Code of Civil Procedure (Zivilprozeßordnung – ZPO)

(1) …

(2) The court should suspend the divorce proceedings ex officio if according to its free conviction there are prospects to continue the marriage. If the spouses have been separated for more than one year, the proceedings may not be suspended against the opposition of both spouses.

(3) If the petitioner has moved to suspend the proceedings, the court may not … grant a divorce before the proceedings have been suspended.

(4) Suspension may only be repeated once. All in all, it may not exceed the duration of one year, in case of a separation of more than three years it may not exceed the duration of six months.

(5) With the suspension, the court should as a rule suggest to the spouses to avail themselves of the services of a marriage guidance agency.

The family court must decide on the divorce and on the consequences of the divorce, in principle in combined hearings and combined rulings (§ 23b of the Courts Constitution Act (*Gerichtsverfassungsgesetz* – GVG); §§ 623 and 628 of the Code of Civil Procedure).
…

II.

1. a) Those concerned in the original proceedings which led to the judge's submission (1 BvL 136/78) have been married since December 1972, the wife, who was born in 1938, in her second marriage, and the husband, who was born in 1922, in his third marriage. They have a joint child, who was born in 1967. The wife filed for dissolution of the marriage by divorce in May 1975 for serious marital miscon-

duct on the part of her husband. After the legal dispute had been suspended at her motion for six months in June 1975, the wife pursued her action, asserting that her husband had struck her several times and also otherwise physically mistreated her. The Regional Court (*Landgericht*) took evidence and assigned the proceedings to the family court after entry into force of the First Marriage Law Reform Act. After the wife had left the marital home in January 1978, she asserted as grounds for her divorce petition that her marriage had broken down and that the continuation of the marriage constituted an unreasonable hardship for her for reasons lying in the person of her husband.

b) After taking further evidence, the Local Court suspended the proceedings according to Article 100.1 of the Basic Law and submitted to the Federal Constitutional Court (*Bundesverfassungsgericht*) the question of whether § 1565.1 sentence 1 and § 1566 of the Civil Code were compatible with Article 6 and Article 14 of the Basic Law insofar as, accordingly, a spouse could bring about the breakdown of the marriage arbitrarily against the will of the other spouse by virtue of his or her conduct. It was said to have been established on the basis of the taking of evidence that the spouses had been living apart for more than one year, but not yet for three years, and that the marriage had broken down because of the wife's conduct.

It was said to contradict the core of the institution of marriage guaranteed by Article 6 of the Basic Law that the spouse who was seeking divorce could "cast out" the other partner according to the new divorce law. Marriage may not be left at the disposal of one spouse. The principle of life-long marriage was said to have lost its content according to the new divorce law. Whilst the population's attitude towards marriage and the family was said to have changed, the legislature was said nonetheless not to have been entitled to create a divorce law which clearly contradicted the original values.

2. a) The marriage of the complainant re II 1, who was born in 1921, was concluded in 1946; four children issued from it, who were born in 1947 to 1955. After the spouses had initially lived apart in the marital dwelling from 1959 onwards, the husband, who was also born in 1921, left it at the end of 1961. He has been living with another woman since then; a son, who was born in 1969, issued from that union. After the husband had unsuccessfully petitioned for the dissolution of the marriage by divorce in 1960, 1964 and 1975, the marriage was dissolved by the Local Court in response to his motion lodged in July 1977. The Higher Regional Court rejected the complainant's appeal on points of fact and law because the breakdown of the marriage was irrefutably presumed as a result of the separation which had lasted since July 1959 and the hardship clause contained in § 1568.1 of the Civil Code was no longer applicable according to § 1568.2 of the Civil Code.

b) With her constitutional complaint, the complainant is complaining of a violation of Article 6.1 and Article 20 of the Basic Law. It was said to be not compatible with the principle of life-long marriage, and to be equivalent to "casting out", that a marriage could be dissolved against the will of one spouse on the basis of a presumption of breakdown following a three-year or five-year separation. Since it was said that marriage and family were to be traditionally understood in a Christian sense, the Basic Law was said to be based on the principle of life-long marriage and its indissolubility. It was said that her faith as a practicing Catholic had been violated by virtue of the dissolution of marriage by divorce imposed on her. Moreover, it was said that she was unable to engage in gainful employment, could only draw a small pension and did not receive any maintenance from her husband. As a result of four difficult births, she was said to suffer from progressive sinistral neuroparalysis, so that her marriage also had to continue for financial reasons. Finally, the application of the new divorce law to marriages which had been concluded prior to 1 July 1977 was said to breach the principle of the rule of law.

3. a) The complainant re II 2, who was born in 1937, has been married since 1965. His wife, who was born in 1942, finally left the marital dwelling in 1971. She became the mother of a daughter in 1975; she applied for the dissolution of her marriage by divorce in August 1977. The complainant, who wishes to have the petition rejected, has unsuccessfully requested legal aid. According to the concurring view of the Local Court and of the Higher Regional Court, his legal defence has no sufficient prospects for success because the spouses lived in separation for more than five years and the separation periods did not only start to run when the First Marriage Law Reform Act entered into force.

b) With the constitutional complaint, the complainant objects to the refusal to grant legal aid. The breakdown principle was said to violate Article 6.1 of the Basic Law insofar as it facilitated the dissolution of marriage by divorce by means of an automatic deadline on the basis of arbitrary acts on the part of a spouse and without any possibility to take court action. § 1565.1 of the Civil Code was said to be interpreted in conformity with the constitution in that a marriage is not to be regarded as having broken down until both spouses had lost the commitment to their marriage, which could not be presumed without exception after a five-year separation. It is hence said that the hardship regulation contained in § 1568.1 of the Civil Code should not have been subjected to a time limit.

4. a) The complainant re II 3, who was born in 1902, concluded a marriage in 1923 with her husband, who was born in 1899. A son was born in 1930. The husband was in prison for more than nine years between 1933 and 1945 because of his membership of the Communist Party of Germany (*Kommunistische Partei Deutschlands* – KPD). During this period, the complainant made a living for herself

and their son from the proceeds of a small detergent shop. On release from Dachau concentration camp, the husband returned to his family in 1945, but left it at the end of 1952; since then, he has been living with a much younger woman. The marriage was dissolved by marriage in response to his motion lodged in February 1977. The Higher Regional Court rejected the appeal on points of fact and law against divorce: The transition from the fault principle to the breakdown principle was said to be constitutional; Article 6.1 of the Basic Law was said not to contain an obligation to maintain marriages which had become devoid of content against the will of a spouse solely for the sake of the institution. The five-year period specified by § 1568.2 of the Civil Code is said to counter the presumption of an arbitrary act or of a unilateral disposition of the marriage and to offer sufficient protection against rash divorces. The application of the new divorce law to marriages which were concluded prior to 1 July 1977 is said not to be unconstitutional. It is said that there is no protection of confidence in the continuation of a statutory provision; rather, it is said to be a matter for the legislature to determine the necessity and time of the reform of a legal field.

b) With her constitutional complaint, the complainant is objecting to a violation of Article 2.1, Article 6.1 and Article 20 of the Basic Law.

She argued that she had been able to trust during the two-and-a-half decades of separation from her husband that the dissolution of her marriage by divorce was not possible according to the divorce law which is based on the fault principle. The concept of marriage which was in principle indissoluble was also said to correspond to the moral philosophical view adopted by the case-law. Hence, it was said that she had been able to expect from the legislature that the latter, when adopting new divorce law provisions, should find differentiating solutions and would bring about a transitional solution, in particular for marriages which had already been in existence for twenty years and more on entry into force of the First Marriage Law Reform Act.

5. a) Two sons born in 1956 and 1958, who suffer from haemophilia, issued from the marriage, concluded in 1954, of the complainant re II 4, who was born in 1924. A divorce petition of the husband, who was born in 1920, and moved out of the marital dwelling in March 1969, was rejected in April 1969. The complainant's husband has been living with another woman since roughly the end of 1969. The complainant has been operating the joint coal trading company alone since the separation. On the motion of the husband, the marriage was dissolved by divorce in 1978 because the breakdown of the marriage was irrefutably presumed after more than three years' separation (§ 1566.2 of the Civil Code) and because it was said to have been established unambiguously that the marriage had broken down de facto. The appeal on points of fact and law was rejected. The breakdown principle was

said to be constitutionally unobjectionable; it was said that the hardship clause could no longer be applied after more than five years of separation (§ 1568.2 of the Civil Code).

b) The complainant complains of a violation of Article 6.1 of the Basic Law. The constitution was said to be bound by the concept of marriage which constituted an independent value in the Creation system, which was in principle indissoluble and may not be dissolved against the will of the spouse who was not at fault. It was said that the legislature, by contrast, had constituted a "calendar divorce" with the new provision. There was said to be basically no need for a judicial ruling to dissolve a marriage after "termination" by the spouse seeking divorce and on expiry of the three-year period. It was said to be sufficient here for a registrar to act. The divorce law contained in the First Marriage Law Reform Act was also said to contradict the general legal principle that no one was to obtain advantages from their own misconduct. Since she had sacrificed years of her life to her family because of the unusually wearing work in the household and in the shop, divorce was said to constitute an unreasonable hardship for her, especially after the long separation from her husband. The dissolution of her marriage by divorce was said, finally, to violate her dignity as a wife and mother and to restrict her right to the free development of her personality as a wife.

III.

1. The German *Bundestag* has acceded to the proceedings. It made its statement in the oral hearing.

2. The Federal Minister of Justice, who made a statement on behalf of the Federal Government, considers §§ 1565.1 sentence 1 and 1566 of the Civil Code, which have been submitted for review, to be compatible with the Basic Law and the constitutional complaints to be unfounded.

…

3. The *Land* Governments of Hesse and North Rhine-Westphalia, as well as the Senates of the Free Hanseatic City of Bremen and of the Free and Hanseatic City of Hamburg, which have acceded to the proceedings, have like the Senate of Berlin concurred with the statement of the Federal Minister of Justice.

4. The Federal Court of Justice (*Bundesgerichtshof*) has pointed to the ruling of the Fourth Civil Senate, which has jurisdiction for family-law cases, on the new di-

vorce law (Decisions of the Federal Court of Justice in Civil Matters (*Entscheidungen des Bundesgerichtshofes in Zivilsachen* – BGHZ) 74, 38; 74, 86).

IV.

…

B. – I.

The submission is admissible.
According to the grounds of the submission order, the ruling of the court on the wife's motion in the original proceedings is contingent on the validity of § 1565.1 sentence 1 of the Civil Code. By contrast, it does not emerge from the facts presented that § 1566 of the Civil Code is material for the ruling on the legal evaluation; according to the findings of the submitting court, the spouses are not petitioning for divorce together (§ 1566.1 of the Civil Code) and also have not yet been separated for three years (§ 1566.2 of the Civil Code).

II.

The constitutional complaints are admissible.
Given that the legal remedies have been exhausted, they directly address the impugned rulings of the Local Courts and of the Higher Regional Courts, and indirectly address provisions of the First Marriage Law Reform Act.

C.

The view of the submitting court cannot be concurred with.
The constitutional complaints are unfounded.

I.

1. The provision contained in § 1565.1 sentence 1 of the Civil Code, according to which a marriage may be dissolved by divorce without regard for fault if the conjugal community of the spouses no longer exists, and it cannot be expected that the spouses restore it, does not violate Article 6.1 of the Basic Law.
a) Marriage and the family enjoy the particular protection of the state order. According to the structural principles guaranteed by Article 6.1 of the Basic Law, which are not at the disposal of the legislature, the pre-defined institution of mar-

riage makes of the union of a husband and wife a comprehensive, fundamentally indissoluble partnership (see Decisions of the Federal Constitutional Court (*Entscheidungen des Bundesverfassungsgerichts* – BVerfGE) 10, 59 (66)). The principle of the life-long nature of marriage, which is explicitly recognised in § 1353.1 of the Civil Code and has been made the guiding principle of the law on marriage, means that the marriage is intended and promised by both parties as a permanent community and that, according to its content, it is also established for a lifetime.

Having said that, the spouses can fail in the task of bringing about the life-long personal community by fateful entanglements and causes, or those for which they are responsible. Marriages can break down without state legislation being able to maintain or restore them. The principle of protection enshrined in the constitution hence does not guarantee a life-long marriage in abstract terms, but in the shape in which it corresponds to the prevailing views which have been expressed in the statutory regulation. Accordingly, the constitution is based on the picture of a "secularised" civil-law marriage, which also entails that the spouses can be divorced under the preconditions prescribed by the statutes, and hence can regain their freedom to conclude marriage (BVerfGE 31, 58 (82-83) with further references).

The legislature has a considerable margin of appreciation when it comes to regulating on the preconditions for the dissolution of marriage, but is bound here by the constitutional guarantee of marriage which is said to be in principle indissoluble (BVerfGE 31, 58 (69-70)). For this reason, divorce law must also contain elements which are to maintain marriage. Divorce must constitute an exception for the legal order.

b) According to these principles, the legislature is empowered to determine the principles according to which divorce law is to be shaped. It is in particular not prevented from taking the breakdown principle, instead of the fault principle, as a basis in regulating the grounds for divorce.

The legislature considered the dependence of the dissolution of marriage on elements of fault to be in need of reform for a variety of reasons. It was said to be seldom successful to establish clearly which of the two spouses had culpably caused the breakdown of the marriage. There were also said to be no sufficient standards which were binding in each case for when the conduct of one of the spouses constituted marital misconduct. Respect for the personality was said to make it appear to be undesirable for the judge to have to research the spouses' inner circumstances. The dispute regarding the establishment of fault as a precondition for divorce and as a basis for the regulation of the consequences of divorce is said to exacerbate the personal tensions between the spouses unnecessarily. Finally, the pronunciation of fault was said to be overvalued because one-off serious marital misconduct would

lead, even after decades of trouble-free marriage, to a loss of maintenance claims (reasoning of the draft Bill of the Federal Government (*Bundestag* printed paper – *BTDrucks.* 7/650 pp. 72 et seq.)).
According to these constitutionally unobjectionable considerations, the breakdown principle, which is fundamentally independent of fault, is not intended to call the institution of marriage established for life into question by making divorce easier, but to shape the process of the dissolution of marriage in a more humane, truthful and factual manner. The transition to the breakdown principle pure and simple does entail major changes in divorce law; the principle of the incurable breakdown of a marriage, which could be established using objective circumstances, could however be made to form the basis of the new divorce law without the boundaries drawn by Article 6.1 of the Basic Law being overstepped.
2. § 1566.2 of the Civil Code does not violate Article 6.1 of the Basic Law.
a) In § 1566.2 of the Civil Code, the legislature established the irrefutable presumption that a marriage had broken down if the spouses had been living apart for three years. According to the definition contained in § 1567.1 sentence 1 of the Civil Code, the spouses are separated if there is no domestic community between them and one spouse recognisably does not intend to create this.
Constitutional reservations have been raised against § 1566.2 of the Civil Code: Taking a specific separation period as a basis, which – independently of the question of the actual breakdown of marriage – was intended in principle, at the wish of only one spouse and against the declared will of the other, to lead to the dissolution of marriage, was said to be comparable to the legal institution of termination, which was said not to be compatible with the concept that marriage is established for life … By contrast, Article 6.1 of the Basic Law was said in substantive-law terms to permit divorce only in the event of an objective breakdown of the marriage. It was said in this respect that a refutable presumption based on a longer separation of homes was constitutionally unobjectionable as a regulation on the burden of proof; that a marriage could be said to have broken down after a three-year separation was said to correspond to experience. However, the irrefutable presumption was said to be unconstitutional; it was said to substitute the breakdown element by the expiry of a separation period, so that marriages which had not broken down would also be dissolved. Article 6.1 of the Basic Law was however said to require very strict individual case justice. Also the possibility of a suspension according to § 614 of the Code of Civil Procedure was said not to eliminate the breach of the constitution; suspension was said to bring about only a delay, but not a refusal of divorce with marriages which had not broken down on expiry of the three-year separation period ….

The problem arising, namely of an irrefutable presumption of breakdown, had been discussed in detail during the legislative procedure. The majority of the members of the Committee on Legal Affairs stated (*Bundestag* printed paper 7/4361 pp. 12-13) that in contradistinction to the initial appearance a refutable presumption had consequences which were inimical to marriage which also did not serve the interest of the spouse who was against divorce. If the party opposing divorce was able to submit objections to the breakdown of his or her marriage without a time limit, then the party seeking divorce would not await the three-year separation period, but would file suit immediately. This would however completely eliminate any remaining chances to restore the marital partnership. The party seeking divorce would avoid desirable contacts with his or her spouse, but in many cases also with the children, during the separation period in order to avoid his or her spouse later presenting the marriage as not having broken down. What is more, were there to be a refutable presumption, the family courts could be forced by the party opposing divorce to penetrate the spouses' private and intimate spheres for an unlimited time although they were seldom able to ascertain the truth on the course taken by and the status of a marriage according to the facilities available to them to obtain knowledge.

b) According to its wording, Article 6.1 of the Basic Law in any case requires the state order to afford special protection to marriage and the family. This broad wording already clearly labels the provision – also – as a fundamental provision for the whole law relating to marriage and the family (BVerfGE 6, 55 (72)). Accordingly, the legislature is constitutionally required to regulate divorce law in such a manner that the dissolution of marriages by divorce which have not broken down is avoided. It has not violated this obligation through the form taken by § 1566.2 of the Civil Code.

The consequence of the provision is as a rule that the judge does not have to establish the breakdown of marriage, but must already grant a divorce when the separation has endured for three years. Nonetheless, this regulation remains within the statutory margin of appreciation. The legislature was able to presume that as a rule a marriage has broken down once the partners have been separated for three years under the preconditions named in § 1567.1 of the Civil Code and that, moreover, the considerations presented previously justify placing any doubts remaining in individual cases in a secondary position. Even in these cases, the three-year period does not merely lead to an "automatic divorce" as a result of the passage of time. Rather, according to the new law, the granting of the divorce, for which the judge is responsible, is not forgone. According to § 614 of the Code of Civil Procedure, the family judge is obliged, by suspending the divorce proceedings, to attempt to maintain a marriage which according to his or her free conviction has not yet ultimately broken down. This by itself is conditional on the judge exploring possibilities for reconciliation and carrying out a clarifying discussion with the spouses once more. In each case, the spouse opposing divorce also still has the possibility to be heard by the court after a three-year separation and to explain for what personal reasons he or she rejects divorce.

What is more, the absoluteness of the three-year arrangement is weakened by § 1568.1 of the Civil Code, which permits the maintenance of even a broken down marriage over and above this period under certain conditions.

3. It cannot be ascertained that § 1568.2 of the Civil Code violates the Basic Law.

a) Four justices whose view carries the ruling consider § 1568.2 of the Civil Code to be compatible with Article 6.1 of the Basic Law.

The hardship arrangement contained in § 1568 of the Civil Code relates to marriages which have already broken down. That a marriage has broken down after a five-year separation of the partners corresponds to experience. The indefinite maintenance of such marriages can also not be derived from Article 6.1 of the Basic Law insofar as this fundamental right guarantees marriage as a legal institution. This guarantee obliges the legislature to guarantee marriage in the shape of a community established for a lifetime as an element of the private legal order. Also, marriage as a legal institution may however not be regarded in isolation from the fact that it is a partnership between two partners which rests on their consensus and that its essence includes the lived realisation of the marital community. In view of this strong personal connection of the institutional guarantee, it is by no means possible to derive from Article 6.1 of the Basic Law the obligation to permanently maintain broken down marriages as a forced community against the sustained rejection of one of the two spouses, and to impose on them a prohibition of re-marriage for life. As Beitzke (*Zeitschrift für Rechtsvergleichung* – ZfRV 1972, p. 1) and also the Matrimonial Law Commission (*Vorschläge zur Reform des Ehescheidungsrechts und des Unterhaltsrechts nach der Ehescheidung*, 1970, p. 34) have explained, such a requirement would be difficult to bring into line with the guiding perception of marriage contained in the Basic Law and its significance, and could be more likely to distort this perception. In any case, the legislature is not prevented from declaring broken down marriages to be dissoluble after a suitable period and accommodating the ongoing personal responsibility of the spouses for one another by an arrangement on the consequences of divorce. With this arrangement on the consequences, but not through refusal of divorce, is it also possible to take account of conduct on the part of a spouse which is calculated to destroy the marriage.

The consequential effects after separation and divorce include the provisions on maintenance and pensions (BVerfGE 22, 93 (96-94)), as well as the division of the joint assets (BVerfGE 42, 64 (77); 47, 85 (100)). Over and above this, an obligation emerges from Article 6.1 of the Basic Law as a consequence of a marriage established for life and to protect the partner who opposes divorce, even with broken down marriages to prevent divorce coming at an inopportune time and to make it easier for the spouse who opposes divorce to become accustomed to the changed situation. Insofar as this obligation exists, the legislature has complied with it by means of the hardship arrangement contained in § 1568 of the Civil Code. Accordingly, with the time limit contained in § 1568.2 of the Civil Code even a broken down marriage should not be dissolved as long as the divorce would constitute such a grievous hardship for the party rejecting it because of extraordinary circumstances that maintenance of the marriage, also taking account of the interests of the other spouse, appears to be necessary by way of exception. The legislature was in principle not obliged to enact a further regulation. The actual hardship linked with the breakdown of a marriage for the parties concerned can in any case not be remedied with a legal hardship clause.

It is however conceivable that the granting of divorce can affect the spouse who opposes divorce at an inopportune time, even on expiry of five years after separation, that is if the circumstances giving rise to the hardship do not occur until after this time. The Agent of the Federal Government also did not rule out this possibility in the oral hearing and admitted on enquiry that a further power of the judge to suspend the proceedings could be justified here. It is not to be ruled upon whether, in the meantime, the current statutory regulation could be constitutionally objectionable for certain case constellations. The circumstances on which the constitutional complaints are based do not provide such an indication.

b) According to the view of the four other justices, the time limit of the hardship clause contained in § 1568.2 of the Civil Code is not compatible with the Basic Law. In their view, a time-limited hardship clause cannot serve its purpose if the hardship which the statute is to avoid lasts beyond the statutory deadline of five years or does not arise until after the deadline has passed. Such cases cannot be ruled out given the diversity of life.

At the same time, despite its restricted area of application, the hardship clause contained in § 1568.1 of the Civil Code still does justice to the constitutional boundaries of the statutory margin of appreciation in the first five years of separation according to Article 6.1 of the Basic Law. Insofar as the provision however relates to hardships in the non-economic area, its time limit as defined by § 1568.2 of the Civil Code is unconstitutional. Also on expiry of a five-year separation period, it remains required to continue to maintain a broken down marriage if, because of extraordinary circumstances, divorce would also constitute thereafter such a serious hardship for the spouse holding onto marriage that the maintenance of the marriage appears necessary by way of exception, even considering the interests of the other

spouse. Such cases may well be rare. Any consideration that the legislature only has to regulate on typical cases is however ruled out when it comes to marriage, as is guaranteed in Article 6.1 of the Basic Law. It may remain unanswered whether a settlement regulation over and above § 614 of the Code of Civil Procedure could suffice in case constellations in which the time limit arrangement contained in § 1568.2 of the Civil Code does not comply with the constitutional requirements; § 1568.2 of the Civil Code is already not compatible with the Basic Law because of the lack of such a regulation.
c) According to the view of two justices who have at the same time constitutional reservations against the irrefutable presumption contained in § 1566.2 of the Civil Code, it may even be necessary for marriages to remain indissoluble until the death of a spouse.
The guarantee of marriage lying in Article 6.1 of the Basic Law does not end when it breaks down. Traditional and current divorce law hence also does not place the broken down marriage at the private disposition of the spouses, but only permits divorce under substantive and formal preconditions which are governed in detail. The legislature has a considerable margin of appreciation in shaping these preconditions. However, the constitution requires that a responsibility of the spouses for one another also going beyond the broken down marriage does not remain entirely unconsidered. Also the confidence of the spouse holding onto the marriage that the other cannot deliberately and maliciously terminate the marriage must be protected. Otherwise, a guarantee of "marriage in principle concluded for life" becomes bereft of any substance for the marriage that has broken down.
The mutual responsibility of the spouses for one another in a marriage that has broken down can also not be considered solely by the valid law on the consequences of divorce corresponding to this fundamental concept. Marriage as an institution related to both spouses still belongs to the area of responsibility of the spouse seeking to leave the marriage. The breakdown of marriage reduces this responsibility. The boundary is however overstepped where the legislature gives to the spouse seeking to leave the marriage the possibility to invoke his or her own action in neglecting marital duties as a lever in order to have the marriage dissolved. The legislature may hence not make the dissolution of marriage already dependent on the one-sided decision of only one spouse.

II.

Article 12 no. 3.1 of the First Marriage Law Reform Act, according to which the provisions of this Act on divorce also apply to the dissolution of a marriage if the marriage was concluded prior to its entry into force, is compatible with the Basic Law.

1. In principle it is a matter for the legislature to determine whether a field of law requires a reform, and from when the new provision is to apply (BVerfGE 47, 85 (93)). It has a broad margin of appreciation for the transition. Many graduations are conceivable, between immediate entry into force of the new law with no transition, and the unrestricted continued application of the existing legal positions. It is necessary to weigh between confidence in the continuation of the legal situation according to the previous statutory provision and the significance of the legislative matter for the good of the public. Only the matter of whether the legislature has overstepped the boundary of what is reasonable is subject to review by the Federal Constitutional Court in an overall weighing between the gravity of the encroachment and the weight and the urgency of the reasons justifying it, taking account of all circumstances (BVerfGE 43, 242 (286 and 288-289) with further references).

2. When adopting new provisions on divorce in the shape of the First Marriage Law Reform Act, the legislature presumed, as stated above, that the fault principle, on which the previous divorce law was largely based, demonstrated grievous shortcomings and led to considerable injustices in many cases, particularly insofar as the legal consequences of divorce were also linked to a party being at fault with regard to the divorce. On the basis of these considerations, which are in line with the values of Article 6.1 of the Basic Law and with the Basic Law as a whole, it would have meant a legal inequality which would have been difficult to tolerate if during a longer period, possibly still after decades, some marriages continued to be dealt with according to the fault-based divorce law, which was regarded as obsolete and suffering from shortcomings, and the question of the dissolubility of marriage, which is of the utmost importance for those concerned, had been ruled on differently, depending on the time of the conclusion of marriage. Avoiding this legal inequality constitutes a major general interest which justifies the new divorce law coming into force for all marriages to be dissolved after 1 July 1977.

On the other hand, the confidence of the spouse holding onto marriage that it was not possible for a marriage which could not be dissolved under the previous law to be dissolved in future by means of an amendment to the law on divorce did not require protection to such a degree as to render maintenance of the previous legal situation necessary for prior marriages. The economic interests of the spouses principally concerned are in principle to be maintained in the form taken by the law on the consequences of divorce. In this sense, the First Marriage Law Reform Act was intended to improve the legal position of the economically dependent spouse in major areas. Whether the valid law on the consequences of divorce and the concomi-

tant transitional provisions meet the constitutional requirements is not to be reviewed in the instant proceedings.
When evaluating the negative interest of spouses who entered into marriage prior to the entry into force of the First Marriage Law Reform Act, it should further be considered that marriages were already largely dissoluble according to the previous law. It is true that, with a divorce petition because of three-year suspension of the domestic community (§ 48 of the Marriage Act (*Ehegesetz* – EheG)), the respondent spouse did have a right of objection under certain circumstances (§ 48.2 of the Marriage Act). This was however linked to the relatively indefinite preconditions, which particularly after a longer separation period could frequently only be established with uncertainty, that the spouse seeking divorce was completely or largely at fault in causing the breakdown of the marriage, and that the respondent spouse did not lack a commitment to the marriage and a reasonable willingness to continue the marriage.
Over and above this, prior to the entry into force of the First Marriage Law Reform Act, a spouse already had to consider the possibility of an amendment to the divorce provisions, namely one towards more stringent implementation of the breakdown principle. Prior to the new provision in the First Marriage Law Reform Act, divorce law had been contentious in legal policy for a long time, and reforms which were to introduce the breakdown principle had been repeatedly called for, and also tackled in part. If, however, divorce law was amended, it was necessary at the same time to expect – in line with the transitional law that was in force until that time in that respect (see Article 201 of the Introductory Act to the Civil Code (*Einführungsgesetz zum Bürgerlichen Gesetzbuch* – EGBGB); §§ 84 and 93 et seq. of the Marriage Act of 6 July 1938 (*Reich* Law Gazette (*Reichsgesetzblatt* – RGBl.) I p. 807)) – that the new law would also apply to marriages concluded during the term of application of the old law.
3. The application of the new divorce law to prior marriages is also constitutionally unobjectionable insofar as these are marriages which have been in existence for longer, for instance those which had already been in existence for twenty years or longer on entry into force of the First Marriage Law Reform Act. Spouses in such marriages, insofar as they have trusted in the continued application of the old divorce law, may admittedly find it more difficult to adjust to the new law. On the other hand, however, particularly with older marriages, especially if the spouses had been separated for a long period and one of them had entered a new union from which children had issued, there was in many cases now a special need to open up the possibility for divorce. That the legislature, taking account of these contradictory interests, has enacted a general transitional regulation, and has not distinguished

between shorter and longer "prior marriages", was within the margin of appreciation at its disposal.
From the point of view of the constitutional protection of legitimate expectations, the legislature was also not obliged with regard to the separation periods which are important according to §§ 1566.2 and 1568.2 of the Civil Code to create a transitional regulation such that the periods did not start to run with the de facto separation, but only after the entry into force of the First Marriage Law Reform Act. The period lying between the proclamation of the Act on 15 June 1976 and the entry into force of the impugned provisions on 1 July 1977 was sufficient for each spouse to become accustomed to the new law.

Justices: Dr. Benda, Dr. Simon, Dr. Faller, Dr. Hesse, Dr. Katzenstein, Dr. Niemeyer, Dr. Heußner; Justice Dr. Böhmer is unable to attend for signing.

No. 11

BVerfGE 55, 171
of 5 November 1980 – 1 BvR 349/80 –
"Custody case"

HEADNOTES:

1. **The arrangement, orientated in line with the child's best interests, that the will of the child is to be taken into account in rulings on custody after the divorce of the parents (§ 1671.2 of the Civil Code), and hence that his or her personal hearing by the court that is handing down the ruling will, as a rule, be required (§ 50b of the Act on Matters of Non-Contentious Jurisdiction), is in compliance with the Basic Law.**
2. **The ruling on which form of the hearing of the child appears to be suited and to have prospects of success is determined according to the circumstances of the individual case; it is a matter for the family courts with jurisdiction and in principle is removed from subsequent constitutional review.**

Order of the First Senate of 5 November 1980
– 1 BvR 349/80 –

in the proceedings regarding the constitutional complaint 1. of Mr. L., 2. of the child L., represented by his father L. – authorised representative: ..., lawyer – against the order of the Munich Higher Regional Court (*Oberlandesgericht*) of 5 March 1980 – 16 UF 868/79 –.

RULING:

The constitutional complaint is rejected as unfounded.

EXTRACT FROM GROUNDS:

A.

The constitutional complaint relates to a judicial arrangement according to which parental custody for the son issuing from the dissolved marriage of the complainant re 1) has been assigned to the mother.

I.

The ruling on parental custody for a child who is the issue of a dissolved marriage is determined according to § 1671 of the Civil Code (*Bürgerliches Gesetzbuch* – BGB).

The provision, originally created by the Act on Equal Rights of Men and Women in the Field of Civil Law (*Gesetz über die Gleichberechtigung von Mann und Frau auf dem Gebiete des bürgerlichen Rechts*) of 18 June 1957 (Federal Law Gazette (*Bundesgesetzblatt* – BGBl.) I p. 609) was re-worded by the First Act Reforming the Law on Marriage and Family (*Erstes Gesetz zur Reform des Ehe- und Familienrechts*) of 14 June 1976 (Federal Law Gazette I p. 1421). This took into account the abolition of the fault principle in the law on divorce. § 1671 of the Civil Code has applied since 1 January 1980 in the version of the Act Reforming the Law on Parental Custody (*Gesetz zur Neuregelung des Rechts der elterlichen Sorge* – SorgeRG) of 18 July 1979 (Federal Law Gazette I p. 1061) – Custody Act –:

> (1) If the parents' marriage is dissolved by divorce, the family court shall determine which parent shall have parental custody for a joint child.
> (2) The court shall make the arrangement which is most beneficial to the child's best interests; the child's ties, in particular to his or her parents and siblings, shall be taken into account here.
> (3) The court should only derogate from an agreed proposal made by the parents if this is necessary in the child's best interests. If a child who has reached the age of 14 makes a derogating proposal, the court shall rule according to subsection 2.
> (4) to (6) …

Prior to the entry into force of the Custody Act, the court was able to "personally get to know the child" according to § 1695.2 of the Civil Code. The personal hearing of the child is now regulated in greater detail in § 50b of the Act on Matters of

Non-Contentious Jurisdiction (*Gesetz über die Angelegenheiten der freiwilligen Gerichtsbarkeit* – FGG):

> (1) The court shall hear the child personally in proceedings relating to the care of the person or of the property of the child if the inclinations, the ties or the will of the child are significant to the ruling, or if it appears suitable that the court obtains a direct impression of the child in order to ascertain the facts.
> (2) If a child has reached the age of fourteen and is not incapable of entering into legal transactions, the court shall always hear the child in person in proceedings related to the care of the person. The child should be heard in person in property matters if this appears to be in keeping with the nature of the matter. Unless disadvantages are to be feared for his or her development or upbringing, the child should be informed at the hearing of the subject-matter and possible outcome of the proceedings in a suitable manner; he or she shall be afforded the opportunity to make a statement.
> 3) In the cases falling under subsection 1 and subsection 2 sentence 1, the court may only refrain from holding the hearing for serious reasons. If the hearing does not take place merely because a delay is likely to jeopardise the success, it shall be subsequently held without delay.
> 4) …

II.

1. The marriage of the complainant re 1) – hereinafter: complainant –, which was concluded in 1965, was dissolved in 1978. Two children issued from the marriage: A daughter who is today fourteen and who has had a walking disability since 1974 because of a bone marrow infection, and a seven-year-old son. The divorced wife of the complainant left the marital home in August 1976, taking the son, who was three years old at that time, and moved in with a man in another town, with whom she has lived since then; she is working in her former profession again. The daughter was in hospital at the time of the separation of the spouses.

Parental power (*elterliche Gewalt*) for both children was assigned to the complainant by means of an injunction in September 1976. The children have lived with him since then. The complainant is a civil servant in a rural community.

Once the divorce judgment had become final, both the complainant and his former wife claimed parental power for both children. After hearing the competent youth welfare offices, which both favoured assigning custody to the parent whom they reported on, the Local Court (*Amtsgericht*) assigned parental power of the daughter to the complainant and that of the son to the mother. The court presumed that both parents were suited to bring up the children, and went on to state: Since the daughter had clearly come out in favour of remaining with her father and, with regard to her continuing disability, a change of environment would entail major difficulties in readjusting, she was to be left with the father. By contrast, the son, who had not opted unambiguously for one or other parent at his court hearing, could be looked after better by the mother, who in future intended to only work half-time. A mother who was able to largely care for her biological child in person was as a rule to be granted preference in assigning parental power. This was said not to run counter to the principle that children from a failed marriage should not be separated wherever possible; one could presume that they had completely different interests because of the age difference between the siblings and of their different genders.

2. The complainant unsuccessfully appealed to the Higher Regional Court against this ruling. The court reasoned its ruling of 5 March 1980 as follows: It was stated to be necessary to assign parental custody of the son to the mother. The complainant, who otherwise had not missed a single opportunity to make derogatory statements about his former wife, had been unable to submit anything against her ability to care for and bring up the child. By contrast, the complainant had shown himself to be quick-tempered and lacking in self-control. These were said to be characteristics that had a disadvantageous impact on bringing up children as a rule. Particular significance was said to attach to the fact that the complainant, as he himself had stated, spoke about the problems of his failed marriage with the children. Even taking into account the circumstances as they stood, it was clearly beyond his ability to bring up a small child with the necessary attention and to protect the child from unnecessary burdens if he weighed the child down with his own disappointments. Finally, it was said to be of vital importance that the son could be better cared for by the mother, who in future was only going to work half-time, rather than in the household of the father, who worked full-time, even taking the help of the sister into account. Even though the father had done his utmost in order to provide the children with the things necessary in everyday life, it could not be overlooked that his son obviously needed special care and attention for his personal development; it had come to note that he was unable to answer the court's question as to "why he was there", and had reacted by crying when practiced phrases had not been accepted as answers.

III.

With the constitutional complaint, the complainant claims for himself and his son a violation of fundamental rights and of rights equivalent to these: The Higher Regional Court was said to have disregarded the impact of fundamental rights on civil

law and to have handed down an arbitrary ruling which was not compatible with Article 3.1 of the Basic Law (*Grundgesetz* – GG). Without sufficient reasoning, it had deviated both from the principles of continuity of upbringing of children, as well as from the prohibition of separation of siblings, and from regard for the external living conditions. The impugned ruling was said to have torn the existing remaining family apart against its will and to have removed the son from his previous, familiar environment. Hence, firstly, the fundamental rights of the son under Article 1.1 and Article 2.1 of the Basic Law were said to have been violated and, secondly, the remaining family, which should have been protected by Article 6.1 of the Basic Law, had been damaged in a manner that was not permissible. Furthermore, the impugned order was said to cause detriment both to the parental right of the complainant under Article 6.2 of the Basic Law and to the fundamental right of the complainant and of his son for the child to remain in the family (Article 6.3 of the Basic Law). Finally, the right of the child to freedom of movement (Article 11 of the Basic Law) was also said to have been impaired.
Over and above this, the complainant claims that the hearing of the son had not been carried out by the judge commissioned by the Senate in a manner suited to a child, but in an unsuitable, inquisitory manner. This was said to have made his son insecure, and his hearing unsuccessful. The form of his hearing, which was said to be incompatible with the dignity of the child, as well as the ruling based thereon, was said to have made it clear that the judge who had been commissioned had not had the necessary personal and factual independence. Hence, the constitutional principle of the lawful judge was said to have been violated (Article 101.1 sentence 2 of the Basic Law). What is more, the son was said in this respect not to have been granted a legal hearing in the manner required by Article 103.1 of the Basic Law.
The complainant goes on to complain that, after the oral hearing by the judge who had been commissioned, the Higher Regional Court had surprisingly ruled without a further oral hearing before the entire Senate; this was said to have violated his right to a legal hearing.
Finally, the complainant complains that the lawful judge had also been removed by virtue of the fact that the Higher Regional Court, in contradistinction to § 546.1 sentence 2 no. 2 of the Code of Civil Procedure (*Zivilprozeßordnung* – ZPO), had not admitted the further complaint although it had deviated from the established supreme court case-law with its ruling.
…

B.

The admissible constitutional complaint is unfounded.

I.

If divorced spouses are unable to agree on exercising the parental responsibility incumbent on them for the joint children after divorce, the state is called upon to decide through the courts on the opposing interests of the parents. This obligation emerges, firstly, from the task to uphold the legal order and legal peace, and secondly from the role of watchdog assigned to it by Article 6.2 sentence 2 of the Basic Law (BVerfGE 31, 194 (205)). This places the child, as a being with his or her own human dignity and a right to the free development of his or her personality, under the special protection of the state (BVerfGE 24, 119 (144)). The children of parents who are fighting for custody are not themselves parties to the custody proceedings. The custody arrangement however has a vital influence on their ongoing lives, and hence affects them directly. Any judicial solution of a conflict between parents which has an impact on the future of the child must hence be orientated towards the child's best interests and take account of the child in his or her individuality as a holder of fundamental rights (see BVerfGE 37, 217 (252)). Because of its obligations to provide protection, which emerge from Article 6.2 sentence 2 and Article 2.1 of the Basic Law, the state has to create statutory provisions for custody proceedings, in substantive and procedural terms, that guarantee adequate consideration of the fundamental rights status of the child in question.

This requirement is met by the provisions of the Custody Act which are material here, and which entered into force on 1 January 1980.

1. Apart from the fact that the term "parental power" (*elterliche Gewalt*) has been replaced by "parental custody" (*elterliche Sorge*) in adjustment to the new linguistic usage, the re-wording of § 1671 of the Civil Code places the child's ties, and those to his or her parents and siblings in particular, more than was previously the case at the centre of the custody ruling which becomes necessary following the failure of a marriage.

The substantive arrangement recognisably orientated towards the child's best interests is supplemented in the field of procedural law. It is according to the provision contained in § 50b of the Act on Matters of Non-Contentious Jurisdiction, introduced by Article 5 no. 2 of the Custody Act, that the court is to hear the child in person in custody proceedings in which inclinations, ties or the will of the child are significant to the ruling, unless serious reasons – such as a risk to the child's best interests (see *Bundestag* printed paper (*Bundestagsdrucksache* – BTDrucks.) 8/2788, p. 74) – are against a hearing. As emerges from § 50b.1 of the Act on Matters of Non-Contentious Jurisdiction, the legislature furthermore presumed that, with children under the age of 14, it was in principle also a matter of the court gaining a direct impression of them (*Bundestag* printed paper 8/2788, p. 73-74).

2. Creation by the legislature of a statutory arrangement for custody rulings, in particular as to the nature of the regulations on hearings, that is in line with the constitutional requirements does not by itself ensure the defence of the child's best interests in custody proceedings. In the legislative proceedings, the Committee on Legal Affairs shared the view of the Committee on Youth, Family Affairs and Health, which was consulted on the matter, that the judges working at family and guardianship courts were to be made familiar with the fundamental principles of education and psychology through basic and further training, and hence enabled to hear the children and juveniles themselves to a greater extent than previously (*Bundestag* printed paper 8/2788, p. 42). The problem of a hearing which is in keeping with the needs of children can hence ultimately not be solved by the legislature. It is, rather, the difficult task of the family judge to structure the hearing as far as possible in line with the individual circumstances (see on this Arntzen, *Elterliche Sorge und persönlicher Umgang mit Kindern aus gerichtspsychologischer Sicht*, pp. 51 et seq.).

II.

The design of the proceedings, the determination and valuation of the facts, as well as the interpretation and application of constitutionally unobjectionable regulations in the individual case, is in principle a matter for the non-constitutional courts with jurisdiction in the field, and is therefore removed from subsequent review by the Federal Constitutional Court. Only if the ruling is based on a fundamentally incorrect view of the significance and scope of a fundamental right is the intervention of the Federal Constitutional Court required (BVerfGE 18, 85 (92-93); 32, 311 (316); 42, 143 (148-149); 49, 304 (314)).
The impugned ruling is ultimately not based on a fundamentally incorrect view of the significance of the fundamental rights which have been complained of as having been violated.
1. It is in the child's best interests that, according to the promotion principle, the parent from whom the child can presumably expect the most support for the formation of his or her personality is to receive parental custody. It would hence not be compatible with the role of the state community as watchdog statuted in Article 6.2 sentence 2 of the Basic Law for the courts to assign custody of a child to a parent who is unable to bring up his or her child. However, the finding that aptitude for bringing up does not apply or only applies to a restricted degree impacts the parent judged in this manner in his or her fundamental rights under Article 6.2 sentence 1 and also under Article 2.1 of the Basic Law. The intensity of the possible impairment of fundamental rights and the seriousness of the impact for the party con-

cerned are manifest and could cause the Federal Constitutional Court to examine the civil law ruling based on this valuation in greater detail (see BVerfGE 35, 202 (219); 42, 143 (148-149); 42, 163 (168)), especially since the long-term fate of the child is determined by the judge's finding. The evaluation of the personality of the complainant by the Higher Regional Court, which recognisably contradicts the findings of the Local Court, of the youth welfare office and of a child psychological report submitted in the proceedings, appears to be objectionable, but does not justify any further review by the Federal Constitutional Court, given that ultimately the impugned ruling is also not constitutionally objectionable if one presumes the unrestricted ability of the complainant to bring up a child.

2. a) As the Federal Constitutional Court has ruled, the protection of fundamental rights largely influences the form and the implementation of procedural law (BVerfGE 53, 30 (65)). The obligation to watch over the care and upbringing of the child assigned to the state community by Article 6.2 sentence 2 of the Basic Law also triggers the constitutional impact on procedural law and the way it is dealt with by the courts in custody proceedings.

b) § 50b of the Act on Matters of Non-Contentious Jurisdiction corresponds to the constitutional principle to take account of the will of the child in custody rulings insofar as this is compatible with his or her best interests. A ruling which does justice to the interests of the child can, as a rule, only be handed down if the child has been afforded the possibility to make clear his or her personal ties to the other family members in the judicial proceedings. In order to guarantee this, the family courts must shape their manner of proceeding in the individual case, taking account of the age of the individual child, and of his or her state of development, above all considering his or her psychological state, which is frequently made particularly tense by the dispute between the parents, so that the court can recognise as reliably as possible the basis of a ruling which is orientated in line with the child's best interests. Which of the available procedural possibilities they select, whether they hear the children in person once or several times, whether they hear siblings individually or together, in the court or in their familiar family environment, in the presence or absence of the parents and of their counsel, and whether they consult a psychologist as an expert witness, must be left to the family courts. The judge handing down the ruling must retain the right to decide as to which path he or she considers suitable to take within the procedural code prescribed to him or her in order to obtain the information necessary for his or her ruling. The outcome and the success of a personal hearing of the child by the court will however depend vitally on the degree to which the judge has the ability to place himself or herself in the particular psychological situation of the child and whether he or she is able to enter into a dialogue with the child.

c) The Higher Regional Court ordered the complainant's children to be heard in person. It hence made it clear that in this set of proceedings, in which objections against the judgment of the Local Court on the ties of the children to their parents and to one another were lodged by both the complaint and by the subsequent complaint of the mother, and in which de facto changes had been claimed, it considered it to be necessary to hear the children in person. The judge who was commissioned however interrupted the hearing of the son, who at that time was six-and-a-half years old, when it emerged that the child was unable to answer her questions. The cause of the child's insecurity – that the hearing by the judge was hardly in keeping with the needs of children, as the complainant opines, or that the child was unable to bear up to the mental strain generally linked with his hearing – is not a matter for review by the Federal Constitutional Court. It can be presumed that insurmountable psychological hindrances at this court session prevented a further hearing of the complainant's son. Whether it was necessary to attempt a further hearing of the child at a later point in time could only be determined by the court. The latter was also to judge whether here, for serious reasons, the hearing of the child should not be repeated (§ 50b.3 of the Act on Matters of Non-Contentious Jurisdiction) or whether it was necessary to consult a psychological expert report. It might be significant for the ruling here that younger children are frequently unable to precisely explain to the court their personal ties to their parents. The child is in a conflict because by opting for one parent he or she must of necessity decide against the other, something which he or she cannot afford to do (see Lempp, *Die Ehescheidung und das Kind*, p. 22).

3. In principle it is in the child's best interests if a court, in its custody ruling relating to a child in need of care, regards the question as to the possibility of care by the parents as a major one. The younger a child is, the more important it is for his or her development that he or she knows himself or herself to be in the care of a person who has time to spend on his or her questions, wishes and needs. However, the ties of the child to his or her parents and siblings, which are particularly to be considered according to § 1671.2 of the Civil Code, must not be disregarded. If the child has nonetheless developed a closer relationship with a parent who, because of full-time employment, can provide less care than the other, this must be taken into account in the custody ruling (see also Lempp, loc. cit., p. 32); there is hence no ex ante primacy of the mother in custody arrangements if she is not employed or is only employed half-time.

The ruling impugned with the constitutional complaint confirms the custody order of the Local Court. It is hence based on the presumption that the son, whose closer tie to father could not be ascertained, will be better cared for in the future by the mother because of her half-time employment rather than by the complainant, and that this is in the child's best interests. This prognosis and the evaluation based thereon are constitutionally unobjectionable.

…

Justices: Dr. Benda, Dr. Böhmer, Dr. Simon, Dr. Faller, Dr. Hesse, Dr. Niemeyer, Dr. Heußner

No. 12

BVerfGE 57, 170

of 5 February 1981 – 2 BvR 646/80 –

"Pre-trial detention II case (correspondence by letter)"

HEADNOTE:

Decision regarding the monitoring of letters during pre-trial detention; written correspondence between adult children and their parents.

Order of the Second Senate of 5 February 1981
– 2 BvR 646/80 –

in the proceedings regarding the constitutional complaint of Mr. G. – authorised representative: …, lawyer – against a) the order of the Düsseldorf Higher Regional Court (*Oberlandesgericht*) of 29 April 1980 – 2 WS 217/80 –, b) the order of the President of the Ninth Criminal Division of the Duisburg Regional Court (*Landgericht*) of 17 September 1979 – IX 6/79 –.

RULING:

1. The order of the Düsseldorf Higher Regional Court of 29 April 1980 – 2 WS 217/80 – violates the fundamental right of the complainant under Article 2.1 of the Basic Law (*Grundgesetz* – GG). It is reversed. The case is referred back to the Düsseldorf Higher Regional Court.
2. The *Land* (state) North Rhine-Westphalia is ordered to refund the complainant's necessary expenses.

EXTRACT FROM GROUNDS:

A. – I.

The complainant was sentenced on 20 August 1979 to five years' imprisonment by judgment of the Ninth Criminal Division of the Duisburg Regional Court because according to the court's findings he had attempted to kill his wife by causing a car to fall onto a lower schoolyard when she had stated that she intended to separate from him permanently. The complainant, who was 23 years old at the time of the offence, is described in the judgment handed down by the chamber of the court sitting with one professional and two lay judges (*Schwurgericht*) as an only child who was extremely spoilt by his parents. It characterises the complainant as having a neurotic, emotionally unstable, immature, infantile and heavily mother-fixated personality with narcissistic disturbances. Because of this mental constitution, of the unresolved marital conflicts, and of the possible after-effects of various psychiatric drugs, the judgment presumes considerably reduced capacity to understand the wrongfulness of his action. After the Federal Court of Justice (*Bundesgerichtshof*) had reversed the conviction as regards the terms of the sentence …, the punishment was reduced to four years' imprisonment by the now final judgment of the Fourteenth Grand Criminal Division of the Duisburg Regional Court of 19 August 1980. Execution of the arrest warrant was subsequently suspended.

The complainant commented on his conviction in a letter of 8 September 1979 written to his parents from pre-trial detention prior to service of the first judgment … He wrote that though innocent he had been sentenced to five years' imprisonment. He regretted "although it is a sin" that he had not really intended to kill his wife; "since if I had wanted to do it, it would have worked, after all I'm not stupid". And now everything was destroyed for him. "I have a boundless hate for six people who have destroyed my life by their arrogance and stupidity." In another place it reads: "… But I feel sorry for the limitedness of the people (meaning the judges handing down the judgment). If stupidity hurt …"

He expresses a request to establish contact with a newspaper reporter to whom he wished to relate his case. In the event of the journalist not being able to obtain a visiting permission because "those mentally limited people are scared", he knew another way. "The public must be told where the evil lies. The terrorists have recognised it, but are using the wrong means …" He said that he could well imagine what it had been like in Hitler's day, "we still seem to have mini Hitlers. But I suppose I have sworn enough now. Now I already feel much better". In another paragraph, the complainant says "Now to us three. You know that I will never give up. To the last second I will tell the pigs that I am innocent, even if it doesn't get

into their stupid skulls. I am and remain innocent! This is how I can put up with it, because my conscience is pure and my soul unburdened! All that remains is for you to hold out! Don't let the slave drivers get you down. There are enough of them giving up in here!" Finally he calls on his parents to gather new strength on holiday "so we can attack again with new strength afterwards!"
By order of 17 September 1979, the president of the Ninth Criminal Division of the Duisburg Regional Court objected to the first two pages of this letter, prohibiting their forwarding because the letter "contains gross insults suited and aimed to disparage and make appear contemptible organs of the administration of justice, and furthermore to endanger order in the prison. ... (§ 119 of the Code of Criminal Procedure (*Strafprozeßordnung* – StPO), no. 34 of the Pre-Trial Detention Code (*Untersuchungshaftvollzugsordnung* – UVollzO))". The President forwarded a duplicate of the letter to the governor of the prison. He forwarded the order to the public prosecution office with a request for a statement on whether a criminal charge would be filed in respect of the content of the impugned letter. The public prosecutor and the chief senior public prosecutor refrained from filing a charge.
On 26 September 1979, the complainant wrote to the President of the chamber of the court sitting with one professional and two lay judges: "I would like herewith to formally apologise for the letter of 8 September 1979. Please accept this apology. I believe that I expressed myself wrongly. Please allow for this circumstance."
The President brought the apology letter to the attention of the associate judges on 1 October 1979, and on 2 October 1979 noted the following in the records:

> The denoted statements ... comply with the elements of the offences under §§ 185 and 186 of the Criminal Code without justification under § 193 of the Criminal Code.
> We – the professional judges of the chamber of the court sitting with one professional and two lay judges involved in the main trial against G. – herewith file a criminal charge.

The note was also signed by the associate professional judges. The President had underlined in red the passages in the complainant's letter by which he felt insulted.
After the President of the Regional Court had refused to file a criminal charge in accordance with § 194.3 of the Criminal Code, the President of the chamber of the court forwarded the letter of the complainant and the order of 17 September 1979 to the public prosecution office, referring to the criminal charges. He submitted the complainant's apology letter to the duplicate files of the pending proceedings. The letter was not designated as evidence in the written charge against the complainant in respect of insult towards the judges. In response to a request by the Local Court

judge to whom the charge was submitted, the public prosecution office stated that the letter could be considered as evidence.

The President of the Criminal Division did not remedy the complaint against the order of the President of the Criminal Division of 17 September 1979. The complaint was essentially based on an allegation that the complainant's letter was a statement in the "insult-free intimate sphere". The public prosecution office stated in its statement that, whilst special significance attached to freedom of contact with one's closest relatives by letter with regard to the constitutional principle of respect for the intimate sphere, the complainant's letter did not limit itself to expressions of his annoyance regarding his conviction, but contained carefully worded insults targeting the judges. Under these circumstances, the President was said to be entitled to seize the letter temporarily and to forward it to the public prosecution office for further examination. …

The complaint was rejected as unfounded by order of the Düsseldorf Higher Regional Court of 29 April 1980. As grounds, the court stated that the impugned ruling was well-founded because the letter posed a danger to order in the prison. The fundamental rights of the complainant were said not to have been violated. The rulings of the Federal Constitutional Court (*Bundesverfassungsgericht*) regarding pre-trial detainees' correspondence by letter were said to relate to correspondence by letter with spouses. This was said not to be the case at hand. The same significance was said not to attach in the relationship of a long-since adult pre-trial detainee with his or her parents to freedom of contact by letter with regard to the constitutional principle of respect for the intimate sphere, this also applying to a case such as the one at hand, in which the pre-trial detainee was not able to turn to his spouse. The Senate had also become convinced that the complainant had not intended to express his annoyance in the letter, which was written almost three weeks after his conviction, but had intentionally taken the opportunity "to brazenly and directly insult" at least the president of the court. This conviction was said to be also based on the fact that the complainant, after having stated in the second paragraph of the intercepted letter that he had now sworn enough, in the third paragraph had "once more used insolent words". There was said to be a risk that, were the letter to be forwarded without complaint, this would encourage other pre-trial detainees to engage in similar insolent behaviour. This risk was said to suggest itself all the more, given that the complainant had established a kind of trusted position among his co-inmates and "knew how to get into the foreground". He was said to be a member of the "broadcasting council", so that there was allegedly no doubt that "this complainant" would boast about his insulting letter having been forwarded without complaint. This would in turn be highly probable to incite others to engage in insulting conduct against prison staff.

…

Once the complaint ruling had been handed down, the Local Court admitted the charge of insult … and opened the main proceedings.

II.

The constitutional complaint received on 14 June 1980 targets the order of the Higher Regional Court in conjunction with the order of the President of the Criminal Division. The complainant alleges a violation of his fundamental right to freedom of opinion (Article 5.1 of the Basic Law). He claims that his relationship with his parents, who are said to be the only persons with whom he has a close relationship, is allegedly equally worthy of protection in accordance with Article 6.1 of the Basic Law as the relationship between spouses. In contradistinction to the view of the Higher Regional Court, [he alleges that] it is the seizure of a letter, and not its unhindered forwarding, which leads to a risk to the image of the judiciary because it allegedly betrays fear and uncertainty, and does not give pre-trial detainees an impression of sovereignty and strength on the part of the judiciary and of its organs. Finally, he alleges that his unimpeachable conduct in pre-trial detention and the confidence of his co-inmates should not lead to further restrictions being imposed on his intimate statements towards his parents.

III.

…

B.

The constitutional complaint gives rise to a new constitutional question; it is therefore admissible. It is also well-founded.

I.

The order of the Düsseldorf Higher Regional Court of 29 April 1980 violates the complainant's fundamental right under Article 2.1 of the Basic Law.

… The freedom of action of an individual is guaranteed on the proviso of the constitutional order. Restrictions which are carried out on the basis of provisions which are constitutional in formal and substantive terms hence do not violate the fundamental right under Article 2.1 of the Basic Law. The Federal Constitutional Court has no reservations that § 119.3 of the Code of Criminal Procedure forms a constitutionally sufficient statutory basis for restrictions on pre-trial detainees' freedoms derived from fundamental rights (Decisions of the Federal Constitutional Court (*Entscheidungen des Bundesverfassungsgerichts* – BVerfGE) 35, 311 (316); established case-law). It has ruled that the correspondence by letter of a pre-trial detainee can be subject to judicial review in order to prevent a risk to the public interests referred to in § 119.3 of the Code of Criminal Procedure (BVerfGE 35, 35 (39-40)). The judge carrying out monitoring of letters must however take account of the fact that in an interpretation of § 119.3 of the Code of Criminal Procedure which allows for fundamental rights and the principle of proportionality, restrictions may only be imposed on pre-trial detainees if concrete indications exist of a disturbance to order in the prison (BVerfGE 35, 5 (10); 42, 234 (236)). With regard to the significance of Article 2.1 of the Basic Law as a fundamental freedom right, it says this for the monitoring of letters: The less concrete the risk to order in the prison, the greater weight attaches to the freedom of action of the pre-trial detainee and the more restrained the judge must be when encroaching on correspondence by letter.

The interpretation of § 119.3 of the Code of Criminal Procedure and its application to the individual case are primarily a matter for the criminal courts with jurisdiction. The Federal Constitutional Court can intervene here only if constitutional law has been violated, in particular if the impugned ruling reveals errors of interpretation indicating a fundamentally erroneous view of the meaning and scope of a fundamental right (BVerfGE 18, 85 (92-93); established case-law). This is the case here. The Higher Regional Court has ignored the scope of Article 2.1 of the Basic Law in the family area.

As the Federal Constitutional Court has ruled, the principle of respect, guaranteed by Article 2.1 of the Basic Law, for the right of development in the private sphere is particularly strengthened by the constitutional guarantee of marriage and the family (BVerfGE 42, 234 (236)). The area protected by Article 6.1 of the Basic Law also includes relations between parents and their major-age children. As defined by law, the relationship between parents and children is not limited to the function of the family of bringing up children. The traditional maintenance law arrangement clearly refers to a life-long obligation between parents and children to afford assistance to one another. By introducing § 1618a of the Civil Code (*Bürgerliches Gesetzbuch* – BGB), the legislature brought onto the statute books a model of a parent-child relationship which constitutes a mutual duty to assist and support, regardless of the age of the children. This was particularly intended to contribute to greater autonomy of families, and to counter risks to the family as an institution (see *Bundestag* printed paper (*Bundestagsdrucksache* – BTDrucks.) 8/2788 p. 43). In restricting the obligation to give testimony, also criminal procedure law has always taken account of the confidential relationship between parents and adult chil-

dren in the same way as of the relationship between spouses (§ 52 of the Code of Criminal Procedure).
The parent-child relationship takes on considerable significance in personality-related crisis situations also when it comes to the mental stabilisation of adult family members. The family provides a space that is free of public scrutiny in which a self-portrayal is possible which serves to reduce strain; it also helps to maintain the individual's ability to remain integrated into society. In this respect, the community of parents and children carries out a task similar to that of a marital community.
The view on which the order of the Düsseldorf Higher Regional Court was based – namely that the principles for the restriction of pre-trial detainees' correspondence by letter derived in the case-law of the Federal Constitutional Court from the fundamental right of Article 2.1 and from the guarantee of marriage and the family were not of equal significance in the case to be ruled on because it was not concerned with the relationship between spouses – misjudges the scope of these constitutional guarantees and also the significance which may attach to them for the relationship of a major-age child with his or her parents, in particular if his or her personality is threatened by incisive events such as the failure of marriage and a first serious conviction in respect of a criminal offence related to this conflict. When evaluating the expressions of a pre-trial detainee by letter, these constitutional guarantees require one to take account of the parent-child relationship as it presents itself in the concrete case, and to evaluate all statements on which the judicial response to the decisive question is based as to the danger to order in the prison mentioned in light of the fundamental rights. This applies here also to the characteristics established in the criminal proceedings forming the personality of the complainant, to his conduct in pre-trial detention, to the circumstances leading to his membership of the inmates' co-responsibility body, to the personal attitude towards his activities there, which will also be reflected in the manner in which they are exercised, and possibly also to the circumstance that the complainant subsequently apologised to the President of the Criminal Division for the contents of his letter.
It cannot be ruled out in the instant case that, when deciding on the question of whether a concrete risk to order in the prison by virtue of the letter was to be feared, the Higher Regional Court would have reached a different legal assessment had it applied the stated constitutional standard. § 119.3 of the Code of Criminal Procedure is an offence under administrative law related to averting dangers. It is not an offence defined under criminal law serving to protect honour; the elements of §§ 185 et seq. of the Criminal Code, and prosecution under this provision as such, remain unaffected. Conduct which for instance complies with the elements of the offence defined by § 185 of the Criminal Code (see Dreher/Tröndle, *StGB*, 40th

ed., *§ 185*, marginal no. 11) need not at the same time signify a concrete danger to order in the prison and vice versa.

…

II.

The order of the Düsseldorf Higher Regional Court was to be reversed in the light of the above and the case referred back to the Higher Regional Court.

…

III.

This decision was passed by five votes to three.

Justices: Rinck, Wand, Hirsch, Dr. Rottmann, Dr. Dr. h.c. Niebler, Steinberger, Träger; Justice Zeidler is unable to attend for signing.

Dissenting opinion of Justice Hirsch
on the order of the Second Senate of 5 February 1981
– 2 BvR 646/80 –

I agree with the ruling, but consider that the Senate should have taken the constitutional questions it raised to a more fundamental solution …

The Senate considered the violation of the constitution by the impugned ruling to lie in a violation of the fundamental right of personal freedom of development, enhanced by the constitutional protection of the family in interpreting § 119.3 of the Code of Criminal Procedure as a statute restricting freedom of action.

1. There is considerable doubt in my view as to whether § 119.3 of the Code of Criminal Procedure can still legitimise encroachments on the fundamental freedoms of pre-trial detainees as an element of the constitutional order: In a parliamentary democracy based on the rule of law, the reservation that the citizen's fundamental rights may be encroached on only by a statute or on the basis of a statute may only have the meaning that the legislature itself is to take responsibility for the fundamental decisions (BVerfGE 33, 303 (346)). A special relationship of subordination, however defined, is not suited to make dispensable a formal statute where the proviso of legality applies by virtue of an explicit constitutional order (BVerfGE 40, 237 (254)).

The provision contained in § 119.3 of the Code of Criminal Procedure does not adequately do justice to these rule-of-law requirements. It does not regulate the content of the pre-trial detainee's legal status, but merely refers to the purposes of pre-trial detention and the needs of the prison [authority] as *limits* to which restrictions on rights, which are not designated, are subject. This merely describes the traditional view of the special relationship of subordination as constituting an adequate basis for encroachments on fundamental rights. The teaching of the special relationship of subordination, in specific subjection relationships between the citizen and the state, derived the content and scope of legal restrictions directly from the purposes and tasks of the institution. According to this teaching, solely the generally recognised purposes of punishment, and the goal to be achieved by detention, could legitimise by themselves restrictions on fundamental rights. The prevalence of this doctrine delayed the creation of a legal basis for criminal detention until the Federal Constitutional Court indicated the necessity in terms of the rule of law to regulate circumstances in detention by means of a law (BVerfGE 33, 1).
In its case-law on implementation of pre-trial detention, the Federal Constitutional Court itself initially invoked the teaching of the special relationship of subordination, and noted as follows on the constitutionality of the former § 116.2 of the Code of Criminal Procedure, the wording of which is identical to § 119.3 of the Code of Criminal Procedure: "§ 116.2 of the Code of Criminal Procedure also correctly outlines the points of view under which the nature of this special relationship of subordination justifies restrictions." After the Federal Constitutional Court had rejected the special relationship of subordination for criminal detention as an entitlement to encroach on rights (BVerfGE 33, 1), this reason was no longer convincing. Doubts as to whether the mere limitation of entitlements to encroach on rights from the purposes of the institution of pre-trial detention *suffices* to legitimise encroachments on fundamental rights in a manner which is in line with the rule of law arise clearly in my understanding, given that BVerfGE 35, 311 (316) reads as follows: "No valid constitutional misgivings exist against § 119.3 of the Code of Criminal Procedure."
In my view, misgivings are also difficult to overcome in light of the fact that the execution of pre-trial detention is based practically on an administrative provision which subjects a judicial order to the restrictions provided for therein: "Insofar as he (the judge) does not make special orders in conjunction with the acceptance request or later, it should be presumed that the regulation generally taken for the execution of pre-trial detention by this execution order in the will of the judge is also to apply in an individual case" (Pre-Trial Detention Code no. 2.2 sentence 2). The judges responsible for matters of pre-trial detention, in turn, frequently refer – as also in the case at hand – to the Pre-Trial Detention Code as grounds for their re-

striction measures. The legal uncertainty is revealed in a large number of constitutional complaints relating to the execution of pre-trial detention, and not lastly also in the mere purpose-related restriction of the entitlements to encroach on rights being able to "justify a large number of measures very different in content" (BVerfGE 35, 311 (316-317)). In the Federal Constitutional Court's view, this "characteristic" of § 119.3 of the Code of Criminal Procedure establishes the possibility of replacing "incorrect reasoning" on the part of the non-constitutional court, which is more familiar with the subject-matter, with its own assessment of the danger of a disturbance to order on the basis of its own assessment of the facts (BVerfGE loc. cit.). Why the pre-trial detainee, who is regarded as innocent, must frequently accept wide-ranging encroachments on fundamental rights because of a provision of such a unique scope and openness is not understandable.

The legislature has concluded from this for the area of criminal detention that the principle of the rule of law requires the shaping of the circumstances in criminal detention within the meaning of a regulated legal status of the detainee: "Which restrictions the detainee must accept must emerge sufficiently clearly from the statutory provisions. The legal relationship between the state and the detainee must be regulated clearly; for this reason, the draft has not been able to limit itself to a small number of general clauses" (official reasoning of the Federal Government on the draft Prison Act, *Bundesrat* printed paper (*Bundesratsdrucksache* – BRDrucks.) 71/73 p. 38).

My more than nine years' experience with largely non-uniform practice in the execution of pre-trial detention, characterised as it has been by legal uncertainty, has strengthened the conviction that it is necessary to help this insight to see the light of day for the execution of pre-trial detention. Outlining points of view from a special relationship of subordination – as the content of the regulation of the execution of pre-trial detention in the Code of Criminal Procedure was rightly characterised (BVerfGE 15, 288 (293)) – is all the more difficult to reconcile with the principle of the rule of law when, in the execution of pre-trial detention, fundamental rights restrictions affect detainees who are constitutionally to be regarded as innocent.

2. The Senate once more indicated that § 119.3 of the Code of Criminal Procedure is not an offence serving to protect honour. If the interception of pre-trial detainees' letters is used as a sanction for the "disparagement of organs of the administration of justice", this is arbitrary because this "application" of § 119.3 of the Code of Criminal Procedure is no longer orientated in line with the purpose and standard of the law, and hence constitutionally no longer appears expedient. All attempts to cause this reason for the restriction of correspondence by letter to appear "furthermore" to be a risk to order in the prison have made this flaw only more apparent.

As the Federal Constitutional Court has found, letters which are addressed outside from prison cannot as a rule disturb order in the prison in the strict sense of the word. Other inmates do not receive the original of such letters. Any discussion about them or the circulation of duplicates is uninfluenced by the question of whether or not the letters have passed scrutiny: If the inmates discuss their letters among themselves, they will certainly concentrate on those which have been intercepted (BVerfGE 33, 1 (16)). This view is confirmed by the information from the Minister of Justice of the *Land* North Rhine-Westphalia, according to which insulting letters have not been observed to have an impact on order in the prison. The complete lack of such information – insofar as also evident in the specialist reference material – cannot be explained by stating that writings with an insulting content are always intercepted. The majority of judges responsible for matters of pre-trial detention engaged in monitoring of letters are unlikely to see it as being their job to examine letters from pre-trial detainees as to whether they impermissibly criticise them or other organs of the administration of justice. Constant monitoring of all letters without exception, consisting of taking note of the content of documents sent, is as such not one of the restrictions imposed on pre-trial detainees which always have to be required by the purpose of the investigation. Rather, unscrutinised correspondence by letter is to be permitted if there is no suspicion of collusion of facts, preparation for escape or disturbances to order. Certainly judges who for instance let family letters pass unscrutinised are by no means neglecting their official duties (Dünnebier in: Löwe-Rosenberg, *StPO, § 119,* marginal no. 82). In view of these facts, the Higher Regional Court has attempted to derive a connection between the insulting statements in the sent letter and order in the prison via the complainant's specific character traits: "This complainant" would boast about his insulting letter having been forwarded without complaint. The court has "no doubt" of this because the complainant is a member of the broadcasting council. The complainant falls foul of the fact that he had mentioned his activity in the broadcasting council in the impugned letter. This fact, which an unbiased observer would not consider at all negative, is used against him without his hearing of this intention. After the Higher Regional Court had taken time from 7 March 1980 until 29 April 1980, following the statement of the public prosecution office, to rule on the complaint of 27 January 1980 on the forwarding of a family letter, the urgency of the ruling could not be the reason why the complainant was not informed that – in the view of the court – his activity in the prison could throw an evil light on his character. Warning of an evaluation of a fact which is in breach of any sensible expectation would in my view have been required by the principle of a fair trial, in line with the rule of law.

The limits also imposed on application of the law by the courts by the general principle of equality are completely overstepped by the manner in which the Düsseldorf Higher Regional Court uses membership of the broadcasting council to the disadvantage of the complainant. It supposes that it is a broadcasting council of the pre-trial detainees which the complainant could only have joined by gaining the trust of his co-inmates. According to the supposition of the court which is indispensable for the sufficiency of the taking of evidence, the complainant has gained this trust by showing tendencies which are inimical to the law. Hence, it is allegedly also to be feared that he will boast about his insulting letter having been forwarded without complaint.
In this assessment the court has not accounted for the circumstance suggesting itself that the broadcasting council of Essen Prison is a facility of inmate co-responsibility in accordance with § 160 of the Prison Act (*Strafvollzugsgesetz* – StVollzG), to which only convicts are elected, whilst pre-trial detainees are selected by a conference of civil servants. The facilities created in accordance with § 160 of the Prison Act are intended to achieve the purpose of detention constituted by re-integration through the assumption of social responsibility (*Bundestag* printed paper 7/3998, p. 46).
Just as the Higher Regional Court has on the one hand concluded from an off-hand remark made in the complainant's letter a complex of facts the untenability of which it could have discovered by enquiring of the prison [authority], it has on the other hand disregarded information which was kept on file when assessing the complainant's personality. The complainant's close tie to his mother ascertained in the criminal proceedings on the basis of a special personality structure, the social commitment expressed through activity in church and charitable institutions, the apology to the chamber president, did not fit the picture of a pre-trial detainee who earns positions in a subculture of criminals by demonstratively showing disrespect of judicial officers. The Senate was hence right to object that neither the concrete relationship of the complainant with his parents, as emerging from his mental constitution ascertained in the criminal proceedings, nor the circumstances and nature of his conduct in pre-trial detention, from which far-reaching conclusions restricting fundamental rights are drawn, have been taken into account by the Higher Regional Court. In my view, this was not only necessary because a ruling had to be handed down on the restriction of the communication in the parent-child relationship. The manner in which the court proceeded, rather, fundamentally violated the minimum requirement of care in effecting an establishment and assessment of the facts, which must characterise adjudication which deserves this name.
The Federal Constitutional Court described the limits imposed on the courts in applying non-constitutional law by the prohibition of arbitrariness such that it must be

possible to find sufficient, plausible reasons for the assessment made, and an erroneous application of the law is constitutionally objectionable if it is no longer understandable on the basis of a sensible evaluation of the concepts prevailing in the Basic Law, and hence the conclusion suggests itself that it is based on irrelevant considerations (BVerfGE 42, 64 (73-74)).

I have not been given a reason why the manner of proceeding of the court in the case at hand appears to make it understandable against the background of the valuations of the Basic Law. The special sensitivity of professional judges already described by Bendix (*Zur Psychologie der Urteilstätigkeit des Berufsrichters*, 1968, p. 145) referring to Hoche (*Das Rechtsgefühl in Justiz und Politik*, Berlin, 1932, p. 63) does make it appear comprehensible that, in contradistinction to the mayor of a city, a judge cannot include the collection of roughly 300 insulting letters among his "valuable assets" (Manfred Rommel, *Theater heute*, 1981, p. 2), and in individual cases even finds unbearable the knowledge of insulting criticism in the family letter of a heavily punished inmate. The view of the judges may also be understandable that they are not sufficiently well protected against disparagement, and that the authority of organs of the administration of justice is placed at risk by the outspokenness of pre-trial detainees.

Nonetheless, the application of a provision serving to maintain order in the prison for the purpose of averting a feared loss of authority objectively constitutes abuse.

I concur with my colleague justice Böhmer when he writes in his dissenting opinion on the ruling of the First Senate of 10 March 1981 (1 BvR 92/71, preliminary print p. 14) that "drawing the conclusion that the end justifies the means, as in a 'police state', has no legitimate place in the Basic Law". If state power nonetheless acts by this principle, the rule of law is at risk. "Nothing can destroy a government more quickly than its failure to observe its own laws, or worse, its disregard of the charter of its own existence." (Mr. Justice Clark, in: *Mapp v. Ohio*, 367 U.S. 643 (659)). Against [the standard of] the Basic Law, which binds the legislature to law and order, and imposes on it protection of human dignity and freedom, concern about the collapse of state authority, whilst it should not be underestimated, cannot justify that, without investigating facts, and disregarding details which are kept on file, a citizen's character is described as inimical to order, and thereby a link is created for encroachments on fundamental rights.

3. The Senate has concluded as follows from the significance of Article 2.1 of the Basic Law as a fundamental freedom right: The less concrete the risk to order in the prison, the greater weight attaches to the freedom of action of the pre-trial detainee, and the more restrained must be the judge in encroachment on correspondence by letter. The Senate has found that the scope of Article 2.1 of the Basic Law in the family sphere has been misjudged in this weighing. I agree with this statement. In

my view, however, there would have been no need for stating the increased protection of privacy in the area of an intimate group. The Federal Constitutional Court has already derived the requirement of "concrete indications" of a "real danger" of a disturbance to order in prison as a precondition for the restriction of the pre-trial detainee from the influence of the fundamental right of general freedom of action on the interpretation of § 119.3 of the Code of Criminal Procedure (BVerfGE 35, 5 (9-10)). If the Senate now also does not permit a concrete danger, depending on the degree of concreteness in proportion to the increased need for protection of the personality in the private sphere, to suffice as a ground for restrictions of freedom that stands up to the constitution, I concur with this completely, but in my view one should have examined first of all whether the impugned ruling is based at all on a concrete indication of a real danger of disturbances to order. This question was to be negated. If activity in an inmates' co-responsibility body which the law provides for re-socialisation purposes can be a concrete indication of the danger posed by an inmate, this definition lending concrete form to the principle of proportionality is devoid of content and ability to provide a distinction.

4. As against the review which I consider necessary by the standard of the general freedom of action and of the prohibition of arbitrariness, the Senate preferred to measure the restriction imposed on the complainant by the guarantee of personal development in the family sphere. In doing so, it has taken into account that the Higher Regional Court had negated the applicability of this specific manifestation of the fundamental freedom right on the grounds that the complainant had allegedly not made expedient use of his right to free communication within the family – insofar as there was one at all. Even if I am of the opinion that such considerations to motivate the exercise of a fundamental right are unable to give rise to a legitimate restriction or even negation of fundamental rights, I do doubt whether they are to be so little taken seriously that they do not require a word of rebuttal. In addition to the "supraconstitutional emergency", the "extra-constitutional reservation" that fundamental rights must be exercised with the right intention could become a dangerous tool to undermine freedoms that are guaranteed by fundamental rights.

a) The Federal Constitutional Court has ruled that the sending of a letter in the knowledge that its content will be taken note of by the judge may not deprive the pre-trial detainee's correspondence by letter of the protection of privacy (BVerfGE 35, 35 (40)). Any other view would subject the pre-trial detainee to public scrutiny in his personal communication, and would force him, even in communication with those close to him, to conduct himself as if the communication took place under public observation. If the pre-trial detainee's protection of family privacy is to be maintained at all, the access of a third party which he is forced to tolerate may not be imputed to him. A view which would see the censorship judge as an interlocutor

of the pre-trial detainee would also not comply with the scope of the negative freedom of opinion which includes the right to be able to select for oneself the addressee of a personal message.
The Federal Constitutional Court has furthermore ruled that the protection of the exercise of a fundamental right does not depend on whether the citizen intends to act to implement the purposes of the fundamental right guarantee (BVerfGE 12, 113 (128-129)). What the Federal Constitutional Court has found in this ruling on protection of expression of opinion in public by Article 5.1 of the Basic Law applies no less to the area of privacy protected in accordance with Article 2.1 of the Basic Law. Also the statements in this area are frequently not determined by the purposes which are to be served by fundamental right protection. It will virtually never be possible to ascertain with certainty the motives on which an act is based that by its external appearance is to be attributed to the private sphere. Motives for an act emerge from interpretations of varied needs, interests, expectations, norms and purposes. As long as an act can be objectively portrayed as an action situated in the area protected by fundamental rights, it cannot forgo this character by virtue of the person acting also being prompted by other motives (see BVerfGE, loc. cit.).
The statements made by the complainant in the impugned letter are in objective terms contributions to his self-portrayal in the family sphere. They are suited to support his claims of innocence with which he had linked them. From the point of view of the complainant, the allegation that the judges are stupid and malicious can explain his conviction for attempted manslaughter, which he fights because he considers it a wrong decision. That the complainant hence provides a picture of his personality which clashes with reality is not a reason to prevent him from making such a portrayal. The content of the right of personality is in particular the free determination of the social validity claim transmitted by self-portrayal (see BVerfGE 54, 208 (217-218)).
In light of this objective factual situation, the scope of protection of the fundamental right and its effectiveness cannot be qualified in accordance with motivations which do not allow of an examination.
b) Insofar as action in the area protected by fundamental rights can, accordingly, at all relate to the intentions pursued thereby, the Federal Constitutional Court would moreover naturally not be bound by the identification of a motive by the state power. If the Federal Constitutional Court has jurisdiction with regard to encroachments on fundamental rights which are of considerable intensity to examine the assessment of statements of the person concerned by the court (BVerfGE 42, 143 (148-149); 42, 163 (168)), it certainly must claim this entitlement if the citizen is quite simply denied invocation of his or her freedom of expression in the private sphere protected by fundamental rights on grounds that he or she had acted with

abusive intention. As a result, it would not be able to suffice itself with the question of whether the impugned ruling contains errors based on a fundamentally erroneous view of the significance of the fundamental right and of the area protected by it. The Federal Constitutional Court would, rather, also examine in detail whether in ascertaining and assessing the facts this ruling has violated the constitutionally guaranteed freedom of expression in the private sphere.
The cunning reasoning of the Higher Regional Court, alleging that the complainant had wished to directly insult the censorship judge since he himself had previously stated that he had sworn enough would have easily proven to be untenable in a serious analysis of the wording of the letter since the Higher Regional Court completely disregarded interpretations suggesting themselves by the context of the statements lying between an expression of annoyance and intentional deliberate insult.
...

Justice: Hirsch

Dissenting opinion of Justice Wand
on the order of the Second Senate of 5 February 1981
– 2 BvR 646/80 –

I cannot concur with the order. The constitutional complaint should have been rejected as unfounded on the merits – assuming it to be admissible.

I.

The Federal Constitutional Court has twice dealt in Senate rulings with constitutional aspects of the scrutiny of letters written by pre-trial detainees to their spouses. Firstly in 1973, and again in 1976, the Second Senate ruled "that freedom of contact by letter with a spouse takes on particular significance in view of the constitutional precept of respect for the intimate sphere" (BVerfGE 35, 35 (Headnote)). The Court held that as a rule, it is irreconcilable with the special significance of freedom of expression of opinion in the area of marital privacy to intercept letters of a pre-trial detainee to his wife because of insults to third parties which they contain. In both cases, the letters impugned and intercepted by the non-constitutional courts in accordance with § 119.3 of the Code of Criminal Procedure contained amongst other things gross insults of the judges who were dealing with the criminal proceedings against the pre-trial detainee. In both cases, the impugned rulings of

the Higher Regional Courts were reversed as being incompatible with the fundamental right of the pre-trial detainee under Article 5.1 sentence 1 in conjunction with Article 2.1 of the Basic Law (BVerfGE 35, 35; 42, 234).
I take a fundamentally different view. This also applies to the result and parts of its grounds in the instant case, albeit I consider the present order of the Senate to be a step in the right direction in the approach of the constitutional argumentation.

II.

…

III.

The prohibition of the forwarding of the impugned letter passage is compatible with the Basic Law.
1. It is based on § 119.3 of the Code of Criminal Procedure, in accordance with which *only* those restrictions may be imposed on an arrested person which are required by the purpose of pre-trial detention or order in the prison. *Both Senates* of the Federal Constitutional Court have examined the reconcilability of this provision with the Basic Law and affirmed it in their established case-law for convincing reasons. I may refer to them in the interest of avoiding repetitions. § 119.3 of the Code of Criminal Procedure is hence a component of the constitutional order within the meaning of Article 2.1 of the Basic Law (see *inter alia* BVerfGE 15, 288 (295) re the identically worded previous § 116.2 of the Code of Criminal Procedure; 34, 369 (379, 381-382); 34, 384 (395 et seq.); 35, 35 (39-40); 35, 307 (309); 35, 311 (316 et seq., 320 et seq.) …; 42, 95 (100)).
2. The interpretation of § 119.3 of the Code of Criminal Procedure and its application in the instant case are constitutionally unobjectionable.
a) (1) The meaning of the constitutional complaint and the special and at the same time limited task of the Federal Constitutional Court in the framework of the judicial power permit judicial rulings to be reviewed only within limited boundaries (BVerfGE 22, 93 (97)). The interpretation of so-called non-constitutional law and its application to the individual case are solely a matter for the non-constitutional courts with jurisdiction, and are removed from subsequent review by the Federal Constitutional Court unless arbitrariness applies or specific constitutional law is otherwise violated (BVerfGE 18, 85 (92); 30, 173 (197)). The Federal Constitutional Court has in particular not to rule on whether a different ruling would have been possible or would deserve preference in accordance with non-constitutional law – in this instance in accordance with § 119.3 of the Code of Criminal Procedure

(BVerfGE 34, 369 (379); see also BVerfGE 21, 209 (216); 29, 413 (424)). And, finally, it cannot already intervene if with a weighing between competing interests imposed on a judge by statutory general clauses the evaluation carried out by him may be questionable because it attaches too much or too little weight to the interests of one side or the other (BVerfGE 18, 85 (93); 35, 311 (316-317)). It is admittedly difficult to delineate clearly the boundaries of the possibilities open to the Federal Constitutional Court to intervene: "In general terms, it will be possible to say that the normal subsumption within non-constitutional law is withdrawn from review by the Federal Constitutional Court insofar as errors of interpretation are not evident which are based on a fundamentally erroneous view of the meaning of a fundamental right, and in particular of the scope of the area protected by it, and are also of some weight in their substantive significance for the concrete legal case" (see BVerfGE 18, 85 (93)). This means for the boundaries imposed on subsequent review by the constitutional court of interpretation of § 119.3 of the Code of Criminal Procedure by the non-constitutional courts: The Federal Constitutional Court must restrict itself to examining "whether the utmost limit of the power to decide afforded by the general clause has been overstepped in light of the fundamental rights restricted by it. This can only be ascertained if the overstepping of that limit is somewhat evident" (BVerfGE 35, 311 (317)).

...

(2) The constitution does not force the non-constitutional courts to interpret narrowly the legal definition of "order in prison" contained in § 119.3 of the Code of Criminal Procedure and to understand it to include for instance only a minimum of order. For instance, also consideration that well-functioning life in prison is not to be placed at risk, be it by disciplinary violations on the part of the detainees, be it by creating tension between pre-trial detainees and the supervisory staff, relates to order in the prison. To maintain this order, the agencies responsible for implementing pre-trial detention, in particular the judges with jurisdiction for imposing restrictions, may exhaust the decision-making powers granted to them by § 119.3 of the Code of Criminal Procedure in a constitutional and unobjectionable manner (BVerfGE 35, 311 (316-317); 42, 95 (100)).

In this interpretation, § 119.3 of the Code of Criminal Procedure evidently permits the judge in principle to prohibit the forwarding of letters by pre-trial detainees which contain criminal offences or which serve to prepare a punishable act. For it is difficult to imagine order in the prison not being disturbed in concrete terms if punishable acts which are not minor in nature could be set in motion from there before the eyes of the judge who has jurisdiction for monitoring in detention. It is not comprehensible that anything else should apply to gross insults, in other words to considerable, unlawful and intentional attacks on the honour of another (and hence at the same time as a rule on their dignity which is protected by the Basic Law!). Particularly because judges and prison staff may not encroach on the dignity of the inmate, but on the contrary must respect and where necessary protect it (Article 1.1 of the Basic Law) and where necessary must even fear criminal prosecution and (or) disciplinary measures if they violate this duty, it would be unbearable for well-functioning prison life, and hence destructive to order in the prison, if letters were not to be intercepted or able to be intercepted in which in communications with the outside world inmates grossly insult the judges and public prosecution officers dealing with their case, the prison staff, as well as third parties, as they see fit. Anyone with half an idea asks themselves in this context not only the question of what mental strain may be heaped on those responsible for maintaining order in prison, but not lastly the perhaps even more weighty question of what degree of state authority – taken for granted as respected by the inmates, where necessary to be enforced – is indispensable to maintain order in prison.

The *Land* administrations of justice which are responsible for the prisons for the implementation of pre-trial detention, imprisonment and measures of correction and prevention involving deprivation of liberty, which for this reason have special knowledge and experience concerning the requirements which are indispensable to maintain order in prison, do not see this differently. In the national Pre-Trial Detention Code agreed by them in the version of 15 December 1976 in knowledge and correct accommodation of the case-law of the Federal Constitutional Court – just as in all earlier versions – they take it for granted that a risk to order in the prison can also be considered if a letter by a detainee which has circulated with the outside world contains gross insults (see no. 34 of the Pre-Trial Detention Code). Also the legislature of the Prison Act determines in § 31.1 no. 4 that such letters may be intercepted; this applies even if they were not intended to endanger the security or order of the prison in the individual case.

If an inmate writes a letter to someone outside the prison containing gross insults, there are in principle reasons to presume a serious risk to order in the prison simply by virtue of its being forwarded. The fundamental rights principle of weighing in the individual case and the principle of proportionality hence as a rule do not require *further* circumstances to be ascertained which heighten the danger to order in the prison. Whether the inmate for instance "boasts" to those around him or her of letters which have passed letter monitoring, and (or) "encourages" others to imitate is hence bereft of significance. If letters with a grossly insulting content in principle were not halted, in all likelihood they would belong to the daily picture of life there, with the intolerable consequences that this would have for the atmosphere in prisons in the foreseeable time.

The fundamental rights-related principle of weighing in the individual case and the prohibition of excessiveness, by contrast, prevent retaining all letters with an insulting content without exception. The pre-trial detention facility is not an authority responsible for protecting honour. Letters are not monitored in the interest of third parties, but in the public interest with the aim of ruling out concrete dangers to the purpose of pre-trial detention and order in the prison. From this point of view, different responses are possible in individual cases. For instance, letters with an insulting content addressing certain authorities (such as the public prosecution office), or letters to family members in which the addressee himself or herself or members of one's own family are degraded, may only be liable to disturb order in the prison in exceptional cases.

(3) The Second Senate considered the prohibition to forward a letter addressed by a pre-trial detainee to his wife, in which he insulted the judges acting in his proceedings, to be an unconstitutional encroachment on the fundamental right of the detainee to "free expression of opinion in the area of marital privacy" (Article 5.1 sentence 1 in conjunction with Article 2.1 of the Basic Law) (BVerfGE 35, 35; 42, 234). This cannot be concurred with. In my view, this case-law is already mistaken in its approach:

Marital and family privacy enjoys the protection of the Basic Law, with the consequence that, from this point of view, statements of a family member are not subject to state encroachment, or only to a limited degree. This is however contingent at least on expressions of opinion the *confidential treatment* of which in the closest family circle is *desired*, which thus are not to be accessible to outsiders; and it is further necessary that under the circumstances one may reasonably presume that third parties may surely not listen in. Only with this state of affairs and to this degree does the constitutional protection of marital and family privacy apply under Article 2.1 in conjunction with Article 6 of the Basic Law, and only under this precondition does the criminal law case-law today correctly see the elements of insult as not having been fulfilled (see *inter alia* Bavarian Highest Regional Court (*Bayerisches Oberstes Landesgericht*), *Monatsschrift für Deutsches Recht* – MDR 1976 p. 1036). Were it to be otherwise, also those who violate the dignity and the reputation of third parties in the presence not only of persons belonging to their close family could invoke the protection of marital and family privacy, *in extremis* indeed those who – whilst being located within the close circle of the family – shout out the insults of others through an open window. It is evident that this could be neither reconciled with the constitutionally required protection of those concerned, nor accepted in the area of criminal law.

If the letter of a pre-trial detainee to his or her spouse or to close family members contains insults directed against third parties, there is obviously a lack of confiden-

tiality which is a prerequisite for attributing such statements to the protection of marital or family privacy; it is established that the judge who watches over correspondence by letter, in other words a third party, will be entitled to take note of the content of the letter (Article 10 of the Basic Law and § 119.3 of the Code of Criminal Procedure).
The fundamental right to freedom of expression of opinion under Article 5.1 sentence 1 of the Basic Law also does not oppose the interception of a letter addressed to a close family member of the pre-trial detainee. This fundamental right is restricted *inter alia* by the right to personal honour, and hence by § 185 of the Criminal Code. However, this provision too is to be interpreted "in light" of the significance of freedom of opinion. At the same time, it is recognised that insulting abuse is certainly not covered by Article 5.1 of the Basic Law. The protection of this fundamental right could only intervene in this context if it did not appear to be ruled out under the circumstances that the inmate acts in exercising justified interests (§ 193 of the Criminal Code), which he may not be hindered from doing by the monitoring of letters.
No other result emerges if one relates the fundamental right of freedom of expression to the constitutional protection of family privacy. If the constitution does not grant protection under fundamental rights from one point of view or from the other, it changes nothing if one interconnects the two constitutional standards, if this is permitted here at all, in order to form a single standard of review.
(4) However, when it comes to deciding whether the forwarding of a letter of a pre-trial detainee may be prohibited in accordance with § 119.3 of the Code of Criminal Procedure, constitutional significance may well attach to the matter of whether it addresses the spouse or a close relative of the detainee, or indeed third parties. In this starting point, I agree with the majority of the Senate for the following considerations: Marriage and the family enjoy the special protection of the state (Article 6.1 of the Basic Law). The Federal Constitutional Court has drawn a number of legal conclusions from this. It is decisive here that the fundamental provision that determines values contained in Article 6.1 of the Basic Law also takes on particular significance in detention. Each instance of longer-term pre-trial detention, as a rule, places a considerable strain on the family relationships of the person concerned. Its execution impairs the necessary communication between the detainee and his or her family members who live in freedom, and can contribute towards their becoming fundamentally alienated from one another. The duty of the state, in fulfilment of its constitutional obligation to ensure the preservation of marriage and the family, is to limit such a detrimental impact of the deprivation of liberty as far as is possible and reasonable, whilst adequately satisfying the interests of the public (BVerfGE 42, 95 (101)). If as a result of the monitoring of letters – necessary for reasons of over-

whelming public interest – the pre-trial detainee may not correspond in confidence with his or her spouse and close family members, it should be considered when *assessing statements* for their potential to disturb order in the prison that the pre-trial detainee must also be able to communicate openly with his or her spouse and (or) with his or her parents or children with regard to the criminal proceedings pending against him or her and to portray the situation from his or her point of view. If in doing so he or she portrays subjectively coloured, objectively incorrect impressions and in this context says things which are *not factually true* about judges acting in the criminal proceedings or commissioned with monitoring in detention, or about prison staff, as a rule this will take on a *lesser weight* for the danger to order in the prison than in other contexts in which family relations are immaterial. To in principle take this into account in favour of the pre-trial detainee requires respect for his or her *freedom of development* in the family area. More than this *required respect* admittedly cannot be derived from this fundamental right in the context at hand. That it may not permit pre-trial detainees to actively counter the public interest – also entrenched in the principle of the rule of law – in maintenance of order in the prison, or to violate the rights of third parties, should be taken for granted.

b) (1) In the instant case, in accordance with the conviction of the Higher Regional Court, it was not – at least not primarily – the complainant's concern to express himself openly about the criminal proceedings in the letter to his parents in the close family circle, in other words to "present matters from his point of view"; in view of the time which had passed between the conviction of the complainant and the sending of the letter, as well as of the repeated seizing on insulting wording, it could also not be presumed that the complainant wished to "spontaneously lend expression to his annoyance in a still understandable manner". In the view of the judge carrying out monitoring in detention, as well as of the Higher Regional Court, the complainant was rather more concerned to use the letter to his parents as an occasion and excuse to express gross insults towards third parties. The impugned rulings establish on this matter that the complainant had *aimed*, by virtue of the impugned letter, to disparage organs of the administration of justice and make them appear contemptible (Order of the President of the Ninth Criminal Division of the Duisburg Regional Court of 17 September 1977); in the knowledge that this letter was subject to judicial scrutiny, he had allegedly "intentionally taken the opportunity" to "brazenly insult the judges of the chamber of the court sitting with one professional and two lay judges dealing with his case, at least the President who carried out the monitoring of letters" (Order of the Düsseldorf Higher Regional Court of 29 April 1980). The Higher Regional Court stated the following as grounds: "The Senate reaches this conviction *also* in view of the fact that, *after* in paragraph 2 of that letter – in which he had used insulting expressions such as 'mentally limited people' and 'mini Hitlers' – he had written: 'But I have sworn enough now. Now I already feel much better', but in the following paragraph 3 the complainant once more used insolent words and, referring to the trial court judge dealing with his case, used the words 'pigs', 'their stupid skulls' and 'slave-drivers'."

The Federal Constitutional Court must base its ruling on these findings of the non-constitutional courts. The finding and the assessment of the offence are solely a matter for the courts which have general jurisdiction for it; they are removed from ex-post review by the Federal Constitutional Court unless they are based on considerations which are factually not comprehensible, and hence violate the Basic Law's prohibition of arbitrariness (BVerfGE 18, 85 (92)). Such non-factual considerations are however manifestly not contained in the assessment of the intercepted letter passage by the non-constitutional courts. It emerges from the letter itself that the complainant *expected* judicial scrutiny of letters; since it says: "I have learned a lot more which I unfortunately cannot write to you *because of the false eyes*". In light of his level of education – he was a student –, if he had been concerned with convincing his parents of his innocence and in doing so making it clear that and why he had allegedly been wronged, he could have easily availed himself *of arguments*. That instead of this, and in the knowledge that his letters would be monitored, he emphasisedly used gutter language although he undoubtedly knows how to express himself suitably certainly suggests – as the non-constitutional courts opine – that the complainant was primarily concerned to grossly and deliberately insult the judges dealing with his criminal case.

(2) Given these facts, the impugned rulings consider, and their actions in doing so were constitutionally unobjectionable, that forwarding the impugned part of the letter would constitute a concrete danger to order in the prison within the meaning of § 119.3 of the Code of Criminal Procedure, particularly since, as a member of the "broadcasting council" – regardless of whether elected to it by the inmates or appointed to this position by the prison governor – the complainant at that time took up a prominent sectoral position among the pre-trial detainees in which an appropriate agreement, *exemplified through the inmate's own life*, with the requirements of order in the prison is indispensable. Disturbances to order in the prison emanating from *such inmates* already have particular weight – as the Higher Regional Court correctly presumes in the result – because of the violation of a certain obligation to set an example towards other inmates. It was therefore justified to prohibit the forwarding of the letter passage in application of § 119.3 of the Code of Criminal Procedure. The principle of proportionality manifestly did not oppose this measure.

I already consider it to be ruled out outright that interception of the letter part could violate the complainant's fundamental right to freedom of development in the family area in view of the established facts – the majority of the Senate might forgive me for this –. This fundamental right does not demand the omission of actually required measures to protect order in the prison only because the inmate undertakes the disturbance of this order *in the external framework* of a letter to close family members. This fact in particular is however ascertained in the impugned rulings. It is rounded off in a passage of the letter not explicitly mentioned by the non-constitutional courts, but certainly not overlooked by them and also not to be disregarded by the Federal Constitutional Court (see BVerfGE 35, 311 (317)): Here, the complainant asks his parents to interest a "newspaper reporter" in his case, and then goes on: "If he doesn't get a visiting permission because those mentally limited people are scared, I know another way." His intention clearly expressed here to contact the press, if necessary circumventing monitoring in detention, additionally underlines how far the letter part impugned by the non-constitutional courts departs from the facts for which the pre-trial detainee can claim fundamental rights protection from the point of view of freedom to develop in the family.

The Senate majority now opines that the Higher Regional Court had misjudged the scope of that fundamental right; it is said not to be ruled out that, on re-examination, this court would adjudge differently the question of whether by passing on the *entire* letter a concrete danger to order in the prison would have had to be feared. The Senate majority bases this view on a passage in the grounds to the order in which the Higher Regional Court considers the previous case-law of the Second Senate on stopping letters written by pre-trial detainees to their spouses (BVerfGE 35, 35; 42, 234) not to apply to the present case; "In the relationship of a long-since adult pre-trial detainee with his or her *parents* the same significance does not attach to freedom of letter contact with regard to the constitutional principle of respect for the intimate sphere, as has been recognised in the referenced rulings for *marital privacy*." Hence, the Senate majority does not do justice to the Higher Regional Court for at least three reasons: Firstly, this consideration recognisably had no primary significance for the ruling handed down in view of the established facts. Secondly, the Second Senate – as shown by its ruling in the instant case – derogated from its earlier (in my opinion erroneous) case-law; it considers the constitutional problem of a certain protection of letters written by pre-trial detainees to close relatives no longer from the point of view of marital (family) privacy in conjunction with the fundamental right of freedom of opinion, but correctly from the point of view of the quite different point of view of the freedom to develop in the family area – which is also important for the practical result –. And thirdly, the Higher Regional Court is indeed right with this remark: Contact by letter of a "*long-since adult*" pre-trial de-

tainee with his wife (and with his children) takes on *as a rule* greater significance for the cohesion of the family than contact with his parents. If this is different in an individual case, the judge admittedly must take account of this in the monitoring of letters. That, moreover, the complainant in the instant case did not reveal to his parents the crisis situations that had preceded the attempted killing of his wife, in other words that he did not seek to discuss this openly with them, emerges clearly from the criminal files consulted.
The grounds for the Senate's ruling … could be understood or misunderstood such that the non-constitutional courts had disregarded the fact that § 119.3 of the Code of Criminal Procedure was "not an offence serving to protect honour" and that "conduct which for instance complies with the elements of the offence defined by § 185 of the Criminal Code … does not at the same time signify a concrete danger to order in the prison and vice versa". There are however no indications of this from the grounds to the impugned ruling.
In accordance with the above, the constitutional complaint is unfounded, insofar as it opposes the interception of the impugned passage decided in application of § 119.3 of the Code of Criminal Procedure; it should have been rejected.
…

Justice: Wand

Dissenting opinion of Justice Prof. Dr. Dr. h.c. Niebler
on the order of the Second Senate of 5 February 1981
– 2 BvR 646/80 –

The constitutional complaint should have been rejected as unfounded since the partial prohibition of forwarding of letters by the impugned orders of the Duisburg Regional Court and of the Düsseldorf Higher Regional Court is compatible with the Basic Law. I concur completely with the detailed grounds of my colleague justice Wand at III. no. 2 of his dissenting opinion.

Justice: Prof. Dr. Dr. h.c. Niebler

No. 13

BVerfGE 60, 79

of 17 February 1982 – 1 BvR 188/80 –

"Case concerning the separation of a child from its family"

HEADNOTES:

It is constitutionally unobjectionable that children can be separated from the family in accordance with § 1666.1 sentence 1 in conjunction with § 1666a of the Civil Code as amended by the Act on Custody of Children, also in case of non-culpable failure of the parents, if it is not otherwise possible to prevent the child's best interests from being jeopardised.
The measure of separating a child from its family, as the strongest encroachment on parental rights, is only consistent with constitutional law if the principle of proportionality is strictly observed.

Order of the First Senate of 17 February 1982
– 1 BvR 188/80 –

in the proceedings concerning the constitutional complaint 1. of Ms. H., 2. of Mr. H. authorised representative: …, lawyer – against the decision of the Higher Regional Court (*Oberlandesgericht* – OLG) of Frankfurt am Main of 15 January 1980 – 20 W 565/79 –.

RULING:

The decision of the Higher Regional Court of Frankfurt am Main of 15 January 1980 – 20 W 565/79 – is in violation of Article 6.2 in conjunction with Article 6.3 of the Basic Law (*Grundgesetz* – GG). The decision is reversed. The case is referred back to the Higher Regional Court of Frankfurt am Main.
The *Land* (state of) Hesse is ordered to reimburse the complainants their necessary expenses.

EXTRACT FROM GROUNDS:

A.

The constitutional complaint concerns the withdrawal of parental custody rights for a legitimate child and the transfer of such custody rights to a municipal youth welfare office that intends to arrange a foster home for the child.

I.

Subject to certain requirements, the guardianship court (*Vormundschaftsgericht*) is entitled to intervene with the right to exercise parental custody that on principle accrues to the parents. The relevant provisions in Article 1 no. 16 of the Act to Revise Parental Custody Rights (*Gesetz zur Neuregelung des Rechts der elterlichen Sorge* – SorgeRG) as amended on 18 July 1979 (Federal Law Gazette (*Bundesgesetzblatt* – BGBl.) I p. 1061) read as follows:

§ 1666 of the Civil Code

> (1) Where the physical, mental or psychological best interests of the child are jeopardised by the abusive exercise of parental custody, by neglect of the child, by non-culpable parental failure or by the conduct of a third party, if the parents are unwilling or unable to avert the danger, the guardianship court shall take the measures necessary in order to avert the danger. The court may also take measures with effect against a third party.
> (2) The court may replace declarations of the parents or of one parent.
> (3) The court may withdraw the right to manage the child's property from a parent if the latter has violated the child's right to receive child maintenance and if the child maintenance could be in jeopardy in future.

§ 1666a of the Civil Code

> (1) Measures which entail a separation of the child from its parental family are admissible only if the danger cannot be countered in another way, including through public support measures.
> (2) The complete care for the person of the child may be withdrawn only if other measures have been unsuccessful or if it is to be assumed that they will not suffice to avert the danger.

Prior to entry into force of the Act on Parental Custody, § 1666 of the Civil Code applied as amended by Article 1 no. 22 of the Act on Equality of Men and Women in the Area of Civil Law (*Gesetz über die Gleichberechtigung von Mann und Frau auf dem Gebiete des bürgerlichen Rechts, Gleichberechtigungsgesetz* – Equal Rights Act, GleichberG) of 18 June 1957 (Federal Law Gazette I p. 609), which cited fault on the part of the parents as being a prerequisite for government measures:

§ 1666 of the Civil Code old

> If the mental or physical best interests of the child are jeopardised in that the father or the mother abuses the right to care for the child, neglects the child or is guilty of dishonourable or immoral conduct, the guardianship court shall take the measures necessary in order to avert the danger. In particular, the guardianship court may order that the child be placed in a suitable family or in an educational institution for the purpose of its upbringing.
> The guardianship court may withdraw the right to manage the child's property from a parent if the latter has violated the child's right to receive child maintenance and if the child maintenance could be in considerable jeopardy in future.

Since corresponding proposals were put forward during consultations on the Act on Equality of Men and Women in the Area of Civil Law and on the Restoration of Legal Unity in Family Law (*Gesetz über die Gleichberechtigung von Mann und Frau auf dem Gebiete des bürgerlichen Rechts und über die Wiederherstellung der Rechtseinheit auf dem Gebiete des Familienrechts, Familienrechtsgesetz* – Family Law Act) in 1952 (see opinion issued by the *Bundesrat* on the relevant draft legislation: Schedule A to *Bundestag* printed paper (BTDrucks) 3802, 1st electoral term, p. 8), with § 1666 of the Civil Code as amended by the Act to Revise Parental Custody Rights, the legislature complied with the demands made in jurisprudence and legal practice to abolish the principle of fault in the area of government encroachment on parental rights, in the interest of affording adequate protection to the child.

II.

1. The (female) complainant who was born in 1947 and the (male) complainant born in 1939 have been married to each other since 1974. Both complainants have been looked after by the municipal social welfare office for many years within the context of care for handicapped persons. The (male) complainant has now taken up work again in a workshop for the handicapped, having been made redundant in 1978 due to frequent absences from work.

When it became clear that the (female) complainant was pregnant, the physicians advised her to have an abortion because in addition to her diagnosed severed deafness and scoliosis, she was feeble-minded in the first to second degree, and since the (male) complainant was severely mentally handicapped and suffered from epilepsy. The (female) complainant refused to have an abortion.

2. After the (female) complainant gave birth to a daughter in the seventh month of her pregnancy (February 1976), the youth welfare office immediately requested that the guardianship court withdraw the parental custody rights from the parents and transfer them to the youth welfare office. The court first decided in line with the request, without hearing the parents since immediate measures were considered essential, by issuing a preliminary order that the sickly baby not be released from hospital into her parents' household. The child was initially placed in a children's home from hospital, where her parents were able to visit her for the first time in late March 1976.

In the further course of the parental custody proceedings, the Local Court (*Amtsgericht*) obtained expert neurological opinions on the complainants from the municipal health authority. The neurologist established that the (male) complainant suffered from a slight mental handicap and a slight degree of feeble-mindedness. He drew the conclusion that owing to the father's low degree of motivation and his work, he was not able to look after the child. The neurologist held that the (female) complainant, the examination of whom revealed a substantial degree of feeble-mindedness, was therefore not capable of looking after the child without severely jeopardising its physical development.

After the court had obtained an opinion from the carers at the children's home, it withdrew the parental custody rights from the complainants with final force, having heard them in person in August 1976, and transferred the rights to the youth welfare office as the guardian on the grounds that the child would be at risk mentally and physically if it were released into the parents' household.

The complainants unsuccessfully filed an objection against this decision, with the aim of causing the (female) complainant's mother to be appointed as the guardian.

Upon a further objection, the Higher Regional Court reversed the decision handed down by the Regional Court and referred the case back to that court for further clarification and a new decision.

3. The Regional Court hereupon obtained expert opinions from medical specialists on the child's development and the ability of the parents to bring her up.

The expert arrived at the conclusion that the child's deficits in the area of basic and fine motor skills had been rectified, but that deficits still existed regarding social behaviour, the use of language and in the meaningful use of objects. It was considered necessary to communicate and sing with the child meaningfully for her further

development. The child must on no account be neglected; at the time, however, special educational therapy was not considered necessary.
The psychiatric and neurological examination of the complainants showed that both were in a position to look after the child without placing her physical or emotional development at risk.
The court thereupon suspended the proceedings for a period of 9 months in May 1978. At the same time it ordered that the child be taken into the parents' home for a trial phase as soon as a place in a certain nursery became vacant. The complainants were ordered to register the child at the nursery and to ensure that she attended it regularly.
After the suspension period, reports were obtained from the youth welfare office, the health authority and the nursery, as well as an expert opinion from another psychologist, on the question whether the parents were able to provide the child with the emotional stability and social sense of security she so urgently needed for her positive mental development.
In May 1979 the expert judged the parents' conduct to be lacking in sensitivity and empathy; attempts to discuss somewhat complex goals and values in upbringing had failed from the outset. The independence of the (female) complainant in particular in house-keeping and in attending external family-related appointments was deemed inadequate. The child's reaction could be interpreted to mean that she had not received the desired reaction from her parents and hence did not expect anything more. The present personality of the child permitted the possibility of an overall positive development; however, the concentrated playing observed could not be traced back to corresponding behaviour of the parents, but, rather, to the influence of the nursery. The expert concluded that despite their emotional ties with the child, the parents were not able to guarantee socialisation within a changing system of standards as well as educational and professional demands. He considered the possibility of a cooperation between advice offices and the family to be unrealistic and hence unfeasible in view of the intellectual potential of both parents.
In July 1979 the Regional Court thereupon rejected the objections again and ordered that the (female) complainant's parental rights be suspended.
4. Upon the objections raised against this decision, the Higher Regional Court fully reinstated the decision of the Local Court by amending the decision handed down by the Regional Court in that the parental rights were to be withdrawn from both complainants. Although this entailed the separation of the child from her parents, it was held that since the guardian intended to place the child in a foster family, the measure was permissible since it was not otherwise possible to prevent the child from being at risk. The expert most recently heard had after all described the previ-

ous proposal from an expert of leaving the child in the parental home and of improving the situation through additional assistance, as being unrealistic.

III.

In their constitutional complaint against the decision of the Higher Regional Court the complainants object to a violation of their constitutional right under Article 6.2 of the Basic Law.
They argue that the Higher Regional Court has failed to take into account adequately that according to § 1666a of the Civil Code, state assistance takes precedence over state encroachment and that the state is under an obligation to support parents through upbringing aids or other educational measures before removing a child from the family. It was argued that the expert opinion on which the decision of the Higher Regional Court was ultimately based, had failed to give sufficient consideration to the possibility of state assistance.

IV.

1. In the opinion of the Federal Minister of Justice, speaking on behalf of the Federal Government, there are objections under constitutional law against the decision contested.
…
2. The youth welfare office presented the opinions of the responsible social worker, which report on details of the child's care by the complainants. The reports essentially cite the principal nursery teacher who looks after the child at the municipal nursery. The youth welfare office considers the withdrawal of parental custody to be justified since the child's best interests are still at risk. …

V.

At the request of the complainants, by way of a preliminary order the Federal Constitutional Court suspended execution of the decision contested, until a decision was made on the constitutional complaint.

B.

The admissible constitutional complaint is well-founded.

I.

Article 6.2 sentence 1 of the Basic Law guarantees parents the right to look after and bring up their children. Hence the child's upbringing is primarily made the parents' responsibility, in which respect this "natural right" is not granted to the parents by the state, but, rather, recognised by the latter as being a given right. The parents may in principle decide without state influence or encroachment, according to their own concepts, how they wish to perform the care and upbringing of their children, thus fulfilling their parental responsibilities. In relations with the child, however, the child's best interests have to be the principal guideline for parental care and upbringing (see judgment of the Federal Constitutional Court of 9 February 1982 – 1 BvR 845/79 – preliminary print p. 18). When parents fail to fulfil their responsibilities, the state's watchdog function pursuant to Article 6.2 sentence 2 of the Basic Law intervenes; the state is not only entitled but also obliged to ensure the care and upbringing of the child. This obligation incumbent on the state arises primarily from the fact that as a holder of fundamental rights, the child is entitled to the protection of the state (see Decisions of the Federal Constitutional Court (*Entscheidungen des Bundesverfassungsgerichts* – BVerfGE 24, 119 (144)). Children may be separated from their families against the will of the parents on the basis of the law only if the parents fail in their duties or if the children are otherwise in danger of serious neglect (Article 6.3 of the Basic Law).

§ 1666.1 sentence 1 and § 1666a of the Civil Code as amended by the Act on Parental Custody are consistent with these constitutional provisions: according to the provisions of civil law, children can be separated from their families in case of non-culpable parental failure, if the risk for the best interests of the children cannot otherwise be prevented.

1. § 1666 old of the Civil Code required a culpable breach of the parental right to bring up the child. However, in case-law and the literature refusal to listen to reason and incorrigibility have been deemed fault, when proceeding on the basis of the thoughts of a reasonable adult (see decision of the German Federal Court of Justice (*Bundesgerichtshof* – BGH, *Zeitschrift für das gesamte Familienrecht* – FamRZ 1956, p. 350-351; Hermann Lange, in: Soergel/Siebert, *BGB*, 10th ed. 1971, *§ 1666*, marginal nos. 14 et seq., with further references; Diederichsen, in: Palandt, BGB, 35th ed. 1976, § 1666, marginal no. 2).

The grounds stated for the inclusion in § 1666 of the Civil Code as amended by the Act on Parental Custody of non-culpable parental failure as the prerequisite for intervention are that the child's best interests could be endangered without the parents being at fault or without their fault being provable (see *Bundestag* printed paper 7/2060 p. 28): It was considered possible that parents might be unable to cope with parental responsibilities despite their best intentions and personal commitment. Determination of fault caused considerable problems especially where the parents' refusal to listen to reason or their incorrigibility was caused by certain intellectual or mental abnormalities. It also had to be taken into account that the express determination of fault in the decision handed down by the guardianship court was often seen as discrimination by the parents, which could considerably impair the cooperation between the parents and the guardianship court or the youth welfare authorities, to the detriment of the child. Finally, it was stated that there was a discrepancy lacking objective justification insofar as measures under § 1666 old of the Civil Code depended on fault on the part of the parents, whereas there was no such requirement even for a particularly severe encroachment on parental rights under the Youth Welfare Act (*Jugendwohlfahrtsgesetz*).

According to these considerations, the revision through the Act on Parental Custody (SorgeRG) serves to create the legal requirements for the most comprehensive protection of the child possible.

2. The legislature assumed in line with Article 6.2 sentence 1 and Article 6.3 of the Basic Law that the separation of children from their parents constitutes the strongest encroachment on parental rights; it may only take place if the principle of proportionality is strictly observed. For this reason, upon a proposal of the Committee on Legal Affairs of the *Bundestag*, diverging from the government draft (*Bundestag* printed paper 8/111), the provision § 1666a was added to the Civil Code. The objective was to clarify that the separation of a child from its parents is only permissible where other measures are not sufficient in order to avert danger from the child. The assistance required was determined solely by the child's best interests and the parental rights, not by the necessary expense. In this context, § 1666a.2 of the Civil Code was intended to clarify that withdrawal of the entire custody rights only came into question where milder measures were insufficient. Hence the courts would have to attempt to avert danger from the child initially by issuing reminders and warnings, by imposing orders and prohibitions. Only where one had to assume that these measures would not be adequate could the most severe measure of withdrawal of the custody rights be applied (see *Bundestag* printed paper 8/2788 pp. 59-60).

Hence, with § 1666.1 sentence 1 in conjunction with § 1666a of the Civil Code, the legislature created a provision which enables the judge at the guardianship court to take sufficient account of the constitutionally guaranteed parental rights when ordering measures for protection of the child.

II.

In principle, the course of the proceedings, the determination and assessment of the constituent elements as well as the interpretation and application of constitutionally unobjectionable provisions in an individual case, are the responsibility of the non-constitutional courts having jurisdiction and are excluded from the scrutiny of the Federal Constitutional Court. The Constitutional Court is merely responsible for verifying whether there are errors in interpretation in the decision being contested, which result from a fundamentally incorrect view taken of the significance of a constitutional right or its scope of protection (see BVerfGE 18, 85 (92); 42, 143 (147 et seq.); 49, 304 (314)). In fulfilling this responsibility, however, the boundaries of the possibilities for intervention by the Federal Constitutional Court are not rigid and set in stone. Rather, they depend specifically on the intensity of the impairment of constitutional rights (established case-law, see BVerfGE 42, 163 (168)).

Where a child is separated from its parents against their will, this amounts to the strongest encroachment on parental rights possible under Article 6.2 sentence 1 of the Basic Law, which also affects the child just as severely. At the same time, the withdrawal of the care for the person of the child also constitutes a finding by the court that the parents have failed in their parental responsibilities. This assessment of their personalities affects the constitutional rights of the parents under Article 2.1 of the Basic Law (see BVerfGE 55, 171 (181)). In this factual situation, in addition to the question whether the decision contested contains errors caused by a fundamentally incorrect view taken of the significance of the constitutional right, especially the scope of protection it affords, individual errors in interpretation also have to be considered (see BVerfGE 42, 163 (169)).

III.

1. The decision of the Higher Regional Court, according to which the separation of the child from her parents can be enforced, is only compatible with the parental rights anchored in Articles 6.2 and 6.3 of the Basic Law if there is severe misconduct – even without fault – and correspondingly if the child's best interests are significantly at risk. Not every failure or inattentiveness by the parents entitles the state to exclude them from caring for and bringing up their child, or to assume this responsibility itself (see BVerfGE 24, 119 (144-145)). In the opinion he issued, the Federal Minister of Justice rightly pointed out that it is not sufficient in this respect for the child to be inadequately looked after within the family. Rather, the extent of

the parental misconduct has to mean that the child's physical, mental or emotional best interests are lastingly at risk.

2. The Higher Regional Court held that the complainants' child had been exposed to parental failures in upbringing in the past, and would be in future, so that parental custody of the child had to be withdrawn from the parents in order to avert the danger:

It was held that the (female) complainant's handicap detrimentally affected her housekeeping and the related physical care of the child, which was not ensured without the aid of third parties, particularly the grandmother. Furthermore, the (female) complainant did not satisfy the fundamental prerequisites for upbringing, namely independence in housekeeping and the ability to attend to external family matters and to plan with foresight. Owing to her mental handicap, she was not in a position either to support her child in its favourable talents. For example, the reduction in the development deficit in the child's social and language behaviour was not due to her influence, but, rather, to attending of the nursery. The (male) complainant especially refused to accept that his daughter was not being looked after as necessary within the family. He left the upbringing of the child wholly to the incapable mother and his mother-in law, and behaved in an irresponsibly passive manner.

a) The findings are not sufficient to justify the separation of the child from the complainants in a manner that is consistent with the requirements of the Basic Law. The restricted ability of the (female) complainant to keep house herself and to attend to other family responsibilities without outside help and to plan with foresight, cannot as such justify the child's removal from the parents. Nor does the (male) complainant's passive behaviour as described in the decision satisfy the requirements under constitutional law for the withdrawal of parental custody rights. In particular, he cannot be expected to agree to placing of the child in a foster family without taking his wife's feelings into consideration.

Even if one were to assume failure by the complainants in the sense of § 1666.1 sentence 1 of the Civil Code, such failure did not lead to an acute or severe risk for the child's physical and mental best interests; the grounds of the decision contested do not permit this conclusion. The expert opinion of May 1979, on which the withdrawal of the complainants' rights of parental custody was ultimately based, confirms that the child "played in a concentrated manner" and only "rarely had deficits and uncertainties in language". It is irrelevant whether the child's positive development can be attributed to the parents' success in bringing up the child or is the result of attending a nursery.

If the parents were unable to provide a sufficient guarantee for the necessary care and upbringing following the child's release from the children's home, the development has shown that the risk for the child's best interests could be countered by a milder measure than that of separating the child from her parents. By making the care and upbringing of the child by the complainants dependent on her attending a nursery, in its provisional decision of May 1978 the Regional Court complied with the obligation incumbent on the state pursuant to § 1666a of the Civil Code, namely to first endeavour to counter parental failure with appropriate assistance and support measures in line with the principle of proportionality (see BVerfGE 24, 119 (145)).

b) Insofar as the decision contested is based on future risks for the child's best interests, the findings are not sufficient to justify separating the child from her parents.

aa) When assessing the future development, the Higher Regional Court (OLG) proceeded on the assumption of "talents" with which the child was equipped, to which the handicapped parents could not do justice.

It is true that the child's best interests in parental relations with it constitute the supreme guideline for parental care and upbringing. However, this does not mean that exercise of the state's watchdog function pursuant to Article 6.2 sentence 2 of the Basic Law, includes the best possible nurturing of the child's abilities against the will of the parents. The Basic Law leaves the decision on the continued education of the child after primary school firstly to the parents as the natural administrators of the child's upbringing. The primary responsibility of the parents for making decisions is based on the consideration that as a rule the child's interests are best exercised by the parents. In this respect the possibility that the child suffers genuine or putative disadvantages through its parents' decisions, which in the context of a selection of talents according to objective standards could have been avoided, is accepted (see BVerfGE 34, 165 (184)).

The separation of a young child from its parents on the grounds that they do not guarantee "the child's socialisation within a changing system of standards as well as educational and professional demands", is therefore incompatible with the Basic Law.

bb) Insofar as the complainants require state assistance in order to bring up their child, in view of their handicaps, it is possible that they were not sufficiently willing to cooperate with the responsible authorities. However, it has to be taken into account in this respect that they gained the impression at the start of the pregnancy that they were considered unsuitable to have and look after a child themselves. Since the child is the focus in the life of the (female) complainant in particular, she would possibly be more receptive towards the authorities if one gave her the feeling that she could look after her child herself with the support of state measures. In view of the strong emotional ties between the (female) complainant and her child,

and her willingness – both aspects are confirmed in the decision contested – one cannot automatically assume that if relations between the youth welfare office and the complainants were relaxed, they would not be able or willing to cooperate with the authorities insofar as necessary in the interest of the child. This assumption is also rebutted by the experience that the parents were willing to cooperate with the nursery school teachers at the nursery attended by the child since 1978, within the scope of their abilities.
Therefore, contrary to the view taken by the Higher Regional Court, it appears possible that dangers to the child's best interests could be averted in future by educational assistance or by ordering specific educational measures while observing the principle of proportionality.

IV.

In view of the above considerations, the Higher Regional Court failed to appreciate the significance and implications of the parental rights anchored in Article 6.2 sentence 1 in conjunction with Article 6.3 of the Basic Law. In particular, the decision contested, through which the complainants were deprived of all parental custody rights as the requirement of the separation of the child from her parents that was intended and prepared by the youth welfare office, does not take sufficient account of the requirement of proportionality that is pivotal in the present context. The decision therefore had to be reversed and the case referred back to the Higher Regional Court.

Justices: Dr. Benda, Dr. Simon, Dr. Hesse, Dr. Katzenstein, Dr. Niemeyer, Dr. Heußner; Justice Dr. Faller is unable to attend for signing.

No. 14

BVerfGE 61, 358
of 3 November 1982 – 1 BvL 25, 38, 40/80, 12/81 –
"Joint custody case"

HEADNOTE:

The provision contained in § 1671.4 sentence 1 of the Civil Code, according to which joint custody of divorced spouses for their children is ruled out even if they are willing and suited to continue to bear parental responsibility together in the child's best interests, violates the parental right contained in Article 6.1 sentence 1 of the Basic Law.

Judgment of the First Senate of 3 November 1982
on the basis of the oral hearing of 8 June 1982
– 1 BvL 25, 38, 40/80, 12/81 –

in the proceedings for constitutional review of § 1671.4 sentence 1 of the Civil Code (*Bürgerliches Gesetzbuch* – BGB) in the version of the Act Reforming the Law on Parental Custody (*Gesetz zur Neuregelung des Rechts der elterlichen Sorge*) of 18 July 1979 (Federal Law Gazette (*Bundesgesetzblatt* – BGBl.) I p. 1061) – submission order of the Königstein Local Court (*Amtsgericht*) of 12 February 1980 – 10 F 94/79 – So – 1 BvL 25/80 –, submission order of the Bielefeld Local Court of 10 June 1980 – 34 F 6/80 – 1 BvL 38/80 –, judgment of the Bergisch Gladbach Local Court of 15 August 1980 – 28 F 135/80 – 1 BvL 40/80 –, and submission order of the Waiblingen Local Court of 7 May 1981 – 11 F 129/81 – 1 BvL 12/81 –.

RULING:

§ 1671.4 sentence 1 of the Civil Code in the version of Article 1 no. 20 of the Act Reforming the Law on Parental Custody of 18 July 1979 (Federal Law Gazette I p. 1061) is incompatible with Article 6.1 sentence 1 of the Basic Law, and hence void.

EXTRACT FROM GROUNDS:

A.

The subject-matter of the proceedings which have been consolidated for a joint hearing and joint adjudication is the question of whether it is compatible with the Basic Law that parental custody for a child who is the issue of a marriage which has been dissolved by divorce must be assigned to one parent alone.

I.

On dissolution of the marriage by divorce, the question has always arisen as to who is to have the care for the person of the joint children in future.
1. According to § 74.4 of the Marriage Act (*Ehegesetz* – EheG) of 20 February 1946 (Act no. 16 of the Allied Control Council (*Kontrollratsgesetz Nr. 16*) – Official Gazette of the Control Council (*Amtsblatt des Kontrollrates* – KRABl.) 1945/48 p. 77), the consequence of the sole or primary fault of a spouse as to the divorce was in principle that custody was not assigned to him or her. By contrast, § 1671.3 of the Civil Code in the version of the Act on Equal Rights of Men and Women in the Field of Civil Law (*Gesetz über die Gleichberechtigung von Mann und Frau auf dem Gebiete des bürgerlichen Rechts – Gleichberechtigungsgesetz*) of 18 July 1957 (Federal Law Gazette I p. 609) – only considered the sole fault of a spouse to constitute as a rule a reason to refuse to assign parental power. Moreover, the court had to make the arrangement corresponding to the child's best interests, taking account of the overall circumstances, priority being given to a joint proposal on the part of the parents. § 1671.4 of the Civil Code went on to provide as follows:

> Parental power should as a rule be assigned to one parent solely. If the child's best interests so require, one parent may be assigned the care for the person of the child, and the other custody of the child's property.

With the First Act Reforming the Law on Marriage and Family – First Marriage Law Reform Act (*Erstes Gesetz zur Reform des Ehe- und Familienrechts* – 1. EheRG) of 14 June 1976 (Federal Law Gazette I p. 1421), in line with the transition from the fault principle to the breakdown principle in divorce law, the priority previously afforded to the parent not at fault with regard to the divorce ceased to apply to the assignment of parental power. The wording of § 1671.4 of the Civil Code remained unchanged.

§ 1671 of the Civil Code took on the following version by virtue of the Act Reforming the Law on Parental Custody of 18 July 1979 (Federal Law Gazette I p. 1061):

§ 1671 of the Civil Code

(1) If the parents' marriage is dissolved by divorce, the family court shall determine which parent shall have parental custody for a joint child.
(2) The court shall make the arrangement which is most beneficial to the child's best interests; the child's ties, in particular to his or her parents and siblings, shall be taken into account here.
(3) The court should only derogate from an agreed proposal made by the parents if this is necessary in the child's best interests. If a child who has reached the age of 14 makes a derogating proposal, the court shall rule according to subsection 2.
(4) Parental custody shall be assigned to one parent alone. If the child's property interests so require, custody of the property may be assigned in full or in part to the other parent.
(5) The court may assign the care for the person of the child and custody of the property to a guardian or curator if this is necessary to avert a danger to the child's best interests. It should assign a curator to the child to assert maintenance claims if this is necessary in the child's best interests.

2. a) The question as to whether joint custody could also be granted to divorced parents was disputed since § 1671.4 of the Civil Code in the version of the Equal Rights Act commenced its application. According to the opinion initially prevailing, such a possibility could not even be considered in case of such a joint motion on the part of the spouses … As reasoning, it was largely pointed out that the wording of § 1671.4 of the Civil Code did not permit this with regard to the context of its sentences 1 and 2. Over and above this, it was objected that joint custody ran counter to the child's best interests, who had to be kept out of the dispute between his or her parents and may not become the subject of an experiment.
After increasing criticism of the prevailing view had been expressed in the literature …, some Local and Regional Courts had initially favoured continuation of joint custody by divorced parents … In the ensuing period, in particular after the entry into force, through the First Marriage Law Reform Act, of the version of § 1671 of the Civil Code which dispensed with fault, Higher Regional Courts had also granted joint custody to divorced parents if such an arrangement was in the best interests of the child in question according to their estimation ….

b) The question of joint custody of divorced parents was also dealt with … at the public hearing of expert witnesses which was carried out during the legislative procedure to reform the law on parental custody. Some of the expert witnesses were in favour of this possibility: If both parents were fully able to bring up the child, had equally strong emotional ties with the child and would like to continue to bear the responsibility, this was said to be in the interest of the child (*Bundestag* printed paper – BT-Drucks. 8/2788, p. 63). In its recommendation for a resolution, which has become law, the Committee on Legal Affairs nonetheless came out against joint custody of divorced parents, the key argument for the Committee being that there was allegedly no practical need for such a regulation and that it was in the interest of the child if unambiguous circumstances were created by his or her affiliation to one parent at the time of the divorce (*Bundestag* printed paper, loc. cit.).
c) The dispute of opinion has also continued in the literature and in the case-law after the unambiguous decision on the part of the legislature against joint custody of divorced parents. Here, the regulation, where it is considered to be unconstitutional, is objected to for a violation of the parental right which is guaranteed by Article 6.2 sentence 1 of the Basic Law (*Grundgesetz* – GG) ….
In the same vein, the Berlin Court of Appeal (*Kammergericht*) considered § 1671.4 sentence 1 of the Civil Code to be unconstitutional (*Zeitschrift für das gesamte Familienrecht* – FamRZ 1980, p. 821): The prohibition to assign joint parental custody to both parents after divorce without permitting exceptions was said to violate the parental right guaranteed in Article 6.2 of the Basic Law as a fundamental right to care and upbringing of children. It was said that, in exercising its watchdog function, the state may only encroach on parental rights and parental responsibility with across-the-board prohibitions if individual measures were not sufficient to avert the danger to the child's best interests; it was said, however, that there was no experience to suggest that the child's best interests were always placed at risk if both parents retained joint custody after divorce.
In view of the fact that a submission to the Federal Constitutional Court (*Bundesverfassungsgericht*) cannot be considered for proceedings being pursued in Berlin, the Berlin Court of Appeal did not apply the provision that was recognised to be unconstitutional, and found in the case to be ruled on that the divorced spouses were jointly entitled to parental custody.

II.

1. a) The parties to the original proceedings which led to the submission by the Königstein Local Court – 1 BvL 25/80 – concluded marriage in 1975. Their son was also born in this year.

In the context of their petitions for divorce by mutual consent, the spouses – the wife is an Egyptologist and the husband a qualified mineralogist – moved for parental custody of the child to be assigned to them jointly. They submitted the following as reasoning: The child would continue to live together with them in the joint detached house after their separation and to be looked after by them alternately. This living arrangement also appeared to them to be desirable for the future in the interest of the child. It was said that he had been cared for by them alternately since his birth, and therefore found in both of them persons to relate to equally, and had equal emotional ties with both of them. They wished by these means to spare the child, for whom their separation had not entailed any tangible change because of the way they had previously lived, from undergoing a change of his environment and lifestyle. It was also possible to implement the alternating care entailed by the joint exercise of custody in professional terms.

The competent youth welfare office which had been heard in the original proceedings had favoured assigning parental custody to both spouses jointly.

b) The Local Court dissolved the marriage by divorce by final judgment of 12 February 1980 and carried out pension sharing. At the same time, it separated and suspended the proceedings to arrange parental custody. It submitted the matter to the Federal Constitutional Court for review of the constitutionality of § 1671.4 sentence 1 of the Civil Code.

With regard to the arrangement on parental custody which has to be made ex officio, the court would like to comply with the proposal of the divorced spouses and to leave joint custody to them, but considers itself prevented from doing so by § 1671.4 sentence 1 of the Civil Code. It considers this provision to be unconstitutional because of a violation of Article 6.2 of the Basic Law. The arrangement is said not to adequately consider the fact that both parents also continue to be entitled to the parental right protected by the Basic Law after dissolution of the marriage by divorce. The parental right may be permissibly restricted in the context of the exercise of the state's watchdog function for reasons of the child's best interests. Also, it is said that there are generally valid considerations making it appear appropriate in the majority of the cases which are to be regulated to assign custody to one spouse alone after divorce. The restriction of the joint parental right of both parents not permitting exceptions is however said not to be compatible with the Basic Law. It is said – as proven by the original proceedings – that case constellations are conceivable in which no concrete aspects of the child's best interests speak against the joint exercise of custody proposed by the parents.

2. a) In the proceedings on which the submission of the Bielefeld Local Court – 1 BvL 38/80 – is based, the parties – a secondary school teacher and a general teacher – had married in 1965. Two children were born within the marriage in 1966

and 1967. The husband left the marital home in the summer of 1976 and has been living with another woman since then. Independently of this, the father's contact with his children and his wife was not discontinued. Decisions in matters concerned with the children continued to be taken by both parents jointly.
In the divorce proceedings initiated by the husband in 1980, the spouses had moved by mutual consent for joint custody of the children to remain with both of them. They pointed out that, during the relatively long period of living separately, they had both accepted and fully shouldered joint responsibility for their children; in their view, there were no tensions or unresolved conflicts. For instance, the father came regularly several times per week to the home of his divorced wife in order to have contact with the children and spend time with them.
b) The Local Court dissolved the marriage by divorce by judgment of 10 June 1980, carried out pension sharing and provisionally assigned parental custody of the children to the wife by means of an injunction. At the same time, it suspended the proceedings for a final arrangement on parental custody and submitted the matter to the Federal Constitutional Court for review of the constitutionality of § 1671.4 sentence 1 of the Civil Code.
The court would like to concur with the parents' proposal made by mutual consent to assign joint custody. This was however said to be opposed by the impugned provision, which it considers to be unconstitutional because of a violation of Article 6.2 sentence 1 of the Basic Law: The across-the-board exclusion of one parent from parental custody after divorce was said not to be covered by the state's watchdog function. This was said to justify, taking account of the principle of proportionality, only such encroachments which were necessary in the child's best interests. However – as in the original proceedings – it was said that individual cases were conceivable in which the one-sided legal assignment of the child to one parent was blatantly counter to the child's best interests because it denied full legal recognition of the continuing natural parent-child relationship. This created a risk that differences of opinion between the parties in matters related to parental custody had to be brought before the courts rather more often than if both parents were still formally entitled holders of parental custody. It was also stated that the impugned provision could not be justified by stating that a "necessary" ruling on custody was only postponed; the outcome of the custody proceedings could never be regarded as final with regard to the further development of the child. Finally, the risk that the statutory combination of the rulings could be circumvented could be prevented by the family court being obliged according to the relevant procedural provisions in any case to hand down a ruling on custody; since this set of proceedings was determined by the principle of official investigations, it was also said to be guaranteed that the court seized of the matter was able to form a precise picture of the situation

of the children in question, and was therefore able to reach an arrangement that was required by the child's best interests.

3. a) In the original proceedings before the Bergisch Gladbach Local Court – 1 BvL 40/80 – the parties – a lawyer and a procura-holder – had married in 1962. A son issued from the marriage, born in 1965, who has been living in the household of his mother since the separation of the spouses in 1979.

In the divorce proceedings initiated by the husband, the parties had proposed to the court by mutual consent to assign parental custody of the son to both parents and to waive an explicit arrangement of the right of access. They had stated as reasoning that this proposal did most justice to the son's best interests. It was said that he could thus expect from both parents the most support for the development of his personality, especially since he had a particular relationship of trust with both parents. It was said to be planned for the mother to care for the son in personal terms, whilst the father was to look after school-related matters.

The competent youth welfare office had favoured an assignment of parental custody to both parties. The son, who was almost 15 years of age at the time of his hearing, had taken the view that the arrangement practiced to date worked; he had good contacts with both parents. For instance, he spent more time during his holidays with his father than with his mother. His living arrangements had actually changed only slightly since his parents' separation.

b) The Local Court dissolved the marriage by divorce by judgment of 15 August 1980, found that pension sharing was not to take place between the parties, and at the same time provisionally assigned custody of the child to the mother. It suspended the consolidated proceedings on the parental custody arrangement and submitted to the Federal Constitutional Court the question of the constitutionality of § 1671.4 sentence 1 of the Civil Code.

The court would like to concur with the parents' joint proposal, which the son did not contradict, and assign parental custody to both parents jointly, since – for reasons explained in detail – this is said to be most beneficial to the son's best interests and such an arrangement is said to be completely practicable in the case at hand according to the court's conviction.

The Local Court however considers itself to be prevented from handing down such a ruling by the unambiguous wording of § 1671.4 sentence 1 of the Civil Code. It considers the provision to be initially unconstitutional because of a violation of Article 6.2 of the Basic Law. The across-the-board exclusion of joint custody by divorced parents is said not to be justified by Article 6.2 sentence 2 of the Basic Law; the regulation is said to be incompatible with the constitutional principle of proportionality. It is said that the legislature could have granted to the judges, whose margin of appreciation had in any case been considerably expanded by the Act Reforming the Law on Parental Custody, more comprehensive jurisdiction for a custody arrangement orientated towards the child's best interests.

Over and above this, the court also considers that the provision put forward for review violates the fundamental value determination of the legislature adopting the constitution expressed in Article 6.1 of the Basic Law. For a child who because of its descent from both parents, and because of the original care and upbringing by both parents, had a tie with the latter deeply determining its personality, the impact of the protection afforded by Article 6.1 of the Basic Law had to be such that it was maintained as far as possible. If joint upbringing and care by both divorced parents was psychologically more beneficial to the child than assignment to one parent, an obligatory regulation according to which only one parent could be legally entitled to care and upbringing would destroy a naturally existing tie between the child and the parent without custody, and hence particularly the elementary family tie protected by the constitution. This could certainly not be accepted without a special justification.

4. a) In the proceedings which led to the submission of the Waiblingen Local Court – 1 BvL 12/81 –, the parties – a procura-holder and an office clerk – concluded marriage in 1969. From this issued a son born in 1974 and a daughter born in 1975, who have been living with their mother since the spouses separated in 1978.

In the divorce proceedings applied for by the husband in 1980, the spouses applied by mutual consent for parental custody of both children to be assigned to them jointly. They had claimed as grounds that all decisions concerned with the future of the children had been discussed and taken jointly. The right of access had not been implemented according to strict rules during the time of living separately, but on an ad hoc basis and without difficulties. The maintenance of the children was arranged such that the mother withdrew as much money from a joint account of the spouses as she needed for herself and the two children.

The competent youth welfare office had no reservations against assigning joint custody.

b) The Local Court dissolved the marriage by divorce by judgment of 19 February 1981, carried out pension sharing and assigned parental custody of the children to the wife by means of an injunction. By order of 7 May 1981, it suspended the proceedings for a parental custody arrangement and submitted the case to the Federal Constitutional Court for review of the constitutionality of § 1671.4 sentence 1 of the Civil Code.

The family court is convinced that joint custody by the parents would be in the children's best interests. It also considers the opposing provision contained in § 1671.4 sentence 1 of the Civil Code to be unconstitutional because of a violation of Article 6.2 of the Basic Law; the legislature was said, in exercising the state's

watchdog function, to have encroached on the parental right in an impermissibly global manner even though cases were certainly conceivable in which joint exercise of the parental right was unlikely to be disadvantageous, but rather advantageous, to the child in question.
The court also considers the provision submitted for review to be incompatible with Article 3.1 of the Basic Law. It complains in this respect that – in contradistinction to existing marriage – an encroachment was made on the parental right after divorce without this being justified by the obligation to protect the child's best interests.

III.

1. The Federal Minister of Justice, who made a statement in the name of the Federal Government, considers the provision contained in § 1671.4 sentence 1 of the Civil Code to be compatible with Article 6.2 of the Basic Law. The decision taken by the legislature was said to be based on a weighing between the child's best interests and parental responsibility.
…
2. The parties to the original proceedings on which the submission of the Königstein Local Court was based have concurred with the view of the submitting court.

IV.

1. In the oral hearing, Prof. Dr. Pechstein, Director of the Rhineland-Palatinate Child Neurological Centre, as well as of the Institute for Social Paediatrics in Mainz, and Prof. Dr. Dr. Fthenakis, Director of the State Institute for Early Childhood Education in Munich, were heard as expert witnesses on a variety of questions from the group of problems related to joint custody by divorced parents. Both also ultimately favoured opening to parents the possibility of joint parental responsibility after dissolution of their marriage by divorce.
…

B.

The provision contained in § 1671.4 sentence 1 of the Civil Code, which cxplicitly prescribes the assignment of custody for a child issuing from a dissolved marriage to one parent and does not even permit the father and mother to continue to be entitled to joint custody of their children after dissolution of the marriage in exceptional cases, is incompatible with the parental right of Article 6.2 sentence 1 of the Basic Law.

I.

1. The constitutional guarantee of the parental right acts primarily to protect the child. It is based on the fundamental concept that as a rule parents are more concerned for the child's best interests than any other person or institution. The parental right is a freedom right in the relationship with the state, which on principle may only encroach on the parents' right to bring up their children if this is permitted by the watchdog function which it is entitled to exercise according to Article 6.2 sentence 2 of the Basic Law. In the relationship with the child, its best interests must be the sine qua non of parental care and upbringing. Article 6.2 sentence 1 of the Basic Law provides – and this is clearly expressed in the wording of the provision – a fundamental right and a fundamental obligation at the same time. The parental right has therefore been designated as a fiduciary right, a serving fundamental right, a freedom assigned in trust that is entrusted in the true sense of the word (see Decisions of the Federal Constitutional Court (*Entscheidungen des Bundesverfassungsgerichts* – BVerfGE) 59, 360 (376-377)). The constitutionally guaranteed parental right is hence contingent on the parents being willing and able to exercise their right of upbringing in the child's best interests; only on this condition may one presume that the responsibility entailed by the parental right is fulfilled (BVerfGE 56, 363 (382)).
2. Article 6.2 sentence 1 of the Basic Law presumes a standard case in which the child lives in a family community with parents who are linked by marriage and in which the father and mother care for and bring up the child jointly (BVerfGE 31, 194 (205)). The upbringing and care of a minor child by a mother and father within a harmonious community best guarantees that the child grows to become an autonomous personality and is able to live in a community (see BVerfGE 24, 119 (144)). As the expert witness Prof. Dr. Pechstein stated, it corresponds to the knowledge in all areas of child science that the longevity of family social relations is regarded today as the key basis for the stable, healthy psychosocial development of a growing person.
3. The child's ties of affection to mother and father can continue regardless of the separation and divorce of its parents. If joint exercise of the parental responsibility by both parents is no longer possible in the previous manner, they are nonetheless obliged to alleviate wherever possible the damage done to the development of the child which as a rule ensues by virtue of their separation and to find a sensible solution which is in the best interests of the child for its care and upbringing, and for its

further personal relations with them (see BVerfGE 31, 194 (205)). In exercising a parental right thus understood and continuing, separated or divorced parents must therefore aspire not to burden the children with their conflicts. This includes in particular also that one parent omits everything which might impair the child's relationship with the other (see § 1634.1 sentence 2 of the Civil Code). By these means, divorced parents can bring about a situation in which residual family ties are preserved which are beneficial to the development of the child.

However, not only the marital community, equipped as it is with rights and obligations, but also the domestic community of the child with the parents, is finally destroyed by divorce. Further, even a child who retains close contact with both parents after the divorce no longer lives with its parents constantly, but with its mother or father, depending on its place of residence, even with the most generous constellation of the right of access. Divorce hence has an impact on the parent-child relationship even in cases in which divorced parents meet their ongoing parental responsibility.

In view of these consequences which are entailed by divorce, the legislature was able to order in a constitutionally unobjectionable manner that a ruling of the family court on custody for joint children in connection with divorce had to take place without exception (§ 1671.1 of the Civil Code and §§ 621.1 no. 1, 623.1 sentence 1 as well as 623.3 sentence 2 of the Code of Civil Procedure (*Zivilprozeßordnung* – ZPO)) and should not for instance be restricted to cases in which a conflict arises. Insofar as the courts here – according to § 1671.3 sentence 1 of the Civil Code – should only derogate from a concurrent proposal on the part of the parents if this is necessary in the child's best interests, this provision does justice to Article 6.2 sentence 1 of the Basic Law; a decision with mutual consent on the part of the parents regarding the person having custody after the breakdown and dissolution of their marriage by divorce as a rule speaks in favour of the fulfilment of their ongoing parental responsibility.

II.

If divorced parents are unable to agree as to which of them is to exercise parental custody for their joint child, it follows from the general task of the state to protect the legal order and the legal peace that it is entitled to decide itself on the equalisation of the parents' contradictory interests (BVerfGE 31, 194 (205)). Since its activity aims in cases of conflict to strike a balance between legal positions of divorced parents, both independent and protected by the parental right, without touching on their priority as educators, it is not bound by the strict preconditions which must apply to an encroachment on the parental right of upbringing (BVerfGE loc. cit. (208)).

In cases however in which both parents are willing to continue to bear joint responsibility for their child after divorce, there is no need for the state to arbitrate as to opposing interests of the parents. If, over and above this, both parents are still fully able to participate in bringing up the child, and if there are no other reasons making it appear to be suited in the child's best interests to assign custody to one parent, the state is also not required in exercising its watchdog function to exclude one parent from the care and upbringing of the child and to restrict him or her to a right of access. If it nonetheless rules out without exception the continued existence of joint parental responsibility after divorce, this constitutes an encroachment on a legal position of the parents protected by Article 6.2 sentence 1 of the Basic Law which requires special justification.

In this respect, other conditions apply than with parents whose child grows up in their non-marital community. Here, because of the deliberate refusal of the parents to conclude marriage with one another, the state is within the limits of the margin of appreciation incumbent on it if it refuses legal participation in custody to the non-marital father and has placed the minor child born out of wedlock solely in the parental custody of the mother (BVerfGE 56, 363 (385-386)). The legislature is certainly not constitutionally required to create a regulation opening up the possibility of joint custody for unmarried parents. By contrast, married parents obtain joint care for the person of their children on the birth of their child according to § 1626.1 sentence 1 of the Civil Code which they also carry out with joint responsibility as a rule, up to separation, and which according to the provision submitted for review is removed from one parent on divorce.

III.

No reason can be identified justifying the nature of this regulation in not permitting exceptions.

1. This applies, first and foremost, in view of the constancy in the development and upbringing of the child. As is recognised in youth psychiatry and psychology, this takes on considerable significance … This was also what the legislature sought to do justice to in its ruling against joint custody of divorced parents. It presumed here that the agreement reached by the parents on carrying out their joint parental responsibility would not be permanent, so that assignment of custody to one parent was only delayed. Hence, nothing was however said to be gained for the continuity of upbringing. The latter was said to be guaranteed solely if unambiguous circumstances were created, and hence by assigning the child to one parent at the time of

divorce (*Bundestag* printed paper 8/2788, p. 61). These considerations on the part of the legislature are however unable to provide grounds for the regulation not permitting any exceptions.

a) The question as to the persistence of the agreement of divorced parents regarding the exercise of joint care for the person of the child was not resolved in the hearing of the expert witnesses held in the legislative proceedings. Prof. Dr. Pechstein answered it at the oral hearing by stating that divorced parents – albeit a restricted number – are indeed able to exercise parental custody in the long term.

It can certainly not be ruled out that the situation of the spouses after their divorce may develop in such a way that responsible cooperation in the upbringing and care of their child is no longer possible, so that it becomes necessary for the court to make a ruling to assign the child to one parent. Also in such a case, it may however be that the particular phase of the child's life in which the parents were still able to shoulder their parental responsibility jointly proves to be key to the development of the child, and that the joint effort of the parents for their child has had a positive impact in this respect. Continuity of parental upbringing guaranteed by the joint exercise of parental custody for a temporary period may hence be in the child's best interests in some cases.

Moreover, it is not rare for new rulings to become necessary, even in those cases in which custody of the child is assigned to only one parent from the outset. This is caused by the difficulty of the prognosis as to the development of the circumstances which are important for a growing child, and by the length of the regulatory period … The legislature has considered this and opened up to the guardianship and family courts in § 1696 of the Civil Code the possibility to be able to change their orders at any time during the duration of parental custody if they consider this to be appropriate in the interest of the child.

b) According to the continuity principle, however, not only such a custody solution is to be aspired to which guarantees for the future that the child receives an upbringing which is as uniform and uncomplicated as possible after the dissolution of its parents' marriage by divorce. Rather, the emotional ties of the child to its parents and siblings at the time of the custody ruling are also to be taken into account (see BVerfGE 55, 171 (184)). The legislature also presumed this to be the case when it explicitly ordered in § 1671.2 second half-sentence of the Civil Code that the child's ties were to be considered because the transition to an incomplete family with only one parent was said to be least detrimental to the child if its ties were impaired as little as possible (*Bundestag* printed paper 8/2788, p. 61).

Such an impairment is however unavoidable if the child has equally strong emotional ties with the father and the mother and is to nonetheless opt for one parent although it is in its interest to have a parent-child relationship which is indissoluble lasting throughout childhood. As Prof. Dr. Dr. Fthenakis has stated, the joint custody of divorced parents for their children permits a high degree of continuity in this respect.

2. a) The danger of alien motives for the desire of the spouses to leave joint custody for their children to them after divorce also does not entail any adequate legitimation for the assignment of parental custody to one parent without exception.

Concern was expressed in the legislative proceedings that the possibility of joint custody for parents wishing to divorce could be a major incentive to feign unity in this matter towards the court in order to accelerate the divorce proceedings, whilst avoiding having the matter of custody ruled on together with the divorce (*Bundestag* printed paper 8/2788, p. 63). Over and above this, the Federal Minister of Justice pointed out in his statement that parents might propose to the courts to retain joint custody because they shied away from an argument, and thus in the final analysis merely wished to avoid a dispute, and their decision in this respect was not orientated towards the child's best interests. The literature considers a further risk to lie in the fact that the parents might reach agreements regarding joint custody that were detrimental to the children if the alleged agreement between the parents was based in the final analysis on blackmail of the economically, mentally or emotionally inferior parent …

Manipulated custody decisions must be avoided in the child's best interests. Considerations of this nature may however not lead from the outset and without exception to a rejection of joint custody by divorced spouses. The child must take priority where there is any conflict between the interests of the parents and the best interests of their child (see BVerfGE 37, 217 (252)). Such conflicts must however be solved in the individual case; this may not be prevented by a statutory regulation which is able to prevent abuse only by accepting possible violations of fundamental rights (see BVerfGE 29, 104 (118)).

b) According to § 1671.2 first half-sentence of the Civil Code, the court must bring about the arrangement which is most beneficial to the child's best interests. The difficult task faced by the judge in taking account of this standard in conjunction with the divorce (§§ 621 and 623.1 of the Code of Civil Procedure) to clarify who is to have the right and the obligation to care for the minor children after divorce, exists regardless of whether only one parent or both can be considered entitled to custody. The objection that a judge might lean towards concurring with the parents' proposal as to joint custody in order to simplify the proceedings without carrying out the review incumbent on him or her as to the child's best interests … cannot take on constitutional significance. Moreover, this objection would have to be raised in the same way against the material provision contained in § 1671.2 of the Civil Code;

here too, the judge may not satisfy himself or herself with an agreed proposal made by the parents.

3. The other considerations asserted against joint custody of divorced spouses are also unable to justify the impugned provision.

a) The ruling against joint custody is reasoned *inter alia* by stating that parents are certainly able to achieve the outcome which they wished for in practical terms by means of private arrangements (*Bundestag* printed paper 8/2788, p. 63). The parent exercising parental custody was said to need only to involve the other in this implementation. The other was said to then contribute towards upbringing and able to help towards all matters related to the child. It was said that the proxy of the parent with custody was required in a number of cases. It was however not an unreasonable burden to issue and submit such a proxy.

That the necessities of everyday life do not require joint custody if the child's parents are divorced … is however without significance for the question of the constitutionality of § 1671.4 sentence 1 of the Civil Code. If, accordingly, the across-the-board exclusion of joint custody is reasoned by alleging that parents could neutralise the impact of the encroachment on their parental right by taking suitable measures, in other words by acting other than as provided for by the law, this is not a justification which is able to stand up to the constitution.

b) The "mass appeal" feared by the Federal Minister of Justice of permission of joint custody of divorced parents could solely consist, were there to be a corresponding statutory regulation, of a larger number of spouses filing applications for joint custody for their children in divorce proceedings. Even if there were to be a tangible increase in the number of such applications, however, these would only have to be allowed if the continuation of joint parental responsibility was in the child's best interests. Concurring with the Federal Minister of Justice, one must presume that a detailed judicial review of the individual case is needed here which might be able to delay a ruling on custody for longer than if it were a matter of assigning the child to one parent. This certainly applies to a comparison with cases in which spouses agree as to which of them is to assume custody of the children after divorce. Regardless of the fact that in frequently contentious custody proceedings the rapid clarification of custody which is desirable in the interest of the child can also not be achieved, the argument of the long duration of the proceedings is not suited to justify the impugned regulation. The same applies to the objection that the statutory possibility of joint custody after the divorce of the parents could lead to undermining the current regulation which is said to constitute the suitable solution to the typical situation on divorce. Insofar as such undermining cannot already be countered by an interpretation of the existing provisions, the legislature is at liberty to work by means of a suitable regulation towards the assignment of joint custody remaining the exception.

c) In a certain contrast to the "undermining effect" forecast on opening up the possibility to leave divorced spouses with joint custody, it is the consideration of the Federal Minister of Justice that experience shows that there would only be a very small number of cases in which the preconditions for practicing joint custody after divorce were met. These were said not to be suited to allow constitutional conclusions to be drawn; hence, the legislature was permitted to neglect them in its generalising regulation.

As Prof. Dr. Pechstein stated in the oral hearing, the assignment of custody to one parent is a suitable solution in the majority of impending divorce proceedings. This is concurred with by the fact that schematic custody rulings are to be avoided in the child's best interests after a motion had been filed by the spouses. The leaving of joint custody, rather, is contingent on the conviction of the judge that the spouses can continue to exercise the care and upbringing of their child jointly in the child's best interests, albeit in a form that is modified by divorce. On this premise, the presumption may be justified that even on opening the statutory possibility of joint custody, rulings in which both parents are assigned joint responsibility for their children after their divorce will remain the exception. This however does not justify the regulation of § 1671.4 sentence 1 of the Civil Code not permitting exceptions. A generalising regulation is only permissible if the encroachment on fundamental rights which it entails is not very intensive (see BVerfGE 45, 376 (390)). This cannot be presumed in this instance. Here, the encroachment on the parental right must be considered in a close connection with the obligation incumbent on divorced spouses to ensure that the damage to the child as a rule caused by divorce remains as slight as possible (see BVerfGE 31, 194 (205)). Insofar as parents are able to treat divorce largely as their own concern, so that the relationships between the child and both parents remain as intact as possible, they meet this obligation. It is hence primarily the child who is affected by the refusal to allow joint custody to his or her divorced parents in such cases. Even with a cautious assessment of the favourable impact on the development of a child from a marriage that has been dissolved by divorce had by the legalisation on the continuance of joint parental responsibility, the invocation of a necessary generalisation does not do justice to the problem under these circumstances; moreover, it does not adequately satisfy the fundamental-right claim of the child already impaired by the divorce of his or her parents to an arrangement which is orientated towards his or her best interests (see BVerfGE 55, 171 (179)).

d) Finally, the fear also cannot justify the impugned provision that it allegedly could not be ensured that the custody ruling would be amended in good time if the preconditions for joint custody of divorced parents for their child subsequently ceased to apply. Even if the child were to be assigned to one parent, changes in the circumstances cannot be ruled out which make a correction of the custody ruling appear urgently necessary in the child's best interests. Insofar as, however, the parent without custody – for whatever reason – is not interested in the fate of his or her child and, moreover, the conditions for deprivation of custody do not apply, the original ruling also remains. It is hence not evident that the best interests of the child who is in the joint custody of its divorced parents are at greater risk because a necessary change to the original custody ruling does not take place in an individual case.

Justices: Dr. Benda, Dr. Böhmer, Dr. Simon, Dr. Faller, Dr. Hesse, Dr. Katzenstein, Dr. Niemeyer, Dr. Heußner

The legislature did not initially substitute § 1671.4 sentence 1 of the Civil Code, which was declared void, by a new provision. With Article 1 no. 19 of the Act Reforming the Law of Parent and Child (Gesetz zur Reform des Kindschaftsrechts – KindRG) *of 16 December 1997 (Federal Law Gazette I p. 2942), § 1671 of the Civil Code was changed such that, with joint parental custody continuing in principle after separation or divorce, each parent can apply for assignment of sole custody.*

No. 15

BVerfGE 66, 84
of 10 January 1984 – 1 BvL 5/83 –
"Maintenance priority case"

HEADNOTE:

It is compatible with Article 6.1 in conjunction with Article 3.1 of the Basic Law (*Grundgesetz* – GG) if, in cases where the disposable income of the person liable for maintenance is insufficient to meet the minimum needs of all persons entitled to maintenance (case of shortfall), the legislature gives priority to the claim to maintenance of the divorced spouse who is in need by virtue of caring for a child, even if the new spouse is prevented from working by the care and upbringing of a child (§ 1582.1 sentence 2 of the Civil Code (*Bürgerliches Gesetzbuch* – BGB)).

Order of the First Senate of 10 January 1984
– 1 BvL 5/83 –

in the proceedings for the constitutional review of § 1582.1 sentence 2 of the Civil Code inserted by Article 1 no. 20 of the First Act for the Reform of Matrimonial and Family Law (*Erstes Gesetz zur Reform des Ehe- und Familienrechts* – 1. EheRG) of 14 June 1976 (Federal Law Gazette (*Bundesgesetzblatt* – BGBl.) I p 1421) – suspension of proceedings and submission order of the Schleswig-Holstein Higher Regional Court (*Schleswig-Holsteinisches Oberlandesgericht*) of 4 January 1983 (8 UF 309/79) –.

RULING:

§ 1582.1 sentence 2 of the Civil Code, inserted by Article 1 no. 20 of the First Act for the Reform of Matrimonial and Family Law of 14 June 1976 (Federal Law Gazette I p 1421), is compatible with the Basic Law in so far as the claim to maintenance of the divorced spouse is based on § 1570 of the Civil Code and the disposable income of the person liable for maintenance is insufficient to meet the minimum maintenance needs of all persons entitled to maintenance.

EXTRACT FROM GROUNDS:

A.

The submission concerns the question of whether priority under the law of maintenance for the divorced spouse over the new spouse of the person liable for maintenance is compatible with the Basic Law where both of them care for a child and the ability to pay of the person liable for maintenance is insufficient to meet the minimum needs of the person entitled to maintenance (“case of shortfall”).

I.

1. The First Act for the Reform of Matrimonial and Family Law of 14 June 1976 (Federal Law Gazette I p. 1421) – hereinafter: “the First Matrimonial Law Reform Act” (*Erstes Eherechtsreformgesetz* – 1. EheRG) – put the law on maintenance of spouses on a no-fault basis in line with the new rules of divorce law (for details see Decisions of the Federal Constitutional Court (*Entscheidungen des Bundesverfassungsgerichts* – BVerfGE) 57, 361 et seq.)). A claim to maintenance on account of need arising from the marriage exists where there is care of children:

§ 1570 of the Civil Code

> One divorced spouse may demand maintenance from the other as long and in so far as he or she cannot be expected to undertake gainful employment by reason of care for or upbringing of a child of the spouses.

Pursuant to § 1578.1 of the Civil Code, the amount of maintenance, which includes all the necessities of life, is in principle determined by the matrimonial circumstances. The cases in which the person liable for maintenance is not in a position to afford maintenance appropriate to the marriage are regulated as follows:

§ 1581 of the Civil Code

> If the person liable, with regard to his earnings and property situation, taking into account his other obligations, is unable without endangering his own appropriate maintenance to pay maintenance to the person entitled, he need pay main-

> tenance only to the extent that is equitable taking into account the needs and the earnings and property situation of the divorced spouses. He need not realise the basic assets to the extent that the realisation would be uneconomical or, taking into account the financial circumstances of both spouses, inequitable.

Subject to the requirements of § 1581 of the Civil Code, the following applies to the order of priority between concurrent maintenance claims of a divorced spouse and a new spouse:

§ 1582 of the Civil Code

> (1) In determining the maintenance of the divorced spouse under § 1581, the divorced spouse has priority over a new spouse if the latter would not be entitled to maintenance on application *mutatis mutandis* of §§ 1569 to 1574, § 1576 and § 1577.1. If the new spouse would have a claim to maintenance under those provisions, the divorced spouse nevertheless has priority over him or her if, under § 1570 or § 1576, he or she is entitled to maintenance or the marriage to the divorced spouse was of long duration. The period during which one spouse was entitled to maintenance under § 1570 by reason of the care or upbringing of a child of the spouses is equal to the duration of the marriage.
> (2) § 1609 remains otherwise unaffected.

§ 1609 of the Civil Code determines the order of priority of all persons entitled to maintenance if and in so far as the ability to pay of the person liable for maintenance is limited. Under § 1609.2 of the Civil Code, the claim to maintenance of the spouse is equal to that of the minor, unmarried children. The position of the divorced spouse in relation to the minor, unmarried children is not expressly regulated; however, in this regard, all marital partners of the person liable are deemed to be spouses because otherwise the priority of the divorced spouse over the new spouse could not be given effect …

II.

1. The original proceedings concern the actions for maintenance of a wife born in 1954 and divorced from the defendant in 1979 – the first plaintiff – and a daughter of the spouses, born in 1973 – the second plaintiff –. Custody of the daughter was granted to the mother, who is raising the child and does not work. The defendant remarried shortly after the divorce. A child has also resulted from this marriage, who is in the care of the non-working wife.

The Family Court (*Familiengericht*) awarded the divorced wife DM 530 and the daughter DM 200 in maintenance per month for the period from 1 January 1981. In his appeal, the defendant seeks a reduction of his liability for maintenance. In her cross-appeal, the second plaintiff seeks an increase in her maintenance.
The submitting court takes as basis a minimum need of DM 750 per month for the divorced spouse and a "large retention amount" of DM 1100 for the defendant, which is reduced as against the maintenance claims of his children to DM 850 ("small retention amount"). To meet the claims of all persons entitled to maintenance, the court calculates that DM 711.84 is available per month, which is then increased by DM 250 in respect of the children. On application of § 1582.1 sentence 2 of the Civil Code, the defendant would have to pay to his divorced wife DM 494 per month. Taking account of half of the child benefit in assessing the claim for maintenance, the first child would be able to claim DM 203 and the second DM 128. The defendant would be left with DM 987 per month; a claim for maintenance by the second wife would fail in its entirety.
2. The Higher Regional Court (*Oberlandesgericht*) stayed the proceedings and submitted the matter in accordance with Article 100.1 of the Basic Law for a decision as to whether § 1582.1 sentence 2 of the Civil Code is compatible with the Basic Law to the extent that it provides that the divorced wife is to take priority over the new wife even if both have a claim to maintenance on account of caring for a child (§ 1570 of the Civil Code) and the ability to pay of the husband liable for maintenance is insufficient to meet the minimum needs of each of them (case of shortfall).
The court takes the view that the provision objected to infringes Article 6.1 and Article 2.1 of the Basic Law. According to the court, the new marriage, although intact, in contrast to the failed marriage, is treated in an unconstitutional fashion as a lesser-ranking marriage. Article 6.1 of the Basic Law guarantees the right to be able to enter into a marriage and to found a family. Therefore, the financial consequences of the dissolution of a marriage ought not to restrict unduly the freedom to marry.
The court argues that if the new wife is forced to claim public funds, that represents considerable psychological strain for the spouses in the new marriage, which could cause the marriage to break down. The forgoing of children, expected of the spouses on account of the higher priority for entitlement to maintenance of the former partner of the person liable for maintenance, interferes excessively in the sphere of their private lives and does not take account of the fact that remarriage frequently occurs because of existing further children.
The court further argues that § 1582.1 sentence 2 of the Civil Code also infringes the principle of proportionality, as the spouse liable for maintenance is compelled to make payments, even below the "limit of sacrifice" under the law of mainte-

nance, which is fixed by the "small retention amount" exclusively in favour of minor children. In a case of shortfall, in view of the mutual responsibility of the spouses under the law of maintenance, as laid down in § 1360 of the Civil Code, he must share his remaining funds with his wife, even though they are just sufficient for himself.

III.

1. The Federal Minister of Justice, who has made a statement on behalf of the Federal Government, considers § 1582.1 sentence 2 of the Civil Code to be compatible with the Basic Law. …

2. The Federal Court of Justice (*Bundesgerichtshof* – BGH) has advised that no questions of law relating to the provision submitted have been decided previously or are pending.

B.

The submission is admissible.

The court has limited the question submitted to the application of § 1582.1 sentence 2 of the Civil Code in cases where the claim to maintenance of the divorced spouse is based on § 1570 of the Civil Code, the new spouse him or herself would be entitled to maintenance on account of care of a child and there is a "case of shortfall". If there is no case of shortfall, the court is able, according to its own observations (see *Zeitschrift für das gesamte Familienrecht* – FamRZ 1982, pp. 705-706), to interpret the provision submitted for review in conformity with the constitution. Since the question submitted can be confined solely to the facts relevant to the decision in this case (see BVerfGE 36, 41 (44)), the constitutionality of § 1582.1 sentence 2 of the Civil Code is to be reviewed only in so far as it provides for priority for maintenance for the divorced spouse even if the new spouse also cares for a child and the person liable for maintenance is not in a position to meet the minimum needs of all persons entitled to maintenance.

C.

To that extent, § 1582.1 sentence 2 of the Civil Code is compatible with the Basic Law.

I.

The provision submitted is to be reviewed on the basis of Article 6.1 in conjunction with Article 3.1 of the Basic Law.

Article 6.1 of the Basic Law contains a fundamental provision for the whole area of private and public law concerning marriage. It must be presumed here that every marriage is equal before the law. Constitutionally, this follows from the fact that Article 6.1 of the Basic Law places every marriage under the protection of the state without distinction, whether entered into by the partners as a first marriage or after a divorce (see BVerfGE 55, 114 (128-129)).

Although the mutual obligations of marriage are certainly altered by separation and the dissolution of the marriage, they are not ended (see BVerfGE 53, 257 (297)). It follows that not only the existing marriage, but also the consequential effects of a dissolved marriage, of which the maintenance system forms part, are protected by Article 6.1 of the Basic Law (BVerfGE, loc. cit. p. 296). It is therefore necessary to take as a starting point two fundamental-rights positions based on that guarantee, so that the question of whether the priority for maintenance of the divorced spouse represents an unconstitutional disadvantage for the spouses in a new marriage cannot be reviewed on the basis of Article 6.1 of the Basic Law in isolation. Rather, regard must additionally be had to the general principle of equality (Article 3.1 of the Basic Law) as a standard of review.

II.

§ 1582.1 sentence 2 of the Civil Code – in so far as it is the subject-matter of the constitutional review – does not infringe Article 6.1 in conjunction with Article 3.1 of the Basic Law.

1. a) Article 6.1 of the Basic Law prohibits the state from undermining or otherwise impairing marriage. This also applies to the material and economic aspects of marriage (see BVerfGE 55, 114 (126-127)). In this context, the legislature must, wherever possible, avoid regulations which would be capable of interfering in the spouses' free determination of the allocation of tasks within the marriage (see BVerfGE 39, 169 (183); 48, 327 (338)). An autonomous lifestyle includes, on the one hand, the decision of the spouses to have children, and, on the other, the matter of whether one spouse alone should earn the family income and the other devote him or herself to the care of the children (see BVerfGE 61, 319 (347)).

Equally, the divorced spouses were free to organise their family life in such a way that the wife managed the household as well as undertaking the care and upbringing of the children. Having regard to Article 3.2 of the Basic Law, those functions were equal in value to the divorced husband's maintenance functions which he performed by providing the necessary money (see BVerfGE 37, 217 (251) with further references). According to the case-law of the Federal Constitutional Court (*Bundesverfassungsgericht*), the legislature had to proceed on the basis that the equal entitlement of both partners, which continues to affect their relationship under the law of maintenance after the dissolution of the marriage, also formed part of the nature of this marriage – intended to be for life – for the purposes of the guarantee laid down in Article 6.1 of the Basic Law (see BVerfGE 53, 257 (296) with further references).

b) The legislature had to solve the problem of regulating the claims to maintenance of the divorced and the new wife in accordance with the Basic Law, while the application of the principle of equality is influenced by the personal and material sphere in question (see BVerfGE 60, 123 (134); established case-law), which in this case is determined by Article 6.1 of the Basic Law. However, the original situation is characterised by the fact that it involves two conflicting legal positions, both of which are protected by Article 6.1 of the Basic Law. Because of that equal status in the eyes of the Basic Law, no specific requirements concerning the legislature's regulatory power can be derived from Article 6.1 of the Basic Law. Instead, it must merely be examined whether there are sufficient grounds for the difference in treatment required by the legislature as between the divorced and the new wife. The Federal Constitutional Court does not have to decide whether the legislature has adopted the fairest and most suitable system in each case, but merely whether the legislature has kept within the utmost limits of its freedom of action (see BVerfGE 52, 277 (281); established case-law).

2. The legislature has not overstepped those limits in § 1582.1 sentence 2 of the Civil Code with respect to the case of shortfall. As the legislative process shows, the difference in treatment is based on sufficient grounds.

a) The First Matrimonial Law Reform Act was preceded by many years of research which also covered the problem of concurrent claims to maintenance of divorced and new spouses. To justify priority under the law of maintenance for the divorced spouse, the report of the Matrimonial Law Commission (*Eherechtskommission*) drew attention, *inter alia*, to the difficulties which existed in enforcing maintenance claims of divorced spouses, in particular the divorced wife, and which could be countered at least in part by priority for maintenance …

However, the Matrimonial Law Commission had pronounced itself in favour of a hardship clause under which a claim to maintenance of the divorced spouse would not apply if and in so far as the demands on the other spouse would be extremely harsh and inequitable in view of the particular personal circumstances of the spouses or the short duration of the marriage. This hardship clause was intended not to operate only in the first three months after the divorce … The *Bundesrat* also wanted to restrict the divorced spouse's claim to maintenance with the hardship clause proposed by it where this was necessary in order to avoid inequitable hardships for the new spouse … Whether the courts would be in a position, with an additional hardship clause, to find more satisfactory solutions in individual cases than is possible under the existing statutory position is not to be decided here.

b) In the legislative process, it was assumed that a divorced spouse who cares for children from the dissolved marriage thereby fulfils a task for which the person liable for maintenance, as the other parent, should also pay. It was argued that this gives his or her claim to maintenance a particularly strong basis, so that equity required that priority be conferred on him or her …

aa) The factual precondition for maintenance of caring for children (§ 1570 of the Civil Code), which gives rise to priority for the claim to maintenance of the divorced spouse, is intended to release the parent with whom the child lives from gainful employment, for as long and in so far as the child requires care or upbringing. From this point of view, the needy parent's claim to maintenance is intended, first, to ensure the discharging of his or her own parental responsibility, which forms a characteristic and integral part of the parental right (see BVerfGE 57, 361 (383)). In addition, however, there is still room for the legislative consideration that the maintenance payments to the divorced partner should at the same time be viewed as the financial discharge of the obligations in respect of care and upbringing peculiar to the person liable for maintenance (see BVerfGE loc. cit., pp. 382 and 385); this points towards a resolution of the maintenance conflict in favour of the divorced spouse. In that regard, it must be presumed, according to the case-law of the Federal Constitutional Court, that the parents' joint responsibility for their child continues beyond the dissolution of the marriage (see BVerfGE 31, 194 (205)), even if custody has been granted solely to the parent caring for the child.

bb) § 1582.1 sentence 2 of the Civil Code has been objected to on the ground that the legislature's concern to ensure the care and upbringing of the children is confined to those of the first marriage, but does not apply to the children of a second marriage … The latter are denied the personal care provided by one parent. As a result they are placed in a worse position than other legitimate children, without any objective reason. …

It is conceivable that, because of the priority for maintenance for the divorced spouse, married couples will be unable to exercise their freedom of decision in respect of the allocation of tasks within the marriage because they are both forced to work as a result of the low income of the person liable for maintenance and for this reason their children will need to be cared for by other people or fend for themselves. It does not however follow that the rule objected to is unconstitutional. On the one hand, in a case of shortfall, as shown in the original proceedings, the payments of the person liable for maintenance will in any event not cover the maintenance needs of the divorced spouse, so that in principle he or she will have to find – albeit limited – employment, during which he or she will be unable to care for the child him or herself. On the other hand, children in an existing marriage generally grow up in more favourable circumstances than children who now live in a family with only one parent (see BVerfGE) 57, 361 (382)).

c) The question of the constitutionality of priority for maintenance for the divorced spouse was not overlooked in the legislative process. The view that the rule infringes Article 1.1, Article 2.1, Article 3.1 or Article 6.1 of the Basic Law was not shared … Each spouse is only able to undertake new duties within the limits of what he or she can afford financially, which could also be limited by obligations undertaken at some time in a first marriage.

The submitting court clearly considers this argument unconvincing. In its observations on the considerable psychological strain placed on the new spouse by being forced to claim social assistance, the court follows the discussion paper of the Federal Ministry of Justice. The rejection by that paper of lower-ranking priority for the new spouse was based on the argument that, in such a case, if the new spouse is forced to rely on social assistance, this, even more than equal entitlement for the former spouse, would be likely to bring discord into the new relationship and place a burden on the matrimonial circumstances (loc. cit., p. 112; …). A family in which the wife suffers such economic discrimination from the outset tends to be doomed to break up …

By contrast, the Matrimonial Law Commission rightly attached special importance to the new spouse's knowledge of the maintenance claims which generally arise from marriage:

> The second spouse whom the person liable for maintenance marries knows of the former marriage. He or she also knows, in particular, that his or her marriage is encumbered with an "economic mortgage", namely, a duty to provide maintenance to the spouse of the first marriage. He or she can and must be prepared for this situation …

The Matrimonial Law Commission also proposed priority for maintenance for the divorced spouse on the further ground that a spouse in need of maintenance is unable successfully to resist the other spouse's petition for divorce indefinitely under the divorce law of the First Matrimonial Law Reform Act … The legislature was entitled to take this consideration into account by means of § 1582.1 sentence 2 of the Civil Code, with the result that the rule objected to cannot be deemed unfit for purpose. It is therefore also not inconsistent with an approach orientated towards the notion of fairness for the new spouse to be expected, if the worst comes to the worst, to claim social assistance. Making available public funds can help to ensure that the marriage to a new partner of a person liable for maintenance can in fact take place and that the new spouses are not forced to forgo having children.

d) The rule objected to is also not unconstitutional because the person liable for maintenance is obliged to share his "retention amount" with his wife.

In the case of an existing marriage, it is equally incumbent on both spouses to maintain the family appropriately through their work and with their assets (§ 1360 sentence 1 of the Civil Code). The maintenance duty of the spouses is therefore reciprocal; each spouse is, in relation to the other, both a person entitled to maintenance and a person liable for maintenance (see BVerfGE 17, 38 (53); …). It would be incompatible with the concept of the marital relationship to treat the maintenance obligations of the spouses as performance and consideration in the manner of bilateral contractual obligations (BVerfGE 17, 1 (11)). On the contrary, it accords with the rationale underlying § 1360 of the Civil Code that the burden of upkeep of the family is borne jointly by the spouses (Federal Court of Justice, (*Zeitschrift für das gesamte Familienrecht* – FamRZ) 1967, p. 380 (381); 74, p. 366 (367)). At the same time, the person liable cannot refuse to give his or her partner his or her contribution to the upkeep of the family on the ground that he or she is not in a position to pay maintenance without prejudicing his or her own needs. Such conduct would be out of keeping with the principle of marriage partnership and contrary to the system of maintenance under family law, according to which spouses are mutually obliged, irrespective of the matrimonial property regime, to contribute to the common upkeep as best they can without one spouse being able to keep back for him or herself a certain proportion of his or her income for his or her own needs (see BVerfGE 12, 180 (190)). In such a case, however, a spouse liable for maintenance, whose partner is disregarded in a case of shortfall on account of the priority for maintenance for the divorced spouse, cannot be "pushed below the limit of sacrifice under the law of maintenance" in contravention of Article 6.1 in conjunction with Article 3.1 of the Basic Law if he or she has to share his or her retention amount with his or her marriage partner on account of the spouses' mutual responsibility under the law of maintenance.

e) If § 1582.1 sentence 2 of the Civil Code is applied in the original case, a claim to maintenance of the divorced wife of DM 494 per month arises. Taking into account child maintenance (including child benefit), the one-parent family then has DM 722 DM per month available to it to meet its needs and the person liable for maintenance has DM 1175 for himself and his new family. Assuming that both women's claims to maintenance rank equally – a solution which the submitting court clearly considers constitutionally imperative – the claim to maintenance of each woman would amount to DM 291. The one-parent family would then have to get by on DM 519 while the two-parent family would be left with DM 1377 per month. This result proves that the rule objected to does not have, in a case of shortfall, consequences which would be obviously incompatible with the notion of fairness (see BVerfGE 24, 104 (109)).

Justices: Dr. Herzog, Dr. Simon, Dr. Hesse, Dr. Katzenstein, Dr. Niemeyer, Dr. Heußner, Niedermaier, Dr. Henschel

No. 16

BVerfGE 72, 122
of 18 June 1986 – 1 BvR 857/85 –
"Withdrawal of custody rights case"

HEADNOTE:

Decision regarding the representation of minors in constitutional complaint proceedings where the parents having custody of the child are prevented from representing their child's interests.

Order of the First Senate of 18 June 1986
pursuant to § 24 of the Federal Constitutional Court Act
(*Bundesverfassungsgerichtsgesetz* – BVerfGG)
– 1 BvR 857/85 –

in the proceedings regarding the constitutional complaint 1. of the minors a) Albert L., b) Alwine L., 2. of the Social Services of Catholic Women (*Sozialdienst Katholischer Frauen*) in B., 3. of the St. Vinzenz Children's Home, registered society – authorised representatives: …, lawyers – against a) the order of the Hamm Higher Regional Court (*Oberlandesgericht*) of 19 June 1985 – 15 W 175/85 –, b) the order of the Bochum Regional Court (*Landgericht*) of 19 March 1985 – 7 T 366/84 –.

RULING:

The constitutional complaint is dismissed as inadmissible.

EXTRACT FROM GROUNDS:

A.

The constitutional complaint concerns orders which reversed a decision of the Local Court in the temporary injunction proceedings, by means of which custody rights for the complainants in 1) were withdrawn from their unmarried mother and transferred to the complainant in 2).

I.

The mother is in principle entitled to the right and the duty to care for an illegitimate minor (§ 1705 sentence 1 of the Civil Code (*Bürgerliches Gesetzbuch* – BGB)). She may require surrender of the child from every person who is unlawfully withholding it from her (§ 1632.1 of the Civil Code). Where, however, the physical, mental or psychological best interests of the child are endangered by abusive exercise of the custody rights, by neglect of the child or by non-culpable failure of the unmarried mother, the guardianship court may even take measures which entail separating the child from its mother. These are, however, only permissible if the danger cannot be countered in another way (§ 1666.1 sentence 1, § 1666a.1 of the Civil Code; see Decisions of the Federal Constitutional Court (*Entscheidungen des Bundesverfassungsgerichts* – BVerfGE) 60, 79 (80 et seq.)).
A complaint against an order containing a decision on a matter affecting the custody rights for a child may be brought by any person with a justified interest in exercising such matters (§ 57.1 no. 9 of the Act on Matters of Non-Contentious Jurisdiction (*Gesetz über die Angelegenheiten der freiwilligen Gerichtsbarkeit* – FGG)).

II.

1. In December 1981 the unmarried mother of the complainants in 1) entered the Federal Republic of Germany from Zaire as an asylum-seeker with the children, who were eight and five years old at the time. The application for asylum has in the meantime been refused with final effect.
The family was initially accommodated in a hotel, but in early September 1982 was then put in an apartment in which relatives of theirs were already living. Following arguments with those living in the apartment the mother left the accommodation with her children after only a few days, went to the Social Welfare Office and asked for another apartment. A heated argument broke out, which culminated in the mother leaving the authority without her children. The children were taken to a

child welfare centre, from which their mother collected them again after she had managed on her own authority to find an apartment which happened to be empty but which she had to vacate again soon. She then took the complainants to a police station and told them to go inside; they would get help there, she said. After being temporarily accommodated elsewhere, the complainants in 1) were taken to the home run by the complainant in 3).

For a time the mother drew social welfare benefits, but according to the Youth Welfare Office had other income too. On one occasion she was seen in a bar, but she staunchly denies having engaged in prostitution. For the rest, she allegedly attempted to obtain social welfare benefits surreptitiously under a false name.

Criminal proceedings were instituted against the mother of the complainants in 1) on suspicion of street robbery of a woman from Ghana. Because she did not appear at the trial, a warrant was issued for her arrest. After her arrest she was first taken into pre-trial detention and then into detention awaiting deportation. She stated that she did not wish to leave the Federal Republic of Germany without her children. The Foreigners' Office twice in vain tried to fly her to Zaire alone. Each time she offered considerable resistance, so that the pilot refused to allow her to board the plane.

After the detention awaiting deportation was reversed, the woman refused to leave the detention facility because she was worried that she would be arrested by the police and deported without the complainants. In the end, she was removed from the detention facility by force. On account of her behaviour during her discharge from detention she was temporarily admitted to a psychiatric hospital and was then taken to a reception facility for asylum-seekers.

2. When the complainant in 3) was informed in May 1984 by the foreigners' authority that the complainants in 1) were to be taken to Zaire with their mother, it applied for a custody curatorship order and for the complainant in 2) to be appointed as curator. The application was supported by submissions made by a certified psychologist.

a) Custody of the complainants in 1) was thereupon withdrawn from the mother and transferred to the complainant in 2).

After the mother lodged a complaint, the Regional Court revoked the order. The preconditions for §§ 1666, 1666a of the Civil Code were not met, it found. It was not apparent that the physical, mental or psychological best interests of the complainants in 1) were in danger if the mother was able to determine their place of residence and was able to care for them in other respects as well. The mere fact that the mother had taken the complainants with her to the Federal Republic of Germany was evidence of her natural maternal instincts and her close attachment to them. The complainants had confirmed that their mother had never treated them

badly or even ill-treated them, but that she had always provided for them. Even taking account of those instances in which she had "abandoned" them could not prove the opposite. The incidents had only occurred because the mother had not felt able to provide for the complainants. In this context it was irrelevant that she had possibly brought about the difficulties herself. The fact that the mother had visited the children only infrequently in the children's home in the months prior to her detention was – insofar as could be ascertained – not to be put down to her indifference towards them. Rather, she had credibly, at least irrefutably, stated that she had been afraid that she would be arrested by the police on account of her illegal status.
The application for asylum was refused because the mother did not have to fear persecution in her home country. It was therefore to be assumed that she and the complainants in 1) could return to Zaire without being placed in any danger. The mother had declared that she would be killed in Zaire because she had a "problem" there. However, this was entirely unbelievable. There were no serious indications for the assumption made by the complainant in 2) that the mother wanted the complainants in 1) to die together with her.
The fact that the complainants in 1) had developed well in their current environment did not, in the opinion of the Chamber, provide sufficient grounds to withdraw custody from the mother. This favourable development would in all probability be interrupted if they had to leave the Federal Republic of Germany. However, given the mother's strong emotional attachment to the complainants, they would soon get used to being in their home country again.
Following a further complaint lodged by the complainants in 2) and 3), the Higher Regional Court revoked the order of the Regional Court and referred the case back to the Regional Court, because further investigations were necessary. The Higher Regional Court thereby assumed that the German courts had jurisdiction under international law, at least for the temporary injunction proceedings (Articles 1 and 8 of the Hague Convention concerning the Powers of Authorities and the Law Applicable in Respect to the Protection of Infants) of 5 October 1961 (Federal Law Gazette (*Bundesgesetzblatt* – BGBl.) II 1971, p. 217)).
b) The Regional Court did not amend its decision that the ascertained facts did not justify the permanent separation between the complainants and their mother which would be associated with her deportation. The street robbery was highly likely to have been an act of revenge on the part of the mother and her twin sister against the lover of the sister's husband. Even if – and this had not been proved – the mother had engaged in prostitution, this did not constitute a violation of her parental duty of care and protection. The fact that she had apparently attempted to obtain social welfare benefits under a false name was irrelevant in the present proceedings.

After spending two-and-a-half years living with the complainant in 3), the complainants in 1) had no doubt found people other than their mother to whom they could closely relate. However, they would be taken away from them even if they were to remain in the Federal Republic of Germany; since the intention was to put them into foster care. Even if the complainants did not wish to return to Zaire with their mother and the daughter did not even wish to encounter her mother in the court room, it was not to be feared that the complainants would suffer psychological harm on account of being returned to their mother. They were, after all, now nearly 12 and nine years of age; they had been separated from their mother at a time when they had already formed a close attachment to her.
c) The renewed further appeal on the part of the complainants in 2) and 3) was unsuccessful.
Contrary to the opinion expressed by these complainants, § 1666 of the Civil Code did not permit interference with parental custody after every impairment or endangering of the child's best interests. This could also hardly be reconciled with Article 6.2 and 6.3 of the Basic Law (*Grundgesetz* – GG). The mother could not be blamed for being unable to raise and provide for the complainants in 1) to such an extent which could justify further separating her from her children. The reference to the fact that if a child was given into foster care the duration of the foster care alone could lead to the guardianship court ordering that it remain there according to § 1632.4 of the Civil Code if serious and permanent harm to the child's physical or psychological best interests was to be expected if it were surrendered to the parents (see BVerfGE 68, 176) was erroneous; the complainants in 1) were living in a home and not in foster care. No indications were apparent that there was such a serious disruption in the complainants' relationship with their mother that even returning them to her would cause them psychological harm. For that reason no more supplementary expert opinions were required in respect of this issue.
Where the laws of the state giving residence required that the person having custody leave, the return to his or her home country was thus deemed reasonable and, if necessary, carried through by force, it could not be evaluated as an abuse of parental custody if the person having custody did not wish to be separated from his or her children. The Regional Court had, for the rest, correctly pointed out that the fate which awaited the complainants on their return to Zaire was unclear; but in the eyes of the mother their development were they to remain in the Federal Republic of Germany was equally uncertain. This too ruled out that the mother's insistence that the complainants be surrendered to her could be viewed as an abuse of custody.
3. In the constitutional complaint lodged against the latter orders of the Regional Court and of the Higher Regional Court the complainants complain of a violation

of Article 1.1, Article 2.1 and 2.2, Article 3.3, Article 6.2 and Article 103.1 of the Basic Law.

a) Based on the analogous application of § 57.1 no. 9 of the Act on Matters of Non-Contentious Jurisdiction, the complainants in 2) and 3) believe they are authorised to assert the fundamental rights of the complainants in 1). The mother had no interest in appealing the decisions, which were in her favour, by lodging a constitutional complaint. It therefore had to be possible for third parties to exercise the constitutional rights of the complainants in 1).

The constitutional complaint lodged by the complainants in 1) was also admissible. The current authorised representatives had not represented the complainants in 1) in the custody proceedings. However, that had already not been possible because they had not formally been parties to the temporary injunction proceedings. As the fundamental rights of the complainants in 1) could be violated on account of the contested decision, they had to have the right to lodge a constitutional complaint. The complainants in 2) and 3) had borne responsibility for the underage complainants for a longer period of time. As a result, they were authorised, in exercising the interests of the complainants in 1), to issue the effective power of attorney in regard to the lodging of the constitutional complaint.

b) The constitutional complaint was also well-founded.

The Higher Regional Court assumed that the complainants in 1) would face grinding economic and social hardship in Zaire. In addition, as a result of their previous history they would be subjected to ill-treatment in their home country. Nevertheless, the court had granted the mother custody rights and thus violated the fundamental rights of the complainants in 1) in respect of the safeguarding of human dignity and the free development of one's personality. The courts had not exercised the state's watchdog function (*Wächteramt des Staates*) [as regards the exercise of the parental duty of to care for and bring up their children] in the manner required by the constitution. Comparable court decisions involving a German unmarried women with two small children were not conceivable. Thus, Article 3.3 of the Basic Law had been violated. The courts had ignored the will of the children, which should have been taken into account. The complainants no longer had a close relationship with their mother. They had both stated that they did not wish to accompany their mother to Africa. The daughter was even afraid of her mother.

The complainants further complain that as well as the facts not being clarified, they had not received written submissions made by the authorised representative of the mother of the complainants in 1) until after the Higher Regional Court had issued its decision. The written submissions had contained incorrect legal explanations in respect of the interpretation of § 1666 of the Civil Code, which was decisive in the present case, and on which the contested decisions were also based. They had not been given the opportunity to respond to the written submissions.

III.

1. In the opinion of the Federal Minister of Justice, who submitted observations on behalf of the German Government, the constitutional complaint is inadmissible.

…

B. – I.

1. The constitutional complaint lodged by the complainants in 2) and 3) is inadmissible insofar as they complain of the violation of the fundamental rights of the complainants in 1) in their own name, since only those who have themselves been affected by an act of state can lodge a constitutional complaint. They are not affected in this manner because the complainants in 3) had instituted the proceedings for the withdrawal of custody rights and the subsequent court proceedings had been carried through by the complainants in 2) and 3). § 57.1 no. 9 of the Act on Matters of Non-Contentious Jurisdiction also grants third parties the right to lodge an appeal in their own name in custody proceedings insofar as there is a justified interest in the exercise of this matter. However, this rule is tailor-made to suit the needs of proceedings involving matters of non-contentious jurisdiction and cannot readily be transferred to constitutional complaint proceedings. Its application would be tantamount to allowing the fundamental rights of others to be asserted in one's own name. However, the constitutional complaint cannot be lodged by way of representative action (see BVerfGE 25, 256 (263); 31, 275 (280) with further references).

2. The constitutional complaint lodged by the complainants in 2) and 3) is also inadmissible insofar as it complains of a violation of Article 103.1 of the Basic Law. They can in principle refer to this fundamental procedural right, since according to the provisions of the Act on Matters of Non-Contentious Jurisdiction they were parties to the proceedings which led to the contested decisions (see BVerfGE 21, 362 (373)). However, this complaint was not sufficiently substantiated (§ 92 of the Federal Constitutional Court Act).

The complainants assert that the court had not given them the opportunity before making its decision to submit a statement regarding the written submissions made by the mother of the complainants in 1), which contained incorrect legal explanations in respect of § 1666 of the Civil Code. However, the grounds for the order issued by the Higher Regional Court show that the court was aware of the complainants' divergent legal opinion and that it had been informed thereof and had taken it into consideration. Given this state of affairs, the complainants would have had to explain what it was they would have wanted to submit over and above their previous submissions had they been given a time-limit within which to make written submissions. This is the condition which must be met for a complaint of a violation of Article 103.1 of the Basic Law to be admissible (see BVerfGE 66, 155 (175)).

II.

Insofar as the constitutional complaint was lodged by the complainants in 1), it can be assumed to be admissible, as it must in any case be rejected pursuant to § 24 of the Federal Constitutional Court Act on the grounds of substantive law. It can, thereby, be assumed without a final decision that the complainant in 3) was allowed to appoint the authorised representatives for the children. The complainant took the complainants in 1) into its care for a not inconsiderable period of time after the mother had recognisably, by "abandoning" them, declared that she agreed to her children being cared for in a suitable facility.

1. Decisions in child custody cases which have a decisive influence on the future life of children affect them directly and can violate their fundamental rights. Regardless of that, however, an answer must be found to the question of how complaints can be admissibly lodged in the constitutional complaint procedure against violations of the fundamental rights of minors.

a) The Federal Constitutional Court Act contains no provisions governing the capacity to conduct proceedings in one's own name. It is thus down to the court to find the legal basis for creating an appropriate procedure by way of analogy with other procedural law (BVerfGE 1, 109 (110); 28, 243 (254); 51, 405 (407)). As regards the capacity to conduct proceedings in one's own name, the relevant rules of procedure create the connection to legal capacity according to the provisions of the Civil Code. In regard to the procedural law which is decisive in respect of the original proceedings, there is no provision governing who has the capacity to exercise his or her rights him or herself. However, according to prevailing opinion in proceedings on matters of non-contentious jurisdiction, the provisions of the Civil Code regarding legal capacity are in principle to be applied *mutatis mutandis* ... In personal matters, a child aged 14 years and over, however, can exercise the right of appeal independently without the involvement of his or her legal representative (§ 59.1 and 59.3 of the Act on Matters of Non-Contentious Jurisdiction). No decision need be taken here regarding the question of whether minors below the age of 14 years can be recognised as having the capacity to conduct proceedings in one's own name in regard to the constitutional complaint procedure against decisions in child custody cases …; since the complainants in 1) do not meet this condition.

b) Parental custody includes the representation of the child (§ 1629.1 sentence 1 of the Civil Code) and thus in principle includes the authority to lodge a constitutional complaint on behalf of minors and to represent them in proceedings before the constitutional court. To what extent this right also exists when a conflict of interests cannot be excluded between the parent holding custody rights and the child is a question the Federal Constitutional Court has not answered thus far (BVerfGE 68, 176 (184)).

In the present case it is apparent that such a conflict exists between the complainants in 1) and their mother. In addition, the mother had no reason to lodge a constitutional complaint on behalf of her children against the decision on custody rights, which is in her favour, in order to remain separated from them against her own wishes.

Given this state of affairs, it was out of the question for the mother, who according to the Civil Code is competent to represent them, to lodge a constitutional complaint on behalf of the complainants in 1).

2. That cannot, however, mean that the complainants in 1) are denied the opportunity to assert violations of their fundamental rights by means of a constitutional complaint.

Decisions in custody proceedings are characterised by the fact that the decisive factor in respect of state action is the child's best interests. The courts' decisions must be guided entirely by the best interests of the child within the meaning of the general principles as developed in the case-law of the Federal Constitutional Court in regard to the state's "watchdog" function (see BVerfGE 31, 194 (208-209)). The close link between the custody proceedings and the child's right, as guaranteed under the Basic Law, to claim the protection of the state (see BVerfGE 24, 119 (144)) at any rate prevents a minor being denied access to the Federal Constitutional Court if his or her legal representative is not willing or not in the position to lodge a constitutional complaint on his or her behalf.

a) On account of its duties of protection resulting from Article 6.2 sentence 2 and Article 2.1 of the Basic Law, the state must also create provisions under procedural law in respect of custody proceedings to guarantee that sufficient consideration is given to the concerned child's status as a holder of fundamental rights (see BVerfGE 55, 171 (179)). Whether the existing legal situation does sufficient justice to the child's "status as subject" in those proceedings in which its fate is being decided has been the subject-matter of in-depth discussions … In this context some have called for a separate person to represent the minor's interests. However, the matter of the "counsel for the child" will not be dealt with in any more detail here.

Such an institution does not currently exist, and so it cannot come into question as a representative for the complainants in 1) in proceedings before the constitutional court.
b) A person who is subject to parental custody or guardianship is given a curator for matters which the parent or guardian is prevented from carrying out (§ 1909.1 sentence 1 of the Civil Code). Whether and under what conditions a child who has not yet reached the age of 14 years requires a curator in proceedings on matters of non-contentious jurisdiction concerning parental custody has hardly been dealt with in the case-law and literature … The other question regarding the need to appoint a supplementary curator for constitutional complaint proceedings when parents are prevented from lodging a constitutional complaint on behalf of their underage children on account of a conflict of interests has neither been discussed in the case-law of the Federal Constitutional Court nor in the relevant commentaries.
In future, a supplementary curator will have to be appointed in cases such as the present one where the legislature does not take sufficient account of the child's interests in the constitutional complaint proceedings in another way.
Children who are not yet able to protect themselves must be protected against the harm which can ensue when custody decisions violate their personality right and they cannot contest that violation themselves by means of a constitutional complaint on account of their being minors. The legislature at present provides a solution to those cases in which there is a conflict of interests between parents and their child, namely the appointment of a supplementary curator (§ 1909.1 sentence 1 of the Civil Code), which is an appropriate means of preventing the child's interests not being sufficiently taken into consideration. This statutory regulation gives that person who feels called to act as the child's trustee the possibility of prompting the guardianship court to appoint a supplementary curator for the purposes of lodging a constitutional complaint. That way the question of whether there exists a conflict of interests between the child and the holder of custody rights can be examined in advance by the non-constitutional courts, and the Federal Constitutional Court does not, in addition, have to make the authorisation to lodge a constitutional complaint on behalf of a minor dependent on criteria which are not based in civil law and in general procedural law.
c) In the present case the omission which was made was that no supplementary curator was appointed for the complainants in 1). This may be explained by the fact that up until now the possibility of appointing and the need to appoint a curator have not been sufficiently recognised. This also raises the question of whether this omission forces the constitutional complaint lodged by the complainants in 1) to be dismissed as inadmissible. That would seem unsatisfactory, since the complainants in 1) had no influence on the appointment of the curator, on the other hand, how-

ever, the children, who are not yet in a position to protect themselves, must be protected against harm which could arise on account of the fact that they cannot lodge a constitutional complaint against custody decisions which violate their personality right because they are minors. Taking account of Article 6.2 sentence 2 of the Basic Law, this consideration could possibly justify permitting, by way of exception, representatives in constitutional complaint proceedings who have not been formally appointed. These could include persons who – as in the present case of the complainants in 3) – had been authorised to have the child in their care for a not inconsiderable period of time. Thus, the responsible care of the father who did not have custody of the child living in his household was, ultimately, the reason why the child's constitutional complaint, through his father as representative, was deemed to be admissible (see BVerfGE 55, 171 (176, 178)). Finally, § 57.1 no. 9 of the Act on Matters of Non-Contentious Jurisdiction is also based on the idea that minors require special protection. This provision permits an appeal, among other things, against a decision regarding the child by any person who has a justified interest in exercising this matter. This precondition is met where the complainant has understandable reason, on account of his or her personal relationship with the child, to speak up for the child´s personal best interests …

C.

The constitutional complaint is at any rate unfounded.

I.

1. The complainants have a right to the free development of their personality (Article 2.1 of the Basic Law), although this is subject to the delimitations set out in this constitutional provision. That is contrasted with their mother's position as a holder of fundamental rights, which is based on the guarantee under Article 6.2 sentence 1 of the Basic Law.

The relationship between the parental right and the child's personality right is characterised by the special structure of the parental right. This is essentially a right which is in the child's interests, as already results from the wording of Article 6.2 sentence 1 of the Basic Law, which refers to the right of care and upbringing and by definition alone includes the child's interests in the parental right. This corresponds to the fact that the less care and upbringing the child needs and the more its ability to decide for itself increases, the more the authorities rooted in the parental right are pushed back, until, ultimately, they expire when the child reaches the age of majority (BVerfGE 59, 360 (382)).

2. Where conflicts of interests arise between the child and its parent, priority is in principle given to the child's interests (see BVerfGE 61, 358 (378)). However, insofar as the matter involves the child being separated from its parents, the strongest encroachment on the parental right, this is only permissible if the conditions under Article 6.3 of the Basic Law are met. Accordingly, children may only be separated from the family against the will of the persons entitled to their upbringing pursuant to a statute where those so entitled have failed or where, for other reasons, the children are in danger of serious neglect. § 1666.1 sentence 1 and § 1666a of the Civil Code, according to which children may also be separated from their family in the event of non-culpable failure by the parents if no other measures can be taken to counter the danger posed to the child's best interests, conform to this constitutional provision (see BVerfGE 60, 79 (88)).

II.

The contested decisions are based on the application of § 1666 of the Civil Code. They are constitutionally unobjectionable.

1. In principle the form of the proceedings, the ascertainment and evaluation of the facts of the case, as well as the interpretation and application of regulations which are unobjectionable for constitutional reasons is in each individual case a matter for the competent non-constitutional courts, and the Federal Constitutional Court is divested of the opportunity to review them. The Federal Constitutional Court is merely obligated to control whether the contested decision shows evidence of errors of interpretation based on a fundamentally erroneous view of the significance of a fundamental right or of the extent of its area of protection (see BVerfGE 18, 85 (92); 42, 143 (147 et seq.); 49, 304 (314)). However, in fulfilling these tasks the boundaries of the Federal Constitutional Court's means of interfering cannot be drawn up rigidly and unchangeably. In particular, they are dependent on the intensity of the interference with the fundamental right (established case-law, see BVerfGE 42, 163 (168)).

In the case of court decisions to withdraw the parents' custody rights for their child, the objective significance of the interference with the parents' fundamental rights under Article 6.2 sentence 1 and Article 2.1 of the Basic Law gives reason to go beyond the basic scope of the review, especially since the interference in the parental right affects the child with the same intensity (see BVerfGE 60, 79 (91)). However, the same must then also apply when decisions are contested by means of the constitutional complaint which deem lawful that the child should remain in the family against the children's will. For such a judgment is of the same existential significance in regard to the child's future as its being separated from its parents.

2. Even taking account of the extended scope of the review, the contested decisions do not reveal any violation of a fundamental right.

That the economic living conditions in the Federal Republic of Germany are disproportionately better than in Zaire is a matter which requires no further discussion. The question can remain unanswered of whether it in fact would serve the children's best interests if the complainants were to be permitted to remain in Germany, although they would be well cared and provided for, but would lose contact with their relatives and their culture for good. At any rate the courts did not ignore the impact of the parental right, which is also associated with duties, when they came to the conclusion that the mother's wish to take her children with her to Zaire when she is deported does not represent an abuse of her custody rights. Any other decision would inevitably mean that even the parents' restricted financial circumstances could lead to their custody rights being withdrawn if they do not voluntarily hand their children over to people who are better off.

Even taking account of the aspect of the more favourable educational opportunities and career advancement of the obviously talented complainants, it is not constitutionally required that their stay in the Federal Republic of Germany be guaranteed by withdrawing the mother's custody rights. The same rules must apply here as do to German parents. The child's best interests are the supreme guideline in respect of parental care and upbringing. However, that does not mean that the exercising of the state's watchdog function according to Article 6.2 sentence 2 of the Basic Law includes ensuring the child's skills are promoted in the best possible way against the parents' wishes. The Basic Law has primarily left the decision regarding a child's education to the parents, as the natural trustees with responsibility for the child's upbringing. The parents' primary decision-making competence is based on the consideration that the child's interests are as a general rule best safeguarded by its parents. The possibility is thereby accepted that the child may suffer actual or purported disadvantages on account of their parents' decision which could perhaps be avoided if gifted children were exclusively selected according to objective standards (BVerfGE 60, 79 (94)).

The courts did not have to conclude from the incidents in Zaire that the mother – who, incidentally, was not actively involved in the incidents – was incapable of bringing up and caring for her children, all the less so since these incidents could not be verified.

Nor did the state's watchdog function obligate the courts to withdraw the mother's custody rights for the complainants in 1) on account of her conduct after entering the Federal Republic of Germany and to transfer them to the complainants in 2). The mother did not "abandon" her children in a manner which gave rise to the fear that they would be in danger, but rather she entrusted them in a targeted fashion into the care of the authorities of whom she could expect that they would look after her children. The courts rightly made reference to the fact that the mother found herself in exceptional psychological circumstances since she had to take existential decisions while living in a foreign environment with two small children – obviously without any help from relatives. They concluded therefrom that the mother's conduct did not permit any conclusions to be drawn regarding any current or future endangering of the children's best interests on account of her failing in the children's upbringing or care.

Nevertheless, the child's best interests may require that children be separated from their parents even if the conditions under § 1666 of the Civil Code are not met. This may be the case when the child has found new people to closely relate to and would experience the separation from them as a severe psychological shock (see BVerfGE 68, 176). The contested decisions also dealt with and addressed the fact that the complainants were living in a home and not in foster care. Insofar as the complainants had found people in the children's home they could closely relate to, they would anyway have to be separated from them – a fact to which the Regional Court referred – since they were to be given into foster care if they were able to remain in the Federal Republic of Germany.

The contested decisions were thus issued in accordance with the Basic Law in that respect too.

Justices: Dr. Herzog, Dr. Simon, Dr. Hesse, Dr. Katzenstein, Dr. Niemeyer, Dr. Henschel

No. 17

BVerfGE 76, 1

of 12 May 1987 – 2 BvR 1226/83, 101, 313/84 –

"Entry of aliens to join family members living in the Federal Republic"

HEADNOTES:

1. **Neither Article 6.1 nor Article 6.2, first sentence, of the Basic Law establishes a fundamental right allowing foreign spouses or family members to claim that they are entitled to join their foreign spouses or family members legitimately living in the Federal Republic of Germany.**
2. **The duty of the state to protect marriage and the family is fulfilled when persons entitled to fundamental rights are able to claim under Article 6.1 and 6.2, first sentence, of the Basic Law that in deciding on a request for residency under § 2.1, second sentence, of the Aliens Act, the responsible authorities and courts pay regard to the existing marital and familial ties to persons living in the Federal territory, and this in a manner corresponding to the great weight that the Basic Law unequivocally assigns to the protection of marriage and the family.**
3. **The impairment of the concerns of marriage and the family by way of the requirement of three years of marriage as a prerequisite to joining spouses living in the Federal Republic exceeds the degree that those affected must tolerate, even with regard to opposing public interests.**

Order of the Second Senate of 12 May 1987
– 2 BvR 1226/83, 101, 313/84 –

in the proceedings relating to the constitutional complaints 1. of Mrs. S., 2. of minor F., legally represented by complainant 1), – authorised representatives: …, lawyers – against the order of the Baden-Württemberg Higher Administrative Court (*Verwaltungsgerichtshof*) of 23 June 1983 – 13 S 878/83 –, b) the order of the Freiburg Administrative Court (*Verwaltungsgericht*) of 17 March 1983 – 4 K 233/82 – 2 BvR 1226/83 –; of 1. Mrs. D., 2) of minor D., 3) of minor D., complainants 2) and 3) being represented by complainant 1), – authorised representatives: ..., lawyers – against a) the order of the Higher Administrative Court (*Oberverwaltungsgericht*) for the *Länder* (states of) Lower Saxony and Schleswig-Holstein of 13 December 1983 – 11 OVG B 1201/83 – b) the order of the Schleswig-Holstein Administrative Court of 20 October 1983 – 14 D 129/83 – 2 BvR 101/84 – of Mrs. P. – authorised representatives: ..., lawyers – against a) the order of the Baden-Württemberg Higher Administrative Court of 27 January 1984 – 1 S 2190/83 –, b) the order of the Stuttgart Administrative Court of 21 July 1983 – VRS 7 K 1250/83 – and application for the issuance of a temporary injunction – 2 BvR 313/84 –.

RULING:

1. The constitutional complaint in the proceedings 2 BvR 101/84 is hereby rejected as unfounded.
2. The orders of the Freiburg Administrative Court of 17 March 1983 – 4 K 233/82 – and the Baden-Württemberg Higher Administrative Court of 23 June 1983 – 13 S 878/83 – violate Article 6.1 and 6.2, first sentence, of the Basic Law. They are hereby quashed. The matter is referred back to the Freiburg Administrative Court.
3. The orders of the Stuttgart Administrative Court of 21 July 1983 – VRS 7 K 1250/83 – and the Baden-Württemberg Higher Administrative Court of 27 January 1984 – 1 S 2190/83 – violate Article 6.1 of the Basic Law. They are hereby quashed. The matter is referred back to the Stuttgart Administrative Court.
4. The *Land* Baden-Württemberg is ordered to reimburse the complainants in the proceedings 2 BvR 1226/83 and 2 BvR 313/84 their necessary expenses.

EXTRACT FROM GROUNDS:

A.

The complainants are Turkish and Yugoslavian nationals. They object to the imposition of waiting periods prior to being able to join their Turkish and Yugoslavian family members living in the Federal territory. The Senate has consolidated their constitutional complaints for joint adjudication.

I.

1. As the economic recovery in the Federal Republic of Germany following World War II began to stabilise in the mid-1950s, this was accompanied by the full employment of German nationals available to the labour market at that time. The sustained economic growth led to the situation where the German labour market was no longer capable of fully covering the workforce requirements of the state and industry. For this reason, the Federal Republic of Germany subsequently concluded agreements with a variety of European states – in particular, Turkey and Yugoslavia – as well as non-European states for the recruitment of "guest workers" (*Gastarbeitnehmer*).

In these so-called "recruiting states" (*Anwerbestaaten*), commissions of the Federal Agency for Job Placement and Unemployment Insurance (today, the Federal Institute for Employment; *Bundesanstalt für Arbeit*) were set up and charged with selecting the workers to be recruited. If they fulfilled the health requirements and were able to be placed in a German job listed with the Federal Agency, the nationals of these states interested in gainful employment in the Federal Republic of Germany were issued a so-called identity card (*Legitimationskarte*), which enabled them without any additional visa to enter the Federal territory in order to take up work.

2. With the approval of the Federal Government, the Federal Minister of Labour and Social Affairs terminated the guest worker recruitment by way of the so-called "recruitment stop" (*Anwerbestopp*) *of* 23 November 1973. Since then, entry for the purpose of employment by nationals of a state which is not a member of the European Community (EC) is no longer allowed.

3. The Aliens Act (*Ausländergesetz* – AuslG), stemming from the year 1965, contains no provisions regarding the admissibility of entry into the Federal Republic by spouses or children under an obligation to obtain a residency permit in order to join foreigners lawfully living in the Federal territory. The only provision of relevance here is the general rule found in § 2.1 of the Aliens Act, which governs the initial issuance of a residency permit. The rule reads:

> Aliens who enter the area covered by the operation of this Act and wish to reside there are in need of a residency permit. The residency permit may be issued when the presence of the alien does not interfere with the concerns of the Federal Republic of Germany.

Shortly after promulgation of the Aliens Act, the Conference of State Ministers of the Interior adopted the "Principles of Alien Policy", which also took up the issue of family members joining foreign workers. Accordingly, the, permission to join a worker from a recruiting state (so-called first-generation aliens) living in the Federal territory was to be made dependent on one year of domestic residency by the affected party. Further-reaching restrictions were initially not imposed.

II.

1. The continued steady climb in the number of foreigners in the Federal territory that was registered in spite of the recruiting stop in the late 1970s and early 1980s – which, in addition to the increased influx of persons seeking asylum, was primarily attributed to family members joining foreigners (especially, Turkish nationals) – initially prompted the Ministers of the Interior of several states, and then ultimately the Federal Government as well, to take action.
a) The Aliens Decree by the Baden-Württemberg Minister of the Interior of 20 October 1981 (Joint Official Gazette (*Gemeinsames Amtsblatt* – GABl.) p. 1613) made permission for spouses to join first-generation aliens dependent on the observance of a three-year waiting period beginning with the marriage itself (*Ehebestandszeit*).
b) On 2 December 1981, the Federal Government passed the following resolution (*Informationsbrief Ausländerrecht* – InfAuslR 1981, p. 306; see also *Zeitschrift für Ausländerrecht und Ausländerpolitik* – ZAR 1981, p. 159):

> 1. The Federal Government hereby requests the states, as immediate regulation for the social control of families joining aliens from non-EC states (with the exception of those entitled to seek asylum and quotas of refugees), immediately to exclude by way of federally uniform state resolutions the following groups of persons from entry in order to join aliens:
>
> a) young aliens of ages 16 and 17,
>
> b) alien children, when only one parent resides in the Federal Republic of Germany (exception for half orphans and children of divorced or single persons)
>
> c) …
>
> d) spouses of aliens who entered the Federal Republic of Germany as children of aliens or were born here, when they have not lived here at least eight years without interruption, have not yet reached the age of 18 and the marriage has not been in existence for one year.
>
> Exceptions are provided to these restrictions for hardship cases. The restrictions are only not to be applicable in those areas where there are no doubts

with regard to integration policy. In addition, for the restriction on spouses joining aliens, a transitional regulation is to be provided for.

The Federal Government charges the Federal Minister of the Interior with urging upon the state Ministers of, the Interior the need for prompt realisation of the foregoing recommendations.

2. The Federal Minister of the Interior is charged with preparing legislation on the recommendations under 1b) and c) with express regulation in the Aliens Act.

No restrictive measures were recommended for spouses joining first-generation aliens. For these aliens, the requirement of a period of one-year residency by the spouse living here prior to entry into the Federal territory was to remain unchanged.
2. On the basis of a proposal by the Federal Government, the states thereafter issued corresponding administrative regulations or amended existing ones. However, federally uniform control of the decisions of state authorities on alien matters, specifically, spouses joining aliens living in the Federal territory, did not come about.
a) In Baden-Württemberg, the Aliens Decree of 20 October 1981 was replaced by the Decree of 30 March 1982 (GABl. p. 383). In the version of 1 August 1984 (GABl. p. 725), it provides for the following regulation:

2.6.2	Principle
2.6.2.1	When a family intends to join an alien who is legitimately living in the Federal territory and will apparently be residing here for some time, this is – insofar as not opposed by Number 2.6.2.2 or Number 2.6.2.3 – permissible when he is in possession of adequate housing and is able to support the family from his own income.
2.6.2.2	In principle, it is not permissible for a family to join an alien who himself has entered the Federal Republic of Germany in the course of joining his family or was born here. Exceptions can be made when the alien who is living in the Federal territory – is at least 18 years of age, – has lawfully resided in the Federal territory for 8 years without interruption, – is in possession of unlimited residency permit,

– can support the family from his own income, and when
– adequate housing is available, as well as
– the marriage has existed for tat least three years.

2.6.2.3 …

2.6.3 Conditions for familial entry

2.6.3.1 Circle of persons entitled to enter

In principle, only the spouse of the alien and his unmarried children younger than 16 years of age are able to enter to join the alien. Children will not be allowed to join a parent living alone in the Federal territory when the other parent is living abroad.

2.6.3.2 …

2.6.3.3 …

2.6.3.4 Waiting period

2.6.3.4.1 It is only possible for families to join aliens who have been lawfully residing in the Federal territory for at least three years since the marriage. If family members enter the Federal Republic prior to this period and, following a three-month tourist residency, apply for the issuance of a permit for continued residency, this is as a rule to be denied. Renewed tourist residency is only possible following an interruption of at least three months.

The Alien Authorities may – apart from the cases listed in Number 2.6.2.2 – make exceptions for the entry of families to join
– nationals of European states, and
– nationals of the non-European states of Australia, Israel, Japan, Canada, New Zealand and the USA …

2.6.3.4.2 …

2.6.3.5 In cases of extreme hardship, further exceptions may be made with the approval of the District Chief Administrative Office (*Regierungspräsidium*).

2.6.4 …

b) In Bavaria, the area of spouses joining second-generation aliens from recruiting states was likewise made subject to the requirements of a three-year marriage and eight-year residency of the spouse living in the Federal territory. For spouses joining first-generation aliens from recruiting states, the Bavarian State Ministry of the Interior continued only to require one year of residency in the Federal territory (see nos. 3.1 and 3.2 of the decree of 17 May 1983, published in *Ausländerrecht der Bundesländer-Familienzusammenführung (Übersicht), Mitteilungen der Beauftragten der Bundesregierung für Ausländerfragen*, March 1986, pp. 4-5).

c) The remaining states basically followed the recommendations of the Federal Government. They elected not to require a marriage period for entry to join first-generation aliens. In the area of entry to join second-generation aliens, they introduced the requirement of a one-year marriage and eight-year residency of the spouse living here; in Hesse, a minimum residency of five years was demanded (see *Ausländerrecht der Bundesländer-Familienzusammenführung (Übersicht), Mitteilungen der Beauftragten der Bundesregierung für Ausländerfragen*, March 1986, pp. 7-8)
d) Efforts by the Baden-Württemberg Ministry of the Interior to introduce a federally uniform requirement of three years of marriage met with no success.

III.

The complainants object to the judicial confirmation of the immediate enforcement of the denial of their requests to join their spouses/fathers with respect to the requirements of eight-year residency and, in Baden-Württemberg, three-year marriage.

1. Constitutional complaint 2 BvR 1226/83
a) Complainant 1), born in 1949, and her son from a previous marriage, complainant 2), born in 1969, are Yugoslavian nationals. Complainant 1) received a divorce from her first husband in Yugoslavia in 1978. Custody of complainant 2) was awarded to complainant 1). On 28 July 1982, complainant 1) was married in Yugoslavia to her present husband, a Yugoslavian national born in 1949. On 1 April 1971, he had entered the Federal territory with an identity card to take up work. He is presently employed as a steel worker with a steel and metal company in Freiburg im Breisgau, and is not under notice. On 25 January 1982, he received an unlimited residency permit. He is living together with a son from a previous marriage and with complainant 1) and complainant 2) in a 65-m^2 apartment.
b) Complainant 1) and complainant 2) entered the Federal territory on 30 July 1982. On 6 September 1982, complainant 1) indicated her residency to the City of Freiburg, as responsible authority for aliens. At the same time, she applied for the issuance of a residency permit for the purposes of family unification. By order of 12 October 1982, the Alien Authority denied the application, placed a deadline of one month following delivery of the order on complainant 1) to leave the country, and threatened her with deportation plus costs in the event of failure to observe the deadline. At the same time, the Authority restricted complainant 2)'s permit-free residency to a period of one month following delivery of the order and directed im-

mediate enforcement of these measures. The complainants filed an objection to these actions, which was rejected by a decision of 14 December 1982.
c) The complainants lodged a complaint with the Administrative Court in Freiburg against the denial of the residency permit; at the same time, they applied for suspensive effect for their appeal. By order of 17 March 1983, the Administrative Court refused the complainants' applications. By order of 23 June 1983, the Higher Administrative Court rejected the complainants' remedy to the foregoing order, stating:
When the public interest in a temporary delay in joining spouses is basically given priority to the interest in an immediate joining; this is based on material reasons corresponding to the purpose of the Aliens Act. …
d) With their constitutional complaint, the complainants object to the orders of the Administrative Courts. They assert a violation of their fundamental rights under Article 6.1 and 6.2 of the Basic Law. …
e) Following expiry of the three-year period, complainant 1) received the residency permit for which she had applied. The complainants assert a continuing interest in a decision on the merits with regard to their constitutional complaint.

2. Constitutional complaint 2 BvR 101/84
a) The husband of complainant 1), born in 1961 and father of complainants 2) and 3), is, as are the complainants, a Turkish national. On 25 February 1978, he entered: the Federal Republic for the purpose of family reunification in order to join his father, who was living in the Federal territory as a recruited worker. He was subsequently granted a limited residency permit, which was repeatedly extended. On 10 February 1983, he received an unlimited residency permit. He is employed as a chemical worker in a company in Neumünster (Schleswig-Holstein). On 7 September 1981, he married complainant 1), born in 1964, in Turkey. On 16 July 1982, a daughter, complainant 2), was born to the couple in Turkey.
b) On 19 October 1982, complainant 1) applied for the issuance of a three-month visitor's visa at the Embassy of the Federal Republic of Germany in Ankara. On 7 December 1982, complainant 1)'s application was granted, and on 1 January 1983, she entered Federal territory and resided with her husband. Prior to expiry of her visa, complainant 1) applied with the City of Neumünster, as responsible Alien Authority, for the issuance of a residency permit in order to be able to remain with her husband, along with complainant 2). On 25 April 1983, she notified the Alien Authority that she was expecting another child; delivery date was to be 20 December 1983.
By order of 16 May 1983, the Alien Authority turned down the application and gave complainant 1) one month following delivery of the order to leave the coun-

try, threatening her with deportation in the event of refusal. At the same time, the Alien Authority limited the permit-free residency of complainant 2) to the point at which complainant 1) was to leave the country. Immediate enforcement of this limitation was not directed.

c) The complainants filed an objection to this order. At the same time, they applied to the Schleswig-Holstein Administrative Court for suspensive effect for their appeal. The Court held that complainant 2)'s application was inadmissible; her objection was said to have suspensive effect in the concrete case. Complainant 1)'s application was held to be unsubstantiated, since the appeal applied for in the principal proceedings lacked prospect for success. In any event, the issuance of a residency permit is opposed by the application (without errors of discretion) of the Guidelines of the Schleswig-Holstein Ministry of the Interior for Family Entry, according to which eight years of domestic residency on the part of complainant 1)'s husband is a prerequisite to her being able to join her husband. …

The complaint lodged by complainant 1) alone was rejected by the Higher Administrative Court for the *Länder* Lower Saxony and Schleswig-Holstein by order of 13 December 1983. In its reasoning, the court basically referred to the comments of the lower court.

On 23 November 1983, complainant 1) delivered her second child, complainant 3).

d) With their constitutional complaint, the complainants assert a violation of their fundamental rights under Article 6 of the Basic Law. …

e) Complainant 1) has since received a (limited) residency permit, since the requirement of eight years of residency on the part of her husband has been fulfilled. The complainants claim a continuing interest in a determination of the unconstitutionality of the attacked decisions.

3. Constitutional complaint 2 BvR 313/84

a) The husband of the complainant, born in 1954, is, as is the complainant, a Turkish national. In 1966 he entered the Federal territory to join his parents, who were living here as workers. At age 16, he received a residency permit. Since March 1976, the complainant's husband has been employed as a machinist with an automobile company in Sindelfingen, and is not under notice. On 9 July 1982, he married the complainant, born in 1966, in Turkey. On 13 September 1982, the complainant applied for the issuance of a three-month visa with the General Consulate of the Federal Republic of Germany in Istanbul in order to visit her husband. Following this granting of this application, the complainant entered the Federal territory in mid-December 1982.

b) On 3 March 1983, she applied for the issuance of a residency permit. By way of order of 18 March 1983, the City of Sindelfingen denied the application, ordered the complainant to exit the country by 10 April 1983 and threatened her with deportation in the event that she failed to fulfil her obligation to exit.

c) The complainant lodged an objection to this order, which has since been rejected. At the same time, she applied with the Stuttgart Administrative Court for suspensive effect for her appeal.

By order of 21 July 1983, the court granted the application due to the inappropriate shortness of the exit deadline, to the extent that the objection was directed at the threat of deportation; in all other respects, the application was rejected.

d) To the extent that the relief sought by her had not been granted, the complainant filed an appeal with regard to the rejection with the Baden-Württemberg Higher Administrative Court, which was rejected by order of 27 January 1984. The Higher Administrative Court made reference to the consistent holdings of all of its Senates dealing with the law of aliens, according to which the Guidelines at issue do not give concrete form to the so-called negative barriers of § 2.1, second sentence, of the Aliens Act ("concerns of the Federal Republic of Germany") but rather merely contain regulations binding as to discretion. As such, they were held to be compatible with higher-ranking law, especially with Article 6.1 of the Basic Law:

…

With respect to these decisions, the City of Sindelfingen placed by order of 20 February 1984 a deadline on the complainant of exit by 31 March 1984, at the same time, it threatened the complainant with deportation in the event of failure to adhere to this deadline.

e) With the constitutional complaint, the complainant asserts a violation of her fundamental rights under Articles 1.1, 3.1 and 6.1 of the Basic Law. …

IV.

In the name of the Federal Government, the Federal Minister of the Interior entered a statement on the constitutional complaints; in the proceedings 2 BvR 1226/83 and 2 BvR 313/84, the Baden-Württemberg Ministry of the Interior and the opponents of the original proceedings have rendered opinions. In the proceedings 2 BvR 101/84, the Minister-President of the *Land* Schleswig-Holstein submitted an opinion. The President of the Federal Administrative Court submitted opinions regarding the three constitutional complaints on behalf of the First Appellate Senate responsible for the law of aliens.

…

V.

The Federal Constitutional Court has requested that the Federal Government and the governments of the *Länder* provide information on certain issues of spousal entry, in particular: on the bases of the prognoses made in 1981 with respect to the number of requests for entry, on possible alternatives regarding measures undertaken, on development in entry conduct since 1982, and on present expectations for future developments in this conduct. The governments have submitted the requested information to the extent possible.

...

B.

The constitutional complaints are admissible.

1. From the submissions of the complainants, it does not appear to be ruled out that the connection between them and their family members living in the Federal territory, as well as their desire for residency, is covered by the factual scope of protection afforded by Article 6 of the Basic Law, that the personal scope of protection afforded by Article 6 of the Basic Law extends to them, and that the attacked decisions impermissibly interfere with the connection with their family members protected by Article 6 of the Basic Law.

2. In addition, complainants 2) and 3) in the proceedings 2 BvR 101/84 are affected by the attacked judicial decisions. Although these decisions establish only a duty on the part of the mother, complainant 1), to leave the Federal territory at once, the case-law of the Federal Constitutional Court recognises that an alien's duty to exit also affects his family members entitled to stay – such as complainants 2) and 3) – and can permissibly be attacked with a constitutional complaint (Decisions of the Federal Constitutional Court (*Entscheidungen des Bundesverfassungsgerichts* – BVerfGE) 51, 386 (395)). Complainants 2) and 3) are affected by way of the fact that they have been expected under the complained-of court decisions to live separated from a parent for a considerable length of time or at least that they are prevented from living with both parents together in the Federal territory for an unlimited period of time.

3. The original interest in a decision on the merits has not been removed in light of the fact that the waiting period imposed on the complainants has expired following filing of the constitutional complaints and that complainants 1) in the proceedings 2 BvR 1226/83 and 2 BvR 101/84 have received the residency permits for which they had applied. The Federal Constitutional Court has consistently held that the issue of how a change in the facts affects a pending constitutional complaint is to be

decided on a case-by-case basis with reference to the type of sovereign act attacked, the significance of the asserted constitutional guarantee and the purposes of the constitutional complaint (see BVerfGE 33, 247 (257); 50, 244 (247-248)). Under these aspects, there is a continued interest in a decision on the merits in the instant cases. It would not be consistent with the fundamental significance of the issues raised by the constitutional complaints if the requirements for a ruling by the court on these issues were no longer to be present with expiration of the waiting period. Moreover, the burdens to which aliens seeking entry are exposed in the event that they do not fulfil the waiting-period requirements – the confirmation by the Administrative Court of their duty to exit the Federal Republic of Germany immediately – are often restricted to a period within which a decision on the merits is unable to be reached in the ordinary course of procedures before the Federal Constitutional Court. The possibility for clarifying the constitutionality of this requirement by the Federal Constitutional Court would therefore be dependent on the time requirements in an individual case. This would be inappropriate. As long as a fundamental decision by the Federal Constitutional Court is lacking with regard to the constitutionality of waiting periods for permitting familial entry, this would be tantamount also for those affected by these deadlines to an unreasonable shortening of their legal protection if they were forced to accept the fact that time factors beyond their control determine whether they will be able to obtain the sought-after decision on the merits by the Federal Constitutional Court (see BVerfGE 74, 163 (172-173)).

4. a) The requirements of § 90.2, first sentence, of the Federal Constitutional Court Act (*Bundesverfassungsgerichtsgesetz* – BVerfGG) have been fulfilled. In each of the disputes, all legal remedies had been exhausted with the decisions by the two Higher Administrative Courts (see BVerfGE 59, 63 (82)). In the proceedings 2 BvR 101/84, however, not all of the complainants sought provisional legal protection in all available instances. On the contrary, only complainant 1) has submitted an application under § 80.5 of the Code of Administrative Court Procedure and attacked the Administrative Court's decision of denial with a complaint. Nevertheless, this exhaustion of remedies is also effective for complainants 2) and 3). Their assertions have been adequately brought forward by complainant 1) in the original proceedings for review and decision by the non-constitutional courts. Sense and purpose of the requirement of exhaustion of remedies has thus also been satisfied in that complainants 2) and 3) seek the granting of legal protection by the Federal Constitutional Court (see BVerfGE 51, 386 (395-96)).

b) The complainants also need not surmount the general principle of subsidiarity of the constitutional complaint on which § 90.2, first sentence, of the Federal Constitutional Court Act is based. According to this principle, a constitutional complaint is as a rule inadmissible when the complainant is or was able to eliminate in some other manner the alleged constitutional violation or to achieve this other than by introducing a constitutional complaint (see BVerfGE 33, 247 (258); established case-law). Under this aspect, the Federal Constitutional Court has ruled restrictively on the admissibility of constitutional complaints against decisions by administrative courts in proceedings regarding provisional legal protection; it has held that a complainant can be required to exhaust remedies in the principal proceedings prior to resorting to the Federal Constitutional Court (see BVerfGE 51, 130 (138 et seq.) – regarding proceedings under § 123 of the Code of Administrative Court Procedure; BVerfGE 53, 30 (52 et seq.) – regarding proceedings under § 80.5 of the Code of Administrative Court Procedure; BVerfGE 70, 180 (187-188) – regarding proceedings under § 80.6 of the Code of Administrative Court Procedure). The extent to which the principle of subsidiarity of constitutional complaints places limits on the admissibility of constitutional complaints against decisions of administrative courts in urgent cases is not in need of a definitive ruling here. In the instant proceedings, it does not prevent a decision on the merits for the following reasons:

The complainants assert that they should at least have been accorded provisional legal protection; by way of Article 61 of the Basic Law, they allege a claim to be able to conduct their family life without interruption in the Federal territory. The complaints are or were unable to realise with the remedies available to them in the principal proceedings the objective pursued with the constitutional complaints, i.e. no time limits on setting up a family unit in the Federal territory. By forgoing resort to the Federal Constitutional Court prior to a definitive decision on there remedies, they would have had to accept a lengthy separation from their family members living in the Federal territory or to forgo familial life together with them in the Federal territory at least for a considerable period of time. Furthermore, for the evaluation of the issues raised by the constitutional complaints, there is no need for further clarification of the actual circumstances in the individual case. The administrative courts conducted in the attacked decisions more than only a summary review of the facts. With regard to the state of the law as well, they conducted an extensive review, including constitutional law. Moreover, the Federal Administrative Court, as supreme competent tribunal, dealt with the issues raised, basically approving the standpoint of the administrative courts in a number of fundamental decisions (see A. IV. 5 above as well as *Neue Juristische Wochenschrift* – NJW 1985, p. 2099; InfAuslR 1985, p. 129). Finally, the constitutional complaints are of general importance (see BVerfGE 53, 30 (53-54)).

C.

The constitutional complaints BvR 1226/83 and 2 BvR 313/84 are well-founded. The constitutional complaint 2 BvR 101/84 is unfounded.
Article 6 of the Basie Law provides marriage and the family with the special protection of the state, in addition to a fundamental right functioning as a defensive right (*Abwehrrecht*) in the classic sense, Article 6 contains both an institutional guarantee and a fundamental provision that determines values (BVerfGE 6, 55 (71 et seq.); established case-law). With regard to the three-year marriage requirement, the duty to protect and support marriage and the family following from this constitutional provision has not been adequately taken into consideration; in all other respects, there are no constitutional reservations to the attacked decisions.

I.

1. The scope of applicability of the constitutional guarantee afforded by Article 6.1 of the Basic Law extends to the complainants and their marital and familial communities.
a) From the standpoint of the German legal system, these communities have, however, international aspects on account of the nationality of the complainants. The extent to which Article 6.1 of the Basic Law is applicable to such communities must be ascertained from the Constitution itself; in so doing, the rules of German conflicts law, which is secondary to the Constitution, on the recognition of foreign judgments – by way of which or due to which such communities are established or dissolved – can only be drawn upon for a point of reference (see BVerfGE 31, 58 (77)). The scope of protection afforded by Article 6.1 is not limited to marriages and families with purely domestic contacts; on the contrary, it covers marital and familial communities regardless of where and under which legal system's standards they were established and whether the legal effects of the marital or familial bond are to be judged according to German or foreign law (see BVerfGE 62, 323 (330)). This does not, however, mean that marital and familial communities such as polygamous marriages – which are entered into pursuant to foreign law and which do not comport with the concept of marriage and the family under the Basic Law – fall in all cases within the scope of protection afforded by Article 6.1 of the Basic Law. A conclusive ruling on this matter is nevertheless not necessary here, since the complainants – each of whom is living in *one* marriage and family – are bonded in communities that are not contrary to the concept of marriage and the family prevailing under the Basic Law.

b) The protection afforded by Article 6.1 of the Basic Law covers the freedom to marry and set up a family (see BVerfGE 31, 58 (67)) and the right to marital and familial life.

aa) The waiting-period regulations to be reviewed here do not interfere with Article 6.1's scope of protection insofar as this Article guarantees the right to marry and set up a family. Although they may lead to the situation where an alien living in the Federal territory forgoes marriage and the establishment of a family with an alien living in his native country or elsewhere outside the Federal Republic of Germany, their effect represents at most an indirect impairment of the freedom to marry and set up a family that does not touch upon this freedom as such. This effect is a consequence of the burden borne by aliens in general from time immemorial that they may not reside in the Federal territory when they are not in possession of a corresponding legal entitlement only attainable upon fulfilment of specific conditions.

bb) On the other hand, the scope of protection afforded by Article 6.1 of the Basic Law is affected to the extent that it covers the right to marital and familial life.

(1) The complainants and their family members are seeking this sort of life. Thus, one of the essential conditions for the development of the protective effects offered by Article 6.1 of the Basic Law vis-à-vis residency law comes into view. Only when, in addition to legal, actual bonds between spouses and their family members (this being normally expressed as care for a household community) exist or are (re)established within a reasonable period is an application of Article 6.1 of the Basic Law factually justified from the aspect of residency law. To this extent, the reach of the protective effects of Article 6.1 of the Basic Law is determined by the rules found in §§ 1353.1, second sentence, and 1626 et seq. of the Civil Code (*Bürgerliches Gesetzbuch* – BGB), which also have a general impact on the concept of marriage and the family under the Basic Law; these rules are based on the notion that spouses are bound with one another in a marital community and that minority-age children receive care and upbringing in household life together with their parents (see BVerfGE 48, 327 (339)).

(2) Article 6.1 of the Basic Law is not applicable in the instant cases simply because, for instance, the complainants, whose family members are living in the Federal territory on account of a specific status of residency, seek to exercise their right to marital and familial life in the Federal Republic of Germany, even though the marital and familial unit could be established in the respective native country. The decisions made by the Authorities in applying the contested waiting-period regulations did not rescind, but rather kept intact, the entry and residency prohibition (with permit reservation) under § 2.1, second sentence, of the Aliens Act. The permanent establishment of a familial community would only have been possible for the complainants during the period in which the prohibition applied if the spouse/

father living in the-Federal territory had returned to the native country and cut his ties to Germany, e.g., to the economic and social position he had achieved, as well as personal ties. From a legal standpoint, such a return would have meant the definitive extinguishment of any residency permit or right he may have had. In attempting to re-enter, he would then be treated like other aliens seeking entry and residency for the first time; in particular, he would be covered by the recruiting stop. Consequently, the complainants as well would no longer be able to receive the permit for permanent residency in the Federal territory. The pressure laid upon the affected party to accept for a lengthy period a physical separation from his family members or to renounce conclusively an existing right to residency and leave the Federal Republic of Germany is capable of interfering with marital and familial life and must therefore be measured against Article 6.1 of the Basic Law. The situation is no different than in those cases in which the residency of an alien married to a German national is, contrary to the will of the spouses, terminated or from the outset not allowed by way of deportation or non-extension of a residency permit (see BVerfGE 19, 394 (397); 35, 382 (408); 51, 386 (397-938).

c) In that they represent aliens seeking to join family members in the Federal Republic of Germany, the complainants are not precluded from the possible protective effect of Article 6.1 of the Basic Law vis-à-vis residency law.

aa) Since Article 6.1 of the Basic Law makes reference to "marriage" and "family", its protection runs to communities of persons who as such basically do not appear in legal relations under civil law or public law. Instead, the relevant legal norms of civil law and public law normally refer only to the individual members of these communities. Against this background, it appears to be unreasonable to assume that the protection afforded by Article 6.1 of the Basic Law applies only the community as a whole (see BVerfGE 6, 55 (71) et seq.; 13, 290 (297-298)). The personal scope of protection afforded by Article 6.1 thus covers also the spouses and family members affected by an act of public authority.

In addition, it is to be assumed that each individual member of the community protected by Article 6.1 is included in the provision's personal scope of protection and is therefore entitled to assert this with regard to a decision by administrative authorities or courts affecting the marital or familial community (see BVerfGE 51, 386 (395); 31, 58 (68)). Article 6.1 of the Basic Law protects marriage and the family not merely in the interest of *individual freedom* of the spouses and family members but also for the sake of the freedom of the individual *in the community* and the maintenance of this community, as is made clear by the designation "marriage" and "family" in Article 6.1. This protection in favour of the community covers all of its members, even when the measure by public authority is addressed only to an individual member. With respect to spouses and family members, there is only one, joint marriage or family. It would be contrary to the essence of the ideal of unity of marriage and the family and the equal rights of spouses set down in Article 3.2 of the Basic Law (see BVerfGE 10, 59 (67)) when the scope of protection afforded by Article 6.1 were to be substantively and procedurally restricted to a certain marital partner or family member with regard to a sovereign act falling within the norm's material scope of protection. The unity of marriage and the family and the equal rights of spouses would be no less disturbed when protection under Article 6.1 of the Basic Law were only to be available to a spouse or family member by way of a derived right, i.e. pursuant to and within the limits of the legal position or legal actions of the other spouse or some other family member.

For the present context of spousal and familial entry, this means:

First, the spouse currently living in the Federal territory and any children living with him are affected in the scope of protection afforded by Article 6.1 of the Basic Law if and to the extent that the other spouse/parent is denied residency in the Federal territory for the purpose of marital and familial life. Such a denial also prevents those persons living here from maintaining marital or familial life. It is irrelevant whether their own residency status thereby remains unaffected.

Second, the spouse/parent seeking entry, as well as any children seeking to join a parent in the Federal territory, are not precluded from this scope of protection insofar as the issue is that one of them has been prevented from setting up marital and familial life in the Federal Republic of Germany.

bb) However, it may appear basically questionable whether the scope of protection afforded by constitutional guarantees also extends to those aliens seeking entry and residency who have not yet made their way into the territorial sovereign area of the Federal Republic of Germany (*see* Isensee, *Veröffentlichungen der Vereinigung der Deutschen Staatsrechtslehrer* – VVDStRL 32 (1974), pp. 61 et seq.). Although the complainants have established contact with the territory of the Federal Republic of Germany through their visits with family members, with the expiration of their visas, they are on the same level as aliens living outside the Federal territory seeking entry and permit to permanent residency with their family members. However, an alien's lack of contact with the sovereign territory of the Federal Republic of Germany does not result in the inapplicability of Article 6 of the Basic Law when the affected party is bound in marriage and family – thus in a constitutionally protected manner – with another person who, for his part, has already established contact with the sovereign territory of the Federal Republic of Germany. This is precisely the case when – as here – what is sought is spousal or familial entry to join an alien lawfully living in the Federal territory.

d) It can be left aside whether the fundamental right in Article 6.1 of the Basic Law is interfered with when an alien, married to a German national, an alien married

couple, an alien family or an individual member of such a community of persons is placed under a duty to leave the Federal Republic of Germany and thus a – tacit or express – right of residency is terminated, at least for the purpose of marital or familial life in the Federal territory. The complainants were (originally) not granted such a right. They were initially only permitted to reside for a limited period of time for the purpose of a visit with their family members in the Federal Republic of Germany. An interference with the right to marital and familial life guaranteed by Article 6.1 of the Basic Law could thus only be made out in the denial of continued residency if Article 6.1 were to establish a fundamental-rights claim for alien spouses and family members to entry and residency for the purpose of joining their alien family members living in the Federal territory. The wording, history and sense and purpose of Article 6.1 of the Basic Law provide no basis for such a claim. Moreover, the contrary opinion would be difficult to harmonise with Article 11 and Article 16.2, second sentence, of the Basic Law. Article 11 guarantees the right of access to and residency in the Federal territory only to German nationals. Article 16.2, second sentence, protects only persons persecuted on political grounds. In the absence of special points of reference, it is not possible to derive a claim to entry and residency from other norms of the Constitution. Article 6.1 of the Basic Law offers just as few points of reference as do other comparable fundamental-rights guarantees. Thus, for example, no one seriously considers that Article 5.3, first sentence, of the Basic Law provides a foreign scientist seeking entry into the Federal territory because the object of his research is located here with a direct claim to entry and residency. The Basic Law instead widely leaves it to the legislature and the executive to determine to what extent and under what conditions aliens are to be provided with access to the Federal territory. This neither prohibits generous admission of aliens nor requires such a practice. Within the wide framework comprised by it, the legislature and – within the permissible limits set by the latter – the executive branch are to decide on whether and at what number of non-Germans among the overall population the immigration of aliens into the Federal territory is restricted or whether and up to what extent such immigration is tolerated or assisted; in particular, according to the Constitution, it is initially a matter for the legislature and the executive to decide on whether and to what number aliens are recruited to work in the Federal territory and whether children of recruited workers are provided with a right to residency following a certain period of time that is independent of existing familial bonds, or whether for social, economic or other reasons, such a procedure, which forms the likely basis for a multi-generation immigration of aliens into the Federal territory, is not undertaken.
2. The scope of protection of Article 6.2, first sentence, of the Basic Law is likewise affected by the attacked decisions. Article 6.2, first sentence, guarantees the

exercise of parental responsibility for the sake of the child's best interests (see BVerfGE 51, 386 (398); 59, 360 (381-382)). The constraint on spouses set up by the denial of residency at issue here to accept a separation from their families or to terminate existing residency in the Federal territory was suited to placing substantial burdens on the care and upbringing of their children, Such burdens are covered by the scope of application of Article 6.2, first sentence, of the Basic Law. Protective effects vis-à vis residency law that are capable of arising under Article 6.2, first sentence, and that can be asserted by each of the affected spouses do not however extend beyond those under Article 6.1 of the Basic Law; in particular, Article 6.2, first sentence, also does not guarantee any fundamental-rights claim to entry into the Federal territory.

3. On the other hand, the relative prohibition of separation under Article 6.3 of the Basic Law, which forms a limitation for measures in the exercise of the state's watchdog function under Article 6.2, second sentence, of the Basic Law (see BVerfGE 60, 79 (88-89)), does not come into consideration as a standard of review in the present context. Article 6.3 of the Basic Law affects interference that is aimed at a separation of children from their parents in favour of the establishment of state influence in bringing them up when parents have failed to do so (see BVerfGE 24, 119 (142); 74, 102 (122 et seq.).

4. The same goes for Article 6.4 of the Basic Law, which entitles every mother to the protection and care of the community. This claim is available to the mother regardless of whether there exists or is sought a complete, familial community between her, the child and the father of the child. Since in the present context, the issue is the setting up of such a community and not the position of complainants 1) as mothers, the attacked decisions are exclusively to be measured against Article 6.1 and 6.2, second sentence, and not against Article 6.4.

5. In addition to the above-mentioned subjective rights, Article 6 of the Basic Law also contains an institutional guarantee and a "fundamental provision that determines values" (see BVerfGE 6, 55 (71 et seq.); 24, 119 (135); 31, 58 (67 et seq.); 51, 386 (396-397); 62, 323 (329)).

a) The waiting-period requirements at issue here are as such not capable of interfering with marriage and the family as constitutionally recognised institutions. The institutional guarantee of Article 6 of the Basic Law is not only affected when the provisions forming the core of marriage and family law, namely those of civil law, are widely restructured or rescinded. It may also be violated when determinative features of the ideal of marriage and the family on which the Constitution is based are indirectly interfered with. However, this is not the case here. A regulation such as the one at issue here, which prevents a limited circle of persons for a lengthy but reasonable period of time from realising the desire to live together as spouse or family at a clearly defined location without absolutely preventing such life together or unreasonably expecting that the unity of marriage and family be set up under worse conditions, is not capable of calling into question the essential elements of the ideal of marriage and the family underlying Article 6.1 and 6.2, second sentence.

b) Nevertheless, the waiting-period regulations at issue here are in part incompatible with the "fundamental provision that determines values" found in Article 6 of the Basic Law, which – as is normatively set forth in the wording of Article 6.1 of the Basic Law – places on the state the duty to protect and support marriage and the family (see BVerfGE 6, 55 (72); 55, 114 (126); established case-law).

This duty corresponds to a claim by the holder of the fundamental rights under Article 6.1 and 6.2, first sentence, that when making a decision on a request for residency under § 2.1, second sentence, of the Aliens Act, the competent authorities and courts give consideration to the existing marital and familial bonds of the applicant to persons living in the Federal territory in such a way as comports with the great importance attached by the Basic Law in Article 6 to the protection of marriage and the family. The affected person need not accept that these aspects are unreasonably neglected and that he is prevented from taking up permanent residence with close family members living in the Federal territory. The attacked decisions and the underlying administrative provisions do not take adequate account of this; the waiting-period regulations submitted for review here are only partly compatible with § 2.1, second sentence, of the Aliens Act in the interpretation required by Article 6.1 and 6.2, first sentence, of the Basic Law. The complainants' fundamental rights under Article 6.1 and 6.2, first sentence, are thus violated by the attacked decisions insofar as they affect these waiting-period regulations.

aa) In exercising their duty to take appropriate consideration of existing marital and familial relations in making general rules on the issuance of residency permits, the competent organs are often faced with competing public interests or interests of private third parties. If this is the case, then familial concerns of the applicant and the contrary public or private concerns are to be weighed with the objective of a "gentle compromise". The Federal Constitutional Court may review whether such a weighing took place and whether basis and results of the weighing have met the requirements arising under Article 6.1 and 6.2, first sentence, of the Basic Law, that the marital and familial bonds of aliens seeking residency with their family members living in the Federal territory be given due regard. The regulations to be enacted must comport with the principles of proportionality and the prohibition of excessiveness, which necessarily result as guiding rules of all state action from the principle of the rule of law and, in essence, from the very nature of fundamental rights themselves (see BVerfGE 19, 342 (348-349); 23, 127 (133), with further references). Interference in the sphere of freedom is accordingly only permissible when it is indispensable to protect public interests (see BVerfGE 35, 382 (401)). The means selected must thus be suited and necessary to paying regard to the guaranteed public and private concerns to the requisite extent, but the degree of burden on the individual – here, through the denial of a residency permit – must also stand in a reasonable relationship to the advantages for the public interest (see BVerfGE 38, 281 (302)). In applying these standards, the Federal Constitutional Court must pay regard to the discretion possessed by the competent organs in fulfilling their duties of protection and support (see BVerfGE 21, 1 (6); 48, 346 (366); 62, 323 (333); see also BVerfGE 56, 54 (80-81), with further references). This does not mean, however, that the Federal Constitutional Court is limited to the mere review of whether an apparent violation of the duties of protection and support under Article 6.1 and 6.2, first sentence, is present. The extent of review of the court instead corresponds to the rank and significance of the object to be protected by fundamental rights at issue and the special features and the affected area under scrutiny.

The personal quality that marriage and the family as affected objects of fundamental-rights protection display, as well as the high rank attributed to them in the structure of the Basic Law, argues in favour of a more extensive review by the court. Marriage is the legal form of a wide-ranging bond between man and woman; it is the sole basis for a complete familial community, and as such the condition for the best possible physical, mental and spiritual development of children (see BVerfGE 25, 167 (196). Marriage and the family correspond to the mental nature of humans, which is set up on the basis of dialogue. In addition, assistance in life which an individual is able to receive in marriage and family is of fundamental importance for the system of community life.

On the other hand, the competent state organs are, as has been explained, provided with wide discretion in the area of aliens law. This discretion can, however, also be taken into account in a manner other than by a limitation of constitutional review to an apparent violation of the protection and support duties arising under Article 6.1 and 6.2, first sentence, of the Basic Law. The discretion with regard to aliens law, provided under the Constitution to the legislature and the executive, is to be observed in the following manner: the circle of public and private interests that may be pursued with the aid of residency regulations to the detriment of the protection and support of marriage and family is not to be unreasonably constricted, and political organs' power to appraise with respect to future circumstances and developments is to remain intact as is necessary in order to weigh the concerns of marriage and the family against contrary public or private concerns. In this regard, the Federal Constitutional Court only reviews such determinations, as with the appraisals underlying the instant cases, merely, but in any event at least, for whether they are tenable. A mere review of whether they are not apparently untenable would ignore the rank and significance of the objects of legal protection served by Article 6.1 and 6.2, first sentence, of the Basic Law that are at stake; on the other hand, an intensive review would not comport with the special qualities of the area at issue or with the possibilities for forming a judgment of adequate certainty (see BVerfGE 50, 290 (332-333)).

bb) The opinions submitted by the Federal Government and the government of the *Land* Schleswig-Holstein indicate that the introduction of the requirement of eight-year residency, which is decisive for the proceedings 2 BvR 101/84, was preceded by a weighing of the public interests pursued by it and the concerns of marriage and the family. The bases and result of this weighing are not constitutionally objectionable.

(1) The demand of an eight-year, uninterrupted residency by the spouse living in the Federal territory as a prerequisite for the other spouse and children to enter is to ensure that the marital and familial community is only established in the Federal territory once the spouse seeking to be joined has formed a secure basis in the Federal territory for providing for his needs and those of his family members and, from a social standpoint, has become integrated into local conditions; advanced integration by the spouse living here is to aid the spouse joining him in a rapid, secure integration, this also serving the good of the public. The objective that this requirement is to serve has been adequately defined.

(2) It also withstands appraisal against the Constitution. The demand for far-reaching economic and social integration is not directed at complete adoption of German lifestyles and habits which would encompass the overall personality of the affected alien; rather, the objective is merely his integration in the sense of alignment within the external order of the Federal Republic of Germany. This takes account of a possible interest of the affected person protected by Article 1.1, Article 2.1, Article 4.1 and Article 5.1 of the Basic Law in being able to preserve one's national and cultural identity.

Whether public interests pursued with residency regulation enjoy a constitutional rank is irrelevant for the instant context. The Basic Law does not preclude the protection of objects of fundamental-rights protection from being downgraded to a certain extent in favour of other concerns that are not of a constitutional rank.

(3) The regulation at issue here is based on the assumption that eight-year residency by an alien in the Federal territory normally results in his far-reaching alignment with the economic and social life of the Federal Republic of Germany. This assumption involves the appraisal of future events. On the basis of the above-described standard of tenability, the pertinent regulation is not constitutionally objectionable. The rule maker and the Alien Authority that took action in the case of the

complainants under 2 BvR 101/84 operated under the assumption that a lengthy period of residency is necessary in order to achieve the desired integration. The establishment of this period has been, as is to be drawn from the comments submitted by the Federal Government on the constitutional complaint, set up according to the eight-year period under no. 4a of the General Administrative Regulations Relating to the Implementation of the Aliens Act (*Allgemeine Verwaltungsvorschrift zur Ausführung des Ausländergesetzes* – AuslVwV) on § 8. This does not appear materially unreasonable with regard to the high degree of integration required to attain a residency permit. It is not apparent that the experience of the authorities or otherwise has revealed that following an eight-year, uninterrupted residency by aliens in the Federal territory, extensive integration cannot, at least typically, be noted. Therefore, the competent organs were under no duty to "take a second look" with regard to their appraisal of the effects of the requirement at issue (see BVerfGE 49, 89 (130); 65, 1 (55-56), with further references).

(4) It also cannot be established that some means were or could have become available that would have allowed the objective to be achieved in some other manner less burdensome to the marriage and family of the affected persons without substantial detriments for other public or private concerns. In particular, the requirement of residency of at least eight years cannot be opposed by reference to the fact that § 8.1 of the Aliens Act is based on a residency of five years for the issuance of a residency permit. The requirement of five-year domestic residency in § 8.1 of the Aliens Act is a minimum requirement that must be fulfilled if the issuance of a residency permit is not to be legally precluded; in the event that this requirement is satisfied and the affected person is integrated into the economic and social life of the Federal Republic of Germany, the Act confers on him only a claim that a decision on the issuance of a residency permit is made within mandatory bounds of discretion. § 8.1 of the Aliens Act thus is not based on any legislative assessment that would be incompatible with the appraisal on the part of the executive at issue here.

The same applies to the objection that no regulation is necessary since the requirements for entry also include the – constitutionally unobjectionable – requirement that the spouse living here possess an unlimited residency permit, as well as his ability to provide for the support of the marital and familial life from his own income. It is correct that the demand of an unlimited residency permit is constitutionally not objectionable. Article 6.1 and 6.2, first sentence, of the Basic Law normally does not require that the desire of an alien for marital and familial life in the Federal territory must be met when the focus of his life or that of his spouse does not lie here. The fact that the focus of an alien's life is the Federal Republic of Germany can, despite that notions and desires of the affected persons, only be assumed when his domicile is assured in the Federal territory in the long term with regard to residency or when he has a claim to a right of permanent residency (see Baden-Württemberg Higher Administrative Court, InfAuslR, pp.177-178). It is however not untenable to assume that an unlimited residency permit alone in not sufficient in order to achieve the objective pursued with the requirement of eight-year residency for familial entry. The issuance of an unlimited residency permit pursuant to § 7.1 of the Aliens Act presupposes a fundamentally lower degree of integration than that upon which familial entry is based (see no 4.1 to 4.3 AuslVwV on § 7). It is also tenable to assume that the requirement of a residency permit on the part of the spouse living here together with the additional requirement that the affected person must be capable of providing for the common support of the family from his own income is not sufficient for attaining the purpose on which the attacked regulation is based.

Finally, it may be tenably assumed that an investigation of the individual case of whether certain aspects of advanced integration are present alone does not permit an adequately certain conclusion as to whether the degree of integration has been attained that normally is reached with eight-year residency.

(5) The weighing undertaken by the competent organs between the concerns of marriage and family and the public interests on which the attacked regulation is based fulfils the objective weight of the requirement of protection and support under Article 6.1 and 6.2, first sentence. With regard to Article 6.1 and 6.2, first sentence, it is not unreasonable to expect a so-called second-generation alien living in the Federal territory and seeking entry for his spouse and children to forgo family unification in the Federal territory prior to the expiration of eight years of residency or to set up the family unit in the relevant native country. Article 6.1 in no respect obligates the competent organs to make permission for such entry dependent on a degree of integration in the economic and social relations of the Federal Republic of Germany lower than that which can be attained within a period of eight years. It is true that aliens who have made use of the possibility, open to them of setting up an economic and social existence in the Federal Republic of Germany often view the conditions in their native countries as increasingly foreign the longer they live here and the more they become rooted in local conditions. This also applies when their integration is only external. Even a maintenance of their bonds to their cultural, religious, national and other traditions does nothing to change the fact that the actual focus of their life has shifted to the Federal Republic of Germany. On the other hand, family members of this circle of persons have spent a considerable part of their lives in their respective native countries and have normally been raised for lengthy periods in the Federal Republic of Germany by their parents, who share their heritage. In addition, a marriage occurring during this eight-year period with a

person not living in the Federal territory and integrated in the living conditions of the native country is connected with this country.
As a result of the foregoing and in view of the weight that must be assigned to the concerns pursued with the regulation, it is not in violation of the protection and support requirement of Article 6.1 and 6.2, first sentence, of the Basic Law when the affected parties are expected to resettle in their native countries insofar as they wish-to set up *at once* a community with their spouses without any limitation as to time. Article 6.1 and 6.2, first sentence, is not capable of providing protection against the economic difficulties that may be associated with such a resettlement. Extraordinary circumstances which would have made unreasonable a return to the common native country by the husband of complainant 1) in the case based on the constitutional complaint 2 BvR 101/84 have neither been demonstrated nor are they evident. The fact that two children were born to him and complainant 1) prior to expiration of the eight-year period does not lead to the assumption that an atypical fact pattern would have been made out. The regulation at issue was also made with respect to the interests of children of aliens seeking entry. Under Article 6.1 and 6.2, first sentence, it is normally not unreasonable to deny entry in order to avoid possible detriments for the development of the child that could arise when neither of the parents is familiar with the living conditions in the Federal Republic of Germany.
cc) The comments by the Baden-Württemberg Ministry of the Interior on the constitutional complaints 2 BvR 1226/83 and 2 BvR 313/84 indicate that also the demand for *a three-year marriage* as prerequisite to entry was based on a weighing of the concerns of marriage and family with the public interests pursued with the waiting-period requirement.
The result of this weighing does not fulfil the familial concerns protected by Article 6.1 and 6.2, first sentence, of the Basic Law. The impairment of these concerns by the regulation at issue exceeds the degree that must be accepted by the affected persons with regard to the principle of reasonableness. The public concerns at stake do not justify such a far-reaching neglect of their interests protected by fundamental rights.
(1) According to information provided by the Federal Government, the Baden-Württemberg Ministry of the Interior and the head of the Bavarian State Chancellery, the requirement of a three-year marriage is to aid in preventing aliens from acquiring a permit to enter as well as for residency and work by means of a "specious marriage", i.e. a bond not aimed at marital life; in addition, the requirement is to prompt married couples to consider whether, instead of accepting a separation for the duration of the waiting period, they might not prefer to set up the marital and familial community from the outset in the relevant native country and

permanently to forgo marital and familial life in the Federal territory. These objectives are not, as indicated by the above-mentioned information provided by the Federal Government, the Baden-Württemberg Ministry of the Interior and the head of the Bavarian State Chancellery, self-serving; rather, their pursuit aids in limiting (further) entry of aliens into the Federal territory, which in turn is to prevent a looming intensification of existing economic and social problems.

(2) No reliable data has been supplied on the probable effects of the marriage requirement on partners of "specious marriages" who seek entry and residency as well as a permit for work; furthermore, it is not apparent that such data could have been gained or become available, if at all, within a reasonable period of time and with a justifiable effort. The competent organs therefore had to content themselves with an estimation on the basis of assumptions regarding the presumed intentions and desires of "specious spouses". In do doing, they apparently operated under the assumption that since "specious marriages" were concluded with the goal of prompt realisation of the underlying residency objectives, the imposition of a waiting period of three years following marriage would thus thwart the conclusion of such marriages. This estimation is just as tenable as the assumption that at least the partner to a "specious marriage" living in the Federal Republic of Germany is normally interested in avoiding a long-term legal bond with his partner seeking entry into the Federal territory, from whom is demanded a waiting period of three years.

The same applies with respect to the effects of the regulations at issue on alien spouses who desire to set up a marital community. Here as well, reliable data is neither attainable nor able to be attained in a reasonable period of time and with a justifiable effort. The competent organs therefore had to rely on estimations, which were based on their own experiences and opinions. The expectation that the imposition of a waiting period of three years following marriage would result in a curtailment of entry in a not insubstantial number of cases was based on the not untenable estimation of the reaction of the married couples affected to the prospect of having to live apart for the duration of this period, aside from short-term visits. It is true that in view of the poor economic situation in the most important countries of origin of aliens living in the Federal territory, it may seem doubtful whether more than just a very low number of them – particularly with regard to longer periods of residency – would leave the Federal Republic of Germany and drop out of the local working life in order to live in a marital community immediately following the marriage. However, the essence of the matter is a period of three years, a time frame that is so substantial that it seems at least tenable to assume that a considerable number of affected persons would not accept a separation from their spouses for this period – in spite of the possibility of visits – and would opt to resettle abroad.

From the standpoint of the Constitution, there are no objections to the fact that the competent organs adhered to this estimation. Even when one assumes that the above-described doubts are not without weight, a duty to examine these doubts would only have arisen if this had been occasioned by experiences in the practices of administrative authorities or by data generated elsewhere. According to the comments submitted at the request of the Federal Constitutional Court of 12 February 1985, this was not the case; the Baden-Württemberg Ministry of the Interior and the head of the Bavarian State Chancellery have asserted that the general development – namely, a decrease in the share of aliens among the overall population between 1982 and 1983 and the drop in the number of alien immigrants into the Federal Republic of Germany in 1982, 1983 and 1984 – allows one to assume that the measures for the control of familial entry "took hold". This standpoint is at least not untenable in the sense that some other standpoint must clearly be given preference.
(3) It also cannot be established that for limiting alien entry, a waiting period beginning with marriage would not be necessary or that it would be possible to achieve the objective of limiting entry with measures that would be less burdensome for the affected marriages and families and would not have substantial detriments for other public or private concerns.
(i) According to the comments submitted here, it is and was to be expected on the basis of earlier experience that in a number of cases, aliens would only offer the pretence of the desire to set up a marital community in the Federal territory when applying for a residency permit. It is not apparent that this estimation is untenable. A basis for the contrary assumption is also not offered by the fact that the Federal Minister of the Interior and the Baden-Württemberg Ministry of the Interior did not or could not give precise figures as to their statement that the number of cases in which marriages were concluded for non-marital, i.e. residency, purposes had occurred with increasing frequency.
The demand of a three-year marriage is a general instrument, which is applied without regard for whether in the individual case a "specious marriage" is actually present. Although this does not mean that true marriages have been made a tool in "battling specious marriages", the requirement of a three-year marriage might nevertheless be constitutionally impermissible when the applications for residency permits submitted under false pretences of a desire to establish a marital community could effectively be countered with an instrument that did not measure each individual case against one and the same standard. The opinion of the competent organs that such an instrument does not exist is in any event not untenable. Arguing in favour of this is, in particular, that a review by the authorities in the individual case would only uncover the presence of a "specious marriage" upon awareness of circumstances stemming from the highly personal sphere. It would, however, be diffi-

cult to harmonise with Article 1.1 of the Basic Law, in conjunction with Article 2.1 of the Basic Law, if the administrative authorities were to undertake to obtain this information officially. The result would be the same if affected parties were unconditionally burdened with demonstrating that their marriage is not a "specious marriage". Furthermore, it is at least not untenable to assume that it is far beyond the possibilities of the administrative authorities for the alien authorities to conduct a review of each application for a residency permit, submitted with the (apparent) objective of marital life in the Federal territory, for whether a "specious marriage" is present.

It is also not necessary to do away with the requirement of a certain marriage length with respect to the fact that a "specious marriage" often become quickly evident – e.g., through the affected persons' permanently living apart – and that the residency of the "specious spouse" may normally be terminated following entry by way of a subsequent limitation on the residency permit issued to him (§ 7.4 of the Aliens Act) or by deportation due to violation of the provisions of residency law (§ 10.1 no. 7 of the Aliens Act). The constitutionally unobjectionable goal of the marriage-length requirement is to prevent from the outset the residency of aliens based on the false pretence of the desire to marry. In order to achieve this, regulatory measures under §§ 7.4 and 10.1 no. 7 of the Aliens Act are inappropriate.

The competent organs were also not required to dispense with a marriage length of three years for the reason that it is to be presumed that "specious marriages" of spouses seeking entry into the Federal territory are typically concluded with the aim of, in addition to obtaining a right of residency, acquiring as soon as possible a permit to work in the Federal territory. It is indeed possible – notwithstanding contrary obligations under international law – to grant residency permits for the purpose of spousal entry with the special notation under § 7.3 of the Aliens Act "employment not permitted" and to maintain this over lengthy periods of time. Nevertheless, it is not untenable to assume that such a procedure does not assist in effectively battling "specious marriages" since "specious spouses" seeking entry to the Federal territory normally also desire to take up employment even though this is forbidden and therefore the lack of prospects for a work permit in the near future will not have any appreciable effects on the readiness to conclude such marriages.

On the issue of whether to alleviate entry based on "specious marriages", a less burdensome instrument such as a waiting period of less than three years comes under consideration, the *Länder* Baden-Württemberg and Bavaria merely stated in the comments submitted with regard to the constitutional complaints that a waiting period of less than three years is incapable of guaranteeing the effective "battling of specious marriages". This assumption sharply contrasts with the appraisal by the Federal Government and the other states, which have held a period of one year, in any event less than three years, to be sufficient. Although the contrary standpoint is subject to not insubstantial reservations, this is insufficient for declaring it as being unconstitutional. It does not transcend the boundaries of tenability when it is assumed that a waiting period of less than three years, at least for spouses of "specious marriages" seeking entry, is not appreciably long enough in order to exercise lasting effect on the affected persons.

(ii) To the extent that the requirement of a certain marriage length serves the objective of countering entry into the Federal territory in cases involving "proper marriages", it might be considered unconstitutional if in view of a small number of entry requests to be expected, public authorities were not required to take action with regard to the aim of countering an increase in existing economic and social problems threatened by a rise in the share of aliens among the overall population. In the opinion of the competent organs, this was however not the case: despite the ending of the recruitment of alien workers in 1973, the number of aliens in the Federal Republic of Germany subsequently climbed considerably; cause for this was alleged to be primarily the increased immigration of persons seeking asylum and a growing number of spousal and familial entries; an end to this development was unable to be expected and is presently unable to be seen. This appraisal is not untenable:

There is no indication that the growth in the share of aliens among the overall population in the Federal Republic of Germany since 1973 was only to be attributed to a minor degree to the entry of spouses and families and that the main cause lay – beyond the climb in the number of persons seeking asylum – in other circumstances, such as higher birth rates among aliens living here. Findings that could have facilitated a reliable determination or estimation of entries that had to be expected in 1981 were lacking, as is to be taken from the comments submitted upon the request by the Federal Constitutional Court. The cause for this absence of findings is not only lack of statistical data, which can be remedied only in part, but also – and especially – the fact that it is difficult to record or estimate the circumstances that influence the tendency of aliens living here to choose as spouses nationals of their native countries or some other foreign state that do not permanently reside in the Federal territory, as well as the efforts of the affected persons to gain entry into the Federal territory. These include, in particular, cultural influence to which the circle of persons at issue here is subject, economic and social developments within and without the Federal Republic of Germany and the corresponding expectations of the affected persons and their particular individual qualities.

It was therefore impossible for the competent organs to ascertain on the basis of existing, incomplete statistical data exactly what "entry potential" had to be expected and to derive an estimate of foreseeable entries from this. As is to be seen from the submitted comments, the Federal Government came to the opinion in this manner that by the year 2000, the Federal Republic of Germany could expect that 200,000 future spouses of second-generation aliens would seek entry (see also *Bundestag* printed paper (*Bundestagsdrucksache* – BTDrucks.) 9/1629, p. 3); Baden-Württemberg expects for its territory 90,000 future spouses of young aliens by 1997. It cannot be determined that this estimation was untenable – for instance, due to arbitrarily exceeding, or remaining below, the underlying assumptions. Furthermore, it is not constitutionally objectionable that the competent organs relied on these and continue to expect a considerable immigration strain in the area of spousal and familial entry (see Report by the Commission "Alien Policy", composed of representatives of the Federal Government, the *Länder*, and communities, of 24 February 1983, p. 8). It is in any event tenable to take the drop in the number of entries and in the share of aliens among the overall population since 1981 as an indication for the "taking hold" by the measures to control familial entry but not as an indication of a dwindling number of entry desires by alien spouses and family members. It is not apparent that findings had become known that could have or did facilitate a reliable evaluation of future developments in this area or that such findings – at least with a justifiable effort in time and resources – were to be or could have been obtained. On account of the above-described uncertainties typical for this area, statistical recording of both residency-permit applications made for the purpose of marital and familial life in the Federal territory since 1981 and decisions on these by the competent authorities would also have been unable to assist in making such an evaluation.

(iii) Also constitutionally unobjectionable is the appraisal that entry-limiting measures less burdensome to aliens seeking marital and familial life than the requirement of a three-year marriage and not accompanied by detriments for other concerns were not or are not available.

It is clear that the complete exclusion of spousal entry – even with simultaneous easing of naturalisation conditions – would not be such a measure. Subjecting spousal entry to a "quota" would meet with objections with a view to Article 6.1 and 6.2, first sentence, of the Basic Law. Dealing with aliens seeking entry according to the "waiting-line principle" would hardly be appropriate to the mandate of protection and promotion established under Article 6.1 and 6.2, first sentence, of the Basic Law because it would not be guaranteed that due account is taken of the circumstances of the individual case and because the affected persons would be exposed to the risk of long waiting periods.

The fact that the exclusion of spouses seeking entry from the possibility of taking up employment was not given priority to the requirement of a three-year marriage is also constitutionally unobjectionable. This is because it is not untenable to assume that such exclusion would hardly have an entry-limiting effect because the affected persons primarily seek to establish the marital community; as a general rule, the lacking prospect of a possible employment would thus not keep them from entry. The same applies to the requirement of a three-year waiting period which does not start to run from the conclusion of the marriage but from the affected persons' engagement or the notification of such engagement to a competent authority. It is not inappropriate to assume that such a requirement is unsuitable to achieve the objective intended with the marriage-length requirement because difficulties of proving the point in time of the engagement would have to be expected and because a postponement of marriage would in general be perceived as less burdensome compared to a postponement of marital life.

Furthermore, it is not constitutionally objectionable that the requirement of a three-year marriage is given priority to terminating the residency of second- and subsequent-generation aliens when the affected persons reach majority age on the grounds that the objective of their residency, i.e. their living with their parents, has ceased to exist because an end of the domestic community of parents and children is to be expected now. Proceeding in this manner would considerably impair the concerns of the affected aliens. Unlike at present, they, as a general rule, could not expect to be granted the right of permanent residency in the Federal Republic of Germany irrespective of their familial circumstances; they would, in principle, be excluded from the possibility of conducting a marriage with a partner from their native country in Germany. The competent organs were not constitutionally obliged to expect of the second- and subsequent-generation aliens living here to tolerate such considerable disadvantages instead of the waiting-period requirement.

Financial incentives for forgoing spousal entry and for a return of the spouses living here would place a not inconsiderable burden on the budgetary situation of the competent bodies; they thus did not have to be given priority for constitutional grounds over the marriage-length requirement either.

Finally, the fact that the Federal Government and most Federal *Länder* obviously regarded the requirement of a one-year marriage as sufficient for having a considerable entry-limiting effect in cases of "proper marriages", is not sufficient for proving untenable the diverging assessment under review here. The assumption that the prospect of separation of less than three years – interrupted by visits – would not prompt the affected spouses to consider the possibility of conducting the marriage in the (common) native country does not transcend the boundary of untenability. Even the reliance by the competent organs on this standpoint is ultimately not constitutionally objectionable. This also applies when one assumes that states requiring a marriage length of only one year have noted a decrease in immigration and in the share of aliens among the overall population since 1981. This circumstance merely involves an indication for the assumption that a demand for a marriage length of less than three years is also suited to limiting entry to a noticeable degree. A minimum of certainty here can only be achieved – if at all – with an expense of time and resources that without representing a constitutional violation, is to be considered as untenably high.

(4) The competent organs have nevertheless failed to weigh the affected persons' marriage and family concerns against the public interests underlying the requirement of a three-year marriage in a manner comporting with the protection and support requirement of Article 6 of the Basic Law, thus violating their fundamental rights under Article 6.1 and 6.2, first sentence, of the Basic Law.

The highly predominant number of marriages between aliens involves true marriages and not "specious marriages". Accordingly, the principal objective of the marriage-length regulations under review here is the limitation of entry by alien spouses who do not simply give the pretence of desiring marital life in the Federal territory. The evaluation of these regulations' propriety is thus primarily to be measured against the normal case of a marriage corresponding to the understanding of Article 6.1 and 6.2, first sentence, of the Basic Law. The objective of limiting the entry of aliens may be accorded considerable weight under the Constitution. It may be expected of a foreigner who has married a non-German national living abroad – even if he has resided in the Federal territory more than eight years – that, by way of the imposition of a waiting period beginning with the marriage as a condition of entry, he seriously consider whether he may not decide to set up the marital community in the relevant native country. By the selection of his spouse, he has demonstrated a (continuing) association with this country. The length of the waiting period for entry must therefore be bounded by the scope of that which is still reasonable under the protection and promotion requirement of Article 6 of the Basic Law. This scope is substantially exceeded by the requirement of a waiting period of three years.

In those cases turning on this requirement, the spouse seeking to be joined normally has not only acquired a right to permanent residency in the Federal territory and established a well-ensured economic and social existence, but he has also spent a considerable portion of his life in the Federal Republic of Germany, For first-generation aliens, this results from the fact that they normally entered the Federal territory prior to 1973, the year of the so-called recruiting stop; for second- and subsequent-generation aliens, this stems from the requirement of residency of eight years or from the fact that they joined their parents at a pre-school age or were born here. As the length of residency grows, integration in the local lifestyle increases; at the same time, alienation from the native country becomes more marked. The desire by an alien seeking entry for marital and familial life in the Federal Republic of Germany, a desire protected by Article 6.1 and 6.2, first sentence, of the Basic Law, is thus to be accorded growing weight with increasing length of residency by the spouse in the Federal territory.

The degree of integration typically attained by a second-generation alien after eight years is not – in keeping with the objective of this residency requirement – to be considered insignificant. Even for first-generation aliens, it may be assumed that residency of eight years leads to lasting integration in the lifestyle of the Federal Republic of Germany.

Moreover, of decisive relevance is that in contrast to the above-described residency requirement, young marriages are without exception affected by the requirement of a three-year marriage. The demand placed upon the married couple to decide between accepting a lengthy separation or resettling abroad falls in the initial phase of the (intended) marital life, which is often characterised by the birth of children and in which the demands placed on the affected persons by the marital community and parenthood are for the first time experienced and must be overcome. It therefore normally represents a heavy burden and threat to a young marriage when the couple is forced to decide between only being able to live together for short intervals during visits over a period of three years or having to resettle abroad and forgo completely an economic and social position that had been built up over years. The requirement of a three-year marriage is also able to lead to a threat to a young marriage in that young married couples are often not in a position to assess the consequences of a lengthy separation and it recognition of these dangers, to decide against the establishment of the marital community in the native country. Finally, the regulation at issue can pose a threat to marriages because it can occasion young couples to marry too early in order to avoid a separation of more than three years.

In those cases affecting first-generation aliens, the weight accorded to the desire, protected under Article 6.1 and 6.2, first sentence, of the Basic Law, to enter the Federal territory is increased by the fact that the Federal Republic of Germany had recruited these aliens to work in the Federal territory. Although the recruitment as such did not establish a constitutionally protected claim of the affected persons to rely on the permission for entry of their spouses and children, the Federal Republic of Germany nevertheless assumed a certain degree of responsibility vis-à-vis the recruited persons, one which the requirement of a three-year marriage does not comport with.

All the same, the imposition of a waiting period beginning with marriage for entry is not absolutely ruled out. In cases involving "specious marriages", the competent organs are thus not limited to taking action with regulatory means following entry by the relevant spouses. But since the objective of entry limitation in the area of "regular marriages" is of high-ranking importance, the concerns of "battling specious marriages" are incapable of changing the fact that a three-year marriage length unreasonably interferes with the constitutionally protected interests of residency in the Federal territory by spouses seeking entry and thus their sphere of freedom protected by Article 6.1 and 6.2, first sentence, of the Basic Law.

II.

1. The denial of the right of residency sought by the complainants also affects the protective sphere of Article 2.1 of the Basic Law. Since Article 2.1 is a more general provision in comparison with Article 6 of the Basic Law, it would only come under consideration as a standard of review if it were appropriate of providing protective effects under residency law in the instant context that go beyond those offered by Article 6 of the Basic Law. This is, however, not the case. In particular, Article 2.1 of the Basic Law does not establish a claim to entry and residency in cases involving intended entries by spouses and family members. It is nearly uncontested that Article 2.1 of the Basic Law does not result in a fundamental right to *entry*. The Federal Constitutional Court has also thus far only applied Article 2.1 to the "residency of persons living in the Federal Republic" (BVerfGE 35, 382 (399). Although the instant cases do not involve a permit for entry into the Federal territory, the complainants were, following expiration of their visas, as explained equivalent to aliens seeking entry into the Federal Republic of Germany. Their requests aimed at enabling them to remain in the Federal territory; this is fundamentally different in purpose and length from their previous presence in the Federal Republic of Germany. At least in such a situation, Article 2.1 of the Basic Law does not provide the affected persons with a fundamental-rights claim to *residency in* the Federal territory.

2. The denial of the entry requests at issue here also does not represent a constitutionally relevant interference with the residency status of the complainants' spouses/fathers living here. Their right of residency has been provided to them as individuals; residency permits are issued *ad personam.* Moreover, the granting of an unlimited residency permit does not mean that marital and familial life thus far unfeasible in the Federal territory is now permitted or able to be permitted (see Federal Administrative Court, *Neue Zeitschrift für Verwaltungsrecht* – NVwZ 1986, p. 44). It is not apparent that an exception is called for with regard to the complainants.

The temporary impairment to entry sought by the complainants did not affect the right to residency attained by the family member living in the Federal territory. To the extent that this impairment was aimed at prompting a married couple to conduct their marital and familial life in the common native country, existing residency positions were not sought to be impaired with legal effect but rather were merely in fact impaired. Such an effect does not fall within the scope of protection afforded by Article 2.1 of the Basie Law. Whether Article 2.1 of the Basic Law were appropriate whatsoever for providing protective effects under residency law in favour of the complainants, which they could then assert by way of a constitutional complaint, thus need not be ruled upon.

III.

The complainants have not, as asserted, been placed at a disadvantage in violation of the requirement of equal treatment by the denial of their desire for residency.

1. The ban on unfavourable treatment in violation of the requirement of equal treatment has found particular expression in Article 6.1 of the Basic Law (see BVerfGE 28, 104 (112); established case-law). According to this Article, organs of state sovereign power are prohibited from linking legal disadvantage particularly to marriage and the family. Because the waiting-period regulations under review here exclusively relate to spouses and family members of alien nationality and not to single adult aliens, the special ban on unfavourable treatment comes into consideration as a standard of review. It is, however, not violated. While spouses and children of aliens resident in the Federal Republic of Germany are, after expiration of the waiting period and upon compliance of the other entry requirements, exempted from the general administrative practice according to which aliens who strive to enter the Federal territory are, in principle, denied permanent residency, a foreigner who seeks access to the Federal territory in order to live together unmarried with another alien here, is, as a general rule, not granted permanent residency according to this practice. The ban on unfavourable treatment under Article 6.1 of the Basic Law only rules out the unequal treatment, which would be contrary to the value determination of Article 6.1 of the Basic Law, of spouses and family members on the one hand and of single persons and non-family members on the other hand if they are in a comparable situation. This is not the case with a married alien living in the Federal territory who wants to conduct his marriage and family life in the Federal territory and an alien staying in the Federal territory who does not seek the entry of other persons to the Federal Republic of Germany in order to live together with them.

2. The decisions impugned by the complainants also do not infringe the ban on unfavourable treatment in violation of the equality requirement simply because familial entry is granted in other federal *Länder* after shorter waiting periods. Article 3.1 of the Basic Law, which is the only standard of review that comes into consideration in this context, is not violated by these differences in administrative practice. For the individual only has a right to equal treatment vis-à-vis the holder of public authority with concrete competence according to the distribution of competences

(BVerfGE 21, 54 (68). Because the administrative regulations of the supreme *Land* authorities in the area of familial entry ensure uniform execution of administrative tasks for the entire *Land* in question, due account is taken of Article 3.1 of the Basic Law. It can therefore remain undecided whether the right to equal treatment following from Article 3.1 of the Basic Law with regard to the residency permit applied for by complainants 1) is only due to the complainants themselves and whether it could be successfully asserted by means of a constitutional complaint solely by them.

IV.

When a constitutional complaint is lodged in a permissible manner, the Federal Constitutional Court is not limited to reviewing whether the complained-of interference with fundamental rights indeed is present. On the contrary, it may review the attacked sovereign act from any constitutional aspect coming under consideration (BVerfGE 42, 312 (325-326); 53, 366 (390); 54, 53 (67)).
1. § 2.1, second sentence, of the Aliens Act, on which the Alien Authorities based their denial of the complainants' request for entry, is compatible with the constitutional principles of precision of law and proviso of legality.
a) The Senate shares the opinion held by the First Senate of the Federal Constitutional Court that § 2.1, second sentence, of the Aliens Act comports with the minimum requirements of statutory precision (BVerfGE 49,168 (181 et seq.)). Admittedly, the Senate holds that in view of the numerous state administrative regulations on the Aliens Act deviating from one another, the consideration that the provision can be assumed to be sufficiently precise since the Federal Government's administrative guidelines provide for uniform application of § 2.1, second sentence, of the Aliens Act is hardly tenable any longer. As has also been emphasised by the First Senate (BVerfG 49, 168 (181-182, 183-184), the fact that the normative characteristics of the provision have been given concrete shape by court holdings on aliens law, in particular by the Federal Administrative Court, thereby assuring that both the individual and the administrative authorities a minimum of legal certainty, decisively speaks in favour of § 2.1, second sentence, of the Aliens Act still comporting with the requirement of statutory precision.
b) The constitutional principle of a general proviso of legality does not give rise in the present context to requirements going beyond those under the rule-of-law precept of statutory precision. The general proviso of legality obligates the legislature itself to make all essential decisions affecting fundamental rights in fundamental normative areas – irrespective of the element of "encroachment". Whether and to what extent legislative action is required here is to be measured against the effects

that might arise in the relevant area for the affected person's fundamental rights; at the same time, such action depends on the area's special qualities, in particular, on whether and to what extent such area can be regulated whatsoever by the state and can be made subject to legislation in an appropriate fashion (see BVerfGE 49, 89, (126-127)).

If the area at issue here is reviewed under these aspects, then the result is: state decisions on the admission of aliens into the Federal territory have varying effects on the fundamental rights area of affected persons; in cases of spousal and familial entry, they may place a heavy burden on objects protected by Article 6.1 of the Basic Law. On the other hand, the admission of aliens is capable – regardless of for what purpose – of affecting a number of interests of the general public. It influences – in a manner and to an extent often difficult to predict – the Federal Republic of Germany's economic and social structure, placing on governmental authorities in numerous areas (provision, education, labour market, public security, etc.) a variety of duties unable to be described in advance. Moreover, often inevitable changes in the economic or foreign-policy situation or needed changes in objectives and forms of foreign policy require quick, flexible action on the part of Alien Authorities. On the other hand, aliens seeking residency often possess unique individual qualities that are unable to be covered with the aid of general regulations and that can only be appropriately taken into account by way of individual, case-by-case decisions. These reasons justify leaving the executive with considerable discretion in the area of admission of aliens (see BVerfGE 49, 168 (181-182)). As measured against this, § 2.1, second sentence, of the Aliens Act withstands the requirements of the general proviso of legality, even if it may seem desirable that a more extensive legal regulation be undertaken for the area at issue than that accomplished with § 2.1, second sentence, of the Aliens Act.

2. The decisions by the Alien Authorities to which the attacked judicial decisions make reference are also not incompatible with objective constitutional law simply because the administrative regulations underlying them violate Article 84.1 and 84.2 of the Basic Law.

a) The *Länder* were authorised to steer and to bind the discretion in the area of spousal and familial entry available to the Alien Authorities under § 2.1, second sentence, of the Aliens Act by administrative regulations of their own. It is irrelevant that they do not have legislative competence in this respect. According to Article 83 of the Basic Law, the law regarding aliens is executed by the *Länder* in their own right. By virtue of Article 84 of the Basic Law, this authorises them to regulate administrative procedure. The authorisation encompasses not least the right for higher authorities to give technical instructions to subordinate authorities also with regard to dealing with discretionary provisions. § 51 of the Aliens Act does not provide for anything different in this regard. Neither the wording nor the history or the sense and purpose of the provision support the assumption that the provision was intended to restrict the authority of the *Länder* to enact administrative regulations.

b) The area of spousal and familial entry lacks administrative regulations of the Federation which have a blocking effect on the relevant administrative regulations issued by the *Länder*. The General Administrative Regulations of the Federation Relating to the Implementation of the Aliens Act of 7 July 1967 in the version of 7 July 1978 (Joint Ministerial Gazette p. 368) do not contain a regulation on spousal and familial entry which would have such an effect. The Federal Government's resolution on the socially responsible steering of familial entry of 2 December 1981 did not prevent the *Länder* from filling this gap. The resolution is not a general administrative regulation within the meaning of Article 84.2 of the Basic Law. It is not intended for the authorities entrusted with the execution of the Aliens Act; instead, it contains a recommendation for the *Länder* to uniformly enact certain administrative regulations as "immediate regulations". Apart from this, it was enacted without the consent of the *Bundesrat*, which would have been required for general administrative regulations.

3. a) The manner in which the Alien Authorities exercised the discretion provided to them by § 2.1, second sentence, of the Aliens Act in the cases 2 BvR 1226/83 and 2 BvR 313/84 does not violate the principle of federal comity (*Bundestreue*). According to this principle, the organs of a *Land* may make use of their competences only in such a way that the concerns of the state as a whole and of the other *Länder* are not injured or impaired in an unacceptable manner (BVerfGE 34, 9 (44)). The waiting-period regulations introduced by the *Land* Baden-Württemberg for the area of spousal and familial entry integrate into the aim of limiting the entry of aliens pursued by the Federal Government. Without particular other circumstances, the assumption that the particularly far-reaching restriction of the entry of aliens by these regulations will possibly prompt a not inconsiderable number of aliens to shift their domicile to *Länder* which – unlike Baden-Württemberg – have fully complied with the Federal Government's recommendation of 2 December 1981 cannot be regarded as an unacceptable impairment of the concerns of these *Länder*.

b) The requirement of a three-year marriage also does not lead to discrepancies in the application of the Aliens Act among the states of such a variety that the duty to essentially enforce Federal laws uniformly (BVerfGE 11, 6 (18)) would have to be considered as violated. This particularly applies with a view to the fact that the assessment of discrepancies in the execution of Federal laws may not leave possible differences of the living conditions in the individual *Länder* out of account; thus, it must thus be taken into consideration in the present context that the *Land* Baden-

Württemberg is the non-city state of the Federal Republic of Germany with the highest share of aliens in the overall population and that an above-average number of aliens lives in its conurbations.

V.

Neither general international law nor treaty law binding on the Federal Republic of Germany, to which the Federal Constitutional Court is empowered to extend its review (see BVerfGE 58, 1 (34-35); BVerfGE 59, 63 (89)), contain rules that direct a contrary ruling,

1. Notwithstanding opposing provisions of treaty law, states are normally able to decide on the admission or deportation of aliens under their own discretion. Accordingly, the European Court of Human Rights found in its judgment of 28 May 1985, which dealt with the application by alien husbands for entry into Great Britain to join their wives living there, that under an established principle of general international law, a state is empowered, subject to its treaty commitments, to control the entry of aliens into its sovereign territory (Case Abdulaziz et al., Publications de la Cour Européenne des Droits de l'Homme, Série A, Arrets et décisions, Vol. 94, p. 34, no. 67; reproduced in *Europäische Grundrechte-Zeitschrift* – EuGRZ 1985, pp. 567 et seq.; *Neue Juristische Wochenschrift* 1986, pp. 3007 et seq.). Although in the practice of states, a certain tendency can be noted toward a self-limitation of this power with respect to spouse and family members of aliens already admitted (see Nafziger, *The General Admission of Aliens under International Law, American Journal of International Law* – AJIL, Vol. 77 (1983), pp. 804 et seq.; 834), an international obligation to permit the entry of alien spouses and family members within certain periods and without any additional conditions does not, however, follow from this. A corresponding conclusion is also prohibited on account of the fact that numerous states only permit familial entry under specified conditions pursuant to their fundamental decisions on alien policy. For instance, in immigration countries like the United States of America, spouses and family members of immigrants are only accepted, although with preference, within the scope of quotas (see Aleinikoff, in: Frowein/Stein, *Die Rechtsstellung von Ausländern nach staatlichem Recht und Völkerrecht*, Vol. 2, pp. 1572 et seq. (1573), 1591-1592). The Swiss Confederation does not permit the entry of family members of so-called seasonal workers, makes it contingent on a twelve-month waiting period for persons holding a one-year residency title (so-called *Jahresaufenthalter*) and in principle permits it without further preconditions only for persons with a permanent residency title (*Niedergelassene*), a legal position which, as a general rule, can only be attained after a ten-year residency (see Thürer, in: Frowein/Stein, loc. cit., Vol. 2, p.

1374 (1375)). Finally, the Kingdom of Belgium, by means of an Act adopted on 28 June 1984, in principle ruled out the entry of spouses and family members of second-generation aliens with effect of 16 August 1984 to prevent family reunifications "en cascade" (see Melchior/Lecrenier, in: Frowein/Stein, loc. cit., Vol. 1, pp. 122 et seq. (124)).

2. The Federal Republic of Germany is not subject to any international commitments that would require an appraisal of the eight-year residency regulation and the requirement of a three-year marriage in a manner more favourable to the complainants.

a) In particular, Article 8.1 of the European Convention on Human Rights does not compel such an appraisal. The European Commission on Human Rights has consistently maintained the opinion that the Convention – i.e. Article 8.1 as well – does not guarantee an alien the right to enter the territory of a member state and to reside in it; the Commission stated that the control of spousal and familial entry of aliens must nevertheless take place in harmony with the obligations established by the Convention; the exclusion of a person from entry into the territory of a member state in which members of his family live touches upon the scope of application of Article 8 of the Convention, said the Commission (see Frowein/Peuker, *EMRK-Kommentar*, 1985, *Art. 8*, marginal nos. 23-25). In its decision of 28 May 1985 in *Abdulaziz et al.,* the European Court of Human Rights determined that the basic objective of Article 8 of the Convention is the protection of the individual against arbitrary interference by public authorities with private and family life. Although Article 8 could in addition also give rise to positive obligations that are components of effective respect for family life, member states nevertheless have been provided with wide regulatory discretion. This also applies in cases involving entry to join an immigrant. In such instances the reach of the positive obligation of the member states depends on the affected person's situation. The Court held that Article 8 basically does not give rise to a duty on the part of the member state to respect the married couple's choice of residency and to facilitate residency for alien spouses. The Court therefore found no objection under Article 8 "in and of itself" to the British regulation under review, which precluded entry of alien husbands to join their wives living in Great Britain with unlimited residency permits or as naturalised citizens.

b) Art, 12 of the Agreement establishing an Association between the European Economic Community and Turkey of 12 September 1963 (O.J. Eur. Comm. (No. L) pp. 3685, 3702 (1964)); Federal Law Gazette (*Bundesgesetzblatt* – BGBl.) 1964 II p. 510) determines that the contracting parties are to allow free movement of workers, in accordance with Articles 48 et seq. of the EEC Treaty. Article 36 of the Additional Protocol to this Agreement O.J. Eur. Comm. (No. L) p. 293 (1972);

Federal Law Gazette 1972 II p. 386), concluded on 23 November 1970, provides that the free movement of workers is to be completed by the end of the 22nd year following entry into force of the Agreement on the basis of regulations by the Association Council, set up under Article 6 of the Agreement. The Association Council has not adopted any resolutions that pertain to residency law in a narrower sense. There was no duty under the Agreement and the Additional Protocol of the Alien Authorities and the administrative courts that took action in the proceedings 2 BvR 101/84 and 2 BvR 313/84 to fulfil the residency requests by the complainants (see European Court of Justice, Judgment of 30 September 1987, Case 12/86). This duty also did not arise simply because the treaty parties undertook pursuant to Article 7 of the Agreement to adopt all measures to fulfil their obligations under the Agreement and to forgo every measure that might endanger the realisation of the objectives of the Agreement. This provision does not give rise to the situation where, with entry into force of the Agreement, the member states are prohibited from changing the state of the law in the area of residency law, even absent corresponding resolutions by the Association Council, to the detriment of workers and their spouses and family members. Such a prohibition also does not follow from other provisions of the Agreement or the Additional Protocol. In particular, the treaty does not contain any provisions comparable to Articles 44 et seq. of the Act on the Conditions for the Accession of the Republic of Greece to the European Economic Community, to the European Atomic Community, and to the European Coal and Steel Community that would allow one to draw such a prohibition under residency law (see European Court of Justice, Judgment of 23 March 1983, Case 77/82) The Association Agreement and the Additional Protocol only prevent a change in valid residency law to the extent that the required establishment of freedom of movement is later precluded or called into question. This is not the case with regard to the change in regulations on familial entry with regard to the resolutions by the Federal Government on 2 December 1981.

c) That which the European Court of Human Rights stated with regard to Article 8 of the European Convention on Human Rights applies also to Article 17.1 and Article 23.1 of the International Charter on Civil and Political Rights of 19 December 1966. Likewise, no obligations result for the Federal Republic of Germany from Article 19 no. 6 of the European Social Charter of 18 October 1961 or from Article 2.1 and Article 10 no.1 of the International Charter on Economic, Social and Cultural Rights of 19 December 1966, such that a ruling more favourable to the complainants' residency requests would be required.

d) The residency agreement between the German Reich and the Turkish Republic of 12 January 1927 (Reich Law Gazette (*Reichsgesetzblatt* – RGBl.) 1927 II p. 76; Federal Law Gazette 1952 II p. 608) makes entry and residency by members of the treaty parties subject to national immigration law. This reservation rules out commitments by the Federal Republic of Germany that would have required a different ruling on the complainants' requests in the proceedings 2 BvR 101484 and 2 BvR 313/84 by the Alien Authorities and the administrative courts (on this, see Randelzhofer, *Der Einfluß des Völker- und Europarechts auf das deutsche Ausländerrecht*, 1980, pp. 32 et seq., 38 with note 106).

VI.

The constitutional complaint in the proceedings 2 BvR 101/84 is, in view of the foregoing, unfounded. On the contrary, the administrative courts' decisions attacked in the proceedings 2 BvR 1226/83 and 2 BvR 313/84 violate the complainants' fundamental rights under Article 6 of the Basic Law. These decisions have not paid the required attention to the obligation to protect and promote marriage and the family arising from Article 6 of the Basic Law.
Therefore the decisions rendered in the original proceedings 2 BvR 1226/83 and 2 BvR 313/84 had to be quashed; the matters had to be referred back to the administrative courts (§ 95.2 of the Federal Constitutional Court Act).
The decision on the reimbursement of expenses is based on § 34a.2 of the Federal Constitutional Court Act.

D.

This decision is rendered with seven votes in favour and one vote against.

Justices: Zeidler, Dr. Dr. h.c. Niebler, Steinberger, Träger, Mahrenholz, Böckenförde, Klein, Graßhof

No. 18

BVerfGE 79, 51

of 12 October 1988 – 1 BvR 818/88 –

"Foster parents case"

HEADNOTES:

1. **A child may be removed from a foster family and transferred to a designated adoptive family (care prior to adoption) even if psychological impairment as a consequence of the separation cannot be entirely ruled out (further development of a previous decision, Decisions of the Federal Constitutional Court (*Entscheidungen des Bundesverfassungsgerichts* – BVerfGE) 75, 201).**
2. **Where the courts assume in such a case that separating the child from his foster parents will cause psychological impairment, they must examine whether the designated adoptive parents are in a position to integrate the child into their family without any permanent damage arising (Article 6.2 sentence 2 of the Basic Law (*Grundgesetz* – GG)).**

Order of the First Senate of 12 October 1988
– 1 BvR 818/88 –

in the proceedings regarding the constitutional complaint 1. of Mrs. Sch., 2. of Mr. Sch., 3. of the minor R. – authorised representatives: …, lawyers – against a) the order of the Celle Higher Regional Court (*Oberlandesgericht*) of 24 May 1988 – 21 W 9/88 –, b) the order of the Hanover Regional Court (*Landgericht*) of 28 April 1988 – 9 T 95/88 –, c) the order of the Hanover Local Court (*Amtsgericht*) of 25 April 1988 – 64 X R 15/88 –.

RULING:

I. The constitutional complaint of the complainants in 1) and 2) is rejected as unfounded.
II. The orders of the Hanover Local Court of 25 April 1988 – 64 X R 15/88 –, of the Hanover Regional Court of 28 April 1988 – 9 T 95/88 – and of the Celle Higher Regional Court of 24 May 1988 – 21 W 9/88 – violate the fundamental right of the complainant in 3) under Article 2.1 in conjunction with Article 1.1 of the Basic Law. The matter is hereby referred back to the Local Court.
III. The *Land* (state) Lower Saxony is ordered to reimburse the complainant in 3) his necessary expenses.

EXTRACT FROM GROUNDS:

A.

The subject-matter of the constitutional complaint is the court decisions according to which the complainants in 1) and 2) – foster parents – are to surrender the complainant in 3) – foster child – to the Youth Welfare Office, which has custody of the child.

I.

The care for the person of a child includes the right to require surrender of the child from every person who is unlawfully withholding it from the parents or from one parent (§ 1632.1 of the Civil Code (*Bürgerliches Gesetzbuch* – BGB)). Where the right and the duty to care for the person of the child has been transferred to a guardian – in this case the Youth Welfare Office – the right to request surrender falls to him (§ 1800 of the Civil Code). However, where the child has lived in foster care for a period of time, the guardianship court may, pursuant to § 1632.4 of the Civil Code, of its own motion or on the application of the foster carer, order that the child remains with the foster carer if and as long as – especially in regard to the reason for and duration of the foster care – the preconditions therefor are met (§ 1666.1 sentence 1 of the Civil Code). According to the wording of the provision, these preconditions are met in the event of, among other things, the endangering of the physical, mental or psychological best interests of the child by means of the abusive exercise of parental custody, by neglect of the child or by non-culpable failure by the parents. It is thereby compatible with the Basic Law that where the preconditions under § 1666.1 sentence 1 of the Civil Code are not met when the child is given into foster care in a family the duration of the foster relationship alone can lead to the issuing of an order for the child to remain with the foster family according to § 1632.4 of the Civil Code if serious and permanent impairment of the physical or mental best interests of the child is to be expected upon its removal from the foster family (see BVerfGE 68, 176).

II.

1. The complainant in 3) was born in wedlock on 7 June 1987. Shortly after his birth the mother was committed to a psychiatric clinic suffering from a psychosis. As the father was not in a position to look after the child, the Youth Welfare Office on 24 July 1987 placed him in the family of the complainants in 1) and 2). These have already adopted two children and have a third child in permanent foster care. Initially, the foster care in regard to the complainant in 3) was only to last for a period of around one to two months. However, in agreement with the Youth Welfare Office it was extended.

In late January 1988 the father wanted to take the complainant in 3) to live with him. The complainants in 1) and 2) initially prevented this by means of temporary injunction proceedings.

In March 1988 the parents gave the complainant in 3) up for incognito adoption. The Youth Welfare Office, acting as his guardian (§ 1751.1 sentence 2 of the Civil Code), first wanted to place the child in care prior to adoption with a family of its own choice (§ 1744 of the Civil Code). The complainants in 1) and 2) were, however, not prepared to surrender the child.

2. The Youth Welfare Office thereupon succeeded in getting the court to issue an order that the complainants in 1) and 2) are to surrender the complainant in 3) so that he can be taken to the designated adoptive family. At that time the complainants in 1) and 2) did not wish to adopt the child. The court rejected their application to issue an order according to § 1632.4 of the Civil Code after it had heard the foster parents, their authorised representatives, a representative of the German Association of Foster and Adoptive Parents, as well as two representatives from the Youth Welfare Office.

It was the court's view that the child's best interests would not be endangered if it was surrendered to the Youth Welfare Office. Undisputedly, the fact that the complainant in 3) was to be transferred from the foster parents to the chosen adoptive parents would place a considerable psychological burden on the child. Social ties had been formed during his nearly 10-month stay with the foster parents which would impair the psychological development of the complainant in 3) following the separation. However, the court did not believe that any permanent damage would be done. No expert opinion needed to be obtained from a child psychologist as had been applied for.

In the present case particular consideration had to be given to the fact that the child was to be given into a family who wished to adopt him. It could therefore be assumed that the adoptive parents would keep the psychological impairment to the child to a minimum by establishing contact in a loving and careful manner. Such impairment was acceptable in the present case as the child would gain a legal status on account of the planned adoption which would be considerably better than that of a foster child.

In addition, were the child to remain in the foster family it had to be assumed that the natural parents could attempt to make contact with the child and possibly even attempt to have him returned to their family. Furthermore, on account of the lack of name giving the child would not be integrated into the family of the complainants in 1) and 2) to the same extent as it would be in the case of an adoption.

The Court did not believe it was necessary to establish with sufficient certainty that the endangering of the child's best interests upon his removal from the foster family could be ruled out. The Federal Constitutional Court had only required such a high degree of certainty when the application for surrender merely served the purpose of transferring a child from one set of foster parents to another (see BVerfGE 75, 201). Where, however, the purpose of the application for surrender – as in the present case – was to transfer the child to his future adoptive parents, the same standards were to be applied as in the case of returning him to his original family. Thus, after weighing all the circumstances, the planned adoption of the complainant in 3) by the designated adoptive family was in his interests.

3. The complaint lodged by the foster parents was unsuccessful. The Regional Court explained that even after the complaint had been brought it could not be assumed that if the child acquired new persons to whom it would closely relate, which in the interests of the child was, however, to occur without delay, the developmental deficit of the complainant in 3) would be unjustifiably great and irreversible. His age, the relatively short stay with the foster parents and the fact that he was not to be put in another foster family or, for instance, to go to a dysfunctional original family, but rather to adoptive parents, who had no doubt been carefully selected, spoke against that.

4. The further complaint was rejected. In the meantime the complainants in 1) and 2) had themselves applied to the competent Local Court to adopt the complainant. The Higher Regional Court denied that this application was relevant to the issue, stating as grounds that it concerned a new fact which could not be taken into consideration in the further complaint. For the rest, the Higher Regional Court also en-

dorsed the action taken by the Regional Court insofar as it had not obtained the expert opinion from a child psychologist as applied for. As regards the issue of the danger to the child on account of his “relocation”, the complainants had not submitted any facts that required clarifying. The generalised hypothesis they had put forward, namely the impairment to the infant on account of having new persons to whom to relate closely, did not require an expert opinion.

III.

In their constitutional complaint against the contested decisions the complainants in 1) and 2) complain of a violation of Article 6.1 and Article 103.1 of the Basic Law. The complainant in 3) believes there has been a violation of both Article 6.1 of the Basic Law and of his fundamental right under Article 2.1 in conjunction with Article 1.1 of the Basic Law.

Although the complainant in 3) is not the natural child of the complainants in 1) and 2), they were able to invoke Article 6.1 of the Basic Law because they constitute a “social” family. By contrast, however, there was no relationship worthy of protection between the complainant in 3) and the selected adoptive parents.

The complainants in 1) and 2) believe that especially the rejection of their application for a psychological expert opinion on the impact of the separation on the child violates their right to a hearing in court. Even the courts had believed the question of the possible impairment on account of the separation to be an important one.

The order for surrender and the disregarding of the application for the obtaining of an expert opinion violated the fundamental right of the complainant in 3) to observance of his human dignity and the free development of his personality. The fact that the courts had found it reasonable for the child to be transferred to another family was based on a number of legal errors. The Higher Regional Court appeared to accept that the complainant in 3) was endangered, but erroneously assumed that the preconditions under § 1666.1 of the Civil Code had to be met for an order for the child to remain to be issued according to § 1632.4 of the Civil Code. Contrary to this view, according to the decision of the Federal Constitutional Court of 14 April 1987 (BVerfGE 75, 201) and given the present facts of the case, the endangering of the child’s best interest must be ruled out with sufficient certainty. Even if there was only a low probability of physical or mental impairment, every other interest in removing the complainant in 3) from his current foster family had to take second place.

IV.

1. …
2. The Hanover Youth Welfare Office believes the constitutional complaint is unfounded.
…

V.

Upon application by the complainants, the Federal Constitutional Court by way of a temporary injunction suspended the execution of the order of the Local Court until a decision was taken concerning the constitutional complaint, but instructed the complainants in 1) and 2) to permit the designated adoptive parents to make and take up contact with the child upon the request and mediation of the Youth Welfare Office.

B.

The constitutional complaint lodged by the complainants in 1) to 3) is admissible.
1. The complainant in 3) (foster child) is properly represented by a supplementary curator. According to the established case-law of the Federal Constitutional Court, the legal representative cannot lodge a constitutional complaint if it cannot be ruled out that there exists a conflict of interests between him and the underage child (BVerfGE 72, 122 (133)). This precondition is met in the present case. The Youth Welfare Office, acting as the child's guardian, requests the surrender of the child by the foster parents. The foster parents and the child feel that this in particular constitutes the endangering of the child's best interests. For that reason, pursuant to § 1909.1 sentence 1 of the Civil Code a supplementary curator had to be appointed to carry through the constitutional complaint proceedings on behalf of the complainant in 3).
2. Concerns in respect of the admissibility of the constitutional complaint of the complainant in 3) do not even arise from the fact that he has not exhausted the legal remedies (§ 90.2 sentence 1 of the Federal Constitutional Court Act (*Bundesverfassungsgerichtsgesetz* – BVerfGG). Given the legal situation in the present case, the legal remedies in the original proceedings before the guardianship court were only lodged by the foster parents in their own name. The question of whether, in view of the requirement that the legal remedies be exhausted, a supplementary curator should already have been appointed for the complainant in 3) pursuant to § 1909.1 sentence 1 of the Civil Code in the original proceedings on account of a conflict of

interests can remain unanswered; since pursuant to § 90.2 sentence 2 of the Federal Constitutional Court Act a decision must already be taken on a constitutional complaint before the legal remedies have been exhausted if the complainant would otherwise suffer a serious and unavoidable disadvantage. This condition is met in the present case. The complainant would otherwise first himself have to conduct the proceedings before the guardianship court after a supplementary curator had been appointed and, possibly, lodge the admissible legal remedies. However, the unforeseeable temporal delay associated with invoking the Federal Constitutional Court's jurisdiction is not reasonable in the case of the complainant in 3). He has an urgent interest in having the question of the constitutionality of his transfer to the designated adoptive family clarified as quickly as possible.

C.

The constitutional complaint of the complainants in 1) and 2) is unfounded.
The constitutional complaint of the complainant in 3) is well-founded. The contested decisions violate his fundamental right under Article 2.1 in conjunction with Article 1.1 of the Basic Law.

I.

The Federal Constitutional Court has found that where the foster relationship continues over a period of time and a bond develops between the foster parents and the foster child, the foster family is also protected by Article 6.1 of the Basic Law, so that Article 6.3 of the Basic Law cannot be entirely disregarded when taking a decision on whether the child is to be removed from its "social" family (see BVerfGE 68, 176 (187)). Accordingly, the complainants in 1) and 2) can invoke their own position as holders of fundamental rights. However, the review of the contested decisions does not reveal any violation of Article 6 of the Basic Law. Nor has there been any violation of the complainants' right to a hearing in court (Article 103.1 of the Basic Law).
1. a) When introducing § 1632.4 of the Civil Code the legislature was less interested in enhancing the status of the foster parents than in seeking to act in the child's best interests. A foster family relationship which has existed for a long period between the child and the foster parents should not be severed to the detriment of the child. In the case of foster children, who have often already suffered an unhappy fate prior to being taken into foster care, the legislature wanted to ensure that they did not end up without any close relationships without good cause … Account was taken in the legislative procedure of the fact that the foster person who takes the

child into his care deserves respect; the main concern was, however, to create a legal provision – § 1632.4 of the Civil Code – which prevented the child's removal from the foster family at inopportune moments when it was in the child's best interests (see *Bundestag* printed paper (*Bundestagsdrucksache* – BTDrucks.) 8/2788, p. 40).

b) In the course of the constitutional review of the contested decisions account must be taken of the fact that Article 6.1 and Article 6.3 of the Basic Law must be seen in the context of the parental rights under Article 6.2 sentence 1 of the Basic Law, which foster parents cannot invoke. For natural parents being separated from their child is the strongest encroachment imaginable on parental rights and only compatible with the Basic Law if the principle of proportionality is strictly observed (see BVerfGE 60, 79). The separation carries less weight in the case of foster relationships. Such relationships are temporary by institutional design, so that in the case of the removal of the foster child from the foster parents' family they can in principle be expected to bear the loss associated with the separation. A violation of Article 6.1 and 6.3 of the Basic Law can only be assumed in exceptional cases where, for example, the foster parents have looked after the child for many years or other crucial circumstances prohibit breaking up the foster family, along with the separation from the foster child associated therewith, on constitutional grounds.

This cannot be presumed to be the case here. The relatively short duration of the foster relationship already speaks against that. Furthermore, this relationship would already have ended in spring 1988 if the complainants in 1) and 2) had not prevented the complainant in 3) being transferred to the designated adoptive family. It may well be the case that the foster parents' affection for the child had been influential in that, but it does not alter the fact that the further consolidation of their relationship with the child is a consequence of their own conduct, which must thus be ascribed to them.

As, for the rest, there are no other serious reasons which speak against the complainants in 1) and 2) being separated from the child, their own position as holders of fundamental rights under Article 6.1 and 6.3 of the Basic Law has not been violated.

2. As parties to the original proceedings, the complainants in 1) and 2) in principle have a right under Article 103.1 of the Basic Law to a hearing in court. This also applies without restrictions to proceedings subject to the principle of official investigation by the public prosecution office (see BVerfGE 75, 201 (215) with further references). The complainants complain that their submissions and their references in regard to the question of the endangering of the child's best interests had not been taken into consideration and their motion to obtain an expert opinion from a psychologist had not been complied with.

a) According to the established case-law of the Federal Constitutional Court, Article 103.1 of the Basic Law obligates the non-constitutional courts to take note of the submissions made by the parties to the proceedings and to take them into consideration (BVerfGE 69, 141 (143)). However, the courts are not required to explicitly address every submission made in their grounds of judgment. For that reason, in order that the Federal Constitutional Court can establish that Article 103.1 of the Basic Law has been violated, the special circumstances in a specific case must make it clear that either no note at all has been taken of the actual submissions made by a party to the proceedings or that they were not taken into consideration in the decision (BVerfGE 65, 293 (295-296) with further references). Such circumstances do not exist in the present case. The courts took note of the submissions made by the complainants in 1) and 2). The considerations quoted in the grounds of judgment show that the courts also dealt with the question of the endangering of the child's best interests on account of the impairment of the psychological development of the complainant in 3) as a consequence of his removal from the foster family. The question of whether all points of the evaluation must be followed is irrelevant in the context of procedural law. Article 103.1 of the Basic Law does not grant protection against the courts entirely or partly ignoring the submissions made by the parties for formal or substantive law reasons (BVerfGE 69, 141 (143-144)). Therefore, no violation of the constitution is recognisable in that respect.
b) The Federal Constitutional Court further found that Article 103.1 of the Basic Law in conjunction with the principles of the Code of Civil Procedure (*Zivilprozeßordnung* – ZPO) requires that relevant motions for evidence be taken into consideration (BVerfGE, loc. cit.). However, this principle, which was established for proceedings on matters of contentious jurisdiction under the Code of Civil Procedure, cannot be transferred to proceedings on matters of non-contentious jurisdiction, where the principle of official investigation applies. Pursuant to § 12 of the Act on Matters of Non-Contentious Jurisdiction (*Gesetz über die Angelegenheiten der freiwilligen Gerichtsbarkeit* – FGG*)*, the court itself must institute the necessary investigations and gather the evidence it deems appropriate. The extent of the investigations and of the collection of evidence is geared to the constituent facts of the legal provisions relevant to the case. The court is not obligated to take motions for evidence into account if it does not deem the preferred evidence useful on the basis of the other results of the investigations or deems them irrelevant for legal reasons (see Keidel/Kuntze/Winkler, *FGG*, 12th ed., *§ 12*, marginal nos. 85 and 86 with further references). The latter is the case here. The courts did not further investigate and clarify the facts of the case in regard to the question of the child's best interests because, applying and interpreting § 1632.4 of the Civil Code, they did not believe this was necessary. That can, especially since no irrelevant considerations

are recognisable, not be queried in the context of Article 103.1 of the Basic Law on constitutional grounds.

II.

As regards the complainant in 3), when applying § 1632.4 of the Civil Code the courts did not take sufficient account of the requirements resulting from Article 2.1 in conjunction with Article 1.1 of the Basic Law.

1. The Federal Constitutional Court need not review the interpretation and application of non-constitutional law per se. It is only required to decide whether the competent courts have correctly evaluated the scope and effect of the fundamental rights in the field of civil law. In the execution of this task, however, the boundaries of the Federal Constitutional Court's means of interfering cannot be drawn up rigidly and unchangeably; a certain amount of scope must remain to allow consideration to be given to the specific facts of each individual case. The extent of the impairment suffered by the complainant is of particular importance.

The surrender of the complainant to the Youth Welfare Office, which has custody, goes along with his being separated from the foster parents, after which he is to be placed with another family. This measure is of existential importance to the complainant's future. Strict requirements are thus to be made in regard to the constitutionality of such interference: Along with the question of whether the contested decisions evince errors which are based on a fundamentally incorrect notion of the significance of the fundamental right, in particular the extent of its area of protection, individual errors of interpretation can also not be ignored (see BVerfGE 75, 201 (221-222) with further references).

2. The child is a being with its own human dignity and its own right to development of its personality within the meaning of Article 1.1 and Article 2.1 of the Basic Law (BVerfGE 24, 119 (144)). It needs protection and help in order to develop into an autonomous personality with its own place in society. The upbringing and care of a minor by mother and father within a harmonious community is best suited to guaranteeing that that goal is achieved (see BVerfGE 56, 363 (384)). However, this ideal is not always achieved; in particular it will not be achieved when children grow up in a foster family (see BVerfGE 75, 201 (219)), irrespective of the reasons why they cannot live with their parents. Where parents are unable to live with their children and themselves exercise their parental responsibility, the child's best interests require that harmful consequences which could result therefrom be ruled out wherever possible. For that reason, new bonds which the child has formed to other people must not be severed unless there are weighty reasons for doing so. Correspondingly, in the case of the removal of a child from its foster family, physical, mental

or psychological impairment as the consequence of being separated from those to whom he previously related closely must still be acceptable, taking the child's position as a holder of fundamental rights into account.

3. a) If the removal of the child from the previous foster family does not serve to reunite the original family, but rather to transfer the child from one set of foster parents to another, then no violation of Article 2.1 in conjunction with Article 1.1 of the Basic Law will only have occurred where any endangering of the child's best interests can be ruled out with sufficient certainty (see BVerfGE 75, 201). The contested decisions did not assume such narrow limits. The courts did not ignore the fact that the complainant in 3) and the foster parents had formed bonds which, if they are separated, will impair the child's psychological development, although in their view that impairment will not be permanent. However, on account of the planned adoption they believe that to be acceptable. In assessing the risk, the decisive issue for them was not that the complainant was first to be put in care prior to adoption, rather they regard the ultimate goal – the adoption – as the decisive factor, because the complainant can thereby achieve the same status as a child in wedlock. This legal assessment does not violate the personality rights or the human dignity of the complainant in 3).

b) The purpose of adoption is to give a child who has not had a healthy home environment a family. Following the amendment to adoption law made on account of the Act on Adoption and to Amend other Provisions (Adoption Act) (*Gesetz über die Annahme als Kind und zur Änderung anderer Vorschriften* (*Adoptionsgesetz*)) of 2 July 1976 (Federal Law Gazette (*Bundesgesetzblatt* – BGBl.) I p. 1749), the new parent-child relationship is very hard to break up. The parents and the child are to be given that certainty which is necessary for prosperous family life … In accordance with this objective, adoption law is based on the principle of full adoption; by adopting a child, kinship with its previous relations and the rights and obligations resulting therefrom are extinguished (§ 1755.1 sentence 1 of the Civil Code). The precondition for adoption is that it serves the child's best interests and it is to be expected that a parent-child relationship will be established between the child and the adoptive parent (§ 1741.1 of the Civil Code).

The courts can be followed in regard to the fact that the complainant in 3) will gain a better legal status through adoption than he would have as a foster child. Further, the child's best interests require a decision which guarantees him the greatest feeling of security. In this respect, too, the adoption of a child is to be preferred over a foster relationship. Taking these circumstances into account, the courts were not required only to grant the Youth Welfare Office's application for surrender if any endangering of the child's best interests was to be ruled out with sufficient certainty. They were thereby also within their margin of discretion to decide whether they wanted to achieve certainty as regards the extent of the possible impairment to the complainant in 3) by obtaining an expert opinion from a psychologist; at any rate the assessment of the child over and above the decision according to § 1632.4 of the Civil Code was not required on constitutional grounds.

4. a) Care prior to adoption (§ 1744 of the Civil Code), into which the complainant in 3) is also first to be given, is provided for in order to make it easier to predict whether a parent-child relationship will grow between the adoptive parent and the child to be adopted. Normally, where an adoption is envisaged such foster relationships are not burdened by the fact that the people who were previously important to the child fight the separation with all available means. Rather, adoptive children generally come from troubled family circumstances and not from an intact foster family. However, this is why in such exceptional cases within the context of proceedings according to § 1632.4 of the Civil Code the question gains weight of whether the prospective adoptive parents are suited to minimising the psychological impairment associated with separating the child from his foster parents if in the view of the courts such impairment is to be expected.

b) The Local Court holds the view that on account of the child's nearly 10-month stay in the family of the complainants in 1) and 2) bonds have been established which will impair the psychological development of the complainant in 3) on his being separated from the foster parents' family. However, it also rules out permanent impairment after the complainant has been placed with the designated adoptive parents, because it can be assumed that these will keep the child's psychological impairment to a minimum by taking up contact with him in a loving and careful manner. The Regional Court assumes that the adoptive parents have most likely been carefully selected.

c) These assumptions are not sufficient to guarantee that by rejecting the order to remain according to § 1632.4 of the Civil Code a decision was taken which is consistent with the child's best interests and therefore does not violate Article 2.1 in conjunction with Article 1.1 of the Basic Law.

aa) As the Federal Constitutional Court has found, the protection of fundamental rights largely influences the form and application of procedural law. The obligation imposed on the state on the basis of Article 6.2 sentence 2 of the Basic Law, namely to supervise the exercise of the care and upbringing of the child, leads to the constitution influencing procedural law and its implementation by the courts in the case of proceedings regarding decisions which are of existential importance to a child's development (see BVerfGE 55, 171 (182)). As a result, when applying the provisions of the Act on Matters of Non-Contentious Jurisdiction the courts must obtain certainty regarding whether the designated adoptive parents are suited to helping the child to overcome the harmful consequences of being separated from its foster parents if they themselves assume such consequences or are at least not able to rule them out.

bb) The Adoption Procedures and Implementation Act (*Gesetz über die Vermittlung der Annahme als Kind – Adoptionsvermittlungsgesetz* – AdVermiG) of 2 July 1976 (Federal Law Gazette I p. 1762) and the European Convention on the Adoption of Children of 24 April 1967 (transposed by federal act of 25 August 1980 – Federal Law Gazette II p. 1093 –) must be observed in adoption proceedings. In the child's best interests, great demands are made as regards the suitability of those applying for the adoption. The task of arranging the adoption is entrusted to the adoption arrangement centres to be established by the youth welfare and district youth welfare offices (§ 2 of the Adoption Procedures and Implementation Act); only experts suited on account of their training and experience may be entrusted with the task of arranging adoptions (§ 3 of the Adoption Procedures and Implementation Act). According to § 7 of the Adoption Procedures and Implementation Act, when preparing the arrangement particular attention must be paid to examining whether those applying for adoption are suitable to adopt the child, taking the child's personality and its specific needs into account.

In the present case it has not been clarified whether it was established in the course of the adoption arrangement procedure that the designated adoptive parents are able to do justice to the exceptional psychological situation of the complainant in 3) if he is separated from his foster family. Also, the contested decisions do not show evidence that the courts closely examined this precondition, whose fulfilment they themselves feel is relevant to avoid the complainant in 3) suffering permanent harm. In the context of an application in accordance with § 1632.4 of the Civil Code, this examination cannot only be left to the Youth Welfare Office's adoption arrangement centre without any court oversight whatsoever, especially since the Youth Welfare Office, acting as the child's guardian, is itself the complainant and party to the original proceedings.

cc) In the case of a planned incognito adoption, the clarification of whether the adoptive parents can do justice to the special requirements of the specific case can be made more difficult on account of § 1758 of the Civil Code. However, even within the context of this provision the courts have means of clarifying matters which they must exhaust (§ 12 of the Act on Matters of Non-Contentious Jurisdiction). It may, in certain circumstances, be sufficient for the court to obtain an expert statement from the adoption arrangement centre in accordance with the provision under § 56d of the Act on Matters of Non-Contentious Jurisdiction or, if no such centre is involved in the matter, to obtain an expert statement from the youth welfare office regarding whether the designated adoptive parents are suitable, from the point of view of their personality, to reduce the burden on the child on account of the separation. Such expert statements can be made anonymously. According to Article 103.1 of the Basic Law and according to § 34.2 of the Act on Matters of Non-Contentious Jurisdiction, the court would not be required to inform the remaining parties to the proceedings – for instance the foster parents – of all the details of the results of its investigations if that would jeopardise the incognito adoption. Finally, obtaining such a statement would also not unreasonably delay the decision on an application in accordance with § 1632.4 of the Civil Code.

Justices: Herzog, Niemeyer, Seidl, Söllner, Dieterich; Justice Henschel is unable to attend for signing.

No. 19

BVerfGE 80, 81
of 18 April 1989 – 2 BvR 1169/84 –
"Case concerning the adoption of an adult foreigner"

HEADNOTE:

If a German has adopted an adult foreigner, the protection of a family thereby established, as guaranteed by Article 6.1 of the Basic Law (*Grundgesetz* – GG), does not as a rule give rise to a right of residence for the foreigner.

Order of the Second Senate of 18 April 1989
– 2 BvR 1169/84 –

in the proceedings regarding the constitutional complaints 1. of Mr. O., 2. of Ms. O. – authorised representative: …, lawyer – against a) the judgment of the Federal Administrative Court (*Bundesverwaltungsgericht*) of 10 July 1984 – 1 C 11.82 – and b) the judgment of the Higher Administrative Court (*Oberverwaltungsgericht*) for the *Land* North Rhine-Westphalia of 26 February 1981 – 17 A 942/80 –.

RULING:

The constitutional complaints are rejected as unfounded.

EXTRACT FROM GROUNDS:

A.

The constitutional complaints relate to the question of whether an adult foreigner who has been adopted as a child by a German national may be refused a residence permit.

I.

1. … A major may be adopted as a child if the adoption is morally justified (§ 1767.1, 1st half of the sentence of the Civil Code (*Bürgerliches Gesetzbuch* – BGB)). This is to be presumed in particular where a parent-child relationship has already come about between the adopter and the adoptee (§ 1767.1, 2nd half of the sentence of the Civil Code). The adoption of a major may only be granted if there is no doubt that, as well as a personal relationship between those concerned, there is an unconditional willingness to assist one another in all situations and in the long term. Reasons which are not family-related, in particular economic reasons or the concern of preventing expulsion, do not justify adoption in accordance with the case-law of the Higher Regional Courts (see most recently Düsseldorf Higher Regional Court (*Oberlandesgericht* – OLG), *Zeitschrift für das gesamte Familienrecht* – FamRZ 1985, p. 832).

2. a) A major becomes the marital child of the adopter on being adopted (§ 1767.2 of the Civil Code in conjunction with § 1754 of the Civil Code); the provisions of the Civil Code which regulate the relationship between parents and children apply to the family-law relationship created by virtue of adoption. The effect of adoption does not include the relatives of the adopter (§ 1770.1 sentence 1 of the Civil Code). The family relation of the adoptee to his or her biological relatives is – in contradistinction to the standard case of the adoption of minors (see § 1755 of the Civil Code) – in principle not affected by adoption (§§ 1770.2 and 1772 of the Civil Code).

b) Adult adoption does not give rise to acquisition of nationality in accordance with German nationality law. The Adoption Act (*Adoptionsgesetz*) of 1976 only introduced acquisition of German nationality via minor adoption (§ 3 no. 3 in conjunction with § 6 of the Nationality Act (*Reichs- und Staatsangehörigkeitsgesetz* – RuStAG)). The exclusion of the adopted major foreigner from acquisition of German nationality by force of law aimed *inter alia* to permit the residence law restrictions for foreigners to continue to apply after adoption (see reasoning of the Federal Government, *Bundestag* printed paper (*Bundestagsdrucksache* – BTDrucks.) 7/3061, p. 65).

c) The law on residence contains no particular regulation of the right of residence for a foreigner adopted by Germans. His or her right of residence is hence determined in accordance with the general provision contained in § 2.1 of the Aliens Act (*Ausländergesetz* – AuslG):

> Foreigners who wish to enter and reside in the area of application of the present Act shall require a residence permit.

The residence permit may be issued if the presence of the foreigner in Germany does not impair the interests of the Federal Republic of Germany.

…

II.

1. a) The complainant re 1., who was born in 1953, is a stateless Palestinian from Lebanon. His biological parents live in Lebanon and are divorced. He entered the Federal Republic of Germany in February 1976 and applied for recognition as a person entitled to asylum. The aliens authorities issued him with time-limited and individually extended temporary suspensions of removal for the duration of the asylum proceedings. An application filed in 1976 to grant a residence permit for the implementation of the asylum proceedings was rejected by final notice. The complainant re 1. withdrew his asylum application in February 1982.
b) The complainant re 2. is a German national, born in 1937, divorced since 1971 and childless. She has taken care of the complainant re 1. and other asylum-seekers since November 1976, helping them in all personal and economic matters. She took the complainant re 1. into her home in January 1977.
c) By order of 13 February 1979, the Local Court (*Amtsgericht*), sitting as a guardianship court, granted the adoption of the complainant re 1. by the complainant re 2. in response to an request filed to this end by the complainants. …
The immigration authority filed a complaint against this order on grounds that, in a previous application to grant a residence permit, those concerned had declared their intention to enter into marriage with one another and were currently striving not to become a family, but merely wished to prevent the removal of the complainant re 1. from the Federal Republic of Germany. This complaint was rejected as inadmissible, referring to § 56e sentence 3 of the Act on Matters of Non-Contentious Jurisdiction (*Gesetz über die Angelegenheiten der freiwilligen Gerichtsbarkeit* – FGG).
2. a) The complainant re 1. applied on 5 March 1979 for a residence permit not dependent on the asylum proceedings and to permit him thereby to remain permanently with his mother. The immigration authority rejected the application by order of 19 March 1979, set the complainant re 1. a deadline to leave the country by 31 March 1979 and threatened that he would be removed to Lebanon in the event of his not leaving the country on time. Against this the complainant re 1. filed an objection, which was rejected by order of 1 June 1979.
b) The complainant re 1. filed an action with the Administrative Court against the rejection of the requested residence permit and against the threat of removal. By judgment of 3 April 1980, the Administrative Court granted the relief sought on grounds that the immigration authority had allegedly wrongly not allotted any de-

cisive significance to the adoption of the complainant re 1. by the complainant re 2., and had denied him protection of the family in accordance with Article 6.1 of the Basic Law.

c) In response to the appeal on points of fact and law (*Berufung*) submitted against this by the immigration authority, after previously summoning the complainant re 2. as an interested party, the Higher Administrative Court amended the first instance ruling by judgment of 26 February 1981, and rejected the action. …

d) In response to the complainants' appeals on points of law (*Revision*), the Federal Administrative Court rescinded the judgment of the Higher Administrative Court insofar as it relates to the threat of removal, but rejected the appeals on points of law in other respects. The Federal Administrative Court found as follows when reasoning its ruling confirming refusal to grant the residence permit:

… Article 6.1 of the Basic Law also protects a family created via adoption, but does not necessarily give rise to a right to the issuance of a residence permit. Rather, it is necessary to decide on this matter by weighing, in accordance with the principle of proportionality, whether the public interests against the residence of a family member are so weighty that, on rejection of the permit, they clearly outweigh the anticipated detriment to the family; is this the case, refusal of the residence permit is compatible with Article 6.1 of the Basic Law. There is a public interest that immigration into Germany should certainly not take place, and in unsuccessful asylum-seekers leaving German territory. The principle of proportionality does not prohibit in principle granting a residence permit to an adult foreigner who has been adopted by a German national, but demands that it should be weighed to what degree those concerned depended on living together as a family. In contradistinction to marriage, the relationship between adult (adoptive) children and their (German or foreign) parents is typically not dependent on such co-habitation. In a decision on the residence permit, adult adoption can only be assigned similar significance as marriage between a foreigner and a German if either the German adoptive parents or the foreign adoptive children depend on receiving assistance from the family in a manner that requires them to live together. The German nationality of the adoptive mother would only be liable to give rise to a right of residence for the foreign son if – as is the case in marriage – it were necessary for them to live together in order to maintain the family relationship in question, and as a result it would be material that German nationals in principle could not be required to move abroad to maintain family co-habitation.

…

3. With their constitutional complaints, the complainants oppose the judgments of the Higher Administrative Court and of the Federal Administrative Court. They

complain of a violation of their fundamental rights under Article 6.1 and Article 2.1 of the Basic Law. They submit the following as reasoning:

The impugned rulings misjudge the significance and scope of these fundamental rights. The Federal Administrative Court has confirmed in its ruling that Article 6.1 of the Basic Law also has an effect on the relationship between a major and his or her (adoptive) parents. It had however reduced the effects of this protection in that it considered a residence permit necessary only insofar as a member of the family was dependent on the family community for special reasons … Article 6 of the Basic Law protects a family living arrangement as it exists according to the decision of the family members; it is immaterial how the relations between parents and adult children are customarily manifested. The domestic community between the parent and an adult child corresponds to the "guiding model" of the family, which enjoys protection, even if those concerned live together on the basis of a voluntary, uninfluenced decision. Denial of the residence permit forces the complainants to renounce their existing domestic community, and hence violates Article 6.1 of the Basic Law.

4. As to the constitutional complaints, statements were made by the Federal Minister of the Interior in the name of the Federal Government, and by the chief administrative officer (*Oberkreisdirektor*) for the Minden-Lübbecke district:

…

B.

The constitutional complaints are unfounded.

I.

1. The family within the meaning of Article 6.1 of the Basic Law is the community of parents and children. In addition to a family which is established by birth, also any other community of parents and children recognised by the state legal order is protected in principle (see Decisions of the Federal Constitutional Court (*Entscheidungen des Bundesverfassungsgerichts* – BVerfGE) 18, 97 (105-106)).

If § 1767 of the Civil Code provides for adoption as a child, and also permits the adoption of a major, the manner in which such a family is established remains within the requirements of Article 6.1 of the Basic Law. A family thus formed enjoys the special protection of the state system in accordance with Article 6.1 of the Basic Law.

...

2. Article 6.1 in conjunction with Article 6.2 of the Basic Law protects the family first and foremost as a living arrangement and child-raising community. The physical and emotional development of the children finds an essential foundation in families and in parental child-raising. A family formed by responsible parenthood is determined by the fundamental need to protect the growing child. As the child's ability to take action and decisions increases, the responsibility and custody of the parent are reduced. The living arrangement can thus become a mere domestic community which retains common features of co-habitation, but in other respects permits each family member to lead an independent life. On dissolution of the domestic community, the family can then become a mere "meeting community" in which the parent and children only see one another on occasion. The domestic or living arrangement continues by force of law in the family among adults if further maintenance or assistance is provided and this takes place within a domestic community (see §§ 1612.2 and 1618a of the Civil Code). Independently of this, the family offers the adult family members scope for encouragement and establishes the ability to live a responsible life in the community (see BVerfGE 57, 170 (178)). Furthermore, for the adult the family is a community that corresponds to the intellectual nature of human beings, which is geared towards dialogue (see BVerfGE 76, 1 (51)).

3. A family which comes into being through the adoption of an adult can no longer be considered as a child-raising community; as a rule it is not intended to be a living arrangement, but only as a meeting community, and possibly as a domestic community. The Civil Code has accommodated these factual differences and assigned fewer legal effects to the adoption of a major (§ 1770.1 of the Civil Code). § 6 in conjunction with § 3 no. 3 of the Nationality Act links acquisition of German nationality only to the adoption of a minor by a German. This is based on the experience that a family created by adult adoption as a rule does not consist of a living arrangement, so that the family does not need to live together.

Regardless of the provisions of the law on nationality, which do not define the area protected by Article 6.1 of the Basic Law, but only modify and restrict the resulting protective effect, an adult foreigner who is outside Germany or who is in Germany without a residence permit who is adopted by a German may invoke the protective effect exerted by Article 6.1 of the Basic Law under residence law if he or she requests permission to take up permanent residence with his or her family members living in Germany and applies for entry permission to this end (see BVerfGE 76, 1 (46)). The parents living in Germany are affected in the personal protected area of Article 6.1 of the Basic Law if their child is refused residence in Germany for the purpose of living together as a family (see BVerfGE 76, 1 (45-46)).

4. Article 6.1 of the Basic Law does not have a protective effect under the law on residence for an adopted adult foreigner as an institutional guarantee (a) or as a freedom right (b), but as a fundamental provision that determines values (c).
a) As an institutional guarantee, Article 6.1 of the Basic Law ensures the core of the provisions which constitute the law on families, in particular of civil law, against rescission or against the remodelling of its essential features, and provides protection against state measures which impair specific characteristics of the model of the family on which the constitution is based (BVerfGE 76, 1 (49)). This constitutional core is not impaired if a family with German members is separated or remains separated from an adopted adult foreign family member because the residence permit requested has not been issued to this person; the institutional guarantee of Article 6.1 of the Basic Law does not apply to a family of this nature in relation to the place in which the family community is based. This guarantee accordingly assures a right to such a community *in Germany* only if all the members of the family have legal permanent residence in Germany.
b) As a freedom right, Article 6.1 of the Basic Law constitutes an obligation incumbent on the state to forgo incursions on the family. It entitles family members to form their community freely *inter se* in exercising their family responsibility and in consideration for one another. The impact of family freedom expressed towards others, in particular on professional life, schooling, the property order and public community life, must however concur with the constitutional legal order. In this framework, the Basic Law largely assigns the decision on the number and preconditions under which aliens are to be permitted to enter Germany to the legislative and executive power; this also applies to incursions on the place of residence of an adopted adult foreigner.
c) The "fundamental provision that determines values" contained in Article 6.1 of the Basic Law, in accordance with which the state is to protect and promote the family (see BVerfGE 6, 55 (72); 76, 1 (49); established case-law) does not reach the degree of bindingness which is inherent in the institutional guarantee or the freedom right. The obligation of protection which is incumbent on the state to allow for family ties however has an impact on the entire legal order affecting the family, be it that it entitles it to make incursions, to provide benefits and participation or that it obliges to act, tolerate or omit.
aa) § 2.1 of the Aliens Act makes the residence of aliens on the territory of the Federal Republic of Germany dependent on a permit, the issuance of which is at the discretion of the administrative authorities insofar as the presence of the alien does not impair the interests of the Federal Republic of Germany. This arrangement concurs with the protective obligation of Article 6.1 of the Basic Law because it is accessible both in its open element and in granting discretion for the valuations of the

obligation of protection contained in Article 6.1 of the Basic Law. The deciding authority must accordingly include in its consideration the family ties of the applicant with persons lawfully present in Germany in examining the public interests and in exercising its duty bound discretion, i.e. in accordance with the weight of those ties. This constitutional duty which is incumbent on the state to protect the family corresponds to a claim of the holder of the fundamental right under Article 6.1 of the Basic Law that the competent authorities and courts, when ruling on a residence request in accordance with § 2.1 sentence 2 of the Aliens Act, must make suitable allowance for his or her family ties with persons living in Germany (see BVerfGE 76, 1 (49-50); see also BVerfGE 77, 170 (214)).

bb) The Federal Constitutional Court (*Bundesverfassungsgericht*) does not merely examine such rulings for manifest violations of the obligation of protection emerging from Article 6.1 of the Basic Law (see BVerfGE 21, 1 (6); 76, 1 (51)). The intensity of the constitutional review corresponds rather to the rank and the significance which the Basic Law attaches to the family in its various manifestations and functions as an autonomous area which is protected from the state and which supports the diversity of the freedoms which are guaranteed by the rule of law.

II.

In accordance with this standard, the denial of the residence permit impugned by the complainants does not violate Article 6 of the Basic Law as a fundamental provision that determines values.

1. The denial of the residence permit applies the public interests of restriction on entry without thereby endangering the continuation of the family among the complainants. Adult adoption establishes a family which in its constitutional core does not constitute a living arrangement or domestic community, but as a rule is designed as a meeting community, and hence can be maintained by virtue of regular visits, through letter and telephone contacts, as well as by gifts. Insofar as a family established between a mother and her foreign son who was adopted as an adult is to be maintained as a living arrangement over and above a meeting community, refusal of a residence permit with regard to Article 6.1 of the Basic Law is certainly unobjectionable insofar as no living arrangements exist which appear to give rise to family-law protection over and above the maintenance of the meeting community.

Such living arrangements do not apply in the instant case. In particular, they cannot be derived from the complainants' submission that they must live together in domestic community in order to be able to establish the confidential relationship thus far missing in their family. This is merely an expression of the fact that their relationship under family law is not based on the existence of a parent-child relationship, which as a rule is a fundamental element of adult adoption. The aspired subsequent creation of the conditions justifying adult adoption at all can as a rule give rise at best to continuing protective effects of Article 6.1 of the Basic Law under residence law if the moral justification, which is always required for adult adoption (§ 1767.1 of the Civil Code), existed for other reasons despite the (as yet) missing parent-child relationship, and this relationship can be brought about by a living or assistance community. Nothing has been submitted, nor is anything else manifest, to suggest that this situation applies in the instant case.

2. Regardless of this, Article 6.1 of the Basic Law could give rise to further protective effects under residence law if one of the complainants depended on the assistance of the other, and this assistance could be provided only in the Federal Republic of Germany. Under these conditions, the family complies with the core function of an assistance community. If the assistance can only be provided in the Federal Republic of Germany because it is not reasonable to expect a family member involved to leave Germany, the obligation incumbent on the state to protect the family as a rule overcomes immigration policy interests. In such cases, the relationship between parents and adult children is to be evaluated under residence law in the same way as marriage between a foreigner and a German.

The Higher Administrative Court presumed that neither the complainant re 1. nor the complainant re 2. is dependent on family assistance requiring the residence of the complainant re 1. in the Federal Republic of Germany. The submission of the constitutional complaint contains nothing which would prove this view to be constitutionally erroneous. The Federal Constitutional Court does not review whether it is also correct in other respects (see BVerfGE 18, 85 (92-93); established case-law).

III.

Refusal to grant the residence permit requested by the complainant re 1. does not affect the area protected by Article 2.1 of the Basic Law. Since Article 2.1 of the Basic Law contains the more general provision in comparison with Article 6.1 of the Basic Law, it could only be considered as a standard of review if it had a protective effect under residence law beyond that of Article 6.1 of the Basic Law. Article 2.1 of the Basic Law, however, does not contain a provision on entry and residence. Article 2.1 of the Basic Law regulates the free development of the personality for people resident in the Federal Republic of Germany, but does permit within the constitutional order restricting this freedom provisions regarding the residence of aliens (see BVerfGE 35, 382 (399); 76, 1 (71)).

The complainant re 1., who no longer has a right to remain subsequent to the termination of his asylum proceedings, is on the same footing as an alien requesting entry. Based on this starting situation, Article 2.1 of the Basic Law does not grant a right to take up residence in Germany to the complainant re 1.

…

Justices: Mahrenholz, Träger, Böckenförde, Klein, Graßhof, Kruis, Franßen, Kirchhof

No. 20

BVerfGE 82, 6

of 3 April 1990 – 1 BvR 1186/89 –

"Unmarried civil partner as tenant case"

HEADNOTE:

Decision regarding the constitutional permissibility of analogous application of the law.

Order of the First Senate of 3 April 1990
– 1 BvR 1186/89 –

in the proceedings regarding the constitutional complaint of the company X. – authorised representatives: …, lawyers – against the judgment of the Hamburg Regional Court (*Landgericht*) of 11 August 1989 – 11 S 398/87 –.

RULING:

The constitutional complaint is rejected as unfounded.

EXTRACT FROM GROUNDS:

A.

The constitutional complaint opposes a judgment in which the unmarried civil partner of the deceased tenant has been regarded as "another family member" within the meaning of § 569a.2 sentence 1 of the Civil Code.

I.

1. The contractual relationship with the landlord is not terminated by the death of the tenant. Rather, the tenant's heir takes on his or her position in accordance with §§ 1922.1 and 1967 of the Civil Code. With regard to the personal character of the legal relationship, § 569.1 of the Civil Code affords to the landlord and to the heirs an extraordinary time-limited right of termination. The area of application of this provision is however restricted by the special provisions contained in §§ 569a and 569b of the Civil Code, in accordance with which spouses and other family members enter the tenancy arrangement under certain preconditions, regardless of their status as an heir. The only provision that is material here reads as follows:

§ 569a of the Civil Code

> (1) On the death of the tenant, the spouse shall enter tenancy of residential premises in which the tenant has a joint household with his or her spouse. If within one month of gaining knowledge of the death of the tenant the spouse informs the landlord that he or she does not wish to continue the tenancy, he or she shall be deemed not to have taken up tenancy; § 206 shall apply *mutatis mutandis*.
> (2) If a joint household is kept in the residential premises with one or several other family members, the latter shall enter the tenancy on the death of the tenant. The same shall apply if the tenant has kept a joint household with his or her spouse and one or several other family members and the spouse does not enter the tenancy. Subsection 1 sentence 2 shall apply *mutatis mutandis*; if there are several family members, each may file the declaration for themselves.
> …
> (5) The landlord can terminate the tenancy by giving statutory notice if a major reason therefor lies in the person of the spouse or family member who has acceded to the tenancy; …
> (6) If the spouse or other family members do not enter tenancy regarding residential premises, it shall be continued with the heir. Both the heir and the landlord shall be entitled to terminate the tenancy by adhering to the statutory period …
> (7) Any agreement derogating from subsections 1, 2 or 5 shall be null and void.

2. The precursor provision to § 569a of the Civil Code was § 19 of the Act on Tenant Protection and Tenancy Agreement Offices (*Gesetz über Mieterschutz und Mieteinigungsämter* – MSchG). … § 19 of the Act on Tenant Protection and Tenan-

cy Agreement Offices offered the possibility of succession to all persons related to and in-lawed with the tenant, without regard for the degree of this relationship.
§ 19 of the Act on Tenant Protection and Tenancy Agreement Offices was gradually (Article III no. 5 of the Act on the Reduction of Forced Tenancy and on Social Tenancy and Residence Law (*Gesetz über den Abbau der Wohnungszwangswirtschaft und über ein soziales Miet- und Wohnrecht*) of 23 June 1960, Federal Law Gazette (*Bundesgesetzblatt* – BGBl.) I p. 389) replaced by §§ 569a and 569b of the Civil Code (Article I no. 22, Article IV § 1 and § 7.2 of the Second Act Amending Provisions of Tenancy Law (*Zweites Gesetz zur Änderung mietrechtlicher Vorschriften*) of 14 July 1964, Federal Law Gazette I p. 457). The goal of this Act was to not remove the Tenants Protection Act (*Mieterschutzgesetz*) without replacement, which at the time had been created under emergency circumstances, as well as to counter unjustifiable hardships resulting from termination of tenancy (Second Written Report of the Legal Committee of the German *Bundestag* re *Bundestag* printed paper (*Bundestagsdrucksache* – BTDrucks) IV/2195, p. 1). This was said to include adoption of the concept developed in the law on tenant protection to continue tenancy on the death of the tenant in the person of those family members who had belonged to his or her household (*Bundestag* printed paper IV/806, p. 7). Whether unmarried partners were also to be regarded as family members was not – as far as can be ascertained – explicitly discussed in the parliamentary proceedings.

II.

1. The complainant – a non-for-profit cooperative housing association – had let a two-room apartment to Ms. S. in May 1968. Ms. S. died on 5 December 1986. According to the information submitted by the defendant in the original proceedings, he had lived with her in the apartment since 1968. The complainant rejected his request to continue the tenancy with him because sufficient members of the housing association were said to be on the waiting list for such apartments. On being refused vacation of the property, the complainant filed an action for eviction which was successful at first instance. The Local Court (*Amtsgericht*) stated that even if one applied § 569a.2 sentence 1 of the Civil Code analogously to unmarried civil partners, the defendant had not entered the tenancy. Because of the age difference – Ms. S. had died at the age of 76; the defendant was 46 years old at the time of her death – their relationship had not been similar to marriage.
The defendant's appeal on points of fact and law was successful. The Regional Court referred to its legal aid order of 1 February 1988. In this, it had taken the stance that § 569a.2 sentence 1 of the Civil Code was to be applied analogously to

unmarried civil partners. The provision was said to centre on the goal of maintaining the previous geographical focus of the party who had lived with the tenant in the household in order to avoid undue hardships for the party affected. The inclusion of the element "family member" was said to be explained in historical terms on the basis of the fact that unmarried civil partnerships had not yet been a socially relevant element in 1964. This had however fundamentally changed in the ensuing period; also the legislature had taken this phenomenon into account on various occasions. This element should hence become less prominent. Analogous application was also said to be compatible with Article 6.1 of the Basic Law (*Grundgesetz* – GG) and with the principle of sufficient delimitation of the area of application of § 569a of the Civil Code.
In respect of the details, reference is made to the reasoning re-printed in *Wohnungswirtschaft & Mietrecht* – WuM 1989, pp. 304-305.
2. The complainant claims that the Regional Court, in application of § 569a.2 sentence 1 of the Civil Code, has not taken account of the fact that it has been protected against a legal obligation to enter into a contract by Article 14.1 sentence 1 of the Basic Law. The Regional Court is alleged to have, in truth, engaged in impermissible development of the law. The complainant argues that it is the sole preserve of the legislature to shape the legal relationship between the owner and the co-user of the apartment. If it had taken account in other areas, but not in the law on tenancy, of unmarried civil partnerships, which had allegedly only gained in significance in the past 15 years, the courts would have to accept this. This development of the law is also said not to comply with the values set out in the Basic Law (Article 6.1 of the Basic Law).
…

B.

The constitutional complaint is admissible. …

C.

The constitutional complaint is however unfounded. The impugned ruling does not go beyond the restrictions imposed on judicial development of the law by Article 14.1 sentence 1 in conjunction with Article 20.3 of the Basic Law (I.). The restrictions which it imposes also do not violate the guarantee of property (II.).

I.

1. a) The interpretation of non-constitutional law, including the selection of the method to be used therefor, is a matter for the non-constitutional courts and in principle not to be examined by the Federal Constitutional Court (*Bundesverfassungsgericht*) as to its correctness (Decisions of the Federal Constitutional Court (*Entscheidungen des Bundesverfassungsgerichts* – BVerfGE 18, 85 (92)). If the non-constitutional court uses traditional interpretation methods in doing so, there are no constitutional reservations against this (see BVerfGE 11, 126 (130)).
b) The analogous application of non-constitutional provisions is also constitutionally unobjectionable in principle (see BVerfGE 25, 167 (183)). Constitutional barriers do however emerge from the priority of statute set out in Article 20.3 of the Basic Law, which constitutes the standard of review in such cases in conjunction with Article 14.1 sentence 1 of the Basic Law (on the connection between the restricted special fundamental right under Article 20.3 of the Basic Law see BVerfGE 69, 315 (369)). At the same time, it guarantees as an element of the principle of the rule of law the measure of legal certainty which is indispensable in the interest of the freedom rights (see BVerfGE 7, 89 (92); 7, 194 (196); 13, 261 (271); 49, 304 (318)). The citizen must be able to adjust his or her conduct in line with the legal order and act accordingly. If the legislature has enacted a clear decision, the judge may not change this because of his or her own legal policy concepts and substitute it with a judicial solution which it was not possible to achieve thus in Parliament (see BVerfGE 69,315 (372); J. Ipsen, *Richterrecht und Verfassung*, 1975, p. 236).
Developments in fact or law can however lead to a provision which until then was unambiguous and complete becoming incomplete, in need of and also susceptible to supplementation. The constitutional permissibility of seeking out and closing gaps is justified amongst other things by the fact that statutes are subject to an ageing process. They exist in an environment of social circumstances and social policy views which when they change can also change the content of the provision (see BVerfGE 34, 269 (288)). To the extent that gaps form because of such changes, the statute becomes unable to provide a just solution for all cases which its provisions seek to cover. The courts are hence empowered and obliged to examine what is "justice" under the changed circumstances within the meaning of Article 20.3 of the Basic Law.
c) The method of analogy meets these constitutional requirements. It goes beyond interpretation in the strict sense by extending the area of application of a provision to a case not covered by its wording. This development of the law however takes place within the constitutional framework described. It does not constitute the expression of impermissible independent judicial power by means of which the recog-

nisable will of the legislature is pushed aside and substituted by means of an autarkical weighing of interests by the judiciary. Rather, it is decided from the evaluations of the statute whether there is a gap and by what means it is to be closed.
2. a) The non-constitutional court's evaluation of whether the facts justify an analogy is only subject to a restricted degree to the supervision of the constitutional court. The answer to the question of whether a gap or a final provision exists requires to the same degree a legal evaluation and the solution of the problem of the manner in which the gap is to be closed (see Canaris, *Die Feststellung von Lücken im Gesetz*, 2nd ed., 1983, § 84 at the end). It is conditional on a consideration of non-constitutional law, which the Federal Constitutional Court is not called on to investigate (see BVerfGE 18, 85 (93)). It may therefore in principle not substitute the evaluation of the non-constitutional court with its own. The answer to the question of whether the factual conditions have changed since the creation of the provision in a manner justifying its analogous application is initially also a matter for the non-constitutional courts. Even if the problem of the extent to which the judiciary is bound by the law arises to a greater degree in the development of the law, supervision by the constitutional courts of analogous application of the law is restricted to whether the non-constitutional court has been justified in presuming a gap to exist in non-constitutional law, and closing it, and whether this expansion of the area covered by the provision stands in contradiction of evaluations of the constitution, in particular fundamental rights.
b) The impugned ruling meets this standard.
The Federal Constitutional Court already stated in 1958 (BVerfGE 9, 20 (32)) that "communities similar to marriage" are a typical manifestation of social life. This however does not necessarily rule out the supposition of the Regional Court that these communities did not until the end of the seventies become a social phenomenon to a degree which the legislature had not fully foreseen in creating § 569a of the Civil Code. These determinations are not manifestly without a factual basis.
The view of the Regional Court that this change in circumstances within society had to be taken into account by expanding the area of application of § 569a.2 sentence 1 of the Civil Code is also justifiable. It can invoke amongst other things the fact that an agreement legally made in 1964 between parties to a tenancy agreement to enter into a new tenancy agreement after the death of the tenant with his or her surviving unmarried partner would at that time have been at risk of nullity in accordance with § 138.1 of the Civil Code (see Federal Court of Justice, *Zeitschrift für das gesamte Familienrecht* – FamRZ 1964, p. 140 (142); 1965, p. 368 (369)). This legal consequence could hardly be considered today. The same also applies to the question of whether unmarried partners can rent an apartment together. In contradistinction to 1964 (see for instance Cologne Regional Court, *Zeitschrift für*

Miet- und Raumrecht – ZMR 1974, p. 141 (142) on the one hand, Mannheim Local Court, ZMR 1972, p. 193 on the other hand) agreement has largely been reached today that under the preconditions of § 549 of the Civil Code (see on its application Hamm Higher Regional Court, *Sammlung der Rechtsentscheide in Wohnraummietsachen* – RES (vol. II) § 549 of the Civil Code no. 1) the landlord is obliged to tolerate the constant residence of an unmarried partner in the rented apartment; this certainly applies if the latter does not move in soon after conclusion of the agreement (see Federal Court of Justice (*Bundesgerichtshof* – BGH), RES (vol. IV) § 549 of the Civil Code no. 3, p. 47; see also Bavarian Highest Regional Court (*Bayerisches Oberstes Landesgericht*), RES (vol. III) § 549 of the Civil Code no. 2, p. 39). This obligation of tolerance during the life of the tenant is not equivalent to the obligation to continue, after his or her death, the tenancy with the surviving unmarried partner. Nonetheless, this altered legal evaluation shows a change in the views held within society, making the conclusion reached by the Regional Court appear still to be justifiable.

This legal view finds further support by virtue of the fact that the legislature has explicitly accommodated unmarried civil partnerships in various regulatory areas (see § 122 of the Federal Social Assistance Act (*Bundessozialhilfegesetz* – BSHG), § 137.2a of the Employment Promotion Act (*Arbeitsförderungsgesetz* – AFG), § 18 of the Housing Benefit Act (*Wohngeldgesetz* – WoGG). Whether – as opined by the Regional Court (WuM 1989, p. 304 (305)) – it took place with the aim of placing the partner of an unmarried civil partnership on an equal footing with spouses, does not need to be decided here. It is sufficient here solely that the legislature no longer leaves this manifestation of co-habitation unaccommodated.

The impugned adjudication does not impermissibly substitute a fundamental decision of the legislature with a judicial one. Rather, in several instances the legislature itself has restricted the power of the landlord to select his or her contractual partner in private autonomy in favour of such persons who had a joint household in the apartment with the deceased tenant. The impugned ruling hence did not in principle constitute a fundamentally new judicial provision regulating landlords' powers.

3. The analogy, finally, does not contravene Article 6.1 of the Basic Law. This fundamental right provision does impose on the legislature, in addition to the prohibition to impair marriage, an obligation to protect marriage and the family against harm and to promote them by taking suitable measures (BVerfGE 6, 55 (76)). This however does not give rise to an obligation to refuse unmarried communities any legal recognition at all and to try everything possible to work towards denying them the necessary financial and other means of functioning (see BVerfGE 9, 20 (34-35); *Entscheidungen des Bundesverwaltungsgerichts* – BVerwGE 15,306 (316)). Even

if the legislature were to consider the marital form of co-habitation to be the best solution and to direct an explicit provision on the problem which is contentious in the original proceedings towards this orientation, on the other hand this would not give rise to an obligation under Article 6.1 of the Basic Law to make it more difficult for unmarried communities to function through their exclusion from the possibility of succession contained in § 569a of the Civil Code.

II.

The impugned ruling also does not violate Article 14.1 sentence 1 of the Basic Law.

1. If the development of the law that has been carried out is not constitutionally objectionable, the question only arises as to Article 14.1 sentence 1 of the Basic Law of whether, by expanding its area of application, the Regional Court inserted content into § 569a.2 sentence 1 of the Civil Code which even the legislature would not have been able to determine in shaping property (Article 14.1 sentence 2 of the Basic Law) without violating the guarantee of property (see BVerfGE 79, 283 (290)). The question is to be negated.

a) Property, which is protected by fundamental rights, is characterised by private utilisation and fundamental freedom of disposal (see BVerfGE 52, 1 (30)). This rules out the fundamental rights freedom of the owner being reduced, having once let his or her object, to the power to derive a financial profit from this form of utilisation. The owner may also not be obliged to accept all co-habitors of the respective tenant as successors without being able to influence the identity of the contracting partner in any way (see BVerfGE 79, 292 (304) referring to BVerfGE 52, 1 (36-37)).

On the other hand, it must however be taken into account that the owner of let residential premises is under a considerable obligation to accommodate the interests of those fellow citizens who are unable to purchase residential premises for themselves using their own financial resources, and hence rely on using property belonging to others (see BVerfGE 37, 132 (140); 38, 348 (370)). This point of view not only justifies restricting the powers of the owner in tenancy, which the landlord has himself or herself established by contract. It rather provides at the same time – within the limits to be discussed below – a constitutionally adequate basis for partly restricting the free selection of the contractual partner.

b) A dwelling is the spatial centre of private life. The tenant's entitlement to establish and continue an unmarried civil partnership derives from the general freedom of action (Article 2.1 of the Basic Law). Because of the social obligation arising from property, the legislature would be permitted to take into account that the tenant's partner, by virtue of also using the apartment, had established his or her geographical focus in these premises, at least in the event of long-term co-utilisation; it would hence be able to establish compensation in the event of the death of the tenant, who had sole entitlement under the law on obligations. It could however be questionable whether it would be compatible with the owner's private utilisation and freedom of disposal to grant this possibility of succession to each person who only lived there for a short period. In each case, the fact would have to be accommodated that reasons may lie in the person of the third party making it impossible for the owner to be expected to continue the tenancy.

2. The legislature would not have exceeded its regulatory competence (Article 14.1 sentence 2 of the Basic Law) in evaluating these contradictory interests if in cases such as those of the original proceedings it had explicitly afforded a possibility of succession to the civil partner. In accordance with the findings of the Regional Court, which are not impugned by the constitutional complaint, the defendant had been united with Ms. S by an eighteen-year partnership. Such a duration would certainly entitle the legislature to oblige the landlord to take account of the survivor by restricting liberty to enter into a contract. Aspects of acceptability for the landlord could be accommodated here in the context of § 569a.5 of the Civil Code.

…

Justices: Herzog, Henschel, Seidl, Grimm, Söllner, Dieterich, Kühling, Seibert

No. 21

BVerfGE 84, 168
of 7 May 1991 – 1 BvL 32/88 –
"Case regarding custody rights for children born out of wedlock"

HEADNOTES:

1. **Article 6.2 of the Basic Law (*Grundgesetz* – GG) is violated when the joint exercise of parental custody (*elterliche Sorge*) by the father and the mother of a child born out of wedlock is ruled out by force of law after the child's declaration of legitimacy even when the parents are living together with the child, are both willing and able to take on parental responsibility together, and this is in the child's best interests.**
2. **It is not compatible with Article 6.5 of the Basic Law to either deny the legal advantages associated with the declaration of legitimacy to children born out of wedlock who are living with their mother and father and who are being cared for by both parents or to permit them only with the legal consequence that the mother loses the right and the duty to exercise her parental custody.**

Order of the First Senate of 7 May 1991
– 1 BvL 32/88 –

in the proceedings on the constitutional review of § 1738.1 of the Civil Code (*Bürgerliches Gesetzbuch* – BGB) as amended by Article 9.2 no. 3 of the Act to Amend the Right to Exercise Parental Custody (*Gesetz zur Neuregelung des Rechts der elterlichen Sorge*) of 18 July 1979 (Federal Law Gazette (*Bundesgesetzblatt* – BGBl.) I p. 1061) – suspension of proceedings and submission order of the Hamburg Local Court (*Amtsgericht Hamburg*) of 16 September 1988 (113 X K 15575) with a supplementary order of 6 June 1989 (112 VIII K 15575) –.

RULING:

§ 1738.1 of the Civil Code as amended by Article 9.2 no. 3 of the Act to Amend the Right to Exercise Parental Custody of 18 July 1979 (Federal Law Gazette I p. 1061) is incompatible with Article 6.2 and 6.5 of the Basic Law insofar as the mother also loses the right and the duty to exercise parental custody in those cases in which the father and mother are living with the child, both are seeking the declaration of legitimacy on condition that they are both awarded custody rights and this exercise of custody rights is in the child's best interests.

EXTRACT FROM GROUNDS:

A.

The submission concerns the constitutionality of § 1738.1 of the Civil Code, according to which the mother of a child born out of wedlock loses the right and the duty to exercise her parental custody without exception upon the declaration of legitimacy of the child.

I.

1. Up until the reform of the law on the legal status of children born out of wedlock, the child born out of wedlock and its father were not deemed to be related (§ 1589.2 of the Civil Code). The mother was initially only entitled to the care for the person of the child, for whom a guardian was appointed. Other than by means of the act of marriage between the parents or the father's adoption of the child, kinship could be established between the child and the father by means of the declaration of legitimacy. By declaration of legitimacy upon application from the father, which constituted an act of clemency, the mother lost the right and duty of the care for the person of the child.
The first key changes were brought about by the Act to Standardise and Amend Family Law Provisions (Family Law Amendment Act) (*Gesetz zur Vereinheitlichung und Änderung familienrechtlicher Vorschriften* (*Familienrechtsänderungsgesetz*)) of 11 August 1961 (Federal Law Gazette I p. 1221), which made it possible for the mother to apply for parental power (*elterliche Gewalt*) to be assigned to her, provided the grounds for the jurisdiction of the guardianship courts in regard to the declaration of legitimacy, and provided detailed regulations governing the substantive conditions therefor.

2. The Act Governing the Legal Status of Children Born out of Wedlock (*Gesetz über die rechtliche Stellung des nichtehelichen Kindes* (*Nichtehelichengesetz* – NEG) of 19 August 1969 (Federal Law Gazette I p. 1243) reorganised the legal relationships under family law between the child born out of wedlock and its mother and its father. The provisions governing custody rights were again amended by the Act to Amend the Right to Exercise Parental Custody of 18 July 1979 (Federal Law Gazette I p. 1061) such that the term "parental custody" replaced the term "parental power".

a) According to § 1705 of the Civil Code, the mother is now entitled to exercise parental custody for children born out of wedlock. An ex officio curator is appointed in those cases listed in § 1706 of the Civil Code, although, on application from the mother, the curatorship can be cancelled or the sphere of activities of the curator restricted (§ 1707 of the Civil Code).

§ 1589.2 of the Civil Code was repealed. Special regulations apply in part to the legal consequences resulting from the kinship between the child and the father. For instance, §§ 1615b et seq. of the Civil Code contain special regulations governing maintenance and §§ 1934a to 1934e of the Civil Code contain special regulations governing the right of inheritance. In the majority of cases no distinction is drawn between whether the child is living with its father or not; only § 1615f.1 sentence 1 half-sentence 1 of the Civil Code attaches importance to this circumstance in regard to the duty to pay maintenance. The father's involvement in the exercise of parental custody is not provided for. Nor does the possibility exist of separately assigning parental custody to the father. He does, however, still have the possibility of declaring the child legitimate.

When amending the Act Governing the Legal Status of Children Born out of Wedlock, the legislature assumed that the unequivocal, definite and permanent legal assignment of the child born out of wedlock to one parent is in the child's best interests, arguing as follows: It was not possible for both parents to be entitled to exercise parental power, as in most cases they were not living together and in the remaining cases often only living together temporarily. It was in the nature of the matter that only the definite and permanent legal assignment to the mother could be allowed, because the mother and infant had already established a physical and psychological bond. Priority must therefore be given to the mother over the father; neither should the bonds between mother and child be severed later on when circumstances changed. The father was only to be granted parental power in special cases. The declaration of legitimacy had the advantage over merely assigning parental power to the father that the child thereby obtained a new, firmly delimited and safeguarded legal position, which also included the full right of inheritance and to a compulsory portion in relation to its father. The possibility of separately assigning parental power to the father was not provided for at the same time, because the child's best interests were best served by permanently legally assigning the child to either the mother's or the father's family (see *Bundestag* printed paper (*Bundestagsdrucksache* – BTDrucks.) V/2370, p. 63).

b) The institution of the declaration of legitimacy was modified and the German term *Ehelicherklärung* replaced the previously used term *Ehelichkeitserklärung*. According to § 1723 of the Civil Code new, a child born out of wedlock is to be declared legitimate upon application by its father if this is consistent with the child's best interests and there are no serious reasons against it. As well as the consent of the child, the consent of the mother is required if the child is a minor (§ 1726.1 sentence 1 of the Civil Code). The father's application and the consent of the mother and of the child require notarial authorisation (§ 1730 of the Civil Code). The child attains the legal status of a legitimate child by means of the declaration of legitimacy (§ 1736 of the Civil Code). The child receives the surname of the father (§ 1737 of the Civil Code). The father's obligation to furnish maintenance to the child and its descendants takes precedence over that of the mother and of the relatives on the maternal side (§ 1739 of the Civil Code).

According to § 1738.1 of the Civil Code, the mother loses the right and the duty of exercising parental custody. This right may be retransferred to her by the guardianship court according to § 1738.2 of the Civil Code if the parental custody of the father terminates or is suspended, or if the care for the person of the child has been withdrawn from the father. This provision is also based on the assumption that the unequivocal, definite and permanent legal assignment of the child to one parent is in the child's best interests. As the father gains parental power with the declaration of legitimacy, according to § 1736 in conjunction with § 1626 of the Civil Code, in analogy with the previous regulation the mother must lose the right and duty of exercising parental power. The possibility that the mother could also retain sole parental power after the declaration of legitimacy was not provided for, because there could be undesirable consequences. For instance, if such a regulation were permitted, the declaration of the legitimacy of children could be promoted whose parents were living together but were not married; aiding and abetting cohabitation would, however, not be compatible with the protection of marriage and the family (*Bundestag* printed paper V/2370, p. 75).

These are the currently applicable provisions of the Civil Code which are relevant to the proceedings:

§ 1723

> An illegitimate child may, upon application by its father, be declared legitimate by the guardianship court if the declaration of legitimacy is consistent with the child's best interests and there are no serious reasons against it.

§ 1738

> (1) Upon the declaration of legitimacy the mother loses the right and the duty of exercising the parental custody.
> (2) The guardianship court may retransfer the exercise of parental custody to the mother if the parental custody of the father terminates or is suspended or if the care for the person of the child has been withdrawn from the father.

II.

1. The original proceedings concern the declaration of legitimacy of a child born out of wedlock in November 1979, whose parents have been living together since early 1979 and have been looking after and raising the child together since its birth. The father acknowledged paternity in January 1980; in April of the same year the ex officio curatorship was cancelled on application by the mother. In 1988 the father conferred his surname on the child according to § 1618.1 of the Civil Code.
By notarial authorisation of 31 May 1988 the father applied to have the child declared legitimate with the proviso that parental custody be assigned jointly to him and to the mother. In the same document the mother declared in her own name and as the child's legal representative that she consented to the declaration of legitimacy with the legal consequence applied for. The Social Services Office responsible for submitting a declaration according to § 48a of the Youth Welfare Act (*Jugendwohlfahrtsgesetz* – JWG) was of the view that a declaration of legitimacy was only in the child's best interests if the parents were jointly given parental custody.
2. The guardianship court suspended the proceedings and submitted the matter to the Federal Constitutional Court (*Bundesverfassungsgericht*) for a decision regarding whether § 1738.1 of the Civil Code was unconstitutional, arguing as follows:
a) The decision concerning the application for the declaration of legitimacy was dependent on the constitutionality of this provision. Applicable law did not provide for the legal consequence that parental custody was to be assigned jointly to the father and the mother, as applied for. However, in the present case the child's best

interests would only be safeguarded if parental custody was assigned to both parents jointly, as applied for – contrary to § 1738.1 of the Civil Code. If the mother lost the right to exercise her parental custody as a consequence of the declaration of legitimacy, there was a risk that continuity in the safeguarding of its interests, which was key to the welfare of the child, would be broken.

b) § 1738.1 of the Civil Code was compatible neither with Article 6.2 and 6.5 of the Basic Law, nor with Article 6.1 and 6.4, or with Article 2.1 in conjunction with Article 1.1 of the Basic Law.

It violated parental rights when the legislature only permitted the declaration of legitimacy with the consequence that the mother, without consideration of her willingness and ability to continue to bear responsibility for the child, lost the right to exercise parental custody. This mandatory legal consequence went beyond the state's watchdog function [as regards the exercise of the parental duty to care for and bring up their children] (*Wächteramt des Staates*) under Article 6.2 sentence 2 of the Basic Law and violated the principle that any restrictions on parental rights were to be guided by what was in the child's best interests. When shaping the legal consequences of the declaration of legitimacy the legislature was obviously also pursuing the objective of preventing any form of cohabitation of the parents and thus accepted the loss, in the legal sense, of the maternal parent, although it was especially the community which the child formed with both responsible parents which provided the preconditions for as favourable a development on the part of the child as possible. It was in the child's best interests to create the possibility that the father and mother could jointly exercise parental custody after the declaration of legitimacy if they were living together with the child and were suited to and willing to bear parental responsibility together.

The mandatory legal consequence under § 1738.1 of the Civil Code could not be justified by means of the consideration that legally assigning the child born out of wedlock to one parent protected it against its parents` separation having no consequences and that it thus served the child's best interests. The child born out of wedlock's special need of protection in the event that its parents separate only resulted from the fact that the legislature did not attach any consequences to the separation. For the rest, the risk of a possible separation without consequences could not justify the unilateral legal assignment of the child to only one parent whilst the parents were living together harmoniously.

The view that the provision in § 1738.1 of the Civil Code was unconstitutional, insofar as it covered cases of this nature, could also not be contradicted by the fact that in these cases the declaration of legitimacy according to § 1723 of the Civil Code was to be rejected because it was not in the child's best interests. The incompatibility with the child's best interests here solely resulted from the legal conse-

quence ordered by the § 1738.1 of the Civil Code without exception, whilst the declaration of legitimacy as such afforded the child legal advantages. Therefore, justice could not be done to the child's best interests by refraining from the declaration of legitimacy but rather by relinquishing the rigidly applied legal consequence.
The mandate to establish rules which resulted from Article 6.5 of the Basic Law obligated the legislature to make allowances for any changes in the circumstances. Since the passing of the Act Governing the Legal Status of Children Born Out of Wedlock, the number of children born out of wedlock who were living with their parents in a permanent community had risen considerably. A provision which had possibly still been adequate in the past was now inadequate and unconstitutional on account of this development. Exclusively assigning the child to the father was not compatible with the need to create the same conditions for children born out of wedlock as for children born in wedlock. The legislature denied those children who had been declared legitimate the protection it granted legitimate children. That applied in particular when a cohabiting couple split up. In order to put children declared legitimate on an equal footing with those born in wedlock it was necessary to provide for the possibility, in the child's best interests, of a decision to be made in favour of the father or of the mother when the parents separated without having to take recourse to the conditions set out in § 1666 of the Civil Code.
The provision under review also denied the mother of the child born out of wedlock the protection required under Article 6.4 of the Basic Law. The protective obligation had not already been satisfied when the declaration of legitimacy could only be made with the mother's consent; since she found herself in a conflict situation. As the declaration of legitimacy today still gave the child a considerably better social and legal standing, the mother had to "choose" between the child's best interests and her own interest in retaining the right to exercise parental custody. Even the legislature's bringing about of this conflict situation violated Article 6.4 of the Basic Law.
§ 1738.1 of the Civil Code violated the child's personality right since the child's best interests had been neglected on the grounds of the falsely understood protection of marriage and the family. Furthermore, any indirect promotion of marriage to the detriment of the family was incompatible with Article 6.1 of the Basic Law.
c) The unconstitutionality of § 1738.1 of the Civil Code created an unintended loophole, which had to be closed in analogy with § 1671 of the Civil Code. As the legislature had assumed that custody rights would be assigned, the guardianship court had to find a custody regulation in the context of the declaration of legitimacy. Assigning joint parental custody in analogous application of § 1671 of the Civil Code also permitted a regulation in line with the child's best interests even in cases when the cohabiting parents separated later on, because in analogous application of

§ 1696.1 of the Civil Code an amendment was possible on application from one parent.

III.

1. The Federal Minister of Justice, who made submissions on behalf of the Federal Government, believes that § 1738.1 of the Civil Code is constitutional. …
2. The President of the Federal Court of Justice (*Bundesgerichtshof*) forwarded a statement from the Senate responsible for family-law matters. In regard to the matter addressed in the submission it declared that the declaration of legitimacy provided the child with the legal status of a child born in wedlock to his father. That was a benefit which was not necessarily required by Article 6.5 of the Basic Law. That alone meant that the view that the declaration of legitimacy had to be reorganised again by force of the constitution so that both parents were entitled to custody of the child was not very convincing. The question of whether it was compatible with Article 6.5 of the Basic Law that applicable law did not give unmarried parents the opportunity to be jointly given parental custody for their child was surely not the subject-matter of the proceedings.

B.

The submission is admissible.

I.

The judgment of the Federal Constitutional Court of 24 March 1981 (Decisions of the Federal Constitutional Court (*Entscheidungen des Bundesverfassungsgerichts* – BVerfGE) 56, 363) does not stand in the way of its admissibility. That judgment confirms the compatibility of § 1705 of the Civil Code with the Basic Law, as the legislature by force of the constitution was not obligated to create distinct rules for the area of parental custody for children born out of wedlock. Nevertheless, it does not make reference to the legal provision under review here, which concerns the loss of the mother's parental custody as a consequence of the declaration of legitimacy, and does not rule out a review of § 1738.1 of the Civil Code (see BVerfGE 79, 256 (264)).

II.

The decision to make a submission meets the conditions set out in Article 100.1 of the Basic Law and § 80.1 of the Federal Constitutional Court Act (*Bundesverfassungsgerichtsgesetz* – BVerfGG). The grounds of the decision show that, contrary to the text of the operative part, it is not § 1738.1 of the Civil Code as a whole which is subject to a review. The Court only negated the constitutionality of this provision insofar as the mother also loses the right and the duty to exercise parental custody if she is living with the father and is willing and able to exercise parental responsibility together with the father following the declaration of legitimacy.

C.

The provision set out in § 1738.1 of the Civil Code is not compatible with Article 6.2 and 6.5 of the Basic Law insofar as it also applies to cases in which the father and the mother are living together with the child, both are willing and able to jointly take on parental responsibility, and this is in the child's best interests. The provision means that the father of a child born out of wedlock can only gain parental responsibility with all the legal consequences of the declaration of legitimacy to the detriment of the mother or that he does not attain full parental status because the mandatory loss of the maternal custody rights is not in the child's best interests. There is no justification for the associated restriction of parental rights and discrimination against children born out of wedlock.

I.

1. Under Article 6.2 sentence 1 of the Basic Law, parental rights are due to "the parents". The constitutional provision assumes the normal case in which the child is living in a family community with the parents who are bound by marriage and that the father and mother are caring for and bringing up the child together (BVerfGE 56, 363 (382); 61, 358 (372)). However, the protection afforded under Article 6.2 of the Basic Law also applies when these preconditions are not met. Thus, it is also due the mother of the child born out of wedlock (see BVerfGE 24, 119 (135)). The question of whether the father of the child born out of wedlock can also generally invoke parental rights need not be examined here. Parental status within the meaning of this fundamental provision can at any rate not be revoked when he is living with the child and the mother and thus fulfils the preconditions for the exercising of his parental responsibility (see BVerfGE 56, 363 (384); 79, 203 (210)).

2. On account of the regulation in § 1738.1 of the Civil Code, to which there are no exceptions, the legislature denies one parent full legal parental status even in those cases in which the father has proved his willingness to take on full parental responsibility by filing the application for the declaration of legitimacy and the mother is willing and able to continue exercising parental custody. The mother and father who are living with the child do in fact have the option of caring for and bringing up the child together. However, the parental right of both parents is not already satisfied when the legislature does not prevent them from actually fulfilling their parental duties. Rather, this fundamental right is also encroached upon when the legal authorities which are necessary for the exercising of parental responsibility are withheld from one parent.

Parental rights need to be given concrete legal form, as the care and upbringing of a child presupposes legal authority in relation to the child, especially vis-à-vis third parties. The legislature invests the parents of children born in wedlock and the parent with custody rights for children born out of wedlock with these authorities in the form of a number of individual rights which together comprise parental custody. The legislature may not withhold the relevant authorities from other holders of parental rights under Article 6.2 of the Basic Law without justified reason. That does not mean that the civil-law provisions concerning parental custody are guaranteed in their concrete form by Article 6.2 of the Basic Law. However, the protection of parental rights, which include the trusteeship of the child's interests, covers the key elements of custody rights without which parental responsibility cannot be exercised.

The legislature is here not divested of the duty to grant the holder of parental rights the necessary legal status because the parent having custody can enable the parent without custody to exercise full parental responsibility by means of private arrangements, in particular by granting them powers of attorney; since the neutralisation of the legal encroachment by means of suitable measures initiated by those concerned cannot justify the encroachment itself (see BVerfGE 61, 358 (379)).

3. In those cases to which the question submitted is restricted, the legislature's decision to only ever assign the child born out of wedlock to one parent and to deny the other parent custody rights – or the right to exercise parental custody – cannot rely on the consideration that both parents' positions as the holders of fundamental rights need to be balanced and that therefore the strict conditions for encroachment on parental rights do not have to be fulfilled (see BVerfGE 31, 194 (208)).

Nevertheless, the preconditions which apply in the case of the parents of children born out of wedlock differ from those which apply to the parents of children born in wedlock. As they are not united by the bond of marriage, the legislature can neither assume that they are living in the same household, nor that the father and mother wish to and are able to jointly take on personal responsibility for the child. It can, therefore, initially assign the child born out of wedlock, which has a right to have its personal circumstances regulated at the time of its birth, to one parent. It would seem obvious as a matter of principle to assign custody rights to the mother, because a relationship has already been established between her and the child during pregnancy and birth and the baby is especially dependent on her (see BVerfGE 56, 363 (389-390)).

No decision need be taken here regarding the question of whether, in view of the considerable increase since the enactment of the Act Governing the Legal Status of Children Born out of Wedlock in the number of cases in which the parents of a child born out of wedlock are living together and are prepared to jointly take on parental responsibility, the legislature still wishes to presume, as a general rule, that a conflict arises between the parents of the child born out of wedlock and need not provide for the possibility of a procedure to obtain joint custody in the event that they are in agreement. At least in those cases in which a father applies for the declaration of legitimacy with the proviso that parental custody be assigned to him jointly with the mother and the mother consents to his application it is clear that there is no conflict between the parents in which the state needs to mediate. The legal consequence ordered under § 1738.1 of the Civil Code, to which there are no exceptions, can therefore in these cases not rely on the task of the state, namely to safeguard the legal order and undisturbed administration of the law, and to take decisions concerning the balancing of the parents' contentious interests (see BVerfGE 61, 358 (374)).

4. Neither are the preconditions for encroachment on parental rights in the state's exercising of its watchdog function met. The generalised exclusion of joint custody rights for the parents of children born out of wedlock is not required for reasons associated with the child's best interests; by contrast, the mandatory assignment of the child to only one parent can considerably impair the child's best interests.

a) Where the father and mother are living with the child and both are willing and able to take on parental responsibility it is as a general rule in the child's best interests to grant both parents custody rights. It can, in particular, be of considerable importance as regards the child's best interests that the father and mother are able to exercise parental custody in school matters. Further, joint custody rights are suitable for making the joint responsibility for the child clear to the parents and for contributing to the continuity of the relationship. A child which grows up with a cohabiting couple therefore has a considerable interest in the legal safeguarding of the emotional bonds to both its parents …

b) The legislature's decision to legally assign the child to only one parent without exception and not to permit joint custody rights in those cases at issue here can also not be justified by means of the consideration that the cohabiting couple could split up and the child should not become the focus of the dispute between its parents following their separation (deviating from BVerfGE 56, 363 (387)). Rather, it is especially in cases in which the parents separate that the legal safeguarding of joint parental custody takes on special significance.

The child which grows up with its cohabiting parents develops a relationship with both parents. The aspect of the continuity in the child's development and upbringing (see BVerfGE 61, 358 (375-376)) requires that its emotional bonds be taken into account when its parents separate. Therefore, the parents' joint custody can prove to be just as decisive in regard to the best interests of a child born out of wedlock after the separation as it is in regard to the best interests of a child born in wedlock following its parents' divorce (see BVerfGE 61, 358 (376, 377)).

But also in cases in which joint custody rights are not an option after the parents separate, permanently assigning the child to one parent is not a suitable means of preventing the child from suffering after they separate. Quite the contrary, the assignment which is decided without consideration being given to the concrete circumstances makes it impossible to do justice on a case-by-base basis to the bonds the child has established … Where a conflict arises between the parents concerning the relationships with the joint child when a cohabiting couple splits up, the resolution of this conflict must be guided by the child's best interests irrespective of the previous legal assignment and must take account of the child's individuality as a holder of fundamental rights (see BVerfGE 55, 171 (179)). However, that is only possible if a decision on custody rights can be taken which does justice to the concrete situation. To that end it is not sufficient at that point in time at which the decision is taken regarding the declaration of legitimacy to predict which parent the child would be best placed with if the cohabiting couple splits up; since at that point in time the child's further development cannot be adequately predicted nor is it possible to assess whether the parents will actually split up and when that might be. The fear that it might not be possible to guarantee that the assignment of parental custody to both parents will be reversed in good time if the conditions for their joint exercise cease to exist can also not be used to justify excluding joint custody rights altogether (see BVerfGE 61, 358 (382)).

c) The fact that § 1738.1 of the Civil Code does not provide for an exception in cases like the present one can also not be justified by the need to define typical facts. A regulation which defines typical facts is only admissible when the encroachment on fundamental rights associated therewith is not very intensive (see BVerfGE 79, 87 (100)). However, that is not the case here. Both the encroachment on parental rights associated with the denial of joint custody rights and the impairment of the child's best interests carry considerable weight (see BVerfGE 61, 358 (381)).

5. The complete exclusion of joint custody rights after the declaration of legitimacy of the child can also not be based on other constitutional provisions.
Article 6.1 of the Basic Law obligates the state to protect marriage and the family from interference and to promote them by appropriate means. However, that does not lead to the obligation to treat cohabiting couples less favourably than married ones in every respect (see BVerfGE 82, 6 (15)). The question of what specific consequences are to be drawn from Article 6.1 of the Basic Law as regards statutory regulations concerning cohabiting couples can remain unanswered. An obligation to refuse to legally recognise the parental rights of the father and mother of a child born out of wedlock which are protected by Article 6.2 sentence 1 of the Basic Law under the preconditions given in the present case does not at any rate result from this constitutional provision. The admissibility of joint custody rights in these cases would not give concrete shape to the community as such, only to the parent-child relationship.
Legally safeguarding parental status in such a manner can also not be denied on the grounds that parents who consciously reject a legally binding arrangement for their relationship with each other in the form of the institution of marriage have no right to be legally granted parental authorities (deviating from BVerfGE 56, 363 (385-386); 61, 358 (374-375)). It would not be compatible with the constitutional significance of parental rights as the rights of trusteeship, which differ from the other fundamental rights on account of the association with rights and duties (see BVerfGE 56, 363 (381-382); 64, 180 (189); 72, 155 (172)), to deny the parents the rights required to exercise their parental responsibility because they have decided not to marry; since this personal decision on the part of the parents must not have any consequences which are to the detriment of the child (see BVerfGE 56, 363 (384-385)).

II.

1. By giving more concrete form to the general principle of equality and as a protective provision in favour of children born out of wedlock, Article 6.5 of the Basic Law sets limits to legislative discretion (see BVerfGE 25, 167 (190); 74, 33 (38)). Furthermore, the constitutional provision obligates the legislature to create the same conditions by means of positive rules for the mental and physical development of children born out of wedlock as for children born in wedlock. This constitutional mandate sets the legislature a clear objective. The "normal case" of a child born in wedlock which grows up within a stable marriage represents the standard in regard to equal treatment (see BVerfGE 58, 377 (392-393)). There must always be convincing reasons for any unequal treatment of children born out of wedlock

which constitutes discrimination in comparison to children born in wedlock. Deviations from provisions applicable to children born in wedlock are therefore in principle only admissible if formal equality would not do justice to the different social situation of the child born out of wedlock or other legal positions which are equally protected would thereby be impaired (see BVerfGE 74, 33 (39)). The constitutional mandate can therefore also fail where a regulation leads to individual groups of children born out of wedlock being placed at a disadvantage (see BVerfGE 22, 163 (172)).

2. According to these standards, § 1738.1 of the Civil Code is not compatible with Article 6.5 of the Basic Law in regard to the aforementioned cases. The constitutional provision does not obligate the legislature to afford children born out of wedlock the status of children born in wedlock under the conditions referred to under §§ 1723 et seq. of the Civil Code. If it permits further approximation to the status of children born in wedlock for children whose father is prepared to take on full parental responsibility by means of the institution of the declaration of legitimacy, it cannot, however, deny that approximation without sufficient factual grounds for a group of children born out of wedlock or to link them to considerable legal disadvantages.

On account of the mandatory legal consequence set out in § 1738.1 of the Civil Code, which applies without exception, children born out of wedlock whose parents have decided to live in a free partnership and who are seeking a declaration of legitimacy are regularly discriminated against. Either the legal advantages associated with the declaration of legitimacy – especially full equality with children born in wedlock with regard to the law of inheritance in their relationship with their father and the father's custody rights – are denied them on the grounds that it is not in their best interests if the mother loses her custody rights. But if the declaration of legitimacy is in fact made, the child must accept the disadvantage that the mother will no longer be able to fully exercise her parental responsibility because she lacks the legal authorities thereto.

There is no justification for this discrimination against children born out of wedlock who are living with their father and mother. The situation of these children not only does not stand in the way of giving them largely the same legal status as children born in wedlock, it practically requires it. Thus in particular the mandatory assignment to only one parent, the purpose of § 1738.1 of the Civil Code, cannot be justified with the different initial position in relation to children born in wedlock. Rather, this legal consequence, as explained in the above (I 4), leads to considerable discrimination against children born out of wedlock who are living with their parents, because their emotional bonds with both parents are not legally safeguarded and in the event of the parents separating no decision can be taken on a case-by-case basis concerning custody rights which is geared to the child's best interests. The state's duty to protect marriage and the family can likewise not justify the disadvantageous consequences of the regulation under review in the cases discussed here. No concrete marriage is endangered on account of the declaration of legitimacy if the mother retains her custody rights; if the father is still married, the other preconditions for the declaration of legitimacy, in particular the requirement that his wife give her consent, provide sufficient protection. Nor is any impairment of the institution of marriage obvious.

D. – I.

Where a legal provision is not consistent with the Basic Law, it must in principle be declared null and void (§ 82.1 in conjunction with § 78 sentence 1 of the Federal Constitutional Court Act (*Bundesverfassungsgerichtsgesetz* – BVerfGG)). However, that does not apply where several possibilities are available for eliminating the constitutional violation and the declaration of nullity would encroach on the legislature's legislative discretion (see BVerfGE 39, 316 (332-333); 77, 308 (337)). Accordingly, a declaration of nullity is ruled out in the present case. The legislature can remedy the unconstitutionality in various ways. For instance, it can provide for the possibility within the institution of the declaration of legitimacy for the mother and father to have joint custody under the conditions discussed here; whether joint custody rights need to be specified more precisely and whether individual legal consequences of the declaration of legitimacy – for example as regards the child's surname (§ 1737 of the Civil Code) or as regards the right to claim maintenance vis-à-vis the mother and her relatives (§ 1739 of the Civil Code) – need to be modified for these cases are matters which must be reviewed. However, the legislature can also introduce joint custody rights for parents of children born out of wedlock outside of the sphere of the declaration of legitimacy and link it to similar consequences as regards the law of inheritance or further approximate the legal status of children born out of wedlock overall to that of children born in wedlock.

II.

Where the Federal Constitutional Court establishes that a legal provision is incompatible with the Basic Law, the legislature is obligated to immediately make the legal situation consistent with the Basic Law. The courts and administrative authorities may no longer apply the legal provision to the extent that it has been declared incompatible (see BVerfGE 37, 217 (261); 82, 126 (155)). No exception from this principle need be made in the present case. Correspondingly, in those cases in which the child is living with its father and mother and the parents apply for a declaration of legitimacy with the proviso that they wish to exercise joint parental custody, the guardianship courts can neither pronounce the declaration of legitimacy with the legal consequence provided for under § 1738.1 of the Civil Code nor deny it on the grounds that it is not in the child's best interests on account of this legal consequence. Rather, such proceedings must be stayed until the legal amendment enters into force.

Justices: Herzog, Henschel, Seidl, Grimm, Söllner, Dieterich, Kühling, Seibert

§ 1738.1 of the Civil Code and the institution of the declaration of legitimacy of children born out of wedlock were revoked by means of the Reforming the Law of Parent and Child (Gesetz zur Reform des Kindschaftsrechts) *of 16 December 1997 (Federal Law Gazette I p. 2942). Since that time § 1626a of the Civil Code has applied in regard to the parental custody of parents who are not married to each other:*

> *"(1) Where the parents, at the date of the birth of the child, are not married to each other, they have joint parental custody if they*
>
> 1. *declare that they wish to take on parental custody jointly (declarations of parental custody), or*
> 2. *marry each other.*
>
> *(2) Apart from this, the mother has parental custody."*

No. 22

BVerfGE 87, 1

of 7 July 1992 – 1 BvL 51/86, 50/87, 1 BvR 873/90, 761/91 –

"Rubble women case"

HEADNOTES:

1. **The legislative competence of the Federation with regard to the recognition of child-raising periods in statutory pensions insurance emerges from Article 74 no. 12 of the Basic Law (*Grundgesetz* – GG). The Federation was empowered in accordance with Article 74 no. 7 of the Basic Law to enact the Child-Raising Benefits Act (*Kindererziehungsleistungs-Gesetz*).**
2. **The Surviving Dependants' Pensions and Child-Raising Periods Act (*Hinterbliebenenrenten- und Erziehungszeiten-Gesetz* – HEZG) and the Child-Raising Benefits Act did not violate the Basic Law by not placing periods of child-raising, in general terms, on the same footing as contribution periods to statutory pensions insurance. The legislature is, however, obliged to compensate for the deficiency in the pensions insurance system resulting from the disadvantages in old-age pensions caused by child-raising, in accordance with Article 3.1 of the Basic Law in conjunction with Article 6.1 of the Basic Law, to a greater degree than has so far taken place.**
3. **The exclusion of mothers born before 1921 from the allowance of child-raising periods in statutory pensions insurance in accordance with the Surviving Dependants' Pensions and Child-Raising Periods Act was compatible with Article 3.1 of the Basic Law. In addition, the only gradual granting of benefits for child-raising to mothers born before 1921, and at the same time the exclusion of fathers from any benefits in the framework of the Child-Raising Benefits Act, were justified on factual grounds with regard to Article 3.1 of the Basic Law.**

Judgment of the First Senate of 7 July 1992
on the basis of the oral hearing of 28 April 1992
– 1 BvL 51/86, 50/87, 1 BvR 873/90, 761/91 –

in the proceedings I. for the constitutional review 1. of § 28a.1 sentence 1 of the Salaried Employees Insurance Act (*Angestelltenversicherungsgesetz* – AVG) in the version of the … Surviving Dependants' Pensions and Child-Raising Periods Act of 11 July 1985 (Federal Law Gazette (*Bundesgesetzblatt* – BGBl.) I p. 1450), … Article 5 of the Act on Benefits of Statutory Pensions Insurance for Child-Raising to Mothers Born Before 1921 (Child-Raising Benefits Act) (*Gesetz über Leistungen der gesetzlichen Rentenversicherung für Kindererziehung an Mütter der Geburtsjahrgänge vor 1921 – Kindererziehungsleistungs-Gesetz* – KLG) of 12 July 1987 (Federal Law Gazette I p. 1585) – suspension of proceedings and submission order of the Detmold Social Court (*Sozialgericht*) of 4 July 1986, … – 1 BvL 51/86 –, …; II. on the constitutional complaints 1. of Ms. W. – authorised representatives: …, lawyers – a) directly against aa) the judgment of the Federal Social Court (*Bundessozialgericht*) of 29 November 1990 …, b) indirectly against the pension law provisions of the Reich Insurance Code (*Reichsversicherungsordnung*), insofar as child-raising is not accommodated by any "contribution equivalent", but is only accommodated in the form of a so-called child-raising year, this also being subject to further restrictive preconditions, – 1 BvR 873/90 –; 2. a) of Ms. R., b) of Mr. R. – authorised representatives: …, lawyers – a) directly against the judgment of the Federal Social Court of 29 November 1990 – 5 RJ 36/88 –, b) … – 1 BvR 761/91 –.

RULING:

I. 1. § 28a.1 sentence 1 of the Salaried Employees Insurance Act, inserted by Article 2 no. 8 of the Act Reforming Surviving Dependants' Pensions and on the Recognition of Child-Raising Periods in the Statutory Pensions Insurance (*Gesetz zur Neuordnung der Hinterbliebenenrenten sowie zur Anerkennung von Kindererziehungszeiten in der gesetzlichen Rentenversicherung*) (Surviving Dependants' Pensions and Child-Raising Periods Act) of 11 July 1985 (Federal Law Gazette I p. 1450), in the version of Article 7 no. 2 of the 1992 Act Reforming Statutory Pensions Insurance (Pensions Reform Act) (*Gesetz zur Reform der gesetzlichen Rentenversicherung – Rentenreformgesetz 1992* – RRG 1992) of 18 December 1989 (Federal Law Gazette I page 2261) and Article 2 § 6c of the Act Reforming the Law on the Pensions Insurance of Salaried Employees (Salaried Employees Insurance Reform Act) (*Angestelltenversicherungs-Neuregelungsgesetz* – AnVNG),

inserted by Article 5 of the Surviving Dependants' Pensions and Child-Raising Periods Act, in the version of Article 5 of the Act Amending Provisions of Statutory Pensions Insurance (Sixth Pensions Insurance Amendment Act) (*Gesetz zur Änderung von Vorschriften der gesetzlichen Rentenversicherung – Sechstes Rentenversicherungs-Änderungsgesetz* – 6. RVÄndG) of 24 April 1986 (Federal Law Gazette I p. 569), were, taking into account the provisos that are contained in the grounds, compatible with the Basic Law insofar as, accordingly, child-raising periods were not to be allowed in the calculation of old-age pensions paid on the occasion of their reaching the age of 65 for mothers born before 1921.
2. …
3. Article 2 § 61.1 and § 61.2 of the Act Reforming the Law on the Pensions Insurance of Salaried Employees (Salaried Employees Insurance Reform Act), inserted by Article 3 no. 2 of the Act on Benefits of Statutory Pensions Insurance for Child-Raising to Mothers Born Before 1921 (Child-Raising Benefits Act) of 12 July 1987 (Federal Law Gazette I p. 1585) in the version of Article 8 of the Act Reforming Statutory Pensions Insurance (1992 Pensions Reform Act) of 18 December 1989 (Federal Law Gazette I p. 2261), was compatible with the Basic Law.
4. …
II. 1. …
2. …

EXTRACT FROM GROUNDS:

A.

The constitutional complaints and submissions relate to the question of the degree to which child-raising periods are to be allowed in the statutory pensions insurance of wage-earners and salaried employees.

I.

1. Statutory pensions insurance was regulated in a largely identical manner for wage-earners and salaried employees in different statutes until the 1992 Pensions Reform Act came into force. The Reich Insurance Code applied to wage-earners; the Salaried Employees Insurance Act to salaried employees. …
Pensions insurance operates in line with the principle of a wage-indexed pension. Since the 1957 pensions reform, its aim has been to enable those who were insured during their entire working lives to maintain a suitable standard of living should an

insured event occur. A pension takes on a wage-substitution function. The pensions insurance system is funded through earnings-related contributions made by the insured parties and their employers, as well as from a federal subsidy. Since the 1957 pensions reform, the expenditure disbursed by the pensions insurance system has been covered in principle by the income of the same calendar year. Thus, the contributions made by the respective gainfully employed generation finance the pensions that are payable in the same period by means of a contribution procedure (so-called intergenerational contract).
The Sixth Book of the Code of Social Law (*Sechstes Buch Sozialgesetzbuch* – SGB VI), which came into force on 1 January 1992 on the basis of Article 1 and Article 85 of the 1992 Pensions Reform Act, adheres to the existing pensions insurance system which has been in force since 1957. Pensions insurance remains determined by the principle of wage and contribution linking, as well as by that of ensuring the standard of living. The pensions insurance system is funded through a contribution procedure in accordance with § 153 of the Sixth Book of the Code of Social Law, as was the case under the predecessor law. Statutory pensions insurance remains determined by the intergenerational contract.
2. … The Act Reforming Surviving Dependants' Pensions and the Recognition of Child-Raising Periods in the Statutory Pensions Insurance (Surviving Dependants' Pensions and Child-Raising Periods Act) of 11 July 1985 (Federal Law Gazette I p. 1450), which came into force on 1 January 1986, has introduced, in addition to the fundamental reform of surviving dependants' pensions, an allowance for child-raising years which serves to establish pension expectancies and to increase pensions. This Act was caused by the ruling of the Federal Constitutional Court (*Bundesverfassungsgericht*) on widowers' pensions (Decisions of the Federal Constitutional Court (*Entscheidungen des Bundesverfassungsgerichts* – BVerfGE) 39, 169), with which the legislature was instructed to reform surviving dependants' pensions. …
Because of the Surviving Dependants' Pensions and Child-Raising Periods Act, periods of child-raising from 1 January 1986 onwards were allowed in pensions insurance for wage-earners and salaried employees insofar as the legislature valued the first twelve calendar months after the end of the birth month as an element of obligatory insurance (§ 1227a.1 of the Reich Insurance Code; § 2a.1 of the Salaried Employees Insurance Act). The child-raising periods prior to 1 January 1986 attained significance under the law on pensions insurance by the fact that the legislature qualified periods of child-raising in the first twelve calendar months after the end of the birth month as an insurance period in their own right (§ 1251a.1 sentence 1 of the Reich Insurance Code; § 28a.1 sentence 1 of the Salaried Employees Insurance Act). The possibility to allow child-raising periods in pensions insurance was, however, restricted (§§ 1255.6a and 1255a.5 of the Reich Insurance Code; §§ 32.6a and

32a.5 of the Salaried Employees Insurance Act). If the child-raising period coincided with an assessed obligatory contribution period, a period of non-contribution or a supplementary period, it was not separately assessed. Statutory security hence only guaranteed a value of 6.25, which corresponded to 75 per cent of average earnings, within the meaning of a minimum allowance. If the obligatory contribution periods included in the assessment were higher than the above value, child-raising periods were not included in the pension formula.
The additional expenditure emerging from the allowance of child-raising periods as a consequence of the Surviving Dependants' Pensions and Child-Raising Periods Act was to be funded by the Federation in accordance with § 1395c of the Reich Insurance Code, § 117c of the Salaried Employees Insurance Act and the Child-Raising Periods Refund Ordinance (*Kindererziehungszeiten-Erstattungsverordnung*) of 2 January 1986 (Federal Law Gazette I p. 31), which was issued by the Federal Minister of Labour and Social Affairs.
3. a) The Act on Benefits of Statutory Pensions Insurance for Child-Raising to Mothers Born Before 1921 of 12 July 1987 (Federal Law Gazette I p. 1585), which came into force on 17 July 1987, introduced a separate benefit for child-raising for mothers born before 1921, who were not covered by the Surviving Dependants' Pensions and Child-Raising Periods Act, and who were frequently referred to in the public debate as "rubble women" (*Trümmerfrauen*).
In contradistinction to the Surviving Dependants' Pensions and Child-Raising Periods Act, child-raising periods for the birth years affected by the Child-Raising Benefits Act were treated neither as an element of obligatory insurance, nor as an insurance period in their own right. Without regard to such preconditions under the law on pensions insurance, child-raising benefits were accordingly to be granted as a percentage (1.125 per cent) of the respectively applicable general assessment base. Hence there initially emerged a child-raising benefit of DM 27.10 per child per month favouring younger mothers in accordance with the calculations made on the basis of the Surviving Dependants' Pensions and Child-Raising Periods Act.
In contradistinction to the Surviving Dependants' Pensions and Child-Raising Periods Act, child-raising benefits were, however, granted from 1 October 1987 onwards at the earliest. Furthermore, the Act provided for the benefits to start in four phases, depending on the age of the beneficiaries. Accordingly, mothers born from 1917 to 1920 received benefits from 1 October 1990 onwards. The later start of the benefit had a particularly strong impact on mothers of the year 1920. Whilst the latter only received child-raising benefits from 1 October 1990 onwards, it was possible under certain circumstances for mothers born in 1921 to draw an equivalent pension amount from as early as from 1 January 1986 onwards, in accordance with the Surviving Dependants' Pensions and Child-Raising Periods Act.

In accordance with Article 2 no. 2 and Article 3 no. 2 of the Child-Raising Benefits Act and the Child-Raising Periods Refund Ordinance of 18 December 1987 (Federal Law Gazette I p. 2814), which was issued by the Federal Minister of Labour and Social Affairs, the amounts expended by the insurers for child-raising benefits were to be paid by the Federation.

…

b) The Federal Government had opined in the reasoning of the draft Bill (*Bundesrat* printed paper (*Bundesratsdrucksache* – BRDrucks.) 60/87) that the Bill recognised the child-raising activity that was carried out by mothers born before 1921, whilst at the same time improving the social security of these women. It reasoned the phased regulation provided for in the draft Bill, and taken on board in the Child-Raising Benefits Act, by stating that immediate inclusion of all mothers of the birth years in question would have endangered the consolidation of the federal budget. Whilst for older mothers the provision was said to be, in principle, in agreement with the provisions of the Surviving Dependants' Pensions and Child-Raising Periods Act, since the pension biographies of the mothers in question were already completed and were not to be re-written because of the allowance of child-raising periods, the provisions were however said to be designed in a more generalised manner and to be more strongly categorised into types. The Child-Raising Benefits Act was only to apply to mothers because fathers typically did not take on child-raising at that time, and hence were said not to have incurred disadvantages in old-age pensions as a result of child-raising. The draft was said to comply with the roles assumed within families that were typical of that time. Over and above this, it was said to be no longer possible, or only possible with an irresponsibly large administrative effort, to ascertain who had actually brought up the child. The benefits provided for were said to be granted regardless of whether the mothers in question had drawn a pension from the statutory pensions insurance or not. The benefit was said to be granted as a benefit in its own right by an organisation of statutory pensions insurance. In deviation from the regulatory system of the Surviving Dependants' Pensions and Child-Raising Periods Act, the benefit claim was said here not to be contingent on the mother complying with the waiting period for an old-age pension; equally, the benefit was said to be paid regardless of whether the mother herself or her spouse was insured in statutory pensions insurance. It was said here to be a benefit of the equalisation of family burdens, which was funded by the Federation. Hence, the expenditure was said to be payable by all taxpayers (see *Bundesrat* printed paper 60/87, pp. 19 et seq.).

…

4. …The inclusion of child-raising periods in pensions insurance and the recognition of child-raising activities have been governed since 1 January 1992 on the ba-

sis of the provisions of the 1992 Pensions Reform Act in the Sixth Book of the Code of Social Law. Accordingly, for the raising of a child born after 31 December 1991, child-raising time is allowed for its first three years of life. In this respect, "obligatory contributions are deemed to have been paid" (§ 56.1 sentence 1 of the Sixth Book of the Code of Social Law). As in accordance with the previous law, contributions are not payable for the child-raising periods. Equally, the pension law valuation of child-raising periods is in line with the previously applicable law. § 70.2 of the Sixth Book of the Code of Social Law retains the previous provision in that periods of insurance because of child-raising are only valued at 75 per cent of average earnings if they coincide with contribution periods or other periods that are governed by pension law. The exclusion of the birth years before 1921 from the allowance of child-raising time in pensions insurance is retained (§ 249.4 of the Sixth Book of the Code of Social Law). Child-raising benefits are provided for by the new arrangement only transitionally. With the provision contained in § 294 of the Sixth Book of the Code of Social Law, the legislature has essentially taken over the system created by the Child-Raising Benefits Act.

…

II.

The constitutional complaints impugn as a whole the statutory provision on the recognition of child-raising periods in the Surviving Dependants' Pensions and Child-Raising Periods Act, and in the Child-Raising Benefits Act, because it is alleged not to allow that child-raising, because of its significance for the so-called intergenerational contract, constitutes a form of contribution equivalent to monetary contributions to statutory pensions insurance. The submissions claim that child-raising periods should also have been allowed in statutory pensions insurance for the birth years prior to 1921; or at least they should have been granted corresponding benefits at the same time. The constitutional complaints pursue the same goal with alternative motions.

…

B.

…

The provisions on the recognition of child-raising periods in the Surviving Dependants' Pensions and Child-Raising Periods Act, and in the Child-Raising Benefits Act, were within the framework of the legislative competence of the Federation and were, in accordance with the following considerations, also compatible with the Basic Law in substantive terms.

I.

The provisions submitted for review came about constitutionally in formal terms.

1. By including child-raising periods in the framework of the Surviving Dependants' Pensions and Child-Raising Periods Act, the Federation was able to draw on its legislative competence under Article 74 no. 12 of the Basic Law.

The broad constitutional term of social insurance (see BVerfGE 75, 108 (146-147) with further references; established case-law) permits one to include new social benefits in its overall system if these correspond to the picture characterised by classical social insurance in terms of their essential structural elements and, in particular, in the organisational implementation and the risks to be covered. What is decisive is that social insurance is understood within the meaning of "joint coverage of a possible requirement, which can be completely estimated, by distribution among an organised multitude" (BVerfGE 75, 108 (146)). In addition to this characteristic, the manner in which the task is dealt with in organisational terms is also characteristic. Organisations of social insurance are independent institutes or corporations under public law which acquire their funds from the contributions of those concerned (see BVerfGE 11, 105 (111 et seq.); 75, 108 (146) with further references; established case-law).

It is decisive that child-raising periods exert an impact on pension entitlements in accordance with the Surviving Dependants' Pensions and Child-Raising Periods Act. Hence, not only an organisational attribution, but also a factual attribution applies to statutory pensions insurance, and hence to social insurance. In contrast, the point of view of funding by the Federation, which must obtain its funds from the public, is a secondary consideration.

2. The legislative competence of the Federation for the Child-Raising Benefits Act is based on Article 74 no. 7 of the Basic Law. Article 74 no. 12 of the Basic Law cannot be used [here] as a provision granting competences. Over and above the fact that the organisational tasks are attributed to the pensions insurance organisations, there was no further factual attribution to statutory pensions insurance.

The Child-Raising Benefits Act provided for a benefit to the mothers concerned regardless of whether or not they were drawing a pension from statutory pensions insurance. The entitlement to child-raising benefits did not depend on the waiting period for an old-age pension being complied with. Equally, no statutory pensions insurance was required for either the mother or for her spouse. The direct goal of the Child-Raising Benefits Act consisted in the security of the mothers concerned, funded by the Federation, by means of granting a benefit which is to be attributed to the equalisation of family burdens (see *Bundesrat* printed paper 60/87, pp. 19 et seq.; *Bundestag* printed paper (*Bundestagsdrucksache* – BTDrucks.) 11/4124, p. 142). This goal of the child-raising benefits as a part of the general equalisation of family burdens leads to the attribution of the provision to the field of public welfare within the meaning of Article 74 no. 7 of the Basic Law.

II.

The Surviving Dependants' Pensions and Child-Raising Periods Act and the Child-Raising Benefits Act did not violate the Basic Law by not placing periods of child-raising, in general terms, on the same footing as contribution periods to statutory pensions insurance. The legislature is however obliged to compensate for the deficiency in the pensions insurance system resulting from the disadvantages in old-age pensions caused by child-raising to a greater degree than has so far taken place.

1. In the context of old-age pensions, it is not possible to derive from Article 6.1 of the Basic Law an obligation on the part of the legislature to provide higher benefits for child-raising than occurred in the Surviving Dependants' Pensions and Child-Raising Periods Act and in the Child-Raising Benefits Act.

As a freedom right, Article 6.1 of the Basic Law constitutes an obligation incumbent on the state to forgo incursions on the family (see BVerfGE 6, 55 (76); 80, 81 (92)). Over and above this, Article 6.1 of the Basic Law contains a "fundamental provision that determines values", which entails the duty incumbent on the state to protect and promote marriage and the family (see BVerfGE 6, 55 (76); 82, 60 (81); established case-law). However, the state is not under an obligation to compensate for any or all of the burdens affecting the family or any party obliged to pay maintenance (see BVerfGE 82, 60 (81) with further references). Equally, it does not follow from Article 6.1 of the Basic Law that the state should promote the family without regard for other public interests. State family promotion through financial benefits is subject to what is possible in terms of what the individual can sensibly expect to receive from society. In addition to family promotion, the legislature must, in the interests of general welfare, also account for other community interests in its budgeting, and in so doing must ensure above all the proper functioning and equilibrium of the entire system. Only if these principles are adhered to is it possible to ascertain whether family promotion by the state is manifestly unsuitable and no longer complies with the promotion principle of Article 6.1 of the Basic Law (see Federal Constitutional Court, loc. cit., pp. 81-82). Accordingly, it is possible to derive, from the value determination contained in Article 6.1 of the Basic Law, in conjunction with the principle of the social welfare state, the general duty of the state to provide equalisation of family burdens, but not the decision on the degree to or manner in which such social compensation is to be implemented. No concrete conclusions can be drawn from the constitutional mandate to bring about effective equalisation of family burdens for the individual legal areas and sub-systems in which the equalisation of family burdens is to be carried out. In this respect, rather, the legislature has in principle a certain degree of latitude (see BVerfGE 39, 316 (326); 82, 60 (81) with further references).

2. The standard for the review is, rather, first and foremost Article 3.1 of the Basic Law, which however must be taken into account in conjunction with Article 6.1 of the Basic Law.

a) Article 3.1 of the Basic Law requires that all people are treated equally before the law. This does not however prohibit the legislature all differentiation. The principle of equality is, rather, intended to rule out a situation where one group of persons addressed by a provision is treated differently in comparison to another, although there are no differences between the two groups of such a nature and weight that they could justify the unequal treatment (BVerfGE 55, 72 (88)). The legal distinction must hence find sufficient support in factual differences. The application of this principle requires the comparison of circumstances that are never completely identical to one another, but may only be the same with regard to individual characteristics. Under these conditions, in principle it is a matter for the legislature to decide which of these characteristics it regards as material to equal or unequal treatment (see BVerfGE 83, 395 (401)). Article 3.1 of the Basic Law only prohibits the legislature from improperly failing to consider the nature and weight of the actual differences. It is free in its decision-making within these limits. However, a further restriction can emerge from other constitutional provisions. If the legislature makes a distinction which is to the disadvantage of the family, the special protection which the state owes to families must be adhered to in accordance with Article 6.1 of the Basic Law (see BVerfGE 18, 257 (269); 67, 186 (195-196)).

b) The old-age pensions system which is in practice places at a disadvantage persons who devote themselves to child-raising within the family, compared to childless persons who are able to engage in gainful employment without interruption. It is true that the law on pensions does not distinguish between persons with and without a family. Pension benefits are, rather, linked solely to the previous contribution payments from working wages, regardless of family status. This determines the pension entitlement. The reasons leading to leaving work and as a result to the lack of contribution payments are not material. Under pension law, a person who leaves work because of child-raising is treated in the same way as any other person who is not engaged in gainful employment.

As opposed to the other reasons that lead to unemployment, and hence to a lack of contribution payments, child-raising is however important because it ensures ongoing population for the system of old-age pensions. Pensions insurance designed as an intergenerational contract cannot be maintained without the future generation. The latter contributes the funds for the old-age pensions of the now gainfully employed generation. Without a future generation, they would have paid contributions to pensions insurance, but would not be able to expect any benefits from pensions insurance. Here, in view of the broad effect of pensions insurance it can be ignored that every child does not become a contributor later.
The previous design of pensions insurance leads to a disadvantage for the family, namely for families with several children. The family in which one parent leaves work in favour of child-raising accepts, in comparison to the childless, not only loss of income, but also that they must share the lower income between several persons. If the children have entered work, and thus contribute towards the old-age pensions of their parents' generation, the parents themselves can expect a lower pension.
c) The disadvantaged position of families in which one parent devotes himself or herself to child-raising is compensated for neither by state benefits nor by other means.
The old-age pension which was guaranteed by one's own children prior to the introduction of pensions insurance is considerably reduced particularly by the obligatory insurance system. The obligation to pay insurance contributions impairs the children's contributory capacity. Funds which, were there to be no obligatory contributions, they could contribute towards the maintenance of their parents who are no longer in gainful employment, are taken from them and transferred to the solidarity community, which uses them to pay pensions to the insured parties as a whole.
Surviving dependants' pensions, which at a time when women typically were not gainfully employed created a certain degree of compensation for those forgoing their own old-age pension by taking on child-raising, has become largely bereft of this function following the increase in the number of cases in which both parents work, and the fall in the number of children. Also, the various benefits in the context of the equalisation of family burdens (child-raising benefit, child benefit, child allowance, educational assistance) do not compensate for the losses in old-age pensions suffered by parents compared to the childless. The same applies to the provisions on the "baby year" contained in the Surviving Dependants' Pensions and Child-Raising Periods Act and in the Child-Raising Benefits Act. These have also compensated only relatively slightly for the disadvantage affecting families.
In essence, despite the state's efforts to bring about equalisation of family burdens, it remains the case that child-raising is regarded as a private matter, whilst old-age

pensions are considered to be a concern for society. In addition, the disadvantage at which families are placed, as presented by the complainants on the basis of a transfer law view, has not been fundamentally denied in the oral hearing.

d) In view of the obligation of promotion under Article 6.1 of the Basic Law, which restricts the remaining latitude provided by Article 3.1 of the Basic Law, there are no sufficient grounds for the disadvantage to the family caused by the law as it stands. In fact, the current pensions insurance system, which is based on the insurance principle as well as on the wage-substitution function, and in which the pension benefit is funded in a contribution procedure, is not an adequate reason to result in the considerable impairment of people raising children as against the childless. As is shown by the provisions of the Surviving Dependants' Pensions and Child-Raising Periods Act, there are ways to include the recognition of child-bearing benefits in the pensions insurance structure. This statement, however, does not lead to the provisions of the applicable pension law submitted for a review and impugned with the constitutional complaints being constitutionally objectionable, but only to an obligation of the legislature to gradually reduce the disadvantage to a greater degree than has so far taken place.

The ascertained disadvantages are not solely rooted in pension law, and consequently also do not only need to be remedied there. The circumstance placed in the foreground by the complainants, namely that because of the current legal situation, transfer payments are made from families with several children to families with one child and to the childless, who are anyway already better off, relates not only to the law on pensions, but over and above this also to equalisation of family burdens in general terms. It does permit one to reach the conclusion that the legislature has so far inadequately complied with the protection mandate of Article 6.1 of the Basic Law. Concrete conclusions for statutory pensions insurance can however not be derived from this. Rather, in principle the legislature is free in its decision as to how it intends to remedy the disadvantage to the family.

Insofar as the disadvantage is reflected particularly in the old-age pensions of the child-raising family members, it is primarily to be compensated for by pension law provisions. However, here too the legislature has not inconsiderable latitude at its disposal. In particular, no obligation is incumbent on the legislature from Article 3.1 in conjunction with Article 6.1 of the Basic Law as to the establishment of pension expectancies in which child-raising would be placed on the same footing as contribution payments. In view of the contribution procedure that has been practiced in pensions insurance since 1957, which is constitutionally unobjectionable, child-raising and contribution payment are not equivalent. In contradistinction to the monetary contributions of those in gainful employment, the contribution towards the maintenance of pensions insurance which is provided in the shape of child-raising cannot be immediately disbursed once more to the older generation in the shape of pension payments. The different function of both benefits for the pension system also justifies its unequal treatment in establishing pension expectancies.

On the other hand, the allowance of child-raising under pension law constitutes a suitable means, which is compatible with the pension insurance system, to compensate for the disadvantage in old-age pensions. By recognising child-raising periods as a pension-establishing and pension-increasing element in the Surviving Dependants' Pensions and Child-Raising Periods Act, the legislature has already taken a first step towards improving old-age pensions for child-rearers in the context of statutory pensions insurance, even though no factual reason is inherently obvious for the restriction to a value of 75 per cent of average income. An additional step consists of the extension of allowable child-raising periods, which was introduced by the 1992 Pensions Reform Act. That this reform, which does not lead to higher old-age pensions until the distant future, was not intended to complete the efforts towards further compensation is shown by the motion for a resolution introduced by the parliamentary groups of the CDU/CSU, SPD and F.D.P. parties of 21 June 1991 (*Bundestag* printed paper 12/837), accepted by the *Bundestag*, according to which the period until the expiry of the regulations for the protection of the status quo in the framework of the Pensions Transfer Act (*Renten-Überleitungsgesetz* – RÜG) is to be used to improve, in particular, the old-age pensions of women in benefit-related pensions insurance. To this end, above all, an expansion of the recognition of child-raising periods is to be included.

e) The legislature is allowed sufficient adjustment time in meeting the constitutional mandate (see BVerfGE 54, 11 (37); 80, 1 (26)). This applies in particular to reforms which – as here – require a high degree of regulation in various legal areas and considerable funds. The latitude available to the legislature would be impermissibly restricted if it were denied the possibility of realising such a complex reform as the allowance of child-raising periods in old-age pensions in several phases in order to limit the regulatory effort, as well as the financial consequences, and to remain amenable to the experience obtained in the course of the reform (see Federal Constitutional Court – BVerfG, Order of 5 November 1991 – 1 BvR 1256/89 –, *Zeitschrift für das gesamte Familienrecht* – FamRZ 1992, p. 157 (160)).

In establishing the reform steps, the legislature may accommodate the respective budget situation and the financial situation of statutory pensions insurance. However, the Federal Government and legislative bodies must comply with the constitutional mandate in refining pensions insurance and in both medium and longer term financial planning. Here they are not constitutionally restricted to applying only the funding of the Federation for the compensation. The protection of pension expectancies by Article 14.1 of the Basic Law does not oppose a moderate re-distribution within statutory pensions insurance against those with few or no children. Equally, the Basic Law provides latitude for a change to surviving dependants' pensions aiming in the case of widows' and widowers' pensions to concentrate more on the duration of the marriage and on whether the surviving spouse was prevented from acquiring his or her own old-age pension through child-raising or by providing long-term care services in the family. Regardless of the manner in which the funds are collected for compensation, it is certainly to be ensured that the disadvantage to the family is actually reduced with each phase of the reform. This must be recognisably taken into account by the legislature which is bound by the constitutional mandate.

3. Article 6.4 of the Basic Law cannot be applied as a review standard. Whether this provision provides protection to mothers beyond the time of pregnancy, and beyond the first months after birth, is immaterial. Certainly no special rights may be derived from it for elements which affect not only mothers. An interpretation of Article 6.4 of the Basic Law in the sense that (only) mothers are to be granted compensation for their child-raising activities in statutory pensions insurance is also opposed by Article 3.2 of the Basic Law, which prohibits a stipulation of traditional role distributions (see BVerfG, Judgment of 28 January 1992 …, *Europäische Grundrechte-Zeitschrift* – EuGRZ 1992, p. 17 (21)).

Having said that, the insufficient allowance of child-raising in statutory pensions insurance does work mainly to the disadvantage of mothers because mothers still largely take on child-raising today, and hence restrict, interrupt or give up altogether their gainful employment. These consequences, however, do not affect the area protected by Article 6.4 of the Basic Law. That women are affected to a much greater degree gives rise to the obligation ensuing from Article 3.2 of the Basic Law incumbent on the legislature to strive towards equalising the circumstances of women and men (see BVerfG, loc. cit.). The legislature will also have to take this into account.

4. With the impugned provisions, the legislature has not encroached on legal positions protected by Article 14.1 of the Basic Law. The protection of property is conditional on a legal position which is recognised by law (see BVerfGE 83, 201 (208-209)). Prior to the issuance of the Surviving Dependants' Pensions and Child-Raising Periods Act, however, there was no individual legal position on which the legislature could have encroached as to the allowance of child-raising periods. The Surviving Dependants' Pensions and Child-Raising Periods Act created these positions in the first place. The same applies to the child-raising benefits in accordance with the Child-Raising Benefits Act.

5. Details of the provisions which were enacted in the Surviving Dependants' Pensions and Child-Raising Periods Act and which do not impact the Child-Raising Benefits Act such as the provisions regulating the coincidence of child-raising periods with contribution periods, are not to be ruled on here. The complainants and the petitioners in the original proceedings of the judges' submissions have been constitutionally removed from the area of application of the Surviving Dependants' Pensions and Child-Raising Periods Act. Only the Child-Raising Benefits Act applies to them.

III.

The provisions of the Surviving Dependants' Pensions and Child-Raising Periods Act were also compatible with the Basic Law insofar as child-raising periods were not allowed for mothers born before 1921 in the calculation of their old-age pension paid on the occasion of their reaching the age of 65, and also no flat-rate benefits for child-raising were provided for this group of individuals. The Child-Raising Benefits Act was compatible with the Basic Law insofar as benefits for child-raising were not granted in accordance with it for the above group of individuals until times later than 1 January 1986. The unequal treatment of mothers born before 1921, on the one hand, and after 1921, on the other, is constitutionally unobjectionable.

1. The provision of the Surviving Dependants' Pensions and Child-Raising Periods Act (§ 1251a.1 of the Reich Insurance Code and § 28a.1 of the Salaried Employees Insurance Act) to be examined in this respect is a qualifying date regulation. Periods of child-raising were accordingly only to be allowed in the system of statutory pensions insurance for mothers and fathers born after 31 December 1920. In connection with this, Article 2 § 5c of the Wage-Earners' Pensions Insurance Reform Act (*Arbeiterrentenversicherungs-Neuregelungsgesetz* – ArVNG) and Article 2 § 6c of the Salaried Employees Insurance Reform Act permitted the allowance of child-raising performed prior to 1 January 1986 only with regard to insured events occurring after 30 December 1985.

The legislature is not prevented in principle by Article 3.1 of the Basic Law from introducing qualifying dates to provide for specific circumstances, even though each qualifying date unavoidably entails certain hardships. The selection of the time must however be orientated in line with the stated circumstance (BVerfGE 75, 108 (157)). This is the case here.

a) Since the legislature intended to gradually eliminate a deficiency in the system of statutory pensions insurance, it seemed obvious, and was factually justified, to place the provision in the area of pensions insurance. This was to allow for the structures of the pensions insurance system. This corresponded to the fact that the provision of the Surviving Dependants' Pensions and Child-Raising Periods Act was to be restricted to new pensions, and hence to birth years from 1921 onwards, whilst completed pension biographies were no longer to be re-activated. Mothers born before 1921 had, moreover, frequently not been in work because of the traditional distribution of roles between men and women, and hence had not acquired any pension expectancies (see *Bundesrat* printed paper 60/87, p. 20). The statutory goal to pay them a benefit for child-raising could hence only have been insufficiently realised with the solution contained in the Surviving Dependants' Pensions and Child-Raising Periods Act, which serves to establish pension expectancies and to increase pensions, and which – as has been explained – was justified as such for factual reasons. Whilst also women born from 1921 onwards in some cases do not have a pension entitlement, they were however still able to close gaps in their pension biographies by making voluntary contributions (see § 1233 of the Reich Insurance Code and § 10 of the Salaried Employees Insurance Act; now: § 7 of the Sixth Book of the Code of Social Law) and at least by these means would, on occurrence of the insured event, enjoy the benefits in accordance with the Surviving Dependants' Pensions and Child-Raising Periods Act. However, there was no such possibility for mothers born before 1921, who had already reached retirement age.

The pensions insurance organisations would also have been faced by almost insurmountable practical difficulties in the event of a qualifying date regulation other than that adopted by the legislature. At the time of the entry into force of the Surviving Dependants' Pensions and Child-Raising Periods Act on 1 January 1986, the pension biographies of mothers and fathers born before 1921 had already been concluded. As can be inferred from the statement of the Federation of German Pension Insurance Institutes (*Verband Deutscher Rentenversicherungsträger* – VDR), a total of 1,624,671 cases were ascertained in September 1989 of the payment of child-raising benefits for the birth years 1907 to 1911 inclusively. Allowing for the further birth years until the end of 1920, one had to presume 3.7 million cases. The pensions insurance organisations would not have had the staff to re-open such a large number of already concluded pension files in order to implement a pension re-calculation allowing for child-raising periods or, in cases of insured mothers not yet in statutory pensions insurance, to ascertain a pension for the first time.

b) If it was possible to select a pensions insurance law solution in the shape of the Surviving Dependants' Pensions and Child-Raising Periods Act, the circumstance of a lack of funding, which the legislature has presumed in the framework of its estimation prerogative, is a factual reason for not including in this provision mothers born before 1921. Financial considerations are particularly permissible in benefit statutes (see BVerfGE 75, 40 (72) with further references).

A provision that only covers the group of individuals which does not yet draw pensions (new pensions), only has a gradual effect. It is only when the insured event occurs (as a rule reaching the age of 65) that the provision has a direct impact on the individual. The benefits then to be granted only occur gradually. If, by contrast, the beneficiaries of pension payments (pension stock) were also to be included in such a provision, it would be necessary to grant the benefits to this group of individuals from entry into force of the statute onwards. The expenditure on this would be much higher than in the event of a provision that was restricted to new pensions. This also justifies the Surviving Dependants' Pensions and Child-Raising Periods Act not yet providing for flat-rate child-raising benefits for the birth years before 1921 – as later took place in the Child-Raising Benefits Act.
2. The provision that was created with the Child-Raising Benefits Act grants a child-raising benefit right to mothers of the birth years in question, corresponding to the amount granted in allowance of period of child-raising in the Surviving Dependants' Pensions and Child-Raising Periods Act. In contrast to the Surviving Dependants' Pensions and Child-Raising Periods Act, which came into force on 1 January 1986, the Child-Raising Benefits Act, however, provides for benefits to start on 1 October 1987 at the earliest. Hence, there is a benefit gap of at least 21 months for the group of individuals concerned. Since the legislature had provided for a phased arrangement within the birth years favoured by the Child-Raising Benefits Act orientated to the start of the benefit, furthermore, only mothers born before 1907 received the child-raising benefit from 1 October 1987 onwards. By contrast, mothers born later could only draw benefits for child-raising at a later time. Within the group of individuals favoured by the Child-Raising Benefits Act, the legislature had therefore distinguished in the start of benefit payment by the age of the mothers concerned. These distinctions too are factually justified.
One must proceed on the basis of the assessment reached by the legislature, namely that only limited funds were available for the period up to 1991, estimated at DM 6.05 billion. With the phased arrangement that was implemented, the legislature favoured the oldest birth years within the birth year groups affected, and accordingly placed in particular the group of the birth years from 1917 to 1920 at a disadvantage. Even if the fiscal efforts to save expenditure are not sufficient per se to justify differentiating treatment of different groups of individuals as a rule (see BVerfGE 19, 76 (84)), the solution must be accepted here because no other practicable solutions suggest themselves. The legislature could otherwise only have distributed the limited public funds in accordance with the principle of "something for everyone" (see BVerfGE 75, 40 (72) with further references). The possible benefits per child would have been much lower with such a provision than provided for by the Child-Raising Benefits Act. As the Federal Minister of Labour and Social Affairs af-

firmed in his statement, the introduction of the benefit for child-raising from 1 January 1986 onwards for all mothers concerned for 1986 would only have led to a benefit of DM 1.13 per month. The benefit amount would have only increased slightly for the ensuing years, and would have taken until 1990 to reach the amount provided for by the Child-Raising Benefits Act when it came into force. Something similar applies to the case of an equal granting of the benefit for child-raising to all the mothers concerned from 1 October 1987 onwards.

Ultimately, an even spread of the available funds to all mothers of the birth years in question for the implementation of the Child-Raising Benefits Act for 1986 to 1989 would not have entailed comparability with the allowance of child-raising periods within the meaning of the Surviving Dependants' Pensions and Child-Raising Periods Act since the benefits would have been much lower for a long time. Because of their lower life expectancy, the mothers born prior to 1907 would, in practical terms, have been placed at a great disadvantage compared to the younger mothers had the funds been distributed in this manner. The legislature, however, over and above merely fiscal considerations, used the available funds deliberately in order to benefit first chronologically the oldest among the birth years concerned as to their advanced age. This is not objectionable.

The phased arrangement contained in the Child-Raising Benefits Act is admittedly particularly disadvantageous for mothers born in 1920 in comparison to mothers born in 1921, who were already placed at an advantage by the Surviving Dependants' Pensions and Child-Raising Periods Act. However, a qualifying date regulation entails such hardships of necessity, and this must therefore be accepted (see BVerfGE 3, 58 (148); 49, 260 (275); 80, 297 (311)). One must however examine whether the legislature has properly used the latitude to which it is entitled, whether it has sufficiently taken into consideration the time-related factors and whether, with regard to the stated facts and to the system of the overall arrangement, the solution found can be justified by factual reasons, or whether it appears to be arbitrary (see BVerfGE 44, 1 (21-22); 80, 297 (311)). The provision, however, also stands up to a review using these criteria with regard to mothers born from 1917 to 1920. When handing down the Act, the legislature was able to take account of the fact that this group of individuals presumably would enjoy the child-raising benefits for longer, whilst this could not be presumed to the same degree among mothers of the earlier birth years because of the general life expectancy.

IV.

Finally, the regulation also does not violate Article 3.1 and Article 3.3 of the Basic Law in that fathers born before 1921 do not have a right to benefits in accordance

with the Child-Raising Benefits Act, whilst mothers of these years receive child-raising benefits and younger fathers are included in the area of the Surviving Dependants' Pensions and Child-Raising Periods Act.
The legislature presumed in this differentiating regulation that, in the cases covered by the Child-Raising Benefits Act, fathers typically did not take on child-raising, and that they had hence not incurred disadvantages in old-age pensions as a result of child-raising; this was said to be in line with the roles assumed within families that were typical of that time (*Bundesrat* printed paper 60/87, pp. 20-21). This view does not permit one to recognise a mistaken assessment (see also BVerfGE 39, 169 (187-188)). It justifies the exclusion of fathers from child-raising benefits in accordance with the Child-Raising Benefits Act, in particular in view of the goal pursued by the legislature to implement this Act with the least possible administrative effort.
…

Justices: Herzog, Henschel, Seidl, Grimm, Söllner, Dieterich, Kühling, Seibert

No. 23

BVerfGE 93, 373
of 16 January 1996 – 2 BvL 4/95 –
"Case involving a divorced couple's simultaneous membership of a municipal council"

HEADNOTE:

A prohibition of simultaneous membership of former spouses of a municipal council, as is provided for in the Municipal Code of Baden-Württemberg (*Gemeindeordnung für Baden-Württemberg* – GemO BW) in the case of municipalities with not more than 20,000 inhabitants, is incompatible with Article 28.1 sentence 2 of the Basic Law (*Grundgesetz* – GG).

Order of the Second Senate of 16 January 1996
– 2 BvL 4/95 –

in the proceedings for constitutional review as to whether § 29.2 sentence 1 in conjunction with § 18.1 no. 1 of the Municipal Code of Baden-Württemberg is compatible with Article 28.1 sentence 2 of the Basic Law to the extent that it does not permit former spouses to simultaneously be councillors in municipalities with not more than 20,000 inhabitants – suspension of proceedings and submission order of the Karlsruhe Administrative Court (*Verwaltungsgericht*) of 25 April 1995 (1 K 3231/94) –.

RULING:

§ 29.2 sentence 1 in conjunction with § 18.1 no. 1 of the Municipal Code of the *Land* (state) Baden-Württemberg (Law Gazette 1983 p. 578) is incompatible with the Basic Law and void to the extent that it does not permit former spouses in municipalities with not more than 20,000 inhabitants to be councillors simultaneously.

GROUNDS:

A. – I.

§ 29.2 of the Municipal Code of Baden-Württemberg in the version promulgated on 3 October 1983 (Law Gazette p. 578), most recently amended by Article 1 of the Act on the Amendment of Municipal Election Law and Municipal Law (*Gesetz zur Änderung des Kommunalwahlrechts und des Kommunalrechts*) of 8 November 1993 (Law Gazette p. 657), states:

> Persons who are personally liable members of the same commercial partnership/company may not be councillors simultaneously; in municipalities with not more than 20,000 inhabitants, persons whose relationship could give rise to bias pursuant to § 18.1 nos. 1 to 3 may also not be councillors simultaneously. If such persons are elected at the same time, the candidate with the most votes will become a municipal councillor. Where candidates receive the same number of votes, lots will be drawn to determine the successful candidate.

§ 18.1 nos. 1 to 3 of the Municipal Code of Baden-Württemberg lays down:

> Citizens who work on a voluntary basis may not advise on nor participate in decisions on matters which directly affect them or the following persons positively or negatively:
> 1. their spouse, former spouse or fiancé,
> 2. persons related either directly or up to the third degree by consanguinity,
> 3. persons related by either direct or second-degree affinity.

There is no equivalent of the prohibition of simultaneous municipal council membership by *divorced* spouses in the municipal constitutions of the other federal *Länder* (states). Bavarian municipal law excludes joint membership of spouses of a municipal council – in municipalities of up to 10,000 inhabitants – only *during an existing marriage.* The municipal codes of the other *Länder* are content with excluding municipal councillors *in specific cases* from involvement in matters which directly affect their spouses negatively or positively; this specific prohibition of involvement also affects *former* spouses in Hesse, Mecklenburg-West Pomerania, Rhineland-Palatinate, Saarland, Saxony and Schleswig-Holstein.

II.

In the municipal elections held in Baden-Württemberg on 12 June 1994, the plaintiff in the original proceedings and her divorced husband were elected to the municipal council in the municipality of Ketsch (12,451 inhabitants), which was sued in the original proceedings; the plaintiff was a candidate for the *Grün-Bunte Liste* and received 1,380 votes and her divorced husband was a candidate for the SPD and received 2,278 votes. The council resolved on 22 August 1994 that the previous marriage of the plaintiff was an obstacle to her membership of the council and thus that a substitute would become a member of the council in her place.
After the plaintiff was unsuccessful in administrative review proceedings, she commenced proceedings before the Karlsruhe Administrative Court. She alleged that the rule in § 29.2 sentence 1 in conjunction with § 18.1 no. 1 of the Municipal Code of Baden-Württemberg was not in conformity with the equal treatment of votes guaranteed by Article 28.1 sentence 2 of the Basic Law. According to the plaintiff, unlike in the cases where the fact that persons are related or still married is an obstacle to membership of the council, there is no objective reason preventing membership when persons are no longer married.

III.

The Karlsruhe Administrative Court suspended the proceedings in its order of 25 April 1995 and submitted to the Federal Constitutional Court (*Bundesverfassungsgericht*) for decision the question of whether § 29.2 sentence 1 in conjunction with § 18.1 no. 1 of the Municipal Code of Baden-Württemberg is compatible with Article 28.1 sentence 2 of the Basic Law in that the Code leads to former spouses not being able to be municipal councillors simultaneously in municipalities with not more than 20,000 inhabitants.
According to the Administrative Court, the question submitted for decision is essential for deciding this case. The plaintiff, who had received fewer votes than her divorced husband, was prevented from becoming a municipal councillor on the basis of § 29.2 sentence 1 of the Municipal Code of Baden-Württemberg. In the Administrative Court's view, if § 29.2 sentence 1 in conjunction with § 18.1 no. 1 of the Municipal Code of Baden-Württemberg is constitutional, then the challenged decisions were lawful and the claim will have to be dismissed. If on the other hand the provision submitted for review is incompatible with Article 28.1 sentence 2 of the Basic Law and void, then the decisions had no legal basis and the claim will have to be successful.

According to the Administrative Court, § 29.2 sentence 1 in conjunction with § 18.1 no. 1 of the Municipal Code of Baden-Württemberg is unconstitutional to the extent described in the suspension of proceedings and submission order. The Administrative Court is of the opinion that the formal character of the equal treatment of votes guaranteed by Article 28.1 sentence 2 of the Basic Law only gives the legislature a small amount of latitude for making distinctions when regulating voting rights; distinctions always require special, justifying and compelling reasons. No such reasons are said to be present here. In the Court's view, the risk of "cronyism and cliquism", which § 29.2 sentence 1 of the Municipal Code of Baden-Württemberg is supposed to prevent, is substantially less in the case of dissolved marriages than in the case of existing marriages. At all events, in municipalities whose number of inhabitants is just below 20,000 and whose municipal council has 22 members after all, the joint interests of (divorced) spouses are said to pose no danger. Furthermore, § 29.2 sentence 1 of the Municipal Code of Baden-Württemberg is said not to take into account that still existing ties weaken as the length of separation increases. The Administrative Court argues that since in addition the purpose of the provision submitted for review can be achieved by an exclusion from involvement in a specific case according to § 18.1 no. 1 of the Municipal Code of Baden-Württemberg, the right of divorced spouses to be elected (*passives Wahlrecht*) is excessively limited by the general prohibition of simultaneous membership of the council. The Court puts forward that also the fact that there are no such provisions in other *Länder* proves that such a prohibition is not necessary.
The *Land* government of Baden-Württemberg gave a statement on the referred case. It considers the provision submitted for review to be constitutional. The parties to the original proceedings have not given their opinions.

B. – I.

The submission is admissible. The Administrative Court has provided evidence satisfying the requirements of Article 100.1 of the Basic Law and § 80.2 sentence 1 of the Federal Constitutional Court Act (*Bundesverfassungsgerichtsgesetz* – BVerfGG) that its decision depends on the validity of § 29.2 sentence 1 in connection with § 18.1 no. 1 of the Municipal Code of Baden-Württemberg. It has also submitted evidence and provided reasons sufficient to justify its opinion that the provision is unconstitutional.

II.

§ 29.2 sentence 1 of the Municipal Code of Baden-Württemberg in conjunction with § 18.1 no. 1 of the Municipal Code of Baden-Württemberg is incompatible with Article 28.1 sentence 2 of the Basic Law and void to the extent that it does not permit former spouses in municipalities with not more than 20,000 inhabitants to be municipal councillors simultaneously.

1. The principle that each vote must be treated equally in the municipalities is guaranteed by Article 28.1 sentence 2 of the Basic Law. It applies in the same way to the right to vote for others (*aktives Wahlrecht*) and the right to be elected (see Decisions of the Federal Constitutional Court (*Entscheidungen des Bundesverfassungsgerichts* – BVerfGE 11, 266 (272); 48, 64 (81); 57, 43 (56)). According to the principle every person should be able to exercise his or her right to vote in a way which is as similar as possible in formal terms (see BVerfGE 11, 266 (272); 41, 399 (413); 69, 92 (105-106); 71, 81 (94); 82, 322 (337); 85, 148 (157); most recently 89, 266 (270)). Of course distinctions based on the views and circumstances considered significant in the relevant legal communities (see BVerfGE 1, 208 (249); 82, 322 (338)) can also not be completely excluded in this area. Nevertheless, the legislature has only a small amount of latitude given the fact that the principle that each vote should be treated equally is of great significance for the free democratic fundamental order. Compelling reasons are always needed for distinctions (established case-law, see BVerfGE 4, 375 (382-383); 6, 84 (94); most recently 82, 322 (338)).

The principle that each person should be able to formally exercise his or her rights as a citizen in as similar a way as possible does not just apply to the exercise of the right to vote for others and the right to be elected in a narrow sense, but also to the acceptance and exercise of a mandate won (see BVerfGE 38, 326 (338); 40, 296 (317); 48, 64 (88); 57, 43 (67); Decisions of the Bavarian Administrative Court, *Entscheidungen des Bayerischen Verfassungsgerichtshofs* – BayVerfGHE new, 29, 143 (147)). The principle excludes also at the municipal level the possibility of denying an elected candidate the right to accept and exercise a mandate that he or she has won (Article 28.1 sentence 2 of the Basic Law) if there is no compelling reason for doing so.

2. No compelling reason exists for discriminating against divorced spouses pursuant to § 29.2 sentence 1 in conjunction with § 18.1 no. 1 of the Municipal Code of Baden-Württemberg.

a) It is generally thought that the prohibition of the simultaneous council membership of persons who are related by affinity or consanguinity will prevent the risk of unfair protective practices resulting from the excessive influence of individual families ("cronyism and cliquism") and thus avoid from the start inhabitants' mistrusting the work of the municipal council (see State Court (*Staatsgerichtshof* – StGH) of Baden-Württemberg, ESVGH 31, 167 (168-169); Judgment of the Karlsruhe Administrative Court of 15 January 1982, – 5 K 248/80 –, p. 8; Kunze/Bronner/Katz/von Rotberg, *Gemeindeordnung für Baden-Württemberg*, 4th ed. (loose-leaf), *§ 29,* marginal no. 8; similarly for the comparable provision in Article 31.3 of the Municipal Code of Bavaria (*Bayerische Gemeindeordnung* – BayGemO): BayVerfGHE new, 14, 77 (83-84); 29, 143 (148); 36, 83 (90); Hölzl/Hien, *Gemeindeordnung mit Verwaltungsgemeinschaftsordnung, Landkreisordnung und Bezirksordnung für den Freistaat Bayern*, 1994, *§ 31*, comment 6; Widtmann/Grasser, *Bayerische Gemeindeordnung*, 5th ed., marginal no. 9; Masson/Samper, *Bayerische Kommunalgesetze*, 1994, marginal no. 7). In this connection, there can only be an attempt to prevent risks that arise especially from the joint council membership of persons who are related in such a way. On the one hand, such risks can arise from the possibility of promoting jointly and thus *with greater force* one's own interests or the interests of third parties (see on this BayVerfGHE new, 14, 77 (83) (re Article 31.3 of the Municipal Code of Bavaria). On the other hand, the possibility cannot be excluded that members of the municipal council who are closely connected will be influenced in consultations and votes through their taking existing personal ties into account and thus not be guided by their own convictions alone.

b) It is not necessary to decide here whether the goal of preventing these risks in municipalities with less than 20,000 inhabitants through a general exclusion is a compelling reason for a prohibition of joint council membership for *married, engaged* or *closely related* persons. At all events, these risks in respect of *divorced* couples of which there has been no special discussion during the legislative process (see Publication of the *Land* parliament (*LTDrucks.*) supplement 1060 of 4 December 1954, p. 1376 as well as the debates of the *Land* parliament (*Landtag*) of Baden-Württemberg 1/3203 et seq. (3212-3213)) are so low that – even if one takes into account a certain scope of assessment which the principles that formally each vote should be treated in the same way allow the legislature – they cannot be a *compelling* reason for a general prohibition of simultaneous council membership.

aa) Experience shows that spouses no longer jointly pursue personal interests to any mentionable extent after a divorce since marital union, which can be a reason for joint action in a municipal council, has ceased. At all events, the risk of their jointly promoting their own foreign interests or the foreign interests of third parties can be regarded as much lower in such cases than in the case of members of a municipal council who have a close personal or professional relationship to one another. Such joint interests will give citizens of the municipality more reason to be mistrustful than any continuing ties between divorced spouses after the dissolution of their

marriage. The prohibition of involvement in § 18.1 no. 1 of the Municipal Code of Baden-Württemberg may take account of bias based on such reasons; however it does not justify allowing an exception to the principle that formally each vote should be treated in the same way.
bb) The risk that a council member might vote in the municipal council against his or her own political conviction because of his or her personal ties must be assessed as low in the case of divorced spouses. Usually the reason couples divorce is precisely because those kind of personal ties no longer exist. If in an individual case a "personal relationship with a negative character" (see Masson/Samper, loc. cit, *§ 31*, marginal no. 7) should continue to exist, the idea that a divorced spouse would against his or her own convictions reject decisions favoured by the other spouse because of his or her dislike for such other person is nevertheless far-fetched. An exceptional situation of such kind in which a municipal council member would violate in a special manner the commitment to the public good imposed on him or her by § 32.3 of the Municipal Code of Baden-Württemberg cannot be a reason to assume that there is a compelling reason to allow an exception to the principle that each vote should be treated in the same way.
cc) In Baden-Württemberg too no legal view has been handed down to the population nor is one currently held by it that could be suitable for justifying a different assessment with regard to *divorced* spouses. A tradition of such kind is ascertainable only for the prohibition of simultaneous council membership for closely related persons and also spouses *during an existing marriage.*

> § 6.3 and § 6.4 of the Württemberg Administrative Edict for Municipalities, Government Administrations and Foundations (*Württembergisches Verwaltungsedikt für die Gemeinden, Oberämter und Stiftungen*) of 1 March 1822 and § 13 no. 4 sentences 1 and 2 of the (Baden) Act on the Constitution and Administration of Municipalities (*(Badisches) Gesetz über die Verfassung und Verwaltung der Gemeinden*) of 31 December 1831 had prohibited the simultaneous membership of close relatives in a municipal council (see Engeli/Haus, *Quellen zum modernen Gemeindeverfassungsrecht in Deutschland*, 1975, p. 164 (165); p. 208 (210)); § 20.2 of the Baden Municipal Code (*Badische Gemeindeordnung*) of 5 October 1921 (Law Gazette (*Gesetz- und Verordnungsblatt* – GVBl) pp. 347 et seq., 414), Article 59.1 of the Municipal Code (*Gemeindeordnung*) of 19 March 1930 (Government Law Gazette (*Regierungsblatt*) of the *Land* Württemberg pp. 45 et seq.), § 28.1 of the Municipal Code of the *Land* Württemberg-Hohenzollern (*Gemeindeordnung für das Land Württemberg-Hohenzollern*) of 14 March 1947 (Government Law Gazette of the *Land* Württemberg-Hohenzollern 1948, pp. 1 et seq.), § 28.1 of the Baden Municipal Code of 23 Septem-

ber 1948 (Baden Law Gazette pp. 177 et seq.), Article 10.1 of the Act on the Preliminary Approximation of Municipal Law (*Gesetz zur vorläufigen Angleichung des Kommunalrechts*) of 13 July 1953 (Baden-Württemberg Law Gazette pp. 97 et seq.) and finally § 29.2 of the Municipal Code of Baden-Württemberg of 25 July 1955 have continued this tradition uninterrupted (except during the National Socialist era) into the present. Since the introduction in 1919 of the right of women to vote for others and the right of women to be elected, the relevant criteria have included without exception spouses during an existing marriage.

There is also no comparable legal tradition for *divorced* spouses apparent in Baden-Württemberg. Prior to the Municipal Code of 25 July 1955 there had never been a prohibition of simultaneous council membership of divorced spouses in the municipal laws of Baden and Württemberg. Even at the time the "Act on the Preliminary Approximation of Municipal Law" was created in 1953, the *Land* constitutional convention had expressly rejected the extension of the prohibition contained in the legislative draft (see supplement no. 852 of 13 June 1953 on the protocols of the sittings of the *Land* constitutional convention) due to doubts about its constitutionality in view of Article 3.1 of the Basic Law (see Vol. III of the Protocol of the Debates of the *Land* Constitutional Convention of Baden-Württemberg (*Protokolle der Verhandlungen der Verfassunggebenden Landesversammlung von Baden-Württemberg*), 47th sitting of 7 July 1953, pp. 2152-2153).
Finally, the legislature in also including divorced spouses in the prohibition of 1955 was not guided by any legal policy demands raised publicly, but solely by considerations related to the structure of the legal system.

Since already according to the law in force at the time (Article 10.1 no. 3 of the Act on the Preliminary Approximation of Municipal Law), persons *related by marriage* were by virtue of the *mutatis mutandis* application of § 1590.2 of the Civil Code (*Bürgerliches Gesetzbuch*) still considered biased within the meaning of § 18.1 of the Municipal Code of Baden-Württemberg irrespective of the dissolution of the marriage leading to the affinity, it appeared necessary to the legislature for reasons of logic that the situation should be no different for *divorced spouses* as "directly involved parties" (see on this Publication of the *Land* parliament of Baden-Württemberg, supplement 1060 of 4 December 1954, p. 1373). This extension which was tailored to the specific prohibition of involvement in § 18.1 no. 1 of the Municipality Code of Baden-Württemberg was then carried over to the general prohibition of simultaneous council membership without any further discussion (see Publication of the *Land* parliament supplement 1060 of 4 December 1954, p. 1376, as well as the debates of the *Land* parliament of Baden-Württemberg 1/3203 et seq. (3212-3213)).

Justices: Limbach, Böckenförde, Klein, Graßhof, Kruis, Kirchhof, Winter, Sommer

As a result of the Federal Constitutional Court's decision, the legislature of the Land *Baden-Württemberg, by Article 1 no. 3 of the Act on the Amendment of the Municipal Constitution* (Gesetz zur Änderung der Kommunalverfassung) *of 16 July 1998 (Baden-Württemberg Law Gazette 1998, p. 418), deleted "former spouse" from the list of grounds giving rise to bias in § 18 of the Municipal Code.*

No. 24

BVerfGE 96, 56
of 6 May 1997 – 1 BvR 409/90 –
"Case concerning information about father's identity"

HEADNOTES:

1. **A certain outcome for the question whether an illegitimate child has a claim against its mother for identification of the father is neither prescribed on the basis of the child's right to know its descent that is protected under Article 2.1 in conjunction with Article 1.1 of the Basic Law (*Grundgesetz* – GG), nor under Article 6.5 of the Basic Law.**
2. **The courts have substantial discretion when weighing between the conflicting constitutional rights of the mother and the child respectively, when applying general clauses under civil law – such as § 1618a of the Civil Code (*Bürgerliches Gesetzbuch* – BGB) invoked by the court in the present case.**

Order of the First Senate of 6 May 1997
– 1 BvR 409/90 –

in the proceedings concerning the constitutional complaint filed by Ms. B. – authorised representatives: …, lawyers – against the judgment of the Münster Regional Court (*Landgericht*) of 21 February 1990 – 1 S 414/89.

RULING:

1. The judgment of the Münster Regional Court of 21 February 1990 – 1 S 414/89 – violates the complainant's constitutional rights under Article 2.1 in conjunction with Article 1.1 of the Basic Law. The judgment is reversed. The case is referred back to the Regional Court.
2. …

EXTRACT FROM GROUNDS:

A.

The constitutional complaint concerns the question whether and, if so, subject to what requirements the mother has to provide information about the identity of the biological father to an adult illegitimate child.

1. a) In the original proceedings the complainant was sued by her illegitimate daughter born in 1959 for information about the name and address of her biological father. The daughter had been placed in a children's home shortly after her birth and had later been brought up by foster parents. In the grounds for her request she stated that she wanted to learn of her father's identity for personal reasons and in order to assert inheritance claims or substitutional claims in the estate that accrue to illegitimate children (*Erbersatzansprüche*). She also wanted her father to be identified in the registers and deeds of civil status.

In contrast, the complainant argued in particular that she had had sexual relations with several men during the period of conception by statutory presumption, who in the meantime were married and living in intact families. She argued that she therefore did not need to identify these men.

b) The Local Court (*Amtsgericht*) affirmed the plaintiff's claim for identification of her biological father. It was held that the claim arose under § 1618a in conjunction with §§ 1934a et seq. of the Civil Code, while taking into account the constitutional requirement of equality under Article 6.5 of the Basic Law. In order to assert its inheritance claims, the illegitimate child depended on its mother's support since it could only raise such claims with knowledge of its biological father's identity. However, in an individual case it was considered necessary to examine whether the child's duty to take the mother's interests into account conflicted with a claim for information. It was held that the plaintiff's interests superseded the complainant's right to safeguard her general right of personality. The duty to identify a sexual partner is by no means a minor intervention. However, it was held that the complainant was not entitled to avoid her obligation towards her daughter. The principle that the child's interest take precedence over those of the parents on the grounds that the parents are responsible for the existence of the illegitimate child apply here especially because the personal mother-child relationship ended through the placement of the child in a children's home and subsequently in a foster family so that the daughter's obligation to take the mother's interests into account was to be deemed very minor.

2. In the decision being challenged, in accordance with the plaintiff's auxiliary request, the Regional Court amended the judgment of the Local Court insofar as it

ordered the complainant to provide information, including the names and addresses, about the men with whom she had had sexual relations in the period between the 181st day and the 302nd day before her daughter's birth.
An order to identify the biological father was not possible because the court was not convinced that the complainant knew precisely who the plaintiff's father was. However, she had stated that she knew the men who came into question as the father. It was held that the claim for information accrued under § 1618a of the Civil Code in conjunction with Article 6.5, Article 2.1 and Article 14.1 of the Basic Law. According to the statutory material, § 1618a of the Civil Code was intended to be a guideline without sanctions. In individual cases, however, the provision could establish directly enforceable rights and obligations, in particular obligations to provide information. Interests protected by constitutional rights are required however for recognition of a legal obligation based directly on § 1618a of the Civil Code, in order to prevent an overly broad interpretation of the provision. Such interests were given in the present context, it was held.
The plaintiff's financial claims to be asserted with the aid of the information are protected by Article 14.1 of the Basic Law, it was held. Furthermore, her right to know her descent based on Article 2.1 in conjunction with Article 1.1 of the Basic Law as well as her claim for equality under Article 6.5 of the Basic Law were also affected. The plaintiff depended on information from her mother in order to realise her interests protected by constitutional law, it was held.
The weighing of this interest against the complainant's interest in protecting her private sphere resulted in the plaintiff's interest taking precedence. Insofar as the previous case-law of the highest courts assumed that the mother did not have to reveal the father's identity in view of protection of her private sphere, the matters concerned fiscal interests of the state or the continuation of official guardianship. Here, in contrast, the mother's rights of personality conflicted with the interests of the illegitimate child that were protected by constitutional law. In this relationship the mother's interests were secondary in rank. Discriminatory treatment of the illegitimate child in relation to a legitimate child only came into question if it was indicated by fundamental interests of the mother which superseded those of the child. It was held that since enforcement of one right was only possible by restricting the other right, the matter depended on who was responsible for the conflict between the different interests, in which respect discriminatory treatment of the illegitimate child was to be avoided as far as possible. It was held that this applied especially to the pecuniary interests of the child, which could only be pursued with knowledge of the father's identity. Denial of a claim for identification of the father would de facto result in renunciation of a future inheritance.

The argument presented by the complainant that several – in the meantime married – men came into question as the father, had to be taken into account in her favour when weighing the interests; however, it was held not to justify discriminatory treatment of the child through refusal of the claim for information. Consideration did have to be given to the fact that several men could be involved in a procedure to determine paternity although they were not the plaintiff's father. It was however held that there was a general risk in life of being exposed to unjustified claims. Even after 30 years, the father of an illegitimate child could not demand that his paternity be kept secret.

II.

1. With her constitutional complaint the complainant objects to a violation of her constitutional right under Article 2.1 of the Basic Law through the appeal judgment rendered by the Regional Court.

…

2. The plaintiff in the original proceedings defends the challenged decision.

B.

The admissible constitutional complaint is well-founded.

I.

The judgment ordering the complainant to identify the men with whom she had sexual relations during the period of conception by statutory presumption encroaches upon her privacy that is protected by Article 2.1 in conjunction with Article 1.1 of the Basic Law.

1. The general right of personality based on Article 2.1 in conjunction with Article 1.1 of the Basic Law protects the closer personal sphere and preservation of its fundamental terms (see Decisions of the Federal Constitutional Court (*Entscheidungen des Bundesverfassungsgerichts* – BVerfGE) 54, 148 (153-154); 79, 256 (268)). It includes, *inter alia*, the right to respect of privacy (see BVerfGE 89, 69 (82-83)). This includes the family sphere and personal, also sexual, relations with a partner (see BVerfGE 27, 344 (350-351)). Moreover, the general right of personality protect the power of an individual person to decide him- or herself the extent to which and to whom he or she will disclose personal matters (see BVerfGE 65, 1 (43-44)).

2. However, the general right of personality is not guaranteed unreservedly. Unless the inviolable sphere of private life is affected, individuals have to accept restric-

tions imposed in the overriding public interest or in view of third-party interests that are protected by constitutional law, yet subject to strict safeguarding of proportionality (see BVerfGE 65, 1 (44)).
In the present context there is no interference with the inviolable sphere of private life since the relationship about which information is being demanded yielded the daughter who filed suit as the third party whose privacy is severely affected.

II.

The Regional Court based its decision on § 1618a of the Civil Code in conjunction with Article 6.5, Article 2.1 and Article 14.1 of the Basic Law. This does not amount to an inadmissible further development of the law (1.). However, the Regional Court failed to recognise the discretion that the competent government bodies have when exercising their protective obligations under Article 2.1 in conjunction with Article 1.1 of the Basic Law as well as when fulfilling their responsibilities under Article 6.5 of the Basic Law (2.).
1. The question whether an illegitimate child has a claim against its mother for identification of the father is not explicitly regulated by law. § 1618a of the Civil Code, the provision taken as the basis of the claim by the Regional Court, only stipulates generally that parents and children owe one another support and consideration. This merely serves to clarify that in relations between parents and children, performance and claim are reciprocal depending on the capabilities and needs involved. The legislature refused to impose sanctions for violations of the provision; it was to serve as a principle while also being capable of filling gaps in family law (see *Bundestag* printed paper (*Bundestagsdrucksache* – BTDrucks.) 8/2788, p. 36).
In the past a claim for information accruing to the child was denied in the case-law of the highest courts; however, the mother's refusal to identify the father could have other legal consequences, especially the continuation of official guardianship (see Decisions of the Federal Court of Justice in Civil Matters (*Entscheidungen des Bundesgerichtshofes in Zivilsachen* – BGHZ 82, p. 173).
In judgments of the Passau Local Court and of the Passau Regional Court from 1987, § 1618a of the Civil Code was taken as the basis of a claim accruing to an illegitimate child against its mother for identification of the biological father (see *Zeitschrift für das gesamte Familienrecht* – FamRZ 1987, p. 1309; 1988, p. 210). A constitutional complaint against these decisions was not admitted for decision by a Chamber of the Constitutional Court (FamRZ 1989, p. 147).
In deriving the claim for information against the mother from § 1618a of the Civil Code, the Regional Court did not exceed the bounds of an inadmissible further development of the law. The court addressed both the previous case-law of the high-

est courts which denied a claim for information of the youth welfare offices and government bodies, and also took into account the legislative history of the provision when interpreting § 1618a of the Civil Code. The considerations of the court are plausible and do not permit the conclusion that it was objectively unwilling to subject itself to law and justice, but, rather, from playing the role of a body applying provisions became an instance that determines provisions (see BVerfGE 87, 273 (280)).

2. However, the complainant's right of personality has been violated by the judgment being contested, because the Regional Court failed to recognise at her expense that it had further scope for consideration of the interests.

a) A certain outcome for the question whether an illegitimate child has a claim against its mother for identification of the father is neither prescribed on the basis of the child′s right to know its descent that is protected under Article 2.1 in conjunction with Article 1.1 of the Basic Law, nor under Article 6.5 of the Basic Law. Rather, the question whether such a claim accrues has to be decided by the legislature or by the courts when fulfilling their protective obligation ensuing from constitutional rights.

The general right of personality does include the right to know one's own descent. However, Article 2.1 in conjunction with Article 1.1 of the Basic Law does not grant a right to obtain such knowledge, but, rather, only affords protection against the refusal of government bodies to provide obtainable information (see BVerfGE 79, 256 (269)).

Likewise, one cannot infer from Article 6.5 of the Basic Law how the equality of illegitimate children regarding knowledge of their biological fathers, against whom claims for maintenance or inheritance claims could be directed, can be realised. Absolute equality with legitimate children is impossible simply because a child born within a marriage has a legal father according to statutory provisions, who is not necessarily the child's biological father.

No specific standards can be derived from Article 14.1 of the Basic Law for provisions of substantive and procedural law in order to enable an illegitimate child to realise its claim for a share in the inheritance of its biological father.

b) However, a protective obligation incumbent on government bodies does follow from Article 2.1 in conjunction with Article 1.1 of the Basic Law, which obligation also relates to the guarantee of constitutive conditions for personal development (see BVerfGE 54, 148 (153); 79, 256 (268)).

The subjective rights of defence against government interference on the one hand, based primarily on constitutional rights, and protective obligations ensuing from the objective significance of constitutional rights, on the other hand, are fundamentally different from one another in that the object and substance of the right of defence calls for certain conduct of the state, whereas the protective obligation is indefinite in principle. The government bodies themselves decide at their own responsibility as to how they will fulfil their protective obligations (see BVerfGE 46, 160 (164)). As a matter of principle, this applies not only to cases in which there are several possibilities of realising the protection required by the Basic Law. Rather, it is the responsibility of the competent government bodies in each case to weigh the conflicting constitutional rights and to take into account the potential negative consequences of a certain form of fulfilling the protective obligation.

In its established case-law the Federal Constitutional Court has therefore emphasised that the establishment and normative implementation of a concept of protection is the legislature's responsibility, which in principle has scope for assessment, valuation and action even where it is under an obligation to take measures in order to protect legal interests (see BVerfGE 88, 203 (262)).

The same applies where the courts of civil law fulfil the protective obligation by further developing the law or by interpreting undefined legal terms in the absence of a decision by the legislature (see on this point BVerfGE 84, 212 (226-227)), or where this obligation has to be fulfilled by an executive organ (see BVerfGE 46, 160 (164)). Only in exceptional cases can specific regulatory obligations be derived from constitutional rights. There is regulatory scope especially where conflicting constitutional rights have to be taken into account. This also applies where – as in the present case – the protection of a constitutional right necessarily encroaches upon the constitutional right of another person because the competent government bodies in the relevant case are primarily responsible for weighing the interests involved.

Similar considerations apply to the responsibility assigned primarily to the legislature under Article 6.5 of the Basic Law, which has to be taken into account by the courts when applying the law in force. It follows from Article 6.5 of the Basic Law that illegitimate children may not be treated worse than legitimate children on principle, unless grounds justifying unequal treatment arise from their particular situation. However, absolute equality is not possible in the present context simply because the statutory provisions concerning legitimate children depend on the mother's marriage, not on who the biological father is. On the other hand, in these cases the present conflict of interests does not arise for the mother.

c) The Regional Court failed to recognise its scope for weighing the interests. The court did not derive the illegitimate child's claim for information against her mother directly from the Basic Law, but, rather, from a provision of civil law. However, in applying § 1618a of the Civil Code, the court assumed a constitutionally protected interest of the illegitimate child which only permits a weighing with the mother's interests within narrow confines. In particular, the question considered decisive by the Regional Court, namely "who is responsible for the conflict of different interests," excludes the possibility of sufficient consideration of the conflicting interests, because the child is never responsible for the conflict created through its conception by its parents.

The Regional Court also saw a very narrow scope when weighing the specific interests involved. It did acknowledge that the complainant had a heightened interest in not having to identify the men with whom she had had sexual relations during the period of conception by statutory presumption. Ultimately, however, the court did not lend significant weight to this aspect since it granted precedence to the interests of the illegitimate child over those of the mother and the men concerned, without specifically weighing the interests.

It is possible that the Regional Court would have reached a different conclusion if it had fully utilised its scope for weighing the interests involved.

III.

The decision contested therefore has to be reversed and the case referred back to the Regional Court. The Federal Constitutional Court does not have to decide the question, disputed in the literature, as to whether a lawsuit seeking the provision of information such as the present one has to be qualified as a case concerning parents and child, the consequence being that the Higher Regional Court would have jurisdiction for the appeal.

Justices: Seidl, Grimm, Kühling, Seibert, Jaeger, Haas, Hömig, Steiner

No. 25

BVerfGE 97, 332
of 10 March 1998 – 1 BvR 178/97 –
"Graduated kindergarten contributions case"

HEADNOTE:

Kindergarten fees can in principle be graduated by family income.

Order of the First Senate of 10 March 1998
– 1 BvR 178/97 –

in the proceedings regarding the constitutional complaint I. of Ms. S., II. of Mr. R. – authorised representatives: ..., lawyers – 1) directly against a) the order of the Federal Administrative Court (*Bundesverwaltungsgericht*) of 20 February 1996 – BVerwG 8 NB 1.96 –, b) the order of the Hesse Higher Administrative Court (*Hessischer Verwaltungsgerichtshof*) of 26 October 1995 – 5 N 1791/94 –, c) § 2 of the Statutes on Fees for Utilisation of the Kindergartens of the town of Idstein (*Satzung über die Gebühren für die Benutzung der Kindergärten der Stadt Idstein*) of 11 March 1994, 2. indirectly against a) § 10 of the Hesse Kindergarten Act (*Hessisches Kindergartengesetz*) in the version of the Third Act Amending the Hesse Kindergarten Act (*Drittes Gesetz zur Änderung des Hessischen Kindergartengesetzes*) of 21 June 1993 (Law and Ordinance Gazette (*Gesetz- und Verordnungsblatt* – GVBl) I p. 256), b) § 90.1 sentence 2 of the Eighth Book of the Code of Social Law (*Achtes Buch Sozialgesetzbuch* – SGB VIII) in the version promulgated on 3 May 1993 (Federal Law Gazette (*Bundesgesetzblatt* – BGBl) I p. 637).

RULING:

The constitutional complaint is rejected as unfounded.

EXTRACT FROM GROUNDS:

A.

The constitutional complaint relates to the levying of kindergarten fees which are graduated by family income.

I.

1. The complainants are parents of a child who attended a kindergarten in the town of Idstein. The town levied a fee for this. No decision has yet been handed down with regard to the objection filed against this fee. They challenged the Fee Statutes (*Gebührensatzung*) on which the notice is based in administrative-court proceedings on the constitutionality of a statute.
2. The relevant provisions of the Kindergarten Fee Statutes (*Kindergartengebührensatzung* – KiGaGebS) of the town of Idstein of 11 March 1994 read as follows:

§ 1
General

(1) The legal representatives of the children shall pay fees for the use of the kindergartens. Several parties obliged to pay fees shall be liable as joint and several debtors. The fees shall be broken down into the fee for care and the fee for meals.
(2) The fee for care shall be payable for attendance at the kindergarten.
(3) …
(4) …

§ 2
Care fees

(1) The fee for care per month for the care of a child shall be, for the period from 1 April 1994 to 31 December 1995, DM 217.00 in a half-day place, DM 263.00 in a six-hour place, DM 309.00 in a morning-afternoon place and DM 355.00 in an all-day place.
For the period from 1 January 1996 …
(2) …
(3) Over and above this, the care fee shall be reduced according to the number of the children of a family entitled to child benefit not attending a kindergarten.

The fee rate in accordance with the Fees Code shall be reduced in such cases if so requested by the persons with parental rights:
a) 10 per cent for families with one child,
b) 20 per cent for families with two children,
c) 30 per cent for families with three children,
d) 50 per cent for families with four and more children.
(4) The fee set in subsections 1 and 2 can be reduced on request. The care fee shall be reduced for the period from 1 April 1994 to 31 December 1995 according to monthly gross family income as follows:

Monthly gross family income	Half-day place	Six-hour place	Morning-afternoon place	All-day place
DM	DM	DM	DM	DM
>= 10,001	217.00	263.00	309.00	355.00
9,501-10,000	208.00	252.00	296.00	340.00
...				
4,001-4,500	109.00	131.00	153.00	175.00
<= 4,000	100.00	120.00	140.00	160.00

The care fee shall be reduced as follows for the period from 1 January 1996:
...
(5) Monthly gross family income within the meaning of subsection 4 shall be deemed to be the gross annual income of the previous calendar year of all family members divided by twelve. Offsetting against losses shall not be permissible.
(6) ...
(7) ...

In accordance with § 10.1 of the Hesse Local Authority Levies Act (*Hessisches Kommunalabgabengesetz* – KAG), the local authorities can levy usage fees in counter payment for the use of their public facilities which is to be measured by the nature and extent to which the facility is used (§ 10.3 sentence 1 of the Hesse Local Authority Levies Act). By contrast, § 10 of the Hesse Kindergarten Act (*Hessisches Kindergartengesetz* – KiGaG) of 14 December 1989 in the version of the Act of 21 June 1993 (Law and Ordinance Gazette I p. 256) provides for a levy for the use of kindergartens which is graduated by income group and number of children. The provision reads as follows:

Attendance contributions and fees, special support for parents

The attendance contributions or fees payable for attendance at kindergartens can be graduated by income group and number of children.

§ 90.1 of the Eighth Book of the Code of Social Law in the version promulgated on 3 May 1993 (Federal Law Gazette I p. 637) contains the following provision on this matter:

Attendance contributions or fees can be set for the utilisation of services

1. of youth work in accordance with § 11,
2. of the general promotion of child-raising within the family in accordance with § 16.1 and 16.2 nos. 1 and 3, and
3. of the promotion of children in day facilities in accordance with §§ 22 and 24. *Land* law may prescribe graduation of the attendance contributions and fees payable for the utilisation of the day facilities for children, by income group and number of children, or by the number of family members, or may itself set accordingly graduated contributions.

3. The Hesse Higher Administrative Court rejected the application for proceedings on the constitutionality of a statute. The Kindergarten Statutes were said to be lawful in formal and substantive terms. The general empowerment of the town of Idstein to enact statutes was said to emerge from § 5 of the Hesse Municipal Code (*Hessische Gemeindeordnung*). The levy at dispute was said to be a utilisation fee the levying of which was permitted in accordance with § 10 of the Hesse Local Authority Levies Act. The town of Idstein was said to have been able to graduate this fee by the respective family income. In principle, a strictly service-based assessment principle was said to apply in accordance with § 10.3 of the Hesse Local Authority Levies Act which in the previous case-law of the Senate had been referred to as a principle of specific quid pro quo. This principle was however said to have been effectively modified by § 10 of the Hesse Kindergarten Act for the assessment of kindergarten fees.

The graduation of fees by income and number of children was said to comply with the federal law provision contained in § 90.1 sentence 2 of the Eighth Book of the Code of Social Law. It was said that the federal legislature had wished by means of this provision to explicitly avert the differences of opinion regarding the permissibility of such a graduation and to create a possibility for appropriate *Land* law provisions. Accordingly, the *Land* legislature was said to be able either to set the concrete structure of the graduation of fees itself or to leave them for regulation by the local authorities according to their own duty-bound discretion.

The possibility granted by § 90.1 sentence 2 of the Eighth Book of the Code of Social Law and § 10 of the Hesse Kindergarten Act to differentiate the attendance contributions and fees according to income was also said to violate neither Article 3.1 or Article 6.1 of the Basic Law (*Grundgesetz* – GG). That erroneous use could be made of the empowerment in individual cases, and that the concrete implementation could violate fundamental rights, was said not of itself to make the empowerment constitutionally objectionable. It was said to be based on expedient considerations. § 10 of the Hesse Kindergarten Act in conjunction with § 90.1 sentence 2 of the Eighth Book of the Code of Social Law was said to be intended to guarantee that lower-income families could also send their children to kindergarten. The provisions were hence said to serve the protection of the family required by Article 6.1 of the Basic Law.

The Statutes were also said not to be objectionable in other respects. The cost coverage principle was said to leave scope for social considerations. In accordance with § 93.2 no. 1 of the Hesse Municipal Code, the local authority only had to acquire the income necessary to implement its tasks from the fees for its services "where justifiable and necessary". In accordance with the comprehensible calculation carried out by the town, the statutory fee rates for the kindergartens of the town of Idstein were said to give rise to an amount which was far below the maintenance costs …

Neither the *Land* legislature nor the local authorities were said to be bound by a specific definition of income. It had therefore not been necessary to effect an assessment of income based on fiscal law. The definition of income taken as a basis in § 2.5 of the Kindergarten Fee Statutes was said to correspond sufficiently typically to feepayers' economic ability to pay. It was said to serve the purposes of calculating the amount of the fee in a manner that was rapid and simple in administrative terms. The matter was said to require no further differentiation. It was also said to be unobjectionable that the income of all family members was taken as a basis. This term could also be given sufficiently precise form by proper interpretation such that as a rule the income of the parents obliged to grant maintenance was material. An obligation to submit the income tax notice was said to apply only when an application for a reduction was filed. This was said to be unobjectionable in terms of data protection if handled properly.

4. The Federal Administrative Court rejected the complaint against non-submission of the case …

II.

The complainants complain with their constitutional complaint of a violation of Article 2.1, Article 3.1, Article 6.1 as well as Article 14 of the Basic Law.

They submit that the fee demanded for the kindergarten care of their son is by its legal nature neither a fee nor a contribution, but a local income tax. A tax is said to be distinct from non-fiscal levies (fees and contributions) *inter alia* by virtue of the fact that it is not countered by individually attributable counter services. In the area covered by the Local Authority Levies Act, the character of a non-fiscal levy is hence said not to be lost only if the fee is imposed on the occasion of individually attributable public services and is intended, being linked to these services, to cover their costs wholly or partly. Such a link between expenditure and a fee, which is necessary for delimitation from tax, is said to be renounced in the Kindergarten Fee Statutes of the town of Idstein, since the levy is no longer to be determined on the basis of the concrete costs, but only on the basis of the family income. The complainants hence allege that a levy is imposed on them not solely because of the utilisation of the kindergarten place, but specifically because of their family income.

The Hesse Higher Administrative Court is alleged to have renounced the cost coverage principle and the principle of specific quid pro quo which is alleged to be important for delimitation from tax. Hence, the local authorities can now levy income-related fees for the measurement of which local budget deficits and political majorities are said to be relevant, and not the costs arising from providing the public service. Such an encroachment on the ability of the complainants to pay with regard to the funding of public expenditure is however said to be only permissible by means of tax. However, in accordance with Article 105.2 in conjunction with Article 106.3 of the Basic Law, the *Land* Hesse is said not to have competence for levying such a tax, since the Federation has made conclusive use of its concurrent legislative power in the field of income taxation by enacting the Income Tax Act (*Einkommensteuergesetz*).

…

The impugned Statutes are further said to encroach on the principle of equality enshrined in Article 3.1 of the Basic Law. Firstly, it is said to be in breach of equality that the complainants have to pay considerably more than other parents whilst making identical use of the kindergarten. Secondly, the impact of the income-related determination is alleged to be that the income of the complainants is taxed higher than that of childless taxpayers with identical income.

The unequal treatment is said to be arbitrary since there are alleged to be no material reasons for it. In particular, it is allegedly also not possible to refer to the principle of the social welfare state since its concrete shape in the context of income tax is exclusively a matter for the Federation. Otherwise, support from the social welfare state at federal level – such as financial allocations in accordance with the Child Benefit Act (*Kindergeldgesetz*) – would be relativised at local authority level. This is said to be prohibited because taxation and support are said to be balanced out.

Instead, the fundamental provision of Article 6.1 of the Basic Law that determines values, which demands relief when measuring local authority fees in order to protect families, should also be adhered to with local authority levies. Accordingly, the utmost reserve has to be applied with precisely those levies which pose additional burdens on families with children. Their structure may certainly not serve to compensate for general local authority budget deficits.

Encroachment on family income by local authorities is further said to impinge on the area protected by Article 14 of the Basic Law since the family income that has already been acquired, and which has already been burdened by income tax, was a linking point for the obligation to pay imposed on the complainants without considering the extent of the counter service provided by the town of Idstein. The Kindergarten Fee Statutes are said to determine the content and limits of property in a non-permissible manner because of the issuance of a local tax on family income for which jurisdiction is alleged to be lacking. The obligation to pay that was imposed on the complainants is said to lead to an excessive fiscal burden since their income was subject not only to this levy, but also to income tax in accordance with the Income Tax Act. Article 14 of the Basic Law is hence said to require local authorities to keep strictly to the system of federative finance in introducing and structuring their levies. Citizens' ability to pay might otherwise be arbitrarily encroached upon.

III.

The Hesse State Chancellery (*Staatskanzlei*) and the President of the Federal Administrative Court have made statements with regard to the constitutional complaint.

...

B. – I.

The constitutional complaint is inadmissible insofar as it addresses the order of the Federal Administrative Court regarding non-submission of the case. The written complaint does not reveal to what degree the complainants' fundamental rights might have been violated by this order.

The constitutional complaint is admissible in other respects. ...

II.

The constitutional complaint is unfounded.

The fundamental rights of the complainant re I and of the complainant re II have not been violated by the ruling of the Higher Administrative Court. The Fee Statutes of the town of Idstein being reviewed in the proceedings on the constitutionality of a statute in accordance with § 47 of the Code of Procedure of the Administrative Courts (*Verwaltungsgerichtsordnung* – VwGO), and the *Land* and federal law provisions on which these Statutes are based, are in compliance with the Basic Law.

1. The provisions named do not encroach upon the complainants' general freedom of action (Article 2.1 of the Basic Law) in an unconstitutional manner.

a) Article 2.1 of the Basic Law guarantees the general freedom of action in a comprehensive meaning (see Decisions of the Federal Constitutional Court (*Entscheidungen des Bundesverfassungsgerichts* – BVerfGE 6, 32 (36); 80, 137 (152); established case-law). In particular, the claim not to be burdened by state powers with a financial disadvantage not based on the constitutional order is also protected (see for instance BVerfGE 19, 206 (215-216); established case-law). The impugned local authority Fee Statutes imposed burdens on the complainants who used a municipal kindergarten for one of their children in respect of a fee demand, and hence placed them at a disadvantage in terms of their general freedom of action.

b) The encroachment is, however, justified. The Higher Administrative Court has correctly recognised that the statutory bases for the fee demand are within the constitutional order. They violate neither the competence regulation of the Basic Law (aa) nor constitutional provisions on the financial system (bb) nor rule of law principles on the definiteness of powers (cc). They also do not violate the general principle of equality or other fundamental rights of the complainants (nos. 2-4).

aa) The federal legislature had competence to issue § 90.1 no. 3 of the Eighth Book of the Code of Social Law. The provision relates to a matter concentrating on the area of public welfare, which the Federation has power to regulate in accordance with Article 74.1 no. 7 and Article 72.1 of the Basic Law.

The term "public welfare" is not to be narrowly interpreted (see BVerfGE 88, 203 (329-330)). It includes not only welfare work for the young in the strict sense, but also youth services, which seek to promote the physical, emotional and moral interests of all juveniles without there needing to be a danger in the individual case. Youth services are intended to counter the juveniles' developmental difficulties, and thus also avert risks (see BVerfGE 22, 180 (212-213)). The same goals are also served by kindergarten care. It helps parents in bringing up their children, promotes and protects children and helps to create positive conditions for families with chil-

dren (see § 1.3 nos. 1-4 of the Eighth Book of the Code of Social Law). This care, which in most instances is the first care experienced outside the parental home, is highly character-forming for children's subsequent social conduct. The goal of youth services, namely preventive conflict avoidance, is hence effectively served. This was also striven for by the legislature. The latter wished to create a prevention-orientated benefit statute (see *Bundestag* printed paper (*Bundestagsdrucksache – BTDrucks*) 11/5948, p. 1; *Bundestag* printed paper 11/6748, p. 1; *Bundestag* printed paper 12/2866, p. 15; *Bundestag* printed paper 12/3711, p. 38).
However, kindergarten is at the same time an educational facility in the elementary area. The educational mandate has found its reflection in the relevant statutes. § 22.2 of the Eighth Book of the Code of Social Law, as also § 1 of the Hesse Kindergarten Act, called education and upbringing of children a task to be performed by kindergartens. § 2.1 sentence 2 of the Hesse Kindergarten Act provides *inter alia* for promotion by educational offerings. In this sense, § 90 of the Eighth Book of the Code of Social Law also touches on the legislative competence of the *Länder*. In the view of the Bavarian Constitutional Court (*Bayerischer Verfassungsgerichtshof*), hence, the Bavarian Kindergarten Act (*Bayerisches Kindergartengesetz*) finds its basis in the law on jurisdiction in the legislative competence of the *Länder* for the educational system (see BayVerfGH, BayVBl 1977, p. 81 (82 et seq.)).
This connection with education however does not remove the provision from the legislative competence of the Federation. The caring and educational tasks of kindergartens are inseparably connected. Splitting the legislative competence using these aspects cannot be considered for material reasons. This also applies to the cost provisions, without which it would be impossible to effectively safeguard welfare services. The focus of the kindergarten system, on which the determination of the legislative competence depends in such a case (see BVerfG, Judgment of 17 February 1998 – 1 BvF 1/91 –, preliminary print p. 35), remains on the provision of care with the aim of promoting modes of social conduct, and hence preventive conflict avoidance. The pre-school educational mandate takes second place to this task, which is to be allotted to the area of public welfare. A uniform attribution to the area of public welfare within the meaning of Article 74.1 no. 7 of the Basic Law is hence to be affirmed (see also Federal Administrative Court, Order of 14 February 1995 – BVerwG 8 B 19.95 –, Buchholz 401.84 *Benutzungsgebühren* no. 73, p. 27 with further references; North Rhine-Westphalia Higher Administrative Court (*Oberverwaltungsgericht*), *Neue Zeitschrift für Verwaltungsrecht* – NVwZ 1995, p. 191 (192); NVwZ 1995, p. 195; Berlin Higher Administrative Court, *Neue Juristische Wochenschrift* – NJW 1982, p. 954-955).

bb) The impugned provisions of *Land* law also do not violate, as claimed by the complainants, the competence of the Federation to issue income tax laws (Article 105.2 in conjunction with Article 106.3 of the Basic Law). The kindergarten fee is not to be regarded as a tax because it is graduated according to income. It remains linked to the individual use of a state infrastructure facility, and in this sense is not, as is a tax, owed with no preconditions (see BVerfGE 50, 217 (226)). Since according to the findings of the Higher Administrative Court its amount is clearly within the boundaries set by the general law on fees, there is also no reason to investigate the question as to whether with regard to a surplus amount it could be regarded as concealed taxation on income.

cc) In contradistinction to the view of the complainants, § 10 of the Hesse Kindergarten Act is not insufficiently well-defined. The standards set by Article 80.1 sentence 2 of the Basic Law for statutory powers to issue legal ordinances cannot be transferred to powers to issue local authority statutes. In contradistinction to secondary legislation by means of ordinances, general principles of the rule of law and of democracy do not require the content, purpose and extent of the provisions to be issued by corporate bodies under public law in the context of their autonomy to be laid down for them in an equally definite manner (see BVerfGE 21, 54 (62-63)).

The legislature may not fully divest itself of its legislative powers, but must also – above all with regard to possible encroachments on fundamental rights – impose expedient limits on the statutory power of self-administrative bodies (see BVerfGE 33, 125 (157 et seq.)). Where these lie in individual cases does not need to be clarified here, however. Certainly, § 10 of the Hesse Kindergarten Act, in conjunction with § 10.1 of the Hesse Local Authority Levies Act, regulates with sufficient clarity the content, nature and scope of the powers transferred to the local authorities. The provisions make it sufficiently evident to which preconditions the levy links, who is to pay the levies, and – in conjunction with general principles applying to fees – also to what extent it may be levied. Insofar as § 10 of the Hesse Kindergarten Act permits graduation derogating from the general principles, the appropriate preconditions for this – namely income and number of children – are also sufficiently well described.

2. The impugned provisions are in compliance with the principle of equality (Article 3.1 of the Basic Law). There are material reasons for the graduation of kindergarten fees by number of children and family income permitted by the federal and *Land* legislatures and by the town of Idstein which justify placing at a disadvantage users with a higher income.

a) The general principle of equality requires to apply equal treatment to what is essentially alike and unequal treatment to what is essentially different. If groups of individuals are treated unequally, Article 3.1 of the Basic Law is violated if one group is treated differently than another although there are no differences between them of such a nature and weight as to justify the unequal treatment (established case-law; most recently BVerfGE 82, 126 (146); 88, 87 (96-97); 91, 389 (401); 92, 26 (51-52)).

b) Different income situations can also be considered as a difference which can justify unequal treatment. This is recognised in many areas. The tax rate is in line with the amount of income. Social benefits are granted dependent on income or assets. It cannot be derived from Article 3.1 of the Basic Law that the fees levied for the use of state benefits must without exception be structured independently of income. From a point of view of equality, the question arising can only be whether or not the graduation granted by the legislature appears to be expedient. This question can however only be answered by looking at the overall system of state levies and benefits because only on this basis is it possible to derive the extent of the unequal treatment requiring justification in an individual case.

Income-linked unequal treatment of feepayers is not already ruled out by general constitutional principles of the law on fees. The Basic Law does not contain a separate definition of a fee from which criteria emerge directly for the constitutionality of fee standards, fee rates or amounts of fees. Fees are monetary payments under public law which are imposed in respect of individually attributable public services on feepayers by a provision of public law or other sovereign measures and are amenable, in terms of this service, to wholly or partly cover its costs. Its special purpose of attaining income in order to wholly or partly cover the costs of the individually attributable public services distinguishes it from a tax. It follows from this purpose that fees for state services may not be imposed in complete independence from the actual costs of state services which are provided on a for-a-fee basis; the link between the amount of costs and fees must be expedient (see BVerfGE 50, 217 (225 et seq.); 85, 337 (346)).

This does not however rule out graduation orientated to social aspects. No constitutionally founded limitation of the amount of the fee by the actual costs of a state service emerges from linking the fee to a particular purpose. Article 3.1 of the Basic Law opposes neither underpayment nor overpayment of the costs by the fees from the outset (see BVerfGE 50, 217 (226)). The cost coverage principle and similar principles of the law on fees are not principles with constitutional rank. A fee regulation may also pursue other purposes in addition to cost coverage; furthermore, the value of a state benefit for its recipients may be reflected in fee standards (see BVerfGE 50, 217 (225-226); 79, 1 (27-28); 85, 337 (346)). Within its respective regulatory competences, the legislature imposing the fees has broad decision-making and discretionary scope as to which individually attributable public services it subjects to an obligation to pay fees, which fee standards and fee rates it sets up for this, and which purposes over and above cost coverage, such as influencing conduct to a limited degree in certain areas of activity, it intends to pursue with a fee regulation (see BVerfGE 50, 217 (226-227)).

An income-related graduation of kindergarten contributions also does not violate the principles of fairness in the imposition of levies.

These principles have taken on a specific role in fiscal law. Fiscal justice within the meaning of Article 3.1 of the Basic Law requires equal taxation. Income tax law accommodates this principle of equal treatment, amongst other things by means of progressive taxation rates (see BVerfGE 61, 319 (343-344) with further references). Thus, the citizen liable to income tax contributes towards funding the burdens imposed on the community in line with his or her individual and hence relatively equal ability to pay. This equal treatment is broken insofar as public burdens are imposed on individual citizens. The unequal treatment may however be compensated for by a special advantage or equivalent benefit from the administration (see BVerfGE 55, 274 (302 et seq.); 93, 319 (343-344)). Fairness in the imposition of levies is hence maintained.

Income-related fee graduations are hence certainly unobjectionable from the specific point of view of fairness in the imposition of levies as long as even the maximum fee does not cover the actual costs of the facility and is suitably related to the administrative service paid for thereby. In these terms, all users are as a result afforded an advantage in terms of assets. Even users who pay the full fee are not [thereby] additionally, and without preconditions applying, called on to contribute towards the financing of general burdens, and above all to support socially more vulnerable users. According to the findings of the Higher Administrative Court, the fee rates set in the Statutes of the town of Idstein only cover roughly one-third of the actual costs. Those kindergarten users who pay the full fee also enjoy a public infrastructure service the value of which is considerably higher than the amount of the fee.

When a graduation of fees by income is expedient does not require a general decision here. The fee elements are too varied for this. Graduation however can at all events be considered when even the maximum fee does not exceed the proportionate mathematical costs of the facility and relates to a service with which the state accommodates both the principles of the social welfare state and the weighty fundamental rights of those in need of protection, and must be accessible for constitutional reasons to all relying on the benefit. In such a case, the state is not restricted to initially demanding a fee which is the same for all, and then granting financial aid to those users who are in need of assistance. Instead, it is already fundamentally justified in assessing the charge to take account of social aspects and in graduating

the fee imposed according to ability to pay, unless such procedure is opposed by other constitutional reasons.
c) The unequal treatment of the parents in the imposition of kindergarten fees is justified by sufficiently weighty material reasons.
In establishing kindergartens, the state provides equal opportunities with regard to children's opportunities in terms of their lives and education, thereby taking account of concerns of the social welfare state (Article 20.1 of the Basic Law). Kindergarten education provides and promotes elementary knowledge and skills such as use of language and interaction with others. Kindergarten is to support parents in bringing up their children (see also *Bundestag* printed paper 11/5948, p. 42). In this respect, kindergartens are also major elements of the educational system. They are to be available to all parents with small children. This is one of the most important goals of state youth services.
The establishment of kindergartens at the same time meets obligations of protection and support giving rise to fundamental rights. The availability of a kindergarten place can encourage women not to abort an unwanted pregnancy. Kindergartens hence serve to protect unborn life, which the state has undertaken to protect by virtue of Article 2.2 sentence 1 of the Basic Law. By helping families in childcare and child-raising, kindergartens also help meet the duty of promotion entrenched in Article 6.1 of the Basic Law. Finally, by creating kindergartens the state also supports women's equality at work. Mothers are frequently provided with the freedom that enables them to take part in working life, and are helped to achieve greater equality at work, only by their children being cared for in a kindergarten. Also in this sense, the state pursues a requirement to protect fundamental rights. In accordance with Article 3.2 sentence 2 of the Basic Law, it must ensure that family activities and work can be reconciled and that the performance of the family educational duty does not lead to disadvantages at work (see BVerfGE 39, 1 (44-45); 88, 203 (260)).
For the reasons mentioned above, children of lower-income parents may not be deprived of kindergarten places. This requirement can be met by socially graduated tariffs. By contrast, it is however not necessary to extensively subsidise kindergartens in a manner equally benefiting all parents regardless of their income situation in order to ensure that they are open to all.
In view of the important community interests served by creating kindergarten places, and of the need to keep these generally available in all areas, legally founded income-graduated imposition of the costs on users cannot be contested from a point of view of equal treatment. Insofar as public authorities are not obliged to provide subsidies, they can refrain from doing so for budgetary reasons. This is favoured above all by the fact that in a tense budgetary situation equally reducing

kindergarten fees to the level of the minimum fee would in practice further restrict the scope to create and maintain kindergartens.
3. Article 6.1 of the Basic Law is not violated by the impugned provisions.
a) The complainants wrongly claim that the fee arrangement additionally burdens families with children in order to cover local authority budget deficits. This claim is even factually incorrect. The town of Idstein makes available to all users of its kindergartens, including the complainants, kindergarten places for which it charges non-cost-covering fees. They therefore also receive an advantage in terms of assets as a result of budgetary funding provided by the local authority.
b) With its kindergarten fees, the local authority also does not fail to meet the duty of promotion of the family imposed on it in accordance with Article 6.1 of the Basic Law. The state is not obliged by the principle of protection contained in Article 6.1 of the Basic Law to compensate for all burdens concerning the family, or to promote the family regardless of other public interests. The state's promotion of the family is contingent on the possibilities in the sense of what the individual can sensibly claim from society (BVerfGE 87, 1 (35); established case-law).
It is not manifest that, taking account of these points of view, the promotion of the complainants does not comply with the protection principle enshrined in Article 6.1 of the Basic Law. A duty to promote all families equally regardless of their need cannot be derived from Article 6.1 of the Basic Law.
4. Article 14.1 of the Basic Law has also not been violated. It does not provide protection against imposing financial payments which are levied for the use of public facilities (see BVerfGE 78, 214 (230)).

Justices: Papier, Grimm, Kühling, Jaeger, Haas, Hömig, Steiner

No. 26

BVerfGE 99, 145
of 29 October 1998 – 2 BvR 1206/98 –
"Hague Child Abduction Convention case"

HEADNOTES:

1. **The Hague Child Abduction Convention guarantees respect for the child's best interests in the interaction between return as the standard procedure and exceptions in accordance with Articles 13 and 20 of the Hague Child Abduction Convention. The restrictive interpretation of these exception clauses is constitutionally unobjectionable.**
2. **In the special case of converse return applications, more detailed review of the child's best interests is constitutionally necessary using Article 13 of the Hague Child Abduction Convention.**
3. **From the constitutional entrenchment of the child's best interests in Articles 6.2 and 2.1 of the Basic Law (*Grundgesetz – GG*) in conjunction with the right to a hearing in court (Article 103.1 of the Basic Law) emerges the obligation to ensure the child's best interests in procedural terms by appointing a *curator ad litem* to defend the interests of the children already in family court proceedings if there are fears that the interests of the parents might clash with those of the children.**

Order of the Second Senate of 29 October 1998
– 2 BvR 1206/98 –

in the proceedings regarding the constitutional complaints 1. of Mr. T., 2. of the minor T., 3. of the minor T. – authorised representatives re 1.: …, lawyers – authorised representative and supplementary curator re 2. and 3.: …, lawyer – against the order of the Celle Higher Regional Court (*Oberlandesgericht*) of 9 July 1998 – 21 UF 88/98 –.

RULING:

The order of the Celle Higher Regional Court of 9 July 1998 – 21 UF 88/98 – violates the fundamental right of the complainant re 1. under Article 6.2 sentence 1 of the Basic Law and the fundamental rights of the complainants re 2. and 3. under Article 6.2 sentence 2 in conjunction with Article 2.1 and Article 103.1 of the Basic Law. The ruling is reversed and the case is referred back to the Celle Higher Regional Court.

EXTRACT FROM GROUNDS:

A.

The constitutional complaints relate to proceedings in accordance with the Hague Convention of 25 October 1980 on Civil Aspects of International Child Abduction (Federal Law Gazette (*Bundesgesetzblatt* – BGBl) II 1990 p. 206), based on two converse abductions of two children. The children were first of all abducted from Germany to France by the mother and brought back by force nine months later from France to Germany by the father.

I.

1. The abducting parent not infrequently attains a factual advantage with child abductions to another state because return of the children as soon as possible to their original place of residence meets with legal and organisational obstacles in international cooperation, and the international jurisdiction for a rights of custody ruling is determined in line with the "habitual residence" of the child according to the provisions of the Hague Convention of 5 October 1961 concerning the powers of authorities and the law applicable in respect of the protection of minors – (Federal Law Gazette II 1971 p. 217). The Hague Child Abduction Convention hence facilitates cooperation among the Contracting States, and on this basis calls for the immediate return of the child.

Article 3

The removal or the retention of a child is to be considered wrongful where
a) it is in breach of rights of custody attributed to a person, an institution or any other body, either jointly or alone, under the law of the State in which the child was habitually resident immediately before the removal or retention;
and
b) at the time of removal or retention those rights were actually exercised, either jointly or alone, or would have been so exercised but for the removal or retention.
The rights of custody mentioned in sub-paragraph a above, may arise in particular by operation of law or by reason of a judicial or administrative decision, or by reason of an agreement having legal effect under the law of that State.

Article 12

Where a child has been wrongfully removed or retained in terms of Article 3 and, at the date of the commencement of the proceedings before the judicial or administrative authority of the Contracting State where the child is, a period of less than one year has elapsed from the date of the wrongful removal or retention, the authority concerned shall order the return of the child forthwith.
The judicial or administrative authority, even where the proceedings have been commenced after the expiration of the period of one year referred to in the preceding paragraph, shall also order the return of the child, unless it is demonstrated that the child is now settled in its new environment.
Where the judicial or administrative authority in the requested State has reason to believe that the child has been taken to another State, it may stay the proceedings or dismiss the application for the return of the child.

Article 13

Notwithstanding the provisions of the preceding Article, the judicial or administrative authority of the requested State is not bound to order the return of the child if the person, institution or other body which opposes its return establishes that,
a) the person, institution or other body having the care of the person of the child was not actually exercising the custody rights at the time of removal or retention, or had consented to or subsequently acquiesced in the removal of retention;
or

b) there is a grave risk that his or her return would expose the child to physical or psychological harm or otherwise place the child in an intolerable situation.

The judicial or administrative authority may also refuse to order the return of the child if it finds that the child objects to being returned and has attained an age and degree of maturity at which it is appropriate to take account of its views.

In considering the circumstances referred to in this Article, the judicial and administrative authorities shall take into account the information relating to the social background of the child provided by the Central Authority or other competent authority of the child's habitual residence.

In accordance with Article 19 of the Hague Child Abduction Convention, a decision under this Convention concerning the return of the child is not to be taken to be a determination on the merits of any custody issue. The return is to ensure that the custody proceedings are implemented at the child's original place of habitual residence. Article 20 of the Hague Child Abduction Convention makes it possible to refuse to return the child if this would not be permitted by the fundamental principles of the requested State relating to the protection of human rights and fundamental freedoms.

2. The Act Reforming the Law of Parent and Child (*Gesetz zur Reform des Kindschaftsrechts* – KindRG) came into force on 1 July 1998 (Federal Law Gazette I 1997 p. 2942). This Act added the following provision to the Act on Matters of Non-Contentious Jurisdiction (*Gesetz über die Angelegenheiten der freiwilligen Gerichtsbarkeit* – FGG):

§ 50 of the Act on Matters of Non-Contentious Jurisdiction

(1) The court may appoint a children's guardian (*curator ad litem*) to the minor child for proceedings concerning him or her insofar as this is necessary to defend his or her interests.

(2) The appointment shall be deemed necessary as a rule if

1. the interest of the child is markedly in contradiction with that of his or her legal representatives,
2. the proceedings relate to measures in respect of a risk to the child's best interests, entailing the separation of the child from his or her family or the removal of the entire care for the person of the child (§§ 1666 and 1666a of the Civil Code), or

3. the proceedings relate to the removal of the child from the carer (§ 1632.4 of the Civil Code) or from the spouse or person with right of access (§ 1682 of the Civil Code).

If the court refrains from appointing a children's guardian for the proceedings in such cases, it shall provide reasoning for this in the ruling relating to the person of the child.

(...)

II.

1. The complainant re 1. has been married to the applicant of the original proceedings, a French national, since August 1989. The marriage produced a son, born on 31 October 1990, and a daughter, born on 22 July 1994. The spouses are separated. Divorce proceedings have been initiated.

a) In the context of proceedings before a German court on parental custody during the period of separated living in accordance with § 1672 of the Civil Code (*Bürgerliches Gesetzbuch* – BGB), the mother stated in the oral hearing, which took place on 17 February 1997, for the court record that she would not unlawfully leave the Federal Republic of Germany with her children, but would await a final ruling in the custody proceedings.

Nonetheless, on 7 July 1997 she travelled to France with both children, the complainants re 2. and 3., against the will of the father, the complainant re 1. The Local Court (*Amtsgericht*) – Family Court – thereupon assigned to the complainant re 1. the right to determine the place of residence for the children. At the same time, it instructed the mother to surrender both children to the father.

b) Attempts on the part of the father to obtain from the French courts with jurisdiction the return of the children in accordance with the Hague Child Abduction Convention were unsuccessful at first and second instance. The courts did consider the abduction of the children by the mother to be unlawful, but accepted an exception in accordance with Article 13.1 (b) of the Hague Child Abduction Convention, since any renewed change in the present circumstances would place the children in an "intolerable situation". The proceedings have not yet been finally concluded; the Court of Cassation (*Cour de Cassation*) has so far not yet ruled on an appeal on a point or points of law (*pourvoi en cassation)* submitted by the complainant re 1.

c) Within the framework of divorce proceedings initiated by the mother in France, the Blois *Tribunal de Grande Instance* [translator's note: First-instance civil court dealing with claims above 10,000 euros and having exclusive jurisdiction for family matters] awarded an injunction to the effect that both parents are jointly entitled

to parental custody and that the children's place of residence was with their mother. The father appealed this provisional rights of custody ruling. The appeal has not yet been ruled on.
d) On 28 March 1998, the father had the children brought from France to Germany to his place of residence by appointed persons. The kidnappers used force on the mother of the children in doing so. …
e) The mother, the applicant of the original proceedings, thereupon applied before the court with jurisdiction in Germany to recognise the provisional rights of custody ruling of the Blois *Tribunal de Grande Instance* of 10 November 1997 and to declare it provisionally enforceable, as well as to order the surrender of the children to her or to a person appointed by her. The applications were rejected. In response to the immediate complaint, the ruling of the Higher Regional Court was handed down, which is impugned with the constitutional complaints, in which the return of the children to the mother was ordered on the basis of the Hague Child Abduction Convention.
2. The Higher Regional Court considers the actions of the complainant re 1. to constitute unlawful abduction within the meaning of Article 3 of the Hague Child Abduction Convention. For this reason, the children were to be returned to their place of habitual residence in accordance with Article 12.1 of the Hague Child Abduction Convention. The children had had their "habitual residence" in France immediately prior to their abduction to Germany. At that time, they had already lived in France for almost nine months; the son had attended school there, the daughter had attended kindergarten. Both children had been integrated in France. The establishment of the habitual residence at the mother's place of residence was also not opposed by the fact that the mother had abducted the children to France against the will of the complainant re 1.
There were said to be no indications justifying an exception in accordance with Article 13.1 (b) of the Hague Child Abduction Convention. The provision was to be interpreted restrictively. Acceptance of the breaking of the law by means of abduction was only justified in view of extraordinarily grave harm to the child's best interests. Here, also the risk would have to be particularly grievous, concrete and immanent, otherwise the purpose of the Hague Child Abduction Convention would be prevented by applying the exception.
Also Article 13.2 of the Hague Child Abduction Convention was said not to apply. The will allegedly expressed by the four- and seven-year-old children to remain with their father and not to return to their mother in France did not permit the conclusion to be drawn that the children would seriously object to being returned to France. The Senate did not consider a reason to exist to hear the children in order to

ascertain their will, especially since they were subject to the strong influence of their father.

III.

The complainant re 1. filed constitutional complaints against this ruling on 15 July 1998 in his own name as well as in representation of the complainants re 2. and 3. By order of 10 August 1998 the Local Court – guardianship court – ordered a supplementary curator to be appointed for the constitutional complaint proceedings of the complainants re 2. and 3. The supplementary curator filed a "renewed" constitutional complaint by written statement of 17 August 1998 "purely preventively", and made reference to the complete content of the previous reasoning of the constitutional complaints.

1. The complainant re 1. is objecting to a violation of his fundamental rights under Article 6.2 to 6.4 of the Basic Law; the complainants re 2. and 3. are objecting to a violation of their fundamental rights under Article 2.1 in conjunction with Article 1.1 of the Basic Law. It is alleged that an immediate return to France would constitute a grave incursion on the right of personality of the complainants re 2. and 3. and on the best interests of these children, as well as on the parental right of the complainant re 1.

Greater accommodation of the child's best interests was necessary with a converse return than in simple abduction cases. For this reason, the Higher Regional Court had not been permitted to refrain from commissioning a specialist psychological statement. In order to ensure compliance with the children's best interests in material and procedural terms, a generous interpretation of the exception clause was said to be required in the case of a return in order to save the children further burdensome changes of location. Since as yet no final ruling had been handed down by the French courts on the return claim of the complainant re 1., and also the custody proceedings had not yet been concluded, there might be a further change of location after a return. What is more, the Higher Regional Court had allegedly ignored the statement by the youth welfare office that the children had once more become familiar with their customary surroundings within a short period.

Also the parental right of the complainant re 1. was said to be rendered null if only the state that he created unlawfully was assessed and it was disregarded in doing so that the mother had first acted unlawfully and caused the complainant re 1. to choose that course of action. In the result, the Higher Regional Court was said to accept the possibility of the complainant re 1. completely losing his parental right.

It could not be constitutionally accepted in cases of converse child returns that the second abduction served as the sole standard for the ruling, thereby disregarding

the interests of the children and the state now applying. This was alleged to negate the rights of the children and the goals of the Hague Convention.
2. By written statement of 25 September 1998, the supplementary curator supplemented the submission for the complainants re 2. and 3. The latter were said to have been violated by the impugned ruling with regard to their right to a hearing in court in accordance with Article 103.1 of the Basic Law, as well as with regard to their general right of personality in accordance with Article 2.1 in conjunction with Article 1.1 of the Basic Law. The Higher Regional Court had allegedly not sufficiently accounted for the fact that the return application of the children's mother was directed against a return by the children's father, which had been preceded by an initial abduction by the children's mother. Also, the return application of the children's father had been well-founded in accordance with Article 12 of the Hague Child Abduction Convention because of this preceding first abduction by the children's mother. In the negative rulings on the return application of the complainant re 1., the French courts were said to have ignored a partial rights of custody ruling of a German family court on the right to determine the place of residence, which they should have adhered to in accordance with Article 7 of the Hague Convention concerning the powers of authorities and the law applicable in respect of the protection of minors, and allegedly had furthermore ignored the provisions of the Hague Child Abduction Convention. These rulings on the part of the French courts had allegedly caused the second abduction by the complainant re 1.
The Higher Regional Court was said to have not attached sufficient significance to these special circumstances. The mere statement by the courts, namely that, because of their age, the willingness expressed by the children when asked about a return to France should not be overvalued, negated the fundamental rights of the children. The court was said to have been obliged to investigate the will of the children in a suitable manner.
To this end, it should have heard the then 7 ½-year-old son in person, who according to the submission of the complainant re 1. refused to return to France. Even if the court presumed that "both children are exposed to the strong influence of their father", it should have ascertained the seriousness of their will, where necessary through a child psychological report.
Greater participation by the children was also favoured by the amendment to procedural law brought about by the Act Reforming the Law of Parent and Child, which more clearly involved minor children in the proceedings. The ruling of the Higher Regional Court was said to have been handed down after this reform had entered into force. Since the new § 50 of the Act on Matters of Non-Contentious Jurisdiction in principle was said to be applicable to Hague proceedings, the appointment of a *curator ad litem* for the children was said to have been necessary in accordance

with § 50.2 nos. 1 to 3 of the Act on Matters of Non-Contentious Jurisdiction in the proceedings regarding their mother's return application in order to sufficiently guarantee the children's interests. Not appointing a *curator ad litem* was said to constitute a further violation of Article 2.1, Article 1.1 and Article 103.1 of the Basic Law.

IV.

The Federal Constitutional Court (*Bundesverfassungsgericht*) afforded the opportunity to submit a statement to the Federal Government, the *Land* Government of Lower Saxony, the Federal Court of Justice (*Bundesgerichtshof*), the Federal Public Prosecutor General at the Federal Court of Justice as the Central Authority in accordance with the Hague Child Abduction Convention, the Diepholz district youth welfare office and the applicant of the original proceedings. …

B.

The constitutional complaints are admissible.

…

C.

The impugned ruling violates the fundamental right of the complainants re 2. and 3. under Article 6.2 sentence 2 in conjunction with Article 2.1 of the Basic Law and their fundamental right under Article 103.1 of the Basic Law. The fundamental right of the complainant re 1. under Article 6.2 sentence 1 of the Basic Law has been violated.

I.

1. As a holder of fundamental rights, a child has a right to state protection of its fundamental right under Article 2.1 of the Basic Law (see Decisions of the Federal Constitutional Court (*Entscheidungen des Bundesverfassungsgerichts* – BVerfGE) 24, 119 (144); 75, 201 (218)). At the same time, the child's best interests constitute the guide for the state mandate of protection in accordance with Article 6.2 sentence 2 of the Basic Law. In the event of a clash of interests occurring between parents and child, the child's best interests are the determining standard (see BVerfGE 37, 217 (252); 56, 363 (383); 68, 176 (188); 75, 201 (218)).

In principle, marriage as a living arrangement of man and woman is the "precondition for optimum ... development of children" (BVerfGE 76, 1 (51)). Article 6.1 in conjunction with Article 6.2 of the Basic Law protects the family above all as a living arrangement and child-raising community, in which parents have to safeguard their serving fundamental right for the child's best interests (see BVerfGE 80, 81 (90-91)). Insofar as parents are unable to offer such a framework to their children, in allocating the parental responsibility, the parental right is to be understood above all as a parental obligation (Article 6.2 sentence 1 of the Basic Law) to develop the state's "watchdog function" (Article 6.2 sentence 2 of the Basic Law) as an obligation to act in a manner which does justice to the child's best interests (BVerfGE 79, 51 (66-67)) and which is in line with the children's fundamental rights. Here, the parental rights are also restricted by the obligation to abide by the law: Parents have to refrain from unlawful acts towards their children, and in particular are not to involve the children in unlawful conduct as persons concerned.

2. Minors must be represented in proceedings before the Federal Constitutional Court by a supplementary curator if, because of a clash of interests, is not ensured that those entitled to represent them will defend their interests (see BVerfGE 72, 122 (135); 75, 201 (214-215)). The same applies constitutionally to proceedings before the family courts and the guardianship courts, certainly if a decision is taken which is significant for the future of the child and, because of a clash of interests between parents and child, the interests of the child cannot be sufficiently defended by the parents. Accordingly, in the context of the reform of the law of parent and child the institution of a "children's guardian (*curator ad litem*)" (§ 50 of the Act on Matters of Non-Contentious Jurisdiction) has now been introduced as on 1 July 1998 (Federal Law Gazette I 1997 p. 2958).

If the court ruling on a conflict between parents has an impact on the future of the child, it must be aligned to the child's best interests, and must accommodate the child in its individuality as a holder of fundamental rights (see BVerfGE 37, 217 (252)). The obligations of protection emerging from Article 6.2 sentence 2 and Article 2.1 of the Basic Law require precautions to be taken for court proceedings not only under substantive law, but also under constitutional law which guarantee adequate accommodation of the fundamental rights position of the child in question (see BVerfGE 55, 171 (179); 79, 51 (66-67)).

Without a *curator ad litem*, the child in question would rely on the submission of the parents and the investigations carried out by the court, whilst both parents would be able to pursue and defend their interests independently. Such proceedings would not sufficiently ensure that the child's best interests are respected if the parents pursue the proceedings to defend their own interests. Although the judge is obliged to defend the child's best interests, and hence to accommodate the interests

of the children, defending interests within the meaning of representing a party can however not be replaced thereby because the judge must remain neutral.
3. a) The fundamental rights standards also determine the interpretation and handling of international agreements which in accordance with Article 59.2 of the Basic Law have become legally binding by virtue of a law approving an international agreement. International agreements which require interpretation and application by the national courts are to be interpreted in light of national constitutional law. In this framework, the purpose intended by the contracting parties is to be applied as comprehensively as possible. The general rules and principles of international law must also be applied here which relate to the specific area of the contractual regulation (see BVerfGE 46, 342 (361-362) with further references).
b) The Hague Child Abduction Convention is obliged to ensure the child's best interests in the same way as German constitutional law. Its Preamble underlines the significance of the child's best interests, and guarantees that they are served in the interaction between return as the standard procedure (Article 12.1 of the Hague Child Abduction Convention), and exceptions in accordance with Articles 13 and 20 of the Hague Child Abduction Convention, in accordance with which decisions concerning the return of the children do not take place if they are irreconcilable with the child's best interests (see E. Pérez-Vera, *Erläuternder Bericht zum Haager Übereinkommen über die zivilrechtlichen Aspekte internationaler Kindesentführung*, Annex 1 to *Denkschrift der Bundesregierung zum Abkommen*, *Bundestag* printed paper (*Bundestagsdrucksache* – BTDrucks) 11/5314, p. 41, marginal nos. 24-25). A comparison with the case-law of the courts of other Contracting Parties also confirms that the Hague Child Abduction Convention is aligned with the child's best interests (see the statement of the Permanent Bureau of the Hague Conference on Private International Law on proceedings 2 BvR 982/95, *International Legal Materials* – ILM 35 (1996), 529 (544 et seq.)).

II.

1. The Hague Child Abduction Convention contains the presumption that immediate return to the previous place of residence in principle best complies with the child's best interests. This presumption may be refuted in individual cases (Article 13 of the Hague Child Abduction Convention). This provision is intended to bring the fundamental right positions of the parents and children concerned into a proper equilibrium.
a) Immediate return of the child to his or her last place of habitual residence in principle serves the child's best interests because it best preserves the continuity of his or her circumstances. Return to the place of "habitual residence" accommodates the

interests of both parents because the original international jurisdiction for the rights of custody ruling is conserved, and hence a situation is avoided in which a parent draws a factual advantage from the unlawful abduction of the children. Finally, the return order, which obliges the abducting parent to return the child, is likely to have a general preventive impact.

b) The exception clauses in Articles 13 and 20 of the Hague Child Abduction Convention take account of the fact that returning the child to his or her last place of habitual residence may be incompatible with the child's best interests in individual cases. It is possible to refrain from returning a child in particular if such a return would place the child in an intolerable situation, or if the child objects to being returned in a manner which is material, given his or her age and degree of maturity.

2. The restrictive application of the exception clauses by the non-constitutional courts is constitutionally unobjectionable. The purposes of lending constancy to the child's situation, of ensuring a rights of custody ruling at the original place of residence in compliance with the actual circumstances, and of countering child abductions in general, indicate in principle that it is reasonable to order immediate return. For this reason, not all hardships justify the application of the exception clause; rather, only exceptionally do grievous impairments of the child's best interests which are particularly considerable, concrete and immanent oppose return (see Order of the First Chamber of the Second Senate of the Federal Constitutional Court of 15 February 1996 – 2 BvR 233/96 –, *Neue Juristische Wochenschrift* – NJW 1996, p. 1402 (1403)).

3. Hardships for the abducting parent as a rule do not give rise to such a disadvantage. The impairment of the child's best interests, in conjunction with the separation of the child from the abducting parent, can be avoided in most cases by the abducting parent returning together with the child. If return is connected with state sanctions for this parent, these are to be accepted as a consequence of the unlawful abduction (see Order of the Third Chamber of the Second Senate of the Federal Constitutional Court of 18 July 1997 – 2 BvR 1126/97 –, *Zeitschrift für das gesamte Familienrecht* – FamRZ 1997, p. 1269 (1270); Bach, FamRZ 1997, p. 1051 (1056)).

III.

The application of the Hague Child Abduction Convention by the Higher Regional Court violates the fundamental right of the complainants re 2. and 3. under Article 6.2 sentence 2 in conjunction with Article 2.1 of the Basic Law and their claim under Article 103.1 of the Basic Law.

1. Interpretation and application of non-constitutional law are a matter for the non-constitutional courts; the Federal Constitutional Court only objects to the violation of constitutional law. The standards which have been developed by the non-constitutional courts for review of the application of non-constitutional law apply *mutatis mutandis* to the law of international agreements (see BVerfGE 94, 315 (328); see also BVerfGE 58, 1 (34); 59, 63 (89)) The Federal Constitutional Court is to review here whether the impugned ruling is based on a fundamentally erroneous view of the significance of the fundamental rights, and whether the result of the interpretation violates the fundamental rights asserted (see BVerfGE 30, 173 (188); Order of the First Senate of the Federal Constitutional Court of 29 October 1997 – 1 BvR 780/87 –, *Europäische Grundrechte-Zeitschrift* – EuGRZ 1998, p. 330 (335)).
2. The ruling of the Higher Regional Court is accordingly incompatible with the Basic Law. The Hague Child Abduction Convention is applicable to converse abductions. In this sense, the interpretation and application of Article 3 of the Hague Child Abduction Convention by the Higher Regional Court are constitutionally unobjectionable. In the special case of converse return applications, however, a more detailed examination of the child's best interests using Article 13 of the Hague Child Abduction Convention is constitutionally required (a). Moreover, procedural requirements emerge from the state's obligation to ensure the child's best interests to which the proceedings before the Higher Regional Court do not do justice (b).
a) aa) The complainant re 1. brought the children to Germany on his own initiative, after they had been abducted by their mother. In the meantime, they spent a longer period in France. For this reason, the Higher Regional Court should have examined whether a new "habitual residence" within the meaning of Article 3 of the Hague Child Abduction Convention had been established at the destination of the first abduction, and the return hence is to be qualified as re-abduction (see on this the references to US case-law in L. Silberman, Hague Convention on International Child Abduction: A Brief Overview and Case Law Analysis, Family Law Quarterly 28 (1994), pp. 9 et seq. (22-23)). This is the only way to do justice to the synchronism between the decision concerning the return of the child in accordance with the Hague Child Abduction Convention and the jurisdiction for the rights of custody ruling in accordance with Article 1 of the Hague Convention concerning the powers of authorities and the law applicable in respect of the protection of minors.
bb) The ruling of the Higher Regional Court that a new "habitual residence" within the meaning of Article 3 of the Hague Child Abduction Convention was established by reason of the children's integration and the duration of their residence in France is constitutionally unobjectionable. It is aligned to the predominant view that "habitual residence" must be determined in purely factual and not normative terms (see for instance the material re the Hague Child Abduction Convention, *Bundestag*

printed paper 11/5314, p. 48 (marginal no. 66); C. von Bar, *Internationales Privatrecht*, Vol. II, 1991, marginal no. 333), and continues to apply in the context of the case-law on establishment of a new habitual residence in accordance with Article 1 of the Hague Convention concerning the powers of authorities and the law applicable in respect of the protection of minors if a child is taken unlawfully to this new place (see Federal Court of Justice, FamRZ 1997, p. 1070; Federal Court of Justice, NJW 1981, p. 520 (521); Karlsruhe Higher Regional Court, FamRZ 1993, p. 96 (97); Hamm Higher Regional Court, FamRZ 1991, p. 1346 (1347) and p. 1466 (1467-1468); Celle Higher Regional Court, FamRZ 1991, p. 1221 (1222)).

The view of the court that the annual period of Article 12.1 of the Hague Child Abduction Convention does not apply to the determination of the habitual residence within the meaning of Article 3.1 (a) of the Hague Child Abduction Convention is also constitutionally unobjectionable. Analogous application of the annual period (see Staudinger-Pirrung, *Vorb. zu Artikel 19 EGBGB*, marginal no. 647) is not required by a fundamental right, nor is it the only possible interpretation. The decision of the Higher Regional Court not to analogously apply the provision regarding the annual period is particularly favoured by the fact that the presumption linked with the period is intended to formalise the preconditions for the return claim in accordance with Article 12.1 of the Hague Child Abduction Convention, and hence make easier its implementation in practice, but not to favour unilateral self-help measures carried out by a parent.

cc) The ruling of the Higher Regional Court to not examine in greater detail the preconditions of Article 13.1 (b) and 13.2 in conjunction with Article 13.3 of the Hague Child Abduction Convention contradicts the mandate of protection under Article 6.2 sentence 2 of the Basic Law and the fundamental right of the children under Article 2.1 of the Basic Law. At the time of the ruling of the Higher Regional Court, converse return applications were pending in accordance with the Hague Child Abduction Convention. The Higher Regional Court itself had to rule on a return application of the applicant of the original proceedings in respect of the unilateral return of the children by the complainant re 1. At the same time, the appeal on a point or points of law of the complainant re 1. was pending before the Court of Cassation. This does not rule out that, in following on from the order of the Higher Regional Court to return the children to France, the Court of Cassation orders a renewed return to Germany. The purpose of the Hague Child Abduction Convention to lend constancy to the residence of the child until a rights of custody ruling is handed down, to rescind the consequences of unlawful abduction and to return the child to the place of the future rights of custody ruling would hence be missed. Subjecting the children to such a to-and-fro would contradict the child's best interests, and would be intolerable for them if the court does not identify special indications justifying a return despite the risk of a further change of location. The Higher Regional Court did not attach sufficient weight to these special circumstances.

b) Protection of fundamental rights also determines the form and application of procedural law (BVerfGE 53, 30 (65); 55, 171 (182); 79, 51 (66-67)).

aa) From the constitutional entrenchment of the child's best interests in Article 6.2 and Article 2.1 of the Basic Law in conjunction with the right to a hearing in court (Article 103.1 of the Basic Law) emerges the obligation to ensure the child's best interests in procedural terms by appointing a *curator ad litem* to defend the interests of the children even in the family court proceedings.

The decision concerning the return of the child is of considerable significance for the best interests of the children because it determines their social surroundings and can remove the children from the immediate attention of the parent currently taking care of them. For this reason, the constitutional fundamental rights protection of the children and their right to a hearing in court demand that the proceedings be organised in such a way as to ensure independent representation of the interests of the child. This task is in principle a matter for the parents. If, however, the parents have made it abundantly clear through the unlawful abduction of their children that they wish primarily to assert their own interests, their interests may clash with those of their children. In this case, the children must be granted the possibility to assert their own interests, which may perhaps be correctly recognised or formulated by neither the parents nor the court, with a degree of independence in the proceedings which meets the requirements of a legal hearing (Article 103.1 of the Basic Law). For children whose age and maturity do not permit them to defend their procedural rights, this is carried out by a representative who is provided for by § 50 of the Act on Matters of Non-Contentious Jurisdiction as a *curator ad litem*. Such a *curator ad litem* was not appointed for the complainants re 2. and 3. in the proceedings before the Higher Regional Court. For this reason, the fundamental rights of the complainants under Article 6.2 and Article 2.1, in conjunction with Article 103.1, of the Basic Law have been violated.

bb) Article 6.2 sentence 2 of the Basic Law furthermore requires that the children concerned are to be heard in the custody proceedings (see BVerfGE 55, 171 (182)). Decisions concerning the return of children in accordance with Article 19 of the Hague Child Abduction Convention are not to be regarded as rights of custody rulings (see Order of the Third Chamber of the Second Senate of the Federal Constitutional Court of 18 July 1997 – 2 BvR 1126/97 –, FamRZ 1997, p. 1269 (1270)). A hearing of the abducted child is therefore in principle not necessary in the proceedings in accordance with the Hague Child Abduction Convention. Because of the converse return applications, the non-constitutional courts have however to ascertain in the instant case how the children will cope with a return and possible re-return. This may take place via a hearing, where necessary also by an expert witness and by consulting information from the authority which has jurisdiction.

IV.

The violation of the children's best interests at the same time gives rise to a violation of the parental right of the complainant re 1. under Article 6.2 sentence 1 of the Basic Law.

The parental right is a fundamental right to which each parent is individually entitled (see BVerfGE 47, 46 (76)). By virtue of the decision of the Higher Regional Court concerning the return of the child, the area protected by the parental right is affected because the children are removed from the influence of the father and he can no longer determine their place of residence.

When parents separate, it is unavoidable that both parents cannot have the same level of contact with and attention to the children. Since the parental rights of both parents are equivalent, only the child's best interests may justify an incursion on the parental right of the respectively disadvantaged parent (see also BVerfGE 55, 171 (179); 92, 158 (178)).

A state ruling impairing the parental right but not serving the child's best interests therefore violates Article 6.2 sentence 1 of the Basic Law. The ruling handed down by the Higher Regional Court is not compatible with the best interests of the complainants re 2. and 3. At the same time, it violates the parental right of the complainant re 1. under Article 6.2 sentence 1 of the Basic Law.

…

Justices: Limbach, Kirchhof, Winter, Sommer, Jentsch, Hassemer, Broß

No. 27

BVerfGE 99, 216
of 10 November 1998 – 2 BvR 1057, 1226, 980/91 –
"Equalisation of family burdens case"

HEADNOTES:

1. **Article 6.1 of the Basic Law contains a special principle of equality. It prohibits placing marriage and the family on a worse footing in comparison with other partnerships and child-raising communities. This prohibition of discrimination opposes all differentiation imposing burdens linked to the existence of a marriage (Article 6.1 of the Basic Law) or to the exercise of parental rights in a marital child-raising community (Article 6.1 and 6.2 of the Basic Law).**
2. **Over and above the child's existential material needs and the work-related care requirements, parents' ability to pay is reduced in general terms by virtue of the care requirements. The care requirements must remain unburdened by income tax as a necessary element of the minimum family income (see Decisions of the Federal Constitutional Court (*Entscheidungen des Bundesverfassungsgerichts* – BVerfGE) 82, 60 (85); 87, 153 (169 et seq.)) without it being permissible to distinguish how this requirement is met.**
3. **a) In the required revision of compensation for child-related expenses, the legislature must also allow for child-raising requirements regardless of civil status with regard to all parents who receive a child allowance or child benefit.**

   b) Insofar as minimum family income is determined by personal data such as civil status, number of children and age, in accordance with the rule-of-law principle of predictability and calculability, this element must be worded such that the mere statement of these data makes it possible to apply the law.

Order of the Second Senate of 10 November 1998
– 2 BvR 1057, 1226, 980/91 –

in the proceedings regarding the constitutional complaints 1. of Ms. B., authorised representative: Dr. …, lawyer – against a) the judgment of the Federal Finance Court (*Bundesfinanzhof*) of 15 March 1991 – III R 97/89 –, b) the judgment of the Munich Finance Court (*Finanzgericht*) of 18 September 1989 – 13 K 13158/85 –, c) the notice of the Augsburg-Land Tax Office of 4 June 1985, indirectly against § 33c of the Income Tax Act (*Einkommensteuergesetz – EStG*) in conjunction with § 53b.1 and § 32.3 and 32.4 of the Income Tax Act in the version promulgated on 12 June 1985 (Federal Law Gazette (*Bundesgesetzblatt* – BGBl) I p. 977) – 2 BvR 1057/91 –, 2. a) of Ms. L., b) of Mr. B.-L., – authorised representatives re 2. a): …, lawyers – against a) the order of the Federal Finance Court of 14 May 1991 – III B 88/89 –, b) the judgment of the Munich Finance Court of 15 June 1989 – X 188/87 E, X 209/87 E, 10 K 2652/88, 10 K 2651/88, 10 K 3078/88, 10 K 3353/88, 10 K 844/88 and 10 K 845/88 –, indirectly against § 33c of the Income Tax Act in conjunction with § 52.23b and § 32.3 and 32.4 of the Income Tax Act in the version promulgated on 12 June 1985 (Federal Law Gazette I p. 977) as well as § 33c and § 32.7 of the Income Tax Act in the version promulgated on 15 April 1986 (Federal Law Gazette I p. 441) – 2 BvR 1226/91 – and 3. a) of Dr. U. (Ms.), b) of Dr. U. (Mr.), – authorised representatives: …, lawyers – against a) the order of the Federal Finance Court of 22 March 1991 – III B 517/90 –, b) the judgment of the Münster Finance Court of 30 May 1990 – II 5109/88 E –, indirectly against § 33c and § 32.7 of the Income Tax Act in the version promulgated on 15 April 1986 (Federal Law Gazette I p. 441) – 2 BvR 980/91 –.

RULING:

1. § 33c subsections 1 to 4 of the Income Tax Act has been incompatible with Article 6.1 and 6.2 of the Basic Law since its introduction by virtue of Article 3 no. 19 of the 1985 Tax Correction Act (*Steuerbereinigungsgesetz*) of 14 December 1984 (Federal Law Gazette I p. 1493), including all subsequent versions, insofar as it excludes parents unrestrictedly liable to pay tax living in marital community from deduction of childcare costs resulting from gainful employment.
2. § 32.3 and 32.4 of the Income Tax Act has been incompatible with Article 6.1 and 6.2 of the Basic Law since the promulgation of the new version of the Income Tax Act of 24 January 1984 (Federal Law Gazette I p. 113), until the amendment by Article 1 no. 8 of the Act on Performance-Promoting Tax Reduction and on the

Reduction of Family Burdens – 1986/1988 Tax Reduction Act (*Gesetz zur leistungsfördernden Steuersenkung und zur Entlastung der Familie – Steuersenkungsgesetz 1986/1988*) of 26 June 1985 (Federal Law Gazette I p. 1153), as well as § 32.7 of the Income Tax Act, since the promulgation of the new version of the Income Tax Act of 15 April 1986 (Federal Law Gazette I p. 441), including all subsequent versions, insofar as they exclude parents unrestrictedly liable to pay tax living in marital community from the granting of the household allowance.
3. …
4. …
5. The legislature is obliged at the latest with effect as on 1 January 2000 to bring about a new regulation as to the provisions declared unconstitutional at 1., and at the latest with effect as on 1 January 2002 as to the provisions declared unconstitutional at 2. The previous provisions shall remain applicable until that time.
Insofar as no new regulation has yet entered into force with effect as on 1 January 2000, § 33c of the Income Tax Act shall continue to apply on the proviso that, from this time, childcare costs in the amount specified in § 33c.3 of the Income Tax Act shall be deducted from income within the meaning of § 2.4 of the Income Tax Act – regardless of gainful employment and of concrete expenditure – in ascertaining the taxable income of all parents entitled to child allowances or child benefit for the child.
6. …

EXTRACT FROM GROUNDS:

A.

The constitutional complaints relate to the question of whether it is compatible with the Basic Law for parents living in marital community to be excluded from the right to deduct childcare costs resulting from gainful employment as extraordinary expenses from the base for assessment for income tax, as well as from the granting of a household allowance.

I.

1. With regard to the definition and preconditions of the possibilities to offset childcare costs against tax, § 33c of the Income Tax Act contains the following provision in the versions relevant in the instant case:

Childcare costs of single parents

> (1) Expenditure on services for the care of a child who is unrestrictedly liable to income tax, has not yet reached the age of 16 at the beginning of the calendar year, and who belongs to the household of a single parent (§ 32.4 sentence 1), shall be deemed to be an extraordinary expense within the meaning of § 33 insofar as the expenditure arises from gainful employment. The expenditure can only be allowed insofar as it is necessary according to the circumstances and does not exceed a suitable amount. Expenditure for teaching, imparting special skills, sports and other leisure activities shall not be allowed.
> (2) Unmarried persons and married persons who are permanently separated from their spouse shall be deemed to be single parents. Married persons whose spouse is not unrestrictedly liable to income tax shall also be deemed to be single parents.
> (3) The amount to be deducted in accordance with subsection 1 may not exceed 4,000 Deutsche Mark per calendar year for single parents with one child (subsection 1 sentence 1). This amount shall increase by 2,000 Deutsche Mark for each additional child. The maximum amount or additional amount allowable for the child shall be reduced by one-twelfth for each full calendar month in which the preconditions of subsection 1 were not met. If the child belonged to the household of two single parents at the same time, each of them shall be entitled to half the relevant maximum amount or additional amount.
> (4) At least a flat-rate amount of 480 Deutsche Mark per calendar year shall be deducted for expenditure within the meaning of subsection 1 for single parents with one child (subsection 1 sentence 1). The flat rate shall increase by 480 Deutsche Mark for each further child. Subsection 3 sentences 3 and 4 shall apply *mutatis mutandis*.

This provision, which was introduced on the basis of Article 3 no. 19 of the Tax Correction Act 1985 of 14 December 1984 (Federal Law Gazette I p. 1493), was expanded by Article 1 no. 13 of the 1986/1988 Tax Reduction Act of 26 June 1985 (Federal Law Gazette I p. 1153), and then read as follows:

> (1) Expenditure on services for the care of a child who is unrestrictedly liable to income tax, who belongs to the household of a single parent, and who is to be allowed in accordance with § 32.1 to 3, shall be deemed to be an extraordinary expense within the meaning of § 33 insofar as the expenditure arises from

1. gainful employment, or
2. physical, mental or emotional disability, or
3. illness

of the taxpayer. In the case of no. 3, the illness must have existed within a consecutive period of at least three months. Sentence 2 shall not apply insofar as the case of illness arises directly after gainful employment. The expenditure can only be allowed insofar as it is necessary according to the circumstances and does not exceed a suitable amount. Expenditure for teaching, imparting special skills, sports and other leisure activities shall not be allowed.

(2) Unmarried persons and married persons who are permanently separated from their spouse shall be deemed to be single parents. Married persons whose spouse is not unrestrictedly liable to income tax shall also be deemed to be single parents.

(3) The amount to be deducted in accordance with subsection 1 may not exceed 4,000 Deutsche Mark per calendar year for single parents with one child (subsection 1 sentence 1). This amount shall increase by 2,000 Deutsche Mark for each additional child. The maximum amount or additional amount allowable for the child shall be reduced by one-twelfth for each full calendar month in which the preconditions of subsection 1 were not met. If the child belonged to the household of two single parents at the same time, each of them shall be entitled to half the relevant maximum amount or additional amount.

(4) At least a flat-rate amount of 480 Deutsche Mark per calendar year shall be deducted for expenditure within the meaning of subsection 1 for single parents with one child (subsection 1 sentence 1). The flat rate shall increase by 480 Deutsche Mark for each further child. Subsection 3 sentences 3 and 4 shall apply *mutatis mutandis*.

(5) With spouses who are both unrestrictedly liable to income tax are and not permanently separated, subsection 1, subsection 3 sentences 1 to 3 and subsection 4 shall apply *mutatis mutandis* insofar as the expenditure arose from
1. physical, mental or emotional disability, or
2. illness

of a spouse if the other spouse is in gainful employment or also ill or disabled.

…

2. To compensate for the disadvantages of single parent taxpayers with children, the Income Tax Act furthermore provides for a special allowance for increased housing- and household-related expenditure.

The provision contained in § 32.3 and 32.4 of the Income Tax Act applied in the new version of the Income Tax Act promulgated on 24 January 1984 (Federal Law Gazette I p. 113) for the assessment years 1983 and 1984:

Subsection 3:
A taxpayer to whom the preconditions of § 32a.5 or 32a.6 do not apply, and who is not to be assessed separately for income tax in accordance with §§ 26 and 26a, shall be granted a household allowance of 4,212 Deutsche Mark insofar as he or she has at least one child during the assessment period.

Subsection 4:
Children within the meaning of subsection 3 shall be:

1. children who are first-degree relatives of the taxpayer,
2. foster children,
3. stepchildren who the taxpayer has taken into his or her household, as long as the marriage exists by means of which the stepchild relationship has been established.

A child of a parent couple unrestrictedly liable to income tax to whom the preconditions of § 26.1 sentence 1 do not apply shall be allocated to the parent in whose home his or her main residence was first registered in the calendar year. If the child was not registered in a home of a parent, or if his or her main residence was registered in a joint home of the parents, he or she shall be attributed to the mother; he or she shall be attributed to the father if the latter proves by a certification of the competent authority that the child has belonged to his household.

In the assessment years 1986 and 1987, § 32.7 of the Income Tax Act applied in new version of the Income Tax Act promulgated on 15 April 1986 (Federal Law Gazette I p. 441):

A household allowance of 4,536 Deutsche Mark shall be deducted from income in the case of a taxpayer who does not meet the preconditions of §§ 32a.5 or 32a.6, and who is not to be assessed separately for income tax in accordance with §§ 26 and 26a, insofar as he or she receives a child allowance. If the other parent is also unrestrictedly liable to income tax, the taxpayer shall receive the household allowance only if the child for whom a child allowance is deducted is to be attributed to him or her. A child of a parent couple unrestrictedly liable to income tax to whom the preconditions of § 26.1 sentence 1 do not apply shall be allocated to the parent in whose home his or her main residence was first registered in the calendar year. If the child was not registered in a home of a parent, or if his or her main residence was registered in a joint home of the parents, he or she shall be attributed to the mother; he or she shall be attributed to the father instead of to the mother if the father proves by a certification of the competent authority that the child has belonged to his household.

II.

1. In the contentious assessment years 1983, 1984, 1986 and 1987, the complainants lived in a marital family community with their children, who were under 16 years of age. Both parents were gainfully employed for at least some of this period, and were assessed jointly for tax. The complainants applied for the expenditure incurred in these periods for the care of their children to be allowed in accordance with § 33c of the Income Tax Act in the respectively applicable version. These requests were rejected by the competent tax offices. The actions lodged against this were unsuccessful. The finance courts considered themselves prevented from including the complainants in the regulation on the deduction of childcare costs in accordance with § 33c of the Income Tax Act and in the regulation on the household allowance because the respective provisions exclusively entitled single parents with children. …
2. The … appeal on points of law lodged … against this was rejected as unfounded by judgment of the Federal Finance Court of 15 March 1991 …

III.

With their constitutional complaints the complainants … [i]ndirectly … [also] object to § 33c of the Income Tax Act in the respectively applicable versions.
… [They] complain of a violation of their fundamental rights under Article 3.1 in conjunction with Article 6.1 of the Basic Law. … They argue that the legislature may not create unrealistic boundaries to tax allowance for necessary maintenance expenditure … Further, in tax allowance for necessary childcare expenditure, it may not favour single parents over parents living in marital community … Also, only granting the household allowance to unmarried parents was said to give rise to unconstitutional discrimination against spouses with children as against other parents.
…

IV.

The President of the Federal Finance Court submitted to the proceedings statements by two Senates. The Federal Minister of Finance made a statement for the Federal Government.

…

B.

The … constitutional complaints are admissible and well-founded insofar as they oppose exclusion of the complainants from deduction of childcare costs and from a household allowance. In this scope, the impugned court rulings and the statutory provisions on which they are based in this respect are incompatible with Article 6.1 and 6.2 of the Basic Law.

…

I.

1. a) The care and upbringing of children is the natural right of and a duty primarily incumbent on the parents (Article 6.2 sentence 1 of the Basic Law). The parents perform this duty within the family, which is above all a child-raising community (see BVerfGE 80, 81 (90 et seq.)), but also an economic community (see BVerfGE 80, 81 (90); 82, 60 (87)). The parents owe to the children benefits in kind covering the children's economic requirements, as well as care and upbringing meeting the child's need for support, instruction and provision of practical and cultural experience. Article 6 of the Basic Law establishes a comprehensive parental responsibility for the development of the child enabling it to live a responsible life in this society (see BVerfGE 57, 170 (178); 80, 81 (91)).

b) The duty of bringing up their children (Article 6.2 sentence 1 of the Basic Law) affects the parents as a highly personal responsibility which however does not have to be performed by them exclusively in their own person. Article 6.1 of the Basic Law guarantees as a protective right the freedom to decide personally on the shape of marital and family co-habitation (see BVerfGE 61, 319 (347) with further references). For this reason, the state must respect the family community both in the immaterial-personal and in the material-economic sphere with regard to its respective independent, autonomous decisions (BVerfGE 61, 319 (347) with further references). Accordingly, parents may plan and realise their family life ideas as they see fit, and in particular may decide within their responsibility for bringing up their children whether and at what stage of development the child is to be taken care of

largely by one parent alone, by both parents in alternation or by a third party. In particular, the parents determine within their responsibility, on proviso of Article 7 of the Basic Law, whether and to what degree they wish to commission others to exercise their mandate for bringing up their children (see BVerfGE 47, 46 (70)).
c) In accordance with Article 6.1 of the Basic Law, the family enjoys the special protection of the state. The state's watchdog function (Article 6.2 sentence 2 of the Basic Law) however does not entitle the state to enforce on parents a specific manner of bringing up their children. The Basic Law leaves it to the parents to decide on the model for bringing up their children (see BVerfGE 24, 119 (143); 47, 46 (69-70)), to determine the manner in which the child is cared for, its opportunities for social contact or experience, and the content of its education. This primary responsibility of the parents for decision-making is based on the consideration that the interests of the child as a rule are best satisfied by the parents (see BVerfGE 72, 122 (139-140)).
2. a) Article 6.1 of the Basic Law also contains a special principle of equality. It prohibits placing marriage and the family on a worse footing in comparison with other partnerships and child-raising communities (prohibition of discrimination, see BVerfGE 76, 1 (72)). Article 6.1 of the Basic Law prohibits discrimination of spouses as against unmarried persons (see BVerfGE 28, 324 (347); 69, 188 (205-206)), of parents as against the childless (see BVerfGE 82, 60 (80); 87, 1 (37)) as well as of marital as against other child-raising communities (see BVerfGE 61, 319 (355)). This prohibition of discrimination opposes all differentiation imposing burdens linked to the existence of a marriage (Article 6.1 of the Basic Law) or to the exercise of parental rights in a marital child-raising community (Article 6.1 and 6.2 of the Basic Law).
b) Discrimination also exists if spouses or parents are excluded from tax relief because of their marriage or family and the manner in which same is arranged (see BVerfGE 12, 151 (167)). The principle of fiscal equality requires at least for direct taxes a burden that is related to financial ability to pay (see BVerfGE 43, 1 (8 et seq.); 61, 319 (343); 66, 214 (222); 82, 60 (86); 89, 346 (352)). The Federal Constitutional Court makes clear the constitutional principle of income taxation by ability to pay in the duty incumbent on the legislature enacting tax law to exempt from taxation that non-disposable income which is necessary for the minimum family income.
3. a) The constitutional precept follows from Article 1.1 of the Basic Law in conjunction with the principle of the social welfare state contained in Article 20.1 of the Basic Law that the state must exempt the income of the taxpayer from tax insofar as it constitutes a minimum precondition of dignified existence – "minimum income" – (see BVerfGE 82, 60 (85)). When it comes to the taxation of a family, this

applies – Article 6.1 of the Basic Law also being allowed for – to the minimum income of all family members (see BVerfGE 82, 60 (85); 87, 153 (169)). In judging fiscal ability to pay, the state must hence leave out of consideration as taxable income the taxpayer's maintenance expenditure for children insofar as this is necessary to guarantee the minimum income of the children (see BVerfGE 82, 60 (87)). This minimum income is measured by the requirement, not by actual expenditure (see BVerfGE 82, 60 (91); 87, 153 (170)). Over and above this, the court stresses that child maintenance is not to be placed on an equal legal footing with the private meeting of needs, which is why the legislature enacting tax law may not encroach on the indispensable means for the care and upbringing of children such as on financial means used to meet any other needs (see BVerfGE 82, 60 (87); 84, 348 (359-360); 87, 1 (38); 87, 153 (170)).
Over and above the child's existential material needs and the work-related care requirements, parents' ability to pay is hence reduced in general terms by virtue of the care requirements. These care requirements are to be fiscally subsidised as an element of child-related minimum income. Because of the care obligations, which affect their work or their ability to pay, taxpayers with children are able to pay less tax in comparison with childless taxpayers. If this requirement, based on parents' duty to bring up, and care for, their children, were not to be allowed in assessing income tax, the parents would be placed at a disadvantage as against childless taxpayers whose ability to pay is not reduced by meeting parental obligations. The principle of horizontal equality (see BVerfGE 82, 60 (89-90)) would be violated.
b) As a necessary element of minimum family income (see BVerfGE 82, 60 (85); 87, 153 (169 et seq.)), the care requirements must remain unburdened by income tax without it being permissible to distinguish how this requirement is met. The Income Tax Act has always to subsidise the care requirements of a child, whether the parents consider it to be correct in pedagogical terms to care for the child personally, to avail themselves of third-party care for the child for a time, for instance at a kindergarten, or if both parents opt for gainful employment and hence avail themselves of third-party care.
4. In addition to the duty to recognise the decisions made by parents in the service of the child's best interests and not to impose on them any disadvantageous legal consequences, the task of the state to actually facilitate and support childcare in the form respectively selected by the parents also emerges from the duty of protection contained in Article 6.1 of the Basic Law. Childcare is a service also in the interest of the community and which demands to be recognised by the community (see BVerfGE 87, 1 (38-39); 88, 203 (258-259)). Accordingly, the state must ensure that parents are equally able to forgo their own gainful employment, in part and temporarily, in favour of personally taking care of their children, as well as to reconcile

work within the family and gainful employment. The state must also create a situation in which the exercise of bringing up children within the family does not lead to disadvantages at work, in which it is possible to return to work, as well as to reconcile the bringing up of children and gainful employment for both parents, including professional advancement during and after times of bringing up children, and in which the services provided by institutional childcare are improved (see BVerfGE 88, 203 (260)).

II.

1. a) In accordance with this standard, the provisions of § 33c.1 to 33c.4 of the Income Tax Act on the fiscal accommodation of childcare costs resulting from gainful employment violate the complainants' right under Article 6.1 and 6.2 of the Basic Law. They place the marital child-raising community of working parents at a disadvantage when compared to other child-raising communities, and hence run counter to the prohibition of discrimination contained in Article 6.1 and 6.2 of the Basic Law.

§ 33c of the Income Tax Act permits "single parent" taxpayers (§ 33c.2 of the Income Tax Act) to deduct childcare costs resulting from gainful employment. Here, § 33c.2 of the Income Tax Act defines as single parents those who are unmarried, or spouses who are married but permanently separated, as well as married persons whose spouse is not unrestrictedly liable to income tax. Unmarried persons are also "single parents" if they live in a non-marital community. The distinction of § 33c.2 of the Income Tax Act between "single parents" able to deduct and married persons not able to do so can hence not be traced back to a different ability to pay taxes on the part of the two groups. The determination of the party entitled to deduct from tax goes beyond the group of single parents exclusively relying on themselves, and also includes in the fiscal exemption co-habiting and unmarried parents paying maintenance to one another. Apart from cases falling under § 33c.5 of the Income Tax Act, it is only the care costs incurred by parents who are unrestrictedly liable to pay tax, and who live in a marital community, that are subject to income tax.

…

b) Moreover, care costs – beyond the flat rate – can only be claimed in accordance with § 33c.1 sentence 2 (later: § 33c.1 sentence 4) of the Income Tax Act insofar as they are necessary according to the circumstances. This element is alleged not to apply if the taxpayer co-habits with the other parent of the child and the other parent is not in gainful employment … What is more, a need for the care costs is denied if and to the extent that the child cared for or the single parent receive remuneration with which childcare costs are to be paid … Also with this interpretation, single parent taxpayers within the meaning of § 33c.2 of the Income Tax Act may however also deduct childcare costs from the base for assessment for income tax if they are not forced to take up gainful employment because they receive sufficient payments from the other parent for their own maintenance. The childcare costs of such "single parents" are however not more or less necessary than those of parents living in a marital community.

Rather, according to the area protected by Article 6.2 of the Basic Law, it is constitutionally necessary to allow the care expenditure for children with all parents in terms of fiscal law. It arises regardless of whether and if so in what timeframe childcare is provided by third parties. This already finds expression in the statutory provisions on child-raising allowance, on child-raising leave and on the allowance of child-raising periods under pension law. Care expenditure is to be included in the child's minimum income in the same way as material expenditure. This concept also forms the basis for the provisions contained in §§ 1570 and 1615l of the Civil Code (*Bürgerliches Gesetzbuch* – BGB). These provisions afford maintenance to the caring parent with which the latter is not supposed to be able to dispense …

The restriction of the deductibility of childcare costs (§ 33c.1 of the Income Tax Act) and of the imposition of a flat rate on these costs (§ 33c.4 of the Income Tax Act) to single parents within the meaning of § 33c.2 of the Income Tax Act hence violates the marital child-raising community – unrestrictedly liable to pay tax – in terms of its claim to be treated equally under Article 6.1 and 6.2 of the Basic Law. The law denies deduction solely because of the element of marriage, and in this respect violates the prohibition of discrimination contained in Article 6.1 of the Basic Law.

…

d) Nothing has changed as to the unconstitutionality of the impugned legal situation by virtue of the introduction of the deduction amount in accordance with § 10.1 no. 8 of the Income Tax Act. In accordance with this provision, a marital child-raising community could claim expenditure of up to DM 12,000 per calendar year for household employment as special expenditure if there were two children who had not yet reached the age of ten at the beginning of the calendar year. Single parents within the meaning of § 33c.2 of the Income Tax Act could already make use of this deductibility if they only had one child under ten years of age. In this way, this provision too placed marital child-raising communities with one child at a disadvantage in comparison with other child-raising communities with one child.

This differentiation has been abolished in the version of § 10.1 no. 8 of the Income Tax Act applicable since 28 December 1996. By contrast, this deductibility is now equally open to parents liable to pay tax and to childless taxpayers. It is therefore for this reason not to be regarded as compensation for childcare costs.

2. Also the provision contained in § 32.3 and 32.4 of the 1984 Income Tax Act (later: § 32.7 of the Income Tax Act) regarding the deduction of a household allowance violates Article 6.1 and 6.2 of the Basic Law because it places marital communities at a disadvantage in comparison with other child-raising communities. The legislature grants a household allowance to non-marital child-raising communities, even if each parent has a right to a basic allowance, whilst the household allowance is in principle denied to spouses.

The household allowance is to compensate for the increased expenditure of single parent taxpayers who are forced to expand their home and their household because of their children. Single parents with children are to receive an additional allowance similar to a further basic allowance, and hence are to be taxed in the proportional area of income tax in an identical manner to spouses who are assessed jointly (see *Bundestag* printed paper (*Bundestagsdrucksache* – BTDrucks) 7/1470, p. 283 re § 79 and § 80 of the draft, as well as p. 222). The household allowance is linked solely to the household of the single parent taxpayer, but does not increase with the number of children.

The second basic allowance for unmarried parents is not compatible with Article 6.1 and 6.2 of the Basic Law because it is withheld from marital child-raising communities, but is granted to unmarried parents even if they form a child-raising community and both are liable to pay tax. In this case, the respective income is already fiscally subsidised in the amount of the basic allowance (see § 32a.1 sentence 2 no. 1 of the Income Tax Act). The household allowance, as a "third basic allowance", favours such child-raising communities over marital child-raising communities.

This different treatment can also not be traced in this case to a greater child-related increase in household expenditure of the deducting non-marital child-raising community as against a married child-raising community. In principle, the addition of a child increases parents' housekeeping expenditure. This expenditure is the same for each joint household of the parents. If the expenditure to establish a household was also related to marriage with married parents, whereas with single parents by contrast it was at least partly child-related, this one-off requirement is neither the subject nor the reason for the provision contained in § 32.7 (earlier: § 32.3 and 32.4) of the Income Tax Act. The fiscally relevant general additional household requirement recurring in each assessment year, by contrast, which is permitted for deduction here, is the same with married and unmarried parents, so that no different fiscal accommodation is justified.

If a child does not live with his or her parents, but in a third place, it is also not evident why additional child-related expenditure nevertheless arising is not incurred in the same manner in a marital child-raising community. The objection that accommodation of a child in a boarding school, or in medical or other care facilities

is avoidable in a marital community of the parents is not compatible with the parents' right to freely shape family co-habitation emerging from Article 6.1 and 6.2 of the Basic Law.
3. Also the possibility of joint assessment (§§ 26 and 26b of the Income Tax Act) which is available to the parents living in a marital community does not reduce their discrimination by virtue of the impugned provision. The joint assessment can be claimed by all spouses, regardless of whether they have children entitled to maintenance or not; the joint assessment is conditional on a marriage, but not on a child-related requirement. Taking into account the legal consequences of §§ 26 and 26b of the Income Tax Act to compensate for the less advantageous fiscal position hence can already not be considered because it would place married parents at a disadvantage as against spouses without children having a maintenance claim. Moreover, the relief provided by joint assessment depends on the amount of the respective income of both spouses, and on the progression rate. Joint assessment has virtually no impact if both spouses are in gainful employment and have similar income amounts.

C.

In addition to this discrimination of marital as against other child-raising communities, which is not compatible with Article 6.1 and 6.2 of the Basic Law, the fiscal allowance of parents' reduced ability to pay is as a whole less than what is constitutionally required in accordance with Article 6.1 and 6.2 of the Basic Law, and places parents at a disadvantage who are unable to claim the tax relief under § 33c and § 32.7 of the Income Tax Act, including in comparison with childless taxpayers.

I.

Child allowances and child benefit cover in the main only the child's minimum material income. The care requirements of each child are to date only allowed – in violation of equality (see above B.II.1.) – if they arose with single parents within the meaning of § 33c.2 of the Income Tax Act in connection with gainful employment, with illness or disability, or if a parent living in a marital community is ill or disabled and the other is either in gainful employment or is also ill or disabled (§ 33c.1 to 3 and 33c.5 of the Income Tax Act). These provisions do not allow for the fact that the child's care requirements exist regardless of the illness, disability or gainful employment of the parents, and also do not depend on the nature of the provision of the care services.

In the new version of subsidy of the care requirements under the law on income tax, the legislature will hence have to accommodate the same care-related reduction in the fiscal ability to pay with all parents – regardless of the nature of the care and of concrete expenditure – and accordingly increase the child allowance or the child benefit.

II.

In addition to the care requirements (§ 33c of the Income Tax Act), the Income Tax Act also neglects the expenditure of the parents who facilitate the child's personal development and his or her development to become independent and take responsibility (child-raising requirements). It allows in the "household allowance" – incorrectly designated and imposing restrictions constituting a violation of equality (see above B.II.2.) – a child-related additional requirement covering this requirement of the child in the mathematical result. It is not considered here, however, that all parents must meet this additional requirement of the child. In the necessary review of compensation for child-related expenses, the legislature must hence (see ... [BVerfGE 99, 246]) take account of this child-raising requirement of the child regardless of civil status for all parents who receive a child allowance or child benefit.

Also this child-raising requirement is not sufficiently complied with by child allowance and child benefit. Whilst the maintenance necessary for the granting of social assistance, and hence relevant for determining the general fiscal minimum income, also includes personal needs of daily life, in addition to food, accommodation, clothes, physical hygiene, household goods and heating (§ 12.1 sentence 1 and § 22.1 of the Federal Social Assistance Act (*Bundessozialhilfegesetz* – BSHG) in conjunction with § 1.1 sentence 1 of the Ordinance on the Implementation of § 22 of the Federal Social Assistance Act – Standard Rate Ordinance (*Verordnung zur Durchführung des § 22 des Bundessozialhilfegesetzes – Regelsatzverordnung*) of 20 July 1962 (Federal Law Gazette I p. 515), most recently amended by Article 11 of the Act Reforming the Law on Social Assistance (*Gesetz zur Reform des Sozialhilferechts*) of 23 July 1996 (Federal Law Gazette I p. 1088)). This minimum also includes to a justifiable degree social relationships and participation in cultural life (see § 12.1 sentence 2 of the Federal Social Assistance Act). For children and juveniles, the necessary maintenance also includes special requirements, above all those necessitated by their development and growth (see § 12.2 of the Federal Social Assistance Act in the version of the Act Reforming the Law on Social Assistance of 23 July 1996 (Federal Law Gazette I p. 1088) as well as the reasoning of the draft Bill on this (*Bundestag* printed paper 13/3904, p. 44)).

In quantifying this requirement, however, the general costs incurred by parents in order to facilitate the child's development enabling it to live responsibly in this society are not yet sufficiently allowed (see BVerfGE 57, 170 (178); 80, 81 (91)). This includes today for instance – in contradistinction to § 33c.1 sentence 5 of the Income Tax Act – membership of associations as well as other forms of social contact with other children or juveniles outside the domestic sphere, learning and trying out modern communication technologies, access to culture and language, responsible use of free time and the planning of holidays.
To assess this child-raising requirement of children to be met by all parents, the previous household allowance provides a quantitative orientation which is however to be graduated in line with the number of children.
…

D. – I.

The unconstitutionality of the provisions on the deduction of childcare costs resulting from gainful employment (§ 33c.1 to 4 of the Income Tax Act), and on the household allowance (§ 32.3 and 32.4 of the Income Tax Act 1984; later: § 32.7 of the Income Tax Act), on which the impugned court rulings were based covers these provisions in the respective versions.
The unconstitutional provisions on which the rulings impugned with the constitutional complaints are based are only to be declared incompatible with the Basic Law (see § 95.3 sentences 2 and 3, § 79 of the Federal Constitutional Court Act (*Bundesverfassungsgerichtsgesetz* – BVerfGG)). A declaration of nullity would make the constitutionally required allowance of care expenditure and of a household allowance entirely cease to apply, and would hence create a legal situation which would be even less compatible with Article 6.1 and 6.2 of the Basic Law than the provisions of § 33c.1 to 4 and of § 32.3 and 32.4 of the 1984 Income Tax Act (later: § 32.7 of the Income Tax Act). The unconstitutional provisions hence remain temporarily applicable.
1. The provisions of § 33c of the Income Tax Act which have been declared unconstitutional continue to apply until 31 December 1999. … In the framework of this new regulation, the legislature must expand allowance of this care requirement to all parents, regardless of how they provide for this requirement of their children.
2. The provision on the household allowance remains applicable until 31 December 2001. Until this time, the legislature must correct the discrimination of the marital child-raising community brought about by excluding the marital child-raising community from the deduction of a household allowance. …

III.

…

In view of the constitutionally required gradual adjustment of the applicable law, the complainants in the proceedings 2 BvR 1057/91, 2 BvR 1226/91 and 2 BvR 980/91 have a right to the success of their constitutional complaints also having an effect for them, for the respectively pending assessment periods, such that income tax relief should correspond to the constitutional requirements. The Federal Finance Court, to which the proceedings are referred, must hence examine whether by expanding application of the impugned provisions of the Income Tax Act, or by corresponding application of the legal concept of §§ 163 and 227 of the Tax Code, … it can be ensured that the relief envisioned in § 33c, § 32.3 and 32.4 of the 1984 Income Tax Act and § 32.7 of the 1986 Income Tax Act benefits the complainants in the concrete cases. Otherwise, the legislature would have to hand down a retroactive regulation in this respect.

…

E.

…

F.

This decision was passed with 7:1 votes re no. 5 of the ruling, in other respects unanimously as concerns the result.

Justices: Limbach, Kirchhof, Winter, Sommer, Jentsch, Hassemer, Broß, Osterloh

Following the Federal Constitutional Court's decision, the legislature abrogated § 33c of the Income Tax Act by Article 1 no. 13 of the Family Promotion Act (Familienförderungsgesetz) *of 22 December 1999 (Federal Law Gazette I 1999 p. 2552) with effect from 1 January 2000. The Second Family Promotion Act of 16 August 2001 (Federal Law Gazette I 2001 p. 2074) introduced a new version of § 33c of the Income Tax Act with effect from 1 January 2002 to implement the requirements of the Federal Constitutional Court's decision.*
The household allowance provided for in § 32.7 of the Income Tax Act was reduced, with effect from 1 January 2002, by Article 1 no. 7c of the Second Family

Promotion Act of 16 August 2001 (Federal Law Gazette I 2001 p. 2074). The Budget Support Act (Haushaltsbegleitgesetz) *2004 of 29 December 2003 (Federal Law Gazette I 2003 p. 3076) repealed the household allowance with effect from 1 January 2004 and replaced it by an allowance for single parents.*

No. 28

BVerfGE 99, 246
of 10 November 1998 – 2 BvL 42/93 –
"Minimum child income case"

HEADNOTES:

Art 6.1 of the Basic Law (*Grundgesetz* – GG) requires that with regard to the taxation of a family the minimum income of all family members is to be exempt from tax:

a) Here, the minimum income defined by the law on social assistance forms the boundary for minimum income in terms of income tax which may be exceeded, but which must indeed be reached.

b) The full amount of minimum income in terms of income tax is to be exempted from income tax for all taxpayers – regardless of their individual marginal tax rate.

c) The residential requirement is not to be calculated in accordance with the per capita method, but in accordance with the additional requirement.

Order of the Second Senate of 10 November 1998
– 2 BvL 42/93 –

in the proceedings for constitutional review as to whether § 32.6 of the Income Tax Act (*Einkommensteuergesetz*) in the version of the 1986/1988 Tax Reduction Act (*Steuersenkungsgesetz*) of 26 June 1985 (Federal Law Gazette (*Bundesgesetzblatt* – BGBl) I p. 1153, Federal Tax Gazette (*Bundessteuerblatt* – BStBl) I p. 391) is compatible with Article 3.1 in conjunction with Article 6.1 of the Basic Law insofar as according to this provision parents with one child may only claim a (joint) child allowance of DM 2,484 – suspension of proceedings and submission order of the Federal Finance Court (*Bundesfinanzhof* – BFH) of 16 July 1993 - III R 206/90.

RULING:

§ 32.6 of the Income Tax Act in the version of the 1986/1988 Tax Reduction Act of 26 June 1985 (Federal Law Gazette I p. 1153) was incompatible with Article 3.1 in conjunction with Article 6.1 of the Basic Law (*Grundgesetz* – GG) in its application to the 1987 assessment period insofar as according to this provision parents with one child could only claim a joint child allowance of 2,484 Deutsche Mark.

EXTRACT FROM GROUNDS:

A.

The submission concerns the question of whether support for maintenance of a child granted by virtue of child benefit and child income tax allowances in the 1987 assessment period meets the constitutional requirements, as were illustrated in particular in the orders of the Federal Constitutional Court of 29 May 1990 (Decisions of the Federal Constitutional Court (*Entscheidungen des Bundesverfassungsgerichts* – BVerfGE) 82, 60) and of 12 June 1990 (BVerfGE 82, 198).

I.

To compensate for the general burdens associated with the maintenance of children, parents are granted child income tax allowances and child benefit in accordance with the so-called dual system (see BVerfGE 82, 60 (78-79) referring to *Bundestag* printed paper (*Bundestagsdrucksache* – BTDrucks) 9/2140, p. 66).

1. § 32.6 sentence 1 of the Income Tax Act in the version of the 1986/1988 Tax Reduction Act of 26 June 1985 (Federal Law Gazette I p. 1153) provided a child allowance amounting to DM 1,242 for each child of the taxpayer to be allowed for. With spouses who were assessed jointly for income tax in accordance with §§ 26 and 26b of the Income Tax Act, the joint child allowance was doubled to DM 2,484 in accordance with § 32.6 sentence 2 of the Income Tax Act. The child allowance was also granted in this amount if a parental couple unrestrictedly liable to income tax did not meet the requirements of § 26.1 sentence 1 of the Income Tax Act – joint assessment –, but a parent applied for the transfer of the child allowance of the other parent to himself or herself and the other parent consented to this application (§ 32.6 sentence 4 of the Income Tax Act).

§ 32.6 had the following wording in the 1987 assessment period:

> A child allowance of 1,242 Deutsche Mark shall be deducted from income for each child of the taxpayer to be allowed for. Among spouses who are assessed for income tax jointly in accordance with §§ 26 and 26b, a child allowance of 2,484 Deutsche Mark shall be deducted if the child is the child of both spouses. A child allowance of 2,484 Deutsche Mark shall also be deducted if
> 1. the other parent died prior to the commencement of the calendar year or has not been unrestrictedly liable to income tax during the entire calendar year, or
> 2. the taxpayer alone has adopted the child or the child is only his or her foster child.
>
> In derogation from sentence 1, in the case of a parent couple unrestrictedly liable to income tax not meeting the preconditions of § 26.1 sentence 1, on request by one parent the child allowance of the other parent shall be transferred to him or her if he or she meets his or her maintenance obligation towards the child for the calendar year, but the other parent does not do so, or only to an insignificant degree, or if the other parent consents to the application; the consent may not be withdrawn.

2. The child benefit for the first child was DM 50 in accordance with § 10.1 of the Federal Child Benefit Act (*Bundeskindergeldgesetz*) in the version applicable to the 1987 assessment period promulgated on 21 January 1986 (on the legal development see BVerfGE 43, 108 (109-110); 82, 60 (61-62); 91, 93 (94 et seq.)).

II.

The plaintiff in the original proceedings was individually assessed for income tax in 1987, the year under contention. The Tax Office approved a child allowance in the amount of DM 2,484 in respect of the plaintiff's son which the plaintiff had applied for with the consent of the other parent.

In his objection, the plaintiff requested the approval of a higher child allowance. The objection and the action addressed against its rejection were unsuccessful.

The plaintiff continues to pursue his action with the appeal on points of law, and complains that neither the basic allowance nor the child allowance were sufficient in order to exempt his minimum income and that of his son from tax.

III.

1. The Third Senate of the Federal Finance Court suspended the proceedings in order to request a ruling of the Federal Constitutional Court on the legal validity of § 32.6 of the Income Tax Act. § 32.6 of the Income Tax Act was said to be incompatible with Article 3.1 in conjunction with Article 6.1 of the Basic Law insofar as according to this provision parents with one child could only claim a child allowance totalling DM 2,484.

...

IV.

The President of the Federal Finance Court has submitted a statement of the Ninth Senate on the submission order. The Federal Minister of Finance has made a statement for the Federal Government.

1. The Ninth Senate of the Federal Finance Court shares the view of the submitting Third Senate, according to which the child allowance for 1987 does not meet the constitutional requirements. ...

2. In the view of the Federal Government, the submission is unfounded. The amount of the child allowance in 1987 was said to also be in compliance with the constitutional principles which the Federal Constitutional Court had developed in its rulings. Children's fiscal minimum income which was to be exempted was said to be DM 353 per month, DM 4,236 per annum. ... This ... was to be compared for the first child with a child allowance of DM 2,484 and child benefit of DM 600 per annum. If child benefit were to be converted to a child allowance of DM 1,764 and for fiscal reasons rounded off to the amount of DM 1728, which is divisible by 108, it would be sufficient together with the child allowance to cover the minimum income of roughly 78 per cent of all taxpayers with one child. The minimum income for children was hence said to have been allowed for in full up to a taxable income of DM 31,645/DM 62,423 (basic/splitting tax table). The child allowance and child benefit was said to not completely cover the minimum income of roughly 22 per cent of taxpayers with one child from a marginal fiscal burden of roughly 35.4 per cent. Having said that, the increases in the fiscal burden in each case were said to be only small in this instance; with one child, the additional fiscal burden exceeded DM 100 with regard to only roughly 11 per cent of taxpayers, and only exceeded DM 200 per annum in roughly 5 per cent of cases.

The overall provisions of the Income Tax Act were said to be ultimately constitutional within the framework of the uncertainties to be accepted in such an estimate.

B.

The submission is admissible.

…

C.

§ 32.6 of the Income Tax Act in the version of the 1986/1988 of the Tax Reduction Act was incompatible with Article 3.1 in conjunction with Article 6.1 of the Basic Law in its application to the 1987 assessment period insofar as according to this provision parents with one child were only able to claim a child allowance totalling DM 2,484.

I.

In accordance with now established case-law of the Federal Constitutional Court, the Basic Law demands that a suitable, realistic amount of expenditure necessary to maintain a minimum standard of living is to be exempted from income tax. Social assistance law offers a comparative level quantifying the minimum income: The minimum income to be exempted from income tax may at any rate not go below the amount granted by the state to a needy person in the context of state welfare.

1. The constitutional examination standard is the principle emerging from Article 1 in conjunction with Article 20.1 of the Basic Law, namely that the state must exempt the taxpayer's income from tax insofar as it is needed to provide the minimum preconditions for a dignified existence (see BVerfGE 82, 60 (85)). The requirement necessary to maintain a minimum standard of living forms constitutionally the lower limit for encroachment by income tax (see BVerfGE 87, 153 (169)). Article 6.1 of the Basic Law requires over and above this that in the case of taxation of a family the minimum income of all family members must remain tax-free (see BVerfGE 82, 198 (207)).

2. The principle of equality (Article 3.1 of the Basic Law) establishes further constitutional requirements in its manifestation as "horizontal fiscal equality" (see BVerfGE 82, 60 (89-90)). It requires that taxpayers with equal ability to pay should be taxed in the same amounts. Also, recipients of higher incomes must be equally taxed depending on their ability to pay in comparison to recipients of equally high income; reduced ability to pay by virtue of a maintenance obligation towards a child, accordingly, must also be appropriately allowed for in their case in this comparison.

3. The expenditure necessary to maintain a minimum standard of living to be accommodated constitutionally must be measured – realistically – by the actual requirement (see BVerfGE 66, 214 (223); 68, 143 (153); 82, 60 (88)). Its lower limit is lent concrete shape by the social assistance benefits which are to guarantee the minimum income recognised in the social welfare state, calculated in terms of consumption and also regularly adjusted to the changed circumstances. The legislature must as a minimum leave to the income recipient the amount from his or her remuneration that it provides from public funds to a needy party in order to meet a requirement necessary to maintain a minimum standard of living (see BVerfGE 87, 153 (171); 91, 93 (111)).
a) The constitutionally specified standard of the minimum requirement necessary to maintain a minimum standard of living recognised under the law on social assistance is calculated on the basis of the Federal Social Assistance Act (*Bundessozialhilfegesetz*) in the following items:
1. standard rate in accordance with § 22.3 of the Federal Social Assistance Act
2. benefits for housing and heating in accordance with § 3.1 and 3.2 of the Standard Rate Ordinance (*Regelsatzverordnung*)
3. one-off assistance for additional fundamental requirements not covered by ongoing benefits
4. additional requirement in accordance with § 23.4 no. 1 of the Federal Social Assistance Act to account for the increased private needs caused by gainful employment.
b) These items to be accommodated on the basis of constitutional considerations (see BVerfGE 87, 153 (171)) may be typified in a generalising manner making it easier to process high-quantity procedures, but in so doing are to be measured such that the deduction amounts in all cases cover the requirement necessary to maintain a minimum standard of living; no taxpayer is hence required as a result of income taxation to ensure his or her requirement necessary to maintain a minimum standard of living by claiming state benefits (see BVerfGE 87, 153 (172)).
4. a) The fundamental constitutional questions on the reason and amount of the constitutionally required allowance of child maintenance expenditure are largely clarified by the rulings of the Federal Constitutional Court (BVerfGE 82, 60; 87, 153). However, the method of calculating the tax-free maintenance expenditure for the minimum income of children to be exempted from tax by the legislature is a matter for clarification.
The Federal Constitutional Court also previously included in its calculations the residential requirement value which is material to the minimum income, but did not yet consider an occasion to have arisen to explicitly set out the calculation method (left open in the Order of the First Senate, BVerfGE 91, 93 (113 et seq.), see also

Order of the Third Chamber of the First Senate of 13 December 1996 – 1 BvR 1474/88 – *Höchstrichterliche Finanzrechtsprechung* – HFR 1997, p. 251). The Federal Constitutional Court furthermore did not yet state precise figures as to the tax rate with which the child benefit actually paid is to be converted into a fictitious child allowance. In the Order of the First Senate, it merely ruled when unconstitutionality certainly did not arise. In the same ruling, with regard to the scope for assessment and prognosis it specifies a maximum guideline value of 15 per cent by which fiscal law may fall below the average social assistance requirement (see BVerfGE 91, 93 (115-116)). In particular the Federal Finance Court (BFH, *Deutsches Steuerrecht* – DStR 1998, p. 448 (449)) considers that there is still a need for further clarification here.

b) These three sub-values – the assessment technique for the residential requirement, the 15 per cent tolerance limit and the marginal tax rate which is material to the comparison – influence the amount of the minimum child income: The amount of the residential requirement determines the requirement figures as a whole; with the conversion of the child benefit into a child allowance, the applicable marginal tax rate directly determines the amount of the requirement to be accommodated by law; the tolerance limit opens an evaluation framework for the question of constitutionality.

5. a) The residential requirement is not to be calculated in accordance with the per capita method, but in accordance with the additional requirement. This per capita method, as used as a basis with the social assistance values, in principle presumes a proportional expansion of the residential requirement with each further individual; an equal share of the total residential premises is estimated for each person. By contrast, it should however be taken into account that an additional person in an existing household certainly does not give rise to a proportional additional requirement for shared rooms such as kitchen, bathroom or hall. For this reason, the calculation of the residential requirement is to be taken as a basis, using the technique of the additional requirement calculation, in accordance with which the legislature also currently assesses the child income tax allowance (see 1996 Report on the Amount of the Minimum Income of Children and Families (*Bericht über die Höhe des Existenzminimums von Kindern und Familien*), *Bundestag* printed paper 13/381, p. 4 as well as Report on the Amount of the Minimum Income of Children and Families for 1999, *Bundestag* printed paper 13/9561, p. 4). This method covers typical cases of the actual additional expenditure for the residential requirement.

b) The minimum income defined by the law on social assistance forms the boundary for minimum income in terms of income tax which may be exceeded, but which must indeed be reached. The First Senate of the Federal Constitutional Court has put forward, as one of the reasons for a tolerance value of 15 per cent, the circumstance that the residential requirement is alleged to have been calculated with the *guideline values* used there in accordance with the per capita method, and not in accordance with the lower values which merely accommodate the necessary additional requirement of residential premises (BVerfGE 91, 93 (113 et seq.), referring to the statements of the Federal Ministry for Family Affairs and Senior Citizens, the case-law of the Federal Administrative Court (*Entscheidungen des Bundesverwaltungsgerichts* – BVerwGE 79, 17, 20) and the case-law of the Federal Finance Court (Collected Decisions of the Federal Finance Court (*Sammlung der Entscheidungen des Bundesfinanzhofs* – BFHE) 171, 534, 539 et seq.)). The requirement calculation in accordance with the per capita method reaches values which tend to be higher, which can justify a 15 per cent tolerance. In principle, however, also the First Senate requires accommodation of the minimum income "where possible in all cases" within precise, realistic limits (BVerfGE 91, 93 (115)).

aa) In the case at hand, the calculation of the requirement values of 1987 is however based not on the per capita method, but on the additional requirement method. The requirement figures are based not on average guideline values (see BVerfGE 91, 93 (112)), but only on the minimum requirement necessary to maintain a minimum standard of living. These requirement values to determine the minimum standards of living are in each case only statistically documented *minimum* amounts which for this reason may be exceeded, but which must indeed be reached (see Report on the Amount of the Minimum Income of Children and Families of 1996, *Bundestag* printed paper 13/381, p. 4).

bb) Falling below statistically-calculated minimum amounts can also not be justified by the task of setting requirement figures for the future without being able to forecast future developments with certainty. The requirement necessary to maintain a minimum standard of living has thus not fallen in the Federal Republic in the past 50 years, but has regularly increased (Statistical Yearbook (*Statistisches Jahrbuch*) 1994, p. 662). The adjustment of the minimum income under income tax law has as a rule not kept pace with these increases. For this reason, at best it would be necessary to exceed the minimum values – by way of prevention or compensation.

c) Horizontal equality requires the full tax exemption of the minimum requirement necessary to maintain a minimum standard of living for the children of all taxpayers, regardless of their individual marginal tax rate.

aa) The conversion of child benefit into a tax allowance must accommodate the constitutional principle of horizontal fiscal justice, in accordance with which taxpayers whose ability to pay is equal are also to be taxed equally (see BVerfGE 82, 60 (89-90)). An additional fiscal burden on taxpayers with children in need of maintenance, in comparison with childless taxpayers with the same income, cannot be justified by taxpayers with a higher income being able to more easily endure lesser tax relief. This reasoning would permit in circumstances in which only the income of the taxpayer in question is sufficiently high any unequal fiscal treatment as against other recipients of the same amount of income, and would undermine – ultimately to the detriment of the children – the principle of taxation in accordance with ability to pay.

bb) Allowance for the minimum expenditure necessary to maintain a minimum standard of living for child maintenance which is not sufficient in all cases in income tax law is not justifiable with the necessity of a statutory generalisation. Each statutory provision must generalise (see BVerfGE 82, 126 (151); 96, 1 (6)), may in principle be orientated to the standard case, and in particular need not accommodate all possible variants of the respective individual case by means of special regulations. With constitutionally required (see C.I.1.-3. above) allowance for the minimum expenditure necessary to maintain a minimum standard of living for child maintenance, however, no individual case-related specialities are to be taken up in the elements and where appropriate to be typified; rather, a requirement that is equal for all is to be included in the requirements under the law on income tax.

If the legislature structures the compensation for children in accordance with the dual system by combining child allowance and child benefit, it must include on converting child benefit into a child allowance, which then becomes necessary, its own requirements of income tax law. The progressive income tax rate as defined by law applies only to taxable income (§ 2.5 sentence 1 of the Income Tax Act). This assessment base must be reduced by the fiscal minimum income, and is thus not open to imposition of income tax in the respective amount determined by law – be it at the starting or top rate.

cc) The principle of allowing in the assessment base for the minimum expenditure necessary to maintain a minimum standard of living for child maintenance with regard to all taxpayers, regardless of their individual marginal tax rate, also follows from the principle of consistency (see BVerfGE 84, 239 (271); 87, 153 (170); 93, 121 (136)). The legislature may in principle allow for the child-related reduction in ability to pay either in fiscal law, or instead of this in social law by granting sufficient child benefit, or may indeed combine provision of support in fiscal law and in the law on child benefit (see BVerfGE 82, 60 (84) referring to BVerfGE 43, 108 (123-124); 61, 319 (354)). The impact of the respective results from the various methods must however be equivalent. This would be contradicted if in the conversion of child benefit into a fiscal child allowance the child-related reduction in the ability to pay was not equally fully accommodated for each income taxpayer as would be the case if this reduction in ability to pay were to be accommodated solely by a tax allowance (BVerfGE 82, 60 (97)).

6. a) If the amount of the minimum requirement necessary to maintain a minimum standard of living is calculated in accordance with the data transmitted by the Federal Government … and with the calculation method recently used as a basis – housing costs calculated in accordance with the additional requirement method on the basis of a special survey of the Federal Statistical Office (see statement in the proceedings 2 BvR 1852/97 referring to *Bundestag* printed paper 13/9561 p. 4) – but in doing so the minimum requirement for all taxpayers – regardless of their marginal tax rate – is fully allowed for on the basis of constitutional considerations, and also no margin of tolerance is granted, the minimum requirement necessary to maintain a minimum standard of living of a child in the 1987 assessment period is DM 4,416 per child per year. This minimum requirement is calculated from the standard social assistance rate for children amounting to DM 253, one-off benefits of DM 40, an additional rent requirement amounting to DM 62 and heating costs amounting to DM 13 for each child per month. This gives rise to a monthly requirement of DM 368, and an annual requirement of DM 4,416.
b) This minimum income to be allowed for on the basis of constitutional considerations, amounting to DM 4,416, is opposed in accordance with the legislation submitted for a constitutional examination by a minimum requirement of between DM 3,555 and 4,484 recognised by § 32.6 of the 1986/1988 Income Tax Act and the social law. The plaintiff in the original proceedings has a marginal tax rate of 44 per cent; this gives rise for him to a statutory accommodation of the minimum child income amounting to DM 3,847; it is hence DM 569 below the minimum income to be allowed for on the basis of constitutional considerations, amounting to DM 4,416.
7. The derogations from the minimum income recognised by law and required by the constitution are summarised in the table below:

1987 Assessment period 1 child			
Statutory accommodation		Requirement …	Difference
with marginal tax rate			
30 per cent	4,484	4,416	+ 68
40 per cent	3,984	4,416	- 432
44 per cent	3,847	4,416	- 569
50 per cent	3,684	4,416	- 732
56 per cent	3,555	4,416	- 861

…

II.

The Federal Finance Court seeks an examination of the provision contained in § 32.6 of the Income Tax Act, but not also of the provisions of child benefit law included in the requirement calculation (see on this BVerfGE 82, 198 (206)).

The constitutional examination of the provisions of income tax law and child benefit law leads to the result that these provisions do not meet the constitutional requirements in their combination and in the overall allowance for the minimum child income reached thereby. The shortcoming which is material in constitutional terms can hence be caused by too low a child allowance or by child benefit being assessed in an inadequate amount.

Nonetheless, the object of examination is not to be expanded in the sense that both the child benefit law and the individual regulation of income tax law must be examined. In the combination of the child income tax allowance and child benefit under social law, both provisions are per se amenable to an expedient examination. The interrelations to the law on child benefit however also enable the legislature to remedy the constitutional shortcomings such that the provisions of the law on child benefit are adjusted to the constitutional requirements and the impugned income tax law provision of § 32.6 of the Income Tax Act can then ultimately remain unaffected (for instance also BVerfGE 82, 60 (84, 97)).

III.

The Federal Finance Court will have to examine whether, without an amendment of § 32.6 of the 1986/1988 Income Tax Act, it can also remit the income tax for the plaintiff in the original proceedings in accordance with the fundamental concept of §§ 163 and 227 of the Tax Code (*Abgabenordnung* – AO) in the amount which would emerge if the minimum child income to be allowed for on the basis of constitutional considerations in the shape of a child allowance were to be increased by DM 569. Similarly, the Federal Finance Court could find itself required to examine in the original proceedings, and in all sets of parallel proceedings pending before it, a constitutionally required reduction of the tax owed which also without implementing a separate [tax remission] procedure for reasons of equity [§§ 163 and 227 of the Tax Code] would grant to parents pursuing appeal on points of law proceedings their minimum child income as required by the constitution, and hence would eliminate the need for a new statutory regulation with effect for past assessment years and for a small number of cases. Otherwise, the legislature would be obliged in the cases not yet in effect to remedy the discrimination of the affected taxpayers. In any case, it is free to carry out the constitutionally required amendment by increasing the child income tax allowance, by increasing child benefit or by other compensatory regulations (see BVerfGE 82, 60 (97); 82, 198 (208)).

D.

This decision has been passed unanimously.

Justices: Limbach, Kirchhof, Winter, Sommer, Jentsch, Hassemer, Broß, Osterloh

Following the Federal Constitutional Court's decision, Article 1 no. 23 of the Family Promotion Act (Gesetz zur Familienförderung) *of 22 December 1999 (Federal Law Gazette I 1999 p. 2552) introduced, with effect from 1 January 2002, § 53 of the Income Tax Act as a special provision to exempt a child's minimum income from taxes in the 1983 to 1995 assessment periods.*

No. 29

BVerfGE 99, 300
of 24 November 1998 – 2 BvL 26/91, 5, 6, 7, 8, 9, 10/96, 3, 4, 5, 6/97 –
"Civil servants' children case
(state's obligation to take care of civil servants' welfare and family)"

HEADNOTES:

1. **The employer is obliged on the basis of the principle of the state's obligation to take care of civil servants' welfare (Article 33.5 of the Basic Law (*Grundgesetz – GG*)) to pay maintenance to civil servants that is in keeping with their office. This also includes the duty to realistically allow for the maintenance obligations incumbent on a civil servant by virtue of his or her family. Hence, the employer not lastly allows for the task of the permanent civil service to guarantee a stable, law-abiding administration in the interplay of political forces (confirmation of Decisions of the Federal Constitutional Court (*Entscheidungen des Bundesverfassungsgerichts* – BVerfGE 44, 249; 81, 363).**
2. **The remuneration of married civil servants with more than two children entitled to maintenance did not meet these requirements from 1988 to 1996. A general retroactive remedy of the violation of the constitution is however not required with regard to the specific characteristics of employment as a civil servant (as in BVerfGE 81, 363).**

Order of the Second Senate of 24 November 1998
– 2 BvL 26/91, 5, 6, 7, 8, 9, 10/96, 3, 4, 5, 6/97 –

in the proceedings for the constitutional review of
1. a) Article 1 § 1 in conjunction with Annex 2, as well as Article 6 § 5 sentence 1 of the 1987 Act on Adjustment of Salaries and Pensions in the Federation and the *Länder* – 1987 Federal Remuneration and Pensions Adjustment Act (*Gesetz über die Anpassung von Dienst- und Versorgungsbezügen in Bund und Ländern – Bundesbesoldungs- und -versorgungsanpassungsgesetz 1987*) of 6 August 1987 (Fed-

eral Law Gazette (*Bundesgesetzblatt* – BGBl) I p. 2062) in conjunction with Article 14 § 3 of the Act Reforming Public Service Law (*Gesetz zur Reform des öffentlichen Dienstrechts* (*Reformgesetz – Reform Act*)) of 24 February 1997 (Federal Law Gazette I p. 322),
b) Article 1 § 1 in conjunction with Annex 2, as well as Article 10 § 4.1 of the 1988 Act on Adjustment of Salaries and Pensions in the Federation and the *Länder* (1988 Federal Remuneration and Pensions Adjustment Act) of 20 December 1988 (Federal Law Gazette I p. 2363) in conjunction with Article 14 § 3 of the Act Reforming Public Service Law (Reform Act) of 24 February 1997 (Federal Law Gazette I p. 322),
c) Article 1 § 1 in conjunction with Annex 2, as well as Article 10 § 4.1 of the 1988 Act on Adjustment of Salaries and Pensions in the Federation and the *Länder* (1988 Federal Remuneration and Pensions Adjustment Act) of 20 December 1988 (Federal Law Gazette I p. 2363) in the version applicable from 1 January 1990,
d) Article 1 § 1 in conjunction with Annex 2, as well as Article 10 § 5.1 of the 1991 Act on Adjustment of Salaries and Pensions in the Federation and the *Länder* (1991 Federal Remuneration and Pensions Adjustment Act) of 21 February 1992 (Federal Law Gazette I p. 266),
e) Article 1 in conjunction with Annex 2, as well as Article 12.1 of the 1992 Act on Adjustment of Salaries and Pensions in the Federation and the *Länder* (1992 Federal Remuneration and Pensions Adjustment Act) of 23 March 1993 (Federal Law Gazette I p. 342),
f) Article 1 in conjunction with Annex 2, as well as Article 5 § 3.1 of the 1993 Act on Adjustment of Salaries and Pensions in the Federation and the *Länder* (1993 Federal Remuneration and Pensions Adjustment Act) of 20 December 1993 (Federal Law Gazette I p. 2139),
g) Article 1 in conjunction with Annex 2, as well as Article 9 § 3.1 of the 1994 Act on Adjustment of Salaries and Pensions in the Federation and the *Länder* (1994 Federal Remuneration and Pensions Adjustment Act) of 24 August 1994 (Federal Law Gazette I p. 2229) and
h) Article 1 in conjunction with Annex 2, as well as Article 15.1 of the 1995 Act on Adjustment of Salaries and Pensions in the Federation and the *Länder* (1995 Federal Remuneration and Pensions Adjustment Act) of 18 December 1995 (Federal Law Gazette I p. 1942),
insofar as they regard the local cost-of-living allowances of (salary) step 5 and higher of civil servants and judges

– of salary scale B 2 of the Federal Remuneration Ordinance (*Bundesbesoldungsordnung* – BBesO) in the years 1988 and 1989

- of salary scales A 4 to A 13 (not incl. A 5 and A 10), B 2, as well as of R 1 of the Federal Remuneration Ordinance in 1990;
- of salary scales A 4 to A 13 (not incl. A 10), as well as of R 1 of the Federal Remuneration Ordinance in 1991;
- of salary scales A 4 to A 14 (not incl. A 10), as well as of R 1 of the Federal Remuneration Ordinance in 1992;
- of salary scales A 4 to A 14 (not incl. A 10), as well as of R 1 of the Federal Remuneration Ordinance in 1993;
- of salary scales A 4 to A 15 (not incl. A 10), as well as of R 1 of the Federal Remuneration Ordinance in 1994;
- of salary scales A 4 to A 15 (not incl. A 10), as well as of R 1 and R 2 of the Federal Remuneration Ordinance in 1995;
- of salary scales A 4 to A 13 (not incl. A 10), as well as of R 2 of the Federal Remuneration Ordinance in 1996
- suspension of proceedings and submission order of the Freiburg im Breisgau Administrative Court (*Verwaltungsgericht*) of 9 October 1991 in the version of the order of 25 March 1998 (1 K 74/91) – 2 BvL 26/91,
- suspension of proceedings and submission order of the Regensburg Bavarian Administrative Court of 21 February 1996 (RO 1 K 93.2195) – 2 BvL 5/96,
- suspension of proceedings and submission order of the Regensburg Bavarian Administrative Court of 21 February 1996 (RO 1 K 93.0725) – 2 BvL 6/96,
- suspension of proceedings and submission order of the Regensburg Bavarian Administrative Court of 21 February 1996 (RO 1 K 91.2020) – 2 BvL 7/96,
- suspension of proceedings and submission order of the Regensburg Bavarian Administrative Court of 21 February 1996 (RO 1 K 91.0352) – 2 BvL 8/96,
- suspension of proceedings and submission order of the Osnabrück Administrative Court of 27 September 1995 (3 A 140/92) – 2 BvL 9/96,
- suspension of proceedings and submission order of the Frankfurt am Main Administrative Court of 22 January 1996 (9 E 3967/94 (2)) – 2 BvL 10/96,
- suspension of proceedings and submission order of the Koblenz Administrative Court of 22 April 1997 (6 K 2110/94.KO) – 2 BvL 3/97,
- suspension of proceedings and submission order of the Koblenz Administrative Court of 22 April 1997 (6 K 5073/94.KO) – 2 BvL 4/97,
- suspension of proceedings and submission order of the Koblenz Administrative Court of 28 May 1997 (10 K 3076/95.KO) – 2 BvL 5/97,

– suspension of proceedings and submission order of the Koblenz Administrative Court of 28 May 1997 (10 K 464/95.KO) - 2 BvL 6/97 –;

2. of § 2.1 of the Act on the Remuneration of Federal Civil Servants (*Bundesbesoldungsgesetz*), in so far as it denies the courts the opportunity to rule directly and conclusively on a right to constitutionally required care of the welfare of civil servants with more than two children that is in keeping with their office
– suspension of proceedings and submission order of the Frankfurt am Main Administrative Court of 22 January 1996 (9 E 3967/94 (2)) – 2 BvL 10/96 –.

RULING:

1. a) Article 1 § 1 in conjunction with Annex 2, as well as Article 6 § 5 sentence 1 of the 1987 Act on Adjustment of Salaries and Pensions in the Federation and the *Länder* (1987 Federal Remuneration and Pensions Adjustment Act) of 6 August 1987 (Federal Law Gazette I p. 2062) in conjunction with Article 14 § 3 of the Act Reforming Public Service Law (Reform Act) of 24 February 1997 (Federal Law Gazette I p. 322),
b) Article 1 § 1 in conjunction with Annex 2, as well as Article 10 § 4.1 of the 1988 Act on Adjustment of Salaries and Pensions in the Federation and the *Länder* (1988 Federal Remuneration and Pensions Adjustment Act) of 20 December 1988 (Federal Law Gazette I p. 2363) in conjunction with Article 14 § 3 of the Act Reforming Public Service Law (Reform Act) of 24 February 1997 (Federal Law Gazette I p. 322),
c) Article 1 § 1 in conjunction with Annex 2, as well as Article 10 § 4.1 of the 1988 Act on Adjustment of Salaries and Pensions in the Federation and the Länder (1988 Federal Remuneration and Pensions Adjustment Act) of 20 December 1988 (Federal Law Gazette I p. 2363) in the version applicable from 1 January 1990,
d) Article 1 § 1 in conjunction with Annex 2, as well as Article 10 § 5.1 of the 1991 Act on Adjustment of Salaries and Pensions in the Federation and the *Länder* (1991 Federal Remuneration and Pensions Adjustment Act) of 21 February 1992 (Federal Law Gazette I p. 266),
e) Article 1 in conjunction with Annex 2, as well as Article 12.1 of the 1992 Act on Adjustment of Salaries and Pensions in the Federation and the *Länder* (1992 Federal Remuneration and Pensions Adjustment Act) of 23 March 1993 (Federal Law Gazette I p. 342),
f) Article 1 in conjunction with Annex 2, as well as Article 5 § 3.1 of the 1993 Act on Adjustment of Salaries and Pensions in the Federation and the *Länder* (1993

Federal Remuneration and Pensions Adjustment Act) of 20 December 1993 (Federal Law Gazette I p. 2139),
g) Article 1 in conjunction with Annex 2, as well as Article 9 § 3.1 of the 1994 Act on Adjustment of Salaries and Pensions in the Federation and the *Länder* (1994 Federal Remuneration and Pensions Adjustment Act) of 24 August 1994 (Federal Law Gazette I p. 2229), and
h) Article 1 in conjunction with Annex 2, as well as Article 15.1 of the 1995 Act on Adjustment of Salaries and Pensions in the Federation and the *Länder* (1995 Federal Remuneration and Pensions Adjustment Act) of 18 December 1995 (Federal Law Gazette I p. 1942)
were not compatible with Article 33.5 of the Basic Law, insofar as the legislature

- in 1988 and 1989 with civil servants of salary scale B 2 of the Federal Remuneration Ordinance;
- in 1990 with civil servants and judges of salary scales A 4 to A 13 (not incl. A 5 and A 10), B 2, as well as of R 1 of the Federal Remuneration Ordinance;
- in 1991 with civil servants and judges of salary scales A 4 to A 13 (not incl. A 10), as well as of R 1 of the Federal Remuneration Ordinance;
- in 1992 with civil servants and judges of salary scales A 4 to A 14 (not incl. A 10), as well as of R 1 of the Federal Remuneration Ordinance;
- in 1993 with civil servants and judges of salary scales A 4 to A 14 (not incl. A 10), as well as of R 1 of the Federal Remuneration Ordinance;
- in 1994 with civil servants and judges of salary scales A 4 to A 15 (not incl. A 10), as well as of R 1 of the Federal Remuneration Ordinance;
- in 1995 with civil servants and judges of salary scales A 4 to A 15 (not incl. A 10), as well as of R 1 and R 2 of the Federal Remuneration Ordinance;
- in 1996 with civil servants and judges of salary scales A 4 to A 13 (not incl. A 10), as well as of R 2 of the Federal Remuneration Ordinance

having in each case more than two children entitled to maintenance omitted to determine child-related salary elements in an amount corresponding to the principle of the state's obligation to take care of civil servants' welfare in a manner that is in keeping with their office.
2. The legislature must make the legal situation considered to be unconstitutional compatible with the constitution by 31 December 1999.
If the legislature does not comply with this, the following applies, by effect from 1 January 2000:
Remuneration recipients shall have a right to family-related salary elements for the third and each further child entitled to maintenance amounting to 115 per cent of

the average total requirement of a child under the law on social assistance, calculated in accordance with the reasoning re C. III. 3.
3. …

EXTRACT FROM GROUNDS:

A.

The subject-matter of the submissions is the compatibility with the Basic Law of the provisions of the 1987, 1988, 1991, 1992, 1993, 1994 and 1995 Federal Remuneration and Pensions Adjustment Acts detailed in the caption, insofar as they regulate the state's obligation to take care of the welfare of civil servants and judges with more than two children in the period from 1988 to 1996.
…

I.

By means of the 1987, 1988, 1991, 1992, 1993, 1994 and 1995 Federal Remuneration and Pensions Adjustment Acts, the legislature adjusted the remuneration and pensions of civil servants, judges, soldiers and pensioners to developments in the general economic and financial circumstances. In some instances, the increases entered into force with delays in comparison to the collective agreements for the employee area of the public service. This was intended to make a tangible special contribution towards compensating for the cost burdens incurred by economic reconstruction in the new federal *Länder* subsequent to the unification of Germany (see draft Bill of the Federal Government to the 1993 Federal Remuneration and Pensions Adjustment Act, *Bundestag* printed paper 12/5472, p. 21). Additionally, the postponement of the linear increases was to make a special contribution towards reducing the burden on the budget (see draft Bill of the Federal Government to the 1994 Federal Remuneration and Pensions Adjustment Act, *Bundestag* printed paper 12/7706, p. 23). The local cost-of-living allowance from the third child onwards was not increased beyond the general adjustments, although this would have been necessary in accordance with the rulings of the Federal Constitutional Court (*Bundesverfassungsgericht*) of 30 March 1977 (BVerfGE 44, 249) and of 22 March 1990 (BVerfGE 81, 363). In these decisions, the Federal Constitutional Court had found that the child-related salary elements had fallen behind the constitutional requirements from the third child onwards (see BVerfGE 44, 249 (279); 81, 363 (379)). As the reason for its decision not to implement the requirements of the Con-

stitutional Court, the Federal Government put forward the connection between child-related remuneration elements and the reorganisation of the compensation for family burdens, the final structure of which still had to be defined (see reasoning to the draft Bill of the Federal Government to the 1995 Federal Remuneration and Pensions Adjustment Act; *Bundestag* printed paper 13/2210, p. 22).
It was only with the Act Reforming Public Service Law (Reform Act) of 24 February 1997 (Federal Law Gazette I p. 322) that the federal legislature drew conclusions from the order of the Federal Constitutional Court of 22 March 1990 for the period from 1 January 1977 to 31 December 1989. The plaintiffs and objecting parties who asserted their claim within the named period without this already having finally been ruled on receive a monthly increase amount of DM 50.00 for the third and each further child to be included in the local cost-of-living allowance (Article 14 § 3 of the Reform Act).

II.

1. The plaintiffs in the original proceedings are civil servants and judges receiving salaries in salary scales A 4 to A 15 (not incl. A 10), B 2, as well as in R 1 and R 2 of the Federal Remuneration Ordinance. They are married and have more than two children for whom they have received child benefit and child-related local cost-of-living allowances. They consider the remuneration granted to them to be unconstitutional in respect of the number of children. Accordingly, they applied to their respective employers for an increase in their salaries. After the applications had been unsuccessful in the administrative procedure, the plaintiffs in the original proceedings lodged actions with the submitting administrative courts.
The original proceedings relate to the remuneration in specified segments of the period from 1 January 1988 to 31 December 1996.
2. The submitting courts have suspended the action proceedings pending with them in accordance with Article 100.1 of the Basic Law and submitted them to the Federal Constitutional Court for an examination of the question of the compatibility of the provisions of the Federal Remuneration and Pensions Adjustment Acts detailed in the caption with the Basic Law. They take the view that the well-foundedness of the actions depends on the constitutionality of these provisions. If they turn out to be compatible with the Basic Law, the actions would have to be rejected. In the event of their unconstitutionality, the proceedings would have to be further suspended, after a ruling of the Federal Constitutional Court, awaiting a regulation by the legislature. This too was said to be a different ruling than that anticipated in the

event of the validity of the legal provisions within the meaning of materiality for a ruling in accordance with Article 100.1 of the Basic Law.

…

III.

The Federal Government, via the Federal Ministry of the Interior, and the Second Senate Competent for Appeal on Points of Law of the Federal Administrative Court (*Bundesverwaltungsgericht*) have made statements with regard to the submission orders. Additionally, Deutsche Post AG has made a statement as the defendant in the original proceedings in the proceedings 2 BvL 10/96, as have the plaintiffs in the original proceedings in the proceedings 2 BvL 26/91 and 5/96, 7/96, 8/96 and 9/96.

…

B.

The submissions – consolidated for joint adjudication – are admissible insofar as they relate to the provisions of the Federal Remuneration and Pensions Adjustment Acts detailed in the caption …

The submission orders permit one to recognise sufficiently clearly that the submitting courts would reach a different result in the event of the validity of the provisions submitted for an examination than in the event of their invalidity. This has also been sufficiently substantiated (see BVerfGE 7, 171 (173); 37, 328 (333-334); 65, 308 (316)). The orders deal with the non-constitutional legal situation in sufficient detail and explain with which constitutional standard the provisions of the Federal Remuneration and Pensions Adjustment Acts detailed in the caption are not compatible in the view of the submitting courts.

…

C.

The provisions of the Federal Remuneration and Pensions Adjustment Acts detailed in the caption, in conjunction with the respective Annex 2, the 1987 and 1988 Federal Remuneration and Pensions Adjustment Acts also in conjunction with Article 14 § 3 of the Reform Act of 24 February 1997, were not compatible with Article 33.5 of the Basic Law insofar as the legislature omitted to determine the child-related salary elements for married civil servants and judges with more than two children of the individual salary scales referred to in the ruling in an amount corresponding to the principle of the state's obligation to take care of civil servants' welfare in a manner that is in keeping with their office.

I.

The Federal Constitutional Court developed the constitutional standards for the state's obligation to take care of civil servants' welfare in a manner that is in keeping with their office concerning civil servants with more than two children entitled to maintenance in its orders of 30 March 1977 (BVerfGE 44, 249) and of 22 March 1990 (BVerfGE 81, 363). These standards are upheld.

1. a) The principle of the state's obligation to take care of civil servants' welfare belongs to the traditional principles of the permanent civil service within the meaning of Article 33.5 of the Basic Law to be observed by the legislature (see only BVerfGE 81, 363 (375); established case-law). It provides to the individual civil servant an individual right vis-à-vis the state that is similar to a fundamental right (see BVerfGE 8, 1 (17)). The employer is accordingly obliged to pay maintenance to civil servants that is in keeping with their office. This also includes the duty to realistically allow for the maintenance obligations incumbent on a civil servant by virtue of his or her family. Hence, the employer not lastly allows for the task of the permanent civil service to guarantee a stable, law-abiding administration in the interplay of political forces (see BVerfGE 11, 203 (216-217); 39, 196 (201); 44, 249 (265)).

b) In the context of its obligation to take care of civil servants' welfare in a manner that is in keeping with their office, the legislature must establish the attractiveness of employment as a civil servant for qualified staff and the reputation of the office in society, it must allow for the educational level, challenges faced and responsibility undertaken by the office-holder, and ensure that each civil servant can satisfy a "minimum of comfort" over and above basic needs (see BVerfGE 44, 249 (265-266); 76, 256 (324); 81, 363 (376)) and meet his or her maintenance obligations towards his or her family. It hence follows from the safeguarding function which the state's obligation to take care of civil servants' welfare has for the permanent civil service that civil servants may not be confronted with the choice to either satisfy a "minimum of comfort" or forgo having a family and maintaining it in accordance with the accepted obligations. The number of children a civil servant has may hence not be insignificant to an assessment and regulation of what constitutes remuneration that is in keeping with his or her office. Article 33.5 of the Basic Law however leaves the legislature latitude in this respect (see BVerfGE 44, 249 (267); 81, 363 (376-377)).

c) Whether civil servants' salaries are in keeping with their office is judged in accordance with net income. The legislature is hence free to reach the goal pre-defined by the constitution through a corresponding amount of gross salary, to have civil servants participate in generally granted child benefit, to compensate in terms of fiscal law for the ability to pay reduced by child maintenance, or to bring about a combination of these possibilities (see BVerfGE 81, 363 (375-376)).
2. The Federal Constitutional Court assumed in its rulings of 30 March 1977 and of 22 March 1990 that the income of civil servants' families with one or two children at all stages of the remuneration system were at that time largely in keeping with their office, but that the additional requirement incurred by virtue of a larger number of children must be met by means of additional benefits (see BVerfGE 81, 363 (377-378)).
The legislature goes beyond its latitude if it presumes that a civil servant must fall back for the maintenance of a third and further children on the family-neutral elements of his or her salary in order to cover the needs of his or her children. The concomitant advancing erosion of the family-neutral salary elements with a growing number of children is not acceptable because by these means a civil servant with several children cannot achieve the position in life to which he or she is entitled, or can do so only at the expense of his or her family (see BVerfGE 81, 363 (378)).
3. With the measurement of the additional need incurred for the civil servant's third and further children which is to be met by the employer beyond the state's obligation to take care of civil servants' welfare in the case of a two-child-family, the legislature may take as a basis those standard rates for the child's maintenance which are provided by the legal order. These rates are, however, orientated towards the satisfaction of differing needs. The legislature must take account of their unequal authoritativeness for the amount of maintenance owed to the civil servant by his or her employer in keeping with his or her office. For instance, requirement rates orientated to a child's utmost minimum requirement, in other words in particular the social assistance rates, constitute state aid to maintain a minimum degree of social security. In contrast to this, the state's obligation to take care of the welfare of the civil servant and his or her family is a different matter in qualitative terms. This difference must be made clear in the measurement of the child-related elements of the civil servant's salary (BVerfGE 81, 363 (378)).

II.

The objections lodged against this do not hold. The granting of child-related salary elements is neither a "civil servants' privilege", nor is it a "double child benefit" (1). The economic circumstances from 1988 to 1996 do not permit one to conclude that there was a worsening of the general standard of living affecting the "minimum of comfort" to be guaranteed to the civil servant (2). The married civil servant with two children used as a comparison standard was also not overpaid in the period under examination here (3). No consequences emerge for the proceedings at hand from the reduction of the starting salary by the 1984 Budget Support Act (*Haushaltsbegleitgesetz*), to which the Federal Constitutional Court did not object (4). Ultimately, the changed framework resulting from German unification and European Monetary Union did not justify imposing a "special burden" on civil servants with more than two children (5).

1. It does not comply with the special circumstances of employment as a civil servant guaranteed by Article 33.5 of the Basic Law to consider the benefit of child-related salary elements to constitute a "civil servants' privilege" or a "double child benefit". Employment as a civil servant is not an employment contract in the traditional sense; in particular it is not employment for money on the basis of which work is to be performed within limits of content, time and scope, thus giving rise to a right to remuneration. Employment as a civil servant, rather, gives rise to independent duties for the civil servant and the employer respectively. These follow directly from the law; they are not contractually agreed. The civil servant has the duty to provide his or her labour to the employer. The employer is obliged to grant to the civil servant maintenance for himself or herself and for his or her family that is in keeping with his or her office (see BVerfGE 11, 203 (216-216); 39, 196 (201); 44, 249 (265)). Allowance for the number of children in terms of remuneration is hence not a "civil servants' privilege", but is inherent to the obligation incumbent on the state to take care of civil servants' welfare.

2. A new determination of the "minimum of comfort" is not required.

a) Incomes in the Federal Republic of Germany as a rule increased faster than prices in 1978 to 1996. …

As a consequence, the legislature did not react to an alleged worsening of the overall economic situation. Rather, in accordance with the reasoning of the Federal Remuneration and Pensions Adjustment Acts, the remunerations and pensions were also increased in 1993 and 1994 in order to adjust them in line with developments in the general economic and financial situation (see the respective reasoning to the draft Bill of the Federal Government to the 1993 Federal Remuneration and Pensions Adjustment Act (*Bundestag* printed paper 12/5472, p. 21) and to the 1994 Federal Remuneration and Pensions Adjustment Act (*Bundestag* printed paper 12/7706, p. 23)). It is therefore not possible to attribute the statistically calculated increase in income to the increase in civil servants' salaries.

…

3. If in accordance with the above, the "minimum of comfort" is not to be re-defined because of a worsening in the general circumstances, it is also not possible in the period under assessment to assume "overpayment" of a four-person civil servants' family, which still serves as a standard. The remuneration of this group of civil servants was also only increased in line with the general financial and economic situation (see respective reasoning to the draft Bill of the Federal Government to the 1993 Federal Remuneration and Pensions Adjustment Act (*Bundestag* printed paper 12/5472, p. 21) and to the 1994 Federal Remuneration and Pensions Adjustment Act (*Bundestag* printed paper 12/7706, p. 23)).

4. No other conclusion is drawn from the reduction of the starting salary by the 1984 Budget Support Act of 22 December 1983 (Federal Law Gazette I p. 1532), which was not objected to by the Federal Constitutional Court (preliminary examination committee (*Vorprüfungsausschuß*)) in the order of 15 January 1985 – 2 BvR 1148/84 – (*Neue Zeitschrift für Verwaltungsrecht* – NVwZ 1985, p. 333). The Federal Constitutional Court has merely repeated its established case-law there, in accordance with which the legislature has broad latitude (see only BVerfGE 13, 356 (362); 56, 87 (95); 64, 367 (378-379)). The Federal Constitutional Court did not have to address in the referenced order the question of the state's obligation to take care of civil servants' welfare in a manner that is in keeping with their office, which is under consideration in the instant case in relation to civil servants with many children.

5. The state's obligation to take care of civil servants' welfare in a manner that is in keeping with their office is, finally, also not to be re-defined because of the impact on public budgets by German unity, as well as by the Treaty of Maastricht. It is not denied here that the state had to deal with an exceptional historical situation. The legislature may accommodate concerns of public interest of this nature by regulating remuneration in the framework of broad latitude to which it is in principle entitled in this area. Having said that, it must take into account that the state's obligation to take care of civil servants' welfare owed by the employer according to the constitution is not a variable of arbitrary scope (see BVerfGE 44, 249 (264)).

Demanding a "special contribution" only from civil servants with many children is constitutionally impermissible. The state's obligation to take care of civil servants' welfare that is in a manner in keeping with their office can also be achieved without increasing overall expenditure on the remuneration of civil servants.

III.

1. The legislature went beyond the broad latitude to which it is entitled in principle in the law on remuneration and pensions insofar as it demands that a civil servant must fall back on the family-neutral salary elements for the maintenance of his or her third and each further child insofar as related to meeting the need which is considered to be suitable in the standard rates for child maintenance provided by the legal order. The concomitant advancing erosion of the family-neutral salary elements with a growing number of children is not acceptable because by these means a civil servant with several children cannot achieve the position in life to which he or she is entitled, or can do so only at the expense of his or her family (see BVerfGE 81, 363 (378)).

2. The calculations that are necessary for this are based on the respective net income calculated by the Federal Ministry of the Interior (see BVerfGE 81, 363 (376)). The annual remuneration was taken as a basis here. This includes the basic salary (in the final stage), the local cost-of-living allowance, the allowance for special purposes in accordance with no. 27 of the Preliminary Remarks (*Vorbemerkungen*) to Federal Remuneration Ordinances A and B, the annual special payment and the holiday bonus, as well as any one-off payments. The net earnings emerge after deduction of wage tax (in accordance with the special wage tax tables), church tax (church tax rate: 8 per cent) and the solidarity levy (insofar as this was levied in the year in question), and after addition of child benefit.

3. Whether the legislature has sufficiently complied with the state's obligation to take care of the welfare of civil servants with more than two children in the remuneration provisions submitted for examination, is judged on the basis of the overall requirement under the law on social assistance. On this, the Federal Constitutional Court has already stated that the state's obligation to take care of civil servants' welfare is something different in qualitative terms (see BVerfGE 44, 249 (264-265)). This difference must be visible with the assessment of the child-related elements of a civil servant's salary. An amount which is 15 per cent higher than the overall requirement under the law on social assistance ("15 per cent amount") makes sufficiently clear the constitutionally required difference between the satisfaction of an utmost minimum requirement incumbent on social assistance and the maintenance currently owed to the civil servant (and his or her family) (see BVerfGE 81, 363 (382-383)). This calculation method does not lead to an absolute provision of what makes up the remuneration to be granted to the civil servant. If the bonuses granted to the civil servant for his or her third and each further child are not even 15 per cent above the overall requirement under the law on social assistance, the legislature has exceeded the latitude to which it is entitled.

In the case at hand, the overall requirement under the law on social assistance is calculated, initially, by forming an average standard rate in accordance with § 22 of the Federal Social Assistance Act (*Bundessozialhilfegesetz*) for the former federal territory (see the report on this by the Federation/*Länder* remuneration commission on the remuneration law consequences of the income-dependent reduction of child benefit of 30 January 1984, which entered into force on 1 January 1983, (*BLK-Bericht* 1984) p. 9, as well as BVerfGE 82, 60 (94); 91, 93 (112)). To be added to this is an average allowance of 20 per cent to pay for one-off benefits for maintenance (see *Nachrichtendienst des Deutschen Vereins für öffentliche und private Fürsorge* – NDV 1995, p. 1 (p. 10, C. IV. b); BVerwG, Judgment of 20 June 1996 – BVerwG 2 C 7.95 –; *BLK-Bericht* 1984, p. 9), plus the cost of housing on the basis of a residential requirement of 11 m^2 per child (see BVerfG, Order of 10 November 1998 – 2 BvL 42/93 –, preliminary print pp. 26-27, 31; notification by the Federal Government, report on the amount of the minimum income of children and families in 1996, *Bundestag* printed paper 13/381, p. 4). This is based on the average rent in the old Federal *Länder* of DM 9.53 per m^2 calculated by the Federal Statistical Office in the so-called 1993 1 per cent building and apartment survey (*1 %-Gebäude- und Wohnungsstichprobe*) (see Federal Statistical Office, *Bautätigkeit und Wohnungen, 1 %-Gebäude- und Wohnungsstichprobe* 1993, series 5, vol. 3, p. 35). This average rent was reverse projected and updated using the rent index of the Federal Statistical Office (printed in the *Wohngeld- und Mietenbericht* 1997; *Bundestag* printed paper 13/10384, p. 21). Finally, the energy costs for a child are allowed for at 20 per cent of the net rent (see on this *Bundestag* printed paper 13/381, p. 4).

4. The "15 per cent amount", which currently makes clear the constitutionally required difference between the state's obligation to take care of civil servants' welfare and the coverage of an utmost minimum requirement, is compared to the *average* net additional amount which the civil servant receives for his or her third and each further child. This corresponds to the requirement of the legislature according to which the net income must be sufficient in order to provide for a civil servant, including his or her family, in a manner that is in keeping with his or her office. The fact of taking the *average* net additional amount as a basis further accommodates the circumstance that partly because of the income-dependent child benefit reduction from the second child onwards which was applicable until 1995 led – instead of the anticipated smooth course – to fluctuations in the calculation of the net additional amount from child to child. This higher additional amount incurred by the abolition of the income-dependent child benefit reduction cannot however be regarded as a net additional amount for the child due to whom the reduction in

child benefit was discontinued. In this respect, it is to be spread over the third, fourth, fifth (, etc.) child.

IV.

These standards were not met by the provisions detailed in the caption. This is shown by the following comparative calculations per month.

…

These comparative calculations show that the remuneration of married civil servants with more than two children who are entitled to maintenance has not been at least 15 per cent above social assistance as required by the constitution in the salary scales relating to the submission proceedings with regard to the third and each further child. Not even the overall requirement under the law on social assistance was compensated for by the net additional amount granted for a child with an increasing number of children. This applies in 1988 and 1989 to salary scale B 2 to be examined only with regards to these years, even if one adds DM 50.00 per child per month (Article 14 § 3 of the Reform Act).

In accordance with the above, the legislature has exceeded the latitude to which it is entitled in principle. With the provisions submitted for examination, it has remained clearly below the limit imposed by the state's obligation to take care of civil servants' welfare for civil servants in the respective salary scales with more than two children.

This result is confirmed by the "Report of the Federation/*Länder* Remuneration Commission on Remuneration Law Consequences for Constitutional Child-related Remuneration from the Order of the Federal Constitutional Court of 22 March 1990 (2 BvL 1/86)" (*Bericht der Besoldungskommission Bund/Länder über besoldungsrechtliche Folgerungen für eine verfassungskonforme kinderbezogene Besoldung aus dem Beschluß des BVerfG vom 22. März 1990 (2 BvL 1/86)*) from 1992 (*BLK-Bericht* 1992)). This report finds considerable underpayment over the entire period from 1 February 1981 to 31 December 1989, and from 1 January 1990 onwards (see p. 24 of the report). Also in the reasoning of the draft Bill of the Federal Government on the 1995 Federal Remuneration and Pensions Adjustment Act (*Bundestag* printed paper 13/2210, p. 22) it is stated that "it has not yet been possible to implement the increase in the local cost-of-living allowance from the third child onwards required with regard to the order of the Federal Constitutional Court of 22 March 1990 – 2 BvL 1/86 – for the state's obligation to take care of civil servants' welfare in a manner that is in keeping with their office with regard to civil servants with three and more children (...)".

V.

In view of the established violation of Article 33.5 of the Basic Law, it is no longer a matter of whether the legislature has also violated Article 3.1 of the Basic Law. This question may remain open, as in the rulings of 30 March 1977 and of 22 March 1990.

D.

The provisions regarding the time of entry into force of the respective Article I § 1 and Article I of the Federal Remuneration and Pensions Adjustment Act detailed in the caption also do not stand up to a constitutional examination. They too are in breach of Article 33.5 of the Basic Law.

I.

The Federal Constitutional Court found in its order of 22 March 1990 (see BVerfGE 81, 363 (383 et seq.)) that the legislature had been obliged – after the ruling of 30 March 1977 (BVerfGE 44, 249) had become known in July of the same year – to bring the legal situation objected to in that ruling as having been unconstitutional since 1 January 1975 into compatibility with the constitution with effect from 1 January 1977. It was said, however, that a general retroactive elimination of this violation of the constitution had not/no longer been required. Retroactive correction was alleged to have been able to be restricted to civil servants who had soon asserted their claim on the state's obligation to take care of civil servants' welfare in a manner that is in keeping with their office, in other words during the pending budget year, in court or by means of an objection (see BVerfGE 81, 363 (385)). The Federal Constitutional Court has reached this conclusion on the basis of the special circumstances of employment as a civil servant (see BVerfGE 81, 363 (384 et seq.)). This is upheld.

II.

The following conclusions are drawn from this for the proceedings to be ruled on in the instant case:
1. Insofar as remuneration claims from 1988 and 1989 are considered (proceedings 2 BvL 26/91), the legislature was obliged on the basis of the order of the Federal Constitutional Court of 22 March 1990 (BVerfGE 81, 363) towards those civil servants who had soon asserted their claims to create a constitutional legal basis for

remuneration. It did not meet this obligation. The increase amount of DM 50.00 per child per month now envisioned in Article 14 § 3.1 of the Reform Act, which entered in force on 1 July 1997, is not suited to do so.
2. The following applies to remuneration claims from 1990 onwards: The legislature was obliged – after the ruling of the Federal Constitutional Court of 22 March 1990 had become known in July 1990 – to bring the legal situation objected to in this ruling as unconstitutional into compliance with the constitution with effect as on 1 January 1990. This did not take place.
3. The legislature is obliged to bring the legal situation objected to in this ruling as unconstitutional into compliance with the constitution. A general retroactive remedy of the violation of the constitution is not required with regard to the special characteristics of employment as a civil servant already detailed in the order of 22 March 1990. A retroactive remedy is however necessary – at least insofar as the claim on the state's obligation to take care of civil servants' welfare in a manner that is in keeping with their office has been claimed soon in court – both as to the plaintiffs in the original proceedings and also to those plaintiffs on whose claims no conclusive ruling has yet been handed down. No detrimental effect will be had by claims having become legally pending later if the action could not be lodged in time because of the time required for necessary preliminary proceedings.

E.

The ruling re 2. is based on § 35 of the Federal Constitutional Court Act (*Bundesverfassungsgerichtsgesetz* – BVerfGG). The measure is necessary because, despite the mandates for action afforded to it in the rulings of the Federal Constitutional Court of 30 March 1977 and of 22 March 1990, the legislature did not determine the amounts of the child-related salary elements of civil servants with more than two children entitled to maintenance in the period up to 1996 (and possibly thereafter) in a manner compatible with the principle of the state's obligation to take care of civil servants' welfare. If the legislature does not meet its obligation as handed down once more by this ruling by 31 December 1999, the employers are obliged to grant family-related salary elements amounting to 115 per cent of the average overall requirement of a child under the law on social assistance for the third and each further child entitled to maintenance (see C. III. 3. above). The non-constitutional courts are entitled to grant family-related salary elements in accordance with this standard.

Justices: Limbach, Kirchhof, Winter, Sommer, Jentsch, Hassemer, Broß, Osterloh

With the Act to Restructure and Modernise Public Service Law (Gesetz zur Neuordnung und Modernisierung des Bundesdienstrechts) *of 5 February 2009 (Federal Law Gazette I 2009 p. 160, Annex 4), the legislature determined new amounts for the family allowance with effect from 1 July 2009. Until this new legislation came into effect, federal civil servants were paid an increased family allowance on the basis of a circular issued by the Federal Ministry of the Interior.*

No. 30

BVerfGE 101, 361
of 15 December 1999 – 1 BvR 653/96 –
"Caroline of Monaco II case"

HEADNOTES:

1. **Privacy, which is protected by the general right of personality under Article 2.1 in conjunction with Article 1.1 of the Basic Law (*Grundgesetz* – GG), is not restricted to the domestic sphere. It must, in principle, be possible for an individual to move in other places that are recognisably secluded without being disturbed by the activities of photojournalists.**
2. **The general right of personality is not is not meant to serve the interest of the commercialisation of the person of an individual. The protection of privacy from being portrayed comes second to the extent that someone declares his or her consent that specified matters that are usually regarded as private are made public.**
3. **The scope of protection provided by the general right of personality of parents is enhanced by Article 6.1 and 6.2 of the Basic Law to the extent that the publication of images is concerned the subject of which is the specifically parental care of their children.**
4. **The guarantee of the freedom of the press provided by Article 5.1 sentence 1 of the Basic Law also covers entertaining publications and articles as well as the images that they contain. In principle, this applies as well to the publication of images that show persons with roles in public life in everyday or private contexts.**

Judgment of the First Senate of 15 December 1999
on the basis of the oral hearing of 9 November 1999
– 1 BvR 653/96 –

in the proceedings regarding the constitutional complaint of Princess Caroline of Monaco, Monaco Palace, Monaco – authorised representatives: …, lawyers –

against a) the judgment of the Federal Court of Justice (*Bundesgerichtshof*) of 19 December 1995 – VI ZR 15/95 –, b) the judgment of the Hanseatic Higher Regional Court (*Hanseatisches Oberlandesgericht*) of Hamburg of 8 December 1994 – 3 U 64/94 –, c) the judgment of the Regional Court (*Landgericht*) of Hamburg of 4 February 1994 – 324 O 537/93 –.

RULING:

The judgments of the Federal Court of Justice of 19 December 1995 – VI ZR 15/95 –, of the Hanseatic Higher Regional Court of Hamburg of 8 December 1994 – 3 U 64/94 – and of the Regional Court of Hamburg of 4 February 1994 – 324 O 537/93 – violate the complainant's fundamental right under Article 2.1 in conjunction with Article 1.1 of the Basic Law (*Grundgesetz* – GG) to the extent that the relief sought by her had also been rejected as regards three photographs published in the magazine "Bunte" in its numbers 32, of 5 August 1993, and 34, of 19 August 1993, which show the complainant and her children. To this extent and concerning the court order as to costs, the judgment of the Federal Court of Justice is reversed and remanded.
As regards all other points of the constitutional complaint, they are rejected as being unfounded.
The Federal Republic of Germany is ordered to reimburse the complainant one-third of her necessary expenses.

EXTRACT FROM GROUNDS:

A.

The constitutional complaint concerns the publication of photographs from the daily and private life of prominent persons.

I.

1. The defendant in the original proceedings, the company Burda GmbH, publishes the magazines "Freizeit Revue" and "Bunte". Photographs of the complainant, Princess Caroline of Monaco, were published in these magazines to illustrate various articles. The photographs gave rise to the original proceedings, seeking to block their publication.

The original proceedings also dealt with five photographs that were published in the "Freizeit Revue", number 30, on 22 July 1993. In these photographs, the complainant can be seen with the actor Vincent Lindon during an evening together at a table in a garden restaurant in Saint-Rémi (France). On the title page, the photographs are introduced as "Die zärtlichsten Fotos ihrer Romanze mit Vincent" ("The most tender photographs of her romance with Vincent") and they show Vincent Lindon kissing the complainant's hand. These photographs are not at issue in the constitutional complaint because the complainant succeeded in having the Federal Court of Justice block their publication.

Further, on 5 August 1993, the defendant published in the magazine "Bunte", number 32, an article with the title "Caroline: 'Ich glaube nicht, daß ich die ideale Frau für einen Mann sein kann'" ("Caroline: 'I do not believe that I can be the ideal woman for a man'"). The article mostly employs indirect speech and partially reproduces a book about the complainant that had been published in Spain. The article was illustrated with many photographs. One photograph on page 88 shows the complainant riding a horse in a paddock. No other people can be seen in the photograph. It bears the caption "Caroline und die Melancholie. Ihr Leben ist ein Roman mit unzähligen Unglücken, sagt Autor Roig" ("Caroline and melancholy: her life is a novel with countless misfortunes, says author Roig"). Page 89 contains a photograph of the complainant with her children Pierre and Andrea, bearing the caption "Caroline mit Pierre und Andrea, ihren Kindern" ("Caroline with Pierre and Andrea, her children"). In the photograph the three people are visible in the foreground, and automobiles can be seen in the background. The complainant is wearing sunglasses.

In the magazine "Bunte", number 34, of 19 August 1993, an article appears on pages 44 to 52 under the title "Vom einfachen Glück" ("Simple happiness") with several photographs. On the first page of the article is a close-up of the complainant together with her daughter in a paddleboat. The caption at the side of the photograph reads: "Es ist ein heißer Tag in diesem Sommer. Prinzessin Caroline paddelt mit ihrer Tochter Charlotte auf der Sorgues. Das ist ein kleiner Fluß unweit von St-Rémi, dem Dorf in der Provence, wo Caroline lebt. Von New York bis London flüstern die Schönen und Reichen von Le Style Caroline. Kanu statt Jacht. Sandwich statt Kaviar". ("It is a hot day in this summer. Princess Caroline paddles with her daughter on the Sorgues. That is a small river not far from St-Rémy, the Provence village in which Caroline lives. From New York to London, the rich and beautiful people whisper about Le Style of Caroline. Canoe instead of yacht. Sandwich instead of caviar").

Another photograph shows the complainant with a basket-shaped bag hanging from her shoulder on the way to the market. On the photograph, there is a fine-print caption: "Hausfrau Caroline Casiraghi. Sie liebt es, selbst einzukaufen" ("The housewife Caroline Casiraghi. She loves to do her own shopping"). The caption, in larger print, at the side of the photograph reads: "Am Mittwoch ist Markttag. Le Style Caroline wird weltweit kopiert. Ihre Riemchen-Sandalen, mit denen sie zum Blumenmarkt geht, ihr Pareo, den sie als Rock trägt". ("Wednesday is market day. Le Style of Caroline is copied world-wide. The strap sandals that she wears when going to the flower market, the pareo that she wears as a skirt"). Other photographs in this context, which are not covered by the complaint, show two shops in which the complainant allegedly does her shopping, the bistro in which she usually has her coffee, and her country house.

The next photograph that is covered by the constitutional complaint shows the complainant and the actor Vincent Lindon sitting near one another in a cafe surrounded by other patrons. The fine-print text in the lower right corner reads as follows: "Jeden Samstagabend ist hier Tisch Nr. 3 rechts vom Eingang für Caroline reserviert" ("Every Saturday evening table number 3, on the right of the entrance, is reserved here for Caroline"). The larger-format text accompanying the photograph says: "Abends, man sitzt im 'Sous les Micocouliers' und trinkt den leichten Sommer-Rotwein. Caroline und Vincent Lindon sind Gäste wie der Bäcker, der Olivenbauer oder Pfarrer Philippe von der Kirche St. Martin" ("In the evening, people sit in 'Sous les Micocouliers' and drink the light, summer red wine. Caroline and Vincent Lindon are patrons just like the baker, the olive farmer or Father Philippe from the church of St. Martin").

Further, a photograph shows the complainant alone on a bicycle ride on a path through a field. The fine-print text for this photograph reads as follows: "Caroline radelt nach Hause. Ihr 'Mas' liegt am Ende des holprigen Feldwegs 'Chemin de Pilou'" (Caroline rides towards home. Her 'Mas' is situated at the end of the bumpy path 'Chemin de Pilou'"). This text is complemented by the larger accompanying text: "Das Ende der Einsamkeit naht. Le Style Caroline lockt die Schönen und Reichen an. Lady Di soll einen Makler beauftragt haben, ein Grundstück zu finden. Julio Iglesias sucht auch" ("The end of the solitude approaches. Lady Di is said to have commissioned a real estate agent to find a piece of property. Julio Iglesias is also looking") .

The photo on page 51 shows the complainant together with Vincent Lindon, her son Pierre and another child. It is a close-up photograph that captures the identified people from behind or from the side as they turn towards the child. The fine-print text reads as follows: "Carolines Jüngster, Pierre, 6, hat sich gestoßen. Vincent und Caroline trösten ihn" ("Caroline's youngest son, Pierre, 6, hurt himself. Vincent and Caroline comfort him").

The last photo shows the complainant, wearing sunglasses, with a companion near a flower stand at the market. The text accompanying the photo says: "Carolines Bodyguard ist eine Frau. Sie sieht der Prinzessin sogar ähnlich. Meistens gehen sie gemeinsam auf den Markt" (Caroline's bodyguard is a woman. She even looks like the Princess. Most of the time they go to the market together").
2. For the assessment of these photos the civil courts have mainly been guided by § 22 and § 23 of the Act Concerning the Copyright of Works of Visual Art and Photographic Works (*Gesetz betreffend das Urheberrecht an Werken der bildenden Künste und der Photographie*) of 9 January 1907 (Reich Law Gazette (*Reichsgesetzblatt* – RGBl) p. 7, hereinafter referred to as Art Copyright Act (*Kunsturhebergesetz* – KUG)). These regulations have the following wording:

§ 22

> Images may be distributed or presented for public display only with the consent of the subject. In case of doubt, the consent is deemed to have been granted when the subject receives a payment for allowing the images to be made. After the death of the subject and until the expiration of 10 years, the consent of the subject's relatives is required. …

§ 23

> (1) The following images may be distributed and presented for display without the consent required by § 22:
> 1. Images from the sphere of contemporary history;
> 2. Pictures in which the subjects appear only as part of the backdrop in a landscape or other locality;
> 3. Pictures of assemblies, demonstrations and similar events in which the depicted individuals have taken part;
> 4. Images, though not produced by request, in so far as the distribution or display serves a higher interest of art.
>
> (2) The authority does not, however, extend to a distribution and display by which the subject, or in the case the subject is dead, his relatives, suffers an injury to a legitimate interest.

a) The Regional Court granted the complaint to the extent that it dealt with photos published in magazines that are distributed in France. Otherwise, it rejected the complaint.

The court held that unlike in French law, no right to require to publication of the photos to be blocked existed in Germany. According to the court, pursuant to § 23.1 no 1 of the Art Copyright Act, images from the sphere of contemporary history were permitted if they served to illustrate the purpose of contemporary history which was pursued by the report. As the eldest daughter of the Prince of Monaco, the complainant was an absolute person of contemporary history (*absolute Person der Zeitgeschichte*). Reporting about her life referred to a part of the sphere of contemporary history. Here, the degree of banality of the media coverage in a given case was not decisive. Images from the complainant's daily life, as well as images showing her at special occasions, were the illustrating accompaniment of such reports.

In the context of § 23.2 of the Art Copyright Act, the complainant's interest in not being portrayed in the manner in which this had been done had to be weighed against the general public's legitimate interest in being informed. This interest ended at the boundary of privacy, namely "at the front door". Even if it were intended to go beyond this and have the interest in reporting end at the garden fence or at the park wall, this would not lead to the forbearance being sought successfully. All images showed the complainant in public places accessible to everybody, namely in a restaurant, in a kind of riding arena, in streets and places and on a little river that was navigable for canoes. As a result of the weighing, the depicted person's perception that her personality was exploited for purely commercial reasons had to take second place to the general public's interest in the media coverage, which was accommodated by magazines and by the yellow press.

b) The Higher Regional Court rejected the complainant's appeal and, pursuant to the defendant's cross-appeal, it altered the judgment of the lower court, rejecting the complaint to the extent that it had been granted by the regional court (see *NJW-Rechtsprechungs-Report Zivilrecht* – NJW-RR 1995, p. 790).

3. The Federal Court of Justice reversed, in part, the judgment of the Higher Regional Court. The Federal Court of Justice also altered, in part, the judgment of the Regional Court so that the defendant in the original proceedings would be prohibited from again publishing the photographs containing the complainant's image, which had been printed in the magazine "Freizeit Revue". The more expansive claims in the appeal were rejected.

The court held that pursuant to § 22 of the Art Copyright Act, images of a person may, in principle, only be distributed with the person's consent. The right to one's own image was a special manifestation of the general right of personality (*allgemeines Persönlichkeitsrecht*). From this it followed that in principle, the depicted person alone was authorised to judge whether and in what way he or she was pre-

sented to the public in an image. It was undisputed that the complainant had not consented to the images being published.
According to § 23.1 no. 1 and 23.2 of the Art Copyright Act, however, images from the sphere of contemporary history may be distributed and presented for display without the consent of the person concerned unless this would violate a legitimate interest of the subject. Above all, images of persons of contemporary history were part of the sphere of contemporary history, especially of persons who could be regarded as absolute persons of contemporary history. To classify a person as an absolute person of contemporary history, it was decisive that public opinion regarded images of him or her as significant and as worthy of attention for due to the person portrayed, i.e. that the general public could be conceded an interest in a pictorial representation that was justified by a genuine need to be informed. As the eldest daughter of the ruling prince of Monaco, the complainant belonged to this group of persons.
The court further held that, however, images of persons of contemporary history may not be distributed without such persons' consent without any restrictions. According to § 23.2 of the Art Copyright Act, publication was impermissible if was contrary to the depicted person's legitimate interest. Whether this was the case had to be determined by a weighing of legal interests by which it had to be decided in each individual case whether the general public's interest in being informed, which is protected by the freedom of the press, had priority over the right of personality.
In the weighing of the respective legal positions, protection of privacy enjoyed particular importance. The right to respect of one's privacy was a consequence of the general right of personality, which granted everyone an autonomous sphere of shaping their own life in which they can develop and perceive their individuality to the exclusion of others. This included the right to be on one's own and to "belong to oneself". Everyone, the complainant as a person of contemporary history as well, could claim the right to respect of one's privacy. Only by way of exception could the distribution of images from this sphere be permissible in the case of such persons if overriding public interests justified such an encroachment.
To the extent that the appellate court took these principles as a basis but restricted the private area to premises within one's own house that are closed to the public, this assessment could not be shared. The objective and the wording of the Art Copyright Act did not justify such a restriction. Instead, privacy that was worthy of protection could exist outside the domestic sphere as well. This was the case where someone had withdrawn to a local seclusion to be alone, that this wish to be alone is recognisable by an objective person, and that the person, confiding in the seclusion, behaves in a manner in which he or she would not behave in the broad public. Whoever published images of the person affected that, in such a situation, had been

taken secretly or by catching the person unawares encroached upon this area of protection in an impermissible manner.

Like everyone, a person of contemporary history had the right to withdraw in places outside his or her own home in which he or she could be alone or at any rate secluded from a broad public; this right had to be respected by third parties. Such a person could do so also in places that were freely accessible to everyone, i.e. in public places. This, however, required, that the location in question was secluded from the broad public at the specific point in time and that the seclusion from the public was objectively recognisable also by third parties. Examples for this were the secluded premises of a restaurant or of a hotel, sports complexes, phone boxes, possibly even the open country if the person concerned no longer appeared as part of the public.

The claim to respect vis-à-vis third parties furthermore required that the person affected was in a situation which was of a typically private nature. This was the case where someone, confiding in the seclusion, behaved in a manner in which he or she would not behave in the broad public, for instance by following personal impulses which are recognisably not meant for the eyes of third parties, or by letting him or herself go. Only in such a situation could it be assumed that it was objectively recognisable that the person affected did not want others to share it and that he or she could expect others to respect his or her seclusion.

The court held that whoever for their own purposes took advantage of the unawareness of the person affected, who thought him or herself to be unobserved, by taking pictures encroached upon the area of privacy that was worthy of protection in an impermissible manner. This was the case if the person affected was, so to speak, observed through the keyhole and was secretly surprised by pictures being taken. The same applied where the picture was taken openly but catching the person affected so unawares that he or she was unable to prepare to it. The restriction was justified by the consideration that the protection of privacy was claimed at a location access to which was virtually open to everyone and that the privacy of the person affected could therefore only be impermissibly interfered with by secrecy and by catching the person affected unawares.

The result of a weighing of interests that was guided by these principles was that the defendant in the original proceedings had impermissibly encroached upon the complainant's protected privacy by publishing the photos reproduced in the "Freizeit Revue" number 30/93. According to the court, the pictures and the accompanying text showed that the complainant had withdrawn to the secluded atmosphere of a garden restaurant for a private conversation. By doing so, she had exposed herself to a restricted public because the other guests of the restaurant and other persons could have seen and observed her engaging in the conduct that was the subject of the photographs. It made a difference, however, if someone could be seen and observed only by the persons who were incidentally present in his or her surroundings or if in such a situation, photographs were taken of him or her with the purpose of distributing them in the public.

The seclusion and confidentiality of the location and the meeting with her companion, which had been characterised by highly personal conduct, had easily shown that the complainant wanted to be alone during the conversation. The photojournalist had not been allowed to intrude on the privacy determined in that manner. The photos had been taken secretly and unnoticed by the complainant from a large distance with far-reaching telephoto lenses; they were therefore of an intruding nature. On the one hand, secrecy had served to circumvent the complainant's lack of consent and to deprive her of the possibility of resisting the pictures being taken in these moments. On the other hand, it had served to catch highly personal impulses by taking advantage of the complainant's unawareness and unconstrainedness.

However, with regard to the pictures in the other magazines, the appeal on points of law was unsuccessful. These pictures did not affect the complainant's protected privacy. The photos had been taken in public places that had been accessible to everyone. In these cases, the complainant had entered the public sphere and in doing so had become part of the public. Neither had she recognisably withdrawn to an area secluded from the broad public, nor are the situations depicted of a private nature within the meaning that has been described. As a person of contemporary history, the complainant had to tolerate that the general public had a legitimate interest in knowing where she went and how she behaved in public, be it while shopping in a marketplace, in a café, doing sports or engaging in other activities.

This also applied to the picture taken in a restaurant in which the complainant was shown sitting at a table with other persons. This photograph was different from the pictures taken in Saint-Rémy in that it lacked the characteristics which resulted in the publication of the latter being impermissible. Neither had the complainant in this picture in the restaurant withdrawn to a place secluded from the general public, nor was the situation in which the complainant was photographed of a private character within the meaning described above. The fact that the photographs at issue here had been taken unnoticed was in itself not a sufficient reason for demanding the forbearance of the publication. As a general rule, persons of contemporary history had to tolerate photos being taken unnoticed or even secretly if they showed in public.

To refrain from distributing the photographs could not be demanded simply because they did not show the complainant while exercising an official function but concerned her private life in the broader sense. An interest worthy of protection to be presented an absolute person of contemporary history as such in a picture could exist on the part of the general public. A connection to a public function of this person of any kind was not necessary for this. In the context of § 23.1 no. 1 of the Art Copyright Act, an interest on the part of the public in being informed that was worthy of protection had to be recognised already if it was merely focused on how the person affected moved in public as an ordinary person, i.e. outside his or her public functions.

II.

The complainant claims that the collective decisions of the civil courts constituted, to the extent that they do not disallow the future distribution of the photos, a violation of Article 2.1 in conjunction with Article 1.1 of the Basic Law, especially to the extent that these articles concern the right to control over one's own image and the right to enjoy the respect of one's privacy. According to the complainant, the challenged decisions, in applying ordinary statutory (as opposed to constitutional) law to the matter, misjudged the meaning and scope of the fundamental rights. With their classification of the complainant as an "absolute person of contemporary history" the decisions, according to the complainant, abridged the mandatory weighing in an impermissible manner or applied standards that do not stand up to constitutional review when judging the legitimate interests that are to be taken into consideration pursuant to § 23.2 of the of the Art Copyright Act.

The complainant further argues that on viewing these photographs it becomes clear that the situations shown in the respective pictures are part of her privacy. All photographs have in common that they were taken with the knowledge of the complainant's known will to the contrary as "paparazzi photos" from a large distance with powerful telephoto lenses. All photographs show her in private, some in everyday situations in her leisure time outside her domestic sphere. All photographs clearly show that at the point in time in which they were taken, the complainant deliberately did not face the public and that she did not give any occasion whatsoever to attracting public attention.

According to the complainant, it is one of the fundamental prerequisites of the development of one's personality, which is protected by Article 2.1 in conjunction with Article 1.1 of the Basic Law, that the individual has a space in which he or she can be alone and unobserved or in which he or she can meet persons of his or her particular confidence regardless of society's expectations of conduct or other external influences. ...

III.

The defendant in the original proceedings, which had lodged a constitutional complaint against the judgment of the Federal Court of Justice judgment as well but had later on withdrawn it without giving up its legal viewpoint, [regards the constitutional complaint as unfounded].

…

IV.

…

B.

The constitutional complaint is partly founded.

I.

The challenged judgments affect the complainant's general right of personality that follows from Article 2.1 of the Basic Law in conjunction with Article 1.1 of the Basic Law.

1. The constitutional safeguard of the protection of the general right of personality also extends to images of an individual made by third parties.

a) The fundamental right that safeguards the legal protection of the general right of personality has the objective of safeguarding elements of an individual's personality that are not the subject of the freedoms that are especially guaranteed by the Basic Law but do not come second to these freedoms as concerns their importance for the formation of the personality (see Decisions of the Federal Constitutional Court (*Entscheidungen des Bundesverfassungsgerichts* – BVerfGE) 54, 148 (153); BVerfGE 99, 185 (193)). The necessity of such a safeguard for filling gaps in the legislation exists in particular as regards new threats to the free development of one's personality that mostly occur in the wake of scientific and technical progress (see BVerfGE 54, 148 (153); BVerfGE 65, 1 (41)). The standard for ascertaining whether, in the framework of a specific legal action, the general right of personality is affected and if so, which manifestation thereof, is, first and foremost, a question of the threat to one's personality. This must be inferred from the concrete situation.

b) The authority to publish photographs that show individuals in private or everyday contexts depends on the right to one's own image and on the guarantee of privacy that characterise the right to develop one's personality.

aa) Contrary to the complainant's opinion, Article 2.1 of the Basic Law in conjunction with Article 1.1 of the Basic Law does not establish a general and comprehensive individual right to determine the manner in which one is portrayed. To the extent that the complainant would like to infer such a right from former decisions of the Federal Constitutional Court (see BVerfGE 35, 202 (220); BVerfGE 54, 148 (155-156); BVerfGE 63, 131 (142)), this is an incorrect generalisation of the scope of protection of the guarantee provided by the fundamental right, which was formulated in the Court's consideration of the concrete cases. As the Federal Constitutional Court has emphasised on several occasions already, the general right of personality does not confer to the individual the right to be portrayed by others only as he or she views him- or herself or only as he or she wants to be perceived (see BVerfGE 82, 236 (269); BVerfGE 97, 125 (149); BVerfGE 97, 391 (403); BVerfGE 99, 185 (194)). Such a broad protection would not only exceed the aim of protection, i.e. to avoid risks to the development of an individual's personality, but would also extend far into third parties' sphere of freedom.

The complainant does not criticise the way in which she is portrayed in the photographs at issue, which had been regarded as altogether positive by the civil courts that dealt with the case. Rather, the question with which she is concerned is whether images of her may be made and published at all if she does not move in public in an official function but as a private individual or in everyday contexts. The answer to this question can be ascertained from those aspects of the general right of personality that protect the right to control over one's own image as well as privacy.

bb) The right to control over one's own image (see BVerfGE 34, 238 (246); BVerfGE 35, 202 (220); BVerfGE 87, 334 (340); BVerfGE 97, 228 (268-269)) ensures that the individual has the opportunity to influence and decide the taking and the use of photographs or recordings of his or her own person. In principle, it is of no importance whether the photographs or recordings show the individual in private or public contexts. The protection required for the right to control over one's own image is similar to, and developed after, the protection required for the right to control over one's own words. Both find support in constitutional jurisprudence (see BVerfGE 34, 238 (246)). The need for protection, in the case of the right to control over one's own image, results from the fact that it is possible to detach the image of an individual in a specific situation from this individual, to record the image in a data format and to reproduce it at any time for an immeasurable audience. The progress in recording technology, which permits the taking of images from a great distance, most recently even by satellite and under bad lighting conditions, has considerably expanded this possibility.

The existing technology of image and sound reproduction make it possible to change the public setting in which one appears, and the breadth of the public by which one may be observed. In particular, the limited public, in which an individual moves under normal circumstances, can be substituted by a public that is created by the media. The audience that is present in a courtroom, for instance, is the feature that distinguishes the public in court proceedings from the public created by television, because the public in the courtroom witnesses the events itself and can, in turn, be perceived and assessed by the parties to the legal action (see Federal Constitutional Court, Third Chamber of the First Senate, *Neue Juristische Wochenschrift* – NJW 1996, p. 581 (583)). Apart from that, the change of the context in which an image is reproduced can also change, unintentionally or intentionally, the sense of the message that the image conveys.

Among the different aspects of the protection of the right to control over one's own image, only the aspect that concerns the production of specified photographs and their transfer to a broader public is of importance in this context. The proceedings do not deal with manipulated photographs or distortions by a change of context, with which the protection is particularly concerned. The complainant, on the contrary, assumes that the photographs that are at issue in the proceedings and the accompanying text, which is also relevant for the message conveyed by the photographs, correctly depict situations from her life in a way in which observers, had they been present at the occasion when the pictures were taken, could have perceived them. The complainant simply does not want these situations to be captured in photographs and presented to a broader public as these situations, in her opinion, are part of her privacy.

cc) As distinguished from the right to control over one's own image, the protection of privacy, which also flows from the general right of personality, does not refer to images in particular but is determined by the subjects of the images and the places in which they are taken. On the one hand, the protection of privacy comprises matters that, due to the information conveyed, are typically regarded as "private", because their public discussion or display is regarded as unseemly, because they are regarded as embarrassing if they become known, or if they provoke adverse reactions from the environment. This applies e.g. to reflections about oneself in diaries (BVerfGE 80, 367); to confidential communication between husband and wife (BVerfGE 27, 344); to the sphere of sexuality (BVerfGE 47, 46; 49, 286); in the case of socially deviant behaviour (BVerfGE 44, 353) and in the case of diseases (BVerfGE 32, 373). If such matters were not protected from others taking note of them, the reflection about oneself, the uninhibited communication among individuals who are close to each other, the development of one's sexuality and the resort to medical aid could be impaired or made impossible even though these types of behaviour are protected by fundamental rights.

On the other hand, protection extends to a physical space in which the individual can recover, relax and also let him- or herself go (see BVerfGE 27, 1 (6)). It is true that such a space also provides the possibility to behave in a way that is not meant for the public and the observation and display of which by outside observers would be embarrassing or detrimental for the individual affected. In essence, this is a space in which it is possible for the individual to be free from public observation, and thus free from the self-control imposed by the public even if the individual affected does not necessarily behave differently in this space than he or she would in public. If such a possibility of retreating no longer existed, this could overstrain the individual psychically because he or she would always have to be aware of the effect he or she has on others and would always have to consider whether he or she is behaving correctly. This would deprive the individual of phases in which he or she can be alone and recover; such phases are necessary for the development of one's personality, and without them the development of one's personality would be seriously impaired.

Such need for protection also exists in the case of individuals who, on account of their rank or reputation, of their position or influence or of their abilities or actions are the subject of particular public attention. The fact that someone, whether wanted or unwanted, has become a person upon whom the public focuses, does not mean that this person has lost his or her right to a sphere of privacy that is withdrawn from the observation of the public. This also applies to democratically elected office holders. They are certainly accountable to the public for the way in which they administrate their office, and they have to tolerate public attention in this context. They do not, however, have to tolerate the same extent of public attention regarding their private life in so far as their private life does not affect the administration of their office.

By common consent, the domestic sphere constitutes such a protected area. Due to its connection with the free development of one's personality, the area of withdrawal must not, from the outset, be restricted exclusively to the domestic sphere. This holds true if only for the reason that the functions that the area of withdrawal serve do not end at the walls of one's house or at the boundaries of one's property. The free development of an individual's personality would be seriously impaired if the individual could only evade public curiosity in his or her own home. In many cases, it is only possible in the seclusion of a natural environment, e.g. in a holiday resort, for an individual to recover from being a part of the public, which is characterised by compulsions to function in a certain way and by the presence of the media. This is why the individual must also have, in principle, the possibility to move in the

open country, although it is secluded, and in places that are recognisably secluded from the broad public in a manner that is free from public observation. This especially applies with regard to technologies of imaging that overcome physical seclusion without the person affected being able to recognise this.
The physical boundaries of privacy outside the home cannot be determined in a general and abstract manner. Rather, they can be determined only from the particular characteristics of the place visited by the person concerned. The decisive standard is whether the individual finds or creates a situation in which he or she can reasonably, i.e. in a way that is also recognisable for others, assume that he or she is not exposed to the observation of the public.
Whether the prerequisites of seclusion are fulfilled can only be ascertained for each particular situation. In one and the same place, there may be a time in which an individual can, with good reasons, feel unobserved, whereas this is not the case at other points in time. Nor does the fact that an individual stays in a closed room always mean that this place is secluded. The decisive question is whether the individual has good reasons to expect that he or she is unobserved or whether the individual visits places in which he or she moves under the eyes of the public. Therefore, seclusion, which is the prerequisite for the protection of privacy outside the domestic sphere, can be lacking in closed rooms as well.
Places in which the individual is among many people, lack, from the outset, the prerequisites of the protection of privacy within the meaning of Article 2.1 in conjunction with Article 1.1 of the Basic Law. Such places cannot cater to an individual's need of withdrawal, and they therefore do not justify the protection of fundamental rights that this need deserves for reasons of the free development of one's personality. Neither can the individual, by showing a behaviour that would not usually be displayed in public, redefine these places in such a way that they become part of his or her sphere of privacy. It is not the individual's behaviour, whether alone or with others, that constitutes the sphere of privacy but the objective characteristics of the place at the time in question. Thus, if an individual behaves, in places that do not show the characteristics of seclusion, in the manner he or she would behave if he or she were not under observation, this individual eliminates the need for protection of behaviour that is of no concern to the public.
The protection of privacy, over and against the public's observation, is also eliminated if someone declares his or her agreement with the fact that certain matters that are usually regarded as private are made public, e.g. if someone enters into exclusive contracts concerning media coverage of his or her private sphere. The constitutional protection of privacy provided by Article 2.1 in conjunction with Article 1.1 of the Basic Law is not meant to serve the interest of the commercialisation of the person of an individual. Certainly no one is prohibited from opening his or her

private sphere in such a manner. When doing so, however, one cannot claim protection of privacy, because privacy is the status of being removed from the observation of the public. Therefore, someone who expects that others may only to a limited extent or not at all observe matters or behaviour that take place in an area that normally serves for the withdrawal from the observation of the public, must express this expectation in a consistent manner that is not bound to a particular situation. This also applies if someone revokes his or her decision to permit or tolerate reporting about certain issues in his or her private sphere.

dd) There is no previous Federal Constitutional Court case-law about the meaning of the protection of privacy with respect to the family relationship, especially between parents and children. It has been acknowledged, however, that children need special protection because they still have to develop into responsible persons (see BVerfGE 24, 119 (144); BVerfGE 57, 361 (383)). This need for protection extends as well to the protection of children from threats posed by the interest of the media and the consumers of media images of children. This interest can constitute a more severe interference with the development of a child's personality than it does for the development of an adult's personality. The sphere in which children can feel free from observation by the public and develop free from such observation must therefore be protected in a more comprehensive way than in the case of adults.

It is the parents who are first of all responsible for the development of a child's personality. To the extent that education depends on an undisturbed relationship between parents and their children, the special protection of the children's fundamental rights does not have a merely automatic impact in favour of the father or the mother (also see BVerfGE 76, 1 (44 et seq.); BVerfGE 80, 81 (91-92)). Rather, the specifically parental care of their children, in principle, also falls into the sphere of protection provided by Article 2.1 of the Basic Law in conjunction with Article 1.1 of the Basic Law. In this case, the scope of protection provided by the general right of personality is enhanced by Article 6.1 and 6.2 of the Basic Law, which oblige the state to secure the living conditions that are necessary for a child to grow up in a healthy way. Of these conditions, parental care is particularly important (see BVerfGE 56, 363 (384); BVerfGE 57, 361 (382-383); BVerfGE 80, 81 (90 et seq.)).

Article 6 of the Basic Law, thus, enhances the protection to which children are entitled in order to enjoy the general right of personality. The impact that this enhancement has in particular cases cannot be determined in a general and abstract way. As a general rule, there will certainly be no need for protection in cases in which parents deliberately turn towards the public with their children, e.g. if they participate in public functions together or even are the centre of such functions. In such cases, they assent to the conditions of public appearances. As regards all other cases, the protection of the general right of personality as enhanced by the specific relationship between parents and children can, in principle, arise in contexts in which the prerequisite of seclusion is not otherwise fulfilled.

2. The challenged decisions impair the complainant's general right of personality. As the contexts in which the images were made enjoy the protection provided by this fundamental right, the courts' finding that they may be published against the complainant's will diminish the required protection, which the courts in private-law litigation are also obligated to extend to the complainant (see BVerfGE 7, 198 (207)).

II.

The challenged judgments do not fully meet the requirements stipulated by Article 2.1 in conjunction with Article 1.1 of the Basic Law.

1. However, the provisions of § 22 and § 23 of the Art Copyright Act, on which the civil courts based their decisions, are consistent with the Basic Law.

Pursuant to Article 2.1 of the Basic Law, the general right of personality is only guaranteed in the framework of the constitutional order. This also includes the provisions about the publication of photographic images of persons in § 22 and § 23 of the Art Copyright Act. The provision can be traced back to an offensive incident (images of Bismarck on his deathbed, see Decisions of the Supreme Court of the German Reich in Civil Cases (*Entscheidungen des Reichsgerichts in Zivilsachen* – RGZ) 45, 170) and the subsequent discussion on legal policy (see *Verhandlungen des 27. DJT,* 1904, 4th volume, pp. 27 et seq.). The provision seeks to achieve an equitable balance between the respect of an individual's personality and the interest of the general public in being informed (see *Verhandlungen des Reichstages, 11. Legislaturperiode, II. Session, 1. Sessionsabschnitt* 1905/1906, No. 30 p. 1526 (1540-1541)).

Pursuant to § 22 sentence 1 of the Art Copyright Act, images may be distributed or presented for public display only with the consent of the subject. § 23.1 of the Art Copyright Act exempts, *inter alia*, images from the sphere of contemporary history (no. 1) from this principle. Pursuant to § 23.1 of the Art Copyright Act, this exemption does not, however, extend to a distribution by which the subject suffers an injury to a legitimate interest. As this concept of protection consists of several stages, the provision sufficiently takes into account the depicted person's need for protection as well as the public's wish of being informed and the interests of the media that satisfy these wishes. This has already been established by the Federal Constitutional Court on earlier occasions (see BVerfGE 35, 202 (224-225)).

The defendant`s opinion that the regulation violates the freedom of the press as it, in the defendant´s opinion, amounts to a prohibition of publication, with each publication requiring permission in advance (*Verbot mit Erlaubnisvorbehalt*) does not lead to a different assessment. That there is no such prohibition can already be discerned from the fact that the provisions only conciliate different, legally protected interests of individuals. Neither does the regulation favour the protection of an individual's rights to protection of his or her general right of personality in a one-sided manner. It is true that on the first and third stages (§ 22 sentence 1 and § 23.2 of the Art Copyright Act), the regulation is primarily concerned with the depicted person's need for protection. In the second stage (§ 23.1 of the Art Copyright Act), however, the interests of the freedom of the press and of the freedom to form one's own opinion, which is at the background of this fundamental right, are sufficiently taken into account. At the same time, the open wording of the regulation provides enough room for an interpretation and application that is in conformity with the fundamental rights.

2. The interpretation and application of the provisions, however, do not in all respects comply with the requirements established by the fundamental rights.

a) The interpretation and application of constitutional civil-law provisions is the task of the civil courts. In doing so, the civil courts must observe the meaning and the scope of the fundamental rights that are affected by their decisions to assure that their normative content be preserved at the level of judicial application of the law as well (see BVerfGE 7, 198 (205 et seq.); established case-law). This requires a weighing between the conflicting interests that are protected by fundamental rights. This weighing is to take place in the framework of the elements of civil-law provisions that may be interpreted, and it must take the special circumstances of the case into account (see BVerfGE 99, 185 (196); established case-law). Irrespective of the influence of the fundamental rights, the litigation remains a private-law action that finds its solution in private law, the interpretation of which is guided by the fundamental rights. The mission of the Federal Constitutional Court is therefore restricted to reviewing whether the civil courts have taken sufficient account of the influence of the fundamental rights (see BVerfGE 18, 85 (92-93)). It is, however, not the task of the Federal Constitutional Court to prescribe to the civil courts the outcome of their decision in the litigation (see BVerfGE 94, 1 (9-10)).

A violation of fundamental rights that leads to an objection to the challenged decisions only exists if, in the interpretation and application of constitutional provisions of private law, the fact has been overlooked that fundamental rights were to be respected, or if the scope of protection provided by the fundamental rights that are to be respected has not been determined correctly or completely, or if the weight of the fundamental rights that are to be respected has been misjudged in such a way that the weighing of the legal positions of the parties in the framework of the private-law settlement suffers (see BVerfGE 95, 28 (37); BVerfGE 97, 391 (401)), and the decision is based on this mistake.

b) In the present case, the interpretation and application of §§ 22 and 23 of the Art Copyright Act does not only have to consider the general right of personality but also the freedom of the press, which is affected by these provisions as well.

The right to freely determine the nature and tendency, contents and form of an organ of the press is in the centre of the guarantee of the fundamental right of the freedom of the press (see BVerfGE 20, 162 (174 et seq.); BVerfGE 52, 283 (296); BVerfGE 66, 116 (133); BVerfGE 80, 124 (133-134); BVerfGE 95, 28 (35)). This includes, *inter alia*, the decision whether and how to illustrate an organ of the press. The protection is not restricted to specified subjects of illustrations. It also comprises the depiction of persons. The protection does not depend on the nature or the level of the organ of the press or of the reporting (see BVerfGE 34, 269 (283); BVerfGE 50, 234 (240)). Any distinction of this kind would ultimately amount to public authorities assessing and controlling the press, a fact that would plainly contradict this fundamental right (BVerfGE 35, 202 (222)).

The freedom of the press serves to facilitate, for individuals and the public, the free formation of opinions (see BVerfGE 57, 295 (319)). Such formation of opinions can only be successful under the condition that free reporting, i.e. reporting without any prescribed or precluded subjects or manners of presentation, is possible. In particular, the formation of opinions is not restricted to the political sphere. In the interest of a functioning democracy, the formation of opinions with regard to the political sphere is certainly of special importance. The formation of opinions in the political sphere, however, is embedded in a comprehensive, highly interconnected communication process that can neither under the aspect of the development of one's personality nor from the point of view of democratic governance, be split up into relevant and irrelevant areas (see BVerfGE 97, 228 (257)). The press must be allowed to decide according to its own publishing standards what it regards as being worthy of the public interest and what it does not deem to be worthy of such interest.

The fact that the press has to fulfil an opinion-forming mission does not exclude entertainment from the constitutional free press guarantee. The formation of opinions does not stand in opposition to entertainment. Entertaining articles can also contribute to the formation of opinions. Such articles can, under certain circumstances, stimulate or influence the formation of opinions in a more sustainable way than information that is exclusively fact-related. Moreover, in the media, an increasing tendency toward the elimination of the distinction between information and entertainment can be observed both with respect to specific organs of the press as a whole as well as with regard to individual articles, i.e. to disseminate information in an entertaining manner or to mix information and entertainment ("infotainment"). This means that many readers obtain the information that they regard as important or interesting exactly from entertaining articles (see Berg/Kiefer (eds.), *Massenkommunikation*, vol. V, 1996).

Nor can it be denied from the outset that mere entertainment has an influence on the formation of opinions. It would be a narrow view to assume that entertainment only satisfies wishes for amusement, relaxation, distraction and escape from reality. Entertainment can also convey images of reality and provides topics for conversation that can be followed by processes of discussion and integration that refer to views on life, to standpoints concerning values and patterns of behaviour, and in this respect, it fulfils important functions in society (see BVerfGE 97, 228 (257); furthermore: Pürer/Raabe, *Medien in Deutschland*, vol. 1, 2nd ed. 1996, pp. 309-310). For this reason, entertainment in the press cannot be neglected or even be regarded as worthless in the context of the freedom of the press, for which constitutional protection is intended; entertainment is, therefore, also covered by the protection that this fundamental right provides (see BVerfGE 35, 202 (222)).

This also applies to reporting about individuals. Personalising a theme is an important journalistic means for attracting attention. Personalising a theme often awakens the interest in certain problems in the first place and is the basis of the wish for factual information. Sympathy for events and situations is often conveyed by personalising the theme. Moreover, prominent persons also stand for certain ethical positions and views of life. Therefore, prominent persons provide orientation for their own concepts of life to many people. Prominent persons become focuses for approval or rejection and thus fulfil the function of role-models or of examples of lifestyles from which people want to detach themselves. This is the reason for the public interest in the most varied aspects of the lives of prominent persons.

As regards persons from political life, the public's interest has always been recognised as legitimate from the point of view of democratic transparency and control. In principle, however, it cannot be denied that such interest also exists concerning other persons with roles in public life. In this respect, the depiction of individuals that is not restricted to specified functions or events complies with the tasks of the press and therefore also falls under the scope of protection provided by the freedom of the press. Only when a weighing is made between the freedom of the press and colliding rights of personality, can it be of importance whether questions that essentially concern the public are discussed in a serious, fact-related manner or whether merely private matters that only satisfy curiosity are divulged (see BVerfGE 34, 269 (283)).

c) The judgment of the Federal Court of Justice mainly stands up to the review of constitutionality.

aa) It is not objectionable from the constitutional point of view that, in order to determine the elements of § 23.1 no. 1 of the Art Copyright Act, the Federal Court of Justice has taken as its controlling standard the general public's interest in being informed, and that the Federal Court of Justice, for this reason, has regarded the publication of images of the complainant that show her outside her representative function in the principality of Monaco as permissible.

§ 23.1 no. 1 of the Art Copyright Act establishes that the publication of images from the sphere of contemporary history does not require the subject's consent, as otherwise required by § 22 of the Art Copyright Act. As concerns the parliament's intention when establishing this provision (see *Verhandlungen des Reichstages*, *loc. cit.*, pp. 1540-1541) and as regards the purpose of the regulation, it shows consideration for the general public's interest in being informed as well as for the freedom of the press. Therefore, the interest of the public is to be taken into account especially when interpreting the element "images from the sphere of contemporary history", as the public must not be granted free access to images of persons who are not deemed important in the context of contemporary history; such images instead require the subject's consent for publication. The other element of the Art Copyright Act that is open to the influence of fundamental rights, i.e. the "legitimate interest" in § 23.2, refers from the outset only to persons who are of importance in the context of contemporary history and therefore cannot sufficiently take the interests of the freedom of the press into consideration if such interests have before been disregarded when delimiting the group of persons who are considered to be persons of importance in the context of contemporary history.

The concept of contemporary history in § 23.3 no. 1 of the Art Copyright Act is not linked to the proviso of a judicial definition of its contents, by which its coverage might, for instance, be limited to events of historical or political importance; rather, it is determined by the public's interest in being informed (see RGZ 125, 80 (82) already). This takes the importance and the scope of the freedom of the press into account without disproportionately restricting the protection of the general right of personality. The core of the freedom of the press and the freedom of opinion includes that the press has sufficient room to manoeuvre, within the boundaries of the law, so that it may decide, according to its publishing standards, which facts claim public interest, and that it becomes apparent in the process of formation of public opinion which matters are matters of public interest. As has been stated, entertaining articles are not exempt from this.

Moreover, it is not objectionable that the Federal Court of Justice has also assigned to the "sphere of contemporary history" pursuant to § 23.1 no. 1 of the Art Copyright Act images of persons who have not attracted public attention at a certain point through their involvement with a specific event of contemporary history but instead encounter general public attention, independently of single events, on account of their status and their importance. In this context, the increased importance that photojournalism has acquired today in comparison with the time in which the Art Copyright Act was enacted carries weight as well. Certainly, the concept of an "absolute person of contemporary history", to which reference is frequently made in scholarly literature and jurisprudence in this context, imperatively follows neither from the law nor from the Constitution. If this concept is understood, as the Higher Regional Court and the Federal Court of Justice present it, as describing, in an abridged manner, persons whose images the public deems worthy of notice for the depicted person's sake, it is unobjectionable from the constitutional point of view. It is important, however, that a weighing take place, in each individual case, between the public's interest in being informed and the legitimate interest of the depicted person.

The general right of personality does not require that the publication of images of persons who are of importance in contemporary history without the consent of the depicted person, must be limited to images that show them when exercising the function that they discharge in society. Frequently, the public interest that such persons claim is characterised exactly by the fact that it is not restricted to the exercise of this person's public function in the narrower sense. Due to the person's exposed function and to the effect of the function, the interest can also extend to information about how the persons generally move in public, i.e. when they are not exercising their respective public function. The public has a legitimate interest in learning whether such persons, who are often regarded as a role-model or as an example, convincingly bring into agreement the behaviour that they show in their public function and their personal behaviour.

If the publishing of images was limited to the function of a person who is of importance to contemporary history, this would, however, fail to adequately take into account the interest that such persons legitimately arouse in the public. Moreover, this would encourage a selective manner of representation which would deny the public the required opportunity to assess persons from social and political life on account of their functions as role-models and on account of their influence. This does not open the press unlimited access to images of persons of contemporary history. Rather, § 23.2 of the Art Copyright Act provides the courts with sufficient possibilities to bring the requirements of protection to bear that are stipulated by Article 2.1 in conjunction with Article 1.1 of the Basic Law (see BVerfGE 35, 202 (225)).

bb) In principle, the standards that the Federal Court of Justice has developed when interpreting the element of a "legitimate interest" in § 23.2 of the Art Copyright Act are not objectionable from the constitutional point of view.
Pursuant to the challenged judgment, the privacy that is worthy of protection, to which the so-called absolute persons of contemporary history are also entitled, requires (1) a local seclusion to which someone has withdrawn to be alone; (2) that this wish to be alone is recognisable by an objective person; and (3) that the person, confiding in the seclusion, behaves in a manner in which he or she would not behave in the broad public. The Federal Court of Justice assumes that a violation of §§ 22 and 23 of the Art Copyright Act exists if images of the person affected are published that, in such a situation, were taken secretly or by catching the person unawares.
The standard of physical seclusion, on the one hand, takes the sense of the general right of personality into account, i.e. to secure to individuals a sphere outside their home in which they are aware that they are not under constant public observation and therefore do not have to control their behaviour in view of such observation but find it possible to relax and to recover. On the other hand, the standard of physical seclusion does not excessively restrict the freedom of the press, as it does not completely withdraw the daily and private life of persons of contemporary history from photojournalism but makes it accessible to pictorial representation to the extent that it takes place in public. In the case of an outstanding public interest in being informed, the freedom of the press can, pursuant to these rulings, also prevail over the protection of privacy (see Federal Court of Justice, *Juristenzeitung* – JZ 1965, p. 411 (413); Higher Regional Court of Hamburg, Archive of Copyright, Film, Broadcasting and Theatre Law (*Archiv für Urheber-, Film-, Funk- und Theaterrecht* – UFITA) 1977, p. 252 (257); Higher Regional Court of Munich, UFITA 1964, p. 322 (324)).
It is also not objectionable that in its ruling, the Federal Court of Justice took the individual's behaviour in a specific situation as an indicator that he or she is recognisably in a situation of seclusion. The protection against pictorial representations in this sphere, however, is not triggered only if the person affected shows a behaviour in this sphere that he or she would avoid under the eyes of the public. Rather, physical seclusion can fulfil its protective function with respect to its role in the development of someone's personality only if the seclusion ensures the individual, irrespective of the behaviour in which he or she engages in a given moment, a space for relaxation in which he or she need not constantly expect the presence of photographers or camera teams. This, however, is not the decisive question in this case, as pursuant to the findings of the Federal Court of Justice, the first prerequisite for the protection of privacy was lacking in the first place.

Finally, it is not objectionable from the constitutional point of view that the method of obtaining information is regarded as important when weighing the public interest in information and the protection of privacy (see BVerfGE 66, 116 (136)). There are, however, doubts about whether images that are taken secretly or by catching the subject unawares, without more, violate the privacy that exists outside the depicted individual's home. With regard to the function that the Constitution assigns to this sphere, and in view of the circumstance that one often cannot tell whether an image was taken secretly or by catching the subject unawares, an impermissible encroachment upon privacy can, in any case, not only be assumed if these characteristics exist. As the Federal Court of Justice, as concerns the photographs in dispute in these proceedings, denied in the first instance that the context in which the photos were made constituted a sphere of seclusion, the doubts about the manner in which the photographs were taken do not affect the result of its decision.

cc) The constitutional requirements, however, are not met to the extent that the challenged decisions disregarded the circumstance that the complainant's legal position concerning the protection of her right of personality is enhanced by Article 6 of the Basic Law in situations in which she cares for her children.

dd) As regards the different images, this leads to the following conclusions:

The decision of the Federal Court of Justice gives no reason for objection from the constitutional point of view as regards the images that show the complainant on her way to the market, accompanied by a bodyguard at the market and with a companion in a frequented restaurant. In the first two cases, the locations that are shown are not secluded, but are visited by the broad public. Certainly, the location of the third image is a bounded location, the complainant, however, finds herself in this location under the eyes of the public that is present. For this reason, the Federal Court of Justice does not, with its judgment to permit the publication of these photos, act in contradiction to the ban on the photos made at the garden restaurant. This ban is the subject of the challenged decisions but was not raised as part of the constitutional complaint. The seat that the complainant took at the garden restaurant with her companion showed all characteristics of seclusion. The circumstance that the photographs at the garden restaurant were obviously taken from a great distance additionally indicates that the complainant could assume that she was not exposed to the observation of the public.

Neither are there objections to the decision to the extent that it deals with the photos in which the complainant is shown alone, on horseback or riding her bicycle. On the basis of its views, the Federal Court of Justice also did not assign these photographs to the sphere of physical seclusion but to the public sphere. This is not objectionable from the constitutional point of view. The complainant herself also assigns the images to the secluded sphere of privacy only because, in her opinion,

they indicate her wish to be left alone. However, according to the criteria that have been explained, the mere subjective wish is not decisive in this context.
Contrary to this, the three photos that show the complainant together with her children require a new examination under the constitutional standards that were described above. It cannot be excluded that the examination according to these standards leads to a different result as concerns some of the images or all of them. To this extent, the judgment of the Federal Constitutional Court is therefore to be reversed and remanded.
d) As concerns the challenged judgments of the Regional Court and the Higher Regional Court, the violation of a fundamental right already follows from the fact that they – in conformity, however, with case-law at that time – restricted the privacy that is protected by Article 2.1 in conjunction with Article 1.1 of the Basic Law to the domestic sphere. However, it is not required to reverse the decisions because the violation concerning this point was remedied by the Federal Court of Justice and because, with regard to the other points, the case was remanded.

III.

…

Justices: Papier, Grimm, Kühling, Jaeger, Haas, Hömig, Steiner, Hohmann-Dennhardt

No. 31

BVerfGE 103, 89
of 6 February 2001 – 1 BvR 12/92 –
"Marriage covenant case"

HEADNOTE:

Decision regarding the judicial review of the content of agreements in a covenant of marriage concluded with a pregnant woman prior to the conclusion of marriage and affecting the care and maintenance situation of the joint child after a divorce, against the standard of Article 2.1 in conjunction with Article 6.4 of the Basic Law (*Grundgesetz* – GG) and of Article 6.2 of the Basic Law.

Judgment of the First Senate of 6 February 2001
on the basis of the oral hearing of 8 November 2000
– 1 BvR 12/92 –

in the proceedings regarding the constitutional complaint of Ms. L. – authorised representative: …, lawyers – against the judgment of the Stuttgart Higher Regional Court (*Oberlandesgericht*) of 28 November 1991 – 16 UF 280/91 –.

RULING:

1. The judgment of the Stuttgart Higher Regional Court of 28 November 1991 – 16 UF 280/91 – violates the complainant's rights from Article 2.1 in conjunction with Article 6.4, as well as from Article 6.2 of the Basic Law. The judgment is rescinded. The case is referred back to the Stuttgart Higher Regional Court.
2. …

EXTRACT FROM GROUNDS:

A.

The constitutional complaint relates to the question of the degree to which civil courts are constitutionally obliged to subject covenants of marriage to a review of their content insofar as statutory maintenance claims in the event of divorce are waived therein and a spouse is released from paying maintenance for joint children.

…

I.

1. Covenants of marriage may already be concluded prior to marriage, in other words they may be of significance for the conclusion of a marriage. General contract law applies to them, as do individual provisions of family law which pose formal requirements and set limits. Thus, according to § 1614.1 of the Civil Code (*Bürgerliches Gesetzbuch* – BGB), it is not possible to forgo future maintenance from relatives. This provision applies to spouses *mutatis mutandis* according to § 1360a.3 and § 1361.4 sentence 4 of the Civil Code, who may however make agreements according to § 1585c of the Civil Code regarding their mutual maintenance claims for the time after divorce, and in doing so may indeed forgo maintenance altogether. Property law agreements are also permissible according to § 1408.1 of the Civil Code. They are however subject to the formal requirement of § 1410 of the Civil Code, and must therefore be concluded for the record with a notary, and both spouses must attend. Contractual agreements regarding pension sharing, which also require the form of § 1410 of the Civil Code, are ineffective if divorce is applied for within one year after conclusion of the agreement (§ 1408.2 sentence 2 of the Civil Code). If they are made in connection with divorce, they require not only to be certified by a notary, but also the approval of the Family Court over and above this (§ 1587o.2 sentences 1 and 3 of the Civil Code). The contractual obligation of one spouse to release the other from maintenance claims for the child is regarded by the case-law as a permissible assumption of an obligation to perform within the meaning of § 329 of the Civil Code which leaves the maintenance claim of the child unaffected (Federal Court of Justice (*Bundesgerichtshof* – BGH), *Zeitschrift für das gesamte Familienrecht* – FamRZ 1987, p. 934 (935)).

2. …

3. a) The civil court case-law sets limits on the freedom of spouses to privately and autonomously structure their relationships under the law on maintenance in the

event of divorce by virtue of covenants of marriage, invoking § 138.1 of the Civil Code, where the agreement of necessity leads in objective terms to a spouse requiring social assistance (see BGH, FamRZ 1983, p. 137; *Neue Juristische Wochenschrift* – NJW 1991, p. 913 (914); NJW 1992, p. 3164 (3165); Hamm Higher Regional Court, FamRZ 1989, p. 398; Cologne Higher Regional Court, FamRZ 1990, p. 634; Celle Higher Regional Court, (*Niedersächs. Rechtspflege* – NdsRpfl) 1990, p. 250; Hamm Higher Regional Court, *NJW-Rechtsprechungs-Report Zivilrecht* – NJW-RR 1999, p. 950). The Federal Court of Justice considers a waiver of post-marital childcare maintenance according to § 1570 of the Civil Code to be, in principle, not contrary to public policy (see BGH, FamRZ 1985, p. 788). This was said to also apply if a spouse had to engage in gainful employment because of the waiver after the divorce even though he or she had to look after a child. The assessment of whether a covenant of marriage was contrary to public policy was said to depend on its overall character. Also linking waivers of maintenance with property law agreements by itself was said not to lead to the ineffectiveness of the agreement since an economic community was said not to be included in the essence of marriage. Taking account of the child's best interests, a spouse might however be denied liberty in individual cases to invoke the agreed waiver if it was incompatible with the principle of good faith because of the subsequent development, which is also applicable in maintenance law according to § 242 of the Civil Code (see BGH, FamRZ 1985, p. 788 (789); FamRZ 1987, p. 46; FamRZ 1991, pp. 306-307). Also in this context, the Federal Court of Justice took the view that it was not a matter of subjective momenta, in other words of conduct on the part of the party obliged to provide maintenance that was in breach of duty or reproachable, but that the only reason for a maintenance claim should be the needs and legitimate interests of the joint children, despite an effective waiver agreement (see BGH, FamRZ 1987, p. 46; FamRZ 1991, pp. 306-307).

The Federal Court of Justice has thus also considered covenants of marriage to be effective in which prior to concluding marriage pregnant women had waived maintenance to their future husband in the event of divorce (see BGH, FamRZ 1992, p. 1403). The husband was said not to have exploited a coercive situation since he could have refrained from marrying, thus invoking his freedom of conclusion of marriage, and could have withdrawn to the legal obligations of a non-marital father (see BGH, FamRZ 1996, p. 1536; FamRZ 1997, pp. 156 (157-158)). Rather, the economic situation of the woman was said to have improved by virtue of the conclusion of marriage, despite the waiver, since as a single mother she would otherwise only have had a right to a maintenance claim that was limited to one year according to § 1615l of the Civil Code. In another case, the Federal Court of Justice had however invoked § 242 of the Civil Code to grant a maintenance claim to a child-caring mother, for reasons of the child's best interests, which was in contradistinction to the covenant of marriage, but limited the claim to the necessary maintenance. This was said to be sufficient since the child's best interests merely needed to enable the parent with custody to devote himself or herself to caring for and bringing up the child. …

b) The release of one spouse from his or her maintenance obligation towards the joint child by the other spouse was regarded by the Federal Court of Justice as being contrary to public policy if it was agreed in return for refraining to exercise his or her right of access, since such a connection was said to constitute an unauthorised commercialisation of parental custody (see BGH, FamRZ 1984, p. 778). However, it negated that release from a maintenance obligation occurring at the same time as a transfer of parental custody to the releasing party was contrary to public policy if the custody arrangement was in the child's best interests (see BGH, FamRZ 1986, p. 444).

c) …

II.

1. The complainant, who was 26 at the time – that is in the early summer of 1976 –, had to care for a five-year-old child from her first marriage, and had been living with a new partner, later her husband, for two years when she discovered that she was pregnant. … The complainant … pressed for marriage before the birth of the child so that it would be born in wedlock. Her partner's reservations against marriage stemmed from the then immanent reform of the law on divorce and from fear of maintenance claims from his wife in the event of a divorce.

Therefore the complainant had a covenant of marriage drafted, which they both signed at the beginning of July. The agreement reads as follows:

> The parties intend to marry in August 1976 at the latest. Ms. F. is expecting a child who according to medical judgment will be born in November 1976. In the event of the marriage to be concluded being dissolved for reasons not currently apparent, the parties have reached the following agreement in the event of divorce: 1. Ms. B. F. and Mr. W. S. waive towards one another, for the past, present and future, all and any maintenance calculated from the legal force of the divorce, even in the event of need. 2. Mr. S. undertakes, also in the event of divorce, to pay to the expected child maintenance of DM 150.00 per month in advance, calculated from the legal force of the divorce, by the fifth working day of each month at the latest, payable to Ms. F. Ms. F. herewith releases Mr. S.

from all and any further maintenance claims against Mr. S. in respect of the expected child. Stuttgart, 9 July 1976.

The parties concluded the marriage in the same month. Their joint son was born in November 1976. After the end of maternity protection, the complainant returned to her previous employment as an office worker at a much lower remuneration than her husband earned.
The marriage was dissolved in December 1989 and custody for the son assigned to the complainant, who subsequently remarried.
2. In 1990, the son claimed against his father for information and child maintenance by means of an action by stages. After the Local Court (*Amtsgericht*) had sentenced the father by partial judgment to provide information on his income on grounds that the agreement from 1976 was contrary to public policy, the latter filed against the complainant for release from any maintenance claim against him for the child over and above DM 150 per month. The Local Court rejected the action as unfounded. The agreed release claim was said to circumvent the statutory prohibition of a waiver of maintenance between relatives.
In response to the appeal of the divorced husband on points of fact and law, the Higher Regional Court sentenced the complainant as requested, thus amending the ruling that had been handed down at first instance. The covenant of marriage was said to be effective. The child was said to retain his statutory maintenance claim against the father regardless of this agreement. Within the framework of their freedom to make an agreement, spouses could divide the burden of child maintenance between themselves prior to the conclusion of marriage as they wished. Invoking the agreement that had been concluded was said not to constitute a misuse of rights. It was said that the husband could make the marriage contingent on such an agreement since everyone was at liberty with regard to the conclusion of marriage. The agreement was also said not to be contrary to public policy with regard to its content, motives and purpose. The complainant had failed to provide evidence in this respect. It was said that there was neither a link between the release and a custody arrangement, nor an objectionable link with a considerable economic advantage. Given that the complainant was in employment, there was said to be nothing to suggest an agreement based on the coercive situation of economic dependence. The appeal on points of law was not admitted.

III.

The constitutional complaint, with which the complainant complains of a violation of her rights under Article 6.1, 6.2 and 6.4 … of the Basic Law, addresses this ruling of the Higher Regional Court.

In reviewing whether the release agreement was contrary to public policy, the Higher Regional Court is said to have disregarded the mandate of fundamental rights protection from Article 6 of the Basic Law. Giving concrete form to the obligation imposed on parents in Article 6.2 of the Basic Law to care for and bring up their child, the maintenance claim of a child against its parents was said to be indispensable. It was hence said to be incompatible with Article 6.2 of the Basic Law and its protection of the child's best interests if only one parent were to be one-sidedly burdened with this obligation, where that parent also had to provide sole care for the child. The view of the Higher Regional Court that such an agreement was permissible as a condition for conclusion of marriage, since the father had been free to refrain from the conclusion of marriage altogether, was said to be erroneous. The court was said to disregard here the fact that the release, particularly coupled with a waiver of post-marital maintenance on the part of the mother, released the father from all marital and parental obligations in the event of divorce. He was however said to be obliged to pay child maintenance regardless of conclusion of marriage with the mother.

Even if, in principle, the agreement on release from child maintenance was possible according to the case-law of the Federal Court of Justice, the Higher Regional Court should have taken into account the special circumstances applying on conclusion of the agreement and the interplay of the individual contractual agreements. The complainant was said to have waived not only her own maintenance in the event of divorce in the covenant of marriage, but also to have taken on the unpredictable, life-long maintenance obligation of the father towards the unborn child without receiving anything at all in return. Hence, the father was said to have rid himself de facto of his natural tie and relationship with the child to the disadvantage of the mother. This was said not to comply with the protection of marriage and the family and the parental obligation towards the child entrenched in Article 6.1 and 6.2 of the Basic Law.

Over and above this, the impugned ruling was said to violate the complainant's constitutional right as a mother to receive protection and care from the community. This right was said to prohibit legally recognising an agreement with which a pregnant woman in a mentally vulnerable and highly strained personal situation rashly undertook an obligation to largely release the father for life from any maintenance obligations towards their as yet unborn child, and to shoulder this obligation, in addition to her responsibility for bringing up and caring for the child. It was said to be a task for the state to provide expectant mothers with special protection in order to help and encourage them to shoulder responsibility for the new life. Case-law which failed to protect a pregnant woman against making an agreement by means of which she alone took on the overall responsibility for bringing up, caring for and maintaining the child was said not to do justice to this principle of protection. Expectant mothers in particular were said to especially require protection against entering into one-sided agreements that are ill-considered and where nothing material was given in return. The fact that the covenant had enabled the complainant to give the child a father, in line with her wish to bring it into the world in wedlock, and hence to ensure a civil future for it, could not be regarded as a legally recognisable counter payment for the contractual burdens which she shouldered. The Higher Regional Court was said to have disregarded this by imposing on the complainant – with regard to the justification of the breach of public policy – the burden of proof as to whether it had been suggested to her to have an abortion. The negation of the complainant's economic dependence on conclusion of the agreement as an indication that the agreement was contrary to public policy was also said not to take into account the fact that the dependence itself was revealed in the way the agreement entailed a one-sided burden.

…

B.

The constitutional complaint is well-founded. The impugned ruling violates the complainant's right under Article 2.1 in conjunction with Article 6.4 of the Basic Law. Over and above this, it violates Article 6.2 of the Basic Law.

I.

The Higher Regional Court has disregarded the right of the complainant under Article 2.1 in conjunction with Article 6.4 of the Basic Law for protection against unreasonable disadvantage caused by the covenant of marriage.

1. a) The fundamental rights develop their impact in private legal transactions as constitutional value determinations by the medium of the provisions which directly dominate the respective legal field, and also above all by the general clauses of civil law (see BVerfGE 7, 198 (205-206); 42, 143 (148)). Also in this respect, the state has to protect the fundamental rights of the individual and to protect them against violation by others (see BVerfGE 46, 160; 49, 89; 53, 30; 56, 54; 88, 203). It is incumbent on the courts to grant this fundamental right to protection by interpreting

and applying the law and to lend it concrete form in individual cases. The Federal Constitutional Court can only counter the courts' evaluation of fundamental right positions and the balancing of such positions against one another if an impugned ruling reveals errors in interpretation which are based on a fundamentally incorrect view of the significance of a fundamental right, in particular of the scope of its area of protection, and which are also of some import in their substantive significance for the legal case (see BVerfGE 18, 85 (93); 42, 143 (149); established case-law). These preconditions for a correction by the Federal Constitutional Court apply in the instant case.

b) The principle of freedom of action guaranteed by Article 2.1 of the Basic Law is conditional on the prerequisites of the self-determination of the individual actually applying (see BVerfGE 81, 242 (254-255)). The material instrument for the realisation of free action taken on autonomous responsibility in relationships with others is the agreement with which the parties determine for themselves how their individual interests are to be suitably equalised. Mutual ties and the exercise of freedom are hence given their concrete form. Hence, as a rule the agreed decisions, expressed between the parties to the agreement, permit a proper equalisation of interests to be concluded from the agreement which the state must in principle respect (see BVerfGE 81, 242 (254)). If however it is evident from the particularly one-sided burdening of contractual responsibilities and of a highly unequal negotiating position of the partners to an agreement that one partner has such a weight in a contractual relationship that he or she can de facto one-sidedly determine the content of the agreement, it is a matter for the law to work towards maintaining the fundamental right positions of both partners to the agreement in order to prevent one party's self-determination being turned into the other party taking control (see BVerfGE 89, 214 (232)).

c) This also applies to covenants of marriage with which spouses regulate their highly personal relationships for the time of their marriage or thereafter. Article 6.1 of the Basic Law gives them the right here to freely shape their respective community inwardly in marital and family responsibility and respect (see BVerfGE 80, 81 (92)). Having said that, the protection provided by the state system, which is explicitly guaranteed for marriage and the family in Article 6.1 of the Basic Law, is contingent on a statutory structure of marriage (see BVerfGE 31, 58 (69)). It must be taken into account here that the marital and family domain of freedom also receives its constitutional structure through Article 3.2 of the Basic Law. A marriage, in which a man and a woman are in an equal rights partnership towards one another, is therefore constitutionally protected (see BVerfGE 37, 217 (249 et seq.)). As a result, the state must impose limits on the freedom that spouses have, using covenants, to shape their marital relationships and mutual rights and obligations where the covenant is not an expression and outcome of a community based on equal rights, but reflects a one-sided dominance by a spouse based on unequal negotiating positions. In such cases of disturbed agreement parity it is a task for the courts via the general clauses of civil law to subject the content of the agreement to a review for impaired fundamental right positions of a party to a covenant of marriage, and where appropriate to correct them (see BVerfGE 89, 214 (234)).

The Higher Regional Court wrongly presumed that the freedom of conclusion of marriage countered such a content review. It does not follow from the right of the individual to enter into marriage with a partner whom they have chosen themselves, or to refrain from doing so, and hence not to experience any unjustified hindrance in this on the part of the state (see BVerfGE 31, 58 (67)) that the state may not review any covenant of marriage if it contains a promise of marriage. The freedom of conclusion of marriage does not justify the freedom to shape the covenant of marriage without limit, and in particular it does not justify a one-sided distribution of burdens in a covenant of marriage. Accordingly, a part of the law on marriage is traditionally imperative law.

2. a) If a covenant of marriage contains a recognisably one-sided distribution of burdens placing a woman in an unfavourable position, and if it has been concluded prior to marriage and in connection with her pregnancy, the claim to protection and care of the expectant mother from Article 6.4 of the Basic Law also requires that the covenant of marriage is to be subject to a special judicial review of its content. This applies all the more, given that the legislature has refrained, concerning maintenance agreements in prenuptial agreements, unlike agreements regarding the accrued marital gains or pension sharing, from offering a certain protection against disadvantages of a party to the covenant via formal requirements or procedural regulations. In this case, it is primarily incumbent on the courts to implement the constitutional mandate of protection in carrying out the review of the content and to grant to the pregnant woman protection against pressure and distress from her social environment or on the part of the child's father (see BVerfGE 88, 203 (296-297)), in particular if she is pushed thereby to conclude contractual agreements which are extremely counter to her interests.

b) A situation of inferiority can be presumed to exist as a rule if an unmarried pregnant woman is faced in the future with the alternative to either shoulder responsibility and care alone for the expected child, or to include the child's father in the responsibility by conclusion of marriage, albeit at the expense of concluding a covenant of marriage with him which considerably impairs her interests. Her negotiation position will be weakened here by the de facto situation in which she finds herself, by her legal position as a single mother and in particular by the efforts to ensure her own livelihood and that of the expected child.

Pregnancy means existential turbulence in the life of any woman. A pregnant woman undergoes a development process which makes her physically experience changes and which entails risks for her own health and that of the child. She unavoidably incurs a change in her lifestyle and life planning with the child. New tasks, obligations and responsibilities arise. Particularly for unmarried mothers, this frequently occurs hand-in-hand with the failure of the relationship with the child's father (see Vaskovics/Rost/Rupp, *Lebenslage nichtehelicher Kinder*, 1997, pp. 59 et seq.). Over and above this, societal and social coercions also remain today as a result of which an expectant mother may feel herself to be under pressure to justify – not least towards the child – why she is not married. With regard to the time of the conclusion of the covenant of marriage disputed here, scientific studies still speak of the stigma faced by the single mother and of her much greater mental strain compared to married mothers, which also explains the phenomenon of the higher mortality of infants born out of wedlock (see Anthes, *Vorurteile gegenüber ledigen Müttern*, in: Neumann, *Sozialforschung und soziale Demokratie, Festschrift für Blume*, 1979, p. 157 (162 et seq.)).
Added to this, an unmarried pregnant woman faces the certainty of having to bear sole responsibility and care for the child. Also according to the law now applicable, she remains solely responsible for the child if the father is not willing to undertake joint custody. What is more, she had and still has today only a restricted maintenance claim against the father. Whilst, in the period that is material here, this claim was still restricted to the duration of one year after the birth of the child, and then only if the mother is able to engage in gainful employment only to an insufficient degree, or if the child cannot be taken care of by other means, according to § 1615 l.2 sentence 3 of the Civil Code it now applies as a rule for three years, but is not comparable with the safeguarding of married women under the law on maintenance to which children born in wedlock are entitled. An unmarried mother is generally faced in the child's early years with the problem of ensuring childcare and her own livelihood in equal measure.
As a rule, the economic prospects for mothers of children born out of wedlock are particularly poor. After the birth of the child, her income falls in most cases to less than half of its previous level because of bearing sole responsibility for the child. The consequence of this is that roughly one-third of them only have financial security below or at social assistance level for themselves and their children, whilst only 15 per cent of children born in wedlock live in such straightened circumstances (Vaskovics/Rost/Rupp, loc. cit., p. 126). This situation is further exacerbated by a much worse payment morality of fathers towards children born out of wedlock. As a consequence, children born out of wedlock are very much over-represented among beneficiaries according to the Maintenance Advance Act (*Unter-*

haltsvorschussgesetz) (see Federal Ministry for Family Affairs, Senior Citizens, Women and Youth (ed.), *Die wirtschaftlichen Folgen von Trennung und Scheidung*, 2000, pp. 139-140). The special, difficult situation of unmarried pregnant women, which is not comparable with that of married pregnant women or of unmarried women without children, also impacts the circumstances on conclusion of a covenant of marriage that is to be a condition for conclusion of marriage. Particularly because of their concern also about the future of the child and under the pressure of the immanent birth, pregnant women typically find themselves in a position which is far inferior to that of the other partner to the agreement.

c) Having said that, being pregnant on conclusion of a covenant of marriage is only an indication of contractual disparity necessitating subjecting the agreement to a more stringent judicial review. The property situation, vocational skills and outlook, as well as the envisioned sharing of gainful employment and family work in the marriage by the parties to the covenant of marriage, are further material factors determining the situation of the pregnant woman. In an individual case, they may lead to equalising her inferior position, even if statutory legal positions are contracted out by virtue of the covenant of marriage.

d) If however the content of the covenant of marriage also expresses such a position of inferiority of the unmarried pregnant woman, the need of protection becomes manifest. This is the case if the pregnant woman is one-sidedly burdened by the agreement and her interests are not suitably taken into account (see BVerfGE 89, 214 (234)).

Whether the contractual agreements are much more burdensome on the woman than on the man also largely depends on what family constellation the partners to the agreement are striving for and on which they base their agreement. If the spouses waive any mutual post-marital statutory maintenance claims, this does not constitute an unequal burden in marriages in which both partners pursue roughly equivalent gainful employment and share housework and family work. If, however, the life planning of the partners provides that in the marriage one of the two, giving up employment, largely devotes himself or herself to childcare and housekeeping, the waiver of post-marital maintenance constitutes a disadvantage for the person who has devoted himself or herself to the care of the child and to work in the home. The more statutory rights are contracted out in the covenant of marriage or additional obligations assumed, the more this effect of one-sided disadvantage can be amplified.

The promise to marry contained in the covenant of marriage does not outweigh the one-sided burden of a partner to the agreement. The partners are free in their decision as to whether they wish to enter into marriage. If they opt to do so, the marriage entails rights and also obligations for both and shares these equally between the man and the woman; the benefits which they provide to one another are of the same rank (see BVerfGE 37, 217 (251)). The promise to marry as such does not give rise to any one-sided burden on one of the promising parties. It is true that spouses hence assume new obligations as against their former state as single persons, and they are thereby restricted in their own dispositions. This however applies equally to both spouses.

3. The obligation of protection following from Article 2.1 in conjunction with Article 6.4 of the Basic Law was disregarded by the Higher Regional Court in the impugned ruling. It neither took account of the special situation in which the complainant found herself as a pregnant woman already having one child on conclusion of the covenant, nor did it explore the question of whether the covenant of marriage constitutes an unreasonable burden on the complainant, although the content of the agreement gave reason for doing so.

The complainant for one thing waived her own post-marital maintenance in the covenant. In view of the small amount of her income and of the circumstance that both spouses presumed that she would care for the joint child in the event of divorce, she permanently weakened her economic situation by virtue of this waiver. She could not count on considerably improving her income situation through her own efforts, given that she had two children. By contrast, the husband did not give up anything with his own waiver; he could not expect to be able to assert a maintenance claim against the complainant in the event of divorce.

Over and above this, the complainant contractually assumed the obligation to largely release the father from his maintenance obligation towards the joint child despite her comparably poor economic situation. The cash maintenance of the child, which is in line with the father's higher income, had to be financed from her income. Hence, in the event of divorce she was allocated the task of sole care for the child and of ensuring her own maintenance and at the same time that of the joint child. This unambiguous burden on the complainant contrasted with the husband divesting himself of any maintenance claim on the part of the complainant, as well as of any amount over and above DM 150 for the child. Hence, he was in fact in a better situation than the father of a child born out of wedlock in view of the amount that was standard at that time. Invoking the freedom of conclusion of marriage, the court did not take this agreement constellation as a reason for a review of the content of the covenant, thereby disregarding the fact that this freedom does not open up the freedom to contractually establish interests in an unreasonably one-sided manner.

II.

Over and above this, the Higher Regional Court disregarded protection from Article 6.2 of the Basic Law, which imposes limits on contractual agreements between parents in the child's best interests.

1. Article 6.2 sentence 1 of the Basic Law gives rise for the parents in equal measure to the right and the duty to care for and bring up their children (see BVerfGE 24, 119 (143-144)). This responsibility, which is allocated to the parents first and foremost, must serve the child's best interests, and is therefore a fundamental right in the interest of the child (see BVerfGE 59, 360 (382); 75, 201 (218)). The right of the parents to freely organise their care for the child therefore does not deserve protection where parents withdraw from their responsibility towards the child and there is a threat of the child being neglected (see BVerfGE 24, 119 (143-144)). If parental misconduct reaches such a level that the child's best interests are persistently placed in danger, the state is not only entitled, but is indeed obliged to exercise its watchdog function according to Article 6.2 sentence 2 of the Basic Law to ensure the care and bringing up of the child, given that the child, as a holder of fundamental rights, has a right to state protection against the irresponsible exercise of the parental right (see BVerfGE 24, 119 (144); 55, 171 (179); 72, 122 (134)). The protection measures are determined here according to the degree of parental failure and by what is necessary in the interest of the child (see BVerfGE 24, 119 (144-145); 60, 79 (91, 93)).

The responsibility of the parents also includes ensuring maintenance of the child which corresponds to their own ability and at the same time is reasonable, and to ensure the child´s care (see BVerfGE 68, 256 (267); 80, 81 (90-91)). How parents divide these tasks among themselves, and whether in doing so they avail themselves of the support of third-party professionals, is part of their freedom to decide (see BVerfGE 47, 46 (70); 68, 256 (267-268); 99, 216 (231-232)). This also applies in the event of divorce. If parents conclude a contractual agreement for this case, because of the responsibility towards their child they must ensure that the mental burdens on the child which as a rule are linked with the separation of the parents are alleviated wherever possible and a sensible solution is found meeting the interests of the child for its care and upbringing (see BVerfGE 31, 194 (205); 61, 358 (372-372)).

2. If in the event of divorce it is the intention of the parents for one parent to be responsible for custody of the joint child, and also to take on its care, and if the parents agree for this case that the parent who is not the carer is to be released from child maintenance by the parent who is the carer, they do not do justice to their responsibility towards the child, and place its best interests at risk if care which is in

the interest of the child and cash maintenance in line with what both parents can afford is thus no longer ensured.

a) Maintenance payments for the child must be orientated in line with the ability to pay of the party obliged to provide maintenance and the need of the child (see § 1602.2 and §§ 1603 and 1610 of the Civil Code). Its amount is hence also determined by the social situation of the parents and is as such not an indication of a risk to the child's best interests. Even in financially straightened circumstances, a child may experience favourable development due to being cared for and brought up by its parents as they are able, where there are appropriate state benefits guaranteeing the family's basic financial security.

How parents meet their responsibility of bringing up the child, and how they shape the child's circumstances, lies in their primary decision-making responsibility according to Article 6.2 sentence 1 of the Basic Law, which is based on the consideration that they as a rule are best placed to defend the interests of their child. This also applies if the child does not appear to receive optimal promotion according to objective standards (see BVerfGE 34, 165 (184); 60, 79 (94)). If parents keep the standard of living of their child low in relation to their income, for instance as an expression of their ideas for bringing up a child to promote their personality development, this by itself does not justify state interference. If the financial resources available to cover the life needs of the child are however persistently restricted by the parents only because at least one parent wishes to withdraw in financial terms from care for his or her child, this is no longer a form of exercise of parental interest for the child. If the parent wishes to divest himself of herself of the task of defending the interests of the child, Article 6.2 sentence 2 of the Basic Law obliges the state to act to protect the child's best interests.

b) The release of one parent from child maintenance by the other however has no legal impact on the maintenance claim of the child against its parents. In fact, the economic situation of the child undergoes major changes if the carer parent does not have considerable financial resources. If this contractual obligation affects the carer parent, the latter not only does not receive payments to cover the maintenance of the child from the other parent, but at the same time his or her disposable income is reduced by this obligation to cover child maintenance and has de facto the same impact as forgoing maintenance. The income which is at the disposal of the joint household of the carer parent and of the child hence clearly falls as a result. Over and above this, it is necessary to care for the child so that the possibility of further gainful employment is restricted.

c) If the agreement between the parents leads to a situation in which, in the event of divorce, the carer parent is no longer able to cover either his or her maintenance or that of the child through income or assets due to taking on the other parent's burden of child maintenance, this impairs the living conditions of the child in a manner which runs counter to parental responsibility.

If the carer parent wishes to care for the child personally so that after separation from one parent the child does not also have to do without care by the other parent, this necessarily leads with younger children either to a restriction on, or to the impossibility of, the carer parent's return to external gainful employment, and hence to a reduction in, or to the cessation of, his or her own income. Only if the income thus remaining is still sufficient to also cover the maintenance needs of the child, or if the cessation of income can be balanced by assets or by the carer parent's own maintenance claims, in the case of a release agreement both the personal and material care of the child remain safeguarded. If this is however not the case, and if the carer parent, in addition to the release, also forgoes his or her own post-marital maintenance, the circumstances caused by the agreement force him or her either to place the care of the child in the hands of strangers, or to live with the child in circumstances which restrict its possibilities for development much more than would be in keeping with the joint parental assets. Both options are sustainedly detrimental to the interests of the child and are a consequence of a lack of parental responsibility towards the child.

Even if the carer parent is able to engage in gainful employment and would like to place the child in care, an impairment of the child's interests caused by the release agreement can only be ruled out if the income achievable is sufficient to be able to ensure the care costs and the suitable life maintenance for the child without also imposing considerable restrictions on the parent's own maintenance. If this is manifestly not guaranteed on agreeing the release, the parents' contractual agreement is detrimental to the child's best interests here too.

3. The Higher Regional Court did not take this into account in its ruling although the complainant's situation on conclusion of the covenant of marriage required such a review. It satisfied itself with pointing out that the child's right to maintenance is not affected by a release agreement. This is legally correct, but already fails to take into account whether the mother is able to fulfil the concrete claim without excessive effort or a considerable reduction in the family's standard of living. It did not consider, finally, that the release can exert an influence on the establishment of this right of the child, and hence on the interests of the child. Thus, the Higher Regional Court disregarded the fact that the complainant already had her own child to care for at the time of the conclusion of the covenant, and that in the event of divorce the agreement meant that she was burdened with care for the children, as well as with making her own living and with the entire maintenance of both children. In view of her rather modest earning capacity as a commercial clerk, it should have been obvious to the court to ask the question of whether the release

did not violate the interests of the joint child under such circumstances and run counter to the responsibility incumbent on the parents. Hence, it disregarded the scope and significance of the protection provided by Article 6.2 of the Basic Law against irresponsible exercise of the parental right to the disadvantage of the child's best interests.

III.

The impugned ruling is to be rescinded. The case is to be referred back to the Higher Regional Court.

Justices: Papier, Kühling, Jaeger, Hömig, Steiner, Hohmann-Dennhardt, Hoffmann-Riem

No. 32

BVerfGE 103, 242

of 3 April 2001 – 1 BvR 1629/94 –

"Long-term care insurance case"

HEADNOTE:

It is not compatible with Article 3.1 in conjunction with Article 6.1 of the Basic Law (*Grundgesetz* – GG) that members of social long-term care insurance who care for and raise children, and thereby in addition to the monetary contribution make a generative contribution to the functioning of a contributory social insurance system, are burdened with an equally high long-term care insurance contribution as members without children.

Judgment of the First Senate of 3 April 2001
on the basis of the oral hearing of 4 July 2000
– 1 BvR 1629/94 –

in the proceedings regarding the constitutional complaint of Mr. M., – authorised representatives: ..., lawyers – against Article 1 §§ 54, 55, 57, 58 and 60 of the Act on Social Security against the Risk of Need of Long-Term Care (*Gesetz zur sozialen Absicherung des Risikos der Pflegebedürftigkeit* – PflegeVG) (Long-Term Care Insurance Act (*Pflege-Versicherungsgesetz*)) of 26 May 1994 (Federal Law Gazette (*Bundesgesetzblatt* – BGBl) I p. 1014).

RULING:

1. § 54.1 and 54.2, § 55.1 sentence 1 and § 55.2, as well as § 57, of the Eleventh Book of the Code of Social Law (*Elftes Buch Sozialgesetzbuch* – SGB XI) of 26 May 1994 (Federal Law Gazette I page 1014) are not compatible with Article 3.1 in conjunction with Article 6.1 of the Basic Law insofar as members of social long-term care insurance who care for and raise children are burdened with an equally high long-term care insurance contribution as members without children.

2. The provisions of the Eleventh Book of the Code of Social Law quoted at 1. may continue to be applied until a new provision [comes into force], at most until 31 December 2004.
3. The Federal Republic of Germany is ordered to reimburse the complainant his necessary expenses.

EXTRACT FROM GROUNDS:

A.

The constitutional complaint impugns the non-consideration of care for and raising of children in the assessment of the contribution to social long-term care insurance.

I.

The funding of social long-term care insurance is governed by §§ 54 to 68 of the Eleventh Book of the Code of Social Law, which was added to the Code of Social Law by Article 1 of the Act on Social Security against the Risk of Need of Long-Term Care (Long-Term Care Insurance Act) of 26 May 1994 (Federal Law Gazette I p. 1014). It is operated above all by means of contributions (§ 54.1 of the Eleventh Book of the Code of Social Law). Details of the law on contributions are contained in the provisions of §§ 54 to 61 of the Eleventh Book of the Code of Social Law.
1. The contributions are collected from the members of social long-term care insurance (§ 54.2 of the Eleventh Book of the Code of Social Law). Family members are insured free of contributions for the duration of family insurance in accordance with § 25 of the Eleventh Book of the Code of Social Law (§ 56.1 of the Eleventh Book of the Code of Social Law). As is the case with statutory health insurance, the contributions are levied not in accordance with the insured risk, in particular not in accordance with state of health, age and gender, but in accordance with a percentage (contribution rate) of the income of the members on which contributions are levied, up to an assessment limit (§ 54.2 sentence 1, §§ 55 and 57 of the Eleventh Book of the Code of Social Law). As in statutory health insurance, the assessment limit is 75 per cent of the assessment limit of statutory pensions insurance (§ 55.2 of the Eleventh Book of the Code of Social Law), and on 1 January 2000 was 6,450 DM per month in the old *Länder* (states) and 5,325 DM per month in the new *Länder*.
2. The contribution to social long-term care insurance in the period from 1 January 1995 to 30 June 1996 was nationally 1 per cent of the income of the members on

which contributions are levied. Since 1 July 1996, the time when the benefit law provisions on in-patient long-term care entered into force, the contribution has been 1.7 per cent. Wage-earners and salaried employees and those employed in their vocational training on a remunerational basis – individuals who are also subject to obligatory statutory health insurance –, who are subject to obligatory [social long-term care] insurance in accordance with § 20.1 no. 1 of the Eleventh Book of the Code of Social Law, as well as their employers, each pay half the contributions, which are to be assessed in accordance with remuneration (§ 58.1 sentence 1 of the Eleventh Book of the Code of Social Law). Employees covered by voluntary statutory health insurance, who are subject to obligatory social long-term care insurance in accordance with § 20.3 of the Eleventh Book of the Code of Social Law, receive a subsidy from their employer which corresponds to the employer's share for the parties insured in accordance with § 20.1 no. 1 of the Eleventh Book of the Code of Social Law (§ 61.1 sentence 1 of the Eleventh Book of the Code of Social Law). In the Free State of Saxony, in which no statutory *Land* (state) holiday was abolished, the employees bore the full contribution until 30 June 1996 (see § 58.3 of the Eleventh Book of the Code of Social Law). § 58.3 of the Eleventh Book of the Code of Social Law was ultimately amended by Article 2 no. 1 of the Act to Implement the Second Phase of Long-Term Care Insurance (*Gesetz zum Inkraftsetzen der 2. Stufe der Pflegeversicherung*) of 31 May 1996 (Federal Law Gazette I p. 718), such that in Saxony from 1 July 1996 employees pay 1.35 per cent and employers pay 0.35 per cent of remunerations as a contribution burden. In all other *Länder*, the contribution burden continued to be shared in equal halves by employees and employers after 30 June 1996.
The monthly maximum contribution (including the employer's share) has gradually increased in the old *Länder* since 1 January 1995 from 58.50 DM to 109.66 DM in 2000, and in the new *Länder* from 48 DM to 90.52 DM per month.
3. Long-term care insurance does not constitute complete insurance in the sense that all and any need of the person in need of long-term care would be comprehensively covered by benefits in every case. Depending on the long-term care rate, these are not sufficient in the in-patient sector, in some cases in Categories I and II, and very largely in Category III, to cover the cost of long-term care, plus not inconsiderable expenditure on accommodation and food ... As an average per inhabitant in need of long-term care, 4,261 DM needed to be paid per month in the old *Länder* in 1998, while in the new *Länder* it was an average of 3,307 DM (information acc. to Schneekloth/Müller, *Wirkungen der Pflegeversicherung*, Vol. 127 of the series of the Federal Ministry of Health, 2000, pp. 175-176 ... see also *Bundestag* printed paper (*Bundestagsdrucksache* – BTDrucks.) 14/3592, pp. 10-11). This was opposed by the following benefits from statutory long-term care insurance:

	§ 41 of the Eleventh Book of the Code of Social Law	§ 42 of the Eleventh Book of the Code of Social Law	Article 49a § 1 of the Long-Term Care Insurance Act, § 43.5 of the Eleventh Book of the Code of Social Law from 1 July 1996 to 31 December 2001	§ 43a of the Eleventh Book of the Code of Social Law Long-term care in full in-patient facilities of disabled assistance from 25 June 1996
Category	monthly up to	for four weeks per year up to	monthly flat-rate	monthly up to
I	750 DM	2,800 DM	2,000 DM	10 per cent of the home charge agreed in accordance with § 93.2 of the Federal Social Assistance Act (*Bundessozialhilfegesetz* – BSHG), up to a maximum of 500 DM per month
II	1,500 DM from 1 August 1999: 1,800 DM	2,800 DM	2,500 DM	
III	2,100 DM from 1 August 1999: 2,800 DM	2,800 DM	2,800 DM	
Hardship cases	------	------	3,300 DM	

Also in the out-patient sector, the benefits of long-term care insurance do not cover the total cost of care in many cases. In 1998, persons in need of long-term care living in private households on average had regular additional costs which they had to pay themselves in Category I amounting to 210 DM/month, in Category II amounting to 264 DM/month and in Category III amounting to 384 DM/month … Here, the additional cost of out-patient care of the persons most seriously in need of long-term care may be much higher than the average values given above. The benefits of long-term care insurance in the case of domestic care have been as follows since the Act entered into force:

Category	Benefits in kind § 36 of the Eleventh Book of the Code of Social Law per month	Nursing care allowance § 37 of the Eleventh Book of the Code of Social Law per month	Combination benefit § 38 of the Eleventh Book of the Code of Social Law (e.g.: 50/50) per month
I	750 DM	400 DM	575 DM
II	1,800 DM	800 DM	1,300 DM
III	2,800 DM	1,300 DM	2,050 DM
Hardship cases	3,750 DM	-------	2,525 DM

Both for domestic and for in-patient care it is the case that the social assistance organisations must provide benefits for insured persons in need of long-term care if – assuming financial neediness – either the first Category is not yet reached, or the benefits of long-term care insurance are not sufficient to cover the costs.

4. The risk of needing long-term care is determined to a great degree by the age of the insured party. The data available in the legislative procedure (see *Bundestag* printed paper 12/5262, p. 62) and the information provided by the First Report on Trends in Long-Term Care Insurance (*Bundestag* printed paper 13/9528, Annex 2) show that the share of persons in need of long-term care in the age group to 60 is lower than 1 per cent – of whom 0.5 per cent are in the age group under 15 and in domestic care (see *Bundestag* printed paper 13/11460, p. 244), from 60 to 80 years, this increases to 5 per cent, and among the over 80s it is 20 per cent. Among persons in need of long-term care themselves, 17.5 per cent are under 60; 30.3 per cent are aged between 60 and 80, and finally, 52.3 per cent are 80 and older.

II.

The complainant is the father of ten children born between 1982 and 1995. He is in dependent employment, and is a voluntary member of statutory health and social

long-term care insurance. His wife is not in gainful employment. She takes care of the children, and like them is covered by family insurance.
The complainant objects to the contribution law provisions of §§ 54, 55, 57, 58 and 60 of the Eleventh Book of the Code of Social Law concerning him. They are alleged to violate Article 2, 3 and 6 of the Basic Law, as well as the principle of the rule of law and of the social welfare state. Also, the legislature is said to have violated the duties imposed on it by the judgment of the Federal Constitutional Court (*Bundesverfassungsgericht*) of 7 July 1992 (Decisions of the Federal Constitutional Court (*Entscheidungen des Bundesverfassungsgerichts* – BVerfGE) 87, 1).
...

III.

With regard to the constitutional complaint, a joint statement has been made on behalf of the Federal Government by the Federal Ministry of Labour and Social Affairs and the Federal Ministry of Health, as well as by the Federal Association of Local Health Insurance Funds (*AOK-Bundesverband*), the Association of Salaried Employees' Health Insurance Funds (Verband *der Angestellten-Krankenkassen*) and the Association of Workers' Substitute Health Insurance Funds (*Arbeiter-Ersatzkassen-Verband*) – both also for the Federal Association of Company Health Insurance Funds (*Bundesverband der Betriebskrankenkassen*) and the Federal Association of Guild Health Insurance Funds (*IKK-Bundesverband*) – while the German Women Lawyers Association (*Deutscher Juristinnenbund*) has also submitted a statement. The German Families Association (*Deutscher Familienverband*), the Family Federation of German Catholics (*Familienbund der Deutschen Katholiken*) and the Association of Single Mothers and Fathers (*Verband Alleinstehender Mütter und Väter*) have made a joint statement. Over and above this, the German Families Association has submitted a statement of its own in preparation of the oral hearing.
1. The Federal Ministries consider the non-allowance of child-raising in the assessment of contributions for social long-term care insurance to be constitutional.
a) The Long-Term Care Insurance Act is said not to violate Article 3.1 in conjunction with Article 6.1 of the Basic Law. Families with children are said to be particularly accommodated in social long-term care insurance. It is said to provide families with children with considerable advantages in comparison with childless insured parties, both on the contributions and on the benefit side. The Federal Ministries argued that member's children were co-insured in social long-term care insurance free of contributions. The same applied to the spouse if his or her income did not exceed the threshold for insignificant employment. Hence, although paying on-

ly one contribution, families enjoyed multiple insurance protection in line with the number of children, in comparison to childless couples, which started on the birth of the children. Moreover, maternity and child-raising allowance were contribution free. Family members who were co-insured free of contributions received the same benefits as contribution-paying members in an insured event. What is more, caring family members had social insurance by virtue of the contribution payments made to pensions insurance by the long-term care insurance funds. They were also included in statutory accident insurance.

Further benefits for families in the shape of a contribution discount, either standardised or phased in accordance with the number of children, or indeed complete exemption from contributions, were said not to be possible. The financing of long-term care insurance was said to be based on contributions which in principle were to be paid by each insured party. Because of social and family policy considerations, it was possible to justify breaking with this principle. This was however said to be contingent on re-distribution in favour of families falling within the remit of long-term care insurance. However, reducing the financial burden – by whatever form of "family discount" – would not bring about a tangible, expedient improvement in families' economic situations. Even complete exemption from contributions to long-term care insurance could not achieve the goal of an effective burden reduction to which the complainant aspired. The contributions were said to be too low for this.

When comparing the contribution burden incumbent on families against that incurred by the childless, it should, according to the Federal Ministries, also be taken into account that childless people in gainful employment paid with their contributions not only for their own insurance protection, but that they also effected transfer payments for the spouses and children who are co-insured in long-term care insurance free of contributions.

b) Long-term care insurance was said not to be able to compensate in a general manner for the cost of child-raising. This is said rather to be a task for society as a whole within the framework of the equalisation of family burdens, which preferably is to be carried out through fiscal law and child benefit. The Federal Constitutional Court had already confirmed this in its judgment of 7 July 1992 (BVerfGE 87, 1). Insofar as the complainant derived from this ruling a mandate for the legislature to form the contribution regulations in an even more family-friendly manner, he was said to disregard the fact that disadvantages could not accrue in long-term care insurance – in contrast to pensions insurance – if, as a result of child-raising, gainful employment could only be taken up to a limited degree, or was given up altogether. In the event of a need of long-term care, all insured parties were said to receive the same benefits regardless of whether the insurance existed because of membership or on the basis of contribution-free co-insurance as a family member. In particular, interrupting gainful employment because of child-raising was said not to have an impact on the scope of benefits in an insured event. Long-term care insurance was said to be risk insurance independent of the amount of the contributions made. Its benefits were said not to act as a wage replacement, and not to constitute an additional pension. They were said to be intended, rather, to relieve persons in need of long-term care of the burden of expenditure on long-term care. Hence, the system of long-term care insurance was said to be fundamentally different from the system of pensions insurance; there was said to be no need of an additional improvement of the situation of families in the law on contributions under long-term care insurance.

c) Long-term care insurance was said not to violate the principle of the social welfare state. Neither its out-patient nor its in-patient benefits were said to bring about the occasionally claimed "re-distribution from the bottom to the top". Long-term care insurance was said to carry out social compensation both with socially balanced contributions, and with benefits tailored to the need for long-term care. It was said to cause re-distribution benefiting socially weaker individuals. The socially vulnerable, who when in need of long-term care were said otherwise to depend on social assistance benefits, were said to be provided with insurance benefits to the funding of which not only they, but also the financially less vulnerable had contributed.

2. In the view of the Federal Association of Local Health Insurance Funds, the considerations of the Federal Constitutional Court's "rubble women" judgment (BVerfGE 87, 1) are not transferable to social long-term care insurance.

a) In contrast to the situation in statutory pensions insurance, the scope of the benefits was said not to depend on the extent of the contributions made by the member. Furthermore, family members devoting themselves to child-raising, and family-insured children themselves, were said not to be subject to any disadvantages. The contributions made by the children to long-term care insurance after reaching working age were said not to reduce their contributory capacity to meet general maintenance obligations towards their parents. Firstly, the contributions payable to social long-term care insurance were said to be much lower than pensions insurance contributions. Secondly, long-term care insurance was also said not to serve the purpose of old-age security, but to cover the maintenance needs which increased as a result of long-term care.

Insofar as a disadvantage was said nonetheless to remain with regard to the family in that the contributions to social insurance paid by the children were not available to secure the maintenance of the parents, this was said, because of the latitude available to the legislature, not to be objectionable in accordance with Article 3.1

and Article 6.1 of the Basic Law. The introduction of social long-term care insurance was said to have been necessary because of demographic and medical developments. Moreover, the burden on the children of parents in need of long-term care was said to be reduced by long-term care insurance in terms of corresponding maintenance obligations.

b) The family component within the law on contributions called for by family associations was said to be constitutionally unnecessary. It too was said to be neither practicable nor transferable to private obligatory long-term care insurance. The design of the contribution system within long-term care insurance was said also not to be in violation of justice of contributions just because the assessment limit led to a situation in which a disproportionately low burden was imposed on higher incomes, whilst the minimum contribution meant that a disproportionately high burden was imposed on low incomes in terms of the cost of solidarity based insurance. The argument was said to ignore the boundaries imposed by the constitutional subsidiarity of social benefit systems, which favoured an assessment limit. Within the boundaries between the minimum contribution and the assessment limit it was possible for the imposition of a greater burden on insured parties on a high income, in favour of those on a low income, to overstrain the system of social insurance. If at all, an additional family burden component should be considered in fiscal law.

3. The Association of Salaried Employees' Health Insurance Funds and the Association of Workers' Substitute Health Insurance Funds take the view that the contribution provisions of the Eleventh Book of the Code of Social Law do not violate the Basic Law. Already the approach that it was less probable for parents than for a childless couple to have to claim "public care" was said to give rise to reservations. For a variety of reasons, it was said to be by no means certain that parents finding themselves in need of long-term care in old age would be cared for by their children. Moreover, persons in need of long-term care who were cared for by their children also had a right to claim nursing care allowance. That the nursing care allowance was lower than the claim to benefits in kind was said to be factually reasoned in the "windfall effect" feared by the legislature. The contribution made by parents to funding long-term care insurance in the shape of the child maintenance undertaken was said to be sufficiently rewarded by contribution-free family insurance. That the long-term care risk was much lower for those with children did not undermine this consideration. In the case of need of long-term care, the burden on the parents was said to be much greater as a rule than with an illness. The contribution rate was said also not to have had to be degressive. It was said not to be recognisable that any excessive burden had been imposed on the complainant by virtue of the contributions levied in social long-term care insurance.

4. The German Women Lawyers Association considers the assessment of the contributions in social long-term care insurance to be unjust. Social insurance is said to derive its legitimacy from the social compensation which it seeks to achieve. Contributions may hence not be assessed in accordance with the individual risk, but – comparable to fiscal law – solely in accordance with the economic contributory capacity of the individual. In fiscal law, the burden in accordance with economic contributory capacity was said to lead to progressive taxation and to exemption of the minimum income from tax. Strict binding of long-term care insurance contributions to the contributory capacity principle would have to be designed as a levy expressed as a percentage of the individual's tax burden, similar to the solidarity levy. Only the burdening of income from gainful employment and assets implemented in fiscal law was said to accommodate the contributory capacity of the individual vertically in the context of the income distribution within the overall population, and horizontally in the context of the maintenance burden within the respective income grade. It was said to be necessary for the design of social insurance contributions to create if not a progressive, then at least a smooth – linear – contribution levy on higher and lower incomes; those on higher incomes would have to be subject in proportional terms to burdens at least as high as those on lower incomes.
The assessment limit in long-term care insurance was said, by contrast, to have the effect of an allowance for higher incomes; lower incomes were in principle fully assessed. Hence, it was said that the risk of need of long-term care was being differently managed than had been the case prior to the coming into force of the Eleventh Book of the Code of Social Law, no longer by fiscal means on the basis of a tax tariff which imposed a disproportionately high burden on higher incomes, but via contributions on the basis of a social insurance tariff favouring higher incomes. Similar problems were said to emerge with statutory health insurance. Moreover, with long-term care insurance, the lower incomes were not only subject to a disproportionately high burden, but over and above this enjoyed disproportionately low benefits, at least with regard to benefits in the in-patient area. Nothing was said to change as a result of long-term care insurance for the majority of persons in need of long-term care who were accommodated in homes. Because their pensions and assets were too low in comparison to the cost of in-patient care, they were said to continue to depend on drawing social assistance. Beneficiaries of the benefits from the long-term care insurance funds were said to be persons and their heirs who had built up high pension expectancies or other high levels of old-age security during their working lives. Their assets were said to be spared.
5. In their joint statement, the German Families Association, the Family Federation of German Catholics and the Association of Single Mothers and Fathers object to the nature of the funding of social long-term care insurance.

a) The legislature is said to have opted for a contributory solution. By these means, it was said that families were again subject to a two-fold burden in that they paid contributions and at the same time also ensured future long-term care by raising children. The childless were said not to make any contributions to the future long-term care generation, and were said even in future to be more dependent on more costly in-patient care. The concept of social long-term care insurance was said to be all the more dependent on families than was already the case in statutory pensions insurance. In both systems, families were said to raise the stock-ensuring future contributors; in the case of long-term care insurance, today's children furthermore were said to have to take over the function of carer. Since the funding procedure of social long-term care insurance did not recognise the activities of families for this social insurance system, this too was said to lead once more to a provision that was highly questionable in constitutional terms. At the same time, the insurance of carers in statutory pensions insurance was welcome in principle. However, the expectancies that could be achieved were said to be too low if one took as a basis the fact that carers were prevented by their care work from accruing their own old-age pensions. It was proposed in order to equalise the burden on families to introduce a tax allowance of DM 900 per child per month. The allowance was to be granted for each child insured in accordance with § 25 of the Eleventh Book of the Code of Social Law.

b) There were said also to be constitutional reservations insofar as, whilst a spouse who was not in gainful employment and who had no children was insured free of contributions, this was not the case for a divorced mother of several children who was not in gainful employment. The divorced mother was said to contribute to the preservation of the social insurance systems by raising children and to be able to expect to a disproportionately higher degree to be cared for by her children domestically on occurrence of a need of long-term care. If the single mother received maintenance from her divorced husband, the contribution for her was said in fact to have already been made. For maintenance was paid from the income of the party obliged to pay, which had been subject to contributions. With a single parent who was unable to engage in gainful employment because of child-raising, for a solution to be constitutional, his or her activities for the children would have to be valued as a contribution in their own right for as long as the obstacle to gainful employment typically lasted.

6. In its additional statement, the German Families Association submits further reasons in support of its view that long-term care insurance results in exploitation of families by virtue of the fact that benefits are transferred away from them.

a) Long-term care insurance was said to have been introduced with the declared goal of preventing a fall in social status in old age and of protecting the assets of this age group. The childless in particular were said to be able to garner assets, however, as a result of saved maintenance expenditure and a lack of child-related obstacles to earning an income. Poverty was said today to be a problem of families. Despite increases in direct state family benefits, the relationship between the net income of childless young married couples, on the one hand, and of young families, on the other, was said to have remained virtually unchanged in recent years to the disadvantage of families.

Insofar as the income and assets of the current pensioners' generation was protected by long-term care insurance, the whole working-age generation would have to provide the benefits for this pensioners' generation through their contributions. Also here, there was said to be a transfer because a not inconsiderable number of today's pensioners were childless (roughly 10 per cent) or had only brought up one child (20 per cent). This re-distribution from young to old was said to largely equate to a re-distribution from the bottom to the top. Today's pensioners' generation was said to be relatively prosperous on average.

b) The funding of social long-term care insurance via contributions was said to be inimical to families. Higher incomes above the assessment limit were said to be spared. In contrast to tax, with its allowances and progressive tariffs, no regard was given when assessing contributions to the size of a family and its ability to pay. With a single person earning a gross annual income of DM 60,000, the employee share imposed a burden on disposable income of 1.5 per cent. With a four-person family with the same annual income, however, there was said to be a burden of 7 per cent. The contribution system under social insurance law was said to come from a time in which both lifecycles and birth rates had been much more homogeneous than was the case today. The legislature was said to have missed the opportunity to effect an adjustment to the changed conditions.

c) In an overall view of all reservations existing against long-term care insurance, the conclusion was drawn that the contribution provisions contained in the Eleventh Book of the Code of Social Law were unconstitutional. They were already said to violate the mandate to improve the financial situation of families imposed on the legislature by the Federal Constitutional Court in its judgment of 7 July 1992 (BVerfGE 87, 1). Article 3.1 in conjunction with Article 6.1 of the Basic Law was said to be materially violated by the previously indicated "construction error" in long-term care insurance, namely the non-allowance of the financial burdens ensuing from child-raising activities. Contribution payment and child-raising were said to be equivalent. The Federal Constitutional Court had not adopted this point of view in its judgment of 7 July 1992. It had however allegedly failed to sufficiently take into account that the comparability of economic circumstances related to in both cases could only take place on the basis of economic criteria. Contribution payment was said to signify past-orientated forgoing of consumption in order to maintain one's own parent generation, whilst child-raising signified future-orientated forgoing of consumption in favour of the young generation. Also, the Federal Constitutional Court was said not to have sufficiently taken into account that, at macroeconomic level, funding could only be provided via a contribution. The proposal put forward by the German Women Lawyers Association to levy the contribution to social long-term care insurance as a levy on income tax according to the model of the "solidarity levy" was supported explicitly.

...

[B.]

§ 54.1 and 54.2, § 55.1 sentences 1 and 2, as well as § 57, of the Eleventh Book of the Code of Social Law are incompatible with Article 3.1 in conjunction with Article 6.1 of the Basic Law insofar as members of social long-term care insurance who care for and raise children, and who have an equally high contributable income, are burdened with an equally high long-term care insurance contribution as childless members. By contrast, an obligation on the part of the legislature to exempt members of social long-term care insurance who care for and raise children from the obligation to contribute cannot be derived from Article 6.1 of the Basic Law.

I.

As a freedom right, Article 6.1 of the Basic Law constitutes an obligation incumbent on the state to forgo incursions on the family. Over and above this, the provision contains a fundamental provision that determines values, which entails the duty incumbent on the state to protect and promote marriage and the family (see BVerfGE 87, 1 (35) with further references). Article 3.1 of the Basic Law demands that that which is equal is to be regulated on equally, and to regulate unequally on that which is unequal in accordance with its characteristics (see BVerfGE 71, 255 (271); established case-law). It is in principle a matter for the legislature to decide which characteristics it regards as material in comparing circumstances in order to treat them equally or differently in law (see BVerfGE 50, 57 (77); established case-law). Article 3.1 of the Basic Law however prohibits the legislature from improperly failing to consider the nature and scope of the actual differences. The principle of equality is violated if the legislature has omitted to consider inequalities in the circumstances to be ordered which are so significant that they should have been taken into account in accordance with a view that seeks to find a just solution (see BVerfGE 71, 255 (271)). Within these limits, the legislature has latitude in its decision-making (see BVerfGE 94, 241 (260)). Having said that, a further restriction may emerge from other constitutional provisions. In particular, when examining the constitutionality of contribution regulations which treat equally persons with and without children, the special protection which the state owes to the family is to be adhered to in accordance with Article 6.1 of the Basic Law (see BVerfGE 87, 1 (36)).

II.

Article 6.1 of the Basic Law is not violated by virtue of the fact that members of social long-term care insurance are subject to the contribution obligation even if they care for and raise children.

1. Families are as a rule more financially affected by financial burdens which the legislature imposes on citizens in general. This is the result of the special economic burden on families, which emerges from the responsibility of parents for the physical and emotional best interests of their children stipulated in Article 6.2 of the Basic Law and is lent concrete form by family law. For instance, parents must firstly provide maintenance for their children, and secondly they may incur loss of income or care expenditure. A spouse is frequently prevented by caring for and raising the children from taking up gainful employment or unrestrictedly continuing previous gainful employment during the first years after the birth of children. If both parents are in gainful employment, considerable costs are not infrequently incurred from child care provided by third parties. Financial burdens incurred by families by virtue of social insurance contributions hence restrict their [financial] scope more than does the obligation to contribute of married or unmarried individuals without children.

2. The special protection of the family, which Article 6.1 of the Basic Law obliges the state to provide, does not however constitutionally oblige the legislature to avoid every additional financial burden on the family. The latter is not placed at a disadvantage in an unconstitutional manner by virtue of the fact that contributions are also levied for social insurance from a parent who is in gainful employment which to a considerable degree covers the financial risk of need of long-term care for him or her, his or her children, as well as his or her spouse who is not in gainful employment, and which additionally to a large degree exempts them from contributions (see § 25 of the Eleventh Book of the Code of Social Law). The state is also not obliged to compensate for this contribution burden by virtue of the obligation to promote the family contained in Article 6.1 of the Basic Law (see BVerfGE 23, 258 (264); 82, 60 (81); 87, 1 (35); 97, 332 (349)). State family promotion through financial benefits is subject to what is possible and is to be regarded within the frame-

work of other promotion requirements. In the interest of general welfare, in addition to family promotion, the legislature must also account for other community interests in its budgeting, and in so doing must ensure above all the proper functioning and equilibrium of the system as a whole. Only by weighing all interests is it possible to ascertain whether family promotion by the state is manifestly unsuitable and no longer complies with the promotion principle of Article 6.1 of the Basic Law. Accordingly, it is possible to derive, from the value determination contained in Article 6.1 of the Basic Law, in conjunction with the principle of the social welfare state, the general duty of the state to provide equalisation of family burdens, but not the decision on the degree to or manner in which such social compensation is to be implemented. No concrete conclusions can be drawn from the constitutional mandate to bring about an effective equalisation of family burdens for the individual legal areas and sub-systems in which the equalisation of family burdens is to be carried out. In this respect, rather, the legislature in principle has latitude (see BVerfGE 87, 1 (35-36) with further references). It operates within this latitude if it also burdens families with contributions to social long-term care insurance.

III.

The impugned provisions do not violate Article 3.1 in conjunction with Article 6.1 of the Basic Law by not accommodating the special contribution which insured parties with children entitled to maintenance make to the system of social long-term care insurance in this insurance in such a way as to increase benefits.

1. Married parents who completely or largely forgo gainful employment because of caring for and raising their children suffer no disadvantages in claiming the benefits granted by social long-term care insurance, in contrast to the situation in statutory pensions insurance, which is characterised by wage and contribution linking (see on this BVerfGE 87, 1 (5, 37-38)), as against childless insured parties who are in gainful employment. The nature and scope of the benefits granted by the latter depend solely on the person in need of long-term care being insured or co-insured in long-term care insurance, and not upon the degree to which they have made contributions. Social long-term care insurance has benefits without contributions. In this way, for instance, a spouse who is insured free of contributions in accordance with § 25 of the Eleventh Book of the Code of Social Law receives in the context of family insurance in the same Category the same benefits as an insured party who has always paid maximum contributions.

2. Having said that, the monetary burden on the long-term care insurance system may be less with parents than with childless members because the former may receive long-term care from their children in place of long-term care by third parties.

a) Considerable differences in expenditure with in-patient care cannot be demonstrated when comparing parents with the childless. The expert Professor Dr. Schmähl stated that there were currently no representative empirical data as to whether in-patient care was claimed more frequently by the childless than by persons in need of long-term care who had children. There were said to be certain indications that older persons in need of long-term care without children were relatively more frequently in in-patient than in domestic care in comparison to persons in need of long-term care with children, but that the difference did not appear to be significant.

This picture is not likely to change much for the overall group of persons in need of in-patient long-term care, given that the share of residents of in-patient care facilities who are under 60 is in any case only 7 per cent … It can hence not be ascertained for these benefits of long-term care insurance that parents in need of long-term care pose a significantly lower financial burden on long-term care insurance than do childless persons in need of long-term care. What is more – as stated by the expert – having children of one's own is only one of several factors for opting for domestic or in-patient care, and this factor cannot be weighted at present.

b) By contrast, long-term care provided by children exerts an influence on the scope of benefits granted in the out-patient long-term care area. The expert stated convincingly in this respect that the fact of being a parent, although not the number of children, is a decisive element in choosing between the various types of benefit in out-patient long-term care. The evaluation of the data which he collected gives rise to the following picture: A significant difference can be observed in the group of over 60s – accounting for 80 per cent of persons in need of long-term care who are cared for as out-patients. 75.8 per cent of parents in need of long-term care draw nursing care allowance, and only 24.2 per cent draw other, more expensive types of benefit (benefits in kind, combination benefit, day patient benefit). For childless persons in need of long-term care, by contrast, there is a ratio of 66 per cent to 34 per cent. If children – these being overwhelmingly daughters and daughters-in-law – who account for roughly 38 per cent of carers (see Schneekloth/Müller, pp. 52 et seq.), did not care for their parents and parents-in-law, long-term care insurance would have incurred additional costs amounting to DM 3.53 billion in 2000. Even if one were to account for the expense of the pensions insurance contributions payable benefiting carers, the additional costs would still have been DM 2.695 billion. This corresponds to roughly 8 per cent of the current benefit volume of social long-term care insurance.

This is not opposed by the fact that – in relation to all age groups – benefit expenditure in the out-patient area, in particular in Category II, where the data material is most authoritative, is somewhat higher for persons in need of long-term care with children than that for persons in need of long-term care without children. It is decisive that the total benefit expenditure on persons over 60 in need of long-term care without children is 10 per cent higher than for persons of the same age in need of long-term care but with children. The age group of persons in need of long-term care under 60 displays different characteristics, in that it can be presumed that children are less relevant for their long-term care. They are frequently still cared for by their parents. Nursing care allowance is selected for such childcare to a much greater extent than in the case of long-term care of parents. In the view of the expert, this also explains why, in relation to all age groups, childless persons in need of long-term care on average cause slightly lower long-term care expenditure than persons in need of long-term care with children.

3. It is compatible with the principle of equality in Article 3.1 of the Basic Law, also in conjunction with Article 6.1 of the Basic Law, if the legislature, which has major latitude in designing social security systems, does not accommodate the child-raising activities of parents on the benefit side although the latter have a long-term influence on the amount of expenditure on social long-term care insurance. The additional expenditure of social long-term care insurance occurring with childless persons in need of long-term care is not only moderate in degree. It is also justified as a consequence of the legislative goal pursued by virtue of long-term care insurance in solidarity-based compensation also to see to it that those who otherwise have no one to take care of them can nonetheless receive care. Furthermore, it cannot be concluded in generalisation from the circumstance that parents carry out child-raising activities that they are later cared for by their children as persons in need of long-term care, thus claiming the less costly nursing care allowance. This is all the more so since the long-term care potential of daughters and daughters-in-law is less counted upon (see Rückert, *Die demographische Entwicklung und deren Auswirkungen auf Pflege-, Hilfs- und Versorgungsbedürftigkeit*, in: v. Ferber et al. (eds.), *Die demographische Herausforderung*, 1989, pp. 121-122). Already today, the lack of family members is only one reason among several to opt for benefits in kind. Almost 90 per cent of private households in which persons in need of long-term care are cared for give as reasons for opting for long-term care benefits in kind the state of health of the person in need of long-term care or corresponding recommendations of the Medical Advisory Service of Social Health Insurance (*Medizinischer Dienst der Krankenversicherung*). 73 per cent opt for long-term care benefits in kind seeking to avoid imposing excessive burdens on family members …

IV.

Article 3.1 in conjunction with Article 6.1 of the Basic Law is however violated by virtue of the fact that care for and raising of children is not accommodated in the assessment of contributions by insured parties who must pay contributions. This unconstitutionally places at a disadvantage the group of insured parties with children in comparison with childless members of social long-term care insurance who benefit from their care and child-raising activity in the case of their need of long-term care.

1. The child-raising activity of insured parents within a contributory social insurance system, which serves to cover one of the risks which is materially determined by the ageing of the insured parties, specifically favours insured parties without children. It is decisive here that the financial need caused by the occurrence of the insured event occurs disproportionately frequently in the grandparents' generation (60 and older). The probability of needing long-term care increases considerably with age. It initially increases slightly beyond the age of 60, and then beyond 80 becomes a risk which constitutes a material characteristic of the circumstances of the individual (see *Bundestag* printed paper 12/5262, p. 62). If such a general life risk, which as a rule does not occur until old age, is funded by a contribution procedure, the child-raising activity has a constitutive significance for the functioning of this system. On occurrence of the vast majority of insured events, the contribution procedure relies on the contributions of the coming generation.

a) The favourable treatment of the childless becomes manifest if one compares the group of those in need of maintenance who have children with the group of working-age insured parties who have no children. Given that social insurance is funded by a contribution procedure, both rely on sufficient numbers of children growing up. In the contribution procedure, today's contributors of the working-age generation trust that sufficient young persons will be available in future to pay contributions. This can only be today's children, on whom a collective obligation to fund is imposed in future, in favour of those who will then be old and in need of long-term care, by means of obligatory membership entailing contribution burdens which is equivalent to a maintenance obligation related to the special needs of long-term care. This obligation however applies, regardless of the existence of family maintenance obligations, towards all old people who are in need of long-term care. For instance, all persons who will be in need of long-term care in 20 or 30 years' time enjoy the same advantage as a result of the current child-raising activity of parents, namely of being insured and receiving long-term care benefits for their own insured event by means of an obligatory insurance system under public law "of parties ow-

ing maintenance who are jointly linked", regardless of whether or not they themselves have contributed to conserving the stock of contributors by child-raising.
b) Hence, an advantage accrues in the case of an insured event to insured parties without children by virtue of the child-raising activity of other contributors who because of child-raising forgo consumption and asset-formation to their disadvantage. The childless are also called on with their contributions to fund the long-term care risk of spouses and children who are co-insured free of contributions. This however does not outweigh the advantage of childless insured parties against those who take care of the future contributors in order to cover the long-term care risk of all in old age.
This advantage accruing to childless persons subject to obligatory contributions is not called into question by the fact that some of today's children whose parents are currently insured in social long-term care insurance may in future not be contributors subject to obligatory contributions at all, or only temporarily. This is allowed for by the statutory allocation of those subject to obligatory insurance either to social or to private long-term care insurance in accordance with the amount of income or the nature of the gainful employment and the fluctuation existing in this respect between the two insurance sectors. Taking account of the circumstance that, currently, roughly 87 per cent of the population are insured in social long-term care insurance (see for more details … (BVerfGE 103, 197 (198 et seq.)) and that children, as contributors, will not only leave the system of social long-term care insurance, but will also change to it from their parents' private obligatory long-term care insurance, one may certainly presume that child-raising activity in social long-term care insurance will continue to provide sustainable assistance and will benefit childless members of social long-term care insurance.
2. The "system-specific" advantage evident from the conception of social long-term care insurance of childless insured parties differs from the benefit which a society receives by virtue of children and their care and child-raising in general.
Each state community depends on the value added of young generations. There is a general interest in the care and child-raising activity of families (see BVerfGE 88, 203 (258-259)). This alone does not necessitate accommodating this child-raising activity in favour of families in a certain social benefit system (see BVerfGE 87, 1 (35-36)). If however a social benefit system is to cover a risk which above all affects the old generation, and its funding is designed such that essentially it only works via the existence of younger generations who in turn come of working age as contributors and help to pay the costs associated with the previous generations' insured events, not only the insurance contribution, but also child-raising activity is constitutive for such a system. If this generative contribution is no longer provided as a rule by all insured parties, this leads to a specific burden on child-raising in-

sured parties in the long-term care insurance system, the disadvantageous impact of which is also to be compensated for within this system. Child-raising insured parties ensure the functioning of long-term care insurance, therefore, not only by paying contributions, but also through caring for and raising children.

3. The legislature can disregard the disadvantage incurred by insured parties subject to obligatory contributions who have children as against childless members of social long-term care insurance, who respectively belong to the generation of contributors, as long as a clear majority of insured parties has carried out child-raising activities. Under such circumstances, the legislature can avail itself of its right of generalisation and refrain from making a differentiation in contributions that takes account of the child-raising activity. If the overwhelming majority of insured parties subject to obligatory contributions raises children, a social insurance system built on the contributions system, and social long-term care insurance in particular, is in a generative equilibrium. The insured parties subject to obligatory contribution support persons in need of long-term care through their contributions. At the same time, they have taken care of their children. In return, they may trust that, as insured employees, their children will cover their long-term care risk in old age by making contributions, and in turn with child-raising activities create the foundation for their own risk coverage. If in this "three-generational contract" the share of childless persons among the number of members of social long-term care insurance remains in a clear minority, in the context of the latitude open to it the legislature can treat them in relation to contributions as if they were child-raising insured parties. The legislature has however overstepped the boundaries of this latitude in that in 1994 it let the Eleventh Book of the Code of Social Law – apart from the provisions of its §§ 25 and 56 – enter into force without a child-related component to accommodate the contribution burden of parents.

a) If it is regulating complex circumstances, the legislature may take a reasonable period to collect information and gather experience. During this period, it may limit itself to making less precise generalisations. Resulting unfairness only gives rise to a complaint in constitutional terms if the legislature has not reviewed its provisions in the light of newly available information and experience and has failed to attempt to reach a proper solution (see BVerfGE 100, 59 (101) with further references; established case-law).

b) It was however recognisable as long ago as 1994 that the number of persons raising children had fallen dramatically in recent decades. The legislature could no longer presume at that time that an overwhelming majority of insured parties subject to obligatory contributions, in addition to making contributions, would also contribute to the sustainable stabilisation and financing of social long-term care insurance benefits by raising children.

aa) In accordance with the assessment made by the expert Professor Dr. Birg, the population of Germany will age unavoidably and very considerably in the next 50 years. This concurs with other demographic studies, and can be predicted with a high degree of reliability (see [for instance] … *Bundestag* printed paper 13/11460, pp. 69-70). The number of live births per woman has fallen rapidly in Germany since the mid-sixties, from 2.49 to its present level of 1.3. The effect has been observed in most economically developed countries that, as standards of living and per capita income increase, the birth rate in some cases falls far below 2.0. As also stated by the expert, there is no indication that the circumstances which are responsible for this development will change fundamentally in the near future. A rapid increase in the birth rate cannot be expected, especially since the fact of it falling far below the replacement level has already set in motion an unstoppable downward spiral. The population is not shrinking solely by virtue of the fact that fewer children are born than are necessary to maintain the numbers. This development is quite significantly amplified by the fact that, as a result of this development, there are fewer and fewer people who can father, or give birth to, children. Furthermore, more and more women are remaining childless. In accordance with the information provided by the expert, if one intended to stabilise today's age structure purely by increasing the birth rate or immigration, in purely mathematical terms either the birth rate per woman of child-bearing age would have to increase immediately from 1.3 to 3.8, or 188 million younger people would have to immigrate by 2050.
bb) The described development was already recognisable in 1994, and was to be accommodated by the legislature on enacting the Eleventh Book of the Code of Social Law. On the basis of the data already available at this time, it was unable to presume that the ageing of society could be sustainably alleviated by an increase in the birth rate. It had been aware for a long time of the rapid fall in and the consolidation of the birth rate at the present level below 1.5 starting in the mid-seventies (see *Bundestag* printed paper 12/5262, picture 1.1). Regardless of the different presumptions and of the different values to be derived from this, the tendency in demographic developments until the mid-21st century was already clearly recognisable at the start of the nineties. On a database dated 31 December 1989, the Federal Statistical Office forecast in its "seventh co-ordinated population projection" (see the summary of results in Sommer, *Entwicklung der Bevölkerung bis 2030*, WiSta (*Wirtschaft und Statistik*) 1992, pp. 217 et seq.), that the population in Germany would fall by more than 10 per cent by 2030, and that more than one-third of the population would be 60 or over. In the "eighth co-ordinated population projection" of the Federal Statistical Office (see in this instance Sommer, *Entwicklung der Bevölkerung bis 2040*, WiSta 1994, p. 497), which is based on data from 31 December 1992, it was presumed that the birth rate would remain essentially un-

changed, whilst the migration conduct of foreigners could not be assessed with certainty.
Even if the probability of occurrence of the risk of long-term care remains unchanged, the considerable fall in child-raising activity means not only that the ratio between (younger) contributors and (older) persons in need of long-term care becomes worse and worse. There are also no reliable indications that older people will be subject in future to a much lower risk of needing long-term care than is the case today. Equally high, if not indeed increasing, benefit expenditure will have to be funded by fewer and fewer people. This also leads to a situation in which a shrinking number of younger insured persons, in addition to their contribution burdens, will contribute to ensuring the functionality of social long-term care insurance, and bear the cost burden of child-raising. The same burden of insurance contributions leads to a recognisable imbalance between the total contribution which those raising children make to insurance, and the monetary contribution of the childless. Herein lies a disadvantage of child-raising insured parties which is to be compensated for in the law on contributions. A certain degree of compensation is provided by the fact that insured parties who are engaged in caring for and raising children, while making the same contributions as the childless, also receive benefits for the other family members. This favourable situation however does not compensate completely for the generative contribution additionally made through child-raising activity and the concomitant disadvantage of those raising children in terms of the advantage accruing to the childless. Accordingly, the compensation for the disadvantage requires more than the contribution-free acquisition of the right to claim long-term care services by family members.

[C.] – I.

1. The legislature has several possibilities at its disposal to eliminate the unconstitutionality of § 54.1 and 54.2, § 55.1 sentences 1 and 2, as well as § 57, of the Eleventh Book of the Code of Social Law. For this reason, to the degree manifest from the ruling, these provisions are to be only declared incompatible with Article 3.1 in conjunction with Article 6.1 of the Basic Law.
2. A declaration of incompatibility in principle has the consequence that the unconstitutional provisions may no longer be applied. They may continue to be applicable by way of exception. In the interest of legal certainty, and with regard to the fact that the legislature must review which paths are viable and fundable to bring about a constitutional legal situation, it is necessary in the present case to permit the further application of § 54.1 and 54.2, § 55.1 sentences 1 and 2, as well as § 57, of the Eleventh Book of the Code of Social Law until 31 December 2004 (see

BVerfGE 92, 53 (73) with further references; established case-law). The legislature must enact a new constitutional regulation at the latest by this time. In the assessment of the period, the Senate has taken account of the fact that the significance of the instant ruling will also have to be examined for other branches of social insurance.

II.

The legislature has broad latitude in drafting the law on contributions in accordance with Article 3.1 in conjunction with Article 6.1 of the Basic Law in social long-term care insurance. The Basic Law only obliges it to relatively decrease the burden on insured parties subject to obligatory contributions with one or several children in the assessment of contributions in comparison with childless members of social long-term care insurance.
The equalisation accordingly to be carried out between parents and childless persons must however take place by means of provisions which reduce the burden on the parents' generation during the time of care and child-raising, since the contributions made by today's generation of children later as adults also benefit childless insured parties who at that time belong to the years which are vulnerable to needing long-term care, or who are in need of long-term care, and are materially based on the child-raising activities of their parents who are today subject to obligatory insurance. The concomitant burden on parents occurs in their gainful employment phase; it is hence also to be compensated for in this period. The constitutionally necessary compensation between members of social long-term care insurance raising and not raising children can therefore not take place via different benefits in the event of the occurrence of need of long-term care.
It is left to the legislature to decide how to accommodate care and child-raising activity in assessing the contributions of insured parties subject to obligatory contributions with children.
Having said that, it is constitutionally obliged to select a solution which decreases in relative terms the burden on those subject to a maintenance obligation from the first child onwards. The fact of caring for and raising of the first child already leads to a situation in which that which is unequal is treated equally in an unconstitutional manner in the law regulating contributions to social long-term care insurance.
...

Justices: Papier, Jaeger, Haas, Hömig, Steiner, Hohmann-Dennhardt, Hoffmann-Riem; Justice Kühling has retired from office and is hence unable to sign.

As a result of the Federal Constitutional Court's decision, the legislature, with Article 1 no. 1 of the Act for the Consideration of Child-Raising in the Law on Contributions in the Social Long-Term Care Insurance (Gesetz zur Berücksichtigung von Kindererziehung im Beitragsrecht der sozialen Pflegeversicherung) *of 15 December 2004 (Federal Law Gazette I 2004 p. 3448) added, with effect from 1 January 2005, the following subsection 3 to § 55 of the Eleventh Book of the Code of Social Law:*

> *"(3) The contribution rate according to subsection 1 sentences 1 and 2 shall be increased for members after the end of the month in which they reach the age of 23 by an additional contribution to the amount of 0.25 contribution rate points (additional contribution for childless persons). Sentence 1 shall not apply to parents within the meaning of § 56.1 sentence 1 no. 3 and 56.3 nos. 2 and 3 of the First Book. Evidence of the parent status shall be furnished in a suitable manner to the agency remitting the contribution (insured who pay their contribution themselves shall furnish evidence of their parent status to the long-term care insurance fund) if the competent agency did not have knowledge of the parent status for other reasons before. The central associations of the long-term care insurance funds shall jointly adopt recommendations on which supporting documents are suitable as evidence. If the supporting documents are submitted within three months after the birth of the child, the evidence shall be deemed to have been furnished with the beginning of the month of the birth; otherwise, the evidence shall be effective from the beginning of month following the month in which the supporting document has been submitted. Supporting documents for children born before 1 January 2005 which are submitted until 30 June 2005 shall be effective from 1 January 2005. Sentence 1 shall not apply to members born before 1 January 1940, military service draftees, civilian service draftees and recipients of unemployment benefit II."*

Apart from this, the Act of 15 December 2004 contains in its Article 1 further provisions amending the Eleventh Book of the Code of Social Law which implement the Federal Constitutional Court's decision.

No. 33

BVerfGE 104, 373
of 30 January 2002 – 1 BvL 23/96 –
"Double family names case"

HEADNOTE:

Decision regarding the constitutionality of the exclusion of double family names.

Judgment of the First Senate of 30 January 2002
on the basis of the oral hearing of 6 November 2001
– 1 BvL 23/96 –

in the proceedings for a constitutional review of § 1616 subsection 2 sentence 1 and subsection 3 of the Civil Code (*Bürgerliches Gesetzbuch* – BGB) in the version of the Act Reforming the Law on Family Names – Law on Family Names Act (*Familiennamensrechtsgesetz* – FamNamRG) of 16 December 1993 (Federal Law Gazette (*Bundesgesetzblatt* – BGBl) I p. 2054) – suspension of proceedings and submission order of the Hamburg Local Court (*Amtsgericht*) of 6 September 1996 (107 X B 13/95).

RULING:

§ 1616.2 sentence 1 of the Civil Code in the version of the Act Reforming the Law on Family Names (Law on Family Names Act) of 16 December 1993 (Federal Law Gazette I page 2054) and § 1617.1 sentence 1 of the Civil Code in the version of the Act Reforming the Law of Parent and Child – Law of Parent and Child Reform Act (*Kindschaftsrechtsreformgesetz* – KindRG) of 16 December 1997 (Federal Law Gazette I page 2942) are compatible with the Basic Law (*Grundgesetz* – GG).

EXTRACT FROM GROUNDS:

A.

The submission relates to the question of whether it is compatible with the Basic Law that parents with joint custody who do not use a married name may designate as the birth name of their child only either the name of the father or that of the mother, but not a double name consisting of both of their names together. Over and above this, the submission raises the question as to whether the statutory empowerment of the competent court to assign to one parent the right to designate should the parents fail to designate a birth name, with the consequence that the child receives the name of this parent if they persist in not designating a name, is constitutional.

I.

1. According to § 1616 of the Civil Code in the original version of 18 August 1896 (Reich Law Gazette (*Reichsgesetzblatt* – RGBl) p. 195), the birth name of the child born in wedlock followed the name of the father, which on the basis of the conclusion of marriage was at the same time also the name of the mother as joint family name (married name). With the First Act Reforming the Law on Marriage and Family (*Erstes Gesetz zur Reform des Ehe- und Familienrechts* – 1. EheRG) of 14 June 1976 (Federal Law Gazette I p. 1421), spouses were given the right to select either the birth name of the husband or of the wife as the married name. Were the spouses to fail to designate a name, the name of the husband became the married name (§ 1355.2 sentence 2 of the Civil Code in the version of the First Act Reforming the Law on Marriage and Family). A child born in wedlock received the joint family name, in other words the married name of the parents, as birth name according to § 1616 of the Civil Code.
2. By order of 5 March 1991 (Decisions of the Federal Constitutional Court (*Entscheidungen des Bundesverfassungsgerichts* – BVerfGE) 84, 9), the Federal Constitutional Court (*Bundesverfassungsgericht* – BVerfG) ruled that § 1355.2 sentence 2 of the Civil Code was incompatible with Article 3.2 of the Basic Law, and adopted a transitional provision until the entry into force of a new statutory provision for cases in which the spouses did not designate a name according to § 1355.2 sentence 1 of the Civil Code. Accordingly, the spouses were initially to retain the name which they had had prior to the conclusion of marriage. This made it necessary in this respect to also make a temporary provision for the child's name. On the basis of the principle of the possibility of a choice between the father's name and the mother's name, as well as the requirement of selecting a solution – taking

account of the latitude available to the legislature – which encroached as little as possible on the rights of those concerned and which did not make the legal reform difficult, the Federal Constitutional Court expanded the option open to the parents such that they could also choose for the child as birth name a double name combined from the name of his or her parents (BVerfG, loc. cit., p. 24). Here, in the case of a conflict the registrar was to determine the sequence of the names by drawing lots. The broad latitude for the legislature in reforming the law on names was to comprise the option that it could opt on the one hand to retain the uniform family name with a gender-neutral default regulation, whilst on the other hand also permitting exceptions from the principle of uniform names, or could provide for a completely new law on married names (BVerfG, loc. cit., p. 21).

3. With the Act Reforming the Law on Family Names – Law on Family Names Act of 16 December 1993 (Federal Law Gazette I p. 2054), which entered into force on 1 April 1994, both the law on married names and that on birth names was thereupon reformed. Whilst however the draft Bill of the Federal Government (*Bundestag* printed paper (*Bundestagsdrucksache* – BTDrucks) 12/3163) had still provided for the selection of a double married name or that of a double name as the child's birth name, this met with reservations in the *Bundestag*. The CDU/CSU and FDP parliamentary groups supporting the government agreed on the exclusion of double names and on a regulation in the event of the parents not agreeing on the child's name, on the basis of which the Committee on Legal Affairs of the *Bundestag* proposed an amendment of the draft Bill which was adopted in this form by the *Bundestag* and which found the consent of the *Bundesrat*.

In its recommendation for a resolution, the Committee on Legal Affairs provided reasoning for the exclusion of double names by stating that it was necessary to prevent the name structure in Germany undergoing a fundamental change after only several generations had passed because double married names were assigned to children born in wedlock as birth names (see *Bundestag* printed paper 12/5982, p. 18). A solution entailing double and multiple names was said to be absolutely contingent on limiting the number of names, and hence as a consequence two spouses could no longer bring their double name into the next generation, but only a part of it, and hence not really their own names (see *Bundestag* printed paper 12/5982, p. 17).

The spouses were however granted the possibility for the first time not to designate a married name according to § 1355.1 of the Civil Code, in addition to the selection of the name of the husband or of the wife as married name. Where parents had a married name, according to § 1616.1 of the Civil Code the child continued to receive the married name of his or her parents as birth name. For parents without a married name, the selection of the birth name for their child was restricted to the

name of the father or to the name of the mother. If the parents did not designate a name, the guardianship court was charged with assigning the right of designation to one parent.
§ 1616 of the Civil Code was worded as follows:

> (1) A child born in wedlock shall receive the married name of its parents as a birth name.
> (2) If the parents do hot have a family name, they shall designate by declaration to the registrar the name that the father or the mother has at the time of the declaration as the birth name of the child. The declaration must be notarially certified. The designation made by the parents shall also apply to their further children.
> (3) If the parents do not make a designation within one month after the birth of the child, the guardianship court shall assign the right of designation to one parent. Subsection 2 shall apply *mutatis mutandis*. The guardianship court may impose a period of time on the parent for the exercise of the right of designation. If the right of designation has not been exercised after the period has ended, the child shall receive the name of the parent to whom the right of designation was assigned.
> (4) ...

Additionally, the guardianship court was obliged in § 46a of the Act on Matters of Non-Contentious Jurisdiction (*Gesetz über die Angelegenheiten der freiwilligen Gerichtsbarkeit* – FGG) to hear both parents prior to taking a decision according to § 1616.3 of the Civil Code and to strive to bring about an agreement as to the child's name. It was further provided that the ruling of the guardianship court does not require reasoning and is unappealable.
4. The distinction between children born in and out of wedlock under the law on names was also abolished for reasons of equal treatment by the Act Reforming the Law of Parent and Child (Law of Parent and Child Reform Act) of 16 December 1997 (Federal Law Gazette I p. 2942), which entered into force on 1 July 1998. Independently of whether the child was born in or out of wedlock, the right to designate the birth name of a child is now linked to the joint right of custody of the parents or to the sole custody of one parent. The new arrangement has changed the order of the sections and has given to the family court, instead of to the guardianship court, jurisdiction for the assignment of the right to designate the birth name of the child. § 1616 of the Civil Code contains in this respect solely the principle that the child receives the married name of its parents as its birth name.

Subsections 1 and 2 of § 1617 of the Civil Code, which are now material to the selection of the birth name for a child of parents who do not have a married name, read as follows:

> (1) If the parents do not have a family name, and if they have joint parental custody, they shall designate by declaration to the registrar the name that the father or the mother has at the time of the declaration as the birth name of the child. A declaration made after the recording of the birth must be notarially certified. The designation made by the parents shall also apply to their further children.
> (2) If the parents do not make a designation within one month after the birth of the child, the family court shall assign the right of designation to one parent. Subsection 1 shall apply *mutatis mutandis*. The guardianship court may impose a period of time on the parent for the exercise of the right of designation. If the right of designation has not been exercised after the period has ended, the child shall receive the name of the parent to whom the right of designation was assigned.

5. The birth name of the child was also determined according to the married name of the parents according to the Family Code (*Familiengesetzbuch*) of the German Democratic Republic of 20 December 1965 (Law Gazette (*Gesetzblatt* – GBl) 1966 I p. 1). If they were not married, the child received the name of his or her mother (§ 64.1 and 2 of the Family Code). The spouses were able to select as their joint married name the name of the husband or of the wife (§ 7.1 of the Family Code); they had to submit a declaration to this effect prior to conclusion of marriage. This was an absolute precondition for the conclusion of marriage.

II.

1. The parents involved in the original proceedings do not have a married name, and did not designate a birth name according to § 1616.2 of the Civil Code in the version of the Law on Family Names Act (hereinafter: § 1616.2 of the Civil Code old) for their child, who was born in 1995. They agree in wishing their child to receive a double name as a birth name consisting of the name of the father and of the mother. The registry office informed the guardianship court of this, which had jurisdiction for this according to the law applicable at the time, which was now obliged according to § 1616.3 of the Civil Code old to assign the right of name designation to one parent.
2. The guardianship court suspended the proceedings according to Article 100.1 of the Basic Law and submitted the question to the Federal Constitutional Court as to

whether § 1616 subsections 2 and 3 of the Civil Code old is constitutional. The right provided for in § 1616.3 of the Civil Code old for the guardianship court to determine the name is said to conflict with the parents' right as protected by fundamental rights under Article 6.1 and 6.2 of the Basic Law. Over and above this, the prohibition to give a double name regulated in § 1616.2 of the Civil Code old for a child whose parents did not have a married name is alleged to be incompatible with the constitutional guarantees from Article 2.1 in conjunction with Article 1.1 of the Basic Law and from Article 6.1 and 6.2 of the Basic Law.

...

B. – I.

The submission is admissible insofar as it submits the question of the constitutionality of § 1616.2 sentence 1 of the Civil Code old. ...

II.

The review of the submitted question about the constitutionality of § 1616.2 sentence 1 of the Civil Code old is to cover § 1617.1 sentence 1 of the Civil Code in the version of the Law of Parent and Child Reform Act (hereinafter: § 1617.1 sentence 1 of the Civil Code). This provision has replaced § 1616.2 sentence 1 of the Civil Code old since 1 July 1998. Since it too restricts the right of parents who have joint custody but no married name to designate the child's birth name to the name of the father or of the mother, and in this respect rules out the child having a double name, it is necessary to include this new provision in the constitutional review (see BVerfGE 28, 324 (363); 61, 291 (306); 65, 237 (243-244)).

C.

§ 1616.2 sentence 1 of the Civil Code old and § 1617.1 sentence 1 of the Civil Code are compatible with the Basic Law.

I.

The exclusion of a double name for the child does not violate the parental right protected by Article 6.2 of the Basic Law.

1. As a more specific provision in comparison with Article 6.1 of the Basic Law, which obliges the state to respect and promote the unity and self-responsibility of marriage and the family (see BVerfGE 53, 257 (296)), and in doing so to forgo en-

croachments on the free arrangement of family co-habitation, Article 6.2 of the Basic Law protects the parent-child relationship and ensures that parents have the right to care for and bring up their children (see BVerfGE 31, 194 (204)). This freedom right guaranteed to parents by the constitution as against the state primarily serves the child's best interests, which at the same time is the highest guiding principle for the exercise of parents' responsibility (see BVerfGE 61, 358 (371-372); 75, 201 (218)). The right of the parents to care for their child also includes the right to give their child a name.

2. The name of a person is an expression of his or her identity and individuality and accompanies the life story of its bearer, which becomes recognisable under this name as a continuing one (see BVerfGE 78, 38 (49); 84, 9 (22); 97, 391 (399)). It helps the growing up child to find his or her identity and express it towards others. Naming is to open for the child the opportunity for the development of his or her personality and to serve his or her best interests, the maintenance of which is entrusted to the parents as both a right and a duty in equal measure. Naming includes the selection of the name. The decision as to which name the child is to bear is also significant for the child, given that he or she lives from now on with the name designated for him or her and is identified with it. Determining it in exercising the responsibility for the child is a part of the parental right emanating from Article 6.2 of the Basic Law.

a) This applies first and foremost to the selection of a forename for the child, which exclusively lends expression to the individuality of a person, designates the individual and distinguishes him or her from others. It is the primary task of the parents to determine for their child in a free, joint choice a name which he or she cannot yet give himself or herself. A limit may be set on this right of the parents to select a forename for their child solely where its exercise risks impairing the child's best interests (see BVerfGE 24, 119 (143)). In exercising its watchdog function according to Article 6.2 sentence 2 of the Basic Law, the state is not only entitled but is indeed obliged to protect the child as a holder of fundamental rights against irresponsible selection of names on the part of the parents. Article 6.2 of the Basic Law does not offer a basis for an encroachment on the parental right to designate the forename for their child over and above this.

b) Added to this is the selection of the birth name as the family name of the child insofar as the legal order provides for the bearing of a family name and provides an option therefor.

Constituting and giving concrete form to the law on family names is a matter for the legislature (see BVerfGE 78, 38 (49)). The function of the family name need not be restricted solely to providing the individual with an expression of his or her individuality. Rather, the family name can also be used to trace lines of descent, to

portray family ties or to clarify the family status of an individual. The function of the family name is expressed for instance in its designation as a birth name or married name.
If the family name is to carry out functions of allocating its name-bearer within a community, its selection may not remain a matter solely for the free decision of the individual, but there is a need for rules according to which it can be allocated or selected, also taking account of the interests of the public. The goals pursued by the legislature in shaping the law on family names must conform to the value principles of the constitution and to the fundamental rights of those affected by it, and must promote the function of the family name.
3. By virtue of § 1616.2 sentence 1 of the Civil Code old and § 1617.1 sentence 1 of the Civil Code, the legislature has excluded the selection of a double name formed from the name of the parents as a birth name for the child in a constitutionally unobjectionable manner in the context of drafting the law on family names.
a) The family attribution to his or her parents via the birth name of the child is orientated in a permissible manner in line with the valuation of Article 6.1 of the Basic Law to protect marriage and the family in their unity as a community.
In order to be able to express in the name the fact of the child belonging with his or her parents, the legislature may provide for the child's name to be derived from the parental name. The structure of the law on birth names is hence predetermined by the design of the law on names of the parents. Their possibility of using and choosing a name sets the framework within which the birth name of the child can be designated. The right of the parents to designate the birth name of their child under Article 6.2 of the Basic Law is hence to be considered in the light of the entire structure of the law on names and the fundamental rights to be protected in its design.
b) The right of the parents as to their own naming is vital first of all here.
aa) In shaping the law on spouses' names, the legislature must respect the protection of the name that is used, which is covered by the name-bearer`s right of personality under Article 2.1 in conjunction with Article 1.1 of the Basic Law (see BVerfGE 78, 38 (49)). A name change may hence only be required by the legislature for an important reason. It is therefore not constitutionally objectionable that the legislature continues to provide in § 1355.1 of the Civil Code for spouses to use a married name as a standard in order to lend expression to the unity of the family in the joint name. This requires one of the spouses to change their name on conclusion of marriage. However, holding a uniform family name in marriage is not constitutionally required since the family unity protected by Article 6.1 of the Basic Law is borne and lived by its individual members, who in turn receive from Article 6.1 of the Basic Law protection and space for freedom.

In addition to the protection of the name as used, the legislature must also respect the principle of equal treatment under Article 3.2 sentence 1 of the Basic Law, which prohibits for the law on names to grant priority to the husband's name on forming a joint family name or passing on a name to a child (see BVerfGE 48, 327 (337-338); 84, 9 (17-18)). Finally, the legislature must at the same time ensure that the law on names does not disproportionately restrict the freedom available for selecting the name granted by Article 2.1 of the Basic Law, as well as by Article 6.1 of the Basic Law.

bb) These constitutional preconditions for the law on names are met by the law on married names now applicable forming the connection for the law on the birth name of the child.

(1) § 1355.1 of the Civil Code opens to spouses the possibility to have a married name. Neither of the names previously used by the spouses is granted priority in the selection of the joint name. If the spouses do not agree on a married name, or if they do not wish to use one, they continue to use their previous names. Hence, the legislature has lent particular expression to the protection of the name used from Article 2.1 of the Basic Law as an expression of the personality of each individual spouse.

(2) The fact that the legislature has ruled out according to § 1355.2 of the Civil Code the selection of a double name as a married name does not violate the spouses' fundamental rights. The need of spouses to be able to express the mutual bond and identity in the new commonality in the name is adequately taken account of by the possibility to select one of their birth names as a married name. The legislature complied with the desire to be able to also express, in addition to the new joint identity, the identity communicated via the previously held name in the joint name by virtue of the fact that it granted to the spouse whose name is not selected as the married name the right to add their previously used name to the married name. For the spouse whose name is designated as the married name, by contrast, this name expresses both his or her previous individual identity and his or her new identity in the commonality, given that it is his or her own name and at the same time the one which his or her spouse now also uses as a name. The right of personality of the spouses is hence accommodated.

cc) The fact of the family name in principle containing one single element, as prescribed by the legislature, which does not permit spouses to have a married name made up of both of their names, is based on considerations which are constitutionally unobjectionable. The legislature has given consideration here to the consequences which may emerge from the formation of double names as the generations pass. If spouses are granted in general terms the right to combine their two previous names to form the married name, and if furthermore the married name is in principle to become the birth name of the child born in wedlock in order to express his or her belonging to the family, four-fold name chains may already be formed in the next generation as married names which would further potentiate on conclusion of marriage, transferred to the children in each case from one generation to the next. The fact that the legislature intends to avoid such multi-element name chains (see *Bundestag* printed paper 12/5982, p. 17) can be reasoned not only with considerations of practicability, but also serves to protect future name-bearers. Hence, with the increase in the number of names, the function of the name to create an identity in being the point of reference for the bearer of the name is at risk of being lost. Particularly because of this function, however, the name receives constitutional protection. If the legislature attempts to prevent such a development for the name structure by virtue of not limiting the combination of names only for following generations, but from the outset opens to spouses the sole possibility in principle to only designate one of their names as a married name, this is the result of a consideration which complies with the constitution. Authorisation of a double married name would be equally constitutional, but it is not required.

c) The possibility for the spouses to opt between retention of their names and holding a joint name creates different preconditions in each case for a link between the child's birth name and the parental name to identify family affiliation: If the parents have a joint name, or if only one parent has custody for a child, only one name is available for the birth name of the child. By contrast, if married or unmarried parents who have custody use different names for the designation of the child's name, this leads to selection between the respective names of the parents and a combination of both parents' names. One of these possibilities is the double name consisting of the parents' names as the birth name for the child. This has however been ruled out by the legislature. Taking such a path is constitutionally unobjectionable.

aa) This restriction of the parental option is however not factually reasoned in the function which the legislature has allotted to family names in general, and hence also to the birth name. The double name combined from the names of the parents may indeed better express the family affiliation of the child than a birth name selected from among the two names, given that it documents by means of the name the fact of the child being tied to both parents.

bb) The possibility of parents to link their names to become a double name, and hence to pass them on to their children, however leads to practical difficulties if they have more than one name each. If they themselves have double names, the right to combine both parents' names in forming the birth name of the child would lead here to a multiple-element name chain which could become longer from one generation to the next. The legislature is not prevented from taking precautions under the law on names in order to avoid such name chains if it wishes to ensure viable family names for future generations and to guarantee the protection of the name that is used.

cc) The development of name chains could however be countered not only by exclusion of a double name for a child. It would also be possible to generally limit the number of names which may be combined to the formation of double names in designating a child's birth name. This would however in turn restrict the possibility of parents with a double name to also claim for themselves the right to completely document both parents' names in the child's name. Furthermore, for persons who have received a double name as a birth name the choice of names would at the same time have to be restricted on conclusion of marriage. In order to prevent name chains over and above double names, they would not only have to be denied the complete combination of both of their names if they wished to have a married name, but they would also have to be prohibited from adding their complete own names to the married name selected. They would hence at least have to do without one part of their previous double name. This would deprive them of what § 1355 of the Civil Code enables name-bearers with one name: Retention of their own name whilst selecting a married name deviating from this. The expansion of parents' options to include the double name as a birth name for their child hence leads to a restriction of the possibilities to select names for bearers of double names themselves. If however the realisation of one fundamental right at the same time leads to the restriction of others, a suitable balance must be struck between the fundamental rights in question.

d) The legislature complied with these requirements by excluding the selection of a double name for a child in pursuance of its goals borne by Article 6.1 of the Basic Law and Article 2.1 of the Basic Law. By linking the child's name to the joint parents' name or to the name of one parent, the legislature intended to lend expression to the child's family affiliation. At the same time, with the exclusion of the double name it prevented name chains being formed as the generations pass. By these means, it intended to ensure the function of the name to create a personal identity. That it did so by restricting the right to determine the name of the current generation of parents, and not by restricting the following parents' generations, is not required as a legislative decision in terms of constitutionality, taking account of the options still open to parents in determining their own name and the child's name, but it is also not objectionable. It leaves the conflicting fundamental rights a sufficient degree of realisation and leads to a law on family names which is supportive of the legislative goals.

II.

The exclusion of a double name for a child violates neither the right of personality of the child, nor that of the parents under Article 2.1 in conjunction with Article 1.1 of the Basic Law.

1. Not being able to receive as a birth name a double name consisting of the parents' names does not violate the child's right of personality.

The child's own right to develop his or her personality (see BVerfGE 24, 119 (144); 72, 155 (172); 79, 51 (63)) includes protection of his or her name. It helps the child to find his or her identity and to develop individuality. Without a name, the child will find it difficult to develop his or her own personality and to build up a relationship with others. Therefore, the right to receive a name is also covered by the child's right of personality as a major precondition for the development of his or her personality. This relates to the forename and to family names. If the legal order provides for family names to be used, this name is the means with the aid of which the child learns to enter into relationships with others.

Having said that, the child's right of personality does not include a right to personal choice of the birth name. If the birth name of the child is to comply with its function of contributing towards the personality development of the child, the child must receive it shortly after birth, in other words at a time when the child is not yet able to give himself or herself a name. What is more, it is vital for his or her search for an identity that the child receives a name, but not what specific name he or she receives. It is only the self-perception via a name which leads to identification with it as a means to form an identity of his or her own.

2. The exclusion of a double name for a child also does not impact on the right of personality of the parents as protected by Article 2.1 in conjunction with Article 1.1 of the Basic Law.

The wish to give one's offspring one's own name for life may be a human need. The parents' right of personality does, however, not establish a right to compliance with this need. Only one's own identity and personality are covered by protection of personality. Article 2.1 of the Basic Law does not provide a right of determination regarding another person (see BVerfGE 24, 119 (144); 72, 155 (172)). This also applies to parents in relation to their children. The right to give their children a name is granted to parents in fundamental-rights terms not in the interest of their own personality development, but solely in the interest of their children, in the framework of their responsibility as holders of custody according to Article 6.2 of the Basic Law.

III.

1. § 1616.2 sentence 1 of the Civil Code old and § 1617.1 sentence 1 of the Civil Code violate neither Article 3.3 sentence 1 of the Basic Law, nor the principle of equal rights contained in Article 3.2 of the Basic Law.

a) According to Article 3.3 sentence 1 of the Basic Law, no one may be disadvantaged or favoured because of their sex. Sex may in principle not be used as an indication for different treatment under the law. A link to sex may also apply if a provision the wording of which is gender-neutral ultimately largely concerns members of one sex, for instance women, and this is the result of natural or social differences between the sexes (see BVerfGE 97, 35 (43)). Article 3.2 of the Basic Law requires over and above this not only to eliminate legal norms which link advantages or disadvantages to sexual characteristics, but is aimed at approximating the situations in life of men and women (see BVerfGE 85, 191 (207)). This is made explicitly clear in sentence 2 of Article 3.2 of the Basic Law (see BVerfGE 92, 91 (109)). The consequence of this for the parental right to designate names is that both parents are equally entitled to designate the name of their child, and no parent may be awarded priority in the possibility of passing on their own name to the child.

b) These requirements are met by § 1616.2 sentence 1 of the Civil Code old and § 1617.1 sentence 1 of the Civil Code. Accordingly, it is left to the free decision of the parents as to which of their own names is designated as the child's name. That they are to agree on one name and cannot over and above this give the child a name combined from both of their names does restrict the choices available to them. This however affects mothers and fathers in equal measure.

Also the fact that the vast majority of married parents still have a married name which has been determined by the husband's name, and that parents who do not have a married name, but use their own names, also to a very great degree opt for the name of the husband as the birth name of the child when making a selection according to § 1616.2 sentence 1 of the Civil Code old and § 1617.1 sentence 1 of the Civil Code, so that only a small number of children receive the name of their mother as a birth name (according to a dpa survey among registry offices, see *Frankfurter Rundschau* no. 62 of 14 March 2001), does not permit the conclusion to be drawn that the provisions provide equal law, but do not take account of a differing starting position of mothers and fathers in determining their child's name.

The fact that, in selecting the birth name of their child, spouses still largely opt for the name of the husband may be an expression of a traditional understanding of roles and indicate that no equal partnership in this respect in fact exists as yet when it comes to the free decision taken by spouses on their own responsibility regarding the structure of their relationship *inter se* and with their children, as well as on the

distribution of tasks in the marriage, protected by Article 6.1 of the Basic Law (see BVerfGE 66, 84 (94)). However, the mandate of Article 3.2 of the Basic Law to promote the de facto implementation of equal rights of women and men, and to work towards the elimination of existing disadvantages, does not lead to a constitutional requirement to enable parents to select a double name for their children.
Insofar as can be seen, a priority selection of the husband's name as the name of the child is largely not based on a disadvantaged situation of women, but on pre-existing attitudes. With the possibility open to parents to select as the name of their child both the name of the father and that of the mother, space has now also been created in terms of the law on names for a change in such attitudes. The change in attitudes thus facilitated is not considerably promoted by virtue of the ability to give children not only the name of the mother as a birth name, but instead also a name combined from the name of the father and the mother. The possibility of also giving to the child a double name combined from both parents' names could help to avoid a conflict between the parents regarding the child's name, whilst at the same time leading to a situation in which more children also bear that of the mother as a part of their name. This could lead the legislature to amend the law on names, but is not required by Article 3.2 of the Basic Law. Such a provision would already lose at least its full effect in the next generation if, in order to avoid name chains, one part of the parents' name had to be removed once again in the determination of the child's name. In view of the at best slight impact on the implementation of Article 3.2 of the Basic Law, the legislature was permitted to pursue its goal of avoiding double names by virtue of the provision as created.
2. Article 3.1 of the Basic Law is not violated simply because whilst the formation of a double name is ruled out as a birth name for a child, a child may have a double name in exceptional cases. There are sufficient factual reasons for this.
a) If parents may also designate a double name held by one parent according to § 1616.2 sentence 1 of the Civil Code old and § 1617.1 sentence 1 of the Civil Code as the birth name of the child, authorisation of this double name for the child does not signify unequal treatment compared to parents who do not have double names. In both cases, only the name of one parent may be selected as the child's birth name.
b) If a child who lives in a new family community after the separation of his or her parents with the re-married parent who has custody may receive a double name by virtue of the fact that the new married name of his or her parent who has custody may be prefixed or suffixed to his or her previously held name for his or her name change according to § 1618 sentence 2 of the Civil Code, this does not constitute any unconstitutional unequal treatment in relation to parents who are unable to give their child a double name as a birth name. Also with double names resulting from

such name changes, only one name, namely the one which was previously held by the child, refers to the child´s descent from his or her parents. The fact that the child may retain this name serves the protection of personality of the child who has already become identified with his or her previously held name. Additionally, the child is to be enabled by adding the new married name of his or her parent with custody to also lend expression to his or her new social affiliation in the name. The function of the authorisation of the double name thus formed is to document both the descent and his or her social affiliation in the name of the child, even if the family situation of the child no longer shows both attributions. If, in contrast, parents who have joint custody designate the birth name of their child, there is no need to label the physical and simultaneously social affiliation of the child by means of two names and their conjunction to form a double name because both affiliations are unified in the family in which the child lives.
The same factual reasons also justify on adoption of a child to be able to give him or her a double name according to § 1757.4 sentence 1 no. 2 of the Civil Code in the context of the name change which consists of the previous name of the child and of the family name of his or her adoptive parents.
c) Finally, it is also factually justified and does not violate Article 3.1 of the Basic Law that siblings of children who received a double name from 5 March 1991 until 31 March 1994 on the basis of the ruling of the Federal Constitutional Court are also granted this double name as a birth name according to Article 224 § 3.3 of the Introductory Act to the Civil Code (*Einführungsgesetz zum Bürgerlichen Gesetzbuch* – EGBGB). This transitional regulation serves to maintain a common name among siblings also in families in which the first born was given a double name in a legally permissible manner, and at the same time the name protection of the first born from Article 2.1 of the Basic Law.

D.

This decision was rendered with 6:2 votes re C. I., and in other respects unanimously.

Justices: Papier, Jaeger, Haas, Hömig, Steiner, Hohmann-Dennhardt, Hoffmann-Riem, Bryde

No. 34

BVerfGE 105, 1
of 5 February 2002 – 1 BvR 105, 559/95, 457/96 –
"Post-marital maintenance case"

HEADNOTE:

Decision regarding the equivalence of family work and gainful employment in the assessment of post-marital maintenance.

Order of the First Senate of 5 February 2002
– 1 BvR 105, 559/95, 457/96 –

in the proceedings regarding the constitutional complaints 1. of Ms. V., authorised representative: …, lawyer – against the judgment of the Karlsruhe Higher Regional Court (*Oberlandesgericht*) of 30 November 1994 – 16 UF 201/93 – 1 BvR 105/95 –; 2. of Ms. E., – authorised representative: …, lawyer – against the judgment of the Stuttgart Higher Regional Court of 31 January 1995 – 18 UF 361/94 – *and* application to grant legal aid and to assign lawyer … – 1 BvR 559/95 –; 3. of Ms. K.-V., – authorised representative: …, lawyer – against the judgment of the Karlsruhe Higher Regional Court of 19 January 1996 – 20 UF 8/95 – 1 BvR 457/96 –.

RULING:

1. The judgment of the Karlsruhe Higher Regional Court of 30 November 1994 – 16 UF 201/93 – violates the fundamental right of the complainant re 1 under Article 6.1 in conjunction with Article 3.2 of the Basic Law (*Grundgesetz* – GG). The judgment is reversed. The case is referred back to the Karlsruhe Higher Regional Court.
2. The judgment of the Stuttgart Higher Regional Court of 31 January 1995 – 18 UF 361/94 – violates the fundamental right of the complainant re 2 under Article 6.1 in conjunction with Article 3.2 of the Basic Law. The judgment is reversed. The case is referred back to the Stuttgart Higher Regional Court.

3. The judgment of the Karlsruhe Higher Regional Court of 19 January 1996 – 20 UF 8/95 – violates the fundamental right of the complainant re 3 under Article 6.1 in conjunction with Article 3.2 of the Basic Law. The judgment is reversed. The case is referred back to the Karlsruhe Higher Regional Court.
4. …

EXTRACT FROM GROUNDS:

A.

The constitutional complaints, which have been consolidated for joint adjudication, are directed at the manner in which the impugned court rulings have considered the value of the housekeeping and child-rearing performed during marriage in the assessment of post-marital maintenance.

I.

According to § 1578.1 of the Civil Code (*Bürgerliches Gesetzbuch* – BGB), the amount of post-marital maintenance is determined according to the marital circumstances. How the marital circumstances, which are not defined in greater detail by the law, are to be ascertained, and how in particular the post-marital income of the spouse entitled to maintenance who was not employed at all during marriage, or was only in part-time employment, is to be taken into account here is the subject of dispute in the case-law and legal literature.
1. a) Since the entry into force of the valid maintenance law on 1 July 1977 …, the Federal Court of Justice (*Bundesgerichtshof* – BGH) has lent concrete form to the concept of marital circumstances through a large number of rulings. According to its established case-law, the marital circumstances within the meaning of § 1578 of the Civil Code are determined by the income and asset situation which had decisively characterised the standard of living of both spouses during the marriage or indeed the separation period of the spouses. Therefore, the income and assets at the time of divorce are to be decisive as a rule, unless the income of one spouse took on an unexpected development in the period between separation and divorce deviating considerably from the normal course of events (see BGH, *Zeitschrift für das gesamte Familienrecht* – FamRZ 1982, p. 576 (577-578)). By contrast, until the judgment of the Federal Court of Justice of 13 June 2001 (FamRZ 2001, p. 986), changes which did not occur until after divorce could only be taken into account if they were to be expected at the time of the divorce with a high degree of probabili-

ty, and if this expectation already characterised the marital circumstances or materialised at a time close to the divorce (see BGH, FamRZ 1986, pp. 148-149). Accordingly, the Federal Court of Justice distinguished between gainful employment during marriage, and taking up of gainful employment during separation, as well as after divorce.

aa) In contradistinction to the income which was already made during the co-habitation of the spouses, income of the spouse entitled to maintenance from gainful employment taken up between separation and divorce was only to impact the measure of the maintenance if this gainful employment was commenced during the marriage, and hence would also have taken place without the separation. If this could not be ascertained, the resultant income would have to be left out of the assessment of the maintenance requirement since the party pleading for maintenance was said to bear the burden of proof for the shape of the marital circumstances (Decisions of the Federal Court of Justice in Civil Matters (*Entscheidungen des Bundesgerichtshofes in Zivilsachen* – BGHZ 89, 108 (112) = FamRZ 1984, pp. 149-150).

bb) The Federal Court of Justice as a rule has not considered income from gainful employment not taken up until after divorce in determining the marital circumstances (BGH, FamRZ 1985, pp. 161-162 referring to BGH, FamRZ 1981, p. 539 (541) and FamRZ 1982, p. 255 (257)), and also if half-time employment exercised during marriage was expanded to full-time employment (BGH, FamRZ 1985, pp. 161-162). The Federal Court of Justice regarded the economic value of the housekeeping and child-raising of the spouse who was not in gainful employment as not characterising the marital circumstances. These services were said to be in principle equivalent to the gainful employment of the other spouse. However, in terms of cash the family was said to have at its disposal only the income of the spouse who was in gainful employment. This existing income, and not the economic value of the services provided by both spouses, was said to decisively characterise the marital circumstances (BGH, FamRZ 1985, p. 161 (163)).

cc) Income of the person entitled to maintenance which had not characterised the marital circumstances was then taken into account in application of the so-called offsetting method in the calculation of the amount of the maintenance solely in reducing need, whilst income characterising [the marital circumstances] has also been allotted to the income on which the calculation of requirement was to be based in application of the so-called difference method (BGH, FamRZ 1981, p. 539 (541); 1981, p. 752 (754-755); 1982, p. 255 (257); 1983, p. 146 (150); 1988, p. 265 (267)). In the offsetting method, the corrected net income of the person obliged to provide maintenance is divided according to the relevant maintenance ratio; the corrected net income of the person entitled to maintenance is offset against the emerging amount. With the difference method, by contrast, the difference between the corrected net income of the person obliged to provide maintenance and of the person entitled to maintenance is first of all formed, and then sub-divided according to the maintenance ratio.

b) The Federal Court of Justice amended its previous case-law on the offsetting method by its judgment of 13 June 2001 (FamRZ 2001, p. 986). The offsetting method was said not to do justice to the equivalence of child-care and housekeeping, and also to no longer reasonably account for the changed perception of marriage in the majority of cases. Without there being a need for a final ruling on the question of the need to monetarise housekeeping, the income which a spouse entitled to maintenance made or could make after divorce, and which was practically to be regarded as a surrogate of the economic value of his or her previous activity, should be included in calculating the maintenance according to the difference method. The family work carried out during marriage was said to have characterised the marital standard of living, and also to have improved it in economic terms. It was said to be regarded as a service equivalent to gainful employment. The spouses should also be entitled after divorce to the standard of living achieved by the respective work of both spouses in equal parts. If the spouse who had previously done the housekeeping took up gainful employment after divorce, or if he or she extended it beyond the previous extent, apart from exceptional cases of an unusual career development substantially deviating from the normal course of events, the value of his or her housekeeping was reflected in the income made or makeable in gainful employment. The inclusion of this income in the assessment of need with the aid of the difference calculation was said to guarantee that, just as the family work formerly benefited both spouses in equal measure, the mutual income was now shared between them according to the principle of equal participation.

...

II.

The constitutional complaints are based on the following facts:

1st set of proceedings 1 BvR 105/95

The complainant, who married in 1969 and gave birth to a daughter in the same year, took up her employment once more in 1972 on a half-time basis. The spouses separated in June 1991. During the divorce proceedings, the complainant expanded her employment to full-time employment in January 1992. The marriage has been legally dissolved since 29 October 1992.

Whilst the Local Court (*Amtsgericht*) awarded to the complainant maintenance calculated according to the difference method in response to her action, the Higher Regional Court rejected her action, reversing the judgment of the Local Court. An expansion of part-time employment to full-time employment which did not take place until after separation by the spouse demanding maintenance was said to be able to characterise the marital circumstances only if it would also have taken place without the separation. In the case of the complainant, it could not be ruled out on the basis of the information provided by her husband that she had taken up full-time employment once again solely as a result of the separation.

2nd set of proceedings 1 BvR 559/95

The complainant concluded a marriage in 1983 which gave issue to a daughter in 1984. The spouses separated at the beginning of 1988. The marriage was legally dissolved in October 1992. Parental custody for the daughter was assigned to the divorced husband.

As to her career, the complainant submitted in the original proceedings that she had worked as a travel agent prior to giving birth to her daughter. After the birth, she had devoted herself to child-rearing. From 1989 she had then wished to reintegrate into working life, and had commenced re-training as an industrial clerk in January 1990. After her stay in a rehabilitation clinic from December 1992 to March 1993, she had unsuccessfully applied for jobs. She had received a pension for inability to work since July 1994.

The Higher Regional Court amended the first-instance ruling and awarded her a lower maintenance claim with the impugned judgment, and furthermore found that the complainant only had a maintenance claim against her husband until 16 January 1995 since the pension for inability to work which had been granted to her had caused her need for maintenance to cease. The marital circumstances of the complainant were said to have been characterised by the employment of the husband, and not also by her income from gainful employment or pensions. The complainant was said to have wanted to re-commence gainful employment only as a result of separation. There were said to be no indications that she would have taken up employment had the separation not occurred. It was said that she had been able to cover her maintenance requirement since December 1994 by her own pension income, which she had to offset according to § 1577.1 of the Civil Code.

3rd set of proceedings 1 BvR 457/96

Two children, born in 1972 and 1973, had issued from the marriage of the complainant, which had been concluded in 1968. According to her own information, the complainant had worked as a housewife and mother after the birth of her children, as well as occasionally teaching painting courses for children, and had tried to find a job as an architect. After the separation of the spouses in 1982, she worked for a time on a half-time basis as an intern for an architect. Her marriage was legally dissolved in August 1986. In 1987 the complainant started preparatory service to work

in a vocational school, and was later taken on. According to a court agreement concluded between the spouses, a maintenance claim of the complainant beyond August 1993 was to be in line with the legal provisions applicable at that time.
The Local Court rejected the complainant's maintenance claim, with which she applied for maintenance from January 1995. The complainant's appeal on points of fact and law of was also unsuccessful. The Higher Regional Court ruled that no maintenance amount could be calculated in favour of the complainant. The basis of the complainant's maintenance claim was said to be solely the salary income of her divorced husband, which had characterised the marital circumstances. Personal employment income of the complainant should not be considered. Possible income from teaching painting courses had also ceased back in 1981 according to her information. Gainful employment of the complainant had hence only commenced after divorce, so that maintenance was not to be calculated by the difference method. It was said to be calculated by offsetting her income against the maintenance quota based solely on the income of the divorced husband. No maintenance claim was calculated here in favour of the complainant.

III.

With their constitutional complaints addressing in each case the decision of the Higher Regional Court, the complainants complain in particular of the violation of Article 3.1 and 3.2, as well as of Article 6 of the Basic Law. As grounds, they refer to the equivalence of housekeeping and gainful employment in marriage. The protection of marriage is said to also comprise the family work. In particular parents bringing up children may not be placed at a disadvantage in terms of maintenance if they restricted or gave up their employment in the interest of the family. The burdens of the joint decision of spouses regarding their division of tasks may not unilaterally encumber the party who had taken on the family work. Moreover, it is said to be a matter of coincidence according to the case-law on which their proceedings were based in which cases employment income of the housekeeping spouse is categorised as characteristic for the marriage. If divorce takes place at a time when the children were still small, so that the person taking care of the children did not engage in gainful employment, subsequent income is said not to be considered. If it takes place at a time when the children were older, the person taking care of the children has frequently taken up gainful employment once more, which is then included in the calculation of the maintenance requirement. In order to do justice to the protection of marriage and to the equal rights of spouses, in terms of the law on maintenance it should not be a matter of the time when the caring parent has returned to employment once more.

…

B.

The constitutional complaints are well-founded. The impugned court rulings violate the complainants' fundamental rights under Article 6.1 in conjunction with Article 3.2 of the Basic Law.

I.

1. a) Article 6.1 in conjunction with Article 3.2 of the Basic Law protects marriage as a life community of equal partners (see Decisions of the Federal Constitutional Court (*Entscheidungen des Bundesverfassungsgerichts* – BVerfGE) 35, 382 (408); 103, 89 (101)), in which spouses take joint responsibility for determining their personal and economic lives (see BVerfGE 57, 361 (390); 61, 319 (347)). In addition to the decision as to whether the spouses wish to have children, the responsible shaping of their lives in particular includes agreement on the division of labour within the family and the decision as to how the joint family income is to be ensured by gainful employment (see BVerfGE 61, 319 (347); 66, 84 (94); 68, 256 (268)). Spouses are free here to maintain their marriage such that one spouse alone engages in employment and the other devotes himself or herself to family work, just as they can decide for themselves to both engage in employment entirely or partly and to share housekeeping and child-raising or to have this carried out by third parties (see BVerfGE 39, 169 (183); 48, 327 (338); 99, 216 (231)).
b) If spouses have the same rights and the same responsibility in shaping their married and family lives, the services which they provide respectively in the context of the allocation of work and tasks which they made in a joint decision are also to be regarded as equivalent (see BVerfGE 37, 217 (251); 47, 1 (24); 53, 257 (296); 66, 84 (94); 79, 106 (126)). Housekeeping and child-care do not take on a lower value for the joint lives of spouses than income which is available to the household. They equally characterise the marital circumstances and contribute towards the maintenance of the family.
Having said that, the equivalence of the family maintenance contributions of spouses is not calculated by the amount of the employment income which one or both spouses make, or by the economic value of family work and by its scope. It rather expresses the fact that the services provided by each of the spouses for the marital

community are equivalent, regardless of their economic valuation, and hence no contribution by a spouse may be valued higher or lower than that of the other. …

c) If the contributions made by spouses within their joint maintenance community are equivalent, both spouses in principle also have a right to participate equally in what they have earned together, which is to be allotted to them in equal parts. This applies not only to the time of the existence of the marriage, but after the separation and divorce of the spouses also has an impact on their relationship as to maintenance, pensions and division of the joint assets (see BVerfGE 47, 85 (100); 63, 88 (109)). This corresponds to the statutory regulations regarding pension sharing (see BVerfGE 53, 257 (296)) and the equitable division of accrued gains (see BVerfGE 71, 364 (386)) on divorce. In particular, however, the claim to equal participation in what was earned jointly also includes the relationship between the divorced spouses in terms of maintenance (see BVerfGE 63, 88 (109)). When calculating the maintenance, the income which characterised the standard of living in the marriage is in principle to be equally allotted to the spouses. Its amount is calculated as a rule from the total of the income which the spouses had at their disposal for their lives together, regardless of whether it was earned by only one spouse or by both spouses. In general, half this joint total income is the part which – if the other statutory preconditions are met – is to be ensured in terms of the law on maintenance for the spouse who does not have his or her own income in the respective amount after divorce.

2. The established case-law of the civil courts also takes into account when calculating the maintenance increases in income which were not achieved by one or both spouses until after divorce insofar as this increase corresponds to normal income and career development (see A I 1 a above). Such an interpretation of the concept of marital circumstances, according to which the amount of post-marital maintenance is determined pursuant to § 1578.1 of the Civil Code, is constitutionally unobjectionable if both spouses' right to an equal standard of living being ensured also after marriage, arising from the equivalence of the marital maintenance contributions, is in principle protected in the calculation of post-marital maintenance.

3. The impugned rulings, based as they are on the earlier case-law of the Federal Court of Justice, do not do justice to this in that they take account as an element of the total income corresponding to the marital circumstances of the increase in income which the spouse achieves after the divorce who already engaged in full-time employment during the marriage when calculating the maintenance, but not of that which the spouse who was not or only partly in gainful employment during the marriage made by virtue of resuming part-time or full-time employment after divorce. They hence violate Article 6.1 in conjunction with Article 3.2 of the Basic Law.

a) The non-consideration of post-marital income growth resulting from the resumption of gainful employment in the total income on which the maintenance calculation is based leads to a situation in which, measured against the marital income situation, which is based on the contributions of both spouses, the spouse who was already in employment during the marriage experiences a unilateral reduction of his or her financial burden as to his or her maintenance obligation when the other takes up employment. He or she is hence left with a higher share of his or her income than what was at his or her disposal during the marriage. By contrast, the additional income of the spouse who during the marriage was not or only partly in gainful employment in the amount of this income reduces his or her maintenance claim. It does not have an impact on his or her maintenance requirement, but simply reduces his or her need. The income growth which he or she has achieved does not benefit him or her, but only the other divorced spouse. This result does not do justice to the equivalence of the contribution which the non-employed spouse has provided during the marriage. This contribution, in addition to the income of the other spouse, has equally characterised marital life. If this contribution, which is not expressed in a monetary value, made during marriage, is replaced by one which is remunerated, the non-consideration of the income thus made in the determination of the marital income situation leads in hindsight to disregard for the value of the family work which has been performed, to the disadvantage of the person having provided it during the marriage.
b) If in respect of the inclusion of such growth in the total income on which the maintenance calculation is to be based, and which characterises the income situation of the spouses, the impugned rulings require that resumed gainful employment should at least be based on a joint life plan of the spouses which had at least been partly realised prior to divorce, this ignores the protection provided to each spouse by Article 6.1 in conjunction with Article 3.2 of the Basic Law. The spouses may shape their marital relationship freely and in a joint decision which is based on equal rights. The decision on their respective tasks within the marriage determines their marital circumstances. If one spouse takes on the family work here, he or she forgoes personal income, also to the benefit of the other. The reasoning of this waiver lies in marriage. If it is terminated by divorce, the foundation is removed from the marital agreement. To force the spouse forgoing personal income during marriage to adhere to this in terms of the law on maintenance on termination of the marriage means now allocating to him or her alone the ensuing financial disadvantages which both spouses had to bear on the basis of the joint decision that was made in the marriage. This places at a disadvantage the spouse shouldering the family work as against the one who was able to continuously engage in gainful employment also during marriage.

c) What is more, the legal view supposed by the courts with this finality of a division of tasks once decided jointly by the spouses no longer corresponds to the real situation in marriage. The conduct of women in terms of training, gainful employment and family establishment has undergone continuous change since the seventies. Whilst the average age on marriage of single women was as low as 22.7 in 1975, single women in 1998 on average did not marry until they were 28 (*Statistisches Jahrbuch* 1985, p. 72 and *Statistisches Jahrbuch* 2000, p. 69). This permits one to reach the conclusion that women today do not conclude marriage until completing their vocational training and until after several years at work …. Many women also remain in work during child-care … or resume employment once more after the end of the child-care phase. For instance, 74 per cent of women whose youngest child was between 15 and 18 were engaged in gainful employment in May 2000 (result of the Microcensus 2000, see Federal Statistical Office (*Statistisches Bundesamt*), *Zentralblatt für Jugendrecht* 2001, p. 278). Accordingly, the employment rate of married women in the age group of 40-to 45-year olds, i.e. in an age in which child-care has been largely completed, is highest at 78 per cent …. 61 per cent of women with at least one minor child worked part-time in May 2000 …. It is thus shown that the housewife marriage, which was still dominant in the fifties and sixties, has in the meantime given way to a now predominant concept of marriage which is based on reconciliation of work and family in which the type of bread-winner marriage has only largely been retained during the active parenthood phase. Here, the majority of women are looking to combine private child-raising and gainful employment on the basis of temporary part-time work …. One may therefore presume that a spouse temporarily forgoing gainful employment in order to take on the task of child-rearing characterises the marital circumstances, as does previous employment and the subsequent resumption or attempted resumption of gainful employment. The impugned judgments fail to take this into account if they are based solely on the time of the divorce before which gainful employment must be resumed in order to be taken into consideration in calculating the total income characterising the marital circumstances in terms of the law on maintenance.

4. It is a matter for the non-constitutional courts to judge as to how the equivalence of family work and marital income required by Article 6.1 in conjunction with Article 3.2 of the Basic Law is to be brought to bear in the interpretation of the term "marital circumstances" according to § 1578.1 of the Civil Code in assessing post-marital maintenance, and how the maintenance is to be calculated. With its ruling of 13 June 2001 (FamRZ 2001, p. 986), the Federal Court of Justice amended its previous case-law and now carried out an assessment of maintenance which takes account of the equivalence of the maintenance contributions of both spouses. By virtue of having regarded the new employment of the spouse previously not in

gainful employment as a "surrogate" of the housekeeping and child-raising previously carried out, the Federal Court of Justice has demonstrated a possible, constitutionally unobjectionable way to have the value accruing to the marriage from family work make a difference in terms of the law on maintenance.

II.

In their impugned rulings, the courts did not take account of the equivalence of the marital maintenance contributions provided, and based the assessment of post-marital maintenance on a calculation which does not do justice to the value of the family work performed in marriage, thereby applying an unconstitutional interpretation to the term "marital circumstances". In all three sets of proceedings, the resumption of gainful employment by the complainants shortly before or after divorce only had a payment-reducing impact on their maintenance claim, without the family work performed in their marriage having been adequately reflected in the assessment of their maintenance requirement. The rulings are hence to be reversed and the cases referred back to the Higher Regional Courts.

…

Justices: Papier, Jaeger, Haas, Hömig, Steiner, Hohmann-Dennhardt, Hoffmann-Riem, Bryde

No. 35

BVerfGE 105, 313
of 17 July 2002 – 1 BvF 1, 2/01 –
"Civil Partnerships Act case"

HEADNOTES:

1. **Where a statute has been passed and is to be corrected, which is admissible in exceptional cases, it is necessary for the statute to be plainly incorrect. The incorrectness may be shown not only by the text of the statute, but in particular also by taking into account its meaning in context and the parliamentary background materials of the statute.**
2. **If the Federal Government or the *Bundestag* divides a subject-matter between a number of statutes in order to prevent the *Bundesrat* from preventing provisions that in themselves are not subject to its consent, this is constitutionally unobjectionable.**
3. **The introduction of the legal institution of the registered civil partnership for same-sex couples does not infringe Article 6.1 of the Basic Law. The particular protection of marriage in Article 6.1 of the Basic Law does not prevent the legislature from providing rights and duties for the same-sex civil partnership that are equal or similar to those of marriage. The institution of marriage is not threatened by any risk from an institution that is directed at persons who cannot be married to each other.**
4. **It does not infringe Article 3.1 of the Basic Law that persons of different sex cohabiting with each other and groups of people related to each other and living together have no possibility of becoming registered civil partnerships.**

Judgment of the First Senate of 17 July 2002
on the basis of the oral hearing of 9 April 2002
– 1 BvF 1, 2/01 –

in the proceedings on the constitutional review of the Act on the Termination of the Discrimination of Same-Sex Couples: Civil Partnerships (*Gesetz zur Beendigung der Diskriminierung gleichgeschlechtlicher Gemeinschaften: Lebenspartnerschaften*) of 16 February 2001 (Federal Law Gazette, *Bundesgesetzblatt,* BGBl I, p. 266), amended by Article 25 of the Ninth Book of the Code of Social Law (*Neuntes Buch Sozialgesetzbuch* – SGB IX) Rehabilitation and participation in society of disabled persons of 19 June 2001 (Federal Law Gazette I p. 1046), by Article 10 number 7 of the Act on the Reorganisation, Simplification and Reform of Landlord and Tenant Law (*Gesetz zur Neugliederung, Vereinfachung und Reform des Mietrechts*) of 19 June 2001 (Federal Law Gazette I p. 1149) and by Article 11 of the Act on the Improvement of Civil-Court Protection in the case of Violence and Stalking and to Facilitate the Transfer of the Matrimonial Home in Case of Separation (*Gesetz zur Verbesserung des zivilgerichtlichen Schutzes bei Gewalttaten und Nachstellungen sowie zur Erleichterung der Überlassung der Ehewohnung bei Trennung*) of 11 December 2001 (Federal Law Gazette I p. 3513), First Applicants: 1. Government of the Free State of Saxony, represented by the Minister-President ..., 2. *Land* government of the Free State of Thuringia, represented by the Minister-President ..., authorised representatives: 1. Professor Dr. ..., 2. Professor Dr. ... – 1 BvF 1/01 –, Second Applicant: Bavarian state government, represented by the Minister-President ..., – authorised representative: Professor Dr. ... – 1 BvF 2/01 –.

RULING:

The Act on the Termination of the Discrimination of Same-Sex Couples: Civil Partnerships (*Gesetz zur Beendigung der Diskriminierung gleichgeschlechtlicher Gemeinschaften: Lebenspartnerschaften*) of 16 February 2001 (Federal Law Gazette I p. 266) as amended by the Act of 11 December 2001 (Federal Law Gazette I p. 3513) is compatible with the Basic Law (*Grundgesetz* – GG).

EXTRACT FROM GROUNDS:

A.

The applications for the judicial review of a statute relate to the compatibility of the Act on the Termination of the Discrimination of Same-Sex Couples: Civil Partnerships of 16 February 2001 (Federal Law Gazette I p. 266; hereinafter: Civil Partnerships Act, LPartDisBG), which entered into force on 1 August 2001, with the Basic Law.

I.

The aim of the Act is to reduce discrimination against same-sex couples and to give them the opportunity to give their partnerships a legal framework. For this purpose, the registered civil partnership has been created as a family-law institution for a long-term same-sex partnership, with a large number of legal consequences.

1. In the year 2000, at least 47,000 same-sex couples were cohabiting in the Federal Republic of Germany (see Eggen, *Gleichgeschlechtliche Lebensgemeinschaften*, 2nd part, in: *Baden-Württemberg in Wort und Zahl* 12/2001, pp. 579 et seq.). According to a study commissioned by the German Federal Ministry of Justice and carried out by Buba and Vaskovics in the year 2000, same-sex couples do not essentially differ from different-sex couples in their expectations of the partnership, its permanence, their mutual readiness to support each other and assumption of responsibility for each other. More than half of the interviewees living in same-sex partnerships expressed the desire to live in a legally binding partnership (Buba/ Vaskovics, *Benachteiligung gleichgeschlechtlich orientierter Personen und Paare*, study commissioned by the German Federal Ministry of Justice, 2000, pp. 75 et seq., 117 et seq.). Same-sex couples are prohibited from marrying.

2. The first parliamentary initiatives for legislation for homosexual partnerships in the Federal Republic of Germany date back to the 11th parliamentary term of the German *Bundestag* (see the resolution proposal of the parliamentary group of the Green Party of 18 May 1990, *Bundestag* printed paper, *Bundestagsdrucksache* – BTDrucks 11/7197). In 1994, in a resolution, the European Parliament called on the member states of the European Union to avoid unequal treatment of persons of same-sex orientation in their individual legal and administrative provisions, and appealed to the Commission to grant homosexuals access to marriage or to corresponding legal institutions (see Official Journal of the European Communities C 61 of 28 February 1994, 40-41; *Bundestag* printed paper 12/7069, p. 4). There now exist provisions on same-sex partnerships in several European countries (see the study

of the *Max-Planck-Institut für ausländisches und internationales Privatrecht*, ed. von Basedow *et al. Die Rechtsstellung gleichgeschlechtlicher Lebensgemeinschaften*, 2000). They extend from partnerships in the Scandinavian countries that are treated as equal to marriage in their effects to the *pacte civil de solidarité* (PACS) in France with its possibility of the registration of same-sex and different-sex partnerships, which has fewer legal effects than marriage and can be dissolved more easily. In the Netherlands, same-sex couples may now be married.
In July 2000, the parliamentary groups of the SPD (*Sozialdemokratische Partei Deutschlands*) and BÜNDNIS 90/DIE GRÜNEN introduced a bill for an Act on the Termination of the Discrimination of Same-Sex Couples: Civil Partnerships to the legislative procedure (*Bundestag* printed paper 14/3751). The FDP (*Freie Demokratische Partei*) parliamentary group also tabled a bill (*Bundestag* printed paper 14/1259). After the first readings of both bills, referral to the committee stage and the examination of expert witnesses, the Committee on Legal Affairs of the *Bundestag*, which had overall responsibility, on 8 November 2000 recommended that the FDP bill should be rejected and the bill of the governing parliamentary groups should be accepted, but in a version divided into two statutes: firstly, as the Act on the Termination of the Discrimination of Same-Sex Couples: Civil Partnerships with the provisions on registered civil partnerships and on the essential legal consequences associated with them (Civil Partnerships Act, LPartDisBG), and secondly as the Act to Supplement the Civil Partnerships Act and other Acts (*Gesetz zur Ergänzung des Lebenspartnerschaftsgesetzes und anderer Gesetze, Lebenspartnerschaftsgesetzergänzungsgesetz,* Civil Partnerships Act Supplementary Act, LPartGErgG) with in particular procedural-law implementing regulations (*Bundestag* printed paper 14/4545 with annexes). The reason for this was the intention of the governing parliamentary groups to divide the original bill into a bill not requiring the approval of the *Bundesrat* and a bill requiring the approval of the *Bundesrat*. Consequently, the bill of the Civil Partnerships Act was not to name an authority responsible for registering the civil partnership (Committee printed paper (*Ausschuss-Drucksache*) 14/508 (Committee on Family Affairs, Senior Citizens, Women and Youth (*Ausschuss für Familie, Senioren, Frauen und Jugend*)) and 14/944 (Committee on Labour and Social Affairs (*Ausschuss für Arbeit und Sozialordnung*)). This was approved by the majorities in the consulting committees and was also expressed in the report of the Committee on Legal Affairs of 9 November 2000 (*Bundestag* printed paper 14/4550). However, in the text attached to the resolution recommended by the Committee on Legal Affairs of the draft of a Civil Partnerships Act, not all the provisions had been amended in line with this. The Civil Partnerships Act was accepted by the *Bundestag* in this wording (Minutes of plenary proceedings (*Plenarprotokoll*) 14/131, p. 12629 D) and was passed by

the *Bundesrat* unaltered; the *Bundesrat* did not make an application to the Mediation Committee (*Vermittlungsausschuss*) and did not establish that this statute was subject to approval (*Bundesrat*, Minutes of plenary proceedings, 757th session, p. 551 C, D).

When the Federal Ministry of Justice pointed out two obvious errors, in its opinion, in subsections 3 and 4 of Article 1 § 3 of the Civil Partnerships Act, the Presidents of the *Bundestag* and the *Bundesrat* agreed to a correction of the provisions objected to as incorrect. The signing and promulgation of the Act on 16 February 2001 (Federal Law Gazette I p. 266) then followed in the corrected version. The applications for an interim injunction against the entry into force of the Act, made by the governments of the Free State of Bavaria and the Free State of Saxony were unsuccessful before the Federal Constitutional Court (*Bundesverfassungsgericht*; see judgment of 18 July 2001 – 1 BvQ 23/01 and 1 BvQ 26/01 –, *Neue Juristische Wochenschrift* 2001, 2457).

Now there are implementation regulations for the Civil Partnerships Act in all *Länder* (states), establishing jurisdiction in civil partnership matters and associated procedural rules.

The Civil Partnerships Act Supplementary Act, on the other hand, was approved by the *Bundestag* but has not yet been approved by the *Bundesrat* (*Bundestag* printed paper 14/4875). The Mediation Committee applied to by the *Bundestag* (*Bundestag* printed paper 14/4878) has as yet made no resolution thereon.

3. The Act challenged in the applications for judicial review governs the creation and dissolution of a registered civil partnership for same-sex couples. The civil partnership is created by a contract between two persons of the same sex; the statements necessary for this purpose must be made before the competent authority (Article 1 § 1.1). A further requirement for entering into a civil partnership is that both partners make a declaration as to their property status (Article 1 § 1.1 sentence 4). On the application of one or both partners, the civil partnership is terminated by a decree of annulment (Article 1 § 15).

The partners are bound to each other in care and support and committed to plan their lives together. They are responsible for each other (Article 1 § 2). The statute does not require sexual intercourse. The legal consequences of the registered partnership are in part based on the legal consequences of marriage, but they also diverge from the latter. Thus, the partners owe each other support. This applies to a modified extent also to persons living apart and after the termination of the partnership (Article 1 §§ 5, 12 and 16). The partners must make a statement on their financial status; they may choose between a property regime of equalisation of surplus and a contract governing their financial relations (Article 1 §§ 6 und 7). They may choose a joint name (Article 1 § 3). The civil partner or former partner of a parent

who has lived for a long period in domestic community with the child has a right of access (Article 2 number 12, § 1685.2 of the Civil Code). A partner is deemed to be a member of the other's family (Article 1 § 11). A right of intestate succession of the civil partner corresponding to that of the spouse has been introduced (Article 1 § 10). In social security law too, entering into the civil partnership has legal consequences (Article 3 §§ 52, 54 und 56). Thus, for example, in the statutory health insurance scheme civil partners are covered by the family insurance (Article 3 § 52 number 4). In the law concerning foreign nationals, the provisions relating to the right of entry of foreign families that apply to marital relationships are correspondingly extended to same-sex partnerships (Article 3 § 11). In addition the Civil Partnerships Act grants the partner of a parent with sole custody, with the consent of the latter, the authority to make joint decisions in matters of the child's everyday life, known as "limited custody" (Article 1 § 9).
The statute challenged and the supplementary statute that has not yet come into existence provide no adjustment of old-age pension rights between the civil partners if their partnership is annulled, and no rules on pensions in case of death. Similarly, joint adoption of minors is excluded. The supplementary statute contains provisions on tax law and state welfare law, but the Civil Partnerships Act does not.

II.

In their applications for judicial review, the applicants challenge the Act as a whole and individual provisions thereof as incompatible with the Basic Law.
1. They submit that the Act is unconstitutional, firstly, for procedural reasons.
a) The arbitrary division of the original bill into two bills, according to the applicants, circumvented the right of approval of the *Bundesrat*. The division makes the Act a torso and results in its being impossible to implement. Provisions of substantive law that belong together have been abusively torn apart. This is true of the maintenance obligation of partners, which is contained in Article 1 § 5 of the Civil Partnerships Act; because of the division, there is no tax relief provided for this. The two areas of legislation necessarily belong together, and as a result, this provision is not only unconstitutional, but also subject to approval. In addition, the substantive provisions cannot be separated from the procedural provisions. The Civil Partnerships Act needs to be put in effect by the registrar of births, deaths and marriages, for its substantive-law provisions aim at a quite specific organisation of procedure. Thus the *Länder* are largely fettered when they organise procedural law. On the other hand, Article 74.1 number 2 of the Basic Law prevents them from passing their own implementing statutes. Apart from the fact that the Civil Status Act (*Personenstandsgesetz*) governs the law of civil status definitively, the Civil Partner-

ships Act contains no express opening for *Land* legislation. In addition, the Civil Partnerships Act Supplementary Act makes it clear that under Article 72.2 of the Basic Law uniform legislation for the whole of Germany is required. If, contrary to the opinion of the applicants, one is of the opinion that the *Länder* are competent to pass legislation containing implementation provisions, the Act also violates Article 84.1 of the Basic Law because by reason of its substantive-law provisions it requires the *Länder* to create unified procedural law, although under the Constitution this cannot be required of them.

Dividing a statute into one part that requires approval and another part that does not require approval means that the requirement of approval for statutes becomes meaningless. In the Federal Constitutional Court's further development of case-law, a federal statute requires approval if, although it is restricted to provisions on questions of substantive law, these provisions are so determinative that they leave the *Länder* no scope for legislating on administrative procedure on their own responsibility. This is the case in the statute challenged.

b) In addition, the applicants argue, the Act still contains provisions that should have been approved by the *Bundesrat*. This refers to the revision of Article 17a of the Introductory Act to the Civil Code (*Einführungsgesetz zum Bürgerlichen Gesetzbuch,* EGBGB; from 1 January 2002 Article 17b of the Introductory Act to the Civil Code, amended by Article 10 of the Act of 11 December 2001, Federal Law Gazette I p. 3513), whose reference to Article 10.2 of the Introductory Act to the Civil Code establishes a jurisdiction of the registrar of births, deaths and marriages and therefore requires approval, because it allocates to the registrar a legally and qualitatively new administrative activity. The new provisions in the Aliens Act (*Ausländergesetz*) on the subsequent immigration of civil partners now give the provisions of procedure a substantially changed meaning and scope, even if they have not expressly been altered, and lead to qualitatively different activity on the part of the aliens authorities. Whereas previously, when issuing residence permits, these authorities had to take account of Article 6 of the Basic Law in the weighing of proportionality, all that is important in the case of applications of civil partners is the protection of personality, guaranteed by Article 2.1 in conjunction with Article 1.1 of the Basic Law.

c) Finally, the applicants submit, the statute should not have been corrected after the resolutions passed in the *Bundestag* and the *Bundesrat*. It was not a drafting error that Article 1 § 3.3 and 3.4 of the Civil Partnerships Act in the version adopted by the *Bundestag* provide that the registrar of births, deaths and marriages has jurisdiction to accept declarations on the partnership name. The report of the Committee on Legal Affairs reveals that the statute should merely not name the authority that was competent for registering the civil partnership. But Article 1 § 3.3 and 3.4 of the Civil Partnerships Act relate neither to the registration of a civil partnership nor to the stipulation of a name, but to dealing with civil partnerships that have been dissolved. It is appropriate for this purpose to make the declarations before the registrar of births, deaths and marriages, because after the dissolution of the civil partnership the federal Civil Status Act applies again. The provision was the subject of the debate and it became part of the legislature's intention. It was therefore unconstitutional and void to correct the provision. The correction procedure infringes the principle of democracy. The version of the statute promulgated does not correspond to the version adopted. As a result, because the correction is nugatory, the legal provision that was not promulgated, whose allocation of jurisdiction to the registrar made the statute subject to approval, becomes the subject of the proceedings concerning the judicial review of a statute.

2. The applicants submit that the statute is also unconstitutional for substantive reasons.

a) In particular, it is not consistent with the protection of marriage and the family required by Article 6.1 of the Basic Law. It does not comply with the requirement, contained in this fundamental right, of keeping a distance from marriage (*Abstandsgebot*), which is derived in particular from the guarantee of the institution of marriage in Article 6.1 of the Basic Law and from the protection of marriage and the family as a fundamental provision that determines values. The very name of the statute makes it clear that it is intended to give the civil partnership equality of treatment with marriage. The Civil Partnerships Act introduces a family-law institution for same-sex couples largely furnished with the effects of marriage, and in doing so it infringes Article 6.1 of the Basic Law, which prevents the legislature from substantially restructuring the relationships in marriage and the family from the point of view of the law of persons, and which prohibits basing family law in equal measure on marriage and a same-sex civil partnership.

Marriage enjoys special protection as an essential element of state order to guarantee the conditions for the care and upbringing of children in the interest of parents and children, but also of the state community. If parallel institutions are created for other forms of partnership that would be equal to marriage, this levelling out robs marriage of its special protection. Article 6.1 of the Basic Law provides that the relationships between the sexes under the law of persons and family law ought to be organised by the standards of marriage where these are long-term partnerships. The constitutional directive requires that the unity and personal responsibility of marriage are respected and promoted. This has a directive effect for the whole area of public and private law. In this context, Article 6.1 of the Basic Law prohibits not only making marriage available to same-sex partnerships, but also creating beside marriage an institution incorporating structural elements of marriage without objective necessity, since this would amount to a circumvention of the prohibition. The special requirement of protection contained in Article 6.1 of the Basic Law demands a clear distance between the legal form of marriage and that of a civil partnership. Marriage enjoys protection of its exclusivity. The Basic Law grants other partnerships only general protection, but not special protection as institutions. On the basis of this distinction, there is a requirement to differentiate and a prohibition on the reproduction of the legal structure of marriage by other partnerships. They may not be structured on the model of marriage, create a faithful reproduction of marriage or incorporate provisions that shape the core of marriage law. If the registered civil partnership is to a large extent brought into line with marriage, there is an infringement of this requirement. Apparent deviations from marriage law contained in the statute transpired, when examined more closely, to be the same as features of marriage. In contrast, some real differences from marriage contained in the statute did not demonstrate an independent concept. The legislature's intention of copying marriage in the Civil Partnerships Act becomes even clearer as a result of the provisions to be included in the Civil Partnerships Supplementary Act. This applies in particular to the tax-law provisions, whose effect is equivalent to that of a limited joint assessment of spouses.

b) Article 6.1 of the Basic Law is also infringed, according to the applicants, in that the civil partnership is not an impediment to marriage because it is not defined as such in the Civil Partnerships Act. Thus the Act permits a registered civil partnership to exist side-by-side with marriage although the obligations in the registered partnership are incompatible with those of marriage. This constitutes a serious encroachment upon marriage.

c) In addition, in introducing the limited custody in Article 1 § 9, the Act encroaches upon the parental rights of the parent without custody. It infringes Article 14.1 of the Basic Law because without a sufficiently weighty reason it encroaches upon the testamentary freedom of the partners by giving a compulsory portion to the surviving partner, which cannot be justified merely by the need to give financial protection to the surviving partner. In addition, the statute violates Article 3.1 of the Basic Law. Although there are good reasons for providing a comparable legal framework to other long-term relationships based on permanence and mutual support, these other partnerships worthy of protection are not taken into account in the Act. Finally, the Act contains no tax-law provisions, although the duty of maintenance created in the Act is inseparably linked to the need for tax relief.

III.

…

B.

The applications are unfounded. The Civil Partnerships Act is compatible with the Basic Law.

I.

The Civil Partnerships Act was passed in conformity with the Basic Law. It was not subject to the approval of the *Bundesrat*.

1. The Act contains no provisions that require approval under Article 84.1 of the Basic Law.

a) The requirement of approval in Article 84.1 of the Basic Law is intended to protect the Constitution's fundamental decision, with regard to the jurisdiction of the *Länder* in administrative matters, to protect the federal structure of the state and prevent alterations to the federal structure being introduced by way of legislation below the constitutional level bypassing the objections of the *Bundesrat* (see BVerfGE 37, 363, (379 et seq.); 55, 274 (319); 75, 108 (150)). On the basis of this purpose of Article 84.1 of the Basic Law, a statute does not require approval merely because it affects the jurisdiction of the *Länder* to implement it by causing the *Länder* to act or cease to act administratively in a particular sphere. Instead, the requirement of approval by the *Bundesrat* follows from a provision of federal law establishing *Land* authorities or governing their procedure (see BVerfGE 75, 108 (150)). A provision establishing new *Land* authorities does not refer solely to a federal statute providing for new *Land* authorities, but also to a federal statute laying down the duties of a *Land* authority in detail. In contrast, the statute governs the procedure of the *Land* authorities if it bindingly determines the manner and form in which a federal statute is implemented. This includes the case where substantive legal provisions of the statute not merely require the administrative authorities to act, but at the same time prescribe a specific procedural manner of acting in administrative matters (see BVerfGE 55, 274 (321); 75, 108 (152)).

b) Measured against this, the provisions of the Civil Partnerships Act cited by the applicants contain no rules of administrative procedure in the meaning of Article 84.1 of the Basic Law.

aa) Article 1 § 1.1 of the Civil Partnerships Act governs only the substantive-law requirements for the creation of a registered civil partnership. The Act does not contain a federal-law provision governing the administrative procedure when civil partnerships are registered. It does require that the declarations necessary to create a civil partnership must be made to an authority, but it leaves open which authority is competent to receive the declarations. Nor does it make provisions for the procedure when the parties make mutual declarations. It neither specifies a particular registration procedure nor lays down what form the cooperation of the competent authority is to take when a civil partnership is created. Formal requirements on private individuals making declarations of intention such as are contained, for example, in Article 1 § 1.1 sentence 1 of the Civil Partnerships Act, are not provisions governing administrative procedure in the meaning of Article 84.1 of the Basic Law. The *Länder* used the scope they were given and in the implementation provisions passed by them have now created varying jurisdictions of *Land* authorities who have to exercise their administrative activity in registering civil partnerships under the relevant *Land*-law rules.

bb) Article 3 § 25 of the Civil Partnerships Act does not create the jurisdiction of a *Land* authority. Admittedly, Article 17a of the Introductory Act to the Civil Code (now Article 17b of the Introductory Act to the Civil Code), which was newly introduced by this statute and which determines the application of the relevant law for registered civil partnerships, in Article 17a.2 sentence 1, provides that the rule in Article 10.2 of the Introductory Act to the Civil Code applies with the necessary changes. Under sentence 1 thereof, on or after marriage spouses may choose their future name by declaration to the registrar of births, deaths and marriages. However, this reference does not mean that the registrar has mandatory jurisdiction to receive civil partners' declarations as to their name too. Against the background that the Civil Partnerships Act itself has left it open which authority is to have jurisdiction over the creation of registered civil partnerships, the provision that Article 10.2 of the Introductory Act to the Civil Code is to apply merely with the necessary changes is to be understood to mean that the reference is to the substantive-law content of Article 10.2 sentence 1 of the Introductory Act to the Civil Code, but not that a provision as to jurisdiction was made in this way.

cc) Equally, Article 3 § 6 of the Civil Partnerships Act does not give new jurisdiction to the registry offices, but applies their existing jurisdiction to another group of persons when, supplementing § 2 sentence 1 of the Minorities Name Alteration Act (*Minderheiten-Namensänderungsgesetz*), it extends the alteration of the birth name of a person subject to the conditions of § 1 of the Act, that is, by declaration to the registrar of births, deaths and marriages, not only, in the case of a declaration of the spouse to this effect, to the family name, but also to the partnership name, provided the civil partner agrees to the change of name by declaration to the registrar. This does not entail a change of the content of the registrar's duties (see BVerfGE 75, 108 (151)).

dd) The fact that the aliens' authorities under Article 3 § 11 of the Civil Partnerships Act, which relates to §§ 27a, 29.4 and 31.1 of the Aliens Act (*Ausländergesetz*), may now also issue a basic residence permit (*Aufenthaltserlaubnis*), residence

permit for specific purposes (*Aufenthaltsbewilligung*) or residence permit for exceptional purposes (*Aufenthaltsbefugnis*) to foreign civil partners of a foreigner in order to establish and maintain the civil partnership merely extends the factual circumstances subject to which a residence status may be established. As a result of this, the duty of the aliens' authorities is quantitatively increased, but its content is not changed. A requirement for approval can certainly not be derived from the fact that the aliens' authorities are now obliged to base their considerations when exercising their discretion in the case of civil partnerships on Article 2.1 in conjunction with Article 1.1 of the Basic Law, not, as in the case of marriages, on Article 6.1 of the Basic Law. In exercising the discretion granted them, authorities must always taken into account the fundamental rights of those affected, no matter on what fundamental right they may rely.
ee) Finally, Article 3 § 16 number 10 of the Civil Partnerships Act also does not make the Act subject to approval under Article 84.1 of the Basic Law. As a result of the revision of § 661.3 number 1 letter b of the Code of Civil Procedure (*Zivilprozessordnung*), the international jurisdiction of German courts under § 606a of the Code of Civil Procedure now includes the case where a civil partnership is created before a German registrar of births, deaths and marriages. This provision does not impose a duty on the registrar, but by its wording links the jurisdiction of German courts in civil partnership matters to the requirement that a German registrar of births, deaths and marriages was involved when the civil partnership was created. It governs the judicial proceedings, for which Article 84.1 of the Basic Law is not applicable (see BVerfGE 14, 197 (219)). It is conceivable that there could be an objectively unjustified unequal treatment of civil partners whose partnership, by reason of the differing jurisdiction provisions of the *Länder*, was created not before a registrar of births, deaths and marriages but before another competent authority; but this result could be avoided by interpreting § 661.3 number 1 letter b of the Code of Civil Procedure in conformity with the Basic Law.
2. Nor does the fact that in Article 1 § 3.3 and § 3.4 competencies of the registrar of births, deaths and marriages were named before the Civil Partnerships Act was finally consented to and promulgated lead to the statute being subject to approval. This version of the statute was corrected in a manner that is constitutionally unobjectionable.
a) Even if the Basic Law contains no provisions on the correction of adopted bills, the requirements of a functioning legislature, justify, following the traditional government practice, being able to correct printer's errors and other evident errors in the bill without again involving the legislative bodies, as is provided in § 61 of the Joint Rules of Procedure of the Federal Ministries (*Gemeinsame Geschäftsordnung*

der Bundesministerien – GGO) and in § 122.3 of the Rules of Procedure of the *Bundestag* (*Geschäftsordnung des Bundestages*; see BVerfGE 48, 1 (18)).
Admittedly, the correction of adopted bills is admissible only within very narrow limits outside the resolution procedure in Article 76 et seq. of the Basic Law, because of the right of the legislative bodies to respect and to the preservation of their exclusive competence to decide the content of legislation. The criterion for defining such limits in detail and for the admission, in exceptional circumstances, of the correction of an adopted bill, is that it is obviously incorrect. An obvious incorrectness may be shown not only in the text of the statute, but in particular also by taking into account its meaning in context and the parliamentary background materials of the statute. The decisive factor is that the correction does not affect the legally significant substantive content of the statute and with it the identity of the statute (see BVerfGE 48, 1 (18-19)).
b) On the basis of these criteria, the correction carried out of Article 1 § 3.3 and 3.4 of the Civil Partnerships Act did not exceed the limits of what is constitutionally admissible.
aa) The obvious incorrectness of the version of Article 1 § 3.3 and 3.4 of the Civil Partnerships Act passed by the legislative bodies consists in the clear contradiction between on the one hand the text of the statute, which by reason of the recommendation as a resolution by the Committee on Legal Affairs of 8 November 2000 (*Bundestag* printed paper 14/4545) was before the *Bundestag* when it passed resolutions on the second and third reading of the bill and on which the proceedings in the *Bundesrat* were based, and on the other hand the reasons for justification of this statute given by the Committee on Legal Affairs in its report of 9 November 2000 (*Bundestag* printed paper 14/4550), which both equally constitute the basis for the consultation and enactment of the legislative bodies.
At the beginning of November 2000, the SPD and BÜNDNIS 90/DIE GRÜNEN parliamentary parties introduced in the Committee on Legal Affairs responsible and in the committees on Family Affairs, Senior Citizens, Women and Youth (Committee printed paper, *AusschussDrucks* 14/508) and on Labour and Social Affairs (Committee printed paper 14/944), which were co-consulting, a motion for alteration of the bill, which, just as for other provisions, in particular Article 1 § 1 of the bill, for all paragraphs of Article 1 § 3 also provided that the registrar of births, death and marriages should be deleted as the authority competent to receive declarations and the effectiveness of declarations on the partnership name should be made subject to making the declarations before the authority responsible. This motion was the basis of the resolution of the committees and received a majority in favour there. The recommendation for a resolution forwarded to the *Bundestag* by the Committee on Legal Affairs then, however, contained alterations to this effect

only of paragraphs 1 and 2 of Article 1 § 3 of the bill, while it was recommended for paragraphs 3 and 4 that the unchanged previous versions should be accepted, still containing the reference to the registrar of births, deaths and marriages. In the report of the Committee on Legal Affairs, which was also forwarded to the *Bundestag*, to which the recommended resolution referred, in contrast, it was stated with regard to the whole of Article 1 § 3 that the changes recommended here were provisions consequent on the alteration of Article 1 § 1.1 of the Civil Partnerships Act. There was express reference to its reasoning. This included the statement that the bill did not name an authority that is to be responsible for registering the civil partnership.

This reasoning of Article 1 § 3 of the Civil Partnerships Act contradicts the text version of its paragraphs 3 and 4, and when taken into account together with the account of how it originated it shows that the wording of these paragraphs was incorrect. The contradiction between the text and the reasoning also entered the bills approved by the *Bundestag* and the *Bundesrat*. Both of them, on the basis of the resolution recommended by the Committee on Legal Affairs of the *Bundestag*, based their resolutions on the unchanged text of Article 1 § 3.3 and 3.4 of the Civil Partnerships Act. But the resolution was passed subject to the premise that had resulted in the amendment of Article 1 § 1 of the bill; it was intended that there should be no naming whatsoever of a competent authority in the bill.

bb) The version of Article 1 § 3.3 and 3.4 of the Civil Partnerships Act corrected in the proceedings under § 61.2 of the Joint Rules of Procedure of the Federal Ministries and promulgated in this form conforms with the intention of the legislature expressed in the statute.

If Article 1 § 1 of the Civil Partnerships Act, which creates the institution of the registered civil partnership and governs the essential requirements for the creation of this community of persons, in its wording and reasoning does not lay down the authority that is to be responsible for registering the registered civil partnership, and if this failure to mention the authority is consistently repeated not only in the further following statutory provisions but also in the two first paragraphs of Article 1 § 3 of the Civil Partnerships Act, in that references are only to the authority responsible, then this makes it clear that the legislature wishes to leave it to the *Länder* to decide which authority they will determine as responsible for civil partnership matters. It is consistent with this if in the corrected and promulgated version of Article 1 § 3.3 and 3.4 of the Civil Partnerships Act now, taking over the text on which the resolution adopted by the Committee on Legal Affairs was based, there is no attempt whatsoever to make a statement as to the authority to which the civil partners' declarations on names law are to be made.

cc) Furthermore, this is confirmed by the opinions on the correction proceedings. These opinions unanimously state that the statute was not intended to make a decision on the jurisdiction of a particular authority in civil partnership matters. The suggestion of correcting Article 1 § 3.3 and 3.4 of the Civil Partnerships Act came from the office of the Committee on Legal Affairs, with reference to a copying error to this effect made when the recommended resolution was drafted. Thereupon, the Federal Ministry of Justice informed both the President of the *Bundestag* and the President of the *Bundesrat* on the error in copying the resolutions drafted in the Committee on Legal Affairs to the recommended resolution, defined this as an obvious error and commenced the correction procedure under § 61.2 of the Joint Rules of Procedure of the Federal Ministries. In the course of this procedure, the representatives of the parliamentary groups in the Committee on Legal Affairs were involved in the matter. In the oral hearing, the *Bundestag* member Beck (BÜNDNIS 90/DIE GRÜNEN), without contradiction from the members present von Renesse (SPD), Geis (CDU/CSU) and Braun (FDP), submitted that the representatives of all parliamentary groups had agreed to the correction. In letters of 7 and 12 December 2000, the Presidents of the *Bundestag* and the *Bundesrat* approved the correction.

3. The government parliamentary groups first introduced a Bill to End the Discrimination of Same-Sex Partnerships: Civil Partnerships (*Gesetzentwurf zur Beendigung der Diskriminierung gleichgeschlechtlicher Gemeinschaften: Lebenspartnerschaften, Bundestag* printed paper 14/3751); in the course of the legislative procedure, at the recommendation of the *Bundestag* Committee on Legal Affairs, this bill was divided into the Act of the same name that is to be reviewed in the present proceedings, with its substantive provisions on the registered civil partnership, and a bill with predominantly procedural implementation regulations (*Bundestag* printed papers 14/4545 and 14/4550 with annexes); this division does not violate the Constitution. Above all, the division that was carried out does not make the Civil Partnerships Act subject to approval.

a) The *Bundestag* is not constitutionally prevented from dealing with a legislative project in several statutes, in the exercise of its legislative freedom. In doing this, as in the present case, even in the course of the legislative procedure, it may collect the substantive provisions it intends in one statute against which the *Bundesrat* has only a right of objection, and for the provisions intended to govern the administrative procedure of the *Länder* it may design another statute, which requires approval; in practice, this happens quite frequently (see BVerfGE 34, 9 (28); 37, 363 (382)).

The *Bundestag*'s possibility, by dividing the contents of a statute into two or more statutes, of restricting the *Bundesrat*'s right of approval to one part of the intended legislation follows from the *Bundestag*'s right to legislate. Such a division does not inadmissibly restrict the right of the *Länder* to cooperate in the legislation of the Federal Government, nor is there a shift of the constitutionally allocated weights of the *Bundestag* and the *Bundesrat* in legislation (see BVerfGE 37, 363 (379-380); 55, 274 (319); 75, 108 (150)).

aa) In the area of concurrent legislative powers, which under Article 74.1 number 2 of the Basic Law also includes matters of civil status and thus the introduction of the registered civil partnership as a new civil status, the *Länder*, under Article 72.1 of the Basic Law, have power to legislate as long as and to the extent that the Federal Government has not made use of its legislative power by statute. This guarantees the original legislative power of the *Länder* to legislate quantitatively and qualitatively wherever the federal legislature has not yet passed legislation. But if the federal legislature, under the conditions of Article 72.2 of the Basic Law, makes use of its legislative power, the *Bundesrat* merely cooperates in federal legislation under Article 50 of the Basic Law. Here, the requirement that the *Bundesrat* approves a statute under the Basic Law is the exception to the rule (see BVerfGE 37, 363 (381)). *Inter alia*, this requirement exists under Article 84.1 of the Basic Law if the statute exclusively or together with other legislation contains provisions on the establishment of authorities or on administrative procedures and thus encroaches on the competence of the *Länder* under Article 83 of the Basic Law to implement federal statutes as matters of their own concern and to pass the necessary *Land* law provisions for this purpose. The *Bundesrat*'s approval of such a statute is intended to ensure that the *Länder* are not deprived of their legislative competence in the administrative procedure by a federal statute below the constitutional level against the will of the majority of the *Bundesrat*. This blocking effect guarantees that they have influence on the contents of the federal statute as a whole. For the requirement of the approval of the *Bundesrat*, by the case-law of the Federal Constitutional Court, extends to the whole statute as a legislative unit, that is, also to the provisions that in themselves do not require approval (see BVerfGE 8, 274 (294); 37, 363 (381); 55, 274 (319)). In the present case it is not necessary to decide whether, in view of the criticism in the literature (see, for example, Lücke in: Sachs, *Grundgesetz, Kommentar*, 2nd ed. 1999, *Art. 77*, marginal number 15; Maurer, *Staatsrecht I*, 2nd ed. 2001, *§ 17*, marginal numbers 74 et seq.) this case-law should continue to be followed, for in the present case the legislature did not choose this approach.

If the federal legislature, in contrast, omits provisions relating to administrative procedure in a statute, this corresponds to the model of the constitutional allocation of competence between the Federal Government and the *Länder* under Article 83 and Article 84 of the Basic Law. The *Bundesrat*, under Article 77.3 of the Basic

Law, has merely a right of objection to such a statute; under Article 77.4 of the Basic Law, an objection may be rejected by the *Bundestag*.

bb) The same applies to the case where the federal legislature does intend to pass not only legislation under substantive law but also regulations for its implementation in the administrative procedure of the *Länder*, and instead of including both sets of provisions in one statute, it puts each in a separate statute. If, as a result, the requirement of the *Bundesrat*'s approval relates only to the statute that contains the procedural part, this does not constitute a shift detrimental to the *Länder* of the competencies laid down in the Basic Law. For the *Bundesrat* has a right of approval of substantive-law federal legislation – except in the special cases laid down in the Basic Law – only where the federal legislature encroaches upon the area of competence of the *Länder* under Article 83 et. seq. of the Basic Law. But such an encroachment is effected only by the procedural statute, which is separated from the substantive-law content of the legislation.

The division prevents the *Bundesrat* acquiring a right of approval with regard to the substantive-law provisions too, as a result of dealing with substantive-law and procedural-law provision together. At the same time it ensures that the *Bundestag* can legislate on the matters allocated to it that do not require approval without being dependent on the approval of the *Bundesrat*. If the *Bundestag* chooses to proceed in this way, it bases the structure of its legislation precisely on the constitutional division of competence between the Federal Government and the *Land* governments. The *Länder*, as the present case shows, suffer no loss of competence as a result of this. They have now themselves on their own responsibility passed the necessary procedural regulations for the implementation of the Civil Partnerships Act.

b) Whether the *Bundestag*'s right of disposal with regard to the division of legal material into several statutes is subject to constitutional limits in the individual case, and when such limits, if they exist, are overstepped, need not be decided here either (see BVerfGE 24, 184 (199-200); 77, 84 (103)). The decision of the federal legislature to collect the provisions not requiring approval on the new institution of the registered civil partnership in one statute and to make the provisions thereof that are subject to approval the content of a separate state is free of arbitrariness.

aa) If the *Bundestag* is presumed to have had a motive in dividing the material of the statute between two statutes only in order in this way to deprive the *Bundesrat* of the possibility of preventing the intended substantive-law provisions together with the procedural provisions by refusing its approval, this manner of proceeding does not appear to be arbitrary. Under the assumption made until now that a whole statute becomes subject to approval if it contains only one provision that is subject to approval (see BVerfGE 8, 274 (294); 55, 274 (319)), such a division is a legitimate way to prevent a process of extension of the requirement of approval of statutes and to make it possible for parliament to realise its enactment. To conclude from such a motive on the part of the legislature that its procedure was abusive would in the last instance lead to imposing a duty on the *Bundestag* always to pass procedural regulations itself and together with the substantive law. On the one hand this would make it possible for the *Bundesrat* to exercise its influence more strongly on substantive law too, but on the other side it would gradually deprive the *Länder* of legislative competencies where they have original jurisdiction under the Constitution. Such an approach might lead to a general shift of constitutional competencies, which is precisely what Article 84.1 of the Basic Law is intended to prevent, but in contrast, dividing the legal material into two statutes could not have this result.

bb) Nor are the substantive-law provisions contained in the Civil Partnerships Act, contrary to the applicants' opinion, a "torso of a statute". They are comprehensible in themselves and sufficiently definite. They structure the legal position in such a way that the persons affected can allow their conduct to be guided by them. There was in particular no necessity for the legislature to legislate on the right of maintenance for civil partners and the tax treatment of maintenance payments based on this in one and the same statute. The maintenance rights of spouses have also always been defined separately from their treatment under tax law by the legislature in the taxation statutes.

Finally, the Act is also enforceable. This is unequivocally confirmed by the various implementation regulations of the *Länder*.

II.

The Civil Partnerships Act is also constitutional from a substantive point of view.

1. It is compatible with Article 6.1 of the Basic Law. The introduction of the new institution of the registered civil partnership for same-sex couples and its legal structure infringe neither the freedom of marriage guaranteed in Article 6.1 of the Basic Law nor the institutional guarantee laid down there. The registered civil partnership is also compatible with Article 6.1 of the Basic Law in its character as a fundamental provision that determines values.

a) As a fundamental right, Article 6.1 of the Basic Law protects the freedom to enter into a marriage with a partner one has chosen oneself (see BVerfGE 31, 58 (67); 76, 1 (42)). This right to unhindered access to marriage is not affected by the Civil Partnerships Act.

aa) Even after the introduction of the registered civil partnership by the Civil Partnerships Act, the path to marriage is still open to every person who has the capacity to marry. However, marriage is only possible to a partner of the other sex, since the fact that the spouses are of different sexes is an inherent characteristic of marriage (see BVerfGE 10, 59 (66)) and the right of freedom to marry relates only to this. Even after the Civil Partnerships Act, same-sex couples are still unable to marry. The only legal institution open to them for a long-term commitment is the registered civil partnership.

Similarly, the Act neither directly nor indirectly affects the freedom of heterosexual couples to marry. Since they cannot enter into a registered civil partnership, this institution cannot prevent them from marrying.

bb) Access to marriage is not restricted by the Civil Partnerships Act. Under the statute, a civil partnership that has already been entered into does not prevent marriage. The Civil Partnerships Act does not create an express impediment to marriage in this case. However, in the case of such a constellation, the registrar of births, deaths and marriages must examine whether, as a requirement of marriage, the partners have a serious intention to be married, and the registrar must refuse to participate in the wedding if such an intention is missing (§ 1310.1 sentence 2 in conjunction with § 1314.2 number 5 of the Civil Code).

However, the legislature left it open whether a marriage entered into when a registered civil partnership already existed has legal consequences for the continuing existence of the civil partnership and if so, what these would be. The answer to these questions is thus in the last instance left to case-law.

This gap in the statute can be closed constitutionally only if consideration is paid to the protection owed to marriage under Article 6.1 of the Basic Law. Here it is important to take into account that marriage as the form of a close two-person relationship between a man and a woman is characterised by personal exclusivity. Marriage might lose this characteristic if one or both of the spouses remained permitted to keep their civil partnership with another partner, which is also intended to be permanent. The protection of marriage under Article 6.1 of the Basic Law requires that alongside marriage no other legally binding partnership of a spouse should be permitted, and in Article 1 § 1.2 of the Civil Partnerships Act the legislature itself proceeded on this assumption.

For this reason, it is suggested in the literature of legal scholarship that the possibility that the Civil Partnerships Act does not exclude, of entering into a marriage when a civil partnership exists, is linked to the legal consequence that the marriage dissolves the civil partnership by operation of law, so that it no longer legally exists (see Schwab, *Zeitschrift für das gesamte Familienrecht* 2001, p. 385 (389)). This would be a way to close the existing statutory gap in a way that did justice to Article 6.1 of the Basic Law. Admittedly, this solution has a more unfavourable effect on the other partner than an annulment under Article 1 § 15 of the Civil Partnerships Act, but in view of the guarantee in Article 6.1 of the Basic Law it is acceptable.

The requirement of protecting marriage as a way of life between a man and a woman, however, could also be done justice to if entering into a marriage were made subject to the requirements that there is no civil partnership or is no longer a civil partnership. Such an impediment to marriage could not inadmissibly restrict the guarantee of freedom in Article 6.1 of the Basic Law, because its factual reason would lie precisely in the nature and in the form of marriage (see BVerfGE 36, 146 (163)). Just as an existing marriage prevents a new marriage from being entered into (§ 1306 of the Civil Code), in order not to endanger the two-person relationship of marriage, it conforms to the protection of marriage to open it only to those who have not already bound themselves legally in another partnership. This possibility of giving marriage the required protection would, in addition, offer the protection of confidence to those who, in the registered civil partnership, have chosen a way of life that the legislature has now made available to them as a legally binding community of responsibility of a permanent nature. It would be guaranteed for them that their partnership could not be dissolved merely by the unilateral decision to marry of the other partner. It is true that a prohibition of entering into marriage while the civil partnership existed would as a general rule be objectively justified. However, it would restrict the freedom to marry. It need not be decided here whether the present statute also makes it possible for the gap to be filled by case-law in this respect. If one takes into account the far-reaching consequences of the termination or dissolution of a registered civil partnership for the personal life and the financial situation of the individual persons affected, which, depending on what legal construction is chosen in order to exclude marriage and civil partnership existing side-by-side, may be very different in nature, it would seem appropriate for the legislature itself to determine whether an existing civil partnership prevents a marriage taking place or a marriage leads to the dissolution of an existing civil partnership.

b) When the legislature introduced the registered civil partnership in the Civil Partnerships Act, it did not violate the constitutional requirement of Article 6.1 of the Basic Law to offer and protect marriage as a way of life (institutional guarantee, see BVerfGE 10, 59 (66-67); 31, 58 (69-70); 80, 81 (92)). The object of legislation of the Act is not marriage.

aa) The Basic Law itself contains no definition of marriage, but presupposes it as a special form of human cohabitation. The realisation of the constitutional protection of marriage therefore needs a legal provision that structures and restricts what form of partnership enjoys the protection of the Constitution. Here, the legislature has considerable freedom of drafting in determining the form and content of marriage (see BVerfGE 31, 58 (70); 36, 146 (162); 81, 1 (6-7)). The Basic Law guarantees the institution of marriage not in the abstract, but in the form that corresponds to current prevailing opinions, which are expressed definitively in the statutory provisions (see BVerfGE 31, 58 (82-83). However, in shaping marriage, the legislature must take into account the essential structural principles that follow from the application of Article 6.1 of the Basic Law to marriage as it is actually encountered in connection with the nature of the fundamental right guaranteed as a freedom and in connection with other constitutional norms (see BVerfGE 31, 58 (69)). Part of the content of marriage, as it has stood the test of time despite social change and the concomitant changes of its legal structure and been shaped by the Basic Law, is that it is the union of one man with one woman to form a permanent partnership, based on a free decision and with the support of the state (see BVerfGE 10, 59 (66); 29, 166 (176); 62, 323 (330)), in which man and woman are in an equal partnership with one another (see BVerfGE 37, 217 (249 et seq.); 103, 89 (101)) and may decide freely on the organisation of their cohabitation (see BVerfGE 39, 169 (183); 48, 327 (338); 66, 84 (94)).

bb) This protection does not cover the institution of the registered civil partnership. The fact that the partners are of the same sex distinguishes it from marriage and at the same time constitutes it. The registered civil partnership is not marriage within the meaning of Article 6.1 of the Basic Law. It grants rights to same-sex couples. In this way, the legislature takes account of Article 2.1 and Article 3.1 and 3.3 of the Basic Law, by helping these persons to better develop their personalities and by reducing discrimination.

cc) Marriage as an institution is not affected by the Civil Partnerships Act itself in its constitutional structural principles and its organisation by the legislature. There has been no change to its legal foundation. All the provisions that give marriage a legal framework and furnish the institution with legal consequences continue to exist (see Federal Constitutional Court, judgment of 18 July 2001 – 1 BvQ 23/01 and 1 BvQ 26/01 –, *Neue Juristische Wochenschrift* 2001, 2457-2458). No prohibition on giving same-sex partners the possibility of a legally similarly structured partnership can be derived from the institutional guarantee, precisely because it relates only to marriage.

c) Article 6.1 of the Basic Law does not merely guarantee marriage in its essential structure, but also, as a binding value decision, requires special protection by the state order for the whole area of private and public law relating to marriage and the family (see BVerfGE 6, 55 (72); 55, 114 (126)). In order to satisfy the requirement of protection, it is in particular the duty of the state on the one hand to refrain from everything that damages or otherwise adversely affects marriage, and on the other hand to promote marriage by suitable measures (see BVerfGE 6, 55 (76); 28, 104

(113); 53, 224 (248); 76, 1 (41); 80, 81 (92-93); 99, 216 (231-232)). The legislature did not violate this in the Civil Partnerships Act.

aa) Marriage is neither damaged nor adversely affected in another way by the Civil Partnerships Act.

The particular protection accorded to marriage under Article 6.1 of the Basic Law prohibits treating it less favourably than other ways of life (see BVerfGE 6, 55 (76); 13, 290 (298-299); 28, 324 (356); 67, 186 (195-196); 87, 234 (256 et seq.); 99, 216 (232-233)).

(1) There is no such unfavourable treatment if the Civil Partnerships Act gives same-sex couples the possibility of entering into a registered civil partnership with rights and duties that are close to those of marriage.

It is true that in large areas the legislature has modelled the legal consequences of the new institution of the registered civil partnership on provisions of marriage law. But in this way, marriage or spouses are not treated less favourably that previously and not disadvantaged in relation to the civil partnership or civil partners. The institution of marriage is not threatened by any risk from an institution that is directed at persons who cannot be married to each other.

(2) Nor does the Civil Partnerships Act violate the prohibition of discrimination in that the legislature refrained in this Act from at the same time adding to the Federal Social Assistance Act (*Bundessozialhilfegesetz*) provisions that the income and property of both partners should be taken into account in the case of civil partners too in the means test that is a requirement for the grant of social assistance benefits. As a result, at present, in social assistance law, married couples are treated as a financial unit, but civil partners are not expressly also so treated. In the case of spouses, because of the aggregation of income that has to be made, this may lead to the reduction or elimination of the right to social assistance benefits, whereas civil partners without aggregation of income might receive unreduced social assistance benefits. However, any unfavourable treatment of married persons in this procedure was the result not of the Civil Partnerships Act, but of a lack of provisions to remedy this in the Federal Social Assistance Act. The Civil Partnerships Act specifically does not privilege civil partners as against spouses with regard to the obligation to maintain each other. If the proper legal conclusions are not drawn from this in social assistance law, there may be a violation there of the prohibition on discrimination under Article 6.1 of the Basic Law, but not as a result of the provisions of the Civil Partnerships Act, which alone are the subject of these proceedings for the abstract review of a statute.

bb) In introducing the new institution of the registered civil partnership, the legislature also did not violate the requirement of promoting marriage as a way of life.

The Act does not divest marriage of any promotion that it previously enjoyed. It merely gives legal protection to another partnership and gives it rights and duties.
cc) On account of the constitutional protection of marriage under Article 6.1 of the Basic Law, the legislature is not barred from treating marriage more favourably than other ways of life (see BVerfGE 6, 55 (76)). But the admissibility of giving favourable treatment to marriage over other ways of life in fulfilling and structuring the requirement to promote it does not give rise to a requirement contained in Article 6.1 of the Basic Law to disadvantage other ways of life in comparison to marriage. Justice Haas in her dissenting opinion fails to realise this when she understands the requirement to promote marriage in Article 6.1 of the Basic Law as a requirement to disadvantage ways of life other than marriage. Article 6.1 of the Basic Law gives favourable treatment to marriage in a constitutional protection granted only to marriage and imposes on the legislature a duty to promote it with the means appropriate to it. But a requirement to treat other ways of life unfavourably cannot be derived from this. The extent of the legal protection and promotion of marriage is in no way decreased if the legal system also recognises other ways of life that cannot enter into competition with marriage as a community of heterosexual partners. Nor can it be justified constitutionally to derive from the special protection of marriage a rule that such partnerships are to be structured in a way distant from marriage and to be given lesser rights. However, the legislature's duty to protect and promote marriage does require it to ensure that marriage can fulfil the function accorded it by the Constitution.
(1) If Article 6.1 of the Basic Law subjects marriage to special protection, the special element is the fact that marriage alone, in addition to the family, enjoys this constitutional protection as an institution, but no other way of life enjoys it. Marriage cannot be abolished nor can its essential structural principles be altered without an amendment of the Constitution … A constitutional duty of promotion exists for marriage alone. To attach to the special nature of the protection a meaning above and beyond this to the effect that marriage must always be protected more than other partnerships, even in its extent … has no basis either in the wording of the fundamental right or in its genesis.
In the course of the deliberations in the Parliamentary Council, Article 6.1 of the Basic Law underwent a large number of amendments to the text, and here, the wording often alternated between a protection of marriage and a special protection of marriage … It cannot be inferred from these debates that these changes to the wording were made because marriage and the family were to have greater or lesser protection. Instead, there are clear indications that these changes arose solely from the feeling for language of the persons in question. For example, when the *Deutscher Sprachverein* suggested deleting the word "special" (*"besonderen"*) and

choosing the wording "Marriage and the family ... are under the protection of the Constitution" (*"Ehe und Familie ... stehen unter dem Schutze der Verfassung"*), von Mangoldt said that this was exactly the same in content, but worded better ….
In the debates on Article 6.1 of the Basic Law, the question of the protection of new ways of life also played a substantial role … Here, in particular the argument that the special protection of the family excluded the equal treatment of illegitimate children in Article. 6.5 of the Basic Law … was unsuccessful. If Mangoldt, as rapporteur, in his Written Report on Article 6.1 of the Basic Law finally noted that this fundamental right was scarcely more than a declaration in the case of which it was not really evident what effect it had as directly applicable law …, then this reflects that although there was agreement on subjecting marriage and the family to constitutional protection, there was no clarification as to what this means in detail for its relationship to other ways of life. At all events, a requirement of distance cannot be based on this.
(2) Article 6.1 of the Basic Law protects marriage as it is structured by the legislature from time to time, preserving its essential fundamental principles (see BVerfGE 31, 58 (82-83)). As a partnership lived by human beings it is both a sphere of freedom and at the same time part of society, from whose changes it is not excluded. The legislature can react to these and adapt the structure of marriage to changed needs. In this way, the relationship of marriage to other forms of human cohabitation also changes. The same applies if the legislature does not restructure marriage by statute but provides for other partnerships. Therefore ways of life do not stand at a fixed distance from each other, but in a relative relation. At the same time, they may differ from or resemble each other by reason of their given structure not only in the rights and duties allocated to them, but also in their function and with regard to the group of persons who find access to them. Thus the protection of marriage as an institution cannot be separated from the persons who are addressed by the provision, for whom marriage it to be made available as a protected way of life.
(3) The duty of the state to promote marriage must orient itself towards the protective purpose of Article 6.1 of the Basic Law. If the legislature itself, in creating norms, contributed to marriage losing its function, it would violate the requirement of promotion under Article 6.1 of the Basic Law. Such a danger might exist if the legislature created another institution in competition with marriage, with the same function, and, for example, gave it the same rights and lesser duties, so that the two institutions were interchangeable. Such an interchangeability, however, is not associated with the registered civil partnership. It cannot enter into competition with marriage, if for no other reason that that the group of persons for whom the institution is intended does not overlap with the group of married persons. The registered

civil partnership, because of this difference, is also not marriage with a wrong label, as is assumed in the two minority votes, but something different from marriage. Its different nature does not result from its name, but from the circumstance that not man and woman, but two persons of the same sex can create a union in the registered civil partnership. In their totality, the structural principles that characterise marriage give it the form and exclusivity in which it enjoys constitutional protection as an institution. Article 6.1 of the Basic Law, however, does not reserve individual structural elements of this group for marriage alone. It does not prohibit the legislature from offering legal forms for a permanent cohabitation to other constellations of persons than the union of man and woman. The characteristic of permanence does not make such legal relationships marriage. Nor is it discernible in any other way that they could harm the structure of this institution.

2. The Civil Partnerships Act violates neither the special prohibition of discrimination of Article 3.3 sentence 1 of the Basic Law nor the general principle of equality in Article 3.1 of the Basic Law.

a) The fact that the statute opens the registered civil partnership only to same-sex couples (Article 1 § 1.1 of the Civil Partnerships Act) embodies no unfavourable treatment of heterosexual couples on account of their sex under Article 3.3 sentence 1 of the Basic Law.

The Act does not associate rights and duties not with the sex of a person, but takes as its starting point the combination of sexes of a community of persons, and to this community of persons it offers access to the registered partnership. It then allocates rights and duties to the persons in this community. Just as marriage, with its restriction to a two-person relationship between man and woman, does not discriminate against same-sex couples on account of their gender, the civil partnership does not discriminate against heterosexual couples on account of their gender. Men and women are always treated equally. They may enter into marriage with a person of the opposite sex, but not with one of their own sex. They may enter into a civil partnership with a person of their own sex, but not with one of the other sex.

b) It does not infringe Article 3.1 of the Basic Law that persons of different sex cohabiting with each other and communities of mutual support between relatives have no possibility of becoming registered civil partnerships.

Article 3.1 of the Basic Law prohibits treating a group of persons who are addressed by a statute differently from other persons addressed by the statute although there are no differences between the two groups of such a nature and such weight that they could justify the unequal treatment (see BVerfGE 55, 72 (88); 84, 348 (359); 101, 239 (269); established case-law). However, such differences do exist between same-sex couples and the other social communities of persons.

aa) The registered civil partnership makes it possible for same-sex couples to put their partnership on a legally recognised basis and to bind themselves permanently and responsibly together, which has previously been impossible for them because they may not marry. In contrast, the desire of heterosexual couples to join themselves bindingly and permanently is, in the estimation of those concerned, just as important to them as that of same-sex couples is to them, and essentially also similar … But in contrast to same-sex couples, they have access to the institution of marriage for this purpose. The difference, that children of both spouses can be born to a permanent two-person relationship between man and woman, but not to a same-sex partnership, justifies directing heterosexual couples to marriage if they wish to give their relationship a permanent legally binding form. They are not disadvantaged by this.
bb) There are also differences in the relation of the same-sex partnerships to the communities of mutual support between siblings or other relatives, and these differences justify different treatment. This relates even to the exclusivity of the registered civil partnership, which admits no further relationship of the same kind beside itself, whereas communities of mutual support between siblings and other relatives are often part of further comparable relationships and also exist side-by-side with another relationship by marriage or partnership. Communities of mutual support between relatives, in addition, even under existing law in a certain respect contain a guarantee that was opened to same-sex couples only when the civil partnership was created. Thus, in connection with relations, there are rights to refuse to give evidence, rights of succession and in part also rights to a compulsory portion and for it to be given tax relief.
cc) Admittedly, the legislature is not generally prevented from opening new possibilities for heterosexual couples or for other communities of mutual support to put their relationship in a legal form if this can be done without the given legal structure being interchangeable with marriage. However, there is no constitutional requirement to create such possibilities.
3. Nor are the provisions in the statute on the rights to custody and succession of civil partners and on maintenance law objectionable from a constitutional point of view.
a) aa) Under Article 1 § 9 of the Civil Partnerships Act, the civil partner of a parent with sole custody, with the agreement of the latter, has been given the power to share in decisions on matters relating to the child's everyday life if he or she lives together with the parent. At the same time, he or she has been given emergency custody for the situation where there is imminent danger and it is necessary to act for the wellbeing of the child. The same now applies to the spouse of a parent with custody who himself or herself is not a parent (Article 2 number 13 of the Civil

Partnerships Act: § 1687 b of the Civil Code). In creating this "limited custody" for the civil partner, the legislature does not encroach on the parental rights of the parent without custody under Article 6.2 of the Basic Law.

Article 6.2 sentence 1 of the Basic Law protects the care and upbringing of the children as a natural right of the parents and a duty incumbent in the first instance on them. The scope of protection of the parental right here fundamentally also includes the decision as to who has contact with the child and who is permitted to influence the child's education as a result of the transfer of the power to take decisions. Admittedly, the parental right needs to be further refined by the legislature (see BVerfGE 84, 168 (180)). It is incumbent on the legislature to allocate to each parent particular rights and duties if the conditions for a joint exercise of parental responsibility are lacking (see BVerfGE 92, 158 (178-179)), or to refer to the courts the decision as to the parent to whom parental custody is to be transferred in the individual case.

Article 1 § 9 of the Civil Partnerships Act takes up such a constellation where one parent has sole custody. It is not the "limited custody", which is based on the sole custody of the parent living in a civil partnership, that deprives the parent without custody of that custody, but the family-law provisions that give the parent no custody, or the family-court decisions that award sole custody not to this parent, but to the other parent. A parent's rights cannot be affected, if he or she has no custody in any case, if third parties who live together with the child, in agreement with the parent with sole custody, have some joint parental responsibility.

bb) In "limited custody", the legislature has created a new power of custody for spouses and civil partners of a parent with custody who themselves are not parents of the child as part of a permanent legally binding partnership such as marriage or registered civil partnership; this does not constitute a violation of the principle of equality before the law of Article 3.1 of the Basic Law. The provision does not unfairly disadvantage parents without custody who do not live together with the parent with custody in a legally confirmed community. They are granted other legal possibilities of obtaining custody for their child alone or together with the other parent. Whether parents without custody should be given "limited custody" for other reasons need not be decided here.

b) aa) Article 1 § 10.6 of the Civil Partnerships Act, which awards the surviving partner a compulsory portion, does not violate the testamentary freedom protected by Article 14.1 of the Basic Law.

Testamentary freedom is the testator's right in his or her lifetime to provide for his or her property to pass in a different way than it would under the rules of intestate succession (see BVerfGE 58, 377 (398); 99, 341 (350-351). Here the legislature is at liberty to determine the contents and limits of the right of succession. In drafting

this statute in detail, the legislature must safeguard the basic content of the constitutional guarantee of Article 14.1 of the Basic Law, act in harmony with all other constitutional norms and in particular the principle of proportionality and the principle of equality before the law (see BVerfGE 67, 329 (340)). It is not evident that the statutory provision on the surviving partner's right to a compulsory portion oversteps this limit, notwithstanding a general clarification as to which constitutional barriers the right to a compulsory portion is subject to.
The civil partner's right to succeed and right to a compulsory portion are part of the legal institution of the registered civil partnership, which gives the partners mutual rights and duties in a lifelong commitment. In their declaration that they intend to enter into the civil partnership the civil partners commit themselves to mutual care and support and to giving maintenance. This obligation to comprehensive mutual care justifies, just as in the case of spouses, providing a financial basis for the partner even after death by the right to a compulsory portion from the property of the deceased partner.
bb) Nor is Article 14.1 of the Basic Law violated because the inheritance of other persons entitled to inherit is reduced by the partner's statutory right of succession and right to a compulsory portion. Even if Article 6.1 of the Basic Law contained a constitutional prohibition on granting the next of kin a reasonable financial minimum share of the estate, and if in this respect the family member favoured in this way were constitutionally protected as an heir under Article 14.1 of the Basic Law, which may be left open here (see BVerfGE 91, 346 (359-360)), this indicates nothing about the amount or the share owed to the heir from the estate. This is determined solely by the statutory allocation provision, which, in order to be in harmony with the guarantee of a right of succession, must be appropriately structured (see BVerfGE 91, 346 (360, 362)).
The surviving civil partner's right of succession and right to a compulsory portion do not deprive that other relations of the deceased civil partner, who were already entitled to succeed. Another person entitled to inherit merely joins the group of persons entitled to inherit that are to be taken into account when the estate is distributed. In this way, the situation for the relations of the deceased who have rights of succession is no different than it would be if the testator were survived by a spouse or husband and not a civil partner. This structure does not constitute inappropriate treatment of the other persons entitled to inherit.
c) It was intended that the maintenance burdens for civil partners created by Article 1 §§ 5, 12 and 16 of the Civil Partnerships Act should be taken into account in income tax law, but because this provision is part of the draft of the Civil Partnerships Act Supplementary Act, which has not yet been passed, this cannot be done;

this does not makes the maintenance provisions of the Civil Partnerships Act unconstitutional.
Admittedly, the financial burden resulting from maintenance duties is a special and unavoidable burden for the taxpayer, and it is a circumstance that reduces the taxpayer's financial capacity and the failure to take it into account may infringe Article 3.1 of the Basic Law (see BVerfGE 68, 143 (152-153); 82, 60 (86-87)). But the introduction of the maintenance duties for civil partners did not create a legal situation that ignores this burden from an income-tax point of view. Under § 33a of the Income Tax Act (*Einkommensteuergesetz*), on application income tax is reduced by the deduction from a taxpayer's total income of expenses incurred by that taxpayer for the maintenance of a person with a statutory right to support from the taxpayer, in the amount of a sum assessed for the calendar year in question. Since a civil partner's right to maintenance is laid down by statute, it is to be taken into account under § 33a of the Income Tax Act as an extraordinary expense. Whether this form of consideration is adequate in comparison to the tax treatment of spouses is not a question that relates to the Civil Partnerships Act. It would have to be clarified by a constitutional review of the income-tax provisions; the applications for judicial review do not comprise these.

C.

With regard to the compatibility of the Civil Partnerships Act with Article 6.1 of the Basic Law, this decision was passed by five votes to three; with regard to its compatibility with Article 3.1 of the Basic Law, it was passed by seven votes to one; in other respects it was passed unanimously.

Justices: Papier, Jaeger, Haas, Hömig, Steiner, Hohmann-Dennhardt, Hoffmann-Riem, Bryde

Dissenting opinion of Justice Papier
on the judgment of the First Senate of 17 July 2002
– 1 BvF 1, 2/01 –

I am unable to agree with the argument of the majority of the Senate, in particular on the institutional guarantee of marriage laid down in Article 6.1 of the Basic Law and the conclusions following from this.

Article 6.1 of the Basic Law places marriage under the special protection of the state order. Under the established case-law of the Federal Constitutional Court, this constitutional provision – as the majority of the Senate also assume – contains both a fundamental right to protection from encroachments by the state and also an institutional guarantee and a fundamental provision that determines values (see BVerfGE 31, 58 (67); 62, 323 (329)). If marriage, as a partnership between man and woman, needs legislation under non-constitutional law, this by no means gives the non-constitutional legislature the unrestricted authority to structure marriage in accordance with the opinions currently, either in reality or in supposition, predominant in society (see BVerfGE 6, 55 (82); 9, 237 (242-243); 15, 328 (332)). Instead, the provisions of non-constitutional law, notwithstanding the need to recognise a scope of drafting needed by the legislature, must be measured against Article 6.1 of the Basic Law as an overriding guiding norm that itself contains the fundamental principles (see BVerfGE 10, 59 (66); 24, 104 (109); 31, 58 (69-70)). Under this Article, every provision of non-constitutional law must observe the essential principles that define the institution of marriage (see BVerfGE 31, 58 (69)). These structural principles guaranteed by Article 6.1 of the Basic Law, which are removed from the power of disposal of the legislature, include the principle that marriage is the union of one man and one woman in a comprehensive, essentially indissoluble partnership (see BVerfGE 62, 323 (330)). This is also acknowledged by the majority of the Senate, who regard the heterosexuality of the spouses as one of the constitutive characteristics of marriage, so that as a result the legislature would be prevented from including the partnership of two persons of the same sex as a form of marriage by non-constitutional law. But against this background, it is not comprehensible that a mere different name for the newly created legal form of civil partnership should be able to justify regarding the institutional guarantee in Article 6.1 of the Basic Law as not applicable. For the institution of marriage guaranteed in Article 6.1 of the Basic Law is protected not only by name but also in its structural characteristics against arbitrary dispositions by the legislature. If the legislature, albeit under another name, creates a legally defined partnership between two persons of the same sex that in other respects corresponds to the rights and duties of marriage, the legislature in doing this disregards an essential structural principle laid down by Article 6.1 of the Basic Law. It is a false conclusion to assume that precisely because of deviation from an essential structural principle the constitutional institutional guarantee ceases to apply as a standard. When this constitutional standard was applied, the judgment should have set out in detail that the constitutionally enshrined institutional guarantee was not affected in its essential structural principles by the Civil Partnerships Act that was presented for review.

To the extent that the judgment proceeds on the assumption that the institutional guarantee is not affected for the mere reason that the provisions governing marriage are not altered by the Civil Partnerships Act, this assumption is based on a misunderstanding of the nature of an institutional guarantee. This guarantee is not in the first instance intended to ward off unjustified encroachments that disadvantage marriage – in this respect, the defensive function of Article 6.1 of the Basic Law has priority –; instead, the purpose of the institutional guarantee is to oblige the legislature when legislating on marriage to follow certain structural principles, which include the fact that the partners are of different sexes. The legislature is therefore prevented from introducing an institution under another name for same-sex couples that in other respects resembles marriage. Whether the Civil Partnerships Act did this or not the majority of the Senate who support the judgment do not state, precisely because they leave out of account the specifically constitutional effects of the institutional guarantee of Article 6.1 of the Basic Law. On the contrary, it creates no barriers to a substantially equal treatment to marriage.

Justice: Papier

Dissenting opinion of Justice Haas
on the judgment of the First Senate of 17 July 2002
– 1 BvF 1, 2/01 –

1. I agree with the majority of the Senate that there are fundamentally no constitutional objections to introducing a legal form of registered civil partnership for same-sex couples. In this way, everyone (with some exceptions governed by statute) may have his or her partnership with a partner of the same sex registered without a homosexual relationship existing or being intended between these two persons. However, the introduction of the legal form of the registered civil partnership was not constitutionally required.

2. The grounds given by the majority of the Senate on the constitutionality of the concrete legislation on the legal form of the registered civil partnership do not, however, make it possible for me to agree with the decision in the essential elements of its grounds.

a) In particular, the decision does not do justice to the meaning of the institutional guarantee of Article 6.1 of the Basic Law.

It does not take into account in the required degree the significance and effect of the institutional guarantee of marriage. When considering this, the majority of the

Senate should have considered whether the legal form of the registered civil partnership was designed by the legislature to be comparable to marriage and why, in the light of the constitutional guarantee, this does not meet with any constitutional objections.

Article 6.1 of the Basic Law places marriage under the special protection of the state order. Under the established case-law of the Federal Constitutional Court, this constitutional provision – as the majority of the Senate also assume – contains an institutional guarantee, a fundamental provision that determines values, and also a fundamental right to protection from encroachments by the state (see BVerfGE 31, 58 (67); 62, 323 (329)).

Article 6.1 of the Basic Law, as an institutional guarantee, guarantees the existence of the private-law institution of marriage and the family; it provides the legal framework of a way of life (BVerfGE 6, 55 (72)) in which man and woman find themselves in the partnership of marriage and which they can develop further into a family community. Because of this parenthood, which is potentially created in marriage and which promises stability to the community of parents and child, the legislature creating the constitution subjected marriage and the family to the protection of the Constitution. For the sake of the importance of marriage for family and society, Article 6.1 of the Basic Law in its quality of a fundamental provision that determines values in addition contains a requirement to promote marriage directed to the state (BVerfGE 6, 55 (76); established case-law), which has influenced the legislature's design and further development of marriage. Contrary to the opinion of the majority of the Senate, the constitutionally required promotion means more than only preventing marriage from being discriminated against. Promotion means positive consideration beyond the normal degree, and therefore giving marriage privileged treatment. It is therefore not possible to satisfy the requirement of promotion of Article 6.1 of the Basic Law by merely disadvantaging other partnerships either; the requirement to promote marriage is specifically not a requirement to disadvantage third parties.

As an institutional guarantee, Article 6.1 of the Basic Law binds the legislature – beyond the defensive rights of holders of fundamental rights – in structuring provisions of non-constitutional law. The legislature is required to observe the essential structural principles that determine the institution of marriage (see BVerfGE 31, 58 (69)). The essential structural principles of marriage include the fact that the partners are of different sexes.

Whether the institution of marriage enjoys the protection, or as the Constitution words it, the "special" protection, of the state order is virtually immaterial in this context. The express requirement of protection alone, which is found elsewhere in the Constitution in comparable form only in Article 1.1 sentence 2 of the Basic

Law with reference to human dignity, indicates the high value that the legislature creating the Constitution placed on marriage and the family. No other legal community, no community of persons, even if it is designed to provide long-term mutual support, is therefore constitutionally protected as an institution in a comparable way.

The majority of the Senate do not do justice to the significance of the institutional guarantee when they refer only to the fact that marriage is not damaged by the creation of a registered civil partnership. The institutional guarantee is not in the first instance intended to ward off unjustified encroachments that disadvantage marriage – in this respect, the defensive function of Article 6.1 of the Basic Law has priority –; instead, the purpose of the institutional guarantee is to oblige the legislature when legislating on marriage to follow certain fundamental structural principles, which also, in the opinion of the majority of the Senate, include the fact that the partners are of different sexes. There is a contravention of the constitutional requirement that only partners of different sexes may enter into a marriage if in addition to marriage an institution for couples of the same sex is created, the structure of which corresponds to the forms found for marriage in implementation of the constitutional requirement of promotion. The name is not relevant. For the institution of marriage guaranteed in Article 6.1 of the Basic Law is protected not only by name but also in its structuring characteristics against arbitrary dispositions by the legislature. The legislature cannot escape the requirements of Article 6.1 of the Basic Law by avoiding the designation "marriage". If the legislature, without being supported by the grounds justifying the institution of marriage, creates the legal form of a partnership between persons of the same sex, which apart from this in its rights and duties corresponds to those of marriage, the legislature in doing this disregards an essential structural principle, laid down by Article 6.1 of the Basic Law. The majority of the Senate fail to recognise this when they state that the constitutional institutional guarantee does not apply as a standard precisely because of the deviation from an essential structural principle.

The majority of the Senate should therefore have examined whether the legal form of the registered civil partnership has a content that is comparable to that of the institution of marriage. This would be incompatible with Article 6.1 of the Basic Law, since the civil partnership lacks the elements that characterise marriage, restrict its exclusivity to the joining of man and woman, and justify its special promotion. For it is not intended for the partners to have a child of their own, does not create parental responsibilities and therefore makes no contribution to the future viability of state and society.

b) The opinion of the majority of the Senate that Article 3.3 of the Basic Law has not been violated because the decisive factor is the commitment of two persons and

not their gender is not very convincing. For the prerequisite for entering into a registered civil partnership with a particular partner is having the same gender as that partner. Thus, to qualify for registration of the two-person relationship, the main factor is naturally gender. It would therefore have been desirable for the Senate to have made further argument apart from the concise grounds given.
c) The remarks of the majority of the Senate on the constitutionality of excluding siblings and lineal relations entering into the registered civil partnership (Article 1 § 1.2 numbers 2 and 3 of the Civil Partnerships Act) are so general that they are not capable of substantiating the opinion of the majority of the Senate that Article 3.1 of the Basic Law is not violated.
(1) Even the standard applied by the Senate is imprecise. In the review of the unequal treatment of groups of persons, the legislature, according to established case-law, is subject to a strict commitment (see BVerfGE 55, 72 (88); 88, 87 (96)) that is all the stricter the more the personal characteristics approach those set out in Article 3.3 of the Basic Law and the more strongly the negative effect the unequal treatment of the persons may have on the exercise of liberties protected by fundamental rights (see BVerfGE 60, 123 (134); 82, 126 (146); 88, 87 (96)). Just as the majority opinion does not fully describe the standard, there is also no description of the groups with which comparison is made; a defect that has an effect on the review.
(2) Just as the standard is not described in full, the argument of the majority of the Senate is shortened. It is not discernible on the basis of this argument what differences exist between the partners of a registered civil partnership and one between siblings or relations that are of such weight that they could justify the different treatment of the groups of persons.
Thus, to justify the exclusion of relations from entering into a registered civil partnership, weight is attached to the exclusivity of the registered civil partnership; but this "exclusivity" is neither justified nor described in detail. Nor can this be derived from the provision on entering into the registered civil partnership or from the overall context of the statute.
But the facts that relatives are "often" already part of another partnership in the form of a marriage or a civil partnership, which the majority of the Senate refer to, is immaterial in this context, for this is already taken into account in the impediments to creating a partnership in Article 1 § 1.2 number 1 or 4 of the Civil Partnerships Act.
Consequently, the grounds of the judgment do not reveal why unmarried lineal relations and siblings who are not bound by another partnership could not satisfy the principle of "exclusivity" postulated by the majority of the Senate.
In their line of argument, which remains abstract, the majority of the Senate avoid dealing with the comparable group that is genuinely relevant. This comprises sib-

lings and lineal relatives who live together in such a way that their need to be governed by statutory provisions is comparable to that of other partnerships to whom the legal form of the registered civil partnership is now open, because they have a joint household, support each other in emergencies, act together in legal relations or act for each other and emotionally relate primarily to each other, with the same reliability as other relationships intended to be permanent.

Insofar as it is sufficient for the majority of the Senate to point out that communities of mutual support between relatives even under existing law "in a certain respect contain a guarantee that was opened to same-sex couples only when the civil partnership was created," this formulation in itself, which remains absolutely vague and approximate, shows that the majority of the Senate lack a concrete standard to review equality. It remains unclear what circumstances are to be regarded as relevant to the comparison and what degree of difference is required to justify the unequal treatment of partnerships between relatives and between non-relatives. The concept of "guarantee" (*Absicherung*) introduced at this point is also not defined in detail. The reference that then follows to the "rights to refuse to give evidence, rights of succession and in part also rights to a compulsory portion and for it to be given tax relief" that exist in the relationship between relatives is incorrect and also incomplete in this lack of differentiation. This is shown, for example, in the following: siblings have a right to refuse to give evidence, for example under § 52.1 number 3 of the Code of Criminal Procedure (*Strafprozessordnung*). But siblings have only a restricted right of intestate succession (children and parents have priority, § 1924.1, § 1930.1 of the Civil Code and § 1925.1 and 2 of the Civil Code and § 1925.1 and 1925.2 of the Civil Code) and have no right to a compulsory portion whatsoever (§ 2303.1 and 1925.2 of the Civil Code). Above all, the legal effects of the civil partnership are not restricted to the law of succession and legislation for rights to refuse to give evidence, but affect a large number of areas of law. A fundamental characteristic of the civil partnership, for example, is the obligation to pay maintenance, which does not exist between siblings (§ 1601 of the Civil Code). Siblings are also not included in family insurance (§ 10.1 of the Fifth Books of the Code of Social Law); in addition, they cannot adjust their net asset position (Article 1 § 6 of the Civil Partnerships Act) and they are given no "limited custody" as in Article 1 § 9 of the Civil Partnerships Act.

The majority of the Senate, on account of the restricted review carried out by them, were unable to assess the facts adequately in the light of Article 3.1 of the Basic Law. It therefore did not become evident that between communities of mutual support of siblings and relatives in each case of the same sex, and other partnerships which have access to the legal form of the registered civil partnership, there are differences of such weight that it is justified to hold that for the two first-mentioned groups of persons there is no comparable need to provide for their relations and to refuse to permit them to enter into a registered civil partnership.

Justice: Haas

No. 36

BVerfGE 106, 166

of 29 October 2002 – 1 BvL 16, 17/95, 16/97 –

"Case involving the advantage acquired through additional counted children"

HEADNOTE:

Decision regarding the equal treatment of different forms of family under the law on child benefit.

Order of the First Senate of 29 October 2002
– 1 BvL 16, 17/95, 16/97 –

in the proceedings for the constitutional review of § 3.3 sentence 1 of the Federal Child Benefit Act (*Bundeskindergeldgesetz* – BKGG) in the version of the First Act Implementing the Savings, Consolidation and Growth Programme (*Erstes Gesetz zur Umsetzung des Spar-, Konsolidierungs- und Wachstumsprogramms* – 1. SKWPG) of 21 December 1993 (Federal Law Gazette (*Bundesgesetzblatt* – BGBl) I p. 2353) – suspension of proceedings and submission orders a) of the Magdeburg Social Court (*Sozialgericht*) of 31 May 1995 (S 5 Kg 31/94) – 1 BvL 16/95 –, b) of the Magdeburg Social Court of 31 May 1995 (S 5 Kg 33/94) – 1 BvL 17/95 –, c) of the Federal Social Court (*Bundessozialgericht*) of 28 May 1997 (14/10 RKg 22/95) – 1 BvL 16/97 –.

RULING:

§ 3.3 sentence 1 of the Federal Child Benefit Act in the version of the First Act Implementing the Savings, Consolidation and Growth Programme of 21 December 1993 (Federal Law Gazette I p. 2353) was incompatible with Article 3.1 of the Basic Law (*Grundgesetz* – GG).

In the event of the legislature not replacing the unconstitutional provision with a new provision by 1 January 2004 at the latest, it is to be substituted through application of the law applicable until 31 December 1993 to as yet uncompleted sets of proceedings.

EXTRACT FROM GROUNDS:

A.

The proceedings relate to the question of the constitutionality of a provision of the Federal Child Benefit Act applicable from 1994 to 1995, in accordance with which only parents who were married to each other and co-habiting were able to determine to which of them child benefit was to be granted. Parents who did not meet these requirements were unable to make such a "determination of the entitled party", with the consequence that they might forgo advantages with regard to the amount of child benefit. The submitting courts consider this provision to be incompatible with Article 3.1 of the Basic Law, the Social Court also with Article 6.1 and 6.5 of the Basic Law.

I.

1. § 3.1 of the Federal Child Benefit Act has provided since the entry into force, on 1 July 1964, of the Federal Child Benefit Act of 14 April 1964 (Federal Law Gazette I p. 265) that child benefit in each case is granted to only one of the entitled parties, in other words that it cannot be shared. In the event of several persons – as a rule the mother and father – meeting the conditions for a claim, competitions for a claim would have to be resolved. For instance, the legislature stipulated in § 3.2 of the Federal Child Benefit Act the priority of foster parents, grandparents and siblings, as well as of stepparents, before the parents. It regulated the relationship between the parents in § 3.3 of the Federal Child Benefit Act.
§ 3.3 of the Federal Child Benefit Act (in the version of the Unification Treaty (*Einigungsvertrag*) of 31 August 1990 (Federal Law Gazette II pp. 889 and 1093)) read as follows until 31 December 1993:

> (3) If the father and the mother meet the conditions for a claim in respect of a child, child benefit shall be granted to the one whom they determine to be the entitled party. As long as they have not made such a determination, child benefit shall be granted to the one who largely maintains the child; however, it shall be granted to the parent who has the care for the person of the child or the sole parental right to bring up the child.

2. By means of the First Act Implementing the Savings, Consolidation and Growth Programme of 21 December 1993 (Federal Law Gazette I p. 2353), § 3.3 of the Federal Child Benefit Act took on the version which is the subject-matter of the submission proceedings. The provision read as follows from 1 January 1994 to 31 December 1995:

> (3) If spouses who are not permanently separated meet the conditions for a claim in respect of a child, child benefit shall be granted to the one whom they determine to be the entitled party. As long as a determination has not been made, child benefit shall be granted to the one who largely maintains the child; however, it shall be granted to the parent who has the care for the person of the child or the sole parental right to bring up the child.

This new version was based on a draft Bill of the Federal Government (*Bundestag* printed paper (*Bundestagsdrucksache* – BTDrucks) 12/5502). The reasoning read as follows, *inter alia* (loc cit., p. 45):

> "It corresponds to the principle of payment of child benefit in line with the actual maintenance burden if child benefit is paid between unmarried parents to the one who largely maintains the child, or who has the sole care for the person of the child. The previously permissible determination of the entitled party also among unmarried parents facilitates an increase in the child benefit claim through the inclusion of children who a parent does not share with his or her present partner, also if the parent does not largely maintain any of his or her children and he or she also does not have the care for the person of a child. Furthermore, entitled parties who are married but permanently separated from their spouses can to date claim such advantages."

Parents could be interested in freely determining the entitled party if not identical but different circumstances applied to them which had an impact on the amount of child benefit. For instance, the so-called advantage acquired through additional counted children could markedly influence the amount of child benefit. This advantage acquired through additional counted children emerged from § 10 of the Federal Child Benefit Act, in accordance with which the amount of child benefit was graduated according to the ordinal number of the child. In 1992 to 1995, monthly child benefit was DM 70 for the first child, DM 130 for the second child, DM 220 for the third child and DM 240 for the fourth and each further child. From a certain annual income of the entitled party, the amount was reduced to DM 70 for the second child and to DM 140 for each further child. In calculating the ordinal number of the child, in accordance with § 10.1 sentence 2 of the Federal Child Benefit Act all the children of the entitled party (as "additional counted children") were additionally counted, even if another entitled person drew child benefit for such a child with priority. If only one parent had additional counted children, it was advantageous to determine this parent as the entitled party. For unmarried parents, and for parents who were married but separated, the provision submitted for constitutional review eliminated this possibility to determine the party entitled to child benefit, which until then had been available to all parents, but maintained it for married parents who were co-habiting.

3. The 1996 Annual Tax Act (*Jahressteuergesetz*) of 11 October 1995 (Federal Law Gazette I p. 1250) comprehensively re-worded the law on child benefit. § 64.2 sentences 1 to 3 of the Income Tax Act (*Einkommensteuergesetz* – EStG) applied from 1 January 1996 onwards to taxpayers with unlimited tax liability:

> (2) Among several entitled parties, child benefit shall be paid to the one who has accepted the child in his or her household. If a child has been accepted in the joint household of parents, of one parent and his or her spouse, of foster parents or of grandparents, they shall determine the entitled party inter se. If no determination is made, the guardianship court shall determine the entitled party if so requested.

The provision contained in § 3.2 sentences 1 to 3 of the Federal Child Benefit Act applied to taxpayers without unlimited tax liability from 1 January 1996 onwards:

> (2) If several persons meet the conditions for a claim in respect of a child, child benefit shall be granted to the person who has accepted the child in his or her household. If a child has been accepted in the joint household of parents, of one parent and his or her spouse, of foster parents or of grandparents, they shall determine the entitled party inter se. If no determination is made, the guardianship court shall determine the entitled party if so requested.

II.

The plaintiffs in the original proceedings are fathers with several children whose child benefit grants were rescinded by the defendant Federal Institute for Employment (*Bundesanstalt für Arbeit*) on the basis of the provisions contained in § 3.3 of the Federal Child Benefit Act applicable in 1994 and 1995, and whose families thereby lost the advantage acquired through additional counted children.

1. The plaintiff in the original proceedings in the proceedings on the constitutionality of a statute 1 BvL 16/95 has four children. Both older children come from a now dissolved marriage of the plaintiff, and lived with their mother. Both younger children were born out of wedlock. They lived in a household with their mother and the plaintiff. Prior to the amendment of § 3.3 of the Federal Child Benefit Act, the plaintiff, who was determined as the entitled party, received child benefit of DM 220 per month for his third child, the son S., his two older children from the dissolved marriage being taken into account. The mother of S., who had custody of him, her first child, would by contrast only have been entitled to claim child benefit of DM 70. The defendant [authority] rescinded the grant of child benefit for S. on expiry of August 1994, referring to the new wording of § 3.3 of the Federal Child Benefit Act; a determination of the entitled party among unmarried parents was hence said no longer to be possible.
The Social Court suspended the proceedings and submitted to the Federal Constitutional Court the question for a ruling as to whether § 3.3 sentence 1 of the Federal Child Benefit Act in the version applicable from 1 January 1994 is compatible with Article 3.1 in conjunction with Article 20.1 of the Basic Law, as well as with Article 6.1 and 6.5 of the Basic Law.
In the view of the Social Court, this is not the case. The new provision is said to be clear in terms of its wording, position in the legislative system and the declared intention of the legislature, and hence not amenable to an interpretation in conformity with the constitution. The different treatment of the parents is said to be arbitrary, to lead to random results and to prevent the realisation of the highest possible child benefit for a not inconsiderable group of families. Because of the changes which have taken place within society, the group of individuals concerned is said to constitute a not insignificant group whose financial situation is additionally worse on average than the group of parents alleged to be receiving preferential treatment. The unequal treatment is said to be justified neither by the state's need for finances, nor by a lesser legal position of those concerned. All communities of adults with (their) children are said to be equally under the protection of Article 6.1 of the Basic Law, regardless of their legal form. It is said not to be permissible to differentiate by the nature or quality of the relationships between the parents. The abuse concept, which the legislature highlighted according to the reasoning, is said not to be suitable to justify unequal treatment of the two groups.
2. The plaintiff in the original proceedings in the proceedings on the constitutionality of a statute 1 BvL 17/95 is the father of five children. Three older children come from an earlier marriage of the plaintiff, and lived with their mother. The two younger children S. and St. are children of the plaintiff and his partner together. Prior to the new wording of § 3.3 of the Federal Child Benefit Act, the plaintiff,

who was determined as the entitled party for S. and St., drew child benefit totalling DM 480 per month because they were treated under the law on child benefit as his fourth and fifth children. The mother of S. and St., who had sole custody, would only have received a child benefit totalling DM 200. The defendant [authority] rescinded the child benefit grant for the plaintiff on expiry of August 1994 since in accordance with the new wording of the Federal Child Benefit Act a determination of the entitled party among parents who were not married was no longer permissible.

The Social Court suspended the proceedings with the reasoning stated at II 1, and submitted to the Federal Constitutional Court the question for a ruling as to whether § 3.3 sentence 1 of the Federal Child Benefit Act in the version applicable from 1 January 1994 is compatible with Article 3.1 in conjunction with Article 20.1 of the Basic Law, as well as with Article 6.1 and 6.5 of the Basic Law.

3. The plaintiff in the original proceedings in the proceedings on the constitutionality of a statute 1 BvL 16/97 lived with the mother of his son M. in a non-marital community. Furthermore, his daughter K., a child from an earlier marriage, of whom the plaintiff had custody, lived in this household. The plaintiff has another two children from the previous marriage who did not live in his household. The original proceedings relate to the child benefit for the son M., for whom the plaintiff, who was determined as the entitled party, received child benefit amounting to DM 140 per month until February 1994 because M. was treated as the plaintiff's fourth child. The mother would only have been entitled to a child benefit claim of DM 70 because, for her, M. was the first child. The defendant [authority] rescinded the child benefit grant related to M. from 1994 on the basis of the amendment of § 3.3 of the Federal Child Benefit Act because unmarried parents were said now no longer to be able to determine an entitled parent. Objection, action and appeal on points of fact and law proceedings were unsuccessful.

The Federal Social Court suspended the proceedings and submitted to the Federal Constitutional Court the question for a ruling as to whether § 3.3 of the Federal Child Benefit Act in the version applicable from 1 January 1994 is compatible with Article 3.1 of the Basic Law.

In the view of the Federal Social Court, this is to be negated. The provision is said to be arbitrary and to lead to a differentiation between co-habiting married couples on the one hand and separated married couples, as well as non-marital communities, on the other hand, which is alleged to be incompatible with Article 6.1 of the Basic Law. This differentiation is said to be manifestly inexpedient. Already the starting point of the legislature's reasoning, in accordance with which it is allegedly a principle of the payment of child benefit that among unmarried parents the one who largely maintains the child or who is entitled to sole custody is entitled to draw the benefit is alleged to be incorrect. Rather, the entitlement to draw child-related state benefits is said to reflect the fundamental equality of the various forms of maintenance (care or financial allowances). The right to draw benefits of only one parent with priority for the person with custody is said only to be regarded as permissible if it is only a temporary attribution which does not impact the amount of child benefit. With parents who have children from an earlier union, however, the entitlement to draw benefits is said to be a factor determining the amount of child benefit because of utilisation of the advantage acquired through additional counted children.

The goal of the legislature, namely to avoid "unjustified" advantages acquired through additional counted children, is said to be attainable with the new provision only for the group of parents who are not married. The provision however allegedly goes beyond its goal in cases in which additional counted children are not only counted but are also maintained. This is said to be the case of the plaintiff, who had accepted his daughter K. in his household and was taking care of her maintenance. Conversely, married parents with children from earlier relationships are said to continue to benefit from the advantage acquired through additional counted children if neither maintenance obligations exist, nor custody is exercised. In the view of the Federal Social Court, the legislature could only have achieved the goal of eliminating the advantage acquired through additional counted children in cases in which neither maintenance nor custody exist towards a child by restricting the advantage acquired through additional counted children in § 10 of the Federal Child Benefit Act to children for whom maintenance is indeed provided, or with regard to whom custody exists.

The constitutional protection afforded by Article 6.1 of the Basic Law is alleged to apply not only to intact marriages, but to relate equally to the community of parents and children, and also to cover the community of children born out of wedlock with their parents who are not married to each other, or only with one parent. Article 6.1 of the Basic Law may well permit a privilege towards marriage as against non-marital communities. A favourable treatment of the so-called normal family as against that consisting of unmarried parents and their children however is said not to be permissible. An interpretation of the new regulation in conformity with the constitution is said not to be possible.

III.

Statements on the submissions have been made by the Federal Ministry for Family Affairs, Senior Citizens, Women and Youth on behalf of the Federal Government, the Federal Social Court (in the proceedings 1 BvL 16/95 and 1 BvL 17/95), the

Federal Institute for Employment (in the proceedings 1 BvL 16/95 and 1 BvL 17/95), as well as the plaintiff in the original proceedings in the proceedings 1 BvL 17/95.

1. The Federal Ministry considers the provision submitted for examination to be constitutional.

The reason for differentiating is said to emerge from the purpose of graduating child benefit by the child's ordinal number in order to particularly promote families with many children. A disproportionate burden is said however only to occur in family households with a correspondingly large number of children. If the children live in various family households, they form different families. Worthiness for promotion is then determined by the conditions found in the respective individual family. For this reason, the legislature has not been denied the possibility to rule out in general terms the determination of entitled parties among parents belonging to two different households.

The restriction of the determination of the entitled party to married parents co-habiting in a household is said to be permissible because the financial and legal circumstances of married and unmarried co-habiting parents under the law on child benefit is said to be so materially different as to justify the diverging provisions.

It has been open to the legislature to treat unmarried and married couples equally, as indeed took place from 1996 onwards in the law on child-raising benefit and in the law on child benefit. This is however said to have been problematic because child benefit is linked to the income in accordance with § 10.2 and 10.3 of the Federal Child Benefit Act. The amount of child benefit would then have depended on the income of a partner who possibly would not have been entitled to child benefit at all. Therefore, in the legal amendment as in January 1994 the legislature has been guided by the consideration that non-marital communities are not to be regarded as economic communities.

Considerations of the law on custody are also said to justify a differentiation. Attribution to the parent with sole custody is said not to be arbitrary as it is linked to the different degrees of legal relations between the child and his or her parents.

If the Federal Social Court considers discrimination to consist in the customary exclusion of fathers of children born out of wedlock from the advantage acquired through additional counted children, it is said to ignore the other different provisions of compensation for family burdens and income taxation. The treatment of married and unmarried couples is said to have been so different in the period under dispute that the random lower amount of the child benefit claim is said not to be in breach of equality.

2. …

3. The Federal Institute for Employment considers the … new wording of § 3.3 sentence 1 of the Federal Child Benefit Act … to be compatible with the Basic Law. In accordance with Article 6.1 of the Basic Law, marriage and the family are said to enjoy the special protection of the state. A non-marital community with children is however said not to constitute a family within the meaning of Article 6.1 of the Basic Law, but to form two incomplete families. From the point of view of the promotion of marriage and the family, it is said to be justifiable to favour marriage in the sense that in principle only married parents living in an intact marriage are to be granted the possibility to receive the highest child benefit rate. The possibility provided for in § 3.4 sentence 2 of the Federal Child Benefit Act for the guardianship court to determine the entitled party is said to ensure avoidance of unfairness and hardship in individual cases.

B. – I.

§ 3.3 sentence 1 of the Federal Child Benefit Act in the impugned version was incompatible with Article 3.1 of the Basic Law.

1. The general principle of equality (Article 3.1 of the Basic Law) requires all persons to be treated equally before the law. This does not however deny the legislature the possibility to make any differentiation whatever. The legislature has latitude here in the field of benefit-granting state activity for the delimitation of the favoured groups of individuals (see Decisions of the Federal Constitutional Court (*Entscheidungen des Bundesverfassungsgerichts* – BVerfGE 99, 165 (178)). However, the more it is possible for unequal treatment to have a disadvantageous impact on the implementation of freedoms that are protected by fundamental rights, the narrower are the limits that emerge for the legislature from the general principle of equality (see BVerfGE 82, 126 (146); 88, 87 (96)). With unequal treatment of families, which are protected by Article 6.1 of the Basic Law, also including unmarried parents and their children, it should therefore be examined whether reasons of such a nature and weight exist for the envisioned differentiation that they can justify the unequal legal consequences (see BVerfGE 88, 87 (97)).

2. The new wording of § 3.3 sentence 1 of the Federal Child Benefit Act led to unequal treatment between co-habiting spouses and their families on the one hand and other parents and their families on the other to gain a so-called advantage acquired through additional counted children in the drawing of child benefit.

In accordance with § 10.1 of the Federal Child Benefit Act, child benefit increased disproportionately with a higher number of children. In calculating the ordinal number of the child, all children of the entitled party were counted as "additional counted children" in accordance with § 10.1 sentence 2 of the Federal Child Benefit Act, even if a different person entitled to claim took priority in drawing child benefit for such a child. It was hence advantageous for parents to determine as the entitled party the parent who had the most additional counted children.

The provision submitted for review eliminated this possibility open until then to all parents to determine the entitlement to child benefit for unmarried parents and for parents who were married but separated, but maintained the possibility for co-habiting married parents (§ 3.3 sentence 1 of the Federal Child Benefit Act). § 3.3 sentence 2 of the Federal Child Benefit Act, which regulated the consequences of the lack of such a provision, seems by its wording to refer only to the parents named in sentence 1 who had not determined an entitled party. If however § 3.3 sentence 2 of the Federal Child Benefit Act is compared with its predecessor provision, and if furthermore the Federal Government's reasoning of the Act is taken into account (see *Bundestag* printed paper 12/5502, p. 45), sentence 2 can be understood with the non-constitutional case-law such that it was to cover all other cases, in other words both married co-habiting parents who had not made a determination of the entitled party, and all other parents because they were generally excluded from the possibility of determining an entitled party in sentence 1.

Hence, as becomes clear in the original proceedings for different family constellations, the new provision reduced the family income for families in which the parents were not married or were separated, whilst families with married co-habiting parents are unaffected by the amendment. Restricting this impact to cases in which no earlier provision yet existed, or analogous application of § 3.3 sentence 1 of the Federal Child Benefit Act to non-marital communities, cannot be considered against the will of the legislature.

3. This unequal treatment is not justified on the merits.

a) The unequal treatment and the justifying reason must be suitably interrelated. This did not take place – even taking account of the latitude available to the legislature – in the provision contained in § 3.3 sentence 1 of the Federal Child Benefit Act in the impugned version, as no reasons are manifest that would be suitable to justify the different treatment of the groups of parents by the legislature handing down child benefit law in 1994 and 1995.

b) The goal of the new provision was however constitutional in its approach.

The First Act Implementing the Savings, Consolidation and Growth Programme aimed to achieve savings in the social welfare area (see *Bundestag* printed paper 12/5502, pp. 1-2). To this end, the advantage acquired through additional counted children was to be restricted by means of the determination of the entitled party. This is permissible in principle.

The legislature has latitude in deciding on the manner in which it wishes to realise the protection of the family entrusted to it (see BVerfGE 43, 108 (124); 82, 60 (81)). It has other community interests to accommodate in addition to promotion of the family, and in doing so above all to safeguard the smooth functioning and balance of the whole (see BVerfGE 82, 60 (82); 87, 1 (35-36); 103, 242 (259)). Accordingly, the general duty of the state to ensure compensation for family burdens can be derived from the value determination contained in Article 6.1 of the Basic Law in conjunction with the principle of the social welfare state, but not the ruling on the degree to which and the means by which such social compensation is to be carried out (see BVerfGE 87, 1 (36); 103, 242 (259)).
The legislature is hence not obliged to grant an advantage acquired through additional counted children. If it permits child benefit to increase progressively with a higher number of children, it can restrict this impact to those cases in which the older children are in fact largely maintained, live in the household of the entitled party or the entitled party has the care for their person.
c) It is also not constitutionally prohibited to use marital status as a basis for resolving competition between several parties who are entitled to child benefit. Since married co-habiting parents as a rule share maintenance and the care for the person, it suggests itself to carry out entitlement, as a general rule, by joint determination. With other parents the legislature can carry out an attribution which is orientated primarily to the care for the person. Single parents in particular can thus receive the benefit directly and do not depend on receiving compensation through maintenance payments. The different situation of the various groups of parents however does not justify restricting to married co-habiting parents the statutorily granted possibility of changing the determination of the entitled party through agreement. According to the intention of the legislature, the purpose of excluding all other parents by the new provision submitted for review was based not on the different situations of various family types, but on ruling out the advantage acquired through additional counted children if the older children were neither largely maintained and there was no care for their person (see *Bundestag* printed paper 12/5502, p. 45). Compatibility with the principle of equality must be measured by this goal.
d) The differentiation by forms of family is unsuited for the achievement of this legislative goal.
There is no recognisable connection between, on the one hand, the relationship of a person entitled to child benefit and his or her older children from other unions and, on the other hand, the form of co-habitation with the mother or father of the child for whom child benefit is paid.
For parents who are married and co-habiting, the right to determine, and hence the advantage acquired through additional counted children, were maintained also

where the legislature precisely intended to reduce it if the recipient of the increased child benefit neither largely paid maintenance for, nor had the care for the person of, the additional counted children. Conversely, the advantage acquired through additional counted children of the other parents was forgone even if – as in the initial case of proceedings 1 BvL 16/97 – children from the earlier union had been accepted in the household and there was the care for their person.

e) This result also cannot be justified with the power of the legislature to impose a blanket regulation on frequently occurring manifestations (see BVerfGE 96, 1 (6); 101, 297 (309)). There are no indications that the situation in which from the point of view of the legislature the advantage acquired through additional counted children is to be reduced takes place more regularly among unmarried or separated parents than among those who are married and co-habiting.

A constitutionally justifiable provision, as the Federal Social Court correctly finds, would have been able to set in at the advantage acquired through additional counted children directly. The restriction created by the legislature of the determination of entitled persons to married co-habiting parents was by contrast unsuited to achieve the legislative goal.

f) The unequal treatment is also not justified by the special protection of marriage in Article 6.1 of the Basic Law. If the Federal Ministry refers in justification of maintaining the possibility of determination among married couples to the burden of maintenance incumbent on the spouse by virtue of additional counted children which the partner had at least to partly bear through a reduction in standard of living, this runs counter to the legal reasoning that the advantage acquired through additional counted children was in particular not to be granted solely because of maintenance obligations. If however one permits the existence of such maintenance obligations as justification for the advantage acquired through additional counted children, as the legislature did until the new provision, this applies in turn to all families, given that a child born out of wedlock is also indirectly affected by a parent having maintenance obligations for children from other relationships.

g) The unequal treatment is finally also not justified by the determination of the entitled party with unmarried parents in addition to the advantage acquired through additional counted children being able to have other advantages not attainable for married couples.

The amount of the child benefit was determined not only by the ordinal number of the children and the advantage acquired through additional counted children in accordance with § 10.1 sentences 1 and 2 of the Federal Child Benefit Act, but also by the income of the claimant in accordance with §§ 10.2 and 10.3 of the Federal Child Benefit Act. Accordingly, child benefit was gradually reduced to base amounts for the second and each subsequent child if the annual income of the claimant exceeded certain allowances. As a rule, a lower income hence led to a higher child benefit. A determination of the entitled party was hence also able to lead to a larger amount of child benefit because of these income limits. Since the incomes of married co-habiting spouses were added together in assessing the allowances, this possibility was uninteresting for them, whilst with other parents the determination of the parent with the lower income, or who had no income, as the entitled party could increase the child benefit claim.

This conceivable advantage for unmarried parents was however already compensated for by the considerably higher allowances for married persons. Furthermore, the Act determined the entitled parent to be the party with custody, and as a rule this means the mother, who in reality typically also has the lower income, in particular when there are several children – and only with several children were the income limits of § 10.2 and 3 of the Federal Child Benefit Act significant. In contradistinction to the determination of the entitled party because of the advantage acquired through additional counted children, the determination because of different income hence hardly took on significance in practice and also played no role as an argument in the legislative procedure. From a point of view of equality, it is certainly not possible for a rather more rare and atypical advantage for one group to compensate for the group's being placed at a disadvantage in a very much more frequent and typical constellation.

II.

Since the legislature has a variety of possibilities to eliminate the unconstitutional state in the case of violations of the principle of equality, the provision submitted for review is to be declared incompatible with the Basic Law. The original proceedings remain suspended until the legislature has replaced the unconstitutional provision by a provision that is compatible with the constitution (see BVerfGE 28, 324 (363)). In the event of the legislature not having created a new provision by 1 January 2004, the law as applicable until 31 December 1993 is to be applied to as yet uncompleted sets of proceedings.

Justices: Papier, Jaeger, Haas, Hömig, Steiner, Hohmann-Dennhardt, Hoffmann-Riem, Bryde

As a result of the Federal Constitutional Court's decision, the legislature, through Article 4 of the Act for the Implementation of Family-Law Decisions of the Federal

Constitutional Court (Gesetz zur Umsetzung familienrechtlicher Entscheidungen des Bundesverfassungsgerichts) *of 13 December 2003 (Federal Law Gazette I 2003 p. 2547) inserted, with effect from 31 December 2003, the following § 20.3 into the Federal Child Benefit Act:*

"§ 20 Instructions for application

> …
>
> *(3) In cases in which the decision on the amount of the child benefit claim for months in the period between 1 January 1994 and 31 December 1995 has not yet become final, § 3.2 sentences 1 and 2 of this Act in the version applicable on 23 December 2003 shall be applied instead of § 3.3 sentence 1 of this Act in the version of the First Act Implementing the Savings, Consolidation and Growth Programme of 21 December 1993 (Federal Law Gazette I p. 2353)."*

No. 37

BVerfGE 107, 104

of 16 January 2003 – 2 BvR 716/01 –

"Parental involvement in proceedings under the Juvenile Court Act case"

HEADNOTES:

1. **It is part of the parental responsibility, protected by Article 6.2 sentence 1 of the Basic Law (*Grundgesetz* – GG), that parents should protect the rights of their children vis-à-vis the state or third parties. As a result, it is a constitutional necessity for parents to participate early on in criminal proceedings before a juvenile court. Provisions which deprive parents of the right to be involved or which exclude them from the trial are encroachments on their constitutionally protected rights.**
2. **Safeguarding the undisturbed administration of the criminal law and the enforcement of the state's right to punish in judicial proceedings are constitutional tasks which can come into conflict with the parental right to bring up a child. A conflict between parental rights and the constitutional requirement that the criminal law protect legal interests does not lead inevitably to parental rights being overruled; it is to be resolved through a weighing of interests, whereby the parental right concerned and the protection of legal interests by the criminal law must be balanced against each other.**
3. **The right to enforce the state's right to punish may allow encroachment upon the parental right to bring up a child, but this does not make the requirement that such encroachment be based on a sufficiently definite statute dispensable.**

Judgment of the Second Senate of 16 January 2003
on the basis of the oral hearing of 5 November 2002
– 2 BvR 716/01 –

in the proceedings regarding the constitutional complaint of Mr. Z. – authorised representative: Professor Dr. ... – against 1. a) the order of the Karlsruhe Higher Regional Court (*Oberlandesgericht*) of 11 February 2002 – 2 Ss 185/01 –, b) the judgment of the Heidelberg Local Court (*Amtsgericht*) of 2 May 2001 – 5 Ds 36 Js 9126/2000 – AK 132/00 Jug –, 2. a) the order of the Heidelberg Regional Court (*Landgericht*) of 3 April 2001 – 3 Qs 10/01 Jug –, b) the order of the Heidelberg Local Court of 16 March 2001 – 5 Ds 36 Js 9126/2000 – AK 132/00 Jug –, 3. a) the order of the Heidelberg Regional Court of 1 February 2001 – 3 Qs 2/01 –, b) the order of the Heidelberg Local Court of 11 January 2001 – 5 Ds 36 Js 9126/2000 – AK 132/00 Jug –, 4. the order of the presiding judge of the Heidelberg Local Court of 29 June 2000 – 5 Ds 36 Js 9126/2000 – AK 132/00 Jug – and 5. indirectly against § 51.2 of the Juvenile Court Act (*Jugendgerichtsgesetz* – JGG).

RULING:

1. § 51.2 of the Juvenile Court Act is incompatible with Article 6.2 of the Basic Law and void to the extent that the provision allows persons who bear parental responsibility within the meaning of Article 6.2 of the Basic Law to be excluded [from proceedings before a juvenile court].
2. The order of the presiding judge of the Heidelberg Local Court of 29 June 2000 – 5 Ds 36 Js 9126/2000 – AK 132/00 Jug –, the orders of the Heidelberg Local Court of 11 January and 16 March 2001 – 5 Ds 36 Js 9126/2000 – AK 132/00 Jug – and the orders of the Heidelberg Regional Court of 1 February 2001 – 3 Qs 2/01 – and of 3 April 2001 – 3 Qs 10/01 Jug – violate the complainant's fundamental right under Article 6.2 of the Basic Law. Similarly, the judgment of the Heidelberg Local Court of 2 May 2001 – 5 Ds 36 Js 9126/2000 – AK 132/00 Jug – and the order of the Karlsruhe Higher Regional Court of 11 February 2002 – 2 Ss 185/01 – violate Article 6.2 of the Basic Law; they are reversed. The matter is referred back to the Wiesloch Local Court.
3. The *Land* (state) Baden-Württemberg must bear the necessary expenses of the complainant in the constitutional complaint proceedings.

EXTRACT FROM GROUNDS:

A.

The constitutional complaint concerns the sentencing by a juvenile criminal court of a minor whose father had been excluded from the proceedings pursuant to § 51.2 of the Juvenile Court Act. It raises the question of whether § 51.2 of the Juvenile Court Act is compatible with the parental right to bring up a child in Article 6.2 of the Basic Law.

I.

The Juvenile Court Act describes in § 67 the position of the person with parental rights and of the legal representative for the whole of criminal proceedings before a juvenile court. They are granted in principle the same rights as the minor accused of a crime. These rights may, however, be withdrawn to the extent that the above-mentioned persons are suspected of having been involved in the offence of which the minor is accused or there is a justified fear that they could abuse their rights. In these cases, a temporary guardian and, if necessary, counsel must be appointed by the court pursuant to § 68.2 of the Juvenile Court Act to safeguard the interests of the minor in criminal proceedings which are pending.
§ 67 of the Juvenile Court Act states:

§ 67 Position of the person with parental rights and the legal representative

(1) To the extent that the accused has a right to be heard, to submit questions and motions or to be present at investigations, this right shall also be available to the person with parental rights and the legal representative.
(2) Where notice must be given to the accused, a similar notice should be given to the person with parental rights and the legal representative.
(3) The rights of the legal representative to choose defence counsel and to exercise legal remedies shall also be available to the person with parental rights.
(4) The judge may withdraw these rights from the person with parental rights and the legal representative if they are suspected of having been involved in the offence of which the minor is accused or if they have been sentenced for their involvement. Where the person with parental rights and the legal representative satisfy the prerequisites referred to in sentence 1, the judge shall be entitled to withdraw the rights of both of them if there is a fear that they will abuse their

rights. Where the person with parental rights and the legal representative are no longer entitled to their rights, the judge of the court of guardianship shall appoint a temporary guardian to safeguard the interests of the accused in pending criminal proceedings. The trial shall be postponed until a temporary guardian has been appointed.

(5) Where several persons have parental rights, each one of them may exercise the rights of a person with parental rights specified in this statute. At the trial or at another hearing before a judge, an absent person with parental rights shall be regarded as being represented by a person with parental rights who is present. If notifications or summonses have to be sent, it shall be sufficient if they are addressed to one person with parental rights.

… § 51 of the Juvenile Court Act restricts the right to be present since subsection 1 provides for the temporary exclusion of the accused and subsection 2 grants the presiding judge the option of also excluding persons with parental rights and legal representatives from the hearing.

§ 51 of the Juvenile Court Act states:

§ 51 Temporary exclusion of participants

(1) The presiding judge should exclude the accused from the hearing for the duration of discussions which could be disadvantageous to his or her upbringing. The presiding judge must inform him or her of what was said during his or her absence if this is necessary for his or her defence.

(2) The presiding judge should also exclude relatives, the person with parental rights and the legal representative if there are misgivings about whether they should be present.

II.

1. In the challenged judgment the Local Court issued the complainant's son, who is still a minor, with a warning on account of bodily injury and dangerous bodily injury and ordered him to do 50 hours of community service under the instruction of the youth welfare office and to participate in a social training course. The complainant, who has sole custody for his son, was excluded pursuant to § 51.2 of the Juvenile Court Act from participating in the trial. … The course of proceedings prior to sentencing was as follows:

a) The son of the complainant, who was 14 years old at the time of the offence, was prosecuted for bodily injury in two cases in connection with physical fights with other pupils. …

The complainant was initially present at the trial as legal representative. After the court had interviewed a witness who had incriminated the accused son, the juvenile court judge interrupted the hearing of evidence in order to recommend to the accused and the complainant as his legal representative that they enter into "Offender-Victim Mediation" (*Täter-Opfer-Ausgleich*). After consulting with his son the complainant refused to have the proceedings disposed of in this way and insisted that the hearing of evidence be continued.

The details of how the hearing continued are unclear. What is certain is that the complainant was ultimately expelled from the courtroom by the judge. The record does not contain more detailed reasons; there is simply a note:

"The legal representative was expelled from the courtroom pursuant to § 51.II."

The trial was continued thereafter in the absence of the complainant. Ultimately, the proceedings were temporarily discontinued with the consent of the accused and the public prosecutor's office in order to carry out "Offender-Victim Mediation" in both cases in which charges were brought.

b) …

c) The "Offender-Victim Mediation" which had been ordered was only successfully carried out in one case; in the second case, the son of the complainant and the presumable victim rejected this. On 11 January 2001 the juvenile court judge ordered that proceedings be resumed and fixed the oral hearing for 8 February 2001. At the same time, the Local Court dismissed an application of 6 July 2000 to assign court-appointed counsel to the accused and decided to exclude the complainant as legal representative from participating in the new trial (but not from the handing down of judgment) pursuant to § 51.2 of the Juvenile Court Act. …

The complaint directed against this order was dismissed by the Regional Court in its order of 1 February 2001. The court held that neither the seriousness of the offence nor the difficulty of the facts or law made it necessary for defence counsel to be involved. …

d) A private defence counsel for the son of the complainant submitted a pleading on 6 February 2001, which led to the court postponing the trial. After the defence counsel had inspected the court file, the complainant again unsuccessfully rejected the juvenile court judge on the basis that he was concerned that the judge was biased. …

e) The application by the defence counsel of 10 March 2001 that he should be appointed by the court as counsel for the accused and that the complainant should be appointed to advise the accused was rejected by the juvenile court judge in his or-

der of 16 March 2001. … In its order of 3 April 2001 the Regional Court dismissed the complaint submitted by the defence counsel against the rejection; at the time of submitting the complaint, defence counsel also withdrew from the case.
f) The trial at which numerous witnesses were questioned was ultimately held on 19 April and 2 May 2001 in the absence of the complainant.
2. Both the complainant and his son made an appeal against the subsequent judgment which they later described as an appeal on points of law only. The complainant complained in the grounds for his appeal on points of law (which grounds were accepted by his son) that among other things he had been excluded from the trial …
In its order of 11 February 2000 the Higher Regional Court dismissed the appeal on points of law by the accused and the complainant pursuant to § 349.2 of the Code of Criminal Procedure (*Strafprozessordnung*).
3. In the period thereafter the son of the complainant only performed a part of the community service work he had been ordered to perform. With regard to the remainder of the work, the Local Court ordered juvenile detention in the form of "custody during the minor's usual recreation time" (*Freizeitarrest*) in its order of 18 July 2002 pursuant to § 11.3 and § 15.3 of the Juvenile Court Act. The Regional Court dismissed the immediate complaint by the complainant against the above in its order of 8 August 2002.
Until now juvenile detention has not been enforced.

III.

1. Initially, the constitutional complaint of the complainant was directed against the decisions of the Local Court of 29 June 2000 and 11 January 2001 as well as against the decision of the Regional Court of 1 February 2001. To this extent he complained of a violation of Article 6.2 of the Basic Law by the arbitrary application of § 51.2 of the Juvenile Court Act. The complainant alleged that the juvenile court judge had incorrectly exercised his discretion in interpreting the provision where there were no specific facts that could have justified an exclusion.
He argued that this was at the same time a violation of Articles 103.1 and 3.1 of the Basic Law as well as against the principles of a fair hearing. In his opinion, the reasons later given could also not justify an exclusion. The precedence of the parental right to bring up a child would prevent this. … The provision in § 51.2 of the Juvenile Court Act … was also generally objectionable under constitutional law due to its lack of definiteness. According to the complainant, defence counsel should in any case have been assigned to his son applying § 68 no. 2 of the Juvenile Court Act *mutatis mutandis*.

2. In his letter of 14 April 2001 the complainant extended his constitutional complaint to the orders of the Local Court and Regional Court of 16 March and 3 April 2001, which had rejected the appointment of defence counsel and his appointment as adviser. Finally, in his pleading of 26 March 2002 he extended his constitutional complaint to the judgment of the Heidelberg Local Court and the decision of the Higher Regional Court which had dismissed the appeal on points of law. …

IV.

1. The Federal Ministry of Justice (*Bundesministerium der Justiz*) considers the possibility of excluding the person with parental rights from the trial to be constitutionally unobjectionable. In its view, § 51.2 of the Juvenile Court Act does not violate Article 6.2 of the Basic Law. …

2. The *Land* Baden-Württemberg did not make use of its opportunity to present an opinion.

…

B. – I.

The constitutional complaint is admissible.

1. The complainant is permitted to lodge a constitutional complaint against the decisions sentencing his son. According to the case-law of the Federal Constitutional Court, disciplinary measures are in principle permissible in connection with the "state's watchdog function", and do not conflict with the parental right to bring up a child if the measures are intended to respond to and remedy the misbehaviour of minors which persists in spite of parental disciplinary efforts (see Decisions of the Federal Constitutional Court (*Entscheidungen des Bundesverfassungsgerichts* – BVerfGE 74, 102 (124-125)). In principle this is at the same time recognition that a decision by a criminal court – in which the state reacts to the criminal offence of a minor – can affect the scope of protection of Article 6.2 of the Basic Law and that parents may thus assert the infringement of their own rights.

2. The complainant is also entitled to lodge the complaint to the extent that he is challenging the decisions which ordered his exclusion from ongoing proceedings. He is thus asserting with regard to the position in proceedings granted to him by the Juvenile Court Act (§ 50 and § 67 of the Juvenile Court Act) above all a violation of his parental right under Article 6.2 of the Basic Law, and alleging also – even if decisions in criminal proceedings against his son are at issue – a violation of his own rights.

Entitlement to lodge a complaint exists independently of the possibility of the complainant to himself challenge the sentencing of his son with the constitutional complaint. The exclusion of the complainant – irrespective of its effect on the proceedings of the accused juvenile – is a drastic measure which is not only suitable for impairing the complainant's reputation but even goes further by depriving him of his ability to bring up his son with his son's best interests in mind. In this case it can be assumed that a legal interest worthy of protection exists (see BVerfGE 15, 226 (230)).

3. The complainant, who regards the necessity for the court to appoint counsel as a necessary consequence of his exclusion from the entire trial, may also allege violations of his own rights to the extent that he challenges those decisions which do not permit court-appointed counsel to be assigned to his son. This also applies to the decisions which do not permit his appointment as adviser; also to this extent the complainant, who regards the refusal to appoint him as advisor as a violation of Article 6.2 of the Basic Law, is entitled to lodge a complaint.

The admissibility of the constitutional complaint is also not otherwise called into question by the fact that the orders last made were not made directly as a result of action by the complainant, but rather in response to pleadings by the defence counsel who was authorised by the son. They affect nevertheless the legal position of the complainant, which the courts were obliged to consider in the same way as the procedural rights of the son. The spirit and purpose of the requirement that appeals be exhausted did not require the complainant on the facts in this case to first exhaust his appeals to the non-constitutional courts through his own additional applications. This is because it could not be expected that the decision on whether he would be permitted to advise his son would be decided differently as a result of such applications (on this, see BVerfGE 38, 105 (110)).

II.

The constitutional complaint is also well-founded.

§ 51.2 of the Juvenile Court Act, which permits relatives, persons with parental rights and legal representatives to be excluded from the trial if there are misgivings about their being present, is incompatible with Article 6.2 of the Basic Law to the extent that it permits persons to be excluded who bear parental responsibility within the meaning of Article 6.2 of the Basic Law. This provision is not definite enough to be the basis for encroachments on the parental right to bring up a child.

1. a) Article 6.2 sentence 1 of the Basic Law guarantees parents the right to the care and upbringing of their children. They may in principle decide free of state influence and according to their own ideas how they wish to live up to their responsibili-

ty as parents (see BVerfGE 24, 119 (143-144); 59, 360 (376); 60, 79 (88); established case-law). The goal, content and methods of bringing up a child fall within the parents' sphere of responsibility. The constitution does not lay down specific objectives for them in relation to the bringing up of a child. Article 6.2 of the Basic Law protects parents in the exercise of their parental right to bring up a child from state encroachment and combines this with an obligation on the part of parents to make the child's best interests their guiding principle in bringing up a child (see BVerfGE 56, 363 (381-382); see too BVerfGE 59, 360 (376)).

If parents do not live up to this responsibility because they are not willing or not in a position to fulfil their duty to bring up their child or because their own transgressions permanently pose a considerable risk to the child's best interests, then the "state's watchdog function" pursuant to Article 6.2 sentence 2 of the Basic Law takes effect. The state is then not just entitled, but also obliged to guarantee the care and upbringing of the child; the child who requires help in order to develop into a responsible member of a society that corresponds to the Basic Law's concept of society has a right to protection by the state (see BVerfGE 24, 119 (144); 60, 79 (88)). Disciplinary measures for minors pursuant to the Juvenile Court Act are accordingly permissible aids for bringing up children as part of the "state's watchdog function"; they respond to misbehaviour of minors which may persist in spite of their upbringing by their parents and seek to guide minors to a life free of crime (see BVerfGE 74, 102 (124-125)).

Not every failure and not every act of carelessness entitle the state to restrict or even exclude the parents' authority to bring up their child; it is also not part of the "state's watchdog function" to see to it that the child develops in the best possible way if this is contrary to the will of the parents (see BVerfGE 60, 79 (91)). Instead the state must always respect the precedence of the parents' right to bring up their child. In addition, the principle of proportionality also applies here. The type and extent of the encroachment depends on the degree to which the parents have failed and on what is necessary in the interests of the child (see BVerfGE 24, 119 (145)). The separation of a child from its family can only be considered in particularly serious cases; it is the strongest encroachment on the rights of persons with parental rights pursuant to Article 6.3 of the Basic Law, which is directed against the removal of children from their families for the purposes of forcing them to be brought up by the state (BVerfGE 24, 119 (139 et seq.); 31, 194 (210)). It can only be justified where the failure of the persons with parental rights amounts to serious misconduct and where there is a considerable risk to the child's best interests or where the child is on the brink of becoming neglected, which can also be expressed in the commission of serious crimes …

b) The exercise of the parental right is not only limited according to Article 6.2 and 6.3 of the Basic Law; it is subject – in any case as far as the exercise of rights in criminal proceedings against a minor is concerned – to additional limits (see generally on the limitation of parental rights BVerfGE 34, 165 (181-182); 41, 29 (44); 47, 46 (71-72); 96, 288 (304); 98, 218 (244-245)). By way of exception, both conflicting fundamental rights of third persons as well as other legal values that have been given constitutional status are, taking into account the unity of the constitution and the entire value system protected by it, in a position to also limit unrestrictable fundamental rights in individual aspects (see BVerfGE 28, 243 (261); established case-law).
The safeguarding of the undisturbed administration of the law by the criminal law has always been an important task of state authority. The solving of criminal cases, the finding of the perpetrator, the determination of his or her guilt and his or her punishment as well as the acquittal of the innocent are the main tasks of the administration of the criminal law (see BVerfGE 39, 1 (45 et seq.); 88, 203 (257-258); see also BVerfGE 51, 324 (343)), which is supposed to uniformly enforce the state's right to punish in judicial proceedings aimed at ascertaining the truth for the protection of citizens (see BVerfGE 57, 250 (275); 80, 367 (378); 100, 313 (389)). Criminal laws and their application in proceedings governed by the rule of law are constitutional tasks.
Just as the state administration of the criminal law may in making its decision encroach under certain circumstances on the fundamental rights of adult suspects and may encroach on the rights of the perpetrator where there is proof that he or she is guilty of the commission of a crime, it is not prevented from also encroaching on the parental right to bring up a child in criminal proceedings against minors. This does not mean, of course, that the parental right must in principle step back. Conflicts between parental rights on the one hand and the constitutional requirement that the criminal law protect legal interests and their enforcement in proceedings on the other hand must be resolved by weighing the rights and interests. In this connection, a balance must be achieved between the parental right concerned and the protection of legal interests by the criminal law. If it is not possible to achieve this balance, then a decision must be made as to which interest should step back taking into account the peculiarities and special circumstances of the individual case (see on Article 5 of the Basic Law: BVerfGE 35, 202 (225); 59, 231 (261 et seq.); 67, 213 (228); see also BVerfGE 81, 278 (292); 93, 1 (21)). However, the disciplinary concepts at the foundation of the criminal law relating to minors, which does not establish any privilege on the part of the state to bring up children and does not suspend the precedence of the parental right to bring up a child ..., cannot be accorded any special significance, at all events prior to the conclusion of the proceedings.

The disciplinary effect on the minor where the goal is that he or she lead a life free of crime in the future (see BVerfGE 74, 102 (123) on the goal of a reaction under juvenile criminal law) presupposes in principle that there is judicial evidence that the minor is in need of discipline and that this need has become recognisable due to a specific crime; it also presupposes a legal consequence that is geared towards this neediness has been determined. While criminal proceedings are being conducted it will usually not be possible to ascertain the above, so that there is hardly any constitutional scope for justifying the subordination of the parental right to bring up a child on the basis of disciplinary objectives alone.

c) Encroachments on Article 6.2 of the Basic Law require a statutory basis. It is necessary for there to be a sufficiently definite statute; here, the requirements placed on sufficient definiteness will be stricter, the more significant the effects of a rule are (see BVerfGE 49, 168 (181); 59, 104 (114); 86, 288 (311)). The person affected must be able to understand the legal situation (BVerfGE 64, 261 (286)). This applies also to limits on the parental right to bring up a child which result from its limitation inherent in the constitution. The right to enforce the state's right to punish may – over and beyond the prerequisites for state encroachment in the case of parenting failures pursuant to Article 6.2 of the Basic Law – allow encroachment on the parental right to bring up a child, but it does not mean that the necessity for such encroachment to be based on a sufficiently definite statute is also dispensable.

2. Measured by the above, § 51.2 of the Juvenile Court Act only stands up to constitutional examination in part.

a) The exclusion of parents from a trial in respect of a minor affects the constitutionally protected parental right according to Article 6.2 of the Basic Law. However, to the extent that the issue is the removal of relatives, persons with parental rights or legal representatives who are not the parents the scope of protection of Article 6.2 of the Basic Law is not affected …

aa) The parental right is to be understood comprehensively and refers in principle to the whole person of the child. The parents and other persons with parental responsibility within the meaning of Article 6.2 of the Basic Law (according to the decision in BVerfGE 34, 165 (200), this also includes grandparents who are at the same time legal guardians) are entitled to a constitutionally protected influence on all living and developmental conditions of the child, including those outside of the family.

The authority to safeguard ("as trustee") the rights of the child against the state or against third parties derives from the right and the duty to take care of the child … If criminal proceedings are commenced against a minor suspected of committing a crime, this in itself is an encroachment on his or her rights and those of his or her parents … If the protection of the rights of their children belong to the scope of responsibility of parents, from that it follows also that there is a necessity under constitutional law to ensure the participation of the parents in criminal proceedings in a juvenile court early on. This takes into account above all that, due to the fact that they have less experience of life and due to the intense psychological and physical developmental processes to which they are exposed, minors are much less able to safeguard their interests than adults and are therefore particularly in need of protection when they are confronted with the enforcement of the state's right to punish in criminal proceedings …

bb) The parental right to exercise a protective and advisory function for the child also includes the right to assert one's own ideas of how to bring up a child in criminal proceedings in a juvenile court. On the one hand, the question of which statements the minor should make in relation to the offence alleged against him or her and which of the means provided by the Juvenile Court Act and the Code of Criminal Procedure he or she should use to invalidate the allegations made and, on the other hand, the parent's decision on the disciplinary measures he or she should take in response to the (possible commission of an) offence (prior to the state taking action) are both related to the bringing up of a child and thus primarily the task of the parents. The goal of proceedings, i.e. to impose a penalty on the minor under the criminal law relating to minors if the commission of an offence is proven, which can itself encroach on the parental right to bring up a child, also requires the inclusion of the parents in the proceedings. In this connection, it is less important from the point of view of constitutional law that the state measures are likely to be more effective if the understanding and support of the parents can be expected (on this, see already Decisions of the Federal Court of Justice in Criminal Matters (*Entscheidungen des Bundesgerichtshofes in Strafsachen* – BGHSt) 18, 21 (5)). What is decisive in this respect is that it must be possible for parents to present contrary ideas of their own prior to the imposition of a measure that impairs their rights …

cc) The fundamental rights in Article 6.2 of the Basic Law are thus concretised – in non-constitutional law – in the provisions of the Juvenile Court Act on the participation of persons with parental rights and legal representatives in criminal proceedings in a juvenile court (§ 50 and § 67 of the Juvenile Court Act) – to the extent that the parental right is affected … Just as is the case with the withdrawal of rights of participation (§ 67.4 of the Juvenile Court Act), exclusion from the trial (§ 51.2 of the Juvenile Court Act) is thus also an encroachment on the constitutionally protected parental rights.

b) The exclusion of the parents from the trial of their child is a serious encroachment, which can prevent the exercise of parental rights in criminal proceedings in a juvenile court and put the accused minor, who is dependent on his or her parent's advice, in a largely unprotected position. The constitution requires such exclusion to be based on a law which acquaints those affected by it in a clear and comprehensive way with the objectivised intention of the legislature expressed therein (see BVerfGE 34, 293 (301) in connection with the exclusion of a defence counsel; see also BVerfGE 38, 105 (119) on the removal of the person advising a witness). § 51.2 of the Juvenile Court Act does not satisfy this requirement. Nor can clarification of the provision with the aid of traditional methods of interpretation cure this defect.

aa) The wording of § 51.2 of the Juvenile Court Act makes the exclusion of the parents possible within the framework of a directory provision to the extent that there are "misgivings (*Bedenken*) about whether they should be present". If one takes the everyday meaning of "misgivings", i.e. "a thought based on existing doubts, fears or reservations, which make it appear advisable to (still) wait with one's consent or to reconsider a plan" (see *Duden, Das große Wörterbuch der deutschen Sprache*, 3rd edition 1999, Vol. 1, entry: "*Bedenken*") or "a thought which contains doubts, concerns or reservations" (with a reference to the origins of the word in the language used in chanceries in the 15th century: *Etymologisches Wörterbuch des Deutschen*, 2nd edition by Wolfgang Pfeifer, 1993, entry: "*bedenken*"), the grammatical interpretation with the surrounding semantics opens up an extensive encroachment on the parental right in Article 6.2 of the Basic Law.

The wording does not contain any indication as to what the doubts, reservations or objections should relate. There are many possibilities as to the subject of "misgivings": possibly doubts in the willingness or ability of the parents to assert their rights in the child's best interests; concerns that they will abuse their rights in proceedings or that there will be an impairment of the ascertainment of the truth; fear that the work of the agency assisting the juvenile courts outside of the hearing will be made more difficult; reservations about discussing circumstances in the presence of the parents that are unpleasant for them; doubts as to whether one can take effective disciplinary measures in the presence of the parents … The wording allows a judge to use any reservation about the presence of the parents as a reason for excluding them.

In addition, to what degree the judge has to be convinced that there are misgivings is not evident from the provision (see expressly in connection with the exclusion of a defence counsel BVerfGE 34, 293 (301)). The Act does not shed light on whether it is already sufficient for exclusion that it is in the judge's view obvious, possible or probable that, for example, the parents are not in a position to fulfil their duty to bring up their child, or whether it is necessary for the existence a specific ground for exclusion that the judge hold a conviction based on facts.

bb) Having regard to § 51.2 of the Juvenile Court Act's position in the statutory framework narrows on the one hand the scope of application of the provision, but

on the other hand makes it clear that the means that the general law of criminal procedure has of removing legal representatives also remain available in criminal proceedings in a juvenile court.
According to the official heading, § 51 of the Juvenile Court Act permits the "Temporary exclusion of participants". This in itself speaks in favour of the interpretation that a judge cannot base an exclusion for the entire trial on § 51.2 of the Juvenile Court Act …, but only an exclusion for a certain part of proceedings or a certain situation during the proceedings. An indication of the correctness of this result is also provided by § 67.4 of the Juvenile Court Act, which makes it possible to deprive the person with parental rights of all of the rights to which he or she is entitled – including the right to participate in the entire trial – and makes this dependent on the existence of important grounds which call into question in principle and in general the exercise of his or her rights in accordance with the rules of procedure.
The result arrived at by virtue of this interpretation is further confirmed by the consequences that the legislature attaches to the withdrawal of rights pursuant to § 67.4 of the Juvenile Court Act on the one hand, and the exclusion from the trial pursuant to § 51.2 of the Juvenile Court Act on the other hand. While § 67.4 sentence 3 of the Juvenile Court Act makes the appointment of a temporary guardian to safeguard the interests of the accused in criminal proceedings the consequence of a complete withdrawal of rights and § 67.4 sentence 4 of the Juvenile Court Act orders that the trial be stayed until a temporary guardian is appointed and § 68.2 of the Juvenile Court Act even prescribes that counsel be appointed by the court (in the event that all of the legal representatives and persons with parental rights have had their rights withdrawn), § 51.2 of the Juvenile Court Act does not contain any comparable provision which attempts to compensate for disadvantages caused by the exclusion. If the legislature had wanted § 51.2 of the Juvenile Court Act to be understood as a section that also permits exclusion for the entire duration of the proceedings, the obvious thing to do would have been to make exclusion subject to a rule similar to the one in § 67.4 of the Juvenile Court Act.
The general possibilities of excluding the legal representatives remain in principle in existence parallel to § 51.2 of the Juvenile Court Act (see § 2 of the Juvenile Court Act). It is true that the Code of Criminal Procedure does not provide any specific grounds for excluding legal representatives. A general reason for removing a legal representative from the trial can be, however, the fact that he or she is a potential witness; § 58.1 and § 243.2 sentence 1 of the Code of Criminal Procedure allow in this case an oral hearing without the legal representative.
cc) A historical interpretation of § 51.2 of the Juvenile Court Act does not help to further clarify the provision.

Already the previous provision in § 34.2 of the Juvenile Court Act of the German Reich (*Reichsjugendgerichtsgesetz* – RJGG) of 6 November 1943 (Reich Law Gazette (*Reichsgesetzblatt* – RGBl) I p. 635), whose wording was almost identical and which was later adopted without additional discussion as § 51.2 of the Juvenile Court Act, was not intended to allow a complete exclusion … Both the previous statute and the earlier regulations in respect of the statute expressly mentioned a "temporary exclusion".

There are otherwise no statutory materials which could make the intention of the legislature historically clearer. …

dd) Nor does an objective-teleological interpretation serve to more clearly delineate the meaning of § 51.2 of the Juvenile Court Act.

To the extent that the provision, understood according to its purpose, is intended to serve in the broadest sense to exclude the influence of relatives in the trial of a minor and thus ensure that the proceedings run smoothly, this insight still provides insufficient information to answer the question of what may be deemed to be a relevant disturbance according to the statute. This could only be answered if one could ascertain the goals which § 51.2 of the Juvenile Court Act is bound to achieve: the ascertainment of the truth, the protection of a minor or a witness, the support of the work of the agency assisting the juvenile courts, the achievement of any disciplinary objective or perhaps even a number of these objectives in a certain order of priority and combination. This is not the case here.

ee) An interpretation of § 51.2 of the Juvenile Court Act based on its wording, structure in the legal system, drafting history and purpose cannot determine an area of application sufficiently clearly and bindingly. The cases of application which are referred to in the work of legal commentators indeed pursue different objectives; they all fall easily within the provision in view of the broad formulation of the enactment. The term "misgivings" does not provide a precise definition of the prerequisites for encroachment and also does not stand in the way of a possibly expansive interpretation which goes beyond the types of cases previously discussed.

The legislature failed in § 51.2 of the Juvenile Court Act to itself regulate the questions that are important in this connection for the application of the provision – description of the situation in litigation in which exclusion may occur; the degree to which a judge must be convinced that the prerequisite for encroachment exists; measures which are intended to compensate for the encroachment; it left the decision regarding the exclusion to the juvenile court judge.

It would have been possible for the legislature – contrary to the view adopted by the Federal Government – to enact a sufficiently clear and complete provision. This is shown by the provision set forth in § 247 of the Code of Criminal Procedure, which regulates the temporary exclusion of an accused from the trial. It describes the possible cases of application, formulates goals and provides in addition for the accused to be later informed [about proceedings] (when he or she is again present). It succeeds in regulating individual grounds of exclusion and to nonetheless include from a variety of possible cases mention of those that are significant. The legislature should thus not see itself as hindered from identifying from the variety of conceivable cases certain types of cases in which it is permissible to override the parental right to bring up a child within the limits set by the Basic Law; nor should it therefore see itself as hindered from clarifying the goal, conditions of application and consequences of § 51.2 of the Juvenile Court Act – for example, the protection of the accused minor or other parties to proceedings, the ascertainment of the truth or the response to an abuse of rights by parents (see § 67.4 of the Juvenile Court Act).

ff) In view of the lack of definiteness of § 51.2 of the Juvenile Court Act an interpretation in conformity with the Basic Law also does not come into consideration. If the interpretation of a provision leads, as with § 51.2 of the Juvenile Court Act, to the result that one cannot deduce from the provision sufficiently definite terms intended by the legislature, then the necessary prerequisite, pursuant to the case-law of the Federal Constitutional Court, for an interpretation in conformity with the Basic Law, which is that there is, at all events, one interpretation of the provision which is in conformity with the Basic Law (see BVerfGE 88, 145 (166); established case-law), will not be satisfied. An interpretation of a provision encroaching on parental rights set forth in Article 6.2 of the Basic Law, which interpretation is compatible with the Basic Law, would require however – for the satisfaction of the constitutional proviso of legality – that there be a core provision covering all important questions which can be traced back to the clear, objectivised intention of the legislature.

This is missing, however, in the case of a provision such as § 51.2 of the Juvenile Court Act, which does not contain either specific requirements for exclusion or allow the purpose which the provision is intended to fulfil to be clearly recognised. If one nevertheless allowed an interpretation in conformity with the Basic Law, the constitutional necessity for the specific enactment of a statute – which requires that any encroachment on a fundamental right be based on a statutory regulation and have its nature and scope defined by the legislature itself – would be devoid of effect.

3. a) The decision of the Local Court of 29 June 2000, which excluded the complainant from participating in the trial, is incompatible with the Basic Law.

The provision set forth in § 51.2 of the Juvenile Court Act on which the removal was based is unconstitutional and thus it may not be used as an enabling law. Since there is also no other provision which could justify exclusion, the challenged order violates Article 6.2 of the Basic Law.

b) The decisions of 11 January and 1 February 2001, which excluded the complainant from participation in the trial (except for the handing down of the judgment) and at the same time refused the appointment of counsel by the court, are also incompatible with the Basic Law.

This follows – as far as exclusion from the trial is concerned – from the fact that § 51.2 of the Juvenile Court Act, the provision on which the removal was based, violates Article 6.2 of the Basic Law. To the extent that the courts rejected the complainant's application for the appointment of counsel for his son by the court, this too was based on a fundamental misjudgement of the meaning of Article 6.2 of the Basic Law. Already the fact that the courts dealt first and foremost with the prerequisites for the appointment of counsel by the court pursuant to § 140 of the Code of Criminal Procedure (which did not exist in their opinion) and only dealt in passing with the exclusion of the complainant and the possible resulting necessity for appointing defence counsel show that they were not aware of the seriousness of the encroachment on a fundamental right caused by the exclusion and the resulting procedural consequences.

The statement that the son of the complainant was also able to appropriately defend himself at the first hearing in the absence of his father and the idea that the facts and law were quite simple even for a 15-year-old, cannot replace consideration of the necessity according to the Basic Law for compensation of the exclusion of a parent who had taken over the representation of the interests of a minor in the trial. In particular, it was not taken into consideration that the complainant was not just excluded from part of the trial, but completely excluded so that removal pursuant to § 51.2 of the Juvenile Court Act – in any case as far as the exercise of rights at the trial were concerned – was the same as withdrawal of rights pursuant to § 67.4 of the Juvenile Court Act. If the courts had considered the matter along these lines, it cannot be ruled out that they would have – although there was no express statutory provision – appointed counsel.

c) The orders of 16 March and 3 April 2001, in which the appointment of counsel by the court was again rejected and at the same time the appointment of the complainant as advisor was rejected, are also not compatible with the constitution.

With regard to the rejection of the appointment of counsel by the court, the violation of a fundamental right by the previous orders of 11 January and 1 February 2001 is repeated. To the extent that the Local Court bases the rejection of the appointment of the complainant to advise his son primarily on the exclusion pursuant to § 51.2 of the Juvenile Court Act and thus on an unconstitutional provision, the order thus already shows itself to be constitutionally unsound.

The additional consideration of the Local Court not to contemplate the appointment of the complainant to advise his son in view of § 69.2 of the Juvenile Court Act also does not give the rejection order a constitutionally sound basis. In any case, with regard to the parents whom the fundamental right set forth in Article 6.2 of the Basic Law protects, "disadvantages to the child's upbringing", as referred to by the Act in § 69.2 of the Juvenile Court Act, do not unconditionally justify the rejection of the parents' appointment to advise their child. The precedence which the parental rights to bring up a child enjoy vis-à-vis state influence on a minor in criminal proceedings in a juvenile court, which are aimed at solving and prosecuting a crime, requires restraint according to the constitution in assuming that disadvantages to the child's upbringing exist and ordering consequences based on this during ongoing proceedings …

In this case, whether the considerations of the Local Court could support a rejection based on § 69.2 of the Juvenile Court Act can be ultimately left open. This is because the Local Court was in any case just as unaware in its decision as it was in the application of § 51.2 of the Juvenile Court Act of the effect of the parental right to bring up a child, which counters state influence on a minor in criminal proceedings. Thus it cannot in any case be ruled out that the Local Court and subsequently also the Regional Court would have reached different decisions if they had properly evaluated the parental right to bring up a child.

d) The verdict sentencing the son of the complainant also violates the complainant's fundamental right under Article 6.2 of the Basic Law. This right grants him a constitutional right to be present at the trial. The withdrawal of this right to be present on the basis of a provision that does not satisfy constitutional standards and the subsequent trial in the absence of the complainant violate the meaning and scope of the rights guaranteed by Article 6.2 of the Basic Law which the complainant is prevented from exercising.

…

The violation of the parental right also had an effect on the decision of the Local Court sentencing the son of the complainant. At all events, the possibility cannot be excluded that the Local Court would have decided differently if the complainant had had the opportunity to participate at the oral hearing, to exercise his rights and to support his son. The subject of the trial was primarily the hearing of evidence and the interrogation of several witnesses on the accusation of bodily injury, which the son of the complainant had denied on the basis that there had been justifying circumstances. It is obvious that the complainant could have influenced the course and result of the trial by exercising his right to ask questions, by submitting motions to admit evidence, by submitting his comments on particular evidence collected and by making closing arguments.

e) The order of the Higher Regional Court, which dismissed the appeals on points of law by the complainant and his son against the sentence of the Local Court pursuant to § 349.2 of the Code of Criminal Procedure, is also not compatible with Article 6.2 of the Basic Law.

...

4. The decisions that are not compatible with the Basic Law must be reversed and the original proceeding referred back to the Local Court (§ 95.2 of the Federal Constitutional Court Act (*Bundesverfassungsgerichtsgesetz* – BVerfGG)). In doing so the Federal Constitutional Court has made use of the possibility of referring the matter back to a Local Court other than the one which adjudicated previously (see BVerfGE 20, 336 (343)). At the same time, § 51.2 of the Juvenile Court Act is to be declared void on account of being incompatible with Article 6.2 of the Basic Law to the extent that it allows persons to be excluded who take parental responsibility within the meaning of Article 6.2 of the Basic Law (§ 95.3 sentence 2 of the Federal Constitutional Court Act).

...

Justices: Hassemer, Sommer, Jentsch, Broß, Osterloh, Di Fabio, Mellinghoff, Lübbe-Wolff

As a result of the Federal Constitutional Court's judgment, the Second Act to Modernise the Judicial System (Justizmodernisierungsgesetz) *of 22 December 2006 (Federal Law Gazette I 2006 p. 3416), with effect from 31 December 2006, reworded § 51.2 of the Juvenile Court Act as follows:*

> *"(2) The presiding judge can also exclude persons with parental rights and legal representatives of the accused if*
>
> 1. *there is the threat of considerable disadvantage to the upbringing of the accused because it there is a fear that the discussion of the personal circumstances of the accused in their presence will considerably complicate a necessary future cooperation between the persons mentioned and the agency assisting the juvenile courts with regard to the implementation of sanctions that can be expected to be imposed by the juvenile court,*
> 2. *they are suspected of having been involved in the offence of which the minor is accused or if they have been sentenced for their involvement,*

3. *a danger to the life, limb or freedom of the accused, of a witness or another person or another considerable impairment of the best interests of the accused must be feared,*
4. *there is a fear that their presence will impair the ascertainment of the truth, or*
5. *circumstances from the personal sphere of a party to the proceedings, of a witness or of a person injured by an unlawful act will be discussed whose discussion in their presence would violate interests that are worthy of protection, unless there is a predominant interest of the persons with parental right and legal representatives in these circumstances to be discussed in their presence."*

No. 38

BVerfG 107, 150

of 29 January 2003 – 1 BvL 20/99, 1 BvR 933/01 –

"Case regarding parental custody for children born out of wedlock"

HEADNOTES:

1. **The child's best interests require that from its birth the child has a person who can act for the child with legally binding effect. In view of the diversity of the living conditions into which children born out of wedlock are born, it is constitutional that parental custody of a child born out of wedlock is normally attributed to its mother upon the child's birth.**
2. **The possibility of joint custody facilitated by § 1626a.1 no. 1 of the Civil Code (*Bürgerliches Gesetzbuch* – BGB) to the parents of a child born out of wedlock is based on a regulatory concept of custody which, on the basis of the child's best interests, makes the parents' agreement about joint custody the precondition of joint custody. At present there is no evidence to substantiate that this regulatory concept does not take sufficient account of the parental right under Article 6.2 of the Basic Law (*Grundgesetz* – GG) of a father of a child born out of wedlock.**
3. **In cases in which both parents live with the child and both parents have already shown their willingness to cooperate by factually caring for the child jointly, the legislature was justified in assuming that the parents will as a rule make use of the statutory possibility of joint custody that now exists, i.e. that they will legalise their factual care by making declarations of parental custody.**
4. **The legislature is obliged to observe the actual development and to review whether its assumption stands the test of reality. If it becomes apparent that this is normally not the case, it will have to ensure that fathers of children born out of wedlock who live with the mother and a child as a family are opened an access to joint custody that takes sufficient account of their parental right under Article 6.2 of the Basic Law, with due consideration being given to the child's best interests.**

5. **Parents who lived with their child born out of wedlock but who separated before the entry into force of the Act Reforming the Law of Parent and Child on 1 July 1998 must be given the possibility of having judicially reviewed whether joint custody is not contrary to the child's best interests although one parent does not agree with it.**

Judgment of the First Senate of 29 January 2003
on the basis of the oral hearing of 19 November 2002
– 1 BvL 20/99, 1 BvR 933/01 –

in the proceedings I. regarding a constitutional review of whether it is compatible with Article 6.2 sentence 1 of the Basic Law and Article 6.5 of the Basic Law that, according to §§ 1626a and 1672 of the Civil Code, the father of a child born out of wedlock who had lived together with the child's mother and the child for several years in a relationship that was similar to a family cannot be awarded joint custody for his child after the separation of the parents as long as the child's mother withholds her consent, without consideration being given to the circumstances of the individual case – suspension of proceedings and submission order of the Korbach Local Court (*Amtsgericht*) of 16 August 1999 (7 F 10/99 SO) – 1 BvL 20/99 –, II. regarding the constitutional complaint 1. of Mr G., 2. of the minor H. , represented by the complainant re 1 – authorised representative: …, lawyer – a) directly against the order of the Federal Court of Justice (*Bundesgerichtshof*) of 4 April 2001 – XII ZB 3/00 –, the order of the Stuttgart Higher Regional Court (*Oberlandesgericht*) of 2 December 1999 – 18 UF 259/99 –, the order of the Tübingen Local Court of 19 May 1999 – 6 F 60/99 –, b) indirectly against § 1626a.1 no. 1 and § 1626a.2 of the Civil Code – 1 BvR 933/01 –.

RULING:

I. 1. § 1626a of the Civil Code in the version of the Act Reforming the Law of Parent and Child (*Kindschaftsrechtsreformgesetz*) of 16 December 1997 (Federal Law Gazette (*Bundesgesetzblatt* – BGBl) I page 2942) is not compatible with Article 6.2 and 6.5 of the Basic Law insofar as there is no transitional arrangement for parents who separated prior to the entry into force of the Act Reforming the Law of Parent and Child on 1 July 1998.
2. The legislature is instructed to bring a constitutional transitional arrangement into being by 31 December 2003. Until such time as a new statutory provision is

adopted, court proceedings are to be suspended insofar as the ruling depends on the constitutionality of § 1626a of the Civil Code, taking into account the provisos that are contained in the grounds.
II. 1. The order of the Federal Court of Justice of 4 April 2001 – XII ZB 3/00 –, the order of the Stuttgart Higher Regional Court of 2 December 1999 – 18 UF 259/99 – and the order of the Tübingen Local Court of 19 May 1999 – 6 F 60/99 – violate the fundamental right of the complainant re 1 under Article 6.2 of the Basic Law. The orders of the Federal Court of Justice and of the Higher Regional Court are reversed. The case is referred back to the Stuttgart Higher Regional Court.
2. The constitutional complaint of the complainant re 2 is dismissed as inadmissible.
3. …

EXTRACT FROM GROUNDS:

A.

The judge's submission and the constitutional complaint relate to the question of whether it is constitutional that the father of a child born out of wedlock may only have custody of the child together with the mother, who otherwise has sole custody, if both submit appropriate declarations of parental custody or marry each other.

I.

1. Prior to the entry into force of the Act Reforming the Law of Parent and Child (*Kindschaftsrechtsreformgesetz* – KindRG) of 16 December 1997 (Federal Law Gazette I p. 2942) on 1 July 1998, the mother alone was entitled to custody of a child born out of wedlock (§ 1705 sentence 1 of the Civil Code old). There was no statutory provision for joint custody of their child of parents who were not married to each other.
2. The draft Bill Reforming the Law of Parent and Child submitted by the Federal Government in 1996 (*Bundestag* printed paper (*Bundestagsdrucksache* – BT-Drucks) 13/4899), with which in particular also the legal differences between children born in wedlock and children born out of wedlock were to be removed as far as possible (see *Bundestag* printed paper 13/4899, p. 1) contained amongst other things a comprehensive reform of parental custody, and in doing so provided for the first time in § 1626a of the Civil Code for joint custody for parents who were

not married to each other on submission of concurring declarations of parental custody.

It was stated as reasoning that after the Federal Constitutional Court had issued a call (see BVerfGE 61, 358) for a new provision, it was no longer a matter of the pros and cons of joint custody, but of the modalities of the structure of this legal institution. By means of the requirement of declarations of parental custody, it was said to be ensured that joint custody could not come about against the will of one of the parents. Children who are born out of wedlock were said to be born not only into intact out-of-wedlock communities, but also still into volatile, unstable relationships. Imposing joint custody against the will of one parent would harbour the danger here that from the outset conflicts would be carried out at the expense of the child. Joint custody was said not to be made contingent on any prior court review as to whether it was not contrary to the child's best interests because this would express unjustified mistrust of those mothers and fathers who wished to share custody (*Bundestag* printed paper 13/4899, p. 58-59).

In the context of the legislative procedure, the Committee on Legal Affairs of the *Bundestag* responsible for the Bill, together with the Committee for Family, Youth and Senior Citizens, held an expert hearing. In its recommendation for a resolution and in its concluding report, it named as an important goal of the reform to also facilitate joint parental custody, even if parents are not married to each other. Joint parental custody should be promoted if the parents considered themselves able to implement it because this framework could make the best contribution towards the child being able to establish and maintain relationships with both parents. In order to ensure that the establishment of joint custody was not omitted out of ignorance of this possibility, it was recommended that the youth welfare office should point this out in its advisory and support work. There had been diverging views as to whether joint custody should also be possible against the will of one parent, in particular if the child had lived together with both parents for a long period, but joint custody had not been awarded because the mother had rejected this without further reasoning. The retention of the sole custody of the mother could appear to pose problems here if the child had equally built up relationships with both parents and there were no reasons against joint custody from the point of view of the child. The majority of the Committee had however given priority to the consideration that the enforced establishment of joint custody against the will of one parent would generally entail more disadvantages for the child than advantages because the conflict between the parents about this would shift to conflicts on the exercise of custody. These would ultimately do the child more harm than good. The majority of the Committee on Legal Affairs was therefore said to give preference to the willingness of the parents, strengthened by voluntary advisory and assistance services, to cooperate in the best interests of their child instead of enforced commonality (*Bundestag* printed paper 13/8511, pp. 65-66).

3. The regulatory proposal of the Federal Government on joint custody of unmarried parents in § 1626a of the Civil Code remained unchanged in rem in this regard and entered into force on 1 July 1998 with the Act Reforming the Law of Parent and Child, after being adopted by the *Bundestag* and with the consent of the *Bundesrat*.

The provision reads as follows:

§ 1626a of the Civil Code

> (1) Where the parents, at the date of the birth of the child, are not married to each other, they have joint parental custody if they
> 1. declare that they wish to take on parental custody jointly (declarations of parental custody), or
> 2. marry each other.
> (2) Apart from this, the mother has parental custody.

This gives the opportunity to parents who are not married to each other to have joint parental custody, regardless of whether or not they live together, if they intend this and make declarations of parental custody, which may be done even before the child is born (§ 1626b.2 of the Civil Code). If these declarations of parental custody are not made, then in principle the mother has sole parental custody of a child born out of wedlock. The father may only be granted custody against the mother's will if parental custody is withdrawn from her (§ 1680.3 in conjunction with § 1666 of the Civil Code), she is factually prevented from exercising custody (§ 1678.2 of the Civil Code) or dies (§§ 1680 and 1681 of the Civil Code). Parental custody may be withdrawn from the mother according to § 1666 of the Civil Code if the physical, mental or emotional best interests of the child are at risk from abuse of custody, by neglect of the child, by non-culpable failure of the mother or by the conduct of a third party, and if – over and above this – other measures have been unsuccessful or it is to be assumed that they are not sufficient to avert the danger. If custody is withdrawn from the mother, it is transferred to the father if this is in the child's best interests (§ 1680.2 and 1680.3 of the Civil Code).

II.

1. Recent social science studies also confirm that joint parental custody in principle meets the needs of the child for relationships with both parents and makes it clear

to him or her that both parents are equally willing to take responsibility for the child …. Thus, Proksch, who has investigated the implementation of the reform of the law of parent and child, reached the conclusion that joint custody also of separated parents is more suited than sole custody to exert a positive influence on communication and cooperation between the parents, to maintain contact between the child in question and both parents, and to alleviate the adverse effects on the child caused by separation … However, studies also indicate that a lack of willingness to cooperate and a considerable potential for conflict between the parents may impose serious burdens on the child so that there are considerable reservations against joint custody … According to Wallerstein/Lewis/Blakeslee …, it is not so significant for the child's best interests in the case of the separation of his or her parents whether the parents have joint custody or only one of them is entitled to custody. It is rather said to be the quality of the parent-child relationship and the willingness to cooperate between the parents which are decisive.

2. How many children are affected by the statutory provision on joint custody of parents not married to each other can only be documented with figures by approximation. There were 2.1 million non-marital cohabitations in the Federal Republic in 2001, of whom 27.6 per cent lived together with children under the age of 18. This concerned 821,000 children. By contrast, 2.12 million children lived with only one parent … Hence, 19.4 per cent of all 15.1 million minor children lived with their unmarried parent or parents, whilst 12.16 million children, that is 80.5 per cent, lived with their married parents … However, it should be taken into account with these figures that children born out of wedlock become born in wedlock by marriage and children born in wedlock may live in a non-marital cohabitation of one parent. According to the study by Vaskovics et al. from 1997, there was no partnership … between the mother and father of a child born out of wedlock at the time of his or her birth in a total of 17 per cent of the cases investigated … In the first six months after the birth, the share of mothers who no longer had a relationship with the father of the child increased to 35 per cent in the new federal *Länder* (states) and to half in the old federal *Länder*. In approximately 24 per cent of the households surveyed, finally, the children lived with their mother and father, in 51 per cent only with the mother and in 15 per cent with the mother and a man who was not the father of the child; 42 per cent of children living with the mother had contact with their father ….

III.

1. The applicant of the original proceedings that gave rise to proceedings 1 BvL 20/99 lived in non-marital cohabitation from 1983 to 1993 with the respondent and

her two sons from another relationship. Their joint son, for whom the complainant recognised paternity, was born in 1990. The parents separated in 1993. On the basis of a written agreement, the child initially remained with the father, who looked after him for eight months until he released the child at the request of the mother. During the following years, there was frequent contact and joint holidays between the father and the son. When the mother had a stay in hospital, she placed the child in the care of the father. In 1997 the mother then forbade the father any contact to the child. A contact arrangement was however made through the mediation of the youth welfare office.

After one attempt to obtain joint custody together with the mother had already failed, and after the Act Reforming the Law of Parent and Child had entered into force at the end of 1998, the father once more applied to the family court accordingly. He pointed out that he considered the statutory provision to be unconstitutional whereby he could only have custody for his child jointly with the mother with her consent. He had always wanted to be responsible for his son's future. The mother applied for the application to be rejected on grounds that normal communication had no longer been possible between her and the father since their separation.

After hearing the parties to the proceedings, the family court suspended the proceedings and submitted the question to the Federal Constitutional Court for review as to whether it is compatible with Article 6.2 and 6.5 of the Basic Law that according to §§ 1626a and 1672 of the Civil Code the father of a child born out of wedlock who lived together with the child's mother and the child for several years in a relationship that was similar to a family after the separation of the parents, without consideration of the concrete circumstances of the individual case, cannot be awarded joint custody of his child as long as the child's mother withholds her consent (see *Zeitschrift für das gesamte Familienrecht* – FamRZ 2000, p. 629).

…

2. The complainant re 1 of the proceedings 1 BvR 933/01 also lived with the mother of his son, who was born in 1993, in non-marital cohabitation for a long period. After the separation and the mother moving out with the child from the joint home in 1996, the parents agreed on an extensive right of contact of the complainant re 1, enabling him to have the child in his home for half of the week. Furthermore, they agreed to arrange matters relevant to the child by agreement as far as possible. The mother did not however comply with a request of the complainant re 1 to submit a declaration of parental custody.

The Local Court rejected the application of the complainant re 1, submitted in 1999 after the entry into force of the Act Reforming the Law of Parent and Child, to grant joint custody to him together with the mother fully, else partly. The Higher

Regional Court rejected the complaint lodged against this after hearing the parties to the proceedings and permitted a further appeal on points of law (see FamRZ 2000, p. 632). …
The Federal Court of Justice rejected the further appeal against this (see FamRZ 2001, p. 907). It considers § 1626a of the Civil Code to be constitutional. …
This is countered by the constitutional complaint lodged by complainant re 1 also on behalf of his son, the complainant re 2, with which he complains of a violation of Article 1, Article 2, Article 3, Article 6.2 and Article 20.3 of the Basic Law. He considers § 1626a.1 no. 1 and 1626a.2 of the Civil Code to be unconstitutional insofar as this provision makes the establishment of joint custody solely contingent on the consent of the mother. …

IV.

The possibility granted to state an opinion in the proceedings was made use of by the Federal Ministry of Justice on behalf of the Federal Government, by the Federal Court of Justice, by the Academic Association for Family Law (*Wissenschaftliche Vereinigung für Familienrecht*), by the German Women Lawyers Association (*Deutscher Juristinnenbund*), by the German Society for the Protection of Children (*Deutscher Kinderschutzbund*), by the Association of Single Parents (*Verband alleinerziehender Mütter und Väter*), by the Fathers for Children Association (*Verein Väter für Kinder*), as well as by the applicant of the original proceedings that gave rise to the proceedings on the constitutionality of a statute, and these once more submitted their views in the oral hearing. The German Institute for Youth Welfare Services and Family Law (*Deutsches Institut für Jugendhilfe und Familienrecht*) and the respondent of the original proceedings giving rise to the constitutional complaint proceedings also made a statement in the oral hearing.
…

B. – I.

The submission order is admissible. …
However, § 1672 of the Civil Code, also submitted for review, is not relevant to the decision on the underlying case. …

II.

1. The constitutional complaint of the complainant re 1 with which he complains of the incompatibility of § 1626a.1 no. 1 and 1626a.2 of the Civil Code and of the rul-

ings by non-constitutional courts based on this provision with Article 6.2 and 6.5 of the Basic Law, as well as with Article 3.1 of the Basic Law, is admissible. …
2. The constitutional complaint lodged by the complainant re 1 on behalf of his son, the complainant re 2, is inadmissible. …

C.

§ 1626a of the Civil Code is not compatible with Article 6.2 and 6.5 of the Basic Law insofar as there is no transitional arrangement which provides for judicial review of the individual case as to whether the child's best interests are opposed to joint parental custody held by parents who are not married to each other in cases in which the parents have lived with the child but separated before the Act Reforming the Law of Parent and Child entered into force on 1 July 1998. In other respects, no reasons are currently recognisable as to why the regulatory concept of § 1626a of the Civil Code on joint custody of parents not married to each other should not be compatible with the Basic Law.

I.

1. It still does not violate the parental right of the father of a child born out of wedlock under Article 6.2 of the Basic Law that, according to § 1626a.2 of the Civil Code, a child is first awarded legally to the mother alone and care for the person of the child is assigned to her in principle (see BVerfGE 56, 363 (389-390); 84, 168 (181)).
a) The holders of the parental right under Article 6.2 of the Basic Law are also the mother and the father of a child born out of wedlock (see BVerfGE 24, 119 (135); 92, 158 (177-178)). The inclusion of all parents in the scope of protection of this fundamental-rights provision however does not mean that all mothers and fathers must be granted the same rights in the relationship with their child. The parental right needs to be given concrete form by the legislature. Joint exercise of parental responsibility is contingent on the existence of a viable social relationship between the parents, requires a minimum degree of agreement between them and must be in line with the child's best interests. If the preconditions for joint assumption of parental responsibility are not met, the legislature may allocate the principal responsibility for the child to one parent (see BVerfGE 92, 158 (178-179)).
b) Unlike in the case of the parents of children born in wedlock, who legally undertook, when they married, to take responsibility for each other and for their joint children, the legislature even today cannot make a general assumption in the case of

parents who are not married to each other that they are living in domestic community and are willing and able to take joint responsibility for the child.
aa) The number of non-marital cohabitations has continually increased in recent decades. Whilst there were only 137,000 such communities in 1972, there were 2.1 million couples in 2001 who cohabited out of wedlock, 27.6 per cent of whom lived together with children … Equally, the number of children born out of wedlock has increased, whilst the birth figures have fallen further … However, in 2001 of the total of 15.1 million minor children only 5.4 per cent, in other words 821,000 children, lived together with their parents who were united in cohabitation … According to the study by Vaskovics et al. from 1997 on the circumstances of children born out of wedlock, roughly 24 per cent of the children in the cases studied lived with their father and mother after their birth … These figures do not permit one to conclude that the vast majority of children who are born out of wedlock are now born into a domestic community of mother and father.
bb) There are also no adequate factual indications for the assumption that the father of a child born out of wedlock on birth wishes to take responsibility for the child together with the mother as a rule. For instance, on the birth of a child born out of wedlock it had not yet been ascertained in the vast majority of the cases investigated by Vaskovics who the father of the child was. More than 80 per cent of fathers recognised their paternity voluntarily. However, in two-thirds of cases this did not take place until after the birth of the child …
The figures show that children who are born out of wedlock are born into a variety of family configurations even today. There are situations in which the father cannot be established or is not certain, in which he does not want to have anything to do with the child over and above paying maintenance, or would like to remain in touch with the child, but not with the mother, ranging to those in which the father would like to hold custody of the child jointly with the mother in agreement or in cohabitation with her.
c) The child's best interests require that from its birth the child has a person who can act for the child with legally binding effect. In view of the diversity of living conditions into which children born out of wedlock are born, it is justified that parental custody of the child is normally attributed to its mother upon the child's birth and not to the father or to both parents jointly.
A relationship already develops between mother and child during pregnancy, in addition to the biological ties, which continues after birth. Even if the father takes on a considerable significance for the development of the child, he must nonetheless build up a relationship with the child after the birth of the child – assuming he wishes to do so – which already exists between the mother and the child from the outset. Whilst the mother must already deal during pregnancy with the fact that she

is soon to bear responsibility for the child once it has been born, and has as a rule expressed her willingness to do so through pregnancy, the decision of the father as to how to behave towards his child has in many cases not yet been decided at its birth. The mother is the only sure relation whom the child encounters at its birth. If she is given sole custody, this hence ensures that factual and legal responsibility may be borne for the child from the first day of its life.

d) The allocation of custody in principle to the mother of the child born out of wedlock according to § 1626a.2 of the Civil Code is also constitutionally unobjectionable because, with § 1626a.1. no. 1 of the Civil Code, the legislature has now granted the possibility to those parents who wish to have joint custody for their child born out of wedlock by means of concurring declarations of parental custody to also already hold custody jointly in legal terms on the birth of the child.

The fact that the legislature here has regarded the declared concurring will of the parents as a sufficient foundation of a parent-child relationship on which joint custody can be founded, and did not satisfy itself with cohabitation of the parents as circumstance required for joint custody, is justified and reasoned also in the need to create a clear, secure responsibility for the child from the time of its birth. If there is a concurring declaration of will on the part of the parents, there is not only an indication that custody of the child can be held by the parents jointly, but there is also no need to clarify whether they are equally willing to do so. By tying joint custody to cohabitation of the parents, one would have to start by examining whether the parents of the child born out of wedlock in fact live together when the child is born and this cohabitation is able to offer a viable, long-term basis for joint custody. Such a future prognosis can however not yet be made solely from the cohabitation at the time of the birth of the child without a corresponding explicit will on the part of the parents. This is also confirmed by the study by Vaskovics according to which prior to the birth of a child born out of wedlock only a total of 17 per cent of mothers did not have a relationship with the child's father (or no longer had one), whilst this number had increased to roughly 50 per cent in the old and 35 per cent in the new Federal *Länder* in the first six months after the birth … There would therefore be a danger that the circumstances required for joint custody could not yet be finally clarified at the time of the birth of the child, in particular if the parents took different views on this. This would however be at the expense of the child, who at birth would not experience a clear attribution of legal custody.

Also linking the establishment of joint custody to the recognition of paternity would not make it dispensable to initially allocate to the mother sole custody of a child born out of wedlock. In view of the fact that only for one-third of children born out of wedlock paternity is recognised at birth, it is ensured solely by the provision contained in § 1626a.2 of the Civil Code that the child has an established holder of custody at this time.

2. Also § 1626a.1 no. 1 of the Civil Code does not violate Article 6.2 of the Basic Law.

a) The possibility facilitated with the Act Reforming the Law of Parent and Child by § 1626a.1 no. 1 of the Civil Code to the parents of a child born out of wedlock to legally hold joint custody for their child is based on a regulatory concept of custody which, on the basis of the child's best interests, makes the parents' agreement about joint custody the precondition of joint custody. At present there is no evidence to substantiate that with this [regulatory concept], the legislature did not take sufficient account of the parental right under Article 6.2 of the Basic Law of a father of a child born out of wedlock.

aa) The protection of parental rights according to Article 6.2 of the Basic Law, to which the father and the mother of a child are entitled in equal measure, covers the major elements of custody without which parental responsibility cannot be exercised (see BVerfGE 84, 168 (180)). If the father and the mother live together with the child, and if both are willing and able to shoulder parental responsibility, as a rule this is in line with the child's best interests if both parents are granted custody, given that the emotional ties of the child to both of its parents are legally secured thereby. At the same time, this makes it clear to the parents that they have a joint responsibility for their child, and joint custody can contribute towards perpetuating the parent-child relationship (see BVerfGE 84, 168 (182)).

In the child's best interests, however, joint custody is dependent on both parents being willing not only to derive rights from their position as parents, but also to shoulder duties towards the child, in other words to take responsibility for the child. Exercising this joint responsibility in turn makes it necessary for each parent to develop a personal relationship to the child and requires a minimum degree of agreement between the parents (see BVerfGE 92, 158 (178-179)). If this is lacking, and if the parents are neither willing nor able to cooperate, joint custody of the child may run counter to the child's best interests. If the parents carry out their conflict at the expense of the child, the child's ability to maintain relationships may be impaired and its development placed at peril. This insight gained from scientific studies … was confirmed only recently by the long-term studies of Wallerstein/Lewis/Blakeslee …

bb) The legislature was hence able to assume that joint custody enforced against the will of one parent will as a rule entail more disadvantages than advantages for the child (see *Bundestag* printed paper 13/4899, p. 58 et seq.; *Bundestag* printed paper 13/8511, p. 66). Hence, it has accommodated the child's best interests which it is

called upon to accommodate in shaping parental custody by Article 6.2 sentence 2 of the Basic Law.
(1) The legislature lent expression with § 1626a of the Civil Code to the fact that both parents are in principle entitled to joint custody (see *Bundestag* printed paper 13/4899, p. 93). In the case of married parents, the legislature has assumed, by reason of the legal connection they assumed in marrying, that there is agreement between them and willingness to share the care of their child as a requirement for a jointly exercised parental custody serving the child's best interests, and has hence attributed joint custody to them.
In the case of parents not married to each other, this indication is lacking for an assumption that joint custody is wanted by them and could hence also be exercised in the child's best interests. In order to create an equivalent for this which takes account of the statutory presumption of jointly exercised parental custody in the child's best interests even when the parents are not married to each other, the legislature, in § 1626a.1 no. 1 of the Civil Code, has given them the possibility of expressing by means of concurring declarations to lend expression to the fact that they are willing, and prepared to cooperate, to share the care for their child. Hence, on the one hand, it has accommodated the different situations of married and unmarried parents, and on the other hand it has made joint custody available to both sets of parents.
(2) The assumption on the part of the legislature that the wish of both parents to exercise joint custody, shown by conclusion of marriage or explicitly declared, showed their willingness to cooperate and best guaranteed the joint exercise of custody by the parents which corresponded best to the child's best interests, is constitutionally unobjectionable. It has been recognised that the quality of the respective parent-child relationship, as well as the willingness to cooperate of the parents with regard to the child, are highly significant for the child's best interests … If this is lacking, conflicts between the parents may have a major impact on the child. Making the declaration of the will of the parents the decisive precondition for joint custody, and not linking to it any further preconditions, such as cohabitation of the parents, also does justice to the right of parents under Article 6.2 of the Basic Law to decide for themselves how they intend to comply with their parental responsibility towards the child (see BVerfGE 47, 46 (69-70); 60, 79 (88); 98, 218 (244)).
cc) It is not apparent at the present time that the regulatory concept of joint custody of parents who are not married to each other in § 1626a.1 no. 1 of the Civil Code violates the parental right of the father of a child born out of wedlock under Article 6.2 of the Basic Law.
(1) When shaping the rights of parents of children born out of wedlock, the legislature may take the circumstance into account that one may not assume in general

terms the existence of a social relationship between them and the child, and may take into account whether the father shows an interest in the development of the child (see BVerfGE 92, 158 (179)). The legislature has initially allotted custody of the child to the mother in a constitutionally unobjectionable manner. The establishment of joint custody of unmarried parents hence requires a constitutive act opening to the father access to custody for his child together with the mother. Such access has been created for the father by virtue of the possibility to submit corresponding declarations of parental custody together with the mother. Here, the parents' concurring declarations of parental custody as a requirement for joint custody are an expression of the willingness to cooperate in taking care of and bringing up the child; they are at the same time to ensure that joint custody has a basis on which it can be exercised in the child's best interests.

That by these means access of the father of a child born out of wedlock to parental custody also depends on the willingness of the mother to hold joint custody with him is constitutionally unobjectionable. The legislature hence does justice to the fact that the exercise of the parental right requires a minimum degree of agreement between the parents. The mother is initially allocated parental custody of the child from which she cannot withdraw – in contradistinction to the father. However, she can also not share custody of the child with the father unless he is willing. Both parents hence receive equal access to joint custody only if they agree on wanting to do so. This by itself does not constitute an unjustified restriction of the father's parental right. Even with married parents, joint custody is based on concurring declarations submitted in the marriage vows.

(2) The object of the Act Reforming the Law of Parent and Child, with which § 1626a of the Civil Code was introduced, was to also facilitate – in the interest of the children – joint parental custody for parents who are not married to each other, to promote this form of custody and in doing so to strengthen parents' autonomy (see *Bundestag* printed paper 13/8511, pp. 64 et seq.). For this reason, it was rejected to make the establishment of joint custody contingent on a review of the child's best interests in individual cases (see *Bundestag* printed paper 13/4899, p. 58-59). With the Reform Act, the youth welfare offices have been obliged by § 52a of the Eighth Book of the Code of Social Law (*Achtes Buch Sozialgesetzbuch* – SGB VIII) to notify the mother of a child born out of wedlock of the possibility of establishing joint custody.

(a) The legislature has assumed that as a rule joint custody comes about according to § 1626a.1 no. 1 of the Civil Code where the parents are willing to cooperate. This applies in particular to cases in which both parents live with the child and both parents have already shown their willingness to cooperate by factually caring for the child jointly. This provision did adequate justice to the parental right of the father

under Article 6.2 of the Basic Law. The legislature was justified in assuming that the parents will as a rule make use of the statutory possibility of joint custody that now exists, i.e. that they will legalise their factual care by making declarations of parental custody. This is all the more so, given that the legislature has also enabled both unmarried and married parents with joint custody according to § 1671 of the Civil Code in case of subsequent separation and conflicts to have a court review carried out as to whether joint custody is still in the child's best interests.
(b) The legislature has been aware of the fact that there may nevertheless be cases in which the mother does not wish to make a declaration of parental custody, despite living with the father and the child (see *Bundestag* printed paper 13/8511, p. 66). Its assessment that in such cases the mother's refusal expressed a conflict between the parents which has a negative impact on the child in the case of a dispute also occurring with regard to joint custody is justifiable. The legislature was justified in assuming that a mother, particularly when she lives with the father and the child, will only exceptionally reject the father's wish for joint custody, and that she will only do so if she has serious reasons for this based on the defence of the child's best interests, and that she therefore will not misuse the possibility of refusing to submit a declaration of parental custody as a power position against the father. Making such an assumption, it is compatible with Article 6.2 of the Basic Law that the legislature refrained from admitting judicial review of the individual case if no concurring declarations of parental custody were reached. For if the reasons for the failure to reach concurring declarations of parental custody are so serious and the conflict between the parents so major despite living together, it cannot be expected that the courts will consider joint custody of the parents to be beneficial to the child's best interests. The court dispute by itself could once again be to the detriment of the child, quite apart from the other conflicts.
(c) Finally, it is constitutionally unobjectionable that the legislature above all opened joint custody to parents not married to each other by virtue of the requirement of concurring declarations of parental custody de facto above all at the time when the parents are in a relationship with one another and with the child that is marked by agreement, in particular therefore if they live together and in fact take care of the child together, and not only when they have separated.
The study by Proksch … has now confirmed that joint custody is beneficial to the child's best interests in many cases, even if the parents have separated. This finding however relates to the continuance after separation of joint custody already existing during cohabitation. If however joint custody is to be established for the first time after the separation of the parents, there is all the more need of an indication for the assumption that the parents are willing and able to cooperate. If therefore § 1626a.1 no. 1 of the Civil Code also takes concurring declarations of parental custody here

as a precondition for the establishment of joint custody, and where such declarations are not provided indeed does not provide the father with a possibility of joint custody, this is adequately factually justified by consideration of the child's best interests. If the cohabitation of the parents has already not led to their joint custody although the possibility for this was in existence, the assumption on the part of the legislature is all the more justified, if the parents separate and if there is a dispute between them on joint custody, that opening up joint custody as a rule would now entail more disadvantages than advantages for the child for a lack of a basis for co-operation between the parents (see *Bundestag* printed paper 13/8511, p. 66).

(3) (a) If the assumptions of the legislature prove to be correct, the parental right of the father of a child born out of wedlock has been adequately taken into account by § 1626a.1 no. 1 of the Civil Code. If he does not have a social relationship with the child, or at least initially with the mother, there is no basis for joint custody in the child's best interests. If he lives with the mother and the child, or if there is otherwise agreement between the mother and him, this will as a rule lead to joint custody, unless grievous reasons concerned with the child's best interests make it impossible to reach concurring declarations of parental custody. Hence, the father as a rule also continues to have custody jointly with the mother in the case of separation, unless reasons related to the child's best interests require a different kind of custody in an individual case. The father can also still obtain joint custody after separation from the mother if both so wish.

(b) If the assumptions of the legislature were however to be incorrect, in particular were it to emerge that even where the parents live together with the child in a large number of cases no joint custody is attained according to § 1626a.1 no. 1 of the Civil Code for reasons not based on the child's best interests, § 1626a.1 no. 1 of the Civil Code would reveal itself to be incompatible with Article 6.2 of the Basic Law. Then, the statutory definition of typical facts would no longer be justified, and it would violate the parental right of the father of a child born out of wedlock under Article 6.2 of the Basic Law if he is excluded from custody despite living together with the mother of his child and despite factual joint custody of the child although the ability and willingness of both parents to cooperate is proven by factual joint custody of the child, and therefore cannot be the real reason behind the negative stance of the mother.

(4) There have been no indications so far to place the correctness of the assumptions of the legislature in serious doubt. In particular, there is no secure knowledge as to whether despite the possibility which has been created for joint custody of parents of a child born out of wedlock in the long term there is a considerable number of cases in which joint custody does not come about even though the parents live together with the child, and which reasons are relevant for this. No data are

currently available relating to the number of declarations of parental custody submitted since the entry into force of the Act Reforming the Law of Parent and Child. It is also not known how large the share of family communities is in which parents live with their child born out of wedlock who have submitted a joint declaration of parental custody, as against the share in which this has not yet taken place. It should finally be taken into account that parents who are not married to each other have only had the possibility of joint custody since 1 July 1998. Since such a recently created legal form requires to become widely known and more widely publicised in order to become entrenched in society, the time which has passed so far is in fact too short to already be able to make viable statements regarding the impact of the statutory reform.

b) Since the legislature has enacted provisions which safeguard the parental right of the father of a child born out of wedlock under Article 6.2 of the Basic Law only if the legislature's prognostic assumptions are correct, the legislature is obliged to observe the actual development and to review whether its assumptions stand the test of reality. If it becomes apparent that this is not the case, the legislature will have to ensure by means of a correction to the provision that fathers of children born out of wedlock who live with the mother and the child as a family are opened an access to joint custody that takes sufficient account of their parental right under Article 6.2 of the Basic Law, with due consideration being given to the child's best interests.

3. The statutory regulation of joint custody of parents of a child born out of wedlock in § 1626a of the Civil Code is however constitutionally inadequate insofar as the legislature has omitted to make a transitional arrangement for parents who lived with their child born out of wedlock, and took care of the child jointly, but separated before the entry into force of the Act Reforming the Law of Parent and Child on 1 July 1998. They, in particular the fathers, must be given the possibility to have a judicial review carried out as to whether joint custody can be established although the other parent does not agree with it, taking account of the child's best interests. It violates the parental right of the father of a child born out of wedlock under Article 6.2 of the Basic Law if he only does not have access to joint custody for his child because there was no possibility for him and the mother to establish joint custody of the child at the time when he lived with the mother and the child, and after separation the mother is not (or is no longer) willing to submit a declaration of parental custody although joint custody is in the child's best interests.

a) With the legal reform, the legislature has opened up a possibility of joint custody for parents of a child born out of wedlock which is to make joint custody the rule where parents are willing and able to take care of their child together.

If the parents are living together and are taking care of the child together, so that the legislature may assume that they will indeed make use of the possibility of joint

custody facilitated to them, the necessity of a review of the individual case to establish it would on the one hand restrict the parents' freedom without there being indications that joint custody on the basis of the will of both parents was contrary to the child's best interests. On the other hand, recourse to a court would be opened, with the burdens also affecting the children, for such cases in which the courts, taking account of the child's best interests, would as a rule also not be able to establish joint custody because of the conflicts between the parents. This justifies not making joint parental custody contingent on a judicial review of the individual case.
At the same time, the legislature permits joint custody of parents of a child born out of wedlock established by declarations of parental custody to continue to be valid even after their separation unless it emerges on judicial review according to § 1671 of the Civil Code that this is no longer in the child's best interests. For this reason, the legislature was able to assume that, if joint custody was not established even when the parents were living together, the conflicts between them were likely to be all the more serious on their separation, so that a judicial review of the individual case would only lead to further burdens for the child, but not to joint custody between the conflicting parents. This in principle justifies not granting to the father the possibility in the individual case to have a judicial review carried out as to whether the conditions for joint custody are met if the mother refuses to submit a declaration of parental custody.
b) If however there was no possibility at all for the parents to be granted joint custody while they were living together with the child, there are no circumstances from which one could conclude, following a definition of typical facts, that the parents did not have the necessary willingness to cooperate related to custody for their child. The separation of the parents or the refusal of the mother declared after separation to submit a declaration of parental custody is also not an adequate indication of this. It suggests itself that a mother who, just as the father, could not have joint custody during their cohabitation, and who was hence the sole holder of custody during this period, as a rule is not going to be willing to share custody of the child with the father when she and the father of the child have now separated and they have only been given the possibility to have joint custody after separation. It is not possible to absolutely conclude from such conduct that parental conflicts remove the necessary foundation for joint custody, and hence impair the child's best interests. Then it is however not justified, and violates the parental right of the father under Article 6.2 of the Basic Law who in fact took care of his child born out of wedlock for a long period which was relevant to its development, to also continue to exclude him from joint custody simply because the mother is not, or no longer, willing to submit a declaration of parental custody after separation.

c) It may however not be assumed in such cases that joint custody of the parents as a rule serves the child's best interests. Joint custody of the parents may also prove to be decisive for the best interests of the child born out of wedlock after their separation (see BVerfGE 61, 358 (376 et seq.); 84, 168 (182)). Separation and the concomitant conflicts between the parents may however impact their willingness and ability to cooperate in custody of the child to such a degree that joint custody is not in the interest of the child. For cases in which parents separated before the entry into force of the Act Reforming the Law of Parent and Child, after living with the child for a long period, and in which the father now wishes to receive joint custody with the mother, but the mother does not submit a declaration of parental custody, the legislature must hence open up a judicial review of the individual case as to whether the child's best interests stand in the way of joint custody.
d) In contradistinction to the view of the Federal Court of Justice, § 1666 of the Civil Code does not provide in such cases to the father of a child born out of wedlock a way to obtain a judicial review of the individual case adequately taking account of his parental right with regard to joint custody.
§ 1666 of the Civil Code does not aim to balance the parental rights in conflict situations between parents. The provision rather draws a boundary for encroachments on the part of the state on the right of parents, and hence determines under what preconditions the state must carry out its watchdog function under Article 6.2 sentence 2 of the Basic Law. This standard is not suited as a criterion to determine which position in the law on custody each of the parents is to be given if they are unable to agree on custody. The abuse threshold makes the parental right of the father take second place to that of the mother in a disproportionate manner in contradiction to Article 6.2 of the Basic Law if the father is only to participate in custody of the child if the child's best interests are placed at risk by the mother, and not if this is merely in the child's best interests. Also, the mere refusal of the mother to submit a declaration of parental custody cannot be deemed to constitute abusive exercise of her parental responsibility.

II.

1. With the exception of the omitted regulation of the old cases mentioned [i.e. the cases arising prior to the current statutory regulation], for the above reasons § 1626a of the Civil Code also does not violate the requirement addressed to the legislature under Article 6.5 of the Basic Law to create the same conditions for the development of children born out of wedlock as for children born in wedlock.
It follows from Article 6.5 of the Basic Law that children who are born out of wedlock in principle may not be treated less well than those born in wedlock unless

their special situation leads to justifying reasons for unequal treatment (see BVerfGE 84, 168 (185); 96, 56 (65)). The fact that a child born out of wedlock, in contradistinction to a child born in wedlock, cannot necessarily be legally attributed to a father at its birth, and one may also not assume that the father wishes to have custody of the child or will build up a relationship with the child by living with the mother, justifies arranging custody for a child born out of wedlock differently than that for a child born in wedlock as long as the statutory provision creates a suitable framework to bring about joint custody. Apart from the lack of an arrangement on old cases, this has taken place.

The assumption of the legislature that the lack of willingness of parents who live together to legally agree on joint custody allowed the conclusion to be drawn that there are such conflicts between the parents which would be disadvantageous for the child were joint custody to be established against the will of one parent, is comprehensible and currently not refutable. In this sense, it is justified to leave sole custody with the mother in such cases, without a judicial review of the individual case. However, in cases in which the parents did not have the possibility prior to their separation to certify their willingness to hold joint custody, the children born out of wedlock affected by this are placed at a disadvantage in violation of Article 6.5 of the Basic Law until such time as a way is opened up to reach joint custody after all via a judicial review of the individual case.

2. Finally, § 1626a of the Civil Code also does not violate Article 3.1 of the Basic Law. In the case of fathers of children born out of wedlock, as with fathers of children born in wedlock, joint custody with the mother is contingent on her consent, but with the difference that in one case consent is already given on conclusion of marriage, whilst in the other case it is submitted by a declaration of parental custody. This is however founded factually by the different situation in which the fathers of children born out of wedlock find themselves in comparison to fathers who are married to the mother. The further differences in shaping the law on custody which result from this are justified, as has been explained, by the currently unobjectionable assumption of the legislature that this is in the best interests of children born out of wedlock.

D.

The court rulings impugned in the proceedings 1 BvR 933/01 are also not compatible with the Basic Law in terms of the above statements at C.

The ruling of the Federal Court of Justice violates the complainant re 1, who lived for a long period with the mother of his child born out of wedlock and with the child before the parents separated prior to the entry into force of the Act Reforming

the Law of Parent and Child, in his parental right under Article 6.2 of the Basic Law. The ruling is based on § 1626a of the Civil Code, which for such old cases does not provide for judicial review of the individual case, and hence violates Article 6.2 and 6.5 of the Basic Law.
The impugned ruling of the Higher Regional Court is not only based on § 1626a.1 no. 1 of the Civil Code, since the court, regardless of the wording, has carried out a review of the individual case. In doing so, however, it already did not take adequate account of the parental right of the complainant re 1 under Article 6.2 sentence 1 of the Basic Law because it has not done justice to the constitutional reservations existing against the application of the provision to the above old cases.
Finally, the impugned ruling of the Local Court also violates the fundamental right of the complainant re 1 under Article 6.2 of the Basic Law because it is based on the provision of § 1626a of the Civil Code, which is unconstitutional in this respect.

E. – I.

If a provision is not according to the Basic Law, it is to be in principle declared null and void (§ 82.1 in conjunction with § 78 sentence 1, § 95.3 of the Federal Constitutional Court Act (*Bundesverfassungsgerichtsgesetz* – BVerfGG)). The situation is different if the unconstitutionality of the provision is not due to its regulatory content, but to the omission of a transitional arrangement for old cases, if there are several possibilities to eliminate the unconstitutional situation and the declaration of nullity would encroach on the latitude of the legislature (see BVerfGE 84, 168 (186-187); 92, 158 (186)). Accordingly, a declaration of nullity is ruled out in this instance. The legislature may remedy unconstitutionality by a variety of means. For instance, it may grant to each parent to whom these conditions apply a right to apply for a judicial review as to whether joint custody with the other parent is in the child's best interests. The legislature may however also open up to the parent the possibility to have the lack of consent of the other parent reviewed in court by the standard of the child's best interests, and where appropriate have it substituted.

II.

If the Federal Constitutional Court establishes the incompatibility of a provision with the Basic Law, the legislature is obliged to bring the legal situation into accordance with the Basic Law without delay. Because of the significance of the passage of time, particularly in cases of the law of parent and child, the legislature is set a deadline until 31 December 2003 for the supplementary new statutory regulation. Within the scope of the declaration of incompatibility, the provision may no longer be applied by the courts and administrative authorities (see BVerfGE 82, 126 (155); 84, 168 (187)). No exception from this principle is necessary here. In cases in which the parents of a child born out of wedlock have lived with the child for a long period and separated prior to the entry into force of the Act Reforming the Law of Parent and Child, the courts may accordingly not refuse the joint custody striven for by one parent for the child because there is no declaration of parental custody on the part of the other parent according to § 1626a.1 no. 1 of the Civil Code. Rather, such proceedings should be suspended until a new provision enters into force.

...

Justices: Papier, Jaeger, Haas, Hömig, Steiner, Hohmann-Dennhardt, Hoffmann-Riem, Bryde

By Article 1 of the Act for the Implementation of Family-Law Decisions of the Federal Constitutional Court (Gesetz zur Umsetzung familienrechtlicher Entscheidungen des Bundesverfassungsgerichts) *of 13 December 2003 (Federal Law Gazette I 2003 p. 2547), the legislature, with effect from 31 December 2003, enacted the transitional arrangement demanded in the decision by amending Article 224 § 2 of the Introductory Act to the Civil Code* (Einführungsgesetz zum Bürgerlichen Gesetzbuch) *as follows:*

> *"(3) If parents who were not married to each other jointly exercised parental responsibility for their child in domestic community for a long period and separated before 1 July 1998, the Family Court, upon the application of one parent, shall substitute the other parent's declaration of parental custody according to § 16261.1 no. 1 of the Civil Code where joint parental custody serves the child's best interests. As a general rule, joint exercise of parental responsibility exists if the parents lived together with the child for at least six months without interruption."*

No. 39

BVerfGE 107, 205

of 12 February 2003 – 1 BvR 624/01 –

"Family insurance case"

HEADNOTE:

§ 10.3 of the Fifth Book of the Code of Social Law (*Fünftes Buch Sozialgesetzbuch* – SGB V) does not violate Article 3.1 in conjunction with Article 6.1 of the Basic Law (*Grundgesetz* – GG) insofar as it treats marriages and non-marital communities differently with regard to the exclusion of children from family insurance.

Judgment of the First Senate of 12 February 2003
on the basis of the oral hearing of 20 November 2002
– 1 BvR 624/01 –

in the proceedings regarding the constitutional complaint I. of the minor S., represented by the complainant re II and by Mr. S., II. of Ms. G. – authorised representative: …, lawyer – 1. directly against a) the order of the Federal Social Court (*Bundessozialgericht*) of 25 January 2001 … –, b) the judgments of the Bavarian Regional Social Court (*Bayerisches Landessozialgericht*) of 9 December 1999 – …– and of 8 June 1995 – …, c) the judgment of the Augsburg Social Court (*Sozialgericht*) of 26 October 1993 – …, d) the notices of the Barmer Ersatzkasse [a substitute social health insurance fund] of 17 July 1992 and 30 June 1997 in the version of the notices ruling on objection of 11 November 1992 – …– and of 12 August 1997 – …–, 2. indirectly against § 10.3 of the Fifth Book of the Code of Social Law (*Fünftes Buch Sozialgesetzbuch* – SGB V).

RULING:

The constitutional complaint is rejected as unfounded.

EXTRACT FROM GROUNDS:

A.

The constitutional complaint relates to the contribution-free co-insurance of family members, and in particular of children, in statutory health insurance in accordance with § 10 of the Fifth Book of the Code of Social Law, so-called family insurance.

I.

Since the Act on Structural Reform in the Healthcare System (Health Reform Act) (*Gesetz zur Strukturreform im Gesundheitswesen – Gesundheits-Reformgesetz* – GRG) of 20 December 1988 (Federal Law Gazette (*Bundesgesetzblatt* – BGBl) I p. 2477) came into force on 1 January 1989, family insurance has been governed by § 10 of the Fifth Book of the Code of Social Law. Today's regulation, insofar as its fundamental concept is concerned, is part of a long tradition under social insurance law (for more details see Gerlach/Epping, *Die Familienversicherung*, 4th ed. 1994, pp. 10 et seq.). The Reich Insurance Code (*Reichsversicherungsordnung* – RVO) already provided under certain preconditions for benefits to be provided to family members (family assistance). In contradistinction to family assistance, family insurance as set out in the Fifth Book of the Code of Social Law gives rise to independent benefit rights of the co-insured family member. Their status as insured parties is however accessory to the membership of the main insured party. § 10 of the Fifth Book of the Code of Social Law in the version of Article 1 of the Health Reform Act, in so far as it is of significance to the case at hand, reads as follows:

§ 10 Family insurance

(1) Insurance shall cover the spouse and the children of members if such family members

1. have their place of residence or habitual residence within the area of application of this Code,
2. are not insured in accordance with § 5.1 nos. 1 to 8, 11 or 12, or are not voluntarily insured,
3. are not exempt from insurance or are not exempt from obligatory insurance; exemption from insurance in accordance with § 7 shall not be considered here,
4. are not self-employed on a full-time basis, and

5. do not have a joint monthly income regularly in excess of one-seventh of the monthly reference value in accordance with § 18 of the Fourth Book; with pensions, the payment amount shall be authoritative.

(2) Children shall be insured

1. until reaching the age of eighteen,
2. until reaching the age of twenty-three if they are not in gainful employment,
3. until reaching the age of twenty-five if they are in school or vocational training or are rendering a voluntary social year within the meaning of the Act to Promote a Voluntary Social Year (*Gesetz zur Förderung eines freiwilligen sozialen Jahres*); if the school or vocational training is interrupted or delayed by the child fulfilling a statutory duty to render a service, insurance shall also exist for a period corresponding to the duration of this service over and above the age of twenty-five,
4. without an age limit if they are unable to maintain themselves because of physical, mental or psychological disability; the prerequisite shall be that the disability existed at a time when the child was insured in accordance with no. 1, 2 or 3.

(3) Children shall not be insured if the spouse of the member related to the children is not a member of a health insurance fund and his or her total income per month regularly exceeds one-twelfth of the annual remuneration threshold and is regularly higher than the total income of the member; with pensions, the payment amount shall be authoritative.

(4) [to] (5) …

§ 3 sentence 3 of the Fifth Book of the Code of Social Law provides that no contributions are to be levied for insured family members. § 243.2 sentence 2 of the Fifth Book of the Code of Social Law stipulates that contributions graduated by marital status or by the number of the family members who are covered by family insurance in accordance with § 10 of the Fifth Book of the Code of Social Law are not permissible. If a child is excluded from family insurance on the basis of § 10.3 of the Fifth Book of the Code of Social Law, § 9.1 no. 2 of the Fifth Book of the Code of Social Law opens the possibility to take up statutory health insurance. This right to take up cover has been linked since 1 January 2000 to the prerequisite of a prior insurance period. Family insurance benefits 14.6 million children and roughly 7 million spouses. The total annual benefit expenditure paid out by the health insurance funds for family insurance is stated at 15 billion euros and more (Ruland, *Neue Juristische Wochenschrift* – NJW 2001, p. 1673 (1678 marginal no. 35)). § 10 of the Fifth Book of the Code of Social Law has undergone several amendments since coming into force. The Act on the Termination of the Discrimination of Same-Sex Couples: Civil Partnerships (*Gesetz zur Beendigung der Diskriminierung gleichgeschlechtlicher Gemeinschaften: Lebenspartnerschaften*) of 16 February 2001 (Federal Law Gazette I p. 266) gave § 10.3 of the Fifth Book of the Code of Social Law the following version:

> Children shall not be insured if the spouse or civil partner of the member related to the children is not a member of a health insurance fund and his or her total income per month regularly exceeds one-twelfth of the annual remuneration threshold and is regularly higher than the total income of the member; with pensions, the payment amount shall be authoritative.

II.

The complainant re I is the son, born in 1992, of the complainant re II, who is married to the father of the complainant re I. The parents live in domestic community with the son.

Since the birth of the complainant re I, the complainant re II, apart from an interruption of roughly 1 1/2 years, has been subject to obligatory insurance with the defendant in the original proceedings, a substitute social health insurance fund. Her regular monthly total income was roughly DM 3,400 at the time of filing the constitutional complaint. Her husband is a civil servant, has private health insurance and is entitled to government aid for civil servants for the complainant re I at a rate of 80 per cent. The parents have concluded private health insurance for the complainant re I. in respect of the cost of illness not covered by the government aid …

The father of the complainant re I had a monthly total income of between DM 6,375 and DM 7,887 during the period from 1992 to 1999.

The defendant in the original proceedings refused to provide contribution-free family insurance for the complainant re I for the periods in which the complainant re II was an obligatory member, referring to § 10.3 of the Fifth Book of the Code of Social Law. The appeals against this were unsuccessful. The Federal Social Court considers the exclusion regulation of § 10.3 of the Fifth Book of the Code of Social Law to be constitutional. …

III.

With their constitutional complaint the complainants challenge § 10.3 of the Fifth Book of the Code of Social Law and the administrative and court rulings based thereon. The regulation is said to violate Article 3.1 in conjunction with Article 6.1

of the Basic Law because it allegedly does not apply to children whose parents are not married to each other. There are said to be no reasons justifying the unequal treatment constituted thereby. …

IV.

…

V.

…

B.

The constitutional complaint is unfounded.

I.

§ 10.3 of the Fifth Book of the Code of Social Law is compatible with Article 6.1 and Article 3.1 of the Basic Law insofar as it excludes from contribution-free family insurance children of parents who are married to each other if the total income of the parent who is not a member of a statutory health insurance fund is higher than that of the member and than income thresholds established by the law.

1. § 10.3 of the Fifth Book of the Code of Social Law is not in contradiction with Article 6.1 of the Basic Law.

a) Article 6.1 of the Basic Law requires as an binding value determination for the entire area of private and public law relating to marriage and the family special protection through the state system (see Decisions of the Federal Constitutional Court (*Entscheidungen des Bundesverfassungsgerichts* – BVerfGE) 105, 313 (346); established case-law). As a fundamental provision, a general duty can be derived therefrom obliging the state to promote the family by means of suitable measures (see BVerfGE 103, 242 (259)). The legislature however has latitude in deciding on the manner in which it intends to implement the protection which it is obliged to provide. The general duty incumbent on the state can be derived from Article 6.1 of the Basic Law in conjunction with the social welfare state principle to provide compensation for family burdens, but not the decision on the degree to and the manner in which such social compensation is to be effected. Concrete claims in respect of specific state benefits cannot be derived from the promotion requirement of Article

6.1 of the Basic Law (see BVerfGE 82, 60 (81)). This also applies to the design of the statutory health insurance system.

b) In line with these principles, § 10.3 of the Fifth Book of the Code of Social Law is in compliance with Article 6.1 of the Basic Law. The contribution-free insurance of children of the member of a statutory health insurance fund in accordance with § 10.1, 10.2 and 10.4 of the Fifth Book of the Code of Social Law is a measure of social compensation which is intended to relieve the burden on the family. Article 6.1 of the Basic Law does not demand in the design of the family insurance system that its benefits must be provided regardless of the income circumstances of parents who are married to each other. In determining the group of individuals which it includes in family insurance, and in deciding on the preconditions under which it excludes children from it, the legislature may take as a basis the economic ability to pay of those concerned, and in particular of the parents, and hence apply the point of view of the need for social protection. Article 6.1 of the Basic Law does not prohibit it from making the advantages of contribution-free health insurance of the children conditional on such an examination.

2. The characteristics used as a basis by the legislature in § 10.3 of the Fifth Book of the Code of Social Law for the exclusion of children from family insurance meet the requirements of the general principle of equality of Article 3.1 of the Basic Law.

a) Article 3.1 of the Basic Law requires that all people are treated equally before the law. This does not however prohibit the legislature all differentiation. But the legislature violates the fundamental right if it treats one group of persons addressed by a provision differently in comparison to another although there are no differences between the two groups of such a nature and weight that they could justify the unequal treatment (see BVerfGE 104, 126 (144-145); established case-law).

b) § 10.3 of the Fifth Book of the Code of Social Law places married individuals at a disadvantage insofar as their children are excluded from family insurance in accordance with this provision, in contradistinction to those married individuals to whom the preconditions for exclusion do not apply and whose children are hence co-insured contribution-free. Those children who meet the preconditions of § 10.1, 10.2 and 10.4 of the Fifth Book of the Code of Social Law for a right to co-insurance, but – like the complainant re I – fall under the exclusion provision of § 10.3 of the Fifth Book of the Code of Social Law, are also placed at a disadvantage.

c) These disadvantages are however sufficiently justified. In § 10.3 of the Fifth Book of the Code of Social Law, the legislature uses income-related characteristics in the application of which typically the need for social protection of the married parents and their children can be negated. It is expedient to exclude children from contribution-free family insurance if the total income of the parent who is not a member of a health insurance fund exceeds the annual remuneration threshold within the meaning of § 6.1 no. 1 of the Fifth Book of the Code of Social Law. This value corresponds to the amount of the earnings – even if not of the total earnings – upwards of which an employee is no longer subject to obligatory insurance in the statutory health insurance fund because the legislature no longer regards him or her as being in need of protection (§ 5.1 no. 1 in conjunction with § 6.1 no. 1 of the Fifth Book of the Code of Social Law; see BVerfGE 102, 68 (89)).

The link to income in § 10.3 of the Fifth Book of the Code of Social Law is however also expedient insofar as children remain in family insurance if the total income of the member is not less than that of the non-member, regardless of the ratio of the income of the non-member to the annual remuneration threshold. Exclusion from family insurance accordingly takes place only if the parent who does not have statutory health insurance can be made primarily responsible for insuring his or her children against the risk of illness because his or her higher total income exceeds the annual remuneration threshold. If, by contrast, the parent with statutory insurance has a higher income, and the family insurance of the children is therefore retained, this is justified because the member pays correspondingly high contributions up to the assessment limit (§ 223.3 of the Fifth Book of the Code of Social Law) to the community based on solidarity, and at the same time makes a material contribution to the family income.

II.

§ 10.3 of the Fifth Book of the Code of Social Law does not violate Article 3.1 in conjunction with Article 6.1 of the Basic Law insofar as it relates to the different treatment of marriages and non-marital communities with regard to the family insurance of children.

1. Constitutional standard for the unequal treatment of marriages and non-marital communities by the provision contained in § 10.3 of the Fifth Book of the Code of Social Law is Article 3.1 in conjunction with Article 6.1 of the Basic Law (see BVerfGE 67, 186 (195)). It is a matter of the question of placing marriage at a disadvantage in comparison with non-marital communities with regard to the family insurance of the children in statutory health insurance, for whose benefits the community of insured parties must pay. It should be taken into account in this examination of equality that Article 6.1 of the Basic Law imposes limits on the freedom of the legislature as to which circumstances it treats equally and which unequally (see BVerfGE 103, 242 (258)). The legislature is prohibited from discriminating against marriage in comparison with other communities (see BVerfGE 69, 188 (205-206); 75, 382 (393)), in particular against married people as against unmarried people, in

granting legal advantages (see BVerfGE 67, 168 (195-196); 75, 382 (393)). A statutory disadvantage is however to be accepted in some aspects where the general trend of the law aims to compensate for family burdens, and in doing so partly favours married individuals whilst partly placing them at a disadvantage, but in an overall view the statutory provision does not however place married couples at a disadvantage.

2. Accordingly, § 10.3 of the Fifth Book of the Code of Social Law is not objectionable.

a) Insofar as its preconditions are met, the regulation does initially place members of statutory health insurance who are married to the other parent of the joint children at a disadvantage by virtue of the exclusion of the children from family insurance, if the income-related preconditions of § 10.3 of the Fifth Book of the Code of Social Law apply, in comparison to unmarried members with regard to whom such exclusion does not take place. If in a non-marital community the total income of the parent who is not a member of the health insurance fund exceeds the income threshold of § 10.3 of the Fifth Book of the Code of Social Law, this does not – in contradistinction to the situation pertinent to married parents – oppose co-insurance of the child with the parent who has statutory insurance.

b) This different treatment does not however place married people at a disadvantage in an overall view.

aa) The provisions on family insurance contained in § 10 of the Fifth Book of the Code of Social Law provide for legal advantages which apply only in the event of marriage. For instance, in accordance with § 10.1 of the Fifth Book of the Code of Social Law, the spouse who is a member of statutory health insurance can confer contribution-free insurance cover in statutory health insurance on the other spouse who is not himself or herself a member of statutory health insurance. Such a possibility is not open to partners in a non-marital community. Roughly 7 million spouses are co-insured on the basis of this provision. What is more, in accordance with § 10.4 of the Fifth Book of the Code of Social Law, step-children of the spouses who have statutory insurance are also included in family insurance.

bb) The exclusion of the marital child of parents who are married to each other from family insurance under the preconditions of § 10.3 of the Fifth Book of the Code of Social Law in relation to non-marital children is however also justified from the point of view that more effective protection is provided in a marriage for the health insurance cover of a child outside family insurance on the basis of the mutual obligations under maintenance law which arise thereby than is the case in a non-marital community. It is true that maintenance law as it now stands in principle places marital and non-marital children on an equal footing (§§ 1601 et seq. of the Civil Code (*Bürgerliches Gesetzbuch* – BGB)). Also the maintenance right of the

non-marital child includes the cost of suitable health insurance protection … However, the partners of a non-marital community do not owe statutory maintenance to one another, in contradistinction to spouses (see also BVerfGE 75, 382 (395)). The law as it stands only provides for an obligation to furnish family maintenance between spouses (§ 1360 of the Civil Code). This maintenance is owed to the other spouse, but is also orientated towards the needs of the joint children, who are entitled to maintenance …, particularly also in making provision against illness.
The right under § 1615 l of the Civil Code to care maintenance, which also benefits children, cannot compensate for the fact that parents who are not married to each other do not have a right to family maintenance. Care maintenance is time-limited. It is to be provided to the mother in principle only for the period from six weeks before until eight weeks after birth of the child against its father (§ 1615 l.1 of the Civil Code). Insofar as § 1615 l.2 of the Civil Code grants to the mother a maintenance right against the father of the child over and above this for up to three years, and also beyond this period in cases in which such a time limitation would be grossly unfair, this is contingent on the mother being unable for specific reasons to engage in gainful employment, or it being unreasonable to expect her to do so. The degree of maintenance is in line with the circumstances of the mother only (§ 1610.1 of the Civil Code). The spouse and minor unmarried children of the father precede the mother in application of § 1609 of the Civil Code (§ 1615 l.3 2nd half of sentence 3 of the Civil Code).

III.

…

Justices: Papier, Jaeger, Haas, Hömig, Steiner, Hohmann-Dennhardt, Hoffmann-Riem, Bryde

No. 40

BVerfGE 108, 82
of 9 April 2003 – 1 BvR 1493/96, 1724/01 –
"Biological father case"

HEADNOTES:

1. **Article 6.2 sentence 1 of the Basic Law (*Grundgesetz* – GG) protects the natural father who is not at the same time the legal father (known as the biological father) in his interest in taking the legal position of father. He must be given the possibility under procedural law of attaining the legal position of father if the protection of a family relationship between the child and its legal parents does not conflict with this.**
2. **The biological father, together with his child, is also a family of the kind protected by Article 6.1 of the Basic Law if there is a social and family relationship between him and the child. The protection of fundamental rights also includes the interest in preserving this relationship. It is a violation of Article 6.1 of the Basic Law if the biological father who has a relationship of this kind with his child is denied contact with the child even though the contact serves the child's best interests.**
3. **Decision regarding the constitutionality of §§ 1600 and 1685 of the Civil Code and § 1711.2 of the Civil Code (*Bürgerliches Gesetzbuch* – BGB) old.**

Order of the First Senate of 9 April 2003
– 1 BvR 1493/96, 1724/01 –

in the proceedings regarding the constitutional complaints 1. of Mr. L., authorised representative: ..., lawyer – against a) the order of the Cologne Higher Regional Court (*Oberlandesgericht*) of 14 June 1996 – 16 Wx 105/96 –, b) the order of the Cologne Regional Court (*Landgericht*) of 5 September 1995 – 1 T 657/94 –, c) the order of the Cologne Local Court (*Amtsgericht*) of 25 January 1994 – 52 X 138/93 – 1 BvR 1493/96 –, 2. of Mr. A-K.; authorised representatives: ..., lawyers – against a) the judgment of the Cologne Higher Regional Court of 30 August 2001 –

14 UF 119/01 – b) the judgment of the Leverkusen Local Court of 28 February 2001 – 30 (33) F 223/00 – 1 BvR 1724/01 –.

RULING:

I. 1. § 1685 of the Civil Code in the version of the Act Reforming the Law of Parent and Child (*Gesetz zur Reform des Kindschaftsrechts, Kindschaftsrechtsreformgesetz* – KindRG) of 16 December 1997 (Federal Law Gazette, *Bundesgesetzblatt* – BGBl I p. 2942) is incompatible with Article 6.1 of the Basic Law (*Grundgesetz* – GG) to the extent that it excludes from the group of persons permitted contact with the child the natural father who is not the legal father, even if there is or has been a social and family relationship between him and the child.

2. The legislature is instructed to pass a provision in conformity with the constitution by 30 April 2004. Legal proceedings are to be stayed until the statute is amended to the extent that the decision depends on the constitutionality of § 1685 of the Civil Code.

3. The order of the Cologne Higher Regional Court of 14 June 1996 – 16 Wx 105/96 –, the order of the Cologne Regional Court of 5 September 1995 – 1 T 657/94 – and the order of the Cologne Local Court of 25 January 1994 – 52 X 138/93 – violate the complainant's fundamental right under Article 6.1 of the Basic Law. The orders are reversed. The matter is referred back to the Cologne Local Court.

4. …

II. 1. § 1600 of the Civil Code (*Bürgerliches Gesetzbuch* – BGB) in the version as amended by the Act Reforming the Law of Parent and Child is incompatible with Article 6.2 sentence 1 of the Basic Law to the extent that without exception it excludes the natural father of a child who is not the legal father from challenging an acknowledgment of paternity.

2. The legislature is instructed to pass a provision in conformity with the constitution by 30 April 2004. Legal proceedings are to be stayed until the statute is amended to the extent that the decision depends on the constitutionality of § 1600 of the Civil Code.

3. The judgment of the Cologne Higher Regional Court of 30 August 2001 – 14 UF 119/01 – and the judgment of the Leverkusen Local Court of 28 February 2001 – 30 (33) F 223/00 – violate the complainant's fundamental

right under Article 6.2 sentence 1 of the Basic Law. The judgments are reversed. The matter is referred back to the Leverkusen Local Court.

4. …

EXTRACT FROM GROUNDS:

A.

The constitutional complaints relate to the legal position of the (putative) natural father of a child who is not the legal father of the child (known as the biological father). In particular, they relate to the question as to whether such a father enjoys the protection of Article 6.2 sentence 1 and Article 6.1 of the Basic Law and whether it is possible to derive from this a right to challenge the legal paternity in order to determine that he himself is the father and to be granted contact with the child.

I.

1. Since the Act Reforming the Law of Parent and Child (*Gesetz zur Reform des Kindschaftsrechts, Kindschaftsrechtsreformgesetz* – KindRG) of 16 December 1997 (Federal Law Gazette I p. 2942) came into force on 1 July 1998, § 1592 of the Civil Code has provided that the father of a child is either the man who at the date of the birth was married to the child's mother (no. 1) or the man who acknowledged paternity (no. 2), and, finally, the man whose paternity is judicially established under § 1600d of the Civil Code (no. 3). In this respect, there has been no material alteration of the legal position existing until then. Under the previous law too, the father of a child that was born to its mother after her marriage was her husband, if he had cohabited with her during the conception period (§ 1591.1 of the Civil Code old). In the case of illegitimate children, paternity was established by acknowledgment or by judicial decision (§ 1600a of the Civil Code old).
The mother of a child is the woman who bears it (§ 1591 of the Civil Code). The acknowledgment of paternity now no longer requires the consent of the child or of its legal representative (§§ 1600c and 1600d of the Civil Code old), but in principle only the consent of the mother (§ 1595.1 of the Civil Code). The recognition is not effective as long as the paternity of another man exists (§ 1594.2 of the Civil Code). The paternity of the mother's husband and of the man who acknowledged the paternity can be challenged. § 1600.1 of the Civil Code, which governs this today, reads:

(1) Entitlement to challenge the paternity lies with the man whose paternity exists under § 1592 no. 1 and 1592 no. 2 ... above, the mother and the child.

If there is no paternity under § 1592 no. 1 and § 1592 no. 2 of the Civil Code, it is to be established by the Family Court upon an action by the man against the child or upon an action of the mother or of the child against the man (§ 1600d.1 and § 1600e.1 of the Civil Code).

If a man other than the man who was married to the mother at the date of the child's birth, or than the man who has recognised paternity, is the natural father of the child, or if someone claims to be the natural father of the child, then under the law applicable today he can still neither challenge the existing legal paternity nor commence legal proceedings for a determination of his paternity.

The legislature justified its exclusion of the biological father from the right to challenge the paternity on the following grounds: it could not be denied that the biological father had an interest in the challenge, since his own paternity could only be determined after there had been a challenge. In view of the rights of challenge of the other persons involved, however, it considered that the natural father did not have a right of challenge of his own. If the other persons involved did not exercise their rights of challenge, this argued in favour of concluding that a challenge would be at odds with the welfare of the "social family". The natural father must be expected to respect the lack of a right to challenge (see *Bundestag* printed paper, *Bundestagsdrucksache* – BTDrucks 13/4899, pp. 57-58).

2. a) Until the Act Reforming the Law of Parent and Child entered into force, the parent of a legitimate child who did not have the care for the person of the child had a right of contact with the child (§ 1634 of the Civil Code old). But contact with the father of an illegitimate child was normally decided by the child's mother or another person with custody over the child (§ 1711.1 of the Civil Code old). However, the guardianship court was able to grant the father a right of contact under the aspect of the child's best interests.

§ 1711 of the Civil Code old read as follows:

(1) The person who is entitled to the care for the person of the child decides on the contact between the child and the child's father. …

(2) If personal contact with the father serves the child's best interests, the guardianship court may rule that the father has the right to personal contact. …

(3) and (4) …

b) With the Act Reforming the Law of Parent and Child, the legislature has given up the distinction between legitimate and illegitimate children in the right to contact

as elsewhere and has newly structured the law of contact. Now the child, irrespective of its family status, under § 1684.1 of the Civil Code has a right to contact with each parent, and each parent in turn has the right and the duty to have contact with the child. In addition to the parents, § 1685 of the Civil Code also grants the grandparents, siblings, and the spouse or former spouse, or now also civil partners a right of contact with the child subject to specific requirements in each case. The statute contains no more extensive right of contact with the child.
§ 1685 of the Civil Code, in its present version, reads as follows:

> (1) Grandparents, brothers and sisters have a right to contact with the child if this serves the child's best interests.
> (2) The same applies to the spouse or former spouse and the civil partner or former civil partner of a parent, where this person lived for a long period in domestic community with the child, and to persons with whom the child has spent a long period as a foster child.
> (3) …

This extension of the right of contact to persons other than the parents was justified by the legislature on the grounds that, in view of the strengthening of the right of contact for the parents of illegitimate children, it seemed natural no longer to completely exclude other persons apart from the parents to whom the child related from the right of contact. However, the legislature stated that a great increase in contact disputes should be avoided. For this reason, the right of contact was being restricted to those persons to whom the child related who were normally particularly close to the child, and recognised only if the contact served the child's best interests. In examining the question as to whether this was the case, the newly created § 1626.3 sentence 2 of the Civil Code, it stated, might be helpful; this provided that the child's best interests normally also includes contact with persons to whom the child has ties, if it is advantageous for the development of the child to preserve these (see *Bundestag* printed paper 13/4899, pp. 106-107).

II.

1. a) According to a blood group test of the year 1990, the complainant in the proceedings 1 BvR 1493/96 is beyond all doubt the natural father of a child born legitimate in 1989, with whose married mother he had a relationship. Three to four months before the birth of the child, the complainant separated from the mother, but several months after the birth he resumed the relationship, which finally ended in 1992. During this period, the mother lived with the child apart from her husband

in the marital home, and in 1992 the husband returned there. The complainant had his own flat.
It remained disputed how intensive the contact was that existed between the complainant and the child during the time when the complainant had a relationship to the child's mother. While the complainant states that he looked after the child several times a week, and that therefore a close and intensive emotional relationship between him and the child developed, the child's mother submits that the complainant looked after the child only by the hour. Because the complainant was unreliable and behaved high-handedly, and because she wanted to live together with her husband again, she states that she then reduced the contact further. At no time, according to the child's mother, were there family relationships between her, the complainant and the child.
Since March 1993 the complainant has had no further relations with the child. He paid maintenance for the child and took out an insurance policy for the child. The mother states that this was done without her desire and was intended to induce her husband to contest the legitimacy of the child.
In 1994, the Local Court dismissed the complainant's application to be granted a right of contact with the child and ordered him not to remain in the immediate vicinity of the child's current home, to avoid all meetings with the child and not to lie in wait for the child. Because there was no legal connection between the complainant and the child, there was no right of contact under § 1634 of the Civil Code old. Since the complainant was not the father of an illegitimate child either, § 1711 of the Civil Code old did not apply. It could not be found that there had been an abuse of the right of custody, and therefore § 1666 of the Civil Code also did not apply. It was problematical for a child to have to distinguish more than one mother and father when it was very young. The complainant was to keep away from the child, in order that the problems of identification were not aggravated for the child.
The complainant filed an immediate appeal against this decision, and the Regional Court dismissed this on the same grounds. The Higher Regional Court held that the complainant's further appeal was inadmissible. It stated that the complainant could not be permitted to have a more favourable procedural position than the father of a child born illegitimate, for whom a further appeal under § 63a of the Act on Matters of Non-Contentious Jurisdiction (*Gesetz über die Angelegenheiten der freiwilligen Gerichtsbarkeit* – FGG) old was excluded in contact proceedings. This provision, the court held, was at present still constitutional and in the case of the complainant it applied by analogy.
b) The constitutional complaint is directed against the judicial decisions; in it, the complainant challenges a violation of Article 1, Article 2.1, Article 3.1 and 3.2, Article 6.1, 6.2 and 6.3, Article 19.4 and Article 20.3 of the Basic Law and Article

103.1 of the Basic Law in conjunction with Article 6, Article 8 and Article 14 of the European Convention on Human Rights.
A claim of the biological father to contact with his child followed, he submitted, both from Article 8.1 of the European Convention on Human Rights and from Article 6.2 of the Basic Law. He was a holder of parental rights, since this was a natural right and did not depend on recognition under civil law. The refusal of the right of contact was an encroachment upon his right under Article 6.2 of the Basic Law. When the child's best interests and the positions under fundamental rights of the legal parents and of the biological father were weighed against each other, the interest of the child and of the biological father in contact carried greater weight, if it had been established that he was the father and there had been at least regular contact, as there had been in his own case. The claim to contact also rose from Article 6.1 of the Basic Law, since the concept of family also covered the relationship of the biological father to his natural child, and the relationship between himself and the child was close and intensive.
In order to assess whether the requirements of § 1666 of the Civil Code are satisfied, the opinion of a judicially appointed independent expert should have been obtained as requested in his application. There was a violation of the principle of proportionality, since the parties to the original proceedings were given no possibility of coming to an agreement. An expert could have been appointed in this connection too. In addition, neither the Youth Welfare Office (*Jugendamt*) nor the parents or the child had been heard. The child had not had separate representation and had therefore not been adequately represented. It was a violation of Article 6.1 and 6.2 of the Basic Law that the rejection of the application for contact had in particular been made without any time limitation. With regard to the prohibition of contact, the court had failed to establish that the child's best interests were endangered. Finally, the Higher Regional Court ought not to have applied § 63a of the Act on Non-Contentious Matters (old) by analogy.
2. a) The complainant in the proceedings 1 BvR 1724/01, a Palestinian with Israeli nationality, first tried to acknowledge paternity of the child born in November 1998. He was informed that the mother of the child did not want a determination of paternity. Thereupon the complaint made an application to the Local Court for a declaration that he was the father of the child.
Presenting evidence, he submitted that since 1991 he had had a relationship with the child's mother and since 1997 had lived with her. He had been present when the child was born and had cut the umbilical cord. The child had been a planned child. With the mother, he had made all the preparations for the birth and, for example, furnished the nursery. The name of the child, an Arabic name, had also been chosen together with the mother. The mother of the child had never expressed doubts as to

his paternity of the child. With his dark eyes and hair, his skin colour and his features, the child also looked like the complainant. In the first three to four months after the birth, he had looked after the child for the majority of the time, since the mother had worked in the mornings. After this, there had been tensions between them and then he had broken up with her. There had been arguments about, among other things, the fact that the mother had not named him as the father of the child at the registry office.

In the name of the defendant child, the mother pleaded lack of knowledge of all the submissions of the complainant and pointed out that meanwhile, in October 2000, another man had acknowledged the paternity. Hereupon, the complainant petitioned in the alternative for a declaration that this man was not the father of the child.

The Local Court dismissed the action. It stated that a determination of paternity was admissible under § 1600d.1 only if there was no other paternity under § 1592 no. 1 or no. 2 of the Civil Code. But in the present case there now was another paternity, following the acknowledgment of paternity of another man with the consent of the mother. The determination of a different paternity was therefore barred. It was also inadmissible for the complainant to challenge the paternity of the person acknowledging paternity, since under § 1600 of the Civil Code only the man whose paternity exists under § 1592 nos. 1 and 2 and § 1593 of the Civil Code, the mother of the child and the child itself were entitled to challenge. In contrast, the legislature deliberately excluded the biological father from making a challenge. There were no constitutional objections to this provision.

The Higher Regional Court dismissed the complainant's appeal. Positive judicial determination of paternity was not admissible even if, as in the present case, acknowledgment was made by another man and the consent of the mother was given only in the course of the proceedings at first instance. Furthermore, the Federal Court of Justice (*Bundesgerichtshof* (*Zeitschrift für das gesamte Familienrecht* – FamRZ) 1999, p. 716) has already stated that the legislature deliberately restricted the positive determination of paternity to the cases in which there is no other paternity involved. The action of another man, even that of the biological father, as a general rule went directly against the welfare of the social family if the other persons involved did not exercise their rights of challenge. Admittedly, the biological father too was in principle a holder of the right of paternity under Article 6.2 of the Basic Law. But the interest of the biological father conflicted with the interest of the child, which was also constitutionally protected, in being able to grow up undisturbed in its familiar social connections, and the interest of the mother in keeping these social connections undisturbed in her own interest.

This also applied if the mother did not live with the man who had acknowledged the paternity. The legal system was permitted to protect social connections instead of taking a purely biological standpoint. If a man wanted to be a father, he could marry the woman first or, at times of agreement, make a formal acknowledgment of paternity, to which the woman would then consent. This adequately protected his rights. The child's fundamental rights too were protected. The child, represented by its mother or, after reaching the age of majority, itself could challenge the paternity and thereafter file an action for a positive declaratory judgment. It followed from this that the restriction of the persons entitled to file a challenge in § 1600 of the Civil Code was unobjectionable even if the putative biological father wanted to satisfy the requirements for a positive determination of paternity in this way.

b) In his constitutional complaint, the complainant challenges a violation of his fundamental right under Article 6.2 of the Basic Law.

It follows from parental rights, he submits, that the biological father of a child must as a matter of principle be accorded the possibility of challenging the paternity of an ostensible father and having his own paternity determined. This applied at least if there was a personal relationship between him and the child and in contrast there was no personal relationship between the ostensible father and the child or there were no family bonds. In this case, a challenge of paternity and a subsequent acknowledgment by the biological father could not adversely affect the child's best interests. § 1600 of the Civil Code and § 1600d.1 of the Civil Code were unconstitutional in that they did not permit, as an exception, for cases with a particular constellation, the fundamental rights of the biological father to be weighed against those of the child. This reduced the scope of protection under Article 6.2 of the Basic Law and prevented the biological father from enjoying his fundamental right at all. The encroachment upon his parental rights as the biological father was justified neither by the child's best interests nor by the protection of the family as a social institution. Unlike in the case decided by the Federal Court of Justice, in the present case there was neither a marriage relationship between the mother of his child and the person acknowledging paternity, nor a long-term relationship between the child and its legal father. Acknowledgment by another man was not in itself an indication that a social relationship existed. It was constitutionally unacceptable that the parental rights of the biological father depended without exception on the favour of the mother, who was able by consenting to a third party's acknowledgment of paternity to remove the ground from under the parental rights of the biological father.

III.

…

B.

The constitutional complaints are admissible. …

C.

The constitutional complaints are well-founded.

§ 1600 of the Civil Code is incompatible with Article 6.2 sentence 1 of the Basic Law insofar as it excludes the natural father of a child without exception from challenging the paternity of his child that had been acknowledged by another man in order to be granted legal paternity himself (I.).

The contact provision in § 1711.2 of the Civil Code old was compatible with the Basic Law (II.), but in the decisions challenged it was not applied in conformity with Article 6.1 of the Basic Law (III. 1).

In contrast, § 1685 of the Civil Code is not in conformity with Article 6.1 of the Basic Law to the extent that it excludes the natural father of a child who has a social and family relationship to his child from contact with the child even if that contact is in the child's best interests (IV.).

I.

1. The natural father of a child who is not the legal father is also protected by Article 6.2 sentence 1 of the Basic Law. However, merely being the natural father of a child does not make him the holder of the parental right under Article 6.2 sentence 1 of the Basic Law. But this provision containing a fundamental right protects the natural father in his interest in taking the legal position of father of the child. This protection gives him no right to be granted the position of father with higher priority than the legal father in every case. However, the legislature must give him the opportunity to attain the position of legal father if the protection of a family relationship between the child and its legal parents does not conflict with this and it is established that he is the natural father of the child.

a) Under Article 6.2 sentence 1 of the Basic Law, the care for and upbringing of the child are the right and duty of the parents. The concept of parents, by its usage, also includes the natural parents of a child, regardless of the parents' marital status and the closeness of the relationship between them and the child (see BVerfGE 92, 158 (177-178)). When Article 6.2 sentence 1 of the Basic Law speaks of the natural right of the parents, this expresses on the one hand that this right is not granted by the state, but is recognised by the state as pre-existing (see BVerfGE 59, 360 (376)). On the other hand this makes it clear that the persons who give life to a child are by nature fundamentally prepared and called upon to take on responsibility for its care and upbringing (see BVerfGE 24, 119 (150)). The legislature is therefore required to orient its allocation of the legal position of parents to the child's parentage (see BVerfGE 79, 256 (267)).

b) However, the legislature is not under a duty to make legal recognition of parentage always dependent on an examination of the parentage of the child in the individual case. With regard to the protection of family social relationships under Article 6.1 of the Basic Law and the protection of privacy under Article 2.1 of the Basic Law, it is sufficient to conclude what the parentage of a child is from particular facts and circumstances and social situations and to allocate the legal positions of parents on the basis of this presumption, if this as a general rule means that natural and legal parenthood coincide (see BVerfGE 79, 256 (267)). Thus it has always been presumed, not only in our legal culture, on the basis of the relationship entered into on marriage, that the mother's husband is also the natural father of her child, and the legal paternity of the husband is based on this. The same applies if a man, in declared agreement with the mother of an illegitimate child, acknowledges paternity and through this expresses with binding legal effect that he is prepared to take on the responsibility of a parent. The consequence of these statutory provisions on presumption, which are constitutionally unobjectionable, is that in the individual case, contrary to the statutory presumption, legal and natural paternity may be separate. The child then has two fathers, both of whom may rely on their parental rights protected by Article 6.2 sentence 1 of the Basic Law.

2. The protection of Article 6.2 sentence 1 of the Basic Law does not require legal parenthood. The man who fathers a child is the father of the child, even if the legal system does not recognise him as such. Article 6.2 sentence 1 of the Basic Law does not require more than this parenthood based on parentage to include parents in its scope of protection. However, this alone does not make the biological father the holder of parental rights under Article 6.2 sentence 1 of the Basic Law together with the legal father.

a) The holders of parental rights for a child under Article 6.2 sentence 1 of the Basic Law may only be one mother and one father.

aa) Article 6.2 sentence 1 of the Basic Law allocates the child to the parents. Here, the very fact that a child can have only two parents leads to the conclusion that the legislature creating the constitution intended to give the parental rights for a child only to two parents. The parental right is based on this allocation, which at the same time determines its orientation: it is a right that belongs to each parent but corresponds to the right of the other parent, which is of equal value (see BVerfGE 99, 145 (164)), and that relates to the child, for whose best interests it is to be exercised (see BVerfGE 75, 201 (218-219)). The responsibility for the child, which Article 6.2 sentence 1 of the Basic Law in this way both grants to the parents and imposes on them, in turn also requires a clear allocation of the parental role, which must be filled in order for the responsibility to be exercised in the child's interest. It is true that the family relationships into which a child is born, and therefore also the female and male persons with whom the child has close relationships, may change in the course of time. But for the development of the child, in addition to its parentage and the quality of its relationship to the persons to whom it relates most closely at any given time, another factor of decisive importance is the knowledge and certainty of who it belongs to, to what family it is allocated and who is responsible for it as mother or father. Only this creates personal and legal certainty for the child, which the provision on the fundamental right of parenthood is intended to convey to it.

bb) Article 6.2 sentence 1 of the Basic Law excludes a person from enjoying parental rights without at the same time having duties towards the child. From the outset, the parental right is connected with the duty to care for and bring up the child, as the element that determines its nature (see BVerfGE 24, 119 (143); 52, 223 (235); 61, 358 (372)). Those who claim the parental right for themselves may not merely demand rights for themselves, but must also bear duties. Thus the right of contact is also part of parental responsibility. But if the parental right under Article 6.2 sentence 1 of the Basic Law conveys rights only together with duties, the holder of this right may be only a person who at the same time bears the parental responsibility, regardless of whether the parenthood is based only on parentage or on the allocation of a right (see BVerfGE 56, 363 (381 et seq.); 75, 201 (218-219); 79, 203 (210); 80, 286 (295)).

cc) Having two fathers at the same time, each of whom together with the mother bears the same constitutionally allocated parental responsibility for the child, does not correspond to the idea of parental responsibility that is the basis of Article 6.2 sentence 1 of the Basic Law. Nor does the change of family life circumstances require that a child should be subjected to the parental responsibility of two fathers at the same time. It is not a new phenomenon, attributable to the change in family structures, that legal and natural paternity may not coincide. Instead, its cause lies in the legal tradition of presuming paternity on the basis of particular social facts and circumstances, basing the legal allocation of the child on this and then in the individual case establishing natural paternity as the basis for legal paternity only when the statutory presumption does not lead to the desired result. Even if it should appear that natural fathers, where legal and natural paternity do not coincide, increasingly wish to acknowledge their paternity and have a relationship to their children, such a development would not in itself be a reason to recognise the natural father in addition to the legal father as the holder of the parental right under Article 6.2 sentence 1 of the Basic Law.

If Article 6.2 sentence 1 of the Basic Law in the first instance gives the parents the responsibility for the child, this is based on the consideration that, as a general rule, in joint exercise of this responsibility, they usually observe their child's interests best (see BVerfGE 103, 89 (108)). But such a consideration cannot relate to a community consisting of two fathers and one mother; in this case the presumption that the joint exercise of parental responsibility serves the child's welfare best is unreliable. Instead, such a constellation would, so to speak, contain the seeds of role conflicts and disputes as to competence between the parents, and this might have a negative influence on the development of the child. At all events, there would be no guarantee that parental responsibility would be effectively observed in the interests of the child. At the same time, it would become more difficult to attach parental responsibility to persons in order to fulfil the duty of the state community of watching over the exercise of parental rights in order to safeguard the child's best interests. In this way, the content of the parental right limits those who hold it.

b) The legal father of a child who accepts parental responsibility for the child is the holder of the parental rights under Article 6.2 sentence 1 of the Basic Law and does not lose this right and the position as father connected with it merely by virtue of the fact that another man is shown to be the natural father of the child (see BVerfGE 24, 119 (136)). The statutory establishment of paternity creates the possibility for a person to be able as a parent to actually take comprehensive care of the child. It opens the way for parental responsibility and is the requirement for the safeguarding of the constitutionally protected position as a parent. Only the termination of the position as legal father releases the legal father from his position as a holder of parental rights and from his responsibility for the child.

c) Natural paternity also needs to be recognised legally in order that parental rights may be asserted on the basis of it. If it corresponds to the statutory presumption, this gives it its legally binding nature. If this is not the case, then it is usually not automatically apparent who is the natural father of the child in place of the legal father. If the natural father has no interest in accepting parental responsibility for the child, and only then, the circumstance that the child is his natural child and not that of the legal father becomes apparent to outside observers, and this fact becomes important if the legal paternity is challenged by one of the persons entitled to do so and if as a consequence of this determinations are made as to the paternity. But even if a man acknowledges that he, in addition to the legal father, is the natural father of a child, this alone neither establishes that this is actually the case, nor can it be concluded from this that the natural father is also prepared to take on parental responsibility for the child in place of the legal father. But a person`s position as the holder of a fundamental right entailing rights and duties relating to a child may not be established on the basis of such uncertainties. Being able to take this position as a natural father in place of the legal father therefore requires the challenger's natural paternity to be established or confirmed with the intention that he takes on parental responsibility with legally binding effect.

3. Article 6.2 sentence 1 of the Basic Law protects the interests of the natural father of a child in also taking the legal position of father.

a) The statutory fleshing out of the justification and content of family legal relationships must be oriented to the fact that as a general rule the natural parents of a child must also be granted the legal position of parents. If in the individual case the natural and legal paternity of a child do not coincide, the natural father is in the first instance prevented from bearing responsibility for his child. However, this does not leave him unprotected as a parent.

The precept contained in Article 6.2 sentence 1 of the Basic Law that if possible natural and legal parenthood should coincide requires that in such cases too, where there are doubts as to the paternity, proceedings should be commenced in which the parentage is examined and the parental rights, if necessary, are legally adjusted. To this extent, Article 6.2 sentence 1 of the Basic Law in principle grants the biological father too the possibility of obtaining parental rights by legal proceedings.

b) This also applies to a person who can assume by reason of particular facts and evidence that he is the natural father of a child, but who has not yet been able to prove this because the mother has not cooperated. If he were refused the possibility of having his natural paternity examined and confirmed as the requirement for obtaining legal paternity, he would be barred from acquiring his fundamental rights, even if he were indeed the natural father of the child. This would be contrary to the intention of Article 6.2 sentence 1 of the Basic Law to create possibilities for the natural father to take on the position of the legal father in addition. Examining and establishing paternity is therefore part of the procedural guarantee under Article 6.2 sentence 1 of the Basic Law.

c) However, this protection granted to the biological father by Article 6.2 sentence 1 of the Basic Law covers only the possibility of commencing proceedings to be recognised as the legal father too. The desire to obtain merely knowledge and certainty as to the parentage of a child cannot be based on Article 6.2 sentence 1 of the Basic Law, because it has no connection to parental responsibility. Just as the right of the child to know its own parentage arises from its right of personality (see BVerfGE 79, 256 (268 et seq.)), the desire of a man for mere knowledge as to whether a child is his affects his self-image and the possibility of placing himself as an individual in a relationship to others, not only socially, but also genealogically, and therefore it relates to his right protected by Article 2.1 in conjunction with Arti-

cle 1.1 of the Basic Law. It need not be decided here whether his right of personality gives rise to a claim for him to have the parentage of a child judicially resolved, since such a resolution is not the subject of either of the cases to be decided. The right of personality does not give rise to a claim for recognition of legal paternity.
4. It cannot be inferred from Article 6.2 sentence 1 of the Basic Law that natural paternity must always be preferred to legal paternity. This provision containing a fundamental right gives no right for the natural father to be granted the position of father in every case with priority over the legal father and therefore to displace the latter from his position as father.
Article 6.2 sentence 1 of the Basic Law admittedly proceeds on the assumption of natural paternity following from procreation, but it then goes beyond this allocation and protects the parent-child relationship as a comprehensive relationship of responsibility of parents towards their children, who need care and upbringing. The requirement for being able to bear responsibility for the child as part of the parental right in this connection is that parents and child are socially connected (see BVerfGE 56, 363 (382); 61, 358 (372); 103, 89 (107)). Parentage and a social and family community of responsibility can be said to be the content of Article 6.2 sentence 1 of the Basic Law. The legislature should endeavour to bring these two elements together. But if they do not coincide in reality, the provision containing the fundamental right does not lay down a rigid weighting as to which of the two characteristics that are to constitute parenthood should be given priority, and it therefore does not create an order of priority between biological and social parenthood. Instead, the legislature, when deciding to whom the child should be allocated in such a case, must take account of both interests and weigh them against each other. Here it may attach importance not only to parentage, but also to legal and social circumstances (see BVerfGE 92, 158 (178)).
5. In principle, it is constitutionally unobjectionable that the legislature has granted priority to the interests of the child and its legal parents in maintaining an existing social family organisation as against the interest of the natural father to also be recognised legally as the father, and in this connection, in § 1600 of the Civil Code, has excluded the natural father from challenging the legal paternity.
If the natural and legal paternity do not coincide, it must be decided which of the two is to be allocated the parental rights for the child. This decision affects not only the interest of the natural father, but also the interests of the legal parents and in particular the interest of the child.
a) The legislature, as grounds for the access to legal paternity being barred to the natural father in this case and for his having no right of challenge, emphasised in particular the protection of the social family (see *Bundestag* printed paper 13/4899, p. 58). Article 6.1 of the Basic Law too extends its protection to the social family as

a long-term community of responsibility of parents and children (see BVerfGE 80, 81 (90); 99, 216 (231-232)). The social structure and continuation of the family relationship between the legal parents and the child may be adversely affected by the fact that another man claims legal paternity for himself. Protecting it against this adverse effect is a good reason, against which the exclusion of the biological father from challenging the existing legal paternity under § 1600 of the Civil Code is to be measured (see BVerfGE 38, 241 (255)).
At the same time, the interests of the individual members of the family organisation must be taken into account. Since the parental rights are allocated to the parents jointly, the right of the mother corresponds to that of the father. If, against her will, there is a change in the position of that right, the mother must now, outside the existing social family organisation, share the parental rights with a man as the father of her child where she is not (no longer) in a social connection with that man. For the legal father, a change of legal paternity would mean the loss of his legal position with regard to the child protected by Article 6.2 sentence 1 of the Basic Law, although he has taken responsibility for the child and in living together with the mother and the child continues to take care of it in practice, but may no longer take part in making decisions as to its fate. Finally, the child loses its previous father and must adapt to a new one, even if it remains in the existing family organisation. The legal change would ensure that natural and legal parenthood coincide, but at the same time it would mean that legal and social paternity would be separated and it could also lead to loss of the status as a legitimate child. This requires a new orientation from the child, and this may involve the child in conflicts. It is true that a child must also cope with such a change if its mother or its previous legal father challenges the paternity. But in this case there is not only a change on the legal plane in the social parent-child relationship, but the cohesion of the social family is endangered from within itself rather than by the person who claims paternity for himself.
Nor is this change comparable to the cases in which the child, after the separation and divorce of its legal parents, moves to family constellations in which it must live together with new (step-) parents. Here, admittedly, the child has to adapt to a new social context. But it still has the allocation to its legal parents as a security and a constant. In contrast, if the legal paternity were successfully challenged by the natural father, the allocation of the child would change, even if the previous social family organisation was not endangered from inside itself, but might be exposed to a danger only through the challenge.
However, there may also be an interest of the child not only in knowing its natural father, but also in being allocated him as legal father. This interest is served by the child's own right of challenge. It need not be decided here whether the fleshing out

of this right takes sufficient account of the constitutionally protected position of the child (see Wanitzek, FPR (*Familie, Partnerschaft, Recht*) 2002, p. 390 (392)), for this is not relevant to a right of challenge for the natural father. Conflicts of interest between the child and its legal parents, who have custody, as to a challenge of the legal paternity cannot be solved by granting the biological parent the right to undertake the challenge on behalf of the interests of the child. Instead, the child must be put in the position to formulate its own interests and to convert them into legal acts, if necessary with the help of third parties (see BVerfGE 72, 122 (134); 99, 145 (157)).

b) Against this is the justified interest of the biological father not only in knowing that he is the natural father, but also in being legally recognised as the father and having a legal relationship to his child. But a new legal allocation of the child would not lead to the creation of a new social family as the basis for a beneficial cooperation of parents in exercising their responsibility to the child in the child's interest. Instead, the cohesion of the previous family unit in which the child lives would be adversely affected by the dissolution of the legal relationships of its members. The divergence of legal allocation and social and family relationship might give rise to conflicts that on the one hand would endanger the child being brought up in a way conducive to its best interests and on the other hand might make it more difficult for the child to orient itself as to who it belonged to. This justifies the legislature in § 1600 of the Civil Code having in principle granted the natural father no possibility of challenging legal paternity, in the interest of preserving an existing family cohesion between the child and its legal parents.

6. However, § 1600 of the Civil Code is incompatible with Article 6.2 sentence 1 of the Basic Law insofar as it refuses the biological father the right to challenge the legal paternity even if the legal parents do not form a social family together with the child that needs protection under Article 6.1 of the Basic Law.

a) If a man, without being the natural father of the child, has acknowledged paternity but does not live together with the mother and the child, and is merely a "paying father", there is no sufficient reason to refuse the natural father the right to be recognised as the legal father too and to take on the associated duty. Nor do the interests of the mother and the child prevent this.

If there is no social and family relationship to the legal father, the preservation of which might be the basis of the mother's interest, her only remaining interest is not wanting to share the parental rights with the natural father. But this interest is not protected by Article 6.2 sentence 1 of the Basic Law, which makes the position of parent dependent not on the will of the other parent, but solely on the circumstance of presumed or real parenthood. For the child, the challenge by the natural father would mean a change in its allocation to the father, but a change which would not materially affect the child's best interests if there is no relationship between the child and the legal father that developed while the child was living with the latter and that could be adversely affected. On the other hand, the child would now be allocated legally in a way that would not give it a family life together with both parents, but that would now ensure that the legal paternity coincided with the child's parentage.

b) A change in the legal position of the paternity even conforms with the interest of the child in maintaining personal relationships if it has been able in fact to build up a father-child relationship precisely with its natural father, who also wants to be its legal father, while it does not live in a family community with its legal father and its mother. In these circumstances, no good reason justifies refusing to a biological father who is prepared to take on parental responsibility for his child the possibility of also taking on the legal position of parent, and such a refusal injures the biological father's right under Article 6.2 sentence 1 of the Basic Law to be given a possibility through legal action of enjoying the fundamental right of parenthood.

c) Nor can the exclusion of the biological father from the possibility of finding access to the legal position of father in the case where there are no family relations between the legal father and the child be justified by reference to the existence of a social relationship that deserves protection and that would be endangered.

If a marriage exists, it may be concluded in a process of categorisation that the married parents live together as a family with their child, but it may not be concluded from an acknowledgment of paternity that occurs with the consent of the mother that the mother, the child and the legal father live together as a family.

Statistics show that children who were born illegitimate still far more often live with only one parent (usually the mother) and not with both parents together. Thus, for example, in the year 2001, 821,000 minor children lived in a community with their parents as against 2.12 m children who lived with only one parent (see Statistisches Bundesamt 2002, *Leben und Arbeiten in Deutschland, Ergebnisse des Mikrozensus 2001*, pp. 29, 65). In only 36 per cent of the cases investigated by Vaskovics and others was there a long-term relationship between the parents after the birth of an illegitimate child, whereas in far more than 80 per cent of the cases there was a voluntary acknowledgment of paternity, that is, not to a court finding as to the natural and therefore legal paternity (see Vaskovics/Rost/Rupp, *Lebenslage nichtehelicher Kinder, Rechtstatsächliche Untersuchung zu Lebenslagen und Entwicklungsverläufen nichtehelicher Kinder*, 1997, pp. 62, 160). This means than in over half of the cases an acknowledgment of paternity was made where the parents of the child did not live together. These figures give no basis to make an assumption by categorisation that where there is an acknowledgment of paternity, there is usually also a social relationship worthy of protection between father, mother and child.

In general, an acknowledgment of paternity is not made lightly, for it means that the person making the acknowledgment will at minimum be obliged to share responsibility for the maintenance of the child and will be treated in property law and the law of succession as the father of the child. And despite the lack of a family connection to mother and child, there may also be reasons to acknowledge the paternity of a child, even if the person acknowledging is not certain that he is the father of the child. If, in such cases, an acknowledgment of paternity is made, it is possible to counter the danger that mother and child are bombarded with challenge proceedings with less oppressive means than the complete exclusion of challenge by the natural father. Thus, for example, prima facie evidence that the challenger is the natural father may be required in advance, and this evidence may be linked to particular requirements. Time limits for challenge also help contain this risk.

II.

§ 1711.2 of the Civil Code old which provided that the guardianship court could grant the father personal contact with the child if such contact served the child's best interests, did not violate Article 6.1 of the Basic Law.

1. The natural father who is not the legal father of a child also forms a family together with the child which is protected by Article 6.1 of the Basic Law if there is a social relationship between him and the child that arises from the fact that at least for a period of time he did in fact have responsibility for the child. Article 6.1 of the Basic Law protects the natural father and the child in their interest that this social and family relationship is preserved, and therefore in their contact with each other. It is a violation of Article 6.1 of the Basic Law if the biological father who has a relationship of this kind with his child is denied contact with the child even though the contact serves the child's best interests.

a) Article 6.1 of the Basic Law protects the family as a community of parents with children. In this connection it is not significant whether the children are the children by birth of the parents and whether they are legitimate or illegitimate (see BVerfGE 10, 59 (66); 18, 97 (105-106); 79, 256 (267)). Family is the actual long-term and upbringing relationship between children and parents who are responsible for the children. If the child lives together with both parents, they form a family together. If this is not the case, but both parents in fact bear responsibility for the child, the child has two families, which are protected by Article 6.1 of the Basic Law: the family with the mother and the family with the father (see BVerfGE 45, 104 (123)).

b) If the natural father who is not the legal father has actual responsibility for his child, and if a social relationship between him and the child develops from this, the two form a family which is covered by the protection of Article 6.1 of the Basic Law, despite the lack of a legal status as father and despite other family relationships of the child.
Admittedly, the basis may be removed from such a family at any time because of the lack of a legal relationship between the father and the child. While the legal father, even if he does not live (or no longer lives) together with the child and has no right of custody, may nevertheless bear responsibility for the child both legally and in fact, the family relationship between the natural father and his child is based only on his preparedness to take responsibility for the child and on the factual possibility of doing this, which comes to an end if the parents who have custody no longer permit it.
c) When it becomes impossible for the biological father to continue to act with actual responsibility for the child, the protection of Article 6.1 of the Basic Law does not end for the family that has come into existence between the biological father and his child.
It is true that neither Article 6.2 sentence 1 of the Basic Law nor Article 6.1 of the Basic Law gives the natural father who is not the legal father a claim to continue to act with responsibility for the child. But even when this possibility ends, the personal connection that has developed between the biological father and his child continues in existence; it is also still kept in existence by the blood connection between father and child. The interest of the biological father, who has till now been connected in a family with the child, and the interest of his child in the continuation of this relation to each other is protected by Article 6.1 of the Basic Law as an after-effect of the protection that previously covered their family community of responsibility.
d) This protection, which continues to have an effect, gives rise to a right of the biological father to contact with his child, at least if this contact serves the child's best interests.
aa) In order to maintain an existing relationship, the persons between whom the relationship exists must have the possibility of having personal contact and communicating with each other. This applies in particular to the parent-child relationship. The separation of a child from a parent with whom it has previously had a close relationship deprives the child of an important element of orientation and affects its self-assurance and inner sense of security (see Goldstein/Freud/Solnit, *Jenseits des Kindeswohls*, 1974/1991, pp. 33 et seq.; BVerfGE 75, 201 (219)). Because of the particular way in which a child experiences time, such a separation soon appears to the child to be final, for it learns only gradually that people who go away may re-

turn (see Heilmann, *Kindliches Zeitempfinden und Verfahrensrecht*, 1998, p. 26). In order to discover here that the existing relationship did not end as a result of the separation, that is, that the parent did not turn away from the child, the child needs personal contact with the parent, that is, contact, at fairly regular intervals.

bb) On the other hand, as a result of the new family context in which it is placed, the child may find itself in conflict between the old and the new relationship. Here, continuing contact might have the effect that the child is once more exposed to orientation problems that endanger rather than encourage its development (see Klußmann/Stötzel, *Das Kind im Rechtsstreit der Erwachsenen*, 1995, p. 223).

cc) Article 6.1 of the Basic Law protects the relationship between the child and its parent, not the individual family member taken alone (see BVerfGE 78, 38 (49)). The provision containing the fundamental right can therefore give the individual only a right that corresponds to the interest of the other family member who is connected with him or her and that serves the protection of the family relationship. A right of the biological father to contact with his child to maintain the social relationship that exists between them therefore exists only to the extent that this serves the child's best interests.

2. Judged by these standards, § 1711 of the Civil Code old was compatible with Article 6.1 of the Basic Law.

Taking into account the protection that this provision containing a fundamental right also accords to the family relationship between the biological father and his child, it was possible to interpret § 1711.2 of the Civil Code old in conformity with the constitution to mean that the natural father who was not the legal father who has or has had a social and family relationship to his child was able to obtain permission for contact with his child by a judicial decision if this contact serves the child's best interests.

a) It is admittedly necessary to proceed on the assumption that when the legislature created § 1711 of the Civil Code old it used the concept of father to mean the legal father of an illegitimate child. But this does not exclude a more extensive interpretation to include the natural father. It seems likely that at that time the legislature did not contemplate the constellation where a natural father who is not the legal father has a relationship to the child and seeks to maintain this relationship, for it was assumed that the natural father of an illegitimate child often had no interest of his own in his child (see BVerfGE 38, 241 (252) on the challenge of legitimacy). It may therefore not be imputed to the legislature that in § 1711.2 of the Civil Code old, it intended expressly to exclude the natural father, as opposed to the legal father, of an illegitimate child from the judicial examination of a right of contact with his child. The text and parliamentary history of the provision therefore do not prevent it from being interpreted in conformity with the constitution.

b) Nor do the meaning and purpose of that statutory provision prevent it being interpreted in conformity with the constitution. § 1711.2 of the Civil Code old tied the contact of the father of an illegitimate child to the requirement that this served the child's best interests. But if the child's best interests were the conclusive yardstick for opening the possibility of contact, the legal status of the relationship of the father to his child moved into the background. For in order to assess whether contact serves the child's best interests, what is important is not the legal relationship of the child to its father, but the actual relationship. Nor, if the biological father is included in the concept of father of § 1711.2 of the Civil Code old, is this open to the objection that the legislature intended to exclude the biological father from contact in order to ensure that the child was clearly allocated to one father. Because the section created a judicial examination of the individual case by the standard of the child's best interests, all social and family circumstances and ties of the child affected had to be taken into account in every individual case when the decision was made. Here too, however, it was not the legal status of the father, but the concrete social network of relationships in which the child was involved, that was decisive.

III.

The judicial decisions based on § 1600 of the Civil Code and § 1711.2 of the Civil Code old are incompatible with the Basic Law.

1. The complainant in the proceedings 1 BvR 1493/96 suffered no violation of his right under Article 6.2 sentence 1 of the Basic Law as a result of the decisions challenged. But the decisions violate his right to the protection of his social and family relationship to his child under Article 6.1 of the Basic Law.

a) The complainant, who is the natural father of a child, does not wish also to be determined to be the legal father of the child, but to be granted contact with his child. Natural paternity does not have the effect that the complainant is the holder of the parental rights under Article 6.2 sentence 1 of the Basic Law alongside the legal father of the child. Therefore this provision containing a fundamental right cannot give him a right to contact with his child. The parental right of contact is part of parental responsibility and is due only to the person who bears this responsibility with its rights and duties.

b) However, Article 6.1 of the Basic Law has not been adequately taken into account. § 1711.2 of the Civil Code old, on which the courts based their challenged decisions, was admittedly compatible with the Basic Law if it was interpreted in conformity with the constitution. But in their decisions, the courts failed to see the protection of the complainant under Article 6.1 of the Basic Law. They attached no importance to the fact that the complainant, as the natural father of the child, for a long period also took on the role of father for his child and built up a relationship with the child, and therefore they did not examine whether § 1711.2 of the Civil Code old can be interpreted as being in conformity with the constitution. Since the courts declared that this provision cannot be applied to the complainant, there was no examination as to whether giving the complainant contact with his child would serve the child's best interests. In this respect, the courts in their decision did not do justice to the protection that is enjoyed even by an existing family relationship of the natural father to his child under Article 6.1 of the Basic Law.

2. In the proceedings 1 BvR 1724/01, the decisions challenged by the constitutional complaint violate the complainant's right under Article 6.2 sentence 1 of the Basic Law. They are based on § 1600 of the Civil Code, which unconstitutionally excludes the natural father who is not the legal father of a child from challenging paternity, with no exceptions.

a) It is true that the decisions were made in proceedings for the determination of paternity and therefore they are based on § 1600d.1 of the Civil Code, which excludes a determination of paternity as long as another man is deemed to be the father of the child. But in their decisions, the courts also examined whether the complainant may challenge paternity that has been acknowledged by another man, and with reference to § 1600 of the Civil Code they answered this question in the negative, assuming that § 1600 was constitutional.

b) The complainant petitions for his paternity to be determined, so that he can take the position of legal father for the child born in 1998. There are sufficient indications that he may be the natural father of the child. The child has an Arabic name. According to information from the complainant, the complainant chose the child's name together with the mother, also lived together with her in the first months of the child's life and jointly with her cared for the child. The child is said to be similar to the complainant in appearance. The mother denies these statements solely on the basis of lack of knowledge. During the proceedings for the determination of paternity, another man made an acknowledgment of paternity with the consent of the mother, and consequently the complainant is prevented by § 1600 of the Civil Code from challenging the legal paternity in order to be recognised as the father of the child himself, although the man who is deemed to be the father of the child as a result of the acknowledgment does not live together with the child and the mother. The complainant's exclusion from the possibility of challenge under § 1600 of the Civil Code is therefore not justified by the protection of the family under Article 6.1 of the Basic Law and violates the complainant's right under Article 6.2 sentence 1 of the Basic Law to have his paternity established legally too as the natural father.

IV.

§ 1685 of the Civil Code is incompatible with Article 6.1 of the Basic Law to the extent that it does not include in the group of persons entitled to contact the natural father of a child who is not the legal father, if there is or has been a social and family relationship between him and the child.

1. The fact that § 1711.2 of the Civil Code old has been repealed by the Act Reforming the Law of Parent and Child makes it necessary for the Federal Constitutional Court to subject the new law on contact with a child that is to be applied by the courts to a constitutional examination too. Otherwise it could not be ensured that the courts in the proceedings 1 BvR 1493/96 can make decisions on rights of contact that are in conformity with the constitution.

a) If judicial decisions are challenged by a constitutional complaint and if the Federal Constitutional Court comes to the conclusion that the decisions violate a fundamental right of the complainant, they are to be reversed under § 95.2 of the Federal Constitutional Court Act (*Bundesverfassungsgerichtsgesetz* – BVerfGG). If the provision on which the decisions are based has already been repealed, in general it is sufficient to make a declaration that the decisions violated a particular fundamental right of the complainant. But this is out of the question if this does not completely deal with the relief sought in the original proceedings. Then the matter must be referred back to the competent court for a new decision. However, this requires that the court to which the matter is referred back is able to make a new decision while preserving the fundamental rights of the complainant. This is not possible if the courts, with regard to the claim asserted by the complainant, cannot create a situation that is in conformity with the constitution. That is the case here.

b) § 1711.2 of the Civil Code old, in interpreting which the courts in the decisions challenged in the proceedings 1 BvR 1493/96 failed to appreciate the protection of the complainant under Article 6.1 of the Basic Law, was repealed by the Act Reforming the Law of Parent and Child. If these decisions are reversed by the Federal Constitutional Court and the matter is referred back to the competent court, this provision can no longer be used as a basis when the right of contact desired by the complainant is examined. The claim asserted judicially by the complainant to contact with his child has not, however, been rendered invalid by the passage of time. The contact that has been missed to date cannot be replaced, of course, but it could be granted for the future. The child, which was born in 1989, is also still far from the age of majority, and therefore the right of contact has not been terminated by the child having reached the age of majority. The courts, in applying the new law, would therefore have to examine whether the complainant should be granted a right of contact with his child.

c) For this, it is crucial whether the new law grants a right of contact with their children to natural fathers who are not legal fathers or continues to refuse it. In the first case, the Federal Constitutional Court would merely have to make a declaration that the decisions challenged were unconstitutional in that they failed to appreciate the protection of the complainant's fundamental right under Article 6.1 of the Basic Law when they interpreted § 1711.2 of the Civil Code old. But if a right of contact of the natural father is unconstitutionally still excluded, such a declaration does not suffice to give the complainant a way to enforce his rights. Even the reversal of the decisions does not go far enough if the courts, which when making their new decision now have to apply the new law, would be prevented by this law from making a decision in conformity with the constitution. They would then immediately have to submit the matter, which had only just been referred back to them, to the Federal Constitutional Court again for a decision on the constitutionality of the new statutory arrangements. In order on the one hand to be able to determine the scope of the decision to be made, and on the other hand to avoid an unconstitutional state being perpetuated solely as a result of procedural details, the Federal Constitutional Court must in such a case also examine the constitutionality of the new law to be applied by the courts.

2. § 1685 of the Civil Code is not completely compatible with Article 6.1 of the Basic Law.

a) The Act Reforming the Law of Parent and Child fundamentally changed the right of contact. In the case of the right of contact of a parent, which is governed by § 1684 of the Civil Code, a distinction is no longer made between legitimate and illegitimate children. In addition, § 1685 of the Civil Code also opens up the possibility of a right of contact with other persons to whom the child relates. Both sections do not expressly include the natural father of a child in the group of persons entitled to contact.

b) Neither § 1684 of the Civil Code nor § 1685 of the Civil Code can be interpreted to the effect that the natural father of a child is also granted a right of contact.

aa) Under § 1684.1 of the Civil Code, each parent has a right but also a duty to have contact with the child. This provision refers to parental responsibility and defines this for contact with the child as a right entailing duties. But the only person who can be given the duty of contact with the child is the one who has parental responsibility. Someone who has this status is both entitled and obliged to have contact with the child. This excludes the possibility of subsuming the biological father of a child, who by definition does not have the position of legal father, under the definition of parent of § 1684.1 of the Civil Code.

bb) In § 1685 of the Civil Code, the legislature has now in certain circumstances granted a right of contact with the child to grandparents, siblings, stepparents and

foster parents. The ground for granting it here is the relationship of these persons to the child, which gives rise to a right of contact if this serves the child's best interests (see *Bundestag* printed paper 13/4899, pp. 106-107). The requirements contained in § 1685 of the Civil Code of those who are granted the possibility of a right of contact may also be fulfilled by the natural father who is not the legal father of the child, if the child has a personal relationship to him. In addition, like grandparents and siblings, he has connection to the child by parentage.
Nevertheless, it is not permitted to interpret § 1685 of the Civil Code to mean that the biological father too is included in the groups of persons named in subsection 1 or subsection 2 of the provision. Apart from the fact that he is not expressly listed, the legislature clearly expressed that the right of contact was to be restricted to those persons to whom the child has a relationship who are expressly named in the section and of whom the legislature assumes that they are normally very close to the child. It justified this restriction on the basis of the need to prevent disputes on contact being greatly increased (see *Bundestag* printed paper 13/4899, loc. cit.). This prohibits increasing the groups of persons named in § 1685 of the Civil Code by adding the natural father as a result of interpreting the Article in conformity with the constitution.

D. – I.

1. § 1685 of the Civil Code is therefore to be declared incompatible with Article 6.1 of the Basic Law to this extent.
It cannot be annulled, because it is not the content of the provision, but the failure to include the biological father who has a social relationship to his child in the group of the persons entitled to contact named in this provision that violates Article 6.1 of the Basic Law (see BVerfGE 90, 263 (276)).
The legislature is required to put the legal situation into conformity with the constitution by 30 April 2004. The provision may no longer by applied by the courts to the extent that it is incompatible (see BVerfGE 82, 126 (155); 84, 168 (187)).
2. The violation of Article 6.2 sentence 1 of the Basic Law that has been determined makes it necessary to declare that § 1600 of the Civil Code is incompatible with this fundamental right to the extent that it is unconstitutional. There can be no annulment here either, because the violation of the constitution lies in the failure of the legislature to include the biological father in the group of persons entitled to challenge subject to the requirements named. The legislature is required to put the legal situation into conformity with the constitution by 30 April 2004. In doing this, when setting time limits for the exercise of the right of challenge, it must ensure

that the biological fathers for whom challenge has been impossible until now are also put in a position to rely on the right of challenge.

II.

The decisions challenged are to be reversed (§ 95.2 of the Federal Constitutional Court Act). The matters are referred back to the Local Courts. The proceedings are to be stayed until the legislature amends the law.

III.

…

Justices: Papier, Jaeger, Haas, Hömig, Steiner, Hohmann-Dennhardt, Hoffmann-Riem, Bryde

As a result of the Federal Constitutional Court's decision, Article 1 no. 7 of the Act of 23 April 2004 (Federal Law Gazette I 2004, p. 598), with effect from 30 April 2004, reworded § 1685.2 of the Civil Code as follows:

> *"(2) The same applies to persons to whom the child relates closely if these have or have had actual responsibility for the child (social and family relationship). It is in general to be assumed that actual responsibility has been taken on if the person lived for a long period in domestic community with the child."*

No. 41

BVerfGE 108, 351

of 7 October 2003 – 1 BvR 246/93, 2298/94 –

"Case relating to the splitting advantage in case of spousal maintenance"

HEADNOTE:

Decision regarding the consideration of fiscal advantages from spousal splitting in the assessment of the maintenance payable to the former spouse.

Order of the First Senate of 7 October 2003
– 1 BvR 246/93, 2298/94 –

in the proceedings regarding the constitutional complaints I. of Mr. G. – authorised representatives: …, lawyers – against the judgment of the Braunschweig Higher Regional Court (*Oberlandesgericht*) of 13 January 1993 – 1 UF 78/92 – 1 BvR 246/93 –, II. 1. of Mr. K., 2. of Ms. K. – authorised representative: …, lawyer – against a) the judgment of the Stuttgart Higher Regional Court of 27 October 1994 – 16 UF 181/94 –, b) the judgment of the Waiblingen Local Court (*Amtsgericht*) of 21 April 1994 – 11 F 72/94 – 1 BvR 2298/94 –.

RULING:

I. 1. In the proceedings 1 BvR 246/93, the judgment of the Braunschweig Higher Regional Court of 13 January 1993 – 1 UF 78/92 – violates the complainant's fundamental right under Article 6.1 of the Basic Law (*Grundgesetz* – GG). The judgment is reversed. The case is referred back to the Braunschweig Higher Regional Court.
2. …
II. 1. In the proceedings 1 BvR 2298/94, the judgment of the Stuttgart Higher Regional Court of 27 October 1994 – 16 UF 181/94 – and the judgment of the Waiblingen Local Court of 21 April 1994 – 11 F 72/94 – violate the fundamental right of

the complainant re 1 under Article 6.1 of the Basic Law. The judgments are reversed. The case is referred back to the Waiblingen Local Court.
2. The constitutional complaint of the complainant re 2 is dismissed as inadmissible.
3. …

EXTRACT FROM GROUNDS:

A.

The constitutional complaints relate to the consideration of fiscal advantages from a new marriage of a person obliged to provide maintenance in the assessment of the maintenance payable to the former spouse.

I.

1. If a spouse is unable to take care of himself or herself after the divorce, he or she has a maintenance claim against his or her spouse divorced from him or her according to § 1569 of the Civil Code (*Bürgerliches Gesetzbuch* – BGB). According to § 1578.1 sentence 1 of the Civil Code, the scope of the maintenance is determined here by the marital circumstances. The Federal Court of Justice (*Bundesgerichtshof* – BGH) and the case-law concurring with it understand this to mean the circumstances determining the living conditions during the marriage, and hence the marital standard of living until divorce (see BGH, *Zeitschrift für das gesamte Familienrecht* – FamRZ 1982, p. 575 (576); FamRZ 1999, p. 367 (368); established case-law). Subsequent changes in the economic circumstances are hence only to be taken into account if they were very much to be expected at the time of the divorce and the underlying development already contributed towards determining the marital circumstances (see BGH, FamRZ 1987, pp. 459 (460); established case-law).
In calculating the marital income, the case-law takes in principle as a basis the actual net income available on the basis of the concrete fiscal burden which was made by gainful employment during the marriage. The real tax burdening the income is hence said to also remain material for the assessment of the economic circumstances characterising the marriage if it increases or falls after separation or divorce of the spouses by virtue of a change in tax classes prescribed by law or of a change to the statutory tax tariff (see BGH, FamRZ 1990, p. 503 (504); FamRZ 1990, p. 981). This is said to also apply on re-marriage of the spouse obliged to provide maintenance. A splitting advantage thereby brought about would not have to con-

tinue to benefit him or her and his or her new family; rather in this case too, the tax actually paid would have to be deducted from the gross income when calculating the maintenance. If, however, the spouse obliged to provide maintenance has had himself or herself classified in tax class V, the wage tax actually retained is said to be corrected by a deduction by means of which a shift in the fiscal burden linked with this classification to the spouse obliged to provide maintenance is remedied as far as possible (see BGH, FamRZ 1980, p. 984). Something else would however have to apply to a case in which the person obliged to provide maintenance is not left with sufficient means to maintain his or her new spouse. It would be grossly unfair here if the person obliged to pay maintenance had to use the splitting advantage granted for the new marriage for the former spouse. It is hence said to be justified to reduce the maintenance claim according to § 1579 no. 7 of the Civil Code to the amount which is said to emerge without consideration of the splitting advantage (see BGH, FamRZ 1985, p. 911-912). However, one may not presume an actual tax deduction if the fiscal saving was a consequence of actual expenditure incurred to form assets and not taken into account in terms of maintenance law in such a way as to reduce income.

2. a) According to § 26 of the Income Tax Act (*Einkommensteuergesetz* – EStG) as promulgated on 7 September 1990 (Federal Law Gazette (*Bundesgesetzblatt* – BGBl) I p. 1898), spouses may opt between two different types of fiscal assessment if they are not permanently separated: separate assessment, as well as the joint assessment using the splitting tariff (§§ 26b and 32a.5 of the Income Tax Act).

With joint assessment, the taxable annual income of both spouses is first and foremost halved in order to calculate the fiscal burden, and the income tax is hereafter calculated from the basic income tax schedule, and is then in turn doubled. The amount thus calculated according to § 32a.5 of the Income Tax Act constitutes the total tax for the couple. Because of the alleviation of the fiscal progression brought about by splitting, the fiscal advantage emerging for a couple from joint assessment is highest if only one spouse has an income, and is reduced in proportion to the additional contribution made by the other spouse to the household income. If the spouses' income is equal, there is no splitting advantage.

The income tax is initially levied according to §§ 38 et seq. of the Income Tax Act by deduction of wages at source as wage tax. For the implementation of the monthly wage tax deduction, employees who are unrestrictedly subject to income tax are classified in tax classes (§ 38b of the Income Tax Act). If both non-separated spouses receive an income, they are both classified in tax class IV. At their request, they may however opt to combine tax class III (lower tax rate for one of the spouses) with tax class V (higher tax rate for the other spouse). If only one spouse receives a wage, he or she is classified in tax class III. On expiry of the calendar year, for

spouses who have both received a wage, the income tax is assessed according to § 25.1 of the Income Tax Act on the basis of a joint tax declaration to be submitted by both spouses.
If the spouses separate permanently, they no longer have the possibility to be assessed jointly. They are classified in wage tax class I or II as if they were single employees. If a divorced spouse re-marries, he or she and his or her new spouse may also opt for joint assessment according to § 26b of the Income Tax Act, as well as their wage tax class combination according to § 38b of the Income Tax Act, and hence receive the fiscal splitting advantage.
...
c) According to § 10.1 no. 1 of the Income Tax Act, a separated or divorced spouse may claim a tax deduction for maintenance payments made to the other spouse with the consent of the latter up to a maximum prescribed by law as special expenditure. The spouse entitled to maintenance must then pay tax on the maintenance payments (§ 22 no. 1a of the Income Tax Act). This may lead to a tax saving for the person obliged to provide maintenance consisting of the difference between his or her own reduced fiscal burden and the possibly increased fiscal burden of the person entitled to maintenance, from which he or she must release the latter.
This so-called de facto splitting was introduced in 1979 in order to do better justice to the fiscal ability to pay of separated or divorced spouses. The fiscal consideration of the maintenance payments is said to be justified because these are said to constitute not only a greater burden on dissolution of the marriage, but the cessation of splitting is also said to be added (see *Bundestag* printed paper (*Bundestagsdrucksache* – BTDrucks) 8/2100, p. 60).

II.

1. The first marriage of the complainant in the proceedings 1 BvR 246/93 was dissolved in 1980. He re-married. His new wife was in gainful employment. Since his retirement in 1986, the complainant was in ancillary employment. The complainant was obliged to provide maintenance to his former wife. After the latter had drawn an old-age pension from October 1988, the complainant applied for the cessation of his maintenance obligation.
a) The Local Court rejected his corresponding action as unfounded, and sentenced the complainant to continue to pay maintenance in response to the counter-claim of his former wife. The Higher Regional Court amended this ruling, set the maintenance obligation of the complainant for the period of 1 January 1989 to 20 October 1991 and released the complainant from a maintenance obligation for the time after this. In determining the amount of the maintenance, the court took into account tax

refunds which had accrued to the complainant. It found that they were to be taken into account as increasing his income since they were based on the fact that the complainant had opted for tax class IV although he earned much more than his present spouse. Taxation according to classes III and V would be right in fiscal terms. The tax class chosen by the complainant was said to result in an additional burden of DM 260 per month. The splitting advantage which the complainant could achieve in tax class III however also had to benefit his former spouse who was entitled to maintenance. In this sense, she was said to have to also benefit appropriately from the tax refunds which were taken into account from 1989 onwards for the subsequent years at a monthly amount of DM 234.25 as increasing income.

b) The complainant's constitutional complaint, with which he complains of a violation of his rights under Article 2.1, Article 3.1, Article 6.1, Article 12.1 and 12.2, as well as Article 33.5 of the Basic Law, is directed against the ruling of the Higher Regional Court.

In addition to the calculation method, the inclusion of his ancillary income and the non-inclusion of travel expenses, the complainant also considers the consideration of the fiscal splitting advantage in assessing the maintenance to be unconstitutional. The splitting advantage was said to be granted to the existing marriage, not to the one that has been dissolved. If this advantage were to be passed on to the former wife via maintenance, this was said to be in violation of Article 6.1 of the Basic Law. It was said that, in this way, not only the complainant, but also his second wife, to whom the advantage accrued, was called to account to cover the maintenance.

2. The complainant re 1 in the proceedings 1 BvR 2298/94 was divorced in 1989. He was obliged to effect post-marital maintenance payments to his spouse who had been given custody of the child issued from the marriage. The complainant later remarried. After the birth of a joint child, his new wife, the complainant re 2, gave up her gainful employment.

a) The Local Court re-defined the amount of the maintenance payments to the former wife for the period from 2 February 1994. Because of the re-marriage of the complainant re 1, the court used as a base in calculating the maintenance his net income calculated according to tax class III. It did not consider a correction of the maintenance amount thus calculated according to § 1579 no. 7 of the Civil Code to be necessary in view of the income which the complainant still had at his disposal.

The Higher Regional Court ordered the complainant re 1 to make a somewhat higher maintenance payment, and also based the calculation of the net income of the complainant re 1 on tax class III. The fiscal advantage emerging from this was said not to be allocated only to the complainant's new family, but to also benefit his former wife and the child from this marriage. The tax deduction was said not to be a change in the conditions characterising the marital circumstances which was inconsiderable for the assessment of the maintenance requirement. Rather, the fiscal burden was said to be material in its respective real amount. It was said not to be a matter of whether the fall in net income during the relatively long period of living separately caused by the change in tax classes from III to I had been permanent. It was said that the splitting advantage regained as a result of the new marriage should be taken into account since the assessment of the maintenance was determined by the net income. There was said to be no reason for a deviation from this view. Also a reduction of the maintenance according to § 1579 no. 7 of the Civil Code could not be considered since it was not a case of shortfall.

b) The complainants lodged constitutional complaints against both rulings, with which they complain of a violation of Article 6.1 and Article 3.1 of the Basic Law. The complainant re 2 additionally considers that her right under Article 6.4 of the Basic Law has been violated.

…

B. – I.

The constitutional complaint of the complainant in the proceedings 1 BvR 246/93 is admissible. …

II.

1. Only the constitutional complaint of the complainant re 1 is admissible in the proceedings 1 BvR 2298/94. …

2. The constitutional complaint of the complainant re 2, by contrast, is inadmissible. Regardless of the fact that the complainant re 2 was not involved in the original proceedings, she has no grievance necessary for lodging the constitutional complaint. Her legal position has not been directly affected by the impugned rulings (see Decisions of the Federal Constitutional Court (*Entscheidungen des Bundesverfassungsgerichts* – BVerfGE) 24, 289 (295); 51, 386 (395)).

The complainant's fiscal burden is also initially reduced together with her husband by the splitting advantage. The rulings do not oblige her, but only the husband, to effect maintenance payments to the divorced wife of her husband. That her own maintenance claim takes lower priority in principle than that of the divorced wife is a consequence of § 1582 of the Civil Code, not of the rulings. However, the total income available to the new marriage, which is earned by the husband of the complainant re 2 alone, is reduced by virtue of his maintenance obligation towards his former spouse, and in this context also by the consideration of the splitting advantage in the assessment of the maintenance requirement. If this reduces her maintenance claim towards her husband, this is because the maintenance is measured by the actual ability to pay of the person obliged to provide maintenance. In this respect, via their influence on the ability to pay of the husband of the complainant re 2, the rulings indirectly affect her maintenance claim towards the husband. This is however not sufficient for the presumption of a grievance giving rise to the admissibility of the constitutional complaint.

C.

The constitutional complaints which are admissible are also well founded. The impugned rulings do not stand up to the constitutional-court review against the standard of Article 6.1 of the Basic Law.

I.

The protection granted by the legislature on the one hand to the dissolved marriage by the maintenance provisions and on the other hand to the existing marriage by the fiscal-law provisions is compatible with the equality of marriages according to Article 6.1 of the Basic Law (1 and 2). Fiscal advantages which are granted by law only to the existing marriage to give concrete form to the protection mandate from Article 6.1 of the Basic Law may not be removed from it once again by the courts and passed on to the dissolved marriage (3).

1. As a fundamental provision that determines values, Article 6.1 of the Basic Law gives rise to an obligation incumbent on the state to protect and promote marriage for the entire area of private and public law relating to marriage (see BVerfGE 6, 55 (76); 28, 104 (113); 82, 60 (81); 87, 1 (35); 105, 313 (346)). This protection applies to any marriage without distinction (see BVerfGE 55, 114 (128-129)). Not only the existing marriage, but also the subsequent effects of a dissolved marriage are protected by Article 6.1 of the Basic Law (see BVerfGE 53, 257 (296)). Because of the equality and equivalence of a dissolved and a newly concluded marriage with in each case different, indeed conflicting interests emerging from their succession which must be equally protected, no special requirements can be derived from Article 6.1 of the Basic Law for the specific shaping of the respective legal positions by the legislature (see BVerfGE 66, 84 (94-95)). The legislature can in principle determine for itself by what means it intends to bring about the protection of marriage incumbent on it with consideration of the different marriage constellations (see BVerfGE 87, 1 (36)). It is merely to be examined whether there are adequate reasons for different treatment of marriages by the legislature. The Federal Constitu-

tional Court (*Bundesverfassungsgericht* – BVerfG) is not to rule here whether the legislature has brought into being the most fair or expedient arrangement, but whether it has complied with the limits imposed on its latitude (see BVerfGE 52, 277 (281)), which are also subject to the principle of the equivalence of marriages established by Article 6.1 of the Basic Law.

2. a) Since Article 6.1 of the Basic Law also causes protection to be provided to the dissolved marriage which covers post-divorce maintenance claims as a subsequent consequence of the personal responsibility of the spouses for one another, as the Federal Constitutional Court has already ruled (see BVerfGE 66, 84), it is constitutionally unobjectionable for the legislature to grant priority to the divorced person entitled to maintenance in the shape of § 1582 of the Civil Code in case of a conflict of maintenance claims from the dissolved marriage and from the new marriage of a person obliged to provide maintenance. It has hence taken account of the fact that the claim of the divorced spouse already existed before the new marriage was concluded, both new spouses knew about this economic burden from the first marriage and in this respect were able to adjust to this (see Federal Constitutional Court – BVerfG, loc. cit., p. 98). These remain sufficient reasons justifying the different treatment in terms of the maintenance of divorced and married persons entitled to maintenance.

b) Equally, however, the legislature may grant advantages to an existing marriage which it denies to a marriage that has been dissolved. Only when the spouses live together may it presume that they in principle form a community of earning and consumption together in which the each spouse participates in the income and burdens of the other (see BVerfGE 61, 319 (345-346)). Only in this community of earning does the person not in gainful employment also make a contribution to the joint maintenance.

3. Fiscal advantages the coming into being of which are caused by the conclusion of marriage, which are contingent on the spouses living together and which are granted only to the existing marriage by the legislature in giving concrete form to its mandate to protect may not be removed from it once again by the courts by virtue of being assigned to the marriage that has been dissolved and by increasing the maintenance of the divorced spouse via the maintenance calculation.

a) The interpretation and application of statutory provisions is a matter for the non-constitutional courts. The Federal Constitutional Court only reviews them insofar as whether – apart from violations of the prohibition of arbitrariness – the influence of the fundamental rights has been fundamentally misjudged in the interpretation and application of non-constitutional law (see BVerfGE 18, 85 (92-93, 96); 85, 248 (257-258)). This also applies to provisions which have been handed down by the legislature to specify fundamental-rights protection (see BVerfGE 53, 30 (57-58)).

When it comes to provisions intended to meet fundamental right-related protection obligations, the relevant fundamental right has been violated if its interpretation and application fail to fulfil the protective purpose envisaged by the fundamental right (see BVerfGE 89, 276 (285-286)).

If the legislature distinguishes between dissolved and existing marriages in implementing and specifying its obligation under Article 6.1 of the Basic Law, and if it grants them different advantages with which it intends to do justice to their respective needs, the courts must take this into account in their rulings. This emerges from the principle of Article 6.1 of the Basic Law to protect each marriage which takes on its specific form in the respective statutory implementation.

b) With maintenance for divorced parties, the legislature has lent expression to the continuation of the spouses' personal responsibility after divorce, and has also placed the maintenance burden of the person obliged to provide maintenance vis-à-vis his or her divorced spouse on their new marriage. With § 1578.1 sentence 1 of the Civil Code, it has however orientated the standard of the maintenance of a divorced spouse in line with the marital circumstances, and hence restricted it to the respective income situation which characterised the marriage of the former spouses until their divorce. In line with the wishes of the legislature, this rules out taking account of those advantages in the assessment of post-marital maintenance which do not originate from the marriage that has been dissolved and which continue to exist, but which only came into being on conclusion of a new marriage.

c) The original cases do not offer an occasion to make a statement on the constitutional questions concerned with spousal splitting since they are not material to the ruling. The impugned judgments already ignore Article 6.1 of the Basic Law because they have allotted to the marriage that has been dissolved a fiscal advantage which may emerge from tax splitting according to § 32a.5 of the Income Tax Act.

The legislature has allotted the advantage which may emerge from fiscal splitting to the existing marriages of spouses who are assessed jointly for tax and who live together. The splitting tariff hence ceases to apply if the spouses are permanently separated or if they divorce. In order to reduce the tax burden on the person obliged to provide maintenance emerging at the same time as the cessation of the splitting advantage by a maintenance claim of the separated or divorced spouse, the legislature has granted to divorced spouses the possibility of de facto splitting which is available as long as the maintenance obligation exists, regardless of a re-marriage of the person obliged to provide maintenance. If however the latter concludes a new marriage, if the spouses are assessed jointly, this is an element giving rise to the claim for the occurrence of a possible splitting advantage. This is not the resumption of the fiscal splitting advantage which was enjoyed or could have been enjoyed by the divorced spouses when their marriage existed. Rather, with the new marriage a new income constellation arises between the spouses who are now in a union which is material for whether and to what degree their marriage enjoys fiscal advantages by means of the splitting procedure. The new marriage, and not the dissolved marriage of the re-married person obliged to provide maintenance, is hence to see its tax burden reduced. That this reduction of the burden and the income thereby left to the new marriage in fiscal terms may also cover obligations of the spouses, and hence may where appropriate also be subject to pledging, changes nothing about the fact that the legislature has granted the tax burden reduction to the new marriage and not to the dissolved marriage. Had it intended in terms of the law on maintenance to allot it to the dissolved marriage, it should have handed down an explicit statutory provision to this end. However, this is precisely what it did not do, but it exclusively granted the splitting advantage to existing marriages and referred dissolved marriages to de facto splitting. Such a statutory specification is in line with the protective mandate according to Article 6.1 of the Basic Law, which is also to be observed in interpreting § 1578.1 sentence 1 of the Civil Code.

II.

1. The courts fundamentally disregarded this in their interpretation of § 1578.1 sentence 1 of the Civil Code in the rulings impugned by the constitutional complaints. They have deprived the complainants' new marriages of the protection of Article 6.1 of the Basic Law, to which they are entitled by implementation of this Basic Law mandate by the legislature, by virtue of the fact that the income increased by the splitting advantage for the new marriage of the re-married person obliged to provide maintenance has been accommodated in the assessment of the maintenance requirement in real terms or fictitiously because they take the view that this advantage should also benefit the divorced wife of the person obliged to provide maintenance. At the same time, they have allowed the fiscal advantage granted to the new marriage to benefit the marriage that has been dissolved although the legislature particularly wished with this to cause the new marriage now existing to enjoy the protection to which it is indeed entitled according to Article 6.1 of the Basic Law.
a) There is no reason to presume that advantages accruing to the new marriage of a divorced person obliged to provide maintenance had already arisen in his or her previous marriage and had determined the circumstances of the parties now divorced. The divorce rate, and hence also the number of re-marriages, has increased in recent decades. It would however already be inadmissible because of the permanence which in principle characterises marriage, and would also not be supported by indications in reality, if one wished to presume for this reason that, on conclusion of marriage, its possible failure and a subsequent new marriage was concur-

rently taken into consideration and that this would not only determine the conduct of the spouses, but also their income circumstances.
b) The divorced spouse entitled to maintenance also does not suffer any disadvantage by virtue of the new marriage retaining the fiscal advantage. His or her maintenance claim continues to take priority over that of the person now married to the person obliged to provide maintenance, but is solely measured by the income situation in the dissolved marriage. The fact that the fiscal advantage is no longer considered which may have also accrued to the dissolved marriage during its existence is a consequence of the provision according to which joint fiscal assessment may only take place with spouses who live together, and is not the consequence of the re-marriage of the person obliged to provide maintenance.
c) Finally, considerations of practicability may also not justify depriving the new marriage of the person obliged to provide maintenance of the fiscal advantage granted to it in the specific shaping of the protection of Article 6.1 of the Basic Law by the legislature by virtue of the person obliged to pay maintenance also being called to account with this advantage to pay maintenance to his or her divorced spouse. It is simpler for the maintenance calculation to proceed on the basis of the net income actually achieved by the person obliged to provide maintenance, which may be ascertained from the monthly salary statement. The case-law itself however neglects these considerations if the tax class combination selected in the new marriage of the person obliged to provide maintenance does not primarily produce the splitting advantage for the latter already in the monthly tax deduction, and in such cases fictitiously calculates the income on which the maintenance assessment is to be based. It follows the same method if a case of shortfall arises. Also in other aspects, however, a somewhat more difficult calculation, but one which is possible and supported by technology and programs, is not a sufficient reason to allot fiscal advantages in derogation from the intention of the legislature.
2. a) The relief sought by means of the constitutional complaints is therefore to be granted. Insofar as the rulings which they impugn are based on disregard for Article 6.1 of the Basic Law, these are to be reversed according to § 95.2 of the Federal Constitutional Court Act (*Bundesverfassungsgerichtsgesetz* – BVerfGG). The case is referred back to the Higher Regional Court in the proceedings 1 BvR 246/93, and to the Local Court in the proceedings 1 BvR 2298/94. The courts will have to ensure that the complainants' new marriages can indeed retain the splitting advantage which they have been granted. They must decide how they wish to do so.

…

Justices: Papier, Jaeger, Haas, Hömig, Steiner, Hohmann-Dennhardt, Hoffmann-Riem, Bryde

No. 42

BVerfGE 109, 256
of 18 February 2004 – 1 BvR 193/97
"Joint family name case"

HEADNOTE:

It is not compatible with Article 2.1 in conjunction with Article 1.1 of the Basic Law (*Grundgesetz* – GG) that according to § 1355.2 of the Civil Code (*Bürgerliches Gesetzbuch* – BGB) the name of a spouse acquired and held by earlier conclusion of marriage cannot be determined as the married name in his or her new marriage.

Judgment of the First Senate of 18 February 2004
on the basis of the oral hearing of 4 November 2003
– 1 BvR 193/97 –

in the proceedings regarding the constitutional complaint 1. of Ms. A., 2. of Dr. B. – authorised representatives: ..., lawyers – 1. directly against the order of the Berlin Higher Regional Court (*Kammergericht*) of 26 November 1996 – 1 W 7237/95 –, 2. indirectly against § 1355.2 of the Civil Code in the version of the Act Amending the Law on Family Names (*Familiennamensrechtsgesetz* – FamNamRG) of 16 December 1993 (Federal Law Gazette (*Bundesgesetzblatt* – BGBl) I p. 2054).

RULING:

1. § 1355.2 of the Civil Code is not compatible with Article 2.1 in conjunction with Article 1.1 of the Basic Law insofar as it rules out spouses being able to determine as their married name a family name acquired through previous conclusion of marriage which one of them holds at the time of conclusion of marriage.
2. § 1355.2 of the Civil Code is to be applied until the entry into force of a new statutory regulation subject to the proviso that, if the spouses wish to determine on conclusion of marriage a family name acquired by one of the spouses in a previous

marriage as their married name after the date of the publication of this ruling in the Federal Law Gazette, each spouse shall provisionally retain the name held by him or her at the time of conclusion of marriage until such time as a new statutory regulation is adopted.

3. The order of the Berlin Higher Regional Court of 26 November 1996 – 1 W 7237/95 – violates the fundamental right of the complainant re 1 under Article 2.1 in conjunction with Article 1.1 of the Basic Law. The order is reversed and the case referred back to the Berlin Higher Regional Court.

4. The constitutional complaint of the complainant re 2 is dismissed as inadmissible.

5. …

EXTRACT FROM GROUNDS:

A.

The constitutional complaint relates to the question of the constitutionality of § 1355.2 of the Civil Code, according to which spouses who wish to have a joint family name as married name may only determine for this the birth name of the husband or the wife, but not a family name acquired through previous conclusion of marriage held by one of the two at the time of conclusion of marriage.

I.

1. In its original version of 18 August 1896 (Reich Law Gazette (*Reichsgesetzblatt* – RGBl) p. 195), § 1355 of the Civil Code provided that the wife received the family name of the husband as her married name on conclusion of marriage. She was later able to add her birth name to this on the basis of the Equal Rights Act (*Gleichberechtigungsgesetz*) of 18 June 1957 (Federal Law Gazette I p. 609). § 1355 of the Civil Code was amended with the First Act Reforming the Law on Marriage and Family (*Erstes Gesetz zur Reform des Ehe- und Familienrechts*) of 14 June 1976 (Federal Law Gazette I p. 1421) such that the spouses could now select the birth name of the husband or the wife as their married name. However, were the spouses not to agree on the choice of married name, the priority of the husband's name continued to apply. The restriction to the "ancestral" name was to rule out the use of a name acquired through previous conclusion of marriage for designation as the married name. This was reasoned by the wish to prevent abusive name transfers for which the new law on names might provide a certain incentive (see *Bundestag*

printed paper (*Bundestagsdrucksache* – BTDrucks) 7/650, p. 97). At the same time, the husband was deprived of the right to prohibit his divorced wife from continuing to use the name acquired by the conclusion of marriage under certain preconditions. On the other hand, according to § 7.1 of the Family Code (*Familiengesetzbuch* – FGB) of 20 December 1965 (Law Gazette (*Gesetzblatt* – GBl) 1966 I p. 1), the name of the husband or wife used at the time of the conclusion of marriage could be selected as the married name in the German Democratic Republic.

2. a) After the Federal Constitutional Court had declared § 1355.2 sentence 2 of the Civil Code, which determined the prevalence of the husband's name if the spouses were unable to agree on a married name, to be unconstitutional by order of 5 March 1991 (Decisions of the Federal Constitutional Court (*Entscheidungen des Bundesverfassungsgerichts* – BVerfGE) 84, 9), the draft Bill of the Federal Government to reform the law on family names of 14 August 1992 (*Bundestag* printed paper 12/3163) initially provided that the spouses, in addition to their birth names, were also to be able to determine as their married name the respective name used at the time of the conclusion of marriage in order to make it easier to decide on a married name by thus expanding the options available. It was stated as grounds that it had indeed been taken into account that the possibility to determine a name acquired by marriage as the married name of a new marriage might hurt the feelings of the previous spouse or of his or her relatives. Such sensitivities would however of necessity have to be accepted as unavoidable. On conclusion of marriage, the spouse whose family name was not determined as the married name was said to acquire a right to use the family name of the other spouse that was designated as the married name not only for the duration of the marriage. The spouse was, rather, said to be entitled to this name as a right of his or her own on the basis of the joint designation by the spouses. The possibility to pass on a name acquired by marriage to a new marriage was said to avoid difficulties alleged to arise if divorced or widowed spouses married one another. Insofar as both had a family name acquired in the previous marriage, according to the law previously valid they would of necessity have to resort to their birth names, which they might not have used for decades, when determining their married name. Granting to the spouse of the previous marriage the right to prohibit his or her former spouse from taking the name acquired in the previous marriage into the new marriage if this appeared to be abusive was said to counter the independent entitlement of each spouse to his or her family name acquired by conclusion of marriage (see *Bundestag* printed paper 12/3163, p. 11-12).

b) This planned provision was however largely rejected in the deliberations on the draft Bill and in the hearing that was held (see Stenographic Minutes, 12th legislative period, 80th session of the *Bundestag* Committee on Legal Affairs of 30 June

1993). Also the nobility associations made a public statement and protested, invoking the "title inflation" which might then be imminent, against the planned expanded possibility in selecting married names. The Committee on Legal Affairs of the *Bundestag*, finally, recommended in the interest of the divorced spouse or of the surviving dependants of the deceased spouse, and to avert the quite possible danger of abuse in this area, to restrict the selection of a married name once more to the spouse's birth name (see *Bundestag* printed paper 12/5982, pp. 4 and 18).
§ 1355.2 of the Civil Code thus took on the following version by virtue of the Act Reforming the Law on Family Names of 16 December 1993 (Federal Law Gazette I p. 2054), which entered into force in this respect on 1 April 1994:

> The spouses may designate the birth name of the husband or the birth name of the wife as their married name by declaration to the registrar.

3. According to the law as it stands, the name acquired in an earlier marriage cannot hence be passed on to a new spouse as a married name unless the spouses are of mixed-nationality origin and, according to Article 10.2 sentence 1 of the Introductory Act to the Civil Code (*Einführungsgesetz zum Bürgerlichen Gesetzbuch* – EGBGB), can also select for themselves the name of a spouse acquired by previous marriage according to the law of the state to which one spouse belongs. By contrast, the name acquired in a previous marriage held by one parent may be passed on to a child as birth name (§ 1617.1 and § 1617a.1 of the Civil Code). Equally, the adopted child receives the family name of the adopter regardless of whether this name is the birth name of the adopting party or one acquired by marriage (§ 1757.1 of the Civil Code).
4. Those who renounce their birth name on marriage, who take on the name of their spouse as their married name, who retain this name after the death of the spouse or who divorce and re-marry, but cannot determine the name held as the married name for this marriage, are affected by the restriction of the selection of the married name to the birth names of the spouses in § 1355.2 of the Civil Code. The vast majority of these are women. The reason for this is, firstly, that until 1976 the married name was always the name of the husband, so that women had to give up their names on marriage, and that, until 1994, the name of the husband also took statutory priority if there was disagreement between the spouses on the designation of the married name. Secondly, however, even after the reform of the law on family names in 1994, the husband's name was still determined as the married name in most cases. No official statistics are kept on this. Enquiries by the Federal Constitutional Court with the registry offices of Hamburg, Hanover, Frankfurt and Munich however confirm the figures contained in other surveys …, and document for 2001 and 2002

that 85 to 86 per cent of those marrying there selected a joint married name, and in doing so 93 to 97 per cent selected the name of the husband. It is furthermore significant in this context that the share of re-marriages after divorce has increased in recent years as against the total number of conclusions of marriage. It accounted for 36 per cent of Western German and 41 per cent of Eastern German marriages in 2000 ….

II.

1. The complainants married in the USA in 1993. On their return to the Federal Republic of Germany, they expressed to the registrar a wish to designate as their married name the name, acquired in her previous marriage, which the complainant re 1 had held for many years at the time of the conclusion of marriage. The registrar refused to issue such a certificate arguing that it was not the birth name of one of the complainants, and that only this could be designated as their married name. The Local Court (*Amtsgericht*) rejected the complainants' application to instruct the registrar to issue the desired certificate. The complaints directed against this were also unsuccessful. The Regional Court (*Landgericht*) made reference to the unambiguous provision contained in § 1355.2 of the Civil Code, and took the view that no separate right to the name was acquired on assumption of the birth name of the spouse, regardless of the fate of the marriage. Rather, the married name remained only borrowed, and hence could not be passed on to a new marriage. The Berlin Higher Regional Court … confirmed the ruling of the Regional Court ….
2. The constitutional complaint – with which the complainants complain of a violation of their rights of personality under Article 2 of the Basic Law, as well as of their rights under Article 6 of the Basic Law – targets this ruling, and indirectly § 1355.2 of the Civil Code. Furthermore, the complainants consider the general principle of equality under Article 3.1 of the Basic Law to have been violated.
…

B.

The constitutional complaint of the complainant re 1 is admissible. By contrast, the constitutional complaint of the complainant re 2 is inadmissible. He has not substantiated to the degree required by the law (§ 23.1 and § 92 of the Federal Constitutional Court Act (*Bundesverfassungsgerichtsgesetz* – BVerfGG)) to what degree his own fundamental rights could have been violated by not being able to acquire the name held by the complainant re 1 at the time of the conclusion of marriage as his married name according to § 1355.2 of the Civil Code. …

C.

The constitutional complaint of the complainant re 1 is well-founded. § 1355.2 of the Civil Code is not compatible with Article 2.1 in conjunction with Article 1.1 of the Basic Law insofar as it provides that spouses may only select as their joint married name the birth name of the husband or wife, but not the family name acquired through a previous conclusion of marriage which is held by one of the two at the time of conclusion of marriage. The order of the Berlin Higher Regional Court, which is based on § 1355.2 of the Civil Code, violates the general right of personality of the complainant re 1under Article 2.1 in conjunction with Article 1.1 of the Basic Law.

I.

1. Article 2.1 in conjunction with Article 1.1 of the Basic Law protects the name of a person as an expression of his or her identity and individuality. In addition to the forename, the protection also covers the family name (see BVerfGE 78, 38 (49); 84, 9 (22); 97, 391 (399); 104, 373 (385)).

a) When a child receives a birth name as a family name, he or she links this name with his or her individuality. Subsequently, it helps him or her to develop his or her identity and to express it towards others (see BVerfGE 104, 373 (385)). In this function of serving the individual as a means of self-recognition, and at the same time of distinguishability from others, the legal system has to respect and protect the name of its bearer (see BVerfGE 97, 391 (399)).

b) The family name acquired through choice of married name also enjoys the full protection of Article 2.1 in conjunction with Article 1.1 of the Basic Law.

aa) Creating and fleshing out the law on family names is a matter for the legislature (see BVerfGE 78, 38 (49)), which has prescribed in § 1355.1 of the Civil Code in a constitutionally unobjectionable manner for spouses to hold a married name as a standard in order to lend expression to the unity of the family in the joint name (see BVerfGE 104, 373 (387)). If the spouses opt for a joint name in line with this rule, this requires one of the spouses to renounce the previous name and accept the name of the other spouse as a married and family name which he or she should now use and which accompanies him or her in his or her further life. The married name selected by both spouses expresses not only the foundation of a new family unit. Rather, it is a new married name and at the same time a family name for both spouses, with which each of them will be identified from the date of selecting the name. It hence becomes a part and expression of the separate personality of the individual name-bearer which is connected to the name and develops further, and hence enjoys the protection of the general right of personality.

bb) This protection of the name selected and acquired on conclusion of marriage is not restricted to the duration of the marriage. Article 6.1 of the Basic Law requires neither the holding of a uniform family name in marriage (see BVerfGE 104, 373 (387)), nor the renunciation of a name held as married name on dissolution of the marriage. The protection also of the name acquired by selection of a married name arises solely from the right of personality of the name-bearer. A name becomes an expression of the personality of a person by virtue of being held after acquisition by a name-bearer, so that an identity of name and person arises and by these means the person finds themselves reflected in this name and is recognised by others. This identity-creating impact of the name is not influenced by the occasion and reason for acquisition of the name. The latter may hence not restrict its constitutional protection. This also applies to the name acquired by selection of a married name. Even if the name is formed out of the name of the other spouse, it becomes the personal name of its new bearer, supersedes his or her previous name and now becomes a part of the personality of its bearer. As a personal and not only a borrowed name, it therefore enjoys the protection of Article 2.1 in conjunction with Article 1.1 of the Basic Law, regardless of whether the marriage which has been the occasion of the acquisition of the name continues to exist.

2. § 1355.2 of the Civil Code encroaches on the protection of the name which has been acquired by selection of a married name and used since that time.

The general right of personality protects the name-bearer against removal or imposed change of the name used by him or her (see BVerfGE 84, 9 (22)). This right to one's own name and to its retention is respected by the law on married names insofar as the spouses are not forced by § 1355.1 of the Civil Code to determine a joint married name, but are able to also retain the names that they used at the time of conclusion of marriage after conclusion of marriage. If however the spouses wish to use a joint married name, they are prevented by § 1355.2 of the Civil Code from determining the name used by one spouse as their married name if it is no longer the birth name of the spouse, but a name acquired in a previous marriage through statutory name allocation or selection.

With this restriction of the selection of names, the legislature encroaches on the right to bear a name of the bearer of this acquired name. It treats the acquired name as against the birth name as a name used of lower quality by only permitting the choice of the latter, although the protection of personality equally covers the name acquired by marriage and that acquired by birth. Hence, the bearer of the acquired name is forced in selecting a joint married name to once more renounce his or her used name and to take on a new one. He or she can only either acquire the name of his or her spouse or, together with the latter, fall back on his or her birth name which he or she no longer uses, but which has no longer participated in his or her personality development since acquisition of the used name, and in this respect is not an expression of his or her present identity. This is tantamount to a deprivation of name protection, given that this covers as a priority the name which a person has made their own and which he or she uses, and not the one which he or she has renounced and which hence only reminds one of the origins of the person.

3. § 1355.2 of the Civil Code disproportionately encroaches on the right of personality of the name-bearer to protection of the name which he or she has used by excluding the name used as a result of the selection of a married name in determining the married name.

In view of the high value attaching to the right to one's own name, encroachments on the right to bear a name may not take place without significant reasons and only in compliance with the principle of proportionality (see BVerfGE 78, 38 (49)). § 1355.2 of the Civil Code does not meet these requirements.

a) Having said that, one of the grounds on which the statutory provision is based is certainly significant.

aa) With the provision, the legislature has intended to take account of the interests of the divorced spouse and those of his or her surviving dependants (see *Bundestag* printed paper 12/5982, pp. 4 and 18). In doing so it took particular consideration of the feelings of the spouse from the previous family community …, who may find it burdensome or insulting if his or her name is designated as the married name of a new marriage of his or her divorced spouse, and hence is passed on to his or her new partner, so that the latter and he or she have identical names. Because the family name is also used to draw lines of descent, to depict family contexts or to make the family status of an individual clear (see BVerfGE 104, 373 (386)), this might also lead to family ties being concluded where they have in fact been broken and do not exist.

bb) By contrast, the indication of the legislature of an imminent risk of abuse alleged to be linked to the possibility to also select the name acquired in an earlier marriage as the new married name does not justify the encroachment on the right to a name. Neither did it become clear in the legislative procedure which dangers of abuse the legislature envisioned here, nor are such dangers sufficiently recognisable. If the representatives of the Federal Government stated in the oral hearing that an abuse could not be ruled out with particularly "beautiful names", which could take on a special market value were the selection to be free, it is also not evident here what the abuse is likely to be. That it may be the nice sound of a name which tips the scale in the selection of a married name does not make its selection in the second marriage more amenable to abuse than in the first marriage, even if such a

conduct in selection may result in many uses of this name. The use of the possibility to determine, as the name of a new marriage of the name-bearer, a name with a noble designation acquired by means of selection as the married name also does not constitute an abuse. In the event of the abuse to be averted lying in the danger of fictitious marriages being entered into by those concluding them only for the sake of the name in order to divorce after acquiring the name and to take the name into a new marriage …, such a danger can be countered with the means which help to prevent such fictitious marriages, but not with the law on names. Apart from this, the prevention of this danger would not primarily protect the interests of the divorced spouse that the legislature was concerned with, but those of his or her family.
b) The encroachment by § 1355.2 of the Civil Code on the right to bear a name effects a disproportionate impairment of the right of personality of the bearer of an acquired name.
It emerges from the weighing between the severity of the encroachment and the significance of the underlying reasons that the provision is not in compliance with Article 2.1 in conjunction with Article 1.1 of the Basic Law.
aa) The fundamental rights of the bearers of an acquired name which are encroached upon are not opposed by any equivalent interests of others protected by fundamental rights which might justify the provision of § 1355.2 of the Civil Code. The right to one's own name, also accruing to the divorced spouse, ensues from the protection of personality according to Article 2.1 in conjunction with Article 1.1 of the Basic Law, which covers one's own identity and privacy and which is expressed in the name. However, this does not give rise to a right to determine the name of another person (see BVerfGE 104, 373 (392)). For this reason, neither a right to select a name for another person, nor a right to prohibit another person to bear the same name as oneself, may be derived from the right of personality: The constitution does not contain a right to exclusivity of names. The desire of a former spouse for their own name not to be designated as the married name of a new union on the part of his or her divorced spouse, and hence also becomes the name of the new partner, is understandable. It is however not equivalent to the significance of the protection of names under fundamental rights on which § 1355.2 of the Civil Code encroaches.
bb) The encroachment on fundamental rights takes place with the person who has already forgone his or own name as his or her married name in the previous marriage in favour of the name of his or her spouse or had to forgo it because of statutory requirements which have now been recognised as unconstitutional. When remarrying, he or she is forced once more by § 1355.2 of the Civil Code to give up the name which he or she used and to replace it with another one if he or she wishes to use a joint married name with his or her new spouse. By contrast, his or her di-

vorced spouse has been able to continue to use his or her used birth name in marriage as a married name, and over and above this is not prevented by § 1355.2 of the Civil Code from retaining this name as married name for a subsequent marriage and passing it on to the new spouse, although this too may hurt the feelings of the former partner. The burden resulting from a two-fold name change on the bearer of a name acquired by selection of a married name is in this respect only opposed by the unilateral consideration of the interest in not finding his or her name in the name of the new partner of his or her divorced spouse. This interest is only considered by virtue of § 1355.2 of the Civil Code with the party who is able to retain his or her birth name as married name, but not with the person who acquires a new name by selecting a married name. The latter is not protected against the new partner of his or her divorced spouse also acquiring this name.

cc) The unilateral consideration of the interest of the party who has retained his or her birth name as married name is also unable to justify the encroachment on fundamental rights because it establishes ideas which do not do justice to the constitutionally prescribed perception of equal rights of husband and wife contained in the law on married names.

When the law on married names still provided in a manner contrary to equality that the wife received the name of her husband on conclusion of marriage, her interest in not sharing this name with a future wife of her spouse was given no consideration. When the legislature was obliged to also make the name of the wife available for selection for the married name, it then considered it to be necessary to comply with such an interest of the husband with § 1355.2 of the Civil Code. This provision acts in favour of the husband because the restriction of the option to the birth name leaves open to the party who prevails with his or her name in the marriage the possibility to once more also select his or her name in a new marriage as a married name; this was always the husband on conclusion of marriage until 1976 because of the provision valid at that time, which was later declared unconstitutional, since his name became the married name. In this respect, the restriction of § 1355.2 of the Civil Code initially exclusively affected divorced or widowed women whose right to the used name acquired through conclusion of marriage was encroached on by § 1355.2 of the Civil Code on remarriage.

The Reform Act of 14 June 1976 also ultimately brought about little change as to this effect since the husband's name continued to predominate if the spouses were unable to agree on the selection of the married name. In fact, the dominance of the husband's name in the selection of the married name has continued to the present day. The husband's name is still selected as married name in the vast majority of cases of the conclusion of marriage, so that to the present day above all women are affected if § 1355.2 of the Civil Code rules out the name acquired and used by selection of a married name on re-marriage as married name. At the same time, this maintains the idea that if a name becomes the married name, it is not equally the property of both spouses, but continues to primarily belong to the previous bearer of this name, who is hence said to have greater power to dispose of the name.

dd) Finally, also the fact that the spouse who bears a name acquired through previous conclusion of marriage may continue to use it as an additional name in a new marriage according to § 1355.4 of the Civil Code makes the encroachment on the right in the used name unacceptable.

If spouses opt to select a joint married name in which only one of the names of the spouses can be selected, the wish of the spouse whose name is not considered in the selection to also be able to express in the joint name his or her identity as conveyed by the previously used name is accommodated by the right being granted to him or her to add his or her previously-used name to the married name (see BVerfGE 104, 373 (388)). This option however does not sufficiently alleviate the impact of the impugned provision in this respect. § 1355.2 of the Civil Code already deprives spouses of the opportunity to determine a name previously used by a spouse as a married name at all if this is a name acquired by conclusion of marriage. This restriction of the option leads to a situation in which a spouse who has a name acquired by conclusion of marriage is excluded with this from the outset in the selection of the married name, even if he or she is in agreement with the other spouse in his or her wish to select this name as a married name. Such an encroachment on the decision of the spouses in selecting a married name is however not made acceptable for the name-bearer by being able to continue to use it at least as an additional name.

II.

The order of the Berlin Higher Regional Court based on the unconstitutional provision violates the fundamental right of the complainant re 1 under Article 2.1 in conjunction with Article 1.1 of the Basic Law. Since a ruling towards the complainants can only be handed down uniformly, the entire order is to be reversed.

D. – I.

If a provision is not in accordance with the Basic Law, it is in principle to be declared null and void (§ 95.3 sentences 1 and 2 of the Federal Constitutional Court Act). This however does not apply if there are several possibilities to eliminate the breach of the constitution and the declaration of nullity would encroach on the latitude of the legislature (see BVerfGE 77, 308 (337); 84, 168 (186)). Accordingly, a

declaration of nullity is impossible in this respect because it cannot be ruled out that the legislature would take this decision as an occasion to once more reform the law on married names.
The legislature is obliged to bring the law into accordance with the Basic Law by 31 March 2005.

II.

1. Within the scope of the declaration of incompatibility, the provision may no longer be applied by the courts and administrative authorities (see BVerfGE 82, 126 (155); 84, 168 (187)). No exception from this principle is necessary here. Such would lead to new breaches of the constitution which could not be reversed by a subsequent new provision, or only with a further impairment of the right of personality of those concerned, since it cannot be ruled out that a new statutory provision could lead to a further name change.
2. However, the non-applicability of the provision may not lead to a situation in which conclusions of marriage are only carried out until a new statutory provision is passed if the spouses select one of their birth names as their married name. Such an interpretation of the remaining part of § 1355 of the Civil Code cannot be considered in constitutional terms because it would lead to an obstacle to marriage for which there is no statutory provision. Until such time as there is a new statutory provision, a default arrangement is therefore needed for cases in which a name acquired by selection of a married name is to be designated as the married name. It appears here to be the least harmful solution for the spouses to initially retain the names which they had prior to conclusion of marriage. This arrangement does not pre-empt the legislature and avoids multiple name changes. After the statute has entered into force, it will then be necessary to choose which name the spouses will bear in future.
3. For spouses who married prior to the publication of this ruling, the consequences under the law on names initially remain valid which emerged from § 1355.2 of the Civil Code. The legislature must however make a separate arrangement for these cases. It is not necessary here for reasons of legal certainty and legal peace to retroactively eliminate all the consequences of the arrangement. The legislature must however ensure that impacts of the previous unconstitutional legal situation which are disadvantageous for the future can be eliminated (see BVerfGE 84, 9 (24)). The statutory regulation accordingly required is certainly to cover all spouses who were not able to designate as their married name the name held by one of the partners and acquired by conclusion of marriage. They must be enabled in future to hold a name which emerges from an arrangement corresponding to the principle of

equal rights. The more detailed content of the transitional arrangement depends on the structure of the future law on married names.

4. Insofar as proceedings regarding the designation of a name held by one spouse as a married name are pending with the courts, they can be suspended until the new statutory provision is passed in order to avoid cost disadvantages.

The ruling on the costs is based on § 34 a.2 of the Federal Constitutional Court Act.

Justices: Papier, Jaeger, Haas, Hömig, Steiner, Hohmann-Dennhardt, Hoffmann-Riem, Bryde

As a result of the Federal Constitutional Court's decision, the Act Amending the Law on Married Names and Civil Partnership Names (Gesetz zur Änderung des Ehe- und Lebenspartnerschaftsnamensrechts) *of 6 February 2005 (Federal Law Gazette I 2005 p. 203), with effect from 12 February 2005, reworded § 1355.2 of the Civil Code as follows:*

> *"(2) The spouses may designate the birth name of the husband or the wife or the name the husband or wife had at the time of the declaration on the determination of the married name as their married name by declaration to the registrar."*

No. 43

BVerfGE 111, 307

of 14 October 2004 – 2 BvR 1481/04 –

“Görgülü I case”

HEADNOTES:

1. **The principle that the judge is bound by statute and law (Article 20.3 of the Basic Law (*Grundgesetz* – GG)) includes taking into account the guarantees of the European Convention for the Protection of Human Rights and Fundamental Freedoms and the decisions of the European Court of Human Rights (ECHR) as part of a methodologically justifiable interpretation of the law. Both a failure to consider a decision of the ECHR and the “enforcement” of such a decision in a schematic way, in violation of prior-ranking law, may violate fundamental rights in conjunction with the principle of the rule of law.**
2. **In taking into account decisions of the ECHR, the state bodies must include the effects on the national legal system in their application of the law. This applies in particular when the relevant national law is a balanced partial system of domestic law that is intended to achieve an equilibrium between differing fundamental rights.**

Order of the Second Senate of 14 October 2004
– 2 BvR 1481/04 –

in the proceedings regarding the constitutional complaint of the Turkish citizen G., – authorised representative: ..., lawyer – against a) the order of the Naumburg Higher Regional Court (*Oberlandesgericht*) of 30 June 2004 – 14 WF 64/04 –, b) the order of the Naumburg Higher Regional Court of 30 March 2004 – 14 WF 64/04 – *and* the complainant’s application for a temporary injunction.

RULING:

The order of the Naumburg Higher Regional Court of 30 June 2004 – 14 WF 64/04 – violates the complainant's fundamental right under Article 6 of the Basic Law (*Grundgesetz*) in conjunction with the principle of the rule of law and is reversed.
The matter is referred back for a new decision to another civil senate of the Naumburg Higher Regional Court.
Apart from this, the constitutional complaint is rejected as unfounded.
This also disposes of the application for a temporary injunction.
...

EXTRACT FROM GROUNDS:

A.

In his constitutional complaint, the complainant challenges inter alia what he regards as the unsatisfactory enforcement of the judgment of the European Court of Human Rights (ECHR) of 26 February 2004 pronounced in his case and the disregard of international law by the Naumburg Higher Regional Court.

I.

1. a) The complainant is the father of the child Christofer, who was born illegitimate on 25 August 1999. The mother of the child, who at first did not name the complainant to the authorities as the father of the child, gave the boy up for adoption one day after his birth and first declared her prior consent to the adoption by the foster parents in a notarial deed of 1 November 1999; she repeated her consent on 24 September 2002. The boy has been living with the foster parents since 29 August 1999.
The complainant learned in October 1999 of the child's birth and release for adoption; his contact with the mother of the child had broken off in July 1999. Thereupon he began himself to attempt to adopt his son; this encountered difficulties at first, since his paternity was not recognised. Finally, his paternity was established by a judgment of the Wittenberg Local Court (*Amtsgericht*) of 20 June 2000.
b) In an order of 9 March 2001, the Wittenberg Local Court transferred the sole parental custody of Christofer to the complainant in accordance with his application. Before this, there had been a total of four meetings between the child and the complainant by way of access. Upon the appeal of the foster parents and the Wit-

tenberg Youth Welfare Office (*Jugendamt*), which was appointed official guardian after the birth, the Local Court's custody decision was reversed by order of 20 June 2001 of the Naumburg Higher Regional Court, and the complainant's application for transfer of custody was dismissed on the merits. At the same time, the Higher Regional Court, of its own motion, excluded rights of access between the complainant and the boy until 30 June 2002 on the grounds of the best interest of the child.

c) The Third Chamber of the First Senate of the Federal Constitutional Court, by an order not stating grounds of 31 July 2001 – 1 BvR 1174/01 – refused to admit for decision the complainant's constitutional complaint against the order of the Higher Regional Court.

2. a) The complainant had in the meantime commenced new proceedings at the Local Court for the transfer of the rights of custody and access. On seven separate dates he attempted to have contact with Christofer. He submits that these attempts were unsuccessful because the foster parents were not prepared to cooperate or were not present. Two dates for hearings before the Local Court scheduled for February and July 2003 were cancelled. Thereupon, on 22 July 2003, the Local Court appointed a children's guardian in both the custody and access proceedings.

By an order of 30 September 2003, the Naumburg Higher Regional Court dismissed the complainant's application for a temporary injunction to make arrangements for access on the grounds that in the opinion of the court there was continuing tension between the parties and that the legal situation was not clear.

b) On 19 January 2001, the application of the foster parents for the adoption of Christofer was received by the Wittenberg Local Court. The Wittenberg Youth Welfare Office as the official guardian of the boy had already given its prior consent to the adoption. After the complainant refused prior consent to Christofer's adoption, the Local Court, by an order of 28 December 2001, gave prior consent to the adoption in substitution for the complainant's absent consent. On 30 October 2002, the guardianship court at the Dessau Regional Court (*Landgericht*) dismissed the complainant's application for the adoption proceedings to be suspended until the final decision in the custody and access proceedings. Upon the appeal of the complainant, the Naumburg Higher Regional Court, by an order of 24 July 2003, reversed the decision of the Regional Court. Although the Higher Regional Court refused to suspend the adoption proceedings until the decision in the proceedings before the European Court of Human Rights (on this, see under 3. below), in its decision it pointed out that the competent domestic courts were obliged to take a judgment of the European Court of Human Rights into account if applicable. Instead, the Higher Regional Court suspended the appeal proceedings in the adoption proceedings until the final and non-appealable decision of the new custody proceedings, which were now pending at the Higher Regional Court.

3. a) In September 2001, the complainant filed an individual application under Article 34 of the European Convention for the Protection of Human Rights and Fundamental Freedoms (the Convention) at the European Court of Human Rights. He challenged in particular a violation of Article 8 of the Convention, which protects the right to respect for private and family life. He submitted that carrying out a forced adoption in disregard of the rights of the natural father was a flagrant violation of human dignity and the fundamental right to respect for family life. He stated that he had the right to bring up his son himself.

b) In a judgment of 26 February 2004, a chamber of the Third Section of the ECHR declared unanimously that the decision on custody and the exclusion of the right of access violated Article 8 of the Convention. On the basis of Article 41 of the Convention, the ECHR awarded the complainant EUR 15,000.00 in damages and EUR 1,500.00 to reimburse costs and expenses (see ECHR, No. 74969/01, Judgment of 26 February 2004 – Görgülü).

aa) With regard to the right of custody, the ECHR first referred to its case-law, under which in cases where family bonds to a child are shown to exist, the state must act in such a way that these bonds could develop further. According to the ECHR, this gives rise to the duty under Article 8 of the Convention to endeavour to reunite a natural parent with his or her child (ECHR, loc. cit., no. 45, with further references). In consideration of the fact that the complainant is Christofer's natural father and undisputedly willing and able to take care of him, the Higher Regional Court did not examine all possible ways of solving the problem (ECHR, loc. cit., no. 46).

bb) With regard to the right of access, the ECHR came to the conclusion that the grounds on which the Naumburg Higher Regional Court based its decision to exclude the complainant's access to his child for the period of one year were not sufficient to justify such a serious encroachment upon the complainant's family life. It held that notwithstanding the margin of discretion of the domestic authorities, the encroachment was therefore disproportionate with regard to the lawfully pursued goals (ECHR, loc. cit., no. 50). In the present legal matter, it stated, it must be made possible for the complainant at least to have access to his child (ECHR, loc. cit., no. 64).

4. a) Thereupon, in the parallel proceedings on custody, the Wittenberg Local Court transferred sole parental custody to the complainant by an order of 19 March 2004 in accordance with his application. In addition, the Local Court, of its own motion by an order of the same date and with reference to this custody decision, issued a temporary injunction on the access rights of the complainant to his son. He was

given the right, from 3 April 2004, to have access to his son for two hours every Saturday, until there was a final and non-appealable decision in the custody proceedings.

b) The official guardian and the children's guardian appealed against the decision of the Local Court on access rights. The Naumburg Higher Regional Court first, by order of 30 March 2004, suspended the execution of the temporary injunction, and by a further order of 30 June 2004 cancelled the temporary injunction.

It held that arrangements for access could be made only on application. Since this integral requirement had not been satisfied, the order of the Local Court, issued without an application, lacked a basis under procedural law. This applied all the more in view of the fact that the complainant's urgent application had been dismissed as early as in September 2003 and that the reasons for dismissal that were decisive at that time in principle continued in existence unchanged. Granting the right of access of the court's own motion was generally excluded and could have been ordered at most for the welfare of the child, but not in the interest of the child's father, which alone was affected here. The boy was fully integrated in the foster family and was clearly happy there.

The order of the Local Court on access, which was admissibly challenged, also proved to be unjustified on the merits, for there was no need to make arrangements, after the proceedings had been continuing for approximately one and three-quarter years, for an urgent measure that had not been applied for, even taking into account the decision of the ECHR that had been made in the meantime.

Nor could the issuing of a temporary injunction be justified by the decision of the ECHR. It was true that the decision showed that the exclusion of access ordered in June 2001 had violated the rights of the complainant and father of the child under Article 8 of the Convention and that – under no. 64 of the judgment – the Federal Republic of Germany, by reason of its duty under Article 46 of the Convention, was obliged to grant the complainant at least the right of access. But the judgment bound only the Federal Republic of Germany as a subject of public international law, but not its bodies, authorities and the bodies responsible for the administration of justice, which are independent under Article 97.1 of the Basic Law. The effect of the judgment, therefore, subject to a change of domestic law, is limited as a matter of law and as a matter of fact to establishing the sanctioning of what in the opinion of the ECHR was a past violation of law. The judgment of the ECHR remained a judgment that at all events for the domestic courts was not binding, without any influence on the finality and non-appealability of the decision appealed against. Where a decision of the ECHR established that a sovereign German act was contrary to the Convention, neither the European Convention on Human Rights nor the

Basic Law created an obligation to accord to that decision the power to reverse finality and non-appealability.
As a result of the status of the European Convention on Human Rights as ordinary statutory law below the level of the constitution, the ECHR was not functionally a higher-ranking court in relation to the courts of the States parties. For this reason, neither in interpreting the European Convention on Human Rights nor in interpreting national fundamental rights could domestic courts be bound by the decisions of the ECHR.
Furthermore, as a result of the passage of time, both the relevant factual position and the substantive and procedural legal position had since changed with lasting effect. If only for this reason, there could be no binding of any nature to the decision of the ECHR, which did not deal with purely procedural questions of temporary protection of the law.

II.

In his constitutional complaint, the complainant challenges a violation of his fundamental rights under Article 1, Article 3 and Article 6 of the Basic Law, and of the right to fair trial. At the same time he applies for a temporary injunction on access to his son to be issued.
To the extent that the complainant relies on a violation of Article 6 of the Convention (a fair trial), he also considers that there has been a violation of public international law. He submits that he is injured as the child's natural father by the challenged order of the Higher Regional Court of 30 June 2004, because the court, on the basis of an error of law, proceeds on the assumption that the decision of the ECHR relates only to the past. In this, the Higher Regional Court fails to appreciate that the ECHR in its decision unequivocally calls for access in the future. He states that a decision of the ECHR binds the Higher Regional Court for the future too; otherwise the ECHR would not have repeatedly pointed out that the future conduct of the German authorities and courts dealing with the case in future has to orient itself to the ECHR's interpretation of the law.
In addition, he submits, the arguments of the Higher Regional Court are based on an error of law, for example because Article 97.1 of the Basic Law, which is cited, is not relevant to the present case. It is not a question of the independence of the court, but of a specific binding effect of the decision of the ECHR. The ECHR specifically decided that the father of the child should be granted access immediately, in order that the family bonds could be strengthened. The interpretation of law of the Higher Regional Court, he states, is in violation of public international law.

III.

The Federal Ministry of Justice, the State Chancellery of the *Land* of Lower Saxony and the Ministry of Justice of the *Land* of Saxony-Anhalt, and also the Youth Welfare Office, the children's guardian and the foster parents submitted opinions in the proceedings.

B.

The constitutional complaint is inadmissible to the extent that the complainant challenges the order of the Higher Regional Court of 30 March 2004. The time limit in § 93.1 sentence 1 of the Federal Constitutional Court Act (*Bundesverfassungsgerichtsgesetz* – BVerfGG), which provides that the constitutional complaint must be filed and grounds be given within one month after the service or informal notification of the decision, was not complied with.

...

To the extent that the constitutional complaint challenges the order of 30 June 2004, the procedural requirements for the admissibility are satisfied.

C.

The constitutional complaint is well-founded. In its order of 30 June 2004, the Higher Regional Court violated Article 6 of the Basic Law in conjunction with the principle of the rule of law.

The authorities and courts of the Federal Republic of Germany are obliged, under certain conditions, to take account of the European Convention on Human Rights as interpreted by the ECHR in making their decisions (I.). The challenged decision of the Higher Regional Court does not do justice to this obligation, since the court does not pay sufficient attention to the judgment of the ECHR of 26 February 2004 in the case of the complainant (II.).

I.

In the German legal system, the European Convention on Human Rights has the status of a federal statute, and it must be taken into account in the interpretation of domestic law, including fundamental rights and constitutional guarantees (1.). The binding effect of a decision of the ECHR extends to all state bodies and in principle imposes on these an obligation, within their jurisdiction and without violating the binding effect of statute and law (Article 20.3 of the Basic Law), to end a continuing violation of the Convention and to create a situation that complies with the Convention (2.). The nature of the binding effect depends on the sphere of responsibility of the state bodies and on the latitude given by prior-ranking law. Courts are at all events under a duty to take into account a judgment that relates to a case already decided by them if they preside over a retrial of the matter in a procedurally admissible manner and are able to take the judgment into account without a violation of substantive law (3.). A complainant may challenge the disregard of this duty of consideration as a violation of the fundamental right whose area of protection is affected in conjunction with the principle of the rule of law (4.).

1. a) The European Convention on Human Rights and its protocols are agreements under public international law. The Convention leaves it to the States parties to decide in what way they comply with their duty to observe the provisions of the Convention (ECHR, Judgment of 6 February 1976, Series A20, no. 50 – Swedish Engine Drivers Union; ECHR, Judgment of 21 February 1986, Series A98, no. 84 – James and Others; see Geiger, *Grundgesetz und Völkerrecht*, 3rd ed. 2002, 405; Ehlers, in: idem (ed.), *Europäische Grundrechte und Grundfreiheiten*, 2003, § 2 marginal nos. 2-3). The federal legislature consented to the above treaty in each case by a formal statute under Article 59.2 of the Basic Law (Act on the Convention for the Protection of Human Rights and Fundamental Freedoms, *Gesetz über die Konvention zum Schutze der Menschenrechte und Grundfreiheiten* of 7 August 1952, Federal Law Gazette (*Bundesgesetzblatt* – BGBl) II, p. 685; by the proclamation of 15 December 1953, Federal Law Gazette 1954 II p. 14, the Convention entered into force for the Federal Republic of Germany on 3 September 1953; there was a new proclamation of the Convention as amended by the 11th protocol in Federal Law Gazette 2002 II p. 1054). In doing this, the federal legislature transformed the Convention into German law and made an order on the application of the law to this effect. Within the German legal system, the European Convention on Human Rights and its protocols, to the extent that they have come into force for the Federal Republic of Germany, have the status of a federal statute (see BVerfGE 74, 358 (370); 82, 106 (120)).

This classification means that German courts must observe and apply the Convention within the limits of methodically justifiable interpretation like other statute law of the Federal Government. But the guarantees of the European Convention on Human Rights and its protocols, by reason of this status in the hierarchy of norms, are not a direct constitutional standard of review in the German legal system (see Article 93.1 no. 4a of the Basic Law, § 90.1 of the Federal Constitutional Court Act). A complainant can therefore not directly challenge the violation of a human right contained in the European Convention on Human Rights by a constitutional complaint before the Federal Constitutional Court (see BVerfGE 74, 102 (128) with further

references; Order of the First Chamber of the Second Senate of the Federal Constitutional Court of 1 March 2004 – 2 BvR 1570/03 –, *Europäische Grundrechte-Zeitschrift* – EuGRZ 2004, p. 317 (318)). However, the guarantees of the Convention influence the interpretation of the fundamental rights and constitutional principles of the Basic Law. The text of the Convention and the case-law of the European Court of Human Rights serve, on the level of constitutional law, as guides to interpretation in determining the content and scope of fundamental rights and constitutional principles of the Basic Law, provided that this does not lead to a restriction or reduction of protection of the individual's fundamental rights under the Basic Law – and this the Convention itself does not desire (see Article 53 of the Convention; see BVerfGE 74, 358 (370); 83, 119 (128); Order of the Third Chamber of the Second Senate of the Federal Constitutional Court of 20 December 2000 – 2 BvR 591/00 –, *Neue Juristische Wochenschrift* – NJW 2001, pp. 2245 et seq.).
b) This constitutional significance of an agreement under international law, aiming at the regional protection of human rights, is the expression of the Basic Law's commitment to international law (*Völkerrechtsfreundlichkeit*); the Basic Law encourages both the exercise of state sovereignty through the law of international agreements and international cooperation, and the incorporation of the general rules of public international law, and therefore is, if possible, to be interpreted in such a way that no conflict arises with duties of the Federal Republic of Germany under public international law. The Basic Law has laid down in its programme that German public authority is committed to international cooperation (Article 24 of the Basic Law) and to European integration (Article 23 of the Basic Law). The Basic Law has granted the general rules of public international law priority over ordinary statute law (Article 25 sentence 2 of the Basic Law) and has integrated the law of international agreements, by Article 59.2 of the Basic Law, into the system of the separation of powers. In addition, it has opened the possibility of joining systems of mutual collective security (Article 24.2 of the Basic Law), created the duty to ensure the peaceful settlement of international disputes by way of arbitration (Article 24.3 of the Basic Law) and declared that the disturbance of the peace, and in particular preparing a war of aggression, is unconstitutional (Article 26 of the Basic Law). In this complex of norms, the German constitution, as is also shown by its preamble, aims to incorporate the Federal Republic of Germany into the community of states as a peaceful member having equal rights in a system of public international law serving peace (see also BVerfGE 63, 343 (370)).
However, the Basic Law did not take the greatest possible steps in opening itself to international-law connections. On the domestic level, the law of international agreements is not to be treated directly as applicable law, that is, without an Act subject to the consent of the German parliament under Article 59.2 of the Basic

Law, and – like customary international law (see Article 25 of the Basic Law) – not endowed with the status of constitutional law. The Basic Law is clearly based on the classic idea that the relationship of public international law and domestic law is a relationship between two different legal spheres and that the nature of this relationship can be determined from the viewpoint of domestic law only by domestic law itself; this is shown by the existence and the wording of Article 25 and Article 59.2 of the Basic Law. The commitment to international law takes effect only within the democratic and constitutional system of the Basic Law.
The Basic Law aims to integrate Germany into the legal community of peaceful and free states, but does not waive the sovereignty contained in the last instance in the German constitution. There is therefore no contradiction with the aim of commitment to international law if the legislature, exceptionally, does not comply with the law of international agreements, provided this is the only way in which a violation of fundamental principles of the constitution can be averted.
The Basic Law is intended to achieve comprehensive commitment to international law, cross-border cooperation and political integration in a gradually developing international community of democratic states under the rule of law. However, it does not seek a submission to non-German acts of sovereignty that is removed from every constitutional limit and control. Even the far-reaching supranational integration of Europe, which accepts the order to apply a norm, when this order originates from Community law and has direct domestic effect, is subject to a reservation of sovereignty, albeit one that is greatly reduced (see Article 23.1 of the Basic Law). The law of international agreements applies on the domestic level only when it has been incorporated into the domestic legal system in the proper form and in conformity with substantive constitutional law.
c) On this basis, the legal effect of the decisions of an international court that was brought into existence under an international agreement is determined according to the content of the incorporated international agreement and the relevant provisions of the Basic Law as to its applicability. If the Convention law of the European Convention on Human Rights, and with it the federal legislature on the basis of Article 59.2 of the Basic Law, has provided that the legal decisions are directly applicable, then they have this effect below the level of constitutional law. Under domestic law, it is first the duty of the competent non-constitutional courts to establish this legal effect.
2. a) The decisions of the ECHR have particular importance for Convention law as the law of international agreements, because they reflect the current state of development of the Convention and its protocols. Convention law itself accords varying legal effects to the ECHR's decisions on the merits. Under Article 42 and Article 44 of the Convention, the judgments of the ECHR become final and thus formally

non-appealable. In Article 46 of the Convention, the States parties have agreed that in all legal matters to which they are party they will abide by the final judgment of the ECHR. It follows from this provision that the judgments of the ECHR are binding on the parties to the proceedings and thus have limited substantive res judicata (see H.-J. Cremer, in: Grote/Marauhn (eds.), *Konkordanzkommentar*, 2004, *Entscheidung und Entscheidungswirkung*, marginal nos. 56–57 with further references).

The substantive res judicata in individual application proceedings under Article 34 of the Convention is restricted by the personal, material and temporal limits of the matter in dispute (see Order of the Second Senate of the Federal Constitutional Court (preliminary examination committee) of 11 October 1985 – 2 BvR 336/85 – Pakelli, *Europäische Grundrechte-Zeitschrift* 1985, p. 654 (656); see also E. Klein, *Binding effect of ECHR judgments*, *Festschrift für Ryssdal*, 2000, p. 705 (pp. 706 et seq.)). The decisions of the ECHR in proceedings against other States parties merely give the states that are not involved an occasion to examine their domestic legal systems and, if it appears that an amendment may be necessary, to orient themselves to the relevant case-law of the ECHR (see Ress, *Wirkung und Beachtung der Urteile und Entscheidungen der Straßburger Konventionsorgane*, *Europäische Grundrechte-Zeitschrift* 1996, p. 350). In this respect, Convention law has no provision comparable to § 31.1 of the Federal Constitutional Court Act, under which all the federal and *Land* constitutional bodies and all courts and authorities are bound by the decisions of the Federal Constitutional Court. Article 46.1 of the Convention provides only that the State party involved is bound by the final judgment with regard to a specific matter in dispute (res judicata).

b) In the question of fact, the ECHR pronounces a declaratory judgment; the decision establishes that the State party in question – with regard to the specific matter in dispute – complied with the Convention or acted in contradiction to it; however, there is no judgment of cassation that would directly quash the challenged measure of the State party (see Ehlers, loc. cit., § 2 marginal no. 52; Polakiewicz, *Die Verpflichtungen der Staaten aus den Urteilen des Europäischen Gerichtshofs für Menschenrechte*, 1993, pp. 217 et seq.; Steinberger, *Human Rights Law Journal* 1985, p. 402 (407)).

If it is declared that there has been a violation of the Convention, the first consequence is that the State party may no longer hold the view that its acts were in compliance with the Convention (see Frowein, in: Isensee/Kirchhof (eds.), *Handbuch des Staatsrechts*, vol. VII, 1992, § 180 marginal no. 14). In principle, the decision also obliges the State party affected with regard to the matter in dispute to restore, if possible, the state of affairs without the declared violation of the Convention (see Polakiewicz, loc. cit, pp. 97 et seq.; on the possibility of attaining the goal of resti-

tutio in integrum, see the Recommendation of the Committee of Ministers of the Council of Europe No. R (2000) 2 of 19 January 2000). If the violation that has been found is still continuing, for example in the case of continued arrest in violation of Article 5 of the Convention or an encroachment upon private and family life in violation of Article 8 of the Convention, the State party is under an obligation to end this state (see most recently ECHR, No. 71503/01, Judgment of 8 April 2004, no. 198 – Assanidze, *Europäische Grundrechte-Zeitschrift* 2004, p. 268 (275); see also Breuer, *Europäische Grundrechte-Zeitschrift* 2004, p. 257 (259); Grabenwarter, *Europäische Menschenrechtskonvention*, 2003, § 16, marginal no. 3; Polakiewicz, loc. cit., pp. 63 et seq.; Villiger, *Handbuch der Europäischen Menschenrechtskonvention*, 1999, § 13, marginal no. 233). The State party would therefore commit a new violation of the European Convention on Human Rights if it failed to terminate or repeated its conduct that has been established to be contrary to the Convention (see E. Klein, *Binding effect of ECHR judgments*, *Festschrift für Ryssdal*, 2000, p. 705 (708)). However, it should be taken into account that the effect of the decision relates only to the res judicata and that the factual and legal position may change before new domestic proceedings to which the complainant is a party.
c) The fact that the ECHR may award the complainant a "just compensation" in the form of money if the domestic law of the State party involved permits only inadequate compensation (see Article 41 of the Convention) shows that the Convention allows the State party involved some latitude with regard to the correction of decisions that have already been made and that are non-appealable.
However, in its more recent case-law relating to Article 41 of the Convention, the ECHR points out that the States parties, in ratifying the Convention, agreed to ensure that their domestic legal systems are in accordance with the Convention (Article 1 of the Convention). It is therefore, according to the ECHR, for the defendant state to remove every obstacle in domestic law that prevents a redress of the complainant's situation (see ECHR, loc. cit., *Europäische Grundrechte-Zeitschrift* 2004, p. 268 (275) with reference to ECHR, No. 39748/98, Judgment of 17 February 2004, no. 47 – Maestri).
If the State party affected is ordered to pay compensation to the successful complainant under Article 41 of the Convention, this judgment of the ECHR creates an obligation to perform (see Stöcker, *Wirkungen der Urteile des Europäischen Gerichtshofs für Menschenrechte in der Bundesrepublik*, *Neue Juristische Wochenschrift* 1982, p. 1905 (1908)). The granting of compensation is not necessarily part of the decision in the principal proceedings, but may be made at a later date, in order to give the parties the opportunity to reach an amicable agreement. In this way, Convention law recognises that in general only the State party affected can assess

what legal possibilities of action exist in the national legal system for the enforcement of the decision.

d) The legal effect of a decision of the ECHR, under the principles of public international law, is directed in the first instance to the State party as such. In principle, the Convention takes a neutral attitude towards the domestic legal system, and, unlike the law of a supranational organisation, it is not intended to intervene directly in the domestic legal system. On the domestic level, appropriate Convention provisions in conjunction with the consent Act and constitutional requirements (Article 20.3, Article 59.2 of the Basic Law in conjunction with Article 19.4 of the Basic Law) bind all organisations responsible for German public authority in principle to the decisions of the ECHR.

This legal position corresponds to the conception of the European Convention on Human Rights as an instrument for protection and for the enforcement of particular human rights. The obligation of the States parties, integrated into federal law by the consent Act, to create a domestic instance at which the person affected can have an "effective remedy" against particular conduct by the state (Article 13 of the Convention) already extends into the domestic structure of the state system and is not restricted to the executive branch, which is competent to act externally. In addition, the States parties must guarantee the "effective implementation of any of the provisions" of the European Convention on Human Rights in their domestic law (see Article 52 of the Convention), which is possible in a state under the rule of law governed by the principle of the separation of powers only if all the organisations responsible for sovereign power are bound by the guarantees of the Convention (on this, see Order of the Second Senate of the Federal Constitutional Court (preliminary examination committee) of 11 October 1985 – 2 BvR 336/85 – Pakelli, *Europäische Grundrechte-Zeitschrift* 1985, p. 654 (656)). In this view, the German courts too are under a duty to take the decisions of the ECHR into account.

3. The binding effect of decisions of the ECHR depends on the area of competence of the state bodies and the relevant law. Administrative bodies and courts may not free themselves from the constitutional system of competencies and the binding effect of statute and law (Article 20.3 of the Basic Law) by relying on a decision of the ECHR. But the binding effect of statute and law also includes a duty to take into account the guarantees of the Convention and the decisions of the ECHR as part of a methodologically justifiable interpretation of the law. Both a failure to consider a decision of the ECHR and the "enforcement" of such a decision in a schematic way, in violation of prior-ranking law, may therefore violate fundamental rights in conjunction with the principle of the rule of law.

a) The obligation created by the consent Act to take into account the guarantees of the European Convention on Human Rights and the decisions of the ECHR at least

demands that notice is taken of the relevant texts and case-law and that they are part of the process of developing an informed opinion of the court appointed to make a decision, of the competent authority or of the legislature. Domestic law must if possible be interpreted in harmony with public international law, regardless of the date when it comes into force (see BVerfGE 74, 358 (370)).
If there are decisions of the ECHR that are relevant to the assessment of a set of facts, then in principle the aspects taken into account by the ECHR when it considered the case must also be taken into account when the matter is considered from the point of view of constitutional law, in particular when proportionality is examined, and there must be a consideration of the findings made by the ECHR after weighing the rights of the parties (see Order of the First Chamber of the Second Senate of the Federal Constitutional Court of 1 March 2004 – 2 BvR 1570/03 –, *Europäische Grundrechte-Zeitschrift* 2004 p. 317 (319)).
If, in concrete application proceedings in which the Federal Republic of Germany is involved, the ECHR establishes that there has been a violation of the Convention, and if this is a continuing violation, the decision of the ECHR must be taken into account in the domestic sphere, that is, the responsible authorities or courts must discernibly consider the decision and, if necessary, justify understandably why they nevertheless do not follow the international-law interpretation of the law. Precisely in cases in which national courts, as in private law, have to structure multipolar fundamental rights situations, it is always important that various subjective legal positions are sensitively weighed against each other, and if there is a change in the persons involved in the dispute or a change in the actual or legal circumstances, this weighing may lead to a different result. There may therefore be constitutional problems if one of the holders of fundamental rights in conflict with another obtains an ECHR judgment in his or her favour against the Federal Republic of Germany and German courts schematically apply this decision to the private-law relationship, with the result that the holder of fundamental rights who has "lost" in this case and was possibly not involved in the proceedings at the ECHR would no longer be able to take an effective part in the proceedings as a party.
b) aa) If the ECHR has declared a domestic provision to be contrary to the Convention, either this provision may be interpreted in conformity with public international law when applied in practice, or the legislature has the possibility of altering this domestic provision that is incompatible with the Convention. If the violation of the Convention consists in effecting a specific administrative act, the authority responsible has the possibility of cancelling this act under the provisions of the law of administrative procedure (§ 48 of the Administrative Procedure Act (*Verwaltungsverfahrensgesetz* – VwVfG)). Administrative practice that is in violation of the Convention can be amended, and courts may establish the duty to do this.

bb) If judicial decisions violate the Convention, neither the European Convention on Human Rights nor the Basic Law imposes an obligation to accord to a judgment of the ECHR that establishes that a decision of a German court was made in violation of the European Convention on Human Rights the effect of removing the non-appealability of this decision (see Federal Constitutional Court, *Europäische Grundrechte-Zeitschrift* 1985, p. 654). Admittedly, it cannot be concluded from this that decisions of the ECHR need not be taken into account by German courts.

Under Article 20.3 of the Basic Law, judicial decisions are bound by statute and law. The constitutionally guaranteed independence of the judge, who is subject to the law, is not affected by this commitment, which is derived from the principle of the rule of law (Article 97.1 of the Basic Law; see BVerfGE 18, 52 (59); 19, 17 (31–32)). Both the commitment to law and the commitment to statute put into concrete terms the judicial power that is entrusted to the judges (Article 92 of the Basic Law). Since the European Convention on Human Rights – as interpreted by the ECHR – has the status of a formal federal statute, it shares the primacy of statute law and must therefore be complied with by the judiciary.

With regard to the principle of legal certainty, it must be noted that the federal legislature in the year 1998, in § 359 no. 6 of the Code of Criminal Procedure (*Strafprozessordnung* – StPO), introduced into the law of criminal procedure a new ground for reopening criminal proceedings (Act on the Reform of the Reopening of Proceedings under Criminal Law; *Gesetz zur Reform des strafrechtlichen Wiederaufnahmerechts* of 9 July 1998, Federal Law Gazette I p. 1802). This provides that it is admissible to reopen proceedings that ended in a non-appealable judgment if the ECHR has established that there was a violation of the European Convention on Human Rights or its protocols and the German judgment is based on this violation. This amendment of the law is based on the idea that a violation of the Convention whose effect continues in a specific individual case should be terminated, at all events in the area of criminal law, which is a particularly sensitive one for human rights, even if it is already non-appealable (see § 79.1 of the Federal Constitutional Court Act), if the judgment of the ECHR is relevant to the national proceedings. In this way, the competent court is given the opportunity to deal again, on application, with the case which has actually been closed, and to include the new legal facts in its development of an informed opinion. In this connection, the statute expresses the fundamental expectation that the court will change its original decision – which was contrary to the Convention – to the extent that this is based on the violation.

In other rules of procedure, there is no conclusive answer to the question as to how the Federal Republic of Germany, if the ECHR rules against it, is to react, if national court proceedings have been completed and are non-appealable. There may be facts and circumstances in which German courts may make a new decision, not about the res judicata, but about the matter on which the ECHR has established that there has been a violation of the Convention on the part of the Federal Republic of Germany. This may be the case, for example, when the court is intended to consider the matter again on the basis of a new application or changed circumstances, or the court in another constellation is still dealing with the matter. In the last instance, it is decisive whether a court, within the scope of the applicable law of procedure, has the possibility of making a new decision in which it can take account of the relevant decision of the ECHR.

In such case constellations, it would not be acceptable merely to refer the complainant to money damages, although restoration would fail neither for factual nor for legal reasons.

c) In taking into account decisions of the ECHR, the state bodies must include the effects on the national legal system in their application of the law. This applies in particular with regard to a partial system of domestic law whose legal consequences are balanced and that is intended to achieve an equilibrium between differing fundamental rights.

Individual application proceedings under Article 34 of the Convention before the ECHR are intended to decide specific individual cases in the two-party relationship between the complainant and the State party, by the measure of the European Convention on Human Rights and its protocols. The decisions of the ECHR may encounter national partial systems of law shaped by a complex system of case-law. In the German legal system, this may happen in particular in family law and the law concerning aliens, and also in the law on the protection of personality (on this, see, recently, ECHR, No. 59320/00, Judgment of 24 June 2004 – *von Hannover v. Germany*, *Europäische Grundrechte-Zeitschrift* 2004, pp. 404 et seq.), in which conflicting fundamental rights are balanced by the creation of groups of cases and graduated legal consequences. It is the task of the domestic courts to integrate a decision of the ECHR into the relevant partial legal area of the national legal system, because it cannot be the desired result of the international-law basis nor express the will of the ECHR for the ECHR through its decisions itself to undertake directly any necessary adjustments within a domestic partial legal system.

In this respect, it is necessary for the national courts to evaluate the decision when taking it into account; in this process, account may also be taken of the fact that the individual application proceedings before the ECHR, in particular where the original proceedings were in civil law, possibly does not give a complete picture of the legal positions and interests involved. The only party to the proceedings before the ECHR apart from the complainant is the State party affected; the possibility for third parties to take part in the application proceedings (see Article 36.2 of the European Convention on Human Rights) is not an institutional equivalent to the

rights and duties as a party to proceedings or another person involved in the original national proceedings.
4. The constitutional review of the interpretation and application of agreements under international law that have been given by statute the power of domestic German law is governed by the same principles that elsewhere too define the authority of the Federal Constitutional Court to review judicial decisions. The interpretation and application of agreements under international law by the non-constitutional courts can in principle be examined only to assess whether they are arbitrary or are based on a fundamentally incorrect view of the significance of a fundamental right or are incompatible with other constitutional provisions (see BVerfGE 18, 441 (450); 94, 315 (328)).
Admittedly, as part of its competence the Federal Constitutional Court is also competent to prevent and remove, if possible, violations of public international law that consist in the incorrect application or non-observance by German courts of international-law obligations and may given rise to an international-law responsibility on the part of Germany (see BVerfGE 58, 1 (34); 59, 63 (89); 109, 13 (23)). In this, the Federal Constitutional Court is indirectly in the service of enforcing international law and in this way reduces the risk of failing to comply with international law. For this reason it may be necessary, deviating from the customary standard, to review the application and interpretation of international-law treaties by the non-constitutional courts.
This applies in a particularly high degree to the duties under public international law arising from the Convention, which contributes to promoting a joint European development of fundamental rights (*gemeineuropäische Grundrechtsentwicklung*). In Article 1.2 of the Basic Law, the Basic Law accords particular protection to the central stock of international human rights. This protection, in conjunction with Article 59.2 of the Basic Law, is the basis for the constitutional duty to use the European Convention on Human Rights in its specific manifestation when applying German fundamental rights too (see BVerfGE 74, 358 (370)). As long as applicable methodological standards leave scope for interpretation and weighing of interests, German courts must give precedence to interpretation in accordance with the Convention. The situation is different only if observing the decision of the ECHR, for example because the facts on which it is based have changed, clearly violates statute law to the contrary or German constitutional provisions, in particular also the fundamental rights of third parties. "Take into account" means taking notice of the Convention provision as interpreted by the ECHR and applying it to the case, provided the application does not violate prior-ranking law, in particular constitutional law. In any event, the Convention provision as interpreted by the ECHR must be taken into account in making a decision; the court must at least duly consider it.

Where the facts have changed in the meantime or in the case of a different fact situation, the courts will need to determine what, in the view of the ECHR, constituted the specific violation of the Convention and why a changed fact situation does not permit it to be applied to the case. Here, it will always be important how taking account of the decision takes in the system of the field of law in question. On the level of federal law too, the Convention does not automatically have priority over other federal law, in particular if in this connection it has not already been the object of a decision of the ECHR.

Against this background, it must at all events be possible, on the basis of the relevant fundamental right, to raise the objection in proceedings before the Federal Constitutional Court that state bodies disregarded or failed to take into account a decision of the ECHR. In this process, the fundamental right is closely connected to the priority of statute embodied in the principle of the rule of law, under which all state bodies are bound by statute and law within their competence (see BVerfGE 6, 32 (41)).

II.

The challenged decision of the Naumburg Higher Regional Court of 30 June 2004 violates Article 6 of the Basic Law in conjunction with the principle of the rule of law. The Higher Regional Court did not take sufficient account of the judgment of the ECHR of 26 February 2004 when making its decision, although it was under an obligation to do so.

1. The challenged decision does not reveal whether and to what extent the Higher Regional Court considered the fact that the right of access asserted by the complainant is in principle protected by Article 6 of the Basic Law. This constitutional protection is to be seen against the background of the court's remarks on the complementary guarantee in Article 8 of the Convention. The Higher Regional Court should have considered in an understandable way how Article 6 of the Basic Law could have been interpreted in a manner that complied with the obligations under international law of the Federal Republic of Germany.

Here it is of central importance that the Federal Republic of Germany's violation of Article 8 of the Convention established by the ECHR is a continuing violation from the perspective of Convention law, for the complainant still has no access to his son. In its judgment, the ECHR held that the Federal Republic of Germany, in the choice of the means with which the judgment has to be enforced on the domestic level, is free, insofar as these means are compatible with the conclusions from the judgment. In the view of the ECHR, this means that it must at least be possible for the complainant to have access to his child (ECHR, Judgment of 26 February 2004, no. 64). This opinion of the ECHR should have caused the Higher Regional Court to consider the question as to whether and how far personal access of the complainant to his child might precisely be in the best interest of the child and what obstacles that could be documented – if necessary by way of a new expert witness's report – are presented by the consideration of the best interest of the child to the access which the ECHR regards as appropriate and which are protected by Article 6.2 of the Basic Law.

2. The Higher Regional Court in particular assumes in a manner that is not acceptable under constitutional law that a judgment of the European Court of Human Rights binds only the Federal Republic of Germany as a subject of public international law, but does not bind German courts. All the state bodies of the Federal Republic of Germany are – to the extent set out here under C. I. above – bound by operation of law within their jurisdiction by the Convention and the protocols that have entered into force in Germany. They must take into account the guarantees of the Convention and the case-law of the ECHR when interpreting fundamental rights and constitutional guarantees.

In the present case, the Higher Regional Court, by reason of the judgment of the ECHR of 26 February 2004, had particular cause to consider the grounds of that judgment, because the judgment, which established a violation of the Convention by the Federal Republic of Germany, dealt with the matter with which the Higher Regional Court was again concerned. The duty to take the decision into account neither adversely affects the Higher Regional Court's constitutionally guaranteed independence, nor does it force the court to enforce the ECHR decision without reflection. However, the Higher Regional Court is bound by statute and law, which includes not only civil law and the relevant procedural law, but also the European Convention on Human Rights, which has the status of an ordinary federal statute.

In the legal analysis in particular of new facts, in weighing conflicting fundamental rights such as those of the foster family and in integrating the individual case in the overall context of family-law cases relating to the right of access, the Higher Regional Court is not bound in its particular conclusion. The order challenged, however, lacks a discussion of the connections set out above.

3. It is not necessary to decide whether the Higher Regional Court, in a way that is constitutionally unacceptable, proceeded on the assumption that a temporary injunction can be issued only on application and not – as in the present case – also of the court's own motion, and thus that the complaint was admissible (see for example Saarbrücken Higher Regional Court, *OLG-Report* 2001, p. 269 on the one hand, Brandenburg Higher Regional Court, *OLG-Rechtsprechung Neue Länder* – OLG-NL 1994, 159 and Naumburg Higher Regional Court, OLG Naumburg, *Justiz-Ministerialblatt für Sachsen-Anhalt* 2003, p. 346 on the other hand). At all events, the

Higher Regional Court made its procedural remarks too without taking correct account of the judgment of the ECHR of 26 February 2004. However, this was of importance for the question as to whether the Local Court was obliged or entitled of its own motion to examine the granting of a right of access and if the factual requirements were satisfied – as was the case – to make contact by access possible by way of a temporary injunction.

D.

With the decision on the constitutional complaint in the principal proceedings, the application for a temporary injunction is also disposed of.

E.

…

Justices: Hassemer, Jentsch, Broß, Osterloh, Di Fabio, Mellinghoff, Lübbe-Wolff, Gerhardt

No. 44

BVerfGK 4, 339
of 28 December 2004 – 1 BvR 2790/04 –
"Görgülü II case"

HEADNOTE:

–

Order of the Third Chamber of the First Senate of 28 December 2004
under § 32.1 in conjunction with § 93d.2 of the Federal Constitutional Court Act
in the version promulgated on 11 August 1993 (Federal Law Gazette I p. 1473)
– 1 BvR 2790/04 –

in the proceedings regarding the constitutional complaint of Mr. G., – authorised representative: …, lawyer – against a) the order of the Naumburg Higher Regional Court (*Oberlandesgericht*) of 20 December 2004 – 14 WF 234/04 –, b) the order of the Naumburg Higher Regional Court of 8 December 2004 – 14 WF 236/04 –
here: application for a temporary injunction

RULING:

1. The effect of the decision of the Naumburg Higher Regional Court (Order of 20 December 2004 – 14 WF 234/04) excluding the access of the complainant to his son is suspended until the decision on the constitutional complaint.
The decision on access of Wittenberg Local Court of 2 December 2004 – 5 F 463/02 UG – applies, subject to the following:
a) The access begins on 8 January 2005 (see no. 1).
b) The development report on the child must be filed by 6 January 2005 (see no. 2).
c) The warning of an administrative fine does not apply to the fourth party (Youth Welfare Office – *Jugendamt*) and the fifth party (administrative district of Wittenberg) (see no. 5).

2. The *Land* (state) Saxony-Anhalt is ordered to reimburse the complainant the necessary expenses of the temporary injunction proceedings.

EXTRACT FROM GROUNDS:

I.

In his constitutional complaint, the complainant challenges the exclusion of the right of access to his child.

1. The child, who was born in August 1999, was born to the complainant and the mother of the child, who were not married. Immediately after the birth, the mother consented to the adoption of the child, who has since lived with foster parents. In the year 2000, at the instigation of the complainant, the complainant's paternity was judicially established. After the Local Court had granted the complainant a right of access and had also transferred custody, the Fourteenth Civil Senate of the Naumburg Higher Regional Court (Third Senate for Family Matters) reversed these decisions in the year 2001.

Thereupon, the European Court of Human Rights, in its judgment of 26 February 2004 (*Zeitschrift für das gesamte Familienrecht* – FamRZ 2004, p. 1456), upon the complaint of the complainant, ruled *inter alia* that the complainant's right under Article 8 of the European Convention for the Protection of Human Rights and Fundamental Freedoms (European Convention on Human Rights) had been violated by the Higher Regional Court in its exclusion of the right of access. The decision of the Higher Regional Court, it held, had made every form of reuniting of the family and the construction of every more extensive form of family life impossible. It stated that the complainant must at least be enabled to have access to his child.

Following this, the Local Court, in an order of 19 March 2004, issued a temporary injunction making arrangements for access, and the Naumburg Higher Regional Court again reversed this injunction in an order of 30 June 2004.

2. The complainant filed a constitutional complaint challenging this order, and thereupon, in an order of 14 October 2004 –2 BvR 1481/04 – (reprinted in FamRZ 2004, p. 1857), the Federal Constitutional Court (*Bundesverfassungsgericht*) reversed the above decision and referred the matter to another civil senate of the Naumburg Higher Regional Court; the Higher Regional Court, it held, had not taken sufficient account of the judgment of the European Court of Human Rights.

After the Eighth Civil Senate of the Naumburg Higher Regional Court, which was now called upon to decide, stated that a complaint against the temporary injunction

issued by the Local Court was not admissible, the official guardian and the children's guardian withdrew their complaints.
3. On the application of the complainant, the Local Court, on 2 December 2004, once more made arrangements for access. A decision in the temporary injunction proceedings was necessary to clarify the situation, since the last contact in the form of access had been two years earlier and the building up of a father-son relationship had been frustrated to date by the foster parents, supported by the official guardian. The court granted the complainant the right to have access to his child every Saturday in the time from 15.00 to 17.00 hours. For the first four access dates, the Local Court appointed an access guardian, in order to supervise the access.
Upon the appeals against this filed by the official guardian and the children's guardian, the Naumburg Higher Regional Court, now once more through its Fourteenth Civil Senate (Third Senate for Family Matters – hereinafter referred to as Higher Regional Court), in an order of 8 December 2004, suspended the enforcement of the local court order.
4. After the constitutional complaint filed by the complainant against this, together with the application for the issue of a temporary injunction, had been served on those entitled to make a statement, the Higher Regional Court reversed the above order on 20 December 2004 – 14 WF 236/04 – "because the complaint of failure to act filed in the principal proceedings on the right of access is now ripe for judgment".
In an order of the same date, upon the complaint of failure to act filed by the official guardian and the foster parents, it ordered the Local Court to proceed with the principal proceedings on access "with extreme dispatch and bring them to a conclusion". In addition to giving specific instructions on the further course of the proceedings, and altering the temporary injunction of the Local Court of 2 December 2004, it excluded access between the complainant and his son under § 620b.1 sentence 1 and 620b.3 sentence 1 in conjunction with §§ 620a.4 sentence 2 and 621g of the Code of Civil Procedure (*Zivilprozessordnung* – ZPO) until the final decision of the Local Court in the principal proceedings. It stated that contrary to the opinion of the European Court of Human Rights, the decision in the principal proceedings could not be made without an interim clarification of the facts. Access had had to be excluded "in order to avoid endangerment of the best interests of the child, which might otherwise occur" following the "application of the official guardian and the foster parents", which was "at least impliedly made, or alternatively was to be assumed by analogy to § 140 of the Civil Code (*Bürgerliches Gesetzbuch* – BGB) by way of reinterpreting to this effect the complaint, which in this context is of lower priority in the statutory procedural system and therefore is inadmissible".

5. Thereupon, the complainant filed a constitutional complaint against this order too; in the complaint, he challenges *inter alia* a violation of his rights under Article 3 of the Basic Law (*Grundgesetz* – GG), Article 6 of the Basic Law and de facto under Article 101.1 sentence 2 of the Basic Law. He submitted that the decision of the Higher Regional Court was arbitrary. In excluding access in the decision on the complaint of failure to act it had circumvented the provisions of the Code of Civil Procedure, which did not admit a complaint in temporary injunction proceedings relating to access. In addition, there had been no application for this. Finally, the Higher Regional Court had not implemented the decision of the European Court of Human Rights.

At the same time, the complainant upheld his original application for the issue of a temporary injunction. In addition, he stated that the cause of the constitutional complaint against the order of the Higher Regional Court of 8 December 2004 had ceased to exist.

The *Land* government of Saxony-Anhalt, the children's guardian, the foster parents and the official guardian were given an opportunity to give an opinion on the original application for the issue of a temporary injunction.

II.

The application for the issue of a temporary injunction is granted.

Under § 32.1 of the Federal Constitutional Court Act (*Bundesverfassungsgerichtsgesetz* — BVerfGG), the Federal Constitutional Court, in a case of dispute, may provisionally provide for a situation by temporary injunction if this is advisable for the public welfare in order to avert serious detriment, to prevent imminent violence or for another compelling reason. Here, the reasons that are submitted to show that the act of state challenged is unconstitutional must in principle be disregarded unless the constitutional complaint appears from the outset to be inadmissible or patently unfounded (see Decisions of the Federal Constitutional Court (*Entscheidungen des Bundesverfassungsgerichts* – BVerfGE), 88, 185 (186); established case-law). Where the outcome of the principal proceedings is open, the consequences that would occur if the temporary injunction were not issued but the constitutional complaint were later successful must be weighed against the disadvantages that would occur if the temporary injunction desired were issued but the constitutional complaint were unsuccessful (see BVerfGE 88, 185 (186); established case-law).

1. The constitutional complaint is not inadmissible … and … not patently unfounded …, with regard at all events to the order challenged, which excludes the right of access and to which the application for the issue of a temporary injunction solely

relates ... On the contrary: there are many indications that the Higher Regional court violated Article 101.1 sentence 2 of the Basic Law in conjunction with Article 3.1 of the Basic Law (aa). In addition, the Higher Regional Court in all probability once again failed to give sufficient consideration to the instructions of the European Court of Human Rights, and thus violated the complainant's right under Article 6.2 of the Basic Law in conjunction with Article 20.3 of the Basic Law (bb).
aa) (1) There is a violation of Article 101.1 sentence 2 of the Basic Law *inter alia* if a decision of the court, in interpreting and applying a provision on jurisdiction, deviates so far from the constitutional principle that no one may be removed from the jurisdiction of his lawful judge that it is incapable of justification, that is, arbitrary (see BVerfGE 3, 359 (363-364); 29, 45 (49)).
(2) It is likely that these requirements are satisfied in the present case. The objective course of the proceedings to date strongly supports the assumption that in its decision the Higher Regional Court allowed itself to be influenced by irrelevant considerations when it (a) examined the substantive decision of the Local Court on access, which is not part of the complaint of failure to act, which was the subject of the proceedings, and (b) in this way circumvented the provision of § 621g in conjunction with § 620c sentence 2 of the Code of Civil Procedure, which provides that a complaint against a temporary ruling on access is not admissible.
(a) The Higher Regional Court altered the decision on access of the Local Court to the detriment of the complainant without giving comprehensible reasons to show why it is entitled to do this in the proceedings relating to the complaint of failure to act. In its decision, the court relied on § 621g in conjunction with § 620b.1 of the Code of Civil Procedure, under which the court may reverse or alter the temporary injunction "on application". But the Higher Regional Court did not even begin to show why it is competent to make a decision under § 621g in conjunction with § 620b.1 of the Code of Civil Procedure *in the proceedings relating to the complaint of failure to act*. However, it should have considered itself bound to do this, not only by reason of the nature of the complaint of failure to act as an extraordinary legal remedy (aa). An explanation of this nature would also have been advisable because the complainants in the complaint of failure to act clearly themselves did not proceed on the assumption that § 620b.1 of the Code of Civil Procedure applied; they did not make the necessary application – at all events not expressly (bb).
(aa) The complaint of failure to act – which is not governed by statute either in the Code of Civil Procedure or in the Act on Matters of Non-Contentious Jurisdiction (*Gesetz über die Angelegenheiten der freiwilligen Gerichtsbarkeit* – FGG) – was created by case-law as an extraordinary legal remedy. It serves the sole purpose of guaranteeing the right of the parties to the proceedings to effective legal protection (see Karlsruhe Higher Regional Court, FamRZ 2004, p. 53 (54); Dresden Higher

Regional Court, FamRZ 2000, pp. 1422-1423; Saarbrücken Higher Regional Court, *Neue Juristische Wochenschrift – Rechtsprechungs-Report Zivilrecht* – NJW-RR 1999, pp. 1290-1291; Gummer, in: Zöller, *ZPO*, 24th ed., *§ 567*, marginal no. 21; Reichhold, in: Thomas/Putzo, *ZPO*, 26th ed., *§ 567*, marginal no. 10). The subject of the proceedings is exclusively the failure of the court of first instance to act, but not the review of a decision that has already been pronounced (see Gummer, loc. cit., marginal nos. 21, 21a). However, the court of appeal acquires jurisdiction under § 621g in conjunction with § 620b.3 and § 620a.4 of the Code of Civil Procedure only if the subject of the temporary injunction corresponds to the subject of the proceedings pending there, taking into account the nature of the legal protection applied for; correspondence here means direct concurrence (see Hüßtege, in: Thomas/Putzo, *ZPO*, 26th ed., *§ 620a*, marginal no. 15). Precisely this is not the case here. Instead, the access ruling made is the opposite of failure to act. Finally, if the complaint of failure to act is well-founded, then according to the case-law of the nonconstitutional courts and the literature, the courts may merely be instructed to continue the proceedings (see Karlsruhe Higher Regional Court, FamRZ 2004, p. 53 (54); Saarbrücken Higher Regional Court, NJW-RR 1999, pp. 1290-1291; Gummer, loc. cit., marginal no. 21a).

(bb) In this factual and legal situation, it is impossible to follow the remarks of the Higher Regional Court that the application required under § 620b.1 of the Code of Civil Procedure is to be assumed to have been made "at least impliedly ... or alternatively was to be assumed by analogy to § 140 of the Civil Code by way of reinterpreting to this effect the complaint, which in this context is of lower priority in the statutory procedural system and therefore is inadmissible".

(b) In addition, in view of the course of the proceedings to date, it appears not to be out of the question that the Higher Regional Court, in making the ruling challenged, intended to circumvent the provision of § 620c sentence 2 of the Code of Civil Procedure. In its order of 8 December 2004, the Higher Regional Court had already effectively excluded the complainant's access to his child when, in response to the complaint filed against the temporary access ruling of the Local Court, it suspended the enforcement of that ruling. However, the Higher Regional Court was not authorised to do this, for the complaint against a temporary injunction on access, under § 621g in conjunction with § 620c of the Code of Civil Procedure, is patently inadmissible (see Cologne Higher Regional Court, FamRZ 2003, p. 548; Dresden Higher Regional Court, FamRZ 2003, pp. 1306-1307; Naumburg Higher Regional Court (First Family Senate), *Justiz-Ministerialblatt für Sachsen-Anhalt* 2003, p. 346; Philippi, in: Zöller, *ZPO*, 24th ed., *§ 620c*, marginal no. 4 and *§ 621g*, marginal no. 5; Hüßtege, in: Thomas/Putzo, *ZPO*, 26th ed., *§ 620c*, marginal no. 4 and marginal no. 7; Motzer, FamRZ 2003, p. 793 (802)). Despite the unambiguous statutory provision, the Higher Regional Court did not even begin to show, in that order, why it proceeded on the basis that the complaint was admissible. The Fourteenth Senate should have seen all the more reason to give such a justification in that shortly earlier, the Eighth Senate of the Naumburg Higher Regional Court, in the same access proceedings, had expressly stated that the complaint was inadmissible (with regard to the earlier temporary injunction; see also the statement of the Federal Constitutional Court in its order of 14 October 2004, loc. cit., p. 1863).

Admittedly, the Higher Regional Court reversed the order that the enforcement should be suspended after the service on those entitled to make a statement of the constitutional complaint filed against this order together with the application for the issue of a temporary injunction and shortly before the period for submitting opinions expired, on 20 December 2004, on the grounds that the complaint of failure to act was "now ripe for judgment". But the Higher Regional Court made no mention whatsoever in its grounds that it had not been entitled to make this order at all because the complaint was inadmissible. Instead, on the same day, in its order on the complaint of failure to act, the Higher Regional Court once more temporarily excluded the complainant's access to his child when it now in these proceedings, and not in the proceedings on the complaint against the order at first instance, amended that order to this effect.

bb) In addition, it is likely that the complainant's rights under Article 6.2 in conjunction with Article 20.3 of the Basic Law were violated. The European Court of Human Rights held that the complainant's right under Article 8 of the European Convention on Human Rights was violated by the exclusion of the right of access and that he should at least be guaranteed access to his child (see European Court of Human Rights, FamRZ 2004, p. 1456 (1460, no. 64)). According to the order of the Federal Constitutional Court (see Federal Constitutional Court, Order of 14 October 2004, loc. cit., pp. 1858-1859) that was pronounced in response to this decision, the binding effect of a decision of the European Court of Human Rights extends to all state bodies and in principle imposes on them an obligation to terminate a continuing violation of the European Convention on Human Rights and create a situation that complies with the Convention within the scope of their jurisdiction and without violating the binding force of statute and law (Article 20.3 of the Basic Law). Courts are at all events under a duty to take into account a judgment that relates to a case already decided by them if they preside over a retrial of the matter in a procedurally admissible manner and are able to take the judgment into account without a violation of substantive law. In this process, the court must consider, in a comprehensible form, how the fundamental right affected (in this case Article 6 of the Basic Law) can be interpreted in a way that complies with the obligations of the

Federal Republic of Germany under public international law (see Federal Constitutional Court, Order of 14 October 2004, loc. cit., p. 1863).

The Higher Regional Court once again patently did not comply with these requirements. In particular, it did not even begin to consider the question as to how the complainant can succeed in reuniting the family at all if he remains prohibited from building up any contact with his child at all. Nor did the Higher Regional Court sufficiently consider the deliberations of the European Court of Human Rights, under which it is in the best interests of the child to maintain the family relationships, since breaking off such connections means separating the child from his roots, which is justified only in quite extraordinary circumstances. The Higher Regional Court gave as little consideration to the fact that the endangerment of the best interests of the child, indiscriminately postulated by the Higher Regional Court and supported by no concrete facts, may be averted by the presence of a trained person at the meetings, ordered by the Local Court, as it did to the fact that access is planned only for a period of two hours per week in any case. The "specialist medical assessments" mentioned by the Higher Regional Court in its order are not suitable to give rise to an endangerment of the best interests of the child as a result of these very brief access contacts. Thus, for example, the opinion of the paediatrician states that the boy would suffer severe psychological harm if he "is torn out of his family surroundings". In the case of access of two hours per week, however, there can be no question of such a "tearing out".

2. The weighing of consequences that is therefore required results in more weight being given to the reasons that favour the issue of a temporary injunction that guarantees that access takes place.

a) If there were no temporary injunction, but the constitutional complaint were later successful, the complainant would continue to be excluded from contact with his child. Until the complainant could actually have access, taking into account the duration of the constitutional complaint proceedings and the duration of the proceedings in the non-constitutional courts that would follow if the case were possibly rejected as unfounded, up to six months might pass. This is a considerable period of time if one considers that the complainant has made efforts in this respect since the child was born and in view of the increasing age of the child has increasingly less possibility of sharing in the child's development. In addition, the longer the exclusion of access continues, the more unlikely it becomes that the family can be reunited. Moreover, it is of decisive importance here that the European Court of Human Rights has already decided in this matter that the complainant must be granted access to his child (see European Court of Human Rights, FamRZ 2004, p. 1456 (1460, no. 64)), and that this decision, by the order of the Federal Constitutional Court of 14 October 2004 (loc. cit., p. 1857), must also in principle be respected.

b) If, on the other hand, the temporary injunction applied for were issued but the constitutional complaint later had to be refused, the complainant would have access to his child for two hours a week until the decision on the constitutional complaint, and the first four contact sessions would take place with a trained person present. The Higher Regional Court is of the opinion that this would give rise to a severe endangerment of the best interests of the child; this is not apparent. It should not be overlooked that precisely in cases of the present kind the child may experience conflicts as a result of the behaviour of the foster parents on the one hand and the natural parent on the other. However, in its temporary injunction the Local Court counteracted this insofar as it ordered the parties to avoid all statements, in particular derogatory statements, in the presence of the child that might have negative effects on the relationship to the complainant, but also on the relationship to the foster parents. Another argument against an endangerment of the best interests of the child is the fact that the five-year-old child, who has grown up in the home of the foster parents since he was four days old, must have developed a stable relationship to the foster parents that enables him also to enter into contact with people who are not (so) familiar with the child, without his psychological state being endangered (see, for example, Koechel, *Kindeswohl im gerichtlichen Verfahren*, 1995, pp. 23-24, with further references).
In addition, it is not imperative that the access would have to be terminated on the date of the decision on the constitutional complaint. For the courts must orient themselves on the best interests of the child in every stage of the proceedings. If the court came to the conclusion that breaking off the access that had been taking place might be harmful to the child, the necessary measures would therefore have to be taken.
c) The injunction of the Local Court should be brought up to date with regard to the instructions as to times (see no. 1 letters a) and b) of the operative part of the judgment), *inter alia* in order to allow the parties to prepare themselves appropriately. In addition, the Youth Welfare Office and the administrative district of Wittenberg were to be exempted from the threat of an administrative fine (see Zimmermann, in: Keidel/Kuntze/Winkler, *FGG*, 15th ed., *§ 33*, marginal no. 16).
3. The judicial order of the Federal Constitutional Court that the access ruling made by the Local Court was to be observed means that the Local Court ruling continues in force for the duration of the temporary injunction issued by the Federal Constitutional Court failing a change of the factual situation and therefore is not for this time open to a judicial review by the Higher Regional Court.
4. The decision on the reimbursement of expenses is based on § 34a.3 of the Federal Constitutional Court Act (see BVerfGE 82, 310 (315)).

Justices: Papier, Steiner, Hohmann-Dennhardt

No. 45

BVerfGK 5, 161
of 5 April 2005 – 1 BvR 1664/04 –
"Görgülü III case"

HEADNOTE:

–

Order of the First Chamber of the First Senate of 5 April 2005
– 1 BvR 1664/04 –

in the proceedings regarding the constitutional complaint of Mr. G., authorised representative: ..., lawyer – against the order of the Naumburg Higher Regional Court (*Oberlandesgericht* – OLG) of 9 July 2004 – 14 UF 60/04 –.

RULING:

1. The order of the Naumburg Higher Regional Court of 9 July 2004 – 14 UF 60/04 – violates the complainant's fundamental right under Article 6.2 sentence 1 in conjunction with Article 20.3 of the Basic Law (*Grundgesetz* – GG) to the extent that, in reversing the order of the Wittenberg Local Court (*Amtsgericht*) of 19 March 2004 – 5 F 741/02 SO –, it rejects as unfounded the petition of the complainant for custody (number 1 of the operative part of the order). The order is therefore also reversed with regard to the arrangements for costs (number 3 of the operative part). The matter is referred back to a different family senate of the Naumburg Higher Regional Court.
2. In other respects the constitutional complaint is not admitted for decision.
3. The *Land* (state) Saxony-Anhalt is ordered to reimburse the complainant his necessary expenses.

EXTRACT FROM GROUNDS:

I.

In his constitutional complaint, the complainant challenges a decision on custody of the Naumburg Higher Regional Court.

1. The child, who was born in August 1999, was born to the complainant and the mother of the child, who were not married. Immediately after the birth, the mother agreed to the adoption of the child; since that time, the child has been living with foster parents. In the year 2000, at the instigation of the complainant, his paternity was established by judicial decision.

After the Local Court had awarded the complainant a right of contact and had also transferred custody, the Fourteenth Civil Senate (Third Senate for Family Matters) of the Naumburg Higher Regional Court, by an order of 20 June 2001, rejected the complainant's petition for custody and excluded the complainant's right of contact until 30 June 2002. The complainant filed a constitutional complaint with regard to this; the Federal Constitutional Court (*Bundesverfassungsgericht* – BVerfG), by order of 31 July 2001 – 1 BvR 1174/01 – did not accept this constitutional complaint for decision. By judgment of 26 February 2004 (*Zeitschrift für das gesamte Familienrecht* – FamRZ 2004, pp. 1456 et seq.), the European Court of Human Rights, in response to the complainant's individual application, found that there had been a violation of Article 8 of the European Convention for the Protection of Human Rights and Fundamental Freedoms (the Convention). Thereupon, the Local Court again awarded the complainant the right of contact and custody.

The children's guardian and the Youth Welfare Office (official guardian) filed an appeal against this, and thereupon the Higher Regional Court made an order – challenged by the constitutional complaint – reversing the decision on custody and dismissing the complainant's petition for custody. In addition, it dismissed the complainant's applications to divest the official guardian and the children's guardian of their functions. It also dismissed the application for legal aid. As grounds, the Fourteenth Civil Senate stated *inter alia* that neither the Convention nor the Basic Law contained an obligation to accord to a judgment of the European Court of Human Rights an effect that removed the finality and non-appealability of the decision challenged or required proceedings that have been finally and non-appealably completed to be reopened. The judgment of the European Court of Human Rights, it held, did not alter the domestic legal position, nor did it have a binding effect in the sense that it amended the case-law of the supreme federal courts. The court said that it was not possible to establish "even an indirect binding effect, the existence of which might at most be discussed" resulting from a violation of Article 8 of the Convention.

The Regional Court (*Landgericht*) has not yet decided on the appeal filed by the complainant against the order of the guardianship court by which the court gave prior consent to the adoption of the child in substitution for the consent of the complainant.

2. In his constitutional complaint, the complainant challenges *inter alia,* on the merits, a violation of his right under Article 6.2 sentence 1 of the Basic Law in conjunction with Article 20.3 of the Basic Law. If the Higher Regional Court had observed the interpretation of the law of the European Court of Human Rights, it would have had to transfer custody to the complainant in order to carefully reacquaint the child with its father. Because it did not feel it was bound by the decision of the European Court of Human Rights and did not implement the judgment of that court, the Higher Regional Court had violated public international law. In addition, the complainant seeks a determination that the adoption of the child is "unlawful".

...

II.

...

[1.] In other respects, the Chamber accepts the constitutional complaint for decision and grants the relief sought by it under § 93c.1 sentence 1 in conjunction with § 93a.2 letter b of the Federal Constitutional Court Act.

It is appropriate to accept the constitutional complaint for decision to enforce the complainant's fundamental right under Article 6.2 sentence 1 in conjunction with Article 20.3 of the Basic Law (§ 93a.2 letter b of the Federal Constitutional Court Act). The requirements for a chamber decision granting the relief sought by the constitutional complaint are satisfied (§ 93c of the Federal Constitutional Court Act). To the extent that the subject of the constitutional complaint is the question of the binding effect of the decision of the European Court of Human Rights, the element of fundamental importance ceased to exist as a result of the decision of the Second Senate (see Order of 14 October 2004 – 2 BvR 1481/04 –, reprinted in *Zeitschrift für das gesamte Familienrecht* 2004, pp. 1857 et seq.). Apart from this, the Federal Constitutional Court has answered the question as to the relationship in which the parental right stands to the fundamental right of the child under Article 2.1 in conjunction with Article 1.1 of the Basic Law or to the constitutionally protected rights of the foster family under Article 6.1 of the Basic Law (see Decisions of the Federal Constitutional Court (*Entscheidungen des Bundesverfassungs-*

gerichts – BVerfGE) 24, 119 (144); 60, 79 (88-89); 61, 358 (372); 68, 176 (188); 75, 201 (218); 79, 51 (63-64); 88, 187 (195-196)). Similarly, the question of the protection of fundamental rights by the further refining and application of procedural law by the Federal Constitutional Court has already been answered (see BVerfGE 53, 30 (65); 55, 171 (182)).

a) The challenged decision of the Naumburg Higher Regional Court (number 1) violates the complainant's fundamental right under Article 6.2 sentence 1 of the Basic Law in conjunction with Article 20.3 of the Basic Law. The Naumburg Higher Regional Court did not take sufficient account of the judgment of the European Court of Human Rights – pronounced in connection with the custody proceedings, on which the Naumburg Higher Regional Court had to decide – which held that the rejection of the petition for custody is a violation of Article 8 of the Convention.

aa) In principle, a national court must take account of the case-law of the European Court of Human Rights (1). Nor does this in the present case lead to results that are incompatible with the Basic Law (2).

(1) Occasioned by the decision of the European Court of Human Rights of 26 February 2004, the Federal Constitutional Court made an order to the effect that the binding effect of a decision of the European Court of Human Rights extends to all state bodies and in principle obliges them, where this is within their jurisdiction and does not violate the principle of the binding force of law and justice (Article 20.3 of the Basic Law), to end a continuing violation of the Convention and create a state of affairs that is in compliance with the Convention (see Federal Constitutional Court, loc. cit., pp. 1858-1859). Courts are at all events under a duty to take into account a judgment that relates to a case already decided by them if they preside over a retrial of the matter in a procedurally admissible manner and are able to take the judgment into account without a violation of substantive law (see Federal Constitutional Court, loc. cit., p. 1859). In doing this, the court must consider in an understandable manner how the fundamental right affected (in this case Article 6.2 sentence 1 of the Basic Law) may be interpreted in a way that corresponds to the obligations of the Federal Republic of Germany under public international law (see Federal Constitutional Court, loc. cit., p. 1863). The courts must take notice of the Convention provision as interpreted by the European Court of Human Rights and apply it to the case, provided the application does not violate prior-ranking law, in particular constitutional law (Federal Constitutional Court, loc. cit., p. 1862).

(2) Applying the Convention provision (here Article 8 of the Convention) as interpreted by the European Court of Human Rights to the matter would not violate constitutional law in the present case.

The European Court of Human Rights stated that the Higher Regional Court should have examined whether there were possibilities of bringing the father and the child together that were less onerous for the welfare of the child. In addition, it should have taken into account the long-term effects of separating the child from its natural father (see European Court of Human Rights, loc. cit., p. 1459). Measures taken with this in mind comply with the Basic Law; at all events, the Basic Law may be interpreted in this connection in a manner conforming with the obligations of the Federal Republic of Germany under public international law.

(a) When the decision is made as to the conditions under which a child may be removed from a foster family in order to move it to its natural parent, account must be taken – under the case-law of the Federal Constitutional Court too – both of the parental right under Article 6.2 sentence 1 of the Basic Law and of the fundamental right of the child under Article 2.1 in conjunction with Article 1.1 of the Basic Law. Finally, the fundamental right of the foster family under Article 6.1 of the Basic Law must also be taken into account (see BVerfGE 68, 176 (187); 79, 51 (60)). As part of the necessary weighing of interests, when statutory provisions in the area of Article 6.2 of the Basic Law are interpreted, in the same way as in the case of decisions of the legislature, it must be borne in mind that the welfare of the child must in the last instance be the decisive factor (see BVerfGE 68, 176 (188); 75, 201 (218); see also BVerfGE 79, 51 (64)). Even if the separation from the persons to whom it directly relates is normally a considerable emotional burden for the child (see BVerfGE 75, 201 (219)), this alone may not be regarded as sufficient to refuse to release the child, because otherwise bringing a child and its parents together would always be excluded if the child had found its "social parents" (see BVerfGE 75, 201 (219-220)). With regard to the welfare of the child affected, on the contrary, a distinction must be made depending on whether the child is to move from the foster family to the household of its parents or to another foster home. In the former case, the limits of risk are to be defined more generously, whereas in the latter case an endangerment of the child's welfare must be excluded with sufficient certainty (see BVerfGE 75, 201 (217, 220); 79, 51 (64)).

(b) Finally, the protection of fundamental rights also to a large extent affects the drafting and application of procedural law (see BVerfGE 53, 30 (65); 55, 171 (182)). Article 6.2 sentence 2 of the Basic Law transfers to the state community the duty to monitor the care and upbringing of the child; this gives rise to the influence of constitutional law on procedural law and its treatment by the courts in custody proceedings (see BVerfGE 55, 171 (182)). Admittedly, in proceedings based on the principle of official investigation, it must be left to the court of decision which way, within the scope of statutory provisions, it considers appropriate to make the findings necessary for its decision (see BVerfGE 79, 51 (62)). But the proceedings must in principle be appropriate to achieve a basis that is as reliable as possible for a decision oriented on the child's welfare (see BVerfGE 55, 171 (182)).

bb) The challenged decision of the Naumburg Higher Regional Court did not satisfy these requirements.

(1) The Higher Regional Court did not take sufficient account of the judgment of the European Court of Human Rights in its decision. The Fourteenth Civil Senate evidently takes the view that the pronouncement of the European Court of Human Rights does not bind it and that the national courts, in particular, cannot be bound by its decision, either in interpreting the Convention or in interpreting national fundamental rights.

(2) In addition, the Higher Regional Court failed to understand that in the present case no significance attaches to the question – which the court answered in the negative – as to whether the decision of the European Court of Human Rights is to be accorded an "effect that removes the finality and non-appealability of the decision challenged or requires proceedings that have been finally and non-appealably completed to be reopened". Decisions on custody do not acquire the force of a final judgment (see Federal Court of Justice (*Bundesgerichtshof* – BGH), *Neue Juristische Wochenschrift – Rechtsprechungs-Report Zivilrecht* – NJW-RR 1986, p. 1130; Diederichsen, in: Palandt, *BGB*, 64th ed., *§ 1696*, marginal no. 5; Zimmermann, in: Keidel/Kuntze/Winkler, *FGG*, 15th ed., *§ 31*, marginal no. 22a at end). Custody proceedings do not admit the plea of *res judicata*. The care of the minor always has priority over the finality of a decision once taken (see Federal Court of Justice, loc. cit.). § 1696.1 of the Civil Code (*Bürgerliches Gesetzbuch* – BGB) contains a substantive power of amendment which serves not only to adapt the arrangement adopted to a change in the factual circumstances that are decisive for the decision, but also permits the court to take into account such facts as already existed at the time when the decision was made but were not known to the court (see Diederichsen, loc. cit.).

§ 1696.1 of the Civil Code provides that an amending decision requires cogent reasons that have a long-term effect on the welfare of the child; this is equally little an obstacle to taking the decision of the European Court of Human Rights into account. The Higher Regional Court correctly pointed out that an amendment under § 1696.1 of the Civil Code imposes particular requirements on the examination of the child's welfare (see Diederichsen, loc. cit., marginal no. 16). However, the court failed to recognise that this provision of ordinary law may be interpreted in the light of the constitution and therefore in a manner – which at all events to this extent does not contradict the constitution – that complies with the duties of the Federal Republic of Germany under public international law. In addition, the case-law of the non-constitutional courts and the literature recognise that an amendment of case-law may create a reason for amendment in the meaning of § 1696.1 of the Civil Code (see Diederichsen, loc. cit., marginal no. 20 with further references). If

the Higher Regional Court treated the decision of the European Court of Human Rights as an exception to this, it failed to realise that, according to the above statement, the non-constitutional courts too must take the decisions of the European Court of Human Rights into account.
(3) The Higher Regional Court did not in principle exclude an indirect binding effect. However, at the same time it raised the objection that this could "not be established" for lack of plausible reasoning. In this the court – once more – failed to realise that according to the above statements it should have applied the provision of the Convention as interpreted by the European Court of Human Rights to the case.
(a) It is not apparent that the Higher Regional Court considered how Article 6.2 sentence 1 of the Basic Law could have been interpreted in a manner complying with the duties of the Federal Republic of Germany under public international law (on this, see Federal Constitutional Court, loc. cit., p. 1863).
(aa) The Higher Regional Court did not sufficiently consider the question raised by the European Court of Human Rights as to what long-term effects a permanent separation of the child from the complainant might have (on this, see European Court of Human Rights, loc. cit., p. 1459). In this respect, it restricted itself to the mere statement that these effects (in contrast to an endangerment of the child's welfare threatened as a result of removing the child from the foster family) were "certainly to be categorised as less grave, and immaterial from the point of view of custody" if "the foster parents inform C. at the appropriate time and appropriately for the child's age about its origins". However, the court did not in this respect make any determinations that bear up to investigation.
(bb) The Higher Regional Court also failed to take into account the further guideline of the European Court of Human Rights. Under this, it would have been necessary to consider whether there are possibilities of bringing the child and the complainant together in circumstances in which the burden for the child would be less.
If it had taken sufficient account of this guideline, the Higher Regional Court would at least have had to consider whether it might not have been able in a different way to counteract a possible endangerment of the welfare of the child by an immediate removal of the child from the foster family, which in the opinion of the court was intended by the complainant. Thus, for example, it would have been conceivable – as a less forceful intervention – to transfer custody to the complainant, but at the same to link it to an order for the child to remain with the foster family – under § 1632.4 of the Civil Code such an order may also be made by the court of its own motion (on this, see BVerfGE 88, 187 (195-196)).
(cc) The Higher Regional Court correctly pointed out that § 1672 and § 1678.2 of the Civil Code, which apply under § 1751.1 of the Civil Code, permit a transfer of

custody only if "this serves the best interests of the child". But since the Fourteenth Civil Senate did not sufficiently consider whether there are possibilities of bringing the child and its father together that are less onerous for the welfare of the child and what long-term effects a separation of the child from its natural father has, it was also not able to resolve definitively whether the transfer of custody in the meaning of § 1672 and § 1678.2 of the Civil Code serves the welfare of the child. The Higher Regional Court equally little considered whether the above provisions may be interpreted in a way that conforms with the provisions of the Basic Law and is at the same time in compliance with the Convention.

(b) Finally, it is not apparent that the Higher Regional Court initiated the necessary investigations in order to be able to answer the questions raised by the European Court of Human Rights. On the contrary, the proceedings conducted by the Higher Regional Court were not suited to achieve a foundation as reliable as possible for a decision oriented to the welfare of the child. The Fourteenth Civil Senate based its decision on the opinion of the educationalist K.; this in itself is to be criticised because the educationalist based her findings on general academic knowledge without specifically applying this to the case in question by way of an exploration of the complainant or an observation of the interaction of father and child. As far as can be seen, she did not include the complainant himself in her investigations. In addition, this was an opinion commissioned by the Youth Welfare Office (which was appointed official guardian) from the *Land* Youth Welfare Office, and it must therefore be defined as a party opinion. For this reason, it would have been advisable in the present case – from the point of view of constitutional law too – to obtain an independent expert's report, all the more so since it cannot be seen from the grounds of decision that the court itself has enough expert knowledge of its own. Moreover, the Higher Regional Court decided in written proceedings, without hearing the parties in person; as far as the records of the case reveal, the Fourteenth Civil Senate – unlike the Local Court, which heard the parties several times in person – at no time obtained a personal impression of the parties.

b) The decision challenged is based on the violation of a fundamental right set out above. It cannot be excluded that the court, if it had taken sufficient account of the decision of the European Court of Human Rights and if it had taken sufficient account of the complainant's parental right under Article 6.2 sentence 1 of the Basic Law in conjunction with Article 20.3 of the Basic Law, would have reached a different conclusion.

…

Justices: Papier, Hohmann-Dennhardt, Hoffmann-Riem

No. 46

BVerfGE 113, 88
of 7 June 2005 – 1 BvR 1508/96 –
"Parental support case"

HEADNOTE:

Decision regarding the question of the constitutional limits on the interpretation of laws concerning support and social assistance when determining the ability to pay of children who are required by the social assistance funding agency to pay support for their parents as the result of an assigned right.

Judgment of the First Senate of 7 June 2005
on the basis of the oral hearing of 15 March 2005
– 1 BvR 1508/96 –

in the proceedings regarding the constitutional complaint of Ms. B., – authorised representative: …, lawyer – against the judgment of the Duisburg Regional Court (*Landgericht*) of 3 May 1996 – 24 (4) S 285/95 –.

RULING

1. The judgment of the Duisburg Regional Court of 3 May 1996 – 24 (4) S 285/95 – violates the fundamental right of the complainant under Article 2.1 of the Basic Law (*Grundgesetz* – GG).
2. The judgment is reversed and the matter is referred back to the Regional Court.
…

EXTRACT FROM GROUNDS:

A.

The constitutional complaint relates to the determination of the ability to pay of children who are required by the social assistance funding agency to pay support for a parent as the result of an assigned right.

I.

1. Under § 1601 of the Civil Code (*Bürgerliches Gesetzbuch* – BGB), lineal relatives have an obligation to give each other support; consequently, children also have an obligation to support their parents. The requirement for this is, on the one hand, that the parent who claims support is not able to support himself or herself from his or her own means (§ 1602.1 of the Civil Code), and therefore that parent is indigent. On the other hand, the child who is required to pay support must be able, taking into account his or her other obligations, to pay support to the parent without endangering that child's own reasonable support (§ 1603.1 of the Civil Code), that is, the child must be able to pay. In this calculation, the indigence and the ability to pay must exist concurrently. Only if and as long as the person liable for support is able to pay during the time when there is a need for support does a support claim arise. …

The child's own reasonable support therefore constitutes the limit in support law up to which the child liable for support may be required to commit his or her income and assets. The legislature has not defined in detail what the person liable for support would need to have left under these conditions, and therefore this would have to be interpreted by the courts.

…

2. The state too has a duty to help an indigent person in its obligation to establish and maintain a social state, which is laid down in constitutional law. It does this in the form of social assistance, which it also grants as assistance with nursing care – at the time relevant in the present case this was still governed by §§ 68 et seq. of the Federal Social Assistance Act (*Bundessozialhilfegesetz* – BSHG) – to those persons who are in need of care in their old age and cannot afford the full costs for nursing care either from their own means or from the funds of long-term care insurance. However, the support claim of an indigent person against a person liable for support who is able to pay has priority over his or her claim to social assistance (see § 2 of the Federal Social Assistance Act). If the social assistance funding agency grants social assistance despite the fact that a support claim exists, until 26 June

1993, under §§ 90 and 91 of the Federal Social Assistance Act the agency was able to send a notice in writing to the person liable for support with the effect that the support claim passed to the social assistance funding agency up to the amount of social assistance granted. From the date of its amendment by the Act on the Implementation of the Federal Consolidation Programme (*Gesetz zur Umsetzung des Föderalen Konsolidierungsprogramms* – FKPG) of 23 June 1993 (Federal Law Gazette (*Bundesgesetzblatt* – BGBl) I p. 944), § 91 of the Federal Social Assistance Act provided that for the period for which assistance is granted, the support claim of a social assistance recipient existing under private law passes by operation of law to the social assistance funding agency up to the amount of the expenditure incurred.
Social assistance law also contains provisions for taking account of income and assets. § 91.2 of the Federal Social Assistance Act new and § 91.1 sentence 2 of the Federal Social Assistance Act old provided that the support claim of a social assistance recipient passes to the social assistance funding agency, or was permitted to be assigned to the social assistance funding agency, only insofar as a recipient of assistance has to commit his or her own income and assets. This equal treatment of a person liable for support and a recipient of assistance, which restricts the passing of an existing support claim, related to assets pursuant to § 88 of the Federal Social Assistance Act, subsection 2 of which set out what must be left to the recipient of assistance as exempt assets, and subsection 3 of which provided that assets are not to be committed to the extent that this would constitute a hardship for the owner of the assets and his or her relatives entitled to support. This is the case in connection with assistance in particular situations above all if a reasonable standard of living or the maintenance of reasonable old-age provision would otherwise be considerably more difficult (see § 88.3 sentence 2 of the Federal Social Assistance Act). Finally, § 89 of the Federal Social Assistance Act created the possibility for persons who have to commit their assets for their own support under § 88 of the Federal Social Assistance Act and therefore cannot claim social assistance to nevertheless be granted social assistance as a loan if they cannot reasonably be expected to realise their assets immediately.
3. The Act to Integrate Social Assistance Law into the Code of Social Law (*Gesetz zur Einordnung des Sozialhilferechts in das Sozialgesetzbuch*) of 27 December 2003 (Federal Law Gazette I p. 3022) repealed the Federal Social Assistance Act with effect from 1 January 2005. It has been replaced by the Twelfth Book of the Code of Social Law (*Zwölftes Buch Sozialgesetzbuch* – SGB XII) – Social Assistance – which did not alter the contents of the social assistance provisions that are relevant in the present case (see §§ 61 et seq., 93-94 and 90-91 of the Twelfth Book of the Code of Social Law).

However, the fourth chapter of the Twelfth Book of the Code of Social Law integrated basic provision in old age and in the case of reduction of working capacity which those over sixty-five can claim to the extent that they cannot finance their subsistence from their income and assets (§§ 41 et seq. of the Twelfth Book of the Code of Social Law) into social assistance law (governed from 1 January 2003 to 31 December 2004 by § 2.1 of the Basic Provision Law (*Grundsicherungsgesetz*)). Under § 43.2 of the Twelfth Book of the Code of Social Law, this does not take into account support claims of the person eligible for support against children, insofar as their total annual income is less than the amount of EUR 100,000.

II.

1. The mother of the complainant lived in an old people's nursing home from July 1991 until her death in September 1995 because she was in need of long-term care. The costs of the nursing home were much higher than her income, which consisted of her own old-age pension and her widow's pension. The City of B., as the local social assistance funding agency, paid her assistance for long-term care, charged to the supra-local social assistance funding agency, under §§ 68 et seq. of the Federal Social Assistance Act. By the date of the mother's death, the sum of the assistance granted had reached the figure of approximately DM 123,000. By a notice of the same month in which the mother was accepted in the old people's nursing home, the complainant's social assistance funding agency gave notice in due form to the complainant under §§ 90 and 91 of the Federal Social Assistance Act, which was in force at the time, of the statutory assignment of the support claims of the complainant's mother against the complainant, and it later asserted the assigned rights against the complainant in court proceedings.
At this time, the complainant, who was born in the year 1939, was married with no children, and from 1970 on she worked half-time, eventually earning a net monthly income in the amount of approximately DM 1,100. In the year 1994, the married couple separated. The complainant's husband, who had not been gainfully employed since 1990, retired in 1995. The complainant's employment relationship was terminated for redundancy in autumn 1996. Together with her husband, the complainant was and is the co-owner in equal shares of a piece of real estate with a block of four flats erected on it which was intended to provide joint old-age provision. The market value of the real estate was stated as DM 660,000, although at the beginning of 1992 there were encumbrances in the amount of DM 168,000. The complainant and her husband lived in one of the four flats as the matrimonial home until they separated, and after this the complainant lived there alone. The three oth-

er flats were let out. The monthly mortgage repayments for the property were greater than the rental income.

2. In the proceedings before the Local Court (*Amtsgericht*), the social assistance funding agency applied for an order that the complainant pay it support for the period from July 1991 to January 1995 in the amount of DM 104,921.25, and from February 1995 DM 2,640.95 per month for her mother, who was being paid social assistance. It submitted that the complainant had realisable assets in the form of the real estate and building that belonged to her and her husband. It stated that it was not necessary to sell the property, since the complainant could make an acknowledgment of debt with regard to her support debts, and on the basis of this the social assistance funding agency could have a mortgage registered against the real estate in the Land Register.

The action was dismissed by the Local Court on the grounds that the complainant was not obliged to make support payments for lack of ability to pay. Her income from gainful employment and letting out property was less than the amount she would have been allowed to retain, which at all events was more than DM 1,600, according to the court. It held that the complainant did not have to commit her co-owner's share of half of the real estate for the purpose of granting support. It was true that § 1603.1 of the Civil Code in principle created an obligation to commit the capital, but only insofar as the reasonable lifelong support of the person liable was not endangered or the realisation did not result in financially unjustifiable disadvantages. But in the case of the complainant, this would be the result of a realisation of the real estate. Because the block of flats was let out in full and it was therefore not possible for a purchaser to use it himself or herself, the only proceeds of sale that could be expected would be in severe disproportion to the market value. In addition, in the case of a part auction the complainant's husband would also be indirectly forced to sell his property.

The court stated that the complainant could also not reasonably be expected to realise the real estate because it had been purchased for old-age provision. It had to be taken into account that since 1990 her husband had been in early retirement, she herself was threatened with the loss of her job and in view of her age she scarcely had a chance of finding a new job, and therefore, as a result of her unemployment, her income would be appreciably smaller in future. According to the court, every realisation of her share of the real estate would result in considerable financial disadvantages, endangering her own support, for the rest of her life, additionally taking into account the fact that the spouses had separated.

3. The social assistance funding agency appealed against the judgment of the Local Court. By an order of 5 December 1995, the Regional Court presented a settlement proposal to the parties. Under this proposal, the social assistance funding agency

was to agree to grant the support contributions it had asserted as an interest-free loan, applying § 89 of the Federal Social Assistance Act by analogy, in respect of the outstanding payment up to December 1995 in the total amount of DM 132,500 and from January 1996 in the amount of DM 2,500 per month, up to a total maximum loan amount of DM 245,000, the market value of the complainant's share of the real estate less the encumbrances. The loan was to be repayable at the end of three months after the complainant's death. At the same time, the complainant was to agree to secure the repayment of the loan in favour of the social assistance funding agency by consenting to and applying for a land charge to be registered against her co-owner's share.

In justification of this settlement proposal, the court stated that on the one hand it was undisputed that the complainant was not able to pay in the meaning of § 1603 of the Civil Code, since she was not in a position to pay support from regular earnings without endangering her own reasonable support. It was also extremely questionable whether she had a duty to realise her co-owner's share. On the other hand, there was every reason to believe that the complainant was obliged in good faith to accept the offer of a loan from the social assistance funding agency made on the basis of the legal principle of § 89 of the Federal Social Assistance Act, if this merely, without endangering her subsistence, prevented her permanently from realising her real estate.

The complainant did not accept this settlement proposal. Thereupon the social assistance funding agency altered its statement of claim and now applied for a declaration that the complainant owed the total amount of DM 125,527.92 for the long-term care expenses for her mother, who had now died, and an order that the complainant must accept the offer of an interest-free loan in this amount from the social assistance funding agency, repayable three months after the complainant's death – the social assistance funding agency confirmed that it would make this loan – and must consent to an *in rem* security.

By judgment of 3 May 1996, the Regional Court largely granted these applications. It held that the complainant was obliged to pay a support contribution owed to her mother and assigned to the social assistance funding agency in the amount of DM 123,306.88. The court ordered the complainant to accept the interest-free loan offered by the social assistance funding agency in the amount of the sum owed and, in order to secure it, to consent to the registration of a land charge in the amount of DM 123,000 against her co-owner's share. Without endangering her own support and her old-age provision, the complainant, it held, was in the position to commit her co-owner's share with the help of the interest-free loan offered to her by the social assistance funding agency, repayable only after her death, for the arrears of support owed to her mother. The court stated that the obligation of a debtor to pay did not cease if the creditor voluntarily or on the basis of a legal obligation only asserted the claim at a later date. Just as the social assistance funding agency could grant social assistance under § 89 of the Federal Social Assistance Act as a loan to an indigent person who had to commit his or her property, it could also provide the complainant as a person who owed support with the necessary funds in the form of a loan. In order to satisfy obligations to pay support, according to the court, a person liable for support also had to draw on his or her capital, and there was no general equitable limit to the realisation of this. For this reason, the complainant was all the more obliged to commit her assets if she was expected not to realise it immediately but merely to encumber it with a land charge.

It was not necessary to guarantee that the complainant received old-age provision from the property and the capital was ultimately retained for the heirs. On the contrary, the property had to be committed in such a way that it was exhausted by the probable end of the life of the person owing support. Similarly, the court held, it could not be assumed on the basis of the complainant's income situation, her rent-free accommodation and the rental income, which had not been submitted in detail, and her burden of repayment of capital and interest that by reason of the burden of the land charge the complainant was not in a position to guarantee her own support.

4. The constitutional complaint challenges this decision; in it, the complainant submits that her rights under Article 2.1 and Article 14.1 of the Basic Law (*Grundgesetz* – GG) have been violated. …

B.

The constitutional complaint is admissible and is well-founded.

The challenged decision of the Regional Court violates the complainant's fundamental right under Article 2.1 of the Basic Law. There is no basis in law for the obligation imposed on the complainant to accept an interest-free loan and to consent to a land charge being registered against her co-owner's share. The determination made by the court that the complainant is obliged to pay a support contribution owed to her mother and assigned to the social assistance funding agency because she is able to pay by reason of the interest-free loan offered her by the social assistance funding agency cannot be justified from any legal point of view. The decision therefore unconstitutionally restricts the complainant's financial freedom to dispose, protected by Article 2.1 of the Basic Law.

I.

1. Article 2.1 of the Basic Law guarantees personal freedom to act in a comprehensive sense, but only within the limits stated in the provision containing this fundamental right. It is in particular subject to the constitutional order and may be limited by this (see Decisions of the Federal Constitutional Court (*Entscheidungen des Bundesverfassungsgerichts* – BVerfGE) 6, 32 (37 et seq.); 74, 129 (151-152); 80, 137 (152-153)). This includes the legal provisions passed by the legislature or other lawmaker, including their interpretation by the courts, insofar as the provisions and their interpretation are in conformity with the Basic Law (see BVerfGE 57, 361 (378); 74, 129 (152)). In this respect, the law on support and the law on social assistance as interpreted by the courts also impose limits on personal freedom to act. However, the interpretation and application of constitutional provisions of support law and social assistance law may not lead to unconstitutional results (see BVerfGE 80, 286 (294)).

2. The interpretation of non-constitutional legal norms and their application to an individual case are matters for the courts with jurisdiction. It is only if in the process the courts violate constitutional law that the Federal Constitutional Court may intervene in response to a constitutional complaint. The mere fact that a decision is objectively wrong when measured against non-constitutional legal norms is not sufficient for this (see BVerfGE 18, 85 (92-93)). However, if the interpretation is in sharp contradiction to all applicable legal norms, and if this creates claims that have no basis whatsoever in existing law, the courts are laying claim to powers which the constitution has clearly granted to the legislature. In doing this, the courts are assuming the role of lawmakers instead of accepting their true role as administrators of the law, that is, they are ignoring their commitment to law and justice within the meaning of Article 20.3 of the Basic Law (see BVerfGE 96, 375 (394-395)). This results in their imposing a limitation on the personal freedom to act protected in Article 2.1 of the Basic Law which is no longer legitimated by the constitutional order. This is the case here.

3. The Regional Court's interpretation of the law on which the challenged decision is based does not correspond to any of the recognised methods of interpretation (on this, see BVerfGE 93, 37 (81)). Both the interpretation of § 1603.1 of the Civil Code by the Regional Court and that of §§ 90, 91, 88 and 89 of the Federal Social Assistance Act contradict the wording of the provisions and their systematic integration into the context of the provision in question (a), their objective (b), and the legislative intention associated with them (c).

a) The Regional Court's opinion of the complainant's ability to pay was based solely on the view that the complainant was obliged to commit her assets by encumber-ing her co-owner's share with a land charge to secure the interest-free loan offered to her by the social assistance funding agency. The court stated that she must accept this offer in order to fulfil her obligation to support her mother without endangering her own support or her old-age provision. Since the complainant was offered the loan after the settlement proposal of the Regional Court, the complainant's ability to pay, which the court presumed to exist, only arose at this time, that is, after the death of the complainant's mother. The court therefore based a support claim for a past period of time on an ability to pay on the part of the complainant that occurred after the mother's indigence had already ended on her death.

Basing support claims for past periods in such a way on the retroactive creation of the ability to pay in earlier periods when there was a need for support contradicts the very wording and structure of the provisions of support law and social assistance law which are relevant here.

aa) Section 1602.1 and § 1603.1 of the Civil Code contain no express reference to the temporal relationship of the indigence of the person entitled to support and the ability to pay of the person liable for support as the conditions of a support claim. But if the wording of § 1603.1 of the Civil Code is that a person who, taking into account his other obligations, is unable to provide support without endangering his own reasonable support, this shows that for the duration of the inability to pay no support claim can arise. This was even emphasised in the materials to the original Civil Code (*Motive*; loc. cit. (see *Motive zu dem Entwurfe eines Bürgerlichen Gesetzbuches für das Deutsche Reich*, vol. IV, 2nd ed. 1896, pp. 687-688)). But since under § 1602.1 of the Civil Code, on the other hand, a support claim only exists when the person entitled to support is indigent, a support claim under § 1601 of the Civil Code can exist only if both conditions are fulfilled at the same time.

bb) The wording and legislative context of § 90.1 of the Federal Social Assistance Act old and § 91.1 of the Federal Social Assistance Act new also presumed that the statutory assignment of support claims required temporal concurrence of indigence and ability to pay. They permitted the statutory assignment of support claims to which the recipient of assistance is entitled for the period for which assistance is given. This implies that the support claim must exist in the period during which assistance is given, which is subject to the ability to pay of the person liable for support in this period.

Notwithstanding these statutory conditions for the assignment of an existing support claim, the Regional Court assumed that such a claim existed against the complainant, although in the period when social assistance was granted to her mother even in the Regional Court's own opinion she was not yet able to pay, for lack of a loan offer. In this connection, the Regional Court's argument is not convincing when it states that the basic obligation to draw in addition on one's main capital

fund to fulfil obligations to pay support, if appropriate by lending against property and taking a loan, also results in the person liable for support only later paying the support owed and thus fulfilling the obligation only after the end of the periods of indigence. Under §§ 1601 and 1603 of the Civil Code and under §§ 90 and 91 of the Federal Social Assistance Act, what matters is not the manner in which a person liable for support is drawn on to satisfy a support claim against him or her, but solely whether the person liable for support is/was able to pay during the period when the person entitled was indigent, that is, whether the person liable for support was able to satisfy the need for support during this period without endangering his or her own support, for example by taking a loan against his or her property. However, even in the opinion of the Regional Court such a possibility was not available to the complainant until the social assistance funding agency offered her an interest-free loan, and thus only after the end of the period of her mother's need.
cc) § 89 of the Federal Social Assistance Act was also invoked by the Regional Court as the basis of a support claim against the complainant in a manner that is in clear contradiction to the wording of this provision and its systematic integration into the structure of statutes on social assistance law. The provision referred to § 88 of the Federal Social Assistance Act, which determined what assets of a person's own are to be committed before a person may claim social assistance for indigence. If usable assets are available, that is, if there is no indigence, social assistance might nevertheless be granted as a loan under § 89 of the Federal Social Assistance Act, if the assets cannot be realised immediately or if this would constitute a hardship. The application of § 89 of the Federal Social Assistance Act therefore required that there was no indigence. Its application by analogy to a person liable for support with assets may logically be possible at best if the person liable for support too were obliged to commit his or her assets and would therefore be able to pay, but in place of this he or she had, in order to avoid hardship, been offered a loan with the help of which he or she could satisfy the support obligations. Just as the granting of social assistance in the form of a loan cannot end the indigence of a person seeking assistance and thus that person's claim for social assistance, an application of § 89 of the Federal Social Assistance Act by analogy to the situation of a person liable for support by granting a loan cannot give that person the ability to pay.
The inapplicability of § 89 of the Federal Social Assistance Act also follows from § 90.1 sentence 1 of the Federal Social Assistance Act old and § 91.1 sentence 1 of the Federal Social Assistance Act new, which provided that only a support claim which actually existed in the period when assistance was granted might be assigned to the social assistance funding agency. This assignment was further limited by § 91.1 sentence 2 of the Federal Social Assistance Act old and § 91.2 sentence 1 of the Federal Social Assistance Act new, which referred to the fourth section of the

Federal Social Assistance Act and thus also to §§ 88 and 89 of the Federal Social Assistance Act, to the proportion of his or her income and assets which a person seeking assistance is reasonably expected to commit. On the other hand, if there was no support claim, no statutory assignment under §§ 90 and 91 of the Federal Social Assistance Act was possible.

b) The interpretation of the Regional Court also contradicts the purpose of the provisions applied. The support obligation of lineal relatives is laid down in §§ 1601 et seq. of the Civil Code and serves to secure mutual support within the family. The principle that applies here is that in the first instance each person must ensure his or her own support. Thus only persons who are not able to do this are entitled to support (§ 1602.1 of the Civil Code), and only persons who are in the position to pay support over and above their own reasonable needs are liable for support (§ 1603.1 of the Civil Code). At the same time, §§ 1606 et seq. of the Civil Code lay down the order of priority of the persons liable for support in relation to those entitled to support. This establishment and limitation of support obligations between relatives is definitively laid down in the Civil Code. Social assistance law relates the claims it creates to these civil-law support obligations, but it does not alter them, as was expressly emphasised by § 2.2 sentence 1 of the Federal Social Assistance Act. Consequently, the support obligations have no statutory basis in social assistance law. On the contrary, the purpose of social assistance is to make it possible for persons who cannot support themselves and who do not receive the necessary assistance from others, for example from a relative with a support obligation (see § 1.1 of the Federal Social Assistance Act) to lead lives that are in keeping with human dignity (see § 1.2 of the Federal Social Assistance Act).

aa) This subordination of social assistance as against existing support claims is also expressed in §§ 90 and 91 of the Federal Social Assistance Act, which ensured, when support claims of the recipient of assistance were assigned, that the social assistance funding agencies ultimately have to bear only the costs of social assistance for which persons liable to make support payments to the recipient of assistance cannot be called on. But the possibility created here of refinancing social assistance payments that have been granted by asserting assigned support claims does not exist where no support claim whatsoever exists in the absence of ability to pay on the part of the person liable for support. Then social assistance ceases to be subordinate, and the legal claim to social assistance takes effect.

bb) It runs counter to the principle of social assistance law of granting a legal claim to assistance, albeit a claim that is subordinate to a support claim, to justify under social assistance law, by means of a loan given by the social assistance funding agency, a support claim that does not exist in civil law. This legal construction would eventually cause social assistance claims to be extinguished completely. For

if it could be ensured with the help of a loan that a person liable for support had the ability to pay, it would be up to the social assistance funding agency to decide that a social assistance claim was not to take effect. By granting a loan, the agency could have the social assistance payments granted refinanced to itself again and again by the person liable for support paying off the outstanding principal. As a result, the existence of a support claim and therefore also of a social assistance claim of the indigent person would depend on the actions of the social assistance funding agency, with the consequence that although an indigent person would be unsuccessful in asserting a support claim against a person liable for support who by reason of his or her income and assets was not able to pay, the social assistance funding agency could nevertheless substantiate the support claim by offering an appropriate loan and in this way could relieve itself of its obligation to grant social assistance. This would not only result in the removal of the social assistance claim laid down in §§ 1 and 2 of the Federal Social Assistance Act, but it would also contravene the purpose of social assistance law that the granting of assistance should not be left to the free decision of the state social assistance funding agency, but instead a legal claim to social assistance should be created subject to the conditions provided in the statute. In addition, it would run counter to the obligation to establish and maintain a social state of Article 20.1 of the Basic Law in conjunction with Article 1.1 of the Basic Law, which requires persons to be given a claim to assistance from the state in order to ensure that they reach subsistence level.
It was precisely for this reason that the legislature specifically did not make it possible to give an indigent person a loan in order to remove the indigence in this way and thus to end the claim to social assistance and have the payments granted later reimbursed. On the contrary, in § 89 of the Federal Social Assistance Act the legislature permitted social assistance to be granted by way of a loan only where the person seeking assistance was not indigent by reason of property of his or her own which could be committed. The purpose of this legislation is turned on its head if this provision, which existed in favour of a non-indigent person seeking assistance, is used by way of analogy to create a support claim and thus to the detriment of the person liable for support.
c) Finally, the interpretation of the Regional Court also runs counter to the intention of the legislature. Despite the legal policy discussion in the last years on the preservation of parental support …, the legislature did not make any alterations to the family-law provisions on support for relatives in §§ 1601 et seq. of the Civil Code. It still proceeds on the basis of the mutual family responsibility for one another which exists between parents and children, which is laid down in the mutual duty of assistance and respect and the duty to give support in § 1618a of the Civil Code (see BVerfGE 57, 170 (178)).

aa) However, Article 6.2 of the Basic Law expressly creates only the right and duty of the parents to give their children care and bring them up, and thus also to give them support (see BVerfGE 108, 52 (72); …). In contrast, no duty of the children to give their parents support can be derived from the wording of the Basic Law. But Article 6.1 of the Basic Law places the family under the particular protection of the state order. In the structuring of family responsibility, the legislature is not constitutionally prevented from not only imposing on the parents obligations of support towards their children, but also imposing such duties on children towards their parents if the latter are not in a position to secure their own support.
bb) In laying down the order of priority of support claims within lineal family relationships, the legislature defined the relevant support obligations hierarchically. While under § 1609.1 of the Civil Code parents are primarily obliged to give support to their children, and over and above this under § 1603.2 of the Civil Code they also have an obligation to unmarried minor children and unmarried children who have reached the age of majority up to the age of twenty-one to commit all available means equally for their own support and the support of the children, children are liable for the support of their parents before the relatives in the ascending line (§ 1606.1 of the Civil Code). However, the claim of the parents is subordinate to all other claims of the children, the spouses and the other descendants of the person liable for support (§ 1609 of the Civil Code); in addition, the child liable for support may only be called on to pay support to the extent that a reasonable amount remains for the child's own support (§ 1603.1 of the Civil Code).
Here, the legislature indicated that within the structure of support law it attaches differing weight to the two obligations to pay support. It not only gave subordinate weight to parental support in contrast to child support, but also markedly limited the scope of the obligation in contrast to that of the duty to grant child support. The legislature did not merely take account of the differing dependence and role of the indigent persons in the family support system. The subordinate treatment of parental support also, as the Federal Court of Justice (*Bundesgerichtshof* – BGH) emphasised (see BGH, *Zeitschrift für das gesamte Familienrecht* – FamRZ 1992, p. 795), corresponds to the fundamentally different life situation in which the obligation to support takes effect in each case. Parents have to care for their children and must as a general rule expect to give them support even after they reach the age of majority, until the children, after their education and training, are able to support themselves with their own income. In contrast, the obligation to give parental support usually takes effect when the children have long since started their own families, are exposed to support claims of their own children and spouses, and have to provide for themselves and their own old-age security. In addition, one or both par-

ents now have a need for support in old age which cannot be met by their income, in particular their pension, above all if they need long-term care.

The legislature took account of these cumulative demands when it not only gave subordinate priority to parental support, but in § 1603 of the Civil Code also ensured that the child retains reasonable support of his or her own, that is, appropriate to the child's personal circumstances. The Federal Government also pointed out this intention of the legislature in the oral hearing, and stated that the subordinate and limited degree to which children can be called on for parental support was at the same time intended to take account of the circumstance that the children are already called on to cover their parents' old-age support by way of their contributions to pensions insurance.

cc) The latest legislative developments further emphasise the relatively weak legal position accorded by the legislature to parental support.

Through the step-by-step reduction of the benefits provided by the statutory old-age pension scheme and the introduction of private old-age provision promoted by statute (known as the Riester Pension) by the Act for the Reform of the Statutory Old-Age Pension Scheme and to Promote a Funded Old-Age Provision Scheme (Retirement Savings Act – *Gesetz zur Reform der gesetzlichen Rentenversicherung und zur Förderung eines kapitalgedeckten Altersvorsorgevermögens – Altersvermögensgesetz* – AVmG) of 26 June 2001 (Federal Law Gazette I p. 1310) and the Retirement Savings Amendment Act (*Altersvermögensergänzungsgesetz* – AVmEG) of 21 March 2001 (Federal Law Gazette I p. 403), the legislature has emphasised the responsibility each individual has to provide in time and adequately for his or her old age alongside the statutory old-age pension scheme. On the one hand, this emphasises the principle which is also laid down in § 1602.1 of the Civil Code that a person must primarily ensure his or her own support. On the other hand, it is associated with the expectation that provision for oneself also extends to periods in future in which no further earned income is to be expected, and therefore appropriate financial precautions must be taken prior to this in order to ensure one's own old-age support in an amount appropriate to one's previous standard of living, which is no longer guaranteed by the statutory old-age pension scheme alone. In this way, parental support for old-age provision is given still less value, and at the same time it is expected of an adult child liable for support that in addition to the other support burdens and the old-age provision of earlier generations, he or she will also bear the burden of his or her own old-age provision. This must be taken appropriately into account when his or her remaining reasonable support is determined under § 1603.1 of the Civil Code (see BGH, FamRZ 2002, p. 1698; FamRZ 2004, p. 1184).

In particular, however, by introducing a basic provision in old age and in the case of a reduction of earning capacity from 1 January 2003 through the Basic Provision Act (*Grundsicherungsgesetz*) and from 1 January 2005 by §§ 41 et seq. of the Twelfth Book of the Code of Social Law, the legislature has made it clear that burdening adult children with the duty to pay parental support is to be subjected to limits, taking account of their own personal circumstances. § 43.2 of the Twelfth Book of the Code of Social Law has now introduced an income limit of EUR 100,000 per annum, up to which children may receive income without support claims of their parents against them being taken into account in the grant of basic provision in old age. In addition, there is a statutory presumption that the income of a child liable for support does not exceed this limit.

This too clearly shows the intention of the legislature, not to release children completely from the duty to give support to their parents, but in considering whether a support claim against the children exists to take into account the subordination of this claim and also the particular situation of the person liable for support with regard to burdens.

II.

In view of the foregoing, the Regional Court, with its acting as a law-maker in presuming that a support claim exists in contradiction to the wording of all legal provisions that are relevant to the decision, their legislative context and the recognised methods of interpretation, left the firm basis of established law. Its interpretation of the legal provisions applied is inconsistent with the relationship of support law and social assistance law laid down by the legislature and encroaches without a legal basis on a person's personal freedom to act under Article 2.1 of the Basic Law when it calls on that person, who is not able to pay by reason of her own income and assets, to make support payments. The decision of the Regional Court therefore has no basis in the constitutional order, which only sets limits to the personal freedom to act protected in Article 2.1 of the Basic Law, and it violates the complainant's right under Article 2.1 of the Basic Law. The decision is reversed and the matter is referred back to the Regional Court.

…

Justices: Papier, Haas, Hömig, Steiner, Hohmann-Dennhardt, Hoffmann-Riem, Bryde, Gaier

No. 47

BVerfGE 115, 259
of 28 March 2006 – 1 BvL 10/01 –
"Maternity protection period case"

HEADNOTE:

It is incompatible with Article 6.4 of the Basic Law (*Grundgesetz* – GG) if periods in which women interrupt their employment requiring the payment of social security contributions are not, because of the prohibitions of employment under maternity protection law, taken into account in the calculation of the qualifying period in statutory unemployment insurance.

Order of the First Senate of 28 March 2006
– 1 BvL 10/01 –

in the proceedings for constitutional review as to whether the Third Book of the Code of Social Law (*Drittes Buch Sozialgesetzbuch* – SGB III) of 24 March 1997 (Federal Law Gazette (*Bundesgesetzblatt* – BGBl) I p. 594) was compatible with Article 3.1 and Article 6.4 of the Basic Law (*Grundgesetz* – GG) insofar as women who, because of statutory maternity protection, interrupted employment requiring the payment of social security contributions and received maternity pay were not compulsorily insured in this period, unlike persons receiving sickness benefit – suspension of proceedings and submission order of the Federal Social Court (*Bundessozialgericht*) of 20 June 2001 – B 11 AL 20/01 R –.

RULING:

1. It was incompatible with Article 6.4 of the Basic Law that periods in which women interrupted their employment requiring the payment of social security contributions because of the prohibitions of employment under maternity protection law were not, under the law in force from 1 January 1998 to 31 December 2002,

taken into account in the calculation of the qualifying period in statutory unemployment insurance.

2. By 31 March 2007, the legislature must pass provisions that comply with the constitutional requirements. If no provisions are passed within this period, then in proceedings in which there has been no final and non-appealable administrative or judicial decision and in which the grant of unemployment benefit depends on taking into account the period of prohibition of employment under maternity protection law in the calculation of the qualifying period under the law in force from 1 January 1998 until 31 December 2002, the following provision is to be applied mutatis mutandis: § 107 sentence 1 no. 5 letter b of the Employment Promotion Act (*Arbeitsförderungsgesetz* – AFG) in the version of the Budget Support Act 1984 (Act on Measures for the Relief of the Public Budgets and for the Stabilisation of the Financial Situation of the Pension Insurance Scheme and on the Prolongation of the Investment Assistance Levy, *Gesetz über Maßnahmen zur Entlastung der öffentlichen Haushalte und zur Stabilisierung der Finanzentwicklung in der Rentenversicherung sowie über die Verlängerung der Investitionshilfeabgabe, Haushaltsbegleitgesetz 1984* – HBeglG 1984) in force on 31 December 1997.

EXTRACT FROM GROUNDS:

A.

The subject of the proceedings is the question whether it was unconstitutional that under the employment promotion law in force between 1998 and 2002 periods in which mothers interrupted employment requiring the payment of social security contributions because of the prohibitions under maternity protection law were not taken into account in the calculation of the qualifying period for receiving unemployment benefit.

I.

1. Maternity protection under the Act on the Protection of Working Mothers (*Gesetz zum Schutze der erwerbstätigen Mutter, Mutterschutzgesetz* – MuSchG, Maternity Protection Act) of 24 January 1952 (Federal Law Gazette I p. 69) in the version relevant in the present case, as promulgated on 17 January 1997 (Federal Law Gazette I p. 22), is intended to protect a mother who is employed and her child against dangers arising in the workplace, excessive demands and injury to health. In this statute, the legislature also fulfils its mandate of protection under Article 6.4 of

the Basic Law (see Decisions of the Federal Constitutional Court (*Entscheidungen des Bundesverfassungsgerichts* – BVerfGE) 37, 121 (125-126); 109, 64 (85-86)). Women who enjoy the protection of the statute may not be employed for six weeks before and eight weeks after giving birth (§ 3.2, § 6.1 of the Maternity Protection Act). But they should not be obliged to forgo their income from employment in this period. For the period of prohibition of employment, they receive benefit in lieu of income in the form of maternity pay (§ 13 of the Maternity Protection Act) and a contribution to maternity pay from their employer linked to the amount of their pay (§ 14 of the Maternity Protection Act).

2. The periods of prohibition of employment under maternity protection law have been treated in varying ways in German social security law in the calculation of the qualifying period to acquire an entitlement to unemployment benefit (on the legal position until the year 1979 see BVerfGE 60, 68 (69-70)). In the time from 1979 to 1997, § 104.1 sentence 3 of the Employment Promotion Act as amended by the Act Introducing Maternity Leave (*Gesetz zur Einführung eines Mutterschaftsurlaubs* – MuUrlG) of 25 June 1979 (Federal Law Gazette I p. 797) treated receiving maternity pay as equivalent to an employment creating an obligation to pay social security contributions if an employment creating an obligation to pay social security contributions was interrupted by pregnancy or maternity. The mother was not required to pay a contribution to unemployment insurance.

3. In the period relevant in the present case, from 1998 to 2002, § 123 sentence 1 of the Third Book of the Code of Social Law as amended by the First Act to Amend the Third Book of the Code of Social Law and Other Statutes (*Erstes Gesetz zur Änderung des Dritten Buches Sozialgesetzbuch und anderer Gesetze*) of 16 December 1997 (Federal Law Gazette I p. 2970) provided in respect of the qualifying period:

Qualifying period

> The qualifying period has been satisfied by a person who, within the overall qualifying period,
> 1. for a minimum of twelve months,
> 2. in the case of those doing military service or community service as an alternative to military service (§ 25.2 sentence 2, § 26.1 nos. 2 and 3 and § 26.4) for a minimum of ten months or
> 3. in the case of a seasonal worker for a minimum of six months
>
> was in an employment requiring the payment of social security contributions.

The dates and duration of the overall qualifying period in which the employment requiring the payment of social security contributions was required to have existed are laid down in § 124 of the Third Book of the Code of Social Law. The wording of the provision as amended on 16 December 1997, insofar as it is relevant here, was as follows:

Overall qualifying period

(1) The overall qualifying period shall be three years and shall begin on the date before all other conditions of an entitlement to unemployment benefit are fulfilled.
(2) The overall qualifying period shall not extend into an earlier overall qualifying period in which the unemployed person had completed a qualifying period.
(3) The overall qualifying period shall not include

1. periods in which the unemployed person, as a carer, cared for a ... relative ... for at least fourteen hours per week,
2. periods spent looking after and bringing up a child of the unemployed person that is under three years of age,
3. periods of self-employment,
4. periods in which the unemployed person received a maintenance allowance ... under this Book,
5. periods in which the unemployed person received a temporary allowance ... from a rehabilitation organisation.

In the cases in numbers 3 to 5, the overall qualifying period shall end at the latest five years after it commences.

Under § 24.1 of the Third Book of the Code of Social Law, an employment requiring the payment of social security contributions in the meaning of § 123 exists for persons who are compulsorily insured as employees or for other reasons. Under § 25.1 of the Third Book of the Code of Social Law, those who receive pay for employment or are in vocational training are compulsorily insured. § 26 of the Third Book of the Code of Social Law contains the provisions on the other instances of compulsory insurance. The wording of the provision in the version relevant in the present case as amended on 16 December 1997, insofar as it is relevant here, is as follows:

Other compulsorily insured persons

(1) The following are compulsorily insured:
1. disabled young persons …,
2. persons who, by reason of statutory obligation, perform military service or community service as an alternative to military service for longer than three days ...,
3. persons during the period of military service in the "readiness to serve" stage …,
4. prisoners …

(2) Persons are compulsorily insured in the period for which they
1. receive sickness benefit, disabled persons' sick pay or injury grant from a benefit agency, or a temporary allowance from an agency responsible for the provision of medical rehabilitation, if immediately before this benefit commenced they were compulsorily insured or receiving ongoing benefit in lieu of income under this Book.
2. receive daily sickness benefit from a private health insurance company, if immediately before this benefit commenced they were compulsorily insured or receiving ongoing benefit in lieu of income under this Book.

(3) and (4) …

Under these provisions, the receipt of maternity pay did not create a compulsorily insured status. It can be inferred from the legislative reasons that the provision in force until that date on treating periods of receipt of maternity pay as equivalent to employment requiring the payment of social security contributions was to cease because this equal treatment would not have complied with the principle of insurance, which was to be introduced consistently as a result of the reform (see *Bundestag* printed paper (*Bundestagsdrucksache* – BTDrucks) 13/4941, pp. 143, 158).
4. …

II.

…

1. The plaintiff, who was born in 1968, was from 1 February 1991 to 30 September 1994 in employment requiring the payment of social security contributions as a publishers' representative. From 1 October 1994 to 31 January 1995 she was unemployed and received unemployment benefit. From 1 February 1995 to 31 December 1996, she again worked as a publishers' representative. In 1997 she was unem-

ployed again and received unemployment benefit for a total of 312 working days. After this, from 1 January 1998 to 31 January 1999, she worked as a bookseller. In May 1998, she gave birth to a child. The protection periods under § 3.2 and § 6.1 of the Maternity Protection Act ran from 3 April until 12 July 1998 inclusive. During the protection periods, the plaintiff received maternity pay and contributions to maternity pay. From 13 July 1998 to 31 January 1999, she was again employed in a bookshop for 21.5 hours per week, and – in addition to child-raising benefit – she received pay.

2. On 1 February 1999, the plaintiff once more registered for employment and applied for contributory unemployment benefit to be granted. This application was refused by the Federal Institute for Employment (*Bundesanstalt für Arbeit*) of the time, which was the defendant in the original proceedings ... The Institute stated that, after exhausting the entitlement on 30 December 1997, the plaintiff did not establish a new future right to unemployment benefit. During the overall qualifying period that applied to the establishment of her entitlement, she had compulsorily insured status only for 295 days, and thus for less than the twelve months required under § 123 of the Third Book of the Code of Social Law to fulfil the qualifying period. In this calculation, the whole time of the protection periods, when she was receiving maternity pay, was not to be taken into account, for this period did not confer compulsorily insured status. For this reason, it could not contribute to completing the qualifying period.

3. The plaintiff took legal action [– which was unsuccessful at first –] to challenge the rejection of her application. ... The plaintiff appealed to the Federal Social Court (*Bundessozialgericht*), which stayed the proceedings and submitted to the Federal Constitutional Court (*Bundesverfassungsgericht*) the question as to whether the Third Book of the Code of Social Law is compatible with Article 3.1 and Article 6.4 of the Basic Law insofar as women who, because of statutory maternity protection, interrupted employment requiring the payment of social security contributions and received maternity pay were not compulsorily insured in the years from 1998 to 2002, unlike persons receiving sickness benefit.

...

III.

...

B.

It was incompatible with Article of the Basic Law that periods in which women interrupted their employment requiring the payment of social security contributions because of the prohibitions of employment under maternity protection law were not, under the law in force from 1 January 1998 to 31 December 2002, taken into account in the calculation of the qualifying period in statutory unemployment insurance.

I.

1. Article 6.4 of the Basic Law contains a binding mandate that the legislature should allow every mother to enjoy the protection and care of the community. In principle it also commits the legislature to make compensation for financial burdens on the mother that are related to her pregnancy and maternity. To this extent, Article 6.4 of the Basic Law protects mothers in a way comparable to the protection of marriage and the family by Article 6.1 of the Basic Law (see BVerfGE 60, 68 (74)). This also applies to the area of social security (see Federal Constitutional Court, *Neue Juristische Wochenschrift* – NJW 2005, p. 2443 (2447) on the building up of pension expectancies in the professional pension scheme for lawyers) and in particular to social security insurance (see BVerfGE 60, 68 (74) with further references).

2. The mandate of protection of Article 6.4 of the Basic Law admittedly does not mean that the legislature is required to make compensation for every financial burden connected with maternity (see BVerfGE 60, 68 (74)). In exactly the same way as in the case of Article 6.1 of the Basic Law, the legislature is not obliged to comply with the requirement of promotion of employment measures notwithstanding other concerns (see BVerfGE 82, 60 (81) …) But if, as in § 3.2 and § 6.1 of the Maternity Protection Act, the legislature forbids the woman for a certain period of time before and after the birth of a child to continue or resume her employment requiring the payment of social security contributions, it is required to make compensation as far as possible for the disadvantages under social law arising from this prohibition. This includes protection by social security law in the case of unemployment.

The mother who is affected by the prohibition of employment is prevented from building up or continuing to build up a future right in statutory unemployment insurance under § 123 of the Third Book of the Code of Social Law by continuing or resuming her employment requiring the payment of social security contributions. This consequence of the prohibitions of employment under maternity protection law may not be permitted to disadvantage the woman as against other employees who are not affected by such prohibitions. In principle, the legislature has the freedom to decide how it will design the support of mothers imposed on it by Article 6.4 of the Basic Law, but this freedom is in this respect qualified and restricted, by reason of its own legislative acts in protecting mothers-to-be and children by prohibitions of employment. Measured against Article 6.4 of the Basic Law, the protection intended by the prohibitions of employment remains incomplete if it is not accompanied by measures which make compensation as far as possible for the consequent unfavourable treatment of the mother, who is prevented during the maternity protection period from fulfilling the qualifying period (see also BVerfGE 60, 68 (77)).

Article 6.4 of the Basic Law puts the principle of the social welfare state into specific terms for the special area of maternity protection (see BVerfGE 32, 273 (279)), and it is therefore incompatible with Article 6.4 that the periods of prohibition of employment were not taken into account in the calculation of the qualifying period in statutory unemployment insurance during the period relevant in the present case, between 1998 and 2002, and therefore contrary to the law in force before and after this period ... In the case where the mother was unemployed, the legislature, in a way that no longer complied with the mandate of protection of Article 6.4 of the Basic Law, made it more difficult for her to obtain unemployment benefit. Moreover, this was also in contradiction to the treatment under social security law of persons who similarly involuntarily interrupt their employment because of illness and receive sickness benefit; under § 26.2 no. 1 of the Third Book of the Code of Social Law, these persons are compulsorily insured and are able to build up or continue to build up a future right while they are receiving benefits.

a) The need to take into account the period of prohibition of employment before the birth of the child in the calculation of the qualifying period does not cease to apply by reason of the fact that the mother may in principle waive the protection given to her and her child under § 3.2 of the Maternity Protection Act and continue her employment requiring the payment of social security contributions until the birth.

The legislature did not create the special provision in § 3.2 of the Maternity Protection Act in order to give pregnant women the possibility of remaining gainfully employed for financial reasons in the period in question and in this way of avoiding the disadvantage under social security law in the present case. On the contrary, in the combination of maternity pay and employer's contribution to maternity pay it intended to protect mothers during the prohibition of employment, even before they gave birth, in such a way that there was no incentive for them to work in order to secure their livelihood while taking the risk of dangers to their health (see BVerfGE 109, 64 (86)). This circumstance made it easier for the legislature to decide, in the interest of the mother-to-be, whose protection is the particular aim of Article 6.4 of the Basic Law (see BVerfGE 32, 273 (277); 52, 357 (365)), not to introduce an absolute prohibition of employment ... The special provision is based on the experience that it can be psychologically preferable for a pregnant woman to take her mind off other matters with her previous work to which she is accustomed, as long as her health permits (see Decisions of the Federal Labour Court (*Entscheidungen des Bundesarbeitsgerichts* – BAGE) 102, 218 (224)). Under the special provision, as a general rule the prohibition of employment is to continue in effect; this also serves to protect the unborn child.

The detailed drafting of the special provision reflects this. Thus, under § 3.2 half-sentence 2 of the Maternity Protection Act, a woman may at any time notify her employer that she revokes her declaration that she will continue in employment. She may not, even by contract, waive this right of revocation, which may be exercised without stating reasons ... The declaration of the woman that she will be prepared to work during the protection period is, according to unanimous opinion, subject to strict requirements, for going to work during the protection period is relatively dangerous in many cases .... § 3.2 of the Maternity Protection Act requires an express declaration for this purpose. In addition, the prohibition of employment may be varied only by the woman. The employer must comply with it of its own accord as soon as it is aware of the pregnancy. The prohibition of employment is mandatory for the employer ....

b) The three-year overall qualifying period of § 124.1 of the Third Book of the Code of Social Law, during which the qualifying period for the entitlement to benefits must be completed, does not compensate for the disadvantage under social security law described in a manner that complies with the requirements of Article 6.4 of the Basic Law. It must be conceded in favour of the legislature that the extension of the overall qualifying period from two to three years, which was introduced by § 104.3 half-sentence 1 of the Employment Promotion Act of 25 June 1969 (Federal Law Gazette I p. 582) and retained in the Third Book of the Code of Social Law, made it easier to complete the qualifying period; with this justification, the legislature removed the "privilege given to the time of maternity" in employment promotion law (see written report by the Committee on Labour of the German *Bundestag* of 6 May 1969, *Bundestag* printed paper V/4110, p. 18). The extension was suitable above all to benefit insured persons whose employment was particularly often interrupted (see BVerfGE 60, 68 (75, 76)). In this respect, as a general provision, it also benefited the mothers who had interrupted their gainful employment for some time as a result of the prohibitions of employment (see BVerfGE 60, 68 (76)). But the facts on which the original proceedings are based show that in the case of a far from untypical alternation of employment, maternity protection and unemployment, it was not sufficiently suitable to make social security provision for the case of unemployment in a way satisfying the mandate of protection of Article 6.4 of the Basic Law. The three-year overall qualifying period did not give the plaintiff an advantage, because a previous overall qualifying period, by reason of § 124.2 of the Third Book of the Code of Social Law, prevented an extension of the overall qualifying period that was decisive for her repeated entitlement to unemployment benefit.

c) In these and in other sets of circumstances, it was also of no use for the person affected that some of the periods of prohibitions of employment under maternity protection law were at the same time periods of child raising, which under § 124.3 sentence 1 no. 2 of the Third Book of the Code of Social Law indirectly additionally extended the overall qualifying period of § 124.1 of the Third Book of the Code of Social Law. The legislature later also realised this. In the legislative reasons for the Act to Reform the Instruments of Labour Market Policy (*Job-AQTIV-Gesetz*), it is stated that the entitlement to benefit in lieu of income, under the previous law, was dependent on a multiplicity of rigid time limits, which in particular largely disregarded the concerns of mothers. As a result, coincidences in the chronological sequence of qualifying period, maternity protection and child-raising period were decisive for the entitlement to benefits and thus for the promotion of integration into employment (see *Bundestag* printed paper 14/6944, p. 26).

II.

…

C. – I.

The subject of the judicial referral is not the review of the constitutionality of a particular legal provision, but the failure of the legislature to make a provision in the period from 1 January 1998 to 31 December 2002. As a result of this, the only possible conclusion is a declaration of incompatibility.

The legislature must pass a constitutional provision by 31 March 2007. If no provisions are passed within this period, then in proceedings in which there has been no final and non-appealable administrative or judicial decision and in which the grant of unemployment benefit depends on taking into account the periods of prohibition of employment under maternity protection law in the calculation of the qualifying period under the law in force from 1 January 1998 to 31 December 2002, the following provision is to be applied with the necessary modifications: § 107 sentence 1 no 5 letter b of the Employment Promotion Act in the version in force on 31 December 1997 of the Act on Measures for the Relief of the Public Budgets and for the Stabilisation of the Financial Situation of the Pension Insurance Scheme and on the Prolongation of the Investment Assistance Levy (*Gesetz über Maßnahmen zur Entlastung der öffentlichen Haushalte und zur Stabilisierung der Finanzentwicklung in der Rentenversicherung sowie über die Verlängerung der Investitionshilfeabgabe, Haushaltsbegleitgesetz 1984,* Budget Support Act 1984) of 22 December 1983 (Federal Law Gazette I p. 1532).

II.

…

Justices: Papier, Haas, Hömig, Steiner, Hohmann-Dennhardt, Hoffmann-Riem, Bryde, Gaier

The legislature implemented the Federal Constitutional Court's decision by § 427a, which was newly inserted into the Third Book of the Code of Social Law by Article 3 no. 8a of the Older Persons' Employment Opportunities Act (Gesetz zur Verbesserung der Beschäftigungschancen älterer Menschen) *of 19 April 2007 (Federal Law Gazette I 2007 p. 538). It reads as follows:*

"§ 427a Equal treatment of maternity periods

(1) To persons who in the period from 1 January 1998 to 31 December 2002 received special assistance according to the Maternity Protection Act or maternity pay, § 107 sentence 1 no. 5 letter b of the Employment Promotion Act in the version in force until 31 December 1997 shall apply mutatis mutandis with regard to fulfilling the qualifying period required for a claim to unemployment benefit and to the duration of the claim.

(2) The Employment Agency (Agentur für Arbeit) *shall*

1. *ex officio*
    a) *render a new decision on claims to unemployment benefit which were rejected for the sole reason that periods according to § 107 sentence 1 no. 5 letter b of the Employment Promotion Act in the version applicable until 31 December 1997 had not been taken into account if the decision had not yet become unappealable on 28 March 2006,*

b) on claims to unemployment benefit that have not yet, or only provisionally, been decided upon because the claimant received one of the maternity benefits mentioned in subsection 1;

2. as for the remainder, it shall render a new decision upon application."

§ 427a entered into force only on 1 May 2007; thus, the legislature did not observe the time-limit for the implementation of the decision (31 March 2007). As had been ordered by the Federal Constitutional Court, § 107 sentence 1 no. 5 letter b of the Employment Promotion Act in the version of the Budget Support Act 1984 in force on 31 December 1997 was therefore applied mutatis mutandis in the period between 31 March and 1 May 2007.

No. 48

BVerfGE 117, 202
of 13 February 2007 – 1 BvR 421/05 –
"Secret paternity test case"

HEADNOTES:

1. **In order to put into effect the right of a legal father to know that his child is biologically his (Article 2.1 in conjunction with Article 1.1 of the Basic Law (*Grundgesetz* – GG)), the legislature must make available a suitable procedure solely to determine paternity.**
2. **It is in conformity with the Basic Law if the courts, on the ground of violation of the right to informational self-determination of the child involved, protected by Article 2.1 in conjunction with Article 1.1 of the Basic Law, refuse to recognise as evidence secretly obtained genetic paternity test reports.**

Order of the First Senate of 13 February 2007
on the basis of the oral hearing of 21 November 2006
– 1 BvR 421/05 –

in the proceedings regarding the constitutional complaint of Mr. S. – authorised representative: …, law firm – against a) the judgment of the Federal Court of Justice (*Bundesgerichtshof* – BGH) of 12 January 2005 – XII ZR 227/03 –, b) the judgment of the Celle Higher Regional Court (*Oberlandesgericht*) of 29 October 2003 – 15 UF 84/03 –, c) the judgment of the Hildesheim Local Court (*Amtsgericht*) of 4 March 2003 – 37 F 37525/02 Kl –.

RULING:

1. In violation of Article 2.1 in conjunction with Article 1.1 of the Basic Law (*Grundgesetz* – GG), the legislature has failed to provide a procedure in a legal

form which is capable of clarifying whether a child is the biological child of its legal father and in which solely this paternity can be confirmed or denied.
2. The legislature is instructed to make such an arrangement to determine whether or not a child is the biological child of its legal father by 31 March 2008.
3. Apart from this, the constitutional complaint is rejected as unfounded.
4. …

EXTRACT FROM GROUNDS:

A.

The constitutional complaint relates to whether it is possible to use as evidence in judicial proceedings contesting paternity a DNA test report to clarify paternity obtained secretly, without the consent of the child in question or its mother as its legal representative, and thus at the same time it relates to the question as to whether applicable law gives the legal father of a child an adequate possibility of obtaining knowledge and determining that a child is biologically his.

I.

1. § 1592 of the Civil Code (*Bürgerliches Gesetzbuch* – BGB) provides that the father of a child is either the man who at the date of the birth is married to the child's mother (no. 1) or the man who has acknowledged paternity (no. 2), and, finally, the man whose paternity has been judicially determined under § 1600d of the Civil Code or § 640h.2 of the Code of Civil Procedure (*Zivilprozessordnung* — ZPO) (no. 3). The acknowledgment of paternity requires the consent of the mother (§ 1595.1 of the Civil Code).
In the case of later doubts as to the paternity, § 1600.1 no. 1 of the Civil Code provides that in addition the man who has acknowledged paternity, and also the man who, because of his marriage to the mother, is regarded as the legal father of the child she gives birth to, may contest the paternity before the Family Court. Under 1600b.1 of the Civil Code, the contestation must be made within a period of two years from the date when the man learns of circumstances that suggest he is not the father. At the commencement of the proceedings, the child is presumed to be the child of the man (§ 1600c.1 of the Civil Code). If it emerges in the proceedings contesting paternity that the man is not the biological father of the child in question, this is judicially established, with the legal consequence that he is no longer the legal father of the child (§ 1599.1 of the Civil Code). Applicable law does not provide

for a procedure that serves solely to determine whether the child is the biological child of its legal father.

…

II.

1. In 1994, shortly after the birth of the child that was later the defendant, the complainant effectively acknowledged his paternity of this child. He had sexual relations with the mother of the child throughout the statutory period of conception of the child, and after the birth of the child he lived with the child and the mother, who has sole custody of the child, in extramarital cohabitation until the beginning of 1997. …

a) In the year 2002, the complainant, without the knowledge of the mother of the child, obtained a genetic diagnostic report from a private laboratory, based on test samples consisting of his saliva and a piece of chewing gum which he claimed the child had chewed. When the report confirmed that it was 100 per cent impossible for the donors of the two samples to be father and child, he again filed an action contesting paternity, relying on the results of this test. By the judgment of 4 March 2003 that is challenged in the present proceedings, the Family Court dismissed the suit. The court held that the action was unfounded, since the secretly ordered paternity test was unlawful by reason of grave violations of the child's right to informational self-determination and of the Federal Data Protection Act (*Bundesdatenschutzgesetz* – BDSG) and by reason of the infringement of the mother's right of custody, and that it could therefore not be used as evidence. The father's right to knowledge of the parentage of the child, according to the court, could not be regarded as prior-ranking as against the child's right to informational self-determination. …

b) The Higher Regional Court dismissed the appeal against this in its judgment of 29 October 2003. The court stated in its grounds that the test results submitted were not suitable to raise doubts as to the complainant's paternity. Contrary to the Code of Practice for the Provision of Paternity Test Reports, it did not in any way determine the identity of the persons tested. As a result, it was not established whether the samples tested came from the parties to the original proceedings. In addition, a secretly obtained proof of paternity could not be used as evidence in court proceedings because it had been obtained in an unlawful manner. The court stated that a secret DNA test violated the child's general right of personality in its manifestation as the right to informational self-determination, for the decision to disclose a person's genetic data could be made only by the person in question or, if the person did not yet have sufficient understanding and judgment, the person's parent who

had custody. Against this constitutionally protected right of the child was the right of the father to knowledge of paternity. Weighing the protected interests of the parties did not result in the father's interests outweighing the interests of the child. In principle, a private paternity test was suitable to prove paternity. However, this did not apply if the origin of the samples tested was not unequivocally confirmed.
c) Finally, the Federal Court of Justice dismissed the appeal against this in its judgment of 12 January 2005. The refusal of the mother and legal representative of the child to consent subsequently to the DNA test report being obtained and to agree to it being used as evidence did not give rise, the court stated, to an initial suspicion that provided a sufficient cause of action for the proceedings contesting paternity. Nor was it an obstruction of the obtaining of evidence, for such conduct flowed from the child's right to informational self-determination. The court stated that this right would be eroded if such a refusal were to open an action contesting paternity with the result that the information that this fundamental right was intended to protect would then always have to be disclosed, against the will of the person affected, as part of a court's taking of evidence. *A fortiori*, the mother's refusal to consent subsequently to the use as evidence of information that had already been unlawfully obtained could not be deemed a circumstance that opened the action contesting paternity. If the law provided for an obligation to tolerate tests to determine paternity only subject to certain requirements, the mother's refusal could not be invoked to confirm that these requirements were satisfied.
The court held that submitting a secretly obtained DNA test report was also unsuitable to demonstrate circumstances that give rise to an initial suspicion. No importance therefore attached to the complainant's objection that the Higher Regional Court had neglected to take evidence as to whether one of the samples tested actually was from the child. Even if it was established that the DNA tested came from the parties, this report could not be relied on either as evidence or as the submission of a party in the action contesting paternity. The right of the child to know its parentage also included the right not to know it. The Higher Regional Court's decision stood up to an appeal on points of law when it weighed the interests with the result that the child's right to informational self-determination did not have to be given less weight than the father's interest in disproving his paternity. Every DNA test encroached upon the right of personality guaranteed by Article 2.1 in conjunction with Article 1.1 of the Basic Law in its manifestation as the right to informational self-determination. This right could be restricted only in the predominant interest of the general public and paying due regard to the principle of proportionality. The restriction was not permitted to apply further than was indispensable to protect the public interest. The protection of the fundamental right of every human being that in principle the examination of his genome should be subject to his or

her consent, the court stated, was also supported by Article 5 of the Universal Declaration on the Human Genome and Human Rights, Article II-68 of the draft Constitution for Europe, Article 8 of the European Convention for the Protection of Human Rights and Fundamental Freedoms and, insofar as it related to the child's rights, Article 8.1 and Article 16 of the UN Convention on the Rights of the Child. This right must also be observed when evidence and findings were relied on in legal proceedings. For it was a constitutional requirement that the judge must examine whether the application of provisions of civil law affected fundamental rights in the individual case. If this occurred, he must interpret and apply these provisions in the light of the fundamental rights that were affected in their application. The right to informational self-determination of the child had to be weighed against a right of the father, similarly derived from the general right of personality, to knowledge of his own paternity, which was not to be treated as of higher value. This was shown even by the fact that the enforcement of this right in judicial proceedings contesting paternity was materially restricted by the statutory time-limit, whereas the child's right to refuse to permit its genetic data to be collected and relied on was not subject to any time bar. In addition, in the reform of the law on parent and child matters the legislature had decided against a right of the father to clarify the biological paternity of a child in every case. Furthermore, the right to knowledge of one's own paternity, even if it was to be treated as of equal value with the fundamental right of the child to know its own parentage, was not a right to obtain such knowledge.

2. In his constitutional complaint, the complainant challenges a violation of his general right of personality under Article 2.1 in conjunction with Article 1.1 of the Basic Law. He submits that, ultimately, the Federal Court of Justice contents itself with the statement that the (non-) father's general right of personality is not prior-ranking as against the child's right to informational self-determination. According to the complainant, in its abstract discussion of the question of priority, the Federal Court of Justice failed to appreciate that the present case concerns a concrete conflict of fundamental rights, and that the fact that the two holders of fundamental rights do not confront each other in isolation makes it more difficult for this conflict to be solved by way of practical concordance. For this reason, the courts should have clarified the question as to the priority of the fundamental-rights positions of the parties with regard to the individual case to be dealt with. This did not happen.

...

The complainant submits that the facts of the present individual case therefore support the conclusion that the secretly obtained paternity test should be used as evidence. He states that the legislature has neither created the possibility of obtaining knowledge as to the paternity of a child in a different way nor made arrangements as to how the fundamental-rights positions affected in such cases are to be weighed against each other in proceedings contesting paternity. The court rulings exploited the latitude for interpretation thus existing in a manner that is unacceptable to the complainant. With its strict requirements for the onus of presentation and the sufficiency of the submissions on circumstances that give rise to doubts as to paternity, the decision of the Federal Court of Justice is not in keeping with the case-law of the European Court of Human Rights, because these requirements make it practically impossible for a father to have his paternity reviewed and to contest it. …

III.

…

B.

The constitutional complaint is admissible and is well-founded to the extent that the legislature, in violation of Article 2.1 in conjunction with Article 1.1 of the Basic Law, has failed to provide a procedure in a legal form which is capable of clarifying whether a child is the biological child of its legal father and in which this paternity can be confirmed or denied without at the same time attaching consequences to this for the legal status of the child (I.). The proceedings for the contestation of paternity under §§ 1600 et seq. of the Civil Code are not a procedure that takes account in a constitutional manner of the father's right solely to knowledge that the child is his biological child (II.).

Apart from this, the constitutional complaint is unsuccessful.

The decisions that it challenges satisfy constitutional standards. It is in conformity with the constitution not to use as evidence in court proceedings contesting paternity the results of genetic paternity tests obtained secretly, that is, without the consent of the child or of its parent who has sole custody (III.).

I.

Article 2.1 in conjunction with Article 1.1 of the Basic Law guarantees, as a manifestation of the general right of personality, not only the right of a man to know the parentage of the child legally attributed to him, but also the possibility for him to realise this right. In violation of this fundamental right, the legislature has failed to create a statutory arrangement to determine that a child is the biological child of its legal father.

1. Under Article 2.1 in conjunction with Article 1.1 of the Basic Law, the right to the free development of one's personality and the obligation to respect and protect

human dignity ensure that every individual has an independent area of private life, in which his or her individuality can be developed and preserved (see Decisions of the Federal Constitutional Court (*Entscheidungen des Bundesverfassungsgerichts* – BVerfGE) 35, 202 (220)). In this connection, the understanding and development of individuality are closely connected to the knowledge of their constitutive factors. These factors include parentage (see BVerfGE 79, 256 (268)). Parentage occupies a key position in the individual's consciousness for a person to find his or her individuality and for a person's self-perception and family relationship to others. The possibility of entering into a relationship to others as an individual not only socially but also genealogically is therefore comprised in the protection of the right of personality and under Article 2.1 in conjunction with Article 1.1 of the Basic Law it creates a right of the child to know its own parentage, just as it grants a man the right to know whether a child is his biological child (see BVerfGE 108, 82 (105)). This relates both to the assumption of a man that he might be the biological father of a child that is legally not attributed to him and to the suspicion that a child might not be his biological child although the man is legally regarded and treated as the father of that child. Both interests affect the relationship in which a man enters to a child and its mother and the emotional and social relationships that he develops with them. The knowledge of the child's parentage also has a decisive influence on the self-perception of the man and on the role and manner he takes on towards the child and the mother.

2. The right of a man to know whether a child is his biological child also includes the right to be given the possibility of having his paternity of a child clarified and determined in a procedure.

a) Admittedly, the right of personality does not confer a right to obtain knowledge, but it does protect against the withholding of information that can be obtained (see BVerfGE 79, 256 (269)). This protection is only guaranteed if a procedure is made available that makes it possible for a man to have access to the information withheld from him that is necessary to know whether a child is his biological child. By reason of the present state of science, such information is contained in particular in the genetic substance of the child, which, when it is compared with the genetic data of the father by means of a DNA test, leads to confirmed knowledge as to whether the child is the biological child of the man. The genetic information from the child's genetic substance is therefore the key to the man's knowledge as to whether he is the father of the child.

b) However, the fundamental right to the free development of one's personality under Article 2.1 in conjunction with Article 1.1 of the Basic Law, from which the right to knowledge and, connected with this, also to clarification and determination of parentage are derived, is not granted without limits. It may be exercised only within the constitutional order and is subject to legislative formulation, which only violates the fundamental right if the legislature, in drafting, pursues unconstitutional purposes or does not observe the principle of proportionality (see BVerfGE 79, 256 (269-270)).

A violation of the fundamental right to the free development of one's personality also occurs if the legislature fails to put into effect the fundamental right to knowledge of parentage in a procedure which is suitable for that purpose. The fundamental rights not only comprise defensive rights of the individual as against public authority, but at the same time are value determinations of the constitution which create duties of protection for the government institutions. The constitution states that such protection is its aim, but does not lay down its detailed implementation. This is the task of the government institutions responsible in each case; in carrying out their protective duties, they have a wide discretion (see BVerfGE 96, 56 (64)). But what is necessary is a form of protection that is appropriate when account is taken of other objects of legal protection which may conflict, and that is also effective (see BVerfGE 88, 203 (254)).

3. In violation of its duty to protect arising from Article 2.1 in conjunction with Article 1.1 of the Basic Law, the legislature has failed to make a form of procedure available by which the right to knowledge of paternity can be appropriately asserted and enforced.

a) A man who, in the case of doubts as to his paternity, wishes to clarify with regard to a child whether the child is his biological child, does have the possibility of obtaining a paternity test privately, with the consent of the child or of its mother who has custody, relying in part on genetic samples from the child, and in this way attaining knowledge as to paternity. However, this approach is solely dependent on the consent of others and is legally prohibited if the child or the mother refuse their consent. This results from the fact that to date the legislature has created no procedure in which the right to knowledge of parentage can be enforced. The de facto possibility of obtaining knowledge of biological paternity privately is not sufficient to furnish the man with the protection needed. This is apparent specifically in the case where the consent of the child or the mother to obtaining a paternity test is lacking. For a test obtained secretly by a man without their consent violates the child's right of personality under Article 2.1 in conjunction with Article 1.1 of the Basic Law in its manifestation as the right to informational self-determination, and it also violates the mother's right of custody, protected by Article 6.2 of the Basic Law.

aa) The right to informational self-determination, included under Article 2.1 in conjunction with Article 1.1 of the Basic Law, protects the authority of an individual to decide, in principle, personally on the disclosure and use of that individual's personal data (see BVerfGE 65, 1 (43)). These data protected by fundamental rights also include data that contain information on genetic characteristics from which, when they are compared against the data of another person, conclusions can be drawn as to the person's parentage (see BVerfGE 103, 21 (32)).

But the right to informational self-determination is not guaranteed without limits either. In particular, the individual must accept restrictions of this right that are in the predominant interest of others or of the general public. Such restrictions require a statutory foundation from which the requirements and the scope of the restrictions follow and which complies with the principle of proportionality (see BVerfGE 65, 1 (44)). In this way, provisions of procedural law, such as § 372a of the Code of Civil Procedure (*Zivilprozessordnung* – ZPO), may lay down the requirements subject to which even sensitive data that are capable of giving information on a person's parentage must be disclosed by way of the release of the appropriate bodily samples as test samples if this, taking into account the fundamental rights of others, such as the right of the father in the present case to know of the paternity, is justified and not disproportionate. But the right to informational self-determination imposes a duty on the government institutions to give the individual protection against private third parties having access to the data that characterise his or her individuality, without the person's knowledge and without the person's consent. In principle, this applies even if the purpose, the clarification of paternity, is supported by an interest in knowledge that is protected as a fundamental right. The conflict of fundamental rights that exists in such cases cannot be overcome by one of the holders of fundamental rights as he or she thinks fit: it can only be solved by the legislature. A paternity test obtained secretly with the help of genetic samples is based on an unjustifiable violation of the right of the child affected to informational self-determination, against which the government institutions must offer protection.

bb) The mother with custody must also be protected against undesired access to the genetic substance of a child. Article 6.2 of the Basic Law guarantees the parents the right and the responsibility to care for their child. Parental custody also includes making the decision, in the interests of the child, as to whether a person may collect and analyse genetic data from a child. In order that the constitutionally required protection is given to the person with custody in this respect, the legal order may not tolerate that a secretly obtained paternity test serves to obtain knowledge of the parentage of a child.

b) However, the legal order must also make available a procedure to provide the possibility of determining paternity. The lack of such a procedure is not justified solely on the basis of fundamental-rights positions of the child or the mother.

aa) (1) In the present case it is not necessary to decide whether – as the Federal Court of Justice assumes – the child has a right not to know its own parentage. At all events, such a right would not justify withholding a form of procedure in which a man may obtain knowledge of the parentage of the child that has been legally attributed to him without this automatically leading to changes in the child's legal status.

It is certainly questionable whether such a right, as the negative complement of the right to knowledge of parentage, is comprised by the right to free development of the personality under Article 2.1 in conjunction with Article 1.1 of the Basic Law. For unlike the positive knowledge of parentage, ignorance does not give the individual, when the individual receives the information, the possibility of placing himself or herself in relationship to concrete persons and discovering the personal family context in relation to which his or her own identity can align itself. In this respect, in the case of a procedure to clarify the parentage of a child, what is at issue is not the child's lack of knowledge of its parentage, but its possibly only supposed knowledge of the paternity of its legal father, which could be shaken by knowledge of its actual parentage.

But a right that protects an assumption that may be erroneous and preserves the child from a clarification of its actual parentage, even if it were included in the sphere of protection of the right of personality, would in principle be of less weight than the right to knowledge of parentage, because only the latter can ultimately make a long-term contribution to the finding of one's own identity both by the man and by the child. However, particular situations and phases of development in which a child finds itself may in the individual case justify refraining for a limited period of time, by reason of particular endangerment of the child's welfare, from making available a procedure which may help enforce the man's right to knowledge that the child is his biological child.

(2) The child's right to informational self-determination is equally incapable of justifying withholding the knowledge of the child's paternity from its legal father in the long term. The right to informational self-determination protects the self-determined passing on and use of personal data. In the case of doubts as to the paternity, however, only these data, when compared with the genetic data of the legal father, may provide knowledge that the child is his biological child. Unrestricted protection of the genetic data of a child from the legal father would therefore at the same time mean for the father the withholding of the knowledge of his own data and often the impossibility of obtaining knowledge that the child is his biological child, for he cannot necessarily know whether the mother of the child also had sexual relations with other men during the time of conception. The father's justified interest in knowledge of the real parentage of the child is reinforced by the duties for the child that he has as the legal father. If the mother has sole custody of the child, she may also, exercising the child's right to informational self-determination, prevent

the man from lawfully obtaining knowledge that the child is his biological child as long as there is no form of procedure available to the man that serves to clarify the parentage.

(3) Admittedly, the legislature is not under a duty always to make the legal recognition of parentage subject to the determination of the biological parents of the child in the individual case (see BVerfGE 108, 82 (100)). In view of the protection of family social relationships under Article 6.1 of the Basic Law and the protection of privacy under Article 2.1 of the Basic Law, it is sufficient to make conclusions as to the paternity of a child on the basis of particular factual circumstances and social situations, above all including an existing marriage, and to attribute legal parentage on the basis of this presumption, if this as a rule results in biological and legal parentage being united in one person (see BVerfGE 108, 82 (100) with reference to 79, 256 (267)). It is the consequence of these provisions on presumption passed by the legislature in § 1592 nos. 1 and 2 of the Civil Code, which are constitutionally unobjectionable, that they may lead to doubts as to the true paternity of a child. But if the legislature decides to follow this legal route of to a large extent not clarifying biological paternity but instead making presumptions, it must at the same time provide a procedure in which such doubts can be clarified in the individual case. The right of a man to know that a child is his biological child, contained in Article 2.1 in conjunction with Article 1.1 of the Basic Law, requires a procedure to be made available for such cases in which the paternity can be clarified without further legal consequences being inescapably attached. This also applies to a man who has acknowledged the paternity of a child. As long as the legislature has not made a procedure to clarify paternity available and does not in addition make the acknowledgment of paternity legally dependent on the proof that the child is the biological child of the person acknowledging paternity, a man may only base his acknowledgment on his presumption, supported by statute, that he is the father of the child. In doing this, he has not forfeited his right to know that the child is his biological child if doubts later arise.

In making such a procedure for clarification and determination of paternity available, the legislature admittedly restricts the child's right to informational self-determination by granting the access to the child's genetic data that is necessarily entailed. But this is required by the protection that is also given to the man by Article 2.1 in conjunction with Article 1.1 of the Basic Law. Since these are data that may be related to those of the man who is the legal father of the child, the right of the child not to disclose these data is less worthy of protection than the right of the man. In this constellation of fundamental rights, the right of the legal father to know the paternity of the child must be given greater weight than the child's right to informational self-determination, *inter alia* because the legislature can only comply with its duty under Article 2.1 in conjunction with Article 1.1 of the Basic Law if it provides a procedure in which it can be clarified by comparing the genetic data of the child and the data of its legal father whether the child is really the biological child of the latter.

bb) Nor do fundamental rights of the mother run counter to the provision of a procedure to clarify and determine that a child is the biological child of the man that follows from the legal protection of the man's personality under Article 2.1 in conjunction with Article 1.1 of the Basic Law.

It is true that the clarification of whether her child is the biological child of the man who is deemed to be its legal father also affects the mother's right of personality under Article 2.1 in conjunction with Article 1.1 of the Basic Law, which gives her the right to decide for herself whether she permits access to her privacy and her sexual life, and if so to whom and in what form (see BVerfGE 96, 56 (61)). However, this does not entail an impermissible encroachment upon the mother's inviolable sphere of private life. The encroachment has the primary goal of clarifying whether the child is the product of her relationship with its legal father, who in turn has a constitutionally protected right to know whether the child is the product of this relationship and is his biological child (see BVerfGE 96, 56 (61)). When the fundamental-rights positions that conflict in this case are weighed against each other, account must also be taken of the fact that the mother has already allowed the man access to her private sphere, has allowed him to share in her sexual life and as a result has helped create an interest of the man in knowing who is the biological father of her child.

cc) No other fundamental-rights positions of child and mother prevent the enforcement of the right of a man solely to knowledge as to whether a child is his biological child, in a procedure especially intended for this purpose. Even an interest on the part of the legislature in not wishing to disturb the family peace of the legally connected family with a procedure to clarify the paternity of a child does not justify withholding such a procedure, for only such a procedure protects and puts into effect the constitutionally guaranteed fundamental right of the father to the knowledge of the paternity. In addition, the family peace may be disturbed by a legal father merely by doubts expressed by him as to the paternity of his child, long before a procedure that clarifies the doubted paternity.

II.

The proceedings contesting paternity under §§ 1600 et seq. of the Civil Code are not proceedings that constitutionally take into account the father's right solely to knowledge that the child is his biological child. Its goal and its requirements are not restricted to enforcing the right to knowledge of parentage under Article 2.1 in conjunction with Article 1.1 of the Basic Law, but serve to implement the precept contained in Article 6.2 sentence 1 of the Basic Law that if possible biological and legal paternity should be united in one person (see BVerfGE 108, 82 (104)). As a result, these proceedings go beyond the desire for knowledge of paternity and in addition impose excessive conditions on the obtaining of this knowledge; these conditions are not constitutionally necessary for a procedure directed solely to the determination of paternity.

1. The proceedings contesting paternity serve to unite the legal and biological paternity of a child and end the legal paternity if it transpires in the proceedings that the child is not the biological child of its legal father. In the proceedings contesting paternity, the clarification of paternity is merely a means to this end.

a) In this case, therefore, unlike the situation where solely knowledge of the parentage of a child is obtained, the interest of the legal father in having the paternity annulled if it transpires that he is not the biological father of the child, protected by Article 6.2 sentence 1 of the Basic Law, must be weighed against the interest of a child in maintaining its legal and social family attribution, which is protected by Article 6.1 of the Basic Law (see BVerfGE 38, 241 (251); 108, 82 (107-108)). This interest of the child carries great weight, for it is of decisive importance for the development of the child's personality to have a stable family framework in which it can feel that it belongs to a father and a mother. In addition, a successful contestation of paternity in which the child also loses in the legal father a person with responsibility and with a duty of maintenance towards it may have substantial effects on the circumstances of the child's life. This also affects the mother of the child, whose interest in the continuation of the family legal relationship is equally protected by Article 6.1 of the Basic Law (see BVerfGE 108, 82 (107)).

b) The legislature has attempted to achieve a balance between these conflicting fundamental-rights positions of father, child and mother by giving the father the possibility of initiating proceedings contesting paternity in order to safeguard his right, and if it is determined that the biological and legal father is not the same person, the legislature has not provided for a further necessity to weigh the father's rights against the interests of the mother and the child, but allows the fact that the biological and legal father are not the same person to be sufficient to end the legal bond between the child and its current legal father. In contrast, the legislature has taken account of the interests in particular of the child and its mother in stability of the existing legal and social family attribution by making the contestation of paternity subject to special requirements. Thus, in § 1600b of the Civil Code the legislature provides that the contestation must take place within two years, starting at the date on which the legal father learns of the circumstances that argue against his paternity. In addition, in § 1600c of the Civil Code the legislature has created the presumption that the child is the biological child of the man whose paternity exists under § 1592 nos. 1 and 2 and § 1593 of the Civil Code, and in this way has given the legal father the onus of presentation in refuting this presumption. This balancing of interests by the legislature, which manifests itself in the procedural design of the action of contestation, is constitutionally unobjectionable. It takes equal account of both fundamental-rights positions, and its requirements for contesting paternity do not unreasonably encroach upon the father's right under Article 6.2 of the Basic Law to annul his legal paternity if the legal paternity and biological paternity do not coincide.

c) Nor are there constitutional objections to the interpretation in case-law of the requirements for contesting paternity. It is in conformity with the protection of the legal and social family organisation under Article 6.1 of the Basic Law and with the onus of presentation imposed by statute on the legal father who is contesting his paternity if case-law does not regard the mere statement of the legal father that he has doubts as to his paternity or is not the biological father of the child as sufficient for this, but requires him to set forth objective circumstances that give rise to doubts as to his paternity. Without such a de facto criterion, the time-limit for contestation of § 1600b of the Civil Code, which also serves the protection arising from Article 6.1 of the Basic Law, would be ineffective, for without objective circumstances of which the legal father has learned and on which he relies it is impossible to calculate on what date the two-year period within which the father may contest his paternity, which relates precisely to such circumstances, begins to run. If the mere statement that the father is not the biological father of the child were sufficient to satisfy the onus of presentation, the father would be at liberty to time his doubts in such a way that they always fell within the period for contestation. But in this case the balancing by the legislature of the interests of father, child and mother protected by fundamental rights would be one-sidedly shifted in favour of the father's interest in breaking the legal bond between himself and the child, neglecting in particular the interest of the child in maintaining its legal and social family ties.

On the other hand, however, the requirements for the onus of presentation of the legal father may also not be made too strict, in order that his interest in annulling his legal paternity if he is not the biological father may be adequately taken into account in the proceedings contesting paternity. He is therefore only to be required, as the Federal Court of Justice has stated in its case-law (see Federal Court of Justice, *Neue Juristische Wochenschrift* 1998, p. 2976 (2977)) to submit circumstances that make it appear not completely remote that not he but another may possibly be the biological father of the child.

2. In judicial proceedings contesting paternity, after a contesting legal father has made submissions that satisfy the onus of presentation, the court begins the stage of taking evidence and obtaining a DNA report; in the course of this, it is also clarified and determined whether the child is the biological child of its legal father. But because of its further-reaching goal of legally separating the legal father from the child and the stricter procedural requirements that result from this, the proceedings contesting paternity do not do justice to the right of a man, protected by Article 2.1 in conjunction with Article 1.1 of the Basic Law, to mere knowledge as to whether a child is his biological child.

a) In the case of doubts as to his paternity, the legal father will admittedly often have come to the decision that if it transpires that he is not the biological father of the child he will break the legal bond to the child. In these cases, the desire for knowledge of the biological paternity of the child coincides with the desire to end the legal bonds to the child, and therefore as a general rule the proceedings contesting paternity are the suitable route, and the route provided for him, to reach his goal of ending his legal paternity. But the desire of a legal father may also be solely directed to knowing whether the child is really his biological child, without at the same time wanting to give up his legal paternity. This may be because, although he wishes to have clarification as to the parentage of the child, he feels such a close personal connection with the child that even if he is not the biological father of the child he wants to remain its legal father. It is also possible that the legal father would first like to remove his doubts as to the paternity of the child in order that, when he knows the results of a test report to this effect, if this does not confirm that he is the biological father, he will then consider the situation and decide what legal consequences he will draw.

Proceedings contesting paternity which are directed to the goal of ending legal paternity are too broad and not appropriate for this relief sought, which is protected by Article 2.1 in conjunction with Article 1.1 of the Basic Law and which consists in the father obtaining, either solely or in the first instance, merely knowledge as to the parentage of the child whose legal father he is. It forces the legal father, if he pursues his interest in determining that the child is his biological child, at the same time also to take the risk of possibly losing his legal paternity or, if he does not wish to do this, to give up his desire to obtain knowledge of the child's paternity. This neither does justice to the father's interest in knowledge relating solely to the paternity, nor does it serve the interest of the child concerned in maintaining its legal relationship to its father.

b) The statutory requirements subject to which paternity can be contested are also disproportionate, in relation to a father's pursuit of the interest in obtaining knowledge of the paternity of his child. They are designed with regard to the protection to which the child and its mother are entitled with a view to the continuity of the legal and social family relationship with the father, which is endangered when paternity is contested. However, they do not need this protection of legal continuity where the only purpose is to pursue the goal of obtaining certainty as to the child's paternity. In this case, there is no interest of the child and mother equally important and worthy of protection to be weighed against the father's right to knowledge of the paternity, and it would therefore not be justified to subject a procedure for clarification and determination of paternity to the same onus of presentation and time-limits as those for the proceedings contesting paternity. To make a procedure available, it would be sufficient in this case if the legal father submitted doubts as to whether the child is his biological child.

c) The requirements set out above apply to the legal father whose right to the determination of the paternity of the child legally attributed to him is the sole subject of the present proceedings. Insofar as the legislature makes available proceedings for the determination that a child is the biological child of a man who is not the legal father of the child but who assumes that he is the biological father of the child, it may impose stricter requirements on the basis that the child has not been legally attributed to the man. The man can be required to submit circumstances from which it appears possible that he might be the biological father of the child, in order to protect the child and the mother against the disclosure of personal data and of intimate events in proceedings that are initiated without cause by men to whom the mother and child stand in no legal or social relationship.

III.

By these standards, the decisions challenged by the constitutional complaint are constitutionally unobjectionable. In this respect, the constitutional complaint is unfounded. The unsatisfactory legal situation with regard to the interest of a man in obtaining, either solely or in the first instance, merely knowledge as to whether a child is his biological child, which is protected by Article 2.1 in conjunction with Article 1.1 of the Basic Law, cannot be compensated for by the proceedings contesting paternity which the complainant initiated and conducted. In their decisions, the courts interpreted constitutionally the statutory provisions on the contestation of paternity, which safeguard the fundamental rights of the father, the child and the mother, and in this interpretation they rightly refused to use as evidence a secretly obtained paternity test which the complainant submitted.

1. The proceedings contesting paternity under §§ 1600 et seq. of the Civil Code serve to terminate legal paternity. Even if the complainant challenged the fact that no procedure was available to him for prior clarification of the paternity of the child

legally attributed to him and he therefore secretly, by way of a genetic paternity test report, obtained knowledge of this, he did nevertheless initiate proceedings contesting paternity with the aim of annulling his legal paternity. Consequently, the statutory provisions are to be applied to him that, as set out above, constitutionally balance the fundamental-rights positions affected in the contestation of paternity. The courts must observe these legal provisions, in particular those relating to the onus of presentation. They may not disregard them in order to satisfy the right to knowledge of paternity in proceedings that are directed not only to that knowledge, but also to the termination of paternity. The interpretation and application of the statutory provisions on the proceedings contesting paternity in the challenged decisions are constitutionally unobjectionable. Apart from submitting the secret paternity test, all that the complainant stated before the non-constitutional courts to show his doubts as to his paternity was that it could be presumed from the refusal of mother and child to consent to the paternity report obtained that he was not the father of the child. The Federal Court of Justice rightly did not regard this as sufficient to satisfy the onus of presentation of § 1600b of the Civil Code.

2. It is in conformity with the constitution that the courts refused to use as evidence the genetic paternity test report secretly obtained by the complainant.

a) In judicial proceedings, the judge confronts the parties as a person exercising the sovereign power of the state. The judge is, therefore, under Article 1.3 of the Basic Law, bound to take account of the fundamental rights that are relevant in this connection in passing judgment and has a duty to structure the proceedings in accordance with the rule of law (see BVerfGE 52, 203 (207); 106, 28 (48-49)). From the principle of a state under the rule of law follows the duty to handle the law of evidence fairly, in particular the rules relating to the burden of proof (see BVerfGE 52, 131 (145)). In family-law proceedings, too, in which there is a dispute on the legal situations of the parties within a legal relationship governed by family law, the courts are in principle under a duty to take into account evidence or statements of a case submitted by the parties in order to maintain a functionally reliable administration of justice and to reach their decisions in a substantively correct manner.

The substantive fundamental rights such as Article 2.1 of the Basic Law may also give rise to requirements for judicial proceedings (see BVerfGE 101, 106 (122)) in connection with the disclosure and evaluation of personal data that are constitutionally protected against coming to the knowledge of third parties. The court must therefore examine whether the use of secretly obtained personal data on another person and of knowledge that is derived from these data is compatible with the general right of personality of the person affected (see BVerfGE 106, 28 (48)). When the interest in a functionally reliable administration of justice and the protection of the right to informational self-determination as flowing from the general right of personality are weighed against each other, the interest in the use of the data and information submitted is of greater weight only if further aspects extending beyond the mere interest in giving evidence apply and these show that, despite the encroachment upon the right of personality, the interest in the use of the data is in need of protection. The mere interest in securing an item of evidence for oneself is not sufficient for this (see BVerfGE 106, 28 (49-50)).

b) This was taken into account by the Federal Court of Justice and by the lower courts in their challenged decisions. In a manner that is constitutionally unobjectionable, they proceeded on the basis that the complainant's secret obtaining of genetic substance of the child, and thus the impermissible access to its personal data, substantially impaired the child's right to informational self-determination and that the use in the judicial proceedings of the information obtained from this constituted an encroachment on the right of personality of the child. On the other hand, the courts were rightly unable to identify a particular interest worthy of protection of the complainant that the report should be accepted for use in the proceedings, an interest that went beyond the interest in obtaining an item of evidence to show that he did not have paternity in the form of the report made secretly and without the consent of the child.

Nor does the circumstance that to date no procedure is available that makes it possible for a man to have the paternity of a child that is legally attributed to himself clarified and determined enable the court to recognise such an interest of the complainant that is particularly worthy of protection. Thus a man who wants to contest his legal paternity is not in a situation similar to a situation permitting self-defence that could justify the man, without the consent and knowledge of the child or its mother, in obtaining genetic data of the child and these data being used as evidence in family-court proceedings, in violation of the child's right of personality. As has been shown by the practice of the family courts over decades, the submission of a DNA test report is not the only possibility of satisfying the requirements for stating one's case in proceedings contesting paternity and of submitting circumstances that suggest it is not completely remote that the biological father of the child is not the man challenging paternity, but possibly another man. In this respect, the constitutional complaint is unfounded.

C. – I.

The legislature must create a procedural possibility that helps to realise the right to knowledge and determination of paternity under Article 2.1 in conjunction with Article 1.1 of the Basic Law, without tying this mandatorily to proceedings contesting paternity. The legislature has freedom of drafting with regard to the way in which it complies with this duty. Various routes are open to it in this connection. However, for the reasons set out under B.I.3.a) and B.III.2.b), the legislature may not permit secretly obtained genetic diagnostic paternity test reports to be introduced into proceedings contesting paternity nor make it possible for the courts to take account of these.

1. The legislature has more than one possibility of complying with its duty to protect. One possibility would be passing provisions that make the refusal of the child or its mother who has custody to consent to a genetic paternity test being obtained privately subject to review by the courts and that allow the court, by removing or transferring the authority to act for the child, to open the way for such a report to be prepared, as is provided by the Draft Act of the Government of the Free State of Bavaria. Using as evidence a report that had been prepared in this way would be constitutionally unobjectionable. In addition, there could be provision for independent separate proceedings or proceedings prior to the proceedings contesting paternity to clarify and determine paternity; in these proceedings, if the legal father stated that he had doubts that the child was his biological child, the court would be required to examine the case on the merits.

2. However, the legislature has a duty to ensure that in the proceedings contesting paternity the interest protected by Article 6.1 of the Basic Law, in particular the interest of the child in retaining its legal and social family attribution where appropriate, continues to be taken into account. Here too the legislature has discretion. For example, it can ensure that the knowledge of the legal father that he is not the biological father, which is now easier to obtain, does not immediately lead to the annulment of legal paternity in the proceedings contesting paternity, if, on account of the duration of the legal and social connection between the child and its legal father and the particular life situation and phase of development in which the child currently is, this would result in a substantial adverse effect on the welfare of the child.

II.

The legislature is instructed to pass procedural provisions that ensure that, by 31 March 2008, the legal situation is in conformity with the right to knowledge of paternity under Article 2.1 in conjunction with Article 1.1 of the Basic Law. Until these provisions come into force, there will only be the present possibility for the legal father to obtain knowledge of the paternity of a child within proceedings contesting paternity under §§ 1600 et seq. of the Civil Code.

III.

…

Justices: Papier, Steiner, Hohmann-Dennhardt, Hoffmann-Riem, Bryde, Gaier, Eichberger, Schluckebier

No. 49

BVerfGE 118, 45

of 28 February 2007 – 1 BvL 9/04 –

"Childcare maintenance case"

HEADNOTE:

It is in breach of Article 6.5 of the Basic Law to determine the duration of a maintenance claim granted by the legislature to one parent against the other parent because of the care of his or her child differently for children born in and out of wedlock.

Order of the First Senate of 28 February 2007
– 1 BvL 9/04 –

in the proceedings for the constitutional review of § 1615 l.2 sentence 3 of the Civil Code – suspension of proceedings and submission order of the Hamm Higher Regional Court (*Oberlandesgericht*) of 16 August 2004 (5 UF 262/04) –.

RULING:

1. The different arrangement of the maintenance claims because of the care or bringing up of children in § 1570 of the Civil Code, on the one hand, and § 1615 l.2 sentence 3 of the Civil Code, on the other hand, is incompatible with Article 6.5 of the Basic Law.
2. The legislature is instructed to bring a constitutional transitional arrangement into being by 31 December 2008.

EXTRACT FROM GROUNDS:

A.

The submission relates to the question of whether it is compatible with the Basic Law (*Grundgesetz* – GG) that § 1615 l.2 sentence 3 of the Civil Code (*Bürgerliches Gesetzbuch* – BGB) in principle limits the maintenance which a parent may claim from the other parent who is not married to him or her for the care or bringing up of the joint child born out of wedlock to three years after the birth of the child and only provides for an extension in exceptional cases, in particular taking the child's interests into account, whilst § 1570 of the Civil Code, which regulates maintenance owed to one divorced parent by the other parent for the care or bringing up of the joint child born in wedlock, does not contain a time limit and the case-law, on the basis of this statutory provision on claims, grants a maintenance claim in general terms for a considerably longer period than three years.

I.

1. According to § 1570 of the Civil Code, which was created by the First Act Reforming the Law on Marriage and Family Law (*Erstes Gesetz zur Reform des Ehe- und Familienrechts*) of 14 June 1976 (Federal Law Gazette (*Bundesgesetzblatt* – BGBl) I p. 1421), entered into force on 1 July 1977 and has not been amended since then, a divorced parent may demand maintenance from the former spouse as long as and insofar as he or she cannot be expected to take up gainful employment because of the care or bringing up of a joint child.

a) The legislature stated as grounds for this claim that the joint economic basis of the spouses ceased to apply on divorce. Hence, their mutual economic ties were said to end in principle. The joint responsibility of the spouses for one another was however said to continue beyond a divorce in certain cases, for instance if the spouse had to bring up and care for a joint child (see *Bundestag* printed paper (*Bundestagsdrucksache* – BTDrucks) 7/650, p. 60). The maintenance claim granted in this respect in the shape of § 1570 of the Civil Code was said to only apply as long as the spouse is prevented from taking up gainful employment as a result of childcare. It was thus said to cease to apply if the child no longer required care or bringing up (see *Bundestag* printed paper 7/650, p. 123). Here, the legislature deliberately omitted to give instructions or to provide interpretation aids as to the duration of the maintenance claim. It took the view that making a statement on for instance the number and age of the children was inappropriate in view of the diversity of circumstances (see *Bundestag* printed paper 7/4361, p. 29; *Bundestag* printed paper

7/650, p. 122-123). Whether and to what degree one could expect a mother to enter into gainful employment was said to depend not only on the age of the children, but also on other circumstances.

b) It is also already stressed in the case-law in this respect that there are no fixed points in time from which age and from what number of children the divorced spouse has to take up gainful employment (see Federal Court of Justice (*Bundesgerichtshof* – BGH), Judgment of 23 February 1983 – IVb ZR 363/83 –, *Zeitschrift für das gesamte Familienrecht* – FamRZ 1983, p. 456 (458)). Not only the age of a child, but also the child´s state of health, his or her state of development at school and in other respects, or possible behavioural disturbances, are said to play a role here (see BGH, Judgment of 26 October 1984 – IVb ZR 44/83 –, FamRZ 1985, p. 50 (51)).

Nonetheless, standards have been formed in court practice for a standard case of child development for a gradual increase in the obligation of divorced parents taking care of children to take up gainful employment, orientated in line with the child's age, and have been incorporated into the Higher Regional Courts' maintenance guidelines (see Palandt/Brudermüller, *BGB*, 66th ed., 2007, *§ 1570*, marginal nos. 8 et seq. with further references). Even if the information on the child's age, to which the obligation of a parent taking care of children to (re)assume gainful employment is to be orientated, is not completely identical in these guidelines, they nonetheless concur that no obligation to take up gainful employment exists for the parents taking care of children until a child reaches the age of eight or until the end of his or her primary schooling. In principle, part-time employment is considered to be reasonable in addition to his or her care when the child is aged between eleven and fifteen, and it is presumed in a standard case at the latest when the child reaches the age of sixteen that childcare does not stand in the way of full-time employment. This age phase concept is followed by the case-law.

2. a) With the entry into force of the Act on the Legal Status of Children Born out of Wedlock (*Gesetz über die rechtliche Stellung der nichtehelichen Kinder* – NEhelG) (Federal Law Gazette I (1969) p. 1243) on 1 July 1970, the mother not married to the father of her child was granted a claim against the father for the first time by the newly created § 1615 l of the Civil Code for payment of maintenance which could be granted to her for a maximum of one year after the birth of the child and was conditional on the mother either not being in gainful employment or only being restrictedly employed because the child otherwise could not be cared for. The time limit was reasoned by the first year of life being particularly significant to the favourable development of a child according to the state of psychological and pedagogical knowledge (see *Bundestag* printed paper V/2370, p. 56).

b) The Act Amending Assistance for Pregnant Women and Families (*Schwangeren- und Familienhilfeänderungsgesetz* – SFHÄndG) of 21 August 1995 (Federal Law Gazette I p. 1055) amended § 1615 l of the Civil Code such that the duration of the claim for childcare maintenance was extended to three years. This was then no longer permitted only to be granted if the mother was able to prove that there was no other possibility of care for her child, but indeed in all cases in which she could not be expected to take up gainful employment because of the care and bringing up of the child. It was stated as grounds that the father of a child born out of wedlock should shoulder greater responsibility in balancing the opportunities for development of children who are born out of wedlock and in wedlock to make it possible for the child to be cared for by its mother, and hence improve the framework for its development. The extension of the duration of the claim to three years was to facilitate full care of the child by its mother until kindergarten age (see *Bundestag* printed paper 13/1850, p. 24).
c) The Act Reforming the Law of Parent and Child (*Gesetz zur Reform des Kindschaftsrechts* – KindRG) of 16 December 1997 (Federal Law Gazette I p. 2942) brought about another amendment of § 1615 l of the Civil Code. The three-year time limit on the claim was in principle retained, but was expanded to include the possibility to grant maintenance beyond this time insofar as, in particular taking account of the interests of the child, it would be grossly inequitable to refuse a maintenance claim after expiry of the three-year period. The possibility of extension was reasoned with hardships that might arise in exceptional cases if the time limits were to be applied inflexibly and such hardships were to be avoided. The child might for instance have a disability, and hence rely on more intensive care on the part of the mother, so that it would be equitable to also burden the father for the maintenance of the mother over and above the period of three years (see *Bundestag* printed paper 13/4899, p. 89). What is more, the father who cares for his child born out of wedlock has now also been granted a claim for childcare maintenance against the mother.
The *Bundesrat* had criticised in the legislative procedure that the arrangement allegedly continued to maintain the differences between children born in wedlock and out of wedlock with regard to maintenance without any convincing reason. Post-marital solidarity was also said not to be a suitable criterion for the differentiation. Children born out of wedlock should be placed on an equal footing with those born in wedlock with regard to the care opportunities. The *Bundesrat* proposed to apply § 1570 of the Civil Code to the maintenance claim of the mother not married to the father of her child accordingly unless such an expansion of the claim was grossly inequitable for serious reasons (see *Bundestag* printed paper 13/4899, p. 149). The Federal Government opposed this, arguing that the proposal gave too lit-

tle consideration to the fact that the claim was not one of the child, but of the child´s parent taking care of him or her. In realising the constitutional mandate emerging from Article 6.5 of the Basic Law, the time limit on the care-related maintenance claim was favoured by the fact that care of the child was as a rule guaranteed by other means on its reaching the age of three. Special situations could however require the claim to be extended (see *Bundestag* printed paper 13/4899, p. 167). The *Bundestag's* Committee on Legal Affairs had also recommended that the Government Draft be adopted without amendment. The claim of the mother against the father was said to depend on the legal nature of the relationship between the parents. This was said to justify making the claim of the divorced wife stronger in terms of post-marital solidarity than that of a mother who was not married to the father of the child (see *Bundestag* printed paper 13/8511, p. 71).
The relevant subsections of § 1615 l of the Civil Code in the version adopted at that time, which entered into force on 1 July 1998, and updated since then, read as follows:

§ 1615 l

Maintenance claim of mother and father by reason of the birth

> (1) …
> (2) To the extent that the mother is not engaged in gainful employment because as a result of the pregnancy or of an illness caused by the pregnancy or the delivery she is incapable of doing so, the father is obliged to pay her maintenance for a period exceeding the period set out in subsection (1) sentence 1. The same applies to the extent that the mother cannot be expected to be engaged in gainful employment by reason of the care or upbringing of the child. The obligation to maintain begins at the earliest four months before the birth; it ends three years after the birth unless it would be grossly inequitable, taking account of the interests of the child, to refuse a maintenance claim on expiry of this period.
> (3) …
> (4) If the father cares for the child, he has the claim under subsection (2) sentence 2 against the mother. …

d) Case-law has now formed with regard to the question of when gross inequity within the meaning of § 1615 l.2 sentence 3 of the Civil Code exists, distinguishing between “child-related” and “parent-related” reasons (see Frankfurt Higher Regional Court, Judgment of 13 October 1999 – 2 UF 335/98 –, FamRZ 2000, p. 1522 (1523); Celle Higher Regional Court, Judgment of 21 November 2001 – 21 UF 96/01 –, FamRZ 2002, p. 636; Karlsruhe Higher Regional Court, Judgment of 4 September 2003 – 2 UF 6/03 –, *Neue Juristische Wochenschrift* – NJW 2004, p.

523 (524); Hamm Higher Regional Court, Judgment of 4 November 2004 – 3 UF 555/01 –,NJW 2005, p. 297 (298); Düsseldorf Higher Regional Court, Judgment of 23 May 2005 – II-2 UF 125/04 –, FamRZ 2005, p. 1772). Having said that, there are not many among the published rulings in which a maintenance claim has been granted beyond the child's third birthday. If gross inequity is presumed, the claim – where it can be ascertained – has not been granted for longer than until the child's sixth or seventh birthday in most cases.

e) The question of the constitutionality of § 1615 l.2 sentence 3 of the Civil Code is the subject of controversial discussion in legal literature. For instance, the view is taken that the different manifestations of childcare maintenance violate Article 6.5 of the Basic Law in particular. It is said that there is no convincing reason to presume that it was harmless for a child born out of wedlock if, because of gainful employment of the mother, he or she had to forgo the mother's constant attention, whilst it was presumed to be detrimental to the development of children born in wedlock if they were not cared for by a parent in person until the age of at least eight (see Schwab/Borth, *Handbuch des Scheidungsrechts*, 5th ed., 2004, Part IV, marginal no. 1412; Peschel-Gutzeit/Jenckel, *Familie und Recht* – FuR 1996, p. 129; Puls, FamRZ 1998, p. 865; Müller, *Der Amtsvormund* – DAVorm 2000, p. 830; Seidel, *Der Anspruch der Mutter eines nichtehelichen Kindes gegen den Kindesvater auf Betreuungsunterhalt im Lichte des Verfassungsrechts*, 1999, pp. 89 et seq.). In contrast, it is argued that the differentiation in childcare maintenance is justified by there being post-marital solidarity after the failure of a marriage which is said to give rise to an obligation to pay maintenance for a longer period, whilst there is no legal bond between unmarried partners who had children. The constitution was hence said not to require an equal position. With a not too narrow interpretation in conformity with the constitution of the equitability clause contained in § 1615 l.2 sentence 3 of the Civil Code, constitutionally objectionable outcomes could be avoided for individual cases by bringing together the duration of the maintenance claim and the claim regulated by § 1570 of the Civil Code (see Wichmann, FuR 1996, p. 161; Derleder, *Deutsches und europäisches Familienrecht* – DEuFamR 1999, p. 84; Büttner, FamRZ 2000, p. 781; Wever/Schilling, FamRZ 2002, p. 581; Hahne, *Forum Familienrecht* – FF 2006, p. 24).

f) In its judgment of 5 July 2006 – XII ZR 11/04 – (FamRZ 2006, p. 1362), the Federal Court of Justice held § 1615 l of the Civil Code to be constitutional. The different manifestation of the maintenance claim for care of a child after a dissolved marriage according to § 1570 of the Civil Code and of the claim according to § 1615 l.2 sentence 2 of the Civil Code was said to correspond to the different circumstances on which the provisions were based. The claim from § 1570 of the Civil Code was said to also be justified by Article 6.1 of the Basic Law, which protects the ongoing effect of marriage, including the maintenance arrangement. The elements of maintenance contained in § 1570 of the Civil Code and § 1615 l.2 of the Civil Code had in common that the parent with whom the joint child lived was to be released from gainful employment as long as, and to the degree that, the child required care and bringing up. In this respect, the maintenance claim of the needy spouse was also said to serve initially to ensure that parental responsibility was assumed. The vital difference was however said to lie in maintenance also being granted to the divorced spouse for his or her own sake because of post-marital solidarity, emerging from marriage, which was however not correspondingly transferable to partners in non-marital cohabitations. § 1615 l.2 of the Civil Code was said to cover a large number of different circumstances. It was said that the maintenance claim could even arise out of a relationship between the parents which had been restricted to procreation of the child; it was however also said to exist in cases in which the parents had lived together for a prolonged period without marrying, and had indeed had several children. This by itself was said to show that a differentiation was necessary, opposing treating this maintenance claim in exactly the same way as claims under § 1570 of the Civil Code. It was hence said to be constitutionally unobjectionable that, in § 1615 l.2 of the Civil Code – unlike for post-marital maintenance –, the legislature had determined a short minimum period, but one coordinated with state assistance, which could be extended, consideration being given to the individual case. It is said to be not immaterial to the interpretation of this provision whether the joint child had emerged from a community similar to marriage. If the partners of such a community considered themselves to be responsible for one another to such an extent that they initially made certain of their joint livelihood before they used their personal incomes to meet their own needs, their situation was said to be comparable to that of spouses. Parent-related reasons were also said to be able to thus influence the duration of the maintenance claim by these means.

The parental right contained in Article 6.2 of the Basic Law was said to protect the possibility of the parent entitled to bring up the child to ensure the care and bringing up of the child without being prevented from doing so by their own gainful employment. Where personal care by a parent was absolutely necessary, it was said to be therefore necessary to structure the maintenance claims ensuring care in an identical fashion. Particularly during the first three years of life, when the parents could not rely on state assistance in the shape of crèches, a child was said to rely on personal care, whether he or she was born in or out of wedlock. This was said to be allowed for by § 1615 l.2 of the Civil Code. Accordingly, the child was said to be entitled to a statutorily guaranteed kindergarten place. However, insofar as state assistance could not be claimed, it was said to be constitutionally required to enable a

parent to bring up the child in person. This was said to be to be considered in the framework of the interpretation of § 1615 l.2 sentence 3 of the Civil Code.
Article 3.1 of the Basic Law was also said not to require the maintenance claims to be treated equally, given that the claim of a divorced spouse for care of a child, unlike the claim according to § 1615 l.2 of the Civil Code, was said to be simultaneously based on the ongoing impact of a dissolved marriage in addition to the child-related reasons. Article 6.5 of the Basic Law was said to place the legislature under an obligation to create the same conditions for the physical and mental development and status in society of children not born in marriage as children born in wedlock. The child's best interests protected by this fundamental rights-related provision were however said to impact the claim under § 1615 l.2 of the Civil Code only insofar as the maintenance was to enable the caring parent to facilitate the care and bringing up of the child without being prevented from doing so by gainful employment. Only to this degree was it said that the provision was covered by the protective purpose of Article 6.5 of the Basic Law, whilst the interaction in particular regarding Article 6.1 of the Basic Law had to be considered. Since the claim from § 1615 l.2 of the Civil Code was said to impact not the maintenance of the child born out of wedlock, but that of the caring parent, Article 6.5 of the Basic Law was said to require equal treatment only insofar as the maintenance of the parent had a direct impact on the development of the child and its social status. The legal term of gross inequity, to which the possibility of extending the maintenance claim links, was therefore to be interpreted broadly if the circumstances of the individual case, in spite of state assistance, did not offer a guarantee that the physical and mental development of the child was safeguarded. § 1615 l.2 sentence 3 of the Civil Code was said to permit an interpretation in conformity with the constitution, accommodating child-related and parent-related reasons. Since the child-related reasons took on particular significance, an extension of the maintenance claim was said to already be conceivable if the postponement of the mother's gainful employment appeared to be expedient and in the child's best interests either in objective terms because of the special needs of the child, or the child was in particular need of care. Parent-related reasons, by contrast, might apply if the party obliged to provide maintenance had created a special trust towards the beneficiary, for instance because the parents had had the child in an expectation of a lasting co-habitation.

II.

The plaintiff of the original proceedings is the mother of a child born in April 1997, cared for by her, whose father was not and is not married to her. He was sentenced in 1998 to pay maintenance to the plaintiff of DM 1,230 per month until the child reached the age of three according to § 1615 l.2 of the Civil Code, and is the defendant of the original proceedings. In May 2001, the plaintiff had another child born out of wedlock from another man. The father of this child was obliged by the court to pay childcare maintenance to the plaintiff of € 211 per month for the period from February 2002 to May 2004. The plaintiff also has two more children from a dissolved marriage, one of whom lives with the plaintiff.

1. In 2002, the plaintiff applied for legal aid for intended court action against the defendant in respect of payment of childcare maintenance from February 2002 amounting to € 451 per month; she deducted the maintenance payment of the father of her child born in 2001 when calculating the amount of the maintenance. Both the Local Court (*Amtsgericht*) and the Higher Regional Court rejected the application due to lack of prospects of success. The claim according to § 1615 l.2 of the Civil Code was said to be restricted in principle to three years after the birth of the child. This time limit was said not to be unconstitutional. It was said that the plaintiff had not put forward any circumstances making the time limit appear grossly inequitable.

The Federal Constitutional Court rescinded the rulings of the Local Court and of the Higher Regional Court by order of 4 February 2004 (Chamber Decisions of the Federal Constitutional Court (*Kammerentscheidungen des Bundesverfassungsgerichts* – BVerfGK) 2, 275) and referred the case to the Local Court. It held that the constitutionality of § 1615 l.2 sentence 3 of the Civil Code not a simple question or one that could be ruled on clearly or decided on in the summary legal aid proceedings. Childcare maintenance according to § 1570 of the Civil Code, and according to § 1615 l.2 of the Civil Code, was said to serve to facilitate the personal care of the child by a parent. Against this background, the constitutionality of the different manifestation of childcare maintenance with regard to the principle of the equal treatment of children who are born in wedlock and out of wedlock from Article 6.5 of the Basic Law appeared to be at least questionable. The ruling on this question in the legal aid proceedings was said to deny the plaintiff the possibility to put forward her own point of view in greater detail in the principal proceedings and, after exhausting the legal remedies, where appropriate to have § 1615 l.2 of the Civil Code indirectly reviewed for its constitutionality by lodging a constitutional complaint.

2. After granting legal aid, the Local Court rejected the action. It was stated that it was immaterial whether and to what degree, with regard to the childcare maintenance of the plaintiff, there was a part debtorship of her divorced husband or of the father of her other child born out of wedlock, in addition to the defendant, given that § 1615 l.2 sentence 3 of the Civil Code, which caused childcare maintenance to end three years after the birth of the child, was constitutional. The plaintiff was said

not to have put forward any circumstances indicating that refusal of maintenance after three years was grossly inequitable. The plaintiff submitted an appeal on points of fact and law against this, which she reasoned by claiming that the time limit in § 1615 l.2 of the Civil Code was unconstitutional.

III.

By order of 16 August 2004, the Higher Regional Court suspended the proceedings and submitted the question for a ruling to the Federal Constitutional Court of whether § 1615 l.2 second half of sentence 3 of the Civil Code was incompatible with Article 6.5 of the Basic Law.

1. The ruling was said to depend on the validity of the provision. If it were constitutional, the appeal on points of fact and law would have to be rejected. Reasons for gross inequity within the meaning of this provision had not been put forward. If, by contrast, the provision was unconstitutional, the same standard would have to be applied to the question of the degree to which the plaintiff could be expected to engage in gainful employment as under § 1570 of the Civil Code. Given the age of her child born in 1997, this would give rise to a continuing maintenance claim. It would still be necessary to clarify the amount of this claim in such a case, considering any partial liability of the divorced husband and of the father of her other child born out of wedlock. The defendant would however definitely have to shoulder a share of the maintenance.

2. According to Article 6.5 of the Basic Law, the legislation was to create the same conditions for the intellectual and mental development and status in society for children born out of wedlock as for children born in wedlock. The reason for the claim under § 1570 of the Civil Code was said to be to ensure maintenance for a parent in order to enable him or her to take personal care of the child which the legislature, and with it the supreme court case-law, still regarded as the optimum form of care in the interest of the child, and hence as a rule granted a maintenance claim until the child's tenth birthday. By contrast, the maintenance claim was said to be time-limited to three years after the birth for the personal care of a child born out of wedlock by § 1615 l.2 sentence 3 of the Civil Code unless it would be grossly inequitable to refuse a maintenance claim, the burden of presentation and evidence for this lying with the maintenance beneficiary. Hence as a rule, a child born out of wedlock, in contradistinction to a child born in wedlock, was to accept third-party care from the age of three since the caring parent relied on taking up gainful employment because of not having a maintenance claim. The question of until when it was most beneficial for the healthy development of a child that personal care was undertaken by a parent could however only be answered in a uniform

manner already from a scientific point of view, and certainly in the light of Article 6.5 of the Basic Law.

This unequal treatment of children who are born in and out of wedlock could also not be justified with the marital solidarity which survives marriage, which was said to be missing in the case of maintenance claims according to § 1615 l.2 of the Civil Code. Just as this provision, § 1570 of the Civil Code was also said to serve to facilitate the care of the child by a parent. From the point of view of the child, however, it was said to be immaterial to the question of the time until when a parent could care for the child personally whether its parents had been married to each other or not. The unequal treatment was therefore said to be in breach of Article 6.5 of the Basic Law.

3. It was also said that § 1615 l.2 of the Civil Code could not be made to comply with this constitutional standard by interpreting it in conformity with the constitution. It was stated that this would only be possible if gross inequity within the meaning of this provision was presumed whenever and as long as a caring parent of a child born in wedlock was granted maintenance, given that this was the only way to guarantee the necessary equal treatment. However, such a far-reaching conclusion was said not to be drawn by the proponents of an interpretation of § 1615 l.2 of the Civil Code in conformity with the constitution. It was also said to go beyond an interpretation in conformity with the constitution, given that contrary to the clearly expressed intention of the legislature the relationship between rule and exception stated in § 1615 l.2 of the Civil Code would be reversed.

IV.

…

B.

The different legislation on maintenance claims for the care of children in § 1570 of the Civil Code, on the one hand, and in § 1615 l.2 sentence 3 of the Civil Code, on the other, is not compatible with the Basic Law. It is in breach of the principle contained in Article 6.5 of the Basic Law requiring the legislature to create for children born out of wedlock the same conditions for their physical and mental development as children born in wedlock.

I.

1. Article 6.5 of the Basic Law contains a constitutional mandate aiming to bring about equality and equal treatment of all children, regardless of their civil status, and which obliges the legislature to create for children born out of wedlock by means of positive legislation the same conditions for their physical and mental development as children born in wedlock. Here, the legislature may in principle not satisfy itself with merely bringing closer together the status of children born out of wedlock and that of children born in wedlock (see BVerfGE 85, 80 (88)). A child may not be placed at a disadvantage because of being born out of wedlock (see BVerfGE 25, 167 (190)). Article 6.5 of the Basic Law also prohibits children born out of wedlock being placed in an indirectly less favourable position as against children born in wedlock (see BVerfGE 88, 87 (96)). A differentiating legislation for children who are born out of wedlock is constitutionally only justified if it is absolutely necessary because of the different de facto circumstances in order to achieve the goal of the equality of children born out of wedlock with children born in wedlock. If there are no such absolute de facto reasons for the unequal treatment of children born out of wedlock, this can only be justified by colliding constitutional law, which is to be weighed against Article 6.5 of the Basic Law (see BVerfGE 84, 168 (185), as well as re Article 3.3 of the Basic Law BVerfGE 85, 191 (209); 92, 91 (109)).

2. The legislature has acted in breach of this prohibition to place children born out of wedlock in a less favourable position as against children born in wedlock, which is contained in Article 6.5 of the Basic Law, by assessing differently the duration of the maintenance which a parent who takes care of a child may claim from another parent in § 1570 of the Civil Code for the divorced spouse and in § 1615 l.2 sentence 3 of the Civil Code for the parent of a child born out of wedlock.

a) § 1570 of the Civil Code and § 1615 l of the Civil Code however give rise to maintenance claims which are not for the child itself, but for the parent caring for the child. Nonetheless, the question of how long this maintenance is to be paid to the carer relates to and affects the circumstances and care situation of the child. Childcare maintenance is granted for reasons of the child's best interests. It enables the parent to give personal attention to the child insofar as the child requires care or bringing up, and hence the carer cannot be expected to engage in gainful employment, as stated in identical wording in both provisions in this respect. Maintenance is hence orientated towards the child and its needs for personal care, and defines the circumstances in which the child grows up (see BVerfGE 103, 89 (110)). The duration of the maintenance payment to the parent determines how long the child can be personally cared for by this parent. If it is expected, as it is in § 1615 l of the Civil

Code, that the caring mother or the caring father should engage in gainful employment again after the child's third birthday, and if the maintenance claim hence ends, they are as a rule forced from this time to engage in employment in order to ensure their livelihood. The consequence of this is that they must entrust the child to third-party care at least for a time, and are only available to him or her for a restricted period of time. If, by contrast, the maintenance of the mother or of the father is secured by maintenance payments which, as in § 1570 of the Civil Code, are orientated not only as to the reasons, but also in their duration towards the care interests of the child and in this respect reach – according to the case-law – far beyond the child's third birthday, the child may enjoy personal parental care for a considerably longer time. The circumstances of the children in question are hence heavily influenced by the maintenance arrangements.
b) The different assessment of childcare maintenance according to § 1570 of the Civil Code and § 1615 l.2 sentence 3 of the Civil Code, leading to different care situations of children who are born in wedlock and out of wedlock, is a direct consequence of the statutory regulation; it does not emerge solely from the interpretation of the provisions by the case-law.
In enacting § 1570 of the Civil Code, the legislature explicitly omitted to impose a time limit on childcare maintenance or indeed to provide aids for interpretation for the case-law as to the duration of the claim because it considered this incorrect given the diversity of circumstances (see *Bundestag* printed paper 7/650, pp. 122-123). Rather, through the utilisation of the undefined legal term "as long as", and relating the latter to the reason for the claim – because of the care and bringing up of the child –, it tied the duration of the claim to the child's need for care, and hence deliberately permitted the case-law to deal with the special circumstances of the individual case and to develop standards for a uniform case determining a child's need for care according to his or her age phases. Hence, at the same time the parent's obligation to engage in employment is lent concrete form, and the duration of maintenance is determined on that basis. The guidelines of the Higher Regional Courts set out age grades according to which personal full-time care of the child is considered to be necessary until the child reaches the age of between eight and ten, and hence it is presumed that the caring parent is not obliged to enter gainful employment. The full amount of childcare maintenance is therefore payable until then. Thereafter, only partial gainful employment is expected, the income from which is to be counted against maintenance. Only when the child reaches the age of sixteen does the obligation to take up gainful employment apply in full, and the right to childcare maintenance cease to apply as a rule. This concrete form given by the case-law in the shape of an age phase model is based on the openness of the provision, and has also not been corrected by the legislature by making the provision

more precise. By contrast, considering this interpretation of § 1570 of the Civil Code by the case-law, the legislature has generally restricted maintenance to allow care for a child born out of wedlock in § 1615 l.2 sentence 3 of the Civil Code to three years, and has permitted an extension of the claim over and above this only in exceptional cases, namely if refusal would be grossly inequitable after this time has expired, in particular taking the child's interests into account. It considered this time limit to be suitable because it was said to ensure full care of the child by a parent until kindergarten age, after which there was a possibility of third-party care which was not detrimental to the child, but which on the contrary promoted its development. It hence facilitated and approved the granting of different durations of childcare maintenance for the care of children who are born out of wedlock and in wedlock.

c) The legislature places children who are born out of wedlock at a disadvantage as against children born in wedlock by providing unequal security of personal care by a parent under maintenance law.

It is irrelevant here how long it is most beneficial in pedagogical and psychological terms for a child and its physical and mental development to be comprehensively and continually cared for by a parent. The Federal Constitutional Court does not have to find on whether or from what age onwards one must presume that a child does not incur damage if it is at least cared for during a certain period by other persons than its parents, or whether it does not indeed receive additional promotion by virtue of third-party care, for instance in kindergarten, and hence by being together with other children. The specialist scientists continue to discuss these questions controversially, and do not give unambiguous answers to it. It is a matter for the legislature to decide whether it intends to financially safeguard the personal care of a child by a parent, which benefits the child, through maintenance claims, it lying in the legislature's assessment prerogative as to how long it considers it suitable, weighing the child's best interests with the interests of the, in this respect, beneficiary and debtor, to grant such a maintenance claim. If it however considers it to be necessary for and beneficial to the child's best interests to maintain for the child the possibility, at least for a certain time, to experience the full attention of a parent, and thus grants to the caring parent a maintenance claim against the other parent, Article 6.5 of the Basic Law prohibits measuring with two standards and considering much longer personal care to be indicated with children born in wedlock than with children born out of wedlock. How much personal parental care and attention a child needs is not determined by whether he or she was born in or out of wedlock. If, by contrast, the legislature considers it to be non-detrimental, or indeed beneficial, to the child's development for children to attend kindergarten from the age of three, and if as in § 1615 l of the Civil Code it limits the maintenance claim of the caring parent for this reason, so that this parent once more must ensure his or her maintenance through gainful employment, it may equally not apply this point of view to children born out of wedlock only. Rather, in its assessment of how long a child needs the personal care of a parent the legislature must select the same standard for children who are born out of wedlock and in wedlock and measure the duration of the maintenance claims thereby.

It places children who are born out of wedlock in a less favourable position if the caring parent of a child born in wedlock is as a rule granted the possibility on the basis of the statutory decision to give full personal attention to the child at least until its eighth birthday with the aid of a maintenance claim granted until then, whilst the legislature considers it to be sufficient that a child born out of wedlock only receives such personal care in the first three years of life, and hence restricts the maintenance claim of its caring parent to this period in a standard case. Hence, the legislature deprives a parent of a child born out of wedlock, in contradistinction to a parent of a child born in wedlock, from this point in time onwards, of the financial basis for the freedom to decide between personal care and third-party care of the child, and hence of necessity places a child who is born out of wedlock in the situation of being cared for elsewhere earlier than children who are born in wedlock. Even if this does not cause detriment to a child in general, a disadvantage is constituted by virtue of the fact that a child who is born out of wedlock is placed in a disadvantageous position as against a child born in wedlock because of being denied the possibility of being at the centre of parental care just as long as a child born in wedlock.

3. The unequal duration of the maintenance claims under § 1570 of the Civil Code and § 1615 l.2 of the Civil Code, which leads to children born out of wedlock being placed in a less favourable position as against children born in wedlock, is justified neither by different social situations in which the children are found, nor by differences consisting in the relationships between their parents, or by marital solidarity continuing to apply to divorced spouses, in contradistinction to parents not married to each other, which may give rise to claims to which the unmarried are not entitled.

a) The de facto circumstances of the children of divorced parents born in wedlock and of children born out of wedlock are fundamentally only slightly different. They live either in a family situation which the caring parent has created after divorce by virtue of a new partnership or which he or she continues in a non-marital community, or they grow up with only the caring parent. In both family constellations, the caring parent relies on his or her maintenance being safeguarded if he or she wishes to care for the child personally, whether born in or out of wedlock, and hence not to engage in gainful employment. Therefore, children who are born in wedlock and out of wedlock are equally affected if the caring parent is no longer able to claim maintenance from the other parent, and hence must take up gainful employment. They must equally forgo personal care by a parent unless the divorced spouse, the new partner or the other parent is willing to pay for the maintenance of the caring parent with no legal foundation.

b) Also the broad range of different living arrangements mentioned in the legislative procedure which is stated to be found with unmarried parents in contrast to married parents is unable to justify the unequal duration of the maintenance claims of parents caring for children. It is correct to state that the variance of the parental relationships from which a child born out of wedlock arises ranges from a fleeting affair to a lasting community, whilst marriage in which children are born is always planned to last, even if it may fail later. A maintenance claim which is granted because of the care or bringing up of a child is however not determined by this difference. The party obliged to provide maintenance is claimed against by law not for the sake of the other parent, but because of the child so that he or she can be cared for personally by a parent. The diversity of non-marital relationships also does not lead to different parental responsibility towards the child. Each legally identified parent is entitled to the parental right entrenched in Article 6.2 of the Basic Law, which also imposes on him or her the comprehensive responsibility for the living and development conditions of the child, regardless of whether the child was born in or out of wedlock or whether it is the product of a fleeting or established tie between its parents. This responsibility also includes ensuring care for the child, in a manner serving the child's best interests, by paying maintenance to the caring parent. Article 6.5 of the Basic Law prohibits making a distinction here according to the nature of the parental relationship (see BVerfGE 84, 168 (185)), given that it intends precisely to bring about the equality of children whose parents have not undertaken responsibility for one another with those children whose parents take care of one another and of their child by being married.

c) Post-marital solidarity cannot justify that, according to § 1615 l.2 sentence 3 of the Civil Code, the parent of a child born out of wedlock is only entitled to childcare maintenance until its third birthday, whilst according to § 1570 of the Civil Code the parent of a child born in wedlock is granted a much longer childcare maintenance claim, assessed according to age phases of the child.

aa) As a fundamental provision that determines values, Article 6.1 of the Basic Law gives rise to the obligation of the state to protect and promote marriage (see BVerfGE 108, 351 (363)). This protection is enjoyed not only by the existing marriage, but also covers the consequential effects of a dissolved marriage (see BVerfGE 53, 257 (296)) and continues to impact the relationships between the divorced spouses under maintenance law (see BVerfGE 66, 84 (94)). Post-marital solidarity applies in particular where a divorced spouse cannot be expected to rely on his or her fundamental independent economic responsibility after divorce because he or she is unable to ensure his or her own livelihood through reintegration into employment due to the tasks which he or she assumed in marriage (see BVerfGE 57, 361 (379)). This in particular also applies to cases in which the divorced spouse takes care of a joint child. For this reason, in addition to safeguarding divorced spouses under maintenance law in the event that they cannot be expected to engage in gainful employment because of their age (§ 1571 of the Civil Code) or because of illness (§ 1572 of the Civil Code) or if they do not find suitable gainful employment (§§ 1573 and 1574 of the Civil Code), the legislature ensures with § 1570 of the Civil Code that a divorced spouse can claim maintenance as long as and insofar as he or she cannot be expected to engage in gainful employment because of care or bringing up of the joint child.

bb) That the maintenance of a divorced spouse for the care of a joint child is included in the protection provided by Article 6.1 of the Basic Law and is a result of post-marital solidarity is not a justifying reason why the duration of the maintenance orientated in line with the age of the children provides different age categories for the care of children who are born out of wedlock and in wedlock, leading to children who are born out of wedlock and in wedlock being personally cared for by a parent for different lengths of time.

(1) Article 6.5 of the Basic Law demands that the same living conditions are to be created for children born out of wedlock as for children born in wedlock. Hence, the constitutional provision at the same time prohibits giving privileges to children who are born in wedlock which is reasoned by invoking the protection of marriage under Article 6.1 of the Basic Law because this would particularly run counter to the equality principle.

This however does not rule out placing a divorced parent in a more beneficial position under maintenance law than an unmarried parent because of the protection which is enjoyed by virtue of the marital tie through Article 6.1 of the Basic Law, which indirectly may also impact the circumstances of the children living with these parents (see also Federal Constitutional Court (*Bundesverfassungsgericht* – BVerfG), Judgment of 28 February 2007 – 1 BvL 5/03 –, FamRZ 2007, p. 529). Thus, a divorced parent has a maintenance claim against the other parent regardless of the age of the child of whom he or she is taking care if he or she does not find suitable gainful employment, whilst a non-married parent has no maintenance claim against the other parent in the event of unemployment. This may also lead to different social situations for the children affected. The legislature may grant to the divorced spouse, with post-marital spousal maintenance, claims indirectly also benefiting the child for whom he or she cares, whilst children who are born out of wed-

lock are unable to benefit from such claims because their parents do not owe one another such maintenance. The legislature may also take into account here the fact that the division of tasks which the spouses agreed and practiced with one another during the marriage may cause difficulties to one of the spouses when it comes to reintegrating into working life after divorce, and may use this as a reason to grant to the spouse affected by this a maintenance claim for a certain period.
If however the legislature grants a maintenance claim to the divorced spouse solely because of the personal care of the joint child, Article 6.5 of the Basic Law prohibits it from making a different assessment of the duration of the personal care considered necessary for a child born in wedlock than for a child born out of wedlock. How long a child is to receive personal care from a parent is not determined by marital solidarity, but by the needs of children, which in principle do not differ for children who are born in wedlock and out of wedlock.
(2) It is not the case that the claim from § 1570 of the Civil Code has not been granted solely because of childcare, but that rather, over and above this, it is to enable the divorced spouses not to be exposed to an obligation to take up gainful employment for a longer period in order hence to find a later and easier transition and re-entry into working life because of post-marital solidarity on assumption of childcare. The different duration of the maintenance claim granted according to § 1570 of the Civil Code in relation to the duration of the claim according to § 1615 l.2 sentence 3 of the Civil Code can hence not be justified with this.
(a) Such an orientation, over and above childcare, of the maintenance claim which it contains can be derived neither from the wording of § 1570 of the Civil Code, nor from its history.
The wording of the provision states care or bringing up of a joint child as the only reason for granting maintenance. Also the question of the duration of the claim relates solely to this reason. The title to the provision also stresses that maintenance is granted particularly because of care of a child. The ongoing joint responsibility of the spouses for one another has also been cited in the reasoning for the Act as a reason why, despite termination of the economic relationship between the spouses by virtue of divorce, a divorced spouse can nonetheless be granted maintenance claims against the other spouse in certain cases of need. However, exclusively childcare is named in § 1570 of the Civil Code as such a case of need, and hence as a reason for derogating from the general self-responsibility of the divorced spouses, and the duration of the claim made to depend solely on how long the child requires care. For the first time in the material relating to the Act Reforming the Law of Parent and Child of 16 December 1997 (Federal Law Gazette I p. 2942), the view was taken with the amendment of § 1615 l.2 sentence 3 of the Civil Code carried out therein that childcare maintenance according to § 1570 of the Civil Code was also

reasoned by the additional protection purpose of post-marital solidarity, which was said to justify its more detailed elaboration as against § 1615 l.2 sentence 3 of the Civil Code (see *Bundestag* printed paper 13/8511, p. 71).

(b) Also taking account of this reason added subsequently by the legislature, the indication of post-marital solidarity is unable to justify the different durations of the two maintenance claims in light of Article 6.5 of the Basic Law. The decade-long interpretation and application of § 1570 of the Civil Code in case-law established by the legislature through the openness of the provision and accepted by the legislature does not provide any indication that, with the time assessment of this maintenance claim additionally over and above the need for care of the child, the circumstance is taken into account in time terms that a child-caring spouse has permanently adjusted to the jointly agreed division of tasks in marriage and that he or she is hence to be granted a longer period to reintegrate into working life. Rather, the duration of the maintenance claim from § 1570 of the Civil Code which is orientated and assessed exclusively in line with the child's age stands in opposition to the presumption and consideration of such a further reason determining the duration of the claim, and confirms that the different duration of this claim as against the claim from § 1615 l.2 sentence 3 of the Civil Code is based on a different assessment of the need for care of children who are born out of wedlock and in wedlock. This is however prohibited by Article 6.5 of the Basic Law.

(aa) It should now be asked here whether § 1570 of the Civil Code, in the event of its also covering maintenance owed in terms of marital solidarity over and above the child's need for care, would sufficiently clearly express what orientation the duration of this claim stems from, a claim going over and above the period of childcare, enabling the caring parent to exclusively remain in this role. As a standard of the duration, § 1570 of the Civil Code only names the need for childcare. If the legislature is however additionally pursuing a further purpose with the maintenance claim, it not only must make this purpose clear in the provision, but must also state how the scope of this part of the maintenance claim is to be assessed, as the legislature should also state this if it were to create a separate maintenance claim for this purpose. § 1570 of the Civil Code does not do so.

(bb) Certainly, a considerably longer duration of the claim from § 1570 of the Civil Code, exclusively assessed in line with the age of the children, as against the claim under § 1615 l.2 sentence 3 of the Civil Code, cannot be justified with an additional purpose emerging from post-marital solidarity. The age of children is certainly a suitable link in order to determine the need of a child to be provided with personal care by a parent. This is precisely the orientation of the case-law when it assesses the existence and scope of an obligation to take up gainful employment of the caring parent by the age phases of the children and accordingly determines the duration of the maintenance claim under § 1570 of the Civil Code. According to this case-law, it should be possible as a rule for a parent to care for a child personally into primary school years, and then for the child to be under parental care for at least large stretches of the day and not to need any more care during the day from the age of sixteen. This schematic orientation by the age of the children does not permit one to recognise that the case-law grants the maintenance claim under § 1570 of the Civil Code, as against the claim under § 1615 l.2 sentence 3 of the Civil Code, for a longer period for reasons of a special needs situation of the caring parent. The age of a child is not a viable measure for determining how long a parent should be granted maintenance not because of childcare, but because of his or her trust in the role assumed during marriage in caring for the child. This would be assessable more in line with the duration of marriage or with the duration of the interruption of employment because of childcare.

(cc) In its ruling of 5 July 2006 (loc. cit.), the Federal Court of Justice used post-marital solidarity as a reason for the longer claim duration of § 1570 of the Civil Code, and stated that for this reason the provision also granted maintenance to the divorced parent for his or her sake. However, it did not answer the question as to why case-law, also that of the Federal Court of Justice, orientates the maintenance duration exclusively in line with the age of the children. It also left open whether it hence agrees that the three-year period for the necessary personal care of the child by its parent which is considered sufficient in § 1615 l.2 sentence 3 of the Civil Code and is also used as a basis there is also the timeframe in which the claim is granted for the care of the child in § 1570 of the Civil Code, whilst granting maintenance for the time far beyond this then rightly served to safeguard for the divorced parent his or her maintenance "for his or her own sake", even though this time is also measured in line with the child's age.

Taking account of this duration of the maintenance claim according to § 1570 of the Civil Code assessed by the case-law exclusively in line with the child's age, the argument of post-marital solidarity put forward by the Federal Court of Justice proves not to be able to justify the different duration of the maintenance claims according to § 1570 of the Civil Code and § 1615 l.2 sentence 3 of the Civil Code. Article 6.5 of the Basic Law particularly prohibits solely referring to marriage, and hence also to post-marital solidarity, to treat children who are born out of wedlock differently than children who are born in wedlock. If a maintenance claim is granted because of childcare and its duration is exclusively assessed in line with the child's age, and hence by how long a child requires personal care from a parent, it violates Article 6.5 of the Basic Law to categorise the need for care of children who are born out of wedlock as being shorter than for children who are born in wedlock.

4. The violation of Article 6.5 of the Basic Law caused by placing children born out of wedlock in a less favourable position as against children born in wedlock through the different duration of granting maintenance for childcare according to § 1570 of the Civil Code and § 1615 l.2 sentence 3 of the Civil Code cannot be remedied by an interpretation of § 1615 l.2 sentence 3 of the Civil Code in conformity with the constitution.
a) The interpretation of § 1615 l.2 sentence 3 of the Civil Code carried out by the Federal Court of Justice does not remedy the unequal treatment of children born out of wedlock in violation of Article 6.5 of the Basic Law. A broad interpretation of "gross inequity", which opens the possibility to exceptionally grant childcare maintenance beyond the child's third birthday according to § 1615 l.2 sentence 3 of the Civil Code on the assumption of its application, can lead to a situation in which greater consideration can be given to the special circumstances of the individual case with regard to the specific development of the child or to the parental situation in quite a few cases and lead to extended childcare maintenance being granted. However, the possibility remains that maintenance is restricted to three years for children born out of wedlock whose development does not show any special reasons why they need longer care, or whose parents have not lived in a trust-forming community which, in the view of the Federal Court of Justice, could also justify maintenance payment for only three years to be grossly inequitable, in contradistinction to children born in wedlock, who because of the granting of maintenance according to § 1570 of the Civil Code may experience personal care by a parent for a considerably longer period without special reasons applying. This difference, which also continues to apply with a broad interpretation of the exceptional arrangement contained in § 1615 l.2 sentence 3 of the Civil Code, does not stand up to Article 6.5 of the Basic Law since the constitutional provision also prohibits discrimination against individual groups of children born out of wedlock as against children born in wedlock (see BVerfGE 17, 148 (153-154)).
b) An interpretation of § 1615 l.2 sentence 3 of the Civil Code which would make an exception of the restriction of the maintenance claim to three years the rule in order to do justice to Article 6.5 of the Basic Law, and which in general terms would adjust the period covered by childcare maintenance to the duration of the maintenance granted according to § 1570 of the Civil Code, would however overstep the limits of an interpretation in conformity with the constitution.
Such an interpretation would violate, firstly, the will of the legislature which has been expressed clearly and unequivocally to restrict the maintenance claim of a parent caring for a child born out of wedlock to three years in a standard case and only to grant a claim over and above this in exceptional cases (see BVerfGE 90, 263 (275)). Moreover, however, by these means the duration of the claim to bring about

equal treatment of children who are born out of wedlock and in wedlock could only be increased to the duration of the claim granted according to § 1570 of the Civil Code. However, it lies within the sole competence of the legislature as to how to avoid a less beneficial status for children born out of wedlock as against children born in wedlock and how long it considers it to be necessary for it to be possible for children who are born out of wedlock and in wedlock to be equally cared for personally by a parent in order to orientate in line with this the length of time for which it grants a maintenance claim to the caring parent.

II.

1. § 1615 l.2 sentence 3 of the Civil Code, by contrast, does not violate the parental right protected by Article 6.2 of the Basic Law.

Article 6.2 of the Basic Law gives rise for parents in equal measure to the right and the duty to care for and bring up their children. This responsibility for their child is allocated to the parents first and foremost and has to serve the child's best interests. The parental right is in this respect a right serving the interest of the child (see BVerfGE 75, 201 (218)). The maintenance arrangement carried out in § 1615 l.2 sentence 3 of the Civil Code, which grants to the parent of a child born out of wedlock a childcare maintenance claim which as a rule is restricted to three years, does not breach this right. The legislature has ensured with this arrangement that the parent caring for the child does not have to engage in gainful employment during the first three years of the child's life, but can devote himself or herself to the child and hence carry out his or her parental responsibility. The time limit of three years placed as a rule on the maintenance claim is not objectionable in light of Article 6.2 of the Basic Law. It is, firstly, within the legislature's competence of assessment as to how long it considers it to be necessary in terms of the child's best interests and reasonable for the parent obliged to provide maintenance to facilitate the personal care of the child by a parent by granting a maintenance claim to this parent. Secondly, it has granted to each child a right to a kindergarten place from the age of three. It has hence ensured that a child as a rule can experience external care from this age whilst its parent engages in gainful employment. It is a justifiable assessment of the legislature if it hence does not consider it to be necessary to release the caring parent from his or her obligation to take up gainful employment for a longer period, and has rather presumed by evaluating scientific studies that care of the child in kindergarten is not detrimental to the child, but that it promotes important skills on the part of the child. This does not constitute neglect of the parental right. Rather, with the arrangement the legislature has taken into consideration the interests both of the caring parent and of the parent obliged to provide maintenance, as well as those of the child, and has balanced them out. In particular, however, it has created via the equity clause contained in § 1615 l.2 sentence 3 of the Civil Code the possibility to examine in individual cases whether the cessation of the maintenance payment to the caring parent could impair the child's best interests, and for such a case has provided for an extension of the granting of maintenance. This takes sufficient account of the parental right of the caring parent.

2. Given that the different duration arrangement of the maintenance claims according to § 1615 l.2 sentence 3 of the Civil Code and in § 1570 of the Civil Code violates Article 6.5 of the Basic Law, there is no longer scope for the review as to whether it also violates Article 3.1 of the Basic Law because it treats caring parents of children who are born in wedlock and out of wedlock unequally. Article 6.5 of the Basic Law is the material fundamental-rights provision here, to which a violation of the general principle of equality is subordinated.

C. – I.

Since the violation of Article 6.5 of the Basic Law is constituted by the different arrangement of the maintenance claims because of the care of children in § 1570 of the Civil Code, on the one hand, and § 1615 l.2 sentence 3 of the Civil Code, on the other, it is not possible to hand down a nullity declaration of § 1615 l.2 sentence 3 of the Civil Code, or to hand down a declaration of the incompatibility of this provision with Article 6.5 of the Basic Law (see BVerfGE 84, 168 (186-187)). The legislature has several possibilities at its disposal to remedy the unconstitutional situation. For instance, it may bring about equal treatment of the elements regulated on by amending § 1615 l of the Civil Code, by amending § 1570 of the Civil Code or also by a new legislation on both elements. Here, it must only use as a basis an identical standard in each case as to the duration of the maintenance claim granted for childcare with children who are born out of wedlock and in wedlock.

The legislature is obliged to bring a constitutional transitional arrangement into being by 31 December 2008 which satisfies Article 6.5 of the Basic Law.

II.

The unconstitutional situation is to be accepted until the new regulation comes into being. No order is to be handed down suspending the proceedings in which childcare maintenance is claimed according to § 1615 l of the Civil Code or according to § 1570 of the Civil Code because the legislature is not to be influenced in its decision as to how it wishes to carry out the adjustment required by Article 6.5 of the Basic Law. Suspension of all proceedings based on a claim of childcare mainte-

nance according to § 1570 of the Civil Code and § 1615 l of the Civil Code would also lead to a temporary cessation of the granting of rights, a bottleneck of rulings in the family courts and after entry into force of the new regulation to a delay in processing the suspended proceedings. In light of this, it is suitable that the existing regulations continue to apply until the new regulation comes into force. The disadvantage incurred by the parents and their children born out of wedlock as against children born in wedlock until the new legislation enters into force is acceptable since the duration of the maintenance claim because of the care of a child born out of wedlock according to § 1615 l.2 sentence 3 of the Civil Code per se does not violate the child's best interests.
This decision was passed by seven votes to one.

Justices: Papier, Steiner, Hohmann-Dennhardt, Hoffmann-Riem, Bryde, Gaier, Eichberger, Schluckebier

As a result of the judgment of the Federal Constitutional Court, § 1570 and § 1615 l.2 of the Civil Code were re-worded as follows with effect from 1 January 2008 by Article 1 of the Act of 21 December 2007 (Federal Law Gazette. I p. 3189):

§ 1570
Maintenance to care for a child

(1) A divorced spouse may demand maintenance from the other, for the care for or upbringing of a child of the spouses, for at least three years after the birth. The duration of the claim to maintenance is extended as long as and to the extent that this is equitable. Here, the concerns of the child and the existing possibilities of childcare are to be taken into account.
(2) The duration of the maintenance claim is further extended if, taking into account the arrangement of childcare and gainful employment in the marriage and the duration of the marriage, this is equitable.

§ 1615 l
Maintenance claim of mother and father by reason of the birth

(2) To the extent that the mother is not engaged in gainful employment because as a result of the pregnancy or of an illness caused by the pregnancy or the delivery she is incapable of doing so, the father is obliged to pay her maintenance

for a period exceeding the period set out in subsection (1) sentence 1. The same applies to the extent that the mother cannot be expected to be engaged in gainful employment by reason of the care or upbringing of the child. The obligation to maintain begins at the earliest four months before the birth and continues for at least three years after the birth. It is extended, as long as and to the extent that this is equitable. Here, particular account is to be taken of the concerns of the child and the existing possibilities of childcare.

No. 50

BVerfGE 121, 69

of 1 April 2008 – 1 BvR 1620/04 –

"Duty of contact case"

HEADNOTES:

1. **The duty to care for and bring up their child which is imposed on parents by Article 6.2 sentence 1 of the Basic Law (*Grundgesetz* – GG) is not owed exclusively to the state but also to the child. The child's right to parental care and upbringing in Article 6.2 sentence 1 of the Basic Law corresponds with this parental duty. It is for the legislature to elaborate the right and duty.**
2. **The encroachment on the fundamental right to protection of personality contained in Article 2.1 in conjunction with Article 1.1 of the Basic Law, which is associated with the imposition of an obligation on a parent to have contact with his or her child, is justified by the responsibility for his or her child imposed on the parent by Article 6.2 sentence 1 of the Basic Law and the child's right to parental care and upbringing. It is reasonable to oblige a parent to have contact with his or her child if this is in the child's best interests.**
3. **If coercive measures are necessary to force an unwilling parent to have contact with a child, this contact is not usually in the best interests of the child. The encroachment on the parent's fundamental right to protection of his or her right of personality which results from the threat to apply coercive measures is not justified in this context unless there are sufficient indications which suggest that enforced contact will be in the child's best interests in an individual case.**

Enlarged version of the translation published in: Jürgen Bröhmer & Clauspeter Hill (Eds.), 60 Years German Basic Law: The German Constitution and its Court: Landmark decisions of the Federal Constitutional Court of Germany in the area of fundamental rights, Berlin 2010, © Konrad-Adenauer-Stiftung e.V., reproduced with kind permission.

Judgment of the First Senate of 1 April 2008
on the basis of the oral hearing of 21 November 2007
– 1 BvR 1620/04 –

in the proceedings regarding the constitutional complaint of Mr. B., – authorized representatives: ..., lawyers –, 1. directly against the order of the Brandenburg Higher Regional Court (*Oberlandesgericht*) of 21 January 2004 – 15 UF 233/00 –, 2. indirectly against § 33.1 sentence 1 and § 33.3 of the Act on Matters of Non-Contentious Jurisdiction (*Gesetz über die Angelegenheiten der freiwilligen Gerichtsbarkeit* – FGG) –.

RULING:

1. § 33.1 sentence 1 and § 33.3 of the Act on Matters of Non-Contentious Jurisdiction are to be interpreted in conformity with the constitution as meaning that compulsory enforcement of the duty of contact of a parent who refuses to have contact with his or her child must be avoided unless there are sufficient indications in a specific case that enforced contact would be in the child's best interests.
2. The order of the Brandenburg Higher Regional Court of 21 January 2004 – 15 UF 233/00 – violates the complainant's right of personality under Article 2.1 in conjunction with Article 1.1 of the Basic Law to the extent that it threatens to fine the complainant. To this extent the order is reversed and the matter is referred back to the Brandenburg Higher Regional Court for a new decision.
3. The *Land* Brandenburg is ordered to reimburse the complainant his necessary expenses in the proceedings regarding the constitutional complaint.

EXTRACT FROM GROUNDS:

A.

The constitutional complaint relates to the question of whether a parental duty of contact, which is enforceable by execution pursuant to § 1684.1 of the Civil Code (*Bürgerliches Gesetzbuch* – BGB) against a parent who refuses to have contact with his or her child, can be enforced with the aid of coercive measures that may be threatened and imposed by § 33.1 and § 33.3 of the Act on Matters of Non-Contentious Jurisdiction (*Gesetz über die Angelegenheiten der freiwilligen Gerichtsbarkeit* – FGG).

I.

1. a) The Act Reforming the Law of Parent and Child (*Gesetz zur Reform des Kindschaftsrechts (Kindschaftsrechtsreformgesetz* – KindRG)) of 16 December 1997 (Federal Law Gazette (*Bundesgesetzblatt* – BGBl) I p. 2942), which entered into force on 1 July 1998, amended § 1684.1 of the Civil Code to allow children their own right to have contact with their parents. At the same time this provision stipulates that parents do not simply have a right to have contact with their child, but also have an obligation to have such contact. Family courts are required to decide on the scope of the right of contact, how it should be exercised, how it should be restricted and when it may be excluded pursuant to § 1684.3 and § 1684.4 of the Civil Code. The provisions of § 1684 of the Civil Code which are relevant here state:

> (1) A child has the right to have contact with each of its parents; each parent is obliged and entitled to have contact with his or her child.
> (3) The Family Court may determine the scope of the right of contact and elaborate the details of how it should be exercised, including in relation to third parties. …
> (4) The Family Court may restrict or exclude the right of contact or the enforcement of earlier decisions on the right of contact to the extent the child's best interests make this necessary. It may only issue a decision restricting or excluding the right of contact or its enforcement over an extended period or permanently if failure to do so on its part would endanger the child's best interests. The Family Court may in particular order that contact may only take place when a third party who is willing to assist with it is present. The third party may also be a youth welfare agency or an association; in this case the agency or association will select the individual to provide the assistance.

§ 33 of the Act on Matters of Non-Contentious Jurisdiction applies to the compulsory enforcement of a parent's duty of contact imposed by § 1684.1 of the German Civil Code. The relevant provisions of this section state:

> (1) If the court imposes an obligation on a person to undertake an act whose performance depends entirely on his volition …, it may enforce such performance by ordering him to pay a fine unless the law provides otherwise. …
> (3) Prior to ordering payment of the fine (subsection 1), the court must first threaten the party concerned with imposition of a fine. The fine may not exceed twenty-five thousand euros in a single case. …

b) There was dispute during the legislative procedure as to whether contact with a child should be enforceable. The draft legislation of the Federal Government did not initially provide for a right of contact on the part of the child or a duty of contact on the part of parents because it was thought that enforced contact was not in the child's best interests (*Bundestag* printed paper (*Bundestagsdrucksache* – BT-Drucks) 13/4899, p. 68). However, the *Bundesrat* suggested in its own statement that the child should be granted its own right which could not be exercised until the child had turned 14 and which could only be asserted by the child personally. Nevertheless, the *Bundesrat* rejected the inclusion of means of enforcing the right of contact because the use of coercive measures for the enforcement of a personal relationship appeared to it to be very burdensome and not appropriate (*Bundestag* printed paper 13/4899, pp. 153, 161-162). On the other hand, the Committee on Legal Affairs of the *Bundestag* recommended implementing its reform goal of promoting the rights of the child and giving priority to its interests by creating a subjective right of contact for it without attaching a minimum age to the right and without obliging parents to have contact with the child. This it was thought would make it clear to parents that the child's contact with them was of outstanding significance for its development. Children having their own right of contact would alter parents' level of awareness and send them a clear signal. For this reason and because a reduction in enforceability could lead to no further contact whatsoever it was thought that excluding the possibility of enforcement was not justifiable (*Bundestag* printed paper 13/8511, pp. 67-68). Ultimately, the legislature decided to follow this recommendation of the Committee on Legal Affairs.
2. There is disagreement in the case law and among legal scholars as to whether, and if so under what conditions a parental duty of contact may be enforced compulsorily against the will of the parent concerned.
…

II.

The complainant has two children, who are both minors, from his current marriage. The complainant also has a son from an extramarital relationship, who was born in February 1999. The complainant has recognized his paternity and pays child maintenance for his child. The complainant refuses, however, to have contact with his illegitimate son.
1. The Local Court (*Amtsgericht*) dismissed the application by the child's mother for an access arrangement between the child and its father in its order of 6 November 2000. It found that the child had so far not had any contact with the complainant. Enforced contact was not in the child's best interests. Even if the com-

plainant could be persuaded to actually come and collect the child by the imposition of a fine, enforced contact could not under any circumstances be a pleasant affair for the child. The complainant had understandable reasons for assuming that contact with his son would be detrimental to his marriage and could also lead to its disintegration.

2. The Higher Regional Court obtained an opinion from an expert during appeal proceedings. According to the expert's findings contact in the presence of a social worker would not be detrimental to the child if the complainant continued to ignore the child as he claimed he would – at least not for a certain period of time. However, the expert found that the father's hostile attitude would in the long term undermine the child's feelings of self-worth; it would experience the meetings as something to be endured. In this case there was a risk of serious damage to the child.

The complainant and the child did not meet while the expert opinion was being prepared because the Federal Constitutional Court (*Bundesverfassungsgericht*) had on account of the violation of the complainant's general right of personality overturned the order of the Higher Regional Court threatening to fine the complainant if he refused a meeting with the child which would allow the expert to make an assessment and observe the behaviour of the complainant and the child. The Federal Constitutional Court saw no statutory foundation for this (see Chamber Decisions of the Federal Constitutional Court (*Kammerentscheidungen des Bundesverfassungsgerichts* – BVerfGK) 1, 167 et seq.).

Amending the order of the Local Court in its order of 21 January 2004, which has itself been challenged by way of the constitutional complaint, the Higher Regional Court ordered that the complainant should have contact with the child in the presence of a social worker for two hours every three months. It threatened to impose a fine on him of up to 25,000 euros if he did not comply.

The Higher Regional Court grounded its decision in the fact that the legislature had deliberately drafted the child's right of contact as its own subjective right when amending § 1684.1 of the Civil Code through the Act Reforming the Law of Parent and Child. This corresponded with the duty of parents to have contact with their child. The decision of the legislature was based on recognition of the fact that a child's contact with its parents, especially when it does not live with them, is of outstanding significance for its development and in its best interests.

In view of this legislative background, the Family Court's finding that "enforced contact" – that is to say contact between the child and the father that is based solely on a court order – was not in the child's best interests did not reflect the true legal position. The Local Court failed to recognise that restriction or exclusion of the right of contact could in view of the child's subjective right to have contact with both of its parents only be considered insofar as this was necessary in the best interests of the child. As laid down in § 1684.4 of the Civil Code, courts could only issue a decision restricting or excluding the right of contact or its enforcement over an extended period or permanently if failure to do so would endanger the child's best interests. This statutory provision corresponded with the obligation of both parents under § 1684.2 of the Civil Code to refrain from everything that would render the [child's] upbringing more difficult. In light of this the complainant's objection that he did not have a relationship with his son and did not wish to establish one could be disregarded. He failed to recognise that the child's right of contact does not serve solely to maintain an existing relationship between a parent and child, but also has the purpose of establishing a new relationship between them in the interests of the child so that, among other things, the other parent can be a kind of "parent in reserve".

The Higher Regional Court added further that there were no serious constitutional objections to a duty of contact on the part of the father. Article 2 of the Basic Law subjected the right to freely develop one's personality to the condition that this did not violate the rights of others and did not violate public policy. Individuals were required to accept such restrictions. This also applied to the restrictions imposed by the legislature on the father through the duty of contact laid down in § 1684 of the German Civil Code. The legislature's weighing of the interests of the minor child and the father to give the child's interests precedence over the father's right to freely develop his personality were just as unobjectionable from a constitutional perspective in view of the child's need for special protection that was also expressed in Article 6 of the Basic Law as were other duties that followed from fatherhood such as, for example, the duty to pay child maintenance.

Nor was a violation of Article 6.1 of the Basic Law evident. The actual encroachment which the complainant and his family, which is protected by Article 6.1 of the Basic Law, had to accept as a result of the duty to have contact with his illegitimate child was rather minor and not disproportionate. The threat by the complainant's wife that she would leave him if the Court ordered him to have contact with the child in the proceedings was also not sufficient to lead to a different evaluation. No one would seriously contemplate arguing that the child support claim of a child who did not belong to the immediate family should be held unconstitutional if the spouse threatened to dissolve the marriage in the event that the courts were to enforce the claim. The situation could not be any different in relation to the complainant's legitimate children.

The Senate's orders were in keeping with the recommendations in the expert's opinion, whose content was not challenged by either of the parties. Since the legislature did not exclude the assertion of the child's right from the possibility of enforcement, it could be asserted before the courts and enforced by them directly on the basis of § 33 of the Act on Matters of Non-Contentious Jurisdiction. The threat was justified since the complainant repeatedly had categorically refused to have contact with his son.

III.

The complainant's constitutional complaint alleges a violation of his fundamental rights under Article 2.1 in conjunction with Article 1.1 of the Basic Law and of Article 6.1 of the Basic Law; it is directed against the threat of a fine ordered by the Higher Regional Court on 21 January 2004 and indirectly against § 33.1 sentence 1 and § 33.3 of the Act on Matters of Non-Contentious Jurisdiction which authorizes the Court to make such order.

The complainant argues that the right of contact is a strictly personal right which cannot be enforced in execution proceedings. The Committee on Legal Affairs has assumed primarily in its recommendation that the provision would send a clear signal to parents and was a well-meant appeal to them. It is also not possible to enforce the fulfilment of marital duties; the same applies to contracts for personal service. The complainant does not go so far as to allege that the duty of contact was not enforceable; he simply objects to the threat of a fine and its subsequent imposition.

This violates his general right of personality under Article 2.1 in conjunction with Article 1.1 of the Basic Law. It is true that a child's right to have contact with a parent can be compulsorily enforced under § 33 of the Act on Matters of Non-Contentious Jurisdiction. The legislature has, however, contemplated a situation in which the child's right to have contact is to be enforced against the will of the parent caring for the child. Thus its intention has been to give a child the opportunity to foster its relationship with the parent with access rights against the will of the parent caring for the child and to persuade the latter, if necessary by the imposition of a fine, to allow contact with the other parent. This does not entail the violation of a fundamental right because the parent caring for the child is not himself or herself directly affected by the contact between the child and the parent with access rights.

The complainant further argues that in the present case, however, the application is for the enforcement of the child's contact with the parent who has a right as well as a duty to have contact. This directly impairs the complainant's right of personality. § 33 of the Act on Matters of Non-Contentious Jurisdiction cannot be permitted to lead to the duty of contact under § 1684 of the Civil Code being compulsorily enforced against the will of the obligated parent in violation of his or her right of personality. Contact with his son will inevitably lead to his wife separating from him.

He states that he does not feel any bond with the child whom he does not know, whom he has not wanted to have and who has been conceived against his express wish; he states that he also refuses to establish any such bond.
If the minor child were a legitimate child and if the complainant had custody of it, he could at any time transfer his parental rights and duties to a third party either by giving the child up for adoption or by giving it to foster parents or by transferring its care to a third party. These options have not been available to him since the mother has sole custody rights. The enforcement of the duty of contact against his express will can also not be in the child's best interests. The child does not know the complainant who is a stranger to him. The situation would perhaps be different if a longstanding relationship between the child and its parent had already existed.
Furthermore, the threat of a fine is not only a direct fine to himself, but an indirect threat to his legitimate family. It too is protected by Article 6 of the Basic Law. The preservation of the family and its relationships have to be given higher priority when weighing the interests of the child against those of its family. The absence of contact which has not yet existed represents a minimal impairment for the child, while compulsory enforcement of contact would destroy the complainant's existing family.

IV.

…

B.

The complainant's constitutional complaint is admissible (§ 90.1 and § 90.2 sentence 1 of the Federal Constitutional Court Act (*Bundesverfassungsgerichtsgesetz* – BVerfGG)). …

C.

The constitutional complaint is founded.
The order of the Higher Regional Court encroaches on the complainant's fundamental right to protection of his personality under Article 2.1 in conjunction with Article 1.1 of the Basic Law to the extent that it contained the threat of a fine should the complainant refuse to have contact with his child (I.). The statutory duty of a parent to have contact with his or her child in § 1684.1 of the Civil Code concretizes parental responsibility under Article 6.2 sentence 1 of the Basic Law in a manner which is not constitutionally objectionable. Under Article 6.2 sentence 1 of

the Basic Law, a child has a right to parental care and upbringing which corresponds with the parental responsibility and which has also been concretized by the legislature in the right of a child to have contact with its parent in § 1684.1 of the Civil Code. The legislature pursues a legitimate purpose in providing for the possibility of the threat of an imposition of a fine where a parent is unwilling to have contact with his or her child (II.). However, the threat of a fine to enforce the duty of contact of a parent who refuses to have contact with his or her child is not usually in the child's best interests and thus does not justify the encroachment on the parent's right of personality (III.). § 33.1 sentence 1 and § 33.3 of the Act on Matters of Non-Contentious Jurisdiction are thus to be interpreted in accordance with the constitution as meaning that compulsory enforcement of the duty of contact of a parent who refuses to have contact with his or her child must be avoided unless there are sufficient indications in a specific case that enforcement would be in the child's best interests (IV.). The Higher Regional Court failed to take this sufficiently into account in its decision (V.).

I.

The threat of a fine based on § 33.1 sentence 1 in conjunction with § 33.3 sentence 1 of the Act on Matters of Non-Contentious Jurisdiction to enforce the complainant's duty to cultivate contact with his child against his will encroaches on his fundamental right to protection of his right of personality.

1. This fundamental right protects the narrower personal sphere and the prerequisites for it. It extends to the right of respect for one's privacy. This includes the family sphere and personal relationships with other family members (see BVerfGE 96, 56 (61)). The same applies to the relationship between a parent and his or her child. What form their relationship takes will be determined by their respective personal feelings, attitudes and experiences which influence each other. The decision to have or to refuse contact with one's child expresses the parent's personal understanding of parenthood and his or her emotional relationship with the child. Nonetheless, it is not included in the inviolable core area of private conduct of life since it has a significant social connection with the child concerned whose interests and personal sphere are affected by this decision (see BVerfGE 96, 56 (61)).

2. If coercive measures are threatened to force a person to have contact with his child against his will, this constitutes an encroachment on his right to have his private sphere respected. He is compelled to meet with his child and cultivate personal contact with it contrary to his own wishes. This influences his personal relationship with the child and puts him under pressure to behave in a manner towards the child that he does not wish to behave in.

3. The fundamental right to the protection of privacy is not, however, guaranteed without restriction outside the inviolable core area of private conduct of life. It is restricted pursuant to Article 2.1 of the Basic Law through the constitutional order and the rights of others (see BVerfGE 99, 185 (195)). A statutory basis is necessary for such restrictions from which their prerequisites and scope can be determined. Individuals are required to accept the restrictions which are undertaken in the overriding general interest or are undertaken in view of the constitutionally protected interests of third parties subject to the principle of proportionality (see BVerfGE 96, 56 (61)).

§ 33.1 sentence 1 in conjunction with § 33.3 of the Act on Matters of Non-Contentious Jurisdiction is the statutory basis upon which the Higher Regional Court relied in its decision to threaten to fine the complainant if he did not fulfill his duty of contact and with which it encroached on the complainant's fundamental right to protection of his personality. However, this provision itself only provides a general description of a duty to act which is imposed by the court and which depends on the will of the person concerned as the prerequisite for the threat of a fine; furthermore, it states that the purpose of the threat of a fine is to make the person concerned comply with the duty to act ordered by the court. Thus § 1684.1 of the Civil Code must also be included in the examination of whether the purpose pursued by § 33.1 sentence 1 in conjunction with § 3.3 of the Act on Matters of Non-Contentious Jurisdiction is justified. The court ordered the complainant to have contact with his child on the basis of the provision in the Civil Code which obliges a parent to have contact with his or her child; this provision justifies the duty to act referred to in § 33.1 sentence 1 of the Act on Matters of Non-Contentious Jurisdiction. Whether the encroachment on a fundamental right resulting from the threat of a fine can be justified must be measured against this duty of contact.

II.

The legislature pursues a legitimate purpose in providing the courts in § 33.1 sentence 1 in conjunction with § 33.3 of the Act on Matters of Non-Contentious Jurisdiction with the possibility of threatening to fine a parent to enforce a court-imposed obligation to have contact with his or her child.

1. The statutory duty of a parent to have contact with his or her child that is laid down in § 1684 of the Civil Code is a permissible concretization of the responsibility allocated to parents by the Basic Law.

a) Article 6.2 sentence 1 of the Basic Law guarantees parents the right to care for and bring up their child, but at the same time also makes this task a primary duty imposed on them. In this connection, parents may in principle decide free of state influence and according to their own ideas how they wish to live up to their responsibility as parents (see BVerfGE 107, 104 (117)). Nevertheless, their actions must be guided by what is in the best interests of the child since the parental right is a right to be exercised in the interests of the child (see BVerfGE 103, 89 (107)). They are guaranteed it for the sake of the child. The duty of parents to care for and bring up their child is not owed exclusively to the state which must guard the exercise of parental authority and which is obliged to intervene to protect the child if the parents do not live up to this responsibility (see BVerfGE 60, 79 (88); 107, 104 (117)). Parents also directly owe their child a duty to care for it and to bring it up.

The child has its own dignity and rights. As a subject of fundamental rights it is entitled to the protection of the state and the guarantee of its constitutionally anchored rights. When regulating interpersonal relationships, a constitution which places human dignity at the centre of its value system may not in principle grant anyone rights to the person of another which do not have duties attached to them and which do not respect the human dignity of the other person. The same applies to the relationship between a parent and his or her child. The parental right vis-à-vis the child is justified by the fact that the child requires protection and help so that it can develop into a responsible member of society in keeping with the Basic Law's image of man (see BVerfGE 24, 119 (144)). Thus this right cannot be separated from the duty of parents to offer this protection and help to the child for its well-being. In this context, the duty does not merely relate to the child, it is also owed to the child since the child is not the subject of the parental exercise of rights; it is a legal person and a subject of fundamental rights in whose best interests parents are obliged to act.

b) The child's right to parental care and upbringing under Article 6.2 sentence 1 of the Basic Law corresponds with the parental duty to care for and bring up the child which is imposed by Article 6.2 sentence 1 of the Basic Law. If a duty is imposed on one person which relates to another person and which is at the same time connected with a right to influence the other person, a right to make decisions for the other person, a right to represent the other person's interests and a right to have a significant and dominant influence on the development of the other person's personality, this will affect the core of such person's life development and restrict his exercise of free will. The only justification for granting parents such far-reaching influence over the life of their child is the fact that the child cannot bear responsibility for itself and would come to harm if it were not given any help. If the child needs such support from its parents and if as a result its parents have a responsibility to act only in the child's best interests, then the child also has a right to expect its parents to care first and foremost for it and a right to also have its parents fulfill the duty which cannot be separated from their parental right. Thus the right of the child is based on parental responsibility and it is therefore protected by Article 6.2 sentence 1 of the Basic Law. It is closely connected to the fundamental right of the child to protection of its personality under Article 2.1 in conjunction with Article 1.1 of the Basic Law since it guarantees the child family ties which are significant for the development of its personality. The personal relationship with its parents, their care, help and warmth and affection contribute significantly to the child being able to develop into a person who knows that he or she is respected and who learns to respect himself or herself as well as to respect others.

c) Nevertheless, the parental right with its concurrent duty requires statutory regulation as does the right of the child to care and upbringing by its parents under Article 6.2 sentence 1 of the Basic Law. This applies to the parental right in particular because parents are jointly entitled to it. If parents are unable to agree on how to exercise their parental responsibility, then rules must be made which allocate them rights and duties vis-à-vis their child (see BVerfGE 92, 158 (178-179)). In addition, statutory rules are necessary because legal authority in relation to the child is a prerequisite for the care and upbringing of a child also vis-à-vis third parties (see BVerfGE 84, 168 (180)) and, because of the watchdog function established for it by Article 6.2 sentence 2 of the Basic Law, the state has to ensure that the exercise of the parental right is guided by the best interests of the child and that the child's rights are respected. It must therefore regulate, on the one hand, how the child's right to care and upbringing by its parents in accordance with its best interests can be safeguarded and, on the other hand, when and under what circumstances it will limit the free exercise of the parental right for the child's sake.

d) Contact between parent and child is not merely a possible expression of parental upbringing, but a fundamental basis for the parent-child relationship and thus an essential part of Article 6.2 sentence 1 of the Basic Law. Especially in the case of a parent who does not live with his or her child, access to it is a significant prerequisite for personal contact with the child that would allow the parent to establish or maintain a closer relationship with it. Contact ensures that he or she can devote himself or herself to the child and can be involved in its development; it ensures that payment of maintenance is not the only way that the parent can exercise his or her parental responsibility. This is in keeping with the legislature's decision in § 1684.1 of the Civil Code, which grants a right of contact to parents irrespective of whether they have custody rights. Particularly in the case of a non-custodial parent, a right of contact is the main basis for exercising his or her parental right under Article 6.2 sentence 1 of the Basic Law.

On the other hand, the parental right to bring up a child, which is protected by Article 6.2 sentence 1 of the Basic Law, is intended as a right in the interests of the child (see BVerfGE 75, 201 (218); 103, 89 (107) and has as its aim the child's well-being. However, it is in principle in the child's best interests if through contact with its parents it gains the opportunity to get to know its father and mother, to become close with them and with the help of the contact is able to continue a personal relationship with them. Through communication with its parents, the child can experience affection, can learn and can receive inspiration and advice that give it direction, help it to form opinions and aid it in developing into an independent and responsible person. As far as the child and its development are concerned, refusal to have contact with it and thus the severance of personal ties with it represent a significant withdrawal of parental authority; at the same time, it constitutes neglect of one of the significant parts of the duty of upbringing imposed on parents by Article 6.2 sentence 1 of the Basic Law. Article 6.2 sentence 2 of the Basic Law allocates the state a duty to monitor the exercise of parental responsibility in the best interests of the child, and parental contact is an important prerequisite for this; in exercise of this duty, the legislature has therefore obligated parents in § 1684.1 of the Civil Code to have contact with their child and urged them to fulfill their responsibility to their child. In this connection, it has at the same time granted the child a right to have contact with its parents and thus concretized the right of the child under Article 6.2 sentence 1 of the Basic Law to care and upbringing by its parents.

2. It is of course true that – through its regulation of their right to maintain their privacy and their personal relationships – the obligation of parents to have contact with their child does encroach on their fundamental right to protection of their right of personality since it obliges them to enter into a personal relationship with their child even if they do not wish to start or continue such a relationship. This encroachment is, however, justified in particular due to the responsibility for their child guaranteed as well as imposed on parents by Article 6.2 sentence 1 of the Basic Law and due to the child's right to parental care and upbringing, which is also protected by this fundamental right.

The parental duty of contact serves the purpose pursued by the legislature in § 1684.1 of the Civil Code of reinforcing the legally recognized right of the child to parental contact by imposing a corresponding duty on parents in order to enable the child to have the opportunity to meet with its parents. Such contact is of outstanding significance for the development of the child. The assumption of the legislature, when it imposed this duty on parents, that ongoing personal contact between a parent and a child would have a positive influence on the child's development and be in principle in the child's best interests is supported by scientific findings and therefore no objection can be raised in this connection. The duty of contact is also a suitable means of promoting the relationship between a child and its parents. The possibility cannot be ruled out that a parent subject to a duty of contact could be influenced by the duty to have contact with his or her child in § 1684.1 of the Civil Code or a judicial order concretizing such duty, and that the parent could allow himself or herself to be persuaded to fulfill this duty in the interests of the child and thus allow the child to establish or continue a relationship with him or her, even where the parent was initially not interested in regular meetings with the child and did not of his or her own initiative seek personal contact with the child. Since no more lenient means of reinforcing the child's right of contact in its own interests and assisting in the enforcement of same are evident, a parental duty to have contact is also necessary.

After all, it is also reasonable to urge a parent to cultivate contact with his or her child. There is to be sure an encroachment on the parent's fundamental right to protection of his or her right of personality associated with the duty of contact and this encroachment is not slight. As a rule, the parent is not just expected to endure a meeting with his or her child. Instead, the parent is expected to give the child warmth and affection, to communicate with it and to establish or continue a personal relationship with it. This can lead to not insignificant psychological pressure for a parent who is not prepared to do this. However, one has to take into account that under Article 6.2 sentence 1 of the Basic Law parents do not merely have a right, but also a duty to care for and bring up their child. It is true that parents can fulfill this duty by committing their child to the care of another. However, parents do not release themselves from the responsibility that they bear for their child by delegating its upbringing to another. Without contact with a child, it is scarcely possible for a parent to exert the influence that is necessary for its best interests and instrumental for its personal development. Contact with the child is in this respect a significant prerequisite and the basis for the exercise of the parental right in the interests of the child.

If the legislature concretizes the duty of upbringing imposed on parents in Article 6.2 sentence 1 of the Basic Law by raising contact with the child to a parental duty, it makes clear the importance to be attached to contact between a parent and child in the upbringing of a child. Seen in this light the encroachment on the parent's right of personality following from the imposition of a duty of contact does not appear particularly serious. In addition, the parental duty of contact corresponds with the child's right to have contact with its parents that the legislature granted the child in § 1684.1 of the Civil Code. The legislature took into account the child's right to care and upbringing by its parents based on Article 6.2 sentence 1 of the Basic Law by concretizing and securing one significant point in an ordinary law which makes exertion of an influence on the child's upbringing possible. If one weighs the child's interest in having steady contact with both parents against a parent's interest in not wanting or no longer wanting to have personal contact with it, then one should accord the child's desire considerably more weight than the parent's wishes.

This is because as a significant basis for the development and maintenance of a family relationship and for the receipt of parental support and upbringing, the contact of a child with its parents is of considerable importance for the development of its personality and is something that contributes in principle to its well-being.
It is thus reasonable to oblige a parent to have contact with his or her child – even if this entails an encroachment on the parent's personal sphere if this is in the best interests of the child. Thus the legislature followed a legitimate purpose that is supported by the Basic Law by making it possible through § 33.1 sentence 1 in conjunction with § 33.3 of the Act on Matters of Non-Contentious Jurisdiction to threaten parents with a fine for failure to comply with their legal duty to have contact with their own child and with an order from the court instructing them to do so.

III.

However, as a rule, the threat of a fine to enforce the duty of contact of a parent against his or her express will is not suitable for achieving the sought purpose, i.e. to make it possible for the child to have contact with its parent in a way that would benefit the development of its personality and to assist in the enforcement of the child's right to have the parent exercise his or her responsibility in the child's best interests. If coercive measures are necessary to force an unwilling parent to have contact with a child, this contact is not usually in the best interests of the child. Where this is the case, the threat by the court to apply coercive measures constitutes an unjustified encroachment on the parent's fundamental right to the protection of his or her personality.
1. The effect of the threat of a fine may well be to motivate a parent who is actually not willing to have contact with his or her child to have a meeting with the child, even against his or her will. The psychological and financial pressure exerted through the threat of a fine may bend the will of the parent and prompt him or her to exercise his or her right of contact.
Unlike in the case of a judicial duty of contact, which initially only urges the parent concerned to fulfill his or her parental responsibility and which clarifies his or her legal duty with concrete orders and thus gives him or her the option of reconsidering and following the order to have contact with the child without incurring a fine, the threat of a fine pressures him or her to meet the child and be confronted by it against his or her will. However, that which it is intended to compel the parent to do by the use of pressure does not just conflict with the parent's will. The compulsory enforcement of the duty of contact, which requires not just his or her presence, but his or her emotional warmth towards the child, conflicts with the feelings the parent harbours towards the child. Where a parent's rejection of any contact with

the child has been declared and demonstrated in this manner, any contact with the child that eventuates cannot fail to affect the child; the pressure exerted on the parent alone would suffice to have an impact on the child. If the parent does not change his or her hostile attitude towards the child at a forced meeting with it, the child is faced with a situation in which it does not experience the parental warmth and affection which is the purpose of the contact, but instead experiences personal rejection – and this not from just anyone but from, of all people, a parent. This poses a big risk that the child's self-esteem could be damaged. For it can scarcely understand why its parent does not want to know it and why he or she acts in such an unfriendly way and it could therefore blame itself. This usually does not benefit the child's well-being, but instead damages it.
Nevertheless, the possibility that a forced meeting with the child could lead to the parent opening himself or herself to the child and that this would not result in any mentionable damage to the child's well-being cannot be ruled out. However, if a parent does not show cooperation and if he or she still stubbornly refuses to meet the child in spite of a court order stating that he or she has a duty to do so, it is doubtful whether enforced contact can lead him or her to develop a positive attitude to the child. Thus there is much that would suggest that the child's best interests could at least be significantly impaired through contact enforced by applying coercive measures. It is, however, very difficult to predict with certainty whether this will occur in an individual case and whether the child will be damaged since it depends on the feelings of the parent and his or her reactions at the time which are scarcely foreseeable.
2. a) What counts in deciding if it would be suitable to use coercive measures to force a parent to have contact with his or her child in cases where he or she does not want such contact is not whether the contact could endanger the best interests of the child, but whether such contact is in the child's best interests. The legislature imposed a duty on parents to have contact with their child in order to strengthen the child's right of contact with its parents. This right was granted the child as being in its well-understood best interests. The legislature assumed that a child's contact with its parents was of outstanding significance for its development. This is an expression of its view that contact can establish or maintain an emotional relationship between a child and its parents and that the parent's warmth and affection during the contact is beneficial for the child's development so that contact is in the child's best interests. This benefit in relation to the child's best interests justifies the imposition on the parents of a duty to have contact with their child even though this encroaches on their fundamental right to protection of their rights of personality. However, this is only true to the extent that and for as long as contact with its parent actually serves the best interests of the child. If this is not achieved through the

statutory means intended for this purpose, then this purpose cannot justify the encroachment on the parent's right of personality. This applies to not only the duty of contact imposed on parents, but in particular to the possibility offered by the law of enforcing the duty of contact against the parent's declared will through the threat of coercive measures. The proper metric for determining the suitability of contact achieved through coercion is whether the contact is in the child's best interests.

The fact that § 1684.4 of the Civil Code only permits restrictions on and the exclusion of the right of contact if the best interests of the child would otherwise be endangered does not hinder the aforegoing. This provision deals with the limits on the parental right of contact and not with the enforcement of the duty to have contact. Therefore, it does not apply to the relationship between a parent with a duty of contact and his or her child with a right to have contact.

If a parent wishes to exercise his or her right of contact, he or she may only be restricted from doing this over an extended period or permanently pursuant to § 1684.4 of the Civil Code if the child's best interests would otherwise be endangered. By making the existence of a danger to the child's well-being the standard, the legislature has taken the parental right into account and sought to give it as much room as possible for development. Thus a limit on the parental right of contact is set at the point where the exercise of the right of contact threatens to conflict significantly with the best interests of the child.

The situation is different, however, in relation to the compulsory enforcement of a duty of contact against the will of a parent subject to this duty. In this case the function of enforcement is not the realization of the parent's right of contact; it instead represents an encroachment on the parent's right of personality. This kind of encroachment can, however, only be justified if the right of the child to contact with its parent, which is intended to be realized in this way, also achieves its objective of serving the child's best interests. If there is a risk that instead of the effect which the child's right to contact was intended to achieve the opposite will arise, then the exercise of the right is of no use to the child but can instead harm it. In such case the reason for limiting the right of a parent to conduct the relationship with his or her child according to his or her own wishes and needs disappears. Thus in the case of the compulsory enforcement of contact against the will of the parent obliged to have contact, the standard can only be whether this contact serves the child's well-being.

c) In view of the emotional and psychological strain to which a child can be exposed at a meeting with a parent who rejects it and who only attends the meeting under duress, one cannot, as a rule, start by assuming that contact under such circumstances is in the child's best interests. To be sure, there are – as far as can be seen – no social science studies on the reactions and attitudes adopted in relation to his or her child by a parent compelled by coercive measures to have contact with the child or on the effects on the child of a forced meeting with a parent who refuses contact with it which one could use as a basis for assessing whether, and if so, under what circumstances contact of such kind could be in the child's best interests in spite of the unfavourable conditions under which it takes place. The reason for this is presumably that until now only very few cases have occurred or have become known in which contact was brought about by means of coercive measures. For most of the contact disputes brought before the courts relate to cases in which contrary to the will of the other parent, one parent complains about his or her right of contact with the child. On the other hand, the reason might be that the course such meetings take and how they can affect a child's psyche depend on the psychological state of the relevant persons at the time so that it is difficult to make generalizations on the basis of the results in an individual case. However, even if there are no valid scientific findings on the effects of enforced contact on a child to fall back on, it would seem evident that a parent who obviously does not want to have contact with his or her child and who does not allow a court order clarifying his or her duty to affect or change his or her hostile attitude towards the child will exhibit his or her unwillingness and hostility towards the child at a forced meeting. This is confirmed by the German Institute for Youth Research (*Deutsches Jugendinstitut*) which assumes on the basis of its findings that the hostile attitude of a parent is a prognosis factor for difficult or damaging contact for the child. For if the child's own parent really does demonstrate his or her rejection, then this is likely to leave its mark on the child's psyche; especially since the first meeting or a meeting that occurs after a longer period with its parent will be a particularly emotional event which will trigger feelings of fear and expectation in the child. If the child is not only disappointed, but in addition it feels that it is not accepted as a person, then it seems probable that the child will suffer emotional damage. Contact with its parent, during which such detriment to the child is likely, is not in the best interests of the child.

Nevertheless, one cannot rule out the possibility that there are cases in which there is a realistic chance that through its uninhibitedness towards strangers and its psychological stability a child might be able to overcome the resistance of the parent who wants to avoid it thanks to its open and friendly behaviour so that what was initially enforced contact can be in the child's best interests after all. There may also be cases in which forced contact between the child and its parent can be in the child's interests, even if the parent expresses his or her resistance to the meeting. As was stated by the German Institute for Youth Assistance and Family Law (*Deutsches Institut für Jugendhilfe und Familienrecht*) and the German Institute for Youth Research in their opinions, an interest in meeting an unknown parent arises in the course of a child's development, usually in adolescence or early adulthood. If a child or adolescent has developed this strong interest and if he or she is primarily concerned with meeting the parent to make his or her acquaintance – even if it is only a one-time meeting – then the fulfillment of this need can be more important for the child than the possibly associated experience of finding out that the parent wants to have nothing to do with it. This is to be clarified, if necessary, with the help of an expert. In such a case, even an enforced meeting with the parent can be in the best interests of the child. The older a child is and the more developed its own personality is, the more it can be assumed that even the compulsory enforcement of its own express and emphatic wish to have contact with its parent will be in its best interests. In such cases, the encroachment on the right of privacy of the parent concerned which is associated with enforced contact is not only suitable for achieving the sought purpose of allowing the child to have contact which would be in its best interests, but also justified. More weight should be attached to ensuring the child's best interests are met than to the interest of the parent in being spared from having to have contact with his or her child. In such a case, it is reasonable to expect a parent to have contact with his or her child and, if necessary, to use coercive measures to force him or her to do so.

In the case of children who have not yet developed stable personalities, on the other hand, one can usually begin by assuming that forced contact with the reluctant parent will not serve the child's best interests unless there are enough indications to the contrary in a concrete case. Where a parent unwilling to have contact with his or her child is threatened with coercive measures in order to enforce contact and these measures fail to achieve their purpose, then the encroachment on the fundamental right to protection of personality of the parent refusing contact is not justified unless such coercive measures are suitable for achieving contact which is in the best interests of the child (see BVerfGE 99, 145 (164)).

IV.

The fact that pursuant to § 33.1 sentence 1 and § 33.3 of the Act on Matters of Non-Contentious Jurisdiction a parent who is unwilling to have contact with his or her child may be threatened with a fine even though this violates the parent's fundamental right to protection of his or her personality does not lead to a violation of the Basic Law by these provisions. This provision is thus to be interpreted in accordance with the constitution as meaning that compulsory enforcement of the duty of contact of a parent who refuses to have contact with his or her child must be avoided unless there are sufficient indications in a specific case that enforced contact would be in the child's best interests.

§ 33 of the Act on Matters of Non-Contentious Jurisdiction is a general provision on enforcement in non-contentious matters that covers a multitude of court-imposed obligations relating to acts that depend on the will of the person obliged; the provision allows the courts to reinforce such obligations through the threat and imposition of a fine. This also applies, for example, to the duty of the parent with whom the child lives to hand over the child to the other parent who has a right of contact so as to allow contact at the times set down by the court. The provision is discretionary. It leaves the decision as to whether non-compliance with an imposed obligation should result in enforcement to the due discretion of the court. It thus allows the court to refrain from compulsory enforcement of the obligation. Thus the provision can also be interpreted in conformity with the Basic Law in the case of a duty of contact which the court has imposed on one parent. It leads to a finding that the use of coercive measures against a parent who stubbornly refuses contact should be avoided unless there are enough indications in a concrete case that forced contact will serve the child's best interests because as a rule such contact is not in the best interests of the child. In this respect the discretion granted to the courts by § 33.1 sentence 1 of the Act on Matters of Non-Contentious Jurisdiction is restricted by the Basic Law.

V.

The challenged decision of the Higher Regional Court does not satisfy the constitutional requirements and violates the complainant's fundamental right to the protection of his right of personality under Article 2.1 in conjunction with Article 1.1 of the Basic Law insofar as it threatened him with a fine.

When exercising the discretion to use coercive measures to compel a parent to have contact that § 33.1 sentence 1 of the Act on Matters of Non-Contentious Jurisdiction grants the courts, the Court failed to take into account that that it should have examined whether forced contact against the complainant's will would be in the child's best interests. Instead the standard it used for its examination was whether forced contact could endanger the child's best interests and answered this question in the negative. The Court assumed on the basis of the expert opinion it obtained that there was no risk of serious long-term damage to the child if the child had contact with the complainant in the company of a social worker. To this extent it did not exclude the possibility of detrimental effects on the child, but considered them acceptable for the purposes of encouraging the complainant through the threat of coercive measures to comply with his duty of contact and to thus bring about contact between him and his child. However, this is not sufficient to justify an encroachment on the complainant's right of personality. For the Court did not give adequate consideration to the best interests of the child or the complainant's right to protection of its personality. It failed to recognize that contact may only be enforced against a parent who is obliged to have contact when this contact achieves its objective of serving the child's best interests (see BVerfGE 99, 145 (164)).

VI.

The Court must also consider the child's legal position which is constitutionally protected by Article 6.2 and Article 2.1 of the Basic Law and its right to a hearing in court pursuant to Article 103.1 of the Basic Law; it must also examine whether a guardian ad litem should be appointed for the child in the contested access proceedings pursuant to § 50 of the Act on Matters of Non-Contentious Jurisdiction when it again hears and decides the matter (see BVerfGE 99, 145 (162-163)).
The constitutional protection of the fundamental rights of children requires a procedural form which guarantees the independent exercise of the rights of the child and guarantees its interests. In this context, the child's custodial parent is in principle charged with this task. However, if there are indications that the child's interests might conflict with those of the parent representing it, the child must be given an opportunity to assert its own interests independently of its parent in the proceedings. This occurs in the case of children whose age does not yet permit them to exercise their own interests and rights through the guardian ad litem provided for in § 50 of the Act on Matters of Non-Contentious Jurisdiction whom the court must appoint for a child in such a case. The case to be decided gives rise to doubt as to whether the application made for the child concerned by its mother in which she seeks to oblige the complainant to have contact with the child against his clearly evident will and to enforce this, if necessary, with the aid of coercive measures is really in the best interests of the child or if it is instead contrary to them.

VII.

The order by the Higher Regional Court of 21 January 2004 must be overturned because it violates Article 2.1 in conjunction with Article 1.1 of the Basic Law to the extent that it threatens to fine the complainant (§ 95.2 of the Federal Constitutional Court Act). To this extent the matter is referred back to the Higher Regional Court for a new decision.
The decision on the reimbursement of expenses is based on § 34a.2 of the Federal Constitutional Court Act.
Seven judges concurred on points C.III to IV, whilst one judge dissented; otherwise the decision was unanimous.

Justices: Papier, Hohmann-Dennhardt, Hoffmann-Riem, Bryde, Gaier, Eichberger, Schluckebier, Kirchhof

No. 51

BVerfGE 127, 132

of 21 July 2010 – 1 BvR 420/09 –

"Case regarding custody rights of fathers of children born out of wedlock"

HEADNOTE:

The parental right under Article 6.2 of the Basic Law of the father of a child born out of wedlock is violated because he is in principle excluded from the parental custody of his child where the child's mother does not consent and because he cannot obtain a judicial review as to whether, for reasons of the child's best interests, it is appropriate to grant him the parental custody of his child together with the mother or to transfer the sole parental custody of the child to him in place of the mother.

Order of the First Senate of 21 July 2010
– 1 BvR 420/09 –

in the proceedings regarding the constitutional complaint of Mr. F., – authorised representative: …, lawyer in Law Firm … – 1. directly challenging a) the order of the Bad Oeynhausen Local Court (*Amtsgericht*) of 8 January 2009 – 43 F 3/09 –, b) the order of the Hamm Higher Regional Court (*Oberlandesgericht*) of 20 November 2008 – 1 UF 180/08 –, c) the order of the Bad Oeynhausen Local Court of 30 June 2008 – 23 F 109/08 –, 2. indirectly challenging § 1626a, § 1672.1, § 1680.3 of the Civil Code (*Bürgerliches Gesetzbuch* – BGB).

RULING:

1. § 1626a.1 no. 1 and § 1672.1 of the Civil Code as amended by the Act Reforming the Law of Parent and Child (*Gesetz zur Reform des Kindschaftsrechts – Kindschaftsrechtsreformgesetz* – Parent and Child Law Reform Act – KindRG) of 16 December 1997 (Federal Law Gazette (*Bundesgesetzblatt* – BGBl.) I p. 2942) are incompatible with Article 6.2 of the Basic Law (*Grundgesetz* – GG).

2. Until revised legislation enters into effect, § 1626a of the Civil Code is to apply subject to the proviso that the Family Court, on the application of one parent, transfers parental custody or part thereof to the parents jointly where it is to be expected that this serves the child's best interests.
3. Until revised legislation enters into effect, § 1672 of the Civil Code is to apply subject to the proviso that the Family Court, on the application of one parent, transfers parental custody or part thereof to the father where joint parental custody is out of the question and it is to be expected that this best serves the child's best interests.
4. The order of the Bad Oeynhausen Local Court of 30 June 2008 – 23 F 109/08 – violates the complainant's fundamental right under Article 6.2 sentence 1 of the Basic Law. The order is reversed. As a result of this, the order of the Hamm Higher Regional Court of 20 November 2008 – 1 UF 180/08 – and the order of the Bad Oeynhausen Local Court of 8 January 2009 – 43 F 3/09 – no longer apply. The matter is referred back to the Bad Oeynhausen Local Court.
5. The Federal Republic of Germany and the *Land* (state) North Rhine-Westphalia are each ordered to reimburse the complainant for half of his necessary expenses.

EXTRACT FROM GROUNDS:

A.

The constitutional complaint relates to the question as to whether it is compatible with the Basic Law that it is not possible under the relevant provisions of family law for parental custody of children born out of wedlock to be transferred in part or solely to the father against the mother's will, where the situation does not qualify for removal of parental custody under § 1666 of the Civil Code.

I.

When the Act Reforming the Law of Parent and Child (*Gesetz zur Reform des Kindschaftsrechts – Kindschaftsrechtsreformgesetz* – Parent and Child Law Reform Act – KindRG) of 16 December 1997 … entered into effect on 1 July 1998, § 1626a of the Civil Code for the first time gave the opportunity to parents who are not married to each other to have joint parental custody of their children, regardless of whether or not they live together, if they intend this and make declarations of parental custody, which may be done even before the child is born (§ 1626b.2 of the Civil Code). If these declarations of parental custody are not made, then in principle the mother has sole parental custody of a child born out of wedlock.

§ 1626a of the Civil Code reads as follows:

> (1) Where the parents, at the date of the birth of the child, are not married to each other, they have joint parental custody if they
> 1. declare that they wish to take on parental custody jointly (declarations of parental custody), or
> 2. marry each other.
>
> (2) Apart from this, the mother has parental custody.

The Parent and Child Law Reform Act also provided for a transfer of sole parental custody from the mother to the father of a child born out of wedlock where the parents permanently live apart. Such transfer may also only be effected with the consent of the mother.
§ 1672.1 of the Civil Code, which contains this provision, reads as follows:

> (1) If the parents live apart for a period that is not merely temporary and if, under section 1626a.2, the mother has parental custody, the father, with the approval of the mother, may apply for the Family Court to transfer to him alone the parental custody or part of the parental custody. The application is to be granted if the transfer serves the child's best interests.

The father of a child born out of wedlock may be granted the parental custody of the child against the mother's will only if parental custody is withdrawn from the mother on grounds of endangerment of the child's best interests (§ 1680.3, § 1680.2 sentence 2 in conjunction with § 1666 of the Civil Code), if her parental custody is permanently suspended (§ 1678.2 of the Civil Code) or if she dies (§ 1680.2 sentence 2, § 1681 of the Civil Code).

II.

1. As long ago as in the year 2003, the Federal Constitutional Court considered the constitutionality of the legislative concept of § 1626a of the Civil Code on the joint custody of parents not married to each other, and at that time the Court held that § 1626a of the Civil Code was only incompatible with Article 6.2 and Article 6.5 of the Basic Law insofar as there was no transitional arrangement for parents who had separated before the Act Reforming the Law of Parent and Child entered into force on 1 July 1998 (Decisions of the Federal Constitutional Court (*Entscheidungen des Bundesverfassungsgerichts* – BVerfGE) 107, 150 et seq.).

As grounds, the Court stated that it did not violate the parental right of the father of a child born out of wedlock under Article 6.2 of the Basic Law that, according to § 1626a.2 of the Civil Code, a child was first awarded legally to the mother alone, and the care for the person of the child was assigned to her in principle (see BVerfGE 107, 150 (169)). Unlike in the case of the parents of children born in wedlock, who legally undertook, when they married, to take responsibility for each other and for their joint children, the legislature even at that time could not make a general assumption in the case of parents who were not married to each other that they were living in a domestic community and that they were willing and able to take joint responsibility for the child. The child's best interests required that from its birth the child had a person who could act for the child with legally binding effect. In view of the diversity of living conditions into which children born out of wedlock were born, it was justified that parental custody of the child was normally attributed to its mother upon the child's birth and not to the father or to both parents jointly (see BVerfGE 107, 150 (169-170)).
The Court also stated that § 1626a.1 no. 1 of the Civil Code did not violate Article 6.2 of the Basic Law. At that time there was no evidence to substantiate that the provision, which, on the basis of the child's best interests, made the parents' agreement the precondition of joint custody, did not take sufficient account of the parental right of the father of a child born out of wedlock (see BVerfGE 107, 150 (172)).
In the child's best interests, joint custody was dependent on both parents being willing to take responsibility for the child. Exercising this joint responsibility made it necessary for each parent to develop a personal relationship to the child and required a minimum of agreement between the parents. If this was lacking, and if the parents were neither willing nor able to cooperate, joint custody of the child might run counter to the child's best interests (see BVerfGE 107, 150 (173)).
In the case of married parents, the legislature had assumed, by reason of the legal connection they assumed in marrying, that there was agreement between them and willingness to share the care of their child as a requirement for a jointly exercised custody serving the child's best interests. In the case of parents not married to each other, this indication was lacking and therefore no such assumption could be made. In order to create an equivalent for this which took account of the statutory assumption of jointly exercised parental custody in the child's best interests even when the parents were not married to each other, the legislature, in § 1626a.1 no. 1 of the Civil Code, had given them the possibility of expressing by means of concurring declarations that they were willing and prepared to share the care of their child (see BVerfGE 107, 150 (174)).

The Court stated that the legislature had assumed that, where they were willing to cooperate, the parents would as a rule make use of the possibility of joint custody, i.e. that they would legalise their factual care by making declarations concerning custody. The legislature had been aware of the fact that there might nevertheless be cases in which the mother did not wish to make a declaration of parental custody even despite living with the father and the child. Its assessment that in such cases the mother's refusal expressed a conflict between the parents which had a negative impact on the child in a dispute also occurring with regard to joint parental custody was justifiable. The legislature had been justified in assuming that a mother, particularly when she lived with the father and the child, would exceptionally reject the father's wish for joint custody and that she would only do so if she had serious reasons for this based on the defence of the child's best interests, and that she would not misuse the possibility of refusing to submit a declaration of custody as a power position against the father (see BVerfGE 107, 150 (176-177)).
But § 1626a.1 no. 1 of the Civil Code would reveal itself to be incompatible with Article 6.2 of the Basic Law if this assumption of the legislature were to be incorrect and in particular were it to emerge that even where the parents live together with the child in a large number of cases joint declarations of parental custody were not made for reasons not based on the child's best interests. Since the legislature had enacted provisions which safeguarded the parental right of the father of a child born out of wedlock under Article 6.2 of the Basic Law only if the legislature's prognostic assumption was correct, the legislature was obliged to observe the actual development and to review whether its assumption also stood the test of reality. If it became apparent that this was normally not the case, it would have to ensure that fathers of children born out of wedlock who live together with the mother and the child as a family were opened an access to joint custody which took sufficient account of their parental rights under Article 6.2 of the Basic Law, with due consideration being given to the child's best interests (see BVerfGE 107, 150 (178 et seq.)).
2. The European Court of Human Rights (ECHR) also considered the provision of § 1626a of the Civil Code in the year 2009, in the case Zaunegger v. Germany (see ECHR, *Zaunegger v. Germany*, no. 22028/04, judgment of 3 December 2009). In the judgment, a chamber of the Fifth Section of the ECHR held that the general exclusion of judicial review of the initial attribution of sole custody to the mother was disproportionate with regard to the aim pursued, that is, the protection of the best interests of a child born out of wedlock. Consequently there was a violation of Article 14 in conjunction with Article 8 of the European Convention on Human Rights. The Court stated that by permitting the parents of a child born out of wedlock to agree on joint parental custody, the legislature attempted to a certain extent to treat the parents who are not married to each other in the same way as married parents,

who when they married undertook to take responsibility for each other and for their child. In view of the varying life conditions of children born out of wedlock, and in the absence of a joint declaration of parental custody, it was also justified to initially grant the mother parental custody, in order to protect the child's best interests and to ensure that from the child's birth there was one person who could act for the child with legally binding effect (see ECHR, *Zaunegger v. Germany*, ibid., nos. 53, 55).
The Court stated that there might also be sound reasons for refusing an unmarried father the right to share parental custody. This might be the case if disputes or a lack of communication between the parents endangered the child's best interests. However, it was by no means proved that the relations between unmarried fathers and their children were generally characterised by such an attitude. If there were no sound reasons, then under § 1626a.1 no. 1 of the Civil Code the father of a child born out of wedlock was nevertheless from the outset deprived by law of the opportunity to apply for a judicial review as to whether the transfer of joint parental custody would serve the child's best interests, and to initiate legal proceedings to obtain surrogate consent, where the refusal of the mother to consent to joint parental custody might be arbitrary. The argument of the legislature was unconvincing that if the parents lived together but the mother refused to make a joint declaration of parental custody this was an exception to the rule and the mother had serious reasons for this which were based on the child's best interests (see ECHR, *Zaunegger v. Germany*, ibid., nos. 56 et seq.).
The Court stated that it was equally unconvinced by the argument that it could not be ruled out that a court order of joint parental custody would lead to conflicts between the parents and therefore had a negative impact on the child's best interests. Admittedly, court proceedings making arrangements for parental custody always had the potential to result in unsettling the child, but German law always provided for a comprehensive judicial review of the parental custody arrangements if the father had formerly had parental custody, either because the parents were married at the date when the child was born, or because they had married later, or because they had agreed on joint parental custody. No adequate reasons were apparent why the father of a child born out of wedlock had inferior legal protection, and if he recognised his paternity and assumed the role of a father should be treated differently than a father who had originally had parental custody and had later separated or been divorced from the mother (see ECHR, *Zaunegger v. Germany*, ibid., nos. 61-62).

III.

1. In all twenty-seven Member States of the European Union, there is the possibility of joint parental custody of children born out of wedlock subject to the condition that the paternity of the unmarried father is established with legally binding effect. In the concrete formulation of the arrangements for parental custody, seven EU Member States, unlike Germany, give the mother sole parental responsibility by law, but grant a right of parental custody to the father both if the parents agree and also by court decision (Finland: §§ 9, 10 of the Finnish Child Custody and Right of Access Act; Ireland: section 6A (1) of the Guardianship of Infants Act 1964 as amended by section 6 of the Children Act 1997, section 9 of the Guardianship of Infants Act 1964; Luxembourg: Article 380 of the Luxembourg Civil Code; Netherlands: Article 1:253c of the Dutch Civil Code; Sweden: Chapter 6 section 5 of the Swedish Children and Parents Code; United Kingdom: s. 4 (1) (c) of the Children Act 1989; Cyprus: section 6 of the Illegitimate Children Law CAP 278). In eighteen EU Member States, unmarried parents are treated largely or completely equally to married parents and obtain joint parental custody by operation of law (Belgium: Article 373, Article 374 § 1 of the Belgian Civil Code; Bulgaria: Article 68 (1), Article 72 of the Bulgarian Family Code; Denmark: Chapter 2 § 7 of the Danish Act on Parental Responsibility; Estonia: §§ 49, 50 of the Estonian Family Act; France: Article 372 of the French Civil Code; Greece: Article 1515 of the Greek Civil Code; Italy: Article 317bis of the Italian Civil Code; Latvia: Articles 178, 181 of the Latvian Civil Code; Lithuania: Article 3.165 of the Lithuanian Civil Code; Malta: Article 90 (1), Article 86 of the Maltese Civil Code; Poland: Article 93 § 1 of the Polish Family and Guardianship Code; Portugal: Article 1911 in conjunction with Article 1901 of the Portuguese Civil Code; Romania: Article 97 of the Romanian Family Code; Slovakia: § 28 (2) of the Slovakian Family Act; Slovenia: Article 102, Article 105.1 of the Slovenian Act on Marriage and Family Relations; Spain: Article 156 of the Spanish Civil Code; Czech Republic: § 34 (1), § 52 (1) of the Czech Family Act; Hungary: § 72 (1) of the Hungarian Family Act).
2. On account of the instruction to review legislation formulated by the Federal Constitutional Court, pursuant to the Act for the Implementation of Family-Law Decisions of the Federal Constitutional Court (*Gesetz zur Umsetzung familienrechtlicher Entscheidungen des Bundesverfassungsgerichts*) of 13 December 2003 …, since 2004 statistics of validly made joint parental custody declarations have been recorded annually. If the number of joint parental custody declarations made in a given year is set in proportion to the children born alive out of wedlock in the year in question, then in the year 2004 this gives a figure of 44.3 per cent, in the year 2005 a figure of 45.2 per cent, in the year 2006 a figure of 46.6 per cent, in the

year 2007 a figure of 49.1 per cent and in the year 2008 a figure of 50.7 per cent … However, in this connection it should be taken into account that this does not indicate precisely how many parents of children born out of wedlock actually made joint parental custody declarations at a particular survey date. On the one hand, no consideration is given to the fact that parental custody declarations may also be made for older children and that a declaration of joint parental custody may be made even before the birth of the child (§ 1626b.2 of the Civil Code). On the other hand, it is impossible to use the official figures for the birth of children born out of wedlock to make direct conclusions as to the number of children born out of wedlock at a particular survey date, since the status of the child may change, for example as a result of adoption or of the parents marrying.

3. In the year 2006, the Federal Ministry of Justice (*Bundesministerium der Justiz*) carried out a survey on the joint parental custody of parents not married to each other, in which 440 youth welfare offices and 109 lawyers took part: this produced the result that in the opinion of the youth welfare offices and lawyers polled, approximately 25 per cent to 75 per cent of all parents of children born out of wedlock live together or at least have lived together for a fairly long time (at least for a year) without having established joint parental custody (see *Bundestag* printed paper 16/10047, pp. 9, 12). The persons polled were also asked what motives the mothers gave for rejecting joint parental custody. Here, a choice of eight possible motives was given, some of which were oriented towards the child's best interests and some of which took no account of the child's best interests; multiple answers were permitted. The participants most often named the motives "The mother would like to retain sole parental custody so that she can make decisions on her own" and "The mother wants nothing more to do with the father and so she rejects every contact with him, including contact in matters relating to the child". These two motives were named by approximately 80 per cent of all youth welfare offices. Approximately 70 per cent of the youth welfare offices named the motives "There are often conflicts between the parents; peaceful communication is impossible" and "There has never been a relationship between the parents, the relationship was casual or has ended"; among lawyers, only approximately 50 per cent of them chose the two last motives (see *Bundestag* printed paper 16/10047, p. 12). Some of those polled pointed out in addition that parents are often ill-informed on the legal consequences of establishing or rejecting joint parental custody. Accordingly, they said, emotional reasons – such as uncertainty, the need to exercise control and a sense of personal injury – and the influence of third parties played a great role in their decisions. In addition to this, in an intact relationship the decisions relating to the child were in any case made jointly, and therefore many parents did not see the need to establish joint parental custody. This need often only arose when the parents had already sep-

arated (see *Bundestag* printed paper 16/10047, p. 14). After this survey was evaluated, the Federal Ministry of Justice commissioned a research project. The results of this survey to date show the same tendency.

IV.

1. The complainant is the father of a son born out of wedlock in 1998. The parents only lived together for a few weeks, and they separated when the mother was pregnant. Their son has lived in the mother's household since he was born. After the complainant had questioned his paternity, it was established by an expert witness in proceedings before the Family Court. Following this, in December 1998 the complainant recognised his paternity before the youth welfare office. The mother consented to the acknowledgment of paternity. In January 2001, the complainant had a notarial declaration of parental custody prepared; in this he stated that he wished to have joint parental custody with the mother. The mother refused to make a corresponding declaration of parental custody. In November 2002, the parents agreed before the Family Court on a right of contact which makes it possible *inter alia* for the complainant to spend every second weekend, with overnight stays, with the son. Arrangements were also made for holidays, public holidays and birthdays. In the following years, both parents adhered to the agreement made. However, since the birth of the child the relationship between the parents has been marked by disputes and mutual distrust.

2. After the complainant learnt, at the beginning of 2008, that the mother intended to move elsewhere in Germany with the child in the 2008 summer holidays, he applied to the Family Court for the mother to be partially deprived of parental custody and for the right to determine the child's place of abode to be transferred to himself; in addition, in the alternative, he applied for sole parental custody for his son to be transferred to himself or, in order for joint parental custody to be established, for the court to give surrogate consent to his declaration of parental custody in place of the mother.

After the parties were heard, the Family Court, by an order of 30 June 2008, rejected the complainant's applications. It stated that under § 1626a.1 of the Civil Code, the complainant could not obtain sole parental custody or parts thereof against the will of the mother who had parental custody. Nor could there be a transfer of the right to determine the child's place of abode or of the parental custody applied for in the alternative to the complainant under § 1672.1 of the Civil Code. § 1672.1 of the Civil Code mandatorily required the mother's consent to the establishment of sole parental custody. There were no reasons for the mother to be deprived of parental custody under § 1666 of the Civil Code. Since the beginning of the proceedings, the son had expressly desired to live with the father, and to a partial extent rejected the mother; this alone could not justify an intervention under § 1666 of the Civil Code. The father appealed against this order; his appeal was dismissed by the Higher Regional Court (*Oberlandesgericht*) by an order of 20 November 2008 as inadmissible, holding that the complainant had no right to lodge an appeal. The court stated that it was not possible to find that there had been a direct violation of the rights of the complainant, who had no parental custody, until parental custody was withdrawn from the mother under §§ 1666, 1666a, 1680 of the Civil Code, since only then would the question arise as to whether the parental custody should be transferred to the complainant. The father lodged a complaint alleging that his right to a hearing in court had been violated by the Local Court; the Family Court rejected this by an order of 8 January 2009, since it stated that the complainant had been given an extensive fair hearing.

3. This is challenged by the constitutional complaint filed by the complainant, in which he asserts that there has been a violation of Article 2.1, Article 3.1 and 3.2, Article 6.2, Article 20.3 of the Basic Law and of Article 6.2 of the Basic Law in conjunction with Article 1, Article 6, Article 8 and Article 14 of the European Convention on Human Rights. He regards the provisions on which the decisions are based as unconstitutional insofar as they provide that the establishment of joint or sole parental custody for the father of a child born out of wedlock is dependent on the consent of the mother or on parental custody having been withdrawn from the mother. He submits that, for the legislation to be constitutional, joint parental custody should automatically apply from the date when paternity is determined. At least, there should be a judicial review of the mother's refusal to make a declaration of consent in the individual case, and an order of joint parental custody or a transfer of sole custody to the father should be possible even where the situation does not qualify for § 1666 of the Civil Code. In his case, because the requirements of § 1666 of the Civil Code are so stringent, no account was taken of the will of the child; there was no review as to whether the complainant was suited to exercise parental custody and the transfer of parental custody or of parts of parental custody to him was in the child's best interests. If the child had been born in wedlock, sole parental custody could have been transferred to the complainant under § 1696 of the Civil Code where the mother had sole parental custody, and under § 1671.2 of the Civil Code where joint parental custody applied. He submitted that the Higher Regional Court was in error when it denied his entitlement to lodging an appeal.

V.

Opinions were submitted on invitation by the Federal Ministry of Justice in the name of the Federal Government and by the German Family Court Association (*Deutscher Familiengerichtstag e. V.*).

1. In its opinion, the Federal Ministry of Justice proceeds on the assumption that in the present state of investigations the main impetus for the mother not to agree to joint parental custody with the father in a large number of cases probably does not primarily lie in serious considerations of the child's best interests. In view of this and in the light of the latest decision of the European Court of Human Rights, preliminary deliberations were made for a draft statute to amend the legal position with regard to parental custody. The Ministry stated that provisions on the entitlement to lodge an appeal in parental custody matters were amenable to an interpretation that was in conformity with the Basic Law.

2. The German Family Court Association is of the opinion that § 1672.1 of the Civil Code and therefore also § 1626a of the Civil Code and § 1680.3, 1680.2 sentence 2 in conjunction with § 1666 of the Civil Code violate Article 6.2 sentence 1, Article 6.5 and Article 3 of the Basic Law insofar as the provisions do not provide for a judicial review in the individual case where the mother refuses consent. …

B.

The constitutional complaint is admissible and is well-founded.

§ 1626a.1 no. 1 of the Civil Code and § 1672.1 of the Civil Code are incompatible with Article 6.2 of the Basic Law.

It is constitutionally unobjectionable that the legislature initially transfers parental custody of a child born out of wedlock to its mother alone (see BVerfGE 107, 150 (169)). It is also compatible with the constitution that the father of a child born out of wedlock is not granted joint parental custody together with the mother at the same time as his paternity is effectively recognised. Such a provision would indeed be possible, but it is not constitutionally required.

However, the legislature disproportionately encroaches upon the parental right of the father of a child born out of wedlock when it generally excludes the father from parental custody of his child if the child's mother refuses her consent to joint parental custody with the father or to the father's sole parental custody of the child, without the father being given the possibility of a judicial review as to whether, for reasons of the child's best interests, the father should share in parental custody or the sole custody of the child should be transferred to him, on weighing his parental right against that of the mother or otherwise. There has been no confirmation of the legislature's assumption on which current law is based, that mothers' refusal of consent is as a rule based on a conflict between the parents which has a negative impact on the child and has reasons which do not serve the mother's own interests but safeguard the child's best interests.

I.

The parental right granted by Article 6.2 of the Basic Law to mothers and fathers must be further refined by the legislature. Thus, for example, regulations and procedures in a legal form are necessary which clarify, even for children born out of wedlock, who is to be legally recognised as the father of the child and therefore holds the parental right under Article 6.2 of the Basic Law (see BVerfGE 92, 158 (177-178); 108, 82 (101)). Since both parents hold the parental rights, provisions must also be created giving each of them rights and duties towards the child to provide for the case where they cannot agree on the exercise of their parental responsibility. In this connection, the state, because of its watchdog function established for it by Article 6.2 sentence 2 of the Basic Law, has to ensure that the exercise of parental rights is guided by the child's best interests and that the child's rights are respected when parental responsibility is exercised (see BVerfGE 121, 69 (94)). If this does not occur, for lack of a necessary minimum of agreement between the parents, the legislature may allocate the principal responsibility for the child to one parent (see BVerfGE 92, 158 (178-179); 107, 150 (169)).

1. The parental right under Article 6.2 of the Basic Law of the father of a child born out of wedlock is not violated if parental custody of a child is first awarded legally to its mother alone under § 1626a.2 of the Civil Code and the care for the person of the child is transferred to her. As the Federal Constitutional Court stated in its decision of 29 January 2003, children born out of wedlock are born into a variety of family configurations (see BVerfGE 107, 150 (170)). The spectrum ranges from cases in which the identity of the father cannot be established or is not certain, to those in which the father pays maintenance but does not wish to have any part in the custody of the child and sometimes even refuses contact with the child (see BVerfGE 121, 69 et seq.), and to those in which the father wishes to have parental custody of the child, either together with the mother or alone. At the time of the birth of a child born out of wedlock it can therefore not generally be assumed that the child has a father to whom it can legally be assigned and who is willing to take responsibility for the child.

There have been no fundamental changes to this situation since this decision. It is true that the proportion of children who are born out of wedlock has now risen to 32.1 per cent of the total births in Germany … And in addition, the proportion of minor children who grow up in unmarried parental conjugal communities rose from 5.4 per cent in the year 2001 to at least 7.1 per cent in the year 2008. However, at the same time at least 16.1 per cent of the children grow up with only one parent: this also includes children whose parents have divorced … If, on the other hand, the annual figure for joint declarations of parental custody made by parents of children born out of wedlock is set in proportion to the children born out of wedlock in the year in question, then this supports the assessment that there is now joint parental custody of approximately half of all children born out of wedlock … However, it cannot be established when the declarations of parental custody which are conditional on the acknowledgment of paternity are made. Consequently, a study has not yet been disproved which concluded, on the basis of the cases investigated, that although 80 per cent of the fathers voluntary acknowledged their paternity, in two-thirds of the cases they only did this after the child was born … On the basis of the statistics, it is true that there is a development towards establishing families in which parents who are not married to each other have joint parental custody of their children. But even today, at the time of the birth of a child born out of wedlock it is in many cases not legally clarified who their father is and whether he may also wish to have parental custody of the child.

However, the child's best interests require that from its birth the child has a person who can act for the child with legally binding effect. The legislature therefore pursues a legitimate goal when it normally attributes parental custody of a child born out of wedlock to its mother upon the child's birth and not to the father or to both parents jointly (see also ECHR, *Zaunegger v. Germany*, ibid., nos. 53, 55). For the mother is the only sure relation whom the child encounters at its birth and who is confirmed as a parent by reason of § 1591 of the Civil Code. In order to ensure that factual and legal responsibility for the child may be borne from the first day of its life, it is justified in the first instance not to allow the father to share the parental custody of the child (see BVerfGE 107, 150 (170-171)).

2. Nor does the parental right under Article 6.2 of the Basic Law require that the fathers of children born out of wedlock should generally be granted the parental custody of their child together with the mother by operation of law when they effectively acknowledge their paternity under §§ 1594 et seq. of the Civil Code.

Admittedly, a statutory provision for such a legal consequence of the acknowledgment of paternity would be compatible with the constitution provided it were combined with the possibility of obtaining a judicial review as to whether joint parental custody in accordance with statute actually serves the child's best interests in the individual case. But the legislature has sound reasons for not choosing this solution.

a) The acknowledgment of paternity contains the declaration that one is the father of a child born out of wedlock and wishes to take the legal position of father for the child. If the mother of the child consents to this, it is presumed by statute that this corresponds to the facts, and the declarant takes the legal position of father. However, it cannot be generally concluded from this willingness of the father of a child born out of wedlock to be legally assigned to the child as father that the father is also prepared to assume responsibility for the child together with the mother. Similarly, the agreement of the parents on the acknowledgment of paternity does not automatically mean that the parents are willing and in a position to exercise custody of the child jointly, taking sufficient account of the child's best interests. On the one hand, the configurations of relationships between parents into which children born out of wedlock are born are too various to support such a broad assumption. For it may happen that both parents, despite the legal acknowledgment of paternity, reject each other, and this may not be conducive to beneficial joint parental custody in the interests of the child. Nor can the possibility be excluded that although a father acknowledges his paternity, he refuses to take up or continue contact with his child (see BVerfGE 121, 69 et seq.). On the other hand, the fact that after a legal acknowledgment of paternity, in only approximately half of the cases of children born out of wedlock do the parents voluntarily establish joint parental custody under § 1626a.1 no. 1 of the Civil Code speaks against the assumption that when the parents agree on paternity, it can always be inferred that the parents agree on joint parental custody. At all events, it cannot be assumed from this that the father as a general rule wishes to have custody of his child. There is no indication that the failure to establish joint parental custody in approximately half of the cases of children born out of wedlock above all or even solely results from the mother's lack of willingness to agree.

b) However, this does not prevent the legislature, in view of the fact that, after all, joint parental custody is established for half of the children born out of wedlock, from involving the father of a child born out of wedlock, at the time when he legally acknowledges paternity, by operation of law in taking responsibility for the child and from transferring to him joint paternal custody with the mother, particularly since a large number of parents only fail to make a joint declaration of parental custody for lack of adequate information or because they believe that their de facto joint parental custody of the child does not need to be safeguarded by law (see *Bundestag* printed paper 16/10047, p. 14). This would not merely take account of the father's parental right, but the father of a child born out of wedlock would also be more involved in the duty to care for and bring up his child, which is linked to the parental right under Article 6.2 of the Basic Law (see BVerfGE 108, 82 (102); 121, 69 (92)). However, in the case of such a general assignment of rights of joint parental custody to the mother and to the father of a child born out of wedlock it must be taken into account that it may not at all be assumed that there is always a stable relationship between the parents of a child born out of wedlock which guarantees that the exercise of joint parental custody will proceed sufficiently free of conflicts and will not harm the child's best interests. In order to safeguard the child's best interests, therefore, the legislature ought constitutionally, exercising its watchdog function, to grant each parent the possibility of having a judicial review as to whether joint parental custody in the individual case is genuinely in accordance with the child's best interests or whether sole parental custody of the child, for reasons of the child's best interests, should either again be transferred to the mother or now be transferred to the father. For the case of joint parental custody of parents living apart which was established by marriage or by corresponding declarations of parental custody, the legislature has already provided for this in § 1671 of the Civil Code.

c) On the other hand, however, the legislature is also not prevented from taking into account, when parental custody is assigned for a child born out of wedlock, that it cannot be assumed that the fathers of children born out of wedlock are always willing to share responsibility for their child with the mother. For where bearing parental responsibility is coupled to the acknowledgment of paternity, a lack of willingness on the part of the father to share joint parental custody might entail the danger that fathers are then less prepared to acknowledge paternity voluntarily. This might increase the number of proceedings that become necessary for judicial determination of paternity under § 1600d of the Civil Code and adversely affect the relationship between the parents in a manner that is not conducive to the child's best interests. In addition, the legislature is entitled to include in its considerations the fact that a general statutory arrangement for joint parental custody may also include cases in which as a result of very serious conflicts between the parents the child's best interests would be detrimentally affected for at least until the joint parental custody of the parents were terminated and replaced by the sole custody of one parent (see *Bundestag* printed paper 13/8511, p. 66). In order to prevent this, when the child's best interests are weighed against the parental rights of both parents, it is also constitutionally justified and unobjectionable that the legislature refrained from transferring joint parental custody with the mother to the father of a child born out of wedlock upon his effective acknowledgment of paternity by operation of law, as a result of which, even when the acknowledgment of paternity has been made, at first the mother's sole parental custody of the child remains in place.

II.

However, the parental right of the father of a child born out of wedlock under Article 6.2 of the Basic Law is violated by the fact that when the mother refuses to consent to him sharing in the parental responsibility for his child, he is generally prevented from involvement, because § 1626a.1 no. 1 of the Civil Code and § 1672.1 of the Civil Code give him no possibility of obtaining judicial review against the will of the mother as to whether, by reason of his child's best interests, it is appropriate to grant him parental custody of his child together with the mother, or to transfer sole parental custody of the child to him in place of the mother.

1. It is not simply a necessary legislative formulation of the parental right, but is an encroachment upon the parental right of the father of a child born out of wedlock, protected by Article 6.2 of the Basic Law, that in § 1626a.1 no. 1 and § 1672.1 of the Civil Code the legislature makes the possibility of establishing the father's parental custody dependent on the will of the mother, and refuses parental custody to the father if the mother refuses consent in failing to provide for any judicial review of the individual case in this situation. Parental custody is an essential element of the right of the parents to the care and upbringing of their own child, protected by Article 6.2 of the Basic Law (see BVerfGE 56, 363 (382)). If it is generally withheld from one parent, this is an encroachment.

2. With regard to encroachment upon the parental right by the general exclusion of the father from parental custody where the mother does not consent, another reason why this cannot be denied is that subject to certain conditions, § 1680.3 sentence 2 in conjunction with § 1666 of the Civil Code permits, where there is danger to the child's best interests, the parental custody of the child to be withdrawn from the mother and transferred to the father, if this is in the child's best interests. This does not give the father of a child born out of wedlock general access to parental custody. § 1666 of the Civil Code is not a provision that fundamentally assigns rights to the parents in relation to each other or that is aimed at balancing the parental rights. Instead, this provision sets limits to encroachments of the state upon the right of the parents and defines the conditions subject to which the state must comply with its watchdog function under Article 6.2 sentence 2 of the Basic Law (see BVerfGE 107, 150 (182-183)). It is therefore also not permitted to interpret § 1666 of the Civil Code in such a way that the father of a child born out of wedlock has easier access to parental custody. For this would at the same time lower the threshold of the state's right to encroach upon the parental right, and this might result in a disproportionate and therefore unjustified restriction of the personal responsibility of parents for their children, which is protected by Article 6.2 of the Basic Law. § 1680.3 sentence 2 in conjunction with § 1666 of the Civil Code is therefore neither intended by statute nor appropriate as a general provision on access for fathers to parental custody rights.

3. In requiring the consent of the mother as a condition for the access of the father of a child born out of wedlock to parental custody, the legislature pursues a legiti-

mate goal. It intends to avoid danger to the child's best interests, which might arise if joint parental custody were established by reason of the parents' failure to agree on the custody of their child, or which might be established if the mother-child relationship were adversely affected where sole parental custody is transferred to the father against the will of the mother (see *Bundestag* printed paper 13/4899, pp. 58, 60).

a) Exercising joint responsibility for a child requires a minimum agreement between the parents. If this is lacking, and if the parents are neither willing nor able to cooperate, joint parental custody of the child may run counter to the child's best interests. If the parents engage in their argument to the detriment of the child, the child's ability to relate to others may be impaired and its development endangered (see BVerfGE 107, 150 (173)).

If the parents are in agreement on the parental custody of the child, and if this is expressed in a joint consistent declaration, it may be assumed that both parents also have the intention to cooperate in the care and upbringing of their child. But if there is no such agreement, this may indicate a conflict between the parents which may have a major impact on the child (see BVerfGE 107, 150 (174 et seq.)). For lack of agreement to establish joint parental custody suggests that there may also be arguments on exercising it, and these arguments may possibly take place to the detriment of the children. In the opinion of the legislature, it may be assumed that joint parental custody enforced against the will of one parent as a rule entails more disadvantages than benefits for the child (see *Bundestag* printed paper 13/4899, pp. 58 et seq.; *Bundestag* printed paper13/8511, p. 66). In order to avoid such disadvantages and to take account of the child's best interests, the legislature has provided that joint parental custody may be established under § 1626a.1 no. 1 of the Civil Code only where the parents both agree to it, and has excluded it where the parents fail to agree.

b) The fact that the transfer of sole parental custody to the father is made subject to the mother's consent is also intended to serve the child's best interests. In thus providing, the legislature intends to avoid the mother's sense of insecurity because the parental custody of the child could be withdrawn from her against her will and transferred to the father, putting a strain on the existing close relationship between mother and child and thus having an adverse effect on the child. In addition, it intends to avoid the mother's fear that the father might turn out to be the "better" parent having an effect on her willingness to pursue the determination of paternity and also affecting the father's contact with the child to the detriment of the child (see *Bundestag* printed paper 13/4899, pp. 59-60).

4. The provisions of § 1626a.1 no. 1 and § 1672.1 of the Civil Code which subject the access to parental custody of the father of a child born out of wedlock to the

consent of the mother are fundamentally also appropriate to safeguard the child's best interests and to prevent endangerment of the child's best interests. Admittedly, they cannot prevent conflicts between the parents on the parental custody of their child. However, because these conflicts cannot be taken to court, they have no decisive influence on the exercise of parental custody, which may therefore take place without conflicts and may give the child orientation. In addition, the child is also not additionally burdened by a court dispute (see BVerfGE 107, 150 (177)).

5. However, there are doubts as to whether, in order to prevent endangerment of the child's best interests by joint parental custody of the parents or by a transfer of sole custody to the father against the will of the mother, it is necessary for the father of a child born out of wedlock to be generally excluded from parental custody, without the possibility of judicial review, if the mother refuses consent. At all events, the encroachment contained in this upon the father's parental right under Article 6.2 of the Basic Law is disproportionate in the narrow sense and violates the parental right of the father of a child born out of wedlock because the father is unable to subject the exclusion of parental custody to a judicial review of the individual case by the standard of the child's best interests.

a) § 1626a.1 no. 1 of the Civil Code only gives the father of a child born out of wedlock the opportunity to share the joint parental custody of the child with the mother if the mother consents to this. If the mother refuses this consent, the father is permanently excluded from the joint parental custody of his child. Under §§ 1601 et seq. of the Civil Code, he is in fact called upon to pay child maintenance, and under § 1615 l of the Civil Code he must pay maintenance to the mother for the care of the child insofar as he is able to pay, but he may not share in the decisions on the fate of his child and on its upbringing. He retains only the right to contact with the child (§ 1684 of the Civil Code), if and insofar as contact is in the child's best interests. This refusal to allow the father to influence the care and upbringing of the child, without the possibility of judicial review, is a far-reaching encroachment upon the father's parental right.

In contrast, the mother is not only unconditionally granted by statute sole parental custody, which can be withdrawn only if there is danger to the child's best interests. She is also given the competence to decide whether the father is to have access to the parental custody of his child. In this arrangement it is irrelevant whether the exercise of parental custody which the mother desires or rejects is conducive to the child's best interests. In this dependence of the father's sharing in joint parental custody on the will of the mother, the legislature disproportionately provides that generally the father's parental right takes second place to that of the mother, without this being required to safeguard the child's best interests. Admittedly, court proceedings may temporarily constitute an additional burden for the child (see ECHR,

Zaunegger v. Germany, ibid., no. 61). But fundamentally clarifying the question of parental custody is specifically in the child's best interests. Only the child's best interests may justify excluding a parent from the parental custody of the child (see BVerfGE 121, 69 (94)).

(1) One has to agree with the statement of the European Court of Human Rights that the legislature itself did not consistently base its overall concept for the parental custody of children born out of wedlock on its premise justifying the provision of § 1626a.1 no. 1 of the Civil Code, that lack of agreement between the parents on parental custody reveals a conflict between the parents which always leads to an exercise of joint parental custody that is detrimental to the child's best interests (see ECHR, *Zaunegger v. Germany*, ibid., nos. 61-62). For if parents who are not married to each other who once established joint parental custody live apart, and if one parent wishes to be given sole parental custody of the child against the will of the other, then under § 1671 of the Civil Code that parent is given the right to make an application for transfer of sole parental custody to this effect. Here, the legislature does not conclude from this application itself and from the lack of consent of the other parent that the parents are unwilling and unable to cooperate and this will have detrimental effects on the child. On the contrary, the court must then consider whether it is to be expected that the transfer of sole parental custody to the applicant is actually most favourable to the child's best interests. In this case, therefore, it is the child's best interests that decide the assignment of parental custody, not the lack of agreement of the parents, which is only taken into account in the consideration of the individual case if it needs to be clarified whether it arises from the parents' inability to cooperate which gives rise to fear that there may be negative effects on the child ....

In this respect no reason is apparent why the legislature, in connection with the establishment of joint parental custody, was not also primarily guided by the consideration whether this, despite differences of opinion on it between the parents, was in the individual case in the child's best interests, but instead in this case found the mother's contrary intention sufficient to support the general assumption that the child's best interests would be adversely affected, and on this basis excluded a judicial review of the individual case by the standard of the best interests of the child affected. When joint parental custody is terminated, there has at least in the past been a certain degree of willingness to cooperate on the part of the parents, which is not the case when joint parental custody is first established; but this is not a sound reason to treat these cases differently in law. For in both cases there is a disagreement between the parents on the exercise of parental custody for their child, which can in each case be an indication that a newly established or continuing joint parental custody is likely to be detrimental to the child's best interests in future by

reason of the conflicts between the parents. But whether this assumption can really be relied on can also only be clarified by judicial review in the individual case.
(2) Above all, however, recent empirical findings do not confirm the legislature's assumption that mothers' refusal of consent is as a rule based on a conflict between the parents which has detrimental effects for the child and has reasons which do not serve the mother's own interests but safeguard the child's best interests.
In its decision of 29 January 2003, the Federal Constitutional Court conceded that when the legislature provided for the joint parental custody of parents not married to each other, it was justified in assuming that in future parents, where they were willing to cooperate, would as a rule make use of the possibility of joint parental custody and that mothers would only reject the father's wish for joint custody if they had serious reasons for this based on the defence of the child's best interests, that is, mothers would not misuse the possibility of refusing to submit a declaration of parental custody as a power position against the father (see BVerfGE 107, 150 (177)). But the Federal Constitutional Court pointed out that § 1626a.1 no. 1 of the Civil Code would reveal itself to be incompatible with the parental right of the father under Article 6.2 of the Basic Law if this assumption of the legislature were not confirmed, and in particular were it to emerge instead that in a large number of cases where, for reasons not based on the child's best interests, the parents of children born out of wedlock did not establish joint custody (see BVerfGE 107, 150 (178-179)). For this reason it obliged the legislature to observe the actual development and to review whether its assumptions also stood the test of reality. For if this were not the case, the legislature would have to open the fathers of children born out of wedlock an access to joint parental custody that took sufficient account of their parental rights under Article 6.2 of the Basic Law, with due consideration given to the child's best interests (see BVerfGE 107, 150 (180-181)).
There are now sufficient data available showing that the legislature's assumptions at that time have not been confirmed as correct. This relates on the one hand to the number of cases in which parents of children born out of wedlock have established joint parental custody. The statistics gathered show that only slightly over half of the parents agreed to make declarations of parental custody to this effect … Nor are a relevant number of cases of joint parental custody established even when the parents live together (see *Bundestag* printed paper 16/10047, pp. 11-12). On the other hand, there has been no confirmation – as the Federal Government also states in its opinion – of the legislature's assumption that mothers' refusal to consent to joint parental custody is as a rule based on reasons guided by the child's best interests. The surveys on this carried out by institutions and experts which are permanently concerned with the parental custody of parents of children born out of wedlock and therefore have experience of the motivation of mothers who do not consent to joint

parental custody, but also the results of surveys of mothers available to date show that in addition to considerations of the child's best interests personal wishes of the mothers often also lead to the mothers' rejection of joint parental custody with the father of the child. Thus, for example, it has often been given as a reason that the mother wishes to retain sole custody in order to be able to decide alone on the child's affairs, that is, she does not wish to have to reach an agreement with the father or she wants nothing to do with the father (see *Bundestag* printed paper 16/10047, pp. 12 et seq.).

But if the legislature's assumption is therefore not confirmed, and instead it must be assumed that a considerable number of mothers refuse their consent to joint parental custody merely because they do not wish to share their traditional parental custody with the father of their child, then the access to parental custody of fathers of children born out of wedlock depends in a significant number of cases on the dominant will of the mother and is excluded if she is not prepared to consent to it, without it being established by this whether joint parental custody of the parents is beneficial or detrimental to the child's best interests. The fact that when the mother refuses to consent to joint parental custody fathers are not by law given the possibility of having a judicial review as to whether joint parental custody in their individual situation might not actually be advisable for reasons of the child's best interests therefore has an adverse effect on the father's parental right as against that of the mother in a manner that is disproportionate and therefore unjustified.

b) Under § 1672.1 of the Civil Code, the transfer of sole parental custody for a child born out of wedlock which is held by the mother under § 1626a.2 of the Civil Code to the father of a child born out of wedlock is also dependent on the mother's consent. If this consent is not given, the father has no possibility of obtaining a judicial review as to whether his own parental custody might be more conducive to the child's best interests than the parental custody of the mother. This general exclusion of access to parental custody where the mother does not consent is also a serious encroachment, which is disproportionate and unjustified, upon the father's parental right under Article 6.2 of the Basic Law.

(1) Where the parents are unable to cooperate in the parental custody of their child, which may be expressed in the mother's refusal to consent, this cannot justify the exclusion of the father from sole parental custody. For in the opinion of the legislature too, the very unwillingness and inability of the parents to cooperate is an important reason not to establish or continue joint parental custody but to transfer the parental custody of the child to one parent alone, in order that the child does not suffer detriment as a result of the lack of agreement and disputes between the parents. This assessment is at all events the basis of § 1671 of the Civil Code, which

makes it possible to replace the joint parental custody of parents living apart by the sole custody of one parent by reason of the child's best interests.
(2) Insofar as the legislature intends by this provision to avoid placing strain on the existing mother-child relationship as a result of the mother's constant fear that if the father makes an application, the parental custody of her child could be withdrawn from her and transferred to the father (see *Bundestag* printed paper 13/4899, p. 60), this is also not a sufficient reason to generally exclude the father from parental custody where the mother refuses consent and to grant him no possibility of judicial review as to whether, by reason of the child's best interests, it is appropriate to transfer to him the sole parental custody of the child.
However, it must be taken into account that enabling a court transfer of sole parental custody to the father on the one hand takes account of the father's parental right, but on the other hand is a serious encroachment on the mother's parental right if the father's application is granted. For, unlike in the case where the father is admitted to joint parental custody with the mother, the mother does not merely have to share the parental custody of the child with the father, which Article 6.2 of the Basic Law protects as the standard case when it assigns the care and upbringing of the children not to one parent, but to both parents as a natural right. Instead, the parental custody previously exercised by the mother is completely withdrawn from her, and not because she has failed in her duty of upbringing and therefore the child's best interests are endangered, as § 1666 of the Civil Code presumes, but because the father, in competition with her, claims his right to have parental custody of the child in her place. It is also important in this connection that the legislature in the first instance assigns to the mothers of children born out of wedlock the parental custody of these children from their birth. The mothers thus not only obtain the right of parental custody, but are also obliged by statute to take responsibility for their child. Unlike the fathers of children born out of wedlock, they do not have the choice of deciding for or against taking parental responsibility for their child. Depriving them of the parental responsibility imposed on them despite the fact that their exercise of it was unobjectionable therefore weighs heavy and constitutes a serious encroachment on their parental rights.
(3) In addition, a change of parental custody from the mother to the father, unlike the establishment of joint parental custody, as a general rule also entails a removal of the child from the mother's household to the father's household. This not only affects the existing mother-child relationship, but also impinges on the child's need for stability and continuity with regard to its personal ties that have grown up over the years and its social environment.
(4) Taking account of this, and weighing the constitutionally protected interests of both parents and of the child, it is admittedly disproportionate and therefore incom-

patible with Article 6.2 of the Basic Law that the legislature has excluded the father of a child born out of wedlock from parental custody of his child for the mere lack of the mother's consent and has also, because there is no possibility of a judicial review of the individual case, refused him access to sole custody. But if the possibility of a judicial review of the individual case is granted, sufficient account must also be taken of the parental right of the mother of the child born out of wedlock. Withdrawing parental custody from her is justified only if there is no other possibility to safeguard the father's parental right which encroaches less seriously upon the mother's parental right, and if there are important reasons of the child's best interests which suggest withdrawing parental custody from the mother. Joint parental custody by the parents would be less of an encroachment upon the mother's parental right than the withdrawal of parental custody from her. For this reason, in proceedings for the transfer of sole custody to the father of a child born out of wedlock it must also first be examined whether joint parental custody by the parents might be appropriate where it is not detrimental to the child's best interests. Where this is the case, in order to safeguard the mother's parental right, there may be no transfer of sole custody to the father. Otherwise, important concerns of the child and its best interests may justify the transfer of sole custody to the father.

6. Since the provisions challenged even violate Article 6.2 of the Basic Law and have proved to be unconstitutional, there is no need to further investigate whether they also violate Article 3.1 or 3.2 of the Basic Law and Article 6.5 of the Basic Law. Admittedly, when the legislature reforms the law of the parental custody of children born out of wedlock, it must ensure that these fundamental rights are guaranteed too. This also applies in particular to the question as to whether in the case where the fathers of children born out of wedlock are granted a right, when the mother refuses to consent, to apply for the establishment of joint parental custody or transfer of sole custody of their child to themselves, mothers must also be granted such a right if the father of their child is not prepared to share parental custody or to take on sole custody.

III.

The decision of the Local Court of 30 June 2008 challenged by the constitutional complaint violates the complainant's fundamental right under Article 6.2 of the Basic Law, since it is based on § 1626a.1 no. 1, § 1672.1 of the Civil Code, which violate this fundamental right. The decision is therefore reversed. The decision of the Higher Regional Court of 20 November 2008, pronounced only for procedural reasons, and the order of the Local Court of 8 January 2009 relating to the complaint of the complainant alleging that his right to a hearing in court had been violated thus no longer apply. The matter is referred back to the Local Court for a new decision.

C. – I.

If a provision is not compatible with the Basic Law, then it must in principle be declared null and void (§ 95.3 sentences 1 and 2 of the Federal Constitutional Court Act (*Bundesverfassungsgerichtsgesetz* – BVerfGG)). However, this does not apply if the nullity would create a situation which was even further removed from the constitutional order than the previous one (see BVerfGE 119, 331 (382-383)). Consequently, § 1626a.1 no. 1, § 1672.1 of the Civil Code may not be declared null and void here because this would have the consequence that establishing joint parental custody or transferring sole parental custody to the father would no longer be possible even if the parents of a child born out of wedlock unanimously desired it. In addition, it is an obstacle to a declaration of nullity that the legislature has a variety of possibilities of removing the unconstitutional situation (see BVerfGE 109, 256 (273)).

II.

Nor is it possible to treat the provisions as inapplicable (see BVerfGE 84, 9 (21)) because they are incompatible with Article 6.2 of the Basic Law, since this too would only further aggravate the unconstitutional state.

However, it is also not appropriate merely to declare the unconstitutional provisions as continuing in application until the law is reformed by the legislature. This would lead to a perpetuation of the violation of the fundamental rights of the fathers of children born out of wedlock which it might be impossible to reverse when a constitutional provision entered into force, because in parent-and-child law matters the time factor plays an essential role … With the increasing passing of time, the personal ties of a child may change, and as a result it is possible that there would be de facto changes of course which may have effects on later decisions under new law.

But above all, the non-constitutional courts would be obliged to continue to apply provisions which are not only incompatible with the Basic Law, but in the case of § 1626a.1 no. 1 of the Civil Code even a provision which the European Court of Human Rights has declared to be incompatible with the European Convention on Human Rights because it violates Article 14 in conjunction with Article 8 of the European Convention on Human Rights (see ECHR, *Zaunegger v. Germany*, ibid., no. 64). Since the non-constitutional courts are required in the application of the law to take sufficient account of the guarantees of the European Convention on Human Rights and the case-law of the European Court of Human Rights (see BVerfGE 111, 307 (323-324)), and a suspension of relevant parental custody cases might be contrary to the procedural requirement of expediting parent-and-child cases, it is necessary, in order to provisionally ensure a situation complying with the constitution and the Convention, to make a transitional arrangement. Here, a solution should be chosen which does not anticipate the statutory provision and does not put obstacles in its way (see BVerfGE 84, 9 (23)).

III.

It therefore appears appropriate to proceed from the present legislative concept of the legislature, which makes the establishment of joint parental custody of parents of children born out of wedlock dependent on making joint declarations of parental custody. Consequently, supplementing this provision of § 1626a.1 no. 1 of the Civil Code, it is provisionally ordered, until revised legislation enters into effect, that the Family Court, on the application of one parent, shall transfer parental custody or part of parental custody to the parents jointly, provided it is to be expected that this is in the child's best interests. The selected standard of review of the child's best interests is intended to ensure that the concerns of the child are taken decisively into account, but the requirements for access to joint parental custody are not made too stringent.

With regard to the transfer of sole custody to the father, an appropriate arrangement for the transitional period until the reform of the law would follow the provision of § 1671 of the Civil Code. Since this provision also requires that the transfer of sole parental custody is to be made only if the requirements for joint parental custody of the parents are no longer satisfied, and at the same time, as set out under B.II.5.b) (4), the establishment of joint parental custody where the mother previously had sole parental custody is less detrimental to her parental right than a complete change of parental custody from herself to the father, then in supplementation of § 1672.1 of the Civil Code, until a reform of the law enters into effect it is provisionally ordered that the Family Court, on the application of a parent, shall transfer to the father the parental custody or part of the parental custody where joint parental custody is out of the question and it is to be expected that this best serves the child's best interests.

With regard to the provisional arrangement made, the Senate does not fix a period of time for the legislature to pass the necessary reform of the law, particularly since the Federal Government stated in the proceedings that there have already been preliminary deliberations for a reform of the law.

IV.

The decision on costs is based on § 34a.2 of the Federal Constitutional Court Act.

Justices: Kirchhof, Hohmann-Dennhardt, Bryde, Gaier, Eichberger, Schluckebier, Masing

Appendix

Basic Law for the Federal Republic of Germany

Preamble

Conscious of their responsibility before God and man,
Inspired by the determination to promote world peace as an equal partner in a united Europe, the German people, in the exercise of their constituent power, have adopted this Basic Law. Germans in the *Länder* of Baden-Württemberg, Bavaria, Berlin, Brandenburg, Bremen, Hamburg, Hesse, Lower Saxony, Mecklenburg-Western Pomerania, North Rhine-Westphalia, Rhineland-Palatinate, Saarland, Saxony, Saxony-Anhalt, Schleswig-Holstein and Thuringia have achieved the unity and freedom of Germany in free self-determination. This Basic Law thus applies to the entire German people.

I. Basic Rights

Article 1 [Human dignity – Human rights – Legally binding force of basic rights]

(1) Human dignity shall be inviolable. To respect and protect it shall be the duty of all state authority.
(2) The German people therefore acknowledge inviolable and inalienable human rights as the basis of every community, of peace and of justice in the world.
(3) The following basic rights shall bind the legislature, the executive and the judiciary as directly applicable law.

The Basic Law for the Federal Republic of Germany
Translated by: Professor Christian Tomuschat and Professor David P. Currie
Translation revised by: Professor Christian Tomuschat and Professor Donald E. Kommers in cooperation with the Language Service of the German *Bundestag*

Enlarged by the amendment made on 11 July 2012

Article 2 **[Personal freedoms]**

(1) Every person shall have the right to free development of his personality insofar as he does not violate the rights of others or offend against the constitutional order or the moral law.
(2) Every person shall have the right to life and physical integrity. Freedom of the person shall be inviolable. These rights may be interfered with only pursuant to a law.

Article 3 **[Equality before the law]**

(1) All persons shall be equal before the law.
(2) Men and women shall have equal rights. The state shall promote the actual implementation of equal rights for women and men and take steps to eliminate disadvantages that now exist.
(3) No person shall be favoured or disfavoured because of sex, parentage, race, language, homeland and origin, faith, or religious or political opinions. No person shall be disfavoured because of disability.

Article 4 **[Freedom of faith and conscience]**

(1) Freedom of faith and of conscience, and freedom to profess a religious or philosophical creed, shall be inviolable.
(2) The undisturbed practice of religion shall be guaranteed.
(3) No person shall be compelled against his conscience to render military service involving the use of arms. Details shall be regulated by a federal law.

Article 5 **[Freedom of expression, arts and sciences]**

(1) Every person shall have the right freely to express and disseminate his opinions in speech, writing and pictures, and to inform himself without hindrance from generally accessible sources. Freedom of the press and freedom of reporting by means of broadcasts and films shall be guaranteed. There shall be no censorship.
(2) These rights shall find their limits in the provisions of general laws, in provisions for the protection of young persons, and in the right to personal honour.

(3) Arts and sciences, research and teaching shall be free. The freedom of teaching shall not release any person from allegiance to the constitution.

Article 6 **[Marriage – Family – Children]**

(1) Marriage and the family shall enjoy the special protection of the state.
(2) The care and upbringing of children is the natural right of parents and a duty primarily incumbent upon them. The state shall watch over them in the performance of this duty.
(3) Children may be separated from their families against the will of their parents or guardians only pursuant to a law, and only if the parents or guardians fail in their duties or the children are otherwise in danger of serious neglect.
(4) Every mother shall be entitled to the protection and care of the community.
(5) Children born outside of marriage shall be provided by legislation with the same opportunities for physical and mental development and for their position in society as are enjoyed by those born within marriage.

Article 7 **[School system]**

(1) The entire school system shall be under the supervision of the state.
(2) Parents and guardians shall have the right to decide whether children shall receive religious instruction.
(3) Religious instruction shall form part of the regular curriculum in state schools, with the exception of non-denominational schools. Without prejudice to the state's right of supervision, religious instruction shall be given in accordance with the tenets of the religious community concerned. Teachers may not be obliged against their will to give religious instruction.
(4) The right to establish private schools shall be guaranteed. Private schools that serve as alternatives to state schools shall require the approval of the state and shall be subject to the laws of the *Länder*. Such approval shall be given when private schools are not inferior to the state schools in terms of their educational aims, their facilities, or the professional training of their teaching staff, and when segregation of pupils according to the means of their parents will not be encouraged thereby. Approval shall be withheld if the economic and legal position of the teaching staff is not adequately assured.
(5) A private elementary school shall be approved only if the educational authority finds that it serves a special pedagogical interest or if, on the application of parents

or guardians, it is to be established as a denominational or interdenominational school or as a school based on a particular philosophy and no state elementary school of that type exists in the municipality.
(6) Preparatory schools shall remain abolished.

Article 8 [Freedom of assembly]

(1) All Germans shall have the right to assemble peacefully and unarmed without prior notification or permission.
(2) In the case of outdoor assemblies, this right may be restricted by or pursuant to a law.

Article 9 [Freedom of association]

(1) All Germans shall have the right to form corporations and other associations.
(2) Associations whose aims or activities contravene the criminal laws, or that are directed against the constitutional order or the concept of international understanding, shall be prohibited.
(3) The right to form associations to safeguard and improve working and economic conditions shall be guaranteed to every individual and to every occupation or profession. Agreements that restrict or seek to impair this right shall be null and void; measures directed to this end shall be unlawful. Measures taken pursuant to Article 12a, to paragraphs (2) and (3) of Article 35, to paragraph (4) of Article 87a, or to Article 91 may not be directed against industrial disputes engaged in by associations within the meaning of the first sentence of this paragraph in order to safeguard and improve working and economic conditions.

Article 10 [Privacy of correspondence, posts and telecommunications]

(1) The privacy of correspondence, posts and telecommunications shall be inviolable.
(2) Restrictions may be ordered only pursuant to a law. If the restriction serves to protect the free democratic basic order or the existence or security of the Federation or of a *Land*, the law may provide that the person affected shall not be informed of the restriction and that recourse to the courts shall be replaced by a review of the case by agencies and auxiliary agencies appointed by the legislature.

Article 11 [Freedom of movement]

(1) All Germans shall have the right to move freely throughout the federal territory.
(2) This right may be restricted only by or pursuant to a law, and only in cases in which the absence of adequate means of support would result in a particular burden for the community, or in which such restriction is necessary to avert an imminent danger to the existence or the free democratic basic order of the Federation or of a *Land*, to combat the danger of an epidemic, to respond to a grave accident or natural disaster, to protect young persons from serious neglect, or to prevent crime.

Article 12 [Occupational freedom]

(1) All Germans shall have the right freely to choose their occupation or profession, their place of work and their place of training. The practice of an occupation or profession may be regulated by or pursuant to a law.
(2) No person may be required to perform work of a particular kind except within the framework of a traditional duty of community service that applies generally and equally to all.
(3) Forced labour may be imposed only on persons deprived of their liberty by the judgment of a court.

Article 12a [Compulsory military and alternative civilian service]

(1) Men who have attained the age of eighteen may be required to serve in the Armed Forces, in the Federal Border Police, or in a civil defence organisation.
(2) Any person who, on grounds of conscience, refuses to render military service involving the use of arms may be required to perform alternative service. The duration of alternative service shall not exceed that of military service. Details shall be regulated by a law, which shall not interfere with the freedom to make a decision in accordance with the dictates of conscience, and which shall also provide for the possibility of alternative service not connected with units of the Armed Forces or of the Federal Border Police.
(3) Persons liable to compulsory military service who are not called upon to render service pursuant to paragraph (1) or (2) of this Article may, when a state of defence is in effect, be assigned by or pursuant to a law to employment involving civilian services for defence purposes, including the protection of the civilian population; they may be assigned to public employment only for the purpose of discharging po-

lice functions or such other sovereign functions of public administration as can be discharged only by persons employed in the public service. The employment contemplated by the first sentence of this paragraph may include services within the Armed Forces, in the provision of military supplies, or with public administrative authorities; assignments to employment connected with supplying and servicing the civilian population shall be permissible only to meet their basic requirements or to guarantee their safety.
(4) If, during a state of defence, the need for civilian services in the civilian health system or in stationary military hospitals cannot be met on a voluntary basis, women between the age of eighteen and fifty-five may be called upon to render such services by or pursuant to a law. Under no circumstances may they be required to render service involving the use of arms.
(5) Prior to the existence of a state of defence, assignments under paragraph (3) of this Article may be made only if the requirements of paragraph (1) of Article 80a are met. In preparation for the provision of services under paragraph (3) of this Article that demand special knowledge or skills, participation in training courses may be required by or pursuant to a law. In this case the first sentence of this paragraph shall not apply.
(6) If, during a state of defence, the need for workers in the areas specified in the second sentence of paragraph (3) of this Article cannot be met on a voluntary basis, the right of German citizens to abandon their occupation or place of employment may be restricted by or pursuant to a law in order to meet this need. Prior to the existence of a state of defence, the first sentence of paragraph (5) of this Article shall apply mutatis mutandis.

Article 13 [Inviolability of the home]

(1) The home is inviolable.
(2) Searches may be authorised only by a judge or, when time is of the essence, by other authorities designated by the laws, and may be carried out only in the manner therein prescribed.
(3) If particular facts justify the suspicion that any person has committed an especially serious crime specifically defined by a law, technical means of acoustical surveillance of any home in which the suspect is supposedly staying may be employed pursuant to judicial order for the purpose of prosecuting the offence, provided that alternative methods of investigating the matter would be disproportionately difficult or unproductive. The authorisation shall be for a limited time. The order

shall be issued by a panel composed of three judges. When time is of the essence, it may also be issued by a single judge.
(4) To avert acute dangers to public safety, especially dangers to life or to the public, technical means of surveillance of the home may be employed only pursuant to judicial order. When time is of the essence, such measures may also be ordered by other authorities designated by a law; a judicial decision shall subsequently be obtained without delay.
(5) If technical means are contemplated solely for the protection of persons officially deployed in a home, the measure may be ordered by an authority designated by a law. The information thereby obtained may be otherwise used only for purposes of criminal prosecution or to avert danger and only if the legality of the measure has been previously determined by a judge; when time is of the essence, a judicial decision shall subsequently be obtained without delay.
(6) The Federal Government shall report to the Bundestag annually as to the employment of technical means pursuant to paragraph (3) and, within the jurisdiction of the Federation, pursuant to paragraph (4) and, insofar as judicial approval is required, pursuant to paragraph (5) of this Article. A panel elected by the Bundestag shall exercise parliamentary oversight on the basis of this report. A comparable parliamentary oversight shall be afforded by the *Länder*.
(7) Interferences and restrictions shall otherwise only be permissible to avert a danger to the public or to the life of an individual, or, pursuant to a law, to confront an acute danger to public safety and order, in particular to relieve a housing shortage, to combat the danger of an epidemic, or to protect young persons at risk.

Article 14 [Property – Inheritance – Expropriation]

(1) Property and the right of inheritance shall be guaranteed. Their content and limits shall be defined by the laws.
(2) Property entails obligations. Its use shall also serve the public good.
(3) Expropriation shall only be permissible for the public good. It may only be ordered by or pursuant to a law that determines the nature and extent of compensation. Such compensation shall be determined by establishing an equitable balance between the public interest and the interests of those affected. In case of dispute concerning the amount of compensation, recourse may be had to the ordinary courts.

Article 15 **[Socialisation]**

Land, natural resources and means of production may for the purpose of socialisation be transferred to public ownership or other forms of public enterprise by a law that determines the nature and extent of compensation. With respect to such compensation the third and fourth sentences of paragraph (3) of Article 14 shall apply mutatis mutandis.

Article 16 **[Citizenship – Extradition]**

(1) No German may be deprived of his citizenship. Citizenship may be lost only pursuant to a law, and against the will of the person affected only if he does not become stateless as a result.
(2) No German may be extradited to a foreign country. The law may provide otherwise for extraditions to a member state of the European Union or to an international court, provided that the rule of law is observed.

Article 16a **[Right of asylum]**

(1) Persons persecuted on political grounds shall have the right of asylum.
(2) Paragraph (1) of this Article may not be invoked by a person who enters the federal territory from a member state of the European Communities or from another third state in which application of the Convention Relating to the Status of Refugees and of the Convention for the Protection of Human Rights and Fundamental Freedoms is assured. The states outside the European Communities to which the criteria of the first sentence of this paragraph apply shall be specified by a law requiring the consent of the Bundesrat. In the cases specified in the first sentence of this paragraph, measures to terminate an applicant's stay may be implemented without regard to any legal challenge that may have been instituted against them.
(3) By a law requiring the consent of the Bundesrat, states may be specified in which, on the basis of their laws, enforcement practices and general political conditions, it can be safely concluded that neither political persecution nor inhuman or degrading punishment or treatment exists. It shall be presumed that a foreigner from such a state is not persecuted, unless he presents evidence justifying the conclusion that, contrary to this presumption, he is persecuted on political grounds.

(4) In the cases specified by paragraph (3) of this Article and in other cases that are plainly unfounded or considered to be plainly unfounded, the implementation of measures to terminate an applicant's stay may be suspended by a court only if serious doubts exist as to their legality; the scope of review may be limited, and tardy objections may be disregarded. Details shall be determined by a law.
(5) Paragraphs (1) to (4) of this Article shall not preclude the conclusion of international agreements of member states of the European Communities with each other or with those third states which, with due regard for the obligations arising from the Convention Relating to the Status of Refugees and the Convention for the Protection of Human Rights and Fundamental Freedoms, whose enforcement must be assured in the contracting states, adopt rules conferring jurisdiction to decide on applications for asylum, including the reciprocal recognition of asylum decisions.

Article 17 **[Right of petition]**

Every person shall have the right individually or jointly with others to address written requests or complaints to competent authorities and to the legislature.

Article 17a **[Restriction of basic rights in specific instances]**

(1) Laws regarding military and alternative service may provide that the basic right of members of the Armed Forces and of alternative service freely to express and disseminate their opinions in speech, writing and pictures (first clause of paragraph (1) of Article 5), the basic right of assembly (Article 8), and the right of petition (Article 17) insofar as it permits the submission of requests or complaints jointly with others, be restricted during their period of military or alternative service.
(2) Laws regarding defence, including protection of the civilian population, may provide for restriction of the basic rights of freedom of movement (Article 11) and inviolability of the home (Article 13).

Article 18 **[Forfeiture of basic rights]**

Whoever abuses the freedom of expression, in particular the freedom of the press (paragraph (1) of Article 5), the freedom of teaching (paragraph (3) of Article 5), the freedom of assembly (Article 8), the freedom of association (Article 9), the privacy of correspondence, posts and telecommunications (Article 10), the rights of property (Article 14), or the right of asylum (Article 16a) in order to combat the free democratic basic order shall forfeit these basic rights. This forfeiture and its extent shall be declared by the Federal Constitutional Court.

Article 19 [Restriction of basic rights – Legal remedies]

(1) Insofar as, under this Basic Law, a basic right may be restricted by or pursuant to a law, such law must apply generally and not merely to a single case. In addition, the law must specify the basic right affected and the Article in which it appears.
(2) In no case may the essence of a basic right be affected.
(3) The basic rights shall also apply to domestic artificial persons to the extent that the nature of such rights permits.
(4) Should any person's rights be violated by public authority, he may have recourse to the courts. If no other jurisdiction has been established, recourse shall be to the ordinary courts. The second sentence of paragraph (2) of Article 10 shall not be affected by this paragraph.

II. The Federation and the *Länder*

Article 20 [Constitutional principles – Right of resistance]

(1) The Federal Republic of Germany is a democratic and social federal state.
(2) All state authority is derived from the people. It shall be exercised by the people through elections and other votes and through specific legislative, executive and judicial bodies.
(3) The legislature shall be bound by the constitutional order, the executive and the judiciary by law and justice.
(4) All Germans shall have the right to resist any person seeking to abolish this constitutional order, if no other remedy is available.

Article 20a [Protection of the natural foundations of life and animals]

Mindful also of its responsibility toward future generations, the state shall protect the natural foundations of life and animals by legislation and, in accordance with law and justice, by executive and judicial action, all within the framework of the constitutional order.

Article 21 [Political parties]

(1) Political parties shall participate in the formation of the political will of the people. They may be freely established. Their internal organisation must conform to democratic principles. They must publicly account for their assets and for the sources and use of their funds.
(2) Parties that, by reason of their aims or the behaviour of their adherents, seek to undermine or abolish the free democratic basic order or to endanger the existence of the Federal Republic of Germany shall be unconstitutional. The Federal Constitutional Court shall rule on the question of unconstitutionality.
(3) Details shall be regulated by federal laws.

Article 22 [Federal capital – Federal flag]

(1) Berlin is the capital of the Federal Republic of Germany. The Federation shall be responsible for representing the nation as a whole in the capital. Details shall be regulated by federal law.
(2) The federal flag shall be black, red and gold.

Article 23 [European Union – Protection of basic rights – Principle of subsidiarity]

(1) With a view to establishing a united Europe, the Federal Republic of Germany shall participate in the development of the European Union that is committed to democratic, social and federal principles, to the rule of law, and to the principle of subsidiarity, and that guarantees a level of protection of basic rights essentially comparable to that afforded by this Basic Law. To this end the Federation may transfer sovereign powers by a law with the consent of the Bundesrat. The establishment of the European Union, as well as changes in its treaty foundations and comparable regulations that amend or supplement this Basic Law, or make such amendments or supplements possible, shall be subject to paragraphs (2) and (3) of Article 79.
(1a) The Bundestag and the Bundesrat shall have the right to bring an action before the Court of Justice of the European Union to challenge a legislative act of the European Union for infringing the principle of subsidiarity. The Bundestag is obliged to initiate such an action at the request of one fourth of its Members. By a statute requiring the consent of the Bundesrat, exceptions from the first sentence of

paragraph (2) of Article 42, and the first sentence of paragraph (2) of Article 52, may be authorised for the exercise of the rights granted to the Bundestag and the Bundesrat under the contractual foundations of the European Union.
(2) The Bundestag and, through the Bundesrat, the *Länder* shall participate in matters concerning the European Union. The Federal Government shall keep the Bundestag and the Bundesrat informed, comprehensively and at the earliest possible time.
(3) Before participating in legislative acts of the European Union, the Federal Government shall provide the Bundestag with an opportunity to state its position. The Federal Government shall take the position of the Bundestag into account during the negotiations. Details shall be regulated by a law.
(4) The Bundesrat shall participate in the decision-making process of the Federation insofar as it would have been competent to do so in a comparable domestic matter, or insofar as the subject falls within the domestic competence of the *Länder*.
(5) Insofar as, in an area within the exclusive competence of the Federation, interests of the *Länder* are affected, and in other matters, insofar as the Federation has legislative power, the Federal Government shall take the position of the Bundesrat into account. To the extent that the legislative powers of the *Länder*, the structure of *Land* authorities, or *Land* administrative procedures are primarily affected, the position of the Bundesrat shall be given the greatest possible respect in determining the Federation's position consistent with the responsibility of the Federation for the nation as a whole. In matters that may result in increased expenditures or reduced revenues for the Federation, the consent of the Federal Government shall be required.
(6) When legislative powers exclusive to the *Länder* concerning matters of school education, culture or broadcasting are primarily affected, the exercise of the rights belonging to the Federal Republic of Germany as a member state of the European Union shall be delegated by the Federation to a representative of the *Länder* designated by the Bundesrat. These rights shall be exercised with the participation of, and in coordination with, the Federal Government; their exercise shall be consistent with the responsibility of the Federation for the nation as a whole.
(7) Details regarding paragraphs (4) to (6) of this Article shall be regulated by a law requiring the consent of the Bundesrat.

Article 24 [Transfer of sovereign powers – System of collective security]

(1) The Federation may by a law transfer sovereign powers to international organisations.
(1a) Insofar as the *Länder* are competent to exercise state powers and to perform state functions, they may, with the consent of the Federal Government, transfer sovereign powers to transfrontier institutions in neighbouring regions.
(2) With a view to maintaining peace, the Federation may enter into a system of mutual collective security; in doing so it shall consent to such limitations upon its sovereign powers as will bring about and secure a lasting peace in Europe and among the nations of the world.
(3) For the settlement of disputes between states, the Federation shall accede to agreements providing for general, comprehensive and compulsory international arbitration.

Article 25 [Primacy of international law]

The general rules of international law shall be an integral part of federal law. They shall take precedence over the laws and directly create rights and duties for the inhabitants of the federal territory.

Article 26 [Securing international peace]

(1) Acts tending to and undertaken with intent to disturb the peaceful relations between nations, especially to prepare for a war of aggression, shall be unconstitutional. They shall be made a criminal offence.
(2) Weapons designed for warfare may be manufactured, transported or marketed only with the permission of the Federal Government. Details shall be regulated by a federal law.

Article 27 [Merchant fleet]

All German merchant vessels shall constitute a unitary merchant fleet.

Article 28 **[*Land* constitutions – Autonomy of municipalities]**

(1) The constitutional order in the *Länder* must conform to the principles of a republican, democratic and social state governed by the rule of law, within the meaning of this Basic Law. In each *Land*, county and municipality the people shall be represented by a body chosen in general, direct, free, equal and secret elections. In county and municipal elections, persons who possess citizenship in any member state of the European Community are also eligible to vote and to be elected in accord with European Community law. In municipalities a local assembly may take the place of an elected body.
(2) Municipalities must be guaranteed the right to regulate all local affairs on their own responsibility, within the limits prescribed by the laws. Within the limits of their functions designated by a law, associations of municipalities shall also have the right of self-government according to the laws. The guarantee of self-government shall extend to the bases of financial autonomy; these bases shall include the right of municipalities to a source of tax revenues based upon economic ability and the right to establish the rates at which these sources shall be taxed.
(3) The Federation shall guarantee that the constitutional order of the *Länder* conforms to the basic rights and to the provisions of paragraphs (1) and (2) of this Article.

Article 29 **[New delimitation of the federal territory]**

(1) The division of the federal territory into *Länder* may be revised to ensure that each *Land* be of a size and capacity to perform its functions effectively. Due regard shall be given in this connection to regional, historical and cultural ties, economic efficiency, and the requirements of local and regional planning.
(2) Revisions of the existing division into *Länder* shall be effected by a federal law, which must be confirmed by referendum. The affected *Länder* shall be afforded an opportunity to be heard.
(3) The referendum shall be held in the *Länder* from whose territories or parts of territories a new *Land* or a *Land* with redefined boundaries is to be established (affected *Länder*). The question to be voted on is whether the affected *Länder* are to remain as they are or whether the new *Land* or the *Land* with redefined boundaries should be established. The proposal to establish a new *Land* or a *Land* with redefined boundaries shall take effect if the change is approved by a majority in the future territory of such *Land* and by a majority in the territories or parts of territories of an affected *Land* taken together whose affiliation with a *Land* is to be changed in

the same way. The proposal shall not take effect if within the territory of any of the affected *Länder* a majority reject the change; however, such rejection shall be of no consequence if in any part of the territory whose affiliation with the affected *Land* is to be changed a two-thirds majority approves the change, unless it is rejected by a two-thirds majority in the territory of the affected *Land* as a whole.

(4) If in any clearly defined and contiguous residential and economic area located in two or more *Länder* and having at least one million inhabitants one tenth of those entitled to vote in Bundestag elections petition for the inclusion of that area in a single *Land*, a federal law shall specify within two years whether the change shall be made in accordance with paragraph (2) of this Article or that an advisory referendum shall be held in the affected *Länder*.

(5) The advisory referendum shall establish whether the changes the law proposes meet with the voters' approval. The law may put forward not more than two distinct proposals for consideration by the voters. If a majority approves a proposed change of the existing division into *Länder*, a federal law shall specify within two years whether the change shall be made in accordance with paragraph (2) of this Article. If a proposal is approved in accordance with the third and fourth sentences of paragraph (3) of this Article, a federal law providing for establishment of the proposed *Land* shall be enacted within two years after the advisory ballot, and confirmation by referendum shall no longer be required.

(6) A majority in a referendum or in an advisory referendum shall consist of a majority of the votes cast, provided that it amounts to at least one quarter of those entitled to vote in Bundestag elections. Other details concerning referenda, petitions and advisory referenda shall be regulated by a federal law, which may also provide that the same petition may not be filed more than once within a period of five years.

(7) Other changes concerning the territory of the *Länder* may be effected by agreements between the *Länder* concerned or by a federal law with the consent of the Bundesrat, if the territory that is to be the subject of the change has no more than 50,000 inhabitants. Details shall be regulated by a federal law requiring the consent of the Bundesrat and of a majority of the Members of the Bundestag. The law must provide affected municipalities and counties with an opportunity to be heard.

(8) *Länder* may revise the division of their existing territory or parts of their territory by agreement without regard to the provisions of paragraphs (2) to (7) of this Article. Affected municipalities and counties shall be afforded an opportunity to be heard. The agreement shall require confirmation by referendum in each of the *Länder* concerned. If the revision affects only part of a *Land*'s territory, the referendum may be confined to the areas affected; the second clause of the fifth sentence shall not apply. In a referendum under this paragraph a majority of the votes cast shall be decisive, provided it amounts to at least one quarter of those entitled to

vote in Bundestag elections; details shall be regulated by a federal law. The agreement shall require the consent of the Bundestag.

Article 30 [Sovereign powers of the *Länder*]

Except as otherwise provided or permitted by this Basic Law, the exercise of state powers and the discharge of state functions is a matter for the *Länder*.

Article 31 [Supremacy of federal law]

Federal law shall take precedence over *Land* law.

Article 32 [Foreign relations]

(1) Relations with foreign states shall be conducted by the Federation.
(2) Before the conclusion of a treaty affecting the special circumstances of a *Land*, that *Land* shall be consulted in timely fashion.
(3) Insofar as the *Länder* have power to legislate, they may conclude treaties with foreign states with the consent of the Federal Government.

Article 33 [Equal citizenship – Public service]

(1) Every German shall have in every *Land* the same political rights and duties.
(2) Every German shall be equally eligible for any public office according to his aptitude, qualifications and professional achievements.
(3) Neither the enjoyment of civil and political rights, nor eligibility for public office, nor rights acquired in the public service shall be dependent upon religious affiliation. No one may be disadvantaged by reason of adherence or non-adherence to a particular religious denomination or philosophical creed.
(4) The exercise of sovereign authority on a regular basis shall, as a rule, be entrusted to members of the public service who stand in a relationship of service and loyalty defined by public law.
(5) The law governing the public service shall be regulated and developed with due regard to the traditional principles of the professional civil service.

Article 34 [Liability for violation of official duty]

If any person, in the exercise of a public office entrusted to him, violates his official duty to a third party, liability shall rest principally with the state or public body that employs him. In the event of intentional wrongdoing or gross negligence, the right of recourse against the individual officer shall be preserved. The ordinary courts shall not be closed to claims for compensation or indemnity.

Article 35 [Legal and administrative assistance and assistance during disasters]

(1) All federal and *Land* authorities shall render legal and administrative assistance to one another.
(2) In order to maintain or restore public security or order, a *Land* in particularly serious cases may call upon personnel and facilities of the Federal Border Police to assist its police when without such assistance the police could not fulfil their responsibilities, or could do so only with great difficulty. In order to respond to a grave accident or a natural disaster, a *Land* may call for the assistance of police forces of other *Länder* or of personnel and facilities of other administrative authorities, of the Armed Forces, or of the Federal Border Police.
(3) If the natural disaster or accident endangers the territory of more than one *Land*, the Federal Government, insofar as is necessary to combat the danger, may instruct the *Land* governments to place police forces at the disposal of other *Länder*, and may deploy units of the Federal Border Police or the Armed Forces to support the police. Measures taken by the Federal Government pursuant to the first sentence of this paragraph shall be rescinded at any time at the demand of the Bundesrat, and in any event as soon as the danger is removed.

Article 36 [Personnel of federal authorities]

(1) Civil servants employed by the highest federal authorities shall be drawn from all *Länder* in appropriate proportion. Persons employed by other federal authorities shall, as a rule, be drawn from the *Land* in which they serve.
(2) Laws regarding military service shall also take into account both the division of the Federation into *Länder* and the regional loyalties of their people.

Article 37 **[Federal execution]**

(1) If a *Land* fails to comply with its obligations under this Basic Law or other federal laws, the Federal Government, with the consent of the Bundesrat, may take the necessary steps to compel the *Land* to comply with its duties.
(2) For the purpose of implementing such coercive measures, the Federal Government or its representative shall have the right to issue instructions to all *Länder* and their authorities.

III. The Bundesrat

Article 38 **[Elections]**

(1) Members of the German Bundestag shall be elected in general, direct, free, equal and secret elections. They shall be representatives of the whole people, not bound by orders or instructions, and responsible only to their conscience.
(2) Any person who has attained the age of eighteen shall be entitled to vote; any person who has attained the age of majority may be elected.
(3) Details shall be regulated by a federal law.

Article 39 **[Electoral term – Convening]**

(1) Save the following provisions, the Bundestag shall be elected for four years. Its term shall end when a new Bundestag convenes. New elections shall be held no sooner than forty-six months and no later than forty-eight months after the electoral term begins. If the Bundestag is dissolved, new elections shall be held within sixty days.
(2) The Bundestag shall convene no later than the thirtieth day after the elections.
(3) The Bundestag shall determine when its sessions shall be adjourned and resumed. The President of the Bundestag may convene it at an earlier date. He shall be obliged to do so if one third of the Members, the Federal President or the Federal Chancellor so demand.

Article 40 **[Presidency – Rules of procedure]**

(1) The Bundestag shall elect its President, Vice-Presidents and secretaries. It shall adopt rules of procedure.
(2) The President shall exercise proprietary and police powers in the Bundestag building. No search or seizure may take place on the premises of the Bundestag without his permission.

Article 41 **[Scrutiny of elections]**

(1) Scrutiny of elections shall be the responsibility of the Bundestag. It shall also decide whether a Member has lost his seat.
(2) Complaints against such decisions of the Bundestag may be lodged with the Federal Constitutional Court.
(3) Details shall be regulated by a federal law.

Article 42 **[Public sittings – Majority decisions]**

(1) Sittings of the Bundestag shall be public. On the motion of one tenth of its Members, or on the motion of the Federal Government, the public may be excluded by a two-thirds majority. The motion shall be voted upon at a sitting not open to the public.
(2) Decisions of the Bundestag shall require a majority of the votes cast unless this Basic Law otherwise provides. The rules of procedure may permit exceptions with respect to elections to be conducted by the Bundestag.
(3) Truthful reports of public sittings of the Bundestag and of its committees shall not give rise to any liability.

Article 43 **[Right to require presence, right of access and right to be heard]**

(1) The Bundestag and its committees may require the presence of any member of the Federal Government.
(2) The members of the Bundesrat and of the Federal Government as well as their representatives may attend all sittings of the Bundestag and meetings of its committees. They shall have the right to be heard at any time.

Article 44 [Committees of inquiry]

(1) The Bundestag shall have the right, and on the motion of one quarter of its Members the duty, to establish a committee of inquiry, which shall take the requisite evidence at public hearings. The public may be excluded.
(2) The rules of criminal procedure shall apply mutatis mutandis to the taking of evidence. The privacy of correspondence, posts and telecommunications shall not be affected.
(3) Courts and administrative authorities shall be required to provide legal and administrative assistance.
(4) The decisions of committees of inquiry shall not be subject to judicial review. The courts shall be free to evaluate and rule upon the facts that were the subject of the investigation.

Article 45 [Committee on the European Union]

The Bundestag shall appoint a Committee on the Affairs of the European Union. It may authorise the committee to exercise the rights of the Bundestag under Article 23 vis-à-vis the Federal Government. It may also empower it to exercise the rights granted to the Bundestag under the contractual foundations of the European Union.

Article 45a [Committees on Foreign Affairs and Defence]

(1) The Bundestag shall appoint a Committee on Foreign Affairs and a Defence Committee.
(2) The Defence Committee shall also have the powers of a committee of inquiry. On the motion of one quarter of its members it shall have the duty to make a specific matter the subject of inquiry.
(3) Paragraph (1) of Article 44 shall not apply to defence matters.

Article 45b [Parliamentary Commissioner for the Armed Forces]

A Parliamentary Commissioner for the Armed Forces shall be appointed to safeguard basic rights and to assist the Bundestag in exercising parliamentary oversight over the Armed Forces. Details shall be regulated by a federal law.

Article 45c **[Petitions Committee]**

(1) The Bundestag shall appoint a Petitions Committee to deal with requests and complaints addressed to the Bundestag pursuant to Article 17.
(2) The powers of the Committee to consider complaints shall be regulated by a federal law.

Article 45d **[Parliamentary Control Panel]**

(1) The Bundestag shall appoint a panel to scrutinise the intelligence activities of the Federation.
(2) Details shall be regulated by a federal law.

Article 46 **[Immunities of Members]**

(1) At no time may a Member be subjected to court proceedings or disciplinary action or otherwise called to account outside the Bundestag for a vote cast or for any speech or debate in the Bundestag or in any of its committees. This provision shall not apply to defamatory insults.
(2) A Member may not be called to account or arrested for a punishable offence without permission of the Bundestag, unless he is apprehended while committing the offence or in the course of the following day.
(3) The permission of the Bundestag shall also be required for any other restriction of a Member's freedom of the person or for the initiation of proceedings against a Member under Article 18.
(4) Any criminal proceedings or any proceedings under Article 18 against a Member and any detention or other restriction of the freedom of his person shall be suspended at the demand of the Bundestag.

Article 47 **[Right of refusal to give evidence]**

Members may refuse to give evidence concerning persons who have confided information to them in their capacity as Members of the Bundestag, or to whom they have confided information in this capacity, as well as evidence concerning this information itself. To the extent that this right of refusal to give evidence applies, no seizure of documents shall be permissible.

Article 48 [Candidature – Protection of membership – Remuneration]

(1) Every candidate for election to the Bundestag shall be entitled to the leave necessary for his election campaign.
(2) No one may be prevented from accepting or exercising the office of Member of the Bundestag. No one may be given notice of dismissal or discharged from employment on this ground.
(3) Members shall be entitled to remuneration adequate to ensure their independence. They shall be entitled to the free use of all publicly owned means of transport. Details shall be regulated by a federal law.

Article 49 (repealed)

IV. The Bundesrat

Article 50 [Functions]

The *Länder* shall participate through the Bundesrat in the legislation and administration of the Federation and in matters concerning the European Union.

Article 51 [Composition – Weighted voting]

(1) The Bundesrat shall consist of members of the *Land* governments, which appoint and recall them. Other members of those governments may serve as alternates.
(2) Each *Land* shall have at least three votes; *Länder* with more than two million inhabitants shall have four, *Länder* with more than six million inhabitants five, and *Länder* with more than seven million inhabitants six votes.
(3) Each *Land* may appoint as many members as it has votes. The votes of each *Land* may be cast only as a unit and only by Members present or their alternates.

Article 52 [President – Decisions – Rules of procedure]

(1) The Bundesrat shall elect its President for one year.
(2) The President shall convene the Bundesrat. He shall be obliged to do so if the delegates of at least two *Länder* or the Federal Government so demand.

(3) Decisions of the Bundesrat shall require at least a majority of its votes. It shall adopt rules of procedure. Its meetings shall be open to the public. The public may be excluded.
(3a) For matters concerning the European Union the Bundesrat may establish a Chamber for European Affairs, whose decisions shall be considered decisions of the Bundesrat; the number of votes to be uniformly cast by the *Länder* shall be determined by paragraph (2) of Article 51.
(4) Other members or representatives of *Land* governments may serve on committees of the Bundesrat.

Article 53 [Attendance of members of the Federal Government]

The members of the Federal Government shall have the right, and on demand the duty, to participate in meetings of the Bundesrat and of its committees. They shall have the right to be heard at any time. The Bundesrat shall be kept informed by the Federal Government with regard to the conduct of its affairs.

IVa. The Joint Committee

Article 53a [Composition – Rules of procedure]

(1) The Joint Committee shall consist of Members of the Bundestag and members of the Bundesrat; the Bundestag shall provide two thirds and the Bundesrat one third of the committee members. The Bundestag shall designate Members in proportion to the relative strength of the various parliamentary groups; they may not be members of the Federal Government. Each *Land* shall be represented by a Bundesrat member of its choice; these members shall not be bound by instructions. The establishment of the Joint Committee and its proceedings shall be regulated by rules of procedure to be adopted by the Bundestag and requiring the consent of the Bundesrat.
(2) The Federal Government shall inform the Joint Committee about its plans for a state of defence. The rights of the Bundestag and its committees under paragraph (1) of Article 43 shall not be affected by the provisions of this paragraph.

V. The Federal President

Article 54 **[Election – Term of office]**

(1) The Federal President shall be elected by the Federal Convention without debate. Any German who is entitled to vote in Bundestag elections and has attained the age of forty may be elected.
(2) The term of office of the Federal President shall be five years. Re-election for a consecutive term shall be permitted only once.
(3) The Federal Convention shall consist of the Members of the Bundestag and an equal number of members elected by the parliaments of the *Länder* on the basis of proportional representation.
(4) The Federal Convention shall meet not later than thirty days before the term of office of the Federal President expires or, in the case of premature termination, not later than thirty days after that date. It shall be convened by the President of the Bundestag.
(5) After the expiration of an electoral term, the period specified in the first sentence of paragraph (4) of this Article shall begin when the Bundestag first convenes.
(6) The person receiving the votes of a majority of the members of the Federal Convention shall be elected. If after two ballots no candidate has obtained such a majority, the person who receives the largest number of votes on the next ballot shall be elected.
(7) Details shall be regulated by a federal law.

Article 55 **[Incompatibilities]**

(1) The Federal President may not be a member of the government or of a legislative body of the Federation or of a *Land*.
(2) The Federal President may not hold any other salaried office, or engage in any trade or profession, or belong to the management or supervisory board of any enterprise conducted for profit.

Article 56 **[Oath of office]**

On assuming his office, the Federal President shall take the following oath before the assembled Members of the Bundestag and the Bundesrat: "I swear that I will dedicate my efforts to the well-being of the German people, promote their welfare, protect them from harm, uphold and defend the Basic Law and the laws of the Federation, perform my duties conscientiously, and do justice to all. So help me God." The oath may also be taken without religious affirmation.

Article 57 [Substitution]

If the Federal President is unable to perform his duties, or if his office falls prematurely vacant, the President of the Bundesrat shall exercise his powers.

Article 58 [Countersignature]

Orders and directions of the Federal President shall require for their validity the countersignature of the Federal Chancellor or of the competent Federal Minister. This provision shall not apply to the appointment or dismissal of the Federal Chancellor, the dissolution of the Bundestag under Article 63, or a request made under paragraph (3) of Article 69.

Article 59 [Representation of the Federation for the purposes of international law]

(1) The Federal President shall represent the Federation for the purposes of international law. He shall conclude treaties with foreign states on behalf of the Federation. He shall accredit and receive envoys.
(2) Treaties that regulate the political relations of the Federation or relate to subjects of federal legislation shall require the consent or participation, in the form of a federal law, of the bodies responsible in such a case for the enactment of federal law. In the case of executive agreements the provisions concerning the federal administration shall apply mutatis mutandis.

Article 59a **(repealed)**

Article 60 **[Appointment of civil servants – Pardon – Immunity]**

(1) The Federal President shall appoint and dismiss federal judges, federal civil servants, and commissioned and non-commissioned officers of the Armed Forces, except as may otherwise be provided by a law.
(2) He shall exercise the power to pardon individual offenders on behalf of the Federation.
(3) He may delegate these powers to other authorities.
(4) Paragraphs (2) to (4) of Article 46 shall apply to the Federal President mutatis mutandis.

Article 61 **[Impeachment before the Federal Constitutional Court]**

(1) The Bundestag or the Bundesrat may impeach the Federal President before the Federal Constitutional Court for wilful violation of this Basic Law or of any other federal law. The motion of impeachment must be supported by at least one quarter of the Members of the Bundestag or one quarter of the votes of the Bundesrat. The decision to impeach shall require a majority of two thirds of the Members of the Bundestag or of two thirds of the votes of the Bundesrat. The case for impeachment shall be presented before the Federal Constitutional Court by a person commissioned by the impeaching body.
(2) If the Federal Constitutional Court finds the Federal President guilty of a wilful violation of this Basic Law or of any other federal law, it may declare that he has forfeited his office. After the Federal President has been impeached, the Court may issue an interim order preventing him from exercising his functions.

VI. The Federal Government

Article 62 **[Composition]**

The Federal Government shall consist of the Federal Chancellor and the Federal Ministers.

Article 63 [Election of the Federal Chancellor]

(1) The Federal Chancellor shall be elected by the Bundestag without debate on the proposal of the Federal President.
(2) The person who receives the votes of a majority of the Members of the Bundestag shall be elected. The person elected shall be appointed by the Federal President.
(3) If the person proposed by the Federal President is not elected, the Bundestag may elect a Federal Chancellor within fourteen days after the ballot by the votes of more than one half of its Members.
(4) If no Federal Chancellor is elected within this period, a new election shall take place without delay, in which the person who receives the largest number of votes shall be elected. If the person elected receives the votes of a majority of the Members of the Bundestag, the Federal President must appoint him within seven days after the election. If the person elected does not receive such a majority, then within seven days the Federal President shall either appoint him or dissolve the Bundestag.

Article 64 [Appointment and dismissal of Federal Ministers – Oath of office]

(1) Federal Ministers shall be appointed and dismissed by the Federal President upon the proposal of the Federal Chancellor.
(2) On taking office the Federal Chancellor and the Federal Ministers shall take the oath provided for in Article 56 before the Bundestag.

Article 65 [Power to determine policy guidelines – Department and collegiate responsibility]

The Federal Chancellor shall determine and be responsible for the general guidelines of policy. Within these limits each Federal Minister shall conduct the affairs of his department independently and on his own responsibility. The Federal Government shall resolve differences of opinion between Federal Ministers. The Federal Chancellor shall conduct the proceedings of the Federal Government in accordance with rules of procedure adopted by the Government and approved by the Federal President.

Article 65a **[Command of the Armed Forces]**

(1) Command of the Armed Forces shall be vested in the Federal Minister of Defence.
(2) (repealed)

Article 66 **[Incompatibilities]**

Neither the Federal Chancellor nor a Federal Minister may hold any other salaried office, or engage in any trade or profession, or belong to the management or, without the consent of the Bundestag, to the supervisory board of an enterprise conducted for profit.

Article 67 **[Vote of no confidence]**

(1) The Bundestag may express its lack of confidence in the Federal Chancellor only by electing a successor by the vote of a majority of its Members and requesting the Federal President to dismiss the Federal Chancellor. The Federal President must comply with the request and appoint the person elected.
(2) Forty-eight hours shall elapse between the motion and the election.

Article 68 **[Vote of confidence]**

(1) If a motion of the Federal Chancellor for a vote of confidence is not supported by the majority of the Members of the Bundestag, the Federal President, upon the proposal of the Federal Chancellor, may dissolve the Bundestag within twenty-one days. The right of dissolution shall lapse as soon as the Bundestag elects another Federal Chancellor by the vote of a majority of its Members.
(2) Forty-eight hours shall elapse between the motion and the vote.

Article 69 **[Deputy Federal Chancellor – Term of office]**

(1) The Federal Chancellor shall appoint a Federal Minister as his deputy.
(2) The tenure of office of the Federal Chancellor or of a Federal Minister shall end in any event when a new Bundestag convenes; the tenure of office of a Federal Mi-

nister shall also end on any other occasion on which the Federal Chancellor ceases to hold office.
(3) At the request of the Federal President the Federal Chancellor, or at the request of the Federal Chancellor or of the Federal President a Federal Minister, shall be obliged to continue to manage the affairs of his office until a successor is appointed.

VII. Federal Legislation and Legislative Procedures

Article 70 [Division of powers between the Federation and the *Länder*]

(1) The *Länder* shall have the right to legislate insofar as this Basic Law does not confer legislative power on the Federation.
(2) The division of authority between the Federation and the *Länder* shall be governed by the provisions of this Basic Law concerning exclusive and concurrent legislative powers.

Article 71 [Exclusive legislative power of the Federation]

On matters within the exclusive legislative power of the Federation, the *Länder* shall have power to legislate only when and to the extent that they are expressly authorised to do so by a federal law.

Article 72 [Concurrent legislative powers]

(1) On matters within the concurrent legislative power, the *Länder* shall have power to legislate so long as and to the extent that the Federation has not exercised its legislative power by enacting a law.
(2) The Federation shall have the right to legislate on matters falling within clauses 4, 7, 11, 13, 15, 19a, 20, 22, 25 and 26 of paragraph (1) of Article 74, if and to the extent that the establishment of equivalent living conditions throughout the federal territory or the maintenance of legal or economic unity renders federal regulation necessary in the national interest.
(3) If the Federation has made use of its power to legislate, the *Länder* may enact laws at variance with this legislation with respect to:

1. hunting (except for the law on hunting licenses);
2. protection of nature and landscape management (except for the general principles governing the protection of nature, the law on protection of plant and animal species or the law on protection of marine life);
3. land distribution;
4. regional planning;
5. management of water resources (except for regulations related to materials or facilities);
6. admission to institutions of higher education and requirements for graduation in such institutions.

Federal laws on these matters shall enter into force no earlier than six months following their promulgation unless otherwise provided with the consent of the Bundesrat. As for the relationship between federal law and law of the *Länder*, the latest law enacted shall take precedence with respect to matters within the scope of the first sentence.

(4) A federal law may provide that federal legislation that is no longer necessary within the meaning of paragraph (2) of this Article may be superseded by *Land* law.

Article 73 [Matters under exclusive legislative power of the Federation]

(1) The Federation shall have exclusive legislative power with respect to:

1. foreign affairs and defence, including protection of the civilian population;
2. citizenship in the Federation;
3. freedom of movement, passports, residency registration and identity cards, immigration, emigration and extradition;
4. currency, money and coinage, weights and measures, and the determination of standards of time;
5. the unity of the customs and trading area, treaties regarding commerce and navigation, the free movement of goods, and the exchange of goods and payments with foreign countries, including customs and border protection;

5a. safeguarding German cultural assets against removal from the country;

6. air transport;

6a. the operation of railways wholly or predominantly owned by the Federation (federal railways), the construction, maintenance and operation of railroad lines belonging to federal railways, and the levying of charges for the use of these lines;

7. postal and telecommunications services;
8. the legal relations of persons employed by the Federation and by federal corporations under public law;
9. industrial property rights, copyrights and publishing;
9a. protection by the Federal Criminal Police Office against the dangers of international terrorism when a threat transcends the boundary of one *Land*, when the jurisdiction of a *Land's* police authorities cannot be perceived, or when the highest authority of an individual *Land* requests the assumption of federal responsibility;
10. cooperation between the Federation and the *Länder* concerning
    a) criminal police work,
    b) protection of the free democratic basic order, existence and security of the Federation or of a *Land* (protection of the constitution), and
    c) protection against activities within the federal territory which, by the use of force or preparations for the use of force, endanger the external interests of the Federal Republic of Germany, as well as the establishment of a Federal Criminal Police Office and international action to combat crime;
11. statistics for federal purposes;
12. the law on weapons and explosives;
13. benefits for persons disabled by war and for dependents of deceased war victims as well as assistance to former prisoners of war;
14. the production and utilisation of nuclear energy for peaceful purposes, the construction and operation of facilities serving such purposes, protection against hazards arising from the release of nuclear energy or from ionising radiation, and the disposal of radioactive substances.

(2) Laws enacted pursuant to clause 9a of paragraph (1) require the consent of the Bundesrat.

Article 74 **[Matters under concurrent legislative powers]**

(1) Concurrent legislative power shall extend to the following matters:

1. civil law, criminal law, court organisation and procedure (except for the correctional law of pretrial detention), the legal profession, notaries, and the provision of legal advice;

2. registration of births, deaths and marriages;
3. the law of association;
4. the law relating to residence and establishment of foreign nationals;

4a. (repealed)

5. (repealed)
6. matters concerning refugees and expellees;
7. public welfare (except for the law on social care homes);
8. (repealed)
9. war damage and reparations;
10. war graves and graves of other victims of war or despotism;
11. the law relating to economic matters (mining, industry, energy, crafts, trades, commerce, banking, stock exchanges and private insurance), except for the law on shop closing hours, restaurants, game halls, display of individual persons, trade fairs, exhibitions and markets;

11a. (repealed)

12. labour law, including the organisation of enterprises, occupational health and safety, and employment agencies, as well as social security, including unemployment insurance;
13. the regulation of educational and training grants and the promotion of research;
14. the law regarding expropriation, to the extent relevant to matters enumerated in Articles 73 and 74;
15. the transfer of land, natural resources, and means of production to public ownership or other forms of public enterprise;
16. prevention of the abuse of economic power;
17. the promotion of agricultural production and forestry (except for the law on land consolidation), ensuring the adequacy of food supply, the importation and exportation of agricultural and forestry products, deep-sea and coastal fishing, and preservation of the coasts;
18. urban real estate transactions, land law (except for laws regarding development fees), and the law on rental subsidies, subsidies for old debts, home building loan premiums, miners' homebuilding and homesteading;
19. measures to combat human and animal diseases which pose a danger to the public or are communicable, admission to the medical profession and to ancil-

lary professions or occupations, as well as the law on pharmacies, medicines, medical products, drugs, narcotics and poisons;

19a. the economic viability of hospitals and the regulation of hospital charges;

20. the law on food products including animals used in their production, the law on alcohol and tobacco, essential commodities and feedstuffs as well as protective measures in connection with the marketing of agricultural and forest seeds and seedlings, the protection of plants against diseases and pests, as well as the protection of animals;

21. maritime and coastal shipping, as well as navigational aids, inland navigation, meteorological services, sea routes, and inland waterways used for general traffic;

22. road traffic, motor transport, construction and maintenance of long-distance highways, as well as the collection of tolls for the use of public highways by vehicles and the allocation of the revenue;

23. non-federal railways, except mountain railways;

24. waste disposal, air pollution control, and noise abatement (except for the protection from noise associated with human activity);

25. state liability;

26. medically assisted generation of human life, analysis and modification of genetic information as well as the regulation of organ, tissue and cell transplantation;

27. the statutory rights and duties of civil servants of the *Länder*, the municipalities and other corporations of public law as well as of the judges in the *Länder*, except for their career regulations, remuneration and pensions;

28. hunting;

29. protection of nature and landscape management;

30. land distribution;

31. regional planning;

32. management of water resources;

33. admission to institutions of higher education and requirements for graduation in such institutions.

(2) Laws enacted pursuant to clauses 25 and 27 of paragraph (1) shall require the consent of the Bundesrat.

Article 74a **(repealed)**

Article 75 **(repealed)**

Article 76 **[Bills]**

(1) Bills may be introduced in the Bundestag by the Federal Government, by the Bundesrat, or from the floor of the Bundestag.
(2) Federal Government bills shall first be submitted to the Bundesrat. The Bundesrat shall be entitled to comment on such bills within six weeks. If for important reasons, especially with respect to the scope of the bill, the Bundesrat demands an extension, the period shall be increased to nine weeks. If in exceptional circumstances the Federal Government on submitting a bill to the Bundesrat declares it to be particularly urgent, it may submit the bill to the Bundestag after three weeks or, if the Bundesrat has demanded an extension pursuant to the third sentence of this paragraph, after six weeks, even if it has not yet received the Bundesrat's comments; upon receiving such comments, it shall transmit them to the Bundestag without delay. In the case of bills to amend this Basic Law or to transfer sovereign powers pursuant to Article 23 or 24 the comment period shall be nine weeks; the fourth sentence of this paragraph shall not apply.
(3) Bundesrat bills shall be submitted to the Bundestag by the Federal Government within six weeks. In submitting them the Federal Government shall state its own views. If for important reasons, especially with respect to the scope of the bill, the Federal Government demands an extension, the period shall be increased to nine weeks. If in exceptional circumstances the Bundesrat declares a bill to be particularly urgent, the period shall be three weeks or, if the Federal Government has demanded an extension pursuant to the third sentence of this paragraph, six weeks. In the case of bills to amend this Basic Law or to transfer sovereign powers pursuant to Article 23 or 24 the comment period shall be nine weeks; the fourth sentence of this paragraph shall not apply. The Bundestag shall consider and vote on bills within a reasonable time.

Article 77 **[Legislative procedure – Mediation Committee]**

(1) Federal laws shall be adopted by the Bundestag. After their adoption the President of the Bundestag shall submit them to the Bundesrat without delay.
(2) Within three weeks after receiving an adopted bill, the Bundesrat may demand that a committee for joint consideration of bills, composed of Members of the Bun-

destag and of the Bundesrat, be convened. The composition and proceedings of this committee shall be regulated by rules of procedure adopted by the Bundestag and requiring the consent of the Bundesrat. The members of the Bundesrat on this committee shall not be bound by instructions. When the consent of the Bundesrat is required for a bill to become law, the Bundestag and the Federal Government may likewise demand that such a committee be convened. Should the committee propose any amendment to the adopted bill, the Bundestag shall vote on it a second time.
(2a) Insofar as its consent is required for a bill to become law, the Bundesrat, if no request has been made pursuant to the first sentence of paragraph (2) of this Article or if the mediation proceeding has been completed without a proposal to amend the bill, shall vote on the bill within a reasonable time.
(3) Insofar as its consent is not required for a bill to become law, the Bundesrat, once proceedings under paragraph (2) of this Article are completed, may within two weeks object to a bill adopted by the Bundestag. The time for objection shall begin, in the case described in the last sentence of paragraph (2) of this Article, upon receipt of the bill as re-adopted by the Bundestag, and in all other cases upon receipt of a communication from the chairman of the committee provided for in paragraph (2) of this Article to the effect that the committee's proceedings have been concluded.
(4) If the objection is adopted by the majority of the votes of the Bundesrat, it may be rejected by a decision of the majority of the Members of the Bundestag. If the Bundesrat adopted the objection by a majority of at least two thirds of its votes, its rejection by the Bundestag shall require a two-thirds majority, including at least a majority of the Members of the Bundestag.

Article 78 [Passage of federal laws]

A bill adopted by the Bundestag shall become law if the Bundesrat consents to it, or fails to make a demand pursuant to paragraph (2) of Article 77, or fails to enter an objection within the period stipulated in paragraph (3) of Article 77, or withdraws such an objection, or if the objection is overridden by the Bundestag.

Article 79 [Amendment of the Basic Law]

(1) This Basic Law may be amended only by a law expressly amending or supplementing its text. In the case of an international treaty regarding a peace settlement,

the preparation of a peace settlement, or the phasing out of an occupation regime, or designed to promote the defence of the Federal Republic, it shall be sufficient, for the purpose of making clear that the provisions of this Basic Law do not preclude the conclusion and entry into force of the treaty, to add language to the Basic Law that merely makes this clarification.
(2) Any such law shall be carried by two thirds of the Mem-bers of the Bundestag and two thirds of the votes of the Bundesrat.
(3) Amendments to this Basic Law affecting the division of the Federation into *Länder*, their participation on principle in the legislative process, or the principles laid down in Articles 1 and 20 shall be inadmissible.

Article 80 **[Issuance of statutory instruments]**

(1) The Federal Government, a Federal Minister or the *Land* governments may be authorised by a law to issue statutory instruments. The content, purpose and scope of the authority conferred shall be specified in the law. Each statutory instrument shall contain a statement of its legal basis. If the law provides that such authority may be further delegated, such subdelegation shall be effected by statutory instrument.
(2) Unless a federal law otherwise provides, the consent of the Bundesrat shall be required for statutory instruments issued by the Federal Government or a Federal Minister regarding fees or basic principles for the use of postal and telecommunication facilities, basic principles for levying of charges for the use of facilities of federal railways, or the construction and operation of railways, as well as for statutory instruments issued pursuant to federal laws that require the consent of the Bundesrat or that are executed by the *Länder* on federal commission or in their own right.
(3) The Bundesrat may submit to the Federal Government drafts of statutory instruments that require its consent.
(4) Insofar as *Land* governments are authorised by or pursuant to federal laws to issue statutory instruments, the *Länder* shall also be entitled to regulate the matter by a law.

Article 80a **[State of tension]**

(1) If this Basic Law or a federal law regarding defence, including protection of the civilian population, provides that legal provisions may be applied only in accor-

dance with this Article, their application, except when a state of defence has been declared, shall be permissible only after the Bundestag has determined that a state of tension exists or has specifically approved such application. The determination of a state of tension and specific approval in the cases mentioned in the first sentence of paragraph (5) and the second sentence of paragraph (6) of Article 12a shall require a two-thirds majority of the votes cast.
(2) Any measures taken pursuant to legal provisions by virtue of paragraph (1) of this Article shall be rescinded whenever the Bundestag so demands.
(3) Notwithstanding paragraph (1) of this Article, the application of such legal provisions shall also be permissible on the basis of and in accordance with a decision made by an international body within the framework of a treaty of alliance with the approval of the Federal Government. Any measures taken pursuant to this paragraph shall be rescinded whenever the Bundestag, by the vote of a majority of its Members, so demands.

Article 81 [Legislative emergency]

(1) If, in the circumstances described in Article 68, the Bundestag is not dissolved, the Federal President, at the request of the Federal Government and with the consent of the Bundesrat, may declare a state of legislative emergency with respect to a bill, if the Bundestag rejects the bill although the Federal Government has declared it to be urgent. The same shall apply if a bill has been rejected although the Federal Chancellor had combined it with a motion under Article 68.
(2) If, after a state of legislative emergency has been declared, the Bundestag again rejects the bill or adopts it in a version the Federal Government declares unacceptable, the bill shall be deemed to have become law to the extent that it receives the consent of the Bundesrat. The same shall apply if the Bundestag does not pass the bill within four weeks after it is reintroduced.
(3) During the term of office of a Federal Chancellor, any other bill rejected by the Bundestag may become law in accordance with paragraphs (1) and (2) of this Article within a period of six months after the first declaration of a state of legislative emergency. After the expiration of this period, no further declaration of a state of legislative emergency may be made during the term of office of the same Federal Chancellor.
(4) This Basic Law may neither be amended nor abrogated nor suspended in whole or in part by a law enacted pursuant to paragraph (2) of this Article.

Article 82 [Certification – Promulgation – Entry into force]

(1) Laws enacted in accordance with the provisions of this Basic Law shall, after countersignature, be certified by the Federal President and promulgated in the Federal Law Gazette. Statutory instruments shall be certified by the agency that issues them and, unless a law otherwise provides, shall be promulgated in the Federal Law Gazette.
(2) Every law or statutory instrument shall specify the date on which it shall take effect. In the absence of such a provision, it shall take effect on the fourteenth day after the day on which the Federal Law Gazette containing it was published.

VIII. The Execution of Federal Laws and the Federal Administration

Article 83 [Execution by the *Länder*]

The *Länder* shall execute federal laws in their own right insofar as this Basic Law does not otherwise provide or permit.

Article 84 [Länder administration – Federal oversight]

(1) Where the *Länder* execute federal laws in their own right, they shall provide for the establishment of the requisite authorities and regulate their administrative procedures. If federal laws provide otherwise, the *Länder* may enact deviating regulations. If a *Land* has enacted a law pursuant to the second sentence, subsequent federal laws regulating the organisation of authorities and their administrative procedure shall not be enacted until at least six months after their promulgation, provided that no other determination has been made with the consent of the Bundesrat. The third sentence of paragraph (2) of Article 72 shall apply accordingly. In exceptional cases, owing to a special need for uniform federal legislation, the Federation may regulate the administrative procedure with no possibility of separate *Land* legislation. Such laws shall require the consent of the Bundesrat. Federal laws may not entrust municipalities and associations of municipalities with any tasks.
(2) The Federal Government, with the consent of the Bundesrat, may issue general administrative rules.
(3) The Federal Government shall exercise oversight to ensure that the *Länder* execute federal laws in accordance with the law. For this purpose the Federal Government may send commissioners to the highest *Land* authorities and, with their con-

fence or a state of tension, the Armed Forces may also be authorised to support police measures for the protection of civilian property; in this event the Armed Forces shall cooperate with the competent authorities.
(4) In order to avert an imminent danger to the existence or free democratic basic order of the Federation or of a *Land*, the Federal Government, if the conditions referred to in paragraph (2) of Article 91 obtain and the police forces and the Federal Border Police prove inadequate, may employ the Armed Forces to support the police and the Federal Border Police in protecting civilian property and in combating organised armed insurgents. Any such employment of the Armed Forces shall be discontinued if the Bundestag or the Bundesrat so demands.

Article 87b [Federal Defence Administration]

(1) The Federal Defence Administration shall be conducted as a federal administrative authority with its own administrative substructure. It shall have jurisdiction for personnel matters and direct responsibility for satisfaction of the procurement needs of the Armed Forces. Responsibilities connected with pensions for injured persons or with construction work may be assigned to the Federal Defence Administration only by a federal law requiring the consent of the Bundesrat. Such consent shall also be required for any laws to the extent that they empower the Federal Defence Administration to interfere with rights of third parties; this requirement, however, shall not apply in the case of laws regarding personnel matters.
(2) In addition, federal laws concerning defence, including recruitment for military service and protection of the civilian population, may, with the consent of the Bundesrat, provide that they shall be executed, wholly or in part, either by federal administrative authorities with their own administrative substructures or by the *Länder* on federal commission. If such laws are executed by the *Länder* on federal commission, they may, with the consent of the Bundesrat, provide that the powers vested in the Federal Government or in the competent highest federal authorities pursuant to Article 85 be transferred wholly or in part to federal higher authorities; in this event the law may provide that such authorities shall not require the consent of the Bundesrat in issuing general administrative rules pursuant to the first sentence of paragraph (2) of Article 85.

Article 87c [Production and utilisation of nuclear energy]

Laws enacted under clause 14 of paragraph (1) of Article 73 may, with the consent of the Bundesrat, provide that they shall be executed by the *Länder* on federal commission.

Article 87d [Air transport administration]

(1) Air transport administration shall be conducted under federal administration. Air navigation services may also be provided by foreign air navigation service providers which are authorised in accordance with European Community law.
(2) By a federal law requiring the consent of the Bundesrat, responsibilities for air transport administration may be delegated to the *Länder* acting on federal commission.

Article 87e [Rail transport administration]

(1) Rail transport with respect to federal railways shall be administered by federal authorities. Responsibilities for rail transport administration may be delegated by a federal law to the *Länder* acting in their own right.
(2) The Federation shall discharge rail transport administration responsibilities assigned to it by a federal law, above and beyond those regarding federal railways.
(3) Federal railways shall be operated as enterprises under private law. They shall remain the property of the Federation to the extent that their activities embrace the construction, maintenance and operation of the tracks. The transfer of federal shares in these enterprises under the second sentence of this paragraph shall be effected pursuant to a law; the Federation shall retain a majority of the shares. Details shall be regulated by a federal law.
(4) The Federation shall ensure that in developing and maintaining the federal railway system as well as in offering services over this system, other than local passenger services, due account is taken of the interests and especially the transportation needs of the public. Details shall be regulated by a federal law.
(5) Laws enacted pursuant to paragraphs (1) to (4) of this Article shall require the consent of the Bundesrat. The consent of the Bundesrat shall also be required for laws regarding the dissolution, merger or division of federal railway enterprises, the transfer of tracks of federal railways to third parties, or the abandonment of such tracks, or affecting local passenger services.

Article 87f [Posts and telecommunications]

(1) In accordance with a federal law requiring the consent of the Bundesrat, the Federation shall ensure the availability of adequate and appropriate postal and telecommunications services throughout the federal territory.
(2) Services within the meaning of paragraph (1) of this Article shall be provided as a matter of private enterprise by the firms succeeding to the special trust Deutsche Bundespost and by other private providers. Sovereign functions in the area of posts and telecommunications shall be discharged by federal administrative authorities.
(3) Notwithstanding the second sentence of paragraph (2) of this Article, the Federation, by means of a federal institution under public law, shall discharge particular responsibilities relating to the firms succeeding to the special trust Deutsche Bundespost as prescribed by a federal law.

Article 88 [The Federal Bank – The European Central Bank]

The Federation shall establish a note-issuing and currency bank as the Federal Bank. Within the framework of the European Union, its responsibilities and powers may be transferred to the European Central Bank, which is independent and committed to the overriding goal of assuring price stability.

Article 89 [Federal waterways – Administration of waterways]

(1) The Federation shall be the owner of the former Reich waterways.
(2) The Federation shall administer the federal waterways through its own authorities. It shall exercise those state functions relating to inland shipping which extend beyond the territory of a single *Land*, and those functions relating to maritime shipping, which are conferred on it by a law. Insofar as federal waterways lie within the territory of a single *Land*, the Federation on its application may delegate their administration to that *Land* on federal commission. If a waterway touches the territory of several *Länder*, the Federation may commission that *Land* which is designated by the affected *Länder*.
(3) In the administration, development and new construction of waterways, the requirements of land improvement and of water management shall be assured in agreement with the *Länder*.

Article 90 **[Federal highways]**

(1) The Federation shall be the owner of the former Reich motorways and highways.
(2) The *Länder*, or such self-governing corporate bodies as are competent under *Land* law, shall administer the federal motorways and other federal highways used by long-distance traffic on federal commission.
(3) On application of a *Land*, the Federation may assume the administration of federal motorways and other federal highways used by long-distance traffic insofar as they lie within the territory of that *Land*.

Article 91 **[Internal emergency]**

(1) In order to avert an imminent danger to the existence or free democratic basic order of the Federation or of a *Land*, a *Land* may call upon police forces of other *Länder*, or upon personnel and facilities of other administrative authorities and of the Federal Border Police.
(2) If the *Land* where such danger is imminent is not itself willing or able to combat the danger, the Federal Government may place the police in that *Land* and the police forces of other *Länder* under its own orders and deploy units of the Federal Border Police. Any such order shall be rescinded once the danger is removed, or at any time on the demand of the Bundesrat. If the danger extends beyond the territory of a single *Land*, the Federal Government, insofar as is necessary to combat such danger, may issue instructions to the Land governments; the first and second sentences of this paragraph shall not be affected by this provision.

VIIIa. Joint Tasks

Article 91a **[Joint tasks – Responsibility for expenditure]**

(1) In the following areas the Federation shall participate in the discharge of responsibilities of the *Länder*, provided that such responsibilities are important to society as a whole and that federal participation is necessary for the improvement of living conditions (joint tasks):
1. improvement of regional economic structures;
2. improvement of the agrarian structure and of coastal preservation.

(2) Federal laws enacted with the consent of the Bundesrat shall specify the joint tasks as well as the details of coordination.
(3) In cases to which clause 1 of paragraph (1) of this Article applies, the Federation shall finance one half of the expenditure in each *Land*. In cases to which clause 2 of paragraph (1) of this Article applies, the Federation shall finance at least one half of the expenditure, and the proportion shall be the same for all *Länder*. Details shall be regulated by law. The provision of funds shall be subject to appropriation in the budgets of the Federation and the *Länder*.
(4) (repealed)
(5) (repealed)

Article 91b [Education programmes and promotion of research]

(1) The Federation and the *Länder* may mutually agree to cooperate in cases of supraregional importance in the promotion of:
1. research facilities and projects apart from institutions of higher education;
2. scientific projects and research at institutions of higher education;
3. construction of facilities at institutions of higher education, including large scientific installations.

Agreements under clause 2 of paragraph (1) shall require the consent of all the *Länder*.
(2) The Federation and the *Länder* may mutually agree to cooperate for the assessment of the performance of educational systems in international comparison and in drafting relevant reports and recommendations.
(3) The apportionment of costs shall be regulated in the pertinent agreement.

Article 91c [Information technology systems]

(1) The Federation and the *Länder* may cooperate in planning, constructing, and operating information technology systems needed to discharge their responsibilities.
(2) The Federation and the *Länder* may agree to specify the standards and security requirements necessary for exchanges between their information technology systems. Agreements regarding the bases of cooperation under the first sentence may provide, for individual responsibilities determined by their content and scope, that detailed regulations be enacted with the consent of a qualified majority of the Fed-

eration and the *Länder* as laid down in the agreements. They require the consent of the Bundestag and the legislatures of the participating *Länder*; the right to withdraw from these agreements cannot be precluded. The agreements shall also regulate the sharing of costs.
(3) The *Länder* may also agree on the joint operation of information technology systems along with the establishment of installations for that purpose.
(4) For linking the information networks of the Federation and the *Länder*, the Federation shall establish a connecting network. Details regarding the establishment and the operation of the connecting network shall be regulated by a federal law with the consent of the Bundesrat.

Article 91d **[Comparison of performance]**

With a view to ascertaining and improving the performance of their administrations, the Federation and the *Länder* may conduct comparative studies and publish the results thereof.

Article 91e **[Cooperation in respect of basic support for persons seeking employment]**

(1) In the execution of federal laws in the field of basic support for persons seeking employment the Federation and the *Länder* or the municipalities and associations of municipalities responsible pursuant to *Land* law shall generally cooperate in joint institutions.
(2) The Federation may authorise a limited number of municipalities and associations of municipalities, at their request and with the consent of the highest *Land* authority, to discharge the tasks pursuant to paragraph (1) alone. In this case, the Federation shall bear the necessary expenditures including the administrative expenses for the tasks which are to be discharged by the Federation in the execution of laws pursuant to paragraph (1).
(3) Details shall be regulated by a federal law requiring the consent of the Bundesrat.

IX. The Judiciary

Article 92 **[Court organisation]**

The judicial power shall be vested in the judges; it shall be exercised by the Federal Constitutional Court, by the federal courts provided for in this Basic Law, and by the courts of the *Länder*.

Article 93 **[Jurisdiction of the Federal Constitutional Court]**

(1) The Federal Constitutional Court shall rule:

1. on the interpretation of this Basic Law in the event of disputes concerning the extent of the rights and duties of a supreme federal body or of other parties vested with rights of their own by this Basic Law or by the rules of procedure of a supreme federal body;
2. in the event of disagreements or doubts concerning the formal or substantive compatibility of federal law or *Land* law with this Basic Law, or the compatibility of *Land* law with other federal law, on application of the Federal Government, of a *Land* government, or of one fourth of the Members of the Bundestag;

2a. in the event of disagreements whether a law meets the requirements of paragraph (2) of Article 72, on application of the Bundesrat or of the government or legislature of a *Land*;

3. in the event of disagreements concerning the rights and duties of the Federation and the *Länder*, especially in the execution of federal law by the *Länder* and in the exercise of federal oversight;
4. on other disputes involving public law between the Federation and the *Länder*, between different *Länder*, or within a *Land*, unless there is recourse to another court;

4a. on constitutional complaints, which may be filed by any person alleging that one of his basic rights or one of his rights under paragraph (4) of Article 20 or under Article 33, 38, 101, 103 or 104 has been infringed by public authority;

4b. on constitutional complaints filed by municipalities or associations of municipalities on the ground that their right to self-government under Article 28 has been infringed by a law; in the case of infringement by a *Land* law, however, only if the law cannot be challenged in the constitutional court of the *Land*;

4c. on complaints lodged by associations against their non-recognition as a party for the election to the Bundestag;

5. in the other instances provided for in this Basic Law.

(2) At the request of the Bundesrat, a *Land* government or the parliamentary assembly of a *Land*, the Federal Constitutional Court shall also rule whether in cases falling under paragraph (4) of Article 72 the need for a regulation by federal law does not exist any longer or whether in the cases referred to in clause 1 of paragraph (2) of Article 125a federal law could not be enacted any longer. The Court's determination that the need has ceased to exist or that federal law could no longer be enacted substitutes a federal law according to paragraph (4) of Article 72 or clause 2 of paragraph (2) of Article 125a. A request under the first sentence is admissible only if a bill falling under paragraph (4) of Article 72 or the second sentence of paragraph (2) of Article 125a has been rejected by the German Bundestag or if it has not been considered and determined upon within one year, or if a similar bill has been rejected by the Bundesrat.

(3) The Federal Constitutional Court shall also rule on such other matters as shall be assigned to it by a federal law.

Article 94 [Composition of the Federal Constitutional Court]

(1) The Federal Constitutional Court shall consist of federal judges and other members. Half the members of the Federal Constitutional Court shall be elected by the Bundestag and half by the Bundesrat. They may not be members of the Bundestag, of the Bundesrat, of the Federal Government, or of any of the corresponding bodies of a *Land*.

(2) The organisation and procedure of the Federal Constitutional Court shall be regulated by a federal law, which shall specify in which instances its decisions shall have the force of law. The law may require that all other legal remedies be exhausted before a constitutional complaint may be filed, and may provide for a separate proceeding to determine whether the complaint will be accepted for decision.

Article 95 [Supreme federal courts]

(1) The Federation shall establish the Federal Court of Justice, the Federal Administrative Court, the Federal Finance Court, the Federal Labour Court and the Fed-

eral Social Court as supreme courts of ordinary, administrative, financial, labour and social jurisdiction.
(2) The judges of each of these courts shall be chosen jointly by the competent Federal Minister and a committee for the selection of judges consisting of the competent *Land* ministers and an equal number of members elected by the Bundestag.
(3) A Joint Chamber of the courts specified in paragraph (1) of this Article shall be established to preserve the uniformity of decisions. Details shall be regulated by a federal law.

Article 96 **[Other federal courts]**

(1) The Federation may establish a federal court for matters concerning industrial property rights.
(2) The Federation may establish federal military criminal courts for the Armed Forces. These courts may exercise criminal jurisdiction only during a state of defence or over members of the Armed Forces serving abroad or on board warships. Details shall be regulated by a federal law. These courts shall be under the aegis of the Federal Minister of Justice. Their full-time judges shall be persons qualified to hold judicial office.
(3) The supreme court of review from the courts designated in paragraphs (1) and (2) of this Article shall be the Federal Court of Justice.
(4) The Federation may establish federal courts for disciplinary proceedings against, and for proceedings on complaints by, persons in the federal public service.
(5) With the consent of the Bundesrat, a federal law may provide that courts of the *Länder* shall exercise federal jurisdiction over criminal proceedings in the following matters:

1. genocide;
2. crimes against humanity under international criminal law;
3. war crimes;
4. other acts tending to and undertaken with the intent to disturb the peaceful relations between nations (paragraph (1) of Article 26);
5. state security.

Article 97 **[Judicial independence]**

(1) Judges shall be independent and subject only to the law.

(2) Judges appointed permanently to full-time positions may be involuntarily dismissed, permanently or temporarily suspended, transferred or retired before the expiration of their term of office only by virtue of judicial decision and only for the reasons and in the manner specified by the laws. The legislature may set age limits for the retirement of judges appointed for life. In the event of changes in the structure of courts or in their districts, judges may be transferred to another court or removed from office, provided they retain their full salary.

Article 98 **[Legal status of judges – Impeachment]**

(1) The legal status of federal judges shall be regulated by a special federal law.
(2) If a federal judge infringes the principles of this Basic Law or the constitutional order of a *Land* in his official capacity or unofficially, the Federal Constitutional Court, upon application of the Bundestag, may by a two-thirds majority order that the judge be transferred or retired. In the case of an intentional infringement it may order him dismissed.
(3) The legal status of the judges in the *Länder* shall be regulated by special *Land* laws if clause 27 of paragraph (1) of Article 74 does not otherwise provide.
(4) The *Länder* may provide that Land judges shall be chosen jointly by the *Land* Minister of Justice and a committee for the selection of judges.
(5) The *Länder* may enact provisions regarding *Land* judges that correspond with those of paragraph (2) of this Article. Existing *Land* constitutional law shall not be affected. The decision in cases of judicial impeachment shall rest with the Federal Constitutional Court.

Article 99 **[Constitutional disputes within a *Land*]**

A *Land* law may assign the decision of constitutional disputes within a *Land* to the Federal Constitutional Court, and the final decision in matters involving the application of *Land* law to the supreme courts specified in paragraph (1) of Article 95.

Article 100 **[Concrete judicial review]**

(1) If a court concludes that a law on whose validity its decision depends is unconstitutional, the proceedings shall be stayed, and a decision shall be obtained from the *Land* court with jurisdiction over constitutional disputes where the constitution

of a *Land* is held to be violated, or from the Federal Constitutional Court where this Basic Law is held to be violated. This provision shall also apply where the Basic Law is held to be violated by *Land* law and where a *Land* law is held to be incompatible with a federal law.
(2) If, in the course of litigation, doubt exists whether a rule of international law is an integral part of federal law and whether it directly creates rights and duties for the individual (Article 25), the court shall obtain a decision from the Federal Constitutional Court.
(3) If the constitutional court of a *Land*, in interpreting this Basic Law, proposes to deviate from a decision of the Federal Constitutional Court or of the constitutional court of another *Land*, it shall obtain a decision from the Federal Constitutional Court.

Article 101 **[Ban on extraordinary courts]**

(1) Extraordinary courts shall not be allowed. No one may be removed from the jurisdiction of his lawful judge.
(2) Courts for particular fields of law may be established only by a law.

Article 102 **[Abolition of capital punishment]**

Capital punishment is abolished.

Article 103 **[Fair trial]**

(1) In the courts every person shall be entitled to a hearing in accordance with law.
(2) An act may be punished only if it was defined by a law as a criminal offence before the act was committed.
(3) No person may be punished for the same act more than once under the general criminal laws.

Article 104 [Deprivation of liberty]

(1) Liberty of the person may be restricted only pursuant to a formal law and only in compliance with the procedures prescribed therein. Persons in custody may not be subjected to mental or physical mistreatment.
(2) Only a judge may rule upon the permissibility or continuation of any deprivation of liberty. If such a deprivation is not based on a judicial order, a judicial decision shall be obtained without delay. The police may hold no one in custody on their own authority beyond the end of the day following the arrest. Details shall be regulated by a law.
(3) Any person provisionally detained on suspicion of having committed a criminal offence shall be brought before a judge no later than the day following his arrest; the judge shall inform him of the reasons for the arrest, examine him, and give him an opportunity to raise objections. The judge shall, without delay, either issue a written arrest warrant setting forth the reasons therefor or order his release.
(4) A relative or a person enjoying the confidence of the person in custody shall be notified without delay of any judicial decision imposing or continuing a deprivation of liberty.

X. Finance

Article 104a [Apportionment of expenditures – Financial system – Liability]

(1) The Federation and the *Länder* shall separately finance the expenditures resulting from the discharge of their respective responsibilities insofar as this Basic Law does not otherwise provide.
(2) Where the *Länder* act on federal commission, the Federation shall finance the resulting expenditures.
(3) Federal laws providing for money grants to be administered by the *Länder* may provide that the Federation shall pay for such grants wholly or in part. If any such law provides that the Federation shall finance one half or more of the expenditure, it shall be executed by the *Länder* on federal commission.
(4) Federal laws that oblige the *Länder* to provide money grants, benefits in kind or comparable services to third persons and which are executed by the *Länder* in their own right or according to the second sentence of paragraph (3) on commission of the Federation shall require the consent of the Bundesrat if the expenditure resulting therefrom shall be borne by the *Länder*.

(5) The Federation and the *Länder* shall finance the administrative expenditures incurred by their respective authorities and shall be responsible to one another for ensuring proper administration. Details shall be regulated by a federal law requiring the consent of the Bundesrat.
(6) In accord with the internal allocation of competencies and responsibilities, the Federation and the *Länder* shall bear the costs entailed by a violation of obligations incumbent on Germany under supranational or international law. In cases of financial corrections by the European Union with effect transcending one specific *Land*, the Federation and the *Länder* shall bear such costs at a ratio of 15 to 85. In such cases, the *Länder* as a whole shall be responsible in solidarity for 35 per cent of the total burden according to a general formula; 50 per cent of the total burden shall be borne by those *Länder* which have caused the encumbrance, adjusted to the size of the amount of the financial means received. Details shall be regulated by a federal law requiring the consent of the Bundesrat.

Article 104b [Financial assistance for investments]

(1) To the extent that this Basic Law confers on it the power to legislate, the Federation may grant the *Länder* financial assistance for particularly important investments by the *Länder* and municipalities (associations of municipalities) which are necessary to:
1. avert a disturbance of the overall economic equilibrium;
2. equalise differing economic capacities within the federal territory; or
3. promote economic growth.

In deviating from the first sentence, the Federation may grant financial assistance even outside its field of legislative powers in cases of natural disasters or exceptional emergency situations beyond governmental control and substantially harmful to the state's financial capacity.
(2) Details, especially with respect to the kinds of investments to be promoted, shall be regulated by a federal law requiring the consent of the Bundesrat or by an executive agreement based on the federal budget law. The duration of the grants shall be limited and the grants must be reviewed at regular intervals with respect to the manner in which they are used. The financial assistance must be designed with descending annual contributions.
(3) Upon request, the Bundestag, the Federal Government as well as the Bundesrat shall be informed about the implementation of such measures and the improvements reached.

Article 105 [Distribution of powers regarding tax laws]

(1) The Federation shall have exclusive power to legislate with respect to customs duties and fiscal monopolies.
(2) The Federation shall have concurrent power to legislate with respect to all other taxes the revenue from which accrues to it wholly or in part or as to which the conditions provided for in paragraph (2) of Article 72 apply.
(2a) The *Länder* shall have power to legislate with regard to local taxes on consumption and expenditures so long and insofar as such taxes are not substantially similar to taxes regulated by federal law. They are empowered to determine the rate of the tax on acquisition of real estate.
(3) Federal laws relating to taxes the revenue from which accrues wholly or in part to the *Länder* or to municipalities (associations of municipalities) shall require the consent of the Bundesrat.

Article 106 [Apportionment of tax revenue and yield of fiscal monopolies]

(1) The yield of fiscal monopolies and the revenue from the following taxes shall accrue to the Federation:
1. customs duties;
2. taxes on consumption insofar as they do not accrue to the *Länder* pursuant to paragraph (2), or jointly to the Federation and the *Länder* in accordance with paragraph (3), or to municipalities in accordance with paragraph (6) of this Article;
3. the road freight tax, motor vehicle tax, and other taxes on transactions related to motorised vehicles;
4. the taxes on capital transactions, insurance and bills of exchange;
5. non-recurring levies on property and equalisation of burdens levies;
6. income and corporation surtaxes;
7. levies imposed within the framework of the European Communities.

(2) Revenue from the following taxes shall accrue to the *Länder*:
1. the property tax;
2. the inheritance tax;
3. the motor vehicle tax;

4. such taxes on transactions as do not accrue to the Federation pursuant to paragraph (1) or jointly to the Federation and the *Länder* pursuant to paragraph (3) of this Article
5. the beer tax;
6. the tax on gambling establishments.

(3) Revenue from income taxes, corporation taxes and turnover taxes shall accrue jointly to the Federation and the *Länder* (joint taxes) to the extent that the revenue from the income tax and the turnover tax is not allocated to municipalities pursuant to paragraphs (5) and (5a) of this Article. The Federation and the *Länder* shall share equally the revenues from income taxes and corporation taxes. The respective shares of the Federation and the *Länder* in the revenue from the turnover tax shall be determined by a federal law requiring the consent of the Bundesrat. Such determination shall be based on the following principles:

1. The Federation and the *Länder* shall have an equal claim against current revenues to cover their necessary expenditures. The extent of such expenditures shall be determined with due regard to multi-year financial planning.
2. The financial requirements of the Federation and of the *Länder* shall be coordinated in such a way as to establish a fair balance, avoid excessive burdens on taxpayers, and ensure uniformity of living standards throughout the federal territory.

In determining the respective shares of the Federation and the *Länder* in the revenue from the turnover tax, reductions in revenue incurred by the *Länder* from 1 January 1996 because of the provisions made with respect to children in the income tax law shall also be taken into account. Details shall be regulated by the federal law enacted pursuant to the third sentence of this paragraph.

(4) The respective shares of the Federation and the *Länder* in the revenue from the turnover tax shall be apportioned anew whenever the ratio of revenues to expenditures of the Federation becomes substantially different from that of the *Länder*; reductions in revenue that are taken into account in determining the respective shares of revenue from the turnover tax under the fifth sentence of paragraph (3) of this Article shall not be considered in this regard. If a federal law imposes additional expenditures on or withdraws revenue from the *Länder*, the additional burden may be compensated for by federal grants pursuant to a federal law requiring the consent of the Bundesrat, provided the additional burden is limited to a short period of time. This law shall establish the principles for calculating such grants and distributing them among the *Länder*.

(5) A share of the revenue from the income tax shall accrue to the municipalities, to be passed on by the *Länder* to their municipalities on the basis of the income taxes

paid by their inhabitants. Details shall be regulated by a federal law requiring the consent of the Bundesrat. This law may provide that municipalities may establish supplementary or reduced rates with respect to their share of the tax.

(5a) From and after 1 January 1998, a share of the revenue from the turnover tax shall accrue to the municipalities. It shall be passed on by the *Länder* to their municipalities on the basis of a formula reflecting geographical and economic factors. Details shall be regulated by a federal law requiring the consent of the Bundesrat.

(6) Revenue from taxes on real property and trades shall accrue to the municipalities; revenue from local taxes on consumption and expenditures shall accrue to the municipalities or, as may be provided for by *Land* legislation, to associations of municipalities. Municipalities shall be authorised to establish the rates at which taxes on real property and trades are levied, within the framework of the laws. If there are no municipalities in a *Land*, revenue from taxes on real property and trades as well as from local taxes on consumption and expenditures shall accrue to the *Land*. The Federation and the *Länder* may participate, by virtue of an apportionment, in the revenue from the tax on trades. Details regarding such apportionment shall be regulated by a federal law requiring the consent of the Bundesrat. In accordance with *Land* legislation, taxes on real property and trades as well as the municipalities' share of revenue from the income tax and the turnover tax may be taken as a basis for calculating the amount of apportionment.

(7) An overall percentage of the *Land* share of total revenue from joint taxes, to be determined by *Land* legislation, shall accrue to the municipalities or associations of municipalities. In all other respects *Land* legislation shall determine whether and to what extent revenue from *Land* taxes shall accrue to municipalities (associations of municipalities).

(8) If in individual *Länder* or municipalities (associations of municipalities) the Federation requires special facilities to be established that directly result in an increase of expenditure or in reductions in revenue (special burden) to these *Länder* or municipalities (associations of municipalities), the Federation shall grant the necessary compensation if and insofar as the *Länder* or municipalities (associations of municipalities) cannot reasonably be expected to bear the burden. In granting such compensation, due account shall be taken of indemnities paid by third parties and financial benefits accruing to these *Länder* or municipalities (associations of municipalities) as a result of the establishment of such facilities.

(9) For the purpose of this Article, revenues and expenditures of municipalities (associations of municipalities) shall also be deemed to be revenues and expenditures of the *Länder*.

Article 106a **[Federal grants for local mass transit]**

Beginning 1 January 1996 the *Länder* shall be entitled to an allocation of federal tax revenues for purposes of local mass transit. Details shall be regulated by a federal law requiring the consent of the Bundesrat. Allocations made pursuant to the first sentence of this Article shall not be taken into account in determining the financial capacity of a *Land* under paragraph (2) of Article 107.

Article 106b **[*Länder* share of motor vehicle tax]**

As of 1 July 2009, following the transfer of the motor vehicle tax to the Federation, the *Länder* shall be entitled to a sum from the tax revenue of the Federation. Details shall be regulated by a federal law requiring the consent of the Bundesrat.

Article 107 **[Distribution of tax revenue – Financial equalisation among the *Länder* – Supplementary grants]**

(1) Revenue from *Land* taxes and the *Land* share of revenue from income and corporation taxes shall accrue to the individual *Länder* to the extent that such taxes are collected by finance authorities within their respective territories (local revenue). Details regarding the delimitation as well as the manner and scope of allotment of local revenue from corporation and wage taxes shall be regulated by a federal law requiring the consent of the Bundesrat. This law may also provide for the delimitation and allotment of local revenue from other taxes. The *Land* share of revenue from the turnover tax shall accrue to the individual *Länder* on a per capita basis; a federal law requiring the consent of the Bundesrat may provide for the grant of supplementary shares not exceeding one quarter of a *Land* share to *Länder* whose per capita income from *Land* taxes, from income and corporation taxes and from taxes under Article 106b ranks below the average of all the *Länder* combined; with respect to the tax on the acquisition of real estate, the capacity to generate revenue shall be considered.
(2) Such law shall ensure a reasonable equalisation of the disparate financial capacities of the *Länder*, with due regard for the financial capacities and needs of municipalities (associations of municipalities). It shall specify the conditions governing the claims of *Länder* entitled to equalisation payments and the liabilities of *Länder* required to make them as well as the criteria for determining the amounts of such payments. It may also provide for grants to be made by the Federation to financial-

ly weak *Länder* from its own funds to assist them in meeting their general financial needs (supplementary grants).

Article 108 [Financial administration of the Federation and the *Länder* – Financial courts]

(1) Customs duties, fiscal monopolies, taxes on consumption regulated by a federal law, including the turnover tax on imports, the motor vehicle tax and other transaction taxes related to motorised vehicles as from 1 July 2009, and charges imposed within the framework of the European Communities shall be administered by federal finance authorities. The organisation of these authorities shall be regulated by a federal law. Inasmuch as intermediate authorities have been established, their heads shall be appointed in consultation with the *Land* governments.
(2) All other taxes shall be administered by the financial authorities of the *Länder*. The organisation of these authorities and the uniform training of their civil servants may be regulated by a federal law requiring the consent of the Bundesrat. Inasmuch as intermediate authorities have been established, their heads shall be appointed in agreement with the Federal Government.
(3) To the extent that taxes accruing wholly or in part to the Federation are administered by revenue authorities of the *Länder*, those authorities shall act on federal commission. Paragraphs (3) and (4) of Article 85 shall apply, provided that the Federal Minister of Finance shall take the place of the Federal Government.
(4) Where and to the extent that execution of the tax laws will be substantially facilitated or improved thereby, a federal law requiring the consent of the Bundesrat may provide for collaboration between federal and *Land* revenue authorities in matters of tax administration, for the administration of taxes enumerated in paragraph (1) of this Article by revenue authorities of the *Länder*, or for the administration of other taxes by federal revenue authorities. The functions of *Land* revenue authorities in the administration of taxes whose revenue accrues exclusively to municipalities (associations of municipalities) may be delegated by the *Länder* to municipalities (associations of municipalities) wholly or in part.
(5) The procedures to be followed by federal revenue authorities shall be prescribed by a federal law. The procedures to be followed by *Land* revenue authorities or, as provided by the second sentence of paragraph (4) of this Article, by municipalities (associations of municipalities) may be prescribed by a federal law requiring the consent of the Bundesrat.
(6) Financial jurisdiction shall be uniformly regulated by a federal law.

(7) The Federal Government may issue general administrative rules which, to the extent that administration is entrusted to *Land* revenue authorities or to municipalities (associations of municipalities), shall require the consent of the Bundesrat.

Article 109 [Budget management in the Federation and the Länder]

(1) The Federation and the *Länder* shall be autonomous and independent of one another in the management of their respective budgets.
(2) The Federation and the *Länder* shall perform jointly the obligations of the Federal Republic of Germany resulting from legal acts of the European Community for the maintenance of budgetary discipline pursuant to Article 104 of the Treaty Establishing the European Community and shall, within this framework, give due regard to the requirements of overall economic equilibrium.
(3) The budgets of the Federation and the *Länder* shall in principle be balanced without revenue from credits. The Federation and *Länder* may introduce rules intended to take into account, symmetrically in times of upswing and downswing, the effects of market developments that deviate from normal conditions, as well as exceptions for natural disasters or unusual emergency situations beyond governmental control and substantially harmful to the state's financial capacity. For such exceptional regimes, a corresponding amortisation plan must be adopted. Details for the budget of the Federation shall be governed by Article 115 with the proviso that the first sentence shall be deemed to be satisfied if revenue from credits does not exceed 0.35 percent in relation to the nominal gross domestic product. The *Länder* themselves shall regulate details for the budgets within the framework of their constitutional powers, the proviso being that the first sentence shall only be deemed to be satisfied if no revenue from credits is admitted.
(4) A federal law requiring the consent of the Bundesrat may establish principles applicable to both the Federation and the *Länder* governing budgetary law, the responsiveness of budgetary management to economic trends, and long-term financial planning.
(5) Sanctions imposed by the European Community on the basis of the provisions of Article 104 of the Treaty Establishing the European Community in the interest of maintaining budgetary discipline, shall be borne by the Federation and the *Länder* at a ratio of 65 to 35 percent. In solidarity, the *Länder* as a whole shall bear 35 percent of the charges incumbent on the *Länder* according to the number of their inhabitants; 65 percent of the charges incumbent on the *Länder* shall be borne by the *Länder* according to their degree of causation. Details shall be regulated by a federal law which shall require the consent of the Bundesrat.

Article 109a [Budgetary emergencies]

To avoid a budgetary emergency, a federal law requiring the consent of the Bundesrat shall provide for:

1. the continuing supervision of budgetary management of the Federation and the *Länder* by a joint body (Stability Council),
2. the conditions and procedures for ascertaining the threat of a budgetary emergency,
3. the principles for the establishment and administration of programs for taking care of budgetary emergencies.

The decisions of the Stability Council and the accompanying documents shall be published.

Article 110 [Federal budget]

(1) All revenues and expenditures of the Federation shall be included in the budget; in the case of federal enterprises and special trusts, only payments to or remittances from them need be included. The budget shall be balanced with respect to revenues and expenditures.
(2) The budget for one or more fiscal years shall be set forth in a law enacted before the beginning of the first year and making separate provision for each year. The law may provide that various parts of the budget apply to different periods of time, divided by fiscal years.
(3) Bills to comply with the first sentence of paragraph (2) of this Article as well as bills to amend the Budget Law or the budget itself shall be submitted simultaneously to the Bundesrat and to the Bundestag; the Bundesrat shall be entitled to comment on such bills within six weeks or, in the case of amending bills, within three weeks.
(4) The Budget Law may contain only such provisions as relate to federal revenues and expenditures and to the period for which it is enacted. The Budget Law may specify that its provisions shall expire only upon promulgation of the next Budget Law or, in the event of an authorisation pursuant to Article 115, at a later date.

Article 111 **[Interim budget management]**

(1) If, by the end of a fiscal year, the budget for the following year has not been adopted by a law, the Federal Government, until such law comes into force, may make all expenditures that are necessary:

a) to maintain institutions established by a law and to carry out measures authorised by a law;
b) to meet the legal obligations of the Federation;
c) to continue construction projects, procurements, and the provision of other benefits or services, or to continue to make grants for these purposes, to the extent that amounts have already been appropriated in the budget of a previous year.

(2) To the extent that revenues based upon specific laws and derived from taxes, or duties, or other sources, or the working capital reserves, do not cover the expenditures referred to in paragraph (1) of this Article, the Federal Government may borrow the funds necessary to sustain current operations up to a maximum of one quarter of the total amount of the previous budget.

Article 112 **[Extrabudgetary expenditures]**

Expenditures in excess of budgetary appropriations or for purposes not contemplated by the budget shall require the consent of the Federal Minister of Finance. Such consent may be given only in the event of an unforeseen and unavoidable necessity. Details may be regulated by a federal law.

Article 113 **[Increase of expenditures]**

(1) Laws that increase the budget expenditures proposed by the Federal Government, or entail or will bring about new expenditures, shall require the consent of the Federal Government. This requirement shall also apply to laws that entail or will bring about decreases in revenue. The Federal Government may demand that the Bundestag postpone its vote on bills to this effect. In this event the Federal Government shall submit its comments to the Bundestag within six weeks.
(2) Within four weeks after the Bundestag has adopted such a law, the Federal Government may demand that it vote on the law a second time.

(3) If the bill has become law pursuant to Article 78, the Federal Government may withhold its consent only within six weeks and only after having initiated the procedure provided for in the third and fourth sentences of paragraph (1) or in paragraph (2) of this Article. Upon the expiration of this period such consent shall be deemed to have been given.

Article 114 [Submission and auditing of accounts]

(1) For the purpose of discharging the Federal Government, the Federal Minister of Finance shall submit annually to the Bundestag and to the Bundesrat an account of all revenues and expenditures as well as of assets and debts during the preceding fiscal year.
(2) The Federal Court of Audit, whose members shall enjoy judicial independence, shall audit the account and determine whether public finances have been properly and efficiently administered. It shall submit an annual report directly to the Bundestag and the Bundesrat as well as to the Federal Government. In other respects the powers of the Federal Court of Audit shall be regulated by a federal law.

Article 115 [Limits of borrowing]

(1) The borrowing of funds and the assumption of surety obligations, guarantees, or other commitments that may lead to expenditures in future fiscal years shall require authorisation by a federal law specifying or permitting computation of the amounts involved.
(2) Revenues and expenditures shall in principle be balanced without revenue from credits. This principle shall be satisfied when revenue obtained by the borrowing of funds does not exceed 0.35 percent in relation to the nominal gross domestic product. In addition, when economic developments deviate from normal conditions, effects on the budget in periods of upswing and downswing must be taken into account symmetrically. Deviations of actual borrowing from the credit limits specified under the first to third sentences are to be recorded on a control account; debits exceeding the threshold of 1.5 percent in relation to the nominal gross domestic product are to be reduced in accordance with the economic cycle. The regulation of details, especially the adjustment of revenue and expenditures with regard to financial transactions and the procedure for the calculation of the yearly limit on net borrowing, taking into account the economic cycle on the basis of a procedure for adjusting the cycle together with the control and balancing of deviations of actual bor-

rowing from the credit limit, requires a federal law. In cases of natural catastrophes or unusual emergency situations beyond governmental control and substantially harmful to the state's financial capacity, these credit limits may be exceeded on the basis of a decision by a majority of the Bundestag's Members. The decision has to be combined with an amortisation plan. Repayment of the credits borrowed under the sixth sentence must be accomplished within an appropriate period of time.

Xa. State of Defence

Article 115a [Declaration of state of defence]

(1) Any determination that the federal territory is under attack by armed force or imminently threatened with such an attack (state of defence) shall be made by the Bundestag with the consent of the Bundesrat. Such determination shall be made on application of the Federal Government and shall require a two-thirds majority of the votes cast, which shall include at least a majority of the Members of the Bundestag.
(2) If the situation imperatively calls for immediate action, and if insurmountable obstacles prevent the timely convening of the Bundestag or the Bundestag cannot muster a quorum, the Joint Committee shall make this determination by a two-thirds majority of the votes cast, which shall include at least a majority of its members.
(3) The determination shall be promulgated by the Federal President in the Federal Law Gazette pursuant to Article 82. If this cannot be done in time, promulgation shall be effected in another manner; the determination shall be printed in the Federal Law Gazette as soon as circumstances permit.
(4) If the federal territory is under attack by armed force, and if the competent federal authorities are not in a position at once to make the determination provided for in the first sentence of paragraph (1) of this Article, the determination shall be deemed to have been made and promulgated at the time the attack began. The Federal President shall announce that time as soon as circumstances permit.
(5) If the determination of a state of defence has been promulgated, and if the federal territory is under attack by armed force, the Federal President, with the consent of the Bundestag, may issue declarations under international law regarding the existence of the state of defence. Under the conditions specified in paragraph (2) of this Article, the Joint Committee shall act in place of the Bundestag.

Article 115b [Power of command of the Federal Chancellor]

Upon the promulgation of a state of defence the power of command over the Armed Forces shall pass to the Federal Chancellor.

Article 115c [Extension of the legislative powers of the Federation]

(1) The Federation shall have the right to legislate concurrently for a state of defence even with respect to matters within the legislative powers of the *Länder*. Such laws shall require the consent of the Bundesrat.
(2) To the extent required by circumstances during a state of defence, a federal law for a state of defence may:

1. make temporary provisions concerning compensation in the event of expropriation that deviate from the requirements of the second sentence of paragraph (3) of Article 14;
2. establish a time limit for deprivations of freedom different from that specified in the third sentence of paragraph (2) and the first sentence of paragraph (3) of Article 104, but not exceeding four days, for cases in which no judge has been able to act within the time limit that normally applies.

(3) To the extent necessary to repel an existing or imminently threatened attack, a federal law for a state of defence may, with the consent of the Bundesrat, regulate the administration and finances of the Federation and the *Länder* without regard to Titles VIII, VIIIa and X of this Basic Law, provided that the viability of the *Länder*, municipalities, and associations of municipalities, especially with respect to financial matters, is assured.
(4) Federal laws enacted pursuant to paragraph (1) or clause 1 of paragraph (2) of this Article may, for the purpose of preparing for their enforcement, be applied even before a state of defence arises.

Article 115d [Urgent bills]

(1) During a state of defence the federal legislative process shall be governed by the provisions of paragraphs (2) and (3) of this Article without regard to the provisions of paragraph (2) of Article 76, the second sentence of paragraph (1) and paragraphs (2) to (4) of Article 77, Article 78, and paragraph (1) of Article 82.

(2) Federal Government bills that the Government designates as urgent shall be forwarded to the Bundesrat at the same time as they are submitted to the Bundestag. The Bundestag and the Bundesrat shall debate such bills in joint session without delay. Insofar as the consent of the Bundesrat is necessary for any such bill to become law, a majority of its votes shall be required. Details shall be regulated by rules of procedure adopted by the Bundestag and requiring the consent of the Bundesrat.

(3) The second sentence of paragraph (3) of Article 115a shall apply to the promulgation of such laws mutatis mutandis.

Article 115e [Joint Committee]

(1) If, during a state of defence, the Joint Committee by a two-thirds majority of the votes cast, which shall include at least a majority of its members, determines that insurmountable obstacles prevent the timely convening of the Bundestag or that the Bundestag cannot muster a quorum, the Joint Committee shall occupy the position of both the Bundestag and the Bundesrat and shall exercise their powers as a single body.

(2) This Basic Law may neither be amended nor abrogated nor suspended in whole or in part by a law enacted by the Joint Committee. The Joint Committee shall have no power to enact laws pursuant to the second sentence of paragraph (1) of Article 23, paragraph (1) of Article 24, or Article 29.

Article 115f [Use of Federal Border Police – Extended powers of instruction]

(1) During a state of defence the Federal Government, to the extent circumstances require, may:

1. employ the Federal Border Police throughout the federal territory;
2. issue instructions not only to federal administrative authorities but also to *Land* governments and, if it deems the matter urgent, to *Land* authorities, and may delegate this power to members of *Land* governments designated by it.

(2) The Bundestag, the Bundesrat and the Joint Committee shall be informed without delay of the measures taken in accordance with paragraph (1) of this Article.

Article 115g [Federal Constitutional Court]

Neither the constitutional status nor the performance of the constitutional functions of the Federal Constitutional Court or its judges may be impaired. The law governing the Federal Constitutional Court may be amended by a law enacted by the Joint Committee only insofar as the Federal Constitutional Court agrees is necessary to ensure that it can continue to perform its functions. Pending the enactment of such a law, the Federal Constitutional Court may take such measures as are necessary to this end. Determinations by the Federal Constitutional Court pursuant to the second and third sentences of this Article shall be made by a majority of the judges present.

Article 115h [Expiry of electoral terms and terms of office]

(1) Any electoral terms of the Bundestag or of *Land* parliaments due to expire during a state of defence shall end six months after the termination of the state of defence. A term of office of the Federal President due to expire during a state of defence, and the exercise of his functions by the President of the Bundesrat in case of the premature vacancy of his office, shall end nine months after the termination of the state of defence. The term of office of a member of the Federal Constitutional Court due to expire during a state of defence shall end six months after the termination of the state of defence.
(2) Should it be necessary for the Joint Committee to elect a new Federal Chancellor, it shall do so by the votes of a majority of its members; the Federal President shall propose a candidate to the Joint Committee. The Joint Committee may express its lack of confidence in the Federal Chancellor only by electing a successor by a two-thirds majority of its members.
(3) The Bundestag shall not be dissolved while a state of defence exists.

Article 115i [Powers of the *Land* governments]

(1) If the competent federal bodies are incapable of taking the measures necessary to avert the danger, and if the situation imperatively calls for immediate independent action in particular areas of the federal territory, the *Land* governments or the authorities or representatives they designate shall be authorised, within their respective spheres of competence, to take the measures provided for in paragraph (1) of Article 115f.

(2) Any measures taken in accordance with paragraph (1) of this Article may be rescinded at any time by the Federal Government, or, with respect to *Land* authorities and subordinate federal authorities, by Minister-Presidents of the *Länder*.

Article 115k [Rank and duration of emergency provisions]

(1) Laws enacted in accordance with Articles 115c, 115e and 115g, as well as statutory instruments issued on the basis of such laws, shall suspend the operation of incompatible law so long as they are in effect. This provision shall not apply to earlier law enacted pursuant to Articles 115c, 115e or 115g.
(2) Laws adopted by the Joint Committee, as well as statutory instruments issued on the basis of such laws, shall cease to have effect no later than six months after the termination of a state of defence.
(3) Laws containing provisions that diverge from Articles 91a, 91b, 104a, 106 and 107 shall apply no longer than the end of the second fiscal year following the termination of a state of defence. After such termination they may, with the consent of the Bundesrat, be amended by a federal law so as to revert to the provisions of Titles VIIIa and X.

Article 115l [Repeal of emergency measures – Conclusion of peace]

(1) The Bundestag, with the consent of the Bundesrat, may at any time repeal laws enacted by the Joint Committee. The Bundesrat may demand that the Bundestag reach a decision on this question. Any measures taken by the Joint Committee or by the Federal Government to avert a danger shall be rescinded if the Bundestag and the Bundesrat so decide.
(2) The Bundestag, with the consent of the Bundesrat, may at any time, by a decision to be promulgated by the Federal President, declare a state of defence terminated. The Bundesrat may demand that the Bundestag reach a decision on this question. A state of defence shall be declared terminated without delay if the conditions for determining it no longer exist.
(3) The conclusion of peace shall be determined by a federal law.

XI. Transitional and Concluding Provisions

Article 116 [Definition of "German" – Restoration of citizenship]

(1) Unless otherwise provided by a law, a German within the meaning of this Basic Law is a person who possesses German citizenship or who has been admitted to the territory of the German Reich within the boundaries of 31 December 1937 as a refugee or expellee of German ethnic origin or as the spouse or descendant of such person.
(2) Former German citizens who between 30 January 1933 and 8 May 1945 were deprived of their citizenship on political, racial or religious grounds, and their descendants, shall on application have their citizenship restored. They shall be deemed never to have been deprived of their citizenship if they have established their domicile in Germany after 8 May 1945 and have not expressed a contrary intention.

Article 117 [Suspended entry into force of two basic rights]

(1) Law which is inconsistent with paragraph (2) of Article 3 of this Basic Law shall remain in force until adapted to that provision, but not beyond 31 March 1953.
(2) Laws that restrict freedom of movement in view of the present housing shortage shall remain in force until repealed by a federal law.

Article 118 [New delimitation of Baden and Württemberg]

The division of the territory comprising Baden, Württemberg-Baden and Württemberg-Hohenzollern into *Länder* may be revised, without regard to the provisions of Article 29, by agreement between the *Länder* concerned. If no agreement is reached, the revision shall be effected by a federal law, which shall provide for an advisory referendum.

Article 118a [New delimitation of Berlin and Brandenburg]

The division of the territory comprising Berlin and Brandenburg into *Länder* may be revised, without regard to the provisions of Article 29, by agreement between the two *Länder* with the participation of their inhabitants who are entitled to vote.

Article 125 [Continued applicability of law within the scope of concurrent legislative power]

Law regarding matters subject to the concurrent legislative power of the Federation shall become federal law in the area in which it applies:

1. insofar as it applies uniformly within one or more occupation zones;
2. insofar as it is law by which former Reich law has been amended since 8 May 1945.

Article 125a [Continued applicability of federal law – Replacement by *Land* law]

(1) Law that was enacted as federal law but that by virtue of the amendment of paragraph (1) of Article 74, the insertion of the seventh sentence of paragraph (1) of Article 84, the second sentence of paragraph (1) of Article 85 or of the second sentence of paragraph (2a) of Article 105, or because of the repeal of Articles 74a, 75 or the second sentence of paragraph (3) of Article 98 could no longer be enacted as federal law, shall remain in force as federal law. It may be superseded by *Land* law.
(2) Law that was enacted pursuant to paragraph (2) of Article 72 as it stood up to 15 November 1994 but which, because of the amendment of paragraph (2) of Article 72, could no longer be enacted as federal law shall remain in force as federal law. A federal law may provide that it may be superseded by *Land* law.
(3) Law that has been enacted as *Land* law but which, because of the amendment of Article 73, could not be enacted any longer as *Land* law shall continue in force as *Land* law. It may be superseded by federal law.

Article 125b [Continued applicability of framework laws – Deviation power of the *Länder*]

(1) Law that was enacted pursuant to Article 75 as it stood up to 1 September 2006, and which could be enacted as federal law even after this date, shall remain in force as federal law. The powers and duties of the *Länder* to legislate shall in this regard remain unaffected. In the areas referred to in the first sentence of paragraph (3) of Article 72 the *Länder* may enact regulations that deviate from this law; however, in those areas covered by clauses 2, 5 and 6 of the first sentence of Article 72 the

Länder may do so only if and insofar as the Federation has made use of its power to legislate after 1 September 2006, in those areas covered by clauses 2 and 5 beginning at the latest on 1 January 2010, in cases under clause 6 beginning at the latest on 1 August 2008.
(2) The *Länder* may enact regulations deviating from federal regulations enacted pursuant to paragraph (1) of Article 84 as it stood up to 1 September 2006; up to 31 December 2008, however, they may deviate from regulations on administrative procedure only if, after 1 September 2006, regulations on administrative procedure in the relevant federal law have been amended.

Article 125c [Continued applicability of law within the scope of joint tasks]

(1) Law that was enacted by virtue of paragraph (2) of Article 91a in conjunction with clause 1 of paragraph (1) as it stood up to 1 September 2006 shall continue in force until 31 December 2006.
(2) The regulations enacted in the areas of municipal traffic financing and promotion of social housing by virtue of paragraph (4) of Article 104a as it stood up to 1 September 2006 shall remain in force until 31 December 2006. The regulations enacted on municipal traffic financing for special programmes pursuant to paragraph (1) of Article 6 of the Municipal Traffic Financing Act, as well as the other regulations enacted pursuant to paragraph (4) of Article 104a as it stood up to 1 September 2006, shall continue in force until 31 December 2019, provided no earlier repeal has been or is determined.

Article 126 [Determination about continued applicability of law as federal law]

Disagreements concerning the continued applicability of law as federal law shall be resolved by the Federal Constitutional Court.

Article 127 [Extension of law to the French zone and to Berlin]

Within one year after promulgation of this Basic Law the Federal Government, with the consent of the governments of the *Länder* concerned, may extend to the *Länder* of Baden, Greater Berlin, Rhineland-Palatinate and Württemberg-Hohenzollern any law of the Administration of the Combined Economic Area, insofar as it remains in force as federal law under Article 124 or 125.

Article 128 [Continued authority to issue instructions]

Insofar as law that remains in force grants authority to issue instructions within the meaning of paragraph (5) of Article 84, this authority shall remain in existence until a law otherwise provides.

Article 129 [Continued authority to issue legal acts]

(1) Insofar as legal provisions that remain in force as federal law grant authority to issue statutory instruments or general administrative rules or to make administrative decisions in individual cases, such powers shall pass to the authorities that henceforth have competence over the subject matter. In cases of doubt the Federal Government shall decide in agreement with the Bundesrat; such decisions shall be published.
(2) Insofar as legal provisions that remain in force as *Land* law grant such authority, it shall be exercised by the authorities competent under *Land* law.
(3) Insofar as legal provisions within the meaning of paragraphs (1) and (2) of this Article grant authority to amend or supplement the provisions themselves or to issue legal provisions that have the force of laws, such authority shall be deemed to have expired.
(4) The provisions of paragraphs (1) and (2) of this Article shall apply mutatis mutandis to legal provisions that refer to provisions no longer in force or to institutions no longer in existence.

Article 130 [Transfer of existing administrative institutions]

(1) Administrative agencies and other institutions that serve the public administration or the administration of justice and are not based on *Land* law or on agreements between *Länder*, as well as the Administrative Union of South West German Railways and the Administrative Council for Postal and Telecommunications Services for the French Occupation Zone, shall be placed under the control of the Federal Government. The Federal Government, with the consent of the Bundesrat, shall provide for their transfer, dissolution, or liquidation.

(2) The supreme disciplinary authority for the personnel of these administrative bodies and institutions shall be the competent Federal Minister.
(3) Corporations and institutions under public law not directly subordinate to a *Land* nor based on agreements between *Länder* shall be under the supervision of the competent highest federal authority.

Article 131 **[Persons formerly in the public service]**

The legal relations of persons, including refugees and expellees, who on 8 May 1945 were employed in the public service, have left the service for reasons other than those recognised by civil service regulations or collective bargaining agreements, and have not yet been reinstated or are employed in positions that do not correspond to those they previously held, shall be regulated by a federal law. The same shall apply mutatis mutandis to persons, including refugees and expellees, who on 8 May 1945 were entitled to pensions and related benefits and who for reasons other than those recognised by civil service regulations or collective bargaining agreements no longer receive any such pension or related benefits. Until the pertinent federal law takes effect, no legal claims may be made, unless *Land* law otherwise provides.

Article 132 **[Retirement of civil servants]**

(1) Civil servants and judges who enjoy life tenure when this Basic Law takes effect may, within six months after the Bundestag first convenes, be retired, suspended, or transferred to lower-salaried positions if they lack the personal or professional aptitude for their present positions. This provision shall apply mutatis mutandis to salaried public employees, other than civil servants or judges, whose employment cannot be terminated at will. In the case of salaried employees whose employment may be terminated at will, notice periods longer than those set by collective bargaining agreements may be rescinded within the same period.
(2) The preceding provision shall not apply to members of the public service who are unaffected by the provisions regarding "Liberation from National Socialism and Militarism" or who are recognised victims of National Socialism, absent important personal grounds.
(3) Persons affected may have recourse to the courts in accordance with paragraph (4) of Article 19.

(4) Details shall be specified by a statutory instrument issued by the Federal Government with the consent of the Bundesrat.

Article 133 [Succession to the Administration of the Combined Economic Area]

The Federation shall succeed to the rights and duties of the Administration of the Combined Economic Area.

Article 134 [Succession to Reich assets]

(1) Reich assets shall, in principle, become federal assets.
(2) Insofar as such assets were originally intended to be used principally for administrative tasks not entrusted to the Federation under this Basic Law, they shall be transferred without compensation to the authorities now entrusted with such tasks and to the extent that such assets are now being used, not merely temporarily, for administrative tasks that under this Basic Law are now performed by the *Länder*, they shall be transferred to the *Länder*. The Federation may also transfer other assets to the *Länder*.
(3) Assets that were placed at the disposal of the Reich without compensation by *Länder* or municipalities (associations of municipalities) shall revert to those *Länder* or municipalities (associations of municipalities) insofar as the Federation does not require them for its own administrative purposes.
(4) Details shall be regulated by a federal law requiring the consent of the Bundesrat.

Article 135 [Assets in case of territorial changes between the *Länder*]

(1) If after 8 May 1945 and before the effective date of this Basic Law an area has passed from one *Land* to another, the *Land* to which the area now belongs shall be entitled to the assets of the *Land* to which it previously belonged that are located in that area.
(2) The assets of *Länder* or other public-law corporations or institutions that no longer exist, insofar as they were originally intended to be used principally for administrative tasks or are now being so used, not merely temporarily, shall pass to the *Land*, corporation or institution that now performs those tasks.

(3) Real property of *Länder* that no longer exist, including appurtenances, shall pass to the *Land* within which it is located, insofar as it is not among the assets already referred to in paragraph (1) of this Article.
(4) Insofar as an overriding interest of the Federation or the particular interest of a region requires, a federal law may depart from the rules prescribed by paragraphs (1) to (3) of this Article.
(5) In all other respects, the succession to and disposition of assets, insofar as it has not been effected before 1 January 1952 by agreement between the affected *Länder* or corporations or institutions established under public law, shall be regulated by a federal law requiring the consent of the Bundesrat.
(6) Holdings of the former Land of Prussia in enterprises established under private law shall pass to the Federation. Details shall be regulated by a federal law, which may also depart from this provision.
(7) Insofar as assets that on the effective date of this Basic Law would devolve upon a *Land* or a corporation or institution established under public law pursuant to paragraphs (1) to (3) of this Article have been disposed of by or pursuant to a *Land* law or in any other manner by the party thus entitled, the transfer of assets shall be deemed to have taken place before such disposition.

Article 135a **[Old debts]**

(1) Federal legislation enacted pursuant to paragraph (4) of Article 134 or paragraph (5) of Article 135 may also provide that the following debts shall not be discharged, or that they shall be discharged only in part:

1. debts of the Reich, of the former Land of Prussia, or of such other corporations and institutions under public law as no longer exist;
2. such debts of the Federation or of corporations and institutions under public law as are connected with the transfer of assets pursuant to Article 89, 90, 134 or 135, and such debts of these bodies as arise from measures taken by the bodies designated in clause 1;
3. such debts of the *Länder* or municipalities (associations of municipalities) as have arisen from measures taken by them before 1 August 1945 within the framework of administrative functions incumbent upon or delegated by the Reich to comply with orders of the occupying powers or to terminate a state of emergency resulting from the war.

(2) Paragraph (1) of this Article shall apply mutatis mutandis to debts of the German Democratic Republic or its institutions as well as to debts of the Federation or

other corporations and institutions under public law that are connected with the transfer of assets of the German Democratic Republic to the Federation, *Länder* or municipalities, and to debts arising from measures taken by the German Democratic Republic or its institutions.

Article 136 **[First convening of the Bundesrat]**

(1) The Bundesrat shall convene for the first time on the day the Bundestag first convenes.
(2) Until the election of the first Federal President, his powers shall be exercised by the President of the Bundesrat. He shall not have authority to dissolve the Bundestag.

Article 137 **[Right of state employees to stand for election]**

(1) The right of civil servants, other salaried public employees, professional or volunteer members of the Armed Forces, and judges to stand for election in the Federation, in the *Länder* or in the municipalities may be restricted by a law.
(2) The election of the first Bundestag, of the first Federal Convention and of the first Federal President shall be governed by an electoral law to be enacted by the Parliamentary Council.
(3) Until the Federal Constitutional Court is established, its authority under paragraph (2) of Article 41 shall be exercised by the German High Court for the Combined Economic Area, which shall make determinations in accordance with its procedural rules.

Article 138 **[South German notaries]**

Changes in the rules governing the notarial profession as it now exists in the *Länder* of Baden, Bavaria, Württemberg-Baden and Württemberg-Hohenzollern shall require the consent of the governments of these *Länder*.

Article 139 [Continued applicability of denazification provisions]

The legal provisions enacted for the "Liberation of the German People from National Socialism and Militarism" shall not be affected by the provisions of this Basic Law.

Article 140 [Law of religious denominations]

The provisions of Articles 136, 137, 138, 139 and 141 of the German Constitution of 11 August 1919 shall be an integral part of this Basic Law.

Article 141 ["Bremen Clause"]

The first sentence of paragraph (3) of Article 7 shall not apply in any *Land* in which *Land* law otherwise provided on 1 January 1949.

Article 142 [Reservation in favour of basic rights in *Land* constitutions]

Notwithstanding Article 31, provisions of *Land* constitutions shall also remain in force insofar as they guarantee basic rights in conformity with Articles 1 to 18 of this Basic Law.

Article 142a (repealed)

Article 143 [Duration of deviations from the Basic Law]

(1) The law in the territory specified in Article 3 of the Unification Treaty may deviate from provisions of this Basic Law for a period extending no later than 31 December 1992 insofar and so long as disparate circumstances make full compliance impossible. Deviations may not violate paragraph (2) of Article 19 and must be compatible with the principles specified in paragraph (3) of Article 79.
(2) Deviations from Titles II, VIII, VIIIa, IX, X and XI shall be permissible for a period extending no later than 31 December 1995.
(3) Independently of paragraphs (1) and (2) of this Article, Article 41 of the Unification Treaty and the rules for its implementation shall also remain in effect insofar

as they provide for the irreversibility of acts interfering with property rights in the territory specified in Article 3 of this Treaty.

Article 143a [Exclusive legislative power concerning federal railways]

(1) The Federation shall have exclusive power to legislate with respect to all matters arising from the transformation of federal railways administered by the Federation into business enterprises. Paragraph (5) of Article 87e shall apply mutatis mutandis. Civil servants employed by federal railways may be assigned by a law to render services to federal railways established under private law without prejudice to their legal status or the responsibility of their employer.
(2) Laws enacted pursuant to paragraph (1) of this Article shall be executed by the Federation.
(3) The Federation shall continue to be responsible for local passenger services of the former federal railways until 31 December 1995. The same shall apply to the corresponding functions of rail transport administration. Details shall be regulated by a federal law requiring the consent of the Bundesrat.

Article 143b [Privatisation of the Deutsche Bundespost]

(1) The special trust Deutsche Bundespost shall be transformed into enterprises under private law in accordance with a federal law. The Federation shall have exclusive power to legislate with respect to all matters arising from this transformation.
(2) The exclusive rights of the Federation existing before the transformation may be transferred by a federal law for a transitional period to the enterprises that succeed to the Deutsche Bundespost Postdienst and to the Deutsche Bundespost Telekom. The Federation may not surrender its majority interest in the enterprise that succeeds to the Deutsche Bundespost Postdienst until at least five years after the law takes effect. To do so shall require a federal law with the consent of the Bundesrat.
(3) Federal civil servants employed by the Deutsche Bundespost shall be given positions in the private enterprises that succeed to it, without prejudice to their legal status or the responsibility of their employer. The enterprises shall exercise the employer's authority. Details shall be regulated by a federal law.

Article 143c [Compensation for the cessation of joint tasks]

(1) From 1 January 2007 until 31 December 2019, the *Länder* shall be entitled to receive annual payments from the federal budget as compensation for losing the Federation's financial contributions resulting from the abolition of the joint tasks of extension and construction of institutions of higher education, including university hospitals and educational planning, as well as for losing financial assistance for the improvement of municipal traffic infrastructure and for the promotion of social housing. Until 31 December 2013, these amounts are to be determined by averaging the financial share of the Federation for the years 2000 to 2008.
(2) Until 31 December 2013, the payments pursuant to paragraph (1) shall be distributed among the *Länder* in the form of:
1. fixed annual payments the amounts of which shall be determined according to the average share of each *Land* during the period 2000 to 2003;
2. payments earmarked for the functional area of the former joint financing.

(3) Until the end of 2013, the Federation and the *Länder* shall review the extent to which the financing allotted to individual *Länder* pursuant to paragraph (1) is still appropriate and necessary for the discharge of their tasks. Beginning with 1 January 2014, the earmarking pursuant to clause 2 of paragraph (2) of the financial means allotted under paragraph (1) shall cease; the earmarking for the volume of the means for investment purposes shall remain unchanged. Agreements resulting from Solidarity Pact II shall remain unaffected.
(4) Details shall be regulated by a federal law which shall require the consent of the Bundesrat.

Article 143d [Transitional provisions relating to consolidation assistance]

(1) Articles 109 and 115 in the version in force until 31 July 2009 shall apply for the last time to the 2010 budget. Articles 109 and 115 in the version in force as from 1 August 2009 shall apply for the first time to the 2011 budget; debit authorisations existing on 31 December 2010 for special trusts already established shall remain untouched. In the period from 1 January 2011 to 31 December 2019, the *Länder* may, in accordance with their applicable legal regulations, deviate from the provisions of paragraph (3) of Article 109. The budgets of the *Länder* are to be planned in such a way that the 2020 budget fulfils the requirements of the fifth sentence of paragraph (3) of Article 109. In the period from 1 January 2011 to 31 December 2015, the Federation may deviate from the provisions of the second sen-

tence of paragraph (2) of Article 115. The reduction of the existing deficits should begin with the 2011 budget. The annual budgets are to be planned in such a way that the 2016 budget satisfies the requirement of the second sentence of paragraph (2) of Article 115; details shall be regulated by federal law.
(2) As assistance for compliance with the provisions of paragraph (3) of Article 109 after 1 January 2020, the *Länder* of Berlin, Bremen, Saarland, Saxony-Anhalt, and Schleswig-Holstein may receive, for the period 2011 to 2019, consolidation assistance from the federal budget in the global amount of 800 million euros annually. The respective amounts are 300 million euros for Bremen, 260 million euros for Saarland, and 80 million euros each for Berlin, Saxony-Anhalt, and Schleswig-Holstein. The assistance payments shall be allocated on the basis of an administrative agreement under the terms of a federal law requiring the consent of the Bundesrat. These grants require a complete reduction of financial deficits by the end of 2020. The details, especially the annual steps to be taken to reduce financial deficits, the supervision of the reduction of financial deficits by the Stability Council, along with the consequences entailed in case of failure to carry out the step-by-step reduction, shall be regulated by a federal law requiring the consent of the Bundesrat and by an administrative agreement. There shall be no simultaneous granting of consolidation assistance and redevelopment assistance on the grounds of an extreme budgetary emergency.
(3) The financial burden resulting from the granting of the consolidation assistance shall be borne equally by the Federation and the *Länder*, to be financed from their share of the value-added tax. Details shall be regulated by a federal law requiring the consent of the Bundesrat.

Article 144 [Ratification of the Basic Law – Berlin]

(1) This Basic Law shall require ratification by the parliaments of two thirds of the German *Länder* in which it is initially to apply.
(2) Insofar as the application of this Basic Law is subject to restrictions in any *Land* listed in Article 23 or in any part thereof, such *Land* or part thereof shall have the right to send representatives to the Bundestag in accordance with Article 38 and to the Bundesrat in accordance with Article 50.

Article 145 **[Entry into force of the Basic Law]**

(1) The Parliamentary Council, with the participation of the members for Greater Berlin, shall confirm the ratification of this Basic Law in public session and shall certify and promulgate it.
(2) This Basic Law shall take effect at the end of the day on which it is promulgated.
(3) It shall be published in the Federal Law Gazette.

Article 146 **[Duration of the Basic Law]**

This Basic Law, which since the achievement of the unity and freedom of Germany applies to the entire German people, shall cease to apply on the day on which a constitution freely adopted by the German people takes effect.

Extracts from the German Constitution of 11 August 1919 (Weimar Constitution)

Religion and Religious Societies

Article 136

(1) Civil and political rights and duties shall be neither dependent upon nor restricted by the exercise of religious freedom.
(2) Enjoyment of civil and political rights and eligibility for public office shall be independent of religious affiliation.
(3) No person shall be required to disclose his religious convictions. The authorities shall have the right to inquire into a person's membership in a religious society only to the extent that rights or duties depend upon it or that a statistical survey mandated by a law so requires.
(4) No person may be compelled to perform any religious act or ceremony, to participate in religious exercises, or to take a religious form of oath.

Article 137

(1) There shall be no state church.

(2) The freedom to form religious societies shall be guaranteed. The union of religious societies within the territory of the Reich shall be subject to no restrictions.
(3) Religious societies shall regulate and administer their affairs independently within the limits of the law that applies to all. They shall confer their offices without the participation of the state or the civil community.
(4) Religious societies shall acquire legal capacity according to the general provisions of civil law.
(5) Religious societies shall remain corporations under public law insofar as they have enjoyed that status in the past. Other religious societies shall be granted the same rights upon application, if their constitution and the number of their members give assurance of their permanency. If two or more religious societies established under public law unite into a single organisation, it too shall be a corporation under public law.
(6) Religious societies that are corporations under public law shall be entitled to levy taxes on the basis of the civil taxation lists in accordance with *Land* law.
(7) Associations whose purpose is to foster a philosophical creed shall have the same status as religious societies.
(8) Such further regulation as may be required for the implementation of these provisions shall be a matter for *Land* legislation.

Article 138

(1) Rights of religious societies to public subsidies on the basis of a law, contract or special grant shall be redeemed by legislation of the *Länder*. The principles governing such redemption shall be established by the Reich.
(2) Property rights and other rights of religious societies or associations in their institutions, foundations, and other assets intended for purposes of worship, education or charity shall be guaranteed.

Article 139

Sunday and holidays recognised by the state shall remain protected by law as days of rest from work and of spiritual improvement.

Article 141

To the extent that a need exists for religious services and pastoral work in the army, in hospitals, in prisons, or in other public institutions, religious societies shall be permitted to provide them, but without compulsion of any kind.

Index

A

action, freedom of
  170-171,173,178-179, 226, 318, 379, 482
administrative regulations 281-282
adoption 51-56, 58-59, 62-65, 68-74, 290, 297-299, 302-306, 308, 321, 529, 546, 695-697, 715, 725-726, 811, 833
– adoptive children 304
– adoptive family 287, 289-291, 294
– adoptive parents 304
– adult 308
– incognito 51, 58, 61, 72-74, 289, 299-300
– of an adult foreigner as a child 301, 306
– parental consent to, substitution 51, 54, 56, 58-62, 67, 69, 71, 73-74
alien(s)
– entry 309
  · limiting 271, 276, 282
  · entry-limiting effect 274-275
  · entry-limiting measures 274
  · to join family members in the Federal Republic 245
  · of spouses and family members 255, 261, 272, 274-275, 281-282, 284
– life, focus of 267-268
– first generation 248, 251, 276-277
  · spouses of 248
– second generation 251, 268, 275, 276-277
  · spouses of 274
– workers, recruitment of 273, 277
  · stop 247
analogy 315, 317
– analogous application 314-316
application of the law, order on 701
arbitrariness 182, 557
– prohibition of 10, 110, 177, 179, 187, 676

B

bigamy 258
– bigamous marriage 103
  · impediment of 101, 104, 109, 116-117
biological father/parents 642-645, 648-650, 655, 657-659, 661-662, 667-668
– determination of 769
– information about the identity 365-366
– parental rights 650-651
– relations with a child 647-648, 650, 662, 664
– social and family relationship 642-643, 651, 658-660, 662, 665
birth rates 511
blanket regulation, imposed on frequently occurring manifestations 588

C

care

– and upbringing in household life 259
– maintenance 641
– prior to adoption 287, 289, 297-298
child/children
– abduction 387, 397
  · international 387
– ability to pay support for their parents 732-733
– access to 714-722
  · right of 697
– accommodation in care facilities 414
– best interests of 21, 27, 31-39, 51, 54-57, 63, 67, 69, 72-73, 135, 156-157, 161-165, 197, 200-202, 203-219, 232-233, 235, 239, 241-244, 289, 293-299, 320-322, 324-326, 328, 330-331, 333-335, 386, 389, 391-392, 395-398, 400-401, 411, 477-478, 480, 487-490, 504, 521, 597-599, 603, 611, 614-615, 619-620, 622-632, 642, 645-646, 648, 650-651, 653, 658-664, 667, 716, 721-722, 731, 786, 790, 792, 794, 800-802, 804-809, 811-812, 814-824, 826-831, 833, 836-848, 850
  · avert a danger to 205, 615
  · at risk 196, 199
  · being jeopardised 191-193
  · endangering of 288-292, 294-295, 297
  · physical or psychological 235
– born out of wedlock 332-333, 611-617, 620-622, 624, 626-630, 632, 826-833, 835-850
  · bringing up 780
  · discrimination against 328, 333
  · healthy development of, avert a danger to 68
– bringing up of 410
– care 405, 408, 410-412, 487, 504
  · and upbringing of 411, 504, 508, 510, 513, 599
  · costs 403-405, 408-409, 412-413
  · costs resulting from gainful employment 412, 417
  · expenditure 408, 413, 417
  · requirements 402, 411, 415-416
  · fiscally subsidised 411
– child allowance 346, 421-424, 428, 430
  · fictitious 426
– child benefit 346, 421-423, 426, 428, 430-431, 578-589
  · amount influenced by the advantage acquired through additional counted children 579-580, 583-585, 587-589
  · conversion into a child allowance 426-428
  · refusal to grant 45, 49
– child-raising 497-498, 501-503, 505, 509, 512
  · activities 502, 507-510, 512-513
  · allowance 413
  · benefit 346
  · communities 401
  · leave 413
  · periods 756
  · periods in statutory pensions insurance 336-339, 341
  · requirement(s) 402, 416-417
– child-related minimum income 411
– children's guardian 389-390, 395

– claim against its mother for identification of the father 364-366, 368-370
– contact to, right of 645-648, 663, 665-667, 725
– determining whether or not it is the biological child of its legal father 760-761
– duty to care for and bring up 51, 409, 487, 800
– duty to take the mother's interests into account 365
– economic requirements 409
– existential material needs 402, 411
– healthy development, to avert danger to the 68
– hearing of 156-157, 163-164
– income tax allowance(s) 421, 426, 430-431
– interest of the joint 477
– joint responsibility 214
– legal procedure capable of clarifying whether it is the biological child of its legal father 759, 764-765
– liable for support 744-746
– maintenance 411, 421, 428, 478-480, 488-489, 499
  · release of 480, 487-489
  · reasonable 487
– material expenditure 413
– media images of 465
– minimum income of 411, 413, 426, 429-430
  · measured by the requirement, not by actual expenditure 411
  · minimum material income of 415
– optimal promotion 488
– personality of, development 465
– representation of 21, 27, 39, 64, 239
  · by (both) parents 38
  · by the parents 26, 239
– responsibility of bringing up 488
– right to know its descent/parentage 364, 366, 369, 762-763, 765
– right to parental care and upbringing 804, 816
  · in Article 6.2 sentence 1 of the Basic Law, corresponding with the parental duty 804, 814
  · which corresponds with the parental responsibility 812
– separation from the family/the parents 51, 64, 191-192, 195, 197-202, 599
– to avert danger from 198, 200
– unborn, protection of 755
– will of 156, 158, 161, 163, 236, 393, 835
– work-related care requirements 402, 411
civil servants
– state's obligation to take care of the welfare in a manner in keeping with their office 432, 435-436, 440, 443, 445-448
– child-related salary elements 436-439, 441-442, 444, 446
– income 441
– remuneration and pensions
  · adjusted to general economic and financial circumstances 437, 442-443
  · postponement of linear increases as a contribution to reducing the burden on the budget 437

coercive measures
– against a parent who stubbornly refuses contact 823
– for the enforcement of a personal relationship 807
– to force an unwilling parent to have contact with a child 804-805, 812, 818-824
collusion of facts 176
– danger of 123
community/ies
– non-marital 582-583, 585-586, 633, 639-641
  · with children, not constituting a family within the meaning of Article 6.1 of the Basic Law 585
– similar to marriage 316
constitutional complaint
– authorisation to lodge on behalf of a minor 240
– decision on the merits, continued interest in 256
– general principle of subsidiarity 256-257
– constitutional complaint proceedings
  · representation of minors 231
  · supplementary curator for 240
constitutional court, supervision of 315-316
constitutional legal order 307
constitutional review
– intensity of 308
– standard of 701
contribution procedure 339, 347, 508
contributory capacity principles 500
convict 177
counsel, court-appointed 593, 595, 598, 604, 606-607
criminal detention 174-175
criminal proceedings before a juvenile court, participation of the parents 591, 601-602
curator ad litem 386, 389, 392-393, 395, 400
custody 156, 724-731
– assigned to one spouse alone after divorce 207, 211, 214-215, 218
– proceedings 389-399, 392, 400
– right(s) 198, 697
  · for children born out of wedlock 320
  · withdrawal 192, 196, 198, 200, 231, 237

D

declaration of legitimacy 320-335
defence counsel, appointment of 596, 607
demographic developments 511
detention 122
– monitoring in 183, 187, 189
dignified existence 410
discretion 282-283, 307-308
– in the area of admission of aliens 281
– with regards to aliens law 265
discrimination, prohibition of (contained in Article 6.1 and 6.2 of the Basic Law) 410, 412-413
disturbed agreement parity, case of 483
divorce law 138-139, 141-149, 152-154, 221, 228
– fault-based 153
– fault principle 144, 147, 153, 157
– non-economic hardship 151

· clause 138
– transition from the fault to the breakdown principle 38, 140, 144, 204
DNA test (report) 762-763, 765, 773, 776
– to clarify paternity, obtained secretly 759-762, 764, 775-777
domestic law 703
domestic legal system 703
domestic partial legal system 709

E

education 384
– educational assistance 346
– educational system 384
employment, prohibitions of, under maternity protection law 747-749, 753-756
entertainment 468-469
entry
– into the Federal territory
· fundamental-rights claim to 263
· requirements for 267, 279
– permission 306
– potential 273
equal opportunities 384
equal rights
– for men and women 2, 18, 31, 25-26, 42, 528
· in a marriage (and the family) 24-25, 43
– of spouses 261
– partnership (marriage) 482
– requirement of 20, 24, 27, 30
equality
– (general) principle of 1, 10, 28, 49, 80, 177, 225, 332, 345, 377, 379, 382, 503, 507, 565, 585, 587, 589, 638, 685, 801
– horizontal 411, 427
– fiscal 424
– in taxation 9-10, 18
· for married citizens and unmarried citizens 4
– of father and mother/between parents 20, 24, 29, 31, 37
– special principle of 402
– unequal treatment, ban on 279
escape or collusion of facts, danger of 125
European Convention of Human Rights and Fundamental Freedoms
– observing and applying by German courts within the limits of methodically justifiable interpretation 701
– state of affairs in compliance with 727
– violation of 701, 704, 727
European Court of Human Rights 694, 715-718, 720-721, 725-731, 830, 836, 843, 849
– complainant's situation, redress of 705
– decisions of 703
· binding effect 700, 706
· taking into account 694, 706
– individual application 697
excessiveness, prohibition of 71, 185, 264
exhaustion of legal remedies 256
– in the principal proceedings 257
expulsion
– of a foreign national convicted of a criminal offence 127, 129, 132, 134, 136
– of the foreign parent 135

expression, freedom of 180-181, 186
expression of opinion, freedom of 181, 186

F

familial
– community 305
  · complete 265
– entry 250, 268, 271, 279-280, 282-283, 285
  · guidelines for 253
  · waiting periods for permitting 256
family/families 171-172, 179, 185, 189-190, 305, 586
– as an assistance community 309
– as a living arrangement and child-raising community 305, 395, 409
– burdens
  · compensation for 584, 587, 637
  · equalisation of 341, 344-347, 402, 497, 505
– income 372-373, 375, 377-378, 382
  · minimum 402, 410-411
– insurance 496, 505, 633-635, 638-640
  · assessment limit 639
  · benefiting spouses 635
  · contribution-free (co-insurance) 634, 636-638, 640
  · inclusion of step-children 640
– maintenance 641
– members, joining foreigners 248
– name
  · (spouses) 681-684, 686-688
  · uniform 517
– promotion of 385, 504-505, 584, 587, 637
  · duty to 45
– protection of 173, 504
  · obligation of the state of 307-308
– privacy 179, 186
– roles assumed within 341, 354
– social 645, 649, 656-658, 772
– types/forms of 577, 587
– unit, setting up 257, 268
– work 539-540
father
– information on identity 364
– right to knowledge of the parentage of the child/of the paternity 761-765, 774
Federal Constitutional Court proceedings
– capacity to conduct in one's own name 238
federal comity, principle of 282
Federal Institute for Employment 247, 580, 584-585, 752
federal laws, duty to essentially enforce uniformly 282
Federal Statistical Office 511
fees 382-383
– graduation 383
fiscal
– ability to pay 411
– exemption 412
foreign
– law, application of by domestic public authorities 113
– national
  · convicted of a criminal offence 128

· married to a German national 128-129, 133-136
foster family/parents 287, 290-291, 293-294, 296, 298-299, 715-717, 722
– removal from 289-290, 294-297
free movement 284-285
freedom right (Art 6.1 of the Basic Law) 306-307
fundamental provision(s) 1, 10, 149, 328
fundamental provision (Article 6.1 of the Basic Law) 2, 14, 225, 328, 637
– that determines values 10-11, 13, 62, 88, 107, 122, 125-126, 134, 149, 186, 223, 258, 263-264, 306-308, 344, 378, 503, 675, 794
fundamental right(s)
– right to state protection of 394
– protection of 702
– requirement to protect 384
– serving 395

G

gainful employment
– and family work in marriage 536, 538
– in the assessment of the maintenance requirement 532
– of parents as taxpayers 404-406, 413, 415
general public's (legitimate) interest in being informed 455-456, 459, 466, 470-472
generation(s)
– coming 508
– current pensioners' 502
– future long-term care 501
– of contributors 510
– old 509
– parent 346, 503, 512
– previous 509
– working-age 502, 508
– young 503, 509
generative equilibrium (of the social insurance system) 510
gentle compromise 264
good faith, principle of 477
guardianship court 21-22, 27, 31-32, 34-37, 39, 52-53, 57-58, 65, 68-69, 162, 192-194, 198, 232, 235, 240, 288, 292-293, 303, 321, 323-324, 326, 335, 392, 395, 518-520, 580, 585, 645, 660, 696, 726
guest workers, recruitment of 247

H

health insurance, statutory 493, 495, 500, 634-635, 638-640
– annual remuneration threshold 635-636, 639
– fund 637-639
hearing in court 291, 293-294
– right to 386, 392-393, 400
horizontal fiscal justice 427
household
– allowance 404, 407-409, 414, 416-417
  · denied to spouses 414
  · granted to non-marital child-raising communities, even if each parent has a basic allowance 414
– community, care for 259
housekeeping expenditure 414

I

immigration strain 274
income tax 2-3, 7, 377-378, 402, 407, 412, 420, 422, 424, 428, 430, 503, 569
– base for assessment 404, 413, 428
– lower limit for encroachment by 424
– joint assessment of spouses 2-4, 6-9, 14-19, 414-415, 421-422, 549, 671-672, 677
  · not conditional on a child-related requirement 415
informational self-determination, right to 759, 761-763, 766-769, 775-776
individual case, due account of the circumstances 274
information, obtaining of 472
institutional guarantee (Article 6.1 of the Basic Law) 2, 10-12, 24, 62, 107-108, 134, 150, 258, 263, 306-307, 558, 561-562, 570-573
insults, in letters from a pre-trial detainee 168-170, 181-182, 184-185, 187
insurance
– obligatory 346
  · subject to 639
– principle of 751
– solidarity-based 499
– system, obligatory 346
insured event 339, 351-352
integration 249, 266-268, 277
– economic and social 266
– in the local lifestyle 276
– lasting, in the lifestyle of the Federal Republic of Germany 277
intergenerational contract 339, 342, 346
international agreements 396
– law of 398, 702
international law 695
– commitment to 702
– general international law 283
– general rules and principles 396
international private law, German 104, 111
interpretation
– in conformity with the Basic Law 606
– in conformity with public international law 707
– of the law 694
intimate sphere 169, 181, 189

J

joint (parental) custody 206, 611-619, 621-632, 827-836, 838-850
– for a child born out of wedlock 611
– of divorced spouses 203, 205-207, 209, 214, 216-219
– of parents not married to each other 827-828, 833, 838, 844-845
judge, bound by statute and law, principle 694

K

kindergarten 374, 378, 380, 384-385
– fee/s 372-373, 375, 377, 381-382, 384-385
  · ability to pay 376, 378
  · demand 379
  · Statutes 373, 375, 377-379
  · graduation by income 376
– places 385

L

landlord-tenant law
- death of the tenant 311-313, 316, 318
- landlord 311-312, 316-319
- spouses and other family member(s), entering tenancy agreements 311-313
- unmarried civil partners, entering tenancy agreements 311, 313, 316

legal father
- desire to know whether the child is really his biological child 773
- determining that a child is biologically his 760, 764, 766, 770, 773-774
- fundamental right to know of the paternity 767-768, 770
- right to know that a child is biologically his 759, 764, 769, 773

legal representation, right to 65

legality, (constitutional) proviso of 62, 108, 280, 173, 606
- general proviso of 281-282

legislative
- competence (of the Länder) 380
- power 377

legislature
- failure of 756
- latitude left to the 585-587
  - by Article 33.5 of the Basic Law 440-441, 443-444, 446

letters
- monitoring of (during pre-trial detention) 166, 171, 184, 186, 190
- sent from a pre-trial detainee 166, 168-170, 176-189
  - to their spouses 181
  - to their parents 187

levies 378, 382
- fairness in the imposition of 383
- non-fiscal 377

long-term care
- domestic 495, 506
- in-patient 493, 495, 500, 506
- need of 491, 495, 497-501, 504-508, 510, 512-513
  - childless persons 506-507
- out-patient 506
- risk 499, 509-510
- of spouses 509

M

maintenance 40-44, 75, 79-81, 83-84, 86, 91, 95-96, 119, 132, 143, 150, 222, 228-229
- assets, (not) to be committed for paying support 734, 738-739, 741-742
- case of shortfall 220-221, 223-224, 226, 228-230
- claim(s) 476-480, 484, 486, 488-489
  - concurrent, of divorced and new spouses 224, 226
  - granted by the legislature to one parent against the other parent because of the care of his or her child 779, 790
  - of mother and father by reason of birth 783, 802
  - post-marital statutory, waived by the spouses 485
  - release from (in return for refraining to exercise right of access) 478-479

· of the divorced spouse 224, 226-227
· order of priority between concurrent claims of a divorced and a new spouse 222
– expenditure 408, 425
· for children, of the taxpayer 411
– from relatives 476
– higher priority of the former partner of the person liable for 223
– needs 498
– needy parent's claim to 227
– obligation 422, 424, 432, 440, 498-499, 508
· to the joint child, releasing the father of 486
– payable to the former spouse 670
– payments, in line with the ability to pay of the party obliged to pay and the need of the child 488
– post-marital 480, 486, 489, 531, 537, 539-540
· determined according to the marital circumstances at the time of divorce 531
· equivalence of family work and gainful employment in the assessment of 530
· spousal 795
– priority 220, 226
· for the divorced over the new spouse 222, 224-225, 227-229, 676, 679
marital
– and familial communities, international aspects 258
– and familial life, right to 259
– and family privacy 185, 189
· protection of 185-186
– and familial relations, existing, appropriate consideration 264
– child-raising community 414, 417
· claiming household employment as special expenditure 413
· placed at disadvantage compared to other child-raising communities 412-415
· unrestrictedly liable to pay tax 413
– community 150, 171-172, 213, 259, 270, 275, 277
– privacy, area of 181, 185
– standard of living until divorce 670
marriage(s)
– as a living arrangement of man and woman 395
– breakdown
· irrefutable presumption of after a three-year separation of the spouses 138, 140, 144, 148, 152
· principle 143-144, 147-148, 155
– dissolution of, preconditions 147
– equality (and equivalence) of a dissolved and a newly concluded 675-676
– freedom of 100, 103-104, 107-109, 114-119
– freedom of conclusion of 477
– limping 118-119
– normal case corresponding to the understanding of Article 6.1 and 6.2 first sentence of the Basic Law 276
– life-long, principle of 142-143, 147
– protection of 81, 96, 132, 149, 245, 541, 559-561, 563-564, 588, 675, 795
– regular 277

– specious 269-273, 276-277
· battling of 271-272, 277
– weighing the concerns of with the public interests pursued with the waiting-period requirement 269
– young 277
marriage and the family 2, 10-12, 14, 16-18, 35, 43, 62, 125, 133, 142, 149, 171-172, 186, 245, 263, 265-266, 279, 520, 522, 548, 562, 564, 572-573
– assistance in life 265
– automatic responsibility for the state to promote 88
– concept of under the Basic Law 258-259
– constitutional protection of 564, 572
– duty of the state to protect (and promote) 245, 264, 317, 334, 344, 503
– ideal of 264
· determinative features of 263
– prohibition of discrimination 401
– prohibition to place on a worse footing in comparison with other partnerships and child-raising communities 402, 410
– promotion of 585
– protection of 16, 18, 42, 122-124, 131-132, 149, 245, 260, 317, 323, 326, 480, 548, 753
– protection and promotion of 286, 332
– protection and support of 258, 264-265, 286, 332
– special protection of the state 2, 11-13, 24, 42, 146, 186, 258, 585, 637
– unity of, ideal 261
marriage clauses 82, 85-86, 89-98
– in orphan pensions 75-76, 82-84
marriage covenant 475-486, 489
– assumption of an obligation to perform 476
– causing an unreasonable disadvantage 481
– coercive situation 477
– concluded in connection with the pregnancy of the woman 483
– concluded with a pregnant woman prior to the care and maintenance situation of the joint child 475, 477
– containing a promise to marry 485
– content 485
· review 483
– distribution of burdens in 483
– family situation striven for by the partners 485
– freedom to shape without limit 483
– indication of contractual disparity 485
– judicial review of 475-476, 483, 485
– leading to a spouse requiring social assistance 477
– limits
· set by the case-law 476
· on the freedom of spouses in using 482
– one-sided distribution of burdens 480-483, 485-486
– pregnant woman
· life planning 485
· need of protection 485
· negotiation position, weakened by efforts to ensure her own

livelihood and that of the expected child 483
· situation of inferiority 483, 485
marry and set up a family, right to 259
maternity
– pay 747, 749, 751-752, 754
· contribution (of the employer) to 749, 752, 754
– protection 747, 752, 754-755
media coverage 455
minimum income 416, 420, 422-429
– guaranteed by the social assistance benefits 425
minimum requirement necessary to maintain a minimum standard of living 425, 427, 429
multipolar fundamental rights situations 707
municipal council, simultaneous membership of divorced couples/ former spouses, prohibition of 355-362

N

names
– double (family, married) name 516-517, 519-520, 522-526, 528-529
· child having a 520, 525
· exclusion of for a child 515, 517, 520, 525-526
– law on 682-684, 689, 692
– married name 516, 522-524, 681-693
· law on 690
– right to bear a 687-689
national and cultural identity 266
national court(s) 727, 729
national immigration law, subject to 286
national legal system 706
native country, alienation from 276
need to be informed 456
non-constitutional law, interpretation and application 296

O

official investigation, principle of 728
one's own image, right to control over 455, 459-462
opinion
– expression of 180, 185
– freedom of 170, 180, 189
– freedom to form one's own 467
– (free) formation of 468-469
ordre public 102, 104, 109-110, 117-118, 120
orphans
– differentiation between married and unmarried 80, 87, 97
– pensions 76-84, 87, 89-93, 96-98
· extended 76, 86, 88-90, 94, 97-98

P

parliament, act subject to the consent of the German 701
parent(s) 63, 167, 170-171, 189-190
– absolute equality 27
– and major-age children, relations between 171
– as educators, priority over the state 51, 213
– assessed jointly for tax 408

– correspondence by letter with their adult children (pre-trial detention) 166-167
– deduction of childcare costs 403
– divorced 205
– economic ability to pay 638
– granting of household allowance 404
– grievous and persistent failure 51, 69
– non culpable failure of 191-192, 197
– not married to each other 829
– opting for gainful employment 411
– priority as educators 213
– priority in bringing up and caring for the children 62, 64, 67, 73
– reconciliation of work within the family and gainful employment 412
– reduced ability to pay 402, 411, 415, 428
  · child-related 428
– right to represent the child 64
– single 412, 414
– support for 732-733
– (unrestrictedly) liable to pay tax 412-413
– willingness to cooperate 616, 622-624, 628-629

parent-child relationship 51, 57, 62-65, 71, 172, 177, 208, 213, 215, 297-298, 302, 308-309, 332, 520, 616, 621, 623, 656-657, 662, 663, 815

parentage
– clarification of 768-769, 773
– knowledge of 768, 771
– (fundamental) right to knowledge of 766, 768
  · and to clarification and determination 765

parental
– custody 390-391
  · assigned to one parent alone (after divorce of marriage) 204, 217
  · commercialisation of 478
  · for children born out of wedlock 322, 327
  · joint exercise by father and mother of a child born out of wedlock 320
  · right to exercise 192
  · rights for a legitimate child, withdrawal 192, 211
– obligation 395
– power 20-21, 27-30, 32-33, 35-38, 53, 57-58, 62-63, 65-66, 68, 71, 158-159, 161, 204, 321-323
– responsibility 66-67, 71, 135, 161, 203, 206, 211, 213, 215, 217-218, 227, 296, 320, 325, 328-330, 332-333, 395, 409-410, 489, 567, 591-592, 598, 601, 608, 619, 622-623, 629, 632, 653-656, 659, 664, 666-667, 785, 794, 800, 811, 815-816, 818, 832, 837, 840, 847
  · exercise for the sake of the child's best interests 263
– right(s) 33, 51, 57, 66-67, 70-71, 135, 160, 193-194,198, 202, 206-207, 210, 212-213, 217-218, 227, 241-243, 294, 325, 328-332, 392, 395, 40, 487, 490, 520-521, 527, 549, 567, 591, 597, 599-603, 606, 608, 619, 622-624, 626-629,

631, 650, 652-655, 657, 659, 726, 728, 731, 785, 794, 800-801, 811, 814-815, 817, 826, 829-830, 836-841, 843, 845-848
· exercise of 211
· exercised in a marital child-raising community 402, 410
· limits of 601
· of contact 820
· of upbringing 72, 214
· precedence of 597, 599-600, 608
· strongest encroachment on 191, 198-199
· to bring up a/ the child 197, 578-579, 591, 593, 597-598, 601-602, 606, 608
· to look after and bring up their children 197, 598
– support 743-746
paternity 651-660, 664
– acknowledgment of 643-644, 649-651, 660, 664-665, 760-761, 769
· with the consent of the mother, not leading to the conclusion that mother, child and legal father live together as a family 659
– challenge 644-645, 649-650, 655, 657-660, 663, 668
– clarification (and determination) of 763, 765, 767, 769-770, 773-774, 776-777
– contestation 759, 764, 771-776
– determination of 759, 762, 767, 771
– doubts as to 760-761, 764, 766, 768-770, 772-775, 777
– knowledge of the biological 773
– proof, secretly obtained 761
– right to knowledge (and determination) of one's own 763, 775-777
– test, secretly obtained/ ordered 761, 763, 766-767, 774-775
"paying father" 658
pension
– biographies, gaps in 351
– date regulation, qualifying 350-351, 353
– old-age pensions of women 348
– new pensions 351-352
– sharing (in contractual agreements) 476, 483
– stock 352
– wage-indexed, principle of 338
– wage and contribution linking 339
permanent civil service, principle of 440
person of contemporary history 456-458, 471-472
– absolute 455-456, 458-459, 471
– being portrayed 455-456, 461
– reporting about 455
personality
– (free) development of one's 459-460, 463-464, 472
– (general) right of 367, 369, 450, 455-456, 460-461, 465-473
· protection of 460, 465
– respect of 466
– right to develop one's 460, 468
persons of different sex, cohabiting with each other 541, 566
photographs 451-454, 458-459, 462, 473
· publication of 451-452, 454-458, 460, 466, 470-473

place of residence (of a child), right to determine 390, 392-393
precision of law, constitutional principle of 280
press, freedom of 450, 456, 466-470, 472
pre-trial detention 121-122, 124-126, 166, 172, 174-175, 182, 184-186, 233
– facility 185
– judges responsible for matters of 174, 176
– pre-trial detainee 122, 124-125, 169-171, 173-182, 185-188
  · communication with spouse, parents or children 187
  · correspondence by letter 169, 171-172, 175, 179
  · spouses of 122, 125-126
– visiting
  · permission 123, 125, 167, 189
  · rights 123
  · supervision of visits 123-124
prison 123-126, 129-130, 143, 168, 177, 183-184
– dangers, averting of 172
– order in 124-125, 168-169, 171-173, 175-176, 178-179, 182-185, 187-190
privacy 450, 455-462, 465, 471-474
– protection of 450, 456-457, 462, 464-465, 472, 652, 769, 813
– right to respect of 367
– sphere of 463-465
property
– guarantee of 314, 318
– law agreements 476-477
– protection of 349
proportionality, principle of 67-68, 73, 109, 132, 134, 136, 171, 179, 184, 188, 191, 198, 201, 203, 208-209, 221, 223, 264, 294, 304, 568, 599, 648, 688, 762, 766-767, 813
protection, obligation of (following from Article 2.1 in conjunction with Article 6.4 of the Basic Law) 486
protection, mandate of (under Article 6.2 sentence 2 of the Basic Law) 399
protection of the pregnant woman against pressure and distress from her social environment or the child's father, mandate of (Article 6.4 of the Basic Law) 483
protective effects offered by Article 6.1 of the Basic Law vis-à-vis residency law
259-260, 263, 278-279
public international law
– agreements under 701
– obligations of the Federal Republic of Germany under 727-728
– system of 702
– violations of 710
public policy 102, 809
– contrary to 477-481
  · marriage covenant, depending on its overall character 477
– breach of 481
public's wish of being informed 466
publication 466

R

registered civil partnership (for same-sex couples) 541, 543-545, 549, 551, 554-563, 565-568, 571-576
– as a family-law institution 543, 548
relatives
– entitled to support 734
– lineal, obligation to give each other support 733, 742
– support for 743
reporting 468-469
representative action 237
res judicata 704
residency
– residence permit 304
  · for the purposes of family unification 252
– in the Federal territory, fundamental-rights claim to 278
residential requirement 426-427
– not to be calculated in accordance with the per capita method, but with the additional requirement 420, 426
– value 425
rubble women 336, 340
– Federal Constitutional Court's judgment 498
rule of law, principle of 57, 72, 143, 175, 187, 264, 315, 381, 496, 694, 700-701, 706, 708, 711

S

same-sex civil partnership 542-544
same-sex couples, discrimination of 542-544, 565
sickness benefit 747, 751, 754
social assistance
– funding agency 732-738, 740-743
– rate, standard 429
– requirement 426
social insurance
– system 501, 510
  · contributory 491, 508, 510
– term of 343
social long-term care insurance 491-493, 495-510, 513
– assessment limit 499-500, 502
– contribution(s) 491, 501, 503
  · formed in a family-friendly manner 497
– co-insured spouses 497
– employer's share 493
– families falling within the remit, re-distribution in favour of 497
– functionality of 512
– generative contribution 491, 509, 512
– inimical to families 502
– not constituting complete insurance 493
– re-distribution 498, 502
– subsidy from the employer 493
social pensions insurance 75, 79
social protection, need of 638
social welfare state 425, 637
– principle of 344, 378, 384, 496, 498, 505, 587, 754
solidarity levy 500, 503
sovereignty, reservation of 703
splitting advantage 670-674, 677-679
spousal splitting 669, 677
spouse(s) 87-88, 96-97, 103, 106, 117-119, 135, 140-143, 146-147, 150, 152-154, 158, 161, 170, 172, 187, 207-210, 215-216, 218, 221-226, 229, 245, 247, 249,

251-252, 259-260, 263, 269-270, 272-279, 283-285, 317, 390, 486, 536-539, 559, 562-563, 566, 568-569, 579, 589, 780, 785, 793, 795-796, 802
- alien, fundamental-rights claim to entry and residency 262
- additional tax charge 9, 17
- and their family members, actual bondage 259
- assuming new obligations as against their former state as single persons 486
- being of different sexes as inherent characteristic of marriage 559
- birth name of their child 527
- choosing their future name 551
- co-insured 640
- concluding marriage covenants 476, 482
- continuation of personal responsibility after divorce 677
- detriment of 285
- dividing the burden of child maintenance 479
- divorced 207, 676-677, 679
- de-facto splitting 672
- entitled to maintenance 679
- exclusion from tax relief 410
- foreign, joining family members in the Federal Republic 245
  · waiting period 246, 250
- heterosexuality 570
- income made during the co-habitation, in the assessment of maintenance 532
- intimate spheres 149
- joining first-generation aliens 248-249, 251
- joining second-generation aliens 251
- liable to income tax 406
- maintenance 40
- obligation to furnish family maintenance 641, 671
- permanently separated, defined as single parents 412
- post-divorce maintenance claims 676
- releasing the other form maintenance claims 476
- right to shape freely their community 482
- with children, discrimination against other parents 408

standard of living, ensuring of 339
state of the law, prohibition of changing 285
state's right to punish, enforcement of 591, 600-602
statute
- constitutional necessity for the specific enactment of 606
- federal 701
- priority of 315, 711
- sufficiently definite 591, 601

statutory
- generalisation 428
- precision 280

subordination, special relationship of 173-175
support 736-738, 740-742, 745
- ability to pay 736-740, 742-743, 745
- claim(s) 733-735, 740-745
- debts 736
- person liable for 733, 736, 738, 740-745

supranational integration 703
surviving dependants' pension 76, 88-92, 95, 339, 346, 349

T

tax 377, 381
– burden
  · additional 17
  · related to financial ability to pay 410
– charges, additional on spouses 9
– child-related additional requirement 416
– rate, marginal 420, 426-429
– remission procedure for reasons of equity 430
taxation
– additional requirement 425-427, 429
– basic allowance 414
– individual/ of the individual 3, 7, 9, 14
– in accordance with ability to pay, principle of 428
– margin of 429
– non-disposable income, exempt from 410
– of households 1, 3, 7-9
– of spouses 8, 14-15
– per-capita method 426-427
– tolerance limit 426-427
taxpayer(s) 18, 406-407, 410-415, 423
– ability to pay 412, 424, 427
– childless 413
three-generational contract 510
transfer payments from families with several children to families with one child or to the childless 347
treaty law 283

U

unemployment 753, 756
– benefit 748, 751-752, 754, 756-757
– insurance 749, 753-754
  · qualifying period in 747-750, 752-757
unequal treatment 581, 585-586, 588
  · between co-habiting spouses and their families and other parents and their families 585
  · of families 585
utilisation fee 375

V

value determination contained in Article 6.1 of the Basic Law 587

W

waiting period 250
– beginning with the marriage 248, 271, 276-277
– for entry 276
– for joining family members 246
– of three years following marriage 270
– regulations 259, 264, 279, 282
waiver of childcare maintenance, not contrary to public policy 477
watchdog function of the state (Article 6.2 of the Basic Law) 35, 51, 64, 66, 70, 162, 197, 201, 206-207, 210, 212, 214, 236, 239, 243, 263, 325, 330, 395, 410, 487, 521, 597, 599, 629, 815, 837, 839, 841
wife

– divorced and new, difference in treatment 224, 226
– not gainfully employed, protection of 42
windfall effect 499

Y

Youth Welfare Office 725, 731

Index of Statutes

A

Act on Benefits of Statutory Pensions Insurance for Child-Raising to Mothers Born Before 1921 337, 340
Act on the Protection of Working Mothers 748-749, 752-755, 757
Act on the Termination of the Discrimination of Same-Sex Couples: Civil Partnerships 542, 544, 636
Act Reforming Public Service Law 438
Act Reforming the Law of Parent and Child (Law of Parent and Child Reform Act) 389, 643-645, 515, 518, 520, 665-666
Adoption Act
– § 3 no. 3 in conjunction with § 6 of the Nationality Act 302
Agreement establishing an Association between the European Economic Community and Turkey 284
Aliens Act
– § 2.1 of the 247, 302
– § 2.1 sentence 2 of the 245, 259, 280-282
– § 7.3 of the 272
– § 7.4 of the 272
– § 10.1 no 7 of the 272
– § 51 of the 281
Aliens Decree (Baden-Württemberg) 248-251

B

Basic Law
– Article 1.1 of the 51, 67, 123, 160, 184, 228, 236, 252, 254, 266, 296, 364, 394, 410, 743
– Article 1.1 in conjunction with Article 2.1 of the 272
– Article 2.1 of the 51, 67, 160, 170, 199, 228, 236, 266, 278, 296, 304, 377, 379, 386, 393, 732, 738-739, 746
– Article 2.1 sentence 2 of the 264
– Article 2.1 in conjunction with Article 1.1 of the 288, 291, 293, 296-298, 325, 364, 366-369, 392, 394, 450-451, 459-461, 464-466, 471, 474, 520, 522, 526, 547, 552, 656, 681-682, 686-687, 689, 691, 726, 728, 759, 762-766, 768-771, 773-774, 776-777, 804-805, 810-811, 815, 823-824
– Article 2.1 in conjunction with Article 6.4 of the 475
– Article 2.2 of the 123, 236
– Article 3.1 of the 1, 4, 10, 28, 47-50, 80, 87, 160, 211, 225, 228, 252, 254, 279-280, 336, 345, 347, 350, 354, 362, 376-377, 382-383, 424, 498, 503, 528-529, 535, 541, 549, 561, 565-567, 569, 574, 576, 577-578, 581-582, 585, 596, 619, 630, 637-638, 647, 673-674, 685, 718, 747, 752, 786, 801, 835, 847

– Article 3.1 in conjunction with Article 6.1 of the 336, 408, 420-421, 423-424, 491, 496, 502-503, 505, 507-508, 512-513, 633, 636, 639
– Article 3.2 of the 4, 10, 17-18, 22, 24-25, 27-30, 42-43, 225, 261, 349, 482, 516, 527-528, 535, 647, 835, 847
– Article 3.2 sentence 2 of the 384
– Article 3.3 of the 10, 17-18, 24-25, 27-30, 48-49, 103, 106, 236, 354, 561, 574, 790
– Article 5.1 of the 170, 180, 208, 186, 266
– Article 5.1 sentence 1 of the 186, 450
– Article 5.1 sentence 1 in conjunction with Article 2.1 of the 182, 185
– Article 5.3 sentence 1 of the 262
– Article 6 of the 142, 409, 535, 700
– Article 6.1 of the 2, 4, 9-14, 16-18, 24-25, 27, 35-36, 38, 41-43, 48, 50, 51, 62, 64, 70, 75-81, 87-89, 94, 96-97, 100-101, 103-109, 114-117, 119-120, 122-126, 131, 134-137, 138, 143-146, 148-153, 160, 170-171, 186, 210, 223, 225-226, 228, 245-246, 252, 254, 258-269, 274, 276-279, 281, 291, 293-294, 301, 304-309, 314, 317, 325-326, 332, 336, 344-345, 347, 376-378, 384-385, 402-403, 409-415, 417, 420, 424, 450, 465, 480, 482, 499, 503-505, 520, 522-523, 525, 528, 541, 548-549, 552, 558-565, 568-573, 578, 581-583, 585, 588, 637-639, 642-644, 647-648, 651-652, 657, 660-667, 669-670, 673-679, 687, 726, 728, 744, 753, 769, 771-772, 777, 784, 786, 794-795, 809-810
– Article 6.1 sentence 1 of the 203
– Article 6.1 in conjunction with Article 6.2 of the 305, 395
– Article 6.1 in conjunction with Article 3.1 of the 220, 225, 229
– Article 6.1 in conjunction with Article 3.2 of the 44, 530-532, 536-539
– Article 6.2 of the 22, 25, 27, 35-38, 51, 55, 57-59, 61-62, 64, 66, 71-73, 123, 131, 135-136, 160, 196, 199, 206-207, 209-211, 235-236, 252, 320-321, 325, 328-329, 386, 392, 400, 402-403, 409-410, 412-415, 417, 450, 465, 475, 480-481, 487, 490, 504, 520-522, 526, 567, 592-593, 596-599, 601-603, 606-609, 611-613, 617-619, 622-623, 625-628, 631, 647-650, 712, 744, 766-767, 772, 785, 794, 800, 824, 826, 828-830, 835-841, 843, 845-849
– Article 6.2 in conjunction with Article 1 of the 835
– Article 6.2 in conjunction with Article 6.3 of the 191
– Article 6.2 in conjunction with Article 20.3 of the 720
– Article 6.2 sentence 1 of the 57, 66, 70, 162, 197-199, 202, 206, 208, 212-214, 241-242, 245-246, 262-269, 274, 276-278, 294, 328, 332, 387, 394, 401, 409, 487-488, 490, 567, 591, 598, 612, 631, 642-644, 651-659, 661, 663-665,

668, 727-728, 730, 771, 804, 811, 813-817, 827, 836
- Article 6.2 sentence 1 in conjunction with Article 20.3 of the 724, 726-727, 731
- Article 6.2 sentence 2 of the 51, 57, 66, 70, 161-163, 197, 201, 209, 212, 239, 241, 243, 263-264, 287, 298, 387, 394-395, 397, 400, 410, 487-488, 521, 599, 623, 629, 728, 815-816, 837, 841
- Article 6.3 of the 51, 55, 57-59, 62, 64-65, 70, 160, 197-199, 202, 235, 242, 263, 293-294, 599, 647
- Article 6.4 of the 263, 747-748, 752-756
- Article 6.5 of the 320-321, 325-328, 332, 364-366, 368-370, 612, 615, 617, 619, 629-631, 779, 783-784, 786-790, 792, 794-799, 801, 828, 836, 848
- Article 11 of the 131, 160, 262
- Article 14 of the 377-378
- Article 14.1 of the 366, 368-369, 385, 738
- Article 16.2 sentence 2 of the 262
- Article 19.4 of the 706
- Article 20 of the 123, 143-144
- Article 20.3 of the 694, 700, 706, 708, 718, 720, 727
- Article 23 of the 702
- Article 24 of the 702
- Article 25 of the 112, 703
- Article 25 sentence 2 of the 702
- Article 26 of the 702
- Article 33.5 of the 439, 447
- Article 59.2 of the 396, 701, 706
- Article 72.1 of the 379
- Article 74.1 no 7 of the 379, 381
- Article 83 of the 281
- Article 84.1 of the 281
- Article 84.2 of the 281-282
- Article 97.1 of the 708
- Article 100.1 of the 438
- Article 103.1 of the 236-238, 291, 293-296, 300, 387
- Article 104.1 of the 123
- Article 105.2 in conjunction with Article 106.3 of the 377, 381

C

Civil Code
- § 138.1 of the 477
- § 242 of the 477-478
- § 569a.2 sentence 1 of the 311
- § 1355 of the 525, 682
- § 1355.1 of the 517, 522-523
- § 1355.2 of the 523, 681-682, 684-692
- § 1355.2 sentence 1 of the 516
- § 1355.2 sentence 2 of the 516, 683
- § 1355.4 of the 691
- § 1361.2 of the 42
- § 1565.1 of the 138-140, 143
- § 1565.1 sentence 1 of the 138-139, 142, 145-146
- § 1566 of the 140, 142
- § 1566.2 of the 138-139, 144, 146, 148-149, 152, 155
- § 1568.2 of the 138-140, 142, 144-145, 150-152, 155
- § 1570 of the 220-222, 224, 227
- § 1578.1 of the 531
- § 1581 of the 221
- § 1582.1 of the 222
- § 1582.1 sentence 2 of the 220, 223-227, 229

– § 1600 of the 642-643, 649-651, 656-658, 664, 668
– § 1601 of the 733, 741
– § 1601 et seq. of the 742-743
– § 1602.1 of the 740
– § 1602.2 of the 488
– § 1603 of the 488, 737, 741, 745
– § 1603.1 of the 733, 736, 739-740, 742, 744-745
– § 1603.2 of the 744
– § 1609 of the 222
– § 1609.2 of the 22
– § 1610 of the 488
– § 1612.2 of the 306
– § 1615 1.2 sentence 3 of the 484
– § 1616 of the 516
– § 1618a of the 306, 364-366, 368-370
– § 1626a of the 612-613, 615, 617-619, 623-624, 627, 630-631, 826, 836
– § 1626a.1 of the 834
– § 1626a.1 no. 1 of the 611-612, 618, 621-626, 632, 826, 829-831, 836, 839-845, 848-850
– § 1626a.2 of the 612, 618-619, 621-622
– § 1626b.2 of the 615
– § 1628 of the 20-24, 30, 32, 38-39
– § 1628.1 of the 38
– § 1629.1 of the 20-24, 30, 38-39
– § 1632.1 of the 288
– § 1632.4 of the 288-289, 291, 293-296, 298-300
– § 1666 of the 192-193, 233, 235-237, 242, 244
– § 1666.1 of the 232, 291
– § 1666.1 sentence 1 of the 197, 200, 242, 288-289, 291
– § 1666.1 sentence 1 in conjunction with § 1666a of the 191, 198
– § 1666a of the 192, 196-197, 201
– § 1666a.2 of the 198
– § 1671.4 sentence 1 of the 203, 205-211, 217-219
– § 1672 of the 612, 617
– § 1672.1 of the 826, 828, 834, 836, 840-842, 846, 848-850
– § 1685 of the 642-643, 646, 651, 665-667
– § 1711.2 of the 642, 651, 660, 663-666
– § 1723 of the 323-324
– § 1723 et seq. of the 333
– § 1738.1 of the 320-321, 323-331, 333, 335
– § 1754 of the 302
– § 1755 of the 302
Code of Administrative Procedure
– § 80.5 of the 256-257
Code of Civil Procedure
– § 614 of the 141, 148-149, 152
Code of Criminal Procedure
– § 52 of the 172
– § 119 of the 168
– § 119.3 of the 124, 170-175, 179, 181-183, 186, 188, 190
Code of Social Law
– Third Book of the 747, 749-750, 752-757
– Sixth Book of the 339
– Eleventh Book of the 491
Criminal Code
– § 185 of the 168, 172, 186, 190
– § 193 of the 186
– § 194.3 of the 168

E

Employment Promotion Act 748-749, 755-758
European Convention on the Protection of Human Rights and Fundamental Freedoms 694
– Article 8 of the 725-727
– Article 8.1 of the 284
– Article 12 of 103, 107
– Article 34 of 697, 704
– Article 36.2 of the 709
– Article 41 of 697, 705
– Article 42 of the 703
– Article 44 of the 703
– Article 52 of the 706
European Social Charter 285

F

Federal Child Benefit Act
– § 3.3 sentence 1 of the 577
Federal Constitutional Court Act
– § 31.1 of the 704
– § 34a.2 of the 286
– § 90.2 sentence 1 of the 256, 292
– § 95.2 of the 286
Federal Remuneration and Pensions Adjustment Act 437
Federal Social Assistance Act
– § 12.1 sentence 1 of the 416
– § 12.1 sentence 2 of the 416
– § 12.2 of the 416
– § 22.1 of the 416
– § 22.3 of the 425
– § 23.4 no. 1 of the 425
– §§ 68 et seq. of the 733, 735
– § 90 of the 734-735, 739, 741-742
– § 90.1 of the 740
– § 90.1 sentence 1 of the 741
– § 91 of the 740
– § 91.1 of the 734-735, 739, 741-742
– § 91.1 sentence 1 of the 741
– § 91.1 sentence 2 of the 734, 741
– § 91.2 of the 734
– § 91.2 sentence 1 of the 741

G

General Administrative Regulations of the Federation Relating to the Implementation of the Aliens Act 282

H

Hague Child Abduction Convention 386
– Article 3.1(a) of the 399
– Article 12 of the 388, 393
– Article 12.1 of the 391, 396, 399
– Article 13 of the 386
– Article 13.2 in conjunction with Article 13.3 of the 399
– Article 19 of the 389
– Article 20 of the 386, 389
Hague Convention of 5 October 1961 concerning the powers of authorities and the law applicable in respect of the protection of minors 387
– Article 1 of the 398
Health Reform Act 634

I

Income Tax Act
– § 10.1 no 8 of the 413
– § 26 of the 2-4, 6-7, 9-10, 14, 18-19, 421

– § 26.1 sentence 1 of the 407
– § 26b of the 421
– § 32.1 to 3 of the 405
– § 32.3 of the 403
– § 32.4 of the 403
– § 32.6 of the 420
– § 32.7 of the 403
– § 32a.1 sentence 2 of the 414
– § 32a.5 of the 407
– § 32a.6 of the 407
– § 33 of the 405
International Charter on Civil and Political Rights 285
International Charter on Economic, Social and Cultural Rights 285
Introductory Act to the Civil Code
– Article 13.1 of the 100 -101, 103, 115-116, 120

J

Juvenile Court Act
– § 51 of the 594
– § 51.2 of the 592, 598, 602-603, 606
– § 67 of the 593
– § 69.2 of the 607

L

Law on Family Names Act 515, 517, 519, 681, 684
Long-Term Care Insurance Act 491

M

Marriage Act
– Article 10.2 of the 101, 108

P

Parent and Child Reform Act, Law of 515, 518, 520
Pre-Trial Detention Code
– no 2.2.2 of the 174
– no 34 of the 168, 184
Prison Act
– § 160 of the 177

R

Reich Insurance Code 337
Residency agreement between the German Reich and the Turkish Republic
285

S

Salaried Employees Insurance Act
– § 28a.1 sentence 1 of the 337

T

Tax Code
– § 163 of the 430
– § 227 of the 430

W

Weimar Constitution
– Article 119 of the 11
– Article 119.1 of the 25